# The
# Bibliography
# of
# Appraisal Literature

# The Bibliography of Appraisal Literature

**FIRST EDITION**
**1974**

*Editor*
**Dexter D. MacBride FASA, JD.**

*Bibliography Committee Chairman*
MAX P. ARNOLD, FASA

*Publications Committee Chairman*
FRANCIS L. GORKA, ASA

**The American Society of Appraisers**

Dulles International Airport
P.O. Box 17265
Washington, D.C.

The Bibliography of Appraisal Literature

Library of Congress Catalog Card Number 73-92529

Copyright © 1974 by The American Society of Appraisers, an International, non-profit, unaffiliated educational association. All rights reserved. Printed in the United States of America.

Data processed by Aztech Corp., Washington, D.C.

Printed by Corporate Press, Inc., Washington, D.C.

Published by  The American Society of Appraisers
  Dulles International Airport
  P.O. Box 17265
  Washington, D.C. 20041

Price of The Bibliography—$30.00

# Guidelines for Bibliography Use

(1) To research a *Subject* (e.g., Transportation): Refer to the generic Chapter heading; select the specific sub-category desired (e.g., Highways); direct your examination within this area of reference materials.

To research an *Author* and his work: Examine the Author-Index (second portion of the Bibliography). References to Chapters and Categories will be indicated by Chapter and Category numeration.

(2) References are divided into 15 major categories, e.g., *Chapter One — Appraisal Theory and Methods.*

(3) Each Chapter is divided into sub-categories, e.g.,
11-11 Appraisal Theory
11-12 Appraisal Ethics

(4) Reference units are arranged alphabetically by Author, followed by article title in bold letters, where applicable, e.g.

> AARON, H. **Rent Controls and Urban Development: A Case Study of Mexico City**

(5) Reference units also reflect sources of publication in italics, page references and dates where available, e.g.,

> AARON, H., **Rent Controls and Urban Development: A Case Study of Mexico City;** *Social and Economic Studies;* December '66, 314-320.

BIBLIOGRAPHY OF APPRAISAL LITERATURE

# Major Sources, Referenced Appraisal Literature

The forum for appraisal literature has, in general, been provided by major private, non-profit, education-oriented appraisal societies. Publications which constitute a substantial part of this forum are listed below, together with sponsoring societies and addresses.

Complementary to this organizationally established forum of appraisal literature has been the occasional publication by individual authors of major books on appraising. These include, for example, Frederick M. Babcock's early (1932) classic work "The Valuation of Real Estate," "The Appraisal Process" by George L. Schmitz, "Valuation For Real Estate Decisions" by Richard Ratcliff, and the 1968 publication of the outstanding work on general value theory "Appraisal Principles and Procedures" by Henry A. Babcock.

If library resources available to the researcher cannot provide the materials, direct contact with the Societies below-listed will prove helpful. One of the key characteristics of the societal matrix, which has voluntarily created and maintained the posture of appraisal professionalism, is that of a well-established pattern of service and information-sharing.

Parenthetically, the researcher should be reminded that the parameters of this Bibliography are necessarily restricted to works primarily occupied with Appraising. In consequence, general reference works and publications, although indispensable to the practitioner if he is to be perceptively oriented and authoritatively conversant with his field, are necessarily excluded. Thus, despite their importance and generic relevance, the Fine Arts appraiser would not expect to find "The Critical Eye" by Ballo and Boothroyd listed herein, nor will the Right of Way appraiser find "The New Landscape in Art and Science" by Gyorgy Kepes noted in the Chapter on Transportation.

**Appraisal and Valuation Manual Series**
**Monograph Series**
**Valuation**
(Technicalities, Technical Valuation)
**Valutape Series**

The American Society of Appraisers
Dulles International Airport
P. O. Box 17265
Washington, D.C. 20041

**The Appraisal Journal**

The American Institute of Real Estate Appraisers of the National Association of Real Estate Boards
155 E. Superior Street
Chicago, Illinois 60611

**Right of Way**

The American Right of Way Association
3727 W. Sixth Street
Los Angeles, California 90020

**Journal**

The American Society of Farm Managers and Rural Appraisers
470 South Colorado Boulevard
Denver, Colorado 80222

| | |
|---|---|
| **Appraisal Institute Magazine** | The Appraisal Institute of Canada<br>Institut Canadien Des Evaluators<br>502 - 177 Lombard Avenue<br>Winnipeg, Manitoba, Canada<br>R3B 0W5 |
| **The Valuer** | The Commonwealth Institute of Valuers<br>Clarence House, 152 Clarence Street<br>Sydney (2000) Australia |
| **The Valuer** | The Incorporated Society of Valuers and Auctioneers<br>3 Cadogan Gate<br>London SW1X OAS, England |
| **Assessors Journal** | The International Association of Assessing Officers<br>1313 East Sixtieth Street<br>Chicago, Illinois 60637 |
| **Appraisal Digest** | New York State Society of Real Estate Appraisers of the New York Association of Real Estate Boards<br>Executive Park Tower<br>Western Avenue at Fuller Road<br>Albany, New York 12203 |
| **The New Zealand Valuer** | New Zealand Institute of Valuers<br>Braemar Flats, 32 The Terrace<br>P. O. Box 10322, The Terrace<br>Wellington, New Zealand |
| **SOTAVE Boletin** | Sociedad de Tasadores de Venezuela<br>Apartado Postal 2006<br>Caracas, Venezuela |
| **The Real Estate Appraiser** | The Society of Real Estate Appraisers<br>7 South Dearborn Street<br>Chicago, Illinois 60603 |

NOTE:  A supplement to The Bibliography is planned for publication. The Scope and effectiveness of the publication will be materially enhanced by suggestions and reference contributions from practitioners, students, researchers.

Your thoughtful assistance will be appreciated; forms to supply reference data (which may have been unfortunately omitted from this work) or to supply new input, are enclosed in the back of this Bibliography. Please use them, fill in the data notations and mail them to The American Society of Appraisers.

# Structural Outline of the Bibliography of Appraisal Literature

### Appraisal Theory and Methods

11-11-00 Appraisal Theory; 11-12-00 Appraisal Ethics; 11-13-00 Appraisal Terminology and Definitions; 11-14-00 Appraisal Tools; 11-15-00 Appraisal Manuals; 11-16-00 Appraisal Methods and Objectives; 11-17-00 Market Appraisal, Price-Cost, and Value Theories; 11-18-00 Social Trends and Appraisal; 11-19-00 Economic Analysis.

### Appraisal for Special Purposes

12-11-00 Taxation; 12-12-00 Equalization; 12-13-00 Assessments; 12-14-00 Condemnation; 12-15-00 Easements and Eminent Domain; 12-16-00 Rights and Rights of Way; 12-17-00 Re-evaluations; 12-18-00 Partial Acquisitions; 12-19-00 Highest and Best Use; 12-20-00 Expropriation; 12-21-00 Appraisal for Employee Transfers; 12-22-00 Site Selection; 12-23-00 Insurance Purposes; 12-24-00 Obsolescense and Depreciation. 12-25-00 Capitalization; 12-26-00 Legal Aspects of Appraisal.

### Urban Property

13-11-00 City Growth and Planning; 13-12-00 Parking Facility; 13-13-00 Urban Renewal; 13-14-00 Central Business District Property; 13-15-00 Commercial Property and Concerns; 13-16-00 Housing; 13-17-00 Residential Property; 13-18-00 Rent and Rent Control; 13-19-00 Residential Buildings; 13-20-00 Commercial Buildings; 13-21-00 Institutional Property and Building and Concerns; 13-22-00 Subdivisions; 13-23-00 Suburban Property.

### Rural Property

14-11-00 General Agriculture; 14-12-00 Crop Allotment; 14-13-00 Soils; 14-14-00 Irrigated Land; 14-15-00 Dry Farm Land; 14-16-00 Dairy Farms; 14-17-00 Groves and Orchards; 14-18-00 Ranches and Grazing Land.

### Recreational Property

15-11-00 Bowling Alleys; 15-12-00 Camps; 15-13-00 Country Clubs; 15-14-00 Golf Course; 15-15-00 Resort Property; 15-16-00 Lake Property; 15-17-00 Marina; 15-18-00 Aquarium; 15-19-00 Yacht Harbor; 15-20-00 Parks; 15-21-00 Amusement Parks; 15-22-00 Hunting Property; 15-23-00 Swimming Pool; 15-24-00 Skiing Area; 15-25-00 Tourist Industry; 15-26-00 Tennis Club.

### Public Utilities

16-11-00 General Value; 16-12-00 Electric; 16-13-00 Gas; 16-14-00 Water; 16-15-00 Communications Systems; 16-16-00 Sanitary Sewer.

### Natural Resources

17-11-00 Coal; 17-12-00 Timber and Timberland; 17-13-00 Trees and Shrubs; 17-14-00 Minerals; 17-15-00 Oil and Gas; 17-16-00 Water and Reservoirs; 17-17-00 Fisheries and Marine Deposits.

### Fine Arts, Objects of Value, Collector's Items

18-11-00 Paintings; 18-12-00 Graphic Art; 18-13-00 Sculpture; 18-14-00 Crafts; 18-15-00 Collector's Items; 18-16-00 Antiques; 18-17-00 Gems and Jewelry; 18-18-00 Furniture.

### Intangible Property

19-11-00 Loans; 19-12-00 Mortgages and Equities; 19-13-00 Leases; 19-14-00 Capital Formation; 19-15-00 Investments; 19-16-00 Stocks and Bonds; 19-17-00 Cash Flow Analysis; 19-18-00 Securities and Registration of Securities; 19-19-00 Good Will; 19-20-00 Patents; 19-21-00 Copyrights; 19-22-00 Trademarks.

### Machinery and Equipment

20-11-00 Furnishings and Fixtures; 20-12-00 Construction Equipment; 20-13-00 Environmental Control Equipment; 20-14-00 Fabrication Process; 20-15-00 Industrial Machinery.

### Costs

21-11-00 Economic Theory; 21-12-00 Replacement; 21-13-00 Building; 21-14-00 Rising Costs; 21-15-00 Cost Surveys; 21-16-00 Engineering Construction; 21-17-00 Historical; 21-18-00 Forecasting; 21-19-00 Summation; 21-20-00 Indexes; 21-21-00 Cost to Cure.

### Land

22-11-00 Vacant; 22-12-00 Underwater; 22-13-00 Tideland; 22-14-00 Indian; 22-15-00 Hillside; 22-16-00 Acquisition; 22-17-00 Subdivision; 22-18-00 Raw Land; 22-19-00 Urban Land Value; 22-20-00 Rural Land Value; 22-21-00 Utilization; 22-22-00 Lots; 22-23-00 Marshland; 22-24-00 Waterfront Property.

### Industry

23-11-00 Industrial Property; 23-12-00 Industrial Park; 23-13-00 Technology; 23-14-00 Heavy Industry; 23-15-00 Light Industry; 23-16-00 Raw Material Processing; 23-17-00 Dairy Products Processing Plant; 23-18-00 Atomic Energy Plant; 23-19-00 Shipyard

### Transportation

24-11-00 Impact of Transportation; 24-12-00 Traffic; 24-13-00 Airport; 24-14-00 Railroads; 24-15-00 Highways; 24-16-00 Highway Beautification; 24-17-00 Automobiles; 24-18-00 Bridges; 24-19-00 Rapid Transit; 24-20-00 Truck Terminal.

### Government Property and Concerns

25-11-00 Military Installations and Facilities; 25-12-00 Military Reservations; 25-13-00 Firing Ranges; 25-14-00 Missile Sites; 25-15-00 Naval Yards.

# Table of Contents

Guidelines for Bibliography Use . . . . . . . . . . . . . . . . . . . . . . . . . . . . . . . . . . . . . . . . . . .  v

Major Sources, Referenced Appraisal Literature . . . . . . . . . . . . . . . . . . . . . . . . . . . . .  vi

Bibliography Structural Outline . . . . . . . . . . . . . . . . . . . . . . . . . . . . . . . . . . . . . . . . . .  viii

Foreword by MAX P. ARNOLD, FASA . . . . . . . . . . . . . . . . . . . . . . . . . . . . . . . . . . . . .  x

Introduction by DEXTER D. MacBRIDE, FASA, JD. . . . . . . . . . . . . . . . . . . . . . . . . . .  xiv

| | | |
|---|---|---|
| Chapter One — | Appraisal Theory and Methods . . . . . . . . . . . . . . . . . . . . .  Preface by FREDERICK M. BABCOCK, FASA, SRA | 2 |
| Chapter Two — | Appraisal For Special Purposes . . . . . . . . . . . . . . . . . . . .  Preface by C. E. O. WALKER, ASA | 158 |
| Chapter Three — | Urban Property . . . . . . . . . . . . . . . . . . . . . . . . . . . . . . . . .  Preface by PHILIP F. PIERCE, FASA, MAI | 300 |
| Chapter Four — | Rural Property . . . . . . . . . . . . . . . . . . . . . . . . . . . . . . . . .  Preface by JAMES H. TREES, ASA, MAI | 410 |
| Chapter Five — | Recreational Property . . . . . . . . . . . . . . . . . . . . . . . . . . .  Preface by CHARLES N. MacNEAR, JR., FASA | 438 |
| Chapter Six — | Public Utilities . . . . . . . . . . . . . . . . . . . . . . . . . . . . . . . . .  Preface by CARL WHITE, CPA | 448 |
| Chapter Seven — | Natural Resources . . . . . . . . . . . . . . . . . . . . . . . . . . . . . .  Preface by CLEMENT J. SCHWINGLE, FASA | 476 |
| Chapter Eight — | Fine Arts, Objects of Value, Collectors' Items . . . . . . . . . . . . . . . . . . . . . . . . . . . . . . . . . .  Preface by HENRY K. CORDIER, ASA | 490 |
| Chapter Nine — | Intangible Property . . . . . . . . . . . . . . . . . . . . . . . . . . . . .  Preface by JOHN G. RUSSELL, ASA, P.E. | 538 |
| Chapter Ten — | Machinery and Equipment . . . . . . . . . . . . . . . . . . . . . . .  Preface by GEORGE D. SINCLAIR, ASA, MAI, SR/WA  Preface by JOHN ALICO, ASA, PE | 592 |
| Chapter Eleven — | Costs . . . . . . . . . . . . . . . . . . . . . . . . . . . . . . . . . . . . . . . .  Preface by FRANK C. SWIFT, ASA | 606 |
| Chapter Twelve — | Land . . . . . . . . . . . . . . . . . . . . . . . . . . . . . . . . . . . . . . . . .  Preface by EDWIN M. RAMS, BS, JD, LLM | 626 |
| Chapter Thirteen — | Industry . . . . . . . . . . . . . . . . . . . . . . . . . . . . . . . . . . . . . .  Preface by A. D. SHIACH, ASA | 674 |
| Chapter Fourteen — | Transportation . . . . . . . . . . . . . . . . . . . . . . . . . . . . . . . .  Preface by NORMAN E. CARLSON, ASA, P.E. | 688 |
| Chapter Fifteen — | Government Property and Concerns . . . . . . . . . . . . . . .  Preface by NORMAN E. LAUER, ASA, MAI, MBA | 710 |

Index of Authors . . . . . . . . . . . . . . . . . . . . . . . . . . . . . . . . . . . . . . . . . . . . . . . . . . . . . .  721

Input Data Bank Cards . . . . . . . . . . . . . . . . . . . . . . . . . . . . . . . . . . . . . . . . . . . . . . . . .  775

# Foreword

by Max P. Arnold, FASA

Mr. Max Arnold, Chairman of the Appraisal Bibliography Committee (which directed the data assemblage, classification structuring, and related activities leading to the publication of this Bibliography), is a Member of the College of Fellows and a Past International President of the American Society of Appraisers.

He is President of Max P. Arnold and Associates, a Denver-based organization serving as Appraisers and Consultants in Valuation. Recognized for numerous articles which have appeared in technical journals on such subjects as Ad Valorem Tax Appraising and Machinery and Equipment Appraisals for Property Tax Purposes, he is also the author of Appraisal Manuals prepared especially for various political subdivisions.

Formerly with the United States Department of Agriculture as a Management and Mortgage Loan Supervisor, he was Rural Land Specialist for the Colorado State Tax Commission, State Director of Appraisals for Colorado's Re-Appraisal Program, and acted as Consultant to the Utah Tax Commission. Mr. Arnold has lectured on appraisal topics at the University of Wyoming, University of Colorado, Colorado State College, Boise College and at numerous seminars and technical conference programs.

## ▲ Foreword

THE American Society of Appraisers was originally founded upon, and has continued to pursue, the concept that all property, tangible and intangible, capable of being owned, used and enjoyed, must be subject to the same principles of appraisal practice. The expressed intent to be an independent, multi–discipline professional society carried with it an obligation to provide the membership of varied disciplines in the appraisal field equal attention in supplying technical and fact resources to satisfy their needs.

The lack of degree–granting status in the appraisal sciences in all disciplines by our higher educational institutions forced all appraisal professional societies to pursue educational and qualification standards for designations, within the parameters of their own organizations. This lack has created limitations extending to teaching talents and appraisal text materials because our academic institutions were neither structured nor had the qualified teaching talents to satisfy the needs of the appraisers who were committed to providing a needed public service.

The efforts of the appraisal societies to assume the consequent educational burdens in training and granting designations (when adopted standards of excellence have been met by the applicant), manifest the fact that the same requirements of expertise, intellectual honesty and personal integrity are required in the appraisal field as in other professions where academic degrees are available in our colleges and universities.

Historically, the greatest pressures for appraisal talents have been in the real estate field. This has been the area of greatest economic action. It is understandable that it is the real estate appraisal discipline that has received the most attention and where the greatest amount of source documents and technical efforts have been directed.

The position of the qualified appraiser in our society has become increasingly clear with the arrival in the market place of whole and mixed-whole properties composed of a complex of properties and property rights requiring estimates of value. Significantly, these complex properties have sources of economic life in other areas than the traditional real estate concept. It was an awareness of these complex mixtures, along with the American Society of Appraisers' multi-discipline commitment, that dictated the effort to research and publish the first comprehensive bibliography of appraisal literature. While it is acknowledged that levels of talents after grading in the art of writing exist, the quality of the articles and substance of the material is not a part of this effort. We have assumed the position that knowledge may only be derived from complete exposure to all thought and thought processes of those who have been engaged in interpreting the market place.

The idea of researching and developing a bibliography by the American Society of

## Foreword

Appraisers had its first meaningful exposure at a meeting held in Milwaukee, Wisconsin in 1968. Those attending this meeting were the International officers and committee chairmen.

To review the subsequent years' of efforts by those who were dedicated to their profession and a corresponding sense of obligation to the responsibilities of community service that permitted them to pursue their chosen vocation, would be a time-consuming effort and does not have a place in this narrative. It is our hope that this publication will serve as adequate recognition of all the positive efforts extended to the project. To express my total appreciation to all those who gave favorable support to the project in my judgment would not be entirely deserving for it was those who did *not* support the concept that made the effort more determined, thoughtful and productive.

As one consequence of this publication, it is hoped favorable influences and stimuli will have an impact upon the academic community in encouraging recognition that the field of appraisal sciences is a broad and complex one with orientation directed toward many disciplines.

A primary purpose of this publication is to serve the needs of the membership of the American Society of Appraisers for it was their expressed desires and financial support that made it possible.

The Introduction and the Explanatory Commentaries for each of the fifteen sections, prepared by experienced and qualified technicians, lend significance to the publication for those who seek knowledge and reference assistance for their needs, regardless of the purpose of their pursuit.

*Max P. Arnold, FASA*
*Denver, Colorado*
*February 20, 1974.*

# Introduction

by Dexter D. MacBride, FASA, JD.

Mr. MacBride, Executive Vice President of The American Society of Appraisers, is a member of the College of Fellows and also serves the Society as Director of the audio-library "Valutape" program and as Editor of "Valuation" magazine and "Newsline".

A member of the Virginia and American Bar Associations, Mr. MacBride followed his condemnation law practice with right of way experience in California, the last seven years occupied as head of that state's Public Works appraisal staff, specializing in Highways, Rapid Transit and Water Transport systems.

He is a Registered Senior Member of the American Right of Way Association, a Member, National Panel of Arbitrators, American Arbitration Association, and a member, American Society of Association Executives. Mr. MacBride is known for his writings (in Public Administration, Law, Right of Way, Appraising, Land Economic Studies) as well as for his service as lecturer and instructor on behalf of professional organizations and in college/university courses, seminars, conferences.

## ▲ Introduction

## I. Origins and Parallels

Editors of the monumental **Oxford English Dictionary,** aware of the humor which seems to arise from the size of uniquely bulky publications, could not resist the comment:

*"If there is any truth in the old Greek maxim that a large book is a great evil, English Dictionaries have been steadily growing worse ever since their inception more than three centuries ago."*

As if to bring the great work into perspective and reasonable proportion, the editors continued:

*"To set Cawdrey's slim small volume of 1604 beside the completed Oxford Dictionary of 1933 is like placing the original acorn beside the oak that has grown out of it."*

The **Bibliography of Appraisal Literature** is not a dictionary, but it serves a reference/origin need which is analogous and, to the appraisal practitioner who has seen the publication of but a few, slim single-discipline antecedents, the **Bibliography** is unique in both size and multi-discipline content.

These unique aspects are the consequence of an effort to supply a research medium not heretofore available to the profession or the public: a single source-center which provides references to all types of literature in all of the disciplines of appraising: Real Property, Personal Property, Intangibles, Utilities, Machinery and Equipment, Technical Evaluation, Appraisal Administration.

Heretofore, the several reference efforts were confined to Real Property Appraising; with the publication of this **Bibliography,** practitioners in all disciplines are served.

Thus, this is a pioneering effort, a first, within the "universe" of practicing appraisers. It is much like the situation described in an introduction to Samuel Johnson's magnificent work (Johnson's Dictionery, McAdam and Milne):

*"If Shakespeare had wanted to use an English Dictionary, he would have had to compile his own. ... Samuel Johnson, wholly unknown to the public because all his work had been published anonymously, set out in 1746 to produce such a dictionary, and did."*

Johnson's work, a "landmark of literature and learning", is a treasury of pertinency and humor.

Witness this definition, which reveals a surprising insight into the misuse of the appraisal process:

*"Excise: A hateful tax levied upon commodities, and adjudged not by the common judges of property, but wretches hired by those to whom excise is paid."*

The contemplative student well knows that the origins of American reference works reveal (equally with those of England) pertinent stories of pioneering labors.

One may picture Noah Webster, moving

xv

## ▲ Introduction

about his great circular table, evaluating (for a period of ten years!) the masses of data contained in the dictionaries and grammar texts of some twenty languages. He was 70 when the **American Dictionary of the English Language** was first published (2500 copies for the US, 3000 for Great Britain).

Webster's career was one of the most remarkable in our country's history; he authored pamphlets urging the adoption of the Federal Constitution; was owner-editor of a New York City newspaper; authored the famous **American Spelling Book;** as a lawyer, he served in the General Assembly of Connecticut, the General Court of Massachusetts; he served as President of the Board of Amherst Academy. An experimental scientist, he travelled the east coast, urging state legislatures to pass protective copyright laws).

But, it is Webster's **American Dictionary** which appears to be his dominant contribution, and it is fascinating to observe that his herculean accomplishment was "suggested partly by his resentment against the ignorance concerning American institutions shown in contemporary British dictionaries".

Just as "the significance of Noah Webster's **Dictionary** and his **Spelling Book** can be appreciated only when they are viewed against the background spanned by his life", so the significance of **The Bibliography of Appraisal Literature** can be best understood if one comprehends "the appraisal profession"; and its approximate 50-year history in the United States.

For **The Bibliography,** like the **American Dictionary,** was born of a desire to combat ignorance, as well as to strengthen the American institution of appraising.

### II. The Profession of Appraising in the United States

This country's appraisal practitioner emerged in the late 1920's and early 1930's. Early efforts were directed toward identification, achieving organizational structure, establishing educational and ethical criteria, constructing discipline parameters, seeking public recognition for the emergent profession.

As a result of these efforts, there currently exist five major nationwide testing/certifying appraisal societies, together with an additional (approximate) 20 groups also primarily concerned with appraisal practice and procedures. It must be noted and emphasized that these formal organizations represent perhaps 20-25% of the total number of persons who make appraisals for a monetary consideration in the U.S.; there is a "subterranean matrix" of some 75-80% composed of persons who practice appraising but are non-affiliated and hence, contribute in no formal, easily identifiable, way to the development of the profession or the composition of its literature.

From the organizationally recognizable 20-25%, there has been insistence that appraisers could-and would-achieve professional status (as that term is sometimes related to the classic professions of Law, Medicine, Theology). Indeed, constant striving to fulfill professionally-oriented criteria has been thoughtfully urged by appraisal leaders in all groups.

Perhaps the most effective affirmation of the appraiser's status as a professional was made by Dr. H. A. Babcock (*Valuation,* Sept. 1972):

"I believe that appraising is and should be a profession. I believe there are certain characteristics which distinguish a profession from a business and from other forms of human activity. Briefly, these are: 1) A profession is based on an organized accumulation of specific knowledge—knowledge not possessed by laymen. 2) A client, because he does not have the necessary specialized knowledge himself, puts his trust in the professional practitioner and must rely on his advice and findings. The professional practitioner recognizes this fiduciary relationship and puts his professional responsibilities to his clients and the public above any money considerations. 3) Members of a profession feel obligated to preserve, perpetuate, and extend the body of knowledge on which the profession is based and to this end they contribute to the group the new knowledge they have discovered or developed and they provide for the education and training of those who wish to enter the professional ranks."

Despite the fact that most appraisers agree with Dr. Babcock's belief, there are at least four major areas in which substantive improvement must be made, if the appraiser's achievement of professional status is to be secured. Without improvement in these areas, the appraiser's role is, at best, paraprofessional.

Admittedly, one major improvement area (involving the present fragmentation of the profession into some 25 disparate groups) will be little affected by the publication of this **Bibliography**.

Hopefully, the other three improvement areas (Identity, Education, Societal Relationships) may feel some impact, and be beneficially altered, by the very fact of the existence of this multi-disciplinary reference resource.

*(1) The Identity Area* centers upon the principal weakness of today's professional appraisal organizations. These organizations, and nearly all of their members (with the exception of the American Society of Appraisers and its membership) visualize the profession as a single-discipline, trade-oriented activity. Thus, appraisers in the United States are almost exclusively pre-occupied with the "Real Estate Industry", i.e., appraisers have related to Realty Boards, Realty and Condemnation Commissions, Banks, Mortgage and Savings and Loan Institutions.

One of the results of domination by the "realty orientation" has led to Real Estate Brokers/Salesmen license mandates currently reported in at least twelve states: Delaware, Florida, Indiana, Michigan, Mississippi, Nebraska, Oregon, Pennsylvania, Rhode Island, South Carolina, Texas, West Virginia. Some type of Realty license is a pre-requisite to appraisal practice in these states.

No matter how "wedded" the appraiser may be to the Real Estate Industry of the USA, he knows the relationship is both insecure and untenable. The appraiser knows the "Market Place" of Realty is a place for "high asking" and "low offering" — a place of *cave canem* bargaining. He knows he cannot serve the process as a handmaiden, and simultaneously profess that his is a "profession", based on objective analysis without subjection to pressure salesmanship. He knows he must "create a better image through gradual dissociation of appraisal from brokerage and through selection of a more descriptive name for the profession."

Within such a context, there appears a most eloquent aspect of this "bulky" bibliography: the visual demonstration and documentation that the profession of appraising comprehends a much greater spectrum than the single discipline of Real Estate. There is a wealth of literature in all disciplines, bespeaking dynamic activity in the market place undreamed of by the realty-confined appraiser. It should now be clear, to the most parochial or myopic of realty appraisers, that the public buys many properties other than "land" and "buildings", e.g., Machinery and Equipment, Intangibles (Capital Stock, Bonds, Copyrights, Patents, Franchise and Licensing Agreements), and Personal Properties (Fine Arts, Gems and Jewelry, Household Furnishings, Collectibles).

If Appraising is to transcend the narrow

## ▲ Introduction

confines of a realty-oriented trade, if it is to assume the responsibilities and privileges of a Professional occupation, then *the appraiser must now acknowledge that the Public acquires and cherishes many kinds of properties; that the practice of appraisal must embrace many "new" valuation duties if it is to respond adequately to the multitude of community valuation needs.*

This Bibliography is a dramatic affirmation that there is much "market place" activity in the many disciplines of appraising, and that this activity is described by articulate writers who are eager to share experiences and facts. Professional appraisers will understand the need to become aware of this considerable literature, and to profit by it.

As the perceptive Introduction to *The Complete Encyclopedia of Antiques* reminds:

*"In the course of his study, the collector soon discovers the tremendous difficulties of specialization. . . . the collector must read, not only more intensively, but more widely."*

It is interesting to observe one of the results of intensive *and "wide"*, reading: most appraisers quickly appreciate the fact that, regardless of the appraisal discipline (whether Fine Arts, Real Estate, Machinery & Equipment, or other) The *Ethical Criteria* are identical, the *Appraisal Report* writing involves identical problems of documentation. But, it is a shock to many to learn that the *vocabulary* (comparables, maintenance, condition, cost factors, replacement, etc) is virtually identical, the *Principles* (supply and demand, substitution, etc.) have an almost identical applicability, and the *Appraisal purpose* (Acquisition, Tax, Insurance) is generally the same. Only the *Object* to be appraised (residence, painting, patent) differs (*situs,* tangibility, form) materially.

*(2) Education* is an area in which those who have sought professional status for the appraiser have found little comfort.

In general, educational efforts generated by the appraisal organizations have been characterized by in-house, non-academically-accredited training sessions. To this date, no courses in the US lead to an academically recognized degree in Appraising.

Such an absence of formal academic support and recognition has had a debilitating, if not toxic, effect upon the practice of appraisal. Teaching one another, it is as if the halt were guiding the blind. This condition was the subject of the following commentary at the Ninth Panamerican Appraisal Conference held in 1973 at Mexico City (analysis: Desarrollos Substanciales en la Profesion del Valuador en los Estados Unidos de Norte Americana):

"It is a curious fact that nearly all appraisers in the USA entered the profession by "chance"; that is, few initially planned their careers to be in appraising. This directly relates, of course, to the absence of academic stimulus and recognition.

"Researchers in this field have emphasized that appraisers must 'substitute professional education for most of the current reliance upon on-the-job apprenticeship'."

One of the reasons colleges and universities have not assumed a major role in fulfilling this need at the level of a specific Valuation-degree program: the practice of appraising has been pictured *by appraisers themselves* to be at the narrow, single-discipline, trade, level.

Thus, in general, a handful of courses generated by appraisers and taught by appraisers, complemented by appraiser-led seminars, has seemed to meet the need of single-discipline, para-professional groups.

With the recognition of a multi-discipline educational need (and the Bibliography is evidence of the reservoir of activity and research), it should now be possible for leaders of both the appraisal profession and college/university institutions to visualize appraising as a total, complex, many-faceted professional environment.

Such an environment can now, demonstrably, support a four-year undergraduate program leading to a formal academic degree in Valuation Sciences, with possibility for graduate work and correlative recognition in the field.

*(3) Social Relationship* has been a pressing problem area for those who visualize appraising as a profession.

The problem has revealed itself in the strange fact that only one state has yet addressed itself, legislatively, to the concept of establishing a Certification program to assist the appraisal-buying public in identifying professionally-accredited appraisers.

Unfortunately, because of the para-professional aspects herein-before discussed (single-discipline pre-occupation, Real Estate trade dominance, non-acceptance by academic institutions at formal Degree levels), the one state that has legislated expressly for appraisers as of this writing — Nebraska — has reflected all of these para-professional handicaps (even to the nadir-point of establishing the educational level at the equivalency of a High School education).

Unlike the solicitude exhibited for other professions, no concern has been expressed by state legislatures to assist in the adoption of worthy ethical criteria, education, superintendence and discipline of appraisers.

Perhaps because of this absence of governmental concern, or because of the weight of the tasks of Organization, Education and Discipline inevitably imposed upon (and necessarily assumed by) the approximate 25 private appraisal organizations, little evidence of formal Public-Service-oriented contributions to the community has appeared.

Another facet of the Social Relationship problem: other professional groups have acknowledged a Social Relationship and obligation requiring a donation of professional time and skill to the needy (e.g. lawyers and doctors have created "Legal Aid" and "Medical Clinics" for those not financially able to pay for such services); the appraisal organizations have scarcely investigated the concept or developed a professional concern deep enough to encourage discussion of the topic.

Similarly, there has been little visible cognizance of possible opportunity to stimulate wide "minority" interest in the career potential existing in appraisal practice throughout the country.

Remarkably, there has been virtually no formal publicly-oriented effort extended by the Appraisal societies (other than the "Opportunities for Minorities in Appraising" Seminar sponsored by The American Society of Appraisers) to encourage minority members to consider entering the appraisal profession. Surprisingly, government interest has appeared equally low thus far; in those few instances where the topic has been discussed, it appears the central thrust has been: Do appraisers, when valuing the property of minority representatives, render fair and objective appraisals? Such a question may be in part prompted by the fact that the appraisal groups are composed of a majority (say 95%) of male, white practitioners, and by the appearance in some publications of commentaries about the relationship of property values to racial or minority neighborhoods. Such a question and the factors which prompt it, are silent upon an issue of equal social concern: How to involve minority members in the appraisal process itself, so that they may have a meaningful participative involvement with, and impact upon, the value-norms of the community?

It is hoped that, through the publication of this Bibliography, the rich inheritance of appraisal literature now made available to the practitioner, the student and the public, will encourage a general interest in, and respect for, Appraising as a worthy medium for practical public service, as well as a rewarding professional vehicle for a life's work.

▲ Introduction

### III. Purpose, Structure, Typography, Use, Acknowledgements

"The stars are the apexes of what wonderful triangles!" wrote Thoreau. In like manner, we may reflect upon the thousands of writings, each of which is the literary apex of an author and his experience, included in this single volume.

One cannot but muse, appreciatively, upon the time and effort given by these authors, who extended their energies beyond the pragmatics of daily work, with little thought to reward or notice.

Perhaps Thoreau anticipated such thoughts when he said "We might try our lives by a thousand simple tests; as, for instance, that the same sun which ripens my beans illumines at once a system of earth like ours. If I had remembered this it would have prevented some mistakes. This was not the light in which I hoed them".

*Purpose* — The purpose of this publication has been adumbrated in Section II. However, recapitulation of the factors which contributed to the total venture, and description of the light in which the work was nurtured, may be helpful.

This Bibliography has been published to assist in:

(1) presentation to the Profession of a central appraisal reference-source which would give (for the first time) a multi-disciplinary, practical working tool to practitioners, students, researchers, compeer professionals and the public;

(2) demonstration, by documentation, that appraising comprehends a complex of disciplines, each rich in tradition, experience, literature;

(3) implementation of the American Society of Appraisers' current program to secure an educational program which is formally accredited by a recognized college or university and recognized with a degree of Valuation Sciences;

(4) affirmation of the current ASA testing/certifying program by providing a centralized system of study-material references for its membership;

(5) corroboration of the ASA policy position that appraising is a total profession, worthy of state legislative recognition and support in problems of Identification, Licensing/Certification/Registration, Education, Superintendence, Discipline.

*Structure* — The morphology of this publication was dictated, in major part, by those factors described in "Purpose", *supra,* which relate especially to education and academic recognition.

The Society's representatives felt that employment of a structure which would correspond to academic needs and requirements would be of greatest value to the appraisal profession. Hence, the separation of the data into 15 major Subject Classifications, with dependent sub-categories. Numeration employed is appropriate to the technology required for input, arrangement, analysis, correction, publication.

This structure was designed and recommended to the American Society of Appraisers by Dr. Allen O. Baylor, of the University of Texas at El Paso. Upon acceptance of the concept by ASA, Dr. Baylor then undertook the formidable data-gathering responsibility.

Data input and related activities dependent upon computer technology and hardware were the responsibility of Mr. John W. Rollins, President, Aztech Corporation of Washington, D. C.

*Typography* — Page size (8½ X 11") was selected to conform with standard business office usage. (As an amusing parenthetical, the Government of the U.S. is the exception that proves the rule: it insists upon sheet size of 8" by 10½" for business office usage).

The two-column format (19 picas each, with 2-pica gutter) facilitates readability;

tests have demonstrated that the eye tends not to "span" easily more than 1½ times the lower-case alphabet (regardless of type style); most newspapers employ the single column format based on this formula.

An eleven-point type size was chosen, again for readability, and a 60 lb. paper stock provides necessary bulk and opacity, taking into consideration volume size and cost.

The type finally chosen is *Century,* judged by many typography experts to be one of the most readable of types, and employed by educational institutions in such publications as *Century Schoolbooks* because of its easy-to-read, soft characteristics (cf. the "New Style" Type Faces introduced in the early 1900's, characterized by "flat" serifs).

Mr. Paul Wester, representing Corporate Press of Washington, D. C. was in charge of these several typographic areas; Mr. Wester coordinated the many printing details on behalf of the Society and Corporate Press.

*Use* — The major reference source of the Bibliography is structured in fifteen chapters. Dependent sub-categories are employed in each Chapter. Each reference unit within a Subject category is first related to *author* (last name) and placed in alphabetic order. The author's name appears in capital letters; the *title* of the work appears next, in bold type. Then follows, in italics, the *publication source;* next, in *regular* type, the *date* and *page* reference.

A complementary alpha-author section comprises the later portion of the publication; authors' names may be found in the standard dictionary alphabetization order.

*Acknowledgements* — Appreciative recognition, of the expertise and talents of those who assisted in the technical aspects of this publication, has been expressed in preceeding sections of this commentary.

The morphology suggested by Dr. Allen Baylor, together with his data-input of reference units; the work of Mr. John Rollins in processing the data units; the typographic decisions and printing counsel/coordination of Mr. Paul Wester — all have contributed to the concept, content and appearance of *The Bibliography of Appraisal Literature.*

Each of the fifteen authors who reviewed the data sources in a specific subject category at the request of the Society, and who then contributed an Introductory Commentary to assist in providing a transition from Concept to Reference, has done much to make this educational venture a pleasant, useful reality.

Too, acknowledgement must be paid to four International ASA Presidents, each of whom supported and encouraged the five-year-long project during his term of office: Mr. Robert Jackson, FASA; Mr. Philip Pierce, FASA; Mr. Charles MacNear, Jr., FASA; Mr. Olof Olson, FASA. During periods of doubt and uncertainty, these gentlemen provided continuity, reassurance and leadership.

Special responsibility, throughout this 5-year period, was vested in Mr. Max P. Arnold, FASA, as Chairman of the Bibliography Committee. In the last year, his efforts to bring the project to a successful conclusion were given strong support by Mr. C.E.O. Walker, ASA, Chairman of the International Education Committee, and Mr. Francis Gorka, ASA, Chairman of the International Publications Committee.

Beyond all these contributors, there is the bed rock of support: the membership of the American Society of Appraisers. These ladies and gentlemen, not only in the United States but in Canada, the Caribbean, Latin America, The Philippines, made the entire concept and project possible by constant encouragement and the payment of their personal funds.

▲ Introduction

## Conclusion

It is the privilege of all Editors (and one generally exercised) to anticipate criticism; criticism both friendly and unfriendly, which seems to flow inevitably from the inescapable errors, omissions and regretted commissions which swirl about "pioneering" productions.

The *mea culpa* theme does not appear particularly useful in this instance, nor would it come easily from this source. Rather, each reader has been provided (in the back of *The Bibliography*) with data-input sheets which he or she can use as lumber to help in the repair of, or alteration and addition to, this structure which has been erected to house our mutual inheritance and treasure. The American Society of Appraisers will be grateful if you will join this important project, and will appreciatively receive your thoughts, suggestions, data-input.

Dr. Samuel Johnson, in considering the problem, stated in a Preface to his "Dictionary":

*"A large work is difficult because it is large, even though all its parts might singly be performed with facility; where there are many things to be done, each must be allowed its share of time and labour, in proportion only which it bears to the whole; nor can it be expected, that the stones which form the dome of a temple, should be squared and polished like the diamond of a ring."*

After additional exposition of this theme, Dr. Johnson then concluded:

*"In this work, when it shall be found that much is omitted, let it not be forgotten that much likewise is performed."*

This work specifically catalogs the labor of thousands of writers. As a central reference product, it has been prepared by many volunteers, supported by the good wishes of the general membership of a major appraisal society with the encouragement of compeers and friends. It is now dedicated to the Appraisal Profession and the Public the profession serves.

*Dexter D. MacBride, FASA, JD*
*Editor*

*Reston International Center*
*Virginia*
*February 20th, 1974*

# The Bibliography of Appraisal Literature

## CHAPTER ONE

# Appraisal Theory and Methods

by Frederick M. Babcock, FASA, SRA.

Frederick M. Babcock counsels and appraises for private and government clients on urban renewal and redevelopment, acquisitions and disposals, market measurement and analysis, housing programs, and legislative policy. He holds membership in the: American Society of Appraisers, Society of Real Estate Appraisers, Lambda Alpha (land economics).

Mr. Babcock is author of the *Appraisal of Real Estate* (Macmillan 1923), the *Valuation of Real Estate* (McGraw-Hill 1932), and numerous articles and booklets including contributions to the *Appraisal Journal, Valuation,* and other professional publications. He is author of the *FHA Underwriting Manual* and the Navy's technical publications on *Housing Administration* and *Real Estate.*

A Fellow of the American Society of Appraisers, Mr. Babcock is a member of the Special Committee on Education of the American Institute of Real Estate Appraisers; member, the Editorial Board of "The Appraiser" of the American Institute of Real Estate Appraisers; member, the Building Research Advisory Board of the National Academy of Sciences. He has served as Chairman of the Committee on Appraisal Standards of the American Society of Appraisers, is a recipient of a special citation from both the Society of Real Estate Appraisers, and the American Society of Appraisers, and holds honorary membership and special citations from the Society of Appraisers of Venezuela (Sociedad de Tasadores de Venezuela).

Mr. Babcock entered the valuation field in 1920 in Chicago in the firm of Wm. H. Babcock & Son. For one year (1931-32) he was a member of the faculty of the University of Michigan Graduate School of Business Administration. He was Asst. Administrator of the FHA for its first six years (1934-40), created its appraisal and underwriting system, and managed its underwriting staff of several thousand in 68 offices.

## ▲ Appraisal Theory and Methods

THIS CHAPTER lists references of general significance in the many fields of valuation. It presumes that the appraisal of all kinds of property exhibits an indentity and similarity of lines of reasoning, methods, and practices. The diversity of properties that are subject to valuation is indicated by the following list:

**Public and business properties:** Airports, water systems, power transmission lines, corporations, business companies, insurance policies, leases, contracts, stocks and bonds, etc.

**Chattels:** Furniture, furnishings, oriental rugs, textiles, stamps, coins, glass and china, gems, jewelry, pottery, porcelains, primitive artifacts, drawings, prints, engravings, paintings, statuary, machines, tools, vehicles, airplanes, ships, etc.

**Real Property:** Oilwells, mines, forests, fisheries, farms, ranches, orchards, motels, gasoline stations, restaurants, garages, department stores, theaters, chain stores, parking lots, office buildings, billboards, industrial plants, drydocks and piers, marinas, warehouses, apartments, houses, mobile homes, condominiums, townhouses, easements, leaseholds, rights of ways, parks, etc.

Valuation of both chattels and real properties puts primary emphasis on market prices and on investment value, enhancement potentialities, security, or compensation. Both fields tend to require the use of the same method — examination of prices paid in sales transactions and the making of allowance or adjustments for differences in the compared properties. The differences relate to variations in the usefulness or productivity of the properties, to differences in the nature and quality of the future pleasure to be derived from ownership, to variations in the degree of scarcity, rarity, or uniqueness of the item of property within its generic group, to differences in potential yields, and to variations in the self esteem expected by reason of the possession of the property.

Nevertheless the bibliography seems to provide a greater number of references to land and realty valuation than to other kinds of property. Perhaps this merely reflects the facts that the bulk of the literature relating to chattel appraising tends to be the literature describing the characteristics, history, or functioning of the chattels themselves rather than the actual process of value estimation and that real property valuation seems more frequently to involve complicated business, investment, government, and social matters not always directly related to prices available or paid in a market.

In comprehending the scope of appraisal literature, cognizance must be taken of the variety of persons, agencies, institutions, researchers, students, and practitioners that produce and use the literature: Collectors, investors, purchasers, sellers, bankers, lenders, owners, custodians, curators, governments, and attorneys.

The scope of appraisal literature is further indicated by the manifold kinds of problems that are solved entirely or to some degree by the use of value estimation: Sale price setting, tax assessment, analysis of market possibilities, judgment with respect to mortgage risk and security, settlement of estates, investment analysis, decisions in property management, direction of land planning, determination of economic feasibility, market analysis, urban renewal, settlement of damage and insurance claims, compensation in public acquisitions, and innumerable other problems that require decisions.

Value and valuation are central considerations in all economic life. Therefore the literature of valuation is formidable in quantity. The goal of bibliographical completeness of references to pertinent materials is obviously one that could not be reached without establishing some rational limits. Otherwise the bibliography would likely be as voluminous as the general catalogue of a major non-specialized library. The bibliographers have included items that deal with the methods of appraisal of property and with the practice of appraisal in business and government. Even such limitations fail to permit a full recognition of the vast number of subjects and aspects of related fields of professional and occupational activity in which appraisers engage. Further there has been no attempt to classify materials by quality. If the subject matter of a listed item is related to making value judgments or estimates — or to the practices of those who habitually engage in appraisal — it has been included. Generally in Chapter 1 items dealing with the nature of property are not included except when the process of valuation is involved.

The subjects and themes of most of the references included in this Chapter are listed below:

1. **Meaning of Value.** Concept of "value" for various purposes, date of appraisal, cost vs. value. value in use, asset value, value in laws and regulations, controlling law and guidelines, appraisal terminology, just compensation.

2. **Reasoning Processes and Formulas.** (a) Appraisal rationales, valuation principles, logic, standard processes, relation between purpose of appraisal and definition of value, authentication, substitution idea, rules of thumb, problem of accuracy, operating ratios. (b) Methods: Forecasting, economic utility and useful life, comparison techniques, parameters, reasonable proofs of value. (c) Formulas: Cost estimation, income capitalization, risk rating, equalization. (d) Tools and Techniques: Computer models and calculations, data retrieval and data processing. (e) Valuation of fragments. Valuation of fixtures and equipment.

3. **Valuation Mathematics.** Statistical treatments, accounting practices, capital budgeting, compound interest functions, use of computers, probability.

4. **Value Evidences.** Data sources, census and experience data, sales data and verifications, accounting and record sources, capitalization rates, appraisal units, cost data, economic growth data, government control of land use.

5. **Value Considerations.** Usefulness and prospective productivity, appraisal assumptions, architectural and engineering factors, tenure and legal rights, goal of just compensation, condition, earning prospects, plottage, improved value, highest and best use, damages.

6. **Professional practice.** Appraiser's responsibility, demonstrations and proofs, inspection and examination of property, consultation, kinds of appraisal engagements, appraisal contracts, review of appraisals,

appraisal reports and forms, court testimony, appraisal fees, professional specialization, qualifications of appraisers, training and education, instruction courses, relations with property owners and third parties, updatings, codes of ethics, disclosure of appraisals, liability of appraiser, licensing and certification.

# Appraisal Theory and Methods

11-11-00 Appraisal Theory
11-12-00 Appraisal Ethics
11-13-00 Appraisal Terminology and Definitions
11-14-00 Appraisal Tools
11-15-00 Appraisal Manuals
11-16-00 Appraisal Methods and Objectives
11-17-00 Market Appraisal, Price-Cost, and Value Theories
11-18-00 Social Trends and Appraisal
11-19-00 Economic Analysis

# 11-11 Appraisal Theory

ABBOUD, SAMIR, "Usage Des Statistiques En Valuation," *Appraisal Institute Magazine*, Appraisal Institute of Canada, Winnipeg, September 1, 1973.

ABDEL-BADDIE F E, "An Econometric Analysis of Factors Affecting Land Values In Western Oklahoma," *Dissertation Abstracts*, June, 1968, pp. 4780-A.

ABELMANN, WILLIAM W., "Principles of Land Economics Affecting Net Income," *Real Estate Appraisal Practice*, American Institute of Real Estate Appraisers, Chicago, 1958, pp. 1-5.

ABSUAGA, MIGUEL A., "A Practical Approach to Appraisal of Depreciable Property," *The Valuation Manual*, American Society of Appraisers, Washington, 1958, pp. 399.

ACKROYD, P. H., "Changing Values," *Appraisal Institute Magazine*, Appraisal Institute of Canada, Winnipeg.

ADAMS, JOHN F. JR., "Analysis of Factors Influencing Value," *The Appraisal Journal*, April, 1969, pp. 239-240.

ADAMS, PAUL, "The Case of the Property That Paid Too Well," *The Appraisal Journal*, October, 1949, pp. 441-445.

ADELSBERG, HYMAN, "ASA Education Program," *Technical Valuation*, February, 1954, pp. 18.

ADIKES, JOHN, "Appraising the Economic Outlook," *Appraisal Digest*, October, 1953, pp. 10-11.

ADLER, M., "On Risk Adjusted Capitalization Rates and Valuation by Individuals," *Journal of Finance*, September, 1970, pp. 819-835.

AGUAYO, RAMON CARLOS, "Ensenanza De La Valuacion," *Boletin*, Sotave, Caracas, Venezuela, pp. 21-24.

AGUAYO, RAMON CARLOS, "Primer Seminario Instituto Mexicano," *Boletin*, Sotave, Caracas, Venezuela, pp. 15-18.

ALDERFER, EVAN B., "Rounding the Horn of Plenty," *The Appraisal Journal*, July, 1962, pp. 410-413.

ALDIS, GRAHAM, "Appraising Fractional Real Estate Interests," *The Appraisal Journal*, January, 1941, pp. 69-71.

ALDIS, GRAHAM, "Management As a Factor In Appraisal," *The Appraisal Journal*, April, 1936, pp. 188-193.

ALEXANDER, ROBERT H., "The Area Designation," *The Real Estate Appraiser*, November, 1963, pp. 10-12.

ALEXANDER, ROBERT H., "The Need for Proper Public Relations," *The Residential Appraiser*, September 20, 1962, pp. 9-10.

ALLEN, ELLIS S., "Facts Observed-A Critique," *The Appraisal Journal*, April, 1961, pp. 253-255.

ALLES, WAYNE, "Factual Data Means Technical Appraising," *Technicalities*, January, 1949, pp. 14-15.

ALLIN, B. C., "Bill to License Appraisers In California Legislature," *Technical Valuation*, June, 1955, pp. 5-8.

ALLINGHAM, A. P., "Commodity Dollars," *The Appraisal Journal*, April, 1943, pp. 247-248.

ALLINGHAM, A. P., "Preparing the Appraisal Report," *District Appraisal Conference*, New York State Society of Real Estate Appraisers, New York State Society of Real Estate Appraisers, Rochester, April 17, 1941.

ALLISON, NEVILLE F., "Classifying and Interpreting Market Data," *The Appraisal Journal*, pp. 56-567.

▲ **Appraisal Theory and Methods**

ALLISON, NEVILLE F., "Fundamental Appraisal Thinking," *The Appraisal Journal*, October, 1964, pp. 579-588.

ALLISON, NEVILLE F., "Three Approaches to Value," *Proceedings of the Third Institute on Eminent Domain*, Dallas, 1961.

ALLISON, NEVILLE F., "The Hour of Decision," *The Appraisal Journal*, January, 1961, pp. 119-122.

ALVERT, EUGENE, "A Concept of Value," *Technical Valuation*, June, 1958, pp. 41-42.

AMERICAN ECONOMIC ASSOCIATION, *Reading In Price Theory*, R. D. Irwin, Chicago, 1952.

AMERICAN INSTITUTE OF REAL ESTATE APPRAISERS, *Demonstration Appraisal Reports*, American Institute of Real Estate Appraisers, Chicago, 1957.

AMERICAN INSTITUTE OF REAL ESTATE APPRAISERS, *Problems In Rural Real Estate Appraisal*, American Institute of Real Estate Appraisers, 1968.

AMERICAN INSTITUTE OF REAL ESTATE APPRAISERS, *Problems In Urban Real Estate Appraisal*, American Institute of Real Estate Appraisal, 1967.

AMERICAN INSTITUTE OF REAL ESTATE APPRAISERS, *Real Estate Appraisal Practice*, American Institute of Real Estate Appraisers, Chicago, 1958.

AMERICAN INSTITUTE OF REAL ESTATE APPRAISERS, *Selected Readings In Real Estate Appraisal*, American Institute of Real Estate Appraisers, Chicago, 1953.

AMERICAN INSTITUTE OF REAL ESTATE APPRAISERS, *The Appraisal of Real Estate*, American Institute of Real Estate Appraisers, Chicago, pp. 259.

AMERICAN INSTITUTE OF REAL ESTATE APPRAISERS, *The Appraisal of Real Estate*, American Institute of Real Estate Appraisers, 1967.

AMERICAN INSTITUTE OF REAL ESTATE APPRAISERS, "Analysis of Expense," *The Appraisal of Real Estate*, American Institute of Real Estate Appraisers, Chicago, 1967, pp. 244.

AMERICAN INSTITUTE OF REAL ESTATE APPRAISERS, "Annuity Capitalization and Valuation," *The Appraisal of Real Estate*, American Institute of Real Estate Appraisers, Chicago, 1967, pp. 296.

AMERICAN INSTITUTE OF REAL ESTATE APPRAISERS, "Codigo De Etica Profesional," *Boletin*, Sotave, Caracas, Venezuela, pp. 25-43.

AMERICAN INSTITUTE OF REAL ESTATE APPRAISERS, "Some Thoughts on Appraisal Forms-And Appraisal Judgment," *The Appraiser*, March, 1967.

AMERICAN INSTITUTE OF REAL ESTATE APPRAISERS, "The Nature and Purpose of Appraisal," *The Appraisal of Real Estate*, American Institute of Real Estate Appraisers, Chicago, 1967, pp. 1-7.

AMERICAN INSTITUTE OF REAL ESTATE APPRAISERS, "The Nature of Real Property and Value," *Appraisal of Real Estate*, American Institute of Real Estate Appraisers, Chicago, 1967, pp. 7-23.

AMERICAN INSTITUTE OF REAL ESTATE APPRAISERS, "What to Look for In an Appraisal," American Institute of Real Estate Appraisers, 1964.

AMERICAN SOCIETY OF APPRAISERS, "Principios Del Ejercicio De ASA," *Boletin*, Sotave, Caracas, Venezuela, pp. 25-35.

AMERICAN SOCIETY OF FARM MANAGERS AND RURAL APPRAISERS, "Professional Advancement Means More Income," *Journal of the American Society of Farm Managers & Rural Appraisers*, April, 1956, pp. 8-9.

ANDERSON, BENJAMIN MCALESTER, *Social Value a Study In Economic Theory Critical and Constructive*, New York City, 1966.

ANGULO LOPEZ, ALBERTO, "Principios Basicos De Avaluaciones," *Boletin*, Sotave, Caracas, Venezuela, pp. 5-6.

ANTONMATTEI, JOSE E., "Valoracion De Bienes Raices," *Boletin,* Sotave, Caracas, Venezuela, pp. 11-23.

APPEL, JAMES R., "Market Analysis for a Reuse Appraisal," *The Real Estate Analyst Appraisal Bulletin,* 1957, pp. 25-28.

APPRAISAL DIGEST, *Values In Restricted Areas,* January, 1954, pp. 19-20.

APPRAISAL DIGEST, "The Price of Pride," *Urban Land,* January, 1956, pp. 8-9.

APPRAISAL DIGEST, "The Value of Amenities," *Appraisal Digest,* April, 1954, pp. 13.

APPRAISAL INSTITUTE MAGAZINE, "Value a Word of Many Meanings," *Appraisal Institute Magazine,* December, 1959, pp. 13-15.

APPRAISAL JOURNAL, "Serendipity and the Student of Appraisal," *The Appraisal Journal,* April, 1967, pp. 175-180.

APPRAISAL JOURNAL, "The Aftermath," *The Appraisal Journal,* April, 1953, pp. 286-288.

ARCHITECTURAL FORUM, "Business Factors In Architectural Practice," *Architectural Forum,* February, 1923.

ARENA, JOHN J., "Is the United States Pricing Itself Out of World Markets," *The Appraisal Journal,* January, 1966, pp. 58-62.

ARMSTRONG, EDWIN F., "Appraisers or Appeasers," *Freehold,* November, 1941, pp. 40-42.

ARMSTRONG, ROBERT H., "Boom and Bust--The Appraisers Dilemma," *The Appraisal Journal,* July, 1946, pp. 240-246.

ARMSTRONG, ROBERT H., "Capitalization," *The Appraisal Journal,* pp. 134-146.

ARMSTRONG, ROBERT H., "Critical Assumptions In Real Estate Appraising," *The Appraisal Journal,* January, 1947, pp. 66-72.

ARMSTRONG, ROBERT H., "The Continued and Incessant Decline In Real Estate Values," *The Appraisal Journal,* July, 1951, pp. 270-292.

ARMSTRONG, ROBERT H., "The Folklore of Appraising," *National Real Estate Journal,* October, 1939, pp. 34-37.

ARMSTRONG, ROBERT H., "Values and Fetishes," *The Appraisal Journal,* April, 1950, pp. 71-184.

ARMSTRONG, WILLIAM Y., "Is the Cost Approach Necessary," *The Appraisal Journal,* January, 1963, pp. 71-80.

ARNESON, HARRY R. JR., "Appraiser-Client Agreement," *Appraisal Institute Magazine,* September, 1961, pp. 28-29.

ARNOLD, MAX P., "Are Different Appraised Values for Different Purposes Justified," *Technical Valuation,* February, 1954, pp. 9-11.

ARNOLD, ROBERT S., "Ellwood Revisited-And Perhaps Simplified," *The Appraisal Journal,* October, 1966.

ARNOLD, ROBERT S., "Inwood - Friend or Foe," *The Appraisal Journal,* January, 1963, pp. 35-38.

ARNOLD, ROBERT S., "Its What's Up Front That Counts," *The Appraisal Journal,* January, 1964, pp. 68-70.

ARNOLD, RONALD S., "In Rebuttal: Ellwood Pro and Con," *The Appraisal Journal,* 1967, pp. 579-581.

ARROW, KENNETH JOSEPH, *Social Choice and Individual Values,* Wiley and Sons, New York City, 1951.

ARSUAGA, MIGUEL A., "A Practical Approach to the Appraisal of Depreciable Property," *Appraisal and Valuation Manual,* American Society of Appraisers, Washington, D. C, 1958, pp. 399-404.

ARTILES, SEBASTIAN, "Corte Suprema En Materia De Avaluos," *Boletin,* Sotave, Caracas, Venezuela, pp. 16-17.

ASCHER, DAVID B., "International Valuation a New Science," *The Appraisal Journal,* April, 1952, pp. 232-234.

▲ **Appraisal Theory and Methods**

ASH, FRED C., "Appraisal Docket Reasonable, Probable Demand In Valuation," *The Appraisal Journal,* January, 1955, pp. 116-117.

ASH, FRED C., "Factual Basis for Expert Opinion," *The Appraisal Journal,* July, 1956, pp. 428-429.

ASH, FRED C., "Value As a Potential Power Site," *The Appraisal Journal,* April, 1955, pp. 278-279.

ASSOCIATION OF APPRAISAL EXECUTIVES, *Basic Standards of Appraisal Practice and Procedure,* Association of Appraisal Executives, Washington, D. C, 1936.

ATKINS, DAVID, *The Measurement of Economic Value,* Gelber, Lilienthal, Inc, San Francisco, 1925.

ATKINSON HARRY GRANT, "Appraising As a Profession," *The Appraisal Journal,* July, 1936, pp. 271-277.

ATKINSON HARRY GRANT, "The Basis of Creative Brokerage," *The Appraisal Journal,* April, 1961, pp. 165-176.

ATKINSON, HARRY GRANT, "This Is My Judgment," *The Appraisal Journal,* October, 1958, pp. 557-560.

AXKROYD, PETER H., "Changing Values," *The Appraisal Institute Magazine,* March, 1963, pp. 7-11.

BABCOCK, DR. HENRY A., "One Man's Appraisal Philosophy," *Valuation,* American Society of Appraisers, September, 1972, pp. 2.

BABCOCK, FREDERICK, "Appraisals by Income Analysis," *National Real Estate Journal,* February 21, 1927, pp. 19-21.

BABCOCK, FREDERICK M., *The Appraisal of Real Estate,* Macmillan Company, New York City, 1924.

BABCOCK, FREDERICK M., *The Valuation of Real Estate,* Mcgraw-Hill Book Company, Incorporated, New York City, 1932.

BABCOCK, FREDERICK M., "A New Approach to the Solution of the Appraisal Problem," *The Appraisal Journal,* January, 1937, pp. 54-59.

BABCOCK, FREDERICK M., "A New Approach Toward Solution of the Appraisal Problem," *Practical Appraising Methods,* 1940, pp. 2-4.

BABCOCK, FREDERICK M., "Appraisal Procedure," *Valuation of Real Estate,* 1932, pp. 187-224.

BABCOCK, FREDERICK M., "Appraisal Procedure and Methods," *Proceedings of the Brokers Division of the National Association of Real Estate Boards,* 1924, pp. 48-56.

BABCOCK, FREDERICK M., "Business Conditions Stress Importance of Appraisals," *Real Estate Record and Builders Guide.*

BABCOCK, FREDERICK M., "Common Errors In Appraisal Methods and Analysis," *National Real Estate Journal,* November 24, 1930, pp. 17-20.

BABCOCK, FREDERICK M., "Depreciation Obsolescence and Building Life," *Valuation of Real Estate,* 1932, pp. 401-426.

BABCOCK, FREDERICK M., "El Procedimiento De La Valuacion," *Boletin,* Sotave, Caracas, Venezuela, pp. 15-22.

BABCOCK, FREDERICK M., "Las Tres Aproximaciones," *Boletin,* Sotave, Caracas, Venezuela, pp. 23-29.

BABCOCK, FREDERICK M., "On the Annuity System," *Appraisal Journal,* October, 1936, pp. 437.

BABCOCK, HENRY A., *Appraisal Principles and Procedures,* 1968.

BABCOCK, HENRY A., "Appraising Income Property," *The National Real Estate Journal,* March 7, 1927, pp. 33-40.

BABCOCK, HENRY A., "Basic Appraisal Principles and Procedures," *Technical Valuation,* February, 1953, pp. 34-38.

## BIBLIOGRAPHY OF APPRAISAL LITERATURE

BABCOCK, HENRY A., "Recent Developments In Real Estate Appraising," *The National Real Estate Journal,* April 14, 1930, pp. 31-34.

BABCOCK, HENRY A., "Standardized Appraisal Practice," *Proceedings of the 15th Annual Convention of the Bankers Association of America,* 1928, pp. 119-126.

BABCOCK, HENRY A., "The Appraisal of Parts, Fractions and Whole Properties," *Technicalities,* February, 1950, pp. 9-12.

BABCOCK, HENRY A., "The Relation of Income to Value," *The Annals of Real Estate Practice,* 1926, pp. 83-116.

BABCOCK, HENRY A., "Trends Affecting Urban Real Estate Values," *The Economist,* December 16, 1932, pp. 5-12.

BABCOCK, WILLIAM H., "Appraising As a Phase of Salesmanship," *National Real Estate Journal,* November 5, 1923, pp. 22-26.

BABY, RENE, "The Inversion Phenomenon," *Appraisal Institute Magazine,* 1970.

BACK, DENYS H., "Canadian Contrasts," *Residential Appraiser.*

BADEN, POWELL, BADEN, HENRY, *The Land Systems of British India,* Clarendon Press, Oxford, 1892.

BAGLEY, ELEANOR S., "Appraisal Pitfalls," *The Appraisal Journal,* April, 1949, pp. 173-182.

BAILEY, C. DOUGLAS, "The General Rate," *Ratings and Valuation Society,* 1967.

BAILEY, HOP, JR., "Problems In Appraising," *The Appraisal Journal,* August, 1964, pp. 23-28.

BAKER, LLOYD, "The Market As a Yardstick," *The Review,* June, 1950, pp. 18-19.

BALDERSTON, C. CANBY, "Real Estate's Stake In Sound Dollars," *The Residential Appraiser,* March, 1958, pp. 15-18.

BALDWIN, HARRY, "Appraisals," *National Association of Cost Accountants,* 1928, pp. 180-189.

BALLARD, W. H., "Expense As a Factor In Appraising," *National Association of Real Estate Boards,* 1929, pp. 81-84.

BALLARD, WILLIAM S., "How the Appraiser Discharges His Responsibilities," *Technical Valuation,* February, 1963, pp. 24-28.

BALLIM, FRED A., "An Appraisal of Freedom," *The Real Estate Appraiser,* November, 1968, pp. 21-25.

BALLOU, PAUL, "Emerging Valuation Problems with Changing Patterns of Development," *The Assessors Journal,* July, 1966, pp. 9-16.

BARBOUR, SIR DAVID MILLER, *The Standard of Value,* Macmillan and Co, London, 1912.

BARISH, NORMAN N., *Economic Analysis for Engineer and Managerial Decision Making,* Mcgraw Hill Book Company Inc., New York City, 1962.

BARISH, NORMAN N., "Determinations of Minimum Cost and Maximum Profit," *Economic Analysis for Engineer Managerial Decision Making,* New York City, 1962, pp. 063-307.

BARISH, NORMAN N., "Interest and the Time Value of Money," *Economic Analysis for Engineer and Managerial Decision Making,* New York City, 1962, pp. 49-73.

BARISH, NORMAN N., "Methods for Tangible Evaluation of Alternatives," *Economic Annals for Engineer and Managerial Decision Making,* New York City, 1962, pp. 117-176.

BARISH, NORMAN N., "Waiting Time Evaluations," *Economic Analysis for Engineer Managerial Decision Making,* New York City, 1962, pp. 408-420.

BARNARD, BOYD T., "Appraisal Pitfalls," *Freehold,* August, 1941, pp. 48-50.

BARNARD, BOYD T., "Artist or Mechanic: an Appraiser Appraises Appraising," *The Appraiser,* November, 1969.

BARNARD, BOYD T., "How Much More Can the Market Absorb," *The Appraisal Journal,* April, 1964, pp. 172-176.

BARNARD, BOYD T., "Pitfalls In Appraising," *The Appraisal Journal,* October, 1941, pp. 385-392.

BARNARD, BOYD T., "The Future of Appraising," *The Appraisal Journal,* April, 1965, pp. 181-189.

BARONE, RAY R., "How to Get Your Moneys Worth from the Appraiser," *The Appraisal Journal,* July, 1965, pp. 437-439.

BARTLETT, ROLAND W., "Interdependence of Urban and Rural Economies," *The Appraisal Journal,* January, 1950, pp. 63-71.

BASHAW, FREDERICK J., "Value In a Dynamic Land Economy," *The Review,* 1900, pp. 16-22.

BASS, BOYLSTON B., "Tight Money Again," *The Residential Appraiser,* October, 1958, pp. 3-5.

BATCHELOR, HARRY H., "Adequacy of Restrictions," *The Review,* January, 1956, pp. 7-9.

BATCHELOR, HARRY H., "Special Responsibility of Appraisers In Cited Examples," *The Review,* May, 1956, pp. 8-10.

BAUER, M. H., "The Cost and Price of Value," *Appraisal Institute Magazine,* Appraisal Institute of Canada, Winnipeg.

BAYLOR, DR. ALLEN O., "Valuation As a Multi/Disciplinary Field In Our Higher Education," *Appraisal and Valuation Manual,* Corporate Press Incorporated, Washington, D. C., January, 1972, pp. 290.

BEAN, PHILIP R., *Rating Valuation Practice,* Stevens, London, 1952.

BEATON, J WALLACE, "Father Devitt and Mother Hubbard or Valuation Day Meets Frankenstein," *Valuation Magazine,* American Society of Appraisers, Washington D C, December 1, 1973, pp. 2-11.

BEAUBIER, DAVID W., "Appraisers and the White Paper," *Appraisal Institute Magazine,* Appraisal Institute of Canada, Winnipeg, March 1, 1971.

BEAUCHAMP, J. LYLE, "Appraisal Issues In Pre-Loss & Post-Loss Situations," *Papers and Proceedings,* Wisconsin Colloquium on Appraisal Research, 1963, pp. 46-53.

BEETH, CHANNING C., "Today's Appraisal Digest Must Reflect Today's Cost," *Appraisal Digest,* January, 1954, pp. 4-6.

BEMAN, ARTHUR K., "Hazards of Data Interpretation," *The Appraisal Journal,* July, 1944, pp. 237-244, 757-764.

BENNETT, . H., "The Coming Technological Revolution on the Land," *The Appraisal Journal,* January, 1947, pp. 16-21.

BENNETT, S. Z., "La Organizacion Profesional," *Boletin,* Sotave, Caracas, Venezuela, pp. 9-13.

BENNETT, SAUL Z., "Purpose of the Appraisal and Definition of Fair Market Value," *A Student's Report on an Apartment House,* American Institute of Real Estate Appraisers, Chicago, 1966, pp. 9.

BENSON, PHILIP A., NELSON L. NORTH, "The Hoffman and Davies Rules," *Real Estate Principles and Practices,* 1938, pp. 293.

BENSON, PHILIP A., NELSON L. NORTH, "Valuation of Improved Property," *Real Estate Principles and Practices,* 1938, pp. 297-298.

BENSON, W. A., "Canada Land Inventory," *Appraisal Institute Magazine,* Appraisal Institute of Canada, Winnipeg, June 1, 1971.

BERGER, MILES, "Checkmate, Professor Anderson," *The Appraisal Journal,* April, 1965, pp. 199-202.

BERGER, MILES, "Professional Status Needed by Appraisers," *The Real Estate Appraiser,* pp. 15.

BERHOFF, WILLIAM EARL, *Evolution of Values In New Mexico,* State Bureau of Mines, Socorro, 1962.

BERMAN, W. I., "How the Employer Can Get Better Appraisal Reports," *The Real Estate Appraiser,* May, 1967, pp. 21-25.

## BIBLIOGRAPHY OF APPRAISAL LITERATURE

BERNARD, ALFRED D., "Improved Properties," *Principles and Problems of Real Estate Valuation,* Baltimore, 1913.

BERNARD, W. C., "Do Public Improvements Create Special Benefits," *The Appraisal Journal,* January, 1945, pp. 20-23.

BEROES, MARIANO, "Valuacion," *Boletin,* Sotave, Caracas, Venezuela, pp. 33-40.

BIRCK, LAURITS VILHELM, "The Theory of Marginal Value," E.P. Dutton and Co., New York, 1922.

BIRD, F., "Educational Requirements for Valuers," *Appraisal Institute Magazine,* Appraisal Institute of Canada, Winnipeg.

BISHOP, JESSE E., "Legal Responsibilities of the Appraiser," *Appraisal Institute Magazine,* Appraisal Institute of Canada, Winnipeg.

BLAKELY, A. P., "A Profession," *Appraisal Institute Magazine,* Appraisal Institute of Canada, Winnipeg, June 1, 1972.

BLISS, GEORGE L., "Appraisal Protection for Borrowers," *The Review,* September, 1948, pp. 11-12.

BLOOM, GEORGE, "Real Estate Principles and Practices Workbook," *Readings In Business No. 74,* Indiana University, 1971.

BLUMBERG, AARON J., "How Much Credence Can Be Put In Cycle Theory," *The Appraisal Journal,* January, 1949, pp. 61-66.

BLUME, E., "On the Assessment of Risk," *Journal of Finance,* March, 1971.

BODFISH, MORTON, "Narrowing Margins," *The Review,* May, 1955, pp. 16-24.

BODFISH, MORTON, A. D. THEOBALD, "Appraisal Reports," *Real Estate Fundamentals,* 1941, pp. 19.

BODFISH, MORTON, A. D. THEOBALD, "Appraising--Ascertaining Real Estate Value," *Real Estate Fundamentals, Part Xi,* Northwestern University, Chicago, 1941, pp. 1-29.

BODFISH, MORTON, THEOBALD, A. D, "The Rate of Capitalization," *Real Estate Fundamentals,* 1941, pp. 16-71.

BOECKH, EVERARD HEREFORD, "Appraisal Systems and Their Uses," *Boeckh's Manual of Appraisals,* pp. 19.

BOECKH, EVERARD HEREFORD, "Land Valuation," *Manual of Appraisals,* pp. 339.

BOECKH, EVERARD HEREFORD, "Land Valuation," *Manual of Appraisals,* 1937.

BOECKH, EVERARD HEREFORD, "What Is an Appraisal," *Manual of Appraisals,* pp. 315.

BOHANNON, DAVID D., "Building Trends," *The Review,* September, 1948, pp. 3-6.

BONBRIGHT, JAMES C., "Concepts of Property Value," *The Valuation of Property,* New York, 1937.

BONBRIGHT, JAMES C., "May the Same Property Have Different Values for Different Purposes," *National Tax Association,* Proceedings 20th Annual Conference, 1927, pp. 279-295.

BONBRIGHT, JAMES C., "The General Theory of Appraisal Technique," *The Valuation of Property,* 1937, pp. 129-134.

BONBRIGHT, JAMES C., "Valuation of Property," *Appraisal Principles and Procedures,* Mcgraw-Hill Book Co., Inc, New York, 1937, pp. 231.

BONNER, JOHN, "Hazards and Safeguards In Appraisal Work," *The Appraisal Journal,* April, 1966, pp. 177-180.

BONNER, JOHN T. JR., "Bargaining Ability Affects Market Value," *The Review,* September, 1956, pp. 7-8.

BONTJES, JOHN H., "Horse Sense In Appraising," *The Review,* June, 1950, pp. 3-6.

BOWEN, PERCIVAL V., "Buyers, Sellers Not Always Willing," *The Appraisal Digest,* April, 1952, pp. 16-17.

▲ Appraisal Theory and Methods

BOWEN, PERCIVAL V., "Shall Values Be Based on Past, Present or Future," *The Appraisal Journal*, January, 1934, pp. 125-130.

BOWES, WATSON A., "The Future of the Appraisal Profession," *The Residential Appraiser*, May, 1960, pp. 3-7, 24.

BOWES, WATSON A., "Today's Artificial Economics," *The Review*, October, 1951, pp. 7-12.

BOWES, WATSON A., "Your Appraiser---An Aid to Selling," *The Appraisal Journal*, April, 1954, pp. 262-266.

BOWMAN, W. J., "What the Auditor-Examiner Wants In an Appraisal Report," *The Review of the Society of Residential Appraisers*, October, 1941, pp. 8-11.

BOWMAN, WILLIAM J., "The Auditor Look at Appraisals," *The Appraisal Journal*, April, 1942, pp. 156-159.

BOYD, JOHN T. JR, "Standardizing Appraisals," *The Architectural Forum*, April, 1930, pp. 627-630.

BOYKIN, JAMES H., "Evolution of the Subjective Theory of Value," *The Real Estate Appraiser*, March, 1965, pp. 26-28.

BRABENT, DAVIS, "Appraisal Contracts," *The Residential Appraiser*, August, 1960, pp. 8-11.

BRACHMAN, H. J., "Criticism of Standard Appraisal Methods," *The Real Estate Record*, February 20, 1937, pp. 18-20.

BRADFORD, C. R., "25 Steps In Preparing for Appraisal Theory Examinations," *The Appraisal Institute Magazine*, July, 1957, pp. 15-25.

BRADLEY, VINCENT P., "The Need for Educational Courses," *The National Real Estate Journal*, February 11, 1924, pp. 39-40.

BRADY, HOBART C., "Scientific Appraisals As an Aid to Selling," *The Appraisal Journal*, January, 1948, pp. 57-62.

BRAY, JOHN W., "Capitalization Rate," *A. S. A. Valuation Manual*, American Society of Appraisers, Washington, D. C, 1964, pp. 31.

BREWER, T., "Earth Resources," *Datamation*, August 15, 1970, pp. 25-28.

BRIGGS, J., "Sales on Terms-Do They Represent Market Value," *The Appraisal Institute Magazine*, December, 1963, pp. 9-15.

BRINSMADE, ROBERT BRUCE, *El Latifundismo Mexicano, Su Origen Y Su Remedio*, 1916.

BROOKE, R. J., "Appraisal Methods," *The Appraisal of Machinery and Equipment*, pp. 17.

BROOKS, ROBERT B. JR., "Oldest of the Arts and Newest of the Professions," *The Appraisal Journal*, April, 950, pp. 201-204.

BROWN, GEORGE D., "The Effect of Building Height Upon Costs and Value," *The Valuation Manual*, 1964, pp. 271.

BROWN, J. BRUCE, "Our Profession - Viable In a Modern Economy," *Appraisal Institute Magazine*, Appraisal Institute of Canada, Winnipeg, March 1, 1972.

BROWN, JUANITA C, "Attributes of a Professional Appraiser," *Valutapes Audio-Library Series*, American Society of Appraisers, Washington D.C., January 1, 1973.

BROWN, R. K., "The Need for Generalists," *Appraisal Institute Magazine*, Appraisal Institute of Canada, Winnipeg.

BROWN, ROBERT K, "The Need for Generalists In the Appraisal Profession," *The Appraisal Journal*, May, 1960, pp. 219-224.

BROWN, ROBERT L, "The Generalist Revisited," *The Appraisal Journal*, May, 1965, pp. 227-231.

BROWNER, VINCENT, "Public Relations," *Assessment Administration*, Chicago, 1962, pp. 141-146.

BROZEN YALE, "Inflation-Smoke or Fire?," *The Appraisal Journal*, July, 1959, pp. 321-326.

BRUCHE, ALBERT, "What Constitutes Value?," *Technical Valuation*, June, 1958, pp. 45-46.

## BIBLIOGRAPHY OF APPRAISAL LITERATURE

BRUNSON, THEO R., "Responsibilities of Appraisers," *Right of Way*, 1962, pp. 28-31.

BRYSON, LYMAN, "Notes on a Theory of Advice," *The Appraisal Journal*, January, 1956, pp. 8-19.

BUCK, WALTER M. S., "The Theory of Straight Line Depreciation," *The Appraisal Journal*, July, 1948, pp. 317-320.

BUILDING INVESTMENT AND MAINTENANCE, "Problem of Obsolescence," *Building Investment and Maintenance*, October, 1925, pp. 35-36.

BURGESS, GEORGE V. T., "A Case Study of Inflation," *American Society of Appraisers Manual*, 1960, pp. 25.

BURKHEIMER, WILLIAM D., "Significant Ratios," *The Appraisal Journal*, January, 1940, pp. 30-35.

BURNELL, W. V., "The Three Approaches to Property Value," *Appraisal and Valuation Manual*, American Society of Appraisers, 1955, pp. 17-20.

BURNELL, WILLIAM U., "President's Message-Our Place In the Sun," *Technical Valuation*, October, 1954, pp. 5.

BURNELL, WILLIAM U., "Property Value, Three Approaches," *Technical Valuation*, February, 1955, pp. 17.

BURROUGHS, ROY J., "An Appraisal of an Appraiser's Proposals," *The Appraisal Journal*, July, 1933, pp. 340-345.

BURROWS, R. DOUGLAS, "Written Appraisal Policy," *The Review*, April, 1951, pp. 15-16.

BURT, F. P., "The Practical Value of Accurate Appraisals," *Buildings-And Building Management*, July, 1932, pp. 31-33.

BURTCH, THOMAS, "Reconversion," *The Appraisal Journal*, October, 1944, pp. 345-348.

CADENHEAD, G. M., "Net Realizeable Value Redefined," *Journal of Accounting Research*, April, 1970, pp. 138-140.

CALIFORNIA REAL ESTATE ASSOCIATION, "Contract for Employment for Appraisal Service," *The Appraising Manual by S. L. McMichael, Ed. 2*, 1937, pp. 550-551.

CALUSEN, DON H., "The Appraisers Task-Protecting the Public," *Appraisal and Valuation Manual*, Washington, D. C, January, 1972, pp. 4.

CALVIN, BRENDA, "Land and Landscape," Transatlantic Arts Inc., Levittown, N. Y..

CAMERON, C. C., "Appraising In a Time of Ample Credit," *The Appraisal Journal*, April, 1965, pp. 176-180.

CANNON, FERMOR S., "Boom Psychology---The Test of the Appraiser," *The Review of the Society of Residential Appraisers*, October, 1937, pp. 3-8.

CANTWELL, ROBERT C. III, "The Appraisal Process--Outline and Diagram," *The Appraisal Journal*, April, 1961, pp. 200-206.

CAPPER, G. C. F., "Decay, Development and Land Values," *Manchester School of Economic and Social Studies*, January, 1964, pp. 25-41.

CARMAN, LEWIS A., "Hoskold's Formula," *American Accountant*, April, 1931, pp. 104-106.

CARMAN, LEWIS A., "Substitute for Hoskold's Formula," *American Accountant*, May, 1931, pp. 136-139.

CARMICHAEL, D. R., MAYNARD, R. M., "Auditing and Reporting for Security Valuations," *Journal of Accounting*, April, 1971, pp. 67-68.

CARNEY, JOHN J., "The Development and Use of Gross Income Multipliers," *The Appraisal Journal*, April, 1963, pp. 221-227.

CARR, ANTHONY W., "Some Suggestions for Volume Appraisers," *The Real Estate Appraiser*, pp. 37.

CARROLL, WESLEY C., "The Responsibilty of the Independent Appraiser," *Proceedings of the Eighth Annual National Seminar of the American Right of Way Association*, Washington, D. C., 1962, pp. 41-42.

CASE, FRED E., "Lessons from European Appraisals," *The Residential Appraiser*, June, 1959, pp. 3-6.

CASE, FRED E., "New Decision Tools for Appraisers," *The Appraisal Journal*, January, 1967, pp. 21-27.

CASE, FRED E., "Value, Market Value, and Market Price," *The Appraisal Journal*, April, 1953, pp. 217-222.

CASE, FREDERICK E., *Real Estate*, Allyn and Bacon, Boston, 1962.

CASTENHOLZ, WILLIAM B., *Solution to the Appreciation Problem*, Lasalle Extension University, Chicago, 1931.

CAWTHRA, CHARLES E., "Appraisal Assignments," *Valuation*, American Society of Appraisers, September, 1972, pp. 94.

CHADEAYNE, ROBERT O., "Artist to Appraiser," *A. S. A. Valuation Manual*, American Society of Appraisers, Washington, D. C., 1958, pp. 57.

CHAFFE, R. S., "Physical Depreciation," *Review of Society of Residential Appraiser*, August, 1940, pp. 3-6, 16.

CHALMERS, T. G., "Comments on No Appreciation for Appreciation," *Appraisal Institute Magazine*, Appraisal Institute of Canada, Winnipeg.

CHAMBERLAIN, EDWARD, *Toward a More General Theory of Value*, Oxford University, New York, 1957.

CHAMBERS, R. J., "Measures and Values," *Accounting Review*, J, April, 1968, pp. 239-247.

CHANDIAS, MARIO A., "Invitacion Al Dialogo," *Boletin*, Sotave, Caracas, Venezuela, pp. 21-23.

CHANDIAS, MARIO E., "El Problema De Las Mejoras," *Boletin*, Sotave, Caracas, Venezuela, pp. 5-16.

CHANDIAS, MARIO E., "Introduccion Al Aprovechamiento," *Boletin*, Sotave, Caracas, Venezuela, pp. 7-10.

CHANDIAS, MARIO E., "Los Tasadores Concepto Moderno Valuacion," *Boletin*, Sotave, Caracas, Venezuela, pp. 7-16.

CHANDIAS, MARIO E., "Sobre La Ensenanza De La Tasacion," *Boletin*, Sotave, Caracas, Venezuela, pp. 7-9.

CHANDIAS, MARIO E., "Valuacion Por Puntos," *Boletin*, Sotave, Caracas, Venezuela, pp. 9-10.

CHANDLER, K. WILLIAM, "Going Deeper In Depth," *The Real Estate Appraiser*, October, 1964, pp. 27-30.

CHATTERS, CARL H., IRVING TENNER, *Municipal and Government Accounting*, Prentice-Hall, Englwd Cliffs, N. J., 1960.

CHERNEY, RICHARD A., "A New Look at Narrative Reports," *The Real Estate Appraiser*, pp. 14.

CHERNEY, RICHARD A., "The Profession's Responsibility for Training and Education," *Assessment Administration*, IAAO, Chicago, 1963, pp. 51-55.

CHERNEY, RICHARD A., "The Why and How of Deterioration," *The Appraisal Journal*, July, 1957, pp. 404-408.

CHESSMAN, MARK, "The Appraiser and Public Relations," *The Appraisal Journal*, July, 1937, pp. 273-277.

CHILD, JOHN FRANCIS, JR., "A More Direct Approach to Estimating Future Benefits," *The Appraisal Journal*, November, 1951, pp. 443-450.

CHURCH, BYRON, "Are Appraisers Talking to Themselves," *The Appraisal Journal*, July, 1958, pp. 393-396.

CHURCH, BYRON, "How Many Approaches," *The Real Estate Appraiser*, pp. 26.

CHURCH, BYRON, "What Good Is an Appraisal," *The Residential Appraiser*, May, 1961, pp. 9-11.

## BIBLIOGRAPHY OF APPRAISAL LITERATURE

CHURCH, BYRON M., "Consultation-The Appraiser's Ultimate Function," *The Real Estate Appraiser*, October, 1964, pp. 11-14.

CHURCH, BYRON M., "From Appraising to Counseling," *The Real Estate Appraiser*, American Ins. of Real Estate Appraisers, Chicago, January, 1964, pp. 16.

CHURCH, BYRON M., "Guide to a Successful Appraisal Practice," *The Real Estate Appraiser*, May, 1963, pp. 14-25.

CHURCH, BYRON M., "What's In the Bundle," *The Real Estate Appraiser*, August, 1967, pp. 29.

CHURCH, EUGENE B., "The Economic Elements of Buildings," *Real Estate Record and Builder's Guide*, February 27, 1932, pp. 9-10.

CHURCHILL, WINSTON S., "The Valuer and His Profession," *The Appraisal Journal*, July, 1966, pp. 326-328.

CLARK, C. D., "Economic Appraisal of Depreciation Policy," *Journal Of Business,* January, 1956, pp. 28-40.

CLARK, FRANK B., "What Appraisers Should Know and Study," *National Real Estate Journal*, May 7, 1924.

CLARK, HORACE F., "Bibliography," *Appraising the Home*, 1930, pp. 239-240.

CLARK, HORACE F., "How to Develop an Appraisal File: Collecting Information for a Central File on Real-Estate Values," *Appraising the Home*, 1930, pp. 247-251.

CLARK, HORACE F., "Suggestions for Teaching a Course of Study In Appraising the Home," *Appraising the Home*, 1930, pp. 243-246.

CLARK, HORACE F., "Value Analysis," *Appraising the Home*, 1930.

CLAUSEN, DON H., "The Appraiser's Task--Protecting the Public," *Technical Valuation,* American Society of Appraisers, Washington, September, 1966, pp. 32.

CLOPPER, SIMON, "The Annual School and In-Service Training In Maryland," *Assessment Administration,* IAAO, Chicago, 1959, pp. 132-138.

CLURMAN, ALBERT W., "Land Costs Vs. Land Allowance," *The Appraisal Journal*, October, 1964, pp. 604-605.

COES, HAROLD V., "Appraisals and Property Accounting," *National Association of Cost Accountants Bulletin,* May 1, 1932, pp. 1168-1174.

COFFIN, GEORGE H. JR., "The High Cost of Low Cost Appraising Shown to Be Penny-Wise, Pound-Foolish," *California Real Estate Magazine,* October, 1935, pp. 43.

COHN, WALTER W., "The Art of Testifying In Appraisal Cases," *Practical Appraising. Methods,* 1940, pp. 126-128.

COLLINS, G. ROWLAND, "Appraisal Scene," *The Residential Appraiser*, March, 1957, pp. 8-10.

COLLINS, G. ROWLAND, "The Form and Substance of a Dynamic Economy," *The Appraisal Journal,* April, 1951, pp. 165-171.

COMISKEY, E. E., "Market Respones to Changes In Depreciation Accounting," *Accounting Review,* April, 1971, pp. 279-285.

CONAN, ROBERT J., "Educational Groups Answer Advanced Training Need," *Appraisal Digest,* January, 1951, pp. 6-8.

CONAN, ROBERT J., "Should Appraised Value Contain Profits and Commissions," *Appraisal Digest,* July, 1954, pp. 17-18.

CONDICT, HAROLD V., "Appraisal Highlights," *The Review,* April, 1955, pp. 18-19.

CONDICT, HORACE V., "The Appraiser's Yardsticks," *The Appraisal Journal,* April, 1944, pp. 170-172.

CONRAN, C. L., "Valuation of Museum Objects," *Museums Journal.*

▲ **Appraisal Theory and Methods**

CONSER, EUGENE P., "Realtor's Obligation In Appraising," *Realtor's Headlines,* February 9, 1959, pp. 2.

CONSIDINE, CHARLES RAY, "Paper Prices," *The Review,* September, 1956, pp. 3-4.

CONSTAM, E., "Decisions! Decisions! Decisions!," *Appraisal Institute Magazine,* Appraisal Institute of Canada, Winnipeg.

CONSTAM, E., "P. R. for Appraisers," *Appraisal Institute Magazine,* Appraisal Institute of Canada, Winnipeg.

COOKE, JOHN, "One Judge's Views on Appraiser Certification or Licensing," *The Appraiser,* February, 1967.

COOPER, ARTHUR PH. D., *An Appraisal of the Forecasting Performance of the Council of Economic Advisers, Nichols,* Georgia St. University, 1971.

COPPOCK, D. J., "The Alleged Case Against Devaluation," *The Manchester School,* University of Manchester, September, 1965.

CORDIER, HENRY K., *Valuation Problems and the Client,* American Society of Appraisers.

COTTON, W. O., "Appraisals Help Salesmen Get Better Listings," *National Real Estate Journal,* May, 1940, pp. 15-17.

COULSON, ROBERT, *The Arbitration of Valuation Disputes,* American Society of Appraisers, Washington, September, 1968, pp. 52.

COULSON, ROBERT M, "The Professional Appraiser Looks at Arbitration," *Valutape Audio-Library Series,* American Society of Appraisers, Washington D.C., January 1, 1973.

COWLEY, LEONARD M., "The Lay Away Plan," *The Appraisal Journal,* July, 1954, pp. 353-358.

COX, WARREN E., "The Intrinsic Value of Art," *The A. S. A. Valuation Manual,* American Society of Appraisers, 1956, pp. 179.

CRAGIN, RAYMOND T., "Appraiser's Part Important In Figuring Assets of Companies," *Eastern Underwriter,* June 12, 1936, pp. 6.

CRAIG, R. H., "Real Estate In Halifax-Dartmouth," *Appraisal Institute Magazine,* Appraisal Institute of Canada, Winnipeg.

CRAMER, FLOYD, "Does the Price Freeze Affect Values," *The Review,* February, 1951, pp. 5-6.

CRIST, MARION, "History of the American Society of Appraisers," *A. S. A. Valuation Manual,* American Society of Appraisers, 1964, pp. 277.

CROCHERON, CLARENCE, "Appraisal As a Business Tool," *Commerce and Finance,* May, 1928, pp. 1023-1024.

CRONHEIM, DAVID, "Value and Purchase Price," *Newark Realtor,* August, 1941, pp. 1-2.

CUERPO TECNICO DE TASACIONES DEL PERU, "Tasaciones Del Peru: Capitulo V.," *Boletin,* Sotave, Caracas, Venezuela, pp. 45-48.

CUERPO TECNICO DE TASACIONES DEL PERU, **Tasaciones Peru: Capitulos I y II**," *Boletin,* Sotave, Caracas, Venezuela, pp. 15-23.

CUERPO TECNICO DE TASACIONES DEL PERU, **Tasaciones Peru: Capitulos III y IV**," *Boletin,* Sotave, Caracas, Venezuela, pp. 45-58.

CUERPO TECNICO DE TASACIONES DEL PERU, "Tasaciones Peru: Capitulos Vi y Vii," *Boletin,* Sotave, Caracas, Venezuela, pp. 45-56.

CUMMINS, C. R., "Basic Principles Appraisal Process," *Appraisal Institute Magazine,* Appraisal Institute of Canada, Winnipeg.

CUMMINS, C. R., "Notes on the Basic Principles of Valuation and the Appraisal Process," *The Appraisal Institute Magazine,* September, 1958, pp. 24-26.

CUMMINS, CHARLES A., "Faults of Present Appraisal Practice," *Constructor,* April, 1932, pp. 22-24.

D' RUGGIERO, LORENZO, "Indemnizacion En El Avaluo," *Boletin,* Sotave, Caracas, Venezuela, pp. 40-45.

DANGE, M N, "Valuation of Immovable Properties," *Sneh Babrekar Marg,* Dadar Bombay India, January 1, 1974.

DARBY, CLEMENT H., "Alternative Techniques of Appraising Values In an Inflationary Economy," *Appraisal and Valuation Manual,* American Society of Appraisers, 1962, pp. 213-217.

DARIO GONZALEZ, RUBEN, "El Concepto Del Uso Mejor Y Mas Productivo," *Boletin,* Sotave, Caracas, Venezuela, pp. 39-42.

DARM, ADAM EUGENE, *Graduate Appraisal of the Industrial Technology Program at California State College,* University of California, 1971.

DASSO, JEROME, "Economic Base Analysis for the Appraiser," *The Appraisal Journal,* 1969, pp. 374-335.

DAVENPORT, HERBERT JOSEPH, *Value and Distribution,* University of Chicago Press, Chicago, 1908.

DAVIDSON, WILLIAM R., "Retailing: Some Significant Current Developments," *The Appraisal Journal,* January, 1957, pp. 91-98.

DAVIES, CHARLES T., "Appraisal Review," *American Right of Way Association,* 1968, pp. 275-281.

DAVIS, J. CLARENCE, JR., "The Administrator's Requirements for Appraisers Services," *Appraisal and Valuation Manual,* American Society of Appraisers, 1961, pp. 5-9.

DAVIS, W. D., "A Critical Analysis of Government Appraising," *The Residential Appraiser,* January, 1961, pp. 3-5.

DAVIS, W. D., "Evidences of Market Value," *The Appraisal Journal,* April, 1959, pp. 224-253.

DAVIS, W. D., "In This I Believe," *The Appraisal Journal,* October, 1964, pp. 608-609.

DAVIS, W. D., "L'Analyse Du Revenu De La Mise De Fonds," *Appraisal Institute Magazine,* Appraisal Institute of Canada, Winnipeg.

DAVIS, W. D., "Professional Standards and the Appraiser's Future," *The Real Estate Appraiser,* May, 1963, pp. 2-7.

DAVIS, W. D., "What Is Market Value," *The Appraisal Journal,* January, 1960, pp. 42-46.

DAVIS, WILLIAM D., *The Cost Approach,* American Association of State Highway Officials, Washington, D. C., 1962, pp. 337-345.

DAVIS, WILLIAM D., *The Earnings Approach,* American Association of State Highway Officials, Washington, D. C, 1962, pp. 347-360.

DAVIS, WILLIAM D., *The Market Data Approach,* American Association of State Highway Officials, Washington, D. C, 1962, pp. 361-365.

DAVIS, WILLIAM M., "The Question of Value," *Right of Way,* October, 1956, pp. 15-16.

DAWLEY, CHESTER G., "Appraisal Educational Program," *Technical Valuation,* June, 1959, pp. 41-43, 46-50.

DAY DESMOND D., "Personalities of the Profession," *The Valuer,* The Commonwealth Institute of Valuers, Sydney, Australia, October 1, 1973, pp. 587-.

DE NOYELLES F., "Meriting Confidence," *The Review,* May, 1955, pp. 10-11.

DE SALES PEREZ, FRANCISCO, "El Avaluo En La Regulacion De Inmuebles," *Boletin,* Sotave, Caracas, Venezuela, pp. 11-12.

DE SALES PEREZ, FRANCISCO, "Impulso De La Tecnica Avaluatoria En Venezuela," *Boletin,* Sotave, Caracas, Venezuela, pp. 3-4.

DEBOOS, FRANK A., "Appraisals As an Aid In Real Estate Sales," *The Appraisal Journal,* January, 1952, pp. 110-113.

DEBREU, GERARD, "Theory of Value," Yale University Press, 1971.

▲ Appraisal Theory and Methods

DEMARA, CYRIL R., "On Forecasting Income," *The Appraisal Journal,* July, 1933, pp. 362.

DEMARA, CYRIL R., "Various Appraisal Avenues," *The Review,* April, 1947, pp. 9-11.

DEMMERY, JOSEPH, "Uncertainties In Appraising," *The Appraisal Journal,* January, 1943, pp. 35-38.

DENIS, J. W., "Can Present Market Value Be Determined," *Journal American Institute of Real Estate Appraisers,* April, 1934, pp. 253-256.

DERBES, MAX J., "Accrued Depreciation-Classical Method," *The Real Estate Appraiser,* pp. 2.

DERBES, MAX J. JR., "Common Denominators In the Appraisal Process," *The Real Estate Appraiser,* A.I.R.E.A., Chicago, May, 1964, pp. 28.

DERBES, MAX J. JR., "Dangers of the Double Contract," *The Real Estate Appraiser,* February, 1963, pp. 12-14.

DERBES, MAX J. JR., "The Consideration In Deed," *The Real Estate Appraiser.*

DEWEY, EDWARD R., E. F. DAKIN, "Cycles, the Science of Prediction, with 1950 Postscript," Holt, New York, 1949.

DILMORE, G., "Monetizing the Entrepreneurial Factor," *Appraisal Institute Magazine,* Appraisal Institute of Canada, Winnipeg.

DILMORE, GENE, "New Direction In the Income Approach," *The Real Estate Appraiser,*

DISTELHORST, CARL F., "Progress Within Our Tightrope Economy," *The Residential Appraiser,* April, 1957, pp. 7-12.

DITTRICH, N. E., *Accounting Implications of the Relative Objectivity of the Appraisal Process,* Dissertation Abstracts, Ann Arbor, January, 1967.

DOLAN, HARRY T., "Market Value-The Informed Guess," *The Appraisal Journal,* July, 1952, pp. 330-336.

DOLAN, THOMAS A., "Facts and Theories," *The Appraisal Journal,* April, 1946, pp. 165-168.

DOLMAN, JOHN P., "Responsibilities of the Appraiser," *The Appraisal Journal,* January, 1962, pp. 49-54.

DOLMAN, JOHN P., "The Appraiser of Tomorrow," *Right of Way,* April, 1970.

DOLMAN, JOHN P., "The Appraiser of Tomorrow," *The Appraisal Journal,* October, 1969, pp. 582-586.

DOLMAN, JOHN P., "The Appraiser's Dilemma," *The Appraisal Journal,* July, 1967, pp. 384.

DOODHA, KERSI D., "Analytical Study of Value Theory," M, Vora, A. Edition, pp. 62.

DORAU, HERBERT B., "Capitalization Rate Mirage or Wil-O-The-Wisp," *The Appraisal Journal,* January, 1961, pp. 19-29.

DORAU, HERBERT B., "Is Rote Right In Valuation," *Appraisal Digest,* April, 1960, pp. 6-9.

DORION, GUY, "Le Role De L Evaluateur," *Appraisal Institute Magazine,* Appraisal Institute of Canada, Winnipeg, June 1, 1973.

DOWNIE, LEONARD, "The Appraiser's Responsibility Under H. O. L. C. Property Appraisal Report Form," *The Appraisal Journal,* January, 1937, pp. 60-66.

DOWNS, ANTHONY, "Characteristics of Various Economic Studies," *The Appraisal Journal,* July, 1966, pp. 329-338.

DOWNS, JAMES C., *Principles of Real Estate Management,* 3rd Edition, Institute of Real Estate Management, Chicago, 1950.

DUBOIS, AYERS J., "Appraisal Problems," *The Review,* March, 1945, pp. 16-19.

DUBOIS, AYERS J., "Bracketing In Appraising," *The Appraisal Journal,* July, 1936, pp. 254-270.

DUBOIS, AYERS J., "Some Current Trends In Appraisal Thinking," *National Real Estate Journla,* August, 1939, pp. 34-37.

DUBOIS, AYERS J., "Theoretical Versus Practical Appraising," *Appraisal Journal,* April, 1933, pp. 200-203.

DUCK, BERKLEY W., "Determining Professional Fees," *The Appraisal Journal,* October, 1958, pp. 537-541.

DUDLEY, JAMES E., "The Acceptance of Improved Design," *The Residential Appraiser,* September, 1959, pp. 3-6.

DUFFY, GEORGE C., "The Disinterested Appraiser," *Right of Way,* April, 1963, pp. 13-20.

DUHAMEL, L. A., "Land Tenure In Alberta," *Appraisal Institute Magazine,* Appraisal Institute of Canada, Winnipeg.

DUNN, CECIL L., "The Influence of Income Payments Upon the Level Of Real Estate Prices," *The Appraisal Journal,* January, 1948, pp. 15-18.

DUNN, DOMINICK R., "Current Appraisal Perils," *The Real Estate Appraiser,* 1970, pp. 7-8.

DUNN, DOMINICK R., "Exact Science," *The Real Estate Appraiser,* October, 1964, pp. 25.

DUNN, DOMINICK R., "Knowledge of Architecture Valuable to Appraisers," *The Appraisal Journal,* April, 1949, pp. 243-245.

DUNN, DOMINICK R., "Only One Value," *Review of the Society of Residential Appraisers,* January, 1937, pp. 13-16.

DUNN, DOMINICK R., "The Causes of Value," *The Appraisal Journal,* July, 1963, pp. 411-414.

DUNN, DOMINICK R., "What Is Your Solution," *The Appraisal Journal,* October, 1963, pp. 520-521.

DUNN, DOMINICK R., "Why Vs. What," *The Real Estate Appraiser,* September, 1966, pp. 33.

DUNN, DOMINICK R., "Some Reflections on Value In Eminent Domain Proceedings," *The Appraisal Journal,* July, 1956, pp. 415-1.

DYKSTRA, GERALD O., "Bundle of Rights," *Michigan Business Review,* November, 1956, pp. 18-24.

DYKSTRA, GERALD O., AND L. G. DYKSTRA, *Business Law of Real Estate,* Mcmillan, New York, 1941.

EAGAN, LAURENCE J., "Personal Property Valuation," *Assessment Administration,* Institute of American Assessment Officers, Chicago, 1963, pp. 226-229.

EASTBURN, DAVID P., "Capacity and Inflation," *The Appraisal Journal,* January, 1985, pp. 118-120.

EASTWOOD H. W., "Changes In Some Statutory Land Valuation Requirements," *The Valuer,* The Commonwealth Institute of Valuers, Sydney, Australia, October 1, 1973, pp. 607-615.

ECKSTEIN, ARTHUR, "Publicity," *Technical Valuation,* American Society of Appraisers, February, 1954, pp. 7..

EDMAN, J. J., "Lack of Local Experience Not Always Disqualifies. Appraisal Docket," *The Appraisal Journal,* July, 1957, pp. 446-447.

EDMAN, J. J., "The Appraisal Docket. Appraiser Cannot Use Alternative Valuation Methods," *The Appraisal Journal,* January, 1961, pp. 125-126.

EDMAN, J. J., "The Appraisal Docket. Appraiser's Fee Not Part of Award," *The Appraisal Journal,* October, 1960, pp. 550-551.

EGERTON, J. W., "Valuation Day and the Professional Appraiser," *Appraisal Institute Magazine,* Appraisal Institute of Canada, Winnipeg, June 1, 1972.

EILERTS, HOPE, "Let's Get Back to Fundamentals," *The Real Estate Adpraiser,* American Institute of Real Estate Appraisers, pp. 13.

EINSTEIN, EDWIN M., "Suggestions for the Appraiser," *Review of the Society of Residential Appraisers,* July, 1936, pp. 9-12.

EISENLAUER, JACK F., "Mass Versus Individual Appraisers," *The Appraisal Journal*, October, 1968, pp. 533-535.

ELLIS, J. H., "Origin of the A.I.C.," *Appraisal Institute Magazine*, Appraisal Institute of Canada, Winnipeg, June 1, 1972.

ELLWOOD, L. W., "Emphasis on Equity," *Appraisal Institute Magazine*, Appraisal Institute of Canada, Winnipeg.

ELLWOOD, L. W., "Estimacion Capital Propio: Enfoque De Valor," *Boletin,* Sotave, Caracas, Venezuela, pp. 9-11.

ELLWOOD, L. W., "How Many Approaches to Value," *The Appraisal Journal,* October, 1951, pp. 518-525.

ELLWOOD, LEON W., "Artist or Mechanic? -Two More Independent Appraisals," *The Appraiser.*

ELLWOOD, LEON W., "Today's Appraiser Is a Specialist," *The Review,* April, 1945, pp. 14-15.

ELSE-MITCHELL, JUSTICE, "Duties and Liabilities of Valuers," *Appraisal Institute Magazine,* Appraisal Institute of Canada, Winnipeg, September 1, 1973.

ELY, RICHARD T., "Real Estate and National Planning," *Appraisal Journal,* July, 1940, pp. 222-225.

ELY, RICHARD T., AND G. S. WEHRWEIN,, *Land Economics,* B, Macmillan, pp. 470000.

ELY, RICHARD T., AND OTHERS, *Urban Land Economics,* B, Edwards Bros., pp. 220000.

ENGLE, NATHANIEL, "Business Research In the Appraisal Field," *The Appraisal Journal,* October, 1950, pp. 425-430.

ENGLEHORN, V. A., "The American Society Approach to Various Kinds of Value," *Journal of the American Society of Farm Managers and Rural Appraisers,* April, 1960, pp. 4-8.

EZEKIEL, MORDECAI, "Appraisal Data Research and Future Stabilization of Values," *Review of Society of Residential Appraisers,* April, 1938, pp. 7-11.

EZEKIEL, MORDECAI, "Data Research and Future Stabilization of Values," *Proceedings of the General Session and Urban Group Meetings, National Forum, 1937,*

FALLIN, G. H., "Current Appraisal Problems," *National Real Estate Journal,* September, 1940, pp. 15-17.

FALLON, C., "Put Value Back In Design," *Purchasing,* February 19, 1970, pp. 61-62.

FALLOON, WILBUR J., "Appraisal Fundamentals and Appraisal Terms," *The Appraisal Journal,* January, 1951, pp. 106-109.

FARRELL, PAUL B. JR., "Computer-Aided Financial Risk Simulation," *The Appraisal Journal,* January, 1969, pp. 58-73.

FAVA, EDWARD, "Effective Use of Appraisals by Brokers and Salesmen," *Appraisal Digest,* 1904, pp. 1-5.

FAVA, EDWARD, "The Appraisal Process," *Appraisal Digest,* 1907, pp. 13-17.

FEDERAL HOME LOAN BANK REVIEW, *Appraisal Methods and Policies,*

FEDERAL REAL ESTATE BOARD, *Advisory Committee Report of the Secretary,* July 10, 1923, pp. 22-23.

FEDERAL REAL ESTATE BOARD, "Letter to Heads of Departments and Establishments," *National Real Estate Journal,* January 18, 1923, pp. 18.

FEDERAL RESERVE BANK OF CLEVELAND, "Liquidity and Economic Stability," *The Appraisal Journal,* July, 1963, pp. 387-395.

FEDERAL RESERVE BANK OF CLEVELAND, "Potential Economic Growth of the United States During the Next Decade," *The Appraisal Journal,* July, 1955, pp. 413-420.

FEDERAL RESERVE BANK OF CHICAGO, "The Economic Consequences of the Baby Boom," *The Appraisal Journal,* April, 1956, pp. 208-212.

## BIBLIOGRAPHY OF APPRAISAL LITERATURE

FEDERAL RESERVE BANK OF DALLAS, "Economic Recovery," *The Appraisal Journal*, October, 1961, pp. 517-524.

FEDERAL RESERVE BANK OF ST. LOUIS, "Theory of the Determination of the Economic Activity Level," *The Appraisal Journal*, January, 1968, pp. 123-125.

FENTON, HARRY R., "Good Appraisers Have No Emotions," *Selected Readings In Right of Way*, 1968, pp. 197-201.

FENTON, HARRY R., "How to Use Market Data In Making an Appraisal," *The Appraisal Journal*, July, 1958, pp. 371-378.

FENTON, HARRY R., "The Logic--Stics of Appraising," *The Appraisal Journal*, April, 1960, pp. 190-192.

FERGUSON, HILL, "Making the Appraisal Carry Conviction," *The Appraisal Journal*, April, 1938, pp. 257-261.

FERGUSON, HILL, "Mass Appraising," *The Appraisal Journal*, April, 1943, pp. 156-161.

FIELD, RALPH V., "The Land Survey Systems of the United States," *The Appraisal Journal*, October, 1936, pp. 393-399.

FIFER, LOUIS J., "Mr. Appraiser Your P.R. Is Showing," *Appraisal Institute Magazine*, Appraisal Institute of Canada, Winnipeg.

FINBURGH, BERT J., "Using a FormAppraisal for an Out of Town Investor," *The Residential Appraiser*, October, 1960, pp. 15-21.

FINCH, NELSON E., "The Problems of the Broker and Promoter," *Valuation Manual*, 1955, pp. 62.

FISCHER, R. M., "Appraisals and Valuations," *Technical Valuations*, June, 1956, pp. 5.

FISCHER, R. M., "Standards," *Technical Evaluation*, June, 1954, pp. 64.

FISCHER, R. M., "The Use of Standards In Appraisal Practice," *The Appraisal Jouranl*, October, 1936, pp. 379-392.

FISHER, E. M., *Advanced Principles of Real Estate Practice*, Principles of Investment, New York City, 1930.

FISHER, E. M., "The Judgement of the Appraiser," *National Real Estate Journal*, February 20, 1928, pp. 41-42.

FISHER, ERNEST M., *Basic Elements of Appraisal*.

FISHER, ERNEST M., "Perspective In Appraisals," *The Appraisal Journal*, October, 1952, pp. 481-483.

FISHER, ERNEST M., "The Valuation of Real Estate," *Principles of Real Estate*, Macmillan Company, New York City, 1923, pp. 101-132.

FISHER, R. M., "Appraisal Accuracy," *Technical Valuation*, January, 1949, pp. 21-22, 24.

FISHER, R. M., "The Accuracy of Forecasts," *Technical Valuation*, June, 1955, pp. 17.

FISK, ELMORE A., "Appraising Theory and Practice," *Appraisal and Valuation Manual*, American Society of Appraisers, 1959, pp. 1-8.

FISKEN, A. J., *Qualifications of an Appraiser*, Mutual Savings Bank of Seattle, Washington, D. C, September 9, 1925, pp. 241.

FLORES, ORLANDO, "Principios Generales Valoracion De Bienes Raices," *Boletin*, Sotave, Caracas, Venezuela, pp. 27-33.

FOLEY, CLETIS R., "An Architects Guide to Lasting Design," *The Review*, February, 1952, pp. 12-17.

FOSTER, R. D., *An Emperical Investigation of the Kansas Sales-Ratio Study*, Dissertation Abstracts, Vol. Xxix, No. 10.

FREE, VICTOR J., "The Theory of Depreciation," *The Appraisal Journal*, January, 1939, pp. 46-53.

FREE, VICTOR J., "Upon These Things Have I Relied," *The Appraisal Journal*, January, 1938, pp. 30-36.

FRIDAY, DAVID, "An Extension of Value Theory," *Quarterly Journal of Economics*, 1922, pp. 197-219.

FRIEDMAN, ALBERT L., "Appraising the Human Equation," *Appraisal Digest*, July, 1959, pp. 8-12.

FRISSELL, ROBERT N., "The Professional Appraisal and Market Value," *The Appraisal Journal*, October, 1966, pp. 581-584.

FROST, BENNETT H., "Destroyers of Value," *The Real Estate Appraiser*, June, 1963, pp. 29-31.

FULLER, R. S., "Competition Rises Again," *The Review*, February, 1949, pp. 3-5.

FULLERTON, D. H., "National Capital Commission Land Ownership," *Appraisal Institute Magazine*, Appraisal Institute of Canada, Winnipeg.

GADDIS, PERCY A., "Concept of Value," *The Appraisal Journal*, April, 1935, pp. 269.

GADDIS, PERCY A., "On Horizontal Division of Values," *The Appraisal Journal*, July, 1936, pp. 325-328.

GAGE, DANIEL D. JR., PERCY D. BENTLEY, "Architecture In Appraisal Reports," *National Real Estate Journal*, September, 1941, pp. 11-14.

GALLAHER, JOSEPH A. SR., "A Promise Made a Promise Fulfilled," *Technical Valuation*, February, 1956, pp. 41-44.

GAMBLE, W. P., "Current Appraisal Problems," *Journal of the American Society of Farm Managers and Rural Appraisers*, October, 1949, pp. 109-115.

GAMMON, GEORGE W., "Capital Recovery with Changing Price Levels," *Valuation ASA*, September, 1968, pp. 25.

GARRETT, THOMAS M., "Professions, Association, and Codes," *The Appraisal Journal*, October, 1965, pp. 555-562.

GARRISON, BURL L., "The Three Dimensions of Value," *The Real Estate Appraiser*, May, 1963, pp. 29-32.

GEORGE, ALLAN C., "The Economic Pendulum Swings," *The Appraisal Journal*, July, 1944, pp. 253-257.

GIBSON, BRUCE G., "The Professional Appraiser and Public Relations," *American Society of Appraisers*, 1960, pp. 391-398.

GILLESPIE, JOHN, "An Appraisal of the Profession of Appraising," *The Residential Appraiser*, June, 1962, pp. 19-20, 24.

GILLIS, BRUCE D., "In-Service Training South Dakota," *Assessment Administration*, I. A. A. O, Chicago, 1961, pp. 142-144.

GITTERMAN, A. N., "Decrement As an Appraisal Problem," *Review, Society of Residential Appraisers*, June, 1939, pp. 9-12.

GITTERMAN, A. N., "Pointed Suggestions on Appraisals," *National Association of Real Estate Boards*, 1927, pp. 251-262.

GITTERMAN, A. N., "Uniform Appraisal Factors," *Real Estate Record and Builders Guide*, June 17, 1933, pp. 7.

GLASS, EDWARD F., "Common Errors In Appraising," *The Review*, December, 1949, pp. 3-6.

GODIN, C. R., "Income Approach Applied to Mass Appraisals," *American Society of Appraisers*, 1960, pp. 161-168.

GODIN, CAMILLE R., "Professionalism," *Assessors News Letter*, June, 1963, pp. 67-70.

GOLDEN, G. A., "Counteracting the Dollar's Fluctuations," *The Review*, August, 1951, pp. 3-6.

GOLDEN, G. A., "The Reasoning Behind Capitalization of Income," *The Review*, May, 1948, pp. 3-8.

GOLDFARB, MORRIS, "On Entrepreneur's Increment," *The Appraisal Journal*, January, 1936, pp. 82-84.

GOLDFARB, MORRIS, "On the Residual Process In Max Tieger's Appraisal," *The Appraisal Journal*, April, 1933, pp. 250-251.

GOLDSTEIN, GEORGE, "An Appraisal of Property with Improvements Fully Depreciated," *American Institute of Real Estate Appraisers*, 1949.

GOLDSTONE, BRACTON, "The New Deal In Appraising," *The Appraisal Journal*, April, 1933, pp. 199-204.

GONZALES, C. S., "The Future of Professional Appraising, In Spanish Speaking Countries," Corporate Press Inc., pp. 308-312.

GONZALEZ VALE, LUIS, "El Justiprecio Judicial," *Boletin*, Sotave, Caracas, Venezuela, pp. 35-39.

GONZALEZ, CONCHA J., *Tierra Y Valorizacion*, La Reforma Tributaria Municipal, Antares, 1956.

GOSSELIN, JACQUES, "L Avenir Des Evaluateurs Et De La Profession De L Evaluateurs," *Appraisal Institute Magazine*, June, 1962, pp. 18-21.

GOSSELIN, JACQUES, "L'Avenir Des Evaluateurs," *Appraisal Institute Magazine*, Appraisal Institute of Canada, Winnipeg.

GRANT, E. L., P. T. NORTON, *Depreciation*, Ronald, New York City, 1955.

GRAY, GEORGE H., "Relation of Management to Value," *The Appraisal Journal*, April, 1934, pp. 244-246.

GRAY, RICHARD J., "Current Union Policies," *The Review*, October, 1945, pp. 1, 10.

GREENBAUM, MICHAEL, "Appraisals, Appraisers, and the Regulatory Bodies," *Appraisal and Valuation Manual*, Washington, D. C., January, 1972, pp. 10.

GREENEBAUM, MICHAEL, "Appraisals, Appraisers, and the Regulatory Bodies," *Technical Valuation*, A. S. A, Washington, September, 1966.

GREENESTREET, KELVIN, "Why Three Approaches to Value," *The Appraisal Journal*, July, 1957, pp. 391-392.

GRIMES, JOHN A., WILLIAM H. GRAIGUE, *Principles of Valuation*, Prenticehall Incorporated, New York City, 1928, pp. 274.

GROVES, ASA B., "The V. A. -Past and Future," *The Review*, November, 1951, pp. 17-20.

GROVES, HAROLD M., *Financing Government*, Henry Holt and Company, New York, 1964, pp. 618.

GRUNSKY, CARL E., GRUNSKY, CARL E., JR, "Appreciating and the Unearned Increment," *Valuation, Depreciation and the Rate-Base*, New York, 1917, pp. 387.

GRUNSKY, CARL E., GRUNSKY, CARL E., JR, "Expectancy and Remaining Value," *Valuation, Depreciation, and the Rate-Base*, pp. 293-301.

GUATEMALA AUDIENCIA, *Tasaciones De Los Pueblos De La Provincia De Yucatan*, Guatemala, pp. 103.

GUEST, CHRISTOPHER WILLIAM GRAHAM, *Guest on Valuation*, W. Hodte, London, 1954.

GUMP, RICHARD, *Good Taste Costs No More*, Doubleday and Company.

GUTHMANM, H. G., *Financial Arrangements of the Chicago Fraction Plan*, Harvard Business Review, July, 1931.

HAAGLAND, HENRY E., *Real Estate Principles*, Mcgraw-Hill, New York, 1949.

HAAS, DR. ROBERT BARLETT, "All About Collecting and the Adult Learner," *Appraisal and Valuation Manual*, Corporate Press Incorporated, Washington, D. C, January, 1972, pp. 416.

HAGEN, O., "Elements of Value," *Stats Konomisk Tidsskrift*, March, 1967, pp. 39-51.

HAGOOD, WAYNE D., "Professionalism, a Cooperative Effort" *The Residential Appraiser*, March, 1962, pp. 22-23.

HAIG, GRAEME T., "Role of the Appraiser In Arbitration," *Appraisal Institute Magazine,* Appraisal Institute of Canada, Winnipeg.

HAIGHT, JAMES R., "Money---The Measuring Stick of Values," *The Appraisal Journal,* October, 1942, pp. 340-346.

HAIGHT, JAMES R., "Some Factors Determining Future Values," *National Real Estate Journal,* January, 1940, pp. 34-37.

HALE, JAMES R., "Danger In Horseback Appraisals," *Technical Valuation,* February, 1954, pp. 12.

HALL, C. W., "Appraisal Report Card," *Residential Appraisers Review,* August, 1935, pp. 7.

HALL, FRANK D., "Appraising the Future," *National Real Estate Journal,* July, 1941, pp. 25-26.

HALL, FRANK D., "Estimating, Probabilities Called Responsibility of Appraiser," *Appraisal Digest,* January, 1953, pp. 1-3.

HALL, FRANK D., "On the Prophetic Analysis of Future Benefits In Max Tieger's Appraisal," *The Appraisal Journal,* April, 1933, pp. 247-248.

HALL, FRANK D., "What Makes a Good Appraisal?," *The Appraisal Journal,* October, 1938, pp. 323-328.

HALL, HARRY H., "Managing a Nationwide Appraisal Staff," *The Review,* April, 1948, pp. 3-8.

HALL, HARRY H., "Rx for Overworked Appraisers," *The Review,* July, 1946, pp. 3-8.

HALL, JOHN H., "The Public Image of Real Estate," *Appraisal Institute Magazine,* Appraisal Institute of Canada, Winnipeg.

HALL, ROBERT W., "Speak for Yourself," *The Appraisal Journal,* October, 1960, pp. 537-538.

HAMILTON, ANDREW C., "Appraisals Under the Federal Securities Act," *The Appraisal Journal,* January, 1935, pp. 176-179.

HAMILTON, ANDREW C., "Judicial Review of Appraisals," *The Appraisal Journal,* October, 1934, pp. 80-82.

HANCOCK, M. L., "Replot by Value," *Appraisal Institute Magazine,* Appraisal Institute of Canada, Winnipeg.

HANFORD, LLOYD D., "Management and Appraising," *The Appraisal Journal,* January, 1961, pp. 53-56.

HANSON, ALDEN W., "Appraiser's Expenses," *The Real Estate Appraiser,* S.R.E.A., Chicago, July, 1964, pp. 2.

HANSON, PETER, "The Meaning of Market Value," *National Real Estate Journal,* May 11, 1931, pp. 35-36.

HANSON, PETER, "The Meaning of Value," *The Appraisal Journal,* July, 1933, pp. 289-297.

HARVEY, ROBERT O., "Observations on the Cost Approach," *The Appraisal Journal,* October, 1953, pp. 514-518.

HAYES, DOUGLAS, "Economic Characteristics and Managerial Performance-The Quantitative Appraisal," *Appraisal and Management of Securities,* pp. 127.

HAYNES, J. L., "The Appraisal In the Registration Statement," *The Appraisal Journal,* October, 1935, pp. 417-421.

HAYNES, JUSTIN H., "Some Thoughts on Group Depreciation," *Technical Valuation,* February, 1956, pp. 11-21.

HEAD, GEORGE J., "Valuation Under Modern Condition," *The Appraisal Journal,* April, 1935, pp. 212-222.

HEALEY, F.J., "Musing on Multipliers," *The Real Estate Appraiser,* January, 1963, pp. 21-22.

HEER, CLYDE W., "Building a Profitable Appraisal Business," *Address Given at N. Y. State Society of Real Estate Appraisers' District Conference at Syra. Roch.,* April 16, 1941.

HEINEKE, PAUL H., "Appraisers on Trial," *The Review,* July, 1951, pp. 3-7.

HELD, HARRY, "Appraisal Fundamentals," *Appraisal Digest*, 1958, pp. 18-21.

HERZER, T. O. F., "Proper Appraisal Practices," *Journal of the American Society of Farm Managers and Rural Appraisers*, October, 1945, pp. 134-140.

HEWITT, JOHN A., "What Do You Think About Appraisers and Appraising?Appraising," *The Appraiser*, October, 1970.

HIGNETTE, H. W., "Changing Patterns In the Appraisal Profession," *Appraisal Institute Magazine*, Canada, 1970.

HINDS, DUDLEY S., RICHARD HEWITT III, STEVEN D. KAPPLIN, "Professionalism In the Practice of Real Est Apprsl," *Appraisal Institute Magazine*, Appraisal Institute of Canada, Winnipeg.

HITCHINGS, T. C. JR., "Epilogue and Prologue," *The Appraisal Journal*, January, 1965, pp. 15-22.

HOAGLAND, HENRY E., *Real Estate Principles*, Mcgraw-Hill, New York, 1955.

HOAGLAND, HENRY E., "The Appraisal Process," *Real Estate Principles*, 1940, pp. 511.

HODDESON, DAVID, "Cracked Facade," *The Appraisal Journal*, October, 1957, pp. 527-532.

HODGES, M. B. JR., "Professional Appraisal Fees," *The Real Estate Appraiser*, Chicago, June, 1964, pp. 17.

HODGES, M. B. JR., "The Appraiser In Today's Changing Community," *The Appraisal Journal*, January, 1969, pp. 12-14.

HOFFMAN, JUDGE MURRAY, "Hoffman's Depth Rule," *Appraising Manual, Second Edititon*, 1937, pp. 359, 652.

HOGUET, ROBERT LOUIS, "What About the Future of Real Estate," *Real Estate Record*, October 26, 1940, pp. 3-4.

HOLBROOK, JEFFREY, "Who's to Blame for Divergencies In Valuation," *The Residential Appraiser*, May, 1961, pp. 3-4.

HOLCOMB, J. M., "An Academic Approach to Professional Management," *Journal of the American Society of Farm Managers and Rural Appraisers*, October, 1963, pp. 25-27.

HOLDEN, THOMAS S., "The Management Era," *The Appraisal Journal*, October, 1940, pp. 320-324.

HOLDEN, THOMAS S., AND CLYDE SHUTE, "Economy to Expand Under New National Management," *The Appraisal Journal*, April, 1953, pp. 175-180.

HOLLEBAUGH, CLIFFORD W., "Facts Vs. Fallacies In Real Estate Appraising," *The Appraisal Journal*, April, 1951, pp. 246-251.

HOLLEBAUGH, CLIFFORD W., "Market Data -- and Comparable Properties," *The Appraisal Journal*, 1952, pp. 74-79.

HOLLEBAUGH, CLIFFORD W., "The Narrative Report," *The Review*, December, 1949, pp. 12-14.

HOLLEBAUGH, CLIFFORD W., "Watch Your Language," *The Appraisal Journal*, October, 1958, pp. 508-512.

HOLT, DARRELL M., "An MAI's Report on His Impressions of the Fig Congress," *The Appraiser*, October, 1968.

HOOKER, JOHN P., *Correct Appraisal Methods*, Annals of Real Estate Practice, Vol. I, 1927, pp. 174-185.

HOOVER, RICHARD I., "What Is Market Analysis?," *The Appraisal Journal*, December, 1967, pp. 61-63.

HOPKINS, CHARLES I., "The VA Viewpoint," *The Review*, pp. 3-6, 10.

HOPPE, JOHN G. JR., "Serendipity and the Student of Appraisal," *Appraisal Journal*, April, 1967, pp. 177.

HORAN, GEORGE B., *Appraisal Fundamentals*, New York State Association of Real Estate Boards, New York.

HOYT, ELIZABETH ELLIS, *Primitive Trade, It's Psychology and Economics*, A. M. Delley, New York, 1968.

HOYT, GEORGE H., "Round Table Discussion of Fee, Competitive Bidding and Ethics," *Technicalities*, February, 1950, pp. 26-27.

HOYT, HOMER, "Appraisal of Different Types of Real Property," *The Appraisal Journal*, July, 1964, pp. 383-393.

HOYT, HOMER, "Schizophrenia In the Social Sciences," *The Appraisal Journal*, July, 1965, pp. 433-437.

HOYT, HOMER, "The Appraisal Process In a Price-Controlled Economy," *The Appraisal Journal*, April, 1945, pp. 138-147.

HOYT, JOHN R., "On Standards In Appraisal Practice," *The Appraisal Journal*, January, 1937, pp. 72-73.

HUBBARD, CHARLES L., *Theory of Valuation*, International Text Book Company, Scranton, 1969.

HUBIN, VINCENT J., "The Three Approaches to Value," *The Real Estate Appraiser*, January, 1969, pp. 37-42.

HUCK, ROBERT, "La Tecnica Del Avaluo," *Boletin*, Sotave, Caracas, Venezuela, pp. 11-15.

HUDER, K. LEE, "The Administrative Joker In the Federal Securities Act," *The Appraisal Journal*, April, 1935, pp. 223-228.

HUDSEN, H. R., "Knowledge of Appraising Valuable Asset of the Broker," *The Appraisal Journal*, October, 1953, pp. 550-554.

HUFFMAN, WILLIAM H., "Giving the Land Owner a Fair and Square Deal," *Right of Way*, August, 1962, pp. 7-10.

HUGHES, JAMES J., *A Preliminary and Partial Survey of Sources of Appraisal Data and Information*, January, 1960.

HUGHES, RICHARD, "Washington Report," *The Real Estate Appraiser*, pp. 56.

HULTEN, JOHN J., "Appraisal Methods In Hawaii," *Appraisal and Valuation Manual*, ASA, 1960, pp. 97-108.

HUMPHREYS, LESTER W., "Real and Personal Property," *Right of Way*, February, 1958, pp. 37-40.

HUNTER, HAMILTON W., "The Cost of Quality," *The Review*, December, 1952, pp. 3-7.

HURD, RICHARD M., "Observations on Building Obsolescence," *Real Estate Record*, April 12, 1940, pp. 5-7.

HURTADO MARTINEZ, LUIS, ALBERTO ANGULO LOPEZ, "El Valor De Los Terrenos Para Uso Multifamiliar," *Boletin*, Sotave, Caracas, Venezuela, pp. 35-37.

HUTCHINS, ROBERT MAYNARD, "What Man Has Made of His World," *The Appraisal Journal*, April, 1947, pp. 218-220.

HYAM, LESLIE A., "Appraisal of Fine Arts," *Technical Valuation*, ASA, Washington, October, 1953, pp. 11.

HYDER, K. LEE, *A Question of Value*, November 15, 1938, pp. 348.

HYDER, K. LEE, "Appraisals for Purposes of Public Financing," *The Appraisal Journal*, October, 1935, pp. 422-432.

HYDER, K. LEE, "The Appraisal Process," *The Appraisal Journal*, January, 1936, pp. 13-25.

JACKSON, FRAND W., "The Economics of Obsolescence and Inutility," *The Appraisal Journal*, January, 1938, pp. 22-29.

JACKSON, HOWARD F., "Basic Problems In the Income Approach," *The Real Estate Appraiser*, SREA, Chicago, July, 1964, pp. 35.

JACKSON, KENNETH N., "A Little Learning," *The Residential Appraiser*, October, 1962, pp. 15-16.

JACOBS, THEODORE M., "Municipal Finance," *Municiple Finance*, August, 1937, pp. 27-31.

JAMES, M. F., "What Is the Economic Life of Property In Appraising," *National Real Estate Journal,* April, 1939, pp. 49-50.

JAMES, M. H., "Market Influence on Value," *Review of the Society of Residential Appraisers,* July, 1936, pp. 3, 12.

JAMIESON, J. B., "Equity Participation," *Appraisal Institute Magazine,* Appraisal Institute of Canada, Winnipeg.

JARRETT, R. J., "The Future Appraisal Profession," *Appraisal Institute Magazine,* Appraisal Institute of Canada, Winnipeg.

JEFFERY, RICHARD, "Foundation for Success In Appraising," *The Appraisal Journal,* July, 1947, pp. 326-329.

JENKINS, RALPH W., "Something to Think About," *Technical Valuation,* American Society of Appraisers, Washington, December, 1967, pp. 8.

JOHNSON, CLIFFORD R., "The Major Problem In Making and Using Estimates of Market Value," *The Residential Appraiser,* August, 1961, pp. 21-23.

JOHNSON, JESSE W., "Appraising Today - and Every Day," *The Appraisal Journal,* October, 1949, pp. 461-466.

JOHNSON, U. WEBSTER, RALEIGH BARLOW, *Land Problems and Policies,* Mcgraw-Hill, New York, 1954.

JOHNSTON, DOUGLAS, "Gold Movements and Interest Rates - One Individual's Views," *The Appraiser,* February, 1968.

JONES, DR. OLIVER H., "More Storm Warnings Going Up on Accelerating Inflation Rate," *The Appraiser,* December, 1968.

JOUR OF AMER SOC OF FARM MGRS & RURAL APPRAISERS, "Minimum Provisions for an Act to Certify Real Property Appraisers," *Journal of the American Society of Farm Managers and Rural Appraisers,* October, 1962, pp. 62-66.

JOUR OF AMER SOC OF FARM MGRS & RURAL APPRAISERS, "The American Rural Appraisal System," *Journal of the American Society of Farm Managers and Rural Appraisers,* October, 1946, pp. 84-99.

JUDSON, A. R., "Appraising Under Virgin or Changing Conditions," *Journal of the American Society of Farm Managers and Rural Appraisers,* April, 1950, pp. 51-59.

JURETTE, LOUIS J., "History of the American Society of Appraisers," *American Society of Appraisers, Appraisal Institute Magazine,* 1960.

KAHN, SANDERS A., *State Registration of Appraisers,* ASA, Chicago, 1955, pp. 258-263.

KAHN, SANDERS A., "Land, Does it Depreciate," *The Real Estate Appraiser,* January, 1969, pp. 28-31.

KAHN, SANDERS A., "The Entrepreneur --The Missing Factor," *The Appraisal Journal,* October, 1963, pp. 472-476.

KAHN, SANDERS A., "The Return of Feasibility to Lums," *Valuation,* February, 1965, pp. 15-17.

KAHN, SANDERS A., WILLIAM SMITH, "The Need for State Registration of Appraisers," *Technical Valuation,* ASA, Jamaica, June, 1955, pp. 37.

KAMINS, R. M., "Democratic Centralism, Local Finance In the Soviet Union," *National Tax Journal,* December, 1962, pp. 353-367.

KANN, BRUCE E., "Selecting a Value," *Technical Valuation,* December, 1967, pp. 36.

KARKOW, WALDERMAR, "The Sheridan - Karkow Formula In Practice," *Real Estate Record,* April 20, 1935, pp. 24-26.

KAZDIN, S. EDWIN, "Appraising the Techniques of Appraising," *National Real Estate Journal,* November, 1938, pp. 58-60.

KAZDIN, S. EDWIN, "Custom Tailored Appraisals," *Appraisal Digest,* July, 1954, pp. 13.

▲ Appraisal Theory and Methods

KAZDIN, S. EDWIN, "On Land," *The Appraisal Journal*, April, 1938, pp. 166-167.

KAZDIN, S. EDWIN, "The Value Concept In Appraising," *The Appraisal Journal,* January, 1953, pp. 47-53.

KAZDIN, S. EDWIN, "The Zone of Reasonable Doubt," *The Appraisal Journal,* October, 1962, pp. 489-493.

KAZDIN, S. EDWIN, "What Price Market Value," *Appraisal Digest,* October, 1952, pp. 1-4.

KECK, JOHN G., "Obsolescence," *Journal of Certified Property Managers,* December, 1938, pp. 119-127.

KELLER, HARRY K., "Appraisal Review Procedure," *The Appraisal Journal,* October, 1945, pp. 379-389.

KELLEY, ARTHUR C., "Value As an Accounting Concept," *Journal of Accountancy,* July, 1935, pp. 50-52.

KELLOUGH, W. R., "Characteristics of Value," ASA, 1964, pp. 225.

KELLOUGH, W. R., "Critical Essays," *The Appraisal Journal,* October, 1960, pp. 462-464.

KELLOUGH, W. R., "Essays on Land Economics," *The Real Estate Appraiser,* May, 1969, pp. 31-34.

KELLOUGH, W. R., "Motivation," *Technical Valuation,* pp. 13.

KENNEDY, D. A., "Qualifications Appraisal Society of Societies," *Appraisal Institute Magazine,* Appraisal Institute of Canada, Winnipeg.

KENNEDY, R. D., "On Obtaining Accreditation," *Appraisal Institute Magazine,* Appraisal Institute of Canada, Winnipeg.

KENNY, NORMAN W., "Inadequate Improvements," *The Appraisal Journal,* October, 1932, pp. 53-55.

KENT, FRAND W., "A Search Into the Unknown," *Appraisal and Valuation Manual,* Washington, D.C., January, 1972.

KERSHOW WARREN W, "Using the Appraiser Effectively," *The Real Estate Appraiser,* The Society of Real Estate Appraisers, Chicago Illinois, January 1, 1974, pp. 36-39.

KING, BEN E., "Moral and Legal Concepts Governing Appraisals," *Thereview,* January, 1956, pp. 12-17.

KING, PAT, "Market Value-What Is it," *Appraisal Institute Magazine,* Appraisal Institute of Canada, Winnipeg.

KING, WILLFORD I., "Dependence of Real Estate Values Upon National Income," *The Appraisal Journal,* January, 1941, pp. 29-33.

KINNAID, WILLIAM N. JR., "New Thinking In Appraisal Theory," *Creues Reprint Series No. 2,* August, 1966.

KINNARD, W. N., "New Thinking In Appraisal Theory," *Appraisal Institute Magazine,* Appraisal Institute of Canada, Winnipeg.

KINNARD, WILLIAM N. JR., "Income Property Valuation," *Society of Real Estate Appraisers,* Chicago, Illinois.

KINNARD, WILLIAM N. JR., "New Thinking In Appraisal Theory," *Appraisal Institute Magazine,* 1969.

KISSACK, A. B., "Future Income and Present Value," *Real Estate Analyst Appraisal Bulletin,* 1947, pp. 245-248.

KISSACK, A. B., "On Price As a Measure of Value," *The Appraisal Journal,* October, 1936, pp. 439-442.

KISSACK, A. B., "Selling Prices As Indices of Value," *The Appraisal Journal,* April, 1938, pp. 220-226.

KISSACK, A. B., "Unbalanced Markets," *The Appraisal Journal,* April, 1946, pp. 144-147.

KLAASEN, R. L., "Appraised Value," *Appraisal Institute Magazine,* Appraisal Institute of Canada, Winnipeg.

KNISKERN, P. W., "The Appraiser," *Real Estate Appraisal and Valuation,* 1933, pp. 187-204.

KNISKERN, PHILIP W., "Appraisal and Architects," *Architectural Forum,* April, 1934, pp. 291-292.

KNISKERN, PHILIP W., "On the Residual Process In Max Tieger's Appraisal," *The Appraisal Journal,* April, 1933, pp. 249-250.

KNISKERN, PHILIP W., "The Difficulties and Menaces In Professional Practice," *The Appraisal Journal,* July, 1955, pp. 334-340.

KNISKERN, PHILIP W., "Twenty Years by Certificate Number One," *The Appraisal Journal,* October, 1952, pp. 456-462.

KNISKERN, PHILIP W., "Valuations Under Varying Circumstances," *The Appraisal Journal,* July, 1948, pp. 356-359.

KNISKERN, PHILIP W., "Why Appraisals Should Be Based on Income," *National Real Estate Journal,* September 16, 1929, pp. 29-30.

KOSTER, STUART J., "Economic Aspects of Property Appraisals," *Valuation Manual,* 1960, pp. 49.

KOSTERS, STUART F., "Professional Fees for Professional Services," *Technical Valuation,* November, 1955, pp. 16-18.

KRANZ, MARTIN E., "The Three Approaches to Value," *Appraisal and Valuation Manual,* 1958, pp. 27-28.

KREVOR, HENRY H., *A Congressional Study of Just Compensation,* American Society of Appraisers, 1962, pp. 16-27.

KUEHNLE, WALTER R., *Fundamental Approaches,* The Society of Industrial Realtors, 1953, pp. 5-17.

KURTZ, EDWIN B., *Life Expectancy of Physical Property Based on Mortality Laws,* The Ronald Press, New York, 1930.

KURTZ, EDWIN B., *The Science of Valuation and Depreciation,* The Ronald Press, New York, N. Y, 1937, pp. 221.

KYLE, G. IRWIN, "Do You Consider Yourself a Qualified Appraiser," *The Appraisal Digest,* January, 1951, pp. 19-20.

LAHDE, WALTER, MYERS, WILLS, "Reducing Variations In Independent Appraisals," *Assessors News Letter,* July, 1962, pp. 77-81.

LAIRD, JOHN, *The Idea of Value,* A. M. Kelley, New York, 1969.

LALONDE, JEAN G., "Qu Est-Ce Qu Un Evaluateur," *Appraisal Institute Magazine,* Appraisal Institute of Canada, Winnipeg, September 1, 1973.

LAMARRE, JOHN H., "Probable Future of Fine Arts Appraisal," *Technical Valuation,* A. S. A, Washington, November, 1954, pp. 41.

LANDMAN, A., "What'S Wrong with Using Appraisal Values," *Journal of Accountancy,* March, 1971, pp. 81-82.

LANG, RICHARD O., "The Current Economic Scene," *The Review,* July, 1900, pp. 3-5.

LANGLANDS, I. H., "An Engineer Looks at the Appraisal Process," *Appraisal Institute Magazine,* Appraisal Institute of Canada, Winnipeg.

LANGUM, JOHN D., "The Business Cycle Is Not Yet Dead," *The Appraisal Journal,* October, 1959, pp. 509-515.

LANSING, JOHN B., "The Public's Appraisal," *The Review,* November, 1954, pp. 16-17.

LARSEN, A., "Changes In Land Values In the United States 1925-1962," *Dissertation Abstracts,* Ann Arbor, December, 1966, pp. 1492-A.

LARSEN, DAVID R., "Comparable Sales," *The Review,* April, 1945, pp. 5-7.

LARSEN, DAVID R., "The Appraiser'S Tools and Forms," *The Review,* March, 1949, pp. 6-15.

LAUER, ROBERT L., MATHEWS, MYRON L., "American Society of Appraisers-A Reality," *Technical Valuation,* November, 1952, pp. 26-29.

LAUNER, E. J., "Problems on Market and Cash Value," *Technical Valuation,* October, 1958, pp. 25-27.

LAUNER, E. J., "The Development of Appraisal Methods," *Appraisal and Valuation Manual,* American Society of Appraisers, 1958, pp. 1-26.

LAUNER, E. J., "The Significance of the American Society of Appraisers In the Appraisal Field," *Technical Valuation,* February, 1959, pp. 3-4.

LAWRENCE, DAVID M., MAY, HAROLD G, REES, W. H, *Modern Methods of Valuation of Land, Housing, and Buildings,* The Estates Gazette, London, 1949, pp. 2.

LAWRENCE, DAVID M., REES, W. H, *Modern Methods of Land, Houses, and Buildings,* Estates Gazette, London, 1956.

LAWRENCE, THOMAS, "The Economics of Taste," *Review of Market Prices,* New York, pp. 363.

LAYMAN, JOHN J., "National and Local Money Market and Its Effect Upon Real Property," *Proceedings of the Fourth Annual National Seminar,* American Right of Way Association, Washington, D. C, 1959, pp. 72-75.

LEE, ADELBERT W., "The Appraiser and Washington, D. C," *Technical Valuation,* February, 1957, pp. 33-34.

LEHR, WALTER G. JR., "Consultation In Appraising," *The Real Estate Appraiser,* January, 1959, pp. 3-5.

LEIGHLY, WILLIAM LEWIS, "Principles of Capitalization Methods In Appraising Income Property," *National Real Estate Journal,* June, 1939, pp. 44-46.

LEMLEY, B. W., "Value of Appraisals to the Cost Accountant," *Bulletin,* National Association of Cost Accountants, May, 1932, pp. 1175-1181.

LESSINGER, DR. JOCK, "Towards a New Method and Theory of Appraisal," *The Real Estate Appraiser,* pp. 42.

LETCHFIELD, F. T., "Impact of Engineering Upon Our Economy," *The Appraisal Journal,* October, 1953, pp. 487-496.

LEVI, JULIAN H., "Impact of Law and Code Enforcement on Value," *The Appraisal Journal,* January, 1961, pp. 78-82.

LEWIS, H. J., "Land Economic Studies In Alabama," *Selected Papers,* Right of Way Conference, University of Alabama, 1962, pp. 12.

LIANG, FANG-CHUNG, *The Single-Whip Method,* Chinese Economic & Polit Studies, Harvard Univ, Cambridge, 1956.

LIBRARY OF CONGRESS, *Library of Congress Catalog Books Subjects 1950-1954,* Rowman and Littlefiels, New York, 1964.

LIBRARY OF CONGRESS, *Library of Congress Catalog Books Subjects 1955-1959,* Pageant Books, Patterson, 1960.

LIBRARY OF CONGRESS, *Library of Congress Catalog Books, Subjects 1955-1958,* B, Pageant Books, Inc., pp. 600000.

LIETZ, JOHN F. JR., "The Responsible Approach to Value," *The Residential Appraiser,* March, 1961, pp. 23-24.

LINDQUIST, HARRY C., "Appraising Under the Wyatt Program," *The Review,* May, 1946, pp. 3-5.

LOCKYER, ALBERT W., "Appraisal Integrity," *The Review,* March, 1955, pp. 15.

LOCKYER, ALBERT W., "Appraisers Serve Both Buyers and Sellers Equally Well," *Appraisal Digest,* October, 1952, pp. 23-24.

LOEBER, PAUL C., "The Broker and Appraisals," *National Real Estate Journal,* July 16, 1923, pp. 15-23.

LONIM, M. J., "Heterodox Views on Appraising," *The Appraisal Journal,* October, 1951, pp. 530-532.

LORENS, EDWARD R., "The Appraisal Process-Fact Versus Theory," *The Residential Appraiser,* February, 1962, pp. 2-5.

LOS ANGELES REALTY BOARD, "Board's Schedule of Commissions Including Appraisal Fees," *California Real Estate Magazine,* November, 1935, pp. 33-35.

## BIBLIOGRAPHY OF APPRAISAL LITERATURE

LOSTETTER, EARL, "The New Thinking and the Appraisal Process," *The Appraisal Journal,* July, 1963, pp. 343-348.

LOSTETTER, EARL K., "Divergencies---Reasons and Causes," *The Appraisal Journal,* January, 1965, pp. 83-87.

LOSTETTER, EARL K., "The Distinction Between Appraising and Counseling," *Appraisal Digest,* October, 1961, pp. 1-4.

LOSTETTER, EARL K., "The Four-Way Test," *The Appraisal Journal,* October, 1963, pp. 518-520.

LOVE, HAROLD C., "Risk and Uncertainty Factors," *Appraisal Institute Magazine,* Appraisal Institute of Canada, Winnipeg.

LUEBBERT, RAFAEL C., "The Organization, Operating Procedures and Financial Management of an Appraisal Practice," *The Real Estate Appraiser,* pp. 5.

LUM, Y. T., "Basic Considerations of Appraisal Concepts and Value Factors," *The Residential Appraiser,* February, 1962, pp. 14-20.

LUM, Y. T., "Illogical Divergencies of Opinion Values---Some Inconsistencies and Remedies," *The Appraisal Journal,* April, 1964, pp. 192-202.

LUM, Y. T., "Some of the Causes of Divergencies of Value Opinions," *The Real Estate Appraiser,* SREA, Chicago, November, 1967, pp. 17.

LUM, Y. T., "The Meaning, Comparison and Application of Market Data," *The Real Estate Appraiser,* January, 1965, pp. 28-38.

LUNDY, VICTOR R., "A Reviewer's Report," *The Appraisal Journal,* October, 1960, pp. 484-493.

LUNDY, VICTOR R., "Facing Broader Responsibilities," *The Residential Appraiser,* November, 1956, pp. 3-5, 8.

LUNDY, VICTOR R., "New Influence In Appraising," *The Review,* June, 1951, pp. 3-7.

LUNDY, VICTOR R., "The Challenge of the Commonplace," *The Appraisal Journal,* October, 1960, pp. 536.

LUNDY, VICTOR R., "The Doctrine Unity," *The Review,* September, 1956, pp. 3-5.

LYNCH, JOHN R., "The Appraiser's Qualifications," *The Appraisal Journal,* January, 1953, pp. 83-87.

MACBRIDE DEXTER D, "Opportunities In Appraising for Minorities," *Valutape Audio-Library Series,* American Society of Appraisers, Washington D.C., February 1, 1974.

MACBRIDE, DEXTER D, "Decisions That Infuence Value Concepts," *Proceedings Northwest Appraisal Conference,* Society of Real Estate Appraisers, Chicago, September 1, 1966.

MACBRIDE, DEXTER D, "Major Developments In the Appraisal Profession Within the US: Review, Commentary, Prediction," *Valuation Magazine,* American Society of Appraisers, Washington D.C., December 1, 1973, pp. 126-138.

MACBRIDE, DEXTER D, "The American Society of Appraisers," *Valutape Audio-Library Series,* American Society of Appraisers, Washington D.C., January 1, 1973.

MACBRIDE, DEXTER D, "The Profession of Appraising," *Valutape Audio-Library Series,* American Society of Appraisers, Washington D.C., January 1, 1973.

MACBRIDE, DEXTER D., *Power and Process,* Monograph No. 1, American Society of Appraisers.

MACBRIDE, DEXTER D., "Decisions That Influence Value Concepts," *Proceedings,* Portland Oregon, September, 1966.

MACBRIDE, DEXTER D., "Reviewing Certain Appraisal Concepts," *Proceedings,* Detroit, Michigan.

MACBRIDE, DEXTER D., "The Appraisal Process Perspective," *Proceedings,* San Francisco, March, 1965.

MACBRIDE, DEXTER D., "The Appraisal Process, Perspective," *American Society of Appraisers Valuation Manual,* American Society of Appraisers, 1964, pp. 43.

MACBRIDE, DEXTER D., "The Value of Land," *The Appraisal Journal,* March, 1968, pp. 31-39.

MACBRIDE, DEXTER D., "Valuation Concepts," *Proceeding,* Carmel California, May 7, 1966.

MACDONALD, ARTHUR J., "Comprehensive Appraisals," *The Appraisal Journal,* July, 1955, pp. 345-355.

MACGOVERN, JOHN J. JR., "Quality of Credit and the Appraiser," *The Real Estate Appraiser,* December, 1963, pp. 14-19.

MACK, CURT C., "On Land Depreciation," *The Appraisal Journal,* October, 1937, pp. 377-379.

MACKENZIE, DONALD H., *Mathematics of Finance,* Mcgraw-Hill, New York.

MACLEOD, MORTON P., "Horse Sense and Common Sense," *Technical Valuation,* American Society of Appraisers, Washington, January, 1967, pp. 3.

MACLEOD, MORTON P., "If You Want to Know - Go; if Not - Send," *Technical Valuation,* American Society of Appraisers, Washington, February, 1968, pp. 3.

MACLEOD, MORTON P., "Old Bot Bows Out," *Technical Valuation,* American Society of Appraisers.

MACLEOD, MORTON P., "Price Trends---Fact and Fallacy," *American Society of Appraisers Valuation Manual,* American Society of Appraisers, 1960, pp. 217.

MACRAE, CAMERON F., "The Role of Counsel for the Utility Company In Rate Proceedings," *American Society of Appraisers Valuation Manual,* American Society of Appraisers, 1956, pp. 75.

MADGETT, CARL J., *Trends Towards Advanced Education In Property Valuation,* M, Institute of America.

MAIER, E. F., "The Chartered Surveyors Institution of Great Britain," *The Appraisal Journal,* January, 1935, pp. 173-176.

MAIN, L. T., "Occupancy of Public Lands," *Proceedings of the Eighth Annual National Seminar, 1962,* Washington, D. C, 1963, pp. 60-63.

MALE, CHARLES T., "Property Values and Appraisals," *Real Estate Fundamentals,* Van Nostrand, New York, 1932, pp. 473.

MALLARD, WM. F. R., "Civil Planning---Human and Other Values," *Technical Valuation,* pp. 15.

MANN, JACK K., "Analysis of Appraisal Forms," *The Residential Appraiser,* June, 1960, pp. 11-13.

MANN, JACK K., "The Broker's Appraiser," *The Residential Appraiser,* Chicago, July, 1958, pp. 16.

MARQUIS, RICHARD, "Mass Appraisals," *The Review,* December, 1952, pp. 10-14.

MARTENSON, W. J., "No Appreciation for Appreciation," *Appraisal Institute Magazine,* Appraisal Institute of Canada, Winnipeg.

MARTINDELL, JACKSON, "Second Stage---Inflation and Survival," *Technical Valuation,* February, 1953, pp. 47-53.

MASHKE, D. K., "That Question of Fees," *The Real Estate Appraiser,* August, 1963, pp. 12-15.

MATERN, RUDOLPH, "Architecture from the Grass Roots," *The Appraisal Digest,* July, 1950, pp. 17-18.

MATHERLY, WALTER J., "Changing Economy of the South," *The Appraisal Journal,* October, 1950, pp. 440-444.

MATTHEWS, HAROLD WILLIAM, *Accounting for Appraisals,* Austin, Texas, 1933.

MATTHEWS, MYRON L., "American Society of Appraisers Second Mile," *Technical Valuation,* pp. 7.

MATTHEWS, MYRON L., "Fate of the Cost Premium," *The Review,* December, 1947, pp. 19-20.

MATTHEWS, MYRON L., "Grave Beckons Appraisers," *Appraisal Digest,* October, 1950, pp. 4-5.

MATTHEWS, MYRON L., "Licensing Is No Cure-All," *The Review,* July, 1951, pp. 14-15.

MATTHEWS, MYRON L., "The Cost Cycle," *The Review,* January, 1947, pp. 8-11.

MATTHEWS, MYRON L., ROBERT L. LAUER, "American Society of Appraisers—A Reality," *Technical Valuation,* American Society of Appraisers, November, 1952, pp. 26.

MAY, ARTHUR A, *The Estimate of Depreciation,* Valuation of Residential Real Estate.

MAY, ARTHUR A, "Some Nightmares I Have Had," *The Appraisal Journal,* October, 1947, pp. 510-513.

MAY, ARTHUR A., "Beware the Saw-And-Hatchet Men," *The Appraisal Journal,* January, 1940, pp. 50-52.

MAYER, EDWIN, "Land Appraisal Pitfalls," *American Society of Appraisers Valuation Manual,* American Society of Appraisers, 1956, pp. 221.

MC MICHAEL, STANLEY L., "Elementos Administracion Apreciacion Del Valor," *Boletin,* Sotave, Caracas, Venezuela, pp. 45-51.

MCCANDLESS, DONALD C., "Reuse Valuation," New Appraisal Frontier, the Appraisal Journal.

MCCARTHY, JOSEPH R., "Senator McCarthy's Views on GI Appraising," *The Review,* February, 1948, pp. 9.

MCCORMACK, JAMES E., "Valuation Perplexities In Pricing Cleared Land," *The Appraisal Journal,* January, 1959, pp. 41-48.

MCCORMICK, LORING O., SCHMUTZ, HEORGE L, "Fundamental Economic Concepts," *The Appraisal Journal,* July, 1933, pp. 310-318.

MCCORMICK, LORING, SCHMUTZ, GEORGE, *The Economic Approach to Valuation Procedure,* Los Angeles, 1933.

MCCORMICK, M. J., "Effect of Discounting on Retailing," *Appraisal Institute Magazine,* Appraisal Institute of Canada, Winnipeg.

MCDANIEL, G. A., "How to Quickly Evaluate Exploration Projects," *World Oil,* July, 1970, pp. 131.

MCDONALD, A. M., "A Study of Depreciation In Residences," *The Appraisal Journal,* October, 1958, pp. 602-606.

MCDONALD, ADRIAN F., "Appraising Vs. Underwriting," *The Review,* December, 1951, pp. 7-11.

MCDONALD, ADRIAN F., "Today's Market," *The Review,* September, 1954, pp. 14-22.

MCDONALD, ADRIAN F., "Treatment of Accrued Depreciation," *Appraisal Digest,* October, 1953, pp. 1-5, 1-4.

MCDONALD, RAYMOND J., "Appraising the Moral Risk," *National Real Estate Journal,* September 15, 1930, pp. 31-32.

MCGLONE V. P., "Seminar Summary," *Valuer,* The New Zealand Institute of Valuers, New Zealand, August 1, 1973, pp. 135-138.

MCKAY, HERNDON, "Comparison Is Core of Appraising," *The Review,* December, 1950, pp. 15-19.

MCLAUGHLIN, FRANK J., "Is Rote Right In Valuation," *The Appraisal Journal,* October, 1961, pp. 532-534.

MCLEOD, MORTON P., "The Education of the Appraiser," *Technical Valuation,* pp. 11.

MCMANUS, JOSEPH F., "Appraising the Appraiser," *The Appraisal Journal,* October, 1948, pp. 481-482.

MCMICHAEL, STANLEY L., *Appraising Manual,* Prentice-Hall, Inc, New York, 1937.

▲ Appraisal Theory and Methods

MCMICHAEL, STANLEY L., *Mcmichael's Appraising Manual*, Prentice-Hall, New York, 1951.

MCMICHAEL, STANLEY L., "Appraising by the Unit Foot Method-Depth Tables," *Appraising Manual*, 1937, pp. 346-361.

MCMICHAEL, STANLEY L., "Average Density," *Appraising Manual*, 1937, pp. 527.

MCMICHAEL, STANLEY L., "Influence of Governmental Activities on Home Valuation Technique," *Appraising Manual*, 1937, pp. 330-345.

MCMICHAEL, STANLEY L., "New Problems for the Appraiser," *The Appraisal Journal*, July, 1933, pp. 356-361.

MCMICHAEL, STANLEY L., "On Professional Ethics," *The Appraisal Journal*, July, 1933, pp. 336.

MCMICHALL, STANLEY L., *Mcmichaels Appraising Manual*, 1970.

MCMORRAN, J. BURCH, "New York Department of Public Works Appraisal Methods Promise Savings to Taxpayers," *Right of Way*, August, 1963, pp. 933-34.

MCMULLIN J. A., "The Development of Appraisal Standards for Land and Buildings," *Assesment Adminsitration*, 1963, pp. 27-32.

MCPHERSON, JOSEPH F., "The Hindsight Rule," *The Appraisal Journal*, January, 1953, pp. 54-57.

MCSWEENEY, THOMAS F., "Proposed Code of Technical Standards Economic Background of Value," *Technical Valuation*, June, 1959, pp. 27-33.

MCSWEENEY, THOMAS F., "The Deferment Problem," *Technical Valuation*, pp. 35-40.

MCSWEENEY, THOMAS F., "The Precision of the Appraisal," *American Society of Appraisers*, 1959.

MEDICI, GUISEPPE, *Principles of Appraisal*, Iowa State College Pr., Anes, Iowa, 1954.

MEEK, RONALD L., *Studies In the Labor Theory of Value*, Lawrence and Wi Hart, London, 1956.

MEENACH, T. J., "Management Related to Value," *The Real Estate Appraiser*, September, 1963, pp. 26-32.

MELENDY, MERLE C., "Hybrid Approach Being Tested," *The Residential Appraiser*, November, 1960, pp. 13-14.

MERREL, JOHN A., "Professionalism," *The Residential Appraiser*, February, 1962, pp. 6-12.

MERTZKE, ARTHUR J., "Division of Value Between Land and Improvements," *National Real Estate Journal*, March 17, 1930, pp. 62-63.

MERTZKE, ARTHUR J., "Valuation," *National Real Estate Journal*, September 3, 1928, pp. ART, 1-9.

MILISIEWICZ, JANINA, "Dead Ends," *Appraisal Institute Magazine*, Appraisal Institute of Canada, Winnipeg.

MILISIEWICZ, JANINA, "Public Policy - Property - and People," *Appraisal Institute Magazine*, Appraisal Institute of Canada, Winnipeg, March 1, 1973.

MILISIEWICZ, JANINA, "The Merits of Extending Appraisal Education," *Appraisal Magazine*, December, 1961, pp. 26-28.

MILL, JOHN STUART, "Letters on Value," *The Appraisal Journal*, October, 1953, pp. 511-513.

MILLER, R. D., "Short Cut Method to Calculate Declining Balance Depreciation," *Management Accounting*, July, 1970, pp. 68-70.

MINAYA, NICHOLAS J., "Consider the Circumstances," *The Appraisal Journal*, October, 1969, pp. 529-531.

MINWEGEN ROGER P., "Are Cheap Appraisals Really Cheap," *Review of the Society of Residential Appraisers*, November, 1936, pp. 10-13.

# BIBLIOGRAPHY OF APPRAISAL LITERATURE

MITCHELL, A. CROMAR, "Caveat Emptor or Is it Worth it," *The Appraisal Journal,* July, 1962, pp. 408-410.

MONIESON, DAVID DANNY, *Value Added As a Measure of Economic Contribution by Marketing Institutions,* University Microfilms, Ann Arbor, Mich., 1957.

MONTONNA, D. L., "The Appraisal Process," *Appraisal Institute Magazine,* Appraisal Institute of Canada, Winnipeg.

MOORE, MILTON W., "A Yardstick of Value," *The Appraisal Journal,* April, 1934, pp. 238-240.

MOORES, CHESTER A., "Look Westward," *The Appraisal Journal,* April, 1944, pp. 161-169.

MOREHOUSE, E. W., "Land Valuation," *Encyclopedia of Social Sciences,* 1933, pp. 137-139.

MORGAN, BELDEN, "Values In Transition Areas Some New Concepts," *The Review,* March, 1952, pp. 5-10.

MORGAN, JAMES V., "Appraisal Facets," *The Residential Appraiser,* June, 1957, pp. 11.

MORGAN, JAMES V., "Appraisal Fees Restudied," *The Residential Appraiser,* April, 1962, pp. 23-24.

MORGAN, JAMES V., "How Much Is an Appraisal Worth?," *The Review,* August, 1956, pp. 3-6.

MORRISSEY, THOMAS P., "Accounting Reports and the Appraisal Process," *American Society of Appraisers, Appraisal and Valuation Manual,* 1959, pp. 337-346.

MORSEY, NASHAAT, "Effect of Land Tenure on Production In the Near East," *ASA Valuation Manual,* American Society of Appraisaes, 1956, pp. 211.

MORSEY, NASHATT, "Appraisal Profession In Egypt," *Technical Valuation,* American So Cety of Appraisers, Washington, October, 1953, pp. 54.

MORSY, NASHAAT, "The Fifth Arabian Engineering Congress," *Technical Valuation,* June, 1954, pp. 57.

MULHERN, EUGENE S., "Valuation Report," *Technicalities,* January, 1959, pp. 14-18.

MURILLO, ANA J. ECO., G. BAUDILIO, "El Metodo De Incidencias," *Boletin,* Sotave, Caracas, Venezuela, pp. 17-27.

MURPHY J. P., "Anywhere But Here," *The Valuer,* The Incorporated Society of Valuers & Auctioneers, London, December 1, 1973, pp. 430-431.

MURRAY, WILLIAM G., "A Public Appraisal System Open to All Appraisers," *Journal of the American Society of Farm Managers and Rural Appraisers,* April, 1946, pp. 18-23.

MUSCH, HENRY JR., "Current Appraisal Technique," *The Appraisal Journal,* October, 1933, pp. 32-33.

MUSTOE, NELSON EDWIN, *The Complete Valuation Practice,* Estates Gazette, London, 1955.

MYERS, W. I., F. A. PEARSON, AND J. H. LORIE, "Prices Following Wars," *The Appraisal Journal,* October, 1945, pp. 329-338.

NAMAVATI, ROSHAN, *Theory & Practice of Valuation Land & Bldgs for Architects Engineers Surveyors & Tax Practitioners,* Universal Book Corp., Bombay, 1968.

NANCE, JAMES J., "Economic Competition, America'S New Challenge," *The Appraisal Journal,* July, 1962, pp. 341-346.

NATIONAL ASSOCIATION OF ASSESSING OFFICERS, *Urban Land Appraisals,* Chicago, January, 1940.

NATIONAL ASSOCIATION OF ASSESSING OFFICERS, "Land Appraisal Methods," *Urban Land Appraisal,* 1940, pp. 10-57.

NATIONAL ASSOCIATION OF REAL ESTATE BOARDS, "Answers to Appraisal Questions," *National Real Estate Journal,* August 18, 1930, pp. 47-48.

▲ Appraisal Theory and Methods

NATIONAL ASSOCIATION OF REAL ESTATE BOARDS, "Answers to Appraisal Questions," *National Real Estate Journal*, March 30, 1931, pp. 44.

NATIONAL ASSOCIATION OF REAL ESTATE BOARDS, "Answers to Appraisal Questions," *National Real Estate Journal*, October 27, 1930, pp. 43-44.

NATIONAL ASSOCIATION OF REAL ESTATE BOARDS, "Answers to Appraisal Questions," *National Real Estate Journal*, August 4, 1930, pp. 49-50.

NATIONAL ASSOCIATION OF REAL ESTATE BOARDS, "Answers to Appraisal Questions," *National Real Estate Journal*, July 7, 1930, pp. 53-54.

NATIONAL ASSOCIATION OF REAL ESTATE BOARDS, "Appraiser's Code of Professional Ethics," Clark, H. F., *Appraising the Home*, Art, 1-10, 1930, pp. 258-261.

NATIONAL ASSOCIATION OF REAL ESTATE BOARDS, "Canons of Ethics Adopted at the Louisville Conventions," *National Real Estate Journal*, August 6, 1928, pp. 25-26.

NATIONAL REAL ESTATE JOURNAL, *Practical Appraising Methods*, National Real Estate Journal, Chicago, 1940.

NATIONAL REAL ESTATE JOURNAL, "Ohio Appraisal Rates," *National Real Estate Journal*, August, 1929, pp. 63.

NAZARIO, LUIS A, "Compendio De Valuacion De Inmuebles," *Valuacion De Muebles*, Sociedad De Tasadores De Venezuela, Caracas Venezuela, June 1, 1966, pp. 111 PAGES.

NAZARIO, LUIS A., "Evaluacion De Bienes Raices:," *Boletin*, Sotave, Caracas, Venezuela, pp. 61-68.

NAZARIO, LUIS A., "Evaluacion De Bienes Raices: Capitulo Vii," *Boletin*, Sotave, Caracas, Venezuela, pp. 41-47.

NELSON, R. D., A. J. J. POLLAKOWSKI, "Effect of Financing on Value," *Appraisal Journal*, April, 1970, pp. 279-285.

NELSON, RICHRD L., "Who May Act As an Appraiser," *Encyclopedia of Real Estate Appraising*, Friedman, 1959, pp. 777-787.

NELSON, ROLAND D., "New Concepts In Capital Gains Appraising," *The Real Estate Appraiser*, August, 1966, pp. 19.

NELSON, W. L., "Replacement Value," *American Society of Appraisers Valuation Manual*, June 2, 1952, pp. 111.

NEUMAN, RONALD, "A Profession-Knowledge and Control," *Appraisal Institute Magazine*, Appraisal Institute of Canada, Winnipeg.

NEWTON, E. W., "There Is No Shortcut to a Good Appraisal," *Appraisal Institute Magazine*, Appraisal Institute of Canada, Winnipeg.

NICOLLS, J. P., "Real Estate Values In Vancouver-A Reminiscence," *Appraisal Institute Magazine*, Appraisal Institute of Canada, Winnipeg.

NIRENSTEIN, NATHAN, "Build for Peace," *The Appraisal Journal*, April, 1948, pp. 222-226.

NORTH, L. W., "Build it on Paper First," *Appraisal Institute Magazine*, Appraisal Institute of Canada, Winnipeg.

NORTH, L. W., "You Mean it Sold for That Much," *Appraisal Institute Magazine*, Appraisal Institute of Canada, Winnipeg, March 1, 1972.

NOWAK, ARTHUR M., "Appraisal Facts and Fallacies," *Commerce and Finance*, June 22, 1927, pp. 1253-1254.

NOYES, GEORGE I., "Comparisons In Real Estate Appraisals," *The Appraisal Journal*, January, 1940, pp. 53-58.

NUGENT, R. A. L., "Common Errors In Appraisals," *Appraisal Institute Magazine*, Appraisal Institute of Canada, Winnipeg.

NUTTER, C. ARMEL, "The Changing Real Estate Picture," *The Residential Appraiser,* August, 1961, pp. 12-13, 20.

ODELL, H. AUGUSTUS, "Dollars Out of the Depression," *American Architect,* March, 1933, pp. 52-54.

ORORKE, T., "The Intern Program Through English Eyes," *The Appraisal Journal,* January, 1966, pp. 118-122.

O'FLAHERTY, JOHN D., "An Appraiser's Dilemma: the Cost Approach to Value," *The Real Estate Appraiser,* January, 1969, pp. 5-16.

OHIO TAX COMMISSION, "Ohio Appraisal Manual," *Ohio Appraisal Manual,* Columbus, 1930.

OLDAK, P. G., "Analysis of the Concept of Value," *Problems of Economics,* October, 1970.

OLIVER, RUSSELL H., "Depreciation Theory," *The Review,* September, 1946, pp. 18-19.

OLSON, LYLE H., "From the Liability Side," *The Appraisal Journal,* January, 1940, pp. 36-41.

OSTENDORF, E. L., "Appraisal Standards," *The Appraisal Journal,* October, 1937, pp. 325-328.

OSTENDORF, E. L., "Certain Fundamentals of Appraising," *The Appraisal Journal,* January, 1938, pp. 37-39.

OTT, LAWSON R., "The Effect of the Purpose of Appraisal on Value," *Technical Valuation,* pp. 17.

PADILLA GONZALEZ, GILBERTO, "Evaluador Bienes Raices Como Profesional," *Boletin,* Sotave, Caracas, Venezuela, pp. 19-21.

PADILLA GONZALEZ, GILBERTO, "La Aritmetica Tasacion De Bienes Raices," *Boletin,* Sotave, Caracas, Venezuela, pp. 21-26.

PALMA LABASTIDA, M. A., "Conceptos Sobre El Deslinde," *Boletin,* Sotave, Caracas, Venezuela, pp. 25-31.

PALMER, EDWARD DEL, "Fit to Be Compared," *The Appraisal Digest,* April, 1955, pp. 18-21.

PARKER, ELSIE SMITH, "Both Sides of the Color Line," *The Appraisal Journal,* January, 1943, pp. 27-34.

PARKER, ELSIE SMITH, "Both Sides of the Color Line," *The Appraisal Journal,* July, 1943, pp. 231-249.

PARVIN, ROBERT G., "Asset Valuation," *The Appraisal Journal,* October, 1954, pp. 550-560.

PARVIN, ROBERT G., "Market Approach to Value," *Encyclopedia of Real Estate Appraising,* Friedman, 1959, pp. 86-93.

PATCHIN ASA, PETER J., "Multiplicadores Brutos," *Boletin,* Sotave, Caracas, Venezuela, pp. 13-18.

PATINKIN, DON, *Money Interests and Prices An Integration of Monetary and Value Theory,* Row, Peterson, Evanstown, Illinois, 1956.

PEARCEY, F., AND T. G. CHAPMAN, "Aspects of a Computer-Based Land," *Land Evaluation,* Evaluation System, pp. 221.

PEARL, MILTON A., "Reviewing the Public Lands," *The Appraisal Journal,* January, 1967, pp. 28-33.

PEARSON, F. A., W. I. MYERS, AND DON PAARLBERG, "Collusion," *The Appraisal Journal,* April, 1949, pp. 166-167.

PEARSON, F. A., W. I. MYERS, AND DEGRAFF, "Prices, Building, and History," *The Appraisal Journal,* October, 1952, pp. 512-534.

PEARSON, F. A., W. I. MYERS, H. DEGRAFF, "Prices, Building, and History," *The Appraisal Journal,* October, 1952, pp. 512-534.

PENA GARCIA, M. A., "La Tecnica Del Avaluo, Su Evolucion," *Boletin,* Sotave, Caracas, Venezuela, pp. 23-28.

PENA GARCIA, M. A., "Vicios En La Valuacion," *Boletin,* Sotave, Caracas, Venezuela, pp. 14-17.

▲ **Appraisal Theory and Methods**

PERRY, RALPH BARTON, *General Theory of Value*, Longmans Green, New York, 1926, pp. 693.

PERT, WOODBY X., "An Appraiser's Affidavit," *The Appraisal Journal*, October, 1935, pp. 469-470.

PHILIPS, F. M., "The Appraiser and the Realtor," *Appraisal Institute Magazine*, Appraisal Institute of Canada, Winnipeg.

PHIMISTER, Z. S., "Education-Quo Vadit," *Appraisal Institute Magazine*, Appraisal Institute of Canada, Winnipeg.

PHINNEY, G. W., "The Role of the Appraiser," *Appraisal Institute Magazine*, Appraisal Institute of Canada, Winnipeg.

PICKARD, W. C., "When Is a Comparable Comparable," *The Real Estate Appraiser*, October, 1965, pp. 14-17.

PIERCE, PHILIP F, MACBRIDE, DEXTER D, "Licensing/Certification of Appraisers: Pro Bono Publico," *Valuetape Audio-Library Series*, American Society of Appraisers, Washington D.C., January 1, 1973.

PIERCE, PHILIP F., "Land Contract Sales and Their Relationship to Market Value," *Right of Way*, pp. 50-51, 60.

PIERCE, PHILIP F., "The Role of the Appraiser, the Role of ASA In the Years to Come," *Appraisal and Valuation Manual*, Corporate Press Incorporated, Washington, D. C, January, 1972, pp. 278.

PILMER, CHARLES L., "Ethics and Fees," *Journal of the American Society of Farm Managers and Rural Appraisers*, April, 1962, pp. 10-12.

PINKERTON, A. M., "What Is a Profession," *Appraisal Institute Magazine*, Appraisal Institute of Canada, Winnipeg.

PIO, ROBERT, "Round Equals Square," *Technical Valuation*, American Society of Appraisers, Washington, December, 1967, pp. 65.

PITT, JOHN E., "The Value of Fractional Interests," *Technical Valuation*, October, 1959, pp. 39-42.

POINTER, RUSSEL A., "The Appraiser's Part In the Future Development of the Real Estate Business," *Technical Valuation*, American Society of Appraisers, Washington, January, 1967, pp. 9.

POLAK, DR. W. J., "Theories of Depreciation," *Proceedings, International Congress on Accounting, 1929*, New York, 1929, pp. 447-463.

POLLEYS, THOMAS A., "Real Estate Valuations," *Publications*, Minnesota Academy of Social Sciences, 1908, pp. 59-78.

POLLOCK, WALTER W., "A Scientific Approach to Real Estate Valuation," *American Academy of Political and Social Science, Annals*, March, 1930, pp. 96-105.

POLLOCK, WALTER W., "An Equitable Standard for Land Valuation," *National Tax Association Proceedings*, 1913, pp. 234-266, 267-285.

POLLOCK, WALTER W., "Concept of Value for Use," *Certified Public Accountant*, March, 1935, pp. 147-150.

POLLOCK, WALTER W., AND R. W. H. SCHOLZ, *The Science and Practice Of Urban Land Valuation*, Philadelphia, 1926.

POLLOCK, WATER W., "The Science and Practice of Urban Land Valuation," *The Appraisal Journal*, July, 1936, pp. 310-318.

POPE, LONNIE, "Ellwood Makes Sense to Me," *The Real Estate Appraiser*, pp. 13.

PORTER, ROBERT R., "Non-Technical Appraisal Procedure," *Review of the Society of Residential Appraisers*, August, 1937, pp. 3-4.

POTTER, W. E., "The Missouri Basin Plan In Operation," *The Appraisal Journal*, October, 1955, pp. 547-559.

POTTS, W. T. JR., "Problem of the Trainee," *The Real Estate Appraiser*, December, 1936, pp. 26-31.

POWDRELL J. D., "**Land Tenures and Valuation In Papua Guinea**," *The Valuer,* The Commonwealth Institute of Valuers, Sydney Australia, October 1, 1973, pp. 616-619.

PREINREICH, GABRIEL A., *The Theory and General Principles of Depreciation,* The Waverly Press, Inc., Baltimore, Md., 1941.

PRENTICE, PERRY, *The Power to Appraise,* The Residential Appraiser, May, 1960.

PRICE, OLIN, "**Appraising- a Constant Challenge**," *Appraisal and Valuation Manual,* 1956, pp. 17-22.

PROUTY, W. L. AND OTHERS, "**Appraisal of Land**," *Appraisers and Assessors Manual,* 1930, pp. 304-351.

PYE, G., "**Some Lessons In Market Valuation**," *Financial Analysts Journal,* May, 1970, pp. 103-106.

QUIN, GEORGE ROBERT, "**On Probable Income**," *The Appraisal Journal,* January, 1934, pp. 146-147.

QUIN, GEORGE ROBERT, "**Tasa De Capitalizacion**," *Boletin,* Sotave, Caracas, Venezuela, pp. 41-45.

QUINTANA, ISADORO, "**Amenities In Valuation**," *Review of Society of Residential Appraisers,* March, 1940, pp. 8-10.

QUINTANA, ISIDORO, "**Coming to Terms**," *The Appraisal Journal,* January, 1942, pp. 47-51.

QUINTANA, ISIDORO, "**On Rationalizing Appraisal Practice**," *The Appraisal Journal,* October, 1936, pp. 437-439.

QUINTO, OSCAR B., "**Adjusting the Comparative Approach**," *The Review,* September, 1947, pp. 19-21.

RAISON, B. V., "**Can a Valuer Influence the Market**," *Appraisal Institute Magazine,* Appraisal Institute of Canada, Winnipeg.

RAISON, B. V., S. E. WHICKER, "**Errors and Omissions In Valuations**," *Appraisal Institute Magazine,* Appraisal Institute of Canada, Winnipeg.

RAMS, EDWIN M., "**Cost Variables**," *The Review,* October, 1955, pp. 3-5.

RAMS, EDWIN M., "**Economic Size and Value**," *Technical Valuation,* October, 1961, pp. 11.

RAMS, EDWIN M., "**Professional Liability**," *The Review,* November, 1953, pp. 20-23.

RAMS, EDWIN M., "**Valuation of Partial Estates and Interests In Real Estate**," *Technical Valuation,* June, 1956, pp. 16-19.

RANDALL, ROLAND R., "**A Basis for Adequate Fees**," *The Preview,* July, 1947, pp. 10-11.

RAPPORT, RICHARD, "**Is Inflation Inevitable**," *The Review,* May, 1952, pp. 16-18.

RATCLIFF, DR. RICHARD U., "**A Restatement of Appraisal Theory**," *The Appraisal Journal,* January, 1964, pp. 51-67.

RATCLIFF, DR. RICHARD U., "**Economic Life In the Valuation Procedure**," *The Appraisal Journal,* January, 1938, pp. 57-64.

RATCLIFF, DR. RICHARD U., "**Professional Appraisal Education at the University of Wisconsin**," *The Real Estate Appraiser,* June, 1963, pp. 2-6.

RATCLIFF, DR. RICHARD U., "**The Proceedings**," *Paper and Proceedings,* Wisconsin Colloquium on Appraisal Research, 1963, pp. 67-71.

RATCLIFF, DR. RICHARD V., "**A Neoteric View of the Appraisal Function**," *The Appraisal Journal,* April, 1965, pp. 167-175.

RATCLIFF, DR. RICHARD W., "**Market Value Can't Be Estimated**," *The Real Estate Appraiser,* January, 1970, pp. 16-20.

RATCLIFF, R. U., "**A Rationalization of Real Estate Valuation**," *Appraisal Institute Magazine,* Appraisal Institute of Canada, Winnipeg.

RATCLIFF, R. U., "**The Future Education of the Appraiser**," *Appraisal Institute Magazine,* Appraisal Institute of Canada, Winnipeg.

RATCLIFF, R. U., "**The Only Road to Vp**," *Appraisal Institute Magazine,* Appraisal Institute of Canada, Winnipeg.

## Appraisal Theory and Methods

RATCLIFF, R. U., "The Price and Rewards of Professionalization," *Appraisal Institute Magazine,* Appraisal Institute of Canada, Winnipeg.

RATCLIFF, R. U., "Wrong Roads to Vp," *Appraisal Institute Magazine,* Appraisal Institute of Canada, Winnipeg.

RATCLIFF, RICHARD U., "Don't Underestimate the Gross Income Multiplier," *The Appraisal Institute Magazine,* 1970.

RAUBER, EARLE L., "The Money Market and Its Effect on Real Estate Values," *The Appraisal Journal, Vol. Xxvi,* July, 1958, pp. 365-370.

REAL ESTATE ANALYST, THE, "Appraising the Future," *Real Estate Analyst Appraisal Bulletin,* 1959, pp. 101-104.

REAL ESTATE ANALYST, THE, "Inaccessibility of Business," *Real Estate Analyst Appraisal Bulletin,* 1948, pp. 355-362.

REAL ESTATE ANALYST, THE, "Market Prices," *Real Estate Analyst Appraisal Bulletin,* 1960, pp. 403-406.

RECHT, J. RICHARD, LOEWENSTEIN, LOUIS K, "Variations In Rates of Return," *The Appraisal Journal,* April, 1965, pp. 243-248.

REEVE, DOUGLAS W., "Appraisal of a Conversion," *The Review,* September, 1946, pp. 20-24.

REEVE, DOUGLAS W., "Weighing the Components of Value," *Review of Society of Residential Appraisers,* November, 1941, pp. 3-6.

REEVE, DOUGLAS W., "What We Expect from a Competent Appraiser," *Review of Society of Residential Appraisers,* May, 1940, pp. 3-5.

REGISTER, J. ALVIN, "Income As a Factor In Appraising," *National Association of Real Estate Boards,* 1929, pp. 40-47.

REIDY, MAURICE F., "The Changing Scene and Appraisal Progress," *The Appraisal Journal,* January, 1937, pp. 23-29.

REITLINGER, GERALD, *The Economics of Taste,* Holt, Rinehart and Winston, New York, 1961.

RENNE, ROLAND R., *Land Economics,* Harper, New York, 1947.

RESIDENTIAL APPRAISER, "The Meaning of Value," *The Residential Appraiser,* March, 1957, pp. 3-6.

REVIEW OF SOCIETY OF RESIDENTIAL APPRAISERS, "Current Survey on Appraisal Practices and Policies," *Review of Society of Residential Appraisers,* September, 1941, pp. 6-11, 16.

REVIEW, THE, "An Appraisal Brief," *The Review,* May, 1950, pp. 12-14.

REVIEW, THE, "Appraisal Scene," *The Review,* February, 1956, pp. 2.

REVIEW, THE, "Fees-Past and Future," *The Review,* August, 1950, pp. 3-6.

REVIEW, THE, "New Shelter-Income Ratio," *The Review,* March, 1953, pp. 21.

REVIEW, THE, "The Appraisal Process," *The Review,* November, 1949, pp. 12-16.

REVIEW, THE, "Views on Government Appraisals," *The Review,* March, 1948, pp. 17.

RIBETH, WILLIAM C., "Ethics for the Appraiser," *The Review,* April, 1952, pp. 16.

RICARDO, D., "Great 1970 Market Crash," *Financial Analysts Journal,* September, 1970, pp. 22-27.

RICHARDS, JOHN L. JR., "The Principle of Substitution," *Technical Valuation,* February, 1958, pp. 21-22.

RIEMER, RICHARD L., "The Theory of Eminent Domain," *Right of Way,* April, 1971.

RING, ALFRED A., "Appraisal Correlation," *Appraisal and Valuation Manual,* February, 1954, pp. 31.

RING, A. A., "New Look at Market Comparison Approach," *Appraisal Institute Magazine,* Appraisal Institute of Canada, Winnipeg.

RING, A. A., "The Earnings Approach to Value," *Appraisal Institute Magazine,* Appraisal Institute of Canada, Winnipeg.

RING, ALFRED A., "Importance of Cost, Price, Income and Market on Valuation," *The Valuation of Real Estate,* 1970, pp. 43.

RING, ALFRED A., "The Labyrinth of Value," *The Appraisal Journal,* January, 1965, pp. 9-14.

RING, ALFRED A., "What Makes Value," *The Review,* June, 1949, pp. 3-5.

RING, DR. ALFRED A., "Appraising What it Takes to Be an Expert," *The Real Estate Appraiser,* SREA, Chicago.

RINGER, V. P., "Value of an Undivided Interest," *The Appraisal Journal,* July, 1966, pp. 413-418.

ROBERTS, EDWIN A., JR., "Why Freedom of the Seas Policy Is Outdated, Planning Against Anarchy on the Oceans," *The Appraisal Journal,* October, 1968, pp. 595-598.

ROBERTS, RICHARD, "The Appraisers Approach to Market Value," *Appraisal Institute Magazine,* December, 1961, pp. 14-17.

ROBERTSON, FRASER, "The Profession of Duty," *Appraisal Institute Magazine,* Appraisal Institute of Canada, Winnipeg, June 1, 1972.

ROBINS, PHILIP KENNETH, PH. D., "A Theory and Test of Housing Market Behavior," *A Theory and Test of Housing Market Behavior,* University of Wisconsin, 1972, pp. 162.

ROBINSON, WILLIAM K., "Kingswood - a Recreation-Oriented Community," *Urban Land,* Urban Land Institute, Washington, June, 1965.

RODEY, B. S., JR., "Original Cost," *Appraisal and Valuation Manual,* 1955.

RODWIN, LLOYD, "Rejoinder to Dr. Firey and Dr. Hoyt," *The Appraisal Journal,* pp. 454-457.

ROSE, C. W., D. A. THOMAS, "Remote Sensing of Land Surface Temperature and Some Applications," *Land Evaluation,* pp. 367.

ROSS, THURSTON H., "History of Value Theory," *The Appraisal Journal,* April, 1938, pp. 120-132.

ROTHCHILD, SIGMUND, "Appraisal of Contempory Art," *Appraisal and Valuation Manual,* Corporate Press Incorporated, Washington, D. C, January, 1972, pp. 402.

ROTHSCHILD, SIGMUND, "A Theory of Finding Value," *Appraisal and Valuation Manual,* 1958, pp. 39.

ROTHSCHILD, SIGMUND, "Appraisal of Contemporary Art," *Valutape Audio-Library Series,* American Societ of Appraisers, Washington D.C., January 1, 1973.

ROYAL BANK OF CANADA, "Imagination Helps Communication," *Appraisal Journal,* January, 1962, pp. 113-118.

ROYAL, PEYTON K., "Market Data, Cost, and Income Analysis," *The Appraisal Journal,* April, 1962, pp. 245-247.

ROYCE, FRANK A., "New Appraisal Engagements," *Technical Valuation,* June, 1956, pp. 24.

RUAN SANTOS, EDUARDO, "El Tasador: Una Necesidad Nacional," *Boletin,* Sotave, Caracas, Venezuela, pp. 3.

RUGELES, IVAN OLIVER, "Accion Y Proyeccion De Sotave," *Boletin,* Sotave, Caracas, Venezuela, pp. 5-8.

RUGELES, IVAN OLIVER, "Conceptos Generales Sobre Valuacion," *Boletin,* Sotave, Caracas, Venezuela, pp. 7-10.

RUGELES, IVAN OLIVER, "El Proceso De Capitalizacion En El Avaluo," *Boletin,* Sotave, Caracas, Venezuela, pp. 11-14.

RUGELES, IVAN OLIVER, "La Sociedad De Tasadores De Venezuela," *Boletin,* Sotave, Caracas, Venezuela, pp. 9.

RUGGLES, RICHARD, "The Value of Value Theory," *American Economic Review,* May, 1954, pp. 140-160.

RUSSELL, HORACE, "Are Appraisers Employees or Independent Contractors?," *Review of Society of Residential Appraisers*, March, 1941, pp. 3-4.

RUSSELL, HORACE, "The Law of Appraising," *The Review*, March, 1945, pp. 15.

RYAN, JOHN C., "Probate Assignments," *The Review*, December, 1955, pp. 7-8.

SACKMAN, JULIUS L., "Economic Approach to Valuation," *The Appraisal Journal*, October, 1966, pp. 511-530.

SACKMAN, JULIUS L., RUSSELL D. VAN BRUNT, *Valuation*, Mathew Bender and Company, Albany, New York.

SACLES, KENNETH E., "Appraiser's Responsibility In Reporting Substandard New Construction," *The Real Estate Appraiser*, November, 1964, pp. 22.

SANDO, LAURENCE, "Institute Will Study Feasibility of Reciprocity with British," *The Appraiser*, October, 1968.

SARLES, KENNETH E., "Appraisal Fundamentals," *The Appraisal Journal*, October, 1950, pp. 519-525.

SARLES, KENNETH E., "Establishing Marketability of Urban Property," *The Real Estate Appraiser*, December, 1965, pp. 22-28.

SCHARFF, M. R., "Supplemental Note on Valuation and Depreciation," *Appraisal and Valuation Manual*, February, 1957, pp. 1-11.

SCHARFF, MAURICE R., "Depreciation Studies," *Appraisal and Valuation Manual*, 1955, pp. 14.

SCHARFF, MAURICE R., "The Role of the Expert for the Company," *Appraisal and Valuation Manual*, 1956, pp. 67.

SCHLAUCH, WILLIAM S., T. LANG, *Mathematics of Business and Finance*, Ronald, Newyork, 1937.

SCHMID, CALVIN F., *Handbook of Geographic Presentation*, Ronald, New York, 1954.

SCHMUTZ, GEORGE L., *The Appraisal Process*, G. L. Schmutz, Manhattan Beach, Cal, 1959.

SCHMUTZ, GEORGE L., *The Appraisal Process*, G. L. Schmutz, No. Hollywood, Calif, 1953.

SCHMUTZ, GEORGE L., "Appraisal Features," *The Appraisal Process*, 1959, pp. 111-163.

SCHMUTZ, GEORGE L., "Changing Dollar Values," *The Appraisal Journal*, April, 1934, pp. 248-250.

SCHMUTZ, GEORGE L., "History of Value Theories," *The Appraiser Process*, 1959, pp. 7-13.

SCHMUTZ, GEORGE L., "Professional Conduct," *Appraisal Process*, 1941, pp. 1-229.

SCHMUTZ, GEORGE L., "Professional Standards In Appraising," *The Appraisal Process*, 1959, pp. 279-283.

SCHMUTZ, GEORGE L., "Sidelights on Appraisal Methods," *The Appraisal Journal*, June, 1948, pp. 17-21.

SCHMUTZ, GEORGE L., "The Appraisal Problem," *Appraisal Process*, 1941, pp. 1-229.

SCHMUTZ, GEORGE L., "The Evolution of the Interpretation of Appraisal Principles," *The Appraisal Journal*, January, 1948, pp. 40-48.

SCHMUTZ, GEORGE L., "The Factors Affecting Market Price," *The Appraisal Journal*, April, 1934, pp. 181-188.

SCHMUTZ, GEORGE L., "Value and Price Changes," *The Appraisal Process*, 1959, pp. 23-27.

SCHMUTZ, GEORGE L., LORING O. MCCORMICK, *Land Economics As Applied to Appraising*, California Real Estate Association, Los Angeles, 1936, pp. 1-94.

SCHMUTZ, GEORGE L., LORING O. MCCORMICK, "The Doctrine of Surplus Productivity," *The Appraisal Journal*, October, 1933, pp. 56-62.

# BIBLIOGRAPHY OF APPRAISAL LITERATURE

SCHMUTZ, GEORGE L., LORING O. MCCORMICK, "The Relation of Profit to Value," *The Appraisal Journal*, April, 1935, pp. 229-235.

SCHULTE, AUGUST B., "Some Observations on Factors Affecting Prices and Some Sound Value Concepts," *The Appraisal Journal*, April, 1984, pp. 201-202.

SCHULTZ, WILLIAM J., AND C. LOWELL HARRIS, *American Public Finance*, Prentice-Hall, Englewood, N. J, 1965, pp. 1-565.

SCHWARTZ, SIDNEY M., "Analysis of Economic Life," *The Appraisal Journal*, April, 1968, pp. 225-227.

SCHWINGLE, C. J., "What Appraisals Do for the Client," *Technical Valuation*, October, 1961, pp. 7-12.

SCHWULST, EARL B., "A Few Problems and Some Suggestions Concerning Them," *The Appraisal Journal*, April, 1948, pp. 200-204.

SCRIBNER, DAVID JR., "The Appraisers Professional Responsibility to Society," *Appraisal and Valuation Manual*, Corporate Press Incorporated, Washington, D. C, January, 1972, pp. 294.

SEATTLE REAL ESTATE ASSOCIATION, "Reports on City Real Estate Values," The Pacific Press, Seattle, December, 1907.

SELDIN, MAURICE, "Criteria for Evaluating Appraisals," *The Appraisal Journal*, October, 1959, pp. 530-536.

SELDIN, MAURICE, "Does Land Depreciate," *The Appraisal Journal*, July, 1961, pp. 345-351.

SEYMOUR, C. F., "Responsibilities of the Review Appraiser," *Appraisal Journal*, October, 1971, pp. 508-513.

SEYMOUR, CHARLES F., "The Artillery Theory of Market Value," *The Appraisal Journal*, January, 1955, pp. 42-45.

SEYMOUR, CHARLES F., "What Is Effective Age," *The Appraisal Journal*, January, 1960, pp. 39-41.

SHANKLAND, F. J., "The Real Estate Market," *Appraisal Institute Magazine*, Appraisal Institute of Canada, Winnipeg.

SHAPIRO, M., "Purchase-Value Index it Takes More and More Money to Move the Market Up," *Barrons*, November 15, 1971.

SHATTUCK, CHARLES B., "The Realtor and Real Estate Counseling," *The Appraisal Journal*, January, 1962, pp. 33-39.

SHENKEL, WILLIAM M., "Modernizing the Market Data Approach," *The Appraisal Journal*, April, 1967, pp. 181-198.

SHENKEL, WILLIAM M., "Valuation of Leased Fees and Leasehold Interest," *The Appraisal Journal*, October, 1965, pp. 482-498.

SHENKEL, WILLIAM M., ALLAN S. EDISON, "The Analysis of Real Estate Sales and Urban Data The Impact on Resource Allocation," *Review of Regional Studies*, Virginia Polytechnic Institute & State University, April, 1971, pp. 79-92.

SHERIDAN, VINCENT GEORGE, "Establishing the First Rule," *Appraisal Institute Magazine*, Appraisal Institute of Canada, Winnipeg, March 1, 1971.

SHERMAN, H. J., "The Marxist Theory of Value Revisited," *Science and Society*, 1970.

SHERMER, MALCOLM H., "Practical Problems of the Appraiser," *Review of Society of Residential Appraisers*, September, 1938, pp. 11-12.

SHUGRUE, FRANK R., "Basic Steps In the Appraisal of Real Property," *The Appraisal Journal*, January, 1953, pp. 104-111.

SHURBERG, MERWIN, "Economic Factors In Property Valuations," *Appraisal and Valuation Manual*, pp. 65.

SIBERLING, NORMAN J., *Dynamics of Business*, Mcgraw Hill, New York, 1940.

SILVERHERZ, JOSEPH D., "Computing Depreciation and Appreciation," *Real Estate Record*, Metropolitans and National Editions, October 17, 1936, pp. 11-16.

▲ **Appraisal Theory and Methods**

SILVERMAN, BENJAMIN, "Considerations of Authenticity," *Technical Valuation,* February, 1955, pp. 57.

SILVERMAN, BENJAMIN, "Legal Aspects-Value of an Idea," *Technical Valuation,* June, 1954, pp. 54.

SIMMS, S. R., "Legal and Practical Aspects of Appraisal Law," *Appraisal Institute Magazine,* Appraisal Institute of Canada, Winnipeg.

SIMON, ROBERT E., "The Effect of Concepts on the Value of Land," *Appraisal and Valuation Manual,* 1964, pp. 107.

SIMONITE, C. R., "A Record Year," *Appraisal Institute Magazine,* Appraisal Institute of Canada, Winnipeg.

SINGLETON, C. G. JR., AND SCOFIELD, W. H., "Land Syndication In the Rural-Urban Fringe," *The Appraisal Journal,* October, 1962, pp. 494-500.

SLICHTER, S. H., "The Postwar Outlook for Business and Labor," *The Appraisal Journal,* October, 1944, pp. 334-339.

SLICHTER, SUMNER H., "The Business Outlook-Short Run and Long Run," *The Appraisal Journal,* July, 1947, pp. 310-316.

SLONIM, M. J., "Market Value or Market Price," *The Appraisal Journal,* October, 1945, pp. 390-391.

SLONIM, M. J., "The Three Approaches Under Fire," *Technical Valuation,* American Society of Appraisers, Washington, 1966.

SMITH, HALBERT C., AND RONALD L. RACSTER, "Should the Traditional Appraisal Be Restructured," *The Real Estate Appraiser,* 1911.

SMITH, J. H. JR., "Six Ways to Capitalize on a Bad Financial Market," *Business Management,* November, 1970, pp. 29.

SMITH, JAMES J., "Benefits and Problems of an Appraisal Office," *The Real Estate Appraiser,* September 1963, pp. 37-40.

SMITH, LARRY, "Economic Factors and Their Analysis," *Valuation,* June, 1954, pp. 19-35.

SMITH, LEONARD C., "Has Land a Value," *The Appraisal Journal,* 1939, pp. 354-357.

SMITH, LEONARD C., "On Value," *The Appraisal Journal,* October, 1957, pp. 369-371.

SMITH, LEONARD C., "The Appraisal Process," *Review of the Society of Residential Appraisers,* September, 1937, pp. 4-10, 16.

SMITH, LEONARD C., "The Prize In Private Enterprise," *The Appraisal Journal,* July, 1944, pp. 202-203.

SMITH, RALPH M., "The Best Appraisal System," *The Review,* June, 1948, pp. 3-7.

SMITH, WALSTEIN FR., "Value-Verified or Vilfied," *The Real Estate Appraiser,* pp. 2.

SMITH, WALSTEIN JR., "Market Value a Rule of Reasoning," *The Real Estate Appraiser,* pp. 40.

SMITH, WALSTEIN, JR., "Is There More Than One Market Value," *The Residential Appraiser,* September, 1962, pp. 2-13.

SLICHTER, SUMNER H., "The Business Outlook-Short Run and Long Run," *The Appraisal Journal,* July, 1947, pp. 310-316.

SLONIM, M. J., "Market Value or Market Price," *The Appraisal Journal,* October, 1945, pp. 390-391.

SLONIM, M. J. "The Three Approaches Under Fire," *Technical Valuation,* American Society of Appraisers, Washington, 1966.

SMITH, HALBERT C., AND RONALD L. RACSTER, "Should the Traditional Appraisal Be Restructured," *The Real Estate Appraiser,* 1911.

SMYTH, W. A., "Putting Values on Fine Arts," *Technical Valuations,* October, 1953, pp. 35.

SNYDER, BLAKE, AND ROBY, RALPH, *Fundamentals In Real Estate,* Harper and Brothers, New York and London, 1927.

SOCIETY OF RESIDENTIAL APPRAISERS, "Code of Ethics," *Review of the Society of Residential Appraisers,* December, 1936, pp. 15-16.

SOLBERG, ERLING D., "Countryside, USA," *The Residential Appraiser,* October, 1959, pp. 14-24.

SOLOMON, C. FRANCIS, JR., "The Broker's Role In the Appraisal Business," *The Appraisal Journal,* October, 1948, pp. 483-487.

SOTAVE, "Estatutos De La (Sotave)," *Boletin,* Sotave, Caracas, Venezuela, pp. 27-31.

SOTAVE, "La Tecnica Avaluatoria," *Boletin,* Sotave, Caracas, Venezuela, pp. 40-42.

SPAHR, WALTER E., AND OTHERS, *Economic Principles and Problems,* Farrar and Reinhart, New York.

SPEED, A. A., "Courses Being Upgraded," *Appraisal Institute Magazine,* Appraisal Institute of Canada, Winnipeg.

SPILDER, JOHN B., "Errors of Appraisal Thoughts," *Real Estate Business As a Profession,* 1941, pp. 283-288.

SPON, EDWARD, AND F. N. SPON LTD., *Architects and Builders Price Book,* Mcclelland and Steward, Toronto, 1958.

SROUFE, THOMAS A., "Utilizing All Three Approaches to Value," *The Residential Appraiser,* pp. 3..

ST. GEORGE, JOHN F., "Appraising for Government," *Appraisal and Valuation Manual,* American Society of Appraisers, 1960, pp. 381-390.

STAFFORD, L. D., "Depreciation As a Business Expense," *Manufactures News,* August, 1929, pp. 9-10, 65-67.

STEELE, FRANK N., "The Public Image of an Appraiser," *Appraisal Institute Magazine,* Appraisal Institute of Canada, Winnipeg.

STEELE, ROBERT A., "The Impact of Civil Disobedience on Property Values," *The Appraisal Journal,* July, 1908, pp. 342-252.

STEIN, H. L., "The Challenge of Teaching," *Appraisal Institute Magazine,* Winnipeg.

STEINER, JEFFERSON F., "Ethics In the Appraisal Profession," *The Appraisal Journal,* October, 1956, pp. 518-522.

STEINHART, RALPH, "The Look Before the Leap," *The Appraisal Journal,* April, 1964, pp. 297-299.

STERN, OSCAR I., "The End of the Restrictive Covenant," *The Appraisal Journal,* October, 1948, pp. 434-442.

STERZER, HERBERT, "The Approved Appraiser," *The Real Estate Appraiser,* pp. 34.

STEUER, AARON, "Appraisal As a Science," *The Appraisal Journal,* April, 1947, pp. 192-196.

STEUER, AARON, "Appraisers Urged to Better Professionals Standards," *The Review,* October, 1948, pp. 12-16.

STEVENS, FRANCIS K., "The Appraiser's Duties Today As to Value," *The Appraisal Journal,* April, 1933, pp. 204-206.

STEVENS, WILLIAM T., "On Historical Significance As a Factor In Determining Value," *The Appraisal Journal,* July, 1968, pp. 418.

STEVENSON, R. A., "A Revaluation of Our Present Economy," *The Appraisal Journal,* July, 1948, pp. 330-335.

STEWARD, CHARLES L., "Some Aspects of Land Appraisals Abroad," *The Appraisal Journal,* April, 1934, pp. 189-193.

STEWARD, J. A., "Land Evaluation," *Papers of a Csiro Symposium Organized In Cooperation with Unesco,* Mcmillan of Australia, Melbourne, August, 1968, pp. 26-31.

STEWART, DWIGHT A., "University Roles In Professional Adult Education," *Right of Way,* December, 1963, pp. 23-26.

STEWART, J. I., "An Economist Looks at Appraisal Theory," *The Real Estate Appraiser,* July, 1966, pp. 15-28.

▲ Appraisal Theory and Methods

STEWART, J. I., "The Appraiser In Today's Economy," *Appraisal Institute Magazine,* Appraisal Institute of Canada, Winnipeg.

STEWART, JAMES INNES, *Real Estate Appraisal In a Nutshell,* University of Toronto Press, Toronto, 1967.

STEWART, SAMUEL, "Oregon New Certified Appraiser Law," *Assessment Administration,* IAAO, Chicago, 1956, pp. 50-55.

STINSON, CHARLES H., "Ethics--What's the Problem?," *Journal of the American Society of Farm Managers and Rural Appraisers,* April, 1962, pp. 6-9.

STOCKTON, JOHN Q., "Business Statistics," *Technical Valuation,* Southwestern Publishing Co., Cincinnati, Ohio, 1958.

STONE, PETER A., "A Technique for Establishing Relative Values of Realty," *Real Estate Record and Builders Guide,* May 27, 1933, pp. 3-6.

STOTTLE, BURR S., "Reasonable Probability--Exception to the Rule," *The Appraisal Journal,* January, 1962, pp. 55-60.

STOWE, THOMAS C., "The Question of Whole Property : a Comment," *The Real Estate Appraiser,* pp. 29.

STRATHON, ERIC C., "International Problems of Valuation," *New Zealand Valuer,* September, 1961, pp. 417-423.

STRIDE, I. L., "Real Estate Education In B.C.," *Appraisal Institute Magazine,* Appraisal Institute of Canada, Winnipeg.

STUNARD, EUGENE W., "Capitalization Approach and Financing," *Real Estate Appraiser,* May, 1967, pp. 31-36.

SUQIURA, SEIZO, "Real Estate Practice In Japan," *The Appraisal Journal,* January, 1936, pp. 73-75.

SWEPTSON, DWIGHT C., "Pros and Cons of Statutory Controls," *The Appraiser,* April, 1950, pp. 190-200.

SWEZEY, WILLIAM D., "Review and Evaluation of Appraisals," *Appraisal and Valuation Manual,* American Society of Appraisers, 1961, pp. 35-42.

TAEUBER, K. C., "An Argument In Favor of the Acceptance of the Doctrine of One Value for All Purposes," *The Appraisal Journal,* October, 1956, pp. 561-564.

TAIT, STUART C., "The Specific Principles In Appraising Fine Art," *Technical Valuation,* A. S. A., Washington, February, 1952, pp. 16.

TAPP, JESSE W., "Economic Growth and Property Values In the Sixties," *The Appraisal Journal,* July, 1961, pp. 293-299.

TAYLOR, J. J., "Statistical Theory of Depreciation," *Journal American Statistical Association,* December, 1923, pp. 1010-1023.

TAYLOR, JAMES R., "Depreciation Fallacies," *The Review,* April, 1949, pp. 3-4, 8.

TECHNICAL VALUATION, "Appraisal In Israel," *Technical Valuation,* May, 1954, pp. 56.

TECHNICAL VALUATION, "Appraiser Vs. Valuation Engineer Editorial Comment," *Technical Valuation,* September, 1945, pp. 8-9.

TECKEMEYER, E. B., "Modern Management and the Appraisal," *Review of Society of Residential Appraisers,* September, 1938, pp. 14-16.

TECKEMEYER, EARL B., *How to Value Real Estate; the Foremost Factor In Selling,* Prentice-Hall, Englewood Cliffs N J, 1956.

TECKEMEYER, EARL B., "Management's Contributions to Better Appraising," *National Real Estate Journal,* October, 1938, pp. 29-30.

TESTINO G., RICARDO, "Plusvalia," *Boletin,* Sotave, Caracas, Venezuela, pp. 35-37.

THE APPRAISAL JOURNAL, "A Horse of a Different Color," *The Appraisal Journal,* October, 1950, pp. 541-545.

THE APPRAISAL JOURNAL, "Inflation and Your Income," *The Appraisal Journal,* July, 1936, pp. 330.

THE APPRAISAL JOURNAL, "Relief for Hindsight (Appraisal Docket)," *The Appraisal Journal,* July, 1953, pp. 443-444.

THE ECONOMIST, "Business Brief; Money from the Deep," *The Economist,* December 5, 1970, pp. 60-61.

THE REVIEW, "Building Barometers," *The Review,* March, 1946, pp. 12-13.

THEOBALD, A. D., "Uncle Sam's Rubber Dollars," *The Review,* January, 1949, pp. 9-11, 17.

THOMAS, D. L., "Offshore and on Woes Are Piling Up for U. S. Commercial Real Estate," *Barrons,* December 14, 1970, pp. 3.

THOMPSON, BURTON, "On the Prophetic Analysis of Future Benefits In Max Tieger's Appraisal," *The Appraisal Journal,* April, 1933, pp. 245-247.

THOMPSON, BURTON, "On Value Vs. Prices," *The Appraisal Journal,* July, 1936, pp. 320-323.

THOMPSON, PELL, "Real Estate Appraisals by Formula," *Commerce and Finance,* July 20, 1927, pp. 1445-1446.

THOMPSON, R. E., "Income Vs. Physical Value," *National Real Estate Journal,* March 31, 1930, pp. 46-47.

THOMPSON, R. E., "On Entrepeneur's Increment," *The Appraisal Journal,* January, 1936, pp. 82.

THOMPSON, R. E., "This Thing Called Value," *National Real Estate Journal,* December, 1932, pp. 29-32.

THOMSON, CHARLES, "How High to Rise," *The Appraisal Journal,* October, 1966, pp. 585-591.

THOMSSEN, ROHLAND H., "Appraising and Counseling," *The Appraisal Journal,* January, 1960, pp. 17-23.

THORNCROFT, MICHAEL E. T., "The Future of the Professions," *The Appraisal Journal,* January, 1969, pp. 17-24.

THORNDIKE, EDWARD L. AND ELLA WOODYARD, "Individual Differences In American Cities," *American Journal of Sociology,* pp. 191-224.

THORSON, IVAN A., *Simplified Appraisal System,* Realty Research Bureau, Los Angeles, 1949.

THORSON, IVAN A., *Simplified Appraisal System, Land Economic,* Realty Research Bureau, Los Angeles, 1951.

THORSON, IVAN A., "Appraisal Methods In Times of Depression," *Proceedings,* 1933, pp. 310-323.

THORSON, IVAN A., "Confusion Twice Confounded," *The Appraisal Journal,* April, 1952, pp. 162-163.

THORSON, IVAN A., "Essentials of Real Estate Values," *An Appraisal Manual,* Realty Research Bureau, Los Angeles, 1931, pp. 1-96.

THORSON, IVAN A., "On the Capitalization Rate Used In Max Tieger's Appraisal," *The Appraisal Journal,* April, 1933, pp. 244-245.

THORSON, IVAN A., "Our Futile Quest for Exactness," *Review of the Society of Residential Appraisers,* July, 1936, pp. 5-8.

THORSON, IVAN A., "Rationalizing Appraisal Practice," *The Appraisal Journal,* July, 1936, pp. 237-253.

THORSON, IVAN A., "Relation of Value to the Purpose of the Appraisal," *The Appraisal Journal,* January, 1933, pp. 104-122.

THORSON, IVAN A., "The Function of the Appraiser," *Mcmichael's Appraising Manual,* 1937, pp. 123-132.

THORSON, IVAN A., "The Realtor Appraiser's Great Opportunity," *The Appraisal Journal,* February, 1933, pp. 324-339.

THORSON, J. T., "Memorandum on Value to the Owner," *Appraisal Institute Magazine,* Appraisal Institute of Canada, Winnipeg.

THUROW, RAYMOND, "The Pros and Cons of Personnel Testing," *The Assessors Journal,* July, 1966, pp. 1-8.

▲ Appraisal Theory and Methods

TIME, INC., "Instant City," *The Appraisal Journal*, July, 1967, pp. 402-403.

TOLTZMAN, R. J., "Responsibility of the Appraisers In Todays Economy," *Valuation*, September, 1972.

TOMPSON, GEORGE W., *Real Property*, Bobbs Merrill, Indianapolis, Ind..

TOMSON, BERNARD, *Architectural and Engineering Law*, Reinhold, New York, 1951.

TONTZ, ROBERT L., "Land Valuation and the Everyday Land Market," *Journal of the American Society of Farm Managers and Rural Appraisers*, 1955, pp. 24-29.

TORREY, WILLIAM W., "A Long Way to a Short Cut, or the End May Justify the Means," *The Appraisal Journal*, October, 1956, pp. 549-560.

TORREY, WILLIAM W., "The Ellwood Tables, a Critique," *The Appraisal Journal*, July, 1966, pp. 339-352.

TORREY, WILLIAM W., "The Time of Your Economic Life," *The Appraisal Journal*, January, 1955, pp. 46-58.

TOWERS, ALBERT G., "Comparing Property Income with Business Indexes," *National Real Estate Journal*, May, 1940, pp. 24-26.

TOWERS, ALBERT G. JR., "Considerations of Value," *The Appraisal Journal*, January, 1951, pp. 110-112.

TOWERS, ALBERT G. JR., "The Validity of an Appraisal," *The Appraisal Journal*, January, 1949, pp. 36-38.

TRANSOM, G. E. JR., "Current Thoughts on Depreciation," *The Real Estate Appraiser*, July, 1963, pp. 12-18.

TREADWELL, JOHN C., "La Seleccion De La Tasa De Capitalizacion," *Boletin*, Sotave, Caracas, Venezuela, pp. 15-28.

TREASURY DEPARTMENT, *Outline for the Study of Depreciation and Maintenance*, Treasury Department, Washington, 1926, pp. 1-38.

TREVINO, ALBERT F. JR., "Some Insights Into Systems Building," *Urban Land*, July, 1970.

TRITSCHLER, C. A., "Methodology for Asset Valuation by Specific Price Index," *Dissertation Abstracts*, May, 1968, pp. 4314-A.

TROWBRIDGE, CARL R., "The Fallacies of Depreciation," *The Real Estate Appraiser*, pp. 14.

TROWBRIDGE, CARL R., "What Is a Review Appraiser," *The Real Estate Appraiser*, April, 1971.

TROXEL, JAY C., "Expanding the Substitution Theory," *The Appraisal Journal*, July, 1945, pp. 266-270.

TROXEL, JAY C., "Purchaser's Cost Is Value Ceiling," *The Review*, September, 1945, pp. 14-15.

TROXEL, JAY C., "To Market, to Market," *The Appraisal Journal*, April, 1964, pp. 177-182.

TUCKER, GILBERT M., *The Self-Supporting City*, Robert Schalkenbach Foundation, New York, 1958, pp. 1-100.

TURNER, ROBERT C., "Basic Forces for Economic Change," *The Appraisal Journal*, April, 1957, pp. 198-208.

TURNER, ROBERT C., "Economic Impact of the Federal Budget," *The Appraisal Journal*, July, 1961, pp. 300-310.

TURNER, ROBERT C., "Is a Major Depression Coming," *The Appraisal Journal*, July, 1959, pp. 293-297.

TURNER, ROBERT C., "The Ambiguous Economics of Money," *The Appraisal Journal*, January, 1960, pp. 9-16.

TURNER, ROBERT C., "The American Economy In 1970," *The Appraisal Journal*, April, 1956, pp. 165-172.

TURNER, ROBERT C., "The Dilemma of Economic Policy," *The Appraisal Journal*, January, 1958, pp. 9-16.

TURNER, ROBERT C., "The Inventory Recession of 1960," *The Appraisal Journal,* July, 1960, pp. 293-298.

TURNER, ROBERT C., "The Sixty-Four Billion Dollar Question," *The Appraisal Journal,* July, 1958, pp. 325-331.

TURPIE, A., "Rural Appraisal Principles - Town and Farm," *Appraisal Institute Magazine,* January, 1957, pp. 13-15.

TYNAN, PETER, "A Buyer of Appraisals Speaks Out," *Appraisal Institute Magazine,* Appraisal Institute of Canada, Winnipeg, September 1, 1972.

U. P. A. V.,"Estatutos De La UPAV," *Boletin,* Sotave, Caracas, Venezuela, pp. 39-43.

URBAN LAND INSTITUTE, *New Town for California,* Urban Land Institute, Vol. Xxvi, Washington, November, 1966.

URBAN LAND INSTITUTE, "Land, Recreation and Leisure," *Urban Land Institute Special Report, 1970,* Urban Land Institute, Washington.

VAN BUREN, DEWITT, *Real Estate Brokerage and Commission,* Prentice-Hall, New York, 1948.

VAN BUREN, DEWITT, "Appraisal of Estates In Land Less Than the Fee," *The Appraisal Journal,* October, 1943, pp. 327-335.

VAN BUREN, DEWITT, "Legal Requirements Sometimes Modify Property Values," *The Appraisal Digest,* April, 1951, pp. 3-6.

VAN VUUREN, W., *Agricultural Land Prices and Returns In an Advanced Urban and Industrial Economy,* Dissertation Abstracts, Ann Arbor, March, 1969, pp. 2863-A.

VARTY, LEO G., "Reviving the Profit In Obsolete Properties," *National Real Estate Journal,* June, 1934, pp. 23-24.

VAUGHAN, J. H., "The Rule of Thumb," *Appraisal Institute Magazine,* Appraisal Institute of Canada, Winnipeg.

VAUGHAN, J. L. JR., "The Purpose of the Appraisal," *Appraisal And Valuation Manual,* 1956, pp. 23-26.

VEGAS ROLANDO, NICOLAS, "La Experticia En El Proceso Civil Venezolano," *Boletin,* Sotave, Caracas, Venezuela, pp. 11-12.

VEGAS ROLANDO, NICOLAS, "La Propiedad Inmueble," *Boletin,* Sotave, Caracas, Venezuela, pp. 4-5.

VOCKE, DR. WILHELM, "The Future of the Dollar," *The Appraisal Digest,* July, 1959, pp. 15-19.

WADA, S. A., "A Note on Depreciation and Growth," *Bulletin of University of Osaka Prefecture,* 1966, pp. 19-22.

WADDEL, HAROLD H., "The Professional Appraiser's Responsibility To His Client," *The Appraisal Journal,* April, 1958, pp. 227-232.

WAGNER, C. RAY, "Appraisal of Industrial Property," *Assessors Topics,* May, 1957.

WAGNER, J. J., "Standardizing Depreciation and Obsolescence," *National Real Estate Journal,* December 8, 1930.

WAGNER, PERCY E., "A Defense of the Income Approach," *Proceesings of the Third Institute on Eminent Domain,* Dallas, 1961, pp. 151-180.

WAGNER, PERCY E., "Licensing Certification Real Estate Appraisers," *Appraisal Institute Magazine,* Appraisal Institute of Canada, Winnipeg.

WAGNER, PERCY E., "On Economic Concepts of Appraising," *The Appraisal Journal,* January, 1967, pp. 125.

WAGNER, PERCY E., "The Licensing of Real Estate Brokers As Appraisers or the Certification of Real Estate Appraisers," *Appraisal Institute Magazine,* December, 1960, pp. 3-5.

WALDO, FRANCOIS, "An Institutional Investor Evaluates the Appraisal Reports," *The Appraisal Journal,* October, 1967, pp. 550-554.

WALES, T. J., "Estimation of an Accelerated Depreciation Learning Function," *Journal of the American Statistical Association,* December, 1966, pp. 995-1009.

WALLINGFORT, J. WALLINGFORD, "Comments on Comments on Training of Appraisers," *The Appraisal Journal,* January, 1947, pp. 48-50.

WALSH, H. VANDERVOORT, "Finding Reproduction Cost," *The Appraisal Journal,* April, 1934, pp. 228-231.

WALSTEIN, SMITH, JR., "Value-Verified and Vilified," *The Real Estate Appraiser,* September, 1965, pp. 2-11.

WALSTRUM, S. WILLIAM, "Market Analysis," *Journal of Certified Property Managers,* March, 1941, pp. 216-228.

WALTHER, HERMAN O., "Applying Our Principles," *The Review,* June, 1947, pp. 3-7, 12.

WALTHER, HERMAN O., "Professional Standards," *The Appraisal Journal,* April, 1946, pp. 121-123.

WALTHER, HERMAN O., "This Is How Chicago Real Estate Board Appraisals Are Made," *Real Estate,* February 18, 1939, pp. 10-14.

WALTHER, HERMAN O., "Why the Three Approaches Fit Together," *The Review,* June, 1956, pp. 3-7.

WARNER, ARTHUR E., "Creativity In the Appraisal Process," *The Appraisal Journal,* July, 1963, pp. 316-318.

WARREN, G. F., F. A. PEARSON, *Gold and Prices,* John Wiley and Sons, Inc., New York, 1935.

WARREN, ISABELLA, "A Private Eye for Taste," *The Appraisal and Valuation Manual,* 1961, pp. 189.

WARWICK, SAMUEL C., "The Two-Property Concept," *The Real Estate Appraiser,* March, 1965, pp. 23-25.

WATERS, J. M., "Just What Should a Realtor Know," *National Real Estate Journal,* August 13, 1923, pp. 21-22.

WATSON, WILLIAM H., "How Many Values?," *The Review,* March, 1950, pp. 3-6.

WEBB, CLARENCE ALBERT, *Valuation of Real Property,* C. Lockwood and Sons, London 2d Edit V Xii, 1910, pp. 1-332.

WEBB, JAMES A., "Methods of Appraising Improvements," *National Real Estate Journal,* February 26, 1923, pp. 25.

WEBB, JAMES A., "Methods of Appraising Land," *National Real Estate Journal,* February 20, 1923, pp. 23-25.

WEED, KENNETH A., "Market Values Versus Price and Financing," *The Residential Appraiser,* November, 1961, pp. 9-12.

WEIMER, ARTHUR M., "Comments on Training of Appraisers," *The Appraisal Journal,* January, 1947, pp. 42-47.

WEIMER, ARTHUR M., "History of Value Theory for the Appraiser," *The Appraisal Journal,* January, 1953, pp. 8-22.

WEIMER, ARTHUR M., HOYER, HOMER, *Principles of Urban Real Estate,* Ronald, New York, 1948.

WEIR, T. R., "Factors Affecting Land Values," *The Appraisal Institute Magazine,* December, 1959, pp. 28-30.

WEISER, FRIEDRICH, *Natural Value,* Kelley and Millman, New York, 1956.

WELCH, RAYMOND F., "Appraising Real Property In Estates and Trusts," *Appraisal and Valuation Manual,* 1959, pp. 293-298.

WELLS, H. C., "Sure You Can Grow Fast In This Business-Provided You Build a Staff That Can Grow with You," *House and Home,* August, 1970, pp. 28.

WELLS, HENRY W., "A Chartered Surveyor Looks at Soviet Russia-Extracts," *The Appraisal Journal,* July, 1959, pp. 365-374.

WENDT, PAUL F., "An Allegory for the New Year," *The Residential Appraiser,* January, 1957, pp. 3-6.

WENDT, PAUL F., "Economic Growth and Urban Land Values," *The Appraisal Journal,* July, 1958, pp. 427-443.

WENDT, PAUL F., "Ellwood, Inwood, and the Internal Rate of Return," *The Appraisal Journal,* October, 1967, pp. 561-574.

WENDT, PAUL F., "Recent Developments In Appraisal Theory," *Appraisal Institute Magazine,* Appraisal Institute of Canada, Winnipeg.

WENDT, PAUL F., "Theory of Urban Land Value," *Land Economics,* August, 1957.

WENDT, PAUL F., "Urban Land Value Trends," *The Appraisal Journal,* April, 1958, pp. 254-269.

WENDT, PAUL FRANCIS, *Real Estate Appraisal a Critical Analysis of Theory and Practice,* Holt, New York, 1956.

WENGER, RALPH W. JR., "The Easy Way Out," *The Real Estate Appraiser,* pp. 34.

WENZLICK, ROY, "As I See Lessons from the Past," *The Real Estate Analyst Appraisal Bulletin,* 1954, pp. 89-92.

WENZLICK, ROY, "Realty Analyst Predicts Boom Years Ahead," *California Real Estate Magazine,* December, 1940, pp. 9, 42.

WENZLICK, ROY, "Should the Appraiser Be an Advocate?," *Real Estate Analyst Appraisal Bulletin,* 1960, pp. 323-326.

WESCOTT, T. C., "The Inside Story of Outside Help," *The Appraisal Journal,* 1955, pp. 102.

WESTBY, R. L., ALFRED, A. H, SAYNWITTGENSTEIN, L, "The Potential of Large-Scale Air Photographs and Radar Alimetry In Land Evaluation," *Land Valuation,* pp. 376.

WESTERFIELD, RAY B., "Inflation and Real Estate Are Closely Connected," *Appraisal Digest,* January, 1952, pp. 18-19.

WHELDON, GEORGE T., "Publication of Depreciation Theories," *Review of Society of Residential Appraisers,* December, 1939, pp. 3-8.

WHIPPLE, R. T. M., "Teaching of Land Economics," *Appraisal Institute Magazine,* 1968, pp. 22-26.

WHIPPLE, R. T. M., "What Determines Highest and Best Use," *Appraisal Institute Magazine,* Appraisal Institute of Canada, Winnipeg.

WHISTON, FRANK M., "Decentralization In Chicago," *Skyscraper Management,* April, 1936, pp. 3-4, 29-30.

WHITE, JOHN R., "Analyzing Comparable Data," *The Appraisal Digest,* October, 1969, pp. 24.

WHITE, JOHN R., "How Many Approaches to Value?," *Appraisal Digest,* April, 1958, pp. 9-10.

WHITE, JOHN R., "Marking the Discrepancies Between Appraising and Counseling," *The Appraiser,* April, 1969.

WHITE, JOHN R., "New Horizons In Capitalization Rate Selection," *Technical Valuation,* June, 1957, pp. 28-32.

WHITE, JOHN R., "Selection of the Capitalization Rate," *The Appraisal Journal,* October, 1949, pp. 478-489.

WHITE, JOHN R., "The Fallacy of Gross Income Stabilization," *The Appraisal Journal,* July, 1956, pp. 348-350.

WHITE, JOHN ROBERT, "Capitalization Rates and the Current Money Market," *The Appraisal Journal,* July, 1957, pp. 417-420.

WHITE, JOHN ROBERT, "The Past Five Years," *The Appraisal Journal,* January, 1962, pp. 111-113.

WHITE, JOHN ROBERT, "The Real Estate Market In the Past and Future Decade," *The Appraisal Journal,* April, 1959, pp. 189-197.

WHITE, JOHN ROBERT, "This Issue of Professionalism," *The Appraisal Journal,* October, 1960, pp. 539-541.

WHITE, PHILIP H., "Principles and Procedures In the Training of Appraisers," *Wisconsin Colloquium on Appraisal Research, Papers and Proceedings,* 1963, pp. 59-66.

WHITE, PHILIP H., "Some Aspects of the Income Approach," *The Residential Appraiser*, July, 1960, pp. 16-23.

WHITEHEAD, J. B., "How an Appraisal Committee Can Help the Local Board," *Practical Appraising Methods*, 1940, pp. 125-128.

WHITNALL, GORDON, "In Times of War Prepare for Peace," *The Appraisal Journal*, October, 1942, pp. 313-322.

WHITTEN, WILCOX, *Valuation of Public Utilities*, The Banks Law Publishing Company, New York, 1928, pp. 189, 196.

WHYNACHT, C. F., "The Realtor Looks for Value," *The Appraisal Journal*, January, 1963, pp. 56-64.

WICKENDEN, W. E., "The Second Mile-Ethics In Valuation," *Technical Valuation*, October, 1953, pp. 21.

WICKSTEAD, PHILIP HENRY, *The Alphabet of Economic Science*, Kelley and Millman, New York, 1955.

WIGHT, WARD, "Appraising---Past, Present and Future," *The Review*, September, 1947, pp. 9-12.

WILBANKS, RICHARD P., "What Is a Typical Buyer," *The Real Estate Appraiser*, April, 1966, pp. 18.

WILCOX, DONALD A., "Use of Appraisals by Negotiators," *Right of Way*, 1968, pp. 447.

WILDMAN, JOHN R., "Appreciation from the Point of View of the Certified Public Accountant," *Accounting Review*, December, 1928, pp. 396-406.

WILDSMITH, P. D., "The Problem of Value," *Appraisal Institute Magazine*, February, 1958, pp. 5-8.

WILNETT, MCDONNELL, WOLCOTT, "Cost Approach," *Problems In Rural Real Estate Appraisal*, pp. 7.

WILNETT, MCDONNELL, WOLCOTT, "Income Capitalization Techniques," *Problems In Rural Real Estate Appraisal*, pp. 11.

WILNETTE, MCDONNELL, WOLCOTT, "Basic Principles and Procedures," *Problems In Rural Real Estate Appraisal*, pp. 1.

WILNETTE, MCDONNELL, WOLCOTT, "Market Data Approach," *Problems In Rural Real Estate Appraisal*, pp. 20.

WILSON, D. EARL, "On Normal Value," *The Appraisal Journal*, January, 1934, pp. 150-151.

WILSON, GEORGE A., *Depreciation*, Mass Society of Certified Public Accountants, Inc., December 17, 1934, pp. 5-9.

WILSON, P. M., "Canada-Problems and Potential," *Appraisal Institute Magazine*, Appraisal Institute of Canada, Winnipeg.

WINFREY, ROBLEY, KURTZ, EDWIN B, "Life Characteristics of Physical Property," *Iowa Engineering Experiment Station Bulletin, No. 103*, Iowa State College of Agriculture & Mechanic Arts, Ames, June 17, 1931, pp. 1-144.

WINNICK, LOUIS, "Long-Run Changes In the Valuation of Real Estate by Gross Rents," *The Appraisal Journal*, October, 1952, pp. 484-498.

WINSTEAD, ROBERT W., "Market Value, the Old Standby and Zoning," *The Residential Appraiser*, December, 1960, pp. 19-21.

WINSTEAD, ROBERT W., "On Presentation of Conclusions," *The Appraisal Journal*, October, 1962, pp. 544-545.

WINSTON, CAREY, "The Crucial Role of the Appraiser," *The Real Estate Appraiser*, July, 1964, pp. 21.

WINTERHALT, J. H., "So You Want to Buy a House," *Appraisal Institute Magazine*, Appraisal Institute of Canada, Winnipeg.

WISCONSIN PUBLIC SERVICE COMMISSION, *Depreciation, a Review of Legal and Accounting Problems*, The Commission, Madison, 1933, pp. 1-96.

WISCONSIN, UNIVERSITY OF, *Professional Training In Real Estate,* Milwaukee Real Estate Board, Milwaukee, August, 1937, pp. 4.

WOEFF, HELMUT O., "Concepts and Procedures of Arbitration Impact Upon the Community and the Appraisal Profession," *Appraisal and Valuation Manual,* Corporate Press Incorporated, Washington, D. C, January, 1972, pp. 284.

WOLK, H. I., "The Relevant Costing Approach to Asset Valuation and Income Determination, a Critique," *Dissertation Abstracts,* April, 1969, pp. 3265-A.

WOLTZ, SETH P., "Misuse of Comparable Sales," *The Residential Appraiser,* pp. 3.

WOODRUFF, ARCHIBALD MULFORD, *Elementary Appraisal Principles,* Pittsburg Bureau of Business Research, Pittsburg, 1957.

WOODWARD, DONALD B., "Long Term Trends In Industry," *The Appraisal Journal,* April, 1948, pp. 148-155.

WOODWARD, DONALD B., "The Promise of the Future-Can We Muff It?," *The Appraisal Journal,* July, 1945, pp. 225-231.

WOODWORTH, LEO D., "Industrial Appraisers Vs. Mechanical Surveys," *National Real Estate Journal,* June 13, 1927, pp. 24-26.

WORTHINGTON, J. E., "The Theory of Interest," *Appraisal Institute Magazine,* Appraisal Institute of Canada, Winnipeg, March 1, 1973.

WRIGHT, CARROLL, "As Many Values As Uses," *Review of the Society of Residential Appraisers,* October, 1936, pp. 9-10.

WRIGHT, KARL T., "What I See In Present and Future Land Prices," *Journal of the American Society of Farm Managers and Rural Appraisers,* October, 1946, pp. 79-83.

WULFF, EDUARDO J., "Saliendo Del Empirismo," *Boletin,* Sotave, Caracas, Venezuela, pp. 19-23.

WYNACHT, C. F., "The Realtor Looks for Value," *Appraisal Institute Magazine,* Appraisal Institute of Canada, Winnipeg.

YASHANOFF, B. A., "India--Commentary on the Economic Environment," *Technical Valuation,* August, 1967, pp. 15.

ZANGERLE, JOHN A., *Principles of Real Estate Appraising,* Cleveland, 1924.

ZANGERLE, JOHN A., "Appraising Fractional Real Estate Interests," *The Appraisal Journal,* November, 1940, pp. 355-359.

ZANGERLE, JOHN A., "Lot Tables Are Essential In Realty Appraising," *National Real Estate Journal,* 1929, pp. 41-43.

ZECKENDORF, WILLIAM, "Futures In Real Estate," *The Appraisal Journal,* July, 1954, pp. 325-329.

ZEPP, EDWARD G., "Biblical Methods of Valuation," *The Residential Appraiser,* September, 1959, pp. 13-14, 18.

ZEPP, EDWARD G., "Could This Be a Cause?," *The Appraisal Journal,* October, 1963, pp. 522-524.

ZEPP, EDWARD G., "Federalitis, Advocitis, and Sympathesia," *The Appraisal Journal,* April, 1963, pp. 257-258.

ZEPP, EDWARD G., "The Difference Is Up to You," *The Appraisal Journal,* October, 1965, pp. 619-620.

# 11-12 Appraisal Ethics

ADELSBERG, HYMAN, "**ASA Education Program,**" *Technical Valuation,* February, 1954, pp. 18.

ALEXANDER, ROBERT H., "**The Need for Proper Public Relations,**" *The Residential Appraiser,* September 20, 1962, pp. 9-10.

ALLIN, B. C., "**Bill to License Appraisers In California Legislature,**" *Technical Valuation,* June, 1955, pp. 5-8.

AMERICAN INSTITUTE OF REAL ESTATE APPRAISERS, "**Code of Fair Competition for the Profession and Business of Real Estate Appraising,**" *The National Real Estate Journal,* September, 1933, pp. 39-41.

AMERICAN INSTITUTE OF REAL ESTATE APPRAISERS, "**Codigo De Etica Profesional,**" *Boletin,* Sotave, Caracas, Venezuela, pp. 25-43.

AMERICAN SOCIETY OF APPRAISERS, "**Principios Del Ejercicio De ASA,**" *Boletin,* Sotave, Caracas, Venezuela, pp. 25-35.

APPRAISAL DIGEST, "**Committee Suggests Appraisal Fees Be Standardized,**" *Society of Residential Appraisers,* April, 1951, pp. 23-24.

APPRAISAL JOURNAL, "**On Negligent and Fraudulent Appraisals,**" *The Appraisal Journal,* July, 1947, pp. 413-415.

ARMSTRONG, EDWIN F., "**Appraisers or Appeasers,**" *Freehold,* November, 1941, pp. 40-42.

ARNESON JR, H. R., "**Appraiser-Client Agreement,**" *Appraisal Institute Magazine,* Appraisal Institute of Canada, Winnipeg.

ARNESON, HARRY R. JR., "**Appraiser-Client Agreement,**" *Appraisal Institute Magazine,* September, 1961, pp. 28-29.

ASSESSORS NEWSLETTER, "**Beware of Image Over Consciousness,**" *Assessors Newsletter,* May, 1966, pp. 71.

ASSOCIATION OF APPRAISAL EXECUTIVES, *Basic Standards of Appraisal Practice and Procedure,* Association of Appraisal Executives, Washington, D. C, 1936.

ASSOCIATION OF APPRAISAL EXECUTIVES, "**Code of Practice for Independent Public Appraisers,**" *Basic Standards of Appraisal Practice and Procedure,* Association of Appraisal Executives, Washington, D. C, 1936.

ATKINSON HARRY GRANT, "**Appraising As a Profession,**" *The Appraisal Journal,* July, 1936, pp. 271-277.

ATKINSON HARRY GRANT, "**Ethics and Professional Conduct,**" *The Appraisal Journal,* October, 1935, pp. 451-455.

ATKINSON, HARRY GRANT, "**This Is My Judgment,**" *The Appraisal Journal,* October, 1958, pp. 557-560.

BABCOCK, DR. HENRY A., "**One Man's Appraisal Philisophy,**" *Valuation,* American Society of Appraisers, September, 1972, pp. 2.

BABCOCK, HENRY A., "**The Ethics of Appraising,**" *The Annals of Real Estate Practice,* 1928, pp. 118-142.

BABCOCK, WILLIAM H., "**Appraising As a Phase of Salesmanship,**" *National Real Estate Journal,* November 5, 1923, pp. 22-26.

BAGBY, JOHN JR., "**Appraisal Fees Dollars and Cents,**" *The Appraisal Journal,* April, 1961, pp. 251-252.

BALDWIN, H. G., "**Ethics of an Institutional Appraiser,**" *The Real Estate Appraiser,* 1900, pp. 6.

BALLARD, WILLIAM S., "**How the Appraiser Discharges His Responsibilities,**" *Technical Valuation,* February, 1963, pp. 24-28.

BARNARD, BOYD T., "Artist or Mechanic: an Appraiser Appraises Appraising," *The Appraiser,* November, 1969.

BARNARD, BOYD T., "The Future of Appraising," *The Appraisal Journal,* April, 1965, pp. 181-189.

BARONE, RAY R., "How to Get Your Moneys Worth from the Appraiser," *The Appraisal Journal,* July, 1965, pp. 437-439.

BATCHELOR, HARRY H., "Special Responsibility of Appraisers In Cited Examples," *The Review,* May, 1956, pp. 8-10.

BENNETT, S. Z., "La Organizacion Profesional," *Boletin,* Sotave, Caracas, Venezuela, pp. 9-13.

BERGER, MILES, "Professional Status Needed by Appraisers," *The Real Estate Appraiser,* pp. 15.

BISHOP, JESSE E., "Legal Responsibilities of the Appraiser," *Appraisal Institute Magazine,* Appraisal Institute of Canada, Winnipeg.

BLAKELY, A. P., "A Profession," *Appraisal Institute Magazine,* Appraisal Institute of Canada, Winnipeg, June 1, 1972.

BODFISH, MORTON, THEOBALD, A. D, "The Ethics of Appraising," *Real Estate Fundamentals,* 1941, pp. 19.

BOWES, WATSON A., "The Future of the Appraisal Profession," *The Residential Appraiser,* May, 1960, pp. 3-7, 24.

BOWES, WATSON A., "Your Appraiser---An Aid to Selling," *The Appraisal Journal,* April, 1954, pp. 262-266.

BRADY, HOBART C., "Scientific Appraisals As an Aid to Selling," *The Appraisal Journal,* January, 1948, pp. 57-62.

BROWN, JUANITA C, "Attributes of a Professional Appraiser," *Valutapes Audio-Library Series,* American Society of Appraisers, Washington D.C., January 1, 1973.

BROWN, R. K., "The Need for Generalists," *Appraisal Institute Magazine,* Appraisal Institute of Canada, Winnipeg.

BROWN, ROBERT K, "The Need for Generalists In the Appraisal Profession," *The Appraisal Journal,* May, 1960, pp. 219-224.

BROWN, ROBERT L, "The Generalist Revisited," *The Appraisal Journal,* May, 1965, pp. 227-231.

BROWNER, VINCENT, "Public Relations," *Assessment Administration,* Chicago, 1962, pp. 141-146.

BRUNSON, THEO R., "Responsibilities of Appraisers," *Right of Way,* 1962, pp. 28-31.

BURLAKE, J. M., "Conflict of Interest In Appraising," *Technical Valuation,* October, 1961, pp. 35-38.

BURROUGHS, ROY J., "An Appraisal of an Appraiser's Proposals," *The Appraisal Journal,* July, 1933, pp. 340-345.

BURROWS, R. DOUGLAS, "Written Appraisal Policy," *The Review,* April, 1951, pp. 15-16.

BURT, F. P., "The Practical Value of Accurate Appraisals," *Buildings-And Building Management,* July, 1932, pp. 31-33.

CALIFORNIA REAL ESTATE ASSOCIATION, "Contract for Employment for Appraisal Service," *The Appraising Manual* by S. L. McMichael, Ed. 2, 1937, pp. 550-551.

CARROLL, WESLEY C., "The Responsibilty of the Independent Appraiser," *Proceedings of the Eighth Annual National Seminar of the American Right of Way Association,* Washington, D.C., 1962, pp. 41-42.

CHADEAYNE, ROBERT O., "Artist to Appraiser," *A. S. A. Valuation Manual,* American Society of Appraisers, Washington, D. C., 1958, pp. 57.

CHANDIAS, MARIO E., "Introduccion Al Aprovechamiento," *Boletin,* Sotave, Caracas, Venezuela, pp. 7-10.

▲ Appraisal Theory and Methods

CHANDIAS, MARIO E., "Los Tasadores Concepto Moderno Valuacion," *Boletin,* Sotave, Caracas, Venezuela, pp. 7-16.

CHERNEY, RICHARD A., "The Profession's Responsibility for Training and Education," *Assessment Administration,* IAAO, Chicago, 1963, pp. 51-55.

CHESSMAN, MARK, "The Appraiser and Public Relations," *The Appraisal Journal,* July, 1937, pp. 273-277.

CHURCH, BYRON M., "Consultation-The Appraiser's Ultimate Function," *The Real Estate Appraiser,* October, 1964, pp. 11-14.

CHURCH, BYRON M., "From Appraising to Counseling," *The Real Estate Appraiser,* Society of Real Estate Appraisers, Chicago, January, 1964, pp. 16.

CHURCH, BYRON M., "Guide to a Successful Appraisal Practice," *The Real Estate Appraiser,* May, 1963, pp. 14-25.

CHURCHILL, WINSTON S., "The Valuer and His Profession," *The Appraisal Journal,* July, 1966, pp. 326-328.

CLAUSEN, DON H., "The Appraiser's Task--Protecting the Public," *Technical Valuation,* American Society of Appraisers, Washington, September, 1966, pp. 32.

CONAN, ROBERT J., "Should Appraised Value Contain Profits and Commissions," *Appraisal Digest,* July, 1954, pp. 17-18.

CONSER, EUGENE P., "Realtor's Obligation In Appraising," *Realtor's Headlines,* February 9, 1959, pp. 2.

CONSTAM, E., "P. R. for Appraisers," *Appraisal Institute Magazine,* Appraisal Institute of Canada, Winnipeg.

COOKE, JOHN, "One Judge's Views on Appraiser Certification or Liscensing," *The Appraiser,* February, 1967.

CORDIER, HENRY K., *Valuation Problems and the Client,* American Society of Appraisers.

COULSON, ROBERT, *The Arbitration of Valuation Disputes,* American Society of Appraisers, Washington, September, 1968, pp. 52.

COULSON, ROBERT M, "The Professional Appraiser Looks at Arbitration," *Valutape Audio-Library Series,* American Society of Appraisers, Washington D.C., January 1, 1973.

DAVIS, JERRY C., "Current Case Against Licensing," *Appraisal Institute Magazine,* Appraisal Institute of Canada, Winnipeg, September 1, 1972.

DAVIS, W. D., "In This I Believe," *The Appraisal Journal,* October, 1964, pp. 608-609.

DAVIS, W. D., "Professional Standards and the Appraiser's Future," *The Real Estate Appraiser,* May, 1963, pp. 2-7.

DE NOYELLES F., "Meriting Confidence," *The Review,* May, 1955, pp. 10-11.

DOLMAN, JOHN P., "Responsibilities of the Appraiser," *The Appraisal Journal,* January, 1962, pp. 49-54.

DOLMAN, JOHN P., "The Appraiser of Tomorrow," *Right of Way,* April, 1970.

DOLMAN, JOHN P., "The Appraiser of Tomorrow," *The Appraisal Journal,* October, 1969, pp. 582-586.

DOLMAN, JOHN P., "The Appraiser's Dilemma," *The Appraisal Journal,* July, 1967, pp. 384.

DORION, GUY, "Le Role De L Evaluateur," *Appraisal Institute Magazine,* Appraisal Institute of Canada, Winnipeg, June 1, 1973.

DOWNIE, LEONARD, "The Appraiser's Responsibility Under H. O. L. C. Property Appraisal Report Form," *The Appraisal Journal,* January, 1937, pp. 60-66.

DUCK, BERKLEY W., "Determining Professional Fees," *The Appraisal Journal,* October, 1958, pp. 537-541.

DUFFY, GEORGE C., "The Disinterested Appraiser," *Right of Way,* April, 1963, pp. 13-20.

## BIBLIOGRAPHY OF APPRAISAL LITERATURE

DUNN, DOMINICK R., "Some Thoughts on Licensing Appraisers," *The Real Estate Appraiser,* February, 1964, pp. 2..

ECKSTEIN, ARTHUR, "Publicity," *Technical Valuation,* American Society of Appraisers, February, 1954, pp. 7..

EDMAN, J. J., "The Appraisal Docket. Appraiser's Fee Not Part of Award," *The Appraisal Journal,* October, 1960, pp. 550-551.

EGERTON, J. W., "Valuation Day and the Professional Appraiser," *Appraisal Institute Magazine,* Appraisal Institute of Canada, Winnipeg, June 1, 1972.

ELLWOOD, LEON W., "Today's Appraiser Is a Specialist," *The Review,* April, 1945, pp. 14-15.

ELSE-MITCHELL, JUSTICE, "Duties and Liabilities of Valuers," *Appraisal Institute Magazine,* Appraisal Institute of Canada, Winnipeg, September 1, 1973.

FENTON, HARRY R., "Good Appraisers Have No Emotions," *Selected Readings In Right of Way,* 1968, pp. 197-201.

FERGUSON, W. E., "On Professional Ethics," *The Appraisal Journal,* July, 1933, pp. 364-365.

FIFER, LOUIS J., "Mr. Appraiser Your P.R. Is Showing," *Appraisal Institute Magazine,* Appraisal Institute of Canada, Winnipeg.

FISCHER, R. M., "Standards," *Technical Evaluation,* June, 1954, pp. 64.

FISKEN, A. J., *Qualifications of an Appraiser,* Mutual Savings Bank of Seattle, Washington, D. C, September 9, 1925, pp. 241.

FREE, VICTOR J., "Upon These Things Have I Relied," *The Appraisal Journal,* January, 1938, pp. 30-36.

FRIEDMAN, ALBERT L., "Market Comparison As an Appraisal Tool," *Appraisal Digest,* April, 1957, pp. 4-6.

FRISSELL, ROBERT N., "The Professional Appraisal and Market Value," *The Appraisal Journal,* October, 1966, pp. 581-584.

GALLAHER, JOSEPH A. SR., "A Promise Made a Promise Fulfilled," *Technical Valuation,* February, 1956, pp. 41-44.

GARRETT, THOMAS M., "Professions, Association, and Codes," *The Appraisal Journal,* October, 1965, pp. 555-562.

GIBSON, BRUCE G., "The Professional Appraiser and Public Relations," *American Society of Appraisers,* 1960, pp. 391-398.

GILLESPIE, JOHN, "An Appraisal of the Profession of Appraising," *The Residential Appraiser,* June, 1962, pp. 19-20, 24.

GODIN, CAMILLE R., "Professionalism," *Assessors News Letter,* June, 1963, pp. 67-70.

GONZALES, C. S., "The Future of Professional Appraising In Spanish Speaking Countries," Corporate Press Inc., 1966-71, pp. 308-312.

GONZALEZ VALE, LUIS, "El Justiprecio Judicial," *Boletin,* Sotave, Caracas, Venezuela, pp. 35-39.

GOSSELIN, JACQUES, "L Avenir Des Evaluateurs Et De La Profession De L Evaluateurs," *Appraisal Institute Magazine,* June, 1962, pp. 18-21.

HAGOOD, WAYNE D., "Professionalism, a Cooperative Effort," *The Residential Appraiser,* March, 1962, pp. 22-23.

HAIG, GRAEME T., "Role of the Appraiser In Arbitration," *Appraisal Institute Magazine,* Appraisal Institute of Canada, Winnipeg.

HALE, JAMES R., "Danger In Horseback Appraisals," *Technical Valuation,* February, 1954, pp. 12.

HALL, JOHN H., "The Public Image of Real Estate," *Appraisal Institute Magazine,* Appraisal Institute of Canada, Winnipeg.

HALL, JOSEPH B., "On Professional Ethics," *The Appraisal Journal,* July, 1933, pp. 366-367.

HANSON, ALDEN W., "Appraiser's Expenses," *The Real Estate Appraiser,* SREA, Chicago, July, 1964, pp. 2.

▲ Appraisal Theory and Methods

HEAD, GEORGE J., "Advertising by Appraisers," *The Appraisal Journal,* July, 1936, pp. 278-282.

HEAD, GEORGE J., "The Liability of the Appraiser," *The Appraisal Journal,* January, 1933, pp. 143-152.

HEINEKE, PAUL H., "Appraisers on Trial," *The Review,* July, 1951, pp. 3-7.

HENDERSON, JAMES D., "The Modern Appraisal Kit," *The Appraisal Journal,* July, 1933, pp. 335.

HERZER, T. O. F., "Proper Appraisal Practices," *Journal of the American Society of Farm Managers and Rural Appraisers,* October, 1945, pp. 134-140.

HEWITT, JOHN A., "What Do You Think About Appraisers and Appraising? Appraising," *The Appraiser,* October, 1970.

HINDS, DUDLEY S., RICHARD HEWITT III, STEVEN D. KAPPLIN, "Professionalism In the Practice of Real Est Apprsl," *Appraisal Institute Magazine,* Appraisal Institute of Canada, Winnipeg.

HODGES, M. B. JR., "Professional Appraisal Fees," *The Real Estate Appraiser,* Chicago, June, 1964, pp. 17.

HOYT, GEORGE H., "Round Table Discussion of Fee, Competitive Bidding and Ethics," *Technicalities,* February, 1950, pp. 26-27.

HOYT, JOHN R., "On Standards In Appraisal Practice," *The Appraisal Journal,* January, 1937, pp. 72-73.

JEFFERIES, RODNEY L., "Licensing of Appraisers: Problem or Solution," *Appraisal Institute Magazine,* Appraisal Institute of Canada, Winnipeg, March 1, 1972.

JOUR OF AMER SOC OF FARM MGRS & RURAL APPRAISERS, "Minimum Provisions for an Act to Certify Real Property Appraisers," *Journal of the American Society of Farm Managers and Rural Appraisers,* October, 1962, pp. 62-66.

JURETTE, LOUIS J., "History of the American Society of Appraisers," *American Society of Appraisers, Appraisal Institute Magazine,* 1960.

KAHN, SANDERS A., *State Registration of Appraisers,* ASA, Chicago, 1955, pp. 258-263.

KAHN, SANDERS A., WILLIAM SMITH, "The Need for State Registration of Appraisers," *Technical Valuation,* ASA, Jamaica, June, 1955, pp. 37.

KENNEDY, D. A., "Qualifications Appraisal Society of Societies," *Appraisal Institute Magazine,* Appraisal Institute of Canada, Winnipeg.

KENNEDY, R. D., "On Obtaining Accreditation," *Appraisal Institute Magazine,* Appraisal Institute of Canada, Winnipeg.

KING, BEN E., "Moral and Legal Concepts Governing Appraisals," *Thereview,* January, 1956, pp. 12-17.

KNISKERN, PHILIP W., "The Difficulties and Menaces In Professional Practice," *The Appraisal Journal,* July, 1955, pp. 334-340.

KOSTERS, STUART F., "Professional Fees for Professional Services," *Technical Valuation,* November, 1955, pp. 16-18.

KYLE, G. IRWIN, "Do You Consider Yourself a Qualified Appraiser," *The Appraisal Digest,* January, 1951, pp. 19-20.

LALONDE, JEAN G., "Qu Est-Ce Qu Un Evaluateur," *Appraisal Institute Magazine,* Appraisal Institute of Canada, Winnipeg, September 1, 1973.

LAUNER, E. J., "The Significance of the American Society of Appraisers In the Appraisal Field," *Technical Valuation,* February, 1959, pp. 3-4.

LAYDEN, A. L., "On Professional Ethics," *The Appraisal Journal,* July, 1933, pp. 364.

LEHR, WALTER G. JR., "Consultation In Appraising," *The Real Estate Appraiser,* January, 1959, pp. 3-5.

LOCKYER, ALBERT W., "Appraisal Integrity," *The Review*, March, 1955, pp. 15.

LOS ANGELES REALTY BOARD, "Board's Schedule of Commissions Including Appraisal Fees," *California Real Estate Magazine*, November, 1935, pp. 33-35.

LOSTETTER, EARL K., "Ethics of the Professional Appraiser," *The Appraisal Journal*, April, 1953, pp. 269-277.

LOSTETTER, EARL K., "The Distinction Between Appraising and Counseling," *Appraisal Digest*, October, 1961, pp. 1-4.

LUNDY, VICTOR R., "Facing Broader Responsibilities," *The Residential Appraiser*, November, 1956, pp. 3-5, 8.

LYNCH, JOHN R., "The Appraiser's Qualifications," *The Appraisal Journal*, January, 1953, pp. 83-87.

MACBRIDE DEXTER D, "Opportunities In Appraising for Minorities," *Valutape Audio-Library Series*, American Society of Appraisers, Washington D.C., February 1, 1974.

MACBRIDE, DEXTER D, "Major Developments In the Appraisal Profession Within the US: Review, Commentary, Prediction," *Valuation Magazine*, American Society of Appraisers, Washington D.C., December 1, 1973, pp. 126-138.

MACBRIDE, DEXTER D, "The American Society of Appraisers," *Valutape Audio-Library Series*, American Society of Appraisers, Washington D.C., January 1, 1973.

MACBRIDE, DEXTER D, "The Profession of Appraising," *Valutape Audio-Library Series*, American Society of Appraisers, Washington D.C., January 1, 1973.

MACGOVERN, JOHN J. JR., "Quality of Credit and the Appraiser," *The Real Estate Appraiser*, December, 1963, pp. 14-19.

MASHKE, D. K., "That Question of Fees," *The Real Estate Appraiser*, August, 1963, pp. 12-15.

MATTHEWS, MYRON L., "Licensing Is No Cure-All," *The Review*, July, 1951, pp. 14-15.

MAY, ARTHUR A, "Some Nightmares I Have Had," *The Appraisal Journal*, October, 1947, pp. 510-513.

MCMANUS, JOSEPH F., "Appraising the Appraiser," *The Appraisal Journal*, October, 1948, pp. 481-482.

MCMICHAEL, STANLEY L., "On Professional Ethics," *The Appraisal Journal*, July, 1933, pp. 336.

MERREL, JOHN A., "Professionalism," *The Residential Appraiser*, February, 1962, pp. 6-12.

MILISIEWICZ, JANINA, "Public Policy - Property - and People," *Appraisal Institute Magazine*, Appraisal Institute of Canada, Winnipeg, March 1, 1973.

MINWEGEN ROGER P., "Are Cheap Appraisals Really Cheap," *Review of the Society of Residential Appraisers*, November, 1936, pp. 10-13.

MITCHELL, A. CROMAR, "Caveat Emptor or Is it Worth it," *The Appraisal Journal*, July, 1962, pp. 408-410.

MORGAN, JAMES V., "Appraisal Fees Restudied," *The Residential Appraiser*, April, 1962, pp. 23-24.

MORGAN, JAMES V., "How Much Is an Appraisal Worth?," *The Review*, August, 1956, pp. 3-6.

MUSCH, HENRY, JR., "On Professional Ethics," *The Appraisal Journal*, July, 1933, pp. 363-364.

N.A. CONFERENCE OF APPRAISAL ORGANIZATIONS, "Licensing Would Lower Standards," *Appraisal Institute Magazine*, Appraisal Institute of Canada, Winnipeg.

NATIONAL ASSOCIATION OF REAL ESTATE BOARDS, "Appraiser's Code of Professional Ethics," *Clark, H. F., Appraising the Home, Art, 1-10*, 1930, pp. 258-261.

▲ Appraisal Theory and Methods

NATIONAL ASSOCIATION OF REAL ESTATE BOARDS, "Canons of Ethics Adopted at the Louisville Conventions," *National Real Estate Journal*, August 6, 1928, pp. 25-26.

NATIONAL ASSOCIATION OF REAL ESTATE BOARDS, "Committee on Certification of Appraisers," *National Real Estate Journal*, June 8, 1931, pp. 44-48.

NELSON, RICHRD L., "Who May Act As an Appraiser," *Encyclopedia of Real Estate Appraising*, Friedman, 1959, pp. 777-787.

NEUMAN, RONALD, "A Profession-Knowledge and Control," *Appraisal Institute Magazine*, Appraisal Institute of Canada, Winnipeg.

NOLAN, JAMES J., "Professionalism—Licensing Is Not the Answer," *The Real Estate Appraiser*, March, 1963, pp. 26-28, 32.

OSTENDORF, E. L., "Appraisal Standards," *The Appraisal Journal*, October, 1937, pp. 325-328.

OSTENDORF, E. L., "Certain Fundamentals of Appraising," *The Appraisal Journal*, January, 1938, pp. 37-39.

OSTENDORF, E. L., "On Professional Ethics," *The Appraisal Journal*, July, 1933, pp. 365.

PADILLA GONZALEZ, GILBERTO, "Evaluador Bienes Raices Como Profesional," *Boletin*, Sotave, Caracas, Venezuela, pp. 19-21.

PEARSON, F. A., W. I. MYERS, AND DON PAARLBERG, "Collusion," *The Appraisal Journal*, April, 1949, pp. 166-167.

PENA GARCIA, M. A., "Vicios En La Valuacion," *Boletin*, Sotave, Caracas, Venezuela, pp. 14-17.

PHINNEY, G. W., "The Role of the Appraiser," *Appraisal Institute Magazine*, Appraisal Institute of Canada, Winnipeg.

PIERCE, PHILIP F, MACBRIDE, DEXTER D, "Licensing/Certification of Appraisers: Pro Bono Publico," *Valuetape Audio-Library Series*, American Society of Appraisers, Washington D.C., January 1, 1973.

PIERCE, PHILIP F., "The Role of the Appraiser, the Role of ASA In the Years to Come," *Appraisal and Valuation Manual*, Corporate Press Incorporated, Washington, D. C, January, 1972, pp. 278.

PILMER, CHARLES L., "Ethics and Fees," *Journal of the American Society of Farm Managers and Rural Appraisers*, April, 1962, pp. 10-12.

PINKERTON, A. M., "What Is a Profession," *Appraisal Institute Magazine*, Appraisal Institute of Canada, Winnipeg.

PRIMM, HAROLD M., "A New Look at Basis for Charging Farm Management Fees- Pros and Cons," *Journal of the American Society of Farm Managers and Rural Appraisers*, October, 1962, pp. 58-59.

RAISON, B. V., S. E. WHICKER, "Errors and Omissions In Valuations," *Appraisal Institute Magazine*, Appraisal Institute of Canada, Winnipeg.

RAMS, EDWIN M., "Professional Liability," *The Review*, November, 1953, pp. 20-23.

RANDALL, ROLAND R., "A Basis for Adequate Fees," *The Preview*, July, 1947, pp. 10-11.

RATCLIFF, R. U., "The Price and Rewards of Professionalization," *Appraisal Institute Magazine*, Appraisal Institute of Canada, Winnipeg.

REEVE, DOUGLAS W., "What We Expect from a Competent Appraiser," *Review of Society of Residential Appraisers*, May, 1940, pp. 3-5.

REID, GARE B., "Ethics--Fact or Fiction," *The Residential Appraiser*, September, 1960, pp. 15-18.

REVIEW, THE, "Fees-Past and Future," *The Review*, August, 1950, pp. 3-6.

RIBETH, WILLIAM C., "Ethics for the Appraiser," *The Review*, April, 1952, pp. 16.

RING, DR. ALFRED A., "Appraising What it Takes to Be an Expert," *The Real Estate Appraiser*.

## BIBLIOGRAPHY OF APPRAISAL LITERATURE

ROBERTSON, FRASER, "The Profession of Duty," *Appraisal Institute Magazine,* Appraisal Institute of Canada, Winnipeg, June 1, 1972.

RUAN SANTOS, EDUARDO, "El Tasador: Una Necesidad Nacional," *Boletin,* Sotave, Caracas, Venezuela, pp. 3.

RUSSELL, HORACE, "Are Appraisers Employees or Independent Contractors?," *Review of Society of Residential Appraisers,* March, 1941, pp. 3-4.

SANDO, LAURENCE, "Institute Will Study Feasibility of Reciprocity with British," *The Appraiser,* October, 1968.

SAVINGS BANK JOURNAL, *Ethics of Appraisals Defined at Last,* February, 1934, pp. 15.

SCHMUTZ, GEORGE L., "Malpractice by Appraisers Calls for Drastic Action," *National Real Estate Journal,* June, 1940, pp. 1-29.

SCHMUTZ, GEORGE L., "Professional Conduct," *Appraisal Process,* 1941, pp. 1-229.

SCHMUTZ, GEORGE L., "Professional Standards In Appraising," *The Appraisal Process,* 1959, pp. 279-283.

SCRIBNER, DAVID JR., "The Appraisers Professional Responsibility to Society," *Appraisal and Valuation Manual,* Corporate Press Incorporated, Washington, D. C, January, 1972, pp. 294.

SEYMOUR, C. F., "Responsibilities of the Review Appraiser," *Appraisal Journal,* October, 1971, pp. 508-513.

SHATTUCK, CHARLES B., "On Professional Ethics," *The Appraisal Journal,* July, 1933, pp. 365-366.

SILVERMAN, BENJAMIN, "Licensing or Registration for Appraisers," *Technical Valuation,* June, 1955, pp. 23.

SMYTH, WILLIAM A., "State Registration of Appraisers," *Appraisal and Valuation Manual,* American Society of Appraisers.

SOCIETY OF RESIDENTIAL APPRAISERS, "Code of Ethics," *Review of the Society of Residential Appraisers,* December, 1936, pp. 15-16.

SOTAVE, "Estatutos De La (Sotave)," *Boletin,* Sotave, Caracas, Venezuela, pp. 27-31.

STEELE, FRANK N., "The Public Image of an Appraiser," *Appraisal Institute Magazine,* Appraisal Institute of Canada, Winnipeg.

STEINER, JEFFERSON F., "Ethics In the Appraisal Profession," *The Appraisal Journal,* October, 1956, pp. 518-522.

STERZER, HERBERT, "The Approved Appraiser," *The Real Estate Appraiser,* pp. 34.

STEUER, AARON, "Appraisers Urged to Better Professionals Standards," *The Review,* October, 1948, pp. 12-16.

STEVENS, FRANCIS K., "The Appraiser's Duties Today As to Value," *The Appraisal Journal,* April, 1933, pp. 204-206.

STEWART, SAMUEL, "Oregon New Certified Appraiser Law," *Assessment Administration,* Iaao, Chicago, 1956, pp. 50-55.

THOMSSEN, ROHLAND H., "Appraising and Counseling," *The Appraisal Journal,* January, 1960, pp. 17-23.

THORSON, IVAN A., "The Function of the Appraiser," *Mcmichael's Appraising Manual,* 1937, pp. 123-132.

TOLTZMAN, R. J., "Responsibility of the Appraisers In Todays Economy," *Valuation,* September, 1972.

TOWERS, ALBERT G. JR., "The Validity of an Appraisal," *The Appraisal Journal,* January, 1949, pp. 36-38.

U. P. A. V., "Estatutos De La UPAV," *Boletin,* Sotave, Caracas, Venezuela, pp. 39-43.

VEGAS ROLANDO, NICOLAS, "La Experticia En El Proceso Civil Venezolano," *Boletin,* Sotave, Caracas, Venezuela, pp. 11-12.

▲ Appraisal Theory and Methods

WADDEL, HAROLD H., "The Professional Appraiser's Responsibility To His Client," *The Appraisal Journal,* April, 1958, pp. 227-232.

WAGNER, PERCY E., "On Licensing Appraisers," *The Appraisal Journal,* January, 1937, pp. 73-74.

WAGNER, PERCY E., "The Licensing of Real Estate Brokers As Appraisers or the Certification of Real Estate Appraisers," *Appraisal Institute Magazine,* December, 1960, pp. 3-5.

WALTHER, HERMAN O., "Applying Our Principles," *The Review,* June, 1947, pp. 3-7, 12.

WALTHER, HERMAN O., "Professional Standards," *The Appraisal Journal,* April, 1946, pp. 121-123.

WENZLICK, ROY, "Should the Appraiser Be an Advocate?," *Real Estate Alyst Appraisal Bulletin,* 1960, pp. 323-326.

WHITE, JOHN R., "Marking the Discrepancies Between Appraising and Counseling," *The Appraiser,* April, 1969.

WICKENDEN, W. E., "The Second Mile-Ethics In Valuation," *Technical Valuation,* October, 1953, pp. 21.

WINSTON, CAREY, "The Crucial Role of the Appraiser," *The Real Estate Appraiser,* July, 1964, pp. 21.

WISCONSIN, UNIVERSITY OF, *Professional Training In Real Estate,* Milwaukee Real Estate Board, Milwaukee, August, 1937, pp. 4.

ZEPP, EDWARD G., "The Difference Is Up to You," *The Appraisal Journal,* October, 1965, pp. 619-620.

# 11-13 Appraisal Terminology and Definitions

*Appraisal Terminology and Handbook,* American Institute of Real Estate Appraisers, 1967.

AKRON REAL ESTATE BOARD, "Certificate of Appraisal," *Real Estate Appraising,* J. D. Henderson, 1931, pp. 408-410.

ALDIS, GRAHAM, "Management As a Factor In Appraisal," *The Appraisal Journal,* April, 1936, pp. 188-193.

ALEXANDER, ROBERT H., "The Area Designation," *The Real Estate Appraiser,* November, 1963, pp. 10-12.

ALLEN, ELLIS S., "Facts Observed-A Critique," *The Appraisal Journal,* April, 1961, pp. 253-255.

ALLES, WAYNE, "Factual Data Means Technical Appraising," *Technicalities,* January, 1949, pp. 14-15.

ALLISON, NEVILLE F., "Classifying and Interpreting Market Data," *The Appraisal Journal,* pp. 56-567.

ALLISON, NEVILLE F., "Three Approaches to Value," *Proceedings of the Third Institute on Eminent Domain,* Dallas, 1961.

ALVERT, EUGENE, "A Concept of Value," *Technical Valuation,* June, 1958, pp. 41-42.

AMERICAN INSTITUTE OF REAL ESTATE APPRAISERS, *Appraisal Terminology and Handbook,* American Institute of Real Estate Appraisers, Chicago, 1962, pp. 254.

AMERICAN INSTITUTE OF REAL ESTATE APPRAISERS, "Owner of Record," *Demonstration Appraisal Reports,* American Institute of Real Estate Appraisers, Chicago, 1957, pp. 48-83.

AMERICAN INSTITUTE OF REAL ESTATE APPRAISERS, "The Nature and Purpose of Appraisal," *The Appraisal of Real Estate,* American Institute of Real Estate Appraisers, Chicago, 1967, pp. 1-7.

# BIBLIOGRAPHY OF APPRAISAL LITERATURE

AMERICAN INSTITUTE OF REAL ESTATE APPRAISERS, "The Nature of Real Property and Value," *Appraisal of Real Estate,* American Institute of Real Estate Appraisers, Chicago, 1967, pp. 7-23.

AMERICAN SOCIETY OF APPRAISERS, "Principios Del Ejercicio De ASA," *Boletin,* Sotave, Caracas, Venezuela, pp. 25-35.

APPRAISAL DIGEST, "The Value of Amenities," *Appraisal Digest,* April, 1954, pp. 13.

APPRAISAL INSTITUTE MAGAZINE, "Value a Word of Many Meanings," *Appraisal Institute Magazine,* December, 1959, pp. 13-15.

APPRAISAL JOURNAL, "Covenants, Conditions, and Restrictions," *The Appraisal Journal,* January, 1953, pp. 126-217.

APPRAISAL JOURNAL, "Six Points of Evidence. Appraisal Docket," *The Appraisal Journal,* April, 1954, pp. 439-442.

ARDISSONO, ROBERT J., "Checking the Market," *The Review,* March, 1956, pp. 22-23.

ARMSTRONG, ROBERT H., "Prices Vs. Value," *The Appraisal Journal,* October, 1938, pp. 316-322.

ARMSTRONG, ROBERT H., "The Folklore of Appraising," *National Real Estate Journal,* October, 1939, pp. 34-37.

ARMSTRONG, ROBERT H., "Values and Fetishes," *The Appraisal Journal,* April, 1950, pp. 71-184.

ARNOLD, MAX P., "Are Different Appraised Values for Different Purposes Justitied," *Technical Valuation,* February, 1954, pp. 9-11.

ASH, FRED C., "Appraisal Docket Reasonable, Probable Demand In Valuation," *The Appraisal Journal,* January, 1955, pp. 116-117.

ASSOCIATION OF APPRAISAL EXECUTIVES, "Definitions of a Selected List of Words And Terms In Ordinary Use by Appraisers," *Basic Standards of Appraisal Practice and Procedure,* Association of Appraisal Executives, Washington, 1936.

BABCOCK, DR. HENRY A., "One Man's Appraisal Philosophy," *Valuation,* American Society of Appraisers, September, 1972, pp. 2.

BABCOCK, FREDERICK M., *The Appraisal of Real Estate,* Macmillan Company, New York City, 1924.

BABCOCK, FREDERICK M., *The Valuation of Real Estate,* Mcgraw-Hill Book Company, Incorporated, New York City, 1932.

BABCOCK, HENRY A, "Definition of 'Appraisal' 'Valuation' 'Cost Estimation' and 'Earning Forecast'," *Appraisal Principles and Procedures,* Irwin Company, Homewood Illinois, January 1, 1968, pp. 3-11.

BABCOCK, HENRY A., *Appraisal Principles and Procedures,* 1968.

BABCOCK, HENRY A., "Standardized Appraisal Practice," *Proceedings of the 15th Annual Convention of the Bankers Association of America,* 1928, pp. 119-126.

BABCOCK, HENRY A., "The Appraisal of Parts, Fractions and Whole Properties," *Technicalities,* February, 1950, pp. 9-12.

BAILEY, HOP, JR., "Problems In Appraising," *The Appraisal Journal,* August, 1964, pp. 23-28.

BAKER, LLOYD, "The Market As a Yardstick," *The Review,* June, 1950, pp. 18-19.

BARBOUR, SIR DAVID MILLER, *The Standard of Value,* Macmillan and Co, London, 1912.

BARISH, NORMAN N., "Interest and the Time Value of Money," *Economic Analysis for Engineer and Managerial Decision Making,* New York City, 1962, pp. 49-73.

BARNARD, BOYD T., "Appraisal Pitfalls," *Freehold,* August, 1941, pp. 48-50.

BARNARD, BOYD T., "Pitfalls In Appraising," *The Appraisal Journal,* October, 1941, pp. 385-392.

BASS, BOYLSTON B., "Tight Money Again," *The Residential Appraiser,* October, 1958, pp. 3-5.

▲ Appraisal Theory and Methods

BATCHELOR, HARRY H., "Adequacy of Restrictions," *The Review,* January, 1956, pp. 7-9.

BAUER, M. H., "The Cost and Price of Value," *Appraisal Institute Magazine,* Appraisal Institute of Canada, Winnipeg.

BAYLOR, DR. ALLEN O., "Valuation As a Multi/Disciplinary Field In Our Higher Education," *Appraisal and Valuation Manual,* Corporate Press Incorporated, Washington, D. C., January, 1972, pp. 290.

BEAN, PHILIP R., *Rating Valuation Practice,* Stevens, London, 1952.

BEATON, J WALLACE, "Father Devitt and Mother Hubbard or Valuation Day Meets Frankenstein," *Valuation Magazine,* American Society of Appraisers, Washington D C, December 1, 1973, pp. 2-11.

BECK, F. W., "Market Value--So We Define it Correctly," *The Appraisal Journal,* April, 1947, pp. 197-201.

BEETH, CHANNING C., "How to Spot a Sour Loan," *The Review,* July, 1954, pp. 21-24.

BEETH, CHANNING C., "Realistic Appraisals," *The Review,* April, 1953, pp. 13-15.

BENNETT, PHILIP E., "What Is Market Value," *National Real Estate Journal,* September, 1941, pp. 20-22.

BENNETT, S. Z., "La Organizacion Profesional," *Boletin,* Sotave, Caracas, Venezuela, pp. 9-13.

BENSON, PHILIP A., NELSON L. NORTH, "The Hoffman and Davies Rules," *Real Estate Principles and Practices,* 1938, pp. 293.

BEROES, MARIANO, "Valuacion," *Boletin,* Sotave, Caracas, Venezuela, pp. 33-40.

BIRNHOLZ, JACK, "The Appraiser--A Methodology," *Valutape Audio-Library,* American Society of Appraisers, Washington D.C., January 1, 1974.

BLUMBERG, AARON J., "How Much Credence Can Be Put In Cycle Theory," *The Appraisal Journal,* January, 1949, pp. 61-66.

BOECKH, EVERARD HEREFORD, "Appraisal Definitions," *Manual of Appraisals,* pp. 17.

BOECKH, EVERARD HEREFORD, "What Is an Appraisal," *Manual of Appraisals,* pp. 315.

BONNER, JOHN T. JR., "Bargaining Ability Affects Market Value," *The Review,* September, 1956, pp. 7-8.

BOWEN, PERCIVAL V., "Buyers, Sellers Not Always Willing," *The Appraisal Digest,* April, 1952, pp. 16-17.

BOWMAN, W. J., "What the Auditor-Examiner Wants In an Appraisal Report," *The Review of the Society of Residential Appraisers,* October, 1941, pp. 8-11.

BRIGGS, J., "Sales on Terms-Do They Represent Market Value," *The Appraisal Institute Magazine,* December, 1963, pp. 9-15.

BRINSMADE, ROBERT BRUCE, *El Latifundismo Mexicano, Su Origen Y Su Remedio,* 1916.

BROWN, J. BRUCE, "Our Profession - Viable In a Modern Economy," *Appraisal Institute Magazine,* Appraisal Institute of Canada, Winnipeg, March 1, 1972.

BRUNDAGE, PERCIVAL F., "Depreciation an Old Subject with a New Importance," *Harvard Business Review,* 1935, pp. 334-343.

BUCHANAN, ROBERT R., "Is There a Special Value for Antique Buildings?," *Appraisal Institute Magazine,* 1968, pp. 37-42.

CADENHEAD, G. M., "Net Realizeable Value Redefined," *Journal of Accounting Research,* April, 1970, pp. 138-140.

CALIFORNIA REAL ESTATE ASSOCIATION, "Board Appraisals In California," *The National Real Estate Journal,* April 4, 1927, pp. 62-64.

CASE, FRED E., "Value, Market Value, and Market Price," *The Appraisal Journal,* April, 1953, pp. 217-222.

## BIBLIOGRAPHY OF APPRAISAL LITERATURE

CASE, FREDERICK E., *Real Estate,* Allyn and Bacon, Boston, 1962.

CHAMBERS, R. J., "Measures and Values," *Accounting Review,* J, April, 1968, pp. 239-247.

CHANDIAS, MARIO E., "Un Criterio De Depreciacion," *Boletin,* Sotave, Caracas, Venezuela, pp. 5-8.

CHURCH, BYRON, "Let's Adopt Buyer's Terminology for Depreciation," *The Residential Appraiser,* June, 1957, pp. 3-6.

CHURCH, BYRON M., "What's In the Bundle," *The Real Estate Appraiser,* August, 1967, pp. 29.

CLARK, H. F., "Appraisal Terms Glossary," *Appraising the Home,* 1930, pp. 235-238.

CLARK, HORACE F., "Appraisal Forms," *Appraising the Home,* 1930, pp. 291-365.

CLAY, GRADY, "The Good Address," *The Review,* November, 1954, pp. 6-10.

CONAN, ROBERT J., "Should Appraised Value Contain Profits and Commissions," *Appraisal Digest,* July, 1954, pp. 17-18.

CONAN, ROBERT J., "The Fallacy of Future Economic Life," *The Appraisal Digest,* April, 1950, pp. 15.

CRONHEIM, DAVID, "Value and Purchase Price," *Newark Realtor,* August, 1941, pp. 1-2.

CUMMINS, CHARLES A., "Faults of Present Appraisal Practice," *Constructor,* April, 1932, pp. 22-24.

DARIO GONZALEZ, RUBEN, "El Concepto Del Uso Mejor Y Mas Productivo," *Boletin,* Sotave, Caracas, Venezuela, pp. 39-42.

DAVIS, W. D., "Uniformity In Appraisal Reporting Techniques," *Appraisal Institute Magazine,* Appraisal Institute of Canada, Winnipeg.

DERBES, MAX J. SR., "Market Value Vs. Replacement Value," *The Residential Appraiser,* November, 1960, pp. 21-22.

DOLMAN, JOHN P., "Some Reflections on Terminology," *The Appraisal Journal,* July, 1963, pp. 405-407.

DUNN, DOMINICK R., "Common Functional Defects," *The Review,* February, 1947, pp. 12.

DUNN, DOMINICK R., "Only One Value," *Review of the Society of Residential Appraisers,* January, 1937, pp. 13-16.

DYKSTRA, GERALD O., "Bundle of Rights," *Michigan Business Review,* November, 1956, pp. 18-24.

EDMAN, J. J., "The Appraisal Docket. Sales Under Pressure Are Not Evidence of Value," *The Appraisal Journal,* October, 1957, pp. 623-624.

EILERTS, HOPE, "Let's Get Back to Fundamentals," *The Real Estate Appraiser,* American Institute of Real Estate Appraisers, pp. 13.

ELLWOOD, LEON W., "Cost Is Not Value," *The Review,* August, 1951, pp. 3-5.

ENDELMAN, EDWARD, "Value In Reorganization Proceedings," *The Appraisal Journal;* July, 1946, pp. 231-239.

FALLOON, WILBUR J., "Appraisal Fundamentals and Appraisal Terms," *The Appraisal Journal,* January, 1951, pp. 106-109.

FERGUSON, EGBERT R. JR., "Government Appraisals," *The Review,* July, 1954, pp. 15-19.

FERRERO, PAUL E., "Outlook In Appraisals for the Government," *Technical Valuation,* 1900, pp. 23.

FREE, ROBERT L., A. I. BRADLEY, "Common Appraisal Terms," *The Review,* June, 1946, pp. 7-10.

FRYXELL, CARL A., "Should Appreciation Be Brought Into the Account," *Accounting Review,* June, 1930, pp. 157-158.

GADDIS, PERCY A., "Concept of Value," *The Appraisal Journal,* April, 1935, pp. 269.

## Appraisal Theory and Methods

GADDIS, PERCY A., "On Horizontal Division of Values," *The Appraisal Journal*, July, 1936, pp. 325-328.

GRUNSKY, CARL E., GRUNSKY, CARL E. JR., *Definitions*, New York, 1917, pp. 16-31.

HALL, JOSEPH B., "Definition of Terms," *The Appraisal Journal*, October, 1934, pp. 74-79.

HALLIDAY, C. S., "Market Values Versus Sound Values," *Technicalities*, May, 1948, pp. 18-21.

HAMILTON, ANDREW C., "Upset Price Appraisals," *The Appraisal Journal*, April, 1935, pp. 267-268.

HANFORD, EDGAR C., "110 Building Terms Defined," *National Real Estate Journal*, American Society of Appraisers, June 9, 1930, pp. 31-32.

HANSON, PETER, "The Meaning of Market Value," *National Real Estate Journal*, May 11, 1931, pp. 35-36.

HANSON, PETER, "The Meaning of Value," *The Appraisal Journal*, July, 1933, pp. 289-297.

HAWES, A. S., "Value to the Owner," *Appraisal Institute Magazine*, Appraisal Institute of Canada, Winnipeg.

HIEATT, CLARENCE C., "The Difference Between Price and Value," *National Real Estate Journal*, July 11, 1927, pp. 51-52.

HINMAN, ALBERT G., HERBERT G. DORAU, "The Scope of a Useful Economic Survey," Real Estate Merchandising, Chicago, 1926, pp. 363.

HOLBROOK, JEFFREY, "Who's to Blame for Divergencies In Valuation," *The Residential Appraiser*, May, 1961, pp. 3-4.

HOLLEBAUGH, CLIFFORD W., "On Definition Accuracy," *The Appraisal Journal*, October, 1962, pp. 540-541.

HOOVER, RICHARD I., "What Is Market Analysis?," *The Appraisal Journal*, December, 1967, pp. 61-63.

HYDER, K. LEE, *A Question of Value*, November 15, 1938, pp. 348.

HYLTON, G. W., *The Real Estate Dictionary and Appraisal Manual*, Wetzel Publishing Company, Los Angeles, Calif., 1940.

JAMES, M. F., "What Is the Economic Life of Property In Appraising," *National Real Estate Journal*, April, 1939, pp. 49-50.

JAMES, M. H., "How to Lessen Wide Divergency In Appraisals," *Review of Society of Residential Appraisers*, August, 1941.

JONES, FRANCIS E., "The Metes and Bounds System of Land Description," *The Appraisal Journal*, July, 1937, pp. 252-261.

JOSLIN, EDWARD G., "The Future of Value to the Owner," *Appraisal Institute Magazine*, 1963, pp. 32-35.

KANN, BRUCE E., "Machinery Is What You Make it," *Valuation*, September, 1966, pp. 27-31.

KAZDIN, S. EDWIN, "The Value Concept In Appraising," *The Appraisal Journal*, January, 1953, pp. 47-53.

KELLOUGH, W. R., "Characteristics of Value," *Asa*, 1964, pp. 225.

KLAASEN, R. L., "Appraised Value," *Appraisal Institute Magazine*, Appraisal Institute of Canada, Winnipeg.

KNISKERN, PHILIP W., "Appraisal and Architects," *Architectural Forum*, April, 1934, pp. 291-292.

KNISKERN, PHILIP W., "H. O. L. C. Appraisals," *Banking*, November, 1934, pp. 53.

LAIRD, JOHN, *The Idea of Value*, A. M. Kelley, New York, 1969.

LAUNER, E. J., "Problems on Market and Cash Value," *Technical Valuation*, October, 1958, pp. 25-27.

LEVIT, BERT W., "The Expert Witness," *The Appraisal Journal*, July, 1939, pp. 219-226.

# BIBLIOGRAPHY OF APPRAISAL LITERATURE

LITTLETON, A. C., "Value and Price In Accounting," *Accounting Review,* September, 1929, pp. 147-154.

LOVE, HAROLD C., "Risk and Uncertainty Factors," *Appraisal Institute Magazine,* Appraisal Institute of Canada, Winnipeg.

LUNDY, VICTOR R., "Captive Appraisers," *The Review,* November, 1954, pp. 18-19.

MACBRIDE DEXTER D, "Opportunities In Appraising for Minorities," *Valutape Audio-Library Series,* American Society of Appraisers, Washington D.C., February 1, 1974.

MACBRIDE, DEXTER D., "Appraisal Definitions," *The Appraisal of Machinery and Equipment,* American Society of Appraisers, Washington, D. C, 1969, pp. 1.

MACCHESNEY, NATHAN W., *Glossary,* New York, 1927, pp. 835-848.

MACLEOD, MORTON P., "Horse Sense and Common Sense," *Technical Valuation,* American Society of Appraisers, Washington, January, 1967, pp. 3.

MAHAFFY, A. W., "Price Vs. Value and the Theory of Rural Appraisal," *The Appraisal Institute Magazine,* December, 1961, pp. 20-25.

MAIER, E. F., "Market Value," *The Appraisal Journal,* December, 1933, pp. 167-169.

MAISENHELDER, HOWARD, JR., "Historical Value or Hysterical Value," *The Appraisal Journal,* pp. 1-3.

MCDONALD, ADRIAN F., "Appraising Vs. Underwriting," *The Review,* December, 1951, pp. 7-11.

MCMICHAEL, STANLEY L., "Value, Its Meaning and How to Measure it," *Appraising Manual,* 1937, pp. 6-50.

MCMICHALL, STANLEY L., *Mcmichaels Appraising Manual,* 1970.

MEEK, RONALD L., *Studies In the Labor Theory of Value,* Lawrence and Wi Hart, London, 1956.

MITCHELL, A. CROMAR, "Caveat Emptor or Is it Worth it," *The Appraisal Journal,* July, 1962, pp. 408-410.

MOLLAN, WILLIAM W., "Reasonable Normal Value and the G.I.," *The Appraisal Journal,* July, 1945, pp. 263-265.

NELSON, N. B., "Glossary," *Law of Real Estate Brokerage,* Prentice-Hall, Inc., 1928, pp. 489-523.

NOLAN, JAMES J., "Cost Is Not Always Value," *Technical Valuation,* American Society of Appraisers, Washington, D. C., August, 1967, pp. 44.

OPELKA, F. GREGORY, "Technology and Depreciation," *The Real Estate Appraiser,* January, 1964, pp. 23-29.

OSTENDORF, E. L., "Yardsticks for Real Estate," *Banking Digest,* May, 1937, pp. 104.

PAPER INDUSTRY, W. W., "Difference Between Appraisal and Inventory," *The Paper Industry,* October, 1922, pp. 923-924.

PEARSON, F. A., W. I. MYERS, AND DEGRAFF, "Prices, Building, and History," *The Appraisal Journal,* October, 1952, pp. 512-534.

PEARSON, F. A., W. I. MYERS, H. DEGRAFF, "Prices, Building, and History," *The Appraisal Journal,* October, 1952, pp. 512-534.

PELOUBET, MAURICE E., "Is Value an Accounting Concept," *Journal of Accountancy,* March, 1935, pp. 201-209.

PENA GARCIA, M. A., "Valor Probable," *Boletin,* Sotave, Caracas, Venezuela, pp. 5-7.

PENNY, A. L., "Highest and Best Use," *Appraisal Institute Magazine,* Appraisal Institute of Canada, Winnipeg.

PENNY, A. L., "Value to the Owner," *Appraisal Institute Magazine,* Appraisal Institute of Canada, Winnipeg.

PHILIPS, F. M., "The Appraiser and the Realtor," *Appraisal Institute Magazine,* Appraisal Institute of Canada, Winnipeg.

▲ Appraisal Theory and Methods

POLLARD, W. L., "Market Value," *Condemnation Appraisal Procedure,* Hanson, Peter, and Pollard, 1934, pp. 413-434.

POLLARD, W. L., "Terms and Definitions," *Real Estate Brokerage,* California Real Estate Association, Los Angeles, 1936, pp. 61-94.

POLLOCK, WALTER W., "Concept of Value for Use," *Certified Public Accountant,* March, 1935, pp. 147-150.

POST, EDWARD T., "The Appraiser and the Builder," *The Appraisal Journal,* October, 1946, pp. 395-400.

PROUTY, W. L. AND OTHERS, "Architectural Nomenclature; Definitions of Buildings," *Appraisers and Assessors Manual,* 1930, pp. 36-40.

RATCLIFF, R. U., "Capitalized Income Is Not Market Value," *Appraisal Institute Magazine,* Appraisal Institute of Canada, Winnipeg.

RESIDENTIAL APPRAISER, "The Meaning of Value," *The Residential Appraiser,* March, 1957, pp. 3-6.

REVIEW, THE, "Reasonable Normal Value In Congress," *The Review,* February, 1945, pp. 3..

RODEY, B. S., JR., "Original Cost," *Appraisal and Valuation Manual,* 1955.

ROSENWEIG, REUBEN, "Bonus Value Is Taking Bread Out of the Mouths of Appraisers," *Technical Valuation,* June, 1960, pp. 27-30.

SAVINGS BANK JOURNAL, *Ethics of Appraisals Defined at Last,* February, 1934, pp. 15.

SCHMUTZ, GEORGE L., "Cost, Value, Utility and Security," *The Appraiser Process,* 1959, pp. 17-23.

SCHMUTZ, GEORGE L., "The Nature of Property Value," *The Appraisal Process,* 1959, pp. 13-17.

SCHMUTZ, GEORGE L., LORING O. MCCORMICK, "The Relation of Profit to Value," *The Appraisal Journal,* April, 1935, pp. 229-235.

SHANKLAND, F. J., "The Real Estate Market," *Appraisal Institute Magazine,* Appraisal Institute of Canada, Winnipeg.

SHEFFER, H. FRAZIER, "Some Aspects of Market Value," *Appraisal and Valuation Manual,* 1960, pp. 253-258.

SHERMAN, H. J., "The Marxist Theory of Value Revisited," *Science and Society,* 1970.

SILVERMAN, BENJAMIN, "Words and Phrases," *Appraisal and Valuation Manual,* pp. 264.

SIMON, ROBERT E., "The Effect of Concepts on the Value of Land," *Appraisal and Valuation Manual,* 1964, pp. 107.

SLONIM, M. J., "Market Value or Market Price," *The Appraisal Journal,* October, 1945, pp. 390-391.

SMITH, WALSTEIN JR., "Market Value a Rule of Reasoning," *The Real Estate Appraiser,* pp. 40.

SOCIETY OF RESIDENTIAL APPRAISERS, *Real Estate Appraisal: Principles and Terminology,* Chicago, 1960.

STERLING, RAY T., "Terminology," *The Real Estate Appraiser,* May, 1970, pp. 57-59.

STERLING, RAY T., "Terminology," *The Real Estate Appraiser,* March, 1970, pp. 58-59.

STERLING, RAY T., "Terminology," *The Real Estate Appraiser,* January, 1970, pp. 61-62.

STRUNK, NORMAN W., "Shrinking Margins of Error," *The Residential Appraiser,* May, 1959, pp. 8-12.

SWAN, RUSSELL E., "Appraisal Terminology and Its Use," *The Real Estate Appraiser,* pp. 9..

THOMPSON, BURTON, "On the Prophetic Analysis of Future Benefits In Max Tieger's Appraisal," *The Appraisal Journal,* April, 1933, pp. 245-247.

THOMPSON, BURTON, "On Value Vs. Prices," *The Appraisal Journal,* July, 1936, pp. 320-323.

THORSON, J. T., "Memorandum on Value to the Owner," *Appraisal Institute Magazine*, Appraisal Institute of Canada, Winnipeg.

WATSON, WILLIAM H., "How Many Values?," *The Review*, March, 1950, pp. 3-6.

WEED, KENNETH A., "Market Values Versus Price and Financing," *The Residential Appraiser*, November, 1961, pp. 9-12.

WILBANKS, RICHARD P., "What Is a Typical Buyer," *The Real Estate Appraiser*, April, 1966, pp. 18.

WILSON, D. EARL, "On Normal Value," *The Appraisal Journal*, January, 1934, pp. 150-151.

WINSTEAD, ROBERT W., "Market Value, the Old Standby and Zoning," *The Residential Appraiser*, December, 1960, pp. 19-21.

WOODWORTH, LEO D., "Industrial Appraisers Vs. Mechanical Surveys," *National Real Estate Journal*, June 13, 1927, pp. 24-26.

WYNACHT, C. F., "The Realtor Looks for Value," *Appraisal Institute Magazine*, Appraisal Institute of Canada, Winnipeg.

# 11-14 Appraisal Tools

A.I.C., "Demonstration Appraisal Reports," *Appraisal Institute Magazine*, Appraisal Institute of Canada, Winnipeg.

ABBOUD, SAMIR, "Usage Des Statistiques En Valuation," *Appraisal Institute Magazine*, Appraisal Institute of Canada, Winnipeg, September 1, 1973.

ABDEL-BADDIE F E, "An Econometric Analysis of Factors Affecting Land Values In Western Oklahoma," *Dissertation Abstracts*, June, 1968, pp. 4780-A.

ADELSBERG, HYMAN, "ASA Education Program," *Technical Valuation*, February, 1954, pp. 18.

ADLER, M., "On Risk Adjusted Capitalization Rates and Valuation by Individuals," *Journal of Finance*, September, 1970, pp. 819-835.

AGUAYO, RAMON CARLOS, "Ensenanza De La Valuacion," *Boletin*, Sotave, Caracas, Venezuela, pp. 21-24.

AGUAYO, RAMON CARLOS, "Primer Seminario Instituto Mexicano," *Boletin*, Sotave, Caracas, Venezuela, pp. 15-18.

AKRON REAL ESTATE BOARD, "Certificate of Appraisal," *Real Estate Appraising*, J. D. Henderson, 1931, pp. 408-410.

ALEXANDER, ROBERT H., "Narrative Reporting," *The Residential Appraiser*, September, 1961, pp. 9-12.

ALLAN, BRITT H., "A Study of Appraisal Overhead," *The Review*, September, 1956, pp. 9-10.

ALLINGHAM, A. P., "Actual Appraisal Report," *Practical Appraising Methods*, 1940, pp. 45-46.

ALLINGHAM, A. P., "Preparing the Appraisal Report," *District Appraisal Conference, New York State Society of Real Estate Appraisers*, New York State Society of Real Estate Appraisers, Rochester, April 17, 1941.

ALLISON, NEVILLE F., "Converting a VA Form Into a Narrative," *The Review*, March, 1955, pp. 17-24.

AMER INSTITUTE OF REAL ESTATE APPRAISERS, "Appraisal Journal Bibliography, 1932-1969," American Institute of Real Estate Appraisers, pp. 172.

AMERICAN INSTITUTE OF REAL ESTATE APPRAISERS, *Appraisal Reporting Techniques*, American Institute of Real Estate Appraisers, Chicago, 1947.

▲ Appraisal Theory and Methods

AMERICAN INSTITUTE OF REAL ESTATE APPRAISERS, *Demonstration Appraisal Reports,* American Institute of Real Estate Appraisers, Chicago, 1957.

AMERICAN INSTITUTE OF REAL ESTATE APPRAISERS, *Problems In Rural Real Estate Appraisal,* American Institute of Real Estate Appraisers, 1968.

AMERICAN INSTITUTE OF REAL ESTATE APPRAISAL, *Problems In Urban Real Estate Appraisal,* American Institute of Real Estate Appraisal, 1967.

AMERICAN INSTITUTE OF REAL ESTATE APPRAISERS, *Problems In Urban Real Estate with Suggested Solutions,* American Institute of Real Estate Appraisers, Chicago, 1963.

AMERICAN INSTITUTE OF REAL ESTATE APPRAISERS, "Owner of Record," *Demonstration Appraisal Reports,* American Institute of Real Estate Appraisers, Chicago, 1957, pp. 48-83.

AMERICAN INSTITUTE OF REAL ESTATE APPRAISERS, "Some Thoughts on Appraisal Forms-And Appraisal Judgment," *The Appraiser,* March, 1967.

AMERICAN INSTITUTE OF REAL ESTATE APPRAISERS, "Technique of the Cost Approach," *The Appraisal of Real Estate,* American Institute of Real Estate Appraisers, Chicago, 1967, pp. 220.

ANDERSON, MEL, "Mechanics of the One Man Appraisal Office," *Technical,* June, 1962, pp. 38-39.

APPEL JAMES R., "Preparation of the Feasibility Report," *The Real Estate Appraiser,* November, 1964, pp. 33-38.

APPRAISAL DIGEST, "15 Dont's for the Expert," *15 Dont's for the Expert,* October, 1951, pp. 24.

ARDISSONO, ROBERT J., "Checking the Market," *The Review,* March, 1956, pp. 22-23.

ARNOLD, ROBERT S., "Ellwood Revisited-And Perhaps Simplified," *The Appraisal Journal,* October, 1966.

ARNOLD, ROBERT S., "Inwood - Friend or Foe," *The Appraisal Journal,* January, 1963, pp. 35-38.

ARNOLD, ROBERT S., "Its What's Up Front That Counts," *The Appraisal Journal,* January, 1964, pp. 68-70.

ARNOLD, RONALD S., "In Rebuttal: Ellwood Pro and Con," *The Appraisal Journal,* 1967, pp. 579-581.

ASCHER, DAVID B., "The Building-Land Ratio and What You Can Do with it," *Technical Valuation,* October, 1953, pp. 59-60.

ASH, FRED C., "Appraisal Reports Made Available Questioning of Appraiser Limited," *The Appraisal Journal,* January, 1956, pp. 109-111.

ASSOCIATION OF APPRAISAL EXECUTIVES, *Basic Standards of Appraisal Practice and Procedure,* Association of Appraisal Executives, Washington, D. C, 1936.

ASSOCIATION OF APPRAISAL EXECUTIVES, "Definitions of a Selected List of Words And Terms In Ordinary Use by Appraisers," *Basic Standards of Appraisal Practice and Procedure,* Association of Appraisal Executives, Washington, 1936.

ATKINSON HARRY GRANT, "The Three Approaches," Real Estate Appraisal, Chicago, pp. CHICAGO.

ATKINSON, H. G., "The Income Approach (Part 1)," *Appraisal Institute Magazine,* Appraisal Institute of Canada, Winnipeg.

AXFORD, DR. H. M., "Capitalization of Income Property," *The Appraisal Institute Magazine,* May, 1959, pp. 12-18.

BABCOCK, FREDERICK, "Appraisals by Income Analysis," *National Real Estate Journal,* February 21, 1927, pp. 19-21.

BABCOCK, FREDERICK M., "A New Approach to the Solution of the Appraisal Problem," *The Appraisal Journal,* January, 1937, pp. 54-59.

BABCOCK, FREDERICK M., "A New Approach Toward Solution of the Appraisal Problem," *Practical Appraising Methods,* 1940, pp. 2-4.

BABCOCK, FREDERICK M., "Curso Avanzado Lecciones III, IV, V y Vi," *Boletin,* Sotave, Caracas, Venezuela, pp. 43-48.

BABCOCK, FREDERICK M., "Curso Avanzado Xiv, Xi, Xvi, Xvii, Xviii, Xix, Xx," *Boletin,* Sotave, Caracas, Venezuela, pp. 31-39.

BABCOCK, FREDERICK M., "Curso Avanzado: Lecciones X, Xi, Xii y Xiii," *Boletin,* Sotave, Caracas, Venezuela, pp. 31-37.

BABCOCK, FREDERICK M., "Depth Coefficients," *Appraisal of Real Estate,* 1924, pp. 340-357.

BABCOCK, FREDERICK M., "Land Valuation by Comparison," *Valuation of Real Estate,* 1932, pp. 455-476.

BABCOCK, FREDERICK M., "Las Tres Aproximaciones," *Boletin,* Sotave, Caracas, Venezuela, pp. 23-29.

BABCOCK, FREDRICK M., "Curso Avanzado Lecciones Vii, Viii y Ix," *Boletin,* Sotave, Caracas, Venezuela, pp. 43-52.

BAKER, JAMERS S., "Using Computers In County Government," *County Officer,* May, 1964, pp. 219-226.

BALDWIN, H. G., "How to Appraise Buildings by the Inventory Method," *National Real Estate Journal,* April 29, 1929, pp. 54-58.

BALDWIN, H. G., "Inaccuracies of Building Appraisals Based on Unit Foot Costs," *National Real Estate Journal,* April 15, 1929, pp. 57-60.

BALL, JOHN, C. B. WILLIAMS, *Report Writing,* Ronald, New York City, 1955.

BAPPERT, JOSEPH, "Charting Income Properties," *Real Estate Analyst Appraisal Bulletin,* 1956, pp. 507-510.

BARISH, NORMAN N., *Economic Analysis for Engineer and Managerial Decision Making,* Mcgraw Hill Book Company Inc., New York City, 1962.

BARISH, NORMAN N., "Determinations of Minimum Cost and Maximum Profit," *Economic Analysis for Engineer Managerial Decision Making,* New York City, 1962, pp. 063-307.

BARISH, NORMAN N., "Methods for Tangible Evaluation of Alternatives," *Economic Annals for Engineer and Managerial Decision Making,* New York City, 1962, pp. 117-176.

BARISH, NORMAN N., "Waiting Time Evaluations," *Economic Analysis for Engineer Managerial Decision Making,* New York City, 1962, pp. 408-420.

BARNARD, BOYD T., "Practical Use of the New Appraisal Techniques," *National Real Estate Journal,* July, 1939, pp. 32-33.

BAYLOR, DR. ALLEN O., "Valuation As a Multi/Disciplinary Field In Our Higher Education," *Appraisal and Valuation Manual,* Corporate Press Incorporated, Washington, D.C., January, 1972, pp. 290.

BAYNTON-WILLIAMS, *Investing In Maps,* Barrier & Jenkins, London.

BECKER, GEORGE, "Market Data Analysis," *The Appraisal Journal,* October, 1955, pp. 486-494.

BECKETT, P. H. T., "Method and Scale of Land Resource Surveys In Relation to Precision and Cost," *Land Evaluation,* 1900, pp. 53.

BEETH, CHANNING C., "An Inspection Routine," *The Review,* April, 1951, pp. 14-16.

BEETH, CHANNING C., "Narrative Sequence," *The Review,* July, 1950, pp. 10-11.

BEMAN, ARTHUR K., "The Amortization Provision," *The Appraisal Journal,* April, 1942, pp. 160-165.

BENNET, HAZEN, "Capitalization of Income," *Appraisal Institute Magazine,* Appraisal Institute of Canada, Winnipeg.

BENNETT, SAUL Z., "Appraiser's Certificates," *A Student's Appraisal Report on Single-Family Residences,* American Institute of Real Estate Appraisers, Chicago, 1964, pp. 22.

BENNETT, SAUL Z., "Income Approach," *A Student's Report on an Apartment House,* American Institute of Real Estate Appraisers, Chicago, 1966, pp. 31.

## Appraisal Theory and Methods

BENSON, PHILIP A., NELSON L. NORTH, "The Hoffman and Davies Rules," *Real Estate Principles and Practices*, 1938, pp. 293.

BENSON, PHILIP A., NELSON L. NORTH, "Valuation of Improved Property," *Real Estate Principles and Practices*, 1938, pp. 297-298.

BENTLEY, HOWARD H., "The CAP Appraisal Form," *The Residential Appraiser*, September, 1958, pp. 3-6.

BERNARD, BOYD T., "Problems Encountered In Re-Use Appraisal," *Technical Valuation*, 1960, pp. 62.

BILLINGS, VIOLA C., "What the Lender Wants In an Appraisal," *The Appraisal Digest*, October, 1950, pp. 14-16.

BINTLIFF, BENNETT B., "35mm Photography In Appraising," *The Appraisal Journal*, April, 1961, pp. 229-237.

BIRD, F., "Educational Requirements for Valuers," *Appraisal Institute Magazine*, Appraisal Institute of Canada, Winnipeg.

BIRNHOLZ, JACK, "The Appraiser--A Methodology," *Valutape Audio-Library*, American Society of Appraisers, Washington D.C., January 1, 1974.

BLETTNER, ROBERT A., "Mass Appraisals Via Multiple Regression Analysis," *The Appraisal Journal*, October, 1969, pp. 516-521.

BLOOM, GEORGE, *The Appraisal Data Plant*, Indiana University, Bloomington, 1953.

BLOOM, GEORGE, "Real Estate Principles and Practices Workbook," *Readings In Business No. 74*, Indiana University, 1971.

BLOOM, GEORGE F., "Appraisal Data Plant Study," *The Appraisal Journal*, July, 1949, pp. 318-320.

BLOOM, GEORGE F., "Practice of MAI's Regarding the Appraisal Plant," *The Appraisal Journal*, July, 1953, pp. 394-396.

BODFISH, MORTON, A. D. THEOBALD, "Appraisal Reports," *Real Estate Fundamentals*, 1941, pp. 19.

BODFISH, MORTON, THEOBALD, A. D, "Computing Land Value by the Income Approach," *Real Estate Fundamentals*, 1941, pp. 17-18.

BODFISH, MORTON, THEOBALD, A. D, "Forms and Tables," *Real Estate Fundamentals*, 1941, pp. 20-26.

BOECKH, EVERARD HEREFORD, "Appraisal Work-Sheet and Report," *Manual of Appraisals*, 1937, pp. 38-39.

BOECKH, EVERARD HEREFORD, "Boeckh Depreciation Table," *Manual of Appraisals*, 1937, pp. 305-306.

BOECKH, EVERARD HEREFORD, "Individual Costs Section," *Manual of Appraisals*, pp. 287.

BOECKH, EVERARD HEREFORD, "Land Depth Table," *Manual of Appraisals*, 1937, pp. 348.

BOECKH, EVERARD HEREFORD, "Land Valuation," *Manual of Appraisals*, pp. 339.

BOECKH, EVERARD HEREFORD, "Realty, Income Analysis," *Boeckhs Manual of Appraisals*, pp. 324.

BOECKH, EVERARD HEREFORD, "Valuation Based on Income," *Manual of Appraisals*, pp. 322.

BOECKH, EVERARD HEREFORD, "Valuation Based on Income, Valuation by Comparison," *Manual of Appraisals*, 1937, pp. 322-336.

BONBRIGHT, JAMES C., "Concept of Depreciation As an Accounting Category," *Accounting Review*, June, 1930, pp. 117-119.

BONNER, JOHN, "Hazards and Safeguards In Appraisal Work," *The Appraisal Journal*, April, 1966, pp. 177-180.

BONTJES, JOHN H., "Horse Sense In Appraising," *The Review*, June, 1950, pp. 3-6.

BOWES, EUGENE G., "How to Use the Residual Techniques," *The Appraisal Journal*, July, 1957, pp. 27-34.

# BIBLIOGRAPHY OF APPRAISAL LITERATURE

BOWES, W. A., "What Is Market Analysis," *The Real Estate Appraiser,* July, 1968, pp. 11-14.

BOYD, JOHN T. JR, "Standardizing Appraisals," *The Architectural Forum,* April, 1930, pp. 627-630.

BRABENT, DAVIS, "Appraisal Contracts," *The Residential Appraiser,* August, 1960, pp. 8-11.

BRACHMAN, H. J., "Criticism of Standard Appraisal Methods," *The Real Estate Record,* February 20, 1937, pp. 18-20.

BRADFORD, C. R., "25 Steps In Preparing for Appraisal Theory Examinations," *The Appraisal Institute Magazine,* July, 1957, pp. 15-25.

BRADLEY, VINCENT P., "The Need for Educational Courses," *The National Real Estate Journal,* February 11, 1924, pp. 39-40.

BRANDT, L., POPLE, HARRY E, "Chart for Computing Cubic Foot Value of Homes," *The National Real Estate Journal,* June, 1932, pp. 31-34.

BRAY, JOHN W., "Capitalization Rate," *A. S. A. Valuation Manual,* American Society of Appraisers, Washington, D. C, 1964, pp. 31.

BRIGHAM, EUGENE F., MCALLISTER, DONALD M, "Applying Econometric Models," *The Appraisal Journal,* October, 1968, pp. 546-548.

BROWN GEORGE D., "Architectural Analysis of Building Bulk and Height," *Technical Valuation,* pp. 11.

BROWN, R.O., "Using Appraisal Information," *Management Accounting,* October, 1969.

BRUNK, LLOYD S., "Gross Capitalization Rates---Analysis and Synthesis," *The Appraisal Journal,* May, 1962, pp. 200-209.

BUCK, WALTER M. S., "Interpreting the Sale Price," *The Appraisal Journal,* May, 1942, pp. 132-134.

BUCK, WALTER M. S., "The Theory of Straight Line Depreciation," *The Appraisal Journal,* July, 1948, pp. 317-320.

BUNTING, GEORGE R., "Report the Unusual Items," *The Residential Appraiser,* May, 1958, pp. 13-15.

BURKEY, MACK G., "Gross Multipliers," *The Review,* June, 1955.

BURKHARD, EARL E., "Reviewing Our Manuals," *Appraisal and Valuation Manual,* American Society of Appraisers, 1962, pp. 1-4.

BURKHEIMER, WILLIAM D., "Significant Ratios," *The Appraisal Journal,* January, 1940, pp. 30-35.

BURNELL, W. V., "The Three Approaches to Property Value," *Appraisal and Valuation Manual,* American Society of Appraisers, 1955, pp. 17-20.

BURNELL, WILLIAM U., "Property Value, Three Approaches," *Technical Valuation,* February, 1955, pp. 17.

BURNS, E. J., "Gross-Income Multipliers," *Appraisal Institute Magazine,* Appraisal Institute of Canada, Winnipeg, March 1, 1972.

BURNS, WARREN W., "Salvage by Foreclosure," *The Review,* July, 1948, pp. 12-15.

BURROUGHS, ROY J., "The Safe-Risk Rate Formula," *The Appraisal Journal,* October, 1934, pp. 51-51.

BURTCH, THOMAS, "Data Files In the Post-War Period," *The Appraisal Journal,* July, 1947, pp. 375-382.

BUTLER, GORDON, "Getting Ready for the Computer," *Nation's Cities,* September, 1964, pp. 19-22.

CALIFORNIA BUILDING-LOAN LEAGUE, "Appraiser's Field Report Form," *The Review of the Society of Residential Appraisers,* July, 1936, pp. 10-11.

CALIFORNIA REAL ESTATE ASSOCIATION, "Board Appraisals In California," *The National Real Estate Journal,* April 4, 1927, pp. 62-64.

CAMPBELL, BERT, "Methods of Obtaining and Presenting Sales Data In an Appraisal Report," *The Journal of the American Society of Farm Managers and Rural Appraisers,* April, 1960, pp. 83-89.

CAMPBELL, S. J., "The Land Residual Technique," *The Appraisal Institute Magazine,* January, 1957, pp. 11-12.

CANTWELL, ROBERT C. III, "Graphic Aids to Capitalization," *The Appraisal Journal,* July, 1960, pp. 325-331.

CANTWELL, ROBERT C. III, "The Appraisal Process--Outline and Diagram," *The Appraisal Journal,* April, 1961, pp. 200-206.

CAPT, J. C., "Appraisal Significance of Census Statistics," *The Appraisal Journal,* April, 1946, pp. 125-135.

CARDOZA, LEONARD R., "Data Gathering Outline," *The Review,* September, 1956, pp. 11-17.

CARDOZA, LEONARD R., A. ORMSBY DONOUGH, JR., AND WALTER N. GABRIEL, "Depreciation Factors," *The Review,* February, 1950, pp. 3-6.

CAREW, JOHN F., "Inspection Clues," *The Review,* January, 1956, pp. 3-6.

CARMAN, LEWIS A., "Hoskold's Formula," *American Accountant,* April, 1931, pp. 104-106.

CARMAN, LEWIS A., "Substitute for Hoskold's Formula," *American Accountant,* May, 1931, pp. 136-139.

CARMICHAEL, JAMES J., *Preparing the Appraisal Report,* New York State Society of Real Estate Appraisers, Buffalo, N. Y., April 18, 1941.

CARNEY, JOHN J., "The Development and Use of Gross Income Multipliers," *The Appraisal Journal,* April 1963, pp. 221-227.

CARRUTHERS, G. R., "The Two-Part Report," *Appraisal Institute Magazine,* Appraisal Institute of Canada, Winnipeg.

CASE, FRED E., "Electronic Data Processing and the Appraisal Process," *The Real Estate Appraiser,* September, 1966, pp. 2.

CASE, FRED E., "New Decision Tools for Appraisers," *The Appraisal Journal,* January, 1967, pp. 21-27.

CASTENHOLZ, WILLIAM B., *Solution to the Appreciation Problem,* Lasalle Extension University, Chicago, 1931.

CHANDIAS, MARIO E., "Sobre La Ensenanza De La Tasacion," *Boletin,* Sotave, Caracas, Venezuela, pp. 7-9.

CHANDLER, JAMES K., "Safety Check-List," *The Review,* June, 1905, pp. 15-17.

CHENEY, SHELDON, *A New World History of Art,* Viking Press.

CHERNEY, RICHARD A., "A New Look at Narrative Reports," *The Real Estate Appraiser,* pp. 14.

CHICAGO REAL ESTATE BOARD, "Application for Appraisal," *Real Estate Appraising,* J. D. Henderson, 1931, pp. 405.

CHICAGO REAL ESTATE BOARD, "A Prize Winning Appraisal," *National Real Estate Board,* October 3, 1927, pp. 31-33.

CHICAGO REAL ESTATE BOARD, "Appraisal Certificate Reduced Facsimile Blank Form," Henderson, J. D. , *Real Estate Appraising,* 1931, pp. 406.

CHICAGO REAL ESTATE BOARD, MARK LEVY, "Appraisal Which Won the St. Paul Cup," *National Real Estate Journal,* September 2, 1929, pp. 42-46.

CHURCH, BYRON, "How Many Approaches," *The Real Estate Appraiser,* pp. 26.

CHURCH, BYRON, "What Good Is an Appraisal," *The Residential Appraiser,* May, 1961, pp. 9-11.

CHURCH, BYRON M., "Guide to a Successful Appraisal Practice," *The Real Estate Appraiser,* May, 1963, pp. 14-25.

CINCINNATI, OHIO REAL ESTATE BOARD, "Appraisal Certificate," Henderson, J. D. *Real Estate Appraising*, 1931, pp. 455.

CLARK, FRANK B., "Choosing the Cube Unit," *Review of the Society of Residential Appraisers*, June, 1937, pp. 5-6.

CLARK, FRANK B., "What Appraisers Should Know and Study," *National Real Estate Journal*, May 7, 1924.

CLARK, HORACE F., "Appraisal Forms," *Appraising the Home*, 1930, pp. 291-365.

CLARK, HORACE F., "Bibliography," *Appraising the Home*, 1930, pp. 239-240.

CLARK, HORACE F., "Controlling the Valuation During Modernization," *Appraising the Home*, 1930, pp. 122-128.

CLARK, HORACE F., "Cubic Foot Contents," *Appraising the Home*, 1930, pp. 263-273.

CLARK, HORACE F., "How to Develop an Appraisal File: Collecting Information for a Central File on Real-Estate Values," *Appraising the Home*, 1930, pp. 247-251.

CLARK, HORACE F., "Suggestions for Teaching a Course of Study In Appraising the Home," *Appraising the Home*, 1930, pp. 243-246.

CLEVELAND REAL ESTATE BOARD, *Committee on Valuation*, Cleveland.

CLOPPER, SIMON, "The Annual School and In-Service Training In Maryland," *Assessment Administration*, IAAO, Chicago, 1959, pp. 132-138.

CLOPPER, SIMON, "The IAAO Program for Training and Education," *Assessment Administration*, IAAO, Chicago, 1963, pp. 56-60.

COLE, JOHN D., "Performing Appraisal Computations by Data-Processing Equipment," *Assessment Administration*, IAAO, Chicago, 1964, pp. 128-131.

COLWELL, R. N., *Aerial and Space Photographs As Aids to Land Evaluation*, pp. 324.

COMMITTEE FROM FIVE PRINCIPAL FEDERAL AGENCIES, *A Glossary of Housing Terms*, Washington, 1931.

CONAN, ROBERT J., "Educational Groups Answer Advanced Training Need," *Appraisal Digest*, January, 1951, pp. 6-8.

CONDICT, HORACE V., "The Appraiser's Yardsticks," *The Appraisal Journal*, April, 1944, pp. 170-172.

COOPER, J. M., "Percentage Depletion; Abstract," *Valuation Manual*, June, 1956.

COWLEY, LEONARD M., "Appraisal of a Loft Building," *Appraisal Reporting Techniques*, American Institute of Real Estate Appraisers, 1951, pp. 125-151.

COWLEY, LEONARD M., "Assembling the Appraisal," *The Appraisal Journal*, April, 1954, pp. 183-192.

COWLEY, LEONARD M., "Gathering Data for Appraisal," *Encyclopedia of Real Estate Appraising*, 1959, pp. 94-112.

COYLE, JOSEPH A., L. W. ELWOOD, "Capitalization," *Technical Valuation*.

CRAIG, R. H., "Demonstration Appraisal Reports," *Appraisal Institute Magazine*, Appraisal Institute of Canada, Winnipeg.

CRAIGEN, GEORGE J., *Practical Methods for Appraising Lands, Buildings, and Improvements*, New York, 1911.

CRESPO, MANUEL, *Manual De Revaluo Impositivo*, Ediciones Macchi, Ediciones Macchi.

CROSBY, HARRY L., "Real and Personal Property Accounting and Valuation," *Technical Valuation*, February, 1963, pp. 19-21.

CROUSE, EARL F., "Technical Tools of the Appraiser," *The Journal of the American Society of Farm Managers and Rural Appraisers*, April, 1960, pp. 9-15.

CUMMINGS, J. S., AND C. B. RITTER, "Units of Property and the Continuing Property Record," *Technical Valuation*, February, 1957, pp. 7-14.

CURRY, CHARLES F., "Capitalization Rates," *The Appraisal Journal*, July, 1939, pp. 240-244.

DAVIES, CHARLES T., "Appraisal Review," *American Right of Way Association*, 1968, pp. 275-281.

DAVIES, CLARENCE, J., "The Administrative Requirements for Appraisal Services," *Valuation Manual*, American Society of Appraisers, 1961, pp. 5.

DAVIES, MAURICE B. T., "Planning and Selection for Data-Processing Service," *Assessment Administration*, I. A. A. O, Chicago, 1964, pp. 124-128.

DAVIS, IRVING F. JR., *A Statistical Approach to Real Estate Value with Applications to Farm Appraisal*, January, 1965.

DAVIS, J. CLARENCE, JR., "The Administrator's Requirements for Appraisers Services," *Appraisal and Valuation Manual*, American Society of Appraisers, 1961, pp. 5-9.

DAVIS, N. L., "The Appraisers Training and Education," *Appraisal of Machinery and Equipment*, 1969, pp. 99.

DAVIS, W. D., "Evidences of Market Value," *The Appraisal Journal*, April, 1959, pp. 224-253.

DAVIS, W. D., "The Appraisal Review Function," *The Appraisal Journal*, pp. 11-516.

DAWLEY, CHESTER G., "Appraisal Educational Program," *Technical Valuation*, June, 1959, pp. 41-43, 46-50.

DAWNIE, LEONARD, "Are Uniform Appraisal Reports Practical," *Review of Society of Residential Appraisers*, December, 1937, pp. 11-13.

DAWSONS OF PALL MALL, *Art Prices Current*, Wm. Dawson and Sons Ltd, Cannon Hse Kent, Eng.

DE WOLFE, P., "The Depreciation Multiplier," *Review of Economics and Statistics*, November, 1966, pp. 412-418.

DEGRAFF, JOHN T., "Criteria for Use of Cost Approach with Special Purpose Property," *The Appraisal Journal*, January, 1963, pp. 23-27.

DENIS, J. W., "Capitalization Rates and Trends," *The Appraisal Journal*, July, 1941, pp. 276-280.

DENTON JOHN H.,"Depreciation Studies," *Preliminary Report of the Bureau of Internal Revenue*, Government Printing Office, Washington, D. C, 1931.

DERBES, MAX J. JR., "Dangers of the Double Contract," *The Real Estate Appraiser*, February, 1963, pp. 12-14.

DERBES, MAX J. JR., "The Consideration In Deed," *The Real Estate Appraiser*.

DEWEY, EDWARD R., E. F. DAKIN, "Cycles, the Science of Prediction, with 1950 Postscript," Holt, New York, 1949.

DILMORE, GENE, "Elements of Network Analysis," *The Real Estate Appraiser*, March, 1969, pp. 47-52.

DILMORE, GENE, "Market Data Adjustments," *Appraisal Institute Magazine*, Appraisal Institute of Canada, Winnipeg.

DILMORE, GENE, "Multiple Regression Analysis," *Appraisal Institute Magazine*, Appraisal Institute of Canada, Winnipeg, June 1, 1971.

DILMORE, GENE, "New Direction In the Income Approach," *The Real Estate Appraiser*, May 1966, pp. 32-38.

DODDS, R. W., "Advantages and Disadvantages of Various Depreciation Methods," *Valuation Manual*, February 16, 1956, pp. 253-263.

DOIRON, J. CLIFFORD, "Market Data-Bundle of Information," *Technical Valuation*, October, 1956, pp. 31-34.

DOLAN, HARRY T., "Market Value-The Informed Guess," *The Appraisal Journal*, July, 1952, pp. 330-336.

DOLMAN, JOHN P., "Composition of the Professional Appraisal Report," *The Appraisal Journal*, October, 1957, pp. 533-543.

DONOGH, A. ORMSBY, JR., "The Appraisal Plant," *The Review*, October, 1952, pp. 3-7.

# BIBLIOGRAPHY OF APPRAISAL LITERATURE

DORAU, HERBERT B., "Is Rote Right In Valuation," *Appraisal Digest,* April, 1960, pp. 6-9.

DOUGLAS, R. BRUCE., "The Technique of Making Realty Appraisals," *National Real Estate Journal,* November 3, 1924, pp. 27-29.

DOW SERVICE, INC., *Cubic Foot Cost Standard Calculator,* Dow Service, New York, 1937, pp. 76.

DOWNIE, LEONARD, "Choosing the Capitalization Rate," *Review of Society of Residential Appraisers,* May, 1939, pp. 3-7.

DUBOIS, AYERS J., "Bracketing In Appraising," *The Appraisal Journal,* July, 1936, pp. 254-270.

DUBOIS, AYERS J., "The Appraiser Report," *The Appraisal Journal,* April, 1936, pp. 123-135.

DUBOIS, AYERS J., "The Capitalization Process," *The Appraisal Journal,* January, 1935, pp. 109-117.

DUBOIS, AYERS J., "The Data Program," *The Appraisal Journal,* October, 1936, pp. 368-378.

DUNHAM, HOWARD W. JR., "The Adjustment Process Demonstrated," *The Real Estate Appraiser,* 1968, pp. 17-21.

DUNN, DOMINICK R., "Construction Data for the Appraisers," *Review of Society of Residential Appraisers,* August, 1939, pp. 11-13, 10-12,PP.10-12.

DUNN, DOMINICK R., "Knowledge of Architecture Valuable to Appraisers," *The Appraisal Journal,* April, 1949, pp. 243-245.

DUNN, DOMINICK R., "Status of the Torrens Land Registration," *The Appraisal Journal,* April, 1950, pp. 227-230.

DUNN, DOMINICK R., "Why Vs. What," *The Real Estate Appraiser,* September, 1966, pp. 33.

DYKSTRA, GERALD O., AND L. G. DYKSTRA, *Business Law of Real Estate,* Mcmillan, New York, 1941.

DYSON, J. F., "The Use of Digital Computers," *Appraisal Institute Magazine,* Appraisal Institute of Canada, Winnipeg.

ECONOMIC OBSOLESCENCE, *Real Estate Analyst Appraisal Bulletin,* 1963, pp. 193-196.

EDGERTON, WILLIAM H., "The Home of the Diamond Horseshoe-An Analysis," *Appraisal Journal,* October, 1905, pp. 591-603.

EDMAN, J. J., "Admissibility of Drawings and Maps. Appraisal Docket," *The Appraisal Journal,* April, 1960, pp. 265-266.

EDMAN, J. J., "Capitalization of Income As the Standard of Value. Appraisal Docket," *The Appraisal Journal,* January, 1959, pp. 121-122.

EDMAN, J. J., "Capitalization of Income Inappropriate for Vacant Land. Appraisal Docket," *The Appraisal Journal,* July, 1961, pp. 415.

EDMAN, J. J., "The Appraisal Docket. Appraiser Cannot Use Alternative Valuation Methods," *The Appraisal Journal,* January, 1961, pp. 125-126.

EGERTON, J. W., "A New Outlook on Capitalization Rates," *Appraisal Institute Magazine,* Appraisal Institute of Canada, Winnipeg.

EINSTEIN, EDWIN M., "Suggestions for the Appraiser," *Review of the Society of Residential Appraisers,* July, 1936, pp. 9-12.

EISENLAUER, JACK F., "Mass Versus Individual Appraisers," *The Appraisal Journal,* October, 1968, pp. 533-535.

ELLER, HERBERT D., "The Personal Approach of the Inspection," *Appraisal Digest,* October, 1950, pp. 10-11.

ELLWOOD, L. W., "Appraisal Mathematics," *The Appraisal Journal,* April, 1963, pp. 165-168.

ELLWOOD, L. W., "How Many Approaches to Value," *The Appraisal Journal,* October, 1951, pp. 518-525.

ELLWOOD, LEON W., "Capitalization of Income Isn't Enough," *Appraisal Digest, 1901,* pp. 19-21.

EMBREE, WILLIAM L., "Analysis of Financial Statements As Related to Appraising," *The Appraisal Journal,* January, 1952, pp. 30-44, 210-224.

ENGLEHORN, V. A., "Preview 1952 Appraisal," *Journal of the American Society of Farm Managers and Rural Appraisers,* October, 1952, pp. 149-152.

EZEKIEL, MORDECAI, "Appraisal Data Research and Future Stabilization of Values," *Review of Society of Residential Appraisers,* April, 1938, pp. 7-11.

EZEKIEL, MORDECAI, "Data Research and Future Stabilization of Values," *Proceedings of the General Session and Urban Group Meetings, National Forum, 1937,*

FAVA, EDWARD, "Effective Use of Appraisals by Brokers and Salesmen," *Appraisal Digest,* 1904, pp. 1-5.

FEATHERSTON, F. B., "Correlation and Final Value Estimate," *The Real Estate Appraisers,* pp. 40.

FEDERAL HOME LOAN BANK REVIEW, *Building a Modern Appraisal Plant,* December, 1937, pp. 85-86.

FEDERAL POWER COMMISSION, *S 17 Electric Power Statistics,* Supt. of Documents, U. S. Govt. Printing Office.

FEDERAL RESERVE BANK OF BOSTON, "Income Distribution In Federal Grants-In-Aid," *The Appraisal Journal,* 1962, pp. 259-264.

FEDERAL RESERVE BANK OF CLEVELAND, "Interpreting Recent Unemployment Data," *The Appraisal Journal,* January, 1962, pp. 119-123.

FEDERAL RESERVE BANK OF ST. LOUIS, "Recent Employment Trends," *The Appraisal Journal,* January, 1965, pp. 120-125.

FENTON, HARRY R., "How to Plan an Appraisal," *The Appraisal Journal,* January, 1958, pp. 67-74.

FERGUSON, EGBERT R. JR., "Government Appraisals," *The Review,* July, 1954, pp. 15-19.

FERGUSON, HILL, "Making the Appraisal Carry Conviction," *The Appraisal Journal,* April, 1938, pp. 257-261.

FIELD, RALPH V., "How to Build and Maintain an Appraisal Service," *National Real Estate Journal,* June 27, 1927, pp. 40-42.

FIELD, RALPH V., "Inwood and Hoskold and Their Tables," *The Appraisal Journal,* January, 1937, pp. 75-76.

FIELD, RALPH V., "The Land Survey Systems of the United States," *The Appraisal Journal,* October, 1936, pp. 393-399.

FINBURGH, BERT J., "Using a Form Appraisal for an Out of Town Investor," *The Residential Appraiser,* October, 1960, pp. 15-21.

FISCHER, R. M., "Appraisal Accuracy," *Technical Valuation,* January, 1949, pp. 21-22, 24.

FISCHER, R. M., "Appraisals and Valuations," *Technical Valuations,* June, 1956, pp. 5.

FISCHER, R. M., "The Accuracy of Forecasts," *Technical Valuation,* June, 1955, pp. 17.

FISCHER, R. M., "The Use of Standards In Appraisal Practice," *The Appraisal Jouranl,* October, 1936, pp. 379-392.

FISCHER, REINHARD M., "Appraisal Accuracy and the Accountant," *Journal of Accountancy,* May, 1933, pp. 360-367.

FISHER, ERNEST M., "Appraisal Data, Their Compilation and Use," *National Appraisal Forum,* 1937, pp. 22-36.

FISHER, ERNEST M., "Glossary," *Advanced Principles of Real Estate Practice,* 1930, pp. 355-378.

## BIBLIOGRAPHY OF APPRAISAL LITERATURE

FISHER, ERNEST M., "Real Estate Courses for Real Estate Boards and for Educational Institutions," *National Real Estate Journal*, December 31, 1923, pp. 11-13.

FISHER, ERNEST M., "What Should Be Included In a Real Estate Curriculum," *The Appraisal Journal*, July, 1954, pp. 359-362.

FISHER, GEORGE L., "On Sales Verification," *The Real Estate Appraiser*, January, 1970, pp. 41-44.

FITZPATRICK, JOHN S., "How to Get the Most from Appraisals," *The Review*, February, 1963, pp. 3-6.

FLETCHER, C. V., "Appraising by Sound," *Technical Valuation*, February, 1955, pp. 27-28.

FOLEY, CLETIS R., "An Architects Guide to Lasting Design," *The Review*, February, 1952, pp. 12-17.

FOX, NORBERT J., "G. I. Appraisal," *The Review*, May, 1945, pp. 6-9, 20.

FRANKEL, EDWARD T., "Depreciation by Straight Lines and Curves," *Technicalities and Technical Valuation*, February, 1952, pp. 14-15.

FREE, R. L., *Real Estate Appraisal Problem Book*, American Institute of Real Estate Appraisers, Chicago, 1957.

FREE, ROBERT L., *152 Problems In Real Estate Appraisal with Suggested Solutions*, American Institute of Real Estate Appraisers, Chicago, 1954.

FREE, ROBERT L., "The Market Data Approach Applied to Income Properties," *The Appraisal Journal*, pp. 504-509.

FREE, VICTOR J., "Application of Depreciation Theory," *The Appraisal Journal*, April, 1939, pp. 120-127.

FREE, VICTOR J., "The Theory of Depreciation," *The Appraisal Journal*, January, 1939, pp. 46-53.

FREUDENBERGER, JOSEPH N., "Report Writing," *The Appraisal Journal*, July, 1962, pp. 380-385.

FRIEDMAN, ALBERT L., "Market Comparison As an Appraisal Tool," *Appraisal Digest*, April, 1957, pp. 4-6.

FUHRER, MAX, "Our Old Friend Hoskold," *The Appraisal Journal*, January, 1944, pp. 50-51.

FULLER, ROBERT S., "Flexibility In a Large Appraisal System," *The Review*, January, 1952, pp. 3-5.

FULLERTON, D. H., "National Capital Commission Land Ownership," *Appraisal Institute Magazine*, Appraisal Institute of Canada, Winnipeg.

GALIK, ALBERT R., "Derivation of Capitalization Rates," *Assessment Administration*, IAAO, Chicago, 1963, pp. 74-79.

GARDENER, ALAN C., "Present Day Appraisal Practice and Technique," *The Appraisal Journal*, October, 1945, pp. 365-370.

GARRISON, BURL L., "Capitalization-The Interest Rate," *Valuation*, A. S. A, Washington, D. C, February, 1968, pp. 70.

GASTON, JAMES E., "Information Possibilities Available Through Data Processing Equipment," *Assessment Administration*, I. A. A. O, Chicago, 1964, pp. 131-133.

GATES, WILLIAM S. JR., "Can a Property Record Index Be Accurately Controlled," *Technicalities and Technical Valuation*, February, 1952, pp. 25-27.

GIBBONS, JAMES E., "Capitalization Rates and the Money Market," *Appraisal Digest*, October, 1961, pp. 22-24.

GIBBONS, JAMES E., "Income and Capitalization," *The Appraisal Journal*, July, 1962, pp. 347-352.

GIBBONS, JAMES E., "On Operating Ratios," *The Appraisal Journal*, 1962, pp. 535-537.

## ▲ Appraisal Theory and Methods

GILBERT, RICHARD G., "Appraising As a Management Tool," *The Residential Appraiser,* November, 1958, pp. 3-5.

GILL, WILLIAM A., "Accounting Reports and the Appraisal Process," *American Society of Appraisers,* 1900, pp. 337-346.

GILLIS, BRUCE D., "In-Service Training South Dakota," *Assessment Administration,* I. A. A. O, Chicago, 1961, pp. 142-144.

GLOS, HAROLD V., "Actual Appraisal Reports," *National Real Estate Journal,* February, 1938, pp. 30-33, 63.

GLOS, HAROLD V., "Actual Appraisal Reports," *National Real Estate Journal,* August, 1937, pp. 47-49.

GLOS, HAROLD V., "Actual Appraisal Reports," *National Real Estate Journal,* January, 1958, pp. 36-38.

GLOS, HAROLD V., "Appraisal Notations," *Practical Appraisal Methods,* 1940, pp. 9-12.

GLOS, HAROLD V., "Details to Remember In Fixing Property Values," *Real Estate,* May 14, 1938, pp. 7-8.

GOLDSTONE, BRACTION, "Demonstration Appraisal," *The Appraisal Journal,* October, 1932, pp. 56-70.

GOLDSTONE, BRACTON, "On the Capitalization Rate Use In Max Tieger's Appraisal," *The Appraisal Journal,* April, 1933, pp. 242-243.

GOODSPEED, M. J., "Sampling Considerations In Land Evaluation," *Land Evaluation,* 1900, pp. 40.

GRAASKAMP, JAMES, *A Guide to Feasibility Analysis,* Society of Real Estate Appraisers, Chicago, 1900.

GRAASKAMP, JAMES E., "A Practical Computer Service for the Income Approach," *The Appraisal Journal,* January, 1969, pp. 50-57.

GRAHAM, DAVID M., "Loss Adjustment Appraisals," *Valuation,* 1966, pp. 20-24.

GREBLER, LEO, "The Role of the University In Real Estate Research," *The Appraisal Journal,* July, 1959, pp. 353-358.

GREEN, JOHN B., "An Appraisal Report," *The Appraisal Journal,* October, 1935, pp. 456-468.

GREENE, W. L., "The Appraisal School of the Miami Board," *National Real Estate Journal,* March 26, 1923, pp. 31-32.

GRUNSKY, CARL E., GRUNSKY, CARL E., JR., "Amortization and Depreciation Tables," *Valuation, Depreciation and the Rate-Base,* New York, 1917, pp. 387.

GUNNING, WALTER E., "Years' Purchase," *The Appraisal Journal,* April, 1960, pp. 243-250.

GUTHMAN, H. G., "Actuarial Versus Sinking Fund Type Formula for Valuation," *Accounting Review,* September, 1930, pp. 226-230.

HAALAND, ARNE W., "The Market Analysis Approach," *Technical Valuation,* June, 1959, pp. 19-20.

HAAS, DR. ROBERT BARLETT, "All About Collecting and the Adult Learner," *Appraisal and Valuation Manual,* Corporate Press Incorporated, Washington, D. C, January, 1972, pp. 416.

HAGOOD, WAYNE D., "Adjusting Comparable Sales," *The Review,* April, 1956, pp. 15-17.

HAIGHT, JAMES R., "Money---The Measuring Stick of Values," *The Appraisal Journal,* October, 1942, pp. 340-346.

HAINES, HOWARD, "Writing Better Reports," *Valuation Manual,* A. S. A, 1962, pp. 5.

HALL, C. W., "Appraisal Report Card," *Residential Appraisers Review,* August, 1935, pp. 7.

HALL, HARRY H., "Managing a Nationwide Appraisal Staff," *The Review,* April, 1948, pp. 3-8.

HALL, HARRY H., "Rx for Overworked Appraisers," *The Review,* July, 1946, pp. 3-8.

HALL, ROBERT W., "Time and the Appraiser," *The Appraisal Journal,* April, 1965, pp. 294-295.

HAMILTON, H. P., "An Appraisal Education," *Appraisal Institute Magazine,* Appraisal Institute of Canada, Winnipeg.

HAMILTON, H. P., "Six Principles of Report Writing," *Appraisal Institute Magazine,* September, 1963, pp. 23-27.

HAMMAR, CONRAD H., "Land Classification to Aid the Appraiser," *Journal of Land and Public Utility Economics,* August, 1939, pp. 277-286.

HANAO, YOCHIO, "Operating Statement - Income and Expenses," *The Real Estate Appraiser,* July, 1966, pp. 2-14.

HANCOCK, M. L., "Replot by Value," *Appraisal Institute Magazine,* Appraisal Institute of Canada, Winnipeg.

HANES, HERMAN. L., "The Appraiser Installs a Property Ledger," *Appraisal and Valuation Manual,* American Society of Appraisers, 1958, pp. 371-376.

HANFORD, LLOYD B. JR., "New Approaches to the Comprehensive Report," *The Appraisal Journal,* October, 1965, pp. 549-554.

HANFORD, LLOYD D., "Management and Appraising," *The Appraisal Journal,* January, 1961, pp..53-56.

HANFORD, LLOYD D. SR., "The Market Data Approach and Investment Property Appraisal," *The Real Estate Appraiser,* Chicago, December, 1966, pp. 2-10.

HANFORD, LLOYD JR., "Depreciation---Fact of Fiction," *The Real Estate Appraiser,* November, 1965, pp. 19-29.

HANSEN, VIGGO, "The Capitalization Approach," *Appraisal Digest,* October, 1954, pp. 17-18.

HANSON, PETER, "Data Schedules," *Condemnation Appraisal Procedure,* Hanson and Pollard, pp. 259-269.

HARRIS, HARWELL H., "Architectural Trends," *The Review,* February, 1954, pp. 7-11.

HARRISON, LOUIS A., "Do Pictures Lie," *The Residential Appraiser,* June, 1959, pp. 16-17.

HARTMAN, T. W., "Depreciation," *Review of Society of Residential Appraisers,* May, 1940, pp. 6-10.

HARVEY, ROBERT O., "Observations on the Cost Approach," *The Appraisal Journal,* October, 1953, pp. 514-518.

HAYES, DOUGLAS, "Economic Characteristics and Managerial Performance-The Quantitative Appraisal," *Appraisal and Management of Securities,* pp. 127.

HAYES, DOUGLAS A., "Inventory and Depreciation Policies-The Quantitative Appraisal," *Appraisal and Management of Securities,* pp. 207.

HAYNES, J. L., "The Appraisal In the Registration Statement," *The Appraisal Journal,* October, 1935, pp. 417-421.

HAYNSWORTH, CHARLES G., "Effect of Public Ownership on Capitalization Rates," *Appraisal Digest,* 1961, pp. 7-9.

HEALEY, F.J., "Musing on Multipliers," *The Real Estate Appraiser,* January, 1963, pp. 21-22.

HEARLE, EDWARD F. R., AND RAYMOUND J. MASON, *Data Processing for the State and Local Governments, a Rand Corporation Research Study,* Prentice-Hall, Englwd Cliffs, N. J., 1963.

HEER, CLYDE W., "Building a Profitable Appraisal Business," *Address Given at N. Y. State Society of Real Estate Appraisers' District Conference at Syra. Roch.,* April 16, 1941.

HEER, ROBERT R., *Depreciation Tables,* Fallon Lay Book Company, Albany, New York, 1958.

HELLAND, ARTHUR T., "Formal Training for Appraisers," *The Residential Appraiser,* March, 1957, pp. 7, 10.

▲ Appraisal Theory and Methods

HENDERSON, JAMES D., "The Modern Appraisal Kit," *The Appraisal Journal,* July, 1933, pp. 335.

HENDERSON, JAMES D., "Tools and Archives," *Real Estate Appraising,* 1931, pp. 25-49.

HENRY, E. G., "What Price Property Records?," *Technical Valuation,* July, 1945, pp. 3-7.

HERTLEIN, G. C., "Artist Views Discovery Through Computerized Graphics," *Computers and Automation,* August, 1970, pp. 25-26.

HERY, ELMER G., "Property Records," *Valuation Manual,* A. S. A. Valuation Manual, 1959, pp. 17.

HIGGINS WARREN J, "Demolition:Capitalize or Write-Off," *The Real Estate Appraiser,* The Society of Real Estate Appraisers, Chicago Illinois, January 1, 1974, pp. 40-49.

HIMSTREET, WILLIAM C., *Writing Appraisal Reports,* American Institute of Real Estate Appraisers, October, 1971.

HIMSTREET, WILLIAM C., "Writing Letters and Reports," *The Appraisal Journal,* April, 1959, pp. 198-202.

HINMAN, ALBERT G., HERBERT G. DORAU, "The Scope of a Useful Economic Survey," *Real Estate Merchandising,* Chicago, 1926, pp. 363.

HOAGLAND, HENRY E., "The Appraisal Process," *Real Estate Principles,* 1940, pp. 511.

HODGES, M. B., "A Reference Library for Appraisers," *The Real Estate Appraiser,* November, 1968, pp. 5-9.

HODGES, M. B. JR., "Don't Babysit with Your Leica!," *The Appraisal Journal,* July, 1962, pp. 405-407.

HOFFMAN, JUDGE MURRAY, "Hoffman's Depth Rule," *Appraising Manual, Second Edition,* 1937, pp. 359, 652.

HOGAN, JOHN J., "Appraisal Requirements of the General Services Administration," *The Appraisal Journal,* July, 1963, pp. 311-315.

HOLLEBAUGH, CLIFFORD W., "A Logical Approach to Value," *The Review,* November, 1949, pp. 3-6.

HOLLEBAUGH, CLIFFORD W., "Correlation - the Heart Of the Appraisal Process," *The Residential Appraiser,* April, 1962, pp. 17-20.

HOLLEBAUGH, CLIFFORD W., "Facts Vs. Fallacies In Real Estate Appraising," *The Appraisal Journal,* April, 1951, pp. 246-251.

HOLLEBAUGH, CLIFFORD W., "How the Appraiser Collects and Uses Sales Data," *The Review,* January, 1951, pp. 15-19.

HOLLEBAUGH, CLIFFORD W., "The Narrative Report," *The Review,* December, 1949, pp. 12-14.

HOLLEBAUGH, CLIFFORD W., "Watch Your Language," *The Appraisal Journal,* October, 1958, pp. 508-512.

HOLT, A. W., GEORGE P. DELONG, *Holt's Kwick Kost Estimating Systems,* Holt Publishing Co., Minneapolis, Minn., 1939.

HOLZHAUER, JOHN A., "Capitalization and the Income Premise," *The Real Estate Appraiser,* December, 1964, pp. 12-28.

HOME OWNER'S LOAN CORPORATION, "Property Appraisal Report Form," *Appraisal Manual,* 1937, pp. 652.

HONAD, YOSHIO, "Operating Statement - Income and Expenses," *Real Estate Appraiser,* SREA, Chicago, July, 1966, pp. 2.

HOOKER, JOHN P., *Correct Appraisal Methods,* Annals of Real Estate Practice, Vol. I, 1927, pp. 174-185.

HOOKER, JOHN P., "The Importance of Board Appraisal Committees," *National Real Estate Journal,* November 3, 1924, pp. 23-32.

HOPPE, JOHN G. JR., "Post Graduate Education In Real Estate Appraising," *The Real Estate Appraiser,* SREA, Chicago, September, 1964, pp. 34.

HOPPE, JOHN G. JR., "Serendipity and the Student of Appraisal," *Appraisal Journal*, April, 1967, pp. 177.

HORTON, E.B. JR., "How to Use Income and Expense Estimates," *The Appraisal Journal*, July, 1959, pp. 341-348.

HORTON, GEORGE S., "Actual Appraisal Reports," *National Real Estate Journal*, October, 1937.

HOTELLING, HAROLD, "A General Mathematical Theory of Depreciation," *Journal American Statistical Association*, March, 1925, pp. 340-353.

HUBIN, VINCENT J., "Pedestrian Traffic Counts," *The Appraisal Journal*, July, 1953, pp. 397-415.

HUBIN, VINCENT J., "Some Further Remarks on the Nature, Meaning and Use of the Cap Tables," *The Appraisal Journal*, October, 1965, pp. 517-530.

HUBIN, VINCENT J., "The Nature, Meaning Use of 'Cap' Tables," *Appraisal Institute Magazine*, Appraisal Institute of Canada, Winnipeg.

HUBIN, VINCENT J., "The Three Approaches to Value," *The Real Estate Appraiser*, January, 1969, pp. 37-42.

HUCK, ROBERT, "La Tecnica Del Avaluo," *Boletin*, Sotave, Caracas, Venezuela, pp. 11-15.

HUDER, K. LEE, "The Administrative Joker In the Federal Securities Act," *The Appraisal Journal*, April, 1935, pp. 223-228.

HUDSEN, H. R., "Knowledge of Appraising Valuable Asset of the Broker," *The Appraisal Journal*, October, 1953, pp. 550-554.

HUGHES, JAMES J., *A Preliminary and Partial Survey of Sources of Appraisal Data and Information*, January, 1960.

HUHN, G. P., *Method of Figuring Ground Values*, Minneapolis, Minn., 1923, pp. 42.

HULTEN, JOHN J., "The Appraisal Report," *The Appraisal Journal*, July, 1952, pp. 388-393.

HUMPHREY, D. E., "Habits of Failure-The Demonstration Report," *Appraisal Institute Magazine*, Appraisal Institute of Canada, Winnipeg.

HUNTER, WALTER C., "A Calaveras Formula," *Appraisal and Valuation Manual*, Washington, D. C., January, 1972, pp. 10.

HUNTER, WALTER C., "Calaveras Formula," *Valuation*, ASA, Washington, September, 1968, pp. 18.

HUSEMANN, FIELDING L., "Cyclical Valuation Procedure," *The Appraisal Journal*, January, 1942, pp. 9-25.

HYAM, LESLIE A., "Fine Arts - Liquidations," *Technical Valuation*, ASA, October, 1953, pp. 11.

HYDER, K. LEE, HENRY A. BABCOCK, "Fractional and Summation Appraisals," *The Appraisal Journal*, October, 1932, pp. 7-16.

INTERNATIONAL ASSOCIATION OF ASSESSING OFFICERS, *Electronic Data Processing Equipment*, Chicago, Illinois.

JACKS, MORRIS, "Estimating Structural Value, Vol. IV," *Appraisal and Valuation Manual*, ASA, 1959, pp. 99-112.

JACKSON, HOWARD F., "Basic Problems In the Income Approach," *The Real Estate Appraiser*, SREA, Chicago, July, 1964, pp. 35.

JACKSON, KENNETH N., "A Little Learning," *The Residential Appraiser*, October, 1962, pp. 15-16.

JACOBS, THEODORE M., "Municipal Finance," *Municiple Finance*, August, 1937, pp. 27-31.

JAFFE, J. M., "1962 Census of Governments Report on Taxable Property Values," *National Tax Journal*, September, 1963, pp. 267-276.

JAMES, M. H., "How to Lessen Wide Divergency In Appraisals," *Review of Society of Residential Appraisers*, August, 1941.

JARCHOW, ALFRED W., "Appraisals by Computer," *The Real Estate Appraisers*, SREA, Chicago, October, 1966, pp. 37.

▲ Appraisal Theory and Methods

JOACHIM, HARRY J., "For Good Measure, the Appraisers Tools," *The Real Estate Appraiser,* SREA, Chicago, October, 1964, pp. 22.

JOHNSON, CLIFFORD R., "The Major Problem In Making and Using Estimates of Market Value," *The Residential Appraiser,* August, 1961, pp. 21-23.

JOHNSON, E. HOLLAND, "Cost Data In Appraising," *The Appraisal Journal,* July, 1941, pp. 240-247.

JOHNSON, JESSE W., "Appraising Today - and Every Day," *The Appraisal Journal,* October, 1949, pp. 461-466.

JOHNSTON, EARL S., "To Demo or Not to Demo," *Appraisal Institute Magazine,* Appraisal Institute of Canada, Winnipeg.

JONES, FRANCIS E., "The Metes and Bounds System of Land Description," *The Appraisal Journal,* July, 1937, pp. 252-261.

JONES, J. H., "Obsolescence," *Accountant,* September 27, 1930, pp. 427-429.

JOUR OF AMER SOC OF FARM MGRS & RURAL APPRAISERS, "California Society of Farm Managers and Rural Appraisers Suggested Appraisal Outline," *Journal of the American Society of Farm Managers and Rural Appraisers,* October, 1962, pp. 29-30.

KAHN, SANDERS A., "How Good Is the Comparative Sales Approach," *Valuation Manual,* 1958, pp. 51-56.

KAMLET, MARK, "Appraisal Techniques In Restoration Claims," *The Appraisal Journal,* April, 1966, pp. 258-262.

KARKOW, WALDERMAR, "The Sheridan - Karkow Formula In Practice," *Real Estate Record,* April 20, 1935, pp. 24-26.

KAZDIN, S. EDWIN, *Limitations of Appraisal As a Guide In Lending on Income Properties,* Colloquium on Appraisal Research, Wisconsin, 1963, pp. 38-40.

KAZDIN, S. EDWIN, "Custom Tailored Appraisals," *Appraisal Digest,* July, 1954, pp. 13.

KAZDIN, S. EDWIN, "How to Use Income Data In the Appraisal of Apartment Property," *The Appraisal Journal,* July, 1957, pp. 409-416.

KECK, JOHN G., "Obsolescence," *Journal of Certified Property Managers,* December, 1938, pp. 119-127.

KEEFER, E. D., "Estimating Depreciation," *The Review,* July, 1947, pp. 15-19.

KELLER, HARRY K., "Appraisal Reports," *Real Estate Appraisers,* November 29, 1940.

KELLER, HARRY K., "Appraisal Review Procedure," *The Appraisal Journal,* October, 1945, pp. 379-389.

KELLEY, WILLIAM T., "Diagnostic Research," *The Appraisal Journal,* July, 1963, p. 333-337.

KELLEY, WILLIAM T., "Marketing Research and House Design," *The Appraisal Journal,* April, 1960, pp. 235-241.

KELLOUGH, W. R., "Agriculture Economics and Appraisal Sources," *AIREA,* July, 1967, pp. 17-20.

KELLOUGH, W. R., "The Unit In Place Reproduction Cost System," *Technical Valuation,* October, 1958, pp. 37-39.

KENNEDY, D. A., "Qualifications Appraisal Society of Societies," *Appraisal Institute Magazine,* Appraisal Institute of Canada, Winnipeg.

KENT, FREDERICK C., *Compound Interest and Annuity Tables,* New York, 1926.

KERSHOW WARREN W, "Using the Appraiser Effectively," *The Real Estate Appraiser,* The Society of Real Estate Appraisers, Chicago Illinois, January 1, 1974, pp. 36-39.

KESTER, ROY B., *Advanced Accounting,* Ronald, New York, 1946.

KINNARD JR, W. N., "The Ellwood Analysis In Valuation," *Appraisal Institute Magazine,* Appraisal Institute of Canada, Winnipeg.

KISSACK, A. B., "Future Income and Present Value," *Real Estate Analyst Appraisal Bulletin,* 1947, pp. 245-248.

KISSACK, A. B., "On Price As a Measure of Value," *The Appraisal Journal,* October, 1936, pp. 439-442.

KISSACK, A. B., "Selling Prices As Indices of Value," *The Appraisal Journal,* April, 1938, pp. 220-226.

KLAASEN, ROMAIN L., "Feasibility Studies," *Appraisal Institute Magazine,* Appraisal Institute of Canada, Winnipeg.

KLASSEN, ROMAIN L., "Feasibility Studies," *The Appraisal Journal,* December, 1965.

KNISKERN, PHILIP W., "Capitalization Rates, How to Determine the Value of the Income of Various Types of Estates," *National Real Estate Journal,* October 28, 1929, pp. 26-30.

KNISKERN, PHILIP W., 'How to Compute New Income for Appraisal Purposes," *National Real Estate Journal,* September, 1929, pp. 56-58.

KNISKERN, PHILIP W., "On the Residual Process In Max Tieger's Appraisal," *The Appraisal Journal,* April, 1933, pp. 249-250.

KRANZ, MARTIN E., "The Three Approaches to Value," *Appraisal and Valuation Manual,* 1958, pp. 27-28.

KUEHNLE, WALTER R., *Fundamental Approaches,* The Society of Industrial Realtors, 1953, pp. 5-17.

KURTZ, EDWIN B., *Life Expectancy of Physical Property Based on Mortality Laws,* The Ronald Press, New York, 1930.

LAHDE, WALTER, MYERS, WILLS, "Reducing Variations In Independent Appraisals," *Assessors News Letter,* July, 1962, pp. 77-81.

LANDMAN, A., "What's Wrong with Using Appraisal Values," *Journal of Accountancy,* March, 1971, pp. 81-82.

LANE, D. DUFFY, "The Cube Cost Estimate," *The Appraisal Journal,* July, 1942, pp. 237-240.

LARSEN, DAVID R., "The Appraiser's Tools and Forms," *The Review,* March, 1949, pp. 6-15.

LAUSE, CHARLES J., "An Inspection Check List," *The Review,* May, 1951, pp. 7-8.

LAWRENCE, DAVID M., MAY, HAROLD G, REES, W. H, *Modern Methods of Valuation of Land, Housing, and Buildings,* The Estates Gazette, London, 1949, pp. 2.

LAWRENCE, DAVID M., REES, W. H, *Modern Methods of Land, Houses, and Buildings,* Estates Gazette, London, 1956.

LAYDEN, ARTHUR L., "Some Appraisal Mathematics," *The Appraisal Journal,* October, 1934, pp. 5-18.

LEACH, W. A., *Rating Valuation & Appeals a Book on Rating of Ordinary Hereditaments for Gen'l Practitioner & Layman,* Estates Gazette, London, 1961.

LEET, EDMUND, "Demonstration Appraisal of Property Situated at 725 South Dale Street, Denver, Colorado," *Technical Valuation,* February, 1960, pp. 33-44.

LEFEAVER, JAMES H., "A Slightly Different Appraisal," *Technicalities,* January, 1949, pp. 12-13.

LENDRUM, JAMES T., "Heating Research," *The Review,* March, 1948, pp. 11-14.

LESSINGER, DR. JOCK, "Towards a New Method and Theory of Appraisal," *The Real Estate Appraiser,* pp. 42.

LESSINGER, JACK, "Econometrics and Appraisal," *The Appraisal Journal,* October, 1969, pp. 502-509.

LEVY, MARK, "Assembling the Data for Making Appraisals," *National Real Estate Journal,* March, 1941, pp. 20-21.

LEVY, MARK, BROTHER, "Application for Appraisal," *Real Estate Appraising,* 1931, pp. 417.

LEWMAN, HARRY, "**Managing an Appraisal Office**," Amer Institute of Real Estate Appraisers, October, 1971.

LIBRARY OF CONGRESS, *Library of Congress Catalog Books Subjects 1950-1954*, Rowman and Littlefield, New York.

LIBRARY OF CONGRESS, *Library of Congress Catalog Books Subjects 1955-1959*, Pageant Books, Patterson, 1960.

LIBRARY OF CONGRESS, *Library of Congress Catalog Books, Subjects 1955-1958*, B, Pageant Books, Inc., pp. 600000.

LIBRARY OF CONGRESS, *Library of Congress Catalog Books, Subjects 1955-1959*, Pageant Books, Patterson, 1960.

LLOYD, J. P., "**Depth Curves**," *The Appraisal Journal*, April, 1955, pp. 177-189.

LOCKWOOD, A. N., "**How to Write an Appraisal Report**," *Appraisal Reporting Techniques*, American Institute of Real Estate Appraiser, 1947, pp. 3-8.

LOCKYER, ALBERT W., "**Appraisers Serve Both Buyers and Sellers Equally Well**," *Appraisal Digest*, October, 1952, pp. 23-24.

LODGE, RICHARD L., "**Your Crystal Ball--How Sharp a Focus**," *The Appraisal Journal*, July, 1961, pp. 333-336.

LONG BEACH REAL ESTATE BOARD, "**Honorable Mention Award In Appraisal Contest at Seattle**," *National Real Estate Journal*, 1927, pp. 19-22.

LONG, G. B. JR., "**How to Make a Market Analysis**," *The Real Estate Appraiser*, May, 1959, pp. 13-16, 18.

LONIM, M. J., "**Heterodox Views on Appraising**," *The Appraisal Journal*, October, 1951, pp. 530-532.

LORENS, EDWARD R., "**The Appraisal Process-Fact Versus Theory**," *The Residential Appraiser*, February, 1962, pp. 2-5.

LOSTETTER, EARL, "**The New Thinking and the Appraisal Process**," *The Appraisal Journal*, July, 1963, pp. 343-348.

LOUIE, CHARLES F., "**Depreciation and the Cost Approach**," *Appraisal Journal*, October, 1961, pp. 507-516.

LUEBBERT, RAFAEL C., "**The Organization, Operating Procedures and Financial Management of an Appraisal Practice**," *The Real Estate Appraiser*, pp. 5.

LUKENS, C. JR. M. A. I., *The Appraiser and Real Estate Feasibility Studies*, American Institute of Real Estate Appraisers, August, 1972.

LUM, Y. T., "**Applying the Market Data Method**," *The Real Estate Appraiser*, March, 1969, pp. 5-12.

LUM, Y. T., "**Basic Considerations of Appraisal Concepts and Value Factors**," *The Residential Appraiser*, February, 1962, pp. 14-20.

LUM, Y. T., "**Some of the Causes of Divergencies of Value Opinions**," *The Real Estate Appraiser*, SREA, Chicago, November, 1967, pp. 17.

LUM, Y. T., "**The Meaning, Comparison and Application of Market Data**," *The Real Estate Appraiser*, January, 1965, pp. 28-38.

LUNDY, VICTOR R., "**A Reviewer Reports**," *Appraisal Institute Magazine*, Appraisal Institute of Canada, Winnipeg.

LUNDY, VICTOR R., "**A Reviewer's Report**," *The Appraisal Journal*, October, 1960, pp. 484-493.

LUNDY, VICTOR R., "**Market Data**," *The Review*, September, 1955, pp. 3-4, 10.

LUNDY, VICTOR R., "**The Doctrine Unity**," *The Review*, September, 1956, pp. 3-5.

LUTTRELL, RALPH J., "**Some Problems In the Appraisal of Wherry Housing**," *The Appraisal Journal*, April, 1959, pp. 185-188.

LYON, ROBERT L., "**Inspecting New Construction**," *The Review*, November, 1945, pp. 7-10.

MACBRIDE, DEXTER D, "Decisions That Infuence Value Concepts," *Proceedings Northwest Appraisal Conference,* Society of Real Estate Appraisers, Chicago, September 1, 1966.

MACBRIDGE, DEXTER D, "Major Developments In the Appraisal Profession Within the US: Review, Commentary, Prediction," *Valuation Magazine,* American Society of Appraisers, Washington D.C., December 1, 1973, pp. 126-138.

MACBRIDE, DEXTER D., *Power and Process, Monograph No. 1,* American Society of Appraisers.

MACBRIDE, DEXTER D., "The Appraisal Process Perspective," *Proceedings,* San Francisco, March, 1965.

MACBRIDE, DEXTER D., "The Appraisal Process, Perspective," *American Society of Appraisers Valuation Manual,* American Society of Appraisers, 1964, pp. 43.

MACCHESNEY, NATHAN W., *Glossary,* New York, 1927, pp. 835-848.

MACDONALD, ARTHUR J., "Comprehensive Appraisals," *The Appraisal Journal,* July, 1955, pp. 345-355.

MACKENZIE, DONALD H., *Mathematics of Finance,* Mcgraw-Hill, New York.

MACLEOD, MORTON P., "If You Want to Know - Go; if Not - Send," *Technical Valuation,* American Society of Appraisers, Washington, February, 1968, pp. 3.

MACROSSIE, WILLIAM, "Appraising In a War Economy," *The Appraisal Journal,* April, 1943, pp. 107-114.

MADGETT, CARL J., *Trends Towards Advanced Education In Property Valuation,* M, Institute of America.

MANN, JACK K., "Analysis of Appraisal Forms," *The Residential Appraiser,* June, 1960, pp. 11-13.

MANN, JACK K., "Correlation In the Appraisal Process," *The Residential Appraiser,* November, 1960, pp. 10-12.

MANN, JACK K., "Required Courses Revised for Presentation After January 1, 1970," *The Appraiser,* October, 1970.

MANN, JACK K., "The Broker's Appraiser," *The Residential Appraiser,* Chicago, July, 1958, pp. 16.

MARQUIS, RICHARD, "Mass Appraisals," *The Review,* December, 1952, pp. 10-14.

MARSTON, ANSON, ROBLEY WINFREY, J. C. GEMPSTEAD, "Engineering Valuation & Depreciation," Mcgraw-Hill, New York, 1953.

MARSTON, ANSON, THOMAS R. AGG, *Depreciation Accountancy,* M, McGraw-Hill.

MARTLING, W. LOCKWOOD, JR., "Curing Obsolescence," *The Review,* April, 1951, pp. 3-7, 18.

MATTHEWS, HAROLD WILLIAM, *Accounting for Appraisals,* Austin, Texas, 1933.

MATTHEWS, MYRON L., "Fate of the Cost Premium," *The Review,* December, 1947, pp. 19-20.

MAY, ARTHUR A., "The Appraiser's Field Kit," *The Appraisal Journal,* January, 1953, pp. 23-25.

MC MICHAEL, STANLEY L., "Elementos Administracion Apreciacion Del Valor," *Boletin,* Sotave, Caracas, Venezuela, pp. 45-51.

MC MICHAEL, STANLEY L., "Preparacion Del Informe Escrito Tasacion," *Boletin,* Sotave, Caracas, Venezuela, pp. 25-29.

MCCANDLESS, DONALD C., "Reuse Valuation," New Appraisal Frontier, the Appraisal Journa.

MCCUTCHEON, W. B., "Developing Capitalization Rates," *The Review,* April, 1949, pp. 6-8.

MCDONALD, D. L., "The National Capital Commission," *Appraisal Institute Magazine,* Appraisal Institute of Canada, Winnipeg.

▲ Appraisal Theory and Methods

MCFARLEN, T. A., "Demonstration Appraisal Reports," *Appraisal Institute Magazine*, February, 1958, pp. 17-19.

MCGAHEY, ROBERT L., "The Why's What's and How's of Property Records," *Valuation Manual*, American Society of Appraisers, 1964, pp. 119.

MCKAY, HERNDON, "Comparison Is Core of Appraising," *The Review*, December, 1950, pp. 15-19.

MCKEAN, JAMES P., "Appraisal Education," *Papers and Proceedings*, Wisconsin Colloquium on Appraisal Research, 1963, pp. 54-58.

MCKINNEY, HOWARD C., "Wide Variances In Appraisals," *The Appraisal Journal*, October, 1956, pp. 543-548.

MCLEOD, MORTON P., "The Education of the Appraiser," *Technical Valuation*, pp. 11.

MCMICHAEL, JAMES M., *Real Estate Investment Analysis and Programming*, L. A. Exchg Division California Real Estate Assocn, 1968.

MCMICHAEL, STANLEY L., "Appraising by the Unit Foot Method-Depth Tables," *Appraising Manual*, 1937, pp. 346-361.

MCMICHAEL, STANLEY L., "Ascertaining Plottage Value," *Appraising Manual*, 1937, pp. 402-412.

MCMICHAEL, STANLEY L., "Average Density," *Appraising Manual*, 1937, pp. 527.

MCMICHAEL, STANLEY L., "Comparison of Depth Tables," *Appraising Manual*, 1937, pp. 358.

MCMICHAEL, STANLEY L., "Depth Tables," *The Appraisal Journal*, April, 1935, pp. 205-211.

MCMICHAEL, STANLEY L., "Equipment for Appraisal Service," *Appraising Manual*, 1937, pp. 459-464.

MCMICHAEL, STANLEY L., "Land Values Per Front Foot," *Appraising Manual*, 1937, pp. 519.

MCMICHAEL, STANLEY L., "Mathmatical Treatment of Income," *Appraising Manual*, 1937, pp. 115-122.

MCMICHAEL, STANLEY L., "Plottage Applied to Width of Lots," *Appraising Manual*, 1937, pp. 410-412.

MCMICHAEL, STANLEY L., "Relation Between Front Value and Square Foot Value for Various Depths," *Appraising Manual*, 1937, pp. 524-525.

MCMICHAEL, STANLEY L., "Standard Appraisal Certificate Form," *Appraising Manual*, 1937, pp. 530-532.

MCMICHAEL, STANLEY L., "Value, Its Meaning and How to Measure it," *Appraising Manual*, 1937, pp. 6-50.

MCMORRAN, J. BURCH, "New York Department of Public Works Appraisal Methods Promise Savings to Taxpayers," *Right of Way*, August, 1963, pp. 933-34.

MCSWEENEY, THOMAS F., "The Deferment Problem," *Technical Valuation*, pp. 35-40.

MERCER, GEORGE L., "Proper Selection of Capitalization Rates," *The Real Estate Appraiser*, September, 1964, pp. 13.

MERTZKE, ARTHUR J., "A Course In Appraisals," *Annals of Real Estate Practice*, 1925, pp. 217-223.

MERTZKE, ARTHUR J., "Appraisal Contests," *Annals of Real Estate Practice*, 1928, pp. 154-184.

MERTZKE, ARTHUR J., "Board Appraisal Reports," *National Association of Real Estate Boards*, 1930, pp. 672-676.

MERTZKE, ARTHUR J., "Valuation," *National Real Estate Journal*, September 3, 1928, pp. ART, 1-9.

MILISIEWICZ, J., "Extending Appraisal Education," *Appraisal Institute Magazine*, Appraisal Institute of Canada, Winnipeg.

MILISIEWICZ, JANINA, "The Merits of Extending Appraisal Education," *Appraisal Magazine*, December, 1961, pp. 26-28.

MILL, JOHN STUART, "Letters on Value," *The Appraisal Journal*, October, 1953, pp. 511-513.

MINAYA, NICHOLAS J., "Consider the Circumstances," *The Appraisal Journal*, October, 1969, pp. 529-531.

MOLLAN, WILLIAM W., "Reasonable Normal Value and the G.I.," *The Appraisal Journal*, July, 1945, pp. 263-265.

MONTZ, A. S., "New Orleans Appraisal Bureau," *Review of the Society of Residential Appraisers*, May, 1937, pp. 10-129.

MOORE, MILTON W., "A Yardstick of Value," *The Appraisal Journal*, April, 1934, pp. 238-240.

MOREHOUSE, E. W., "Land Valuation," *Encyclopedia of Social Sciences*, 1933, pp. 137-139.

MORGAN, JAMES V., "Appraisal Facets," *The Residential Appraiser*, June, 1957, pp. 11.

MORRISSEY, THOMAS P., "Accounting Reports and the Appraisal Process," *American Society of Appraisers, Appraisal and Valuation Manual*, 1959, pp. 337-346.

MORSE, TRUE D., "Practical Law for Managers and Appraisers," *Journal of the American Society of Farm Managers and Rural Appraisers*, October, 1947, pp. 90-95.

MORSE, TRUE D., "Standard Appraisal Data," *Journal of the American Society of Farm Managers and Rural Appraisers*, April, 1950, pp. 43-48.

MULHERN, EUGENE S., "Valuation Report," *Technicalities*, January, 1959, pp. 14-18.

MUNIC FIN OFFCRS ASSN OF U. S. & CANADA, *Applications of Electronic Data Processing*, Municipal Finance Officers Association, Chicago, 1960.

MURILLO, ANA J. ECO., G. BAUDILIO, "El Metodo De Incidencias," *Boletin*, Sotave, Caracas, Venezuela, pp. 17-27.

MURRAY, WILLIAM G., "A Public Appraisal System Open to All Appraisers," *Journal of the American Society of Farm Managers and Rural Appraisers*, April, 1946, pp. 18-23.

MURRAY, WILLIAM G., "Market Data In Rural Appraising," *The Appraisal Journal*, July, 1956, pp. 385-392.

MUSTOE, NELSON EDWIN, *The Complete Valuation Practice*, Estates Gazette, London, 1955.

NAMAVATI, ROSHAN, *Theory & Practice of Valuation Land & Bldgs for Architects Engineers Surveyors & Tax Practitioners*, Universal Book Corp., Bombay, 1968.

NASARIO, LUIS A., "Curso Evaluacion Bienes Raices, Capitulo Viii," *Boletin*, Sotave, Caracas, Venezuela, pp. 41-46.

NASARIO, LUIS A., "Evaluacion Bienes Raices, IV, V y Vi," *Boletin*, Sotave, Caracas, Venezuela, pp. 41-48.

NASARIO, LUIS A., "Evaluacion De Bienes Raices: Capitulo Ix," *Boletin*, Sotave, Caracas, Venezuela, pp. 49-62.

NASARIO, LUIS A., "Evaluacion De Bienes Raices: Capitulo X," *Boletin*, Sotave, Caracas, Venezuela, pp. 47-56.

NATIONAL ASSOCIATION OF REAL ESTATE BOARDS, *Universities and Colleges Giving Courses In Real Estate*, October, 1936.

NATIONAL ASSOCIATION OF REAL ESTATE BOARDS, "Appraisal Committee," *National Real Estate Journal*, February 12, 1923, pp. 47-48.

NATIONAL ASSOCIATION OF REAL ESTATE BOARDS, "Appraisal Division-Report of Committee Appointed at the Toronto Convention of the Association," *National Real Estate Journal*, February 16, 1931, pp. 38-40.

NATIONAL ASSOCIATION OF REAL ESTATE BOARDS, "New Courses In Appraising and Selling Offered by National Association," *National Real Estate Journal*, pp. 44, 45-46.

NATIONAL ASSOCIATION OF REAL ESTATE BOARDS, "Special Committee Recommends Appraisal Basis for Building and Loan Associations," *National Real Estate Journal*, January 24, 1927, pp. 48.

NATIONAL REAL ESTATE JOURNAL, *California Standard Appraisal Form*, January 6, 1930, pp. 26.

NATIONAL REAL ESTATE JOURNAL, "Ohio Appraisal Rates," *National Real Estate Journal*, August, 1929, pp. 63.

NAZARIO, LUIS A., "Evaluacion De Bienes Raices:," *Boletin*, Sotave, Caracas, Venezuela, pp. 61-68.

NAZARIO, LUIS A., "Evaluacion De Bienes Raices: Capitulo Vii," *Boletin*, Sotave, Caracas, Venezuela, pp. 41-47.

NAZARIO, LUIS A., "Prontuario Para El Curso De Bienes Raices," *Boletin*, Sotave, Caracas, Venezuela, pp. 17-32.

NELSON, N. B., "Glossary," *Law of Real Estate Brokerage*, Prentice-Hall, Inc., 1928, pp. 489-523.

NELSON, R. L., "The Changing Composition of Capitalization Rates," *The Real Estate Appraiser*, October, 1964, pp. 15.

NELSON, RICHARD L., "Capitalization Rates," *The Appraisal Journal*, January, 1958, pp. 34-39.

NELSON, ROLAND D., "New Concepts In Capital Gains Appraising," *The Real Estate Appraiser*, August, 1966, pp. 19.

NELSON, T. R., "An Econometric Model of the Land Market Stressing Effects of Government Programs on Land Values," *Dissertation Abstracts*, Ann Arbor.

NEWLOVE, GEORGE HILLIS, *Mathematics of Valuation*, 1937.

NEWTON, E. W., "There Is No Shortcut to a Good Appraisal," *Appraisal Institute Magazine*, Appraisal Institute of Canada, Winnipeg.

NINDE, HARRY W., "The G. I. Appraisal Process," *Appraisal and Valuation Manual*, 1956-57, pp. 85-91.

NOLAN, JAMES J., "The Certificate of Reasonable Value--A Mandate of Market Value," *The Residential Appraiser*, May, 1962, pp. 15-16.

NORMAN, R. SMITH, MILON BROWN, CHESTER J. KOPEC, *Getting the Most for Your Training Dollar*, Public Personnel Association, Chicago, 1966.

NORTH, L. W., "Build it on Paper First," *Appraisal Institute Magazine*, Appraisal Institute of Canada, Winnipeg.

NOWAK, ARTHUR M., "Appraisal Facts and Fallacies," *Commerce and Finance*, June 22, 1927, pp. 1253-1254.

NOYES, GEORGE I., "Comparisons In Real Estate Appraisals," *The Appraisal Journal*, January, 1940, pp. 53-58.

NUGENT, R. A. L., "Common Errors In Appraisals," *Appraisal Institute Magazine*, Appraisal Institute of Canada, Winnipeg.

ONEIL, THOMAS E., "S. R. W. A. Market Data Center, Inc. : an Actuality," *The Real Estate Appraiser*, September, 1968, pp. 5-13.

ORORKE, T., "The Intern Program Through English Eyes," *The Appraisal Journal*, January, 1966, pp. 118-122.

OAKLAND, CALIF. REAL ESTATE BOARD, "Certificate of Appraisal: Reduced Facsimile Blank Form," Henderson, J. D., *Real Estate Appraising*, 1931, pp. 415.

OCHS, HARRY T., JR., "Application of Price Indexes In Appraisals," *Appraisal and Valuation Manual*, American Society of Appraisers, 1958, pp. 311-322.

OHMAN, ROBERT E., "Demonstration Appraisal of an Industrial Property," *Technical Valuation*, June, 1963, pp. 24-41, 44-54.

## BIBLIOGRAPHY OF APPRAISAL LITERATURE

OLCOTT, MARGARET, AND HELEN E. HENNEFRUND, "Compilers," *Appraisers, and Assessors, Manuals,* 1935, pp. 168-179.

OUTWATER, H. G., "Short Cut by Charts," *Architectural Forum,* December, 1936, pp. 562-563.

PADILLA GONZALEZ, GILBERTO, "La Aritmetica Tasacion De Bienes Raices," *Boletin,* Sotave, Caracas, Venezuela, pp. 21-26.

PARKINSON, G., "Here's a Builder Who Uses the Apartment Buyers Money to Build the Apartments," *House and Home,* January, 1971, pp. 20.

PATT, HERBERT B., "On Capitalization Rates," *The Appraisal Journal,* April, 1938, pp. 170-171.

PEARL, MILTON A., "Appraiser's Guide Under Law Allowing Moving Costs," *The Appraisal Journal,* July, 1953, pp. 327-335.

PENNA LEAGUE OF BLDG & LOAN ASSOCIATIONS, "Real Estate Appraisal Committee," *Review of the Society of Residential Appraisers,* August, 1936, pp. 10.

PEPPIATT, H. G., "The Data Program," *Review of Society of Residential Appraisers,* July, 1940, pp. 10-14.

PERRY, ROBERT D., "New Tool Proves Useful," *The Appraisal Journal,* October, 1960, pp. 465-468.

PERT, WOODBY X., "An Appraiser's Affidavit," *The Appraisal Journal,* October, 1935, pp. 469-470.

PETTY, JOHN A., "Real Estate Lecture Courses," *National Real Estate Journal,* November 5, 1923, pp. 13-14.

PHIMISTER, Z. S., "Education-Quo Vadit," *Appraisal Institute Magazine,* Appraisal Institute of Canada, Winnipeg.

PIDOCK, W. L., "Accounting for Net Salvage," *Management Accounting,* December, 1970, pp. 49-52.

PIERCE, PHILIP F., "Land Contract Sales and Their Relationship to Market Value," *Right of Way,* pp. 50-51, 60.

PILLSWORTH, W. H., "Continuous Learning," *Appraisal Institute Magazine,* Appraisal Institute of Canada, Winnipeg, March 1, 1971.

POLLEY, JOSEPH H., "Simplified Comparable Sales Filing," *The Appraisal Journal,* July, 1966, pp. 449-452.

POPE, LESLIE E., "A Check List of Income and Expenses," *The Review,* September, 1956, pp. 7-11.

POPE, LONNIE, "Ellwood Makes Sense to Me," *The Real Estate Appraiser,* pp. 13.

PORTER, GEORGE D., "Index Numbers and Trending In Public Utility Valuation," *American Society of Appraisers Valuation Manual,* American Society of Appraisers, 1958, pp. 227.

PORTLAND, OREGON, REALTY BOARD, "Application for Appraisal," Henderson, J. D., *Real Estate Appraising,* 1931, pp. 411-413.

POTTS, W. T. JR., "Problem of the Trainee," *The Real Estate Appraiser,* December, 1936, pp. 26-31.

PRACTICAL LAND ECONOMIC STUDY PROGRAMS, *Proceedings of the Fourth Annual National Seminar, 1958,* American Right of Way Association, 1959, pp. 60-71.

PRENTICE HALL EDITORIAL STAFF, *Encyclopedic Dictionary of Real Estate Practice,* Prentice Hall, Englwd Cliffs, N. J., 1962.

PROUTY, W. L. AND OTHERS, "Appraisal Record Systems," *Appraisers and Assessors Manual,* 1930, pp. 253-271.

PROUTY, W. L. AND OTHERS, "Establishing a System for Land Appraisals The Appraisal of Land," *Appraisers and Assessors Manual,* 1930, pp. 285-303.

PRUSSIANO, JOSEPH B., "Blueprint Reading," *The Real Estate Appraiser,* pp. 18.

▲ **Appraisal Theory and Methods**

PUBLIC PERSONNEL ASSOCIATION, *A Guide to Training Practices*, Public Personnel Association, Chicago, 1966.

QUINTANA, ISIDOR, "Actual Appraisal Reports," *National Real Estate Journal*, February, 1932, pp. 63-67.

QUINTO, OSCAR B., "Adjusting the Comparative Approach," *The Review*, September, 1947, pp. 19-21.

QUINTO, OSCAR B., "Selecting Similar Sales," *The Review*, February, 1946, pp. 7-9, 11.

RAMS, EDWIN M., "Some Observations on Appraisal Training," *Right of Way*, December, 1963, pp. 33-38.

RANDALL, WILLIAM J., "Clearly State the Appraisal Premise," *Real Estate Analyst Appraisal Bulletin*, 1958, pp. 49-52.

RATCLIFF, DR. RICHARD U., "Professional Appraisal Education at the University of Wisconsin," *The Real Estate Appraiser*, June, 1963, pp. 2-6.

RATCLIFF, R. U., "The Future Education of the Appraiser," *Appraisal Institute Magazine*, Appraisal Institute of Canada, Winnipeg.

RATCLIFF, R. U., "The Only Road to Vp," *Appraisal Institute Magazine*, Appraisal Institute of Canada, Winnipeg.

RATCLIFF, R. U., "Wrong Roads to Vp," *Appraisal Institute Magazine*, Appraisal Institute of Canada, Winnipeg.

REAL ESTATE ANALYST, THE, "Census Data to Aid the Appraiser," *Real Estate Analyst Appraisal Bulletin*, 1951, pp. 295-298.

REAL ESTATE ANALYST, THE, "Cubic Content and Reproduction Cost," *Real Estate Analyst Appraisal Bulletin*, 1948, pp. 227-230.

REAL ESTATE ANALYST, THE, "Market Prices," *Real Estate Analyst Appraisal Bulletin*, 1960, pp. 403-406.

REAL ESTATE ANALYST, THE, "Multiple Use Depth Chart and Table," *Real Estate Analyst Appraisal Bulletin*, 1949, pp. 313-316.

REAL ESTATE BOARD OF NEW YORK, "Application for Appraisal," *Real Estate Appraising*, 1931, pp. 403.

REAL ESTATE BOARD OF NEW YORK, "Appraisals," *Diary and Manual of the Board*, 1937, p. 135-137.

REAL ESTATE BOARD OF NEW YORK, "Certificate of Appraisement," *Real Estate Appraising*, 1931, pp. 404.

REESE, LOUIE, "Instant Paragraphs--Short Cut to Better Appraisals," *The Appraisal Journal*, April, 1967, pp. 289-294.

REEVES, CUTHBERT E., "Depth Table Based on a Standard of 100 Feet at 100 and Extending to 500 Feet," *Mcmichael S. L. Appraising Manual*, 1937, pp. 357.

REEVES, CUTHBERT E., "Gross Income As an Index of Value," *The Appraisal Journal*, July, 1936, pp. 301-309.

REGISTER, J. ALVIN, "The Appraisal Report," *Jour of Amer Inst of Real Estate Appraisers*, July, 1935, pp. 366-368.

REIDY, MAURICE F., "An Appraisal That Went Sour," *The Appraisal Journal*, July, 1934, pp. 297-302.

RENSHAW, EDWARD F., "Scientific Appraisal," *National Tax Journal*, December, 1958, pp. 314-322.

RESIDENTIAL APPRAISER, "How They Give Appraisers Comparable Sales Data," *The Residential Appraiser*, August, 1962, pp. 7-12.

REVIEW, THE, "An Appraisal Form on Review," *The Review*, April, 1950, pp. 7-11.

REVIEW, THE, "Central Appraisal Bureaus," *The Review*, February, 1947, pp. 14-18.

REVIEW, THE, "Equitable's Appraisal Form," *The Review*, May, 1949, pp. 9-14.

REVIEW, THE, "Guide to Census Data," *The Review*, April, 1952, pp. 17-20.

REVIEW, THE, "New Standards for Narrative Reports," *The Review*, October, 1952, pp. 10-12. , 9-12.,PP.16-20.

REVIEW, THE, "The Appraisal Process," *The Review*, November, 1949, pp. 12-16.

RIHG, ALFRED A., "Appraisal Correlation," *Appraisal and Valuation Manual*, February, 1954, pp. 31.

RING, ALFRED A., "Appraisal Planning and Reporting," *The Valuation of Real Estate*, pp. 346-359.

RING, ALFRED A., "Correlation Is the Secret of Appraisal Success," *The Review*, September, 1952, pp. 20-23.

RING, ALFRED A., "Importance of Cost, Price, Income and Market on Valuation," *The Valuation of Real Estate*, 1970, pp. 43.

RING, ALFRED A., "Narrative Appraisal Report," *The Valuation of Real Estate*, 1970, pp. 457-483.

RING, ALFRED A., "The Market Sales Approach to Value," *The Valuation of Real Estate*, 1970, pp. 131-149.

RODIL, JORGE LAMPORT (LIC), NAVARRO, ARTURO AROCH, "El Proyecto Catastral En Fotografias," *Guatemala*, Division Internacional De Catastro, Guatemala C.A., January 1, 1972.

ROGERS, C. N., "The Comparative Method of Appraisal," *Jour of Amer Soc of Farm Mgs & Rural Appraisers*, October, 1946, pp. 117-122.

ROGERS, RUSSELL R., "On Control Data," *The Appraisal Journal*, October, 1962, pp. 541-542.

ROGERS, RUSSELL R., "Technique of Writing the Narrative Report," *The Appraisal Journal*, October, 1960, pp. 494-500.

ROSE, C. W., D. A. THOMAS, "Remote Sensing of Land Surface Temperature and Some Applications," *Land Evaluation*, pp. 367.

ROSS, THURSTON, "Corner Influence Table In Three Types of Property, Compared with Zangerle Corner Influence Table," *Appraising Manual*, 1937, pp. 382.

ROTH, VINCENT E., "Rule of Measurement," *Technical Valuation*, February, 1956, pp. 23.

ROTHSCHILD, SIGMUND, "Measure of Wealth," *The Appraisal and Valuation Manual*, 1954, pp. 1.

ROUGH NOTES CO., INC., *Inspection and Appraisal Report Work Sheets*, Rough Notes Co., Inc.

ROYAL BANK OF CANADA, "Imagination Helps Communication," *Appraisal Journal*, January, 1962, pp. 113-118.

RUGELES, IVAN OLIVER, "Conceptos Generales Sobre Valuacion," *Boletin*, Sotave, Caracas, Venezuela, pp. 7-10.

RUSSELL, HORACE, "Appraisal Contracts," *The Review*, November, 1951, pp. 7-10.

RUSSELL, JOHN D., "Property Records and Property Values," *Technical Valuation*, 1966, pp. 14.

RYAN, JAMES A., "Improving the Engineering Load Factor of Property Records," *The Appraisal and Valuation Manual*, 1955, pp. 119-126.

SACKMAN, JULIUS L., "The Limitations of the Cost Approach," *The Appraisal Journal*, January, 1968, pp. 55-60.

SANDO, LAURENCE, "Appraisal Review Committee Its Purpose and Function," *The Appraisal Journal*, April, 1966, pp. 228-233.

SCHEIDT, JOHN, "Methods of Determining Value," *Technical Valuations*, October, 1967, pp. 71.

SCHMIDT, WALTER S., "Appraisal Data and the Control of Realty Development," *Proceedings of the General Session and Urban Group Meetings*, 1937, pp. 100-108.

SCHMUTZ, GEORGE L., *Appraisers Interest Tables and Their Uses,* G. L. Schmutz, Los Angeles, 1935, pp. 1-47.

SCHMUTZ, GEORGE L., *Capitalization Tables with Problems and Their Uses,* A.I.R.E.A., Studio City, Calif., 1936.

SCHMUTZ, GEORGE L., *The Appraisal Process,* G. L. Schmutz, No. Hollywood, Calif, 1953.

SCHMUTZ, GEORGE L., *The Appraisal Process,* G. L. Schmutz, Manhattan Beach, Cal, 1959.

SCHMUTZ, GEORGE L., "Appraisal Techniques," *The Appraisal Process,* 1959, pp. 225-249.

SCHMUTZ, GEORGE L., "Appraising by Comparison," *The Review,* November, 1946, pp. 18-20.

SCHMUTZ, GEORGE L., "Construction of Charts and Graphs," *Economic Approach to Valuation Procedure,* 1933, pp. 1-315.

SCHMUTZ, GEORGE L., "The Appraisal Report," *Appraisal Process,* 1941, pp. 1-229.

SCHMUTZ, GEORGE L., "Two Approaches to Land Value," *The Review,* December, 1951, pp. 3-4.

SEGAL, HERBERT I., "Some Practical Guides for the Appraiser," *Appraisal and Valuation Manual,* 1960, pp. 1..

SELDIN, MAURICE, "Criteria for Evaluating Appraisals," *The Appraisal Journal,* October, 1959, pp. 530-536.

SERBEIN, OSCAR N., "The Use of Statistical Methods In Appraisals, Part II," *The Appraisal Journal,* January, 1952, pp. 20-29.

SERBEIN, OSCAR N. JR., "The Use of Statistical Methods In Appraisals, Part I," *The Appraisal Journal,* October, 1951, pp. 423-431.

SHANAHAN, JOHN E., "Statistical Applications for the SREA Market Data Center, Inc., Part II," *The Real Estate Appraiser,* The Society of Real Estate Appraisers, Chicago, Illinois, November 1, 1973, pp. 48-51.

SHENKEL, WILLIAM M., "Characteristics of Gross Income Multipliers," *The Real Estate Appraiser,* pp. 23.

SHENKEL, WILLIAM M., "Modernizing the Market Data Approach," *The Appraisal Journal,* April, 1967, pp. 181-198.

SHUGRUE, FRANK R., "Basic Steps In the Appraisal of Real Property," *The Appraisal Journal,* January, 1953, pp. 104-111.

SILVERMAN, BENJAMIN, "Legal Aspects-Education," *Technical Valuation,* October, 1953, pp. 10.

SIMMS, S. R., "Legal and Practical Aspects of Appraisal Law," *Appraisal Institute Magazine,* Appraisal Institute of Canada, Winnipeg.

SIMONETT, D. S., "Land Evaluation Studies with Remote Sensors In the Infrared and Radar Regions," *Land Evaluation,* pp. 349.

SKOGSTAD, TOR, "Use of Published Trends and Costs Data In Appraisals of Real Estate Improvements," *Appraisal and Valuation Manual,* 1964, pp. 79.

SMELLIE, R. G., "The Manitoba Boundaries Commission," *Appraisal Institute Magazine,* Appraisal Institute of Canada, Winnipeg.

SMITH, CHARLES E., "Inspection Procedure," *The Review,* February, 1954, pp. 3-5.

SMITH, JAMES J., "Benefits and Problems of an Appraisal Office," *The Real Estate Appraiser,*

SMITH, LAMAR, "Wide Disparity In Appraised Values," *Right of Way Conference Selected Papers,* University of Alabama, University, Alabama, 1960, pp. 9-20.

SMITH, LAMAR H., "Appraisal Reports--Their Form and Function," *Technical Valuation,*

SMITH, LEONARD C., "The Appraisal Process," *Review of the Society of Residential Appraisers,* September, 1937, pp. 4-10, 16.

SMITH, LEVIE D. SR., "Assumptions and Limiting Conditions," *The Real Estate Appraiser,* pp. 15.

SMITH, LEWIS R., "Appraisal of the Dixon Block," *The Appraisal Journal*, January, 1934, pp. 131-146.

SMITH, RALPH M., "The Best Appraisal System," *The Review*, June, 1948, pp. 3-7.

SNYDER, DONALD E., "Appraisal Data Banks," *The Real Estate Appraiser*, pp. 19.

SOCIETY OF INDUSTRIAL REALTORS, *Annotated Bibliography of Industrial Real Estate*, Washington, D. C.

SODERQUIST, OSCAR, "A Problem In Appraising," *The Appraisal Journal*, April, 1934, pp. 252-253.

SOLOMON, C. FRANCIS, JR., "The Broker's Role In the Appraisal Business," *The Appraisal Journal*, October, 1948, pp. 483-487.

SOULE, NAT C., "Planning the Appraisal and Writing the Report," *National Real Estate Journal*, September, 1939, pp. 26-28.

SPEED, A., "Revised Guide for Demonstration Reports," *Appraisal Institute Magazine*, Appraisal Institute of Canada, Winnipeg.

SPEED, A. A., "Courses Being Upgraded," *Appraisal Institute Magazine*, Appraisal Institute of Canada, Winnipeg.

SROUFE, THOMAS A., "Utilizing All Three Approaches to Value," *The Residential Appraiser*, pp. 3..

STAFFORD, JAMES G., AND ASSOCIATES, "Unit Foot Value for Square Foot Values and Depths As Indicated," *Appraising Manual, Edition 2*, 1937, pp. 356.

STARKE, GEORGE C., "How to Organize and Operate Appraisal Files," *The Appraisal Journal*, October, 1953, pp. 529-532.

STARKE, GEORGE C., "Utilization of Market Data In the Income-Approach," *Right of Way Conference, Selected Paper*, University of Alabama, 1961, pp. 49-51.

STEIN, H. L., "The Challenge of Teaching," *Appraisal Institute Magazine*, Winnipeg.

STEUER, AARON, "Appraisal As a Science," *The Appraisal Journal*, April, 1947, pp. 192-196.

STEVICK, J. C., "Derive Your Own Formula," *Review of Society of Residential Appraiser*, September, 1940, pp. 14-16.

STEWART, DWIGHT A., "University Roles In Professional Adult Education," *Right of Way*, December, 1963, pp. 23-26.

STONE, PETER A., "A Technique for Establishing Relative Values of Realty," *Real Estate Record and Builders Guide*, May 27, 1933, pp. 3-6.

STRIDE, I. L., "Real Estate Education In B.C.," *Appraisal Institute Magazine*, Appraisal Institute of Canada, Winnipeg.

SUTHERLAND, J. FREDERICK, "On the Appraisal Report," *The Appraisal Journal*, April, 1937, pp. 180-181.

SWAN, J. WILSON, "Appraisal Steps," *The Review*, May, 1958, pp. 3-9.

SWEENEY, HENRY W., "Approximation of Appraisal Values by Index Numbers," *Harvard Business Review*, October, 1934, pp. 108-115.

SWEZEY, WILLIAM D., "Review and Evaluation of Appraisals," *Appraisal and Valuation Manual*, American Society of Appraisers, 1961, pp. 35-42.

TATUM, CHARLES ALVIN, "An Annotated Bibliography of the Professional Appraisers, April 1935-December 1960," *Journal of the Society of Residential Appraisers*, Society of Residential Appraisers, Chicago, 1961.

TAYLOR, CARL, "Milwaukee Appraisal Bureau," *Review of the Society of Residential Appraisers*, May, 1937, pp. 56.

TECKEMEYER, E. B., "Modern Management and the Appraisal," *Review of Society of Residential Appraisers*, September, 1938, pp. 14-16.

TECKEMEYER, EARL B., *How to Value Real Estate; the Foremost Factor In Selling*, Prentice-Hall, Englewood Cliffs N J, 1956.

▲ Appraisal Theory and Methods

TECKEMEYER, EARL B., "Management's Contributions to Better Appraising," *National Real Estate Journal,* October, 1938, pp. 29-30.

TENNER, IRVING, AND EDWARD S. LYNN, *Municipal and Governmental Accounting,* Prentice-Hall, Englwd Cliffs, N. J., 1960.

THAYER, DONALD C., "A New Graphic Method for Determining Values," *National Real Estate Journal,* November, 1940, pp. 24-26.

THE REVIEW, "Building Barometers," *The Review,* March, 1946, pp. 12-13.

THIEL, FLOYD I., "A State-Federal Program of Land Economic Studies," *Right of Way,* June, 1967, pp. 28-31.

THOMPSON, LOREN L., "Exchange of Appraisals--Ripple or Wave," *The Real Estate Appraiser,* p. 2.

THOMPSON, PELL, "Real Estate Appraisals by Formula," *Commerce and Finance,* July 20, 1927, pp. 1445-1446.

THOMPSON, R. E., "Labor-Saving Tables for Computing Depreciation," *National Real Estate Journal,* October 12, 1931, pp. 21-24.

THOMSON, W. F., "Land Registry Systems," *Appraisal Institute Magazine,* Appraisal Institute of Canada, Winnipeg.

THORKELSON, GERALD F., "Rural Appraisals to Meet Users Needs," *Jour of Amer Soc of Farm Mgrs & Rural Appraisers,* April, 1961, pp. 63-76.

THORPE, LAYARD G., "Foreclosure Appraisals," *The Residential Appraiser,* June, 1958, pp. 3-6.

THORSON, IVAN A., *Simplified Appraisal System,* Realty Research Bureau, Los Angeles, 1949.

THORSON, IVAN A., *Simplified Appraisal System, Land Economic,* Realty Research Bureau, Los Angeles, 1951.

THUROW, RAYMOND, "The Pros and Cons of Personnel Testing," *The Assessors Journal,* July, 1966, pp. 1-8.

TOOLEY, R. V., *Maps and Mapmakers,* Batsford, 1970.

TORREY, WILLIAM W., "The Ellwood Tables, a Critique," *The Appraisal Journal,* July, 1966, pp. 339-352.

TOWERS, ALBERT G., "Comparing Property Income with Business Indexes," *National Real Estate Journal,* May, 1940, pp. 24-26.

TOWNSEND, GILBERT, *How to Estimate,* American Technical Society, Chicago, 1939.

TRITSCHLER, C. A., "Methodology for Asset Valuation by Specific Price Index," *Dissertation Abstracts,* May, 1968, pp. 4314-A.

U. S. ARMY CORPS OF ENGINEERS, *Real Property Appraiser's Handbook,* U. S. Army Corps of Engineers, Washington, 1956.

U. S. CENSUS BUREAU, *Real Estate Agencies,* May, 1937.

U. S. DEPARTMENT OF AGRICULTURE, *Yearbook of Agriculture, 1943-1947, Science of Farming,* Govt. Printing Office, Washington, 1949.

VAN CLEEF, EUGENE, "Maps for Appraisals," *The Appraisal Journal,* April, 1949, pp. 219-231.

VAN NOY, C. W., *Guide for Making Costs Estimates for Chemical-Type Operations,* U. S. Bureau of Mines, Washington, 1949.

VAUGHAN, J. H., "The Rule of Thumb," *Appraisal Institute Magazine,* Appraisal Institute of Canada, Winnipeg.

VINCENT, FRED E., "Conversion of Land Prices," *The Appraisal Manual,* 1937, pp. 517-518.

VUKICEVICH, BENJAMIN G., "Four-Page Appraisal Form," *Valuation Manual,* The Residential Appraiser, Chicago, January, 1959, pp. 16.

WAGNER, PERCY E, "Appraisal Procedure of Federal Agencies," *The Appraisal Journal,* July, 1937, pp. 240-247.

# BIBLIOGRAPHY OF APPRAISAL LITERATURE

WALL, NORBERT F., "A Case Study, Land Residual Technique," *The Real Estate Appraiser,* pp. 22.

WALLINGFORT, J. WALLINGFORD, "Comments on Comments on Training of Appraisers," *The Appraisal Journal,* January, 1947, pp. 48-50.

WALTHER, HERMAN O., "Appraisal Quiz," *Freehold,* January 15, 1939, pp. 51-53.

WARE, DORA, *A Short Dictionary of British Architects,* George Allen and Unwin, 1967.

WARNER, ARTHUR J., "Compound Interest and Discount Tables," *Diary and Manual,* New York, pp. 370000.

WARNER, JOHN., "Design and Use of Appraisal Forms," *Municipal Finance,* February, 1937, pp. 7-20.

WARREN, J. STANLEY, "Proprietary Surveys, the Original Title Instruments In the Western Division of New Jersey," *The Appraisal and Valuation Manual,* 1960, pp. 325-332.

WATERMAN, EARL W., "The Sales Yardstick," *The Review,* September, 1946, pp. 13-17.

WEBB, JAMES A., "Real Estate Board Appraisal Committees," *National Real Estate Journal,* March 26, 1923, pp. 27-29.

WEBB, JOHN C., "The Comparative Approach," *Right of Way,* February, 1958, pp. 19-20.

WEIMER, ARTHUR M., "Comments on Training of Appraisers," *The Appraisal Journal,* January, 1947, pp. 42-47.

WELCH, HIRAM, U., "Unit Cost Factors," *The Appraisal Journal,* April, 1934, pp. 194-198.

WELLS, H. C., "Sure You Can Grow Fast In This Business-Provided You Build a Staff That Can Grow with You," *House and Home,* August, 1970, pp. 28.

WELSCH, G. A., "A Fundamental Appraisal of Profit Planning and Control," *Managemt Acctg,* April, 1969.

WENDT, PAUL F., "Ellwood, Inwood, and the Internal Rate of Return," *The Appraisal Journal,* October, 1967, pp. 561-574.

WENZLICK, ROY, "Good Files for Better Appraisals," *The Appraisal Journal,* October, 1958, pp. 599-601.

WESCOTT, T. C., "The Inside Story of Outside Help," *The Appraisal Journal,* 1955, pp. 102.

WESTBY, R. L., ALFRED, A. H, SAYNWITTGENSTEIN, L, "The Potential of Large-Scale Air Photographs and Radar Alimetry In Land Evaluation," *Land Valuation,* pp. 376.

WHELDON, GEORGE T., "Publication of Depreciation Theories," *Review of Society of Residential Appraisers,* December, 1939, pp. 3-8.

WHIPPLE, R. T. M., "Teaching of Land Economics," *Appraisal Institute Magazine,* 1968, pp. 22-26.

WHITE, JOHN R., "Analyzing Comparable Data," *The Appraisal Digest,* October, 1969, pp. 24.

WHITE, PHILIP H., "Principles and Procedures In the Training of Appraisers," *Wisconsin Colloquium on Appraisal Research, Papers and Proceedings,* 1963, pp. 59-66.

WHITEHEAD, J. B., "How an Appraisal Committee Can Help the Local Board," *Practical Appraising Methods,* 1940, pp. 125-128.

WILFRED R., "Statistical Analysis of Industrial Property Retirements," *Engineering Valuation,* 1936.

WILLIAMSON, J. PETER, R. S. BOWER, "Lease Negotiation Using a Time-Sharing Computer," *Appraisal Institute Magazine,* Appraisal Institute of Canada.

WILNETT, MCDONNELL, WOLCOTT, "Cost Approach," *Problems In Rural Real Estate Appraisal,* pp. 7.

WILNETT, MCDONNELL, WOLCOTT, "Income Capitalization Techniques," *Problems In Rural Real Estate Appraisal,* pp. 11.

▲ Appraisal Theory and Methods

WILNETTE, MCDONNELL, WOLCOTT, "Market Data Approach," *Problems In Rural Real Estate Appraisal*, pp. 20.

WINFREY, ROBLEY, "Statistical Analyses of Industrial Property Retirement," *Iowa Engineering Experiment Station Bulletin No. 125*, Iowa State College of Agriculture & Mechanic Arts, Ames, December 11, 1935, pp. 1-176.

WINSTEAD, ROBERT W., *Real Estate Appraisal Desk Book*, Prentice-Hall, Englewood Cliffs, 1968.

WINTER, E. A., SMITH, W. P, "Estimating Aggregate Presidential Real Estate Values from Population-Income Data," *Appraisal and Valuation Manual*, February, 1956, pp. 89-92.

WISCONSIN, UNIVERSITY OF, *Professional Training In Real Estate*, Milwaukee Real Estate Board, Milwaukee, August, 1937, pp. 4.

WITTMAN, FRANK, "The Comparison Method As a Value Indicator," *Appraisal Digest*, January, 1958, pp. 8-11.

WOLTZ, SETH P., "Misuse of Comparable Sales," *The Residential Appraiser*, pp. 3.

WYNGARDEN, HERMAN, "An Index of Local Real Estate Prices," *National Real Estate Journal*, 1927, pp. 26.

YOUNG, ELBERT A., "Depth Tables Used In Cities of the U. S," *Report of the Assessor of St. Paul, Minn.*, 1930.

ZANGERLE, J. A., "Table for Comparing Allotment Property Adjoining Acreage Property," *Appraising Manual, 2nd Edition*, 1937.

ZANGERLE, JOHN, "Cleveland Physical Depreciation of Buildings," *Principles of Real Estate Appraising*,

ZANGERLE, JOHN A., "Appraisal--Building Classification Indispensable," *National Real Estate Journal*, September 24, 1923, pp. 19-20.

ZANGERLE, JOHN A., "Lot Tables Are Essential In Realty Appraising," *National Real Estate Journal*, 1929, pp. 41-43.

# 11-15 Appraisal Manuals

*Appraisal Terminology and Handbook*, American Institute of Real Estate Appraisers, 1967.

*Appraisers & Adjusters Handbook: for Engineers, Architects, Appraisers, Adjusters, Accountants, Etc.*, U. P. C. Book Co., Inc, New York, 1924.

*Manual De Avaluos*, Republica De Guatemala, Guatemala C.A., January 1, 1972, pp. 1-300.

*Marshall Valuation Service*, Marshall and Stevens Publication, Los Angeles.

*Truck Blue Book*, National Market Reports Inc, Chicago Illinois.

*World Collector's Annuary*, Minerua Publishing Co, Amsterdam.

AMER INSTITUTE OF REAL ESTATE APPRAISERS, "Student Outline and Student Reference Manual," Amer Institute of Real Estate Appraisers, pp. 518.

AMERICAN INSTITUTE OF REAL ESTATE APPRAISERS, *Appraisal and Valuation Manuals*, American Institute of Real Estate Appraisers, Chicago, 1956.

AMERICAN INSTITUTE OF REAL ESTATE APPRAISERS, *Appraisal and Valuation Manuals*, American Institute of Real Estate Appraisers, Chicago, 1956.

AMERICAN INSTITUTE OF REAL ESTATE APPRAISERS, *Appraisal Terminology and Handbook*, American Institute of Real Estate Appraisers, Chicago, 1962, pp. 254.

# BIBLIOGRAPHY OF APPRAISAL LITERATURE

AMERICAN INSTITUTE OF REAL ESTATE APPRAISERS, *Real Estate Appraisal Bibliography*, American Institute of Real Estate Appraisers, Chicago.

AUTOMATIC CAR WASH ASSOCIATION, "Cost of Doing Business--Manual," *Cost of Doing Business Manual*, Automatic Car Wash Association, Bellwood, 1900.

BALL, THOMAS L., *Cost Manuals and Cost Data*, American Society of Appraisers, January, 1972.

BOECKH, E. H., *Boeckh's Manual of Appraisals*, The Rough Notes Company, Inc, Indianapolis, 1945.

BOECKH, EVERARD HEREFORD, *Manual of Appraisals*, Rough Notes Co, Indianapolis, 1937.

BOECKH, EVERARD HEREFORD, *Manual of Appraisals*, E. H. Boeckh and Associates, Chicago, 1956.

BOECKH, EVERARD HEREFORD, "Appraisal Definitions," *Manual of Appraisals*, pp. 17.

BOECKH, EVERARD HEREFORD, "Appraisal Systems and Their Uses," *Boeckh's Manual of Appraisals*, pp. 19.

BOECKH, EVERARD HEREFORD, "Individual Costs Section," *Manual of Appraisals*, pp. 287.

BURKHARD, EARL E., "Reviewing Our Manuals," *Appraisal and Valuation Manual*, American Society of Appraisers, 1962, pp. 1-4.

COMMITTEE FROM FIVE PRINCIPAL FEDERAL AGENCIES, *A Glossary of Housing Terms*, Washington, 1931.

DRURY, EUELYN, AND GOULD, R. H., *Builders and Decorators Reference Book*, Hollywood-By-The-Sea, Transatlantic Arts, Florida, 1959.

FISKE, W. P., J. E. BECKETT, *Industrial Accountants Handbook*, Prentice-Hall, Englwood, Cliffs, 1957.

HYLTON, G. W., *The Real Estate Dictionary and Appraisal Manual*, Wetzel Publishing Company, Los Angeles, Calif., 1940.

LORING, A. P., *Trustee's Handbook, Stattuck Revision*, Little, Boston, 1940.

MACHINERY & ALLIED PRODUCTS INSTITUTE, *MAPI Replacement Manual*, Machinery & Allied Products Institute, Washington, 1950.

MACHINERY AND ALLIED PRODUCTS INSTITUTE, *Company Procedural Manual on Equipment Analysis*, Washington, 1951.

MACHINERY AND ALLIED PRODUCTS INSTITUTE, *MAPI Business Investment Manual*, Washington, 1957.

MCMICHAEL, STANLEY L., *Appraising Manual*, Prentice-Hall, Inc, New York, 1937.

MCMICHAEL, STANLEY L., *Mcmichael's Appraising Manual*, Prentice-Hall, New York, 1951.

MCMICHALL, STANLEY L., *Mcmichaels Appraising Manual*, 1970.

OHIO TAX COMMISSION, "Ohio Appraisal Manual," *Ohio Appraisal Manual*, Columbus, 1930.

OLCOTT, MARGARET, AND HELEN E. HENNEFRUND, "Compilers," *Appraisers, and Assessors, Manuals*, 1935, pp. 168-179.

OREGON STATE TAX COMMISSION, VALUATION DIVISION, *Manual of Appraisal Methods for Real Property*, Oregon State Tax Commission, Salem, 1957.

PRENTICE HALL EDITORIAL STAFF, *Encyclopedic Dictionary of Real Estate Practice*, Prentice Hall, Englwd Cliffs, N. J., 1962.

RAUSCHENBUSCH, DR. H., *International Directory of Arts*, 1958.

REAL ESTATE BOARD OF NEW YORK, *Diary and Manual*, The Board, New York, 1937.

SEELYE, EDWIN E., *Data Book for Civil Engineers*, Wiley, New York.

▲ Appraisal Theory and Methods

SOCIETY OF INDUSTRIAL REALTORS, *Annotated Bibliography of Industrial Real Estate,* Washington, D. C.

TATUM, CHARLES ALVIN, "An Annotated Bibliography of the Professional Appraisers, April 1935-December 1960," *Journal of the Society of Residential Appraisers,* Society of Residential Appraisers, Chicago, 1961.

THE AMER INSTITUTE OF ARCHITECTS JOUR, "Boeckh Building Valuation Manual," *The Amer Institute of Architects Jour,* October, 1969, pp. 104.

TIPTON, BALLARD B., "The Iowa Real Property Appraisal Manual," *Assessment Administration,* IAAO, Chicago, 1959, pp. 89-95.

U. S. ARMY CORPS OF ENGINEERS, *Real Property Appraiser's Handbook,* U. S. Army Corps of Engineers, Washington, 1956.

USHER, THOMAS B., *Assessor's Manual,* Newark, 1911, pp. 1-101.

WALKER, FRANK R., "Building Estimator's Reference Book," *Building Estimator's Reference Book,* Chicago, 1957.

WARNER, ARTHUR J., "Compound Interest and Discount Tables," *Diary and Manual,* New York.

WASHINGTON TAX COMMISSION, *Building Appraisal Manual.*

WENZLICK, ROY, RESEARCH CORP., *Residential Appraisal Manual,* Roy Wenzlick Research Corp., St. Louis, 1958.

WESTBROOK, RONALD WILLIAM, *Valuer's Case Book of Approved Valuations,* Estates Gazette, London, 1968.

WINSTEAD, ROBERT W., *Real Estate Appraisal Desk Book,* Prentice-Hall, Englewood Cliffs, 1968.

WORKMASTER, H. C., *Appraisers and Assessors Manual of Taxable Subjects,* Unit Value Appraisal Co, Pittsburg:, 1935, pp. 1-578.

## 11-16 Appraisal Methods and Objectives

A.I.C., "Demonstration Appraisal Reports," *Appraisal Institute Magazine,* Appraisal Institute of Canada, Winnipeg.

AKRON REAL ESTATE BOARD, "Application for Appraisal," *Real Estate Appraising,* J. D. Henderson, 1931, pp. 407.

ALLAN, BRITT H., "A Study of Appraisal Overhead," *The Review,* September, 1956, pp. 9-10.

ALLINGHAM, A. P., "Actual Appraisal Report," *Practical Appraising Methods,* 1940, pp. 45-46.

ALVERT, EUGENE, "A Concept of Value," *Technical Valuation,* June, 1958, pp. 41-42.

AMER INSTITUTE OF REAL ESTATE APPRAISERS, "Problems In Urban Real Estate Appraisal," American Institute of Real Estate Appraisers, 1971.

AMERICAN INSTITUTE OF REAL ESTATE APPRAISERS, *Appraisal Reporting Techniques,* American Institute of Real Estate Appraisers, Chicago, 1947.

AMERICAN INSTITUTE OF REAL ESTATE APPRAISERS, *Selected Readings In Real Estate Appraisal,* American Institute of Real Estate Appraisers, Chicago, 1953.

AMERICAN INSTITUTE OF REAL ESTATE APPRAISERS, *The Appraisal of Real Estate,* American Institute of Real Estate Appraisers, Chicago, pp. 259.

# BIBLIOGRAPHY OF APPRAISAL LITERATURE

AMERICAN INSTITUTE OF REAL ESTATE APPRAISERS, *The Appraisal of Real Estate,* American Institute of Real Estate Appraisers, 1967.

AMERICAN INSTITUTE OF REAL ESTATE APPRAISERS, "Technique of the Cost Approach," *The Appraisal of Real Estate,* American Institute of Real Estate Appraisers, Chicago, 1967, pp. 220.

AMERICAN INSTITUTE OF REAL ESTATE APPRAISERS, "The Nature of Real Property and Value," *Appraisal of Real Estate,* American Institute of Real Estate Appraisers, Chicago, 1967, pp. 7-23.

AMERICAN INSTITUTE OF REAL ESTATE APPRAISERS, "What to Look for In an Appraisal," American Institute of Real Estate Appraisers, 1964.

APPEL, JAMES R., "Preparation of the Feasibility Report," *The Real Estate Appraiser,* November, 1964, pp. 33-38.

APPRAISAL DIGEST, "Fed Survey Reveals Facts of Importance to Appraisers," *The Appraisal Digest,* January, 1953, pp. 4-5.

APPRAISAL JOURNAL, "Covenants, Conditions, and Restrictions," *The Appraisal Journal,* January, 1953, pp. 126-217.

ARMSTRONG, ROBERT H., "Boom and Bust--The Appraisers Dilemma," *The Appraisal Journal,* July, 1946, pp. 240-246.

ARMSTRONG, ROBERT H., "Capitalization," *The Appraisal Journal,* pp. 134-146.

ARMSTRONG, ROBERT H., "Critical Assumptions In Real Estate Appraising," *The Appraisal Journal,* January, 1947, pp. 66-72.

ARMSTRONG, ROBERT H., "Values and Fetishes," *The Appraisal Journal,* April, 1950, pp. 71-184.

ASCHER, DAVID B., "International Valuation a New Science," *The Appraisal Journal,* April, 1952, pp. 232-234.

ATKINSON HARRY GRANT, "The Basis of Creative Brokerage," *The Appraisal Journal,* April, 1961, pp. 165-176.

ATKINSON HARRY GRANT, "The Income Approach," *The Appraisal Journal,* April, 1954, pp. 207-224.

ATKINSON, HARRY GRANT, "The Significance of Real Estate Appraisals," *The Appraisal Journal,* October, 1952, pp. 504-511.

BABCOCK, DR. HENRY A., "One Man's Appraisal Philosophy," *Valuation,* American Society of Appraisers, September, 1972, pp. 2.

BABCOCK, FREDERICK M., *The Appraisal of Real Estate,* Macmillan Company, New York City, 1924.

BABCOCK, FREDERICK M., *The Valuation of Real Estate,* Mcgraw-Hill Book Company, Incorporated, New York City, 1932.

BABCOCK, FREDERICK M., "Common Errors In Appraisal Methods an Analysis," *National Real Estate Journal,* November 24, 1930, pp. 17-20.

BABCOCK, FREDERICK M., "Curso Avanzado Lecciones III, IV, V y Vi," *Boletin,* Sotave, Caracas, Venezuela, pp. 43-48.

BABCOCK, FREDERICK M., "Curso Avanzado Xiv, Xi, Xvi, Xvii, Xviii, Xix, Xx," *Boletin,* Sotave, Caracas, Venezuela, pp. 31-39.

BABCOCK, FREDERICK M., "Curso Avanzado: Lecciones X, Xi, Xii y Xiii," *Boletin,* Sotave, Caracas, Venezuela, pp. 31-37.

BABCOCK, FREDERICK M., "El Procedimiento De La Valuacion," *Boletin,* Sotave, Caracas, Venezuela, pp. 15-22.

BABCOCK, FREDERICK M., "Land Valuation by Comparison," *Valuation of Real Estate,* 1932, pp. 455-476.

BABCOCK, FREDERICK M., "Las Tres Aproximaciones," *Boletin,* Sotave, Caracas, Venezuela, pp. 23-29.

## Appraisal Theory and Methods

BABCOCK, FREDRICK M., "Curso Avanzado Lecciones Vii, Viii y Ix," *Boletin,* Sotave, Caracas, Venezuela, pp. 43-52.

BABCOCK, HENRY A., *Appraisal Principles and Procedures,* 1968.

BABCOCK, HENRY A., "Basic Appraisal Principles and Procedures," *Technical Valuation,* February, 1953, pp. 34-38.

BABCOCK, HENRY A., "Recent Developments In Real Estate Appraising," *The National Real Estate Journal,* April 14, 1930, pp. 31-34.

BABCOCK, HENRY A., "The Appraisal of Parts, Fractions and Whole Properties," *Technicalities,* February, 1950, pp. 9-12.

BAGLEY, ELEANOR S., "Appraisal Pitfalls," *The Appraisal Journal,* April, 1949, pp. 173-182.

BALDWIN, H. G., "How to Appraise Buildings by the Inventory Method," *National Real Estate Journal,* April 29, 1929, pp. 54-58.

BALDWIN, H. G., "Inaccuracies of Building Appraisals Based on Unit Foot Costs," *National Real Estate Journal,* April 15, 1929, pp. 57-60.

BALL, JOHN, C. B. WILLIAMS, *Report Writing,* Ronald, New York City, 1955.

BALLOU, PAUL, "Emerging Valuation Problems with Changing Patterns of Development," *The Assessors Journal,* July, 1966, pp. 9-16.

BARISH, NORMAN N., "Interest and the Time Value of Money," *Economic Analysis for Engineer and Managerial Decision Making,* New York City, 1962, pp. 49-73.

BARNARD, BOYD T., "Practical Use of the New Appraisal Techniques," *National Real Estate Journal,* July, 1939, pp. 32-33.

BARONE, RAY R., "How to Get Your Moneys Worth from the Appraiser," *The Appraisal Journal,* July, 1965, pp. 437-439.

BARTLETT, ROLAND W., "Interdependence of Urban and Rural Economies," *The Appraisal Journal,* January, 1950, pp. 63-71.

BATCHELOR, HARRY H., "Special Responsibility of Appraisers In Cited Examples," *The Review,* May, 1956, pp. 8-10.

BAYLOR, DR. ALLEN O., "Valuation As a Multi/Disciplinary Field In Our Higher Education," *Appraisal and Valuation Manual,* Corporate Press Incorporated, Washington, D. C., January, 1972, pp. 290.

BAYNTON-WILLIAMS, *Investing In Maps,* Barrier & Jenkins, London.

BEAUCHAMP, J. LYLE, "Appraisal Issues In Pre-Loss & Post-Loss Situations," *Papers and Proceedings,* Wisconsin Colloquium on Appraisal Research, 1963, pp. 46-53.

BEETH, CHANNING C., "Narrative Sequence," *The Review,* July, 1950, pp. 10-11.

BEETH, CHANNING C., "Realistic Appraisals," *The Review,* April, 1953, pp. 13-15.

BEMAN, ARTHUR K., "Hazards of Data Interpretation," *The Appraisal Journal,* July, 1944, pp. 237-244, 757-764.

BEMAN, ARTHUR K., "The Amortization Provision," *The Appraisal Journal,* April, 1942, pp. 160-165.

BENGE, ROLAND, A., "Appraising Economic Trends," *The Review,* February, 1948, pp. 3-8.

BENNETT, SAUL Z., "Purpose of the Appraisal and Definition of Fair Market Value," *A Student's Report on an Apartment House,* American Institute of Real Estate Appraisers, Chicago, 1966, pp. 9.

BERMAN, W. I., "How the Employer Can Get Better Appraisal Reports," *The Real Estate Appraiser,* May, 1967, pp. 21-25.

BERNARD, ALFRED D., "Improved Properties," *Principles and Problems of Real Estate Valuation,* Baltimore, 1913.

BERNARD, BOYD T., "Problems Encountered In Re-Use Appraisal," *Technical Valuation,* 1960, pp. 62.

BINTLIFF, BENNETT B., "35mm Photography In Appraising," *The Appraisal Journal,* April, 1961, pp. 229-237.

BLETTNER, ROBERT A., "Mass Appraisals Via Multiple Regression Analysis," *The Appraisal Journal,* October, 1969, pp. 516-521.

BLISS, GEORGE L., "Appraisal Protection for Borrowers," *The Review,* September, 1948, pp. 11-12.

BLOOM, GEORGE, *The Appraisal Data Plant,* Indiana University, Bloomington, 1953.

BLOOM, GEORGE F., "Appraisal Data Plant Study," *The Appraisal Journal,* July, 1949, pp. 318-320.

BLOOM, GEORGE F., "Practice of MAI's Regarding the Appraisal Plant," *The Appraisal Journal,* July, 1953, pp. 394-396.

BODFISH, MORTON, A. D. THEOBALD, "Appraising--Ascertaining Real Estate Value," *Real Estate Fundamentals, Part XI,* Northwestern University, Chicago, 1941, pp. 1-29.

BOECKH, EVERARD HEREFORD, "Appraisal Work-Sheet and Report," *Manual of Appraisals,* 1937, pp. 38-39.

BOECKH, EVERARD HEREFORD, "Boeckh Depreciation Table," *Manual of Appraisals,* 1937, pp. 305-306.

BONBRIGHT, JAMES C., "The General Theory of Appraisal Technique," *The Valuation of Property,* 1937, pp. 129-134.

BONBRIGHT, JAMES C., "Valuation of Property," *Appraisal Principles and Procedures,* Mcgraw-Hill Book Co., Inc, New York, 1937, pp. 231.

BOWEN, PERCIVAL V., "Shall Values Be Based on Past, Present or Future," *The Appraisal Journal,* January, 1934, pp. 125-130.

BOWES, EUGENE G., "How to Estimate Gross Income and Operating Costs," *The Real Estate Appraisal Practice,* American Institute of Real Estate Appraisers, 1958, pp. 173-181.

BOWES, EUGENE G., "How to Use the Residual Techniques," *The Appraisal Journal,* July, 1957, pp. 27-34.

BOWMAN, W. J., "What the Auditor-Examiner Wants In an Appraisal Report," *The Review of the Society of Residential Appraisers,* October, 1941, pp. 8-11.

BOWMAN, WILLIAM J., "The Auditor Look at Appraisals," *The Appraisal Journal,* April, 1942, pp. 156-159.

BOYKIN, JAMES H., "Evolution of the Subjective Theory of Value," *The Real Estate Appraiser,* March, 1965, pp. 26-28.

BRACHMAN, H. J., "Criticism of Standard Appraisal Methods," *The Real Estate Record,* February 20, 1937, pp. 18-20.

BROOKE, R. J., "Appraisal Methods," *The Appraisal of Machinery and Equipment,* pp. 17.

BROWN GEORGE D., "Architectural Analysis of Building Bulk and Height," *Technical Valuation,* pp. 11.

BROWN, R.O., "Using Appraisal Information," *Management Accounting,* October, 1969.

BROWNSTEIN, PHILIP N., "Potential Volume In V.A.," *The Residential Appraiser,* July, 1959, pp. 7-9.

BRUCHE, ALBERT, "What Constitutes Value?," *Technical Valuation,* June, 1958, pp. 45-46.

BRUNK, LLOYD S., "Gross Capitalization Rates---Analysis and Synthesis," *The Appraisal Journal,* May, 1962, pp. 200-209.

BRYSON, LYMAN, "Notes on a Theory of Advice," *The Appraisal Journal,* January, 1956, pp. 8-19.

BUCK, WALTER M. S., "Interpreting the Sale Price," *The Appraisal Journal,* May, 1942, pp. 132-134.

BULLOCK, C. L., "Depreciation Practice- an Independent Accountants Viewpoint," *Public Utility,* February 17, 1972.

BUNTING, GEORGE R., "Report the Unusual Items," *The Residential Appraiser*, May, 1958, pp. 13-15.

BURTCH, THOMAS, "Data Files In the Post-War Period," *The Appraisal Journal*, July, 1947, pp. 375-382.

BUTLER, GORDON, "Getting Ready for the Computer," *Nation's Cities*, September, 1964, pp. 19-22.

CALIFORNIA BUILDING-LOAN LEAGUE, "Appraiser's Field Report Form," *The Review of the Society of Residential Appraisers*, July, 1936, pp. 10-11.

CAMPBELL, BERT, "Methods of Obtaining and Presenting Sales Data In an Appraisal Report," *The Journal of the American Society of Farm Managers and Rural Appraisers*, April, 1960, pp. 83-89.

CAMPNEY, ALBERT E., "How to Sell a Re-Appraisal Program," *Assessor News Letter*, July, 1957, pp. 78-82.

CANNON, FERMOR S., "Boom Psychology---The Test of the Appraiser," *The Review of the Society of Residential Appraisers*, October, 1937, pp. 3-8.

CANTWELL, ROBERT C. III, "The Appraisal Process--Outline and Diagram," *The Appraisal Journal*, April, 1961, pp. 200-206.

CARDOZA, LEONARD R., "Data Gathering Outline," *The Review*, September, 1956, pp. 11-17.

CAREW, JOHN F., "Inspection Clues," *The Review*, January, 1956, pp. 3-6.

CARMICHAEL, JAMES J., *Preparing the Appraisal Report*, New York State Society of Real Estate Appraisers, Buffalo, N. Y., April 18, 1941.

CARR, ANTHONY W., "Some Suggestions for Volume Appraisers," *The Real Estate Appraiser*, pp. 37.

CARRUTHERS, G. R., "The Two-Part Report," *Appraisal Institute Magazine*, Appraisal Institute of Canada, Winnipeg.

CASE, FRED E., "Electronic Data Processing and the Appraisal Process," *The Real Estate Appraiser*, September, 1966, pp. 2.

CASE, FRED E., "Lessons from European Appraisals," *The Residential Appraiser*, June, 1959, pp. 3-6.

CAWTHRA, CHARLES E., "Appraisal Assignments," *Valuation*, American Society of Appraisers, September, 1972, pp. 94.

CHAMBERLAIN, EDWARD, *Toward a More General Theory of Value*, Oxford University, New York, 1957.

CHANDIAS, MARIO A., "Invitacion Al Dialogo," *Boletin*, Sotave, Caracas, Venezuela, pp. 21-23.

CHANDIAS, MARIO E., "Introduccion Al Aprovechamiento," *Boletin*, Sotave, Caracas, Venezuela, pp. 7-10.

CHANDIAS, MARIO E., "Los Tasadores Concepto Moderno Valuacion," *Boletin*, Sotave, Caracas, Venezuela, pp. 7-16.

CHANDIAS, MARIO E., "Valuacion Por Puntos," *Boletin*, Sotave, Caracas, Venezuela, pp. 9-10.

CHANDLER, K. WILLIAM, "Going Deeper In Depth," *The Real Estate Appraiser*, October, 1964, pp. 27-30.

CHERNEY, RICHARD A., "A New Look at Narrative Reports," *The Real Estate Appraiser*, pp. 14.

CHICAGO REAL ESTATE BOARD, "A Prize Winning Appraisal," *National Real Estate Board*, October 3, 1927, pp. 31-33.

CHICAGO REAL ESTATE BOARD, "Contract with HOLC Under Which the Board Makes All Appraisals for Chicago Metropolitan Area," *National Real Estate Journal*, December, 1933, pp. 21-22.

CHICAGO REAL ESTATE BOARD, MARK LEVY, "Appraisal Which Won the St. Paul Cup," *National Real Estate Journal*, September 2, 1929, pp. 42-46.

CHILD, JOHN FRANCIS, JR., "A More Direct Approach to Estimating Future Benefits," *The Appraisal Journal,* November, 1951, pp. 443-450.

CHURCH, BYRON M., "What's In the Bundle," *The Real Estate Appraiser,* August, 1967, pp. 29.

CINCINNATI, OHIO REAL ESTATE BOARD, "Appraisal Certificate," *Henderson, J. D. Real Estate Appraising,* 1931, pp. 455.

CLARK, FRANK B., "What Appraisers Should Know and Study," *National Real Estate Journal,* May 7, 1924.

CLARK, HORACE F., "How to Develop an Appraisal File: Collecting Information for a Central File on Real-Estate Values," *Appraising the Home,* 1930, pp. 247-251.

CLARK, RAMSEY, "The Appraiser's Role In Federal Lands," *The Real Estate Appraiser,* The Real Estate Appraiser, M, pp. M.

COFFIN, GEORGE H. JR., "The High Cost of Low Cost Appraising Shown to Be Penny-Wise, Pound-Foolish," *California Real Estate Magazine,* October, 1935, pp. 43.

COLLINS, G. ROWLAND, "Appraisal Scene," *The Residential Appraiser,* March, 1957, pp. 8-10.

CONDICT, HAROLD V., "Appraisal Highlights," *The Review,* April, 1955, pp. 18-19.

CONSTAM, E., "Decisions! Decisions! Decisions!," *Appraisal Institute Magazine,* Appraisal Institute of Canada, Winnipeg.

CORDIER, HENRY K., *Valuation Problems and the Client,* American Society of Appraisers.

COWLEY, LEONARD M., "Assembling the Appraisal," *The Appraisal Journal,* April, 1954, pp. 183-192.

COWLEY, LEONARD M., "Gathering Data for Appraisal," *Encyclopedia of Real Estate Appraising,* 1959, pp. 94-112.

COWLEY, LEONARD M., "The Lay Away Plan," *The Appraisal Journal,* July, 1954, pp. 353-358.

CROCHERON, CLARENCE, "Appraisal As a Business Tool," *Commerce and Finance,* May, 1928, pp. 1023-1024.

CUMMINGS, J. S., AND C. B. RITTER, "Units of Property and the Continuing Property Record," *Technical Valuation,* February, 1957, pp. 7-14.

CUMMINS, C. R., "Basic Principles Appraisal Process," *Appraisal Institute Magazine,* Appraisal Institute of Canada, Winnipeg.

CUMMINS, C. R., "Notes on the Basic Principles of Valuation and the Appraisal Process," *The Appraisal Institute Magazine,* September, 1958, pp. 24-26.

D' RUGGIERO, LORENZO, "Indemnizacion En El Avaluo," *Boletin,* Sotave, Caracas, Venezuela, pp. 40-45.

DARM, ADAM EUGENE, *Graduate Appraisal of the Industrial Technology Program at California State College,* University of California, 1971.

DAVIES, CLARENCE, J., "The Administrative Requirements for Appraisal Services," *Valuation Manual,* American Society of Appraisers, 1961, pp. 5.

DAVIS, W. D., "A Critical Analysis of Government Appraising," *The Residential Appraiser,* January, 1961, pp. 3-5.

DAVIS, W. D., "The Appraisal Review Function," *The Appraisal Journal,* pp. 511-516.

DAVIS, W. D., "Uniformity In Appraisal Reporting Techniques," *Appraisal Institute Magazine,* Appraisal Institute of Canada, Winnipeg.

DAWNIE, LEONARD, "Are Uniform Appraisal Reports Practical," *Review of Society of Residential Appraisers,* December, 1937, pp. 11-13.

DE SALES PEREZ, FRANCISCO, "El Avaluo En La Regulacion De Inmuebles," *Boletin,* Sotave, Caracas, Venezuela, pp. 11-12.

▲ Appraisal Theory and Methods

DEBOOS, FRANK A., "Appraisals As an Aid In Real Estate Sales," *The Appraisal Journal,* January, 1952, pp. 110-113.

DEMARA, CYRIL R., "Various Appraisal Avenues," *The Review,* April, 1947, pp. 9-11.

DEMMERY, JOSEPH, "Uncertainties In Appraising," *The Appraisal Journal,* January, 1943, pp. 35-38.

DENTON, JOHN H., *The Valuation of Amenities,* American Society of Appraisers, Washington, D. C, 1964, pp. 217.

DERBES, MAX J. JR., "Common Denominators In the Appraisal Process," *The Real Estate Appraiser,* SREA, Chicago, May, 1964, pp. 28.

DILMORE, GENE, "Elements of Network Analysis," *The Real Estate Appraiser,* March, 1969, pp. 47-52.

DITTRICH, N. E., *Accounting Implications of the Relative Objectivity of the Appraisal Process,* Dissertation Abstracts, Ann Arbor, January, 1967.

DOIRON, J. CLIFFORD, "Market Data-Bundle of Information," *Technical Valuation,* October, 1956, pp. 31-34.

DOLMAN, JOHN P., "Composition of the Professional Appraisal Report," *The Appraisal Journal,* October, 1957, pp. 533-543.

DONOGH, A. ORMSBY, JR., "The Appraisal Plant," *The Review,* October, 1952, pp. 3-7.

DORAU, HERBERT B., "Is Rote Right In Valuation," *Appraisal Digest,* April, 1960, pp. 6-9.

DOWNS, ANTHONY, "Characteristics of Various Economic Studies," *The Appraisal Journal,* July, 1966, pp. 329-338.

DOWNS, JAMES C., *Principles of Real Estate Management, 3rd Edition,* Institute of Real Estate Management, Chicago, 1950.

DUBOIS, AYERS J., "Appraisal Problems," *The Review,* March, 1945, pp. 16-19.

DUBOIS, AYERS J., "The Appraisal Report," *The Appraisal Journal,* April, 1936, pp. 123-135.

DUBOIS, AYERS J., "The Data Program," *The Appraisal Journal,* October, 1936, pp. 368-378.

DUBOIS, AYERS J., "Theoretical Versus Practical Appraising," *Appraisal Journal,* April, 1933, pp. 200-203.

DUNN, DOMINICK R., "Common Functional Defects," *The Review,* February, 1947, pp. 12.

DUNN, DOMINICK R., "Current Appraisal Perils," *The Real Estate Appraiser,* 1970, pp. 7-8.

DUNN, DOMINICK R., "Exact Science," *The Real Estate Appraiser,* October, 1964, pp. 25.

DUNN, DOMINICK R., "Only One Value," *Review of the Society of Residential Appraisers,* January, 1937, pp. 13-16.

DUNN, DOMINICK R., "What Is Your Solution," *The Appraisal Journal,* October, 1963, pp. 520-521.

DYKSTRA, GERALD O., "Bundle of Rights," *Michigan Business Review,* November, 1956, pp. 18-24.

DYSON, J. F., "The Use of Digital Computers," *Appraisal Institute Magazine,* Appraisal Institute of Canada, Winnipeg.

EDWARDS, FRANK M., "Landscaping As an Offset to Depreciation," *The Appraisal Journal,* October, 1935, pp. 4378440.

EILERTS, HOPE, "Let's Get Back to Fundamentals," *The Real Estate Appraiser,* American Institute of Real Estate Appraisers, pp. 13.

ELLER, HERBERT D., "The Personal Approach of the Inspection," *Appraisal Digest,* October, 1950, pp. 10-11.

ELLWOOD, L. W., "Appraisal Mathematics," *The Appraisal Journal,* April, 1963, pp. 165-168.

ELLWOOD, LEON W., "The Amount to Be Capitalized," *The Appraisal Journal,* April, 1948, pp. 178-188.

ELLWOOD, LEON W., "Today's Appraiser Is a Specialist," *The Review,* April, 1945, pp. 14-15.

EMBREE, WILLIAM L., "Analysis of Financial Statements As Related to Appraising," *The Appraisal Journal,* January, 1952, pp. 30-44, 210-224.

ENDELMAN, EDWARD, "Value In Reorganization Proceedings," *The Appraisal Journal,* July, 1946, pp. 231-239.

ENGLEHORN, V. A., "The American Society Approach to Various Kinds of Value," *Journal of the American Society of Farm Managers and Rural Appraisers,* April, 1960, pp. 4-8.

EZEKIEL, MORDECAI, "Appraisal Data Research and Future Stabilization of Values," *Review of Society of Residential Appraisers,* April, 1938, pp. 7-11.

EZEKIEL, MORDECAI, "Data Research and Future Stabilization of Values," *Proceedings of the General Session and Urban Group Meetings, National Forum, 1937,*

FALLIN, G. H., "Current Appraisal Problems," *National Real Estate Journal,* September, 1940, pp. 15-17.

FAVA, EDWARD, "The Appraisal Process," *Appraisal Digest,* 1907, pp. 13-17.

FEDERAL HOME LOAN BANK REVIEW, *Building a Modern Appraisal Plant,* December, 1937, pp. 85-86.

FEDERAL RESERVE BANK OF BOSTON, "Income Distribution In Federal Grants-In-Aid," *The Appraisal Journal,* 1962, pp. 259-264.

FEDERAL RESERVE BANK OF CLEVELAND, "Interpreting Recent Unemployment Data," *The Appraisal Journal,* January, 1962, pp. 119-123.

FENTON, HARRY R., "How to Plan an Appraisal," *The Appraisal Journal,* January, 1958, pp. 67-74.

FENTON, HARRY R., "How to Use Market Data In Making an Appraisal," *The Appraisal Journal,* July, 1958, pp. 371-378.

FENTON, HARRY R., "The Logic--Stics of Appraising," *The Appraisal Journal,* April, 1960, pp. 190-192.

FERGUSON, EGBERT R. JR., "Government Appraisals," *The Review,* July, 1954, pp. 15-19.

FERGUSON, HILL, "Making the Appraisal Carry Conviction," *The Appraisal Journal,* April, 1938, pp. 257-261.

FERRERO, PAUL E., "Outlook In Appraisals for the Government," *Technical Valuation,* 1900, pp. 23.

FIELD, RALPH V., "How to Build and Maintain an Appraisal Service," *National Real Estate Journal,* June 27, 1927, pp. 40-42.

FINCH, NELSON E., "The Problems of the Broker and Promoter," *Valuation Manual,* 1955, pp. 62.

FISCHER, R. M., "Appraisal Accuracy," *Technical Valuation,* January, 1949, pp. 21-22, 24.

FISCHER, R. M., "The Use of Standards In Appraisal Practice," *The Appraisal Journal,* October, 1936, pp. 379-392.

FISCHER, REINHARD M., "Appraisal Accuracy and the Accountant," *Journal of Accountancy,* May, 1933, pp. 360-367.

FISHER, E. M., *Advanced Principles of Real Estate Practice,* Principles of Investment, New York City, 1930.

FISHER, ERNEST M., *Basic Elements of Appraisal.*

FISHER, ERNEST M., "Appraisal Data, Their Compilation and Use," *National Appraisal Forum,* 1937, pp. 22-36.

FISHER, ERNEST M., "Perspective In Appraisals," *The Appraisal Journal,* October, 1952, pp. 481-483.

▲ **Appraisal Theory and Methods**

FISHER, ERNEST M., "Real Estate Courses for Real Estate Boards and for Educational Institutions," *National Real Estate Journal*, December 31, 1923, pp. 11-13.

FISHER, ERNEST M., "The Valuation of Real Estate," *Principles of Real Estate*, Macmillan Company, New York City, 1923, pp. 101-132.

FISHER, ERNEST M., "What Should Be Included In a Real Estate Curriculum," *The Appraisal Journal*, July, 1954, pp. 359-362.

FISHER, R. M., "Appraisal Accuracy," *Technical Valuation*, January, 1949, pp. 21-22, 24.

FISK, ELMORE A., "Appraising Theory and Practice," *Appraisal and Valuation Manual*, American Society of Appraisers, 1959, pp. 1-8.

FITZPATRICK, JOHN S., "How to Get the Most from Appraisals," *The Review*, February, 1963, pp. 3-6.

FLETCHER, C. V., "Appraising by Sound," *Technical Valuation*, February, 1955, pp. 27-28.

FLORES, ORLANDO, "Principios Generales Valoracion De Bienes Raices," *Boletin*, Sotave, Caracas, Venezuela, pp. 27-33.

FOSTER, R. D., *An Emperical Investigation of the Kansas Sales-Ratio Study*, Dissertation Abstracts, Vol. Xxix, No. 10.

FOX, NORBERT J., "G. I. Appraisal," *The Review*, May, 1945, pp. 6-9, 20.

FREE, R. L., *Real Estate Appraisal Problem Book*, American Institute of Real Estate Appraisers, Chicago, 1957.

FREE, ROBERT L., *152 Problems In Real Estate Appraisal with Suggested Solutions*, American Institute of Real Estate Appraisers, Chicago, 1954.

FREE, VICTOR J., "Upon These Things Have I Relied," *The Appraisal Journal*, January, 1938, pp. 30-36.

FREUDENBERGER, JOSEPH N., "Report Writing," *The Appraisal Journal*, July, 1962, pp. 380-385.

FRIDAY, DAVID, "An Extension of Value Theory," *Quarterly Journal of Economics*, 1922, pp. 197-219.

FRIEDMAN, ALBERT L., "Appraising the Human Equation," *Appraisal Digest*, July, 1959, pp. 8-12.

FRYXELL, CARL A., "Should Appreciation Be Brought Into the Account," *Accounting Review*, June, 1930, pp. 157-158.

FULLER, ROBERT S., "Flexibility In a Large Appraisal System," *The Review*, January, 1952, pp. 3-5.

FULLERTON, PAUL, "A New Dimension In Depreciation Practice," *The Appraisal Journal*, July, 1961, pp. 319-327.

GADE, RICHARD B., *Valuation by Capitalization of Earnings*, University of Kentucky, Lexington, 1939.

GADDIS, PERCY A., "On Horizontal Division of Values," *The Appraisal Journal*, July, 1936, pp. 325-328.

GARDENER, ALAN C., "Present Day Appraisal Practice and Technique," *The Appraisal Journal*, October, 1945, pp. 365-370.

GARDINER, MAC., "Explanation and Demonstration of the Back Land Theory," *Right of Way*, June, 1959, pp. 29-31.

GARRISON, BURL L., "The Three Dimensions of Value," *The Real Estate Appraiser*, May, 1963, pp. 29-32.

GATES, WILLIAM S. JR., "Can a Property Record Index Be Accurately Controlled," *Technicalities and Technical Valuation*, February, 1952, pp. 25-27.

GIBBONS, JAMES E., "On Operating Ratios," *The Appraisal Journal*, 1962, pp. 535-537.

GILBERT, RICHARD G., "Appraising As a Management Tool," *The Residential Appraiser*, November, 1958, pp. 3-5.

# BIBLIOGRAPHY OF APPRAISAL LITERATURE

GILL, MCCUNE, "Title Decisions," *Technical Valuation,* February, 1959, pp. 58, 62, 70.

GILL, WILLIAM A., "Accounting Reports and the Appraisal Process," *American Society of Appraisers,* 1900, pp. 337-346.

GILLETTE, H. P., "Appraiser Outlines Method of Figuring Building Depreciation," *California Real Estate Magazine,* March, 1940, pp. 9.

GITTERMAN, A. N., "Decrement As an Appraisal Problem," *Review, Society of Residential Appraisers,* June, 1939, pp. 9-12.

GITTERMAN, A. N., "Pointed Suggestions on Appraisals," *National Association of Real Estate Boards,* 1927, pp. 251-262.

GITTERMAN, A. N., "Uniform Appraisal Factors," *Real Estate Record and Builders Guide,* June 17, 1933, pp. 7.

GLASS, EDWARD F., "Common Errors In Appraising," *The Review,* December, 1949, pp. 3-6.

GLOS, HAROLD V., "Actual Appraisal Reports," *National Real Estate Journal,* February, 1938, pp. 30-33, 63.

GLOS, HAROLD V., "Actual Appraisal Reports," *National Real Estate Journal,* August, 1937, pp. 47-49.

GLOS, HAROLD V., "Actual Appraisal Reports," *National Real Estate Journal,* January, 1958, pp. 36-38.

GLOS, HAROLD V., "Appraisal Notations," *Practical Appraisal Methods,* 1940, pp. 9-12.

GLOS, HAROLD V., "Details to Remember In Fixing Property Values," *Realestate,* May 14, 1938, pp. 7-8.

GOLDFARB, MORRIS, "On the Residual Process In Max Tieger's Appraisal," *The Appraisal Journal,* April, 1933, pp. 250-251.

GOLDSTONE, BRACTION, "Demonstration Appraisal," *The Appraisal Journal,* October, 1932, pp. 56-70.

GOLDSTONE, BRACTON, "The New Deal In Appraising," *The Appraisal Journal,* April, 1933, pp. 199-204.

GOODSPEED, M. J., "Sampling Considerations In Land Evaluation," *Land Evaluation,* 1900, pp. 40.

GRAASKAMP, JAMES, *A Guide to Feasibility Analysis,* Society of Real Estate Appraisers, Chicago, 1900.

GRAY, GEORGE H., "Relation of Management to Value," *The Appraisal Journal,* April, 1934, pp. 244-246.

GREAT BRITAIN MINISTRY OF HOUSING AND LOCAL GOVERN, *Distribution of Rateable Values Between Different Classes of Property In England and Values,* H. M. Stationery Offices, London, 1956.

GREENE, W. L., "The Appraisal School of the Miami Board," *National Real Estate Journal,* March 26, 1923, pp. 31-32.

GREENESTREET, KELVIN, "Why Three Approaches to Value," *The Appraisal Journal,* July, 1957, pp. 391-392.

GRIMES, JOHN A., WILLIAM H. GRAIGUE, *Principles of Valuation,* Prenticehall Incorporated, New York City, 1928, pp. 274.

GROVES, ASA B., "The V. A. -Past and Future," *The Review,* November, 1951, pp. 17-20.

GRUNSKY, CARL E., GRUNSKY, CARL E., JR, "Appreciating and the Unearned Increment," *Valuation, Depreciation and the Rate-Base,* New York, 1917, pp. 387.

GUATEMALA AUDIENCIA, *Tasaciones De Los Pueblos De La Provincia De Yucatan,* Guatemala, pp. 103.

GUEST, CHRISTOPHER WILLIAM GRAHAM, *Guest on Valuation,* W. Hodte, London, 1954.

GUTHMAN, H. G., "Actuarial Versus Sinking Fund Type Formula for Valuation," *Accounting Review,* September, 1930, pp. 226-230.

▲ Appraisal Theory and Methods

HAAGLAND, HENRY E., *Real Estate Principles*, Mcgraw-Hill, New York, 1949.

HAALAND, ARNE W., "The Market Analysis Approach," *Technical Valuation*, June, 1959, pp. 19-20.

HAGEN, O., "Elements of Value," *Stats Konomisk Tidsskrift*, March, 1967, pp. 39-51.

HAGOOD, WAYNE D., "Adjusting Comparable Sales," *The Review*, April, 1956, pp. 15-17.

HAGOOD, WAYNE D., "Making Appraisals for the Layman," *The Residential Appraiser*, December, 1961, pp. 17, 22.

HAINES, HOWARD, "Writing Better Reports," *Valuation Manual*, A. S. A, 1962, pp. 5.

HALEY, JOHN L., "Perilous Remainder Studies," *The Appraisal Journal*, October, 1966, pp. 22-24.

HALL, FRANK D., "Appraisal Problems In War Times," *Review of Society of Residential Appraisers*, May, 1941, pp. 3-5, 12.

HALL, FRANK D., "Estimating, Probabilities Called Responsibility of Appraiser," *Appraisal Digest*, January, 1953, pp. 1-3.

HALL, FRANK D., "On the Prophetic Analysis of Future Benefits In Max Tieger's Appraisal," *The Appraisal Journal*, April, 1933, pp. 247-248.

HALL, FRANK D., "What Makes a Good Appraisal?," *The Appraisal Journal*, October, 1938, pp. 323-328.

HALL, HARRY H., "Managing a Nationwide Appraisal Staff," *The Review*, April, 1948, pp. 3-8.

HALL, JOSEPH B., "Why Appraisals Should Be Based on Income," *National Real Estate Journal*, February 3, 1930, pp. 47.

HALL, ROBERT W., "Speak for Yourself," *The Appraisal Journal*, October, 1960, pp. 537-538.

HALL, ROBERT W., "Time and the Appraiser," *The Appraisal Journal*, April, 1965, pp. 294-295.

HALLIDAY, C. S., "Market Values Versus Sound Values," *Technicalities*, May, 1948, pp. 18-21.

HAMILTON, ANDREW C., "Appraisals Under the Federal Securities Act," *The Appraisal Journal*, January, 1935, pp. 176-179.

HAMILTON, ANDREW C., "Upset Price Appraisals," *The Appraisal Journal*, April, 1935, pp. 267-268.

HAMILTON, H. P., "Six Principles of Report Writing," *Appraisal Institute Magazine*, September, 1963, pp. 23-27.

HANES, HERMAN L., "The Appraiser Installs a Property Ledger," *Appraisal and Valuation Manual*, American Society of Appraisers, 1958, pp. 371-376.

HANFORD, LLOYD B. JR., "New Approaches to the Comprehensive Report," *The Appraisal Journal*, October, 1965, pp. 549-554.

HANSON, PETER, "Data Schedules," *Condemnation Appraisal Procedure*, Hanson and Pollard, pp. 259-269.

HARRISON, LOUIS A., "Do Pictures Lie," *The Residential Appraiser*, June, 1959, pp. 16-17.

HART, ALAN F., "New Jersey Revisited Journey to Tomorrow," *Assessment Administration*, IAAO, Chicago, 1960, pp. 91-93.

HATHAWAY, PAUL L., "Current VA Aims," *The Review*, June, 1947, pp. 20-22.

HAWES, A. S., "Value to the Owner," *Appraisal Institute Magazine*, Appraisal Institute of Canada, Winnipeg.

HAYES, DOUGLAS, "Economic Characteristics and Managerial Performance-The Quantitative Appraisal," *Appraisal and Management of Securities*, pp. 127.

HEAD, GEORGE J., "Valuation Under Modern Condition," *The Appraisal Journal*, April, 1935, pp. 212-222.

HEER, CLYDE W., "Building a Profitable Appraisal Business," *Address Given at N. Y. State Society of Real Estate Appraisers' District Conference at Syra. Roch.,* April 16, 1941.

HELD, HARRY, "Appraisal Fundamentals," *Appraisal Digest,* 1958, pp. 18-21.

HELLAND, ARTHUR T., "Formal Training for Appraisers," *The Residential Appraiser,* March, 1957, pp. 7, 10.

HENDERSON, J.D., "Do Sales Prove Value," *National Real Estate Journal,* September 14, 1931, pp. 21-22.

HENDERSON, JAMES D., "The Modern Appraisal Kit," *The Appraisal Journal,* July, 1933, pp. 335.

HENDERSON, JAMES D., "Tools and Archives," *Real Estate Appraising,* 1931, pp. 25-49.

HENRY, E. G., "What Price Property Records?," *Technical Valuation,* July, 1945, pp. 3-7.

HERTLEIN, G. C., "Artist Views Discovery Through Computerized Graphics," *Computers and Automation,* August, 1970, pp. 25-26.

HERY, ELMER G., "Property Records," *Valuation Manual,* A. S. A. Valuation Manual, 1959, pp. 17.

HERZER, T. O. F., "Proper Appraisal Practices," *Journal of the American Society of Farm Managers and Rural Appraisers,* October, 1945, pp. 134-140.

HIEATT, CLARENCE C., "The Difference Between Price and Value," *National Real Estate Journal,* July 11, 1927, pp. 51-52.

HIMSTREET, WILLIAM C., *Writing Appraisal Reports,* American Institute of Real Estate Appraisers, October, 1971.

HIMSTREET, WILLIAM C., "Writing Letters and Reports," *The Appraisal Journal,* April, 1959, pp. 198-202.

HOAGLAND, HENRY E., *Real Estate Principles,* Mcgraw-Hill, New York, 1955.

HOAGLAND, HENRY E., "The Appraisal Process," *Real Estate Principles,* 1940, pp. 511.

HODDESON, DAVID, "Cracked Facade," *The Appraisal Journal,* October, 1957, pp. 527-532.

HODGES, M. B., "A Reference Library for Appraisers," *The Real Estate Appraiser,* November, 1968, pp. 5-9.

HODGES, M. B. JR., "Don't Babysit with Your Leica!," *The Appraisal Journal,* July, 1962, pp. 405-407.

HOFFMAN, JUDGE MURRAY, "Hoffman's Depth Rule," *Appraising Manual,* Second Edition, 1937, pp. 359, 652.

HOGAN, JOHN J., "Appraisal Requirements of the General Services Administration," *The Appraisal Journal,* July, 1963, pp. 311-315.

HOLBROOK, JEFFREY, "The Thinking Man's Capitalization Rate," *The Real Estate Appraiser,* October, 1963, pp. 2-8.

HOLLEBAUGH, CLIFFORD W., "A Logical Approach to Value," *The Review,* November, 1949, pp. 3-6.

HOLLEBAUGH, CLIFFORD W., "Correlation - the Heart Of the Appraisal Process," *The Residential Appraiser,* April, 1962, pp. 17-20.

HOLLEBAUGH, CLIFFORD W., "How the Appraiser Collects and Uses Sales Data," *The Review,* January, 1951, pp. 15-19.

HOLLEBAUGH, CLIFFORD W., "Income Approach to Value," *Encylopedia of Real Estate Appraising,* 1959.

HOLLEBAUGH, CLIFFORD W., "Market Data -- and Comparable Properties," *The Appraisal Journal,* 1952, pp. 74-79.

HOLLEBAUGH, CLIFFORD W., "The Narrative Report," *The Review,* December, 1949, pp. 12-14.

HOLZHAUER, JOHN A., "Capitalization and the Income Premise," *The Real Estate Appraiser,* December, 1964, pp. 12-28.

▲ Appraisal Theory and Methods

HOME OWNER'S LOAN CORPORATION, "Property Appraisal Report Form," *Appraisal Manual,* 1937, pp. 652.

HOOKER, JOHN P., *Correct Appraisal Methods,* Annals of Real Estate Practice, Vol. I, 1927, pp. 174-185.

HOOKER, JOHN P., "The Importance of Board Appraisal Committees," *National Real Estate Journal,* November 3, 1924, pp. 23-32.

HOOVER, RICHARD I., "What Is Market Analysis?," *The Appraisal Journal,* December, 1967, pp. 61-63.

HOPKINS, CHARLES I., "Future 'GI' Assignments," *The Review,* September, 1948, pp. 17-19.

HOPKINS, CHARLES I., "The Fee Appraiser's Future In the V.A. Program," *The Review,* November, 1952, pp. 3-7.

HOPKINS, CHARLES I., "The VA Viewpoint," *The Review,* pp. 3-6, 10.

HOPPE, JOHN G. JR., "Post Graduate Education In Real Estate Appraising," *The Real Estate Appraiser,* SREA, Chicago, September, 1964, pp. 34.

HOPPE, JOHN G. JR., "Serendipity and the Student of Appraisal," *Appraisal Journal,* April, 1967, pp. 177.

HORAN, GEORGE B., *Appraisal Fundamentals,* New York State Association of Real Estate Boards, New York.

HORTON, GEORGE S., "Actual Appraisal Reports," *National Real Estate Journal,* October, 1937.

HOYT, HOMER, "Appraisal of Different Types of Real Property," *The Appraisal Journal,* July, 1964, pp. 383-393.

HOYT, HOMER, "The Appraisal Process In a Price-Controlled Economy," *The Appraisal Journal,* April, 1945, pp. 138-147.

HOYT, JOHN R., "On Standards In Appraisal Practice," *The Appraisal Journal,* January, 1937, pp. 72-73.

HUBIN, VINCENT J., "Some Further Remarks on the Nature, Meaning and Use of the Cap Tables," *The Appraisal Journal,* October, 1965, pp. 517-530.

HUBIN, VINCENT J., "The Determination of Realty Income Quality," *The Appraisal Journal,* 1959, pp. 254-257.

HUBIN, VINCENT J., "The Nature, Meaning Use of 'Cap' Tables," *Appraisal Institute Magazine,* Appraisal Institute of Canada, Winnipeg.

HUCK, ROBERT, "La Tecnica Del Avaluo," *Boletin,* Sotave, Caracas, Venezuela, pp. 11-15.

HUGHES, RICHARD, "Washington Report," *The Real Estate Appraiser,* pp. 56.

HUHN, G. P., *Method of Figuring Ground Values,* Minneapolis, Minn., 1923, pp. 42.

HULTEN, JOHN J., "Appraisal Methods In Hawaii," *Appraisal and Valuation Manual,* ASA, 1960, pp. 97-108.

HUMPHREY, D. E., "Habits of Failure-The Demonstration Report," *Appraisal Institute Magazine,* Appraisal Institute of Canada, Winnipeg.

HUNTER, WALTER C., "A Calaveras Formula," *Appraisal and Valuation Manual,* Washington, D. C., January, 1972, pp. 10.

HUNTER, WALTER C., "Calaveras Formula," *Valuation,* ASA, Washington, September, 1968, pp. 18.

HUSEMANN, FIELDING L., "Cyclical Valuation Procedure," *The Appraisal Journal,* January, 1942, pp. 9-25.

HYAM, LESLIE A., "Appraisal of Fine Arts," *Technical Valuation,* ASA, Washington, October, 1953, pp. 11.

HYDER, K. LEE, "Appraisals for Purposes of Public Financing," *The Appraisal Journal,* October, 1935, pp. 422-432.

HYDER, K. LEE, "The Appraisal Process," *The Appraisal Journal,* January, 1936, pp. 13-25.

INTERART PUBLISHERS INC., *International Art Market,* New York, March, 1961.

JACKSON, HOWARD F., "Basic Problems In the Income Approach," *The Real Estate Appraiser,* SREA, Chicago, July, 1964, pp. 35.

JAMES, M. H., "Market Influence on Value," *Review of the Society of Residential Appraisers,* July, 1936, pp. 3, 12.

JAMESON, MARY ETHEL, "Obsolescence of Buildings," *The Appraisal Journal,* January, 1935, pp. 180-183.

JARCHOW, ALFRED W., "Appraisals by Computer," *The Real Estate Appraiser,* SREA, Chicago, October, 1966, pp. 37.

JEFFERY, RICHARD, "Foundation for Success In Appraising," *The Appraisal Journal,* July, 1947, pp. 326-329.

JELLIS, WILLIAM, "Income Approach-Back Door to Market Value," *Appraisal Institute Magazine,* Appraisal Institute of Canada, Winnipeg.

JOHNSON, CLIFFORD R., "The Major Problem In Making and Using Estimates of Market Value," *The Residential Appraiser,* August, 1961, pp. 21-23.

JOHNSON, E. HOLLAND, "Cost Data In Appraising," *The Appraisal Journal,* July 1941, pp. 240-247.

JOHNSON, U. WEBSTER, RALEIGH BARLOW, *Land Problems and Policies,* Mcgraw-Hill, New York, 1954.

JONES, FRANCIS E., "The Metes and Bounds System of Land Description," *The Appraisal Journal,* July, 1937, pp. 252-261.

JOSLIN, EDWARD G., "The Future of Value to the Owner," *Appraisal Institute Magazine,* 1963, pp. 32-35.

JOUR OF AMER SOC OF FARM MGRS & RURAL APPRAISERS, "California Society of Farm Managers and Rural Appraisers Suggested Appraisal Outline," *Journal of the American Society of Farm Managers and Rural Appraisers,* October, 1962, pp. 29-30.

JOUR OF AMER SOC OF FARM MGRS & RURAL APPRAISERS, "The American Rural Appraisal System," *Journal of the American Society of Farm Managers and Rural Appraisers,* October, 1946, pp. 84-99.

KAFFENBERGER, KARL G. JR., "Market Data In the Appraisal of Income Property," *The Appraisal Journal,* January, 1960, pp. 57-62.

KAHN, SANDERS A., "How Good Is the Comparative Sales Approach," *Valuation Manual,* 1958, pp. 51-56.

KAHN, SANDERS A., "The Return of Feasibility to Lums," *Valuation,* February, 1965, pp. 15-17.

KALISH, JACOB, "Use As a Factor In Determining Fair Market Value," *The Appraisal Journal,* October, 1959, pp. 565-571.

KAMLET, MARK, "Appraisal Techniques In Restoration Claims," *The Appraisal Journal,* April, 1966, pp. 258-262.

KANN, BRUCE E., "Machinery Is What You Make it," *Valuation,* September, 1966, pp. 27-31.

KANN, BRUCE E., "Selecting a Value," *Technical Valuation,* December, 1967, pp. 36.

KAZDIN, S. EDWIN, "Appraising the Techniques of Appraising," *National Real Estate Journal,* November, 1938, pp. 58-60.

KAZDIN, S. EDWIN, "How to Use Income Data In the Appraisal of Apartment Property," *The Appraisal Journal,* July, 1957, pp. 409-416.

KAZDIN, S. EDWIN, "On Land," *The Appraisal Journal,* April, 1938, pp. 166-167.

KAZDIN, S. EDWIN, "What Price Market Value," *Appraisal Digest,* October, 1952, pp. 1-4.

KELLEY, ARTHUR C., "Value As an Accounting Concept," *Journal of Accountancy,* July, 1935, pp. 50-52.

KELLEY, JOHN F., "Fine Arts Appraisals," *Technical Evaluation,* June, 1954, pp. 41.

KELLEY, WILLIAM T., "Diagnostic Research," *The Appraisal Journal,* July, 1963, pp. 333-337.

KELLOUGH, W. R., "Essays on Land Economics," *The Real Estate Appraiser,* May, 1969, pp. 31-34.

KINNAID, WILLIAM N. JR., "New Thinking In Appraisal Theory," *Creues Reprint Series No. 2,* August, 1966.

KINNARD, W. N., "New Thinking In Appraisal Theory," *Appraisal Institute Magazine,* Appraisal Institute of Canada, Winnipeg.

KNISKERN, PHILIP W., "H. O. L. C. Appraisals," *Banking,* November, 1934, pp. 53.

KNISKERN, PHILIP W., "How to Compute New Income for Appraisal Purposes," *National Real Estate Journal,* September, 1929, pp. 56-58.

KNISKERN, PHILIP W., "Valuations Under Varying Circumstances," *The Appraisal Journal,* July, 1948, pp. 356-359.

KNISKERN, PHILIP W., "Why Appraisals Should Be Based on Income," *National Real Estate Journal,* September 16, 1929, pp. 29-30.

KOSTER, STUART J., "Economic Aspects of Property Appraisals," *Valuation Manual,* 1960, pp. 49.

KUEHNLE, W. R., "Public Utility Valuation," *Appraisal Journal,* April, 1972, pp. 195-237.

LAHDE, WALTER, MYERS, WILLS, "Reducing Variations In Independent Appraisals," *Assessors News Letter,* July, 1962, pp. 77-81.

LANGLANDS, I. H., "An Engineer Looks at the Appraisal Process," *Appraisal Institute Magazine,* Appraisal Institute of Canada, Winnipeg.

LARSEN, DAVID R., "Comparable Sales," *The Review,* April, 1945, pp. 5-7.

LARSEN, DAVID R., "The Appraiser's Tools and Forms," *The Review,* March, 1949, pp. 6-15.

LAUNER, E. J., "The Development of Appraisal Methods," *Appraisal and Valuation Manual,* American Society of Appraisers, 1958, pp. 1-26.

LAUNER, E. J., "The Significance of the American Society of Appraisers In the Appraisal Field," *Technical Valuation,* February, 1959, pp. 3-4.

LAYDEN, ARTHUR L., "Some Appraisal Mathematics," *The Appraisal Journal,* October, 1934, pp. 5-18.

LEACH, W. A., *Rating Valuation & Appeals a Book on Rating of Ordinary Hereditaments for Gen'L Practitioner & Layman,* Estates Gazette, London, 1961.

LEET, EDMUND, "Demonstration Appraisal of Property Situated at 725 South Dale Street, Denver, Colorado," *Technical Valuation,* February, 1960, pp. 33-44.

LEFEAVER, JAMES H., "A Slightly Different Appraisal," *Technicalities,* January, 1949, pp. 12-13.

LEVY, MARK, "Assembling the Data for Making Appraisals," *National Real Estate Journal,* March, 1941, pp. 20-21.

LEVY, MARK, BROTHER, "Application for Appraisal," *Real Estate Appraising,* 1931, pp. 417.

LEWIS, H. J., "Land Economic Studies In Alabama," *Selected Papers,* Right of Way Conference, University of Alabama, 1962, pp. 12.

LEWMAN, M.A.I. HARRY, "Managing an Appraisal Office," Amer Institute of Real Estate Appraisers, October, 1971.

LIANG, FANG-CHUNG, *The Single-Whip Method,* Chinese Economic & Polit Studies, Harvard Univ, Cambridge, 1956.

LIETZ, JOHN F. JR., "The Responsible Approach to Value," *The Residential Appraiser,* March, 1961, pp. 23-24.

LITTLETON, A. C., "Value and Price In Accounting," *Accounting Review,* September, 1929, pp. 147-154.

LLOYD, J. P., "Depth Curves," *The Appraisal Journal,* April, 1955, pp. 177-189.

LOCKWOOD, A. N., "Appraising Property In Wartime," *The Appraisal Journal,* January, 1945, pp. 37-41.

LOCKWOOD, A. N., "How to Write an Appraisal Report," *Appraisal Reporting Techniques,* American Institute of Real Estate Appraiser, 1947, pp. 3-8.

LONG BEACH REAL ESTATE BOARD, "Honorable Mention Award In Appraisal Contest at Seattle," *National Real Estate Journal,* 1927, pp. 19-22.

LOSTETTER, EARL, "The New Thinking and the Appraisal Process," *The Appraisal Journal,* July, 1963, pp. 343-348.

LOSTETTER, EARL K., "Divergencies---Reasons and Causes," *The Appraisal Journal,* January, 1965, pp. 83-87.

LOSTETTER, EARL K., "The Distinction Between Appraising and Counseling," *Appraisal Digest,* October, 1961, pp. 1-4.

LOSTETTER, EARL K., "The Four-Way Test," *The Appraisal Journal,* October, 1963, pp. 518-520.

LUEBBERT, RAFAEL C., "The Organization, Operating Procedures and Financial Management of an Appraisal Practice," *The Real Estate Appraiser,* pp. 5.

LUKENS, C. JR. M. A. I., *The Appraiser and Real Estate Feasibility Studies,* American Institute of Real Estate Appraisers, August, 1972.

LUM, Y. T., "Applying the Market Data Method," *The Real Estate Appraiser,* March, 1969, pp. 5-12.

LUM, Y. T., "Basic Considerations of Appraisal Concepts and Value Factors," *The Residential Appraiser,* February, 1962, pp. 14-20.

LUM, Y. T., "The Meaning, Comparison and Application of Market Data," *The Real Estate Appraiser,* January, 1965, pp. 28-38.

LUNDY, VICTOR R., "A Reviewer Reports," *Appraisal Institute Magazine,* Appraisal Institute of Canada, Winnipeg.

LUNDY, VICTOR R., "A Reviewer's Report," *The Appraisal Journal,* October, 1960, pp. 484-493.

LUNDY, VICTOR R., "Captive Appraisers," *The Review,* November, 1954, pp. 18-19.

LUNDY, VICTOR R., "Market Data," *The Review,* September, 1955, pp. 3-4, 10.

LUNDY, VICTOR R., "The Challenge of the Commonplace," *The Appraisal Journal,* October, 1960, pp. 536.

MACBRIDE DEXTER D, "Opportunities In Appraising for Minorities," *Valutape Audio-Library Series,* American Society of Appraisers, Washington D.C., February 1, 1974.

MACBRIDE, DEXTER D, "Major Developments In the Appraisal Profession Within the US: Review, Commentary, Prediction," *Valuation Magazine,* American Society of Appraisers, Washington D.C., December 1, 1973, pp. 126-138.

MACBRIDE, DEXTER D, "The Profession of Appraising," *Valutape Audio-Library Series,* American Society of Appraisers, Washington D.C., January 1, 1973.

MACBRIDE, DEXTER D., "Decisions That Influence Value Concepts," *Proceedings,* Portland Oregon, September, 1966.

MACBRIDE, DEXTER D., "Reviewing Certain Appraisal Concepts," *Proceedings,* Detroit, Michigan.

MACBRIDE, DEXTER D., "Valuation Concepts," *Proceeding,* Carmel California, May 7, 1966.

MACDONALD, ARTHUR J., "Comprehensive Appraisals," *The Appraisal Journal,* July, 1955, pp. 345-355.

MACLEOD, MORTON P., "If You Want to Know - Go; if Not - Send," *Technical Valuation,* American Society of Appraisers, Washington, February, 1968, pp. 3.

▲ **Appraisal Theory and Methods**

MACROSSIE, WILLIAM, *The Marketing of Large Estates,* Freehold, June 15, 1940, pp. 409-411.

MAISENHELDER, HOWARD, JR., "Historical Value or Hysterical Value," *The Appraisal Journal,* pp. 1-3.

MALE, CHARLES T., "Property Values and Appraisals," *Real Estate Fundamentals,* Van Nostrand, New York, 1932, pp. 473.

MANN, JACK K., "Correlation In the Appraisal Process," *The Residential Appraiser,* November, 1960, pp. 10-12.

MANN, JACK K., "Required Courses Revised for Presentation After January 1, 1970," *The Appraiser,* October, 1970.

MARQUIS, RICHARD, "Mass Appraisals," *The Review,* December, 1952, pp. 10-14.

MATTHEWS, MYRON L., "Grave Beckons Appraisers," *Appraisal Digest,* October, 1950, pp. 4-5.

MATTHEWS, MYRON L., ROBERT L. LAUER, "American Society of Appraisers-A Reality," *Technical Valuation,* American Society of Appraisers, November, 1952, pp. 26.

MAY, ARTHUR A., "The Appraiser's Field Kit," *The Appraisal Journal,* January, 1953, pp. 23-25.

MAY, OLIVER, "A Defense of the Straight-Line Method," *Journal of Accountancy,* October, 1935, pp. 282-284.

MAYER, EDWIN, "Land Appraisal Pitfalls," *American Society of Appraisers Valuation Manual,* American Society of Appraisers, 1956, pp. 221.

MC MICHAEL, STANLEY L., "Preparacion Del Informe Escrito Tasacion," *Boletin,* Sotave, Caracas, Venezuela, pp. 25-29.

MCCORMICK, LORING O., SCHMUTZ, GEORGE L, "Fundamental Economic Concepts," *The Appraisal Journal,* July, 1933, pp. 310-318.

MCDONALD, D. L., "The National Capital Commission," *Appraisal Institute Magazine,* Appraisal Institute of Canada, Winnipeg.

MCFARLEN, T. A., "Demonstration Appraisal Reports," *Appraisal Institute Magazine,* February, 1958, pp. 17-19.

MCFARLEN, T. A., "The Rural Appraisal Report," *Appraisal Institute Magazine,* January, 1957, pp. 16-17.

MCGAHEY, ROBERT L., 'The Why's What's and How's of Property Records," *Valuation Manual,* American Society of Appraisers, 1964, pp. 119.

MCGLONE V. P., "Seminar Summary," *Valuer,* The New Zealand Institute of Valuers, New Zealand, August 1, 1973, pp. 135-138.

MCKEAN, JAMES P., "Appraisal Education," *Papers and Proceedings,* Wisconsin Colloquium on Appraisal Research, 1963, pp. 54-58.

MCKINNEY, HOWARD C., "Wide Variances In Appraisals," *The Appraisal Journal,* October, 1956, pp. 543-548.

MCLAUGHLIN, FRANK J., "Is Rote Right In Valuation," *The Appraisal Journal,* October, 1961, pp. 532-534.

MCMICHAEL, JAMES M., *Real Estate Investment Analysis and Programming,* L. A. Exchg Division California Real Estate Assocn, 1968.

MCMICHAEL, STANLEY L., *Appraising Manual,* Prentice-Hall, Inc, New York, 1937.

MCMICHAEL, STANLEY L., *Mcmichael's Appraising Manual,* Prentice-Hall, New York, 1951.

MCMICHAEL, STANLEY L., "Building Appraisals," *Appraising Manual,* 1937, pp. 296-316.

MCMICHAEL, STANLEY L., "Business Frontage," *Appraising Manual,* 1937, pp. 506-512.

MCMICHAEL, STANLEY L., "Comparison of Depth Tables," *Appraising Manual,* 1937, pp. 358.

MCMICHAEL, STANLEY L., "Depth Tables," *The Appraisal Journal*, April, 1935, pp. 205-211.

MCMICHAEL, STANLEY L., "New Problems for the Appraiser," *The Appraisal Journal*, July, 1933, pp. 356-361.

MCMICHAEL, STANLEY L., "Plottage Applied to Width of Lots," *Appraising Manual*, 1937, pp. 410-412.

MCMICHAEL, STANLEY L., "Relation Between Front Value and Square Foot Value for Various Depths," *Appraising Manual*, 1937, pp. 524-525.

MCMICHAEL, STANLEY L., "Standard Appraisal Certificate Form," *Appraising Manual*, 1937, pp. 530-532.

MCMORRAN, J. BURCH, "New York Department of Public Works Appraisal Methods Promise Savings to Taxpayers," *Right of Way*, August, 1963, pp. 33-34.

MCMULLIN J. A., "The Development of Appraisal Standards for Land and Buildings," *Assesment Adminsitration*, 1963, pp. 27-32.

MCPHERSON, JOSEPH F., "The Hindsight Rule," *The Appraisal Journal*, January, 1953, pp. 54-57.

MCSWEENEY, THOMAS F., "Proposed Code of Technical Standards Economic Background of Value," *Technical Valuation*, June, 1959, pp. 27-33.

MCSWEENEY, THOMAS F., "The Precision of the Appraisal," *American Society of Appraisers*, 1959.

MEDICI, GUISEPPE, *Principles of Appraisal*, Iowa State College Pr., Ames, Iowa, 1954.

MEENACH, T. J., "Management Related to Value," *The Real Estate Appraiser*, September, 1963, pp. 26-32.

MELENDY, MERLE C., "Hybrid Approach Being Tested," *The Residential Appraiser*, November, 1960, pp. 13-14.

MERCER, GEORGE L., "Proper Selection of Capitalization Rates," *The Real Estate Appraiser*, September, 1964, pp. 13.

MERRELL, JOHN H., "Appraising on a Staff Basis," *The Residential Appraiser*, May, 1962, pp. 17-18.

MERTZKE, ARTHUR J., "A Course In Appraisals," *Annals of Real Estate Practice*, 1925, pp. 217-223.

MERTZKE, ARTHUR J., "Appraisal Contests," *Annals of Real Estate Practice*, 1928, pp. 154-184.

MERTZKE, ARTHUR J., "Board Appraisal Reports," *National Association of Real Estate Boards*, 1930, pp. 672-676.

MERTZKE, ARTHUR J., "Division of Value Between Land and Improvements," *National Real Estate Journal*, March 17, 1930, pp. 62-63.

MERTZKE, ARTHUR J., "How Capitilization Rates Are Determined," *National Real Estate Journal*, October 13, 1930, pp. 42-44.

MILISIEWICZ, J., "Extending Appraisal Education," *Appraisal Institute Magazine*, Appraisal Institute of Canada, Winnipeg.

MILISIEWICZ, JANINA, "Dead Ends," *Appraisal Institute Magazine*, Appraisal Institute of Canada, Winnipeg.

MOLLAN, WILLIAM W., "Reasonable Normal Value and the G.I.," *The Appraisal Journal*, July, 1945, pp. 263-265.

MONTONNA, D. L., "The Appraisal Process," *Appraisal Institute Magazine*, Appraisal Institute of Canada, Winnipeg.

MONTONNA, DAVID L., "Gross Income and Expenses," *Appraisal Institute Magazine*, July, 1957, pp. 5-9.

MONTZ, A. S., "New Orleans Appraisal Bureau," *Review of the Society of Residential Appraisers*, May, 1937, pp. 10-129.

MORGAN, JAMES V., "Appraisal Facets," *The Residential Appraiser*, June, 1957, pp. 11.

## Appraisal Theory and Methods

MORRISON, E. R., "Bench Marks In Finding Value," *Journal American Society of Farm Managers and Rural Appraisers,* April, 1960, pp. 16-21.

MORRISSEY, THOMAS P., "Accounting Reports and the Appraisal Process," *American Society of Appraisers, Appraisal and Valuation Manual,* 1959, pp. 337-346.

MORSE, TRUE D., "Practical Law for Managers and Appraisers," *Journal of the American Society of Farm Managers and Rural Appraisers,* October, 1947, pp. 90-95.

MORSE, TRUE D., "The American Rural Appraisal System," *The Appraisal Journal,* July, 1940, pp. 23-235.

MORSEY, NASHATT, "Appraisal Profession In Egypt," *Technical Valuation,* American Society of Appraisers, Washington, October, 1953, pp. 54.

MORSY, NASHAAT, "The Fifth Arabian Engineering Congress," *Technical Valuation,* June, 1954, pp. 57.

MROTER, RAYMOND D., "Aspects of Possessory Interest Valuation In California," *The Appraisal Journal,* July, 1965, pp. 383-390.

MULHERN, EUGENE S., "Valuation Report," *Technicalities,* January, 1959, pp. 14-18.

MURPHY J. P., "Anywhere But Here," *The Valuer,* The Incorporated Society of Valuers & Auctioneers, London, December 1, 1973, pp. 430-431.

MURRAY, WILLIAM G., "A Public Appraisal System Open to All Appraisers," *Journal of the American Society of Farm Managers and Rural Appraisers,* April, 1946, pp. 18-23.

MURRAY, WILLIAM G., "Market Data In Rural Appraising," *The Appraisal Journal,* July, 1956, pp. 385-392.

MUSCH, HENRY JR., "Current Appraisal Technique," *The Appraisal Journal,* October, 1933, pp. 32-33.

MUSTOE, NELSON EDWIN, *The Complete Valuation Practice,* Estates Gazette, London, 1955.

NAMAVATI, ROSHAN, *Theory & Practice of Valuation Land & Bldgs for Architects Engineers Surveyors & Tax Practitioners,* Universal Book Corp., Bombay, 1968.

NASARIO, LUIS A., "Curso Evaluacion Bienes Raices, Capitulo Viii," *Boletin,* Sotave, Caracas, Venezuela, pp. 41-46.

NASARIO, LUIS A., "Evaluacion Bienes Raices, IV, V y Vi," *Boletin,* Sotave, Caracas, Venezuela, pp. 41-48.

NASARIO, LUIS A., "Evaluacion De Bienes Raices: Capitulo Ix," *Boletin,* Sotave, Caracas, Venezuela, pp. 49-62.

NASARIO, LUIS A., "Evaluacion De Bienes Raices: Capitulo X," *Boletin,* Sotave, Caracas, Venezuela, pp. 47-56.

NATIONAL ASSOCIATION OF ASSESSING OFFICERS, "Land Appraisal Methods," *Urban Land Appraisal,* 1940, pp. 10-57.

NATIONAL ASSOCIATION OF REAL ESTATE BOARDS, *Universities and Colleges Giving Courses In Real Estate,* October, 1936.

NATIONAL ASSOCIATION OF REAL ESTATE BOARDS, "Answers to Appraisal Questions," *National Real Estate Journal,* October 27, 1930, pp. 43-44.

NATIONAL ASSOCIATION OF REAL ESTATE BOARDS, "Answers to Appraisal Questions," *National Real Estate Journal,* August 18, 1930, pp. 47-48.

NATIONAL ASSOCIATION OF REAL ESTATE BOARDS, "Answers to Appraisal Questions," *National Real Estate Journal,* March 30, 1931, pp. 44.

NATIONAL ASSOCIATION OF REAL ESTATE BOARDS, "Answers to Appraisal Questions," *National Real Estate Journal,* August 4, 1930, pp. 49-50.

NATIONAL ASSOCIATION OF REAL ESTATE BOARDS, "Answers to Appraisal Questions," *National Real Estate Journal*, March 30, 1931, pp. 44.

NATIONAL ASSOCIATION OF REAL ESTATE BOARDS, "Answers to Appraisal Questions," *National Real Estate Journal*, July 7, 1930, pp. 53-54.

NATIONAL ASSOCIATION OF REAL ESTATE BOARDS, "New Courses In Appraising and Selling Offered by National Association," *National Real Estate Journal*, pp. 44, 45-46.

NATIONAL REAL ESTATE JOURNAL, *California Standard Appraisal Form*, January 6, 1930, pp. 26.

NATIONAL REAL ESTATE JOURNAL, *Practical Appraising Methods*, National Real Estate Journal, Chicago, 1940.

NAZARIO, LUIS A, "Compendio De Valuacion De Inmuebles," *Valuacion De Muebles*, Sociedad De Tasadores De Venezuela, Caracas Venezuela, June 1, 1966, pp. 111.

NAZARIO, LUIS A., "Evaluacion De Bienes Raices:," *Boletin*, Sotave, Caracas, Venezuela, pp. 61-68.

NAZARIO, LUIS A., "Evaluacion De Bienes Raices: Capitulo Vii," *Boletin*, Sotave, Caracas, Venezuela, pp. 41-47.

NELSON, ROLAND D., "New Concepts In Capital Gains Appraising," *The Real Estate Appraiser*, August, 1966, pp. 19.

NELSON, T. R., "An Econometric Model of the Land Market Stressing Effects of Government Programs on Land Values," *Dissertation Abstracts*, Ann Arbor.

NESSER, RICHARD S., "Sinking Fund -Validity of Capitalization Method," *Technical Valuation*, February, 1960, pp. 17-22.

NEUMAN, RONALD, "A Profession-Knowledge and Control," *Appraisal Institute Magazine*, Appraisal Institute of Canada, Winnipeg.

NEWLOVE, GEORGE HILLIS, *Mathematics of Valuation*, 1937.

NINDE, HARRY W., "The G. I. Appraisal Process," *Appraisal and Valuation Manual*, 1956-57, pp. 85-91.

NOLAN, JAMES J., "Cost Is Not Always Value," *Technical Valuation*, American Society of Appraisers, Washington, D. C., August, 1967, pp. 44.

NOLAN, JAMES J., "The Certificate of Reasonable Value--A Mandate of Market Value," *The Residential Appraiser*, May, 1962, pp. 15-16.

NORMAN, R. SMITH, MILON BROWN, CHESTER J. KOPEC, *Getting the Most for Your Training Dollar*, Public Personnel Association, Chicago, 1966.

NORTH, L. W., "Build it on Paper First," *Appraisal Institute Magazine*, Appraisal Institute of Canada, Winnipeg.

NORTH, L. W., "You Mean it Sold for That Much," *Appraisal Institute Magazine*, Appraisal Institute of Canada, Winnipeg, March 1, 1972.

NOWAK, ARTHUR M., "Appraisal Facts and Fallacies," *Commerce and Finance*, June 22, 1927, pp. 1253-1254.

ONEIL, THOMAS E., "S. R. W. A. Market Data Center, Inc. : an Actuality," *The Real Estate Appraiser*, September, 1968, pp. 5-13.

O'FLAHERTY, JOHN D., "An Appraiser's Dilemma: the Cost Approach to Value," *The Real Estate Appraiser*, January, 1969, pp. 5-16.

OCHS, HARRY T., JR., "Application of Price Indexes In Appraisals," *Appraisal and Valuation Manual*, American Society of Appraisers, 1958, pp. 311-322.

OLDAK, P. G., "Analysis of the Concept of Value," *Problems of Economics*, October, 1970.

OLSON, LYLE H., "Appraising As an Economic Factor," *The Appraisal Journal*, July, 1935, pp. 310-315.

OLSON, LYLE H., "Reappraisals and Major Adjustments In Property Values," *National Association of Cost Accountants, Bulletin,* May 1, 1932, pp. 1155-1167.

OSTENDORF, E. L., "Certain Fundamentals of Appraising," *The Appraisal Journal,* January, 1938, pp. 37-39.

OSTENDORF, E. L., "Yardsticks for Real Estate," *Banking Digest,* May, 1937, pp. 104.

OTT, LAWSON R., "The Effect of the Purpose of Appraisal on Value," *Technical Valuation,* pp. 17.

OUTWATER, H. G., "Short Cut by Charts," *Architectural Forum,* December, 1936, pp. 562-563.

PALMA LABASTIDA, M. A., "Conceptos Sobre El Deslinde," *Boletin,* Sotave, Caracas, Venezuela, pp. 25-31.

PALMER, EDWARD DEL, "Fit to Be Compared," *The Appraisal Digest,* April, 1955, pp. 18-21.

PARVIN, ROBERT G., "Market Approach to Value," *Encyclopedia of Real Estate Appraising,* Friedman, 1959, pp. 86-93.

PATINKIN, DON, *Money Interests and Prices An Integration of Monetary and Value Theory,* Row, Peterson, Evanstown, Illinois, 1956.

PEARL, MILTON A., "Reviewing the Public Lands," *The Appraisal Journal,* January, 1967, pp. 28-33.

PENA GARCIA, M. A., "La Tecnica Del Avaluo, Su Evolucion," *Boletin,* Sotave, Caracas, Venezuela, pp. 23-28.

PENA GARCIA, M. A., "Valor Probable," *Boletin,* Sotave, Caracas, Venezuela, pp. 5-7.

PENNY, ALFRED L., "The Structure and Development of Capitalization Rates," *Appraisal Institute Magazine,* September, 1958, pp. 17-23.

PERRY, RALPH BARTON, *General Theory of Value,* Longmans Green, New York, 1926, pp. 693.

PICKARD, W. C., "When Is a Comparable Comparable," *The Real Estate Appraiser,* October, 1965, pp. 14-17.

PIO, ROBERT, "Round Equals Square," *Technical Valuation,* American Society of Appraisers, Washington, December, 1967, pp. 65.

PITT, JOHN E., "The Value of Fractional Interests," *Technical Valuation,* October, 1959, pp. 39-42.

PLUMMER, ALVIN S., "Marketing Special Purpose Properties," *Appraisal and Valuation Manual,* American Society of Appraisers, 1958, pp. 365-370.

POLLEYS, THOMAS A., "Real Estate Valuations," *Publications,* Minnesota Academy of Social Sciences, 1908, pp. 59-78.

POLLOCK, WALTER W., "A Scientific Approach to Real Estate Valuation," *American Academy of Political and Social Science, Annals,* March, 1930, pp. 96-105.

POLLOCK, WALTER W., "An Equitable Standard for Land Valuation," *National Tax Association Proceedings,* 1913, pp. 234-266, 267-285.

POLLOCK, WALTER W., AND R. W. H. SCHOLZ, *The Science and Practice Of Urban Land Valuation,* Philadelphia, 1926.

POLLOCK, WATER W., "The Science and Practice of Urban Land Valuation," *The Appraisal Journal,* July, 1936, pp. 310-318.

POPE, LESLIE E., "A Check List of Income and Expenses," *The Review,* September, 1956, pp. 7-11.

PORTER, ROBERT R., "Non-Technical Appraisal Procedure," *Review of the Society of Residential Appraisers,* August, 1937, pp. 3-4.

POST, EDWARD T., "The Appraiser and the Builder," *The Appraisal Journal,* October, 1946, pp. 395-400.

PRACTICAL USE OF OUR LAND ECONOMIC STUDIES, *Proceedings of the Seventh Annual National Seminar, 1961,* American Right of Way Association, 1962, pp. 20-24.

PRENTICE, PERRY, *The Power to Appraise,* The Residential Appraiser, May, 1960.

PUBLIC PERSONNEL ASSOCIATION, *A Guide to Training Practices,* Public Personnel Association, Chicago, 1966.

PYE, G., "Some Lessons In Market Valuation," *Financial Analysts Journal,* May, 1970, pp. 103-106.

QUINTANA, ISIDOR, "Actual Appraisal Reports," *National Real Estate Journal,* February, 1932, pp. 63-67.

QUINTANA, ISIDORO, "Coming to Terms," *The Appraisal Journal,* January, 1942, pp. 47-51.

QUINTANA, ISIDORO, "On Rationalizing Appraisal Practice," *The Appraisal Journal,* October, 1936, pp. 437-439.

QUINTO, OSCAR B., "Selecting Similar Sales," *The Review,* February, 1946, pp. 7-9, 11.

RAMS, EDWIN M., "Cost Variables," *The Review,* October, 1955, pp. 3-5.

RAMS, EDWIN M., "Economic Size and Value," *Technical Valuation,* October, 1961, pp. 11.

RAMS, EDWIN M., "Some Observations on Appraisal Training," *Right of Way,* December, 1963, pp. 33-38.

RAMS, EDWIN M., "Valuation of Partial Estates and Interests In Real Estate," *Technical Valuation,* June, 1956, pp. 16-19.

RANDALL, WILLIAM J., "Age, Depreciation, Future Life, and Net Condition," *Real Estate Analyst Appraisal Bulletin,* 1962, pp. 25- 2.

RANDALL, WILLIAM J., "Capitalization Rates Are Increasing," *Real Estate Analyst Appraisal Bulletin,* 1951, pp. 323-326.

RANDALL, WILLIAM J., "Clearly State the Appraisal Premise," *Real Estate Analyst Appraisal Bulletin,* 1958, pp. 49-52.

RANDALL, WILLIAM J., "Land Value As a Percentage of Total Sales Price of Residences," *Real Estate Analyst Appraisal Bulletin,* 1962, pp. 251-254.

RANDALL, WILLIAM J., "Time Factor Adjustments for Comparable Sales," *Real Estate Analyst Appraisal Bulleitn,* 1958, pp. 291-294.

RANDALL, WILLIAM J., "Treatment of Demolition Costs In the Appraisal Process," *Real Estate Analyst Appraisal Bulletin,* October, 1959, pp. 439 -42.

RATCLIFF, DR. RICHARD U., "A Restatement of Appraisal Theory," *The Appraisal Journal,* January, 1964, pp. 51-67.

RATCLIFF, DR. RICHARD U., "Economic Life In the Valuation Procedure," *The Appraisal Journal,* January, 1938, pp. 57-64.

RATCLIFF, DR. RICHARD U., "Net Income Can't Be Split," *The Appraisal Journal,* April, 1950, pp. 168-172.

RATCLIFF, DR. RICHARD U., "The Proceedings," *Paper and Proceedings,* Wisconsin Colloquium on Appraisal Research, 1963, pp. 67-71.

RATCLIFF, DR. RICHARD V., "A Neoteric View of the Appraisal Function," *The Appraisal Journal,* April, 1965, pp. 167-175.

RATCLIFF, DR. RICHARD W., "Market Value Can't Be Estimated," *The Real Estate Appraiser,* January, 1970, pp. 16-20.

RATCLIFF, R. U., "Capitalized Income Is Not Market Value," *Appraisal Institute Magazine,* Appraisal Institute of Canada, Winnipeg.

RATCLIFF, R. U., "The Only Road to Vp," *Appraisal Institute Magazine,* Appraisal Institute of Canada, Winnipeg.

REAL ESTATE ANALYST, THE, "Census Data to Aid the Appraiser," *Real Estate Analyst Appraisal Bulletin,* 1951, pp. 295-298.

REEVE, DOUGLAS W., "Weighing the Components of Value," *Review of Society of Residential Appraisers,* November, 1941, pp. 3-6.

REEVES, CUTHBERT E., "Gross Income As an Index of Value," *The Appraisal Journal,* July, 1936, pp. 301-309.

REIDY, MAURICE F., "An Appraisal That Went Sour," *The Appraisal Journal,* July, 1934, pp. 297-302.

RENSHAW, EDWARD F., "Scientific Appraisal," *National Tax Journal,* December, 1958, pp. 314-322.

REVIEW OF SOCIETY OF RESIDENTIAL APPRAISERS, "Current Survey on Appraisal Practices and Policies," *Review of Society of Residential Appraisers,* September, 1941, pp. 6-11, 16.

REVIEW, THE, "New Standards for Narrative Reports," *The Review,* October, 1952, pp. 10-12. pp. 16-20.

REVIEW, THE, "The Appraisal Process," *The Review,* November, 1949, pp. 12-16.

REYNOLDS, ANTHONY, WILLIAM D. WALDRON, "Historical Significance... How Much Is it Worth," *The Appraisal Journal,* July, 1969, pp. 401-410.

RICKS, R. BRUCE, "Valuation of Lessor and Lessee Interests In a Physical Asset," *The Appraisal Journal,* April, 1966, pp. 268-272.

RING, A. A., "New Look at Market Comparison Approach," *Appraisal Institute Magazine,* Appraisal Institute of Canada, Winnipeg.

RING, ALFRED A., "Appraisal Planning and Reporting," *The Valuation of Real Estate,* pp. 346-359.

RING, ALFRED A., "Correlation Is the Secret of Appraisal Success," *The Review,* September, 1952, pp. 20-23.

RING, ALFRED A., "The Labyrinth of Value," *The Appraisal Journal,* January, 1965, pp. 9-14.

RING, ALFRED A., "Updating the Earnings Approach to Value," *The Real Estate Appraiser,* April, 1963, pp. 2-9.

RING, ALFRED A., "What Makes Value," *The Review,* June, 1949, pp. 3-5.

ROBERTS, RICHARD, "The Appraisers Approach to Market Value," *Appraisal Institute Magazine,* December, 1961, pp. 14-17.

ROGERS, RUSSELL R., "On Control Data," *The Appraisal Journal,* October, 1962, pp. 541-542.

ROSS, THURSTON H., "History of Value Theory," *The Appraisal Journal,* April, 1938, pp. 120-132.

ROTH, VINCENT E., "Rule of Measurement," *Technical Valuation,* February, 1956, p. 23.

ROTHSCHILD, SIGMUND, "Measure of Wealth," *The Appraisal and Valuation Manual,* 1954, pp. 1..

RUGELES, IVAN OLIVER, "Accion Y Proyeccion De Sotave," *Boletin,* Sotave, Caracas, Venezuela, pp. 5-8.

RUGELES, IVAN OLIVER, "Conceptos Generales Sobre Valuacion," *Boletin,* Sotave, Caracas, Venezuela, pp. 7-10.

RUGELES, IVAN OLIVER, "El Proceso De Capitalizacion En El Avaluo," *Boletin,* Sotave, Caracas, Venezuela, pp. 11-14.

RUGGLES, RICHARD, "The Value of Value Theory," *American Economic Review,* May, 1954, pp. 140-160.

RUPERT, JOHN F., "The Appraiser Prepares for Testimony," *The Real Estate Appraiser,* November 10, 1963, pp. 32-38.

RYAN, JOHN C., "Probate Assignments," *The Review,* December, 1955, pp. 7-8.

SACKMAN, JULIUS L., "Economic Approach to Valuation," *The Appraisal Journal,* October, 1966, pp. 511-530.

SACKMAN, JULIUS L., "The Limitations of the Cost Approach," *The Appraisal Journal,* January, 1968, pp. 55-60.

SARLES, KENNETH E., "Appraisal Fundamentals," *The Appraisal Journal*, October, 1950, pp. 519-525.

SARLES, KENNETH E., "Establishing Marketability of Urban Property," *The Real Estate Appraiser*, December, 1965, pp. 22-28.

SCHARFF, MAURICE R., "The Role of the Expert for the Company," *Appraisal and Valuation Manual*, 1956, pp. 67.

SCHEIDT, JOHN, "Methods of Determining Value," *Technical Valuations*, October, 1967, pp. 71.

SCHMUTZ, GEORGE L., *The Appraisal Process*, G. L. Schmutz, Manhattan Beach, Cal, 1959.

SCHMUTZ, GEORGE L., "Other Factors Affecting Market Price," *The Appraisal Journal*, July, 1935, pp. 351-359.

SCHMUTZ, GEORGE L., "Property Considerations In Appraisal," *The Appraisal Process*, 1959, pp. 163-225.

SCHMUTZ, GEORGE L., "Purposes and Functions of Appraisals," *The Appraisal Process*, 1959, pp. 3-7.

SCHMUTZ, GEORGE L., "The Appraisal Problem," *Appraisal Process*, 1941, pp. 1-229.

SCHMUTZ, GEORGE L., "The Appraisal Process," *Appraisal Process*, 1941, pp. 1-229.

SCHMUTZ, GEORGE L., "Writing Reports," *The Appraisal Journal*, July, 1937, pp. 248-251.

SCHOEN, HARRY, "Chattel Appraising and Its Application," *Appraisal and Valuation Manual*, pp. 353.

SCHOEN, HARRY, "Establishing Financial Evaluation for Specialty Properties," *Appraisal and Valuation Manual*, 1964, pp. 253.

SCHOEN, HARRY, "Specialty Financing and Valuation," *Appraisal and Valuation Manual*, 1959, pp. PP, 299-308.

SCHROPP, T. L., "Appraisal Identification," *The Appraisal of Machinery and Equipment*, 1969, pp. 31.

SEGAL, HERBERT I., "Some Practical Guides for the Appraiser," *Appraisal and Valuation Manual*, 1960, pp. 1..

SEYMOUR, CHARLES F., "The Artillery Theory of Market Value," *The Appraisal Journal*, January, 1955, pp. 42-45.

SHEFFER, H. FRAZIER, "Some Aspects of Market Value," *Appraisal and Valuation Manual*, 1960, pp. 253-258.

SHENKEL, WILLIAM M., "Valuation of Leased Fees and Leasehold Interest," *The Appraisal Journal*, October, 1965, pp. 482-498.

SHERIDAN, V. G., "Water Rights: Real, Personal or Imagined," *Appraisal Institute Magazine*, Appraisal Institute of Canada, Winnipeg.

SHERMER, MALCOLM H., "Practical Problems of the Appraiser," *Review of Society of Residential Appraisers*, September, 1938, pp. 11-12.

SHUGRUE, FRANK R., "Basic Steps In the Appraisal of Real Property," *The Appraisal Journal*, January, 1953, pp. 104-111.

SILVERMAN, BENJAMIN, "Legal Aspects-Education," *Technical Valuation*, October, 1953, pp. 10.

SIMONETT, D. S., "Land Evaluation Studies with Remote Sensors In the Infrared and Radar Regions," *Land Evaluation*, pp. 349.

SLONIM, M. J., "The Three Approaches Under Fire," *Technical Valuation*, American Society of Appraisers, Washington, 1966.

SMITH, CHARLES E., "Inspection Procedure," *The Review*, February, 1954, pp. 3-5.

SMITH, HALBERT C., AND RONALD L. RACSTER, "Should the Traditional Appraisal Be Restructured," *The Real Estate Appraiser*, 1911.

SMITH, LAMAR, "Wide Disparity In Appraised Values," *Right of Way Conference Selected Papers,* University of Alabama, University, Alabama, 1960, pp. 9-20.

SMITH, LAMAR H., "Appraisal Reports--Their Form and Function," *Technical Valuation,*

SMITH, LEONARD C., "The Appraisal Process," *Review of the Society of Residential Appraisers,* September, 1937, pp. 4-10, 16.

SMITH, LEVIE D. SR., "Assumptions and Limiting Conditions," *The Real Estate Appraiser,* pp. 15.

SMITH, RALPH M., "The Best Appraisal System," *The Review,* June, 1948, pp. 3-7.

SMITH, WALSTEIN FR., "Value-Verified or Vilfied," *The Real Estate Appraiser,* pp. 2..

SMITH, WALSTEIN, JR., "Is There More Than One Market Value," *The Residential Appraiser,* September, 1962, pp. 2-13.

SNYDER, BLAKE, AND ROBY, RALPH, *Fundamentals In Real Estate,* Harper and Brothers, New York and London, 1927.

SNYDER, DONALD E., "Appraisal Data Banks," *The Real Estate Appraiser,* pp. 19.

SOCIETY OF RESIDENTIAL APPRAISERS, *Real Estate Appraisal: Principles and Terminology,* Chicago, 1960.

SODERQUIST, OSCAR, "A Problem In Appraising," *The Appraisal Journal,* April, 1934, pp. 252-253.

SOTAVE, "La Tecnica Avaluatoria," *Boletin,* Sotave, Caracas, Venezuela, pp. 40-42.

SOULE, NAT C., "Planning the Appraisal and Writing the Report," *National Real Estate Journal,* September, 1939, pp. 26-28.

SPAHR, WALTER E., AND OTHERS, *Economic Principles and Problems,* Farrar and Reinhart, New York.

SPEED, A., "Revised Guide for Demonstration Reports," *Appraisal Institute Magazine,* Appraisal Institute of Canada, Winnipeg.

SPILDER, JOHN B., "Errors of Appraisal Thoughts," *Real Estate Business As a Profession,* 1941, pp. 283-288.

SROUFE, THOMAS A., "Utilizing All Three Approaches to Value," *The Residential Appraiser,* pp. 3..

STAFFORD, JAMES G., AND ASSOCIATES, "Unit Foot Value for Square Foot Values and Depths As Indicated," *Appraising Manual,* Edition 2, 1937, pp. 356.

STANFORD, MELVIN J., "Forecasting Future Land Values," *Appraisal Institute Magazine,* Appraisal Institute of Canada, Winnipeg, September 1, 1973.

STARKE, GEORGE C., "How to Organize and Operate Appraisal Files," *The Appraisal Journal,* October, 1953, pp. 529-532.

STEVENS, WILLIAM T., "On Historical Significance As a Factor In Determining Value," *The Appraisal Journal,* July, 1968, pp. 418.

STEVICK, J. C., "Derive Your Own Formula," *Review of Society of Residential Appraiser,* September, 1940, pp. 14-16.

STEWART, J. I., "An Economist Looks at Appraisal Theory," *The Real Estate Appraiser,* July, 1966, pp. 15-28.

STEWART, JAMES INNES, *Real Estate Appraisal In a Nutshell,* University of Toronto Press, Toronto, 1967.

STOCKTON, JOHN Q., "Business Statistics," *Technical Valuation,* Southwestern Publishing Co., Cincinnati, Ohio, 1958.

STOTHART, JACK, "Trends Affecting Land Value," *Appraisal Institute Magazine,* September, 1961, pp. 16-18.

STOWE, THOMAS C., "The Question of Whole Property : a Comment," *The Real Estate Appraiser,* pp. 29.

STRUNK, NORMAN, "Purposes of 'GI' Appraisal," *The Review,* September, 1946, pp. 8-11.

STRUNK, NORMAN W., "Shrinking Margins of Error," *The Residential Appraiser,* May, 1959, pp. 8-12.

SWAN, J. WILSON, "Appraisal Steps," *The Review,* May, 1958, pp. 3-9.

SWAN, RUSSELL E., "Appraisal Terminology and Its Use," *The Real Estate Appraiser,* pp. 9..

SWEENEY, HENRY W., "Approximation of Appraisal Values by Index Numbers," *Harvard Business Review,* October, 1934, pp. 108-115.

TAEUBER, K. C., "An Argument In Favor of the Acceptance of the Doctrine of One Value for All Purposes," *The Appraisal Journal,* October, 1956, pp. 561-564.

TAEUBER, K. G., "Current Valuation Problems," *Appraisal Institute Magazine,* Appraisal Institute of Canada, Winnipeg.

TECHNICAL VALUATION, "Appraiser Vs. Valuation Engineer Editorial Comment," *Technical Valuation,* September, 1945, pp. 8-9.

TECKEMEYER, EARL B., "Management's Contributions to Better Appraising," *National Real Estate Journal,* October, 1938, pp. 29-30.

TESTINO G., RICARDO, "Plusvalia," *Boletin,* Sotave, Caracas, Venezuela, pp. 35-37.

THAYER, DONALD C., "A New Graphic Method for Determining Values," *National Real Estate Journal,* November, 1940, pp. 24-26.

THE APPRAISAL JOURNAL, "Relief for Hindsight (Appraisal Docket)," *The Appraisal Journal,* July, 1953, pp. 443-444.

THIEL, FLOYD I., "A State-Federal Program of Land Economic Studies," *Right of Way,* June, 1967, pp. 28-31.

THOMPSON, LOREN L., "Exchange of Appraisals--Ripple or Wave," *The Real Estate Appraiser,* pp. 2..

THOMPSON, PELL, "Real Estate Appraisals by Formula," *Commerce and Finance,* July 20, 1927, pp. 1445-1446.

THOMPSON, R. E., "Income Vs. Physical Value," *National Real Estate Journal,* March 31, 1930, pp. 46-47.

THOMSON, W. F., "Land Registry Systems," *Appraisal Institute Magazine,* Appraisal Institute of Canada, Winnipeg.

THOMSSEN, ROHLAND H., "Appraising and Counseling," *The Appraisal Journal,* January, 1960, pp. 17-23.

THORPE, E. EVERETT, "On Valuation of Old Structures on Building Plots," *The Appraisal Journal,* January, 1938, pp. 70-71.

THORPE, LAYARD G., "Foreclosure Appraisals," *The Residential Appraiser,* June, 1958, pp. 3-6.

THORSON, IVAN A., *Simplified Appraisal System,* Realty Research Bureau, Los Angeles, 1949.

THORSON, IVAN A., *Simplified Appraisal System, Land Economic,* Realty Research Bureau, Los Angeles, 1951.

THORSON, IVAN A., "Appraisal Methods In Times of Depression," *Proceedings,* 1933, pp. 310-323.

THORSON, IVAN A., "Appraising Properties Involving Both Contract Rent and Economic Rents--Reversion Rights," *Technicalities,* February, 1950, pp. 23-25.

THORSON, IVAN A., "Essentials of Real Estate Values," *An Appraisal Manual,* Realty Research Bureau, Los Angeles, 1931, pp. 1-96.

THORSON, IVAN A., "Our Futile Quest for Exactness," *Review of the Society of Residential Appraisers,* July, 1936, pp. 5-8.

THORSON, IVAN A., "Rationalizing Appraisal Practice," *The Appraisal Journal,* July, 1936, pp. 237-253.

THORSON, IVAN A., "Relation of Value to the Purpose of the Appraisal," *The Appraisal Journal,* January, 1933, pp. 104-122.

THORSON, J. T., "Memorandum on Value to the Owner," *Appraisal Institute Magazine*, Appraisal Institute of Canada, Winnipeg.

TIERNEY, JOHN L, "Real Estate Appraisal In Foreclosure Cases," *The Appraisal Journal*, July, 1940, pp. 226-229.

TONTZ, ROBERT L., "Land Valuation and the Everyday Land Market," *Journal of the American Society of Farm Managers and Rural Appraisers*, 1955, pp. 24-29.

TORREY, WILLIAM W., "A Long Way to a Short Cut, or the End May Justify the Means," *The Appraisal Journal*, October, 1956, pp. 549-560.

TOWERS, ALBERT G. JR., "Considerations of Value," *The Appraisal Journal*, January, 1951, pp. 110-112.

TOWERS, ALBERT G. JR., "The Validity of an Appraisal," *The Appraisal Journal*, January, 1949, pp. 36-38.

TOWNSEND, GILBERT, *How to Estimate*, American Technical Society, Chicago, 1939.

TREDWELL, JOHN C., "The Selection of Capitalization Rates," *The Appraisal Journal*, October, 1938, pp. 343-353.

TROWBRIDGE, CARL R., "What Is a Review Appraiser," *The Real Estate Appraiser*, April, 1971.

TROXEL, JAY C., "Expanding the Substitution Theory," *The Appraisal Journal*, July, 1945, pp. 266-270.

TYNAN, PETER, "A Buyer of Appraisals Speaks Out," *Appraisal Institute Magazine*, Appraisal Institute of Canada, Winnipeg, September 1, 1972.

VAN BUREN, DEWITT, "Appraisal of Estates In Land Less Than the Fee," *The Appraisal Journal*, October, 1943, pp. 327-335.

VARTY, LEO G., "Reviving the Profit In Obsolete Properties," *National Real Estate Journal*, June, 1934, pp. 23-24.

VAUGHAN, J. L. JR., "The Purpose of the Appraisal," *Appraisal And Valuation Manual*, 1956, pp. 23-26.

VEGAS ROLANDO, NICOLAS, "La Propiedad Inmueble," *Boletin*, Sotave, Caracas, Venezuela, pp. 4-5.

VINCENT, FRED E., "Conversion of Land Prices," *The Appraisal Manual*, 1937, pp. 517-518.

VUKICEVICH, BENJAMIN G., "Four-Page Appraisal Form," *Valuation Manual*, The Residential Appraiser, Chicago, January, 1959, pp. 16.

WAGNER, PERCY E., "Appraisal Procedure of Federal Agencies," *The Appraisal Journal*, July, 1937, pp. 240-247.

WALL, NORBERT F., "A Case Study, Land Residual Technique," *The Real Estate Appraiser*, pp. 22.

WALSH, H. VANDERVOORT, "Finding Reproduction Cost," *The Appraisal Journal*, April, 1934, pp. 228-231.

WALSTEIN, SMITH, JR., "Value-Verified and Vilified," *The Real Estate Appraiser*, September, 1965, pp. 2-11.

WALSTRUM, S. WILLIAM, "Market Analysis," *Journal of Certified Property Managers*, March, 1941, pp. 216-228.

WALTHER, HERMAN O., "Appraisal Quiz," *Freehold*, January 15, 1939, pp. 51-53.

WALTHER, HERMAN O., "This Is How Chicago Real Estate Board Appraisals Are Made," *Real Estate*, February 18, 1939, pp. 10-14.

WALTHER, HERMAN O., "Why the Three Approaches Fit Together," *The Review*, June, 1956, pp. 3-7.

WARNER, ARTHUR E., "Creativity In the Appraisal Process," *The Appraisal Journal*, July, 1963, pp. 316-318.

WARNER, JOHN., "Design and Use of Appraisal Forms," *Municipal Finance*, February, 1937, pp. 7-20.

WATKINS, J. OLIVER, "Appraisal Practices In Great Britain," *The Appraisal Journal*, April, 1953, pp. 251-257.

WEBB, CLARENCE ALBERT, *Valuation of Real Property*, C. Lockwood and Sons, London 2d Edit V Xii, 1910, pp. 1-332.

WEBB, JAMES A., "Methods of Appraising Improvements," *National Real Estate Journal*, February 26, 1923, pp. 25.

WEBB, JAMES A., "Methods of Appraising Land," *National Real Estate Journal*, February 20, 1923, pp. 23-25.

WEBB, JOHN C., "The Comparative Approach," *Right of Way*, February, 1958, pp. 19-20.

WEIMER, ARTHUR M., "History of Value Theory for the Appraiser," *The Appraisal Journal*, January, 1953, pp. 8-22.

WEIMER, ARTHUR M., HOYER, HOMER, *Principles of Urban Real Estate*, Ronald, New York, 1948.

WELCH, RAYMOND F., "Appraising Real Property In Estates and Trusts," *Appraisal and Valuation Manual*, 1959, pp. 293-298.

WENDT, PAUL F., "Recent Developments In Appraisal Theory," *Appraisal Institute Magazine*, Appraisal Institute of Canada, Winnipeg.

WENDT, PAUL FRANCIS, *Real Estate Appraisal a Critical Analysis of Theory and Practice*, Holt, New York, 1956.

WENZLICK, ROY, "As I See Lessons from the Past," *The Real Estate Analyst Appraisal Bulletin*, 1954, pp. 89-92.

WENZLICK, ROY, "Good Files for Better Appraisals," *The Appraisal Journal*, October, 1958, pp. 599-601.

WHITE, JOHN R., "Analyzing Comparable Data," *The Appraisal Digest*, October, 1969, pp. 24.

WHITE, JOHN R., "Economic Conditions Affecting Capitalization Rate Selection," *Appraisal Digest*, October, 1956, pp. 1-3.

WHITE, JOHN R., "How Many Approaches to Value?," *Appraisal Digest*, April, 1958, pp. 9-10.

WHITE, JOHN R., "New Horizons In Capitalization Rate Selection," *Technical Valuation*, June, 1957, pp. 28-32.

WHITE, JOHN R., "Selection of the Capitalization Rate," *The Appraisal Journal*, October, 1949, pp. 478-489.

WHITE, JOHN ROBERT, "Capitalization Rates and the Current Money Market," *The Appraisal Journal*, July, 1957, pp. 417-420.

WHITE, PHILIP H., "Principles and Procedures In the Training of Appraisers," *Wisconsin Colloquium on Appraisal Research, Papers and Proceedings*, 1963, pp. 59-66.

WHITE, PHILIP H., "Some Aspects of the Income Approach," *The Residential Appraiser*, July, 1960, pp. 16-23.

WHITTEN, WILCOX, *Valuation of Public Utilities*, The Banks Law Publishing Company, New York, 1928, pp. 189, 196.

WIDEN, E. N., "Technique of Fore Casting the Growth of a Community," *National Real Estate Journal*, June 28, 1926, pp. 17-23.

WILDSMITH, P. D., "The Problem of Value," *Appraisal Institute Magazine*, February, 1958, pp. 5-8.

WILNETT, MCDONNELL, WOLCOTT, "Cost Approach," *Problems In Rural Real Estate Appraisal*, pp. 7.

WILNETT, MCDONNELL, WOLCOTT, "Income Capitalization Techniques," *Problems In Rural Real Estate Appraisal*, pp. 11.

WILNETTE, MCDONNELL, WOLCOTT, "Basic Principles and Procedures," *Problems In Rural Real Estate Appraisal*, pp. 1.

WILNETTE, MCDONNELL, WOLCOTT, "Market Data Approach," *Problems In Rural Real Estate Appraisal*, pp. 20.

▲ Appraisal Theory and Methods

WINFREY, ROBLEY, KURTZ, EDWIN B, "Life Characteristics of Physical Property," *Iowa Engineering Experiment Station Bulletin, No. 103,* Iowa State College of Agriculture & Mechanic Arts, Ames, June 17, 1931, pp. 1-144.

WINNICK, LOUIS, "Long-Run Changes In the Valuation of Real Estate by Gross Rents," *The Appraisal Journal,* October, 1952, pp. 484-498.

WINSTEAD, ROBERT W., "On Presentation of Conclusions," *The Appraisal Journal,* October, 1962, pp. 544-545.

WINTER, E. A., SMITH, W. P, "Estimating Aggregate Residential Real Estate Values from Population-Income Data," *Appraisal and Valuation Manual,* February, 1956, pp. 89-92.

WISCONSIN BUREAU OF RECLAMATION, *Recreation Site Evaluation,* Madison, 1968, pp. 1-50.

WITKOWSKY, JACK, "Mass Appraisal Techniques," *The Appraisal Journal,* April, 1952, pp. 206-209.

WITTMAN, FRANK, "The Comparison Method As a Value Indicator," *Appraisal Digest,* January, 1958, pp. 8-11.

WOLTZ, SETH P., "Misuse of Comparable Sales," *The Residential Appraiser,* pp. 3.

WOODRUFF, ARCHIBALD MULFORD, *Elementary Appraisal Principles,* Pittsburg Bureau of Business Research, Pittsburg, 1957.

WRIGHT, CARROLL, "As Many Values As Uses," *Review of the Society of Residential Appraisers,* October, 1936, pp. 9-10.

ZANGERLE, JOHN, "Cleveland Physical Depreciation of Buildings," *Principles of Real Estate Appraising,*

ZANGERLE, JOHN A., *Principles of Real Estate Appraising,* Cleveland, 1924.

ZANGERLE, JOHN A., "Appraisal--Building Classification Indispensable," *National Real Estate Journal,* September 24, 1923, pp. 19-20.

ZANGERLE, JOHN A., "Appraising Fractional Real Estate Interests," *The Appraisal Journal,* November, 1940, pp. 355-359.

ZECKENDORF, WILLIAM, "Futures In Real Estate," *The Appraisal Journal,* July, 1954, pp. 325-329.

ZEPP, EDWARD G., "The Difference Is Up to You," *The Appraisal Journal,* October, 1965, pp. 619-620.

# 11-17 Market Appraisal, Price Cost and Value Theories

ANGULO LOPEZ, ALBERTO, "Principios Basicos De Avaluaciones," *Boletin,* Sotave, Caracas, Venezuela, pp. 5-6.

APPRAISAL DIGEST, "The Value of Amenities," *Appraisal Digest,* April, 1954, pp. 13.

ARDISSONO, ROBERT J., "Checking the Market," *The Review,* March, 1956, pp. 22-23.

ARMSTRONG, ROBERT H., "Prices Vs. Value," *The Appraisal Journal,* October, 1938, pp. 316-322.

ARMSTRONG, ROBERT H., "Valuation Problems In an Unbalanced Economic World," *The Appraisal Journal,* January, 1941, pp. 41-47.

ATKINSON HARRY GRANT, "Professional Ethics," *The Appraisal Journal,* April, 1939, pp. 159-161.

# BIBLIOGRAPHY OF APPRAISAL LITERATURE

BABCOCK, FREDERICK M., *The Appraisal of Real Estate*, Macmillan Company, New York City, 1924.

BABCOCK, FREDERICK M., *The Valuation of Real Estate*, McGraw-Hill Book Company, Incorporated, New York City, 1932.

BABCOCK, FREDERICK M., "A New Approach to the Solution of the Appraisal Problem," *The Appraisal Journal*, January, 1937, pp. 54-59.

BABCOCK, FREDERICK M., "A New Approach Toward Solution of the Appraisal Problem," *Practical Appraising Methods*, 1940, pp. 2-4.

BABCOCK, FREDERICK M., "Appraisal Procedure," *Valuation of Real Estate*, 1932, pp. 187-224.

BABCOCK, FREDERICK M., "Appraisal Procedure and Methods," *Proceedings of the Brokers Division of the National Association of Real Estate Boards*, 1924, pp. 48-56.

BABCOCK, HENRY A., "Recent Developments In Real Estate Appraising," *The National Real Estate Journal*, April 14, 1930, pp. 31-34.

BABCOCK, HENRY A., "Standardized Appraisal Practice," *Proceedings of the 15th Annual Convention of the Bankers Association of America*, 1928, pp. 119-126.

BABCOCK, HENRY A., "The Relation of Income to Value," *The Annals of Real Estate Practice*, 1926, pp. 83-116.

BAILEY, HOP, JR., "Problems In Appraising," *The Appraisal Journal*, August, 1964, pp. 23-28.

BALL, THOMAS B., "Construction Adjustment Factors," *Church Valuation*, Church Valuation Consultants, 1968, pp. 11.

BARBOUR, SIR DAVID MILLER, *The Standard of Value*, Macmillan and Co, London, 1912.

BARNARD, BOYD T., "How Much More Can the Market Absorb," *The Appraisal Journal*, April, 1964, pp. 172-176.

BAYLOR, DR. ALLEN O., "Valuation As a Multi/Disciplinary Field In Our Higher Education," *Appraisal and Valuation Manual*, Corporate Press Incorporated, Washington, D.C., January, 1972, pp. 290.

BECKER, GEORGE, "Market Data Analysis," *The Appraisal Journal*, October, 1955, pp. 486-494.

BEETH, CHANNING C., "Today's Appraisal Digest Must Reflect Today's Cost," *Appraisal Digest*, January, 1954, pp. 4-6.

BERHOFF, WILLIAM EARL, *Evolution of Values In New Mexico*, State Bureau of Mines, Socorro, 1962.

BEROES, MARIANO, "Valuacion," *Boletin*, Sotave, Caracas, Venezuela, pp. 33-40.

BIRCK, LAURITS VILHELM, "The Theory of Marginal Value," E.P. Dutton and Co., New York, 1922.

BODFISH, MORTON, WITTAUCSH, WILLIAM, "The Consumer's Housing Dollar," *The Residential Appraiser*, June, 1957, pp. 16-18.

BOECKH, EVERARD HEREFORD, "Land Depth Table," *Manual of Appraisals*, 1937, pp. 348.

BOECKH, EVERARD HEREFORD, "Valuation by Comparison," *Manual of Appraisals*, pp. 334.

BONBRIGHT, JAMES C., "Concepts of Property Value," *The Valuation of Property*, New York, 1937.

BOWEN, DELBERT, "Relation of Financing to Market Value," *The Residential Appraiser*, December, 1961, pp. 12-16.

BOWES, W. A., "What Is Market Analysis," *The Real Estate Appraiser*, July, 1968, pp. 11-14.

CHALMERS, T. G., "Comments on No Appreciation for Appreciation," *Appraisal Institute Magazine*, Appraisal Institute of Canada, Winnipeg.

CHURCH, EUGENE B., "The Economic Elements of Buildings," *Real Estate Record and Builder's Guide,* February 27, 1932, pp. 9-10.

CHURCH, EUGENE B., "The Relations of Building Cost and Income," *Real Estate Record and Builder's Guide,* January 30, 1932, pp. 5-6.

CONRAN, C. L., "Valuation of Museum Objects," *Museums Journal.*

DAVENPORT, HERBERT JOSEPH, *Value and Distribution,* University of Chicago Press, Chicago, 1908.

DAVIS, WILLIAM D., *The Market Data Approach,* American Association of State Highway Officials, Washington, D. C, 1962, pp. 361-365.

DENAPOLI, CHARLES, "Sales Prices Are Appraisal Facts," *The Review,* July, 1945, pp. 15-16.

DENIS, J. W., "Can Present Market Value Be Determined," *Journal American Institute of Real Estate Appraisers,* April, 1934, pp. 253-256.

DILMORE, GENE, "Market Data Adjustments," *Appraisal Institute Magazine,* Appraisal Institute of Canada, Winnipeg.

DUNHAM, HOWARD W. JR., "The Adjustment Process Demonstrated," *The Real Estate Appraiser,* 1968, pp. 17-21.

DUNN, DOMINICK R., "The Causes of Value," *The Appraisal Journal,* July, 1963, pp. 411-414.

FULLERTON, PAUL, "People, Not Time, Determine Depreciation," *The Real Estate Appraiser,* February, 1963, pp. 2-3.

GARDENER, ALAN C., "Present Day Appraisal Practice and Technique," *The Appraisal Journal,* October, 1945, pp. 365-370.

GARRISON, BURL L., "Physical Deterioration," *The Residential Appraiser,* October, 1962, pp. 17-20.

GRIMES, JOHN A., WILLIAM H. GRAIGUE, *Principles of Valuation,* Prentice hall Incorporated, New York City, 1928, pp. 274.

HENDRIE, ROBERT E., "Depreciation As it Relates to Appraisal Practices," *Technical Valuation,* February, 1958, pp. 27-32.

HIGGINS WARREN J, "Demolition:Capitalize or Write-Off," *The Real Estate Appraiser,* The Society of Real Estate Appraisers, Chicago Illinois, January 1, 1974, pp. 40-49.

HUNTER, HAMILTON W., "The Cost of Quality," *The Review,* December, 1952, pp. 3-7.

HYDER, K. LEE, "The Appraisal Process," *The Appraisal Journal,* January, 1936, pp. 13-25.

KAHN, SANDERS A., "Land, Does it Depreciate," *The Real Estate Appraiser,* January, 1969, pp. 28-31.

KENNY, NORMAN W., "Inadequate Improvements," *The Appraisal Journal,* October, 1932, pp. 53-55.

LAIRD, JOHN, *The Idea of Value,* A. M. Kelley, New York, 1969.

LAUNER, E. J., "The Development of Appraisal Methods," *Appraisal and Valuation Manual,* American Society of Appraisers, 1958, pp. 1-26.

LAUNER, E. J., "The Significance of the American Society of Appraisers In the Appraisal Field," *Technical Valuation,* February, 1959, pp. 3-4.

LONG, G. B. JR., "How to Make a Market Analysis," *The Real Estate Appraiser,* May, 1959, pp. 13-16, 18.

MEEK, RONALD L., *Studies In the Labor Theory of Value,* Lawrence and Wi Hart, London, 1956.

SCHEIDT, JOHN, "Building Appraisals," *Appraisal and Valuation Manual,* 1964, pp. 271.

SCHUMACHER, DAVID T., "Determining Physical Depreciation, Functional and Economic Obsolescence," *Technical Valuation,* October, 1956, pp. 19-24.

SHURBERG, MERWIN, "Economic Factors In Property Valuations," *Appraisal and Valuation Manual,* pp. 65.

SMITH, LARRY, "Economic Factors and Their Analysis," *Valuation,* June, 1954, pp. 19-35.

SMITH, LEONARD C., *Economic Life,* August 1, 1938.

SPAHR, WALTER E., AND OTHERS, *Economic Principles and Problems,* Farrar and Reinhart, New York.

STEVENS, WILLIAM T., "On Historical Significance As a Factor In Determining Value," *The Appraisal Journal,* July, 1968, pp. 418.

THORPE, E. EVERETT, "On Valuation of Old Structures on Building Plots," *The Appraisal Journal,* January, 1938, pp. 70-71.

## 11-18 Social Trends and Appraisal

ADELSBERG, HYMAN, "Sectionalization of the New York Chapter," *Technical Valuation,* February, 1956, pp. 45.

AGUAYO, RAMON CARLOS, "Ensenanza De La Valuacion," *Boletin,* Sotave, Caracas, Venezuela, pp. 21-24.

AKSTON, J. J., "Editorial to Sell or Not to Sell," *Art,* May, 1972, pp. 29.

ALDERFER, EVAN B., "Rounding the Horn of Plenty," *The Appraisal Journal,* July, 1962, pp. 410-413.

ALLIN, B. C., "Bill to License Appraisers In California Legislature," *Technical Valuation,* June, 1955, pp. 5-8.

ALLISON, VEVILLE F., "The Hour of Decision," *The Appraisal Journal,* January, 1961, pp. 119-122.

AMERICAN INSTITUTE OF REAL ESTATE APPRAISERS, *The Appraiser a Monthly Round-Up of Appraisal News and Views,* The American Institute of Real Estate Appraisers, Chicago, 1900.

AMERICAN INSTITUTE OF REAL ESTATE APPRAISERS, "Codigo De Etica Profesional," *Boletin,* Sotave, Caracas, Venezuela, pp. 25-43.

ANDERSON, BENJAMIN MCALESTER, *Social Value a Study In Economic Theory Critical and Constructive,* New York City, 1966.

ANON., "This Could Happen to Appraisers!," *Appraisal Institute Magazine,* Appraisal Institute of Canada, Winnipeg.

APPRAISAL DIGEST, "Committee Suggests Appraisal Fees Be Standardized," *Society of Residential Appraisers,* April, 1951, pp. 23-24.

APPRAISAL DIGEST, "Fed Survey Reveals Facts of Importance to Appraisers," *The Appraisal Digest,* January, 1953, pp. 4-5.

APPRAISAL DIGEST, "Trend of the Times There's a Set of New Buyers," *Business Week,* April, 1955, pp. 1-3.

APPRAISAL JOURNAL, "Peter to Paul," The Appraisal Journal, Vol. Xviii.

APPRAISAL JOURNAL, "Serendipity and the Student of Appraisal," *The Appraisal Journal,* April, 1967, pp. 175-180.

ARCHITECTURAL FORUM, "Business Factors In Architectural Practice," *Architectural Forum,* February, 1923.

ARENA, JOHN J., "Is the United States Pricing Itself Out of World Markets," *The Appraisal Journal,* January, 1966, pp. 58-62.

▲ **Appraisal Theory and Methods**

ARGENTINE REPUBLIC, *Law, Statutes, Etc. Revaluo Inpositivo Ley Y Su Reglamentacion*, Abeledo-Perrot, Buenos Aires, 1960.

ARMSTRONG, ROBERT H., "Forecasting the Future," *The Appraisal Journal*, Vol. Xv.

ARMSTRONG, ROBERT H., "The Continued and Incessant Decline In Real Estate Values," *The Appraisal Journal*, July, 1951, pp. 270-292.

ARMSTRONG, ROBERT H., "Valuation Problems In an Unbalanced Economic World," *The Appraisal Journal*, January, 1941, pp. 41-47.

ARNESON JR, HARRY R., "The Future of Appraising and Appraisers," *Appraisal Institute Magazine*, Appraisal Institute of Canada, Winnipeg.

ARROW, KENNETH JOSEPH, *Social Choice and Individual Values*, Wiley and Sons, New York City, 1951.

ARTHAND, CLAUDE, *Homes of the Great*, Weidenfeld and Nicolson, London.

ARTILES, SEBASTIAN, "Corte Suprema En Materia De Avaluos," *Boletin*, Sotave, Caracas, Venezuela, pp. 16-17.

ASCHER, DAVID B., "International Valuation a New Science," *The Appraisal Journal*, April, 1952, pp. 232-234.

ASCHMAN, FREDERICK T., "Appraisal Scene," *The Review*, April, 1956, pp. 2.

AXKROYD, PETER H., "Changing Values," *The Appraisal Institute Magazine*, March, 1963, pp. 7-11.

AYRES, LEONARD P., "Two War Periods," *The Review*, June, 1945, pp. 6-8.

BABCOCK, FREDERICK M., "Business Conditions Stress Importance of Appraisals," *Real Estate Record and Builders Guide*.

BABCOCK, FREDERICK M., "Influence of Social and Racial Factors on Value," *Valuation of Real Estate*, 1932, pp. 86-92.

BABCOCK, WILLIAM H., "Appraising As a Phase of Salesmanship," *National Real Estate Journal*, November 5, 1923, pp. 22-26.

BACK, DENYS H., "Canadian Contrasts," *Residential Appraiser*, pp. 580700, 3.

BADEN, POWELL, BADEN, HENRY, *The Land Systems of British India*, Clarendon Press, Oxford, 1892.

BARNARD, BOYD T., "The Future of Appraising," *The Appraisal Journal*, April, 1965, pp. 181-189.

BEATON, J WALLACE, "Father Devitt and Mother Hubbard or Valuation Day Meets Frankenstein," *Valuation Magazine*, American Society of Appraisers, Washington D C, December 1, 1973, pp. 2-11.

BEAUBIER, DAVID W., "Appraisers and the White Paper," *Appraisal Institute Magazine*, Appraisal Institute of Canada, Winnipeg, March 1, 1971.

BEMAN, ARTHUR K., "One Quarter Century of Depreciation Change In Value," *The Appraisal Journal*, January, 1948, pp. 72-76.

BLOCK, ALEXANDER, "Currency Inflation In Germany," *The Appraisal Journal*, January, 1936, pp. 62-66.

BODFISH, MORTON, "The Road Ahead," *The Review*, April, 1945, pp. 3-4.

BODFISH, MORTON, THEOBALD, A. D, "The Rate of Capitalization," *Real Estate Fundamentals*, 1941, pp. 16-71.

BOWERS, RAYMOND A., "Home Planning Trends," *The Review*, September, 1945, pp. 8-12.

BRABENT, DAVIS, "Appraisal Contracts," *The Residential Appraiser*, August, 1960, pp. 8-11.

BRACELAND, JOSEPH J., "Tight Money and Its Effect on Real Estate Values," *The Residential Appraiser*, February, 1960, pp. 11-13.

## BIBLIOGRAPHY OF APPRAISAL LITERATURE

BRADLEY, VINCENT P., "The Need for Educational Courses," *The National Real Estate Journal,* February 11, 1924, pp. 39-40.

BRENNER, MARSHALL H., *Impact of Corporate Moving, Real Estate Trends of the Real Estate Broker,* University of Southern California, September, 1971.

BRINSMADE, ROBERT BRUCE, *El Latifundismo Mexicano, Su Origen Y Su Remedio,* 1916.

BROOKS, ROBERT B. JR., "Oldest of the Arts and Newest of the Professions," *The Appraisal Journal,* April, 1950, pp. 201-204.

BROWNSTEIN, PHILIP N., "Potential Volume In V.A.," *The Residential Appraiser,* July, 1959, pp. 7-9.

BRUNSON, THEO R., "Responsibilities of Appraisers," *Right of Way,* 1962, pp. 28-31.

BURGESS, GEORGE V. T., "A Case Study of Inflation," *American Society of Appraisers Manual,* 1960, pp. 25.

BURNELL, WILLIAM U., "President's Message-Our Place In the Sun," *Technical Valuation,* October, 1954, pp. 5.

CALVIN, BRENDA, "Land and Landscape," Transatlantic Arts Inc., Levittown, N. Y..

CASE, FRED E., "Lessons from European Appraisals," *The Residential Appraiser,* June, 1959, pp. 3-6.

CASEMENT, R., "Pay As You Go: Moving People In the 1970's," *The Economist,* March 27, 1971.

CHADEAYNE, ROBERT O., "Artist to Appraiser," *A. S. A. Valuation Manual,* American Society of Appraisers, Washington, D. C., 1958, pp. 57.

CHAMBERLAIN, NARCISSA, *Old Rooms for New Living,* Hastings House.

CHANDIAS, MARIO E., "Sobre La Ensenanza De La Tasacion," *Boletin,* Sotave, Caracas, Venezuela, pp. 7-9.

CHESSMAN, MARK, "The Appraiser and Public Relations," *The Appraisal Journal,* July, 1937, pp. 273-277.

CHURCH, BYRON, "What Good Is an Appraisal," *The Residential Appraiser,* May, 1961, pp. 9-11.

CHURCHILL, WINSTON S., "The Valuer and His Profession," *The Appraisal Journal,* July, 1966, pp. 326-328.

COOKE, JOHN, "One Judge's Views on Appraiser Certification or Liscensing," *The Appraiser,* February, 1967.

COOPER K. J., "The Impact of Technology and Changing Social Patterns on Property Values," *Valuer,* The New Zealand Institute of Valuers, New Zealand, August 1, 1973, pp. 124-134.

COOPER, ARTHUR PH. D., *An Appraisal of the Forecasting Performance of the Council of Economic Advisers,* Nichols, Georgia St. University, 1971.

COULSON, ROBERT, *The Arbitration of Valuation Disputes,* American Society of Appraisers, Washington, September, 1968, pp. 52.

COULSON, ROBERT M, "The Professional Appraiser Looks at Arbitration," *Valutape Audio-Library Series,* American Society of Appraisers, Washington D.C., January 1, 1973.

CRIST, MARION, "History of the American Society of Appraisers," *A. S. A. Valuation Manual,* American Society of Appraisers, 1964, pp. 277.

CUERPO TECNICO DE TASACIONES DEL PERU, "Tasaciones Del Peru: Capitulo V.," *Boletin,* Sotave, Caracas, Venezuela, pp. 45-48.

CUERPO TECNICO DE TASACIONES DEL PERU, **Tasaciones Peru: Capitulos I y II,**" *Boletin,* Sotave, Caracas, Venezuela, pp. 15-23.

CUERPO TECNICO DE TASACIONES DEL PERU, "Tasaciones Peru: Capitulos III y IV," *Boletin,* Sotave, Caracas, Venezuela, pp. 45-58.

CUERPO TECNICO DE TASACIONES DEL PERU, "Tasaciones Peru: Capitulos Vi y Vii," *Boletin,* Sotave, Caracas, Venezuela, pp. 45-56.

▲ Appraisal Theory and Methods

DE SALES PEREZ, FRANCISCO, "El Tribunal Inquilinato," *Boletin,* Sotave, Caracas, Venezuela, pp. 4-5.

DE SALES PEREZ, FRANCISCO, "Impulso De La Tecnica Avaluatoria En Venezuela," *Boletin,* Sotave, Caracas, Venezuela, pp. 3-4.

DENTON, JOHN H., *The Valuation of Amenities,* American Society of Appraisers, Washington, D. C, 1964, pp. 217.

DISTELHORST, CARL F., "Progress Within Our Tightrope Economy," *The Residential Appraiser,* April, 1957, pp. 7-12.

DOLMAN, JOHN P., "Responsibilities of the Appraiser," *The Appraisal Journal,* January, 1962, pp. 49-54.

DOLMAN, JOHN P., "The Appraiser of Tomorrow," *Right of Way,* April, 1970.

DOLMAN, JOHN P., "The Appraiser of Tomorrow," *The Appraisal Journal,* October, 1969, pp. 582-586.

DORION, GUY, "Le Role De L Evaluateur," *Appraisal Institute Magazine,* Appraisal Institute of Canada, Winnipeg, June 1, 1973.

DRURY, EUELYN, AND GOULD, R. H., *Builders and Decorators Reference Book,* Hollywood-By-The-Sea, Transatlantic Arts, Florida, 1959.

DUBOIS, AYERS J., "Some Current Trends In Appraisal Thinking," *National Real Estate Journal,* August, 1939, pp. 34-37.

DUDLEY, JAMES E., "The Acceptance of Improved Design," *The Residential Appraiser,* September, 1959, pp. 3-6.

DUNN, DOMINICK R., "Appraising In 1930," *The Real Estate Appraiser,* pp. 20.

DUNN, DOMINICK R., "Some Thoughts on Licensing Appraisers," *The Real Estate Appraiser,* February, 1964, pp. 2..

DUNN, DOMINICK R., "Status of the Torrens Land Registration," *The Appraisal Journal,* April, 1950, pp. 227-230.

EASTWOOD H. W., "Changes In Some Statutory Land Valuation Requirements," *The Valuer,* The Commonwealth Institute of Valuers, Sydney Australia, October 1, 1973, pp. 607-615.

EDMAN, J. J., "Admissibility of Drawings and Maps. Appraisal Docket," *The Appraisal Journal,* April, 1960, pp. 265-266.

EDMAN, J. J., "Lack of Local Experience Not Always Disqualifies. Appraisal Docket," *The Appraisal Journal,* July, 1957, pp. 446-447.

ELLIS, J. H., "Origin of the A.I.C.," *Appraisal Institute Magazine,* Appraisal Institute of Canada, Winnipeg, June 1, 1972.

FALLON, C., "Put Value Back In Design," *Purchasing,* February 19, 1970, pp. 61-62.

FEDERAL RESERVE BANK OF NEW YORK, "A Year of Expansion," *The Appraisal Journal,* January, 1956, pp. 87-94.

FEDERAL RESERVE BANK OF ST. LOUIS, "Recent Employment Trends," *The Appraisal Journal,* January, 1965, pp. 120-125.

FERRERO, PAUL E., "Outlook In Appraisals for the Government," *Technical Valuation,* 1900, pp. 23.

FISCHER, R. M., "The Future of Prices," *The Appraisal Journal,* January, 1944, pp. 66-72.

FROST, BENNETT H., "Destroyers of Value," *The Real Estate Appraiser,* June, 1963, pp. 29-31.

FULLER, R. S., "Competition Rises Again," *The Review,* February, 1949, pp. 3-5.

FULLERTON, D. H., "National Capital Commission Land Ownership," *Appraisal Institute Magazine,* Appraisal Institute of Canada, Winnipeg.

FURBAY, JOHN H., "Spotlight on Our Changing World," *The Appraisal Journal,* October, 1961, pp. 501-506.

GAGE, DANIEL D. JR., PERCY D. BENTLEY, "Architecture In Appraisal Reports," *National Real Estate Journal,* September, 1941, pp. 11-14.

# BIBLIOGRAPHY OF APPRAISAL LITERATURE

GARRETT, THOMAS M., "Professions, Association, and Codes," *The Appraisal Journal*, October, 1965, pp. 555-562.

GEORGE, ALLAN C., "The Economic Pendulum Swings," *The Appraisal Journal*, July, 1944, pp. 253-257.

GIBSON, BRUCE G., "The Professional Appraiser and Public Relations," *American Society of Appraisers*, 1960, pp. 391-398.

GONZALES, C. S., "The Future of Professional Appraising In Spanish Speaking Countries," Corporate Press Inc.

GOSSELIN, JACQUES, "L Avenir Des Evaluateurs Et De La Profession De L Evaluateurs," *Appraisal Institute Magazine*, June, 1962, pp. 18-21.

GREAT BRITAIN MINISTRY OF HOUSING AND LOCAL GOVERN, *Distribution of Rateable Values Between Different Classes of Property In England and Values*, H. M. Stationery Offices, London, 1956.

GREBLER, LEO, "The Role of the University In Real Estate Research," *The Appraisal Journal*, July, 1959, pp. 353-358.

GROVES, ASA B., "The V. A. -Past and Future," *The Review*, November, 1951, pp. 17-20.

GUMP, RICHARD, *Good Taste Costs No More*, Doubleday and Company.

HAGOOD, WAYNE D., "Making Appraisals for the Layman," *The Residential Appraiser*, December, 1961, pp. 17, 22.

HAIG, GRAEME T., "Role of the Appraiser In Arbitration," *Appraisal Institute Magazine*, Appraisal Institute of Canada, Winnipeg.

HAIGHT, JAMES R., "Money---The Measuring Stick of Values," *The Appraisal Journal*, October, 1942, pp. 340-346.

HALL, FRANK D., "Appraisal Problems In War Times," *Review of Society of Residential Appraisers*, May, 1941, pp. 3-5, 12.

HALL, FRANK D., "Appraising the Future," *National Real Estate Journal*, July, 1941, pp. 25-26.

HALL, JOHN H., "The Public Image of Real Estate," *Appraisal Institute Magazine*, Appraisal Institute of Canada, Winnipeg.

HALL, ROBERT W., "Time and the Appraiser," *The Appraisal Journal*, April, 1965, pp. 294-295.

HANSBERGER, R. V., "Big Business In the Big Housing Market of the 70's," *The Real Estate Appraiser*, May, 1970, pp. 43-47.

HANSEN, HENRY H., "Costume and Styles," Hacker Art Books Inc., New York, 1956, pp. 160.

HARGROVE, M. M., "Cities BC--AD," *The Review*, December, 1946, pp. 18-20.

HARRIS, HARWELL H., "Architectural Trends," *The Review*, February, 1954, pp. 7-11.

HART, ALAN F., "New Jersey Revisited Journey to Tomorrow," *Assessment Administration*, IAAO, Chicago, 1960, pp. 91-93.

HARTWIG, O. J., "The Next Decade In Design," *The Review*, March, 1953, pp. 3-7.

HARVEY, ROBERT O., "Political Economic Forecast," *The Review*, January, 1953, pp. 3-7.

HEINEKE, PAUL H., "Appraisers on Trial," *The Review*, July, 1951, pp. 3-7.

HEWITT, JOHN A., "What Do You Think About Appraisers and Appraising?Appraising," *The Appraiser*, October, 1970.

HIGNETTE, H. W., "Changing Patterns In the Appraisal Profession," *Appraisal Institute Magazine*, Canada, 1970.

HINDS, DUDLEY S., RICHARD HEWITT III, STEVEN D. KAPPLIN, "Professionalism In the Practice of Real Est Apprsl," *Appraisal Institute Magazine*, Appraisal Institute of Canada, Winnipeg.

HODGES, M. B. JR., "The Appraiser In Today's Changing Community," *The Appraisal Journal,* January, 1969, pp. 12-14.

HOGUET, ROBERT LOUIS, "What About the Future of Real Estate," *Real Estate Record,* October 26, 1940, pp. 3-4.

HOLDEN, THOMAS S., "For a Sustained Prosperity," *The Appraisal Journal,* October, 1945, pp. 371-378.

HOLDEN, THOMAS S., "The Management Era," *The Appraisal Journal,* October, 1940, pp. 320-324.

HOLDEN, THOMAS S., AND CLYDE SHUTE, "Economy to Expand Under New National Management," *The Appraisal Journal,* April, 1953, pp. 175-180.

HOLT, DARREL M., "An MAI's Report on His Impressions of the Fig Congress," *The Appraiser,* October, 1968.

HOPKINS, CHARLES I., "Future 'GI' Assignments," *The Review,* September, 1948, pp. 17-19.

HOPKINS, CHARLES I., "The Fee Appraiser's Future In the V.A. Program," *The Review,* November, 1952, pp. 3-7.

HOYT, ELIZABETH ELLIS, *Primitive Trade, It's Psychology and Economics,* A. M. Delley, New York, 1968.

HOYT, HOMER, *One-Hundred Years of Land Values In Chicago,* The University of Chicago Press, Chicago Illinois, 1933.

HOYT, HOMER, "War and Real Estate," *The Appraisal Journal,* April, 1942, pp. 115-119.

HURD, RICHARD M., "Forces Creating Cities," *Principles of City Land Values,* Chapters 2-4, 1924, pp. 159.

HURD, RICHARD MELANCTHON, "Principles of City Land Values," New York, 1911.

JARRETT, R. J., "The Future Appraisal Profession," *Appraisal Institute Magazine,* Appraisal Institute of Canada, Winnipeg.

JEFFERIES, RODNEY L., "Licensing of Appraisers: Problem or Solution," *Appraisal Institute Magazine,* Appraisal Institute of Canada, Winnipeg, March 1, 1972.

JENKS, ALDRO, "Trends In Value," *The Review,* May, 1950, pp. 14-16.

JONES, DR. OLIVER H., "More Storm Warnings Going Up on Accelerating Inflation Rate," *The Appraiser,* December, 1968.

JUDSON, A. R., "Appraising Under Virgin or Changing Conditions," *Journal of the American Society of Farm Managers and Rural Appraisers,* April, 1950, pp. 51-59.

KAHN, SANDERS A., "The Entrepreneur --The Missing Factor," *The Appraisal Journal,* October, 1963, pp. 472-476.

KAMINS, R. M., "Democratic Centralism, Local Finance In the Sovietunion," *National Tax Journal,* December, 1962, pp. 353-367.

KATONA, GEORGE, EVA MUELLER, "Buyers Attitudes," *The Residential Appraiser,* April, 1958, pp. 8-13.

KEITH, JOHN H., "The Role of Institute of American Appraisers Officers, In the Years Ahead," *Assessment Administration,* Institute of American Appraisers Officers, Chicago, 1963, pp. 10-15.

KELLEY, CHARLES B., "Observed Trends In Design," *The Review,* January, 1954, pp. 3-8.

KELLY, ORR, "A Nation Can Dry Up," *The Appraisal Journal,* January, 1966, pp. 106-115.

KISSACK, A. B., "Unbalanced Markets," *The Appraisal Journal,* April, 1946, pp. 144-147.

KUEHNLE, WALTER R., "An MAI's View of the Pan American Valuation Congress," *The Appraiser,* February, 1968.

L. ALBRECHT, "Priority Decoration In the Home," *Supervisory Management,* August, 1970, pp. 22-24.

LALONDE, JEAN G., "Qu Est-Ce Qu Un Evaluateur," *Appraisal Institute Magazine,* Appraisal Institute of Canada, Winnipeg, September 1, 1973.

LAMARRE, JOHN H., "Probable Future of Fine Arts Appraisal," *Technical Valuation,* A. S. A, Washington, November, 1954, pp. 41.

LANG, RICHARD O., "The Current Economic Scene," *The Review,* July, 1900, pp. 3-5.

LANGUM, JOHN D., "The Business Cycle Is Not Yet Dead," *The Appraisal Journal,* October, 1959, pp. 509-515.

LANGUM, JOHN K., "Fiscal and Credit Aspects of the War Economy," *The Appraisal Journal,* April, 1951, pp. 202-207.

LARSEN, A., "Changes In Land Values In the United States 1925-1962," *Dissertation Abstracts,* Ann Arbor, December, 1966, pp. 1492-A.

LAUER, ROBERT L., MATHEWS, MYRON L., "American Society of Appraisers-A Reality," *Technical Valuation,* November, 1952, pp. 26-29.

LAUNER, E. J., "The Significance of the American Society of Appraisers In the Appraisal Field," *Technical Valuation,* February, 1959, pp. 3-4.

LAWRENCE, THOMAS, "The Economics of Taste," *Review of Market Prices,* New York, pp. 363.

LEE, ADELBERT W., "The Appraiser and Washington, D. C," *Technical Valuation,* February, 1957, pp. 33-34.

LEVI, JULIAN H., "Impact of Law and Code Enforcement on Value," *The Appraisal Journal,* January, 1961, pp. 78-82.

LEVITT, CHARLES H., *Law of the Construction Industry In New York State,* Northeastern Retail Lumbermen's Association, Rochester, 1943.

LEVY, MARK, "1932-1952," *The Appraisal Journal,* October, 1952, pp. 463-464.

LEWIS, JOHN F., "1905-1976, Review of Market Price," *The Economics of Taste,* New York, pp. 369.

LOCKWOOD, A. N., "Appraising Property In Wartime," *The Appraisal Journal,* January, 1945, pp. 37-41.

LOCKYER, ALBERT W., "Appraisers Serve Both Buyers and Sellers Equally Well," *Appraisal Digest,* October, 1952, pp. 23-24.

LODGE, RICHARD L., "Your Crystal Ball--How Sharp a Focus," *The Appraisal Journal,* July, 1961, pp. 333-336.

LOEBER, PAUL C., "The Broker and Appraisals," *National Real Estate Journal,* July 16, 1923, pp. 15-23.

LOVERING, T. G., "Commonwealth Institute of Valuers 2000 A.D.," *Appraisal Institute Magazine,* Appraisal Institute of Canada, Winnipeg.

LUNDY, VICTOR R., "New Influence In Appraising," *The Review,* June, 1951, pp. 3-7.

LUNDY, VICTOR R., "The Key to Economic Progress," *The Review,* June, 1952, pp. 10-15.

MACBRIDE DEXTER D, "Opportunities In Appraising for Minorities," *Valutape Audio-Library Series,* American Society of Appraisers, Washington D.C., February 1, 1974.

MACBRIDE, DEXTER D, "The American Society of Appraisers," *Valutape Audio-Library Series,* American Society of Appraisers, Washington D.C., January 1, 1973.

MACBRIDE, DEXTER D., "The Value of Land," *The Appraisal Journal,* March, 1968, pp. 31-39.

MACLEOD, MORTON P., "Price Trends---Fact and Fallacy," *American Society of Appraisers Valuation Manual,* American Society of Appraisers, 1960, pp. 217.

MACROSSIE, WILLIAM, "Appraising In a War Economy," *The Appraisal Journal,* April, 1943, pp. 107-114.

MAIER, E. F., "The Chartered Surveyors Institution of Great Britain," *The Appraisal Journal,* January, 1935, pp. 173-176.

▲ Appraisal Theory and Methods

MARTINDELL, JACKSON, "Second Stage—Inflation and Survival," *Technical Valuation*, February, 1953, pp. 47-53.

MARTINI, EUGENE R., "Landscape Architecture," *The Review*, November, 1954, pp. 3-5.

MATERN, RUDOLPH, "Architecture from the Grass Roots," *The Appraisal Digest*, July, 1950, pp. 17-18.

MATHERLY, WALTER J., "Changing Economy of the South," *The Appraisal Journal*, October, 1950, pp. 440-444.

MATTHEWS, MYRON L., "American Society of Appraisers Second Mile," *Technical Valuation*, pp. 7.

MATTHEWS, MYRON L., ROBERT L. LAUER, "American Society of Appraisers-A Reality," *Technical Valuation*, American Society of Appraisers, November, 1952, pp. 26.

MCCARTHY, JOSEPH R., "Senator McCarthy's Views on GI Appraising," *The Review*, February, 1948, pp. 9.

MCDONALD, ADRIAN F., "Today's Market," *The Review*, September, 1954, pp. 14-22.

MERRELL, JOHN H., "Appraising on a Staff Basis," *The Residential Appraiser*, May, 1962, pp. 17-18.

MOORES, CHESTER A., "Look Westward," *The Appraisal Journal*, April, 1944, pp. 161-169.

MORGAN, BELDEN, "Charting the Future," *The Review*, March, 1948, pp. 3-8.

MORSEY, NASHAAT, "Effect of Land Tenure on Production In the Near East," *ASA Valuation Manual*, American Society of Appraisers, 1956, pp. 211.

MORSEY, NASHATT, "Appraisal Profession In Egypt," *Technical Valuation*, American Society of Appraisers, Washington, October, 1953, pp. 54.

MYERS, W. I., F. A. PEARSON, AND J. H. LORIE, "Prices Following Wars," *The Appraisal Journal*, October, 1945, pp. 329-338.

NANCE, JAMES J., "Economic Competition, America's New Challenge," *The Appraisal Journal*, July 1962, pp. 341-346.

NEILSON, CHARLESWORTH K., "Inflation and Utility Earnings," *Technical Valuation*, October, 1962, pp. 26-30.

NICOLLS, J. P., "Real Estate Values In Vancouver-A Reminiscence," *Appraisal Institute Magazine*, Appraisal Institute of Canada, Winnipeg.

NIRENSTEIN, NATHAN, "Build for Peace," *The Appraisal Journal*, April, 1948, pp. 222-226.

NORCROSS, CARL, "What Buyers Think of Reston," *Urban Land*, ULI, Washington, D.C., February, 1966.

NUTTER, C. ARMEL, "The Changing Real Estate Picture," *The Residential Appraiser*, August, 1961, pp. 12-13, 20.

NUTTER, C. ARMEL, "The Market Ahead," *The Residential Appraiser*, November, 1959, pp. 23-24.

ODELL, H. AUGUSTUS, "Dollars Out of the Depression," *American Architect*, March, 1933, pp. 52-54.

PALYI, MELCHIOR, "Why Prices Keep Rising," *The Review*, December, 1947, pp. 3-6.

PAQUET, HENRI, "One of the Best Years Yet," *Appraisal Institute Magazine*, Appraisal Institute of Canada, Winnipeg.

PARKER, ELSIE SMITH, "Both Sides of the Color Line," *The Appraisal Journal*, January, 1943, pp. 27-34.

PARKER, ELSIE SMITH, "Both Sides of the Color Line," *The Appraisal Journal*, July, 1943, pp. 231-249.

PIERCE, PHILIP F, MACBRIDE, DEXTER D, "Licensing/Certification of Appraisers: Pro Bono Publico," *Valuetape Audio-Library Series*, American Society of Appraisers, Washington D.C., January 1, 1973.

PIERCE, PHILIP F., "The Role of the Appraiser, the Role of ASA In the Years to Come," *Appraisal and Valuation Manual*, Corporate Press Incorporated, Washington, D. C, January, 1972, pp. 278.

POINTER, RUSSEL A., "The Appraiser's Part In the Future Development of the Real Estate Business," *Technical Valuation*, American Society of Appraisers, Washington, January, 1967, pp. 9.

POLLARA, F., "Trends In U. S. Population," *American Federationist*, June, 1970, pp. 9-13.

POWDRELL J. D., "Land Tenures and Valuation In Papua Guinea," *The Valuer*, The Commonwealth Institute of Valuers, Sydney Austrailia, October 1, 1973, pp. 616-619.

PRICE, OLIN, "Appraising- a Constant Challenge," *Appraisal and Valuation Manual*, 1956, pp. 17-22.

PROUTY, W. L. AND OTHERS, "Union Wage Scales," *Appraisers and Assessors Manual*, 1930, pp. 33.

PUGIN, A. W. N., *The Present State of Ecclesiastical Architecture In England*, Basil Blackwell, Oxford.

QUINTANA, ISADORO, "Amenities In Valuation," *Review of Society of Residential Appraisers*, March, 1940, pp. 8-10.

RAPPORT, RICHARD, "Is Inflation Inevitable," *The Review*, May, 1952, pp. 16-18.

REAL ESTATE ANALYST, THE, "Appraising the Future," *Real Estate Analyst Appraisal Bulletin*, 1959, pp. 101-104.

REIDY, MAURICE F., "The Changing Scene and Appraisal Progress," *The Appraisal Journal*, January, 1937, pp. 23-29.

REITLINGER, G. R., "Economics of Taste, the Rise and Fall of Objects D Art Prices Since 1750," *Apollo*, December, 1963, pp. 528.

REITLINGER, GERALD, *The Economics of Taste*, Holt, Rinehart and Winston, New York, 1961.

REVIEW, THE, "Age of Typical Buyers," *The Review*, June, 1955, pp. 14.

REVIEW, THE, "New Products for Builders," *The Review*, February, 1952, pp. 7-9.

REYNOLDS, ANTHONY, WILLIAM D. WALDRON, "Historical Significance... How Much Is it Worth," *The Appraisal Journal*, July, 1969, pp. 401-410.

RING, ALFRED A., "Impact of Urban Forces Upon Property Value," *The Valuation of Real Estate*, 1970, pp. 68-78.

ROYCE, FRANK A., "New Appraisal Engagements," *Technical Valuation*, June, 1956, pp. 24.

RUGELES, IVAN OLIVER, "La Sociedad De Tasadores De Venezuela," *Boletin*, Sotave, Caracas, Venezuela, pp. 9.

SANDO, LAURENCE, "Institute Will Study Feasibility of Reciprocity with British," *The Appraiser*, October, 1968.

SCHMUTZ, GEORGE L., "Trends In Appraisal Thinking," *California Real Estate Magazine*, July, 1941, pp. 14.

SCHMUTZ, GEORGE L., LORING O. MCCORMICK, "Effect of Credit and Production on Prices," *The Appraisal Journal*, January, 1935, pp. 130-137.

SHERMAN, ARTHUR B., *How to Exploit Amenities and Hidden Values In Selling Real Estate*, Prentice-Hall, Englewood Cliffs, 1959.

SIMONITE, C. R., "A Record Year," *Appraisal Institute Magazine*, Appraisal Institute of Canada, Winnipeg.

SLICHTER, S. H., "The Postwar Outlook for Business and Labor," *The Appraisal Journal*, October, 1944, pp. 334-339.

▲ **Appraisal Theory and Methods**

SLICHTER, SUMNER H., "The Business Outlook-Short Run and Long Run," *The Appraisal Journal,* July, 1947, pp. 310-316.

SMITH, JAMES J., "Benefits and Problems of an Appraisal Office," *The Real Estate Appraiser,*

SMITH, RALPH ELBERTON, *Customs Valuation In the United States A Study In Tarriff Administration,* University of Chicago Press, Chicago, 1948.

SPRINKEL, BERLY W., "The Economic Picture--Now and Tomorrow," *The Appraisal Journal,* October, 1962, pp. 471-480.

ST. GEORGE, JOHN F., "Appraising for Government," *Appraisal and Valuation Manual,* American Society of Appraisers, 1960, pp. 381-390.

STAHL, SHELDON W., "On Economic Forecasting," *The Appraisal Journal,* April, 1968, pp. 291-298.

STEELE, ROBERT A., "The Impact of Civil Disobedience on Property Values," *The Appraisal Journal,* July, 1908, pp. 342-252.

STERN, OSCAR I., "The End of the Restrictive Covenant," *The Appraisal Journal,* October, 1948, pp. 434-442.

STEWARD, CHARLES L., "Some Aspects of Land Appraisals Abroad," *The Appraisal Journal,* April, 1934, pp. 189-193.

STEWARD, J. A., "Land Evaluation," *Papers of a Csiro Symposium Organized In Cooperation with Unesco,* Mcmillan of Australia, Melbourne, August, 1968, pp. 26-31.

STEWART, J. I., "The Appraiser In Today's Economy," *Appraisal Institute Magazine,* Appraisal Institute of Canada, Winnipeg.

STOTHART, JACK, "Trends Affecting Land Value," *Appraisal Institute Magazine,* September, 1961, pp. 16-18.

STRATHON, ERIC C., "International Problems of Valuation," *New Zealand Valuer,* September, 1961, pp. 417-423.

SUQIURA, SEIZO, "Real Estate Practice In Japan," *The Appraisal Journal,* January, 1936, pp. 73-75.

SWEPTSON, DWIGHT C., "Pros and Cons of Statutory Controls," *The Appraiser,* April, 1950, pp. 190-200.

TAPP, JESSE W., "Economic Growth and Property Values In the Sixties," *The Appraisal Journal,* July, 1961, pp. 293-299.

TECHNICAL VALUATION, "Appraisal In Israel," *Technical Valuation,* May, 1954, pp. 56.

THE APPRAISAL JOURNAL, "International Federation of Surveyors," *The Appraisal Journal,* January, 1936, pp. 88-94.

THE APPRAISAL JOURNAL, "Twelfth International Congress of Surveyors," *The Appraisal Journal,* January, 1969, pp. 85-104.

THOMAS, D. L., "Offshore and on Woes Are Piling Up for U. S. Commercial Real Estate," *Barrons,* December 14, 1970, pp. 3.

THOMPSON, LOREN L., "Exchange of Appraisals--Ripple or Wave," *The Real Estate Appraiser,* pp. 2..

THORNCROFT, MICHAEL E. T., "The Future of the Professions," *The Appraisal Journal,* January, 1969, pp. 17-24.

THORSON, IVAN A., "Appraisal Methods In Times of Depression," *Proceedings,* 1933, pp. 310-323.

TRUE, WALLACE W., "Problems of 1949," *The Review,* November, 1948, pp. 3-8.

TURNER, ROBERT C., "Basic Forces for Economic Change," *The Appraisal Journal,* April, 1957, pp. 198-208.

TURNER, ROBERT C., "Economic Vulnerability, the Lesson of 1957-1958," *The Appraisal Journal,* January, 1959, pp. 8-14.

TURNER, ROBERT C., "Is a Major Depression Coming," *The Appraisal Journal,* July, 1959, pp. 293-297.

TURNER, ROBERT C., "The American Economy In 1970," *The Appraisal Journal*, April, 1956, pp. 165-172.

TURNER, ROBERT C., "The Inventory Recession of 1960," *The Appraisal Journal*, July, 1960, pp. 293-298.

WARREN, ISABELLA, "A Private Eye for Taste," *The Appraisal and Valuation Manual*, 1961, pp. 189.

WATKINS, J. OLIVER, "Appraisal Practices In Great Britain," *The Appraisal Journal*, April, 1953, pp. 251-257.

WEIR, T. R., "Factors Affecting Land Values," *The Appraisal Institute Magazine*, December, 1959, pp. 28-30.

WELLS, HENRY W., "A Chartered Surveyor Looks at Soviet Russia-Extracts," *The Appraisal Journal*, July, 1959, pp. 365-374.

WENDT, PAUL F., "Urban Land Value Trends," *The Appraisal Journal*, April, 1958, pp. 254-269.

WENZLICK, ROY, "Realty Analyst Predicts Boom Years Ahead," *California Real Estate Magazine*, December, 1940, pp. 9, 42.

WESTERFIELD, RAY B., "Inflation and Real Estate Are Closely Connected," *Appraisal Digest*, January, 1952, pp. 18-19.

WHITE, JOHN ROBERT, "The Past Five Years," *The Appraisal Journal*, January, 1962, pp. 111-113.

WHITE, JOHN ROBERT, "The Real Estate Market In the Past and Future Decade," *The Appraisal Journal*, April, 1959, pp. 189-197.

WHITNALL, GORDON, "In Times of War Prepare for Peace," *The Appraisal Journal*, October, 1942, pp. 313-322.

WIGHT, WARD, "Appraising---Past, Present and Future," *The Review*, September, 1947, pp. 9-12.

WILSON, P. M., "Canada-Problems and Potential," *Appraisal Institute Magazine*, Appraisal Institute of Canada, Winnipeg.

WINSTEAD, ROBERT W., "Market Value, the Old Standby and Zoning," *The Residential Appraiser*, December, 1960, pp. 19-21.

WOLFF, HELMUT O., "Concepts and Procedures of Arbitration Impact Upon the Community and the Appraisal Profession," *Appraisal and Valuation Manual*, Corporate Press Incorporated, Washington, D. C, January, 1972, pp. 284.

WOOD, CHARLES P., "Postwar Employment Prospects," *The Appraisal Journal*, April, 1944, pp. 154-160.

WOODWARD, DONALD B., "Long Term Trends In Industry," *The Appraisal Journal*, April, 1948, pp. 148-155.

WOODWARD, DONALD B., "Outlook for Interest Rates," *The Appraisal Journal*, July, 1946, pp. 259-263.

WOODWARD, DONALD B., "The Promise of the Future-Can We Muff It?," *The Appraisal Journal*, July, 1945, pp. 225-231.

WRIGHT, HENRY, "Trends In Architecture," *The Appraisal Journal*, October, 1948, pp. 429-433.

WRIGHT, KARL T., "What I See In Present and Future Land Prices," *Journal of the American Society of Farm Managers and Rural Appraisers*, October, 1946, pp. 79-83.

YASHANOFF, B. A., "India--Commentary on the Economic Environment," *Technical Valuation*, August, 1967, pp. 15.

ZEPP, EDWARD G., "Biblical Methods of Valuation," *The Residential Appraiser*, September, 1959, pp. 13-14, 18.

▲ Appraisal Theory and Methods

# 11-19   Economic Analysis

ABBOUD, SAMIR, "Usage Des Statistiques En Valuation," *Appraisal Institute Magazine*, Appraisal Institute of Canada, Winnipeg, September 1, 1973.

ABELMANN, WILLIAM W., "Principles of Land Economics Affecting Net Income," *Real Estate Appraisal Practice*, American Institute of Real Estate Appraisers, Chicago, 1958, pp. 1-5.

ACKROYD, P. H., "Changing Values," *Appraisal Institute Magazine*, Appraisal Institute of Canada, Winnipeg.

ADAMS, JOHN F. JR., "Analysis of Factors Influencing Value," *The Appraisal Journal*, April, 1969, pp. 239-240.

ADAMS, PAUL, "The Case of the Property That Paid Too Well," *The Appraisal Journal*, October, 1949, pp. 441-445.

ALLISON, NEVILLE F., "Classifying and Interpreting Market Data," *The Appraisal Journal*, pp. 56-567.

ALLISON, NEVILLE F., "Converting a VA Form Into a Narrative," *The Review,* March, 1955, pp. 17-24.

ALLISON, NEVILLE F., "Three Approaches to Value," *Proceedings of the Third Institute on Eminent Domain*, Dallas, 1961.

AMERICAN INSTITUTE OF REAL ESTATE APPRAISERS, "Analysis of Expense," *The Appraisal of Real Estate*, American Institute of Real Estate Appraisers, Chicago, 1967, pp. 244.

AMERICAN INSTITUTE OF REAL ESTATE APPRAISERS, "Annuity Capitalization and Valuation," *The Appraisal of Real Estate*, American Institute of Real Estate Appraisers, Chicago, 1967, pp. 296.

ANGULO LOPEZ, ALBERTO, "Principios Basicos De Avaluaciones," *Boletin,* Sotave, Caracas, Venezuela, pp. 5-6.

ANTONMATTEI, JOSE E., "Valoracion De Bienes Raices," *Boletin,* Sotave, Caracas, Venezuela, pp. 11-23.

ARGENTINE REPUBLIC, *Law, Statutes, Etc. Revaluo Inpositivo Ley Y Su Reglamentacion*, Abeledo-Perrot, Buenos Aires, 1960.

ARMSTRONG, ROBERT H., "Capitalization," *The Appraisal Journal,* pp. 134-146.

ARMSTRONG, ROBERT H., "Critical Assumptions In Real Estate Appraising," *The Appraisal Journal*, January, 1947, pp. 66-72.

ARMSTRONG, ROBERT H., "Forecasting the Future," The Appraisal Journal, Vol. Xv.

ARMSTRONG, ROBERT H., "The Continued and Incessant Decline In Real Estate Values," *The Appraisal Journal*, July, 1951, pp. 270-292.

ARMSTRONG, ROBERT H., "Valuation Problems In an Unbalanced Economic World," *The Appraisal Journal*, January, 1941, pp. 41-47.

ART DIGEST, "Prices on the European Art Mart," *Art Digest,* May 15, 1944.

ASSOCIATION OF CERTIFIED AND PUBLIC ACCOUNTANTS, *Accounting for Inflation: a Study of Techniques Under Conditions of Changing Price Levels*, Gee, London, 1952.

ATKINS, DAVID, *The Measurement of Economic Value,* Gelber, Lilienthal, Inc, San Francisco, 1925.

ATKINSON HARRY GRANT, "The Income Approach," *Appraisal Institute Magazine*, January, 1957, pp. 5-10.

ATKINSON HARRY GRANT, "The Income Approach," *The Appraisal Journal*, April, 1954, pp. 207-224.

ATKINSON HARRY GRANT, "The Three Approaches," Real Estate Appraisal, Chicago.

# BIBLIOGRAPHY OF APPRAISAL LITERATURE

ATKINSON, H. G., "The Income Approach (Part 1)," *Appraisal Institute Magazine*, Appraisal Institute of Canada, Winnipeg.

AYRES, LEONARD P., "Two War Periods," *The Review*, June, 1945, pp. 6-8.

BABCOCK, FREDERICK, "Appraisals by Income Analysis," *National Real Estate Journal*, February 21, 1927, pp. 19-21.

BABCOCK, FREDERICK M., *The Appraisal of Real Estate*, Macmillan Company, New York City, 1924.

BABCOCK, FREDERICK M., *The Valuation of Real Estate*, Mcgraw-Hill Book Company, Incorporated, New York City, 1932.

BABCOCK, FREDERICK M., "Appraisal Procedure," *Valuation of Real Estate*, 1932, pp. 187-224.

BABCOCK, FREDERICK M., "Appraisal Procedure and Methods," *Proceedings of the Brokers Division of the National Association of Real Estate Boards*, 1924, pp. 48-56.

BABCOCK, FREDERICK M., "Common Errors In Appraisal Methods an Analysis," *National Real Estate Journal*, November 24, 1930, pp. 17-20.

BABCOCK, FREDERICK M., "Curso Avanzado Lecciones III, IV, V y Vi," *Boletin*, Sotave, Caracas, Venezuela, pp. 43-48.

BABCOCK, FREDERICK M., "Curso Avanzado Xiv, Xi, Xvi, Xvii, Xviii, Xix, Xx," *Boletin*, Sotave, Caracas, Venezuela, pp. 31-39.

BABCOCK, FREDERICK M., "Curso Avanzado: Lecciones X, Xi, Xii y Xiii," *Boletin*, Sotave, Caracas, Venezuela, pp. 31-37.

BABCOCK, FREDERICK M., "Depreciation Obsolescence and Building Life," *Valuation of Real Estate*, 1932, pp. 401-426.

BABCOCK, FREDERICK M., "Depth Coefficients," *Appraisal of Real Estate*, 1924, pp. 340-357.

BABCOCK, FREDERICK M., "Influence of Social and Racial Factors on Value," *Valuation of Real Estate*, 1932, pp. 86-92.

BABCOCK, FREDERICK M., "On the Annuity System," *Appraisal Journal*, October, 1936, pp. 437.

BABCOCK, FREDRICK M., "Curso Avanzado Lecciones Vii, Viii y Ix," *Boletin*, Sotave, Caracas, Venezuela, pp. 43-52.

BABCOCK, HENRY A., "Appraising Income Property," *The National Real Estate Journal*, March 7, 1927, pp. 33-40.

BABY, RENE, "The Inversion Phenomenon," *Appraisal Institute Magazine*, 1970.

BAKER, JAMERS S., "Using Computers In County Government," *County Officer*, May, 1964, pp. 219-226.

BAKER, LLOYD, "The Market As a Yardstick," *The Review*, June, 1950, pp. 18-19.

BALDERSTON, C. CANBY, "Real Estate's Stake In Sound Dollars," *The Residential Appraiser*, March, 1958, pp. 15-18.

BALDWIN, HARRY, "Appraisals," *National Association of Cost Accountants*, 1928, pp. 180-189.

BALLARD, J. W., "Accounting Recognition of Fact That Land Does Depreciate," *American Accountant*, March, 1931, pp. 74-75.

BALLARD, W. H., "Expense As a Factor In Appraising," *National Association of Real Estate Boards*, 1929, pp. 81-84.

BARISH, NORMAN N., "Determinations of Minimum Cost and Maximum Profit," *Economic Analysis for Engineer Managerial Decision Making*, New York City, 1962, pp. 063-307.

BEMAN, ARTHUR K., "Hazards of Data Interpretation," *The Appraisal Journal*, July, 1944, pp. 237-244, 757-764.

BEMAN, ARTHUR K., "The Amortization Provision," *The Appraisal Journal*, April, 1942, pp. 160-165.

BENGE, ROLAND, A., "Appraising Economic Trends," *The Review,* February, 1948, pp. 3-8.

BENNET, HAZEN, "Capitalization of Income," *Appraisal Institute Magazine,* Appraisal Institute of Canada, Winnipeg.

BENNETT, SAUL Z., "Income Approach," *A Student's Report on an Apartment House,* American Institute of Real Estate Appraisers, Chicago, 1966, pp. 31.

BENTLEY, HOWARD H., "The CAP Appraisal Form," *The Residential Appraiser,* September, 1958, pp. 3-6.

BERNARD, ALFRED D., "Improved Properties," *Principles and Problems of Real Estate Valuation,* Baltimore, 1913.

BILLINGS, VIOLA C., "Special Notes for the Lender," *The Review,* August, 1950, pp. 23-24.

BLOCK, ALEXANDER, "Currency Inflation In Germany," *The Appraisal Journal,* January, 1936, pp. 62-66.

BLOOD, J., "Chicago Stores Cram Maxi Profit Into Mini Appliances," *Merchandising Week,* Chicago Stores Cram Maxi Profit Into Mini Appliance, Merchandising Week.

BODFISH, MORTON, "Narrowing Margins," *The Review,* May, 1955, pp. 16-24.

BODFISH, MORTON, THEOBALD, A. D, "Appraisal of Income Property," *Real Estate Fundamentals,* 1941, pp. 10-11.

BODFISH, MORTON, THEOBALD, A. D, "Computing Land Value by the Income Approach," *Real Estate Fundamentals,* 1941, pp. 17-18.

BOECKH, EVERARD HEREFORD, "Depreciation---A Reserve for Rehabilitation," *National Real Estate Journal,* October, 1934, pp. 44.

BOECKH, EVERARD HEREFORD, "Realty, Income Analysis," *Boeckh's Manual of Appraisals,* pp. 324.

BOECKH, EVERARD HEREFORD, "Valuation Based on Income," *Manual of Appraisals,* pp. 322.

BOECKH, EVERARD HEREFORD, "Valuation Based on Income, Valuation by Comparison," *Manual of Appraisals,* 1937, pp. 322-336.

BOND, F. A., "On Landscaping," *The Appraisal Journal,* January, 1936, pp. 78-79.

BOWES, WATSON A., "Today's Artificial Economics," *The Review,* October, 1951, pp. 7-12.

BRAY, JOHN W., "Capitalization Rate," *A. S. A. Valuation Manual,* American Society of Appraisers, Washington, D. C, 1964, pp. 31.

BRIGHAM, EUGENE F., MCALLISTER, DONALD M, "Applying Econometric Models," *The Appraisal Journal,* October, 1968, pp. 546-548.

BURGESS, GEORGE V. T., "A Case Study of Inflation," *American Society of Appraisers Manual,* 1960, pp. 25.

BURKEY, MACK G., "Gross Multipliers," *The Review,* June, 1955.

BURNELL, W. V., "The Three Approaches to Property Value," *Appraisal and Valuation Manual,* American Society of Appraisers, 1955, pp. 17-20.

BURNELL, WILLIAM U., "Property Value, Three Approaches," *Technical Valuation,* February, 1955, pp. 17.

BURNS, E. J., "Gross-Income Multipliers," *Appraisal Institute Magazine,* Appraisal Institute of Canada, Winnipeg, March 1, 1972.

BURNS, WARREN W., "Salvage by Foreclosure," *The Review,* July, 1948, pp. 12-15.

BURROUGHS, ROY J., "The Safe-Risk Rate Formula," *The Appraisal Journal,* October, 1934, pp. 51-51.

CAMPBELL, S. J., "The Land Residual Technique," *The Appraisal Institute Magazine,* January, 1957, pp. 11-12.

CANTWELL, ROBERT C. III, "Graphic Aids to Capitalization," *The Appraisal Journal*, July, 1960, pp. 325-331.

CARDOZA, LEONARD R., A. ORMSBY DONOUGH, JR., AND WALTER N. GABRIEL, "Depreciation Factors," *The Review*, February, 1950, pp. 3-6.

CARNEY, JOHN J., "The Development and Use of Gross Income Multipliers," *The Appraisal Journal*, April 1963, pp. 221-227.

CASTENHOLZ, WILLIAM B., *Solution to the Appreciation Problem*, Lasalle Extension University, Chicago, 1931.

CHANDIAS, MARIO E., "El Problema De Las Mejoras," *Boletin*, Sotave, Caracas, Venezuela, pp. 5-16.

CHANDIAS, MARIO E., "Un Criterio De Depreciacion," *Boletin*, Sotave, Caracas, Venezuela, pp. 5-8.

CHATTERS, CARL H., IRVING TENNER, *Municipal and Government Accounting*, Prentice-Hall, Englwd Cliffs, N. J., 1960.

CHERNEY, RICHARD A., "The Problem of Depreciation," *The Appraisal Journal*, January, 1964, pp. 87-90.

CHILD, JOHN FRANCIS, JR., "A More Direct Approach to Estimating Future Benefits," *The Appraisal Journal*, November, 1951, pp. 443-450.

CHURCH, BYRON, "How Many Approaches," *The Real Estate Appraiser*, pp. 26.

CHURCH, EUGENE B., "The Economic Elements of Buildings," *Real Estate Record and Builder's Guide*, February 27, 1932, pp. 9-10.

CLARK, C. D., "Economic Appraisal of Depreciation Policy," *Journal Of Business*, January, 1956, pp. 28-40.

COES, HAROLD V., "Appraisals and Property Accounting," *National Association of Cost Accountants Bulletin*, May 1, 1932, pp. 1168-1174.

COLLINS, G. ROWLAND, "The Form and Substance of a Dynamic Economy," *The Appraisal Journal*, April, 1951, pp. 165-171.

CONAN, ROBERT J., "The Fallacy of Future Economic Life," *The Appraisal Digest*, April, 1950, pp. 15.

CONSIDINE, CHARLES RAY, "Paper Prices," *The Review*, September, 1956, pp. 3-4.

COOPER, J. M., "Percentage Depletion; Abstract," *Valuation Manual*, June, 1956.

COPPOCK, D. J., "The Alleged Case Against Devaluation," *The Manchester School*, University of Manchester, September, 1965.

COX, WARREN E., "The Intrinsic Value of Art," *The A. S. A. Valuation Manual*, American Society of Appraisers, 1956, pp. 179.

COYLE, JOSEPH A., L. W. ELLWOOD, Capitalization," *Technical Valuation*, Feb., 1965, pp. 21-25.

CRAIG, R. H., "Real Estate In Halifax-Dartmouth," *Appraisal Institute Magazine*, Appraisal Institute of Canada, Winnipeg.

CRAIGEN, GEORGE J., *Practical Methods for Appraising Lands, Buildings, and Improvements*, New York, 1911.

CRAMER, FLOYD, "Does the Price Freeze Affect Values," *The Review*, February, 1951, pp. 5-6.

CROSBY, HARRY L., "Real and Personal Property Accounting and Valuation," *Technical Valuation*, February, 1963, pp. 19-21.

CUMMINS, C. R., "Basic Principles Appraisal Process," *Appraisal Institute Magazine*, Appraisal Institute of Canada, Winnipeg.

CURRY, CHARLES F., "Capitalization Rates," *The Appraisal Journal*, July, 1939, pp. 240-244.

DANGE, M N, "Valuation of Immovable Properties," *Sneh Babrekar Marg*, Dadar Bombay India, January 1, 1974.

▲ Appraisal Theory and Methods

DARBY, CLEMENT H., "Alternative Techniques of Appraising Values In an Inflationary Economy," *Appraisal and Valuation Manual,* American Society of Appraisers, 1962, pp. 213-217.

DARM, ADAM EUGENE, *Graduate Appraisal of the Industrial Technology Program at California State College,* University of California, 1971.

DASSO, JEROME, "Economic Base Analysis for the Appraiser," *The Appraisal Journal,* 1969, pp. 374-335.

DAVIS, W. D., "L'Analyse Du Revenu De La Mise De Fonds," *Appraisal Institute Magazine,* Appraisal Institute of Canada, Winnipeg.

DAVIS, WILLIAM D., *The Earnings Approach,* American Association of State Highway Officials, Washington, D. C, 1962, pp. 347-360.

DEMARA, CYRIL R., "On Forecasting Income," *The Appraisal Journal,* July, 1933, pp. 362.

DENAPOLI, CHARLES, "Sales Prices Are Appraisal Facts," *The Review,* July, 1945, pp. 15-16.

DENIS, J. W., "Capitalization Rates and Trends," *The Appraisal Journal,* July, 1941, pp. 276-280.

DENTON JOHN H., "Depreciation Studies," *Preliminary Report of the Bureau of Internal Revenue,* Government Printing Office, Washington, D. C, 1931.

DENTON, JOHN H., "Depreciation," *The Appraisal Journal,* October, 1935, pp. 405-416.

DENTON, JOHN H., "Depreciation on Modern Buildings," *The Appraisal Journal,* July, 1961, pp. 406-407.

DERBES, MAX J., "Accrued Depreciation-Classical Method," *The Real Estate Appraiser,* pp. 2..

DERBES, MAX J. JR., "Accrued Depreciation-Practical Consideration," *The Real Estate Appraiser,* April, 1906, pp. 21-26.

DERBY, LOUIS F., "Analysis of Some of the Factors Involved In Economic Valuation of Income Property," *Technicalities,* October, 1948, pp. 17-21.

DEVELOPMENT VALUE, "Town and Country," *Development Value,* April, 1971, pp. 176.

DIERKER, GERALD J., "Accounting for Depreciation," *ASA Valuation Manual,* American Society of Appraisers, Washington, D. C., 1955, pp. 87.

DIERKER, GERALD J., "Accounting for Depreciation," *Technical Valuation,* October, 1950, pp. 18-21.

DIETZ, P. O., G. P. WILLIAMS, "Influence of Pension Fund Asset Valuations on Rate of Return," *Financial Executive,* May, 1970, pp. 32-35.

DILMORE, G., "Monetizing the Entrepreneurial Factor," *Appraisal Institute Magazine,* Appraisal Institute of Canada, Winnipeg.

DILMORE, G., "The Estimate of Accrued Depreciation," *Appraisal Institute Magazine,* Appraisal Institute of Canada, Winnipeg.

DILMORE, GENE, "Multiple Regression Analysis," *Appraisal Institute Magazine,* Appraisal Institute of Canada, Winnipeg, June 1, 1971.

DILMORE, GENE, "New Direction In the Income Approach," *The Real Estate Appraiser,* May 1966, pp. 32-38.

DOLMAN, JOHN P., "Composition of the Professional Appraisal Report," *The Appraisal Journal,* October, 1957, pp. 533-543.

DORAU, HERBERT B., "Capitalization Rate Mirage or Wil-O-The-Wisp," *The Appraisal Journal,* January, 1961, pp. 19-29.

DOWNIE, LEONARD, "Choosing the Capitalization Rate," *Review of Society of Residential Appraisers,* May, 1939, pp. 3-7.

DUBOIS, AYERS J., "Depreciation--Past and Anticipated," *The Appraisal Journal,* January, 1936, pp. 35-51.

## BIBLIOGRAPHY OF APPRAISAL LITERATURE

DUBOIS, AYERS J., "The Capitalization Process," *The Appraisal Journal,* January, 1935, pp. 109-117.

DUNN, CECIL L., "The Influence of Income Payments Upon the Level Of Real Estate Prices," *The Appraisal Journal,* January, 1948, pp. 15-18.

DUNN, DOMINICK R., "Contradictions In Economic Obsolescence," *The Residential Appraiser,* September, 1957, pp. 3-4.

EDMAN, J. J., "Capitalization of Income As the Standard of Value. Appraisal Docket," *The Appraisal Journal,* July, 1961, pp. 415.

EDMAN, J. J., "Capitalization of Income Inappropriate for Vacant Land. Appraisal Docket." *The Appraisal Journal,* July, 1961, pp. 415.

EGERTON, J. W., "A New Outlook on Capitalization Rates," *Appraisal Institute Magazine,* Appraisal Institute of Canada, Winnipeg.

ELLWOOD, L. W., "Estimacion Capital Propio: Enfoque De Valor," *Boletin,* Sotave, Caracas, Venezuela, pp. 9-11.

ELLWOOD, LEON W., "Capitalization of Income Isn't Enough," *Appraisal Digest,* 1901, pp. 19-21.

ELLWOOD, LEON W., "The Amount to Be Capitalized," *The Appraisal Journal,* April, 1948, pp. 178-188.

ELY, O., "Accelerated Depreciation," *Public Utilities Fortnightly, American Society of Appraisers Valuation Manual,* May 10, 1956, pp. 680-683.

ELY, O., "Accelerated Depreciation and Share Earnings," *Public Utilities Fortnightly, American Society of Appraisers Valuation Manual,* December 20, 1956, pp. 992-995.

FARRELL, PAUL B. JR., "Computer-Aided Financial Risk Simulation," *The Appraisal Journal,* January, 1969, pp. 58-73.

FEATHERSTON, F. B., "Correlation and Final Value Estimate," *The Real Estate Appraisers,* pp. 40.

FEDERAL RESERVE BANK OF DALLAS, "Economic Recovery," *The Appraisal Journal,* October, 1961, pp. 517-524.

FEDERAL RESERVE BANK OF SAN FRANCISCO, "Seward's Folly-A Cold Look," *The Appraisal Journal,* July, 1959, pp. 394-405.

FEDERAL RESERVE BANK OF ST. LOUIS, "Theory of the Determination of the Economic Activity Level," *The Appraisal Journal,* January, 1968, pp. 123-125.

FEDERAL RESERVE BANK OF ST. LOUIS, "Trends In Government Expenditures," *The Appraisal Journal,* January, 1961, pp. 115-119.

FIELD, RALPH V., "How to Treat Depreciation," *The Appraisal Journal,* July, 1935, pp. 369-371.

FRANKEL, EDWARD T., "Depreciation by Straight Lines and Curves," *Technicalities and Technical Valuation,* February, 1952, pp. 14-15.

FREE, ROBERT L., "The Market Data Approach Applied to Income Properties," *The Appraisal Journal,* pp. 504-509.

FUHRER, MAX, "Our Old Friend Hoskold," *The Appraisal Journal,* January, 1944, pp. 50-51.

GADE, RICHARD B., *Valuation by Capitalization of Earnings,* University of Kentucky, Lexington, 1939.

GALIK, ALBERT R., "Derivation of Capitalization Rates," *Assessment Administration,* IAAO, Chicago, 1963, pp. 74-79.

GAMMON, GEORGE W., "Capital Recovery with Changing Price Levels," *Valuation ASA,* September, 1968, pp. 25.

GARRISON, BURL L., "Capitalization-The Interest Rate," *Valuation,* A. S. A, Washington, D. C, February, 1968, pp. 70.

GEORGE, ALLAN C., "The Economic Pendulum Swings," *The Appraisal Journal,* July, 1944, pp. 253-257.

▲ **Appraisal Theory and Methods**

GIBBONS, JAMES E., "Capitalization Rates and the Money Market," *Appraisal Digest,* October, 1961, pp. 22-24.

GIBBONS, JAMES E., "Income and Capitalization," *The Appraisal Journal,* July, 1962, pp. 347-352.

GIBBONS, JAMES E., "Income Forecast," *The Appraisal Journal,* October, 1960, pp. 505-509.

GODIN, C. R., "Income Approach Applied to Mass Appraisals," *American Society of Appraisers,* 1960, pp. 161-168.

GOLDEN, G. A., "The Reasoning Behind Capitalization of Income," *The Review,* May, 1948, pp. 3-8.

GOLDFARB, MORRIS, "On Entrepreneur's Increment," *The Appraisal Journal,* January, 1936, pp. 82-84.

GOLDFARB, MORRIS, "On the Residual Process In Max Tieger's Appraisal," *The Appraisal Journal,* April, 1933, pp. 250-251.

GOLDSTONE, BRACTON, "On the Capitalization Rate Use In Max Tieger's Appraisal," *The Appraisal Journal,* April, 1933, pp. 242-243.

GRAASKAMP, JAMES E., "A Practical Computer Service for the Income Approach," *The Appraisal Journal,* January, 1969, pp. 50-57.

GROGAN, JAMES J., "Depreciation," *The Appraisal Journal,* October, 1934, pp. 42-45.

GROVES, HAROLD M., *Financing Government,* Henry Holt and Company, New York, 1964, pp. 618.

GUTHMAN, H. G., "Actuarial Versus Sinking Fund Type Formula for Valuation," *Accounting Review,* September, 1930, pp. 226-230.

GUTHMANM, H. G., *Financial Arrangements of the Chicago Fraction Plan,* Harvard Business Review, July, 1931.

HALL, FRANK D., "On the Prophetic Analysis of Future Benefits In Max Tieger's Appraisal," *The Appraisal Journal,* April, 1933, pp. 247-248.

HALL, JOSEPH B., "Why Appraisals Should Be Based on Income," *National Real Estate Journal,* February 3, 1930, pp. 47.

HANAO, YOCHIO, "Operating Statement - Income and Expenses," *The Real Estate Appraiser,* July, 1966, pp. 2-14.

HANSEN, VIGGO, "The Capitalization Approach," *Appraisal Digest,* October, 1954, pp. 17-18.

HANSON, PETER, "Valuation of Income Property," *Annals of Real Estate Practice,* National Association of Real Estate Boards, 1929, pp. 76-80.

HARVEY, ROBERT O., "Political Economic Forecast," *The Review,* January, 1953, pp. 3-7.

HAYES, DOUGLAS A., "Inventory and Depreciation Policies-The Quantitative Appraisal," *Appraisal and Management of Securities,* pp. 207.

HAYNSWORTH, CHARLES G., "Effect of Public Ownership on Capitalization Rates," *Appraisal Digest,* 1961, pp. 7-9.

HENSON, C. B., "Progress In Depreciation Thinking," *Technical Valuation,* ASA, Washington, October, 1953, pp. 41.

HIGGINS WARREN J, "Demolition:Capitalize or Write-Off," *The Real Estate Appraiser,* The Society of Real Estate Appraisers, Chicago Illinois, January 1, 1974, pp. 40-49.

HOFFMAN, ARNOLD J., "Depreciation Pitfalls for New Real Estate Owners," *Taxes,* May, 1962, pp. 399-407.

HOLBROOK, JEFFREY, "The Thinking Man's Capitalization Rate," *The Real Estate Appraiser,* October, 1963, pp. 2-8.

HOLLEBAUGH, CLIFFORD W., "This Thing Called Depreciation," *The Residential Appraiser,* January, 1962, pp. 9-13.

HOLZHAUER, JOHN A., "Capitalization and the Income Premise," *The Real Estate Appraiser,* December, 1964, pp. 12-28.

HONAD, YOSHIO, "Operating Statement - Income and Expenses," *Real Estate Appraiser*, SREA, Chicago, July, 1966, pp. 2.

HORNE, DONALD, "Allowance for Depreciation," *The Appraisal Journal*, July, 1941, pp. 248-252.

HORTON, E.B. JR., "How to Use Income and Expense Estimates," *The Appraisal Journal*, July, 1959, pp. 341-348.

HOSSACK, A. B., "Development of a Sound Depreciation Policy," *Bulletin, No. 924*, American Appraisal Company, 1941, pp. 11.

HUBIN, VINCENT J., "Some Further Remarks on the Nature, Meaning and Use of the Cap Tables," *The Appraisal Journal*, October, 1965, pp. 517-530.

HYDER, K. LEE, "Accrued Depreciation," *The Appraisal Journal*, October, 1936, pp. 353-367.

HYDER, K. LEE, HENRY A. BABCOCK, "Fractional and Summation Appraisals," *The Appraisal Journal*, October, 1932, pp. 7-16.

JACKSON, FRAND W., "The Economics of Obsolescence and Inutility," *The Appraisal Journal*, January, 1938, pp. 22-29.

JARCHOW, ALFRED, WALDSMAR WEICHBROTT, "Carpeting and Permanent Floors, Effect on Mortgage and Risk," *The Real Estate Appraiser*, September, 1968, pp. 40-47.

JELLIS, WILLIAM, "Income Approach-Back Door to Market Value," *Appraisal Institute Magazine*, Appraisal Institute of Canada, Winnipeg.

JOACHIM, HARRY J., "For Good Measure, the Appraisers Tools," *The Real Estate Appraiser*, SREA, Chicago, October, 1964, pp. 22.

JOHNSTON, DOUGLAS, "Gold Movements and Interest Rates - One Individual's Views," *The Appraiser*, February, 1968.

JONES, J. H., "Obsolescence," *Accountant*, September 27, 1930, pp. 427-429.

KAFFENBERGER, KARL G. JR., "Market Data In the Appraisal of Income Property," *The Appraisal Journal*, January, 1960, pp. 57-62.

KAZDIN, S. EDWIN, "How to Use Income Data," *The Appraisal Journal*, July, 1957, pp. 409-416.

KAZDIN, S. EDWIN, "On Depreciation," *The Appraisal Journal*, April, 1936.

KEEFER, E. D., "Estimating Depreciation," *The Review*, July, 1947, pp. 15-19.

KINNARD JR, W. N., "The Ellwood Analysis In Valuation," *Appraisal Institute Magazine*, Appraisal Institute of Canada, Winnipeg.

KINNARD, WILLIAM N. JR., "Income Property Valuation," *Society of Real Estate Appraisers*, Chicago, Illinois.

KLAASEN, R. L., "Capitalization Rate Conflicts," *Appraisal Institute Magazine*, Appraisal Institute of Canada, Winnipeg.

KLAASEN, ROMAIN L., "Feasibility Studies," *Appraisal Institute Magazine*, Appraisal Institute of Canada, Winnipeg.

KLASSEN, ROMAIN L., "Feasibility Studies," *The Appraisal Journal*, December, 1965.

KNISKERN, PHILIP W., "Capitalization Rates, How to Determine the Value of the Income of Various Types of Estates," *National Real Estate Journal*, October 28, 1929, pp. 26-30.

KNOWLES, JEROME, JR., "Estimating Accrued Depreciation," *The Appraisal Journal*, January, 1967, pp. 34-43.

KOSTERS, STUART F., "An Appraisal Engineer's Review of a Much Reviewed Subject Depreciation," *Appraisal and Valuation*, 1956, pp. 111-120.

KURTZ, EDWIN B., *The Science of Valuation and Deprecation*, The Ronald Press, New York, N. Y, 1937, pp. 221.

LASSERS, WILLARD J., "The New Depreciation Regulations," *Valuation Manual*, A. S. A., November, 1956, pp. 741-745.

LAUNER, E. J., "The Significance of the American Society of Appraisers In the Appraisal Field," *Technical Valuation*, February, 1959, pp. 3-4.

LEAKE, PERCY DEWE, *Depreciation and Wasting Assets and Their Treatment In Computing Annual Profit and Loss*, London, 1923.

LEIGHLY, WILLIAM LEWIS, "Principles of Capitalization Methods In Appraising Income Property," *National Real Estate Journal*, June, 1939, pp. 44-46.

LESSINGER, DR. JOCK, "Towards a New Method and Theory of Appraisal," *The Real Estate Appraiser*, pp. 42.

LESSINGER, JACK, "Econometrics and Appraisal," *The Appraisal Journal*, October, 1969, pp. 502-509.

LEWIS, JOHN F., "1905-1976, Review of Market Price," *The Economics of Taste*, New York, pp. 369.

LOUIE, CHARLES F., "Depreciation and the Income Approach," *The Appraisal Journal*, January, 1962, pp. 40-47.

LUNDY, VICTOR R., "Depreciation," *The Review*, June, 1953, pp. 3-4.

LUNDY, VICTOR R., "The Key to Economic Progress," *The Review*, June, 1952, pp. 10-15.

LUNDY, VICTOR R., "The Why of Depreciation," *The Appraisal Journal*, January, 1965, pp. 41-46.

MACLEOD, MORTON P., "Allowing for Depreciation In Building Appraisals," *Appraisal and Valuation Manual*, 1958, pp. 289-300.

MARSTON, ANSON, ROBLEY WINFREY, J. C. GEMPSTEAD, "Engineering Valuation & Depreciation," Mcgraw-Hill, New York, 1953.

MARSTON, ANSON, THOMAS R. AGG, *Depreciation Accountancy*, M, McGraw-Hill.

MARTENSON, W. J., "No Appreciation for Appreciation," *Appraisal Institute Magazine*, Appraisal Institute of Canada, Winnipeg.

MAY, ARTHUR A, *The Estimate of Depreciation*, Valuation of Residential Real Estate, M.

MAY, OLIVER, "A Defense of the Straight-Line Method," *Journal of Accountancy*, October, 1935, pp. 282-284.

MCANLY, H. T., "Recognizing the Deficiency of Depreciation Provisions Based Upon Historical Costs," *N. A. A. Bulletin*, American Society of Appraisers, February, 1958, pp. 5-15.

MCCORMICK, LORING O., SCHMUTZ, GEORGE L, "Depreciation and Obsolescence," *Economic Approach to Valuation Procedure*, 1933, pp. 146-182.

MCCORMICK, LORING, SCHMUTZ, GEORGE, *The Economic Approach to Valuation Procedure*, Los Angeles, 1933.

MCCORMICK, M. J., "Effect of Discounting on Retailing," *Appraisal Institute Magazine*, Appraisal Institute of Canada, Winnipeg.

MCCUTCHEON, W. B., "Developing Capitalization Rates," *The Review*, April, 1949, pp. 6-8.

MCDONALD, A. M., "A Study of Depreciation In Residences," *The Appraisal Journal*, October, 1958, pp. 602-606.

MCDONALD, ADRIAN F., "Treatment of Accrued Depreciation," *Appraisal Digest*, October, 1953, pp. 1-5, 1-4.

MCLAUGHLIN, FRANK J., "Proper Capitalization Rates," *Residential Appraiser*, October, 1960, pp. 2-7.

MCLAUGHLIN, WALTER W., "A Comparison of Landlord and Tenant Earnings on 50-50 Livestock Lease and Crop Share Lease," *Journal of the American Society of Farm Managers and Rural Appraisers*, October, 1947, pp. 86-89.

MCMICHAEL, STANLEY L., "Depreciation," *Appraising Manual*, 1937, pp. 51-70.

MCMICHAEL, STANLEY L., "Mathmatical Treatment of Income," *Appraising Manual*, 1937, pp. 115-122.

MCSWEENEY, THOMAS F., "Depreciation Factors and Special Purpose Properties," *American Association of State Highway Officials,* 1962, pp. 471-494.

MCSWEENEY, THOMAS F., "Proposed Code of Technical Standards Economic Background of Value," *Technical Valuation,* June, 1959, pp. 27-33.

MERCER, GEORGE L., "Proper Selection of Capitalizationrates," *The Real Estate Appraiser,* September, 1964, pp. 13.

MERTZKE, ARTHUR J., "How Capitilization Rates Are Determined," *National Real Estate Journal,* October 13, 1930, pp. 42-44.

MERTZKE, ARTHUR., "Determining Capitalization Rates In Appraising Income Properties," *National Association of Real Estate Boards,* 1930, pp. 111-121.

MILLER, R. D., "Short Cut Method to Calculate Declining Balance Depreciation," *Management Accounting,* July, 1970, pp. 68-70.

MONIESON, DAVID DANNY, *Value Added As a Measure of Economic Contribution by Marketing Institutions,* University Microfilms, Ann Arbor, Mich., 1957.

MONTONNA, DAVID L., "Accrued Depreciation," *Appraisal Institute Magazine,* December, 1957, pp. 5-20.

MONTONNA, DAVID L., "Gross Income and Expenses," *Appraisal Institute Magazine,* July, 1957, pp. 5-9.

MONYEK, R. H., "New Depreciation Rev Raises Ques As to Prior Yrs," *Journal of Taxation,* March, 1971, pp. 182-183.

MORGAN, BELDEN, "The Depreciation Controversy," *The Review,* July, 1952, pp. 12-17.

MOSER, A. W., "Depreciation Based on Unit Cost," *Journal of Accountacy,* July, 1931, pp. 25-39.

NELSON, R. L., "The Changing Composition of Capitalization Rates," *The Real Estate Appraiser,* October, 1964, pp. 15.

NELSON, RICHARD L., "Capitalization Rates," *The Appraisal Journal,* January, 1958, pp. 34-39.

NELSON, ROLAND D., "Discounting Fractional Interests," *The Appraisal Journal,* October, 1969, pp. 522-528.

NELSON, ROLAND D., "Overall Rate-Band of Investment Style," *The Appraisal Journal,* January, 1969, pp. 25-30.

NELSON, W. L., "Amortization and Depreciation Rates," *American Society of Appraisers.*

NESSER, RICHARD S., "Sinking Fund -Validity of Capitalization Method," *Technical Valuation,* February, 1960, pp. 17-22.

NEWLOVE, G. H., "Depreciation," *Journal of Accountancy,* November, 1927, pp. 432-437.

NOLAN, PRESTON M., "Determining Cost and Capitalization Rate," *National Real Estate Journal,* July, 1925, pp. 33-35.

NORTH, LINCOLN W., "What Interest Rate Are You Talking About," *Appraisal Institute Magazine,* Appraisal Institute of Canada, Winnipeg, September 1, 1972.

NORTHUP, GRAHAM T., "Caps Success Story," *The Residential Appraiser,* August, 1959, pp. 21-24.

NORTHUP, GRAHAM T., "Test-Flying Cap," *The Residential Appraiser,* March, 1958, pp. 19-20.

NUETZMAN, R. A., "Cost, Income, Market," *The Real Estate Appraiser,* pp. 23.

NURNBERG, H., "Present Val Deprec & Income Tax Allocation," *Accounting Review,* October, 1968.

OLIVER, RUSSELL H., "Depreciation Theory," *The Review,* September, 1946, pp. 18-19.

OPELKA, F. GREGORY, "Technology and Depreciation," *The Real Estate Appraiser,* January, 1964, pp. 23-29.

OSTERGREN, C. N., AND L. SZABO, AND G. G. HENTER, "Equal Life Group Method of Depreciation," *Valuation, Engineering Economist,* 1967.

PALYI, MELCHIOR, "Why Prices Keep Rising," *The Review,* December, 1947, pp. 3-6.

PATON, WILLIAM A., "Accrued Depreciation on Seasoned Properties," *Certified Public Accountant,* July, 1927, pp. 206-210.

PATT, HERBERT B., "On Capitalization Rates," *The Appraisal Journal,* April, 1938, pp. 170-171.

PELOUBET, MAURICE E., "Insufficient Depreciation What Can the Appraiser Do About it," *Appraisal and Valuation Manual,* American Soicety of Appraisers, 1959, pp. 227-234.

PELOUBET, MAURICE E., "Practical Method for Applying Current Value Depreciation," *American Society of Appraisers Manual,* January, 1958, pp. 21-25.

PENNY, A. L., "Structure and Development of Capitalization Rates," *Appraisal Institute Magazine,* Appraisal Institute of Canada, Winnipeg.

PENNY, ALFRED L., "The Structure and Development of Capitalization Rates," *Appraisal Institute Magazine,* September, 1958, pp. 17-23.

PERRY, HORACE B., "Depreciation-Public Utilities Properties," *Appraisal and Valuation Manual,* American Society of Appraisers, 1956, pp. 121-136.

PETERSON, CARL H., "The Depreciation Reserve," *Technical Valuation,* February, 1957, pp. 19-26.

POLAK, DR. W. J., "Theories of Depreciation," *Proceedings, International Congress on Accounting, 1929,* New York, 1929, pp. 447-463.

POPE, LONNIE, "Depreciation In the Cost Approach," *The Real Estate Appraiser,* American Institute of Real Estate Appraisal, June, 1964, pp. 2.

PREINREICH, GABRIEL A., *The Theory and General Principles of Depreciation,* The Waverly Press, Inc., Baltimore, Md., 1941.

PROUTY, W. L. AND OTHERS, "Physical Depreciation of Buildings," *Appraisers and Assessors Manual,* 1930, pp. 58-72.

PROUTY, W. L. AND OTHERS, "St. Paul Life and Physical Depreciation of Buildings," *Appraisers and Assessors Manaul,* 1930, pp. 120.

QUIN, GEORGE ROBERT, "On Probable Income," *The Appraisal Journal,* January, 1934, pp. 146-147.

QUIN, GEORGE ROBERT, "Tasa De Capitalizacion," *Boletin,* Sotave, Caracas, Venezuela, pp. 41-45.

RANDALL, WILLIAM J., "Age, Depreciation, Future Life, and Net Condition," *Real Estate Analyst Appraisal Bulletin,* 1962, pp. 25- 2.

RANDALL, WILLIAM J., "Capitalization Rates Are Increasing," *Real Estate Analyst Appraisal Bulletin,* 1951, pp. 323-326.

RANDALL, WILLIAM J., "Selection of Capitalization Rates," *Real Estate Analyst Appraisal Bulletin,* 1952, pp. 105-108.

RANDALL, WILLIAM J., "Two Frequent Errors In Capitalizing an Income Stream," *Real Estate Analyst Appraisal Bulletin,* M, pp. 461-464.

RATCLIFF, DR. RICHARD U., "Net Income Can't Be Split," *The Appraisal Journal,* April, 1950, pp. 168-172.

RATCLIFF, RICHARD U., "Don't Underestimate the Gross Income Multiplier," *The Appraisal Institute Magazine,* 1970.

RAUBER, EARLE L., "The Money Market and Its Effect on Real Estate Values," *The Appraisal Journal, Vol. Xxvi,* July, 1958, pp. 365-370.

RECHT, J. RICHARD, LOEWENSTEIN, LOUIS K, "Variations In Rates of Return," *The Appraisal Journal,* April, 1965, pp. 243-248.

REGISTER, J. ALVIN, "Income As a Factor In Appraising," *National Association of Real Estate Boards*, 1929, pp. 40-47.

RING, A. A., "The Earnings Approach to Value," *Appraisal Institute Magazine*, Appraisal Institute of Canada, Winnipeg.

RING, ALFRED A., "Depreciation Theory and Practice In Valuation," *The Valuation of Real Estate*, 1970, pp. 184.

RING, ALFRED A., "Pitfalls of Capitalization," *The Appraisal Journal*, April, 1948, pp. 131-138.

RING, ALFRED A., "Updating the Earnings Approach to Value," *The Real Estate Appraiser*, April, 1963, pp. 2-9.

ROSS, THURSTON H., "Rate of Capitalization," *The Appraisal Journal*, July, 1937, pp. PP, 211-218.

ROSS, THURSTON H., "Tasa De Capitalizacion," *Boletin*, Sotave, Caracas, Venezuela, pp. 23-29.

ROYAL, PEYTON K., "Market Data, Cost, and Income Analysis," *The Appraisal Journal*, April, 1962, pp. 245-247.

RUGELES, IVAN OLIVER, "La Tasa De Capitalizacion," *Boletin*, Sotave, Caracas, Venezuela, pp. 11-13.

RYAN, JOHN, "Current Depreciation Allowance, an Evaluation and Criticism," *Appraisal and Valuation Manual*, 1958.

SALIERS, EARL A., *Depreciation Principles and Applications*, Ronald Press, New York, 1939, pp. 482.

SALIERS, EARL A., *Depreciation Principles and Applications*, Ronald Press Company, New York, 1922, pp. 1-59.

SARLES, KENNETH E., "Bases for Capitalization Rates," *The Residential Appraiser*, November, 1960, pp. 5-9.

SARLES, KENNETH E., "Flexibility of Depreciation," *The Real Estate Appraiser*, January, 1963, pp. 14-18.

SARLES, KENNETH E., "Practical Application of Capitalization Theory," *The Real Estate Appraiser*, January, 1966, pp. 22-25.

SCAFF, HAROLD H., "Accounting for Economic Depreciation," *Technical Valuation*, October 1953, pp. 7-9.

SCHARFF, M. R., "Supplemental Note on Valuation and Depreciation," *Appraisal and Valuation Manual*, February, 1957, pp. 1-11.

SCHARFF, MAURICE R., "Valuation and Rate Regulation Overseas," *Technical Valuation*, June, 1963, pp. 4-6.

SCHLAUCH, WILLIAM S., T. LANG, *Mathematics of Business and Finance*, Ronald, New York, 1937.

SCHMIDT, FRITZ, "Basis of Depreciation Charges," *Harvard Business Review*, April, 1930, pp. 257-264.

SCHMIDT, WALTER S., "Appraisal Data and the Control of Realty Development," *Proceedings of the General Session and Urban Group Meetings*, 1937, pp. 100-108.

SCHMUTZ, GEORGE L., *Some Problems In Capitalizing Income*, California Real Estate Association, Los Angeles, 1936, pp. 1-16.

SCHMUTZ, GEORGE L., "Analyzing Depreciation," *The Review*, May, 1947, pp. 12-15.

SCHMUTZ, GEORGE L., "Depreciation," *Appraisal Process*, 1941, pp. 1-229.

SCHMUTZ, GEORGE L., "Depreciation and Replacemant Reserves," *California Real Estate Magazine*, October, 1936, pp. 43.

SCHMUTZ, GEORGE L., "Economic Factors," *The Appraisal Journal*, January, 1934, pp. 98-103.

SCHMUTZ, GEORGE L., "The Discount for Hazard In the Capitalization Rate," *The Appraisal Journal*, July, 1953, pp. 336-340.

SCHMUTZ, GEORGE L., LORING O. MCCORMICK, "Capitalization Rate Affected by Quality of Income," *The Appraisal Journal,* April, 1940, pp. 147-152.

SCHMUTZ, GEORGE L., LORING O. MCCORMICK, "Effect of Credit and Production on Prices," *The Appraisal Journal,* January, 1935, pp. 130-137.

SCHULTE, AUGUST B., "Some Observations on Factors Affecting Prices and Some Sound Value Concepts," *The Appraisal Journal,* April, 1984, pp. 201-202.

SCHUMACHER, DAVID T., "Determining Physical Depreciation, Functional and Economic Obsolescence," *Technical Valuation,* October, 1956, pp. 19-24.

SCHUMACHER, RAY J., "Depreciation Studies by the Appraiser," *Technical Valuation,* February, 1961, pp. 35-36.

SHAPIRO, M., "Purchase-Value Index it Takes More and More Money to Move the Market Up," *Barrons,* November 15, 1971.

SHENKEL, WILLIAM M., "Characteristics of Gross Income Multipliers," *The Real Estate Appraiser,* pp. 23.

SHENKEL, WILLIAM M., "The Depreciation Estimate a Reconsideration," *The Real Estate Appraiser,* 1907, pp. 21-33.

SHENKEL, WILLIAM M., ALLAN S. EDISON, "The Analysis of Real Estate Sales and Urban Data The Impact on Resource Allocation," *Review of Regional Studies,* Virginia Polytechnic Institute & State University, April, 1971, pp. 79-92.

SHIPP, ROYAL, "How Much More Room at the Inn. . . for Net Income," *The Real Estate Appraiser,* March, 1969, pp. 15-21.

SHURBERG, MERWIN, "Economic Factors In Property Valuations," *Appraisal and Valuation Manual,* pp. 65.

SILVERHERZ, JOSEPH D., "Computing Depreciation and Appreciation," *Real Estate Record,* Metropolitans and National Editions, October 17, 1936, pp. 11-16.

SILVERMAN, BENJAMIN, "Some Aspects of Depreciation," *Technical Valuation,* October, 1954, pp. 38.

SIMMONDS, H. H., "Design to Avoid Depreciation," *The Review,* January, 1949, pp. 3-5.

SLONIM, M. J., "The Three Approaches Under Fire," *Technical Valuation,* American Society of Appraisers, Washington, 1966.

SMAILS, R. G. H., "Some Aspects of Depreciation," *Accounting Review,* June, 1927, pp. 101-110.

SMITH, DAVID H., "Depreciation (Cost or Replacement Value)," *Technicalities,* October, 1951, pp. 11-13.

SMITH, LARRY, "Economic Factors and Their Analysis," *Valuation,* June, 1954, pp. 19-35.

SMITH, LEONARD C., *Economic Life,* August 1, 1938.

SMITH, LEONARD C., "Has Land a Value," *The Appraisal Journal,* 1939, pp. 354-357.

SPAHR, WALTER E., AND OTHERS, *Economic Principles and Problems,* Farrar and Reinhart, New York.

SPRINKEL, BERLY W., "The Economic Picture--Now and Tomorrow," *The Appraisal Journal,* October, 1962, pp. 471-480.

STAFFORD, L. D., "Depreciation As a Business Expense," *Manufactures News,* August, 1929, pp. 9-10, 65-67.

STANFORD, MELVIN J., "Forecasting Future Land Values," *Appraisal Institute Magazine,* Appraisal Institute of Canada, Winnipeg, September 1, 1973.

STARKE, GEORGE C., "Utilization of Market Data In the Income-Approach," *Right of Way Conference, Selected Paper,* University of Alabama, 1961, pp. 49-51.

STARRETT, PAUL, "How to Estimate Depreciation," *The Appraisal Journal,* January, 1951, pp. 85-88.

STAUB, WALTER A., "Depreciation of Appraised Values," *American Accountant,* January, 1932, pp. 6-10.

STEVENSON, R. A., "A Revaluation of Our Present Economy," *The Appraisal Journal,* July, 1948, pp. 330-335.

STUNARD, EUGENE W., "Capitalization Approach and Financing," *Real Estate Appraiser,* May, 1967, pp. 31-36.

SWEENY, HENRY W., "Stabilized Depreciation," *Accounting Review,* September, 1931, pp. 165-178.

TAYLOR, J. J., "A Statistical Theory of Depreciation'," *Journal American Statistical Association,* December, 1923, pp. 1010-1023.

TAYLOR, JAMES R., "Depreciation Fallacies," *The Review,* April, 1949, pp. 3-4, 8.

TERBORGH, GEORGE, *Realistic Depreciation Policy,* Machinery and Allied Product Institute, Chicago, 1955.

THEOBALD, A. D., "Uncle Sam's Rubber Dollars," *The Review,* January, 1949, pp. 9-11, 17.

THOMPSON, BURTON, "On the Prophetic Analysis of Future Benefits In Max Tieger's Appraisal," *The Appraisal Journal,* April, 1933, pp. 245-247.

THOMPSON, R. E., "Labor-Saving Tables for Computing Depreciation," *National Real Estate Journal,* October 12, 1931, pp. 21-24.

THOMPSON, R. E., "On Entrepeneur's Increment," *The Appraisal Journal,* January, 1936, pp. 82.

THOMPSON, R. E., "This Thing Called Value," *National Real Estate Journal,* December, 1932, pp. 29-32.

THORSON, IVAN A., "On the Capitalization Rate Used In Max Tieger's Appraisal," *The Appraisal Journal,* April, 1933, pp. 244-245.

TRANSOM, G. E. JR., "Current Thoughts on Depreciation," *The Real Estate Appraiser,* July, 1963, pp. 12-18.

TREADWELL, JOHN C., "La Seleccion De La Tasa De Capitalizacion," *Boletin,* Sotave, Caracas, Venezuela, pp. 15-28.

TREASURY DEPARTMENT, *Outline for the Study of Depreciation and Maintenance,* Treasury Department, Washington, 1926, pp. 1-38.

TREDWELL, JOHN C., "The Selection of Capitalization Rates," *The Appraisal Journal,* October, 1938, pp. 343-353.

WADA, S. A., "A Note on Depreciation and Growth," *Bulletin of Universityof Osaka Prefecture,* 1966, pp. 19-22.

WAGNER, J. J., "Standardizing Depreciation and Obsolescence," *National Real Estate Journal,* December 8, 1930.

WAGNER, PERCY E., "On Economic Concepts of Appraising," *The Appraisal Journal,* January, 1967, pp. 125.

WALES, T. J., "Estimation of an Accelerated Depreciation Learning Function," *Journal of the American Statistical Association,* December, 1966, pp. 995-1009.

WEBSTER, S. S. JR., "New Deal In Depreciation," *Certified Public Account,* August, 1934, pp. 463-467.

WEEKES, ROBERT E., "The Capitalization Rate," *The Appraisal Journal,* April, 1954, pp. 203-206.

WENDT, PAUL F., "Depreciation and the Capitalization of Income Method," *The Appraisal Journal,* April, 1963, pp. 185-193.

WENDT, PAUL F., "Ellwood, Inwood, and the Internal Rate of Return," *The Appraisal Journal,* October, 1967, pp. 561-574.

WHITE, JOHN R., "Economic Conditions Affecting Capitalization Rate Selection," *Appraisal Digest,* October, 1956, pp. 1-3.

WHITE, JOHN R., "New Horizons In Capitalization Rate Selection," *Technical Valuation,* June, 1957, pp. 28-32.

WHITE, JOHN R., "The Fallacy of Gross Income Stabilization," *The Appraisal Journal,* July, 1956, pp. 348-350.

WHITE, JOHN ROBERT, "Capitalization Rates and the Current Money Market," *The Appraisal Journal,* July, 1957, pp. 417-420.

WHITE, PHILIP H., "Some Aspects of the Income Approach," *The Residential Appraiser,* July, 1960, pp. 16-23.

WILDMAN, JOHN R., "Appreciation from the Point of View of the Certified Public Accountant," *Accounting Review,* December, 1928, pp. 396-406.

WILSON, GEORGE A., *Depreciation,* Mass Society of Certified Public Accountants, Inc., December 17, 1934, pp. 5-9.

WISCONSIN PUBLIC SERVICE COMMISSION, *Depreciation, a Review of Legal and Accounting Problems,* The Commission, Madison, 1933, pp. 1-96.

WOODWARD, DONALD B., "Outlook for Interest Rates," *The Appraisal Journal,* July, 1946, pp. 259-263.

WORTHINGTON, J. E., "The Theory of Interest," *Appraisal Institute Magazine,* Appraisal Institute of Canada, Winnipeg, March 1, 1973.

YARMON, ELLIOTT N., "Net Leases," *Appraisal Institute Magazine,* Appraisal Institute of Canada, Winnipeg.

## CHAPTER TWO

# Appraisal For Special Purposes
by C.E.O. Walker, ASA.

Born in London, C.E.O. Walker received his formal education in England with a degree in civil engineering. Following service with the Royal Air Force in World War II, he spent six years in Canada and then joined The American Appraisal Company, Milwaukee, in 1951. He is a Vice President of that company and Manager of the Financial Valuation Division — Eastern Region. In addition to membership of The American Society of Appraisers, his professional affiliations include membership of the Financial Analysts Society, National Association of Accountants, and the Canadian Association of Business Valuators.

A Senior Member of the American Society of Appraisers, Mr. Walker is Chairman of the ASA International Education Committee and additionally serves the Society as an International Vice President.

## ▲ Appraisal for Special Purposes

THIS SEGMENT of the Bibliography is unique and of special interest in that the subject matter has relevance to virtually all the various disciplines of the profession. As may be expected there is a wealth of material pertaining to real estate appraisal theory and practice but there are also multitudinous references directed to the appraiser whose primary activity lies in the valuation of personal property, natural resources, public utilities, intangible property and other special areas.

The subject "Appraisals for Special Purposes" in essence pertains to valuations performed for purposes other than the more common "open market" exchanges of property. The complex needs of modern society for example, necessitate appraisals of property for tax assessment purposes and for other tax related objectives such as establishment of a new income tax basis for property acquired under certain prescribed conditions.

The expansion of highway and other transportation facilities, public utility systems and governmental properties, involves expropriation of private property. Determination of just compensation in such action calls for competent and informed appraisal service.

Other special purpose valuation needs include appraisals to establish appropriate fire insurance coverage for real and personal property, feasibility studies related to site selection and property development, and appraisals required in connection with employee transfers. In many such appraisals, a critical valuation consideration will be a reasoned and documented determination of depreciation or loss in value due to physical deterioration, functional obsolescence and other causes. Reference sources pertaining to all these varied fields of appraisal activity are provided in depth in this section of The Bibliography of Appraisal Literature.

These divergent legal, tax and other objectives might at first glance appear to require widely different appraisal procedures and it is indeed true that in each category special considerations are involved. Nevertheless, there are several underlying strata of valuation knowledge and data, fundamental to sound appraisal practice in all of these special areas, which need to be stressed.

In a foreword to "The Principles of Appraisal Practice and Code of Ethics" of the American Society of Appraisers, the comment is made that "Because of the specialized knowledge and abilities required of the appraiser which are not possessed by the layman, there has now come to be established a fiduciary relationship between him and those who rely on his findings." This statement, made in 1968, is becoming increasingly true and therefore *the first fundamental for any appraiser is a clear application of ethics to appraisal practice.* The Appraiser's claim to professionalism is based on education and technical ability but must ultimately rest upon his integrity and objectivity. A detailed treatment of this subject is contained in A.S.A.'s Code of Ethics and the importance accorded to this matter by the Society is indicated by the fact that examination thereon is an obligatory part of the ASA testing/certifying process.

*The second fundamental is a thorough knowledge of general valuation theory and practice.* Depending on the nature of the property appraised (employing the term 'property' in the widest sense), appraising may be considered to encompass some or all of the following classes of operation:

1. Estimation of the cost of producing or replacing physical property, and of the degree of depreciation or loss in value applicable to the property under appraisement.

2. Analysis of the market for similar properties.

3. Forecasting of the monetary earning power of certain classes of property.

4. The valuation or determination of the worth of property.

Those of us who specialize in "Appraisals for Special Purposes" do not necessarily have to possess a high degree of expertise in all of these areas (although there might be fewer problems if this were so!) but we must surely have a complete understanding of the basic procedures.

*The third primary element is for recognition of the need for cooperation and data exchange between practitioners in the various disciplines.* In the appraisal of various classes of property for the purpose of allocation of a purchase price for tax purposes, for example, the real estate appraiser, the personal property appraiser and the financial analyst are not separate entities each going their own way but an inter-related group whose activities and conclusions must be correlated. The value of membership in a multi-disciplinary appraisal society providing the means of exchange of ideas and concepts between the various disciplines is evidenced by these considerations.

Equipped with this basic knowledge, the appraiser involved in special purpose studies is then faced with the problem areas unique to his field and to maintain his expertise must be aware of, and research, the published material relevant to his activities. Each appraiser, and the student as part of the learning process, must consult the references peculiar to his discipline in the Bibliography; the tax expert needs to consult a certain group of authorities, the right of way representative another, the relocation counselor a third, and so on.

Prior to the publication of this Bibliography, there existed no single source whereby the practitioner in valuation could achieve his research objectives. The quantity of material now being published is evidenced by the vast number of references contained in this volume and it has been virtually impossible for an individual to keep pace with, or even be aware of, the available information and data.

This barrier to knowledge has now been overcome through the foresight of the American Society of Appraisers in assembling and categorizing this mass of material in a single reference source.

The appraiser now has a practical means of identifying the entire assemblage of published technical information pertaining to his speciality and to other disciplines in which he has an interest. Despite their wide scope, the references in this Bibliography have been arranged in a logical and easily identifiable format, and no matter what the special concern may be, the particular datum can be found expeditiously.

The publication is a major contribution to the profession and is particularly vital to those engaged in appraisals for special purposes since the complexities involved are such that a high degree of professionalism can only be maintained through continued research and expansion of knowledge.

# Appraisal for Special Purposes

| | | | |
|---|---|---|---|
| 12-11-00 | Taxation | 12-19-00 | Highest and Best Use |
| 12-12-00 | Equalization | 12-20-00 | Expropriation |
| 12-14-00 | Assessments | 12-21-00 | Appraisal for Employee Transfers |
| 12-13-00 | Condemnation | 12-22-00 | Site Selection |
| 12-15-00 | Easements and Eminent Domain | 12-23-00 | Insurance Purposes |
| 12-16-00 | Rights and Rights of Way | 12-24-00 | Obsolescence and Depreciation |
| 12-17-00 | Revaluations | 12-25-00 | Capitalization |
| 12-18-00 | Partial Acquisitions | 12-26-00 | Legal Aspects of Appraisal |

## 12-11 Taxation

AARON, H., "The Differential Price Effects of a Value-Add Tax," *National Tax Journal*, June, 1968.

ABRAMS, CHARLES, "Opportunities In Taxation for Achieving Planning Purposes," *Assessors Newsletter*, I.A.A.O., August, 1966, pp. 115-123.

ADAMS, PAUL, "The Case of the Property That Paid Too Well," *The Appraisal Journal*, October, 1949, pp. 441-445.

ADAMS, THOMAS S., *Valuation of Real Estate by the Wisconsin Tax Commission*, Minnesota Academy of Social Science Publications.

ADELSBERG, HYMAN, "Suburban Shopping Centers," *Technical Valuation*, February, 1954, pp. P25.

AHMEN, M.M. A., "An Economic Evaluation of Farmland for Tax Assessment, Tulsa County, Oklahoma," *Dissertation Abstracts*, September, 1965, pp. 1384.

ALAND, ROBERT HARRIS, "Ad Valorem Property Taxation: Equalization by Injunction," *Alabama Law Review*, April, 1962, pp. 389-402.

ALAND, ROBERT HARRIS, "Ad Valorem Property Taxation: Equalization by Injunction," *Alabama Law Review*, April, 1962, pp. 389-402.

ALLEN, EDWIN G., "Assistance In New Brunswick," *Assessment Administration*, IAAO, Chicago, 1961, pp. 127-130.

AMERICAN INSTITUTE OF REAL ESTATE APPRAISERS, "Case Studies In Apartment House Valuation," *Case Studies In Apartment House Valuaion*, American Instiute of Real Estate Appraisers, Chicago, 1900.

AMERICAN INSTITUTE OF REAL ESTATE APPRAISERS, "Commercial and Industrial Functional Utility and Inutility Valuation," *The Appraisal of Real Estate*, American Institute of Real Estate Appraisers, Chicago, 1967, pp. 148.

AMERICAN MUNICIPAL ASSOCIATION, *Constitutional Provisions for Tax Exemption of Publicly Owned Property In Selected States*, American Municipal Association, Washington, 1959, pp. 5.

AMERICAN SOCIETY OF APPRAISERS, *Appraisal and Valuation Manual*, American Society of Appraisers, Washington, D. C, 1955.

AMERICAN SOCIETY OF APPRAISERS, "A Primer In Tax Assessing," *American Society of Appraisers Valuation Manual*, 1964, pp. 25.

AMERICAN SOCIETY OF APPRAISERS, "Appraisal of Machinery and Equipment," *American Society of Appraisers Valuation Manual*, Washington, D. C, 1969.

AMERICAN SOCIETY OF APPRAISERS, "Depreciation Change Urged by Machinery Dealers National Association Iron Age," *American Society of Appraisers Valuation Manual*, January 16, 1958, pp. 124.

ANDERSON, LYN FOSTER, *The State Property Tax In Texas*, Bureau of Municipal Research, Austin, 1948.

ANDERSON, LYNN FOSTER, *Texas Property Taxes, 1949*, Institute of Public Affairs, Austin, 1950.

ANDREWS, R. B., JEROME J. DASSO, "The Influence of Annexation on Property Tax Burdens," *National Tax Journal*, March, 1961, pp. 88-97.

ANGELL, STEPHEN, "How Should a Municipality Assess Developers Property," *The Appraisal Journal*, October, 1935, pp. 446-450.

## Appraisal for Special Purposes

APPELSON, WALLACE B., "Highlights from 4000 Years of Property Taxation," *Assessors News Letter*, September, 1960, pp. 103-107.

ARKANSAS LEGISLATIVE COUNCIL, *Taxation of Personal Property In Several States*, Research Department, Little Rock, 1958.

ARKANSAS RAILROAD COMMISSION, TAX DIVISION, *Assessor's Manual*, Little Rock, 1927, pp. 41.

ARMSTRONG, ROBERT H., "Future Urban Land Valuation," *The Appraisal Journal*, January, 1945, pp. 24-36.

ARMSTRONG, ROBERT H., "In Re: This Matter of Taxes," *The Appraisal Journal*, July, 1940, pp. 236-244.

ARMSTRONG, ROBERT H., "Valuation of Industrial Property Part IV," *The Apraisal Journal*, October, 1953, pp. 519-528.

ARMSTRONG, ROBERT H., "Valuation of Industrial Property, Part II," *The Appraisal Journal*, April, 1953, pp. 211-216.

ARMSTRONG, ROBERT H., "Valuation of Industrial Property, Part I," *The Appraisal Journal*, January, 1953, pp. 35-46.

ARMSTRONG, W. Y., "Insurance Valuations the Property Owners Responsibility," *Insurance Valuations*, The American Society of Appraisers, Washington, D. C, 1971, pp. 8-18.

ARNOLD, JAMES A. JR., "The Personal Property Tax," *New Jersey Municipalities*, October, 1956, pp. 5-8.

ARNOLD, MAX P, "Impact of Property Taxes As a Fixed Charge Against Agricultural Land," *Journal; Proceedings*, Am. Soc. Farm Mgrs-Rural Appraisers, Denver, November 27, 1973, pp. 74-80.

ARNOLD, MAX P., "A Rural Land Appraisal for Ad Valorem Tax Purposes," *The Valuation Manual*, American Society of Appraisers, Washington, 1958, pp. 385-398.

ARNOLD, MAX P., "Machinery and Equipment Appraisal for Property Tax Purposes," *The Appraisal Journal*, 1900, pp. 48-55.

ARNOLD, MAX P., C. N. BLOOMFIELD, JACK HULL, "Urban Land Valuation for Taxation Purposes," *Technicalities and Technical Valuation*, February, 1962, pp. 18-19.

ARNOLD, MAX, C. N. BLOOMFIELD, AND JACK HULL, "Urban Land Valuation for Taxation Purposes," *Technical Valuation*, American Society of Appraisers, Washington, 1952, pp. 18.

ARNOLD, ROBERT S., "Mortgage-Equity Capitalization and After-Tax Equity Yield," *The Appraisal Journal*, January, 1969, pp. 40-49.

ASHTON, R. E., "Valuation for Assessment Purposes," *Appraisal Institute Magazine*, April, 1957, pp. 21-27.

ASSESSORS NEWSLETTER, "Automation In Taxation: Property Taxes and Assessment Rolls," *Assessors Newsletter*, June, 1966, pp. 92.

ASSESSORS NEWSLETTER, "Primary Assessing Area for Local Property Taxation," *Assessors Newsletter*, June, 1966, pp. 83-87.

ASSESSORS NEWSLETTER, "Property Tax Exemption Dilemma," *Assessors Newsletter*, May, 1966, pp. 74.

ASSESSORS NEWSLETTER, "Real Estate Transfer Tax," *Assessors Newsletter*, July, 1966, pp. 103.

ATLAS MARTIN, *Tax Aspects of Real Estate Transactions*, Bureau of National Affairs, Washington, D. C, 1955.

AUSTIN, PECK, "Tax Results of Exchanges and Condemnation Conversions," *Right of Way*, December, 1959, pp. 43-48.

BAB, HERBERT J. G., "Property Taxes Cause Urban Decay," *The Appraisal Journal*, July, 1968, pp. 419-425.

BABCOCK, FREDERICK M., "Approaches to Real Estate Valuation," *Real Estate Appraiser*, pp. 29.

BABCOCK, FREDERICK M., "Balanced Valuation," *National Real Estate Journal*, March 5, 1928, pp. 48-50.

BABCOCK, FREDERICK M., "City Growth and Development," *Valuation of Real Estate*, 1932, pp. 49-78.

BABCOCK, FREDERICK M., "Re-Use Analysis and Valuation," *Technical Valuation*, June, 1963, pp. 18-20.

BABCOCK, FREDERICK M., "The Prediction of Population," *Valuation of Real Estate*, 1932, pp. 79-85.

BABCOCK, FREDERICK M., "Valuation of Returns Details of Valuation Procedure Hotels," *The Valuation of Real Estate, Ed. 1*, 1932, pp. 280-284.

BABCOCK, FREDERICK M., "Valuation of Returns Details of Valuation Procedure Parking Lots," *The Valuation of Real Estate, Ed. 1*, 1932, pp. 276-307.

BABCOCK, FREDERICK M., "Valuation of Returns Details of Valuation Pocedure Houses," *The Valuation of Real Estate, Ed. 1*, 1932, pp. 320-395.

BABCOCK, FREDERICK M., "Valuation of Returns Details of Valuation Procedure Store," *The Valuation of Real Estate, Ed. 1*, 1932, pp. 271-393.

BABCOCK, FREDERICK M., "Valuation of Returns Details of Valuation Procedure Theater," *The Valuation of Real Estate, Ed. 1*, 1932, pp. 306-380.

BABCOCK, FREDERICK M., "Valuation of Returns Factory Details of Valuation Procedure," *The Valuation of Real Estate, Ed. 1*, 1932, pp. 318-329.

BABCOCK, FREDERICK M., "Valuation Process and Appraisal Purpose," *The Real Estate Appraiser*, April, 1965, pp. 9-14.

BABCOCK, HENRY A., "On the Valuation of Land Awaiting Conversion to a Higher Use," *The American Mathematical Monthly*, March, 1933, pp. 147-153.

BABCOCK, HENRY A., "Valuation Methods As Related to Property Classification: Kinds of Value," *Appraisal and Valuation Manual*, Washington, D. C, January, 1972.

BABLER, WAYNE E., "Ad Valorem Tax Appraisals Through Capitalization of Earnings," *Conference Proceedings*, National Tax Association, Columbus, 1962, pp. 575-582.

BADEN, POWELL, BADEN, HENRY, *A Short Account of the Land Revenue and Its Administration In British India*, The Clarendon Press, Oxford, 1907.

BADGER, R. E., "Valuation of Industrial Securities," *Principles of Investment*, New York City, 1925.

BADGER, RALPH, "Valuation of Closely Held Securities," *The Technical Valuation*, 1900, pp. 13.

BAILEY, REX R., "Appraisals for Tax Assessment," *Journal of the American Society of Farm Managers and Rural Appraisers*, April, 1949, pp. 36-42.

BAKER, LLOYD, "Valuation of a Shopping Center from the Lenders Viewpoint," *Right of Way*, December, 1964, pp. 43-45.

BAKER, VERNE A., "Appraising Citrus Groves," *Valuation*, June, 1956, pp. 22-23.

BALL, THOMAS L., *Church Valuation*, Church Valuation Consultants, 1968.

BALLAINE, WESLEY C., "Taxes and the Conservation of Privately Owned Timber," *Land Economics*, August, 1960, pp. 279.

BALLARD, E. D., "Preparation of Tax Maps," *Assessment Administration*, IAAO, Chicago, 1960, pp. 136-150.

BANCROFT, D. A., "The Single Tax and Site Valuation," *Appraisal Institute Magazine*, December, 1962, pp. 21-29.

BARBEAU, JACQUES, *Oil and Gas Production and Taxes*, Canadian Tax Foundation, Toronto, March, 1963.

▲ Appraisal for Special Purposes

BARNARD, BERNARD L., "Property Taxes In Local Finance," *Assessors News Letter*, January, 1966, pp. 6.

BARNES, JOHN W., "A Tax Payer Looks at the Property Tax Today," *Conference Proceedings*, National Tax Association, Columbus, 1963, pp. 594-601.

BARTLETT, CHARLES R., "What Every Appraiser Should Know About the Property Tax," *The Appraisal Journal*, July, 1963, pp. 375-382.

BEATON, WILLIAM R., PHILIP PICKENS, "Estate Appraisals," *The Real Estate Appraisers*, June, 1969, pp. 23-26.

BECK, MORRIS, "Exemption of Business Tangibles from Property," *Conference Proceedings*, National Tax Association, Columbus, 1959, pp. 150-161.

BECK, MORRIS, "Urban Redevelopment: Influence of Property Taxation and Other Factors," *Conference Proceedings*, P, Columbus, 1964, pp. 239-249.

BECKER, GEORGE, "Valuation of Office Buildings," *The Appraisal Journal*, October, 1967, pp. 496-506.

BEECROFT, ERIC, "Site Valuation As a Base for Local Taxation," *Appraisal Institute Magazine*, September, 1962, pp. 13-17.

BENSON, GEORGE C. AND OTHERS, "The American Property Tax: Its History, Administration and Economic Impact, Claremont California," Claremont College's Printing Service, 1965.

BERGER, THEODORE, "Tax Treatment of Property Demolition," *Parking*, 1962, pp. 10.

BIRD, RICHARD M., "Local Property Taxes In Columbus," *Conference Proceedings*, Columbus.

BLASE, M. G., W. G. STAUB, "Real Property Taxes In the Rural Urban Fringe," *Land Economics*, May, 1971, pp. 168 174.

BLDG MGRS & OWNERS ASSN OF NEW YORK, INC, "Taxation Committee, Survey of Depreciation of Office Structures In New York City," *Real Estate Record and Builders Guide*, June 30, 1928, pp. 8.

BOLEY, BERTRAM S., "Increasing Depreciation Allowance Through Tax-Free Exchanges," *Tax Magazine*, February, 1932, pp. 45-46, 66-67.

BONBRIGHT, JAMES C., "May the Same Property Have Different Values for Different Purposes," *National Tax Association*, Proceedings 20th Annual Conference, 1927, pp. 279-295.

BONBRIGHT, JAMES C., "Valuation for Tax Purposes, the General Property Tax," *The Valuation of Property*, 1937.

BONBRIGHT, JAMES C., "Valuation of Public Utilities and Other Enterprises for Tax Purposes," *The Valuation of Property*, 1937.

BONBRIGHT, JAMES C., "Valuation Under the Law of Eminent Domain," *The Valuation of Property*, Mcgraw-Hill, New York, 1937, pp. 407-449.

BOOT, HARRY E., "Problems of Transportation Tax Confronting the Interstate Motor Carrier," *Conference Proceedings*, National Tax Association, Columbus, 1964, pp. 464-470.

BOOTH, ERIC ROWLAND, "Rating Valuation of Residential and Business Premises," *The Estates Gazette*, London, 1951.

BOOTH, ERNEST, *Valuations for Rating*, Butterworth and Co, London, 1932.

BORST, A., "Die Ground-Und Einkommensteuer Des Grossherzogtums Sachsen-Weimar," *Die Ground-Und Einkommensteuer Des Grossherzogtums Sachsen-Neimar*, Jena, G. Fischzr, 1979.

BOSLAND, CHELCIE C., "The Valuation of Public Utility Enterprises by the Securities and Exchange Commission," *The Journal of Finance*, March, 1964, pp. 96-106.

BOWEN, PERCIVAL V., "Valuation of Church Cemeteries," *The A. S. A. Valuation Manual*, American Society of Appraisers, 1964, pp. 205.

BOYCE BYRL N, HIGGINS J WARREN, "Tax Shield Considerations In Real Estate Investment Decisions," *The Real Estate Appraiser,* The Society of Real Estate Appraisers, Chicago Illinois, November 1, 1973, pp. 32-38.

BOYCE, LLOYD M., "Problems In the Valuation of Commercial Properties," *National Real Estate Journal,* June, 1932, pp. 49-50.

BOYLAND, WILLIAM E., "Assessing---New York Real Estate Taxes," *Technical Valuation,* American Society of Appraisers, Washington, D. C, October, 1953, pp. 17.

BRAMS, M. R., "State Assessments & Shared Taxes In Mass. with Spec Attention to Boston," *Dissertation Abstracts,* Ann Arbor, November, 1967.

BRANSCOMB, HARVIE JR., "Postponing Income Taxes on Real Estate Transactions," *The Appraisal Journal,* October, 1957, pp. 598-602.

BRAZER, HARVEY E., "The Value of Industrial Property As a Subject of Taxation," *Canadian Public Administration,* June, 1961, pp. 137-147.

BRENNAN, M. J., "Taxes, Market Valuation, and Corporate Financial Policy," *National Tax Journal,* December, 1970.

BRIDGES, BENJAMIN, JR., "Income Elasticity of the Property Tax Base," *The National Tax Journal,* September, 1964, pp. 253-264.

BRIERLY, HENRY CHARLES, *Valuation Precedents and Principles,* Sidney, 1962.

BRIGHAM, EUGENE F., WESTON, J. FRED, "Valuation and the Cost of Capital," *Managerial Finance,* Holt, Rinehart, and Winston, New York, 1966, pp. 275.

BROEMMEL, BERT W., "Property Tax Assessment," *Concepts and Problems.*

BROOKS, ROBERT PRESTON, "The Georgia Property Tax," *Bulletin of the University of Georgia,* University of Georgia, Athens.

BROTHERS, D. S., "Change In Tax Depreciation Policy and Public Regulation of Business," *Land Economics,* November, 1957, pp. 346-358.

BROUGHTON, A. G. S., "Income Tax Depreciation and the Appraiser," *Appraisal Institute Magazine,* Appraisal Institute of Canada, Winnipeg.

BROWN, E. CAREY, "Depreciation and Taxes, Symposium," *Depreciation and Taxes, Symopium,* Tax Institute, Vol. V, Princeton, 1958.

BROWN, E. R., BROWN, H. G., "Land Value Taxation's Incidence," *American Journal of Economics and Sociology,* January, 1966.

BROWN, HARRY GUNNISON, *Land-Value Taxation Around the World,* Robert Schalkenbach Foundation, New York City, 1955.

BROWN, HARRY GUNNISON, *The Economic Basis of Tax Reform,* Lucas Brothers, Columbia, 1932.

BROWN, HARRY GUNNISON, *Two Essays on the Taxation of Unearned Incomes,* Missouri Book Company, Columbia, 1921.

BROWN, JOHN P., "Certain Provisions In the Internal Revenue Code of 1954 Regarding Depreciation Allowance," *Technical Valuation,* February, 1955, pp. 45-49.

BROWN, LONDO H., "Changes In West Virginia Real Property Tax Law," *West Virginia Law Review,* June, 1964, pp. 271-292.

BROWN, ROBERT KEVIN, "Tax Considerations In Sale-Leaseback Transactions," *The Appraisal Journal,* October, 1969, pp. 564-568.

BUCKLEY, ROBERT, DON M. SOULE, "Effects of Work and Residence Locations on Family Tax Burdens In Kentucky," University of Kentucky, 1971, pp. 22.

BUECHLER, ALFRED G., "Partial Report of the Committee on Intergovernmental Fiscal Relations," *Conference Proceedings,* National Tax Association, Columbus, 1964, pp. 147-148.

BUECHLER, ALFRED G., "Report of the Committee on Intergovernmental Fiscal Relations," *Conference Proceedings,* National Tax Association, Columbus, 1965, pp. 395-397.

BURBANK, DANIEL E., "Some Federal Estate Tax Appraisal Problems," *Technical Valuation*, February, 1960, pp. 11-16.

BUREAU OF BUSINESS AND ECONOMIC RESEARCH, *Industry As a Local Taxbase*, Bureau of Business and Economic Research, Univ of Maryland, June, 1960.

BUREAU OF TAXATION, *Guide for Use of Assessors*, Bureau of Taxation, Augusta, Maine, 1950.

BURKE, WILLIAM J., "The Listing & Valuation of Real Estate In the City of Buffalo, N. Y.," *Proceedings of 17th Annual Conference*, National Tax Association, 1924, pp. 212-217.

BURKHARD, EARL E., "Appraising Supermarket Personal Property," *Case Reports In Assessment Administration*, 1960, pp. 30-32.

BURKHARD, EARL E., "Appraising Supermarket Personal Property," *Case Reports In Assessment Administration*, 1960, pp. 30-32.

BURKHARD, EARL E., "Assessment Appraisals of Personal Property at a Shopping Center," *Assessors Journal*, April, 1966, pp. 47-54.

BURKHARD, EARL E., "How to Appraise Taxable Personal Property," *American Society of Appraisers Valuation Manual*, 1959, pp. 61.

BURKHARD, EARL E., "Personal Property Tax Appraising," *American Society of Appraisers Valuation Manual*, 1961, pp. 215.

BURNELL, WILLIAM U., "A Program for Lower Taxes In Real Estate Improvements," *Valuation Manual*, American Society of Appraisers, 1959, pp. 29.

BURNELL, WILLIAM V., "Are New Laws Necessary for Real Estate Taxation," *Appraisal and Valuation Manual*, American Society of Appraisers, 1961, pp. 261-266.

BURNELL, WILLIAM V., "The Real Estate Tax Burden Versus Property Value," *Appraisal and Valuation Manual*, 1960.

BURROUGHS ADDING MACHINE CO., *Tax Accounting In the City of Detroit*, Burroughs Adding Machine Co., Detroit.

BURTON, JOHN E., "Modifying and Supplementing General Property Taxes a Base for Real Estate Taxes," *National Tax Association-Proceedings 27th Annual Conference*, 1934, pp. 55-74.

BUSHAM, K J, "Valuation of Close Corporation Securities," *Trusts and Estates Xc*, Matthew Bender Co.Inc, New York, April 1, 1951, pp. 152.

BYERS, EUGENE, RANDALL S. STOUT, "The Changing Pattern of State Tax Systems Pennsylvania, New Jersey, Indiana, Michigan and Wisconsin," *Conference Proceedings*, National Tax Association, Columbus, 1964, pp. 198-222.

CAHILL, FRANK P., "Valuation Variations," *Technical Valuation*, October, 1953, pp. 31-32.

CALDWELL, BERNARD L., "Tax Factors Which Affect Real Estate Values," *The Appraisal Journal*, October, 1964, pp. 564-575.

CALIFORNIA OFFICE OF STATE CONTROLLER, "Assessed Valuations Tax Rates & Indebtedness of the Counties of Calif.," *Assessed Valuations Tax Rates and Indebtdness of the Counties of Calif*, Calif. Office of State Controller, Sacramento, 1955.

CAMPNEY, ALBERT E., "How to Sell a Re-Appraisal Program," *Assessor News Letter*, July, 1957, pp. 78-82.

CAPLAN, BENEDICTO, "Economia Del Inpuesto Inmobiliario," Mendoza, Univ. Nacional De Cu, 1948.

CARBERT, LESLIE E., "Property Tax Exemptions As a Tool of Planning," *Conference Proceedings*, National Tax Association, Columbus, 1965, pp. 234.

CARLSON, ALFRED E., "Appraising Acreage In Transition for Tax Assessment Purposes," *Valuation*, June, 1968, pp. 21-25.

CARMAN, H. F., J. G. POLSON, "Tax Shifts Occurring As a Result of Differential Assessment of Farmland California 1968-1969," *National Tax Journal*, December, 1971.

CARR, JAMES E., "Inequitable Property Tax Treatment of Railroads," *Conference Proceedings*, National Tax Association, Columbus, 1964, pp. 471-480.

CARTER, J. H., "Problems In the Regulation and Taxation of Mobile Homes," *The Iowa Law Review*, pp. 16-58.

CARTER, LOCH, "Personal Property Taxes: Valuation on Inventory," *Marquette Law Review*, 1963, pp. 92.

CASEY, JAMES, J., "Cambridge System of Real Estate Valuation," *Bulletin*, National Tax Association, pp. 184-187.

CASEY, W. J., *Tax Shelter In Real Estate*, Institute for Business Planning, Inc., New York, 1957.

CATO, C. JACK, "Assistance In Arkansas," *Assessment Administration*, IAAO.

CHAMPNEY, ALBERT E., "Taxing Private Uses for Profit of Exempt Real Property," *Assessors News Letter*, January, 1960, pp. 4-9.

CHAPMAN, CHARLES M., "Property Taxation of Railroad Properties," *Conference Proceedings*, National Tax Association, Columbus, 1959, pp. 252-265.

CHARBEAU, JULES, "Do You Know What Your Possessions Are Worth," *ASA Valuation Manual*, 1955, pp. 156.

CHARLAND, ROGER, "The Basic Principles of Real Property Value," *Appraisal Valuation Manual*, American Society of Appraisers, 1960, pp. 57-70.

CHEN, Y. P., "Present State and Fiscal Significance of Property Tax Exemptions for the Aged," *National Tax Journal*, June, 1965, pp. 162-174.

CHEN, Y. P., "Taxation of the Aged: Some Issues and Possible Solution," *Conference Proceeding*, National Tax Association, Columbus, 1965, pp. 206-225.

CHENG, PAO L., ALFRED L. EDWARDS, "Compensatory Property Taxation an Alternative," *National Tax Journal*, September, 1959, pp. 270-275.

CHING, C. T. K., "Use Value Assessment on Property Tax Rates," *American Journal of Agricultural Economics*, November, 1970.

CHOLVIS, FRANCISCO, *La Revoluacion De Los Bienes Activos*, Editorial Prometeo, Buenos Aires, 1954.

CHRISTOPHER, S. H., "Aerial Photography As a Low Cost Aid for Equalization Work," *Public Works*, March, 1958, pp. 106-108.

CIMELY, G., "1969 Tax Reform Act Its Effect on Real Estate," *Industrial Development and Manufactures Record*, September, 1970, pp. 7-10.

CLARK, EDWARD L., "Property Tax Aspects of Forest Resource Development In the Rocky Mountain Area," *Assessment Administration*, IAAO, Chicago, 1960, pp. 112-115.

CLARK, LOUIS M., "The Real Estate Condominium, Its Tax Problems And Implications," *The Appraisal Journal*, October, 1967, pp. 481-486, 490-492.

CLARK, ROBERT M., "Civic Tax Exemptions--The Edmonton Civic Center Plan," *The Appraisal Journal*, May, 1951, pp. 172-184.

CLAWSON, MARION, "Should Public Lands Pay Taxes," *American Forests*, March, 1965, pp. 11-13.

CLEMINSHAW, J. M., "The Revaluation of Municipalities for Tax Equalization Purposes," *The Appraisal Journal*, January, 1944, pp. 52-65.

COFFMAN, PAUL B., "Estate of James D. McDermott, Deceased, V. Commissioner of Internal Revenue," *Appraisal and Valuation Manual*, ASA, Washington, 1958, pp. 103-128.

COHEN, LEO, "Recent Railroad Tax Litigations and the Valuation of Railroads," *Conference Proceedings*, National Tax Association, Columbus, 1965, pp. 179-195.

▲ **Appraisal for Special Purposes**

COLOAN, H. BRONSON, "The History of Site Valuation Taxation Used for Municipal Purposes," *Assessment Administration,* IAAO, Chicago, 1961, pp. 12-19.

COLORADO, *Assessment and Property Tax Laws of Colorado, 1961,* Committee on Statute Revision, 1962.

CONLON, CHARLES F., "Judicial Views on Tax Administration," *Western Politician Quarterly,* March, 1963, pp. 5-13.

CONNELLY, WILLIAM F., "The Valuation of Industrial and Commercial Property for Taxation," *National Tax Association, Proceeding 20th Annual Conference,* 1927, pp. 295-308.

CONNETICUT TAX COMMISSION, *Information Relative to the Assessment and Collection of Taxes 1935,* Hartford, June, 1936, pp. 170.

CONSIDINE, CHARLES, "Income Tax Pitfalls In Appraising, Part III," *The Appraisal Journal,* October, 1954, pp. 590-592.

CONSIDINE, CHARLES, "Income Tax Pitfalls In Appraising, Part II," *The Appraisal Journal,* July, 1954, pp. 415-422.

CONSIDINE, CHARLES RAY, JOHN DUROSS O BRYAN, "Income Tax Pitfalls In Appraising, Part I," *The Appraisal Journal,* April, 1954, pp. 256-261.

COOK, BILLY D, "Strengthening the Property Tax Through Relief Policies," *Property Tax Reform,* Int'l Ass'n Assessing Officers, Chicago, June 1, 1973, pp. 135-151.

COOMBS, WHITNEY, *Taxation of Farm Property,* U. S. Printing Office, Washington, 1930.

COYLE, JOSEPH A., "Tax Valuation Problems," *Technical Valuation,* October, 1953, pp. 55-57.

CRAIG, R. H., "Revolution In Assessment and Taxation," *Appraisal Institute Magazine,* Appraisal Institute of Canada, Winnipeg.

CRESPO, MANUEL, *Manual De Revaluo Impositivo,* Ediciones Macchi, Ediciones Macchi, Le.

CURRAN, DONALD J., "General Property Tax and Residential Rehabilitation," *Conference Proceedings,* National Tax Association Association, Columbus, 1964, pp. 250-258.

DALEFIELD, K. S., "Application of Electronic Data Processing to Tax Procedures," *Public Service,* August, 1963, pp. 14-19.

DANNER, E. H., "Property Taxation of Telephone Company Property," *Conference Proceedings,* National Tax Association, Columbus, 1959, pp. 241-247.

DAVID, E. L., R. SKURSKI, "Property Tax Assessment and Absentee Owners," *National Tax Journal,* December, 1966, pp. 421-426.

DAVID, MARTIN, "Evaluating Structural Changes In Capital Gains Taxation," *Conference Proceedings,* National Tax Association, Columbus, 1965, pp. 644-652.

DAVIES, MAURICE B. T., "Planning and Selection for Data-Processing Service," *Assessment Administration,* I. A. A. O, Chicago, 1964, pp. 124-128.

DAVIS, ARTHUR M., "Handling Taxpayer Complaints," *Assessment Administration,* I. A. A. O, Chicago, 1962, pp. 137-140.

DAVIS, R. A., "The Taxpayer's Dilemma," *Appraisal Institute Magazine,* Appraisal Institute of Canada, Winnipeg.

DAVIS, W. D., "Valuation for Federal Taxation," *Journal of the American Society of Farm Managers and Rural Appraisers,* April, 1955, pp. 27-30.

DE SALVO, J. S., "Effects of the Property Tax on Operating and Investment Decisions of Rental Property Owners," *National Tax Journal,* March, 1971, pp. 45-50.

DEAN, J., "Four Ways to Write Off Capital Investment Management Should Have a Wider Tax Choice," *Journal of Business,* April, 1956, pp. 79-89.

DESALVO, J. S., "Effects of the Property Tax on Operating and Investment Decisions," *National Tax Journal,* March, 1971, pp. 45 50.

DIX, W. B., "Some Aspects of Mine Taxation In Ontario," *Canadian Tax Journal*, July, 1957, pp. 263-270.

DONAHOO, JOHN W., "Tax Appraisals," *The Review,* June, 1953, pp. 9-12.

DONOVAN, J., "Bleak Picture The Art Market Is Feeling the Financial Pinch, Too," *Barrons*, July 6, 1970, pp. 11.

DOWNS, GEORGE W., "Baltimore's Time Proven Tax Plats," *Case Reports In Assessment Administration,* September, 1961.

DOWNS, M. D., "The Coordination of Tax Assessments and Zoning," *Planners Journal*, 1935, pp. 23-24.

DOYLE, JOHN P., "Taxation of Way," *Conference Proceedings*, National Tax Association, Columbus, 1964, pp. 482-485.

DOZIER, S. ROBERT, "Alaska Property Tax Structure-Before and After Earthquake," *Assessment Administration,* IAAO, Chicago, 1964, pp. 39-43.

DRAKE LAW REVIEW, "Taxation-Exemption of Charitable, Religious and Educational Institutions from Property Taxes," *Drake Law Review,* December, 1962, pp. 87-91.

DUVALL, LOY CLEVELAND LEE, *The Taxation and Equalization of City, Town and County Real Estate,* W. M. Warlick, Dallas, Texas, 1901.

DWYER, JAY J., "Inheritance Tax Appraisals," *The Review,* October, 1946, pp. 9, 12.

DWYER, JAY J., "Inheritance Tax Appraisals," *The Review,* October, 1946, pp. 9, 12.

EAGAN, LAURENCE J., "Personal Property Valuation," *Assessment Administration,* Institute of American Assessment Officers, Chicago, 1963, pp. 226-229.

ECHANDIA, DEVIS HERNANDO, *Land Taxation In Colombia,* Editorial Minerva, Ltds., Bogota, 1944.

ECKER-RACZ, L LAZLO, "Responsibilities of the States for Property Tax Reform," Int'l Assn Assessing Officers, Chicago, June 1, 1973, pp. 23-27.

ECKER-RACZ, L. L., "Limitations on the Taxation of Property," *Assessment Administration,* Institute of American Assessment Officers, Chicago, 1965, pp. 14-20.

ECKERT, FRED W., "The Relationship of Income Taxes to Property Valuation," *The Appraisal Journal*, April, 1946, pp. 180-186.

EISENLAUER, JACK F., "Mass Versus Individual Appraisers," *The Appraisal Journal*, October, 1968, pp. 533-535.

EITEMAN, DAVID K., "Approaches to Utility Valuation for Ad Valorem Taxation," *Public Utilities Fortnightly,* May, 1963, pp. 19-23.

ELLIOTT ADDUESSING MACHINE CO., *Elliott Addressing Machine Co.,* Elliott Systems Machine Co., Cambridge, Mass.

ETTEMAN, DAVID K., "Utility Tax Valuation from Common Stock Prices," *Public Utilities Fortnightly,* May, 1964, pp. 19-31.

ETTINGER, VIRGIL P., "Treasury Decision 4422," *National Association of Cost Accountants,* pp. 242-253.

EUROPEAN CUSTOMS UNION STUDY GROUP., "Valuation of Goods for Customs Purposes," *Convention on the Valuation of Goods for Customs Purposes,* H. M. Stationery Office, London, 1954.

EVERETTE, C. H., "The Farm Manager's Responsibility on Property Taxes," *Journal of the American Society of Farm Managers and Rural Appraisers,* October, 1955, pp. 33-37.

EVERTS, HENRY P., "69 Act Most Complicated Tax Law Ever Written CPA Tells Chapter," *The Appraiser,* May, 1970.

FEDERAL POWER COMMISSION, *S-205-Statistics for Interstate Natural Gas Pipeline Companies,* Supt. of Documents, U. S. Govt. Printing Office, Washington D. C, 1969.

FEDERAL TAX ADMINISTRATION, *State and Local Tax Status of Military Housing Programs*, Federation of Tax Administrators, Chicago, 1956.

FEDERAL TAX ADMINISTRATION, *State Tax Incentives for Fallout Shelters*, Federation of Tax Administrators, Chicago, 1961.

FEDERATION OF TAX ADMINISTRATORS, *Federal Property Reservations And State and Local Property Taxes*, Federation of Tax Administrators, Chicago, 1960.

FEDERATION OF TAX ADMINISTRATORS, *State Administrative Tax Review Organization and Practices*, Federation of Tax Administrators, Chicago, 1958.

FEINSCHREIBER, R., "New Regulations Liberalize Tax Depreciation," *New York Certified Public Accountant*, September, 1971, pp. 637-640.

FENWICK, D. R., "After Tax Equity Yields," *Appraisal Institute Magazine*, Appraisal Institute of Canada, Winnipeg, June 1, 1973.

FERGUSON, HILL, "Mass Appraising," *The Appraisal Journal*, April, 1943, pp. 156-161.

FINOL, VINCENCIO BAEZ, *El Impuesto Predial Rural Su Institucion En Venezuela*, Consejo De Bienestar Rural, Caracas, 1961.

FISK, KENNETH, "Tree Loss for Tax Reports," *The Review*, November, 1951, pp. 14-16.

FLICK, JOHN E., "State Tax Liability of Servicemen and Their Dependents," *Washington and Lee Law Review*, 1964, pp. 22-47.

FLORIDA WORKS PROGRESS ADMINISTRATION, *Final Report on the Activity of Property and Tax Survey on West Palm Beach*, State Statistical Coordinator WPA, Jacksonville, June 30, 1937, pp. 11, 14, 13, 2.

FOGARTY, JAMES T., "Use of Tax Angles to Help Lose Deals Involving Involuntary Conversions," *Right of Way*, October, 1961, pp. 25-29.

FRANKLIN, R. J., "Tax and Business Considerations In Buying Property," *Taxes*, March, 1964.

FREEMAN, ROGER A., *The American Tax System Does it Need Revision Reform or Reconstruction*, Claremont Men's College, 1961.

FRUITS, S. C., "Recent Cases Show Increasing Impact of State and Local Taxation," *Journal of Taxation*, February, 1964, pp. 116-119.

GABERMAN, HARRY, "Paths Through the Jungle of State and Local Taxation of Defense Contractors," *Federal Bar Journal*, 1963, pp. 61-69.

GAFFNEY, M. MASON, "Property Taxes and the Frequency of Urban Renewal," *Conference Proceedings*, National Tax Association, Columbus, 1964, pp. 272-285.

GAYDON, ALEXANDER THOMAS, *The Taxation of 1297*, Streately Bedfordshire Hist Recds Society Vol Xxxi, 1959.

GAZTAMBIDE, DR. JUAN B., "Valuation of Leasehold In Puerto Rico for Inheritance Tax Purpose," *Appraisal & Valuation Manual*, Corporate Press Inc, Wash D. C., January, 1972, pp. 232.

GEORGE, ERNEST, "Real Estate Exchange and Taxation," *The Residential Appraiser*, December, 1962, pp. 17-23.

GERE, EDWIN A. JR., "Tax Assessing a Growing Profession," *American City*, June, 1958, pp. 97-98.

GERRITY, HARRY J., "Depreciation Allowances for Income Tax Purposes," *Skyscraper Management*, March, 1934, pp. 14, 27.

GERRITY, HARRY J., "Depreciation and the Income Tax Law," *Real Estate Record*, February 15, 1936, pp. 13-17.

GIBBONS, JAMES E., "Mortgage-Equity Capitalization and After Tax Equity Yield," *The Appraisal Journal*, January, 1969, pp. 31-49.

GIBSON, LIOYD C., "Bureau's New Depreciation Policy," *Tax Magazine*, June, 1934. pp. 279-285.

GIBSON, LLOYD, "Valuation and Depreciation In Federal Taxes Cases," *Technical Valuation*, July, 1947, pp. 16-24.

GILBERT, HARRY E., "Valuation of Real Estate for Tax Purposes," *National Real Estate Journal*, October, 1932, pp. 32-34.

GILDEA, C. D., G. K. MUHLBERG, "The Use of Edp and Sampling Techniques In Compiling Data Required for State and Local Tax Returns," *Tax Executive*, July, 1961, pp. 240-251.

GLASER, SIDNEY, "Court Appeal Rights," *Conference Proceedings*, National Tax Association, Columbus, 1964, pp. 4000-409.

GLOVER, CHARLES P., "A New Thesis for Tax Appraisals," *The Appraisal Journal*, July, 1941, pp. 266-275.

GODGREY, EDWARD, "Enforcement of Delinquent Property Taxes In New York," *Albany Law Review*, June, 1962, pp. 201-230.

GODWIN, HOWARD S., "Casualty Deductions for Tax Purposes," *Appraisal Digest*, October, 1956, pp. 4-7.

GOLDMAN, ABRAM F., "Taxation of Possessory Interests by California," *The Appraisal Journal*, April, 1951, pp. 185-201.

GOLDSTEIN, WILLEAM M., "Developments In Tax Depreciation and Related Areas," *Virginia Law Review*, April, 1963, pp. 411-432.

GOOD, WILLIAM CHARLES, *Production and Taxation In Canada from the Farmers Standpoint*, Garden City Press, Toronto, 1919.

GOVERNMENT AFFAIRS FOUNDATION, INCORPORATED, *State Constitutional Restrictions of Local Borrowing and Property Taxing Powers*, Government Affairs Foundation, Incorporated, Albany, 1900, pp. 311.

GRAHAM, DONALD H. JR., "Shopping Center Real Property Taxes," *The Appraisal Journal*, January, 1963, pp. 7-12.

GRAVES, T. J., "A Re-Examination of the 1954 Revenue Code Depreciation Problem," *Valuation Manual*, A. S. A, October, 1956, pp. 43-46.

GREER, GUY, "Tax Exemption Is Poison," *The Appraisal Journal*, January, 1947, pp. 8-15.

GRIMES, J. A., "Income Tax Depletion and Depreciation," *Accounting Review*, June, 1928, pp. 161-176.

GRUNDALD, ADOLPH E., *Stock Valuation In Federal Taxation*, Grad School of Bus Admin., Mich State University, East Lansing, 1961.

GRUNEWALD, ADOLPH E, "Stock Valuation In Federal Taxation," *Occasional Paper #4*, Michigan State University, January 1, 1961.

GRUNEWALD, ADOLPH E., *Stock Valuation In Federal Taxation*, Michigan State University, 1961, pp. 104.

GUPTE, K. S., *Land-Taxation-Maharashtra, India-State*, N. R. Bhalerao, 1962.

HAGMAN, D. G., "Open Space Planning and Property Taxation, Some Suggestions," *Wisconsin Law Review*, July, 1964, pp. 628.

HAGMAN, D. G., "The Single Tax and Land-Use Planning, Henry George Updated," *UCLA Law Review*, March, 1965, pp. 762-788.

HAINES, C. GRODON, "Tax Consequences to Owners As a Result of Public Acquisition," *Proceedings of the Sixth Annual National Seminar*, American Right of Way Association, Washington, D. C, 1961.

HALE, C. W., "Impact of Federal Policy and Technological Change on Regional & Urban Planning Problems," *Land Economics*, February, 1971, pp. 24-35.

HALL, JOSEPH B., "Wholesale Appraising for Taxation Purposes," *National Real Estate Journal*, August 5, 1929, pp. 36-42.

HAMBURG, ALEX M., "Valuation of Real Property for Taxation," *Taxes*, March, 1939, pp. 139.

HAMILTON, ANDREW C., "Tax Appraisals As Evidence of Value," *The Appraisal Journal*, January, 1934, pp. 152-153.

▲ **Appraisal for Special Purposes**

HAMILTON, HOWARD D., "Taxes and Taconite, Iron Ore Tax Legislation In the Lake Superior Region," *National Tax Journal,* December, 1964, pp. 324-354.

HANDEL, MORRIS, "Legal Aspects of Appraisals and Expert Testimony In Tax Certiorari Proceedings," *Technical Valuation,* April, 1947, pp. 23-25.

HANDLER, ALAN B., "The Legal Aspects of Tax Exemptions, an Analysis Of the Second Swity Case," *New Jersey Municipalities,* January, 1963, pp. 16-20.

HANFORD, LLOYD JR., "Forecasting Real Estate Taxes," *The Real Estate Appraisal,* pp. 47.

HANSEN, VICTOR R., "The Expert Appraiser As the Focal Point In Preparation of a Condemnation Case for Trail," *Right of Way,* October, 1955, pp. 7-11, 20.

HARDY, T. F., "Incidence of the Personal Property Tax," *National Tax Journal,* December, 1962, pp. 368-384.

HARRISON & SONS, "Taxation of Land," *Presentation to Both Houses of Parliament by Command of His Majesty,* Harrison & Sons, London, 1909.

HARRISON, DAVID C., "Housing Rehabilitation and the Pittsburgh Graded Property Tax," *Duquesne University Law Review,* 1964, pp. 213-243.

HARRISS, C LOWELL, "Estate Taxes and the Family Owned Business," *California Law Review Xxxviii,* March 1, 1950, pp. 119-128.

HARTWIG, J. D., "Tax Considerations In Real Estate Transactions," *Michigan State Bar Journal,* October, 1961, pp. 14-23.

HARTWIG, JOSEPH D, "Valuation Problems Before the Irs and the Tax Court," *13th Annual Institute on Federal Taxation,* Matthew Bender and Co, New York, January 1, 1955, pp. 1-143.

HARVARD LAW REVIEW, "Inequality In Property Tax Assessments New Cures for an Old Ill," *Harvard Law Review,* May, 1962, pp. 1374-1395.

HARVARD UNIVERSITY LAW SCHOOL, *International Program In Taxation?The Taxation Curriculum of the Harvard University,* Harvard University Law School, Cambridge, February, 1961.

HATFIEND, ROLLAND F., "Property Tax System Need Revitalization," *Minnesota Municipalities,* October, 1962, pp. 293-294.

HEARLE, EDWARD F. R., AND RAYMOUND J. MASON, *Data Processing for the State and Local Governments, a Rand Corporation Research Study,* Prentice-Hall, Englwd Cliffs, N. J., 1963.

HECHT, LEE I., "Appraising for Taxation of Real Estate," *Annals of Real Estate Practice,* National Association of Real Estate Boards, 1928, pp. 143-153.

HECKERLING, P. E., "Latin American Tax Systems," *Kentucky Law Journal,* 1964, pp. 609-627.

HECKMAN, J. W., "A Realistic Approach to Utility Property, Valuation for Tax Purposes," *Valuation,* October, 1964, pp. 7-13.

HEILBRUN, JAMES, "Real Estate Taxes and Urban Housing N.J.," Columbia University Press, 1966.

HELLMUTH, WILLIAM F. JR., "Depreciation and the 1954 Internal Revenue Code," *Valuation Manual,* September, 1955, pp. 326-349.

HELMBERGER, JOHN D., *State and Local Taxation of Banks P. H. D. Thesis,* University of Minnesota, 1960.

HENEBERRY, WILLIAM H., *Assessment of Farm Real Estate for Property Taxes,* Michigan State University, East Lansing, 1960.

HERRINGTON, F. A., "Appraisals for Tax Assessment," *Journal of the American Society of Farm Managers and Rural Appraisers*, April, 1959, pp. 60-64.

HERRINGTON, F. A., "Appraisals for Tax Assessment," *Journal of the American Society of Farm Managers and Rural Appraisers*, April, 1959, pp. 60-64.

HIGGINS J. WARREN, "The Real Estate Tax Corner:Involuntary Conversions," *The Real Estate Appraiser*, The Society of Real Estate Appraisers, Chicago Illinois, November 1, 1973, pp. 52-53.

HIGGINS, WARREN J., *Impact of Federal Taxation on Real Estate Decisions*, University of Connecticut, Real Estate Repts No 11, 1971.

HILLENBRAND, BERNARD F., *A Place Where Uncle Sam Does Not Play Fair--Payments In Lieu of Taxes*, National Association of County Officials, Washington, 1959, pp. 5.

HOAGLAND, HENRY E., "Taxes and Assessments," *Real Estate Principles*, 1940, pp. 450-465.

HODGES, M. B. JR., "Ellwood Plus-Or Equity Yield After Taxes," *Real Estate Appraiser*, September, 1969, pp. 11-22.

HODGES, M. B. JR., "Ellwood, Pro and Con an Analysis," *Appraisal Journal*.

HOGAN, HOWARD T., "Judicial Review of Real Estate Tax Assessments," *New York State Bar Journal*, February, 1963, pp. 51-57.

HOGAN, JOHN D., "Revenue Productivity of the Property Tax," *Conference Proceedings*, National Tax Association, Columbus, 1960, pp. 71-78.

HOGAN, W. T., "Plea for Tax Depreciation Reform to Make Paper Profits Real In Steel," *A. S. A. Manual*, October 28, 1957.

HOLDEN, ARTHUR C., "Taxation As A Factor In Urban Redevelopment," *The Appraisal Journal*, April, 1947, pp. 252-260.

HOLLAND, DANIEL M., "The Taxation of Unimproved Value In Jamaica," *Conference Proceedings*, National Tax Association, Columbus, 1965, pp. 442-470.

HOLMES, LAWRENCE G., "Appraising Real Estate for Tax Purposes, The Income Method," *Journal of Land and Public Utility Economics*, November, 1938.

HOLMES, LAWRENCE G., "Our Real Estate Tax Economy Should Come of Age," *The Appraisal Journal*, October, 1943, pp. 315-326.

HOLZMAN, ROBERT S, "The 'Blockage' Rule," *Taxes (Magazine)*, May 1, 1968, pp. 292-299.

HONEY, GAYLE K., "The Land Tax Squeeze," *Appraisal Institute Magazine*, Appraisal Institute of Canada, Winnipeg.

HORAN, GEORGE B., "Municipal Tax Revaluation," *The Appraisal Journal*, October, 1950, pp. 467-471.

HORVITZ, S. A., "Tax Planning Techniques Under the New Class Life System of Depreciation," *Journal of Taxation*, June, 1972, pp. 338-348.

HOSSACK, A. B., "What Treasury Decision 4422 Means," *System and Business Management*, January, 1935, pp. 10-12, 37-43.

HOTCHKISS, L. M., "Licensing of Appraisers," *Technical Valuation*, October, 1963, pp. 7-11.

HOUSE, PETER, "Partial Tax Exemption for Farmland Properties In the Rural-Urban Fringe," *The Appraisal Journal*, July, 1968, pp. 393-407.

HOWARD, T. HOGAN, "Judicial Review of Real Estate Tax Assessments," *The Real Estate Appraiser*, January, 1963, pp. 28-33.

HOWARDS, I., "Property Tax Rate Limits In Illinois and Their Effect Upon Local Government," *National Tax Journal*, September, 1963, pp. 258-293.

## Appraisal for Special Purposes

HOWORTH, PHILIP H., "Site Value Taxation, a Solution to Allocation Problems In the Taxation of Real Estate," *Massachusetts Law Quarterly,* March, 1962, pp. 28-36.

HUANG, HAN LIANG, *The Land Tax In China,* Columbia University, New York, 1918.

HUBIN, VINCENT J., "Tax Advantages of Realty Investments," *Appraisal Digest,* March, 1959, pp. 16-17.

HUGHES, C. W), "Valuation of Assets for Federal Tax Purposes In Trusts and Estates," *Valuation Manual,* ASA, May, 1956, pp. 416-418.

HULSE, FRED E., *Property Tax Problems In Rural - Urban Fringe Areas,* Dept of Agriculture, College Park, Md., 1952.

HUMPHREY, G. H., "Why We Must Limit Fast Tax Writeoffs In Iron Age," *Valuation Manual,* Asa, April 18, 1957, pp. 67-70.

HUNNICUTT, WARREN P., "Appraising for Federal Tax Purposes," *The Appraisal Journal,* October, 1936, pp. 411-424.

HUNTER, JENEL L., "Appraisal of Marinas, Field Data to Be Obtained, Format of Report," *Valuation,* February, 1964, pp. 10-13.

HURLEY, JAMES J., "In the Matter of Admissions and Examinations," *Technical Valuation,* June, 1957, pp. 55-59.

ICE, WILLARD, "State and Local Tax Changes In 1963," *Illinois Bar Journal,* October, 1963, pp. 124-142.

ILLINOIS STATE TAX COMMISSION, *Property Tax - Illinois,* Illinois State Commission, 1942.

INSTITUTE FOR TAX ASSESSORS, UNIVERSITY OF TEXAS, *Property Tax - Texas,* Institute of Public Affairs, Austin, 1959.

IOWA, *State Tax Commission,* State of Iowa, Des Moines, 1939.

IOWA LAW REVIEW, "Taxation Affecting Agriculture Land Use," *Iowa Law Review,* 1965, pp. 600-618.

IOWA LEGISLATIVE RESEARCH BUREAU, *Taxation of Moneys and Credits,* Iowa Legislative Research Bureau, Des Moines, 1960.

JACOBS, HARDY W., "The Value of the Appraisal Report," *The Appraisal Journal,* October, 1945, pp. 348-351.

JAFFE, J. M., "1962 Census of Governments Report on Taxable Property Values," *National Tax Journal,* September, 1963, pp. 267-276.

JEMING, JOSEPH B., "New Depreciation Provisions of the 1954 Revenue Code," *Technical Valuation,* June, 1955, pp. 13-16.

JENKS, ALDRO, "Certification In Connecticut," *Assessment Administration,* IAAO, Chicago, 1961, pp. 173-177.

JERSEY CITY BUREAU OF TAX ASSESSMENT, *Assessor's Manual,* 1915.

JOHNS, A. B. C. JR., "Writing the Report," *The Real Estate Appraiser,* SREA, Chicago, November, 1964, pp. 26.

JOHNSON, ERNEST H., "Timber Taxation In Maine," *Assessment Administration,* IAAO, Chicago, 1961, pp. 114-115.

JOHNSON, LYLE R, SHAPIRO, ELI, OLMEARA JR, JOSEPH, "Valuation of Closely Held Stock for Federal Tax Purposes: Approach to an Objective Method," *Law Review,* University of Pennsylvania, November 1, 1951, pp. 170.

JOHNSON, RALPH S., "Forest Taxation Alternatives," *Assessment Administration,* IAAO, Chicago, 1961, pp. 98-110.

KANSAS AGRICULTURAL EXPERIMENT STATION MANHATTAN, *The Trend of Real Estate Taxation In Kansas from 1910 to 1923,* Kansas State Printing Plant, Topeka, 1925.

KANSAS LEGISLATIVE COUNCIL, *Ad Valorem Taxation of Oil and Gas Property, 78 Kansas Counties 1958,* Kansas Legislative Council Research Department, Topeka, Kansas, 1959.

KAZDIN, S. EDWIN, "Appraisers Face Testing Period to Learn Market Influences," *Appraisal Digest,* July, 1951, pp. 1-3.

KEESLING, FRANK M., "Property Taxation of Leased and Other Limited Interests," *California Law Review,* August, 1959, pp. 470-490.

KEITH, JOHN H., *Property Tax Assessment Practices,* Highland Publishing Co., Monterey Park, Calif, 1966.

KEITH, JOHN H., "Appraisal for Tax Purposes," *The Appraisal Journal,* October, 1947, pp. 514-520.

KEITH, JOHN H., "The Role of Institute of American Appraisers Officers, In the Years Ahead," *Assessment Administration,* Institute of American Appraisers Officers, Chicago, 1963, pp. 10-15.

KENNEDY, JAMES C., "Railroad Ad Valorem Taxation -- a Current Appraisal," *Conference Proceedings,* National Tax Association, Columbus, 1963, pp. 602-610.

KENTUCKY LEGISLATIVE RESEARCH COMMISSION, *Federal In Lieu Payments to School Districts,* Kentucky Legislative Research Commission, Frankfort, 1958.

KENTUCKY LEGISLATIVE RESEARCH COMMISSION, *Taxation Property Taxes, a Report to the Committees on Functions and Resources of State Government,* Frankfort, 1951.

KILPATRICK, WYLIE, "Tax Exemption and Municipal Finance," *Municipal Finance,* February, 1960.

KING, WILLFORD I., *The Valuation of Urban Realty for Purposes of Taxation, with Cert Secs Espec Applicable to Wisconsin,* Madison, Wisconsin, 1914.

KING, WILLFORD ISBELL, "Valuation of Urban Realty for Purposes of Taxation," Madison, Wis., 1914.

KLAASEN, R. L., "Real Estate Income Taxation," *Appraisal Institute Magazine,* Appraisal Institute of Canada, Winnipeg.

KLEIN, JOSEPH J., "Deductions for Depreciation, Obsolescence, and Amortization, Depletion," *Federal Income Taxation,* 1929, pp. 621-683, 684-739.

KLEIN, JOSEPH J., "Depreciation and Obsolescence from the Standpoint of Federal Income Taxation," *International Congress on Accounting,* 1929, pp. 387-403.

KOENKER, WILLIAM E., "Appropriateness of Property Taxes In an Equitable Tax Structure," *North Dakota Law Review,* May, 1965, pp. 505-529.

KOPLIK, MARILYN S., *Property Tax Assessment In the United States, Preliminary Report to New York State,* Board of Equalization and Assessment, Albany, March, 1961.

KREKSTEIN, I. H., "Pennsylvania Taxation at the State and Local Level: the Pennsylvania Allocation Formula," *Taxes,* February, 1965, pp. 128-137.

KRISTENSON, KRISTEN, *Land Valuation In Denmark,* Internat. Union Land Value Taxation & Free Trade, London, 1946.

KUEHNLE, WALTER R., "Valuation of Real Estate for Ad Valorem Tax Purposes," *The Appraisal Journal,* January, 1953, pp. 26-34.

KUEHNLE, WALTER R., "Valuation of Real Estate for Ad Valorem Tax Purposes," *The Appraisal Journal,* January, 1953, pp. 26-34.

LABOVITZ, I. M., "The Property Tax, Quicksand or Bedrock," *Conference Proceedings,* National Tax Association, Columbus, 1960, pp. 58-70.

LAHNER, W. F., "Report of the National Association of Railway Tax Commissions," Pennsylvania Railroad Company, Philadelphia, 1963.

LAIRD, FREDERICK C., "Accounting for Fixed Assets In Taxes," *A. S. A. Manual,* September, 1958, pp. 629-42.

LAMSON, J. E., "Factors That Will Substantiate the Valuation of a Closely Held Corporation," *Journal of Taxation,* April, 1971, pp. 226-229.

LAND ECONOMICS, "Value-Added Vs. Property Taxation of Business: Effects on Industrial Location," *Land Economics,* May, 1971, pp. 150-157.

LARSON, MARTIN A., "You, the Church and Tax Exempt Wealth," *Assessors Journal*, April, 1966, pp. 10-16.

LASSER, J. K., CASEY, WILLIAM J., "Impact of Taxes on Real Estate Values," *The Appraisal Journal*, January, 1952, pp. 94-100.

LASSITER, ROY L., "Reproduction Cost As a Basis for Ad Valorem Railroad Taxation," *Public Fortnightly*, October, 1961, pp. 667-672.

LAVERNE, THOMAS, "Paying for the Public Schools: the Continuing Role of Property Tax," *Property Tax Reform*, Int'l Ass'n Assessing Officers, Chicago, June 1, 1973, pp. 152-158.

LEDBETTER, HOWARD, "Valuation of Leased Equipment for Ad Valorem Tax Purposes," *Assessment Administration*, I. A. A. O, Chicago, 1963, pp. 90-93.

LEE, HOWARD M., "Assessor-Taxpayer Representative Relations," *Assessment Administration*, I. A. A. O, Chicago, 1963, pp. 156-159.

LEET, EDMUND, "Appraising Commercial Urban Land for Ad Valorem Tax Purposes," *Appraisal and Valuation Manual*, American Society of Appraisers, Washington, D. C, 1959, pp. 165-172.

LEET, EDMUND, "The Use Depreciation In the Valuation of Property for Ad Valorem Tax Purposes," *Technical Valuation*, February, 1958, pp. 51-63.

LEFEAVER, JAMES H., "Use of an Appraisal for Tax Purposes," *Technicalities*, February, 1950, pp. 21.

LELAND, SIMEON E., "Valuing Buildings for Taxation," *National Real Estate Journal*, 1928, pp. 25-27.

LEONG, Y. S., ROBERT M. KAMINS, "Property Taxation In the 50th State," *National Tax Journal*, March, 1961, pp. 59-69.

LEROHL, M. L., "Farm Capital and Farm Taxation," *Appraisal Institute Magazine*, 1967, pp. 2-15.

LEVEL, EDWARD E., "Special Purpose Properties," *Appraisal and Valuation Manual*, Corporate Press Incorporated, Washington, D. C, January, 1972, pp. 346.

LEW, IRVING, "Valuation In Condemnation and In Real Estate Tax Assessment Review Proceedings," *Appraisal and Valuation Manual*, American Society of Appraisers, 1962.

LEWIS, GORDON D., *A Possible Approach to Forest Land Taxation*, Forest & Consvn Expermt Sta University of Montana, Missoula, September, 1962, pp. 15.

LEWIS, HENRY W., "Assessing Forest Land and Timber for Property Taxes," *Popular Government*, May, 1956, pp. 3-7.

LEWIS, HENRY W., "Property Tax Classification and Exemption, a Problem In North Carolina Constitutional Law," *North Carolina Review*, February, 1959, pp. 115-141.

LINDER, THOMAS, "Property Valuations and the Tax Assessor," *Bulletin, National Tax Association*, 1923, pp. 271-275.

LINDHOLM, R. W., "Twenty-One Land Value Taxation Questions and Answers," *American Journal of Economics and Sociology*, 1972.

LOUISIANA TAX COMMISSION, *20th Annual Report*, 1936.

LOVELADY, STEVEN M., "California Measure to Cut Property Taxes Opposed Right and Left, Still May Be Voted," *The Wall Street Journal*, pp. 8.

LUCE, DENNETH K., "Assessment of Real Property for Taxation," *Michigan Law Review*, June, 1937, pp. 1217-1252.

LUCEY, PATRICK J, "Property Tax Reform: a Governor's Perspective," *Property Tax Reform*, Int'l Assn Assessing Officers, Chicago, June 1, 1973, pp. 15-22.

LUNSFORD, C. R., "Valuing a Petroleum Refinery for Ad Valorem Tax Purposes," *Assessment Administration*, I. A. A. O, Chicago, 1965, pp. 112-118.

LYNN, ARTHUR D. JR., "Personal Property Taxation," *New York Certified Public Accountant,* May, 1959, pp. 350-356.

LYNN, ARTHUR D. JR., "Rept of Comm on Model Prop Tax Assesmt & Equalizn Methods on Property Tax Policy," *Conference Proceedings,* National Tax Association, Columbus, 1964, pp. 157-195.

MACDONALD KING R., "New Approaches to Personal Property Assessment," *Assessment Administration,* Institute of American Assessment Officers, Chicago, 1964, pp. 58-61.

MACLEOD, MORTON P., "The Hotel Appraisal for Ad Valorem Tax Assessment," *Appraisal and Valuation Manual,* American Society of Appraisers, pp. 89-98.

MACNAUGHTON, A. E., "Depreciation Under the Income Tax Act," *Appraisal Institute Magazine,* September, 1962, pp. 5-8.

MAGAZINE OF WALL STREET, "Undervalued Utilities Offer Tax-Sheltered Returns," *Magazine of Wall Street,* October 11, 1971, pp. 28.

MALONE, CLARENCE J, "Valuation of Public Utilities for Ad Valorem Tax How Can We Help Him Cope with It?," *Valutape Audio-Library Series,* American Society of Appraisers, Washington D.C., January 1, 1973.

MANN, P. C., J. L. MIKESELL, "Electric Utility Taxes: Incidence Revisited," *Public Utilities Fortnightly,* September 24, 1970, pp. 21-25.

MANN, PATRICK C. AND JOHN L. MIKESELL, "The Public Utility: a Taxpayer or a Tax Collector," *Florida Economic Indicators,* University of Florida, 1971, pp. 4.

MANNING, HAROLD ERNEST, *Assessment and Rating Being the Law of Municipal Taxation In Canada,* Cartwright, Toronto, 1951.

MARGULIES, WILLIAM, "Need for Appraisals Under Tax Laws," *The Appraisal Journal,* July, 1946, pp. 294-298.

MARKLE, SHELDON E., "Property Tax Administration In Michigan," *Assessors News Letter,* December, 1958, pp. 139-143.

MARSELE, PETER R. AND ALFRED CALABRESE, "Taxation of Open Spaces: Its Pros and Cons," *Assessors News Letter,* January, 1965, pp. 3-7.

MARTIN D. W., "Depreciation Policy of the Bureau of Internal Revenue Under T. D. 4422," *National Association of Cost Accounts, Bulletin,* pp. 235-242.

MARTIN, JAMES W., "Progress Toward More Accurate Valuation of Railroads for Taxation," *The Appraisal Journal,* January, 1955, pp. 77-86.

MARTIN, JAMES W., GLENN D. MORROW, *Organization for Kentucky Local Tax Assessments,* The University of Kentucky, Lexington, 1941.

MASSACHUSETTS LEGISLATIVE RESEARCH COUNCIL, *Report on University Payments In Lieu of Local Property Taxes,* Massachusetts Legislative Research Council, Boston, March, 1958.

MATTHEWS, MYRON L., "Why an 18" Yardstick to Measure Taxes," *Technical Valuation,* American Society of Appraisers, Washington, February, 1954, pp. 19.

MAYNARD, E. L., "Property Taxation of Electric and Gas Utilities," *Conference Proceedings,* National Tax Association, Columbus, 1959, pp. 248-251.

MCCARTHY, CLARENCE F., "Depreciation for Federal Income Tax Purposes," *Technical Valuation,* October, 1954, pp. 51-56.

MCDONALD, STEPHEN L., "The Effects of Severance Vs. Property Taxes on Petroleum Conservation," *Conference Proceedings,* National Tax Association, Columbus, 1965, pp. 320-327.

MCDONALD, STEPHEN L., "The Effects of Severance Vs. Property Taxes on Petroleum Conservation," *Conference Proceedings,* National Tax Association, Columbus, 1965, pp. 320-327.

## Appraisal for Special Purposes

MCDONNELL, N. B., "Forest Tax Developments In the Northwest--An Industry View," *Assessment Administration*, Institute of American Assessment Officers, Chicago, 1960, pp. 107-112.

MCDOWELL, HARRY G, *Mechanization of Real Property Assessment Records and Control and Production of Annual Tax Roll*, Office of the Director of Finance, Philadelphia, 1957, pp. 1-40.

MCGREGOR, GWENITH, *Tax Appeals, a Study of the Tax Appeal System of Canada, the United States and the United Kingdom*, Canadian Tax Foundation, Toronto, November, 1960, pp. 1-42.

MCKAY, R. J., "Tax Considerations In the Acquisition and Ownership of Real Estate," *Appraisal Institute Magazine*,

MCKINNON, NEIL J., "Consequences of White Paper for Tax Reform," *Appraisal Institute Magazine*, Appraisal Institute of Canada, Winnipeg.

MCLAUGHLIN, CHARLES J., "Taxation of Real Estate," *The Appraisal Journal*, April, 1940, pp. 153-155.

MCMICHAEL, JAMES M., "An Income Tax 'Motivated' Exchange," *Technical Valuation*, pp. 6.

MCMICHAEL, S. L., "Appraising for Purposes of Taxation," *Appraising Manual*, 1937, pp. 424-443.

MCMORRAN, J. BURCH, "New York Department of Public Works Appraisal Methods Promise Savings to Taxpayers," *Right of Way*, August, 1963, pp. PP933-34.

MCNULTY, J. W., "Amortization of Pollution Control Facilities How the New Election Works," *Journal of Taxation*, April, 1971, pp. 211-214.

MCNULTY, J. W., "Utility Aspects of Antipollution Taxes," *Public Utilities Fortnightly*, September 10, 1970, pp. 21 24.

MEAD, WALTER J., "Effect of Capital Gains Taxation on Timber Resource Allocation," *Conference Proceedings*, 1965, pp. 342-359.

MEANS, ERNEST E., "Assessment Standards and Property Tax Equity In Florida," *University of Florida Law Review*, 1964, pp. 83-108.

MEYER, HAROLD F., "Market Value-Beacon Light of Appraisal for Taxation," *The Appraisal Journal*, October, 1965, pp. 598-574.

MICHIGAN CITIZENS RESEARCH COUNCIL, *The Taxation of Public Utilities*, Citizens Research Council, Detroit, 1958, pp. 9.

MIELDS, HUGH JR., "Payment In Lieu of Taxes New Strength After a Long Struggle," *Virginia Municipal Review*, June, 1960, pp. 81-82.

MILLER, M. E., "On the Value-Added Tax In Denmark and the European Economic Community," *Bulletin for International Fiscal Documentation*, October, 1967, pp. 431-450.

MILLER, MARTIN D., "Mechanization of Major Property Assessment and Property Tax Administration Operation," *Assessment Administration*, 1960, pp. 27-33.

MILLER, WILLIAM STANLEY, "Valuation of Real Estate for Taxation," *The Appraisal Journal*, April, 1941, pp. 123-130.

MILLIMAN, J. W., "Price Policy and Land Value Taxation for Urban Watersupplies," *The American Journal of Economics and Sociology*, October, 1966, pp. 379-398.

MILLMAN, DEANE A., *A Brief History of Iron Ore Mining and Taxation In Minnesota*, Department of Taxation, St. Paul, 1964, pp. 15 PAGES.

MILLS, WILBUR D, "The Federal Government'S Role In Promoting Property Tax Reform," *Property Tax Reform*, Int'l Assn Assessing Officers, Chicago, June 1, 1973, pp. 4-7.

MISSOURI STATE TAX COMMISSION, *Biennial Report 10th For the Years 1935-36*.

MOAK, JAMES E., "Forest Appraisals for Assessment of Ad Valorem Taxes," *Journal of the American Society of Farm Managers and Rural Appraisers,* October, 1966, pp. 60-66.

MONTANA LEGISLATIVE COUNCIL, *Property Taxation and the Montana Property Classification Law,* December, 1964.

MONYEK, R. H., "Asset Deprec Range Reg Adopted with No Maj Chgs," *Journal of Taxation,* September, 1971, pp. 150-152.

MONYEK, R. H., "New Depreciation Rev Raises Ques As to Prior Yrs," *Journal of Taxation,* March, 1971, pp. 182-183.

MORA FERNANDEZ, DANIEL, *El Impuesto a La Propiedad Territorial,* Universidad Nacional Autonoma De Mexico, Mexico, 1961.

MORSS, ELLIOTT R., "Some Thoughts on the Determinants of State and Local Expenditures," *National Tax Journal,* March, 1966, pp. 95.

MUSGRAVE, RICHARD A., *Readings In the Economics of Taxation,* Richard D. Irwin, Homewood, Ill, 1959, pp. 581 PAGES.

MUSKIE, EDMUND S, "Essential Federal Role In Reform of Property Tax," *Property Tax Reform,* Int'l Assn Assessing Officers, Chicago, June 1, 1973, pp. 9-10.

MUSKIN, SELMA J., *Property Taxes the 1970 Outlook,* Council of State Governments, Chicago, 1965, pp. 69.

NAMAVATI, ROSHAN, *Theory & Practice of Valuation Land & Bldgs for Architects Engineers Surveyors & Tax Practitioners,* Universal Book Corp., Bombay, 1968.

NATION'S CITIES, *Are Property Taxes Obsolete,* March, 1965, pp. 17-32.

NATIONAL ASSOCIATION OF ASSESSING OFFICERS, *Construction and Use of Tax Maps,* Chicago, 1937.

NATIONAL ASSOCIATION OF COUNTY OFFICIALS, *Statement of the National Association of County Officials In Support of Payments In Lieu of Taxes,* Wasaington, January, 1956.

NATIONAL ASSOCIATION OF TAX ADMINISTRATORS, *Appraisal of Railroadand Other Public Utility Property for Ad Valorem Tax Purposes,* Chicago, 1954.

NATIONAL REAL ESTATE JOURNAL, "Valuation of Lessor's Interest In Leasehold Estate," *National Real Estate Journal,* March 16, 1931, pp. 22-23.

NATTHEN, LEONARD W., "Is the New Jersey Tax System Changing," *Conference Proceedings,* National Tax Association, Columbus, 1964, pp. 223-229.

NEBRASKA LEGISLATIVE COUNCIL, *Report of Nebr Leg Comm on Taxation of Livestock & Farm Property & Comm on Taxation of Intangibles,* Nebraska Legislative Council Rept No. 141, Lincoln, November, 1964.

NEBRASKA STATE TAX COMMISSIONER, *Uniform Instructions to the County and Precinct Assessors,* Wm. H. Smith, State Tax Commissioner, 1935.

NELSON, ROLAND D., "Real Estate Taxes and Value," *The Appraisal Journal,* January, 1966, pp. 41-43.

NETZER, DICK, *Economics of the Property Tax,* The Brookings Institution, 1966.

NEUTZMAN, R. A., "Current Rates of Return," *Technical Valuation,* American Society of Appraisers, 1967, pp. 3.

NEVINS, RICHARD, "The Taxation of Possessory Interest Intergovernmental Problem," *Assessment Administration,* 1964, pp. 117-119.

NEW JERSEY COMMISSION ON STATE TAX POLICY, *The Railroad Tax Problem,* New Jersey Commission on State Tax Policy, Trenton, New Jersey, May, 1964.

NEW JERSEY DIVISION OF TAXATION, *Real Property Appraisal Manual for New Jersey Assessors,* Trenton, New Jersey, 1963.

NEW JERSEY LOCAL PROPERTY TAX BUREAU, *How to Meet the Demands of Your Taxpayers,* Local Property Tax Bureau, Teenton, 1960.

▲ Appraisal for Special Purposes

NEW YORK CITY CITIZENS BUDGET COMMISSION, *How Real Estate Tax Rates Are Set,* New York, 1960.

NEWHOUSE, WADE J. JR., *Constitutional Uniformity and Equality Instate Taxation,* University of Michigan Law School, Ann Arbor, Michigan, 1959.

NICHOLLS, D. H., "Site Value Taxation," *Appraisal Institute Magazine,* Appraisal Institute of Canada, Winnipeg.

NICHOLLS, DAVID H., "Site-Value Taxation-Yes or No," *Appraisal Institute Magazine,* March, 1962, pp. 3-6.

NICHOLS, GEORGE L., "The Problem of Equity In Property Taxation," *Municipal Finance,* November, 1964, pp. 96-100.

NICHOLS, PHILIP, "Tax Valuation of Stocks: Factors In Determining Market Value for Estate, Income Taxes," *Trusts and Estates Lxxx,* January 1, 1945, pp. 93.

NICHOLS, PHILIP, "Two Problems In Tax Valuation," *The Appraisal Journal,* January, 1954, pp. 48-56.

NICHOLS, PHILIP, "Two Problems In Tax Valuation," *The Appraisal Journal,* April, 1954, pp. 225-235.

NICHOLS, THOMAS S., "Real Property Taxation of Divided Interest In Land," *Kansas Law Review,* March, 1963, pp. 309-329.

NOONAN, ALBERT W., "The Process of Tax Appraisal," *Assessment of Property for Taxation,* Editorial Research Reports, Washington, D. C., 1936.

NORTH DAKOTA TAX COMMISSION, *Assessment Manual for Assessors and Boards of Review and Equalization,* Bismarck, 1935.

NUETZMAN, R. A., "Inter-Interest Operation Expense and Property Tax Allocation Methods," *The Real Estate Appraiser,* January, 1969, pp. 17-28.

NURNBERG, H., "Present Val Deprec & Income Tax Allocation," *Accounting Review,* October, 1968.

ONEILL, JOSEPH HENRY, "Gas Station Taxes and Appraisals," *Appraisal Digest,* July, 1956, pp. 10-12.

OAKLAND, W. H., "Theory of Value-Added Tax: 1-A Compar of Tax Bases," *National Tax Journal,* June, 1967, pp. 119-136.

OFFICE, THE, "How Some Counties In California Process Property Tax Payments," *The Office,* May, 1963, pp. 138.

OGDEN, JAMES N., "Railroads Deserve Tax Equality," *Conference Proceedings,* National Tax Association, Columbus, 1960, pp. 377-388.

OLDMAN, O., AND H. AARON, "Assessment Sales Ratios Under the Boston Property Tax," *National Tax Journal,* March, 1965, pp. 36.

OLDMAN, OLIVER, "Mexico City's Property Tax Problems," *Conference Proceedings,* National Tax Association, Columbus, pp. 471.

OLDMAN, OLIVER, "Tax Reform In El Salvador," *Interamerican Law Review,* July, 1964, pp. 379-409.

OLSON, IRVING J., "A Midwest Experience In Wild Land and Forest Taxation," *Assessment Administration,* IAAO, Chicago, 1960, pp. 103-107.

OLSON, LYLE H., "The Value of Appraisals and Their Use for Sales and Tax Purposes," *Proceedings of the 18th Annual Convention,* National Association of Building Owners & Managers, pp. 250000.

OMLID, KENNETH E., "Pros and Cons of the Proposed 1 1/2 Limitation on Oregon Property Taxes," *Assessors News Letter,* May, 1966, pp. 67.

OREGON STATE TAX COMMISSION, VALUATION DIVISION, *Manual of Appraisal Methods for Real Property,* Oregon State Tax Commission, Salem, 1957.

OREGON STATE TAX COMMISSION, *Oregon Laws Relating to Assessment and Taxation,* Valuation Division, Salem, 1963.

OREGON UNIVERSITY, *Trend of Assessed Value of Taxable Property In Oregon by Classes of Property 1910-1937,* Bureau of Municipal Research and Service, University of Oregon, 1938.

ORR, JOHN, *Taxation of Land Values As it Affects Landowners and Others,* P. S. King and Son, London, 1912.

OTIS, ARTHUR S., *Added Revenue Without Burden A New Plan of Taxation,* Christopher Publishing Publishing House, Boston, 1958.

OXFORD AND ASQUITH, *The Land Values Taxes,* The Liberal Publication Department, London, 1909.

PAGE, GEORGE A. JR., "Massachusetts Real Estate Syndication Tax and Other Pitfalls," *Boston University Law Review,* 1963, pp. 491-521.

PARDUE, BEULAH LEA, *State Supervision of the Property Tax Assessments In Kentucky,* University of Kentucky, Lexington, 1948.

PARHAM, J. R., "Taxation of Property In Illinois," *University of Illinois Law Forum,* 1961, pp. 645-685.

PAUL, RANDOLPH E, "Estate and Gift Taxation Vol II," Little Brown and Co, Boston, January 1, 1942, pp. 1215.

PAUL, RANDOLPH E, "Studies In Federal Taxation," Callaghan and Co, Chicago, January 1, 1937, pp. 171.

PEALY, ROBERT H., *A Comparative Study of Property Tax Administration In Illinois and Michigan,* Institute of Public Administration, Ann Arbor, Michigan, 1956.

PELOUBET, MAURICE E., "Depreciation Under the Revenue Act of 1934," *Journal of Accountancy,* September, 1934, pp. 169-197.

PENNSYLVANIA STATE CHAMBER OF COMMERCE, "Special State Taxes; Exemptions on Forest Products and Forest Crop Lands," *Special State Taxes For Exemptions Forest Products and Forest Crop Lands,* Pennsylvania State Chamber of Commerce, Harrisburg, Pennsylv, July, 1960.

PERCIVAL, JOHN C., *Appraising for Tax Adjustment,* February, 1939.

PERIN, RENE, *Land Taxation-Austria,* Wein, Manz, 1912.

PERKINS, CARROLL M., MARTIN T. FARRIS, "Alternative Tax Depreciation," *Public Utilities Fortnightly,* March, 1960, pp. 456-465.

PESCHEL, J. L., "Oil and Gas Tax Planning Post-Reform Act Impact of CA-5s," *Journal of Taxation,* January, 1971, pp. 54-56.

PETERSON, RONALD S., "Assessment of Leasehold Interests In Tax-Exempt Realty In California," *California Law Review,* December, 1960, pp. 806-815.

PETHERICK J. P., "Valuations of Land Under 12c of the Land Tax Act, 1936-1972," *The Valuer,* The Commonwealth Institute of Valuers, Sydney Australia, October 1, 1973, pp. 602-606.

PHELAN, JAMES, "California Tax Scandal When I Looked In Those Files, My Eyes Popped," *Saturday Evening Post,* September, 1966, pp. 23.

PHILLIPS, BARBARA ASHLEY, "The Oregon Tax Court Some Thoughts on Its First Decisions," *Oregon Law Review,* June, 1963, pp. 292-327.

PICKARD, JEROME P., *Changing Urban Land Uses As Affected by Taxation,* Urban Land Institute, Washington, 1962.

PICKARD, JEROME P., "Using the Property Tax to Achieve Social and Economic Change," *Assessment Administration,* Institute of American Assessment Officers, Chicago, 1965, pp. 33.

PIERCE, J. T., "Tax Equalization by Scientific Appraising," *Review of Society of Residential Appraisers,* March, 1938, pp. 11-13.

PITMAN, HAYDEN W., "Exemption of Institutional Real Estate," *Assessment Administration,* Institute of American Assessments Officers, Chicago, pp. 137-141.

PLEYDELL, "Discussion of the Somers System," *Proceedings, 1913,* National Tax Association, 1913, pp. 267-281.

PODELL, BERTRAM L., AND S. HERBERT, "Valuation of Condominiums for Real Estate Tax Purposes," *Real Estate Forum,* November, 1969.

POLK, JAMES K., "Liberalized Depreciation for Federal Income Tax Purposes," *Technical Valuation,* June, 1954, pp. 49-53.

PRENTICE, P. K., "Case for Taxing Location Values," *The American Journal of Economics and Sociology,* April, 1969.

PRIMMER, JOHN L., "Charitable Exemption from Ad Valorem Taxation In Texas," *Southwestern Law Journal,* December, 1964, pp. 703.

PUBLIC AFFAIRS RESEARCH COUNCIL, *The Property Tax System of Louisiana Summary and Recommendations,* Public Affairs Research Council, Baton Rouge, 1960.

PURDY, VICTOR M., "Market Value of Obsolete Property for Tax Assessment Purpose," *Technical Valuation,* 1965, pp. 18-20.

RALSTON, JACKSON HARVEY, *What's Wrong with Taxation,* Ingram Institute, San Diego, Calif.

RAMS, EDWIN M., "The Single Land Tax Premise Some Concepts and Cases," *The Real Estate Appraiser,* July, 1963, pp. 2-11.

RANDALL, WILLIAM J., "Condemnation and the Income Tax Problem," *Real Estate Analyst Appraisal Bulletin,* 1961, pp. 301-304.

RAWSON, MARY, *Property Taxation and Urban Development,* Urban Land Institute, Washington, 1961.

RAWSON, MARY, "Site Value Taxation," *Appraisal Institute Magazine,* Appraisal Institute of Canada, Winnipeg.

RAWSON, MARY, "Site-Value Taxation--A Comment on Burnaby's Experience," *Appraisal Institute Magazine,* June, 1962, pp. 7-9.

REEVE, DOUGLAS W., "Site-Value Taxation--No," *Appraisal Institute Magazine,* March, 1963, pp. 12-14.

REEVES, CUTHBERT E., "On Net Rentals of Taxpayer Properties," *The Appraisal Journal,* January, 1937, pp. 69-72.

REGISTER, J. ALVIN, "Valuation of Lessor's Interest In Leasehold Estate Made for Purpose of Federal Estate Tax," *Practical Appraising Methods,* 1940, pp. 1-128.

REUTHER, J. L., "Report of Committee on Model Property Tax Assessment and Equalization Methods," *Conference Proceedings,* National Tax Association, Columbus, 1962, pp. 320-324.

REYNOLDS, SAMUEL T., "Appraisal and Assessment of Property for Purposes of Taxation," *Proceedings,* 1928, pp. 112.

RICE, RALPH S, "The Valuation of Close Held Stocks: a Lottery In Federal Taxation," *Law Review Xcvii,* University of Pennsylvania, December 1, 1950, pp. 385-388.

RICHMAN, RAYMOND L., "The Theory and Practice of Site Value Taxation In Pittsburg," *Conference Proceedings,* National Tax Association, Columbus, 1964, pp. PP259-271.

RICKS, R. BRUCE, "Tax Shelter and Annual Cash Flow In Investment Real Estate," *The Appraisal Journal,* April, 1966, pp. 300-303.

RINEHART, MORRIS L., "Reducing Compliance Costs Through More Uniform Tax Returns and Reporting Requirements," *Assessment Administration,* Institute of American Assessment Officers, Chicago, 1965, pp. 50-52.

ROBERTS, GORDON L., "Utah Tax on the Use of Tax-Exempt Property," *Utah Law Review,* 1964, pp. 415.

ROBERTS, JAMES O. JR., "Problems of Property Tax Valuation," *Conference Proceedings,* National Tax Association, Columbus, 1962, pp. 597-602.

ROBERTS, NORMAN L., "Property Taxation Taxable Status of Property Rented to Local Government," *Southern California Law Review*, 1962, pp. 361-367.

ROBERTS, SIDNEY I., "Federal Taxes and Real Estate Appraisals," *The Real Estate Appraiser*, March, 1966, pp. 11-18.

ROBERTS, THOMAS L., "Valuation of the Special Purpose Property," *Appraisal and Valuation Manual*, Corporate Press Incorporated, Washington, D. C, January, 1972, pp. 358.

ROBERTSON, JOHN MACKINNON, *The Great Budget: a Justification Explanation & Examination of the Taxes on Land Values*, The Liberal Publication Department, London, 1910, pp. 1-64.

RODDEWIG, CLARE M., "The Power to Tax," *Conference Proceedings*, National Tax Association, Columbus, 1965, pp. 165-170.

ROETTGER, G. J., "Just Compensation Frustration of an Owners Plans," *Appraisal Journal*, October, 1971, pp. 500-507.

ROGERS, CHARLES G., "Depreciation on Buildings As Defined by the Federal Income Tax Law," *National Association of Real Estate Boards Annuals*, 1925, pp. 183-196.

ROGERS, CHARLES G., "How Federal Income Tax Law Has Defined Building Depreciation," *National Real Estate Journal*, January 11, 1926, pp. 45-46.

ROMNEY, GEORGE W, "Case Against Federal Involvement In Property Tax Reform and Relief," *Property Tax Reform*, Int'l Assn Assessing Officers, Chicago, June 1, 1973, pp. 11-14.

ROSTVOLD, WERHARD N., "Distribution of Property, Retail, Sales, and Property Income Tax Burdens In California," *Assessment Bibliography*.

ROWLANDS, DAVID T., "Commonly Accepted Evidences of Real Estate Value for Purposes of Taxation," *American Academy of Political and Social Science Annals*, March, 1930, pp. 88-96.

RUHE, KARL, "The IRS Position on Allocation of Intangibles In Business Acquisitions," September 1, 1965, pp. 50-54.

RUHE, KARL, "U. S. International Revenue Service Effect of Legislation on Real and Personal Property," *Appraisal and Valuation Manual*, Corporate Press, Incorporated, Washington, D. C, January, 1972, pp. 320.

RUJZ SANCHES, JOSE, *Impuesta Predial Y Leyes De Planificcion*, Universidad Nacional Autonoma De Mexico, Mexico, 1963, pp. 1-133.

RYBECK, WALTER, "Impact of Taxation and Assessments on Urban Development," *The Real Estate Appraiser*, pp. 27.

RYBECK, WALTER, "Making the Property Tax Work for Urban Development," *Property Tax Reform*, Int'l Ass'n Assessing Officers, Chicago, June 1, 1973, pp. 125-134.

SABBADINI, ALEX, "Estate Appraiser: Fine Art,Personal Property; Important Role In the Community," *Valutape Audio-Library Series*, American Society of Appraisers, Washington D.C., January 1, 1973.

SABBADINI, ALEX, "The Estate Appraiser and His Role In His Community," *Appraisal and Valuation Manual*, Corporate Press Incoporated, Washington, D. C, January, 1972, pp. 390.

SANDISON, R. W., C. O. LIVINGSTON, "The Tax Reform Act of 1969 As it Affects Real Estate," *The Real Estate Appraiser*, March, 1970, pp. 5-15.

SANDS, LAWRENCE, "The Effect of Financing and Taxation on Market Value," *Assessment Administration*, Institute of American Assessment Officers, Chicago, 1964, pp. 69-72.

SAZAMA, G. W., "Equalization of Property Taxes for the Nation's Largest Central Cities," *National Tax Journal*, June, 1965, pp. 151-161.

SCAARFF, MAURICE R., "Relation of Income Tax to Engineering Economics and to Valuation of Public Utility Property," *Technical Valuation*, October, 1950, pp. 5-10.

SCARRY, DONALD M. PH. D., *The Effects of Degree of Reliance on Property Taxation on State-Local Expenditures,* Rutgers University, 1971.

SCHAAF, A. H., "Effects of Property Taxation on Slums and Renewal—A Study of Land Improvement Assessment Ratios," *Land Economics,* February, 1969, pp. 111-117.

SCHACKNE, JOHN R., "On Appraising the Business District of Toledo, Ohio for Tax Purposes," *The Appraisal Journal,* January, 1938, pp. 71-73.

SCHEFTEL, YETTA, "A Study of Certain Discriminatory Taxes on Land, Boston and New York," *The Taxation of Land Value,* Houghton Mifflin Company, 1916, pp. 1-489.

SCHIEFFELIN, WILLIAM JAY, "Housing and Taxation," *Architectural Forum,* March, 1939, pp. 206.

SCHIMMEL, ALBERT, "Some Standards for Tax Assessments," *Technical Valuation,* June, 1955, pp. 27.

SCHIMMEL, ALFRED, "Some Standards for the Appraisal of Real Estate for Tax Assessment Purposes," *Appraisal and Valuation Manual,* pp. 232.

SCHLAGENHAUF, PAUL, "The Appraisal of Vacant Subdivision Lots for Taxation Purposes," *The Appraisal Journal,* January, 1934, pp. 93-97.

SCHMIDT, EDWARD BENJAMIN, *Estimated Impact of Retail Sales Tax In Nebraska,* University of Nebraska, Lincoln, Nebraska, 1956, pp. 1-28.

SCHMUTZ, GEORGE L., "Taxes, Assessments and Appraisals," *The Appraisal Journal,* July, 1939, pp. 252-257.

SCHMUTZ, GEORGE L., LORING O. MCCORMICK, "The Influence of Real Estate Taxes on Values," *The Appraisal Journal,* January, 1933, pp. 128-131.

SEASTONE, DOW, AND L. M. HARTMAN, "Resource Transfers and Economic Externalities In the Public Sector," *Conference Proceedings,* National Tax Association, Columbus, 1965, pp. 306-320.

SELL, R., "Tax and Business Considerations In Leasing Property," *Taxes,* March, 1964, pp. 159.

SHANNON, FRANCIS JOHN, *The Conflict Between Law & Admin Practice In Valuation of Property for Taxation In Kentucky,* University of Kentucky, Lexington, Ky., 1957, pp. 1-112.

SHANNON, JOHN, "Commentary on the Advisory Commissions' Suggested Property Tax Legislation," *Assessment Administration,* Institute of American Assessment Officers, Chicago, 1964, pp. 36-39.

SHAPIRO, HARVEY, *Taxation of Tangible Personal Property Used In Agriculture,* U. S. Dept of Agriculture Economic Research Servic, Washington, 1962, pp. 1-45.

SHARP, PHILIP D. JR., "Real Estate Taxation of Fraternities and Faculty Houses," *Washington and Lee Law Review,* 1963, pp. 187-192.

SHEEDY, PAUL, "Veterans' Tax Exemption," *Tax Digest,* February, 1960, pp. 31-37.

SHIPLEY, ROBERT C. JR., "Property Valuation and the Internal Revenue Code," *Valuation,* September, 1972, pp. 32.

SHOOP, CARL S., "Comparative Approaches to Tax Policy Within the Major Countries," *Conference Proceedings,* National Tax Association, Columbus, 1965, pp. 409-416.

SILVERHERZ, JOSEPH D., "Appraisal Systems for Tax Purposes," *Real Estate Record,* National and Metropolitan Editions, July 18, 1936, pp. 30-33.

SIMONEAUX, MERVIN J., *Accelerated Depreciation Tax Advantages and Corporate Income Determination,* Louisiana State University, Baton Rouge, La., 1957.

SLY, JOHN F., *Deep In the Heart of Taxes Property Taxes In the State of Washington*, Research Council, Seattle, 1958.

SMALE, JOHN G., *Recent Developments In General Property Tax Assessment In California*, Boulder Conference Committee, Milwaukee, 1965.

SMITH, DAN T., "Tax Aspects of Depreciation, Commercial and Financial Chronicle," *American Society of Appraisers Manual*, February 1, 1958, pp. 11.

SMITH, R. S., "Property Tax Capitalization In San Francisco," *National Tax Journal*, June, 1970, pp. 177-193.

SMITH, RALPH ELBERTON, *Customs Valuation In the United States A Study In Tarriff Administration*, University of Chicago Press, Chicago, 1948.

SMITH, T. R., "Land Value Vs. Real Property Taxation A Case Study Comparison," *Land Economics*, August, 1970.

SMITH, WALSTEIN JR., "Appraising for Probate and Estates," *The Real Estate Appraiser*, 1907, pp. 9-11.

SMITH, WILEY W., "Exemption of Institutional Real Estate," *Assessment Administration*, IAAO, Chicago, 1957, pp. 142-145.

SODERQUIST, OSCAR, "Appraising for Tax Adjustments," *The Appraisal Journal*, January, 1933, pp. 170-171.

SOUTH DAKOTA LEGISLATIVE RESEARCH COUNCIL, *Oil and Gas Taxation Practices In Selected States*, South Dakota Legislative Research Council, Ltd., Pierre, S. D., 1960.

SOUTHERLAND, EDWIN W., "The Property Tax: Some Observation for the Tax Executive," *Tax Executive*, October, 1964, pp. 25-28.

SPEIDEL, R. E., "State and Local Taxation of the United States and Its Contractors," *Law and Contemporary Problems*, 1964, pp. 160.

SPILKER, JOHN B., "Methods of Appraising Real Estate for Taxation Purposes," *Real Estate Business As a Profession*, 1941, pp. 218.

SPILKER, JOHN B., "Methods of Tax Valuation," *Real Estate Business As a Profession*, 1941, pp. 219-220.

ST. PETERSBURG, FLORIDA FINANCE DEPARTMENT, *Pinelles County Tax Study*, Finance Department, St. Petersburg, 1964.

STATHAM, ROBERT R, "Expenditure Control Through Limitations on the Property Tax," *Property Tax Reform*, Int'l Ass'n Assessing Officers, Chicago, June 1, 1973, pp. 159-167.

STERLING, H. ALBERT, "Neighboring Factors Affecting Residential Values," *The Appraisal Journal*, January, 1960, pp. 81-89.

STEWART, J. S., "Tax Reform-Implications for Appraisers," *Appraisal Institute Magazine*, Appraisal Institute of Canada, Winnipeg, September 1, 1972.

STEWART, SAMUEL B., "Protecting the Taxpayer from Excessive Assessments," *Conference Proceedings*, National Tax Association, Columbus, 1961, pp. 77-84.

STILES, LYNN A., "Financing Government In the Suburbs: the Role of the Property Tax," *Conference Proceedings*, National Tax Association, Colombus, 1960, pp. 52.

STOKES, CHARLES J., "The Property Tax Reconsidered," *American Journal of Economics and Sociology*, October, 1963, pp. 473-482.

STOREY, HAROLD, *Taxation of Land Values*, Liberal Publication, London, 1927.

STRAUSS, GEORGE, "The Effect of Tax on Yield and Value," *The Appraisal Journal*, February, 1969, pp. 389-392.

STUDDARD, KENNETH E., "Tax Aspects of Apartment Ownership," *The Residential Appraiser*, July, 1962, pp. 13-16.

STUETZER JR, HERMAN, "Valuing Business Interests of a Decedent," *The Implication of Revenue Ruling 59-60*, Matthew Bender Co Inc, New York, January 1, 1960, pp. 1196.

SURIANO, HORACIO O., *Revaluo Impositivo, Ley 17.335*, Proinvert, Buenos Aires, 1967.

SUTER, ROBERT C, *The Appraisal of Farm Real Estate (Book)*, Interstate Printers and Publishers Inc, Lafayette Indiana, January 1, 1974.

SUTHERLAND, CHARLES F., AND ELLIS T. WILLIAMS, "Timberland and Taxes In Maine: Property and Federal Income Taxes," *Maine Law Review,* 1965, pp. 227-251.

TARRANT, JOHN F., "The Courts As Tax Value Determinators," *Assessors News Letter,* October, 1955, pp. 112-115.

TAX ADMINISTRATION NEWS, "Federation of Tax Administrators," *Tax Administration News,* October, 1987.

TAX ADMINISTRATION NEWS, "Fifteen States Have Independent Tax Review Agencies," *Tax Administrators News,* June, 1904, pp. 61-62.

TAX ADMINISTRATION NEWS, "State Taxation of Intangible Personal Property," *Tax Administration News,* October, 1960, pp. 1-2.

TAX ADMINISTRATION NEWS, "The Use of Data Processing Equipment by State Tax Departments Tabulated," *Tax Administrators News,* October, 1962, pp. 109-110.

TAX INSTITUTE INCORPORATED, *Depreciation and Taxes,* Princeton, 1959, pp. 248.

TAX INSTITUTE, INCORPORATED, *Management's Stake In Tax Administration,* Princeton, 1961.

TAX INSTITUTE, INCORPORATED, *State and Local Taxes on Business,* Princeton, December, 1965, pp. 357.

TAX POLICY, "The Unpopular Personal Property Tax," *Tax Policy,* January, 1957.

TAYNTON, M., "Effect of Salvage Value on Depreciation Taxes," *A. S. A. Manual,* February, 1958, pp. 97-98/.

TENNESSEE BOARD OF EQUALIZATION, *Rules and Regulations of Practice and Procedure,* Tennessee Board of Equalization, Nashville, 1961.

TERBORGH, GEORGE, "Effect of the New Tax Depreciation Methods on the Earnings of Depreciable Assets," *Effect of the New Tax Depreciation Methods on the Earnings of Depreciable Assets,* Machinery and Allied Products Institute, Washington, 1956.

TEXAS COMMISSION ON STATE AND LOCAL TAX POLICY, "Property Taxation and Local Revenues," *Preliminary Report,* Austin, 1961.

THEISS, WILLIAM R., "The Appraisal Docket. Effect of Owner's Statement of Value In Tax Proceedings," *The Appraisal Journal,* October, 1962, pp. 550-551.

THEISS, WILLIAM R., "The Appraisal Docket. Valuation of Personal Property for Tax Assessment," *The Appraisal Journal,* January, 1965, pp. 126-129.

THEISS, WILLIAM R., "The Appraisal Docket, Tax Assessment--Damages for Failure to Assess Equally," *The Appraisal Journal,* July, 1962, pp. 417-418.

THOMPSON, JOSEPH SEXTON, *Taxation's New Frontier, a Businessman's Study of Dignified Vs. Contemptible Taxation,* Robert Schalkenbach Foundation, New York, 1961, pp. 1-96.

THORSON, IVAN A., "Our Real Estate Tax Problem," *The Appraisal Journal,* October, 1937, pp. 357-364.

THORSON, IVAN A., "Reform In Appraising Property for Taxation," *California Real Estate Magazine,* May, 1935, pp. 28-29.

TUCKER, GILBERT M., "Tax Reduction or Tax Relief-Which?," *The Appraisal Journal,* July, 1947, pp. 392-398.

TUCKETT, HARVEY GARNETT PHIPPS, *The Indian Revenue System As it Is,* Elder and Company, Smith, pp. 1-2.

TURE, NORMAN B, "Shortcomings of the Property Tax," *Property Tax Reform,* Int'l Ass'n Assessing Officers, Chicago, June 1, 1973, pp. 92-98.

U. S. ADVISORY COMM ON INTERGOVERNMENTAL RELATIONS, *State Constitutional and Statutory Restrictions on Local Taxing Powers,* Government Printing Office, Washington, October, 1962, pp. 1-122.

U. S. ADVISORY COMM ON INTERGOVERNMENTAL RELATIONS, *Suggested Property Tax Legislation,* Govt. Printing Office, Washington.

U. S. ADVISORY COMM ON INTERGOVERNMENTAL RELATIONS, *The Intergovernmental Aspects of Documentary Taxes,* Government Printing Office, Washington, September, 1964.

U. S. ADVISORY COMM ON INTERGOVERNMENTAL RELATIONS, *The Roleof the States In Strengthening the Property Tax,* Government Printing Office, Washington, 1963, pp. 1-187.

U. S. AGRICULTURAL RESEARCH SERVICE, *Farm Real Estate Taxes, Recent Trends and Developments,* U. S. Agricultural Research Service, Washington, 1960, pp. 1-14.

U. S. AGRICULTURAL RESEARCH SERVICE, *Taxes Levied on Farm Propertyin the United States and Methods of Estimating Them,* Government Printing Office, Washington, August, 1956, pp. 1-47.

U. S. AGRICULTURAL RESEARCH SERVICE, *Taxes Levied on Farm Real Estate In 1958,* U. S. Agricultural Reaearch Service, Washington, 1959, pp. 1-11.

U. S. AGRICULTURAL RESEARCH SERVICE, *The General Property Tax In State Finances,* U. S. Agricultural Research Service, Washington, April, 1960, pp. 1-18.

U. S. BUREAU OF THE CENSUS, "Census of Governments, 1962," *Taxable Property Values,* 1963.

U. S. DEPARTMENT OF AGRICULTURE, *State Actions Relating to Taxation of Farmland on the Rural-Urban Fringe,* U. S. Department of Agriculture, Washington, August, 1961, pp. 1-23.

U. S. INTERNAL REVENUE SERVICE, "Regulation 51; Retailers Excise Taxes, Chapter 19 I.R.C.," *U.S. Gov't Printers Excise Taxes,* U.S. Internal Revenue Service.

U. S. INTERNAL REVENUE SERVICE, "T. D. 6182 Depreciation," *American Society of Appraisers,* June 12, 1956.

U. S. JOINT COMMITEE ON INTERNAL REVENUE TAXATION, *Preliminary Report on Depletion,* 1929, pp. 1-76.

U. S. URBAN RENEWAL ADMINISTRATION, *Open Space Land, Planning and Taxation,* Govt. Printing Office, Washington, 1963.

UNRUH, JESSE M., "Growing Public Awareness of the Property Tax," *Assessment Administration,* IAAO, Chicago, 1964, pp. 10-17.

URBAN LAND INSTITUTE, *Taxation and the Shopping Center, a Statement of Policy,* Urban Land Institute, Washington, 1959, pp. 1-4.

UTAH FOUNDATION, *Problems In Utah Property Tax Administration,* Utah Foundation, Salt Lake City, 1960, pp. 1-6.

VAN FLEET, J. B., "The Taxation and Valuation of Oil and Gas Resources," *Assessment Administration,* IAAO, Chicago, 1963, pp. 125-131.

VAN HORNE, J., "Interest Rate Risk and the Term Structure of Interestrates," *The Journal of Political Economy,* Stanford University, U. S. A, August, 1965, pp. 344-351.

VAN VUUREN, W., "An Evaluation of Ontarios Farm Assessment Proposals for Property Taxation," *Canadian Journal of Agricultural Economics,* July, 1970.

VAUGHAN, J. L. JR., "Appraisal of Commercial Properties for Purposes of Tax Assessment," *Technicalities,* June, 1951, pp. 40-42.

VEGA, ELIAS E., RALPH B. SHORT, "National Tax Administration In the Philippines," *Washington Law Review,* August, 1965, pp. 579-601.

VERMONT TAX DEPARTMENT, *Timberland Appraisal Guide,* Vermont Tax Department, Montpelier, Vermont, May, 1960, pp. 1-13.

VIEIRO, RAUL OSCAR, *Revaluacion Impositiva,* 1967, pp. 1-214.

VON LEHE, ARTHUR R., "Appraising Industrial Property for Ad Valorem Tax Purposes," *Appraisal and Valuation Manual,* Asa, 1956, pp. 161-168.

WALD, HASKELL P., *Taxation of Agricultural Land In Underdeveloped Economies; a Survey and Guide to Policy,* University Press, Cambridge, 1959, pp. 1-231.

WALKER, MABEL, "Eroding the Tax Base by Exemptions," *Conference Proceedings,* National Tax Association, Columbus, 1965, pp. 226-233.

WALKER, MABEL, "Limitations of the Property Tax," *Conference Proceedings,* National Tax Association, Columbus, 1963, pp. 406-411.

WALKER, MABEL, "Property Tax Expedients In Urban Renewal," *Conference Proceedings,* National Tax Association, Columbus, 1960, pp. 44.

WALKER, MABEL, "Unsettled Questions In Real Estate Taxation," *Tax Policy,* June, 1960.

WALKER, PAUL H., "District of Columbia Taxation of 1964-1965," *Journal of the Bar Association of the District of Columbia,* April, 1965, pp. 139-148.

WALKER, WILLIAM P., *Improving Farm Land Tax Assessments In Maryland Under Nonfarm Use,* Univ of Maryland Agricultural Experiment Station, College Park, June, 1965, pp. 1-38.

WALL, WILLIAM J, "The Appraiser and the Real Estate Tax Shelter," *Valuation Magazine,* American Society of Appraisers, Washington D C, December 1, 1973, pp. 94-101.

WALRATH, ARTHUR J., "Equalization of Property Taxes In an Urban-Rural Area," *Land Economics,* February, 1957, pp. 47-54.

WALTHER, HERMAN O., "The Valuation Base for Ad Valorem Taxation," *The Appraisal Journal,* January, 1939, pp. 9-18.

WARD, STANLEY, "Some Comments on the Valuation of a Federally Regulated Natural Gas Pipeline," *Conference Proceedings,* National Tax Association, Columbus, 1961, pp. 86.

WARD, WILLIAM REGINALD, *The English Land Tax In the Eighteenth Century,* Oxford University Press, London, 1953.

WARWICK, SAMUEL C., "Income Approach In Reality Tax Cases," *The Real Estate Appraiser,* SREA, Chicago, September, 1967, pp. 33.

WASHINGTON STATE TAX COMMISSION, *Washington Rural Land Appraisal Manual,* Washington State Tax Commission, Olympia, 1957.

WASHINGTON TAX COMMISSION, *Building Appraisal Manual,* Washington Tax Comm.

WEDGEWOOD, JOSIAH C., *The Land Question, Taxation and Rating of Land Values,* The Labour Party, London, 1920, pp. 11.

WEILER, R. J., *A Critical Examination of Existing Real Estate Taxation Valuation Procedures,* Dissertation Abstracts, Vol. Xxix, No. 3, Ann Arbor, September, 1968, pp. 711-A.

WEILER, ROBERT J., "Is Downtown Really Overtaxed?," *The Real Estate Appraiser,* March, 1969, pp. 12-15.

WEISS, W. B., "Is Free Mass Transportation In Down-Town's Future," *Stores,* April, 1971, pp. 51-52.

WELCH, R. B., "Some Observation on Assessment Ratio Measurement," *National Tax Journal,* March, 1965, pp. 13-21.

WELCH, RONALD B., "Ad Valorem Taxation of Petroleum Producing Properties," *Assessors News Letter,* February, 1964, pp. 15-17.

WELCH, RONALD B., "Report of the Committee on Model Property Tax Assessment and Equalization Methods," *Assessors News Letter,*

WELTZ, VERNON R., "The Valuation of Branch Inventories and Stock on Consignment for Ad Valorem Tax Purposes," *Assessment Administration,* IAAO, Chicago, 1959, pp. 46-51.

WENDT, P. F., A. R. CERF, "Appraisers Bookshelf, Real Estate Investment Analysis and Taxation," *The Real Estate Appraiser,* March, 1970, pp. 61-62.

WEST VIRGINIA LAW REVIEW, "Taxation and Land Titles Under Article Xiii of the West Virginia Constitution," *West Virginia Law Review,* June, 1963, pp. 263-285.

WEST VIRGINIA TAX COMMISSION, *Assessor's Manual,* Charleston, 1925.

WESTERN KENTUCKY UNIVERSITY, *Tax Research Center,* Legislative Research Commission, Frankfort, 1967, pp. 1-108.

WEYERHAEUSER COMPANY, *Plain Talk About Trees and Taxes,* Weyerhaeuser Company, Tacoma.

WHITTAKER, THOMAS PALMER, *The Ownership, Tenure and Taxation of Land, Some Facts, Fallacies and Proposals Relating Thereto,* Macmillan and Company, Ltd, London, 1914, pp. 1-574.

WILLIAMS, CHARLES A. JR., *Florida Constitution and Legislative Classification for Tax Assessment Purposes,* University of Florida Law Review, 1965, pp. 609-615.

WILLIAMS, ELLIS T., "Forest Tax Alternatives and Trends," *Assessment Administration,* Institute of American Assessment Officers, Chicago, 1960, pp. 97-102.

WILLIAMS, ELLIS T., "Some Aspects of Forest Taxation Under the Forest Crop Law and Under the General Property Tax In Wis," *Land Economics,* February, 1960, pp. 65-78.

WILLIAMS, ELLIS T., "Trends In Forest Taxation," *National Tax Journal,* June, 1961, pp. 113-114.

WILLIAMS, PERCY R., "Pittsburgh Pioneering In Scientific Taxation," *American Journal of Economics and Sociology,* January, 1962, pp. 37-56.

WILSON, D. EARL, "Actual Appraisal Reports Series 11: No 1 Industrial Riverfront Valuation for Tax Reduction Purposes," *National Real Estate Journal,* April, 1934, pp. 40-42.

WINGATE, HAROLD C., "The Assessor's Approach to the Taxpayer," *Assessor's News Letter,* March, 1966, pp. 38-42.

WINSOR, EDWARD H., "Tax Differential Capitalization," *The Appraisal Journal,* October, 1948, pp. 455-458.

WISCONSIN BOARD OF TAX APPEALS, *First Report,* Madison, September 7, 1939.

WISCONSIN LEGISLATIVE REFERENCE LIBRARY, *Taxation of State-Owned Prop Under Genl Prop Tax In Several States with Spec Ref to Wisconsin,* Wisconsin Legislative Reference Library, Madison, April, 1962, pp. 1-20.

WISCONSIN LEGISLATIVE REFERENCE LIBRARY, *The Taxation of State-Owned Property Under the General Property Tax,* Madison, March, 1960, pp. 1-15.

WISCONSIN TAXPAYER, "Property Tax Procedure," *Wisconsin Taxpayer,* June, 1964.

WOLFF, LEWIS, "Real Estate Aspects of the Current Tax Structure," *Real Estate Analyst Appraisal Bulletin,* 1960, pp. 451-454.

WOLITZER, P., "Co-Operative Housing Corporation-Development, Accounting, and Taxation," *New York Certified Public Accountant,* June, 1970, pp. 463-474.

WOODRUFF, A. M., "Land or Site Value Taxation," *Assessment Administration,* Institute of American Assessment Officers, Chicago, 1964, pp. 99-103.

WOODRUFF, A. M., "Tax Laws Affect Land Development," *Appraisal Digest,* January, 1962, pp. 17-22.

WOODRUFF, ARCH, "The Australian, New Zealand, and American Property Tax Systems," *Assessment Administration*, Institute of American Assessment Officers, Chicago, 1965, pp. 195-200.

WOODRUFF, ARCHIBALD, "The Property Tax As a Fiscal Resource for American Municipalities," *Illinois Municipal Review*, August, 1964, pp. 7-12.

WOODRUFF, ARCHIBALD W, "Strengths and Weaknesses of the Property Tax," *Property Tax Reform*, Int'l Ass'n Assessing Officers, Chicago, June 1, 1973, pp. 100-124.

WOODRUFF, ARCHIBALD, JR., "The Property Tax Some Urgent Problems," *Tax Review*, April, 1964.

WOODWARD, DONALD B., "Prices, Taxes, and Inflation," *The Appraisal Journal*, January, 1943, pp. 11-14.

YALE LAW JOURNAL, "Toward an Equitable and Workable Program of Mobile Home Taxation," *Yale Law Journal*, March, 1962, pp. 702-719.

YOUNG, MELVIN A., "Organization and Installation of Method for a Tax Equalization Program," *American Society of Appraisers Valuation Manual*, 1959, pp. 215.

ZANABONI VELAZQUEZ, DINAK, *Reflexiones Sobre La Tasa En Los Impuestos*, Mexico, 1965.

ZAVIN, LOUIS B., *How to Minimize Taxes on Sale of a Business Under Section 337 on the Internal Revenue Code*, 1961, pp. 307.

ZAVIN, LOUIS B., "Corporation Income Taxes," *American Society of Appraisers-Appraisal and Valuation Manual*, 1959, pp. 347-356.

ZAVIN, LOUIS B., "Depreciation In Relation to the 1954 Revenue Act," *American Society of Appraisers-Appraisal and Valuation Manual*, 1958, pp. 283-288.

ZAVIN, LOUIS B., "Tax Opportunities In Real Estate," *Appraisal and Valuation Manual*, American Society of Appraisers, 1960, pp. 309-318.

ZETTLEMOYER, CHARLES L., AND MICHAEL ADES, "Timberlands Taxation In Kentucky," *Timberlands Taxation In Kentucky*, Legislative Research Commission, Frankfort, Kentucky, 1963.

ZIRKEL, WILLIAM, "Excessive Taxation & Its Effect on Real Estate Val," *The Real Estate Appraiser*, September, 1970.

# 12-12 Equalization

*Ad Valorem Taxation: Appraisal Accounting Controlling Assesmt Equalztn & Tax Roll Preparation*, Taylor, William E., San Bernadino, 1956.

ALAND, ROBERT HARRIS, "Ad Valorem Property Taxation: Equalization by Injunction," *Alabama Law Review*, April, 1962, pp. 389-402.

ARNOLD, MAX P., "Colorado Appraisal Program," *Technical Valuation*, February, 1953, pp. 39-40, 56.

BALDWIN, ROSALIND G., "The New York Equalization Rate Programs Progress and Problems," *Conference Proceedings*, National Tax Association, Columbus, 1961, pp. 65-76.

BALLOU, PAUL H., "Maintaining Equalization-A Three Stage Production," *Assessment Administration*, IAAO, Chicago, 1960, pp. 72-77.

BELLS, ZURA E., "The Alameda Equalization Appraisal," *National Real Estate Journal*, October, 1928, pp. 26-30.

BLOUGH, J. ROY, "Recent Developments In Methods of Real Estate Tax Equalization In Wisconsin," *The Journal of Land and Public Utility Economics*, May, 1934, pp. 137-147.

BROWN, UDELL C., "Equalization Problems In the State Assessment of Corporate Property," *Conference Proceedings*, National Tax Association, Columbus, 1964, pp. 410-414.

CAMPNEY, ALBERT E., "How to Sell a Re-Appraisal Program," *Assessor News Letter*, July, 1957, pp. 78-82.

CARR, ANTHONY W., "Some Suggestions for Volume Appraisers," *The Real Estate Appraiser*, pp. 37.

CASETTI, E., "Equilibrium Land Values and Population Densities In an Urban Setting," *Economic Geography*, January, 1971.

CHRISTOPHER, S. H., "Aerial Photography As a Low Cost Aid for Equalization Work," *Public Works*, March, 1958, pp. 106-108.

CLEMINSHAW, J. M., "The Revaluation of Municipalities for Tax Equalization Purposes," *The Appraisal Journal*, January, 1944, pp. 52-65.

COOMBE, J. P., "Maintenance of Equalized Assessments After a Revaluation Program," *Technical Valuation*, June, 1961, pp. 55-57.

COOMBE, J. P., "Means to an End," *Assessment Administration*, IAAO, Chicago, 1960, pp. 74-77.

DUVALL, LOY CLEVELAND LEE, *The Taxation and Equalization of City, Town and County Real Estate*, W. M. Warlick, Dallas, Texas, 1901.

EAGAN, LAURENCE J., "Personal Property Valuation," *Assessment Administration*, Institute of American Assessment Officers, Chicago, 1963, pp. 226-229.

EARLY, ALEXANDER R., "Local Equalization Practice In California," *Santa Clara Lawyer*, 1964, pp. 147-165.

EISENLAUER, JACK F., "Mass Versus Individual Appraisers," *The Appraisal Journal*, October, 1968, pp. 533-535.

FEDERATION OF TAX ADMINISTRATORS, *Equalization Programs and Other State Supervisory Activities In the Property Tax Field*, Federation of Tax Administrators, Chicago, January, 1957.

FERGUSON, HILL, "Mass Appraising," *The Appraisal Journal*, April, 1943, pp. 156-161.

GARCIA, K., "Sales Prices and Cash Equivalents," *Appraisal Journal*, January, 1972.

GASTON, JAMES E., "Information Possibilities Available Through Data Processing Equipment," *Assessment Administration*, I. A. A. O, Chicago, 1964, pp. 131-133.

GIBSON, LIOYD C., "Bureau's New Depreciation Policy," *Tax Magazine*, June, 1934, pp. 279-285.

GOLDMAN, ABRAM F., "California's Intercounty Equalization Program the Appraiser's Viewpoint," *The Appraisal Journal*, April, 1965, pp. 255-260.

INTERNATIONAL CITY MANAGERS ASSOCIATION, *Municipal Finance Administration*, International City Managers Association, Chicago, 1962.

JACOBS, J. L., "Systematic Real Property Appraisal and Assessment Equalization," *Assessors News Letter*, January, 1964, pp. 3-5.

KANS., CITIZENS COMM ON ASSESSMEN. EQUALIZATION, "A Program of Action to Improve Assessment Procedures In Kansas," *A Program of Action to Improve Assessment Procedures In Kansas*, Library of Congress, Topeka, Kansas, 1954.

KEENE, J., "Convert it to a Condominium," *House and Home*, January, 1971, pp. 106-111.

KEITH, JOHN H., "Maintenance of Equalization Between Real and Personal Property," *Assessors News Letter*, March, 1960, pp. 27-33.

KEITH, JOHN H., "The Role of Institute of American Appraisers Officers, In the Years Ahead," *Assessment Administration*, Institute of American Appraisers Officers, Chicago, 1963, pp. 10-15.

KENT, FREDERICK C., "Compound Amount of 1," *Mathematic Principles of Finance,* New York, 1927.

KOPLIK, MARILYN S., *Property Tax Assessment In the United States, Preliminary Report to New York State,* Board of Equalization and Assessment, Albany, March, 1961.

MIDDLEMIST, W. J., "Colorado's Equalization Program," *Technicalities,* June, 1951, pp. 12-14.

MISSISSIPPI STATE TAX COMMISSION, *Rules and Regulation for the Equalization of Assessment Rolls,* Jackson, May 1, 1934.

MORGAN, CECIL L., "Equalizing Assessments of City Properties," *Technicalities and Technical Valuation,* June, 1952, pp. 23-26.

MOURRAY, JAMES W., "Legal, Nonconforming Use Appeal," *The Appraisal Journal,* October, 1966, pp. 592-595.

N. Y. STATE BOARD OF EQUALIZATION & ASSESSMENT, *Principles and Procedures Used In Establishing State Equalization Rates,* Albany, New York, 1961.

NEW JERSEY DIVISION OF TAXATION, *Table of Equalized Valuations,* Trenton, New Jersey, 1954.

NICHOLS, ALAN H., "Comment How Not to Contest Special Assessments In California or You Can T Beat City Hall," *Stanford Law Review,* June, 1965, pp. 267-256.

PIERCE, J. T., "Tax Equalization by Scientific Appraising," *Review of Society of Residential Appraisers,* March, 1938, pp. 11-13.

PIERRE, JOHN A., "Detail on the United States Plywood-Algoma Case," *Assessment Administration,* Institute of American Assessment Officers, Chicago, 1959, pp. 129-131.

REUTHER, J. L., "Report of Committee on Model Property Tax Assessment and Equalization Methods," *Conference Proceedings,* National Tax Association, Columbus, 1962, pp. 320-324.

ROBERTS, FRANCIS R., "Equalization In Kansas-Aid and Achievement," *Assessment Administration,* Institute of American Assessment Officers, Chicago, 1959, pp. 161-183.

ROUNTREY, J. EDWARD, "Equalization at Market Value," *The Appraisal Journal,* April, 1956, pp. 213-222.

SAZAMA, G. W., "Equalization of Property Taxes for the Nation's Largest Central Cities," *National Tax Journal,* June, 1965, pp. 151-161.

SMITH, ALAN H., "Equalization of the Property Tax and Equity," *Conference Proceedings,* National Tax Association, Columbus, 1963, pp. 611.

ST. PETERSBURG, FLORIDA FINANCE DEPARTMENT, *Pinelles County Tax Study,* Finance Department, St. Petersburg, 1964.

ST. GEORGE, JOHN F., WILLIAM A. J. RICHARDSON, "Equalization Rates In Relation to the Level of Assessed Valuation," *ASA Valuations Manual,* ASA, 1958, pp. 377.

STEELE, J., "Depreciation Decimal Equivalents," *Journal of Accountancy,* June, 1972, pp. 84-85.

SUTTON, FRANKLIN P., "Equalization Comparable Sales," *The Review,* August, 1950, pp. 8-9.

THEISS, WILLIAM R., "The Appraisal Docket, Tax Assessment--Damages for Failure to Assess Equally," *The Appraisal Journal,* July, 1962, pp. 417-418.

TRAVIS, BROLEY E., "Assessment and Equalization of Utilities In California," *Conference Proceedings,* National Tax Association, Columbus, 1960, pp. 402-409.

WELCH, RONALD B., "Report of the Committee on Model Property Tax Assessment and Equalization Methods," *Assessors News Letter,*

WORKMASTER, H. C., "Tax Equalization Procedure and Processes," *Appraisal and Valuation Manual,* 1955, pp. 244.

## 12-13 Assessments

ABRAMS, CHARLES, "Opportunities In Taxation for Achieving Planning Purposes," *Assessors Newsletter,* I.A.A.O., August, 1966, pp. 115-123.

ACOLIA, GEORGE R., "Case Reports In Assessment Administration: Valuation of Surplus Income In Apartments," *The Assessors Journal,* December, 1965, pp. 39-44.

ACOLIA, GEORGE R., "Garden Apartment Site," *Case Reports In Assessment Administration,* December, 1960, pp. 46-47.

ALEXANDER, ROBERT P., "Inventory Valuation Based on Trade Levels: the Assessors Viewpoint," *Assessment Administration,* IAAO, Chicago, 1963, pp. 120-122.

ALLEN, ALBERT E., "California," *Assessors Manual,* A. Carlisle and Company, San Francisco, 1931, pp. 60.

ALLPHIN, ROBERT, "Inventory Valuation Based on Trade Level: the Taxpayer's Viewpoint," *Assessment Administration,* IAAO, Chicago, 1963, pp. 122-124.

ALLPHIN, ROBERT, "Trade Level Valuation of Inventories," *Conference Proceedings,* National Tax Association, Columbus, 1964, pp. 383-389.

ALYEA, PAUL E., *Assessment of Public Utilities In Alabama,* University of Alabama, Montgomery, 1952.

AMERICAN SOCIETY OF APPRAISERS, "A Primer In Tax Assessing," *American Society of Appraisers Valuation Manual,* 1964, pp. 25.

ANDREWS, JAMES, "Assessment Problems of Condominium Ownership," *Urban Land,* November, 1963, pp. 1-3.

ANGELL, STEPHEN, "How Should a Municipality Assess Developers Property," *The Appraisal Journal,* October, 1935, pp. 446-450.

APPELSON, WALLACE B., "Essential Contents for Assessment Manuals," *The Appraisal Journal,* October, 1959, pp. 491-496.

APPELSON, WALLACE B., "Highlights from 4000 Years of Property Taxation," *Assessors News Letter,* September, 1960, pp. 103-107.

ARKANSAS DIVISION OF ASSESSMENT COORDINATION, *Legal Section, Real Estate and Personal Property Assessment Manual,* Arkansas Division of Assessment Coordination, Little Rock, 1956.

ARKANSAS RAILROAD COMMISSION, TAX DIVISION, *Assessor's Manual,* Little Rock, 1927, pp. 41.

ARNOLD, MAX P., "Assessors-Appraised Values and Purposes In Technical Valuation," *American Society of Appraisers,* Washington, D. C, February, 1954, pp. 9.

ARNOLD, MAX P., "Colorado Appraisal Program," *Technical Valuation,* February, 1953, pp. 39-40, 56.

ARTHUR, JOHN, "Assessment Personnel - the American Experience," *Assessment Administration,* Chicago, 1965, pp. 149-154.

ASHTON, R. E., "Valuation for Assessment Purposes," *Appraisal Institute Magazine,* April, 1957, pp. 21-27.

ASSESSING OFFICIALS OF CONNECTICUT, *Proceedings of the Annual Meetings,* Tax Commissioner, Hartford, 1900.

ASSESSORS NEWSLETTER, "A Shopping Center Profile," *The Assessors Newsletter,* July, 1966, pp. 107.

ASSESSORS NEWSLETTER, "Air Rights Development Costly In New York," *Assessors Newsletter,* June, 1966, pp. 94.

▲ Appraisal for Special Purposes

ASSESSORS NEWSLETTER, "Automation In Taxation: Property Taxes and Assessment Rolls," *Assessors Newsletter*, June, 1966, pp. 92.

ASSESSORS NEWSLETTER, "Beware of Image Over Consciousness," *Assessors Newsletter,* May, 1966, pp. 71.

ASSESSORS NEWSLETTER, "Primary Assessing Area for Local Property Taxation," *Assessors Newsletter,* June, 1966, pp. 83-87.

ASSESSORS NEWSLETTER, "Property Tax Exemption Dilemma," *Assessors Newsletter,* May, 1966, pp. 74.

ASSESSORS NEWSLETTER, "Real Estate Transfer Tax," *Assessors Newsletter,* July, 1966, pp. 103.

AYCOCKE, J. N., "Reconciling Conflict Between Legal Standards and Assessment Practices," *Assessment Administration,* Chicago, 1965, pp. 25-30.

BAILEY, REX R., "Appraisals for Tax Assessment," *Journal of the American Society of Farm Managers and Rural Appraisers,* April, 1949, pp. 36-42.

BALL, THOMAS L., "New Construction Methods," *Assessment Administration,* IAAO, Chicago, 1964, pp. 191-193.

BALLARD, E. D., "Preparation of Tax Maps," *Assessment Administration,* IAAO, Chicago, 1960, pp. 136-150.

BALLARD, E. D., SAMUEL H. GRAY, "Assessment Ratio and Analysis of a Kentucky County," *Assessment Administration,* IAAO, Chicago, 1962, pp. 37-53.

BALLOU, PAUL, "Modern Motel," *Assessment Administration,* Chicago, 1962, pp. 117-122.

BALLOU, PAUL H., "Emerging Valuation Problems with Changing Patterns of Development," *Assessment Administration,* IAAO, Chicago, 1965, pp. 175-180.

BALLOU, PAUL H., "Maintaining Equalization-A Three Stage Production," *Assessment Administration,* IAAO, Chicago, 1960, pp. 72-77.

BANCROFT, D. A., "The Single Tax and Site Valuation," *Appraisal Institute Magazine,* Appraisal Institute of Canada, Winnipeg.

BARAN, EDWARD S., "Recruiting New Assessing Personnel & Their Training," *Assessment Administration,* IAAO, Chicago, 1963, pp. 61-70.

BARAN, EDWARD S., "The Troublesome Presence of Depreciation," *Assessment Administration,* IAAO, Chicago, 1965, pp. 168-172.

BARNARD, BERNARD L., "Assessment Districts In the United States," *Assessors News Letter,* January, 1966, pp. 9.

BARNARD, BERNARD L., "Property Taxes In Local Finance," *Assessors News Letter,* January, 1966, pp. 6.

BARR, GERALD R., "Assessment Review In Michigan," *Assessment Administration,* Iaao, Chicago, 1961, pp. 161-165.

BARTLETT, CHARLES R., *Assessing and the Appraisal Process,* IAAO, Chicago, 1965, pp. 131.

BARTLETT, CHARLES R., "Appraisal In Relation to Assessment of Farm Land," *The Residential Appraiser,* October, 1960, pp. 7-9.

BARTLETT, CHARLES R., "Demonstration Appraisal a Modern Office Building," *Assessment Administration,* IAAO, Chicago, 1957, pp. 47-67.

BATTLE, THOMAS G., "State Supervision and Assistance--The West Virginia Experience," *Assessment Administration,* IAAO, Chicago, 1963, pp. 33-36.

BEACH, DONALD R., "Property Identification and Permanent Numbering Systems," *Assessors News Letter,* January, 1966, pp. 3-4.

BEAUDRY, PAUL, "Adequate Defense Against Appeals," *Assessment Administration,* IAAO, Chicago., 1962, pp. 54-60.

BEAUDRY, PAUL, "Assessment Review In Montreal," *Assessment Administration,* IAAO, Chicago, 1961, pp. 151-156.

## BIBLIOGRAPHY OF APPRAISAL LITERATURE

BELL, STOUGHTON, "The Cambridge, Mass., System of Real Estate Assessment," National Tax Association, August, 1917, pp. 196-198.

BELLANCA, ALFONSO V., "Proximity to a Power Transmission Line and Market Value Today," *Case Reports In Assessment Administration,*

BELLANCA, ALFONSO V., "Revaluation and After the Buffalo Report," *Assesment Administration,* IAAO, Chicago, 1960, pp. 77-80.

BENSON, PHILIP A., NORTH, NELSON L, "Assessed Valuations," *Real Estate Principles and Practices,* 1938, pp. 30-32.

BERGER, MILES, "Assessment Techniques In Urban Renewal Areas," *Assessment Administration,* IAAO, Chicago, 1965, pp. 87-90.

BERGREN, ARTHUR L., "Assessments of Taxable State Lands," *Assessors Topics,* June, 1962, pp. 1-3.

BERGREN, ARTHUR L., "Assistance In New York," *Assessment Administration,* IAAO, Chicago, 1961, pp. 117-122.

BISHOP, SAMUEL M., "Education's Stake In Good Assessment Administration," *Assessment Administration,* IAAO, Chicago, 1965, pp. 10-14.

BONBRIGHT, JAMES C., "May the Same Property Have Different Values for Different Purposes," *National Tax Association,* Proceedings 20th Annual Conference, 1927, pp. 279-295.

BONE, DAVID M., "The Concept of Highest and Best Use As Applied to Mass Appraisals," *Assessment Administration,* IAAO, Chicago, 1965, pp. 93-95.

BORSAK, GEORGE, "The Influence of Airport Operations on Value of Adjacent Real Estate," *Assessment Administration,* IAAO, Chicago, 1961, pp. 20-26.

BOUCHA, MARVIN E., "Demonstration Appraisals, a Fifty-Year-Old Office Building," *Assessment Administration,* IAAO, Chicago, 1957, pp. 69-77.

BOUCK, ROLLAND, "Interstate Commerce and Imports," *Assessment Administration,* IAAO, Chicago, 1956, pp. 84-90.

BOYD, THOMAS G., "Performance Standards and Quality Control of the Assessment Function," *Assessment Administration,* IAAO, Chicago, 1964, pp. 53-57.

BOYLAND, WILLIAM E., "Assessing---New York Real Estate Taxes," *Technical Valuation,* American Society of Appraisers, Washington, D. C, October, 1953, pp. 17.

BOYLAND, WILLIAM E., "Real Estate Tax Assessing In New York City," *Technical Valuation,* October, 1953, pp. 17-20.

BRAMS, M. R., "State Assessments & Shared Taxes In Mass. with Spec Attention to Boston," *Dissertation Abstracts,* Ann Arbor, November, 1967.

BRASSELL, ROSELYN S., "Making Intangibles Tangible---Some Reflections on Todd and Seagram," *Assessment Administration,* IAAO, Chicago, 1964, pp. 62-64.

BRATTON, ALLEN W., "Assessment of Timberlands," *Valuation,* June, 1955, pp. 33-36.

BREWER, HOMER T., "Allocation Problems In Railroad Assessment," *Conference Proceedings,* National Tax Association, Columbus, 1965, pp. 171-178.

BROWN, C. V., "A Theory of Interest Rates or Asset Prices," *The South African Journal of Economics,* University of Glasgow, United Kingdom, September, 1965.

BROWN, G. FAIRFAX, "Assistance In West Virginia," *Assessment Administration,* IAAO, Chicago, 1961, pp. 135-138.

BROWN, G. FAIRFAX, "Supervision of Revaluation Projects," *Assessment Administration,* IAAO, Chicago, 1962, pp. 96-101.

BROWN, UDELL C., "Equalization Problems In the State Assessment of Corporate Property," *Conference Proceedings,* National Tax Association, Columbus, 1964, pp. 410-414.

## Appraisal for Special Purposes

BROWN, WILBUR L., "Technical Aspects of Timber Valuation," *Assessment Administration*, IAAO, Chicago, 1964, pp. 89-94.

BROWN, WYLIE W., "Field Inventory of Improvements," *Assessment Administration*, IAAO, Chicago, 1960, pp. 133-135.

BUREAU OF TAXATION, *Guide for Use of Assessors*, Bureau Oftaxation, Augusta, Maine, 1950.

BURKHARD, EARL E., "Appraising Supermarket Personal Property," *Case Reports In Assessment Administration*, 1960, pp. 30-32.

BURKHARD, EARL E., "Assessment Appraisals of Personal Property at a Shopping Center," *Assessors Journal*, April, 1966, pp. 47-54.

BURKHARD, EARL E., "Assessment Appraising," *Appraisal and Valuation Manual*, American Society of Appraisers, 1958, pp. 241-248.

BURNS, JOSEPH P., "Photogrammetry As a Tool of the Assessor," *Assessment Administration*, IAAO, Chicago, 1964, pp. 134-136.

BURNSIDE, L. D., "Assessing a Small Shopping Center," *Case Reports In Assessment Administration*, March, 1960, pp. 9-12.

BURTON, JOHN E., "Building Obsolescence and the Assessor," *Journal of Land and Public Utility Economics*, May, 1933, pp. 109-120.

BURTON, JOHN E., "The Fundamental Bases of Value Which the Assessor Could Use to Aid In Appraisal," *Architectural Forum*, pp. 27-28, 32-34.

BYRNE, THOMAS A.,"Management's Stake In Tax Administration-Assessor's Viewpoint," *Assessors News Letter*, January, 1961, pp. 3-7.

BYRNE, THOMAS A., "Urban Renewal Plans and Assessment Policy," *Assessment Administration*, Chicago, 1960, pp. 12-14.

CALIF STATE BOARD OF EDUCATION DIV OF ASSMT STDRDS, *Assessor's Handbook--Appraisal of Buildings*, Calif. State Printing Office, Sacramento, May, 1952.

CALIFORNIA OFFICE OF STATE CONTROLLER, "Assessed Valuations Tax Rates & Indebtedness of the Counties of Calif.," *Assessed Valuations Tax Rates and Indebtdness of the Counties of Calif*, Calif. Office of State Controller, Sacramento, 1955.

CALLAWAY, SAM, "Problems In Atlanta Area," *Assessment Administration*, IAAO, Chicago, 1961, pp. 82-85.

CAMPNEY, ALBERT E., "How to Sell a Re-Appraisal Program," *Assessor News Letter*, July, 1957, pp. 78-82.

CARLSON, ALFRED E., "Appraising Acreage In Transition for Tax Assessment Purposes," *Valuation*, June, 1968, pp. 21-25.

CARMAN, H. F., J. G. POLSON, "Tax Shifts Occurring As a Result of Differential Assessment of Farmland California 1968-1969," *National Tax Journal*, December, 1971.

CARPENTER, MAURICE P., "Assessment of Public Utility Properties," *Assessment Administration*, IAAO, Chicago, 1957, pp. 161-166.

CARPER, RAYMOND E., "Assessment of Business Inventories," *Assessment Administration*, IAAO, Chicago, 1957, pp. 115-118.

CARPER, RAYMOND E., "Problems of the Administrator," *Assessment Administration*, IAAO, Chicago, 1959, pp. 29-39.

CARR, ANTHONY W., "Some Suggestions for Volume Appraisers," *The Real Estate Appraiser*, pp. 37.

CARR, FRANCIS J., "Property Assessments Protest, Appeal, and Judicial Review," *The Journal of the State Bar of California*, November, 1964, pp. 877.

CARR, WAGGONER, "Legislative Needs In Assessment Administration," *Assessment Administration*, IAAO, Chicago, 1965, pp. 30-33.

CHAMPNEY, ALBERT E., "Government Owned Property In Private Use," *Assement Administration*, IAAO, Chicago, 1964, pp. 120-124.

CHANDLER, RICHARD A., "Capitalization, Gross and Net," *Assessment Administration,* IAAO, Chicago, 1959, pp. 71-80.

CHANDLER, RICHARD A., "Is Full Current Market Value a Feasible or Practical Assessment Standard," *Assessment Administration,* IAAO, Chicago, 1963, pp. 153-156.

CHANDLER, RICHARD A., "Market Value and Equity Every Year," *Assessment Administration,* IAAO, Chicago, 1960, pp. 63-71.

CHANDLER, RICHARD A., "Use of Capitalized Income to Determine Assessed Values," *Appraisal Institute Magazine,* March, 1960, pp. 19-22.

CHENG, P. L., "Statistical Control of Assessment Uniformity," *Management Science,* June, 1970.

CHERNEY, RICHARD A., *Appraisal and Assessment Dictionary,* Prentice-Hall, Englwd Cliffs N. J., 1960.

CHERNEY, RICHARD A., "Appraisal Principle of Highest and Best Use In Assessing Urban Vacant Land," *The Assessors Journal,* April, 1966, pp. 27-34.

CHERNEY, RICHARD A., "Assessment Quality Controls," *Assessment Administration,* IAAO, Chicago, 1965, pp. 180-184.

CHERNEY, RICHARD A., "Use of Sales-Assessment Ratios In Assessing Real Property," *The Appraisal Journal,* October, 1955, pp. 516-528.

CHING, C. T. K., "Use Value Assessment on Property Tax Rates," *American Journal of Agricultural Economics,* November, 1970.

CHRISTENSEN, CARL C., "In-Service Training-Minnesota," *Assessment Administration,* Chicago, 1961, pp. 147-150.

CLARK, EDWARD L., "Property Tax Aspects of Forest Resource Development In the Rocky Mountain Area," *Assessment Administration,* IAAO, Chicago, 1960, pp. 112-115.

CLARK, RALPH E., "A Prosperous Farm," *Assessment Administration,* IAAO, Chicago, 1957, pp. 93-102.

CLEMINSHAW, WILLIAM, "Valuation Fundamentals and Motel Appraisal," *Assessment Administration,* IAAO, Chicago, 1960, pp. 250-264.

CLEMINSHAW, WILLIAM, AND THOMAS LOFTUS, "Use of Electronic Data Processing In Assessment Work," *Assessment Administration,* IAAO, Chicago, 1962, pp. 11-15.

CLOPPER, SIMON, "The Annual School and In-Service Training In Maryland," *Assessment Administration,* IAAO, Chicago, 1959, pp. 132-138.

CLOPPER, SIMON, "The IAAO Program for Training and Education," *Assessment Administration,* IAAO, Chicago, 1963, pp. 56-60.

CLOVER, VERNON T., *Trego County Real Estate Assessment Plan,* State Printer, Topeka, Kansas.

COLE, JOHN D., "Keeping the Assessment Role Up-To-Date," *Assessment Administration,* IAAO, Chicago, 1962, pp. 18-20.

COLE, JOHN D., "Performing Appraisal Computations by Data-Processing Equipment," *Assessment Administration,* IAAO, Chicago, 1964, pp. 128-131.

COLLANTE, JOSE, "Recent Developments In Assessment Administration, In the Phillipines," *Assessment Administration,* IAAO, Chicago, 1961, pp. 32-38.

COLLINS, C. F., "The Appraisal of Land for Assessment Purposes," *Appraisal Institute Magazine,* January, 1959, pp. 19-21.

COLORADO, *Assessment and Property Tax Laws of Colorado, 1961,* Committee on Statute Revision, 1962.

COLORADO ASSESSMENT METHODS COMMITTEE, *Colorado Property Assessment Methods,* 1958.

▲ Appraisal for Special Purposes

COLORADO LEGISLATIVE COUNCIL, *Report to the Colorado General Assembly Public Utility Assessments,* Denver, December, 1959.

COLORADO TAX COMMISSION, *Instructions to Assessors,* Denver, 1916.

CONNERY, RUSSELL B., "Gasoline Service Station," *Assessment Administration,* IAAO, Chicago, 1961, pp. 236-244.

CONNETICUT TAX COMMISSION, *Information Relative to the Assessment and Collection of Taxes 1935,* Hartford, June, 1936, pp. 170.

COOMBE, J. P., "Maintenance of Equalized Assessments After a Revaluation Program," *Technical Valuation,* June, 1961, pp. 55-57.

COOMBE, J. P., "Means to an End," *Assessment Administration,* IAAO, Chicago, 1960, pp. 74-77.

COOPER, J. ROBERT, *Alternative Methods and Techniques for the Assessment of Farm Real Estate,* Clemson Agricultural College, Clemson, So. Carolna, 1957.

CORNICK, PHILIP H., "How to Assess Real Estate on Income," *The Appraisal Journal,* April, 1934, pp. 241-243.

COWLES, HERBERT V., *How to Assess Property In Cities and Rural Towns,* Wisconsin Tax Commission, Madison, 1914.

CRAIG, R. H., "Property Assessment at Market Value," *Appraisal Institute Magazine,* Appraisal Institute of Canada, Winnipeg.

CRAIG, ROBERT H., "Assessment and Appraisal of Seasonal Motels," *Assessors Journal,* July, 1970.

CRESPO, MANUEL, *Manual De Revaluo Impositivo,* Ediciones Macchi, Ediciones Macchi, Le.

CROCHERON, CLARENCE, *Control of Fixed Assets and Depreciation,* American Appraisal Co., Milwaukee, Wisc.

DASSO, JEROME, PAUL SWEDNEER, "The Impact of Computers on Assessment Procedures," *The Assessors Journal,* April, 1970.

DAVID, E. L., R. SKURSKI, "Property Tax Assessment and Absentee Owners," *National Tax Journal,* December, 1966, pp. 421-426.

DAVIES, MAURICE B. T., "Planning and Selection for Data-Processing Service," *Assessment Administration,* I. A. A. O, Chicago, 1964, pp. 124-128.

DELGADO, CLARENCE N., "The S. M. A. Designation of New Jersey," *Assessment Administration,* I. A. A. O, Chicago, 1961, pp. 183-185.

DOWNS, JAMES C., "Urban Renewal Will it Influence Assessment Policy," *Assessment Administration,* IAAO, Chicago, 1960.

DOWNS, M. D., "The Coordination of Tax Assessments and Zoning," *Planners Journal,* 1935, pp. 23-24.

DREANEY, LEONARD, *Elementary Assessment Practice and Procedure,* T. Whillier, Ontario, 1954.

DUFFY, GEORGE C., "The Education Docket," *Right of Way,* October, 1963, pp. 65-66.

DUGGIN, MARSHALL E., "Improvement In Tennessee," *Assessment Administration,* Institute of American Assessment Officers, Chicago, 1961, pp. 68-76.

DYKE, JOHN B., "Assessment of Condominiums," *Assessment Administration,* Institute of American Assessment Officers, Chicago, 1963, pp. 239-281.

EAGAN, LAURENCE J., "Personal Property Valuation," *Assessment Administration,* Institute of American Assessment Officers, Chicago, 1963, pp. 226-229.

EAMER A. STANLEY, *Assessment In Great Britain,* London, 1925.

# BIBLIOGRAPHY OF APPRAISAL LITERATURE

ECKHARDT, ROBERT A., "Inventory of a Large Manufacturer Assessment Fundamentals," *Assessment Administration,* Institute of American Assessment Officers, Chicago, 1960, pp. 204-211.

EISENLAUER, JACK F., "Mass Versus Individual Appraisers," *The Appraisal Journal,* October, 1968, pp. 533-535.

ERBACH, GEORGE H., "Assessing Leased Equipment," *Assessors News Letter,* August, 1958, pp. 92-93. , 103-105.

FERGUSON, HILL, "Mass Appraising," *The Appraisal Journal,* April, 1943, pp. 156-161.

FICK, H. G. E., "Appraisal of Farm Land," *Assessment Administration,* Institute of American Assessment Officers, Chicago, 1962, pp. 21-36.

FIELD, SAM HOUSTON, *The Law of Assessing Real Property for Ad Valorem Tax Purposes In Texas,* Sam Houston Filed, Austin, 1941.

FINNIS, FREDERIC H., *Real Property Assessment In Canada,* Canadian Tax Foundation, Toronto, 1962.

FISHER, DONALD M., "The Western States Study of the Stock and Debt Approach to Railroad and Utility Valuations," *Assessment Administration,* Institute of American Appraisers Officers, Chicago, 1964, pp. 80-90.

FLEMING, DONALD P., "Systematic Procedures for Assessment Maintenance," *Assessment Administration,* IAAO, Chicago, 1965, pp. 189-195.

FLEMING, DONALD P., "Systematic Procedures for Assessment Maintenance," *The Assessors Journal,* April, 1966, pp. 35-44.

FORBERG, FRED C., "Aid and Assistance In Virginia," *Assessment Administration,* Institute of American Appraisers Officers, Chicago, 1959, pp. 156-160.

FORREST C. HOLVECK, "Farm Personal Property Discovery and Valuation," *Assessment Administration,* Institute of American Appraisers Officers, Chicago, 1965, pp. 135-133.

FREEMAN, RAOUL J., "Real Estate Assessment and Electronic Computers," *The Appraisal Journal,* April, 1959, pp. 182-184.

FRY, PETER, "The Assessor's Dilemma," *Appraisal Institute Magazine,* June, 1962, pp. 11-12.

G/DIN, CAMILLE R., "Demonstration Appraisal a Modern Hotel;" *Assessment Administration,* 1957, pp. 78-90.

GARCIA, K., "Sales Prices and Cash Equivalents," *Appraisal Journal,* January, 1972.

GARRITY, THOMAS P., "The Role of the Assessor In Achieving Assessment Reform," *Property Tax Reform,* Int'l Ass'n Assessing Officers, Chicago, June 1, 1973, pp. 47-52.

GARZON, JULIAN, "Cost Approach," *Assessment Administration,* I. A. A. O., Chicago, 1962, pp. 61.

GASTON, JAMES E., "Information Possibilities Available Through Data Processing Equipment," *Assessment Administration,* I. A. A. O, Chicago, 1964, pp. 131-133.

GERE, EDWIN A. JR., "Tax Assessing a Growing Profession," *American City,* June, 1958, pp. 97-98.

GIBLIN, EDMUND W., "Assistance In Massachusetts," *Assessment Administration,* I. A. A. O., Chicago, 1961, pp. 123-227.

GIBSON, LLOYD C., "Bureau's New Depreciation Policy," *Tax Magazine,* June, 1934, pp. 279-285.

GILBERT, DEWAYNE E., "Climatic In Rural Irrigation Conditions Factors In Rural Land Valuation," *Assessment Administration,* I. A. A. O, Chicago, 1964, pp. 137-140.

GLASER, SIDNEY, "Professionalization of Assessors," *Appraisal Institute Magazine,* Appraisal Institute of Canada, Winnipeg.

GODIN, C. R., "Income Approach Applied to Mass Appraisals," *American Society of Appraisers,* 1960, pp. 161-168.

▲ Appraisal for Special Purposes

GODIN, C. R., "Municipal Assessor 'Evaluator' of the Future," *Appraisal Institute Magazine*, Appraisal Institute of Canada, Winnipeg.

GODIN, CAMILLE R., "Political Administration and Technical Problems," *Assessment Administration*, I. A. A. O, Chicago, 1959, pp. 25-28.

GODIN, CAMILLE R., "Professionalism," *Assessors News Letter*, June, 1963, pp. 67-70.

GRAHAM, D. H. JR., "Shopping Center Assessment," *Assessors News Letter*, March, 1963, pp. 29-32.

GRAY, A. F. B., "Problems In Metropolitan Toronto," *Assessment Administration*, I. A. A. O, Chicago, 1961, pp. 80-82.

GREENE, ALFRED J. JR., "Correlation of Land and Building Values and the Relative Effort Required to Assess Each," *Assessment Administration*, I. A. A. O, Chicago, 1964, pp. 95-96.

GREENE, ALFRED J. JR., "High Rise Apartment House," *Assessment Administration*, I. A. A. O, Chicago, 1961, pp. 212-219.

GREENE, ALFRED J. JR., "Market Value Concept," *Assessment Administration*, I. A. A. O, Chicago, 1965, pp. 154-162.

GREENSWORD, L. H., "Current Assessment Picture In B. C," *Appraisal Institute Magazine*, Appraisal Institute of Canada, Winnipeg.

GRIMES, ROBERT A., "Reorganization In Boston," *Assessment Administration*, I. A. A. O, Chicago, 1961, pp. 62-63.

GROSSO, ANTHONY P., "Appraisal of a Bowling Alley," *Assessment Administration*, I. A. A. O, Chicago, 1963, pp. 180-189.

GRUNDMEIER, HAROLD H., "Appraisal of a Custom-Built Home," *Assessment Administration*, I. A. A. O, Chicago, 1963, pp. 208-217.

HADLEY, GEORGE C., "The Presentation of the Case," *The Appraisal Journal*, July, 1956, pp. 361-376.

HADY, THOMAS F., "Differential Assessment of Farmland on the Rural-Urban Fringe," *Assessors Journal*, April, 1971, pp. 11-26.

HAISLOP, E. G., "Helping West Virginia Assessors," *Assessment Administration*, I. A. A. O, Chicago, 1959, pp. 147-151.

HALGERSON, J. R., "Alberta Assessment Manual-Urban Section," *Appraisal Institute Magazine*, Appraisal Institute of Canada, Winnipeg.

HARRISON, ROLAND T., "Assessment Review In Des Moines," *Assessment Administration*, IAAO, Chicago, 1961, pp. 156-160.

HART, ALAN F., "Can Individual Assessment Be Effectively Equalized by State Administrative Action," *Assessment Administration*, IAAO, Chicago, 1963, pp. 36-41.

HARTMAN, J. W., "The Appraisal of Oil Properties for Assessment Purposes," *Bulletin*, National Tax Association, 1929, pp. 18-21.

HARVARD LAW REVIEW, "Inequality In Property Tax Assessments New Cures for an Old Ill," *Harvard Law Review*, May, 1962, pp. 1374-1395.

HASTINGS, ROD, *Comparisons of Assessed Valuations In Arizona 1913-1957*, League of Arizona Cities and Towns, Phoenix, 1958.

HAYES, EDWARD R., "Special Assessments for Public Improvements In Iowa," *Drake Law Review*, December, 1964, pp. 3-35.

HEARLE, EDWARD F. R., AND RAYMOUND J. MASON, *Data Processing for the State and Local Governments, a Rand Corporation Research Study*, Prentice-Hall, Englwd Cliffs, N. J., 1963.

HEGGLAND, THUROLOW M., "The Professional Public Administrator Looks at the Assessor's Office," *Assessment Administration*, IAAO, Chicago, 1964, pp. 44-48.

HELM, W. P., "Demonstration Appraisal, an Obsolete Motel," *Assessment Administration*, IAAO, Chicago, 1957, pp. 9-15.

HENDERSON, HAROLD W., "Assessment Principles," *The Review*, April, 1952, pp. 11-15.

HENDON, WS., "Property Assessment In Fort Worth," *Dissertation Abstracts*, September, 1964, pp. 1639.

HENEBERRY, WILLIAM H., *Assessment of Farm Real Estate for Property Taxes*, Michigan State University, East Lansing, 1960.

HENRY, ROSS F., "A Modern Farm," *Assessment Administration*, IAAO, Chicago, 1960, pp. 212-219.

HEPDITCH, G. D., "The Assessment of Property In Canada," *Appraisal and Valuation Manual*, American Society of Appraisers.

HEPDITCH, GORDON D., "Problems In a Smaller Canadian Jurisdiction," *Assessment Administration*, IAAO, Chicago, 1961, pp. 89-92.

HERRINGTON, F. A., "Appraisals for Tax Assessment," *Journal of the American Society of Farm Managers and Rural Appraisers*, April, 1959, pp. 60-64.

HINSHAW, ANDREW J., "The Assessor and Computerization of Data," *The Appraisal Journal*, April, 1969, pp. 283-288.

HINTON, W. L. JR., "A Sound Public Relations Program," *Assessment Administration*, I. A. A. O., Chicago, 1957, pp. 191-195.

HINTON, WALTER L., "How to Propose and Staff for Reassessment Appraisal Projects," *The Residential Appraiser*, pp. 14.

HOAGLAND, HENRY E., "Taxes and Assessments," *Real Estate Principles*, 1940, pp. 450-465.

HOFFMAN, ISREAL, "Recent Developments In Judicial Valuation In Assessment Review and Condemnation Proceedings," *Technical Valuation*, February, 1958, pp. 13-16.

HOGAN, HOWARD T., "Judicial Review of Real Estate Tax Assessments," *New York State Bar Journal*, February, 1963, pp. 51-57.

HOGAN, LEO E., "Appraisal of a Commercial Airline," *Assessment Administration*, I. A. A. O., Chicago, 1963, pp. 218-222.

HOUSE, PETER, *Preferential Assessment of Farmland In the Rural-Urban Fringe of Maryland*, U. S. Dept of Agriculture Economic Research Servic, Washington, 1961, pp. 20.

HOUSE, PETER, "Farm Land Assessment In Rural-Urban Fringe," *The Appraisal Journal*, January, 1961, pp. 57-62.

HOWARD, T. HOGAN, "Judicial Review of Real Estate Tax Assessments," *The Real Estate Appraiser*, January, 1963, pp. 28-33.

HULSE, FRED E., *Improving Farm Building Assessment Techniques*, College Park Department of Agriculture, College Park, Md., 1952.

ILLINOIS DEPARTMENT OF REVENUE, *List of Foreign Corporations Assessed on Tangible Property In Illinois*, Illinois Department of Revenue, Springfield, 1947.

ILLINOIS DEPARTMENT OF REVENUE, *Real Property Assessment Manual*, Illinois Department of Revenue, Springfield, 1952.

ILLINOIS TAX COMMISSION, *Illinois Assessors Manual*, 1935.

ILLINOIS UNIV, INSTITUTE OF GOVT & PUBLIC AFFAIRS, *Proceedings of a Short Course for Illinois Assessing Officials*, Illinois University, Urbana, Illinois, 1957.

INSTITUTE FOR TAX ASSESSORS, UNIVERSITY OF TEXAS, *Property Tax - Texas*, Institute of Public Affairs, Austin, 1959.

INSTITUTE OF PUBLIC SERVICE, *Handbook for Connecticut Assessors*, Inst. of Public Service, University of Connecticut, Storrs, 1963.

INTERNATIONAL ASSOCIATION OF ASSESSING OFFICERS, *Appraisal of a Garden Apartment*, Chicago, Illinois.

INTERNATIONAL ASSOCIATION OF ASSESSING OFFICERS, *Assessing and the Appraisal Process*, International Association of Assessing Officers, 1970.

▲ Appraisal for Special Purposes

INTERNATIONAL ASSOCIATION OF ASSESSING OFFICERS, *Assessment - Us,* National Association of Assessing Officers, Chicago, 1938.

INTERNATIONAL ASSOCIATION OF ASSESSING OFFICERS, *Assessment and Appraisal of Shopping Centers,* Institute of American Assessment Officers, Chicago, 1957.

INTERNATIONAL ASSOCIATION OF ASSESSING OFFICERS, *Assessment Organization and Personnel,* National Association of Assessing Officers, Chicago, 1941.

INTERNATIONAL ASSOCIATION OF ASSESSING OFFICERS, *Assessment Principles and Terminology,* National Association of Assessing Officers, Chicago, 1937.

INTERNATIONAL ASSOCIATION OF ASSESSING OFFICERS, *Assessment Terminology,* Institute of American Appraisers Officers, Chicago.

INTERNATIONAL ASSOCIATION OF ASSESSING OFFICERS, *Committee on Assessment Organization and Personnel,* Chicago.

INTERNATIONAL ASSOCIATION OF ASSESSING OFFICERS, *Electronic Data Processing Equipment,* Chicago, Illinois.

INTERNATIONAL ASSOCIATION OF ASSESSING OFFICERS, *Guidelines for Appraising Condominiums,* Chicago, Illinois.

INTERNATIONAL ASSOCIATION OF ASSESSING OFFICERS, *Leased Equipment,* Chicago.

INTERNATIONAL ASSOCIATION OF ASSESSING OFFICERS, *Minimum Assessment Standards, Report of the Commitee on Minimum Assessment Standards,* IAAO, Chicago, 1963.

INTERNATIONAL ASSOCIATION OF ASSESSING OFFICERS, *Shopping Centers, Analysis and Appraisal for Assessment Purposes,* IAAO, Chicago, 1955.

INTERNATIONAL ASSOCIATION OF ASSESSING OFFICERS, *Assessment - US,* National Association of Assessing Officers, Chicago, 1938.

INTERNATIONAL ASSOCIATION OF ASSESSING OFFICERS, *The Assessment of Leased Equipment,* Institute of American Assessment Officers, Chicago, 1959.

INTERNATIONAL ASSOCIATION OF ASSESSING OFFICERS, *The Certified Assessment Evaluation Program of the Institute of American Assessment Officers,* IAAO, Chicago, 1966.

INTERNATIONAL CITY MANAGERS ASSOCIATION, *Municipal Finance Administration,* International City Managers Association, Chicago, 1962.

INTERNATIONAL CONFERENCE OF ASSESSING OFFICERS, *Assessment Administration, 1955,* National Association of Assessing Officers, Chicago, 1956.

IOWA, *State Board of Assessment and Review,* Des Moines, 1929.

IOWA PROPERTY TAX DIVISION, *Summary of Real Estate Assessment Ratio Study,* Iowa Property Tax Division, Des Moines, 1962.

IRVING, KARL, "Use of Recognized Norms and Standards In Fixed Assets Valuation," *Assessment Administration,* Institute of American Assessment Officers, Chicago, 1959, pp. 40-45.

JACOBS, J. L., *Real Estate Assessment Manual,* Jacobs, J. L., Chicago, February, 1933.

JACOBS, J. L., "Systematic Real Property Appraisal and Assessment Equalization," *Assessors News Letter,* January, 1964, pp. 3-5.

JENKS, ALDRO, "Certification In Connecticut," *Assessment Administration,* IAAO, Chicago, 1961, pp. 173-177.

JENKS, ALORO, *Manual for Texas Assessors,* The University of Texas Press, Austin, 1941.

JERSEY CITY BUREAU OF TAX ASSESSMENT, *Assessor's Manual,* 1915.

JERSEY CITY, NEW JERSEY BUREAU OF ASSESSMENT, "Formula Used to Determine Value Per Front Foot When Lot Value Is Given," *Appraising Manual,* Mcmichael, A. L., 1937, pp. 520-521.

JOHNSON, ERNEST H., "The Merits of Full Value Assessments," *The Appraisal Journal,* January, 1958, pp. 75-80.

JOHNSON, RALPH S., "Forest Taxation Alternatives," *Assessment Administration,* IAAO, Chicago, 1961, pp. 98-110.

JOHNSON, RAYMOND, "Public Relations In Smaller Jurisdiction," *Assessment Administration,* IAAO, Chicago, 1961, pp. 94-97.

KANS., CITIZENS COMM ON ASSESSMENT EQUALIZATION, "A Program of Action to Improve Assessment Procedures In Kansas," *A Programof Action to Improve Assessment Procedures In Kansas,* Library of Congress, Topeka, Kansas, 1954.

KANSAS PROPERTY VALUATION DEPARTMENT, *Assessment Manual,* State Printing Plant, Topeka, 1958.

KEITH, JOHN H., *Property Tax Assessment Practices,* Highland Publishing Co., Monterey Park, Calif, 1966.

KEITH, JOHN H., "Determining the Need for and Updating Assessment Standards," *Assessment Administration,* Institute of American Appraisers Officers, Chicago, 1965, pp. 39-41.

KEITH, JOHN H., "The Assessor and A. C. A. A," *The Appraisal Journal,* July, 1967, pp. 392-397.

KEITH, JOHN H., "The Role of Institute of American Appraisers Officers, In the Years Ahead," *Assessment Administration,* Institute of American Appraisers Officers, Chicago, 1963, pp. 10-15.

KEITH, JOHN H., "The Selection of an Assessor," *County Officer,* June, 1962, pp. 303-304.

KEITH, N.S., "An Assessment of National Housing Needs," *Law and Contemporary Problems,* April, 1967, pp. 209-219.

KELLENBERGER, ALLEN N., "Special Assessment Levied Against Railroad Rights-Of-Way," *Conference Proceedings,* National Tax Association, Columbus, 1965, pp. 197-203.

KENNEDY, DAVID H., "Future Role of the Local Assessor," *Minnesota Municipalities,* September, 1964, pp. 277-279.

KENNEDY, FRANCIS H., "Noise Progress -- Street Cars to Jets, and Beyond," *Assessment Administration,* IAAO, Chicago, 1959, pp. 106-110.

KENNEDY, JOHN P., "The Mounting Assessment Dilemma," *The Residential Appraiser,* December, 1956, pp. 3-5.

KENTUCKY DEPARTMENT OF REVENUE, *Kentucky Real Property Assessment Manual,* Kentucky Department of Revenue, Frankfort, 1950.

KENTUCKY LAW JOURNAL, "100 Assessment In Kentucky," *Kentucky Law Journal,* February 11, 1965, pp. 98-124.

KENTUCKY LEGISLATIVE RESEARCH COMMISSION, *Federal In Lieu Payments to School Districts,* Kentucky Legislative Research Commission, Frankfort, 1958.

KENTUCKY LEGISLATIVE RESEARCH COMMISSION, *The Inequality of Assessments,* Lexington, 1949.

KERR, MAX H., "The Allocation of Apportionment of the Value of Common Carriers," *Assessment Administration,* IAAO, Chicago, 1964, pp. 84-88.

KERRISON, IRVINE L. H., "Motivation -- the Teaching and Learning of Adults," *The Assessors Journal,* December, 1965, pp. 4-8.

KLINDT, HAROLD THOMAS, *Development of Procedures for Quantifying and Assessing the Economic Well Being of Rural Areas,* University of Kentucky, Kentucky, 1971.

KONCEL, EDWARD F., "Railroad Operating Property," *Assessment Administration,* IAAO, Chicago, 1961, pp. 248-256.

▲ Appraisal for Special Purposes

KOPLIK, MARILYN S., *Property Tax Assessment In the United States, Preliminary Report to New York State*, Board of Equalization and Assessment, Albany, March, 1961.

KOSTISHAK, GEORGE, *Assessment Administration*, Institute of American Appraisers Officers, Chicago, pp. 184-188.

KOSTISHAK, GEORGE, "Reconciliation of Value Indicators for Market Value Appraisals," *Assessment Administration*, Institute of American Appraisers Officers, Chicago, 1964, pp. 77-79.

KOSTISHAK, GEORGE, "The Appraisal Report," *Assessment Administration*, Institute of American Appraisers Officers, Chicago, 1963, pp. 114-116.

KRIEGER, LAWRENCE W., "Cost Vs. Value In a Monumental Office Building," *Assessment Administration*, Institute of American Appraisers Officers, Chicago, 1964, pp. 194-202.

KROEGER, LOUIS J., "Improve Personnel Administration and the Assessor's Image," *Assessment Administration*, Institute of American Appraisers Officer, Chicago, 1964, pp. 110-113.

KRUEGER, LEONARD B., "Assessment of Business Inventories," *Assessment Administration*, Institute of American Appraisers Officers, Chicago, 1957, pp. 113-114.

KUEHNLE, JOSEPH G., "The Challenges of Professionalization," *Assessment Administration*, Institute of American Appraisers Officers, Chicago, 1964, pp. 17-22.

KUEHNLE, WALTER R., MAI's Delivery Many Papers at Mexican Appraisal Convention," *The Appraiser*, December, 1970.

KUEHNLE, WALTER R., "The Appraisal of Leaseholds," *The Appraisal Journal*, April, 1951, pp. 208-217.

KUEHNLE, WALTER R., "What the Assessor Can Learn from the Professional Appraiser," *Assessment Administration*, Institute of American Appraisers Officers, Chicago, 1963, pp. 98-101.

LAIDLAW, J. B., "Preparation and Purpose of the Alberta Assessment Manual," Assessment Administration, Chicago, 1959.

LAIDLAW, J. B., "Statutory Authority for Assessments In Alberta," *Appraisal Institute Magazine*, Appraisal Institute of Canada, Winnipeg.

LAIDLAW, J. B., "Statutory Authority Whereunder Real Property Is Assessed In Alberta," *Appraisal Institute Magazine*, December, 1962, pp. 5-8.

LARSON, MARTIN A., "You, the Church and Tax Exempt Wealth," *Assessors Journal*, April, 1966, pp. 10-16.

LAWRENCE, EDWARD R., "Meaning of the Term Comparables In Pennsylvania Real Estate Assessment," *University of Pittsburgh Law Review*, October, 1965, pp. 126-136.

LAYNE, LAWRENCE P, "Market Value Assessments In a Dynamic Economy," *Property Tax Reform*, Int'l Ass'n Assessing Officers, Chicago, June 1, 1973, pp. 83-91.

LEAGUE OF WISCONSIN MUNICIPALITIES, *Readings on the Wisconsin Assessment Process, Fundamentals of the Urban Process*, Madison, October, 1961.

LEE, HOWARD M., "Assessor-Taxpayer Representative Relations," *Assessment Administration*, I. A. A. O, Chicago, 1963, pp. 156-159.

LEE, M. W., "Absence of Zoning and Its Effect on Value," *Assessment Administration*, I. A. A. O, Chicago, 1965, pp. 96-99.

LEGISLATIVE RESEARCH COMMISSION; KENTUCKY, *The Inequality of Assessments*, 1949.

LELAND, SIMEON E., "The Scientific Assessment of Land," *National Real Estate Journal*, October 29, 1928, pp. 46-48.

LEW, IRVING, "Administrative and Judicial Review of Real Estate Tax Assessments," *Appraisal and Valuation Manual*, American Society of Appraisers, 1961, pp. 291-305.

LEW, IRVING, "Judicial Review of Assessed Values," *Appraisal Digest*, October, 1958, pp. 22-23.

LEW, IRVING, "Valuation In Condemnation and In Real Estate Tax Assessment Review Proceedings," *Appraisal and Valuation Manual*, American Society of Appraisers, 1962.

LEWIS, HAROLD M., "Relation of Assessed Value to Zoning," *Preliminary Report, No. 5*, Harold M, Lewis, Washington, 1956.

LEWIS, HENRY W., "Assessing Forest Land and Timber for Property Taxes," *Popular Government*, May, 1956, pp. 3-7.

LILLY, JOSEPH, "Considerations In Real Estate Assessments," *Real Estate Record and Builders Guide*, February 28, 1942, pp. 3-5.

LOGGAN, HARRY, "Use of Assessment-Sales Ratios In Assessment Appeals," *Assessors Newsletter*, March, 1964, pp. 27-30.

LOGGAN, HARRY J., "Designing State Technical Assistance to Meet the Assessor's Needs," *Assessment Administration*, I.A.A.O., Chicago, 1964, pp. 32-36.

LOOZE, THEODORE W. DE., "Formalizing Assessors Duties and Qualifications," *Assessors Newsletter*, October, 1962, pp. 111-117.

LOS ANGELES COMPANY, "County Assessors Office," *California Real Estate Principles and Practice*, New York, 1927, pp. 491.

LUCE, DENNETH K., "Assessment of Real Property for Taxation," *Michigan Law Review*, June, 1937, pp. 1217-1252.

LUEDTKE, WALDEMAR W., "An Appraisal of a Mansion-Type Home," *Assessment Administration*, I. A. A. O, Chicago, 1964, pp. 168-173.

LYNN, ARTHUR D. JR., "Legal Problems and Obstacles In Assessing Land for Site Value Taxation," *Assessment of Land Value*, Ohio State University, 1970, pp. 143-155.

LYNN, ARTHUR D. JR., "Rept of Comm on Model Prop Tax Assesmt & Equalizn Methods on Property Tax Policy," *Conference Proceedings*, National Tax Association, Columbus, 1964, pp. 157-195.

MACDONALD KING R., "New Approaches to Personal Property Assessment," *Assessment Administration*, Institute of American Assessment Officers, Chicago, 1964, pp. 58-61.

MACDOUGALL, WILLIAM R, JAFFE, JACOB M, "Prospects for Assessment Reform: an Overview Property Tax Reform," *Tax Reform*, Int'l Ass'n Assessing Officers, Chicago, June 1, 1973, pp. 28-32.

MACRAE, A. A., "Case Report, Aerial Photography and Timberland Assets," *The Assessors Journal*, July, 1966, pp. 48-52.

MAHONEY, JOSEPH B., "Assessment Review In Massachusetts," *Assessment Administration*, Institute of American Assessment Officers, Chicago, 1961, pp. 165-172.

MAINE BUREAU OF TAXATION, *Assessment Techniques*, Maine Bureau of Taxation, Augusta, 1962.

MAINE BUREAU OF TAXATION, *Assessors Handbook*, Augusta, 1935.

MANDLE, I., "Water Stocks Reach Danger Low," *Industrial Management*, 1971, pp. 54-59.

MANNING, HAROLD ERNEST, *Assessment and Rating Being the Law of Municipal Taxation In Canada*, Cartwright, Toronto, 1951.

MANVEL, ALLEN D., "Development of Assessment Ratios In the 1957 Census of Governments," *Assessment Administration*, Institute of American Officers, Chicago, 1958, pp. 20-23.

MANVEL, ALLEN D., "Problems and Policies In the New Census of Governments," *Assessment Administration*, Institute of American Officers, Chicago, 1956, pp. 1-5.

MARKLE, SHELDON E., "Property Tax Administration In Michigan," *Assessors News Letter*, December, 1958, pp. 139-143.

MARSHALL, TRUETT B., *The Assessment of Real Property, a Manual for Fort Worth, Texas*, Austin, 1962.

MARSHALL, TRUETT B., "Certification In Texas," *Assessment Administration*, Institute of American Officers, Chicago, 1961, pp. 188-192.

MARTIN, JAMES M., "Obsolescence and the Assessment of Public Service Properties," *Conference Proceedings*, National Tax Association, Columbus, 1960, pp. 410-426.

MARTIN, JAMES W., "Limitations on Reproduction Less Depreciation In Mass Valuation," *Assessors News Letter*, September, 1955, pp. 101-102.

MARTIN, JAMES W., GLENN D. MORROW, *Organization for Kentucky Local Tax Assessments*, The University of Kentucky, Lexington, 1941.

MASAD, RIMON NICOLA, *The Effect of Commercial Land Use on Land Value Patterns*, Austin Texas, 1958.

MASON, ROBERT G., "Appraisal Statistics for Assessors," *The Assessors Journal*, April, 1966, pp. 1-9.

MATTER, J. AUBREY, "Appraisal of a Restored Home," *Assessment Administration*, Institute of American Assessment Officers, Chicago, 1963, pp. 190-207.

MATTER, J. AUBREY, "Exemption of Institutional Real Estate," *Assessment Administration*, Institute of American Assessment Officers, Chicago, 1957, pp. 145-153.

MCCOOMBS, IRVINE J., "The Appraisal of Shopping Centres," *Appraisal Institute Magazine*, Appraisal Institute of Canada, Winnipeg, June 1, 1972.

MCCUTCHEON, JAMES T., "Why Should Cities Do Their Own Assessing," *Tax Digest*, 1963, pp. 116-117.

MCDONALD, JOHN A., "Capitalized Income-Sometimes an Assessment Tool," *Assessment Administration*, Institute of American Assessment Officers, Chicago, 1959, pp. 56-62.

MCDONALD, JOHN A., "The Use and Abuse of Depreciation Tables," *Assessment Administration*, 1958, pp. 85-90.

MCDONNELL, N. B., "Forest Tax Developments In the Northwest--An Industry View," *Assessment Administration*, Institute of American Assessment Officers, Chicago, 1960, pp. 107-112.

MCDOWELL, HARRY G, *Mechanization of Real Property Assessment Records and Control and Production of Annual Tax Roll*, Office of the Director of Finance, Philadelphia, 1957, pp. 1-40.

MCGUINESS, EDWARD J., "Assessing Luxury Homes In Beverly Hills," *Assessors Journal*, October, 1968.

MCKAY, JACK F., *Property Assessment In Kansas, a Study In Kansas Administrative History*, Bureau of Government Research, University of Kans., 1950.

MCKEE, GLENN M., "The Effect of a Major Disaster on an Assessment Roll," *Assessment Administration*, Institute of American Assessment Officers, Chicago, 1964, pp. 179-181.

MCNULTY, CHARLES S., "The Appraisal of Super-Adequate Residences," *Assessors Journal*, January, 1969.

MCSWAIN, ROBERT H., "Assessing Versus Appraising," *Assessment Administration*, 1965, pp. 145-148.

MEANS, ERNEST E., "Assessment Standards and Property Tax Equity In Florida," *University of Florida Law Review*, 1964, pp. 83-108.

MELNYK, PETER F., "Improvement Assessments-Depreciation and Obsolescence," *Appraisal Institute Magazine*, December, 1962, pp. 17-20.

# BIBLIOGRAPHY OF APPRAISAL LITERATURE

MILLER, GERALD W., "Assessment Problems In Metropolitan Los Angeles," *Assesment Administration,* 1961, pp. 77-80.

MILLER, GERALD W., "Recruiting and Training Appraisers," *Assessors News Letter,* May, 1962, pp. 51-53.

MILLER, MARTIN D., "Appraisal of Urban-Rural Land for Assessment Purposes," *Assessment Administration,* 1958, pp. 6-15.

MILLER, MARTIN D., "How the Local Assessor Can Most Effectively Usesales Ratio Findings," *Assessment Administration,* 1963, pp. 24-26.

MILLER, MARTIN D., "Mechanization of Major Property Assessment and Property Tax Administration Operation," *Assessment Administration,* 1960, pp. 27-33.

MILLER, MARTIN D. M., "Mass Appraisal Technique," *Assessment Administration,* 1965, pp. 162-168.

MILLER, W. S., "Assessment of Public Utility Properties," *Assessment Administration,* 1957, pp. 166-169.

MILWAUKEE TAX DEPARTMENT, *Manual of Tables and Rules In the Assessment of Real Estate,* Milwaukee, 1926.

MINNESOTA TAX COMMISSION, *Assessor's Manual,* 1936.

MISCHKE, ARTHUR, "Getting Scientific with Soils and Sales," *Assessment Administration,* 1960, pp. 50-52.

MISFELDT, DOUGLAS E., "Appraisal of a Natural Gas Transmission Pipeline," *Assessment Administration,* 1963, pp. 223-225.

MISFELDT, DOUGLAS E., "Electric Utility Property," *Assessment Administration,* 1961, pp. 245-247.

MISFELDT, DOUGLAS E., "Natural Gas Pipe Line," *Assessment Administration,* 1962, pp. 123-127.

MISSISSIPPI STATE TAX COMMISSION, *Rules and Regulation for the Equalization of Assessment Rolls,* Jackson, May 1, 1934.

MISSOURI STATE TAX COMMISSION, *Assessor's Manual,* 1939, pp. 63.

MOAK, JAMES E., "Forest Appraisals for Assessment of Ad Valorem Taxes," *Journal of the American Society of Farm Managers and Rural Appraisers,* October, 1966, pp. 60-66.

MOHR, LARRY R., "Applying Depreciation In Assessments of Gas Pipelines, Railroads and Other Utilities," *Assessment Administration,* 1965, pp. 106-107.

MORGAN, CECIL L., "Equalizing Assessments of City Properties," *Technicalities and Technical Valuation,* June, 1952, pp. 23-26.

MORSE, TRUE D., "The Influence of Special Assessments on Farm Values," *The Appraisal Journal,* July, 1935, pp. 335-341.

MUNIC FIN OFFCRS ASSN OF U. S. & CANADA, *Applications of Electronic Data Processing,* Municipal Finance Officers Association, Chicago, 1960.

MUNICIPAL & LOCAL FINANCE OFFCRS OF PENNSYLVANIA, *Handbook for Pennsylvania Assessors,* The Pennsylvania Government Administration, 1941.

MURRAY, WILLIAM G., "Five Point Spur for Better Rural Assessments," *Assessment Administration,* IAAO, Chicago, 1960, pp. 46-49.

MURRAY, WILLIAM G., "Market Values and Assessments," *Technical Valuation,* June, 1955, pp. 45-46. 52.

N. Y. STATE BOARD OF EQUALIZATION & ASSESSMENT, *Principles and Procedures Used In Establishing State Equalization Rates,* Albany, New York, 1961.

NATIONAL ASSOCIATION OF ASSESSING OFFICERS, *Assessment Principles and Terminology,* National Association of Assessing Officers, Chicago, 1937.

▲ Appraisal for Special Purposes

NATIONAL ASSOCIATION OF ASSESSING OFFICERS, *Assessment Terminology,* National Association of Assessing Officers, Chicago, 1956.

NATIONAL ASSOCIATION OF ASSESSING OFFICERS, *Comittee on Assessment Terminology,* Chicago, September, 1936.

NATIONAL ASSOCIATION OF ASSESSING OFFICERS, *Comittee on Principles of Assessment Practice,* Chicago, 1937.

NATIONAL ASSOCIATION OF ASSESSING OFFICERS, *Urban Land Appraisals,* Chicago, January, 1940.

NATIONAL ASSOCIATION OF TAX ADMINISTRATORS, *Guide for Assessment-Sales Ration Studies,* Federation of Tax Administrators, Chicago, 1954.

NATIONAL COMMITTEE OF R. R. & PUB UTIL TAX REP'S, *State Requirements, Procedures and Level of Assessment for Tangible Property In 50 States,* 1965.

NATIONAL EDUCATION ASSOCIATION OF UNITED STATES, *Valuation Of Property Assessments and Sales Compared,* Washington, D. C., 1969.

NATIONAL MUNICIPAL LEAGUE, *Special Assessments; a Means of Financing Municipal Improvements,* National Municipal League, New York, 1929.

NATIONAL MUNICIPAL LEAGUE, "Special Assessments for Benefit As a Means of Financing Municipal Improvements," *National Municipal Review,* pp. 43-58.

NEBRASKA STATE TAX COMMISSIONER, *Uniform Instructions to the County and Precinct Assessors,* Wm. H. Smith, State Tax Commissioner, 1935.

NESSER, RICHARD S., "Reorganization of New Haven Office," *Assessment Administration,* Institute of American Assessment Officers, Chicago, 1961, pp. 63-67.

NEVADA TAX COMMISSION, *Instructions to County Assessors,* Carson City, 1935.

NEW JERSEY STATE TAX DEPARTMENT, *A Manual of Practice In Appraising Real Estate,* Cuthbert E. Reeves, 1934.

NEW YORK STATE SOCIETY OF REAL ESTATE APPRAISERS, *Real Estate Appraisal Bibliography,* Albany, New York, 1942.

NICHOLS, ALAN H., "Comment How Not to Contest Special Assessments In California or You Can't Beat City Hall," *Stanford Law Review,* June, 1965, pp. 247-256.

NORTH DAKOTA TAX COMMISSION, *Assessment Manual for Assessors and Boards of Review and Equalization,* Bismarck, 1935.

OCONNOR, THOMAS A., "Airports and Adjacent Realty In the Miami Area," *Assessment Administration,* IAAO, Chicago, 1959, pp. 101-106.

OESTERLE, HARRIS, "Railroad Property," *Assessment Administration,* IAAO, Chicago, 1962, pp. 132-136.

OLDMAN, O., AND H. AARON, "Assessment Sales Ratios Under the Boston Property Tax," *National Tax Journal,* March, 1965, pp. 36.

OLSON, IRVING J., "A Midwest Experience In Wild Land and Forest Taxation," *Assessment Administration,* IAAO, Chicago, 1960, pp. 103-107.

OREGON STATE TAX COMMISSION, *Oregon Laws Relating to Assessment and Taxation,* Valuation Division, Salem, 1963.

OREGON UNIVERSITY, *Trend of Assessed Value of Taxable Property In Oregon by Classes of Property 1910-1937,* Bureau of Municipal Research and Service, University of Oregon, 1938.

OSBORN, FRANK K., "Income Approach," *Assessment Administration,* I. A. A. O., Chicago, 1962, pp. 74-81.

OSENBAUGH, CHARLES L., "The Practical Application of the Income Approach In Appraising and Assessing Property," *Assessment Administration,* I. A. A. O., Chicago, 1965, pp. 99-102.

## BIBLIOGRAPHY OF APPRAISAL LITERATURE

PARDEE, CATHERINE E., "Minimum Standards for an Assessment Office," *Assessment Administration,* Institute of American Assessment Officers, Chicago, 1963, pp. 21-24.

PARDUE, BEULAH LEA, *State Supervision of the Property Tax Assessments In Kentucky,* University of Kentucky, Lexington, 1948.

PARK, OLIVER W., "The Challenge In the Boston Predicament," *Assessment Administration,* Institute of American Assessment Officers, Chicago, 1960, pp. 23-26.

PARNELL, WALLACE H., "The Professional Assessor," *Municipal World,* September, 1961, pp. 290-291.

PATTERSON, SAMUEL A., "In-Service Training-Virginia," *Assessment Administration,* Institute of American Assessment Officers, Chicago, 1961, pp. 139-142.

PATTERSON, SAMUEL A., "Special Assessment Problems In Totally Planned Satellite Cities," *Assessment Administration,* Institute of American Assessment Officers, Chicago, 1965, pp. 90-92.

PATTERSON, SAMUEL A. JR., "The Approaches to Value," *Assessment Administration,* Institute of American Assessment Officers, Chicago, 1963, pp. 107-114.

PENDLETON, WILLIAM C., "Statistical Inference In Appraisal and Assessment Procedures," *The Appraisal Journal,* January, 1965, pp. 73-82.

PENNSYLVANIA STATE TAX EQUALIZATION BOARD, *Market Values and Assessed Valuations of Taxable Real Property,* Pennsylvania State Tax Equalization Board, Harrisburg, Penn., 1949.

PENNSYLVANIAN, "Professionalism In Assessment Administration," *The Appraisal Journal,* July, 1963, pp. 18-20.

PEREIRA, WILLIAM L., "Vistas for the Future In Planning and Architecture," *Assessment Administration,* Institute of American Assessment Officers, Chicago, pp. 28-31.

PERK, RALPH J., "Public Relations and the Assessor's Office," *Assessment Administration,* Institute of American Assessment Officers, Chicago, pp. CHICAGO.

PETERSON, RONALD S., "Assessment of Leasehold Interests In Tax-Exempt Realty In California," *California Law Review,* December, 1960, pp. 806-815.

PICKARD, JEROME P., "Using the Property Tax to Achieve Social and Economical Change," *Assessment Administration,* Institute of American Assessment Officers, Chicago, 1965, pp. 33.

PITMAN, HAYDEN W., "Exemption of Institutional Real Estate," *Assessment Administration,* Institute of American Assessments Officers, Chicago, pp. 137-141.

POWERS, RONALD V., "Important Minnesota Cases on Interstate Commerce and Imported Goods," *Assessment Administration,* Institute of American Assessment Officers, Chicago, 1959, pp. 115-123.

PRESSLEY, LESTER N., "Demonstration Appraisal A 1956 Residence," *Assessment Administration,* Institute of American Assessment Officers, Chicago, 1957, pp. 15-21.

PROPERTY TAX BULLETIN, "Assessing Household and Kitchen Furniture-Percentage Rule," *Property Tax Bulletin,* June, 1962.

PROUTY, COLLINS, AND PROUTY, "Appraisers and Assessors Manual," *Engineering Valuation,* Mcgraw-Hill Book Co., New York, 1930.

PUBLIC ADMINISTRATION SERVICE, *Standards for Assessing Real Property In Puerto Rico,* Department of the Treasury, Chicago, 1953.

PURDY, LAWSON, *The Assessment of Real Estate,* National Municipal League, Philadelphia.

PURDY, VICTOR M., "Market Value of Obsolete Property for Tax Assessment Purpose," *Technical Valuation,* 1965, pp. 18-20.

PURNELL, ROBERT L., "In-Service Training In Michigan," *Assessment Administration,* 1959, pp. 139-142.

PURNELL, ROBERT L., "In-Service Training-Michigan," *Assessment Administration,* 1961, pp. 145-147.

RACKHAM, JOHN B, "New Technology: Its Management and Use by the Assessor," *Property Tax Reform,* Int'l Ass'n Assessing Officers, Chicago, June 1, 1973, pp. 68-75.

RAGAN, RICHARD, "Precedents and Prospects for Assessment of Federally Owned and Privately Used Property," *Assessment Administration,* Institute of American Assessment Officers, Chicago, 1960, pp. 177-194.

RATCLIFF, WILBUR S. JR., "Revaluation of Charleston Country," *Assessment Administration,* Institute of American Assesmt Adminis Officers, Chicago, 1961, pp. 39-61.

REAL ESTATE ANALYST, THE, "Equitable Assessment Bench Marks," *Real Estate Analyst Appraisal Bulletin,* 1952, pp. 409-412.

REEVES, CUTHBERT E., *The Appraisal of Urban Land and Buildings, a Working Manual for City Assessors,* Public Administration Service, New York, 1928, pp. 1-160.

REEVES, CUTHBERT E., "The Basis of Building Costs for Assessment Purposes," *Appraisal Digest,* January, 1955, pp. 4-7.

REEVES, H. CLYDE, "Importance of Good Assessment Administration to Effective Local Government," *Assessors News Letter,* December, 1964, pp. 163-166.

REGIS, A. S., *Basic Principles of Urban Assessment,* Des Moines, 1955.

REGIS, A. S., "Concepts of Value and Basic Principles of Valuation," *Assessment Administration,* Institute of American Appraisers Officers, Chicago, 1963, pp. 102-107.

REGIS, ANDREW S., "Causes and Remedies for Mass Appeals from Property Assessments," *Assessment Administration,* Institute of American Appraisers Officers, Chicago, 1965, pp. 41-46.

REGISTER, NORMAN, "IAAO's Professional Designation—The Certified Assessment Evaluator," *Assessor's Journal,* December, 1965, pp. 9-13.

REILLY, GEORGE R., "Appraising for Intercounty Equalization of Assessments," *Valuation Manual,* 1961, pp. 267.

REOK, ERNEST C. JR., "College and University Participation in Assessor's Training Programs," *Assessment Administration,* Institute of American Assessment Officers, Chicago, 1963, pp. 71-73.

REUTHER, J. L., "Report of Committee on Model Property Tax Assessment and Equalization Methods," *Conference Proceedings,* National Tax Association, Columbus, 1962, pp. 320-324.

REYNOLDS, SAMUEL T., "Appraisal and Assessment of Property for Purposes of Taxation," *Proceedings,* 1928, pp. 112.

RILEY, WILLIAM H., "Privately Owned Golf Course," *Assessment Administration,* Institute of American Assessment Officers, Chicago, 1961, pp. 227-235.

RING, ALFRED A., "Assessment Methods for Urban Real Property," *The Appraisal Journal,* October, 1949, pp. 490-496.

ROBERTS, FRANCIS R., "Equalization In Kansas-Aid and Achievement," *Assessment Administration,* Institute of American Assessment Officers, Chicago, 1959, pp. 161-183.

ROBERTS, FRANCIS R., "Rural Assessment: a Commitment to Quality In Kansas," *Assessment Administration,* Institute of American Assessment Officers, Chicago, 1960, pp. 55-62.

ROBERTSON, JAMES M., "Behind and Within the Missouri Manual," *Assessment Administration,* Institute of American Assessment Officers, Chicago, 1959, pp. 84-86.

ROCHE, JOHN K., "The Assessor's View of Depreciation," *The Appraisal Journal,* April, 1967, pp. 223-225.

# BIBLIOGRAPHY OF APPRAISAL LITERATURE

RODEWALD, G. E. JR., C. B. BAKER, "Interim Period Asset Valuation A Method for Making Investment Decisions," *Agricultural Economics Research*, April, 1969.

ROESCH, RICHARD R., "A Discussion of Condominium Legislation with Particular Reference to the Michigan Act," *Assessment Administration*, Instituteof American Assessment Officers, Chicago, 1963, pp. 143-152.

ROSE, J. T. SR., "Training Means and Goals In Virginia," *Assessment Administration*, Institute of American Assessment Officers, Chicago, 1959, pp. 143-146.

ROSTVOLD, WERHARD N., "Distribution of Property, Retail, Sales, and Property Income Tax Burdens In California," *Assessment Bibliography*.

ROUNTREY, EDWARD, "Appraising the Assessment," *The Appraisal Journal*, April, 1957, pp. 236-243.

RUTGERS UNIVERSITY BUREAU OF GOVERNMENT RESEARCH, *Proceedings of the First Annual Institute for Assessing Officers*, New Brunswick, N. J, 1955.

RUTGERS UNIVERSITY BUREAU OF GOVERNMENT RESEARCH, *Proceedings of 3rd Ann Inst for Assessing Officers*, Rutgers University Bureau of Government Research, New Brunswick, N. J., 1957.

RYBECK, WALTER, "Impact of Taxation and Assessments on Urban Development," *The Real Estate Appraiser*, pp. 27.

SANDS, LAWRENCE, "The Effect of Financing and Taxation on Market Value," *Assessment Administration*, Institute of American Assessment Officers, Chicago, 1964, pp. 69-72.

SARLES, KENNETH E., "Economic Results of Industrial Assessment Practice," *The Appraisal Journal*, July, 1948, pp. 321-325.

SCARRY, DONALD M. PH. D., *The Effects of Degree of Reliance on Property Taxation on State-Local Expenditures*, Rutgers University, 1971.

SCHALL, I. D., "Asset Valuation and Firm Investment," *Journal of Business*, January, 1972.

SCHIMMEL, ALBERT, "Some Standards for Tax Assessments," *Technical Valuation*, June, 1955, pp. 27.

SCHIMMEL, ALFRED, "Loft Building," *Assessment Administration*, Institute of American Assessment Officers, Chicago, 1959, pp. 221-229.

SCHIMMEL, ALFRED, "Some Standards for the Appraisal of Real Estate for Tax Assessment Purposes," *Appraisal and Valuation Manual*, pp. 232.

SCHMIDT, EDWARD BENJAMIN, "A Case Study of Scientific Assessment Fortax Purposes," *The 1946 Reappraisal of Real Estate In York Nebraska*, University of Nebraska, Lincoln, Nebraska, 1948, pp. 1-59.

SCHMUTZ, GEORGE L., "Taxes, Assessments and Appraisals," *The Appraisal Journal*, July, 1939, pp. 252-257.

SCHWINDEN, JAMES, "Real Property Assessment-Principles and Principles and Practice," *Minnesota Municipalities*, May, 1962, pp. 124-127.

SESTRIC, JOSEPH P., "Basic Assessment Philosophy," *The Appraisal Journal*, July, 1951, pp. 338-341.

SHADRAWY, BERNARD F., "Demonstration Appraisal on Commercial Property Using Income Approach," *Assessment Administration*, Institute of American Assessment Officers, Chicago, 1965, pp. 103-105.

SHANNON, JOHN, "Commentary on the Advisory Commission's Suggested Property Tax Legislation," *Assessment Administration*, Institute of American Assessment Officers, Chicago, 1964, pp. 36-39.

SHAPIRO, H., "Assessment and Taxation of Tangible Personal Property on Farms," *National Tax Journal*, March, 1965, pp. 25.

▲ Appraisal for Special Purposes

SHAY, HERBERT K., "Reproduction Cost Less Depreciation-An Important Tool In Assessing Real Property," *Assessors News Letter,* January, 1957, pp. 3-6.

SHEPPARD, D. W., "Assessment of Farm Personal Property," *Assessment Administration,* Institute of American Assessment Officers, Chicago, 1957, pp. 154-158.

SHOPLIN, AUGUST, *A Study of Relationships Between Assessments and Selling Price of Real Estate In Wyoming 1957-58,* U. of Wyoming Div of Business & Economic Research, Laramie, 1959.

SHWAYDER, K, "The Capital Maintenance Rule and the Net Asset Valuation Rule," *Accounting Review,* April, 1969.

SIEJA, EDWARD M., "Aerial Mapping Programs," *Assessment Administration,* Institute of American Assessment, Chicago, 1957, pp. 126-128.

SIEJA, EDWARD M., "Airports, Noise and Property," *Assessment Administration,* Institute of American Assessment Officers, Chicago, 1959, pp. 97-101.

SILVERHERZ, JOSEPH D., "Bibliography," *Assessment of Real Property In the United States,* 1936, pp. 352-390.

SILVERHERZ, JOSEPH D., "Full Value As a Basic for Assessments," *Real Estate Record and Builders Guide,* National Edition, August 15, 1936, pp. 42-43.

SILVERHERZ, JOSEPH D., "Record Systems," *Assessment of Real Property In the United States,* 1936, pp. 267-278.

SILVERHERZ, JOSEPH D., "Unit Valuation Buildings," *Assessment of Real Property In the United States,* 1936, pp. 266.

SILVERHERZ, JOSEPH DAVID, *The Assessment of Real Property In the United States,* J. B. Lyon Company, Albany, 1936, pp. 1-396.

SIMPSON, DR. H. D., "Results of Present Methods of Assessing Urban Real Estate for Taxation," *Proceedings 20th Annual Convention National Assoication of Building Owners and Managers,* 1927, pp. 280-288.

SISKA, FRNAK J., "Inventory of a Retail Store," *Assessment Administration,* Institute of American Assessment Officers, Chicago, 1960, pp. 196-203.

SKELTON, JOHN E., "EDP and the Assessor," *Assessment Administration,* Institute of American Assessment Officers, Chicago, 1960, pp. 34-36.

SMITH, PIERCE J., "A Motel Assessment," *American Society of Appraisers Manual, 1964-1965,* 1964, pp. 67.

SMITH, WINIFRED W., "Formula Assessment of Fixed Assets," *Case Reports In Assessment Administration,* December, 1958.

SPREAD, K. J., "Alberta Assessment Manual-Rural Section," *Appraisal Institute Magazine,* Appraisal Institute of Canada, Winnipeg.

ST. GEORGE, JOHN F., "Certification In New York," *Assessment Administration,* Institute of American Assessment Officers, Chicago, 1961, pp. 177.

ST. GEORGE, JOHN F., WILLIAM A. J. RICHARDSON, "Equalization Rates In Relation to the Level of Assessed Valuation," *ASA Valuations Manual,* ASA, 1958, pp. 377.

STATE COMMISSION OF REVENUE AND TAXATION: KANSAS, *Assessor's Manual,* Kansas State Printing Plant, Topeka, 1950.

STERLING, R. R., R. E. FLAHERTY, "Role of Liquidity In Exchange Valuation," *Accounting Review,* July, 1971, pp. 441-456.

STEWART, SAMUEL B., "Protecting the Taxpayer from Excessive Assessments," *Conference Proceedings,* National Tax Association, Columbus, 1961, pp. 77-84.

STOCKER, FREDERICK D, "Value Determination: the Assessor's Staff Vs the Private Appraisal Firm," *Property Tax Reform*, Int'l Ass'n Assessing Officers, Chicago, June 1, 1973, pp. 76-82.

STOLINSKI, JOSEPH C., "Assessment of Farm Personal Property," *Assessment Administration*, IAAO, Chicago, 1957, pp. 158-159.

STUBBS, ROBERT C., "Access Rights of Abutting Landowner," *Proceedings of the 4th Inst on Eminent Domain*, Dallas, 1963, pp. 59-88.

SUTER, ROBERT C, *The Appraisal of Farm Real Estate (Book)*, Interstate Printers and Publishers Inc, Lafayette Indiana, January 1, 1974.

SWEET, HOLLIS A., "Technical Assistance to Local Assessors," *Assessment Administration*, IAAO, Chicago, 1962, pp. 102-107.

SYMONDS, WELSFORD J., "Assessment/Sales Ratio Survey," *Appraisal Institute Magazine*, Appraisal Institute of Canada, Winnipeg.

TALMADGE, M. P., *Manual on Methods of Assessment In New York City*, New Your City, 1917.

TANNERY, FLADGER FREEMAN, "Legalistic Theories of Current Asset Val," *(m.A. Thesis)*, Austin, Texas, 1935.

TAX INSTITUTE OF AMERICA;, "Should the United States Adopt the British System of Assessing Realty?," *Tax Institute of America*, New York, 1944, pp. 31.

TAX POLICY, "Viewpoints on Assessment Standards," *Tax Policy*, 1961.

TECHNICAL VALUATION, "Assessors and Assessing Problems," *Technical Valuation*, February, 1954, pp. 27-29.

TEXAS, COMPTROLLER'S OFFICE, *Circular to County Judges, County Attorneys, and Tax Assessors*, Austin, 1977.

THEISS, WILLIAM R., "The Appraisal Docket. Economic Obsolescence As Factor In Assessed Value," *The Appraisal Journal*, October, 1965, pp. 624-626.

THEISS, WILLIAM R., "The Appraisal Docket. Reliability of Sales--Assessment Method," *The Appraisal Journal*, January, 1964, pp. 121-122.

THEISS, WILLIAM R., The Appraisal Docket, Tax Assessment—Damages for Failure to Assess Equally," *The Appraisal Journal*, July, 1962, pp. 417-418.

THEISS, WILLIAM R., "The Appraisal Docket. Use of Construction Cost for Determining Assessed Value," *The Appraisal Journal*, July, 1965, pp. 440-441.

THOMAS, BERY E., "Assessment of Farm Personal Property," *Assessment Administration*, IAAO, Chicago, 1957, pp. 159-161.

THOMPSON, CLARE R., "Special Assessments for Public Improvements," *Assessment Administration*, IAAO, Chicago, 1957, pp. 201-208.

THOMPSON, GLEN, "Notes at a Situs," *Case Reports In Assessment Administration*, August, 1961, pp. 30-31.

THOMPSON, W. E., "Preparation and Use of an Assessor's Manual," *Assessment Administration*, Institute of American Assessment Officers, Chicago, 1962, pp. 91-95.

THUROW, RAYMOND, "The Pros and Cons of Personnel Testing," *The Assessors Journal*, July, 1966, pp. 1-8.

TIDEMAN, ROBERT, "Fractional Assessments--Do Our Courts Sanction Inequality?," *Hastings Law Journal*, May, 1965, pp. 573-589.

TIPTON, BALLARD B., "The Iowa Real Property Appraisal Manual," *Assessment Administration*, IAAO, Chicago, 1959, pp. 89-95.

TOURTELOT, ROBERT H., "Separate Assessment of Condominiums," *Hastings Law Journal*, February, 1963, pp. 289-301.

TRAUTMAN, PHILIP A., "Assessment In Washington," *Washing Law Review*, April, 1965, pp. 100-132.

TRAVIS, BROLEY E., "Assessment and Equalization of Utilities In California," *Conference Proceedings*, National Tax Association, Columbus, 1960, pp. 402-409.

TURNER, EARL KENNETH, *Design of an Assessor's Manual for a Particular State*, University Microfilms, Ann Arbor, 1960.

U. S. DEPARTMENT OF AGRICULTURE, *Selected Legislative and Other Documents on the Preferential Assessment of Farmland*, U. S. Dept of Agriculture Economic Research Servic, Washington, March, 1963, pp. 1-65.

UNITED STATES BUREAU OF CENSUS, *Assessed Valuation of Property And Amounts and Rates of Levy 1860-1912*, Washington, 1915.

UNRUH, JESSE M., "Growing Public Awareness of the Property Tax," *Assessment Administration*, IAAO, Chicago, 1964, pp. 10-17.

USHER, THOMAS B., *Assessor's Manual*, Newark, 1911, pp. 1-101.

UTAH FOUNDATION, *Assessed Valuations of Utah Counties and School Districts, 1925-1946*, Utah Foundation, Salt Lake City, 1947.

VAN VUUREN, W., "An Evaluation of Ontario's Farm Assessment Proposals for Property Taxation," *Canadian Journal of Agricultural Economics*, July, 1970.

VAUGHAN, J. L. JR., "Appraisal of Commercial Properties for Purposes of Tax Assessment," *Technicalities*, June, 1951, pp. 40-42.

WAGNER, C. RAY, "Appraisal of Industrial Property," *Assessors Topics*, May, 1957.

WAILS, CHARLES E., "Assessment of Public Utility Properties," *Assessment Administration*, IAAO, Chicago, 1957, pp. 169-171.

WALDEN, R. R., "Demonstration Appraisal, a Modern Motel," *Assessment Administration*, Iaao, Chicago, 1957, pp. 7-9.

WALKER, WILLIAM P., *Improving Farm Land Tax Assessments In Maryland Under Nonfarm Use*, Univ of Maryland Agricultural Experiment Station, College Park, June, 1965, pp. 1-38.

WALLACE, J. WAGNER, "Industrial Plant," *Assessment Administration*, IAAO, Chicago, 1961, pp. 194-204.

WALLACE, J. WAGNER, "Use of Appraisal Manual," *Assessment Administration*, IAAO, Chicago, 1960, pp. 124-126.

WALLACE, JOHN, "The Assessor and His Community," *Assessors News Letter*, March, 1966, pp. 35-36.

WALLACE, W. H., "How Mississippi Is Solving Its Assessment Problem," *The Appraisal Journal*, April, 1936, pp. 136-145.

WALLACE, W. H., "Valuation of Public-Service Properties for Assessment Purposes," *The Appraisal Journal*, October, 1940, pp. 309-319.

WALTHER, HERMAN O., "The Principle of Highest and Best Use of Land Valuation," *Assessment Administration*, IAAO, Chicago, 1963, pp. 79-81.

WARDEN, FRANK E., "Problems Involved In Valuing Inventories at The Level of Trade," *Assessment Administration*, IAAO, Chicago, 1965, pp. 139-142.

WARREN, JOHN A., "The Wrentham Method-Relative Appraisal," *Case Reports In Assessment Administration*, Entire Issue, January, 1959.

WARTERFIELD, J. SOULE, "Chicago's Quadrennial Assessment," *The Appraisal Journal*, April, 1940, pp. 156-159.

WATKINS, O. R., "Future Living Patterns and Their Impact on Farm Real Estate Values," *Assessment Administration*, IAAO, Chicago, 1965, pp. 124-126.

WATSON, PHILIP E., "Gaining Public Acceptance for Improved Assessment Practices," *Assessment Administration*, IAAO, Chicago, 1964, pp. 22-27.

WATSON, THOMAS C., "The Effects of Inflation on Assessment Procedure In Multnomah County," *Technicalities*, October, 1948, pp. 5-7.

WATTS, RICHARD C., "A Plan for Consolidated Electronic Data Processing," *Assessment Administration*, IAAO, Chicago, 1960, pp. 43-45.

WAYNE, HAROLD M, "The Role of the Courts In Assessment Administration and Reform," *Property Tax Reform,* Int'l Ass'n Assessing Officers, Chicago, June 1, 1973, pp. 53-57.

WEIL, ANDREW L., KENT MAY WATSMAL, RON N., "Unsettled, Settled Law of Sewer Assessments Simon Appeal," *University of Pittsburgh Law Review,* June, 1964, pp. 653-681.

WELCH, CHARLES E., "Assessment of Business Inventories," *Assessment Administration,* Iaao, Chicago, 1957, pp. 118-123.

WELCH, R. B., "Some Observation on Assessment Ratio Measurement," *National Tax Journal,* March, 1965, pp. 13-21.

WELCH, RONALD B, "Characteristics and Feasibility of High Quality Assessment Administration," *Property Tax Reform,* Int'l Assn Assessing Officers, Chicago, June 1, 1973, pp. 33-46.

WELCH, RONALD B., "Maintenance of Appraisals," *Assessors News Letter,* December, 1961, pp. 147-151.

WELHAVEN, E. R., "Level of Trade Assessments," *Assessors News Letter,* April, 1964, pp. 39-43.

WELTZ, VERNON R., "The Valuation of Branch Inventories and Stock on Consignment for Ad Valorem Tax Purposes," *Assessment Administration,* IAAO, Chicago, 1959, pp. 46-51.

WENDT, PAUL F., "Estimating California's Housing Demand, 1954 to 1965," *The Appraisal Journal,* October, 1954, pp. 561-572.

WENZLICK, ROY, "The Future of Raw Land," *Assessors News Letter,* July, 1961, pp. 79-81.

WHEELER, BAYARD O., "Benefits of Improved Access," *Residential Appraiser,* July, 1957, pp. 13-21.

WHITE, JOHN B., "Citrus Groves," *Assessment Administration,* Institute of American Assessment Officers, Chicago, 1956, pp. 70-71.

WHITE, JOHN ROBERT, "Economic Assessment of Large-Scale Projects," *The Appraisal Journal,* July, 1969, pp. 360-371.

WHITE, ROBERT B., "Case Report In Assessment Administration-Two Apartments Over a Small Store," *Special Publication,* Institute of American Assessment Officers, Chicago, April, 1971, pp. 41-47.

WHITE, WALLACE E., "Assessment of Swimming Pools," *Assessors Topics,* August, 1961, pp. 104.

WILLARD, JAMES FIELD, *Side-Lights Upon the Assessment and Collection of the Medieval Subsidies,* Royal Historical Society, Vol. Vii, London, 1913, pp. 167-189.

WILLIAMS, CHARLES A. JR., *Florida Constitution and Legislative Classification for Tax Assessment Purposes,* University of Florida Law Review, 1965, pp. 609-615.

WILLIAMS, ELLIS T., *State Guides for Assessing Forest Land and Timber,* U. S. Forest Service, Washington, 1956, pp. 1-52.

WILLIAMS, ELLIS T., "What Lies Ahead In Forest Assessment?," *Assessment Administration,* Institute of American Assessment Officers, Chicago, 1958, pp. 43-57.

WILLIAMS, ROBERT M., "Trends In Ratio of Assessed to Market Value of Residences," *The Appraisal Journal,* April, 1963, pp. 213-219.

WILLIAMS, SQUIRE N JR., "Reconciling the Conflict Between the Legal Standard and Assessment Practice-Legal Considerations," *Assessment Administration,* Institute of American Assessment Officers, Chicago, 1965, pp. 20-25.

WILSON, FRED, "The State of Aid In the State of Washington," *Assessment Administration,* Institute of American Assessment Officers, Chicago, 1960, pp. 87.

WILSON, LEWIS E., "Improved Rural Land Assessment; the Morgan County Story," *Assessment Adminsitration,* Institute of American Assessment Officers, Chicago, 1960, pp. 53-55.

WILSON, RALPH G., "Certification In Ontario," *Assessment Administraton*, Institute of American Assessment Officers, Chicago, 1961, pp. 1-185.

WILSON, RALPH G., "Determining Depreciation Allowances," *Assessment Administration*, Institute of American Assessment Officers, Chicago, 1960, pp. 126-132.

WINGATE, HAROLD C., "The Assessor's Approach to the Taxpayer," *Assessor's News Letter*, March, 1966, pp. 38-42.

WISCONSIN TAX COMMISSION, *Assessors Manual*, The Commission, Madison, 1935, pp. 1-232.

WOLDEN, RUSSELL L., "The Assessment Role-Barometer of Local Government," *Technical Valuation*, June, 1956, pp. 6.

WOLDEN, RUSSELL L., "The Impact of Freeways and Redevelopments on the Assessments Roll," *Technical Valuation*, October, 1959, pp. 35-37.

WOOD, DODSON COMPANY, INC., *Assessment Manual City of Troy, New York*, Dodson Wood Company, Inc., New York, 1952.

WOODRUFF, ARCH M., "The Challenge for Assessment Administration," *Assessment Administration*, Institute of American Assessment Officers, Chicago, 1963, pp. 5-9.

WORKMASTER, H. C., *Appraisers and Assessors Manual of Taxable Subjects*, Unit Value Appraisal Co, Pittsburg:, 1935, pp. 1-578.

WRIGHT, W. P., "Public Relations and the Assessor," *Appraisal Institute Magazine*, Appraisal Institute of Canada, Winnipeg.

YOUNG, ELBERT A., "Depth Tables Used In Cities of the U. S," *Report of the Assessor of St. Paul, Minn.*, 1930.

YOUNGER, LEE B., "Electric Power Utility," *Assessment Administration*, IAAO, Chicago, 1962, pp. 128-131.

ZANGERLE, JOHN A., "Assessing Real Estate on Its Income," *Public Management*, July, 1933, pp. 206-209.

ZANGERLE, JOHN A., "Real Estate Assessments In Cities," *National Tax Association Association*, Proceedings 16th Annual Conference, 1923, pp. 46-63.

ZUVER, BERT L., "Basic Assessment Policy," *The Appraisal Journal*, Economics Background, pp. J.

ZUVER, BURT L., "A Sound Public Relations Program," *Assessment Administration*, I. A. A. O., Chicago, 1957, pp. 196-198.

## 12-14 Condemnation

ACCREDITED RURAL APPRAISERS, "Rural Appraisal Requirements In Federal Condemnation," *Journal of the American Society of Farm Managers and Rural Appraisers*, October, 1961, pp. 10-14.

ACKERMAN, ALAN L., "Just Compensation," *The Real Estate Appraiser*, July, 1963, pp. 23-32

ADAMS, WESLEY, "The Appraiser and the Attorney In Condemnation Appraisals," *Appraisal and Valuation Manual*, American Society of Appraisers, Washington D.C., 1960.

ADELSBERG, HYMAN, "Valuation Discrepancies In Court Testimony," *Appraisal Digest*, April, 1961, pp. 1-6.

ALLARD, JOSEPH L., "Is Market Value Just Compensation," *The Appraisal Journal*, July, 1967, pp. 355-359.

ALLISON, NEVILLE F., "A Study of Severance Damages," *The Residential Appraiser*, February, 1959, pp. 18-22.

AMERICAN INSTITUTE OF REAL ESTATE APPRAISERS, "The Appraisal Docket," *Condemnation Appraisal Practice*, American Institute of Real Estate Appraisers, Chicago, 1961, pp. 153-157.

AMERICAN RIGHT OF WAY ASSOCIATION, "Condemnations," *Proceedings of the Fifth Annual National Seminar, 1959*, Washington, D. C, 1960.

AMERICAN SOCIETY OF APPRAISERS, "Power and Process (Eminent Domain)," American Society of Appraisers, Publications, Washington.

ANDERS, DOWELL H., "The Jury's Approach to the Determination of Damages In Land Condemnation Suits," *Right of Way,* October, 1962, pp. 43-46.

ANSON, JOHN B., "Attorney-Appraiser Relationships In Preparation Before Trial," *Technical Valuation*, February, 1959, pp. 63-69.

ANSON, JOHN B., "General Legal Principles In Condemnation," *Appraisal and Valuation Manual,* American Society of Appraisers, 1958, pp. 253-260.

APPEL, JAMES R., "Damages Resulting from Construction of Transmission Line," *Real Estate Analyst Appraisal Bulletin*, pp. 513-516.

APPRAISAL DIGEST, "Condemnation Primer," *Business Week,* Appraisal Digest, January, 1958, pp. 23.

APPRAISAL DIGEST, *Moving Expenses In Condemnation,* January, 1953, pp. 12.

APPRAISAL JOURNAL, "Advice to Those About to Testify," *The Appraisal Journal,* April, 1942, pp. 166-169.

APPRAISAL JOURNAL, "Compensation In the Condemnation of Public Utilities," *The Appraisal Journal,* January, 1947, pp. 125-126.

APPRAISAL JOURNAL, "No Severance Damages for Taking of Leasehold," The Appraisal Journal, January, 1951, pp. 129-130.

APPRAISAL JOURNAL, "Six Points of Evidence. Appraisal Docket," *The Appraisal Journal,* April, 1954, pp. 439-442.

APPRAISAL JOURNAL, "The Appraiser As Expert Witness," *The Appraisal Journal,* October, 1952, pp. 598-604.

ARNESON, HARRY R. JR., "The Real Estate Appraiser As an Expert Witness," *Technical Valuation,* February, 1955, pp. 51-55.

ASH, FRED C., "Condemnation Purchase Price Not Evidence on Market Value," *The Appraisal Journal,* January, 1957, pp. 110-111.

ASH, FRED C., "Denial of Jury Trial Upheld In Condemnation Case," *The Appraisal Journal,* July, 1956, pp. 429-431.

ASH, FRED C., "Factual Basis for Expert Opinion," *The Appraisal Journal,* July, 1956, pp. 428-429.

ASH, FRED C., "The Appraisal Docket. Talk on the Street Not Admissible Evidence of Value," *The Appraisal Journal,* April, 1955, pp. 276-278.

ASH, FRED C., "The Appraisal Docket. The Amount of Consequential Benefits Must Be Stated to Be Deducted," *The Appraisal Journal,* October, 1956, pp. 590-591.

ATHERTON E B, "Appraising Noise Damages on Federal-Aid Highway Projects," *The Real Estate Appraiser,* The Society of Real Estate Appraisers, Chicago Illinois, November 1, 1973, pp. 4-8.

ATHERTON, E. B., "Damages Fact or Fiction? or Eminent Domain As it Is Related to the Fair Market Value Concept," *Technical Valuation,* June, 1962, pp. 40-44.

AUSTIN, PECK, "Tax Results of Exchanges and Condemnation Conversions," *Right of Way,* December, 1959, pp. 43-48.

BABCOCK, FREDERICK M., "Valuation for Specific Purposes to Determine Benefits and Damages In Condemnation Store," *The Valuation of Real Estate, Ed. 1,* 1932, pp. 514.

## Appraisal for Special Purposes

BALFOUR, FRANK C., "Special Benefits," *Right of Way,* February, 1957, pp. 7-18.

BALLARD, W. H., "On the Prophetic Analysis of Future Benefits In Max Tiegers Appraisal," *The Appraisal Journal,* 1933, pp. 248-249.

BARRY, DAVID N., "Legal Aspects of the Condemnation of Electric Transmission Line Easement," *Valuation,* February, 1961, pp. 8-13.

BAUMGARTNER, HAMPTON, JR., "Adequacy of Compensation In Federal Condemnation," *The Appraisal Journal,* January, 1963, pp. 36-47.

BEATTY, CLARENCE W. JR., "On the Witness Stand," *The Review,* June, 1945, pp. 9-11.

BEATTY, CLARENCE W. JR., "The Law Says Just Compensation," *The Review,* May, 1945, pp. 3-5.

BECK, F. W., "Market Value--So We Define it Correctly," *The Appraisal Journal,* April, 1947, pp. 197-201.

BEETH, CHANNING C., "Appraisers In Court," *The Review,* September, 1954, pp. 3-6.

BENNETT, PHILIP E., "What Is Market Value," *National Real Estate Journal,* September, 1941, pp. 20-22.

BENNETT, SAUL Z., "Purpose of the Appraisal and Definition of Fair Market Value," *A Student's Report on an Apartment House,* American Institute of Real Estate Appraisers, Chicago, 1966, pp. 9.

BENSON, PHILIP A., NORTH, NELSON L, *The Work of the Appraiser In Condemnation Proceedings.*

BERNARD, W. C., "Do Public Improvements Create Special Benefits," *The Appraisal Journal,* January, 1945, pp. 20-23.

BERNARD, W. C., "Saving Time and Money for the City In Condemnation Procedure," *American City,* January, 1929, pp. 89-91.

BISHOP, MAURICE F., PHELPS, JOSEPH D, "Enhancement In Condemnation," *Right of Way,* December, 1960, pp. 8-18.

BONBRIGHT, JAMES C., "May the Same Property Have Different Values for Different Purposes," *National Tax Association,* Proceedings 20th Annual Conference, 1927, pp. 279-295.

BONNER, JOHN T. JR., "Appraisal of Short-Term Leaseholds In Condemnation Cases," *The Appraisal Journal,* January, 1955, pp. 59-62.

BONNER, JOHN T. JR., "Bargaining Ability Affects Market Value," *The Review,* September, 1956, pp. 7-8.

BORDLEY, R. C., "A Proposal of a Method of Appraising Proximity Damage," *Right of Way,* August, 1957, pp. 41-44.

BOWEN, PERCIVAL V., "Buyers, Sellers Not Always Willing," *The Appraisal Digest,* April, 1952, pp. 16-17.

BOWES, WATSON A., "The Function of the Appraiser In Condemnation," *The Appraisal Journal,* July, 1958, pp. 407-414.

BOYER, RALPH F., AND JOHN P. WILCOX, "An Economic Appraisal of Leasehold Valuation In Condemnation Proceedings," *The University of Miami Law Review,* April, 1963, pp. 245-275.

BRIGGS, J., "Sales on Terms-Do They Represent Market Value," *The Appraisal Institute Magazine,* December, 1963, pp. 9-15.

BRITTON, THOMAS C., "Effect In Florida of Requiring Condemnor to Pay Condemnee's Entire Litigation Expense," *Right of Way,* October, 1963, pp. 15-20.

BROOKS, J. H., "Condemnation Appraising of Area Flooded for Water Storage," *Journal of the American Society of Farm Managers and Rural Appraisers.*

BROWN, PAT, "Condemnation of Cemetery Land, Factors Determining Valuation," *Valuation,* October, 1957, pp. 39-43.

BRUCHE, ALBERT, "What Constitutes Value?," *Technical Valuation,* June, 1958, pp. 45-46.

BURNS, ROBERT L., "Damages and Benefits from Constitutional Damaging and Partial Taking--Community or Special?," *Proceedings of the Third Institute on Eminent Domain 1961,* Dallas, 1961, pp. 119-138.

BURNS, ROBERT L., "Qualifying a Witness and Admissibility of Evidence," *The Real Estate Appraiser,* November, 1964, pp. 2.

CAHILL, FRANK P., "Some Guides for Estimating the Fee Value of Real Estate for Condemnation Purposes," *Technicalities,* May, 1949, pp. 4-6.

CAMPBELL, CHARLES W., "Preparation for the Condemnation Trial," *Right of Way,* June, 1959, pp. 35-38.

CAMPBELL, COLIN, "Transmission Line Easements In Condemnation," *Right of Way,* October, 1963, pp. 45-52.

CARLL, CLOICE D., "On Easement Costs and Damages Under California Practice," *The Appraisal Journal,* July, 1937, pp. 281-285.

CASE, FRED E., "Value, Market Value, and Market Price," *The Appraisal Journal,* April, 1953, pp. 217-222.

CHATELAIN, LEON, JR., "Cities Will Survive," *The Residential Appraiser,* December, 1957, pp. 13-16.

CHICHESTER, C. H. JR., "Market Data In Condemnation Appraisings," *Right of Way Conference, Selected Papers, 1961,* University, Alabama, 1961, pp. 55-59.

CITIZEN'S UNION, NEW YORK CITY, "Special Committee on Condemnation Procedure," *Real Estate Record and Builders Guide,* October 31, 1931, pp. 5-6, 38.

CLAY, DEANE J., "Practical Approach, Appraisal and Preparation for Trial In Condemnation Proceedings," *Technical Valuation,* June, 1959, pp. 65-68.

CLEMINSHAW COMPANY, *Appraisers Manual,* The Company, Cleveland, Ohio, 1937.

CLEMINSHAW, J. M. CO., *Appraisers Manual,* Cleveland, Ohio, 1947.

COHN, WALTER W., "The Art of Testifying In Appraisal Cases," *Practical Appraising Methods,* 1940, pp. 126-128.

COLE, F. M., "Condemnation Appraisal of Woodlands," *Technical Valuation,* 1967, pp. 62.

COLE, JOHN D., *The Room Unit System a Manual for Appraisers,* The Cole Layer Company, Dayton, Ohio, 1939.

COLLIER, RONALD, "Compulsory Purchase and Condemnation, a Comparison of Procedures," *The Appraisal Journal,* January, 1968, pp. 121.

CONGER, GENE M., "Noise Damage," *The Appraisal Journal,* April, 1968, pp. 253-254.

COON, JEAN M., "The Appellate Lawyer Looks at Opinion Evidence In an Appropriation Case," *The Real Estate Appraiser.*

CORUCH, WILLIAM H., "Pretrial Conference Checklist of Factors Affecting Valuation," *The Appraisal Journal,* October, 1964, pp. 523-530.

COTTON, JOHN, "Market Data, Using and Reporting Adjustment Techniques In Condemnation Appraisals," *The Appraisal Journal,* July, 1966, pp. 365-369.

CRAWFORD, CLAUDE O., "Appraising Damages to Land from Power Line Easements," *The Appraisal Journal,* July, 1955, pp. 367-378.

DADDO, DR. JEROME, "Changing Economic Conditions and the Condemnation Value of Real Property," *The Real Estate Appraiser,* March, 1970, pp. 51-55.

DALGETY, GEORGE S., "Aspects of Condemnation Appraising," *The Appraisal Journal,* April, 1950, pp. 215-222.

DARSEY, GLENN S., "General and Special Benefits," *The Appraisal Journal,* January, 1966, pp. 71-78.

DARSEY, GLENN S., "General and Special Benefits to Remainder In Partial Takings," *Valuation Manual,* American Society of Appraisers, 1961, pp. 329.

DAVIS, R. A., "Expropriation Appraisal-Farm Land," *Appraisal Institute Magazine*, Appraisal Institute of Canada, Winnipeg.

DAVIS, W. D., "Estimation of Severance Damages In Partial Acquisition Following the Law of North Carolina," *Right of Way*, December, 1961, pp. 19-24.

DAVIS, W. D., "Evidences of Market Value," *The Appraisal Journal*, April, 1959, pp. 224-253.

DAVIS, W. D., "Principles and Practices of Condemnation Appraisal," *The Appraisal Journal*, July, 1950, pp. 348-362.

DAVIS, W. D., "Rural Appraisal Requirements In Federal Condemnation," *American Society of Farm Managers and Rural Appraisers*, October, 1963, pp. 58-73.

DAVIS, W. D., "What Is Market Value," *The Appraisal Journal*, January, 1960, pp. 42-46.

DENIS, J. W., "Can Present Market Value Be Determined," *Journal American Institute of Real Estate Appraisers*, April, 1934, pp. 253-256.

DERBES, MAX J. JR., "Procedural Guidelines for Measurement of Proximity Damages," *The Appraisal Journal*, July, 1967, pp. 374-379.

DETROIT BUREAU OF GOVERNMENTAL RESEARCH, *The Condemnation Procedure In 24 Cities*, Detroit.

DEUTSCH, JOSEPH S., "Fundamentals of Appraising for Condemnation," *Appraisal Digest*, July, 1963, pp. 12-16.

DIAMOND, JOSEF, "Condemnation Law," *The Appraisal Journal*, October, 1955, pp. 564-580.

DIAMOND, THOMAS M., "Condemnation Preparation," *Right of Way*, June, 1960, pp. 41-45.

DIAMOND, THOMAS M. JR., "The Appraiser In Court," *The Residential Appraiser*, April, 1961, pp. 6-8, 14.

DILMORE, G., "Reasonable Time to Find a Purchaser," *Appraisal Institute Magazine*, Appraisal Institute of Canada, Winnipeg.

DIX, S. M., "The Problem with Value-In-Place Less Salvage In Determining Fixture Damage," *Right of Way*, April, 1969, pp. 34-36.

DIX, SAMUEL M, "Eminent Domain: Principles of Fixture Appraisal," *Valutape Audio-Library Series*, American Society of Appraisers, Washington D.C., January 1, 1973.

DIX, SAMUEL M., "Fixture Qualification and Valuation for Condemnation of the Major Industrial Complex," *The Appraisal Journal*, April, 1966, pp. 245-257.

DOLAN, HARRY T., *Federal Condemnation and Severance Damage*, A.I.R.E.A., Chicago, 1967, pp. 118-128.

DOLAN, HARRY T., *Federal Condemnation with Special Reference to Severance Damages*, U of Pitt Bu of Bus. Res In Coop with Law School, 1957, pp. 47-57.

DOLAN, HARRY T., "Federal Condemnation Practice," *Appraisal Journal*, January, 1945, pp. 9-19.

DOLAN, HARRY T., "Federal Condemnation Practice," *The Appraisal Journal*, April, 1950, pp. 173-178.

DOLAN, HARRY T., "Federal Condemnation Practice General Aspects," *The Appraisal Journal*, January, 1959, pp. 15-30.

DOLAN, HARRY T., "New Federal Procedure In Condemnation Actions," *The Appraisal Journal*, January, 1954, pp. 26-32.

DOLAN, HARRY T., "Trade Fixtures In Condemnation. Confusion," *The Appraisal Journal*, April, 1968, pp. 263-265, 268-269.

DOLAN, HARRY T., "Trade Fixtures In Federal Condemnation," *The Appraisal Journal*, October, 1965, pp. 499-507.

DOLAN, HARRY T., "Unit Rule of Valuation In Federal Condemnation," *The Appraisal Journal*, January, 1965, pp. 23-28.

DOLLE, HODGE L., "Unusual Developments In Past Condemnation Proceedings," *Technical Valuation*, February, 1961, pp. 37-45.

DRISCOLL, ROBERT L., "Condemnation of Underground Reservoirs for Storage of Natural Gas," *The Appraisal Journal*, January, 1965, pp. 67-72.

DUBOIS, AYERS J., "Severance Damage to an Apartment Site," *The Appraisal Journal*, January, 1933, pp. 153-166.

DUFFEY, EARLE M., "Federal Participation In State Condemnation Settlements and Awards," *Federal Participation In State Condemnation Settlements and Awards*, Right of Way Conference, University, Ala., 1961, pp. 146-150.

DUFFY, GEORGE C., "Damage to the Remainder--Made Simple," *Right of Way*, April, 1963, pp. 13-20.

DUNN, DOMINICK R., "Appraisal In Condemnation Proceedings," Encyclopedia of Real Estate Appraising, 1959.

DUNN, DOMINICK R., "Some Reflections on Value In Eminent Domain Proceedings," *The Appraisal Journal*, July, 1956, pp. 415-1.

EDMAN, J. J., "Admissibility of Drawings and Map. Appraisal Docket," *The Appraisal Journal*, April, 1960, pp. 265-266.

EDMANN, J. J., "Condemnation to Allow Access to Fishing Lake. Appraisal Docket," *The Appraisal Journal*, October, 1957, pp. 622.

EDMAN, J. J., "Condemned Sale Price of Improvements Not Evidence of Value. Appraisal Docket," *The Appraisal Journal*, October, 1959, pp. 579.

EDMAN, J. J., "Condemner's Demand As a Part of Market Value. Appraisal Docket," *The Appraisal Journal*, April, 1960, pp. 263-264.

EDMAN, J. J., "Enhancement In Value Involving Related Condemnations. Appraisal Docket," *The Appraisal Journal*, July, 1959, pp. 411-412.

EDMAN, J. J., "Improvements to Drainage May Result in Condemnation. Appraisal Docket," *The Appraisal Journal*, January, 1960, pp. 125-126.

EDMAN, J. J., "Information Acquired by Hearsay May Be Basis of Expert Testimony. Appraisal Docket," *The Appraisal Journal*, April, 1961, pp. 258-258.

EDMAN, J. J., "Jury Instructions As to Meaning of Fair Market Value. Appraisal Docket," *The Appraisal Journal*, January, 1958, pp. 123-125.

EDMAN, J. J., "Moving Costs As an Element of Value. Appraisal Docket," *The Appraisal Journal*, January, 1959, pp. 119-121.

EDMAN, J. J., "Other Purchases of Similar Property As Evidence of Value. Appraisal Docket," *The Appraisal Journal*, April, 1959, pp. 263-265.

EDMAN, J. J., "Sales Made at or About Same Time May Incl Sales Subsequent to Condemnation. Appraisal Docket," *Condemnation Appraisal Practice*, American Institute of Real Estate Appraisers, 1961, pp. 153-154.

EDMAN, J. J., "Sales Made at or About Same Time May Incl Sales Subsequent to Condemnation. Appraisal Docket," *The Appraisal Journal*, January, 1958, pp. 127.

EDMAN, J. J., "Severance Damages for Division of Farms. Appraisal Docket," *The Appraisal Journal*, April, 1959, pp. 268-269.

EDMAN, J. J., "Severance Damages to One Tract for Taking of Another. Appraisal Docket," *The Appraisal Journal*, July, 1959, pp. 410.

EDMAN, J. J., "The Appraisal Docket. Shrinkage of Lot Is Compensible Damage," *The Appraisal Journal*, January, 1959, pp. 122-123.

**EDMAN, J. J., "The Appraisal Docket. Damages for Loss of Aesthetic Values,"** *The Appraisal Journal*, July, 1961, pp. 415-416.

EDMAN, J. J., "The Appraisal Docket. Damages Occasioned by Change of Water Flow," *The Appraisal Journal*, April, 1958, pp. 293-294.

EDMAN, J. J., "The Appraisal Docket. Damages to Aesthetic Values," *The Appraisal Journal*, January, 1960, pp. 126-127.

EDMAN, J. J., "The Appraisal Docket. Right to Condemn Indian Lands," *The Appraisal Journal,* April, 1959, pp. 265-266.

EDMAN, J. J., "The Appraisal Docket. Sales Under Pressure Are Not Evidence of Value," *The Appraisal Journal,* October, 1957, pp. 623-624.

EDMAN, J. J., "The Appraisal Docket. Use of Commissioners Instead of Jury," *The Appraisal Journal,* January, 1958, pp. 121-123.

EDMAN, J. J., "The Appraisal Docket. Vermont Statute Recognizes Damage to Business," *The Appraisal Journal,* January, 1960, pp. 123-124.

EDMAN, J. J., "The Appraisal Docket. Abutting Landowner Not Entitled to Damages for Change In Street Grade," *The Appraisal Journal,* April, 1966, pp. 261-262.

EDMAN, J. J., "Value Where Condemning Body Improves by Mistake. Appraisal Docket," *The Appraisal Journal,* April, 1958, pp. 292.

EDMUNDS, JOHN T., "What Constitutes Just Compensation," *The Residential Appraiser,* April, 1961, pp. 11-14.

ELLWOOD, L. W., "Wherry Condemnation Spotlights Problem of Equity Valuation," *The Appraisal Journal,* April, 1960, pp. 165-176.

EMPSON, W. JENNINGS, "Condemnation Is a Big Business," *Appraisal and Valuation Manual,* American Society of Appraisers, pp. 11-15.

EMPSON, W. JENNINGS, "Grass Roots Impressions In a Study of Condemnation Procedures," *Appraisal and Valuation Manual,* 1961, pp. 321-328.

ENFIELD, CLIFTON W., AND WILLIAM A. MANSFIELD, *General and Specific Benefits,* Right of Way Magazine.

FARSTAD, E. K., "Expropriation Review Committee Report," *Appraisal Institute Magazine,* Appraisal Institute of Canada, Winnipeg.

FAVA, EDWARD, *Quantity Appraisal Data Market Analysis Requirements In Condemnation,* American Society of Appraisers, 1960, pp. 197-204.

FAVA, EDWARD, *Valuation In Condemnation - Partial Taking,* American Society of Appraisers, 1958, pp. 261-266.

FINKEL, JULIUS, "Condemnation Appraisal of a Cemetery," *The Appraisal Journal,* July, 1955, pp. 379-388.

FOLEY, DAVID A., "Land Damage Cases," *Right of Way,* December, 1957, pp. 41-43.

FORD, JAMES, "Appraising for Multi-Family Housing Projects Appraising for Condemnation," *Slums and Housing,* Harvard University Press, Cambridge, 1936, pp. 529-540.

FRANKLAND, BAMFORD, *Techniques of Remainder Parcel Severance Damage Data Collection In Use by Public Agencies,* Amer Rt of Way Assn Procdgs of 8th Ann Natl Seminr, Washington, D.C., 1962, pp. 49-51.

FREE, ROBERT L., "Preparing a Condemnation Appraisal," *Condemnation Appraisal Practice,* American Institute of Real Estate Appraisers, Chicago, 1967, pp. 525.

FRIEDMANN, LIONEL, "Selection of Appraisers for Condemnation," *The Appraisal Journal,* July, 1955, pp. 363-366.

FRISSELL, ROBERT N., "The Professional Appraisal and Market Value," *The Appraisal Journal,* October, 1966, pp. 581-584.

GALLAGHER, JOSEPH A., "Damages-Severance and Consequential," *Technicalities,* February, 1950, pp. 30-31.

GARDINER, MAC., "An Approach to Proximity Damage," *The Appraisal Journal,* April, 1957, pp. 193-197.

GILBERT, HARRY E., "Condemnation Appraisals," *National Real Estate Journal,* March, 1932, pp. 21-24.

GILBERT, HARRY E., "Condemnations," *The Appraisal Journal,* January, 1933, pp. 123-127.

GILBERT, HARRY E., "Example of a Before and After Appraisal In Condemnation Proceedings," *Appraisal Manual,* 1937, pp. 290-292.

GITELSON, ALFRED, *Legal Concept of Market Value and Just Compensation,* Condemnation Appraisal Seminar, 1958.

GLOS, HAROLD V., "Expert Appraisal Testimony Requires More Knowledge Today," *Real Estate,* February 25, 1939, pp. 10-12.

GOLDSTINE, HARRY, "Acquirement of Property by Condemnatiion," *National Real Estate Journal,* November 19, 1923, pp. 24-26.

GOMEZ, CARLOS EDUARDO, "La Interpretacion Del Proyecto De Reforma," *Boletin,* Sotave, Caracas, Venezuela, pp. 11-14.

GOMEZ, CARLOS EDUARDO, "Naturaleza Juridica Del Avaluo De La O," *Boletin,* Sotave, Caracas, Venezuela, pp. 23-26.

GONZALEZ VALE, LUIS, "Derecho Comparado: La Legislacion Colombiana," *Boletin,* Sotave, Caracas, Venezuela, pp. 3-4.

GOOD, H. A., "Manitoba Expropriation Act," *Appraisal Institute Magazine,* Appraisal Institute of Canada, Winnipeg.

GRACE, ARTHUR B. JR., "Severance Damage Studies," *The Appraisal Journal,* July, 1966, pp. 375-379.

GREEN, ARTHUR W., "An Interesting Case In Condemnation Work-Los Angeles County Vs Wright Et Al," *Technical Valuation,* November, 1952, pp. 11-12.

GREEN, ARTHUR W., "Condemnation Procedures," *Technical Evaluation,* A. S. A, November, 1952, pp. 11.

HADLEY, GEORGE C., "Preparation and Conduct of Highway Condemnation Proceedings," *The Appraisal Journal,* July, 1953, pp. 416-423.

HAGMAN, DONALD C., "The Special Benefit, What Is it How Is it Measured?," *The Real Estate Appraiser,* November, 1967, pp. 11-16.

HAIG, GRAEME T., "Your Husband, the Appraiser - In Court," *Appraisal Institute Magazine,* Appraisal Institute of Canada, Winnipeg, June 1, 1973.

HAMILTON, ANDREW C., "Judicial Review of Appraisals," *The Appraisal Journal,* October, 1934, pp. 80-82.

HANFORD, LLOYD D. SR., "A Conflict of Law," *The Appraisal Journal,* April, 1967, pp. 165-174.

HANLEY, DUDLEY J., "Expert Testimony In Condemnations Trials," *The Residential Appraiser,* September, 1960, pp. 10-12.

HANNOCH, FRANKLIN, "The Element of Damages," *National Real Estate Journal,* December 22, 1930, pp. 29-30.

HANSEN, VICTOR R., "Preparation and Trial of Condemnation Cases," *Technicalities and Technical Valuation,* February, 1952, pp. 36-39.

HANSEN, VICTOR R., "The Expert Appraiser As the Focal Point In Preparation of a Condemnation Case for Trail," *Right of Way,* October, 1955, pp. 7-11, 20.

HANSON, PETER, "Condemnation Appraisals," *National Real Estate Journal,* August 17, 1931, pp. 9-12.

HANSON, PETER, "Data Schedules," *Condemnation Appraisal Procedure,* Hanson and Pollard, pp. 259-269.

HANSON, PETER, "The Meaning of Market Value," *National Real Estate Journal,* May 11, 1931, pp. 35-36.

HANSON, PETER, "The Meaning of Value," *The Appraisal Journal,* July, 1933, pp. 289-297.

HANSON, PETER, W. L. POLLARD, "Condemnation Appraisal Procedure," *An Appraisal Handbook In Two Parts,* Los Angeles, 1934, pp. 467.

HARDING, CARL G., "Appraisal of a Trailer Park Under Condemnation," *Appraisal Reporting Techniques,* American Institute of Real Estate Appraisers, 1954, pp. 85-122.

HARRIS, RICHARD D., "Witness for the Defendant," *The Residential Appraiser.*

HECHT, KENNETH G., "In the Witness Chair," *The Residential Appraiser,* June, 1957, pp. 12-13.

HECHT, LESTER S., "Benefit to the Property Owner As Affecting Assessments for Improvements to Real Estate," *Pennsylvania Bar Association Quarterly,* June, 1965, pp. 399-409.

HELSTAD, ORRIN L., "Appraisal Issues In Highway Condemnation Litigation," *Papers and Proceedings,* Wisconsin Colloquium on Appraisal Research, 1963, pp. 7-12.

HENDERSON, JAMES D., "What's the Damage?," *National Real Estate Journal,* March 3, 1930, pp. 24-27.

HENDRICKS, FORD, AND DEXTER MACBRIDE, *Condemnation Clauses a Right of Way Problem.*

HIGHWAY RESEARCH BOARD, *Valuation and Condemnation Problems Involving Trade Fixtures,* Nchrp Report 94, Washington, D. C..

HODGES, M. B. JR., "Compensation Without Condemnation," *The Appraisal Journal,* October, 1967, pp. 581-582.

HOFFMAN, ISREAL, "Recent Developments In Judicial Valuation In Assessment Review and Condemnation Proceedings," *Technical Valuation,* February, 1958, pp. 13-16.

HOLBROOK, M. JEFFREY, "Appraising for Condemnation," *Right of Way,* February, 1955, pp. 21-26.

HOLDEN, ARTHUR C., "Condemnation and Urban Redevelopment," *Real Estate Record,* April 13, 1940, pp. 4-5.

HOLMAN, RALPH, "Expert Testimony As to Value In Condemnation Cases," *Right of Way,* June, 1959, pp. 21-24.

HOLZ, LEFFERT, "Condemnation Law Defects Revealed," *Appraisal Digest,* October, 1954, pp. 14-16.

HOLZ, LEFFERT, HERMAN SCHRIER, "Real Estate Appraisals In Legal Proceedings," *The Appraisal Journal,* January, 1946, pp. 38-46.

HOPKINS, ROBERT W., "Role of the Expert Witness," *Appraisal Digest,* April, 1955, pp. 16-18.

HUDE, JAMES V., "Condemnation Appraisals," *The Real Estate Appraiser,* May, 1970, pp. 51-56.

HUDSON, RAYMOUND, "Damage Claims and Public Relations," *Right of Way,* August, 1957, pp. 38-40.

HUFFMAN, WILLIAM H., "Giving the Land Owner a Fair and Square Deal," *Right of Way,* August, 1962, pp. 7-10.

HUNTLEY, GENE, "The Community Benefit of By-Pass Highways," *Right of Way,* June, 1957, pp. 29-32.

IBSEN, NORM, "Expropriation Powers Vital So Are Fairness, Tact," *Appraisal Institute Magazine,* Appraisal Institute of Canada, Winnipeg.

INGRAM, DAVID, "The Role of Appraiser and Attorney In Condemnation," *Right of Way,* 1958, pp. 35-36.

JAHR, ALFRED D., "Compensable Damages Due to Construction of Limited Access Highways," *Proceedings of the Second Institute on Eminent Domain, 1960,* Dallas, 1960, pp. 77-93.

JOHNDROE, S. F. FR., "Procedural Pitfalls In a Condemnation Case," *Proceedings,* Institute of Eminent Domain, 1959, pp. 101-149.

JOSLIN, E. G., "Voice of the 'Prudent Man'," *Appraisal Institute Magazine,* Appraisal Institute of Canada, Winnipeg.

KALISH, JACOB, "Use As a Factor In Determining Fair Market Value," *The Appraisal Journal,* October, 1959, pp. 565-571.

KAZDIN, S. EDWIN, "The Zone of Reasonable Doubt," *The Appraisal Journal,* October, 1962, pp. 489-493.

KAZDIN, S. EDWIN, "What Price Market Value," *Appraisal Digest,* October, 1952, pp. 1-4.

## BIBLIOGRAPHY OF APPRAISAL LITERATURE

KEEGAN, NORMAN J., "The Home Owner Vs. the Condemner Appraiser," *The Residential Appraiser*, January, 1962, pp. 21-23.

KEENE, J., "Convert it to a Condominium," *House and Home*, January, 1971, pp. 106-111.

KEENLEYSIDE, A., "Function of the Appraiser In Expropriation," *Appraisal Institute Magazine*, Appraisal Institute of Canada, Winnipeg.

KENNEDY, HAROLD W., "Testimony of Expert Appraisers In Condemnation Actions," *California Real Estate Magazine*, January, 1937, pp. 23.

KING, PAT, "Market Value-What Is it," *Appraisal Institute Magazine*, Appraisal Institute of Canada, Winnipeg.

KING, WILLIAM H., "Expert Testimony from the Viewpoint of an Attorney," *New York State Society of Real Estate Appraisers*, February 26, 1941.

KRAMER, HERMAN N., "Appraising for Condemnation," American Association of State Highway Officials, Washington D. C., 1962, pp. 85-102.

KREVOR, HENRY H., *A Congressional Study of Just Compensation*, American Society of Appraisers, 1962, pp. 16-27.

KUEHNLE, WALTER R., "Valuation Technique In Condemnation, the Comparable Sale," *Condemnation Appraisal Practice*, 1961, pp. 60-67.

LA TRIBUNE, SHERBROOKE, "Les Expropriations," *Appraisal Institute Magazine*, Appraisal Institute of Canada, Winnipeg.

LABRECQUE, THEODORE J., "The Court and the Expert Witness," *The Appraisal Journal*, January, 1961, pp. 87-93.

LANDRY, J., "La Negociation En Cas D'Expropriation," *Appraisal Institute Magazine*, Appraisal Institute of Canada, Winnipeg.

LARONGE, JOSEPH, "The Technique of Preparing for Court Testimony," *The Appraisal Journal*, Col. III, July, 1935, pp. 303-309.

LATCHFORD, GEORGE, "Appraiser Witness In Condemnation Cases," *The Society of Industrial Realtors*, 1953, pp. 105-125.

LAW, RAY E., "Preparing Exhibits for Condemnation Trials," *Right of Way*, February, 1961, pp. 21-28.

LEE, ADELBERT W., "Appraisals for Condemnation," *Selected Readings In Right of Way*, American Right of Way Association, Los Angeles, 1968, pp. 577-581.

LEVEY, IRVING L., "Condemnation," *Technical Valuation*, July, 1950, pp. 4-10.

LEVEY, IRVING L., MANHEIMER, J. F, *Condemnation In New York*, Burland Printing Company, New York, 1937.

LEVIT, BERT W., "The Expert Witness," *The Appraisal Journal*, July, 1939, pp. 219-226.

LEW, IRVING, "Valuation In Condemnation and In Real Estate Tax Assessment Review Proceedings," *Appraisal and Valuation Manual*, American Society of Appraisers, 1962.

LEWIS, HARRISON, "Damage Due to Police Power Exercised In Conjunction with a Taking," *The Appraisal Journal*, October, 1962, pp. 481-488.

LINDAS, LEONARD I., "General and Special Benefits," *Right of Way*, December, 1958, pp. 29-32.

LOCKYER, ALBERT W., "Income In Condemnation Appraisal," *The Residential Appraiser*, April, 1959, pp. 21-24.

LOWREY, R. E. JR., "Principles of Condemnation," *The Real Estate Appraisal*, SREA, Chicago, December, 1964, pp. 2.

LUM, Y. T., "Appraising Leaseholds for Condemnation," *Appraisal Institute Magazine*, Appraisal Institute of Canada, Winnipeg.

LUM, Y. T., "Value Concepts for Condemnation In the United States," *Right of Way*, December, 1959, pp. 33-41.

LUM, Y. T., "Value Concepts for Condemnation In the U. S," *Selected Readings In Right of Way,* American Right of Way Association, Los Angeles, 1968, pp. 152-163.

LUTTRELL, RALPH J., "Federal Condemnation Law, Practice, and Procedure," *The Appraisal Journal,* July, 1963, pp. 349-363.

LUTTRELL, RALPH J., "Federal Rules In a Condemnation Trial," *The Appraisal Journal,* April, 1960, pp. 213-218.

LUTTRELL, RALPH J., "Some Applicable Rules In the Trial of a Condemnation," *The Appraisal Journal,* April, 1960, pp. 213-218.

MACBRIDE, DEXTER D, "History and Meaning of Just Compensation," *Proceedings, 3rd Annual Legal, R/W Seminar,* University of Nevada, August 1, 1966.

MACBRIDE, DEXTER D, "Interface: Condemnation, Appraising, Right of Way, Public Works, Administration," *Valutape Audio-Library Series,* American Society of Appraisers, Washington D.C., January 1, 1973.

MACBRIDE, DEXTER D., "Market Value: a Description of California's Landmark Condemnation Case," *Proceedings International Conference,* American Society of Appraisers, July 1, 1966.

MACBRIDE, DEXTER D, "Trends In Condemnation: Effect on the Appraisal Process," *Proceedings 15th Southwest Region Conference,* American Inst of Real Estate Appraisers, April 1, 1965.

MACBRIDE, DEXTER D., *Power and Process A Commentary on Eminent Domain and Condemnation,* American Society of Appraisers, January, 1969.

MACBRIDE, DEXTER D., "Condemnation, Compensation and the Courts," *Proceedings,* American Bar Association National Institute, St. Louis, September, 1968.

MACBRIDE, DEXTER D., "Market Value A Description of California Landmark Condemnation Case," *Proceedings,* San Francisco, July 27, 1966.

MACBRIDE, DEXTER D., "Recent Trends In Condemnation: Effect on the Appraisal Process," *Proceedings,* San Francisco, April, 1965.

MACBRIDE, DEXTER D., "The Right of Way Agent and Condemnation Appraising," *Right of Way Magazine,* December, 1968.

MACCOLLUM, DAVID V. P. E. C. S. P., "What Is the Value of a Disaster," *Valuation,* American Society of Appraisers, September, 1972, pp. 80.

MACHT, LOIS, *Condemnation In Maryland Research Report, No. 31,* Research Division, Maryland Legislative Council, October, 1958.

MADOLE, ROSS, "Legal Problems of Utilities In Condemnation Proceedings," *Proceedings,* Institute on Eminent Domain, 1962, pp. 127-147.

MAIER, E. F., "Market Value," *The Appraisal Journal,* December, 1933, pp. 167-169.

MALLARD, RAYMOND B., "My Views Concerning Condemnation and Condemnation Trials," *Right of Way,* December, 1962, pp. 50-54.

MANN, J. F., "Valuation of Air Lease, Condemned by Eminent Domain," *Buildings and Building Management,* February 10, 1930, pp. 63-64.

MARKEIM, J. WILLIAM, "Condemnation Phases, Condemnation Appraisals, Expert Testimony," *Technical Valuation,* February, 1956, pp. 25-31.

MARPLES, RICHARD A, "Appraisal Practices In the U.S. Army Corps of Engineers," *Valutape Audio-Library Series,* American Society of Appraisers, Washington D.C., January 1, 1973.

MARSHALL, J. W., "Replacement Cost and Condemnation," *Technical Valuation,* February, 1961, pp. 49-51.

MARTZ, CLYDE O., "The Federal View of Damages and Benefits," *The Appraisal Journal,* April, 1969, pp. 200-209.

MAXWELL, GEORGE I., "Condemnation Appraising and Related Problems," *Journal of the American Society of Farm Managers and Rural Appraisers*, April, 1962, pp. 116-120.

MCCOY, CHARLES R., "Effect of Partial Condemnation and of a Temporary Easement on the Value of a Service Stateon," *Real Estate Analyst Appraisal Bulletin*, 1954, pp. 305-311.

MCDONALD, ADRIAN F., "Rules In Condemnation," *The Residential Appraiser*, January, 1958, pp. 3-7.

MCGARRY, DANIEL F., "Expert Testimony In Condemnation from the Standpoint of the Condemnee," *Right Of Way*, December, 1956, pp. 41-44.

MCGOUGH, B. C., "Analysis of Severance Damages and Special Benefits," *The Real Estate Appraiser*, September, 1966, pp. 10-16.

MCKIBBIN, FRANK B., "Damages to Buildings," *The Appraisal Journal*, January, 1933, pp. 171-172.

MCLAUGHLIN, FRANK, "On Severance Damages to an Apartment Site by Dubois," *The Appraisal Journal*, April, 1933, pp. 254-255.

MCLEOD, V. W., "Utility Line Condemnation Cases," *Proceedings of the Second Institute on Eminent Domain*, Dallas, 1960, pp. 95-109.

MCMICHAEL, S. L., "Appraising for Purposes of Condemnation," *Appraising Manual*, 1937, pp. 264-295.

MCMICHAEL, STANLEY L., "Testifying In Court," *Appraising Manual*, 1937, pp. 444-450.

MELLOR, PHILLIP, "Selected Problems of Procedure and Compensation Encountered In Federal Reservoir Condemnation," *Proceedings of the Fourth Institute on Emident Domain*, 1962, pp. 49-66.

MELTZER, HERMAN, "Appraising and Testifying In Condemnation Proceedings," *Brooklyn Realty Magazine*, December, 1939, pp. 7.

MEYER, EDWIN G., "Severance Damages, Fact or Fantasy," *Right of Way*, December, 1963, pp. 21-22.

MEYER, R. A. JR., "Equipment Replacement Under Uncertainty," *Management Science*, January, 1971, pp. 750-758.

MICAY, A. R., "The Proposed Expropriation Act (Manitoba)," *Appraisal Institute Magazine*, Appraisal Institute of Canada, Winnipeg.

MOEBES, CARL, "Condemnation of Mineral Rights," *Right of Way Conference*, 1960, pp. 41-46.

MORESCO, ENRIQUE, "Expropiaciones," *Boletin*, Sotave, Caracas, Venezuela, pp. 31-35.

MORROW, R. CONRAD, "Leasee Improvements and Condemnation," *The Appraisal Journal*, September, 1966, pp. 15-16.

MORTON, PERRY W., "Basic Principles and Practices In Federal Condemnation," *Proceedings of the Second Institute on Eminent Domain*, Dallas, 1960, pp. 1-30.

MORTON, PERRY W., "The Federal Rule of Severance Damage," *The Appraisal Journal*, pp. 499-506.

MORTON, PERRY W., "The Problem of Severance Damages," *The Appraisal Journal*, October, 1956, pp. 499-506.

MOTT, SEWARD H., "The Benefits of Controlled Neighborhood Planning," *Architectural Record*, November, 1940, pp. 36-37.

NATIONAL INSTITUTE OF MUNICIPAL LAW OFFICERS, "The Problem of Opinion Evidence of Value-A Recommendation for Study and Action," *Right of Way*, February, 1960, pp. 7-10.

NEISWANGER, DAVID, "Experiences As a Court Appraiser In Condemnation Proceedings," *Technical Valuation*, February, 1955, pp. 13-16.

NIXON, T. CARL, "What the Lawyer Expects from the Expert," *Address Given at the District Appraisal Conference*, New York State Society of Real Estate Appraisers, April 18, 1941.

NORVELL, JAMES R., "Recent Trends Affecting Compensable and Noncompensable Damages," *Proceedings of the Fourth Institute on Eminent Domain*, Dallas, 1963.

NORVELL, JAMES R., "The Judicial Background," *The Residential Appraiser*, December, 1958.

NUGENT, R. A., "Compensation for Expropriation," *Appraisal Institute Magazine*, Appraisal Institute of Canada, Winnipeg.

NUGENT, R. A. L., "Expropriation Problems Appraiser In Court," *Appraisal Institute Magazine*, Appraisal Institute of Canada, Winnipeg.

NUGENT, R. A. L., "Market Value and the Courts," *Appraisal Institute Magazine*, Appraisal Institute of Canada, Winnipeg.

O'BIER, RAY E., "Facts on Damage & Benefit Appraisal," *Right of Way*, American Right of Way Association, Los Angeles, 1968, pp. 245-251.

OLIVER, WILLIAM FREDERICK, *Planning Compensation Under the Town and Country Planning Act*, Sweet and Maxwell, London, 1954.

ONTARIO CHAPTER REPORT, "The Basis for Compensation," *Appraisal Institute Magazine*, Appraisal Institute of Canada, Winnipeg.

PARKER, W. C., "Proposed Changes In Expropriation Laws," *Appraisal Institute Magazine*, Appraisal Institute of Canada, Winnipeg.

PARTRIDGE, CHARLES, "Appraising and Court Testimony for Condemnation and Certiorari," *National Real Estate Journal*, September, 1937, pp. 36-38.

PAULSON, PHILIP A., "Replacement Cost No Ceiling on Condemnation Award," *Technical Valuation*, February, 1957, pp. 69-70.

PAWLEY, R. W., N. G. MACARTHUR, "Compensation for the Taking of Marshland," *Appraisal Institute Magazine*, Appraisal Institute of Canada, Winnipeg.

PEARL, MILTON A., "Appraiser's Guide Under Law Allowing Moving Costs," *The Appraisal Journal*, July, 1953, pp. 327-335.

PEARL, MILTON A., "Review of Efforts to Minimize Losses In Condemnation," *The Appraisal Journal*, January, 1958, pp. 17-26.

PECK, AUSTIN, "Tax Results of Exchanges and Condemnation Conversions," *Right of Way*, December, 1959, pp. 43-48.

PENA GARCIA, M. A., "El Avaluo De Expropiacion Con Arreglo," *Boletin*, Sotave, Caracas, Venezuela, pp. 3-5.

PETERSON, CHARLES C. M., "Injunction Vs. Condemnation," *Right of Way*, February, 1957, pp. 47-50.

PICKENS, PHILIP, "Appraising Rural Land for Condemnation," *Technical Valuation*, February, 1961, pp. 28-34.

PINGRY, GEORGE S., "Mock Condemnation Trial," *The Review*, pp. 11-13.

PITTMAN, VIRGIL, "A Look at Right of Way Condemnation Proceedings," *Selected Papers, 1960*, Right of Way Conference, University of Ala., 1960.

POLLARD, W. L., "Market Value," *Condemnation Appraisal Procedure*, Hanson, Peter, and Pollard, 1934, pp. 413-434.

POLLARD, W. L., "On the Expert Witness," *The Appraisal Journal*, January, 1937, pp. 67-69.

POLLARD, W. L., "The Appraiser, His Qualifications Limitations on His Testimony," *Condemnation Appraisal Procedure*, Hanson, Peter, and Pollard, 1934, pp. 399-413.

QUINTANA, ISIDORO, "Valuation for Condemnation Purposes for Damages to Comm Prop Caused by 25-Foot Street Widening," *Practical Appraising Methods*, 1940, pp. 116-120.

RALEIGH, JAMES C., "Compensation Without Condemnation," *The Appraisal Journal*, April, 1967, pp. 256-259.

# BIBLIOGRAPHY OF APPRAISAL LITERATURE

RAMOS MARTINEZ, JOSE A., "Naturaleza Juridica En Procedimiento Exprop," *Boletin*, Sotave, Caracas, Venezuela, pp. 17-19.

RANDALL, WILLIAM J., "Appraisal of Damages to Real Estate Caused by Its Proximity to an Airport Serving Jet Transports," *Real Estate Analyst Appraisal Bulletin*, 1953, pp. 233-236.

RANDALL, WILLIAM J., "Attorney's Condemnation Check Sheet," *The Appraisal Journal*, January, 1967, pp. 103-106.

RANDALL, WILLIAM J., "Condemnation and the Income Tax Problem," *Real Estate Analyst Appraisal Bulletin*, 1961, pp. 301-304.

RANDALL, WILLIAM J., "Measure of Damages to Land Because of Loss of Access," *Real Estate Analyst Appraisal Bulletin*, pp. 461-467.

RANDALL, WILLIAM J., "Reflections of a Condemnation Appraiser," *The Appraisal Journal*, July, 1961, pp. 402-406.

RANDALL, WILLIAM J., "Settling Damages or Loss by Subsidence," *The Appraisal Journal*, January, 1956, pp. 95-98.

RATCLIFF, DR. RICHARD, "Condemnation Awards and Appraisal Theory," *The Real Estate Appraiser*, Society of Real Estate Appraisers, Chicago, May, 1964, pp. 6.

RATCLIFF, DR. RICHARD U., *Real Estate Valuation and Highway Condemnation Awards*, University of Wisconsin, Madison, 1966.

RATCLIFF, R. U., "Condemnation Awards and Appraisal Theory," *Appraisal Institute Magazine*, Appraisal Institute of Canada, Winnipeg.

REAL ESTATE BOARD OF NEW YORK, "Separate Appraisals of Land and Building Condemned by Board," *National Real Estate Journal*, December 26, 1927, pp. 33.

REED, ROBERT D., SANDSTROM, MARC, *Condemnation Proceedings*, American Association of State Highway Officials, Washington, D. C, 1962, pp. 78-84.

REEVES, CUTHBERT E., "Consequential Damage to an Industrial Building," *The Appraisal Journal*, January, 1935, pp. 165-168.

RIEMER, RICHARD L., "The Theory of Eminent Domain," *Right of Way*, April, 1971.

RIGGS, H. E., *Depreciation of Public Utility Properties*, New York, 1922.

RING, ALFRED A., "Condemnation Appraising Practices and Procedures," *The Valuation of Real Estate*, 1970, pp. 330-346.

ROBY, RONALD H., "Police Power In Aid of Condemnation," *The Appraisal Journal*, October, 1967, pp. 507-517.

ROGERS, "The Appraisal Docket, Offsetting Special Benefits Against Severance Damages," *The Appraisal Journal*, April, 1965, pp. 308-310.

ROGERS, HENRY, W., *Law of Expert Testimony*, Bendek, New York.

ROGERS, RUSSELL R., "Appraisal Techniques As Related to Condemnation," *Right of Way*, January, 1958, pp. 9-15.

ROGERS, RUSSELL R., "Appraising for Condemnation," *The Residential Appraiser*, June, 1961, pp. 2-6 9-22.

ROGERS, RUSSELL R., "The Expert Witness," *The Appraisal Journal*, October, 1956, pp. 565-572.

ROSENWEIG, REUBEN, "Bonus Value Is Taking Bread Out of the Mouths of Appraisers," *Technical Valuation*, June, 1960, pp. 27-30.

RUPERT, JOHN F., "The Appraiser Prepares for Testimony," *The Real Estate Appraiser*, November 10, 1963, pp. 32-38.

SACKMAN, JULIUS L., "Proximity Damages," *The Appraisal Journal*, April, 1969, pp. 117-199.

SAXON, FLOYD M., "Guide Posts In Condemnation Appraising," *The Appraisal Journal*, July, 1951, pp. 365-369.

SCHMUTZ, GEORGE L., *An Introduction to Condemnation Appraisals*, M Miller, Los Angeles, 1933, pp. 1-70.

SCHMUTZ, GEORGE L., *Condemnation Appraisal Handbook*, Prentice-Hall, New York, 1955.

SCHMUTZ, GEORGE L., *Condemnation Appraisal Handbook*, Prentice-Hall, New York, 1949.

SCHMUTZ, GEORGE L., *Condemnation Appraisal Handbook*, Prentice-Hall, Englewood Cliffs, 1963.

SCHMUTZ, GEORGE L., *Condemnations and Court Testimony*, G. L. Schmutz, Los Angeles, February 25, 1937, pp. 1-11.

SCHMUTZ, GEORGE L., "Appraising for Condemnation," *The Appraisal Journal*, July, 1952, pp. 306-313.

SCHMUTZ, GEORGE L., "Condemnations and Testimony In Court Procedure Related," *California Real Estate Magazine*, March, 1937, pp. 10-11.

SCHMUTZ, GEORGE L., "Court Testimony," *Condemnation Appraisers Handbook*, 1938, pp. 1-339.

SCHMUTZ, GEORGE L., "Depreciation," *Condemnation Appraisers Handbook*, 1938, pp. 1-339.

SCHMUTZ, GEORGE L., "Easements," *Condemnation Appraisers Handbook*, 1938, pp. 1-339.

SCHMUTZ, GEORGE L., "Ethical Consideration," *Condemnation Appraisers Handbook*, 1938, pp. 1-339.

SCHMUTZ, GEORGE L., "Interest Discount Tables," *Condemnation Appraiser's Handbook*, 1938, pp. 260-277.

SCHMUTZ, GEORGE L., "Interest Tables," *Condemnation Appraisers Handbook*, 1938, pp. 1-339.

SCHMUTZ, GEORGE L., "Leasehold Damage," *Condemnation Appraiser's Handbook*, 1938, pp. 1-339.

SCHMUTZ, GEORGE L., "Leases," *Condemnation Appraiser Handbook*, 1938, pp. 1-339.

SCHMUTZ, GEORGE L., "Rock, Sand and Gravel Deposits," *Condemnation Appraisers Handbook*, 1938, pp. 1-339.

SCHMUTZ, GEORGE L., "The Valuation Process," *Condemnation Appraisers Handbook*, 1938, pp. 1-339.

SCHMUTZ, GEORGE L., "Vertical Divisions of Value," *Condemnation Appraisers Handbook*, 1938, pp. 1-339.

SCHNEIDER, ARTHUR A., "The Expert Witness, His Demeanor and Presentation," *Proceedings of the Fifth Annual National Seminar, 1959*, American Right of Way Association, Washington, D.C., 1960, pp. 50-51.

SCHWARTZ, JAY, "The Appraiser and Condemnation," *The Real Estate Appraiser*, April, 1963, pp. 25-27.

SEARLES, SIDNEY Z., "Condemnation Procedure - Room for Reform," *Appraisal Digest*, January, 1962, pp. 1-6.

SEARLES, SIDNEY Z., AND SIDNEY O. RAPHAEL, "Current Trends In the Laws of Condemnation," *The Appraisal Digest*, October, 1959, pp. 511-529.

SEWARD, D. J., "The Appraiser In Court," *Appraisal Institute Magazine*, Appraisal Institute of Canada, Winnipeg.

SHELL, JOE L., "Trial of Condemnation Actions," *Right of Way*, April, 1955, pp. 26-30.

SHULTIS, ARTHUR, AND B. B. BURLINGAME, "Appraising Damages In Fruit Tree Destruction," *Journal of the Society of American Farm Managers and Rural Appraisers*, April, 1949, pp. 56-62.

SIDERMAN, DAVID, "Expropriation," *Appraisal Institute Magazine*, Appraisal Institute of Canada, Winnipeg.

SIGISMONDI, AUGUSTUS R., "Special Benefits In Sewer Condemnation," *The Appraisal Journal*, April, 1967, pp. 249-250.

SILVERMAN, BENJAMIN, "The Mechanics of Expert Testimony," *Appraisal and Valuation Manual*, pp. 219.

SILVERMAN, BENJAMIN, "The Opinion of Counsel," *Technical Valuation*, October, 1953, pp. 10.

SINNITT, PAUL, "Basic Precepts In Condemnation," *The Residential Appraiser*, December, 1957, pp. 3-4, 12-.

SKEER, DAVID, "A Lessee's Interest In Condemnation," *The Appraisal Journal*, April, 1959, pp. 166-174.

SLONIM, M. J., "Market Value or Market Price," *The Appraisal Journal*, October, 1945, pp. 390-391.

SMITH, JOSEPH R. III, "Preparation and Presentation of Condemnation Cases from the Viewpoint of the Appraiser," *Proceedings of the First Institute on Eminent Domain*, 1959, pp. 165-184.

SMITH, WALSTEIN JR., "Market Value a Rule of Reasoning," *The Real Estate Appraiser*, pp. 40.

SMITH, WALSTEIN, JR., "100 Questions on Direct Examination," *The Residential Appraiser*, June, 1962, pp. 3-6.

SNITZER, EDWARD L., "Condemnation of Trade Fixtures: a Reccurring Problem," *Real Estate Appraiser*, 1971.

SNITZER, EDWARD L., "Increase or Decrease In Fair Market Value Because of a Future Condemnation," *The Real Estate Appraiser*, 1968, pp. 53-55.

SNITZER, EDWARD L., "The Law and Condemnation Appraisal," *The Real Estate Appraiser*, 1968, pp. 54-58.

SNITZER, EDWARD L., "The Law and Condemnation Appraisals," *The Real Estate Appraiser*, 1969, pp. 55-58.

SNITZER, EDWARD L., "The Law and Condemnation Appraising," *The Real Estate Appraiser*, March, 1970, pp. 55-57.

SNITZER, EDWARD L., "Unsightliness of an Electric Transmission Line As Evidence of Severance Damage," *Real Estate Appraiser*, 1970, pp. 35-36.

SNYDER, FREAS B., "Expert Testimony from a Layman's Viewpoint," *The Appraisal Journal*, July, 1950, pp. 318-327.

SOMERVILLE, H. H., "Expropriation Procedures In Alberta," *Appraisal Institute Magazine*, Appraisal Institute of Canada, Winnipeg.

SOUTHARD, MELVILLE, "Expert Witnesses and Testimony," *Appraisal and Valuation Manual*, American Society of Appraisers, 1955, pp. 127-134.

SOUTHARD, MELVILLE, "The Role of the Expert Witness," *Technical Valuation*, October, 1954, pp. 15-17.

SPENCER, CHARLES E. JR., "Case of the Month: Appraisers and Retrials," *Right of Way*, June, 1961, pp. 27-29.

STERLING, RAY T., "The Expert Witness Who Wasn't," *The Real Estate Appraiser*, July, 1966, pp. 32.

STEWARD, WILLIAM A., "Preparing the Appraisal for Condemnation Trial," *Appraisal Digest*, July, 1969, pp. 8-12.

STEWART, C. L., "Condemnation Appraisals and Associated Issues In Illinois," *Journal of the American Society of Farm Managers and Rural Appraisers*, October, 1958, pp. 27-31.

STONE, ROBERT R., "Reviewing Condemnation Appraisal Reports," *Right of Way*, February, 1958, pp. 35-36, 40.

STONE, ROBERT R., "The Right-Of-Way Agent In the Condemnation Trial," *American Association of State Highway Officials*, Acquisition for Right-Of-Way, Washington, D. C, 1962, pp. 103-108.

STRAUB, ROBERT, "The Condemnation Law," *Right of Way Conference,* University of Alabama, 1956, pp. 9-15.

STREUKENS, H. H., "Damages, Fact or Fiction?," *Technical Valuation,* pp. 21.

SWAN, ROGER H., "Courtroom Strategy," *The Review,* October, 1955, pp. 17-22.

SYBRANDT, JOHN L., "Investigating Your Loss--Property Damage," *Insurance Valuations, Monograph No. 4 of the American Society of Appraisers,* Washington, D.C.

TALLIN, C. K., "Expropriation Review Committee Reports," *Appraisal Institute Magazine,* Appraisal Institute of Canada, Winnipeg.

TALLIN, CLIVE K., "Expropriation Committee Reports on the Appraiser In Court Proceedings," *Appraisal Institute Magazine,* September, 1961, pp. 21-23.

TAYLOR, THOMAS L., "Highest and Best Use Factor In Condemnation," *Appraisal and Valuation Manual,* American Society of Appraisers, 1959, pp. 287-292.

TEICHERT, C. O., "The Trials of the Opinion Witness," *Right of Way,* December, 1963, pp. 13-15.

THEISS, WILLIAM R., "The Appraisal Docket. Admissibility of Opinion Partly Based on Second Hand Knowledge," *The Appraisal Journal,* October, 1962, pp. 548-550.

THEISS, WILLIAM R., "The Appraisal Docket. Alleged Severance Damages Due to Use of Land Condemned from Others," *The Appraisal Journal,* April, 1905, pp. 307-308.

THEISS, WILLIAM R., "The Appraisal Docket. Apportionment of Condemnation Award Under 99-Year Lease," *The Appraisal Journal,* April, 1964, pp. 303-305.

THEISS, WILLIAM R., "The Appraisal Docket. Compensation for Impairment of Access," *The Appraisal Journal,* October, 1962, pp. 547-548.

THEISS, WILLIAM R., "The Appraisal Docket. Computing Damages for Restriction of Access for Retail Use Only," *The Appraisal Journal,* October, 1964, pp. 612-613.

THEISS, WILLIAM R., "The Appraisal Docket. Exchange of Property As Just Compensation," *The Appraisal Journal,* April, 1963, pp. 271.

THEISS, WILLIAM R., "The Appraisal Docket. Increase In Value by Special Benefits," *The Appraisal Journal,* April, 1965, pp. 306-307.

THEISS, WILLIAM R., "The Appraisal Docket. Interest Due to Mortgage on Award," *The Appraisal Journal,* July, 1963, pp. 417-419.

THEISS, WILLIAM R., "The Appraisal Docket. Limits of Compensable Matters, Speculative Damages," *The Appraisal Journal,* October, 1963, pp. 526-529.

THEISS, WILLIAM R., "The Appraisal Docket. Mortgage Appraisal As Evidence," *The Appraisal Journal,* February, 1964, pp. 438-439.

THEISS, WILLIAM R., "The Appraisal Docket. Offsetting Special Benefits Against Severance Damages," *The Appraisal Journal,* April, 1965, pp. 308-310.

THEISS, WILLIAM R., "The Appraisal Docket. Probable Future Use of Condemned Property," *The Appraisal Journal,* October, 1961, pp. 543-545.

THEISS, WILLIAM R., "The Appraisal Docket. Right to Consequential Damages Due to Language of Interest Condemned," *The Appraisal Journal,* October, 1965, pp. 621-623.

THEISS, WILLIAM R., "The Appraisal Docket. Use by Landowners of Appraisals Prepared for the Condemning Authority," *The Appraisal Journal,* July, 1965, pp. 442-443.

THEISS, WILLIAM R., "The Appraisal Docket. Use of Appraisers' Testimony by Other Party to Litigation," *The Appraisal Journal,* January, 1962, pp. 127-129.

THEISS, WILLIAM R., "The Appraisal Docket. Valuating Leasehold Measure of Damages," *The Appraisal Journal,* January, 1964, pp. 123-125.

THEISS, WILLIAM R., "The Appraisal Docket-Computing Damages for Restriction of Access for Retail Use Only," *The Appraisal Journal,* October, 1964, pp. 612-613.

THEISS, WILLIAM R., "The Appraisal Docket, Assessed Value As Evidence of Condemnation Value," *The Appraisal Journal,* October, 1901, pp. 541-542.

THEISS, WILLIAM R., "The Appraisal Docket, Distinction Between General and Special Benefits," *The Appraisal Journal,* April, 1963, pp. 267-270.

THEISS, WILLIAM R., "The Appraisal Docket, Relocations As Condition Precedent to Possession by Condemning Authority," *The Appraisal Journal,* July, 1963, pp. 419-420.

THEISS, WILLIAM R., "The Appraisal Docket, Rulings and Precedents on Matters Affecting Real Property Valuation," *The Appraisal Journal,* July, 1968, pp. 438-442.

THEISS, WILLIAM R., "The Appraisal Docket, Tax Assessment--Damages for Failure to Assess Equally," *The Appraisal Journal,* July, 1962, pp. 417-418.

THOMPSON, BURTON, "Some Problems Confronting Appraisers In Condemnation Cases," *The Appraisal Journal,* July, 1937, pp. 270-272.

THOMPSON, NEIL S., "There Is No Magic In Condemnation Appraising," *Journal of the American Society of Farm Managers and Rural Appraisers,* April, 1960, pp. 98-101.

TROWBRIDGE, CARL R., "Convincing the Jury," *The Appraisal Journal,* April, 1958, pp. 201-204.

UGHETTA, HENRY L., "Expert Testimony," *Technical Valuation,* July, 1950, pp. 21-24.

WAGNER, PERCY E., "A Defense of the Income Approach," *Proceedings of the Third Institute on Eminent Domain,* Dallas, 1961, pp. 151-180.

WALLEY, ERSEL, "Condemnation and Appraising for Pipeline Installations," *Journal of the American Society of Farm Managers and Rural Appraisers,* April, 1957, pp. 61-68.

WALLSTEIN, LEONARD, "Recommended Changes In City's Condemnation Practice," *Real Estate Record and Builders Guide,* April 31, 1934, pp. 5-7.

WALSH, DONALD, "Condemnation of a Service Station," *Right of Way,* February, 1961, pp. 9-17.

WALTEMADE, HENRY G., "Expert Testimony In Condemnation," *Real Estate Record,* March 8, 1941, pp. 6..

WARWICK, SAMUEL C., "Appraising the Cemetery In Condemnation," *Thereal Estate Appraiser,* May, 1966, pp. 25-31.

WATSON, JAIRUS H., "Address on Condemnation Appraisals," *Technical Valuation,* October, 1960, pp. 44-50.

WAUGH, ALEXANDER P., "A Judicial Critique on Expert Testimony," *The Real Estate Appraiser,* February, 1964, pp. 16.

WEINGARTEN, EDWARD A., "Condemnation Law and Procedure," *Appraisal Digest,* October, 1959, pp. 1-7.

WEINGARTEN, EDWARD A., "Role of the Appraiser In Condemnation," *Appraisal and Valuation Manual,* 1961, pp. 43-58.

WENDT, PAUL F., "Fair Market Value In Condemnation," *Right of Way,* December, 1957, pp. 7-9.

WENGER, RALPH W. JR., "The Courtroom Loometh," *The Real Estate Appraiser,* October, 1966, pp. 29.

WEST WILLIAM B. III, "Preparation and Trial of a Condemnation Case," *Proceedings of the Fourth Institute on Eminent Domain,* Dallas, 1962, pp. 67-109.

WEWEE, DEWITT, "Value Winesses," *The Residential Appraiser,* May, 1962, pp. 21-22.

WHITESIDE, ALBA, "Inverse Condemnation, Invasion of Air Rights," *Right of Way,* February, 1969, pp. 12-16.

WILBANKS, RICHARD P., "What Is a Typical Buyer," *The Real Estate Appraiser*, April, 1966, pp. 18.

WILCOX, DONALD A., "Use of Appraisals by Negotiators," *Right of Way*, 1968, pp. 447.

WILLISTON, W. B., "Court Testimony," *Appraisal Institute Magazine*, Appraisal Institute of Canada, Winnipeg.

WILNETTE, MCDONNELL, WOLCOTT, "Condemnation," *Problems In Rural Real Estate Appraisal*, pp. 33.

WILSON, WILLIAM, "The Appraiser In Court," *Review of Society of Residential Appraisers*, June, 1939, pp. 14.

WINDER, AMBROSE J., "Severance Damage," *Appraisal and Valuation Manual*, 1956, pp. 317.

WINNER, FRED M., "The Expert Witness from a Lawyer's Viewpoint," *The Appraisal Journal*, April, 1955, pp. 254-260.

WINNER, FRED M., "The Rules of Evidence," *Technical Valuation*, November, 1955, pp. 19-30.

WOOLLEY, R. J., "Expropriation Review Committee Reports," *Appraisal Institute Magazine*, Appraisal Institute of Canada, Winnipeg.

WORKMASTER, H. C., "Pittsburgh Stages Mock Condemnation Trial," *Technical Valuation*, February, 1954, pp. 37.

WORSHAM, JOSEPH I., "Problems Peculiar to Partial Taking In Condemnation," *Proceedings of Fourth Institute on Emt Domain*, 1959.

WYCKOFF, RALPH W. G., "Case of the Month," *Right of Way*, June, 1954, pp. 19-20.

YATES, DONALD H., "Testimony of the Expert Witness In Condemnation Proceedings," *The Appraisal Journal*, July, 1958, pp. 385-389.

YOUNG, G. I. M., "Expropriation Ambiguities Under Canadian Statues," *Appraisal Institute Magazine*, Appraisal Institute of Canada, Winnipeg.

YOUNG, G. I. M., "Report Select Committee Expropriation-Ontario," *Appraisal Institute Magazine*, Appraisal Institute of Canada, Winnipeg.

*Condemnation Appraisal Practice*, American Institute of Real Estate Appraisers, 1967.

*Condemnation Appraising, A Lecture and Case Study Course*, Am. Institute of Real Estate Appraisers, 1964.

*The Appraisers Job In Eminent Domain Proceedings*, Bureau of Business, U. of Pitt Bus Ad Sc, 1957.

"Rulings and Precedents Affecting Real Property and Valuation," *The Appraisal Journal*, January, 1968, pp. 126-128.

"Selected Articles an Eminent Domain Compensation and Valuation Problems," *Virginia Law Review*, April, 1963.

## 12-15 Easements and Eminent Domain

ALDIS, GRAHAM, "Appraising Fractional Real Estate Interests," *The Appraisal Journal,* January, 1941, pp. 69-71.

AMERICAN RIGHT OF WAY ASSOCIATION, "Just Compensation Concepts In Eminent Domain," *Proceeding of the Sixth Annual National Seminar, 1960,* Washington, D. C, 1961.

AMERICAN RIGHT OF WAY ASSOCIATION, "Who Exaggerates the Value of an Easement Take," *Proceedings of the Seventh Annual Seminar,* Washington, 1961.

AMERICAN SOCIETY OF APPRAISERS, "Power and Process (Eminent Domain)," American Society of Appraisers, Publications, Washington.

AMERICAN SOCIETY OF PLANNING OFFICIALS, "Land Use Controls In the Surface Extraction of Minerals," Chicago.

ASH, FRED C., "The Appraisal Docket Valuation of Flowage Rights," *The Appraisal Journal,* January, 1957, pp. 109-110.

ATHERTON E. B., "Valuation Problems Involving Aesthetic Programs," *The Real Estate Appraiser,* March, 1968, pp. 25-30.

ATHERTON, E. B., "Damages Fact or Fiction? or Eminent Domain As it Is Related to the Fair Market Value Concept," *Technical Valuation,* June, 1962, pp. 40-44.

ATHERTON, EDWARD B, "Appraising Noise Damages on Federal-Aid Highway Projects," *Valuation Magazine,* American Society of Appraisers, Washington D.C., December 1, 1973, pp. 44-51.

BARRY, DAVID N., "Legal Aspects of the Condemnation of Electric Transmission Line Easement," *Valuation,* February, 1961, pp. 8-13.

BATTY, HARRY, "Capital Reinvestment Problems Created by Eminent Domain," *Right of Way,* December, 1960, pp. 35-37.

BECCIA, MARTIN, "The Effect of Pipeline Easements on Subdivision Developments," *Right of Way,* August, 1960, pp. 11-16.

BELL, SPURGEON E., "Preserving Error for Appeal of the Eminent Domain Case," *Institute on Eminent Domain,* Proceedings, 1959, pp. 151-163.

BENNETT, SAUL Z., "Income Approach," *A Student's Report on an Apartment House,* American Institute of Real Estate Appraisers, Chicago, 1966, pp. 31.

BICKLEY, N. ALEX, "Compensable and Non-Compensable Damages," *Proceeding of the Second Institute on Eminent Domain,* Dallas, 1960, pp. 31-60.

BICKLEY, N. ALEX, "Statutory Changes In Eminent Domain Proceedings Now Under Consideration," *Proceedings Concerning Texas Laws and Practices,* Institute on Eminent Domain, September, 1956, pp. 18-21.

BISHOP, MAURICE F., "Non-Compensable Damages In Eminent Domain Proceedings," *Selected Papers of a Right of Way Conference,* University of Alabama, 1957, pp. 16-26.

BISHOP, MAURICE F., "Opening and Closing Arguments In Eminent Domain Cases," *Right of Way,* April, 1961, pp. 13-19.

BISHOP, MAURICE F., "Recent Developments In Eminent Domain In Alabama," *Selected Papers of a Right of Way Conference,* University of Alabama, 1961, pp. 89-109.

BLANCHARD, C. F., "Publicly Owned Electric Business," *Public Utilities Fortnightly,* June 18, 1970, pp. 43-45.

BOETTCHER, LLOYD D., "Appraisal of a Flowage Easement," *The Appraisal Journal*, January, 1957, pp. 35-38.

BONBRIGHT, JAMES C., "**Valuation Under the Law of Eminent Domain,**" *The Valuation of Property*, Mcgraw-Hill, New York, 1937, pp. 407-449.

BOWES, WATSON A., "**Relations Between the Appraiser and His Attorney,**" *The Appraiser's Job In Eminent Domain Proceedings*, Univ. of Pittsburgh, Bureau of Business Research, pp. 27-36.

BOYLE, ROBERT P., "**Navigational Easements,**" *Proceedings, 8th Annual Seminar, American Right Of Way Association*, Washington, D. C, 1962, pp. 8-11.

BRADEY, A. I., "**The Value of a Navigation Easement,**" *The Real Estate Appraiser*, pp. 7.

BRESNAHAN, C. A., "**Development of Irrigation Water Rights,**" *Appraisal and Valuation Manual*, The American Society of Appraisers, Washington, D. C, 1956, pp. 227-237.

BRICKMAN, RICHARD I., "**The Compensability of Restrictive Covenants In Eminent Domain,**" *The Appraisal Journal*, July, 1961, pp. 359-376.

BRIGHAM, E. F. P., "**Eminent Domain In Florida,**" *The Appraisal and Valuation Manual*, American Society of Appraisers, Washington, D. C, 1959, pp. 357-392.

BROADBENT, LORIN J., "**Eminent Domain Valuation of Land Containing Minerals,**" *The Appraisal Journal*, January, 1961, pp. 63-77.

BROWNELL, KEITH W., "**Valuation of Pipeline Easements,**" *The Appraisal Journal*, April, 1958, pp. 17-180.

BUREAU OF AGRICULTURAL ENGINEERING, *Land Drainage*, Department of Agriculture, Washington, 1936.

BURNS, ROBERT L., "**Damages and Benefits from Constitutional Damaging and Partial Taking--Community or Special?,**" *Proceedings of the Third Institute on Eminent Domain 1961*, Dallas, 1961, pp. 119-138.

CAMPBELL, COLIN, "**A Study of the Effects of Pipeline Easements on Subdivision Developments,**" *Right of Way*, December, 1960, pp. 23-33.

CAMPBELL, COLIN, "**Transmission Line Easements In Condemnation,**" *Right of Way*, October, 1963, pp. 45-52.

CARLL, C. E., "**Evaluation of Easements,**" *California Real Estate Magazine*, October, 1936, pp. 53.

CARLL, CLOICE D., "**On Easement Costs and Damages Under California Practice,**" *The Appraisal Journal*, July, 1937, pp. 281-285.

CARLL, CLOICE D., "**Preparing to Testify—The Use of Demonstrative Evidence,**" *The Appraiser's Job In Eminent Domain Proceedings*, U of Pitt Bu of Bus Res In Coop with Law School, 1957, pp. 11-25.

CARLL, CLOICE D., "**The Use of Demonstrative Evidence,**" *The Appraisal Journal*, January, 1960, pp. 24-38.

CARPENTER, P. E., "**Experience In Partial Eminent Domain Takings,**" *The Real Estate Appraiser*, July, 1967, pp. 24-28.

CLEMINSHAW COMPANY, *Appraisers Manual*, Company, Cleveland, 1932.

CLEMINSHAW COMPANY, *Appraisers Manual*, The Company, Cleveland, Ohio, 1937.

CLEMINSHAW, J. M. CO., *Appraisers Manual*, Cleveland, Ohio, 1947.

COHN, WALTER W., "**The Appraisal of Easements,**" *The Appraisal Journal*, April, 1936, pp. 181-187.

COLE, JOHN D., *The Room Unit System a Manual for Appraisers*, The Cole Layer Company, Dayton, Ohio, 1939.

COWLEY, LEONARD M., "**How to Make an Avigation Easement Appraisal,**" *Real Estate Appraisal Practice*, American Institute of Real Estate Appraisers, 1958, pp. 571-577.

COWLEY, LEONARD M., "The Value of View," *The Appraisal Journal,* April, 1951, pp. 239-242.

CRAWFORD, CLAUDE O., "Appraising Damages to Land from Power Line Easements," *The Appraisal Journal,* July, 1955, pp. 367-378.

CRAWFORD, CLAUDE O., "Valuation of Easement Rights," *Right of Way,* June, 1956, pp. 23-25.

CRONER, FRED, JR., "History and Nature of Eminent Domain," *Right of Way,* August, 1960, pp. 33-39.

DE VRIES, ROSCOE, "The Relationship of Drainage Easements to R-W Liaison," *Right of Way,* February, 1964, pp. 27-29.

DEBOOS, FRANK A., "Easement Evaluation," *The Review,* August, 1952, pp. 5-6.

DECKMAN, WILLIAM L., "Fee Vs. Easement Updated," *American Right of Way Association,* Proceedings of the Eighth Annual National Seminar, Washington, D. C, 1963, pp. 43-46.

DERBES, MAX J. FR., "The Appraisal of Easements," *Right of Way,* December, 1964, pp. 23-29.

DERBES, MAX J. JR., "The Appraisal of Easements," *Selected Readings In Right of Way,* American Right of Way Association, Los Angeles, 1968, pp. 290-300.

DIX, SAMUEL M., "Fixture Qualification In Eminent Domain," *The Appraisal Journal,* April, 1969, pp. 235-238.

DYE, DEWEY A. JR., "Appraisal Considerations Where an Easement Is Taken," *The Real Estate Appraiser,* December, 1961, pp. 18-22.

EDENS, DAVID, "Eminent Domain, Equity and the Allocation of Resources," *Land Economics,* August, 1970.

EDMAN, J. J., "Improvements to Drainage May Result In Condemnation. Appraisal Docket," *The Appraisal Journal,* January, 1960, pp. 125-126.

EDMAN, J. J., "Loss of Indirect Access Compensable. Appraising Docket," *The Appraisal Journal,* July, 1959, pp. 412-413.

EDMAN, J. J., "The Appraisal Docket. Application of Insurance During Pendency of Eminent Domain Proceedings," *The Appraisal Journal,* October, 1960, pp. 124-125.

EDMAN, J. J., "The Appraisal Docket. Damages for Loss of Aesthetic Values," *The Appraisal Journal,* July, 1961, pp. 415-416.

EDMAN, J. J., "The Appraisal Docket. Damages Occasioned by Change of Water Flow," *The Appraisal Journal,* April, 1958, pp. 293-294.

EDMAN, J. J., "The Appraisal Docket. Damages to Aesthetic Values," *The Appraisal Journal,* January, 1960, pp. 126-127.

ELLIS, ROSS M., "Methods and Practices In Appraising Timber for Eminent Domain," *The Appraisal Journal,* July, 1960, pp. 301-317.

EMMENEGGER, EDWIN F., "Proper Negotiation and Laying Foundation for Easement Aquisition," *Right of Way,* October, 1962, pp. 39-42.

EVANS, MARVIN J., "Power Line Right of Way--Fee or Easement," *Right of Way,* December, 1961, pp. 27-38.

FEDERAL POWER COMMISSION, *P-35-Hydroelectric Power Evaluation,* Supt of Documents, U. S. Govt. Printing Office, Washington D. C, 1968.

FEDERAL POWER COMMISSION, *P-40-World Power Data,* Supt of Documents, U. S. Govt. Printing Office, Washington D. C, 1968.

FEDERAL POWER COMMISSION, "National Power Curve," *National Power Surve,* Federal Pwer Commission, December, 1964.

FISHER, EDMOND C., "Zoning In Eminent Domain a Moral Hazard," *The Appraisal Journal,* July, 1965, pp. 331-335.

FOX, PAUL W., "Avigation Easements," *Valuation Manual,* June, 1952, pp. 16-17.

FPC, "P-36 Hydroel Power Rescs of U. S. Devel & Undevel," Supt Doc Govt Ptg Off, Wash, 1968.

FPC, "P-38 Hydroel Power Eval Supp't No 1 July 69," Supt Doc Govt Ptg Off, Wash.

FPC, "S-184 Fed & State Comm Jurisd & Reg of Elec Gas & Telep Utils 1967," Supt Docs Govt Ptg Off, Wash.

GALE, CHARLES J., *Treatise on the Law of Easements,* Carswell, Toronto, 1951.

GALLAGHER, JOSEPH A., "Flowage Easements," *Right of Way,* October, 1960, pp. 35-45.

GANNON, HENRY F., "The Scenic Easement In New York," *The Real Estate Appraiser,* 1900.

GARRET, H. J., "Reservoirs-Partial Taking and Easements," *Journal of the American Society of Farm Managers and Rural Appraisers,* April, 1962, pp. 121-126.

GLEAVES, MILNOR E., "Lawful Compensation In Eminent Domain," *Technicalities and Technical Valuation,* February, 1952, pp. 40-41.

GRAVES, GLENN F., "Pipelines Is Your Environment Showing," *Right of Way,* February, 1971.

GUITTARD, CLARENCE A., "Discovery and Pre-Trial Procedure In Eminent Domain," *Institute on Eminent Domain,* 1959, pp. 199-231.

GUNNING, WALTER E., "Valuation of Restrictive Easements," *The Appraisal Journal,* January, 1963, pp. 29-33.

HAAS, CHARLES E., "Eminent Domain," *Address Given Before the California Real Estate Association's Appraisal Division,* Los Angeles, December 5, 1940.

HADLEY, GEORGE C., "Demonstrative Evidence In Eminent Domain Proceedings," *Institute on Eminent Domain Proceedings,* 1960, pp. 111-132.

HALL, THOMAS, III, WILLIAM R. BEATON, "A Factor Formula for Valuation of Avigation Easements," *The Appraisal Journal,* January, 1965, pp. 29-40.

HAMBLETON, RAY W., "The Appraisal of Leased Commercial Property In Eminent Domain," *Technical Valuation,* June, 1959, pp. 35-39.

HAMBLETON, RAY W., "Valuation for the Acquisition of Easements In Eminent Domain Cases," *Appraisal and Valuation Manual,* American Society of Appraisers, Washington, D. C, 1962, pp. 56-66.

HANSON, PETER, "Easements," *Condemnation Appraisal Procedure,* Hanson and Pollard, 1934, pp. 213, 467.

HAWKINS, GEORGE C., "A Study of Alabama's Eminent Domain Statutes," *Selected Papers, Right of Way Conference,* University of Alabama, 1961.

HEANEY, DONALD L., "Valuation of Property for Highways Under Eminent Domain," Automotive Safety Foundation, Washington, 1960.

HIGHWAY RESEARCH BOARD, *Scenic Easements--Legal Administrative and Valuation Problems and Procedures,* Washington, D. C..

HODGES, M. B., "Public Relations In Eminent Domain Appraising," *The Residential Appraiser,* March, 1962, pp. 2-10.

HOLLOWAY, JOHN P., "Recent Developments In Colorado Eminent Domain," *Right of Way,* April, 1955, pp. 7-14.

HOWARD, JEROME H., "Valuation of an Avigation Easement," *The Appraisal Journal,* July, 1954, pp. 336-344.

HUTCHINSON, GEORGE, "An Appraisal of Flowage Easements," *Technical Valuation,* June, 1961, pp. 47-49.

HUTCHINSON, IRA K., "Appraisal of Utility Easements In the State of Hawaii," *Appraisal and Valuation Manual,* Corporate Press, Incorporated, Washington, D. C, January, 1972, pp. 314.

## BIBLIOGRAPHY OF APPRAISAL LITERATURE

HUTTS, J. MARSHALL, ALFRED RAWS, JR., "Procedure for Bringing Pipe Line Valuations Down to Date," *Technical Valuation,* May, 1945, pp. 5-13.

INSTITUTE ON EMINENT DOMAIN, *Proceedings of the Annual Institute,* Matthew Bender and Co., Albany, New York, 1959.

INSTITUTE ON EMINENT DOMAIN, "Comparable Sales, Proceedings of a Practical Demonstration," *Proceedings,* Institute on Eminent Domain, 1962.

INSTITUTE ON EMINENT DOMAIN, "In the Court at Law, Southwestern Legal Foundation, State Vs. Anyman, Et. Ux," *Proceedings,* 1960.

INTERNATIONAL ASSOCIATION OF ASSESSING OFFICERS, *Environmental Control Facilities,* Chicago, Illinois.

JAHR, ALFRED D., *The Law of Eminent Domain Valuation and Procedure,* Clark Boardman Co., Ltd., New York, 1953.

JERRETT, HERMAN D., "Eminent Domain," *Theory of Real Property Valuation,* Chapter Xiii, 1938.

JOACHIM, HARRY J., "History, Powers, Procedures and Duties of the Federal Eminent Domain Commission," *Right of Way,* April, 1971.

JOHNSON, ALBERT L., "Flowage Easement Market Analysis," *The Appraisal Journal,* January, 1967, pp. 82-87.

JONES, E. P., "Photography and Mapping In Appraisal and Eminent Domain Work," *Proceedings of the Eighth Annual National Seminar, 1962,* American Right of Way Association, Washington, 1962, pp. 31-37.

JOYCE, W. V., "Elusive Shadows In Eminent Domain," *The Residential Appraiser,* pp. 2-9.

KEAN, R. GORDON, JR., *Proceedings of the Third Institute on Eminent Domain,* Eminent Domain Conference, Dallas, 1961, pp. 99-118.

KIZER, JOHN O., "Valuation of Leasehold Estates In Eminent Domain," *West Virginia Law Review,* February, 1965, pp. 101-115.

KNAPP, DEWITT L., *The Market Looks at Utility Right of Way and Easements,* Proceedings of the Fourth Institute on Eminent Dom, Dallas, 1962, pp. 111-125.

KNOWLES, JEROME, JR., "New Points In Eminent Domain," *The Residential Appraiser,* November, 1956, pp. 11-15.

KREVOR, HENRY H., *Trends of Recent Decisions In Eminent Domain,* Right of Way Conference, 1960, pp. 27-40.

KREVOR, HENRY H., "Legislative Changes and Trends Affecting Compensation In Eminent Domain," *Right of Way,* August, 1961, pp. 23-29.

KUCERA, H. P., *Eminent Domain Versus Police Power---A Common Misconception,* Proceedgs of the 1st Inst on Eminent Domain, Dallas, 1959, pp. 1-34.

KUCERA, H. P., *The Developing Law of the Jet Airport,* Proceedgs of the 4th Inst on Eminent Domain, Dallas, 1962, pp. 171-196.

LANDSTROM, COL. KARL S., "A Review of Appraisal Process In Granting Easements Across Federal Lands," *Selected Readings In Right of Way,* American Right of Way Association, Los Angeles, 1968, pp. 281-283.

LASKA, WALTER J., "Fee Versus Easement," *Right of Way,* February, 1967, pp. 20-23.

LAW, W. V., "Utility Easements and Problems," *Right of Way,* February, 1961, pp. 27-28.

LEE, ADELBERT W., "Non-Compensable Damages In Eminent Domain Proceedings," *Technical Valuation,* February, 1959, pp. 51-53.

LEFEAVER, JAMES H., "Eminent Domain Appraising," *Technical Valuation,* A. S. A., October, 1954, pp. 63.

LEVEL, EDWARD E., "Eminent Domain Concepts, Laws and Limitations," *Acquisition for Right of Way,* American Association of State Highway Officials, Washington, D. C, 1962, pp. 25-32.

LEWIS, JOHN, *A Treatise on the Law of Eminent Domain In the United States,* Callaghan, Chicago, 1909.

LEYDEN, J. WALLACE, "Eminent Domain," *Right of Way,* August, 1957, pp. 18-22.

LONG, JEREMIAH M., "Basic Differences Between Federal and Washington Eminent Domain Practice," *Right of Way,* October, 1960, pp. 9-16.

LUPARDUS, O. L., "Cross Examinations of an Expert Appraisal Witness," *Proceedings of the First Institute on Eminent Domain,* Dallas, 1959, pp. 185-197.

LUTTRELL, RALPH J., "Eminent Domain---The Realtor, the Appraiser, and the Lawyer," *The Appraisal Journal,* October, 1963, pp. 493-500.

MACBRIDE, DEXTER D, "History and Meaning of Just Compensation," *Proceedings, 3rd Annual Legal, R/W Seminar,* University of Nevada, August 1, 1966.

MACBRIDE, DEXTER D., *Power and Process A Commentary on Eminent Domain and Condemnation,* American Society of Appraisers, January, 1969.

MACHAT, SYKES, "Valuation Aspects of the Avigation Easement," *Proceedings of the Eighth Annual National Seminar,* American Right of Way Association, Washington, D. C, 1963, pp. 12-13.

MANN, J. F., "Valuation of Air Lease, Condemned by Eminent Domain," *Buildings and Building Management,* February 10, 1930, pp. 63-64.

MCCOY, CHARLES R., "Effect of Partial Condemnation and of a Temporary Easement on the Value of a Service Station," *Real Estate Analyst Appraisal Bulletin,* 1954, pp. 305-311.

MCFADZEAN, JAMES, "Easement Valuation," *The American Journal,* June, 1964, pp. 15-17.

MCGOUGH, B. C., "Eminent Domain Practices, Their Effect on Acquisition," *The Appraisal Journal,* April, 1965, pp. 203-210.

MCGOUGH, B. C., "The Concepts and Practices for Compensation In Eminent Domain," *The Real Estate Appraiser,* March, 1969, pp. 44-47.

MCLEAN, W. M., "Hints to the Expert Witness," *Appraisal Institute Magazine,* Appraisal Institute of Canada, Winnipeg.

MILLER, REX K., "Oil Pipeline Right of Way, Total Compensation and Easement for Sterling Farm," *Journal of the American Society of Farm Managers And Rural Appraisers,* October, 1961, pp. 22-28.

MOORE, PEYTON H., "Nature and Compensability of Access," *Proceedings of the Third Institute on Eminent Domain,* 1961, pp. 1-20.

MOSER, LEROY C., "Rights of Lessor and Lessee In Eminent Domain Cases," *American Association of State Highway Officials,* Acquisition for Right of Way, Washington, D.C., 1962, pp. 419-444.

MOSES, ALEX I., "Contractors Problems In Obtaining Easement Grants for Extra High Voltage Transmission Lines," *Right of Way,* October, 1964, pp. 27-28.

MULCAHY, JOHN V., "Fact or Fiction?. . . Transmission Line Easement," *The Real Estate Appraiser,* September, 1970, pp. 34-36.

MURPHY J. P., "Easement or Wayleave?," *The Valuer,* The Incorporated Society of Valuers & Auctioneers, London, December 1, 1973, pp. 427.

NICHOLS, PHILIP, *Law of Eminent Domain,* Bender, New York, 1958.

NOEL, ALBERT, "Servitudes Et L'Application Du Bill 16," *Appraisal Institute Magazine,* Appraisal Institute of Canada, Winnipeg.

ORGEL, LEWIS, *Valuation Under the Law of Eminent Domain,* Michie, Charlottesville, Va., 1953.

ORGEL, LEWIS, *Valuation Under the Law of Eminent Domain,* The Michie Company, Charlottesville, Va., 1936.

PATT, H. B., AND DAVIS, "Appraising of Damages to Farm by Power Line Easements," *The Appraisal Journal*, July, 1947, pp. 330-338.

PESCHEL, J. L., "Oil and Gas Tax Planning Post-Reform Act Impact of CA-5s," *Journal of Taxation*, January, 1971, pp. 54-56.

PITTLE, HERBERT, "The Appraisers Role In Federal Eminent Domain," *The Real Estate Appraiser*, pp. 2.

PITTLE, HERBERT, "Valuation of Avigation Easements," *Residential Appraiser*, October, 1962, pp. 6-14.

PRAC DEMONS EXAM & CRSEXAM OF INDEPNDT APPRAISER, *Proceedings of the Fourth Institute on Eminent Domain, 1963*, Dallas, 1963.

PROCDGS OF 4TH INST ON EMINT DOM EVIDENCES OF VAL, *Proceedings of the Fourth Institute on Eminent Domain, 1963*, Dallas, 1963.

PROUTY, W. L., AND CLEM W. COLLINS, AND FRANK H. PROUTY, *Appraisers and Assessors Manual*, Mcgraw Hill Book Co., New York, 1930.

PURNELL, CHARLES G., "The Valuation of the Leasehold Estate," *Proceedings of the First Institute on Eminent Domain, 1959*, Dallas, 1959, pp. 79-99.

RANDALL, FRANK, "Easements," *Right of Way*, December, 1954, pp. 23-26.

RANDALL, FRANK, "Valuations of Easements for Public Utility Purposes," *Technical Valuation*, November, 1955, pp. 9.

RANKIN, DUDLEY L., "Special Problems of Pipiline Rights-Of-Way," *Right-Of-Way*, February, 1959, pp. 7-11.

REESE, LOUIE, "The Puzzle of the Power Line," *The Appraisal Journal*, October, 1967, pp. 555-560.

ROBERTS, T. L., "Eminent Domain and Appraisal," *The Appraisal of Machinery and Equipment*, pp. 73.

ROBERTS, THOMAS L., "Machinery & Equipment Appraisal In Cases of Eminent Domain," *Appraisal & Valuation Manual*, Wash D. C., January, 1972, pp. 170.

ROKES, WILLIS PARK, *An Analysis of Property Valuation Systems Under Eminent Domain*, Montana State University, Missoula, 1961.

ROSENFELD, A. J., "Measuring the Value of Easement," *National Journal Journal of Real Estate*, March, 1933, pp. 33.

SACHS, EARL, "An Apparently Harmless Easement Smashes Subdivision Plans," *The Appraisal Journal*, January, 1966, pp. 117-118.

SACKMAN, JULIUS L., "Access---A Problem In Liability," *Proceedings of the Fourth Institute on Eminent Domain*, 1962.

SACKMAN, JULIUS L., "Compensation Upon the Partial Taking of a Leasehold Interest," *Proceedings of the Third Institute on Eminent Domain*, 1961.

SANDO, LAURENCE, "Appraisal of Leasehold Interests," *Proceedings Ofthe Third Institute on Eminent Domain*, 1961.

SAXON, FLOYD, "Appraising Flowage Easements," *The Appraisal Journal*, October, 1956, pp. 490-498.

SCHMUTZ, GEORGE L., "Easements," *Condemnation Appraisers Handbook*, 1938, pp. 1-339.

SCHMUTZ, GEORGE L., "Rights of Way and Easements," *The Appraisal Journal*, April, 1948, pp. 139-147.

SCHMUTZ, GEORGE L., "Valuation of Avigation Easements," *The Appraisal Journal*, October, 1952, pp. 465-472.

SIEMENS, HENRY T., "The Value of Pipeline Easements," *Appraisal Institute Magazine*, 1968, pp. 17-21.

SLONIM, M. J., "Injustices of Eminent Domain," *The Appraisal Journal*, July, 1957, pp. 421-425.

SMITH, LEVIE D., "Avigation Easements," *The Real Estate Appraiser,* May, 1964, pp. 16-23.

SNITZER, EDWARD L., "Increase or Decrease In Fair Market Value Because of a Future Condemnation," *The Real Estate Appraiser,* 1968, pp. 53-55.

SOLO, RICHARD D., "Some Observation on the Laws of Eminent Domain," *American Society of Appraisers Valuation Manual,* September, 1968, pp. 9..

STEWART, TOM, "Development of Eminent Domain," *The Review,* May, 1954, pp. 19-24.

STORY, BEN H. JR., "Appraisal Fees In Eminent Domanin," *The Residential Appraiser,* October, 1962, pp. 2-5.

STRUNCK, JAMES E., "Avigational Easements--Case Studies," *The Appraisal Journal,* April, 1963, pp. 194-206.

STUBBS, ROBERT C., "Access Rights of Abutting Landowner," *Proceedings of the 4th Inst on Eminent Domain,* Dallas, 1963, pp. 59-88.

SULLIVAN, J. BURKE, "Reproduction Cost, Less Depreciation and Obsolescence, In Cases of Eminent Domain," *The Technical Valuation,* February, 1957, pp. 57-59, June 1957, pp. 33-35.

SUTTE, DONALD T. JR., "Scenic Easements," *The Appraisal Journal,* October, 1966, pp. 531-548.

THE AMERICAN INSTITUTE OF REAL ESTATE APPRAISERS, *Case Studies In Air Rights and Subsurface Tunnel Road Easements,* American Institute of Real Estate Appraisers, Chicago, 1900.

THEIS, C KENNETH, "The Law of Eminent Domain, Its Origin and Development," *The Appraisal Journal,* January, 1957, pp. 54-64.

THEISS, WILLIAM R., "The Appraisal Docket. Condemnation of Air Easement--Liability of County," *The Appraisal Journal,* July, 1962, pp. 415-416.

THEISS, WILLIAM R., "The Appraisal Docket. Valuation of Underground Pipe Easement," *The Appraisal Journal,* February, 1962, pp. 416-417.

TRENHOLM, KENNETH M., "Right of Way Agent and Appraiser Relationship In Eminent Domain Proceedings," *Technical Valuation,* February, 1961, pp. 21-23.

UNIVERSITY OF PITTSBURGH, *The Appraiser's Job In Eminent Domain Proceedings,* University of Pittsburgh, Pittsburgh, 1957.

VAN BUREN, DEWITT, "Appraisal of Estates In Land Less Than the Fee," *The Appraisal Journal,* October, 1943, pp. 327-335.

VANDERPOOL, TOM, FRED L. HUNT, "Flowage Easement Appraisals," *The Appraisal and Valuation Manual,* 1961, pp. 147-154.

VINCENT, GERARD, "Les Servitudes Et Leur Evaluation," *Appraisal Institute Magazine,* September, 1962, pp. 9-12.

WALTHER, HERMAN O., "Witness Stand Performance," *The Appraiser's Job In Eminent Domain Proceedings,* University of Pittsburgh, Pittsburgh, 1957, pp. 37045.

WEBB, WILLIAM E., "The Problem of Restrictive Easements," *The Appraisal Journal,* December, 1968, pp. 18-25.

WHEELER, A. J., "Valuation of Easements," *Appraisal Institute Magazine,* Appraisal Institute of Canada, Winnipeg.

WILCOX, JOHN P., "Valuation of Leasehold Interest Under Law of Eminent Domain," *The Appraisal Journal,* October, 1963, pp. 453-471.

WILLIAMS, HOWARD L., DAVIS, W. D, "Effect of Scenic Easements on the Market Value of Real Property," *The Appraisal Journal,* January, 1968, pp. 15-24.

WILLIAMS, HOWARD L., DAVIS, W. D, "Two Studies of Scenic Easements In North Carolina," *Right of Way,* October, 1968, pp. 58-60.

BIBLIOGRAPHY OF APPRAISAL LITERATURE

## 12-16 Rights and Rights of Way

ABBOT, ACTOR T. JR., "Joint Utility Corridors," *Right of Way*, June, 1970, pp. 47-50.

ALEXANDER, LAURENCE A., "Problems and Potentials of Downtown," *Right of Way*, August, 1967, pp. 37-38.

AMERICAN ASSOCIATION OF STATE HIGHWAY OFFICIALS, *Acquisition for Right of Way*, The Association, Washington, 1962.

AMERICAN RIGHT OF WAY ASSOCIATION, INC., *Selected Readings In Right of Way*, American Right of Way Association, Inc., 1968.

AMERICAN RIGHT OF WAY ASSOCIATION, "Co-Ordination of Engineering, Right of Way Acquisition and Construction," *Proceedings of the Second National Seminar, 1956*, Washington, D. C, 1957.

AMERICAN RIGHT OF WAY ASSOCIATION, "Condemnations," *Proceedings of the Fifth Annual National Seminar, 1959*, Washington, D. C, 1960.

AMERICAN RIGHT OF WAY ASSOCIATION, "Joint Occupancy of Railroad Right of Way," *Proceedings of the Seventh Annual National Seminar*, Washington, 1961.

AMERICAN RIGHT OF WAY ASSOCIATION, "Modern Techniques In Public Land Acquistion," *Proceedings of the Sixth Annual National Association, 1960*, Washington, D. C, 1961.

AMERICAN RIGHT OF WAY ASSOCIATION, "Right of Way Valuation," *Proceedings of the Fifth Annual National Seminar, 1959*, Washington, D. C, 1960.

AMERICAN RIGHT OF WAY ASSOCIATION, "Roadside Merchandising Problems," *Proceedings of the Third Annual National Seminar, 1957*, Washington, D. C, 1958.

AMERICAN RIGHT OF WAY ASSOCIATION, "The Appraiser and the Frontage Road," *Proceedings of the First Annual National Seminar, 1955*, Washington, D. C, 1956.

AMERICAN RIGHT OF WAY ASSOCIATION, "The Federal Highway Program and Its Impact," *Proceedings of the Second Annual National Seminar, 1956*, Washington, D. C, 1957.

AMERICAN RIGHT OF WAY ASSOCIATION, "Title Companies and the Expanded Right of Way Problems," *Proceedings of the Third Annual National Seminar*, Washington, 1957.

AMERICAN RIGHT OF WAY ASSOCIATION, "Who Exaggerates the Value of an Easement Take," *Proceedings of the Seventh Annual Seminar*, Washington, 1961.

AMERICAN SOCIETY OF PLANNING OFFICIALS, *Air Rights*, Chicago.

AMERICAN SOCIETY OF PLANNING OFFICIALS, "Land Use Controls In the Surface Extraction of Minerals," Chicago.

ANDERSON JAMES A., "The New Highway Program," *Right of Way*, December, 1956, pp. 34-36.

ANGEL, CARLOS JULIO, GUILLERMO SANZ MAZUERA, *Regimen Fiscal De La Propiedad Raiz, Codificacion*, Imprenta Municipal, Bogota, 1944.

ANGERS, A. G., "Valuation of Pipeline Servitudgs," *Appraisal Journal*, January, 1972.

APPEL, JAMES R., "Damages Resulting from Construction of Transmission Line," *Real Estate Analyst Appraisal Bulletin*, pp. 513-516.

APPRAISAL JOURNAL, "Compensable Deprivation of Riparian Rights," *The Appraisal Journal*, October, 1954, pp. 603.

▲ Appraisal for Special Purposes

APPRAISAL JOURNAL, "Land Acquisition for Right of Way Purposes," *Appraisal Journal*, January, 1944, pp. 38-41.

ARKANSAS LEGISLATIVE COUNCIL, *Reimbursement of Public Utlities for Relocation Facilities on State Highway Rights of Way*, Arkansas Legislative Council, Little Rock, 1958.

ARNOLD, VERN L., "Title Evidence In Washington State," *Right of Way*, 1960, pp. 47-50.

ASH, FRED C., "The Appraisal Docket, Right of Access to Limited Access Highway," *The Appraisal Journal*, 1956, pp. 589-590.

ASHLEY, ROGER H., "Distribution and Use of Case Studies," *Right of Way*, October, 1966, pp. 32-36.

ASSESSORS NEWSLETTER, "Air Rights Development Costly In New York," *Assessors Newsletter*, June, 1966, pp. 94.

BABCOCK, FREDERICK M., "Highest and Best Use," *Right of Way*, June, 1958, pp. 31-32.

BAKER, VERNE, "Farm Appraising," *Right of Way*, December, 1954, pp. 13-16.

BALDWIN, H. G., "Acquisition of Rights of Way for the New York State Thruway," *Right of Way*, June, 1955, pp. 6-10.

BALFOUR, FRANK C., "Appraisal of Access Rights In California," *The Appraisal Journal*, January, 1951, pp. 26-41.

BALFOUR, FRANK C., "Land Economic Studies: Result of Interchanges on Limited Access Highways, Effect of Traffic Changes," *Right of Way Conference Selected Papers*, University of Alabama, 1959.

BALFOUR, FRANK C., "Special Benefits," *Right of Way*, February, 1957, pp. 7-18.

BANGO, HENRY L., "A Timbermans Look at Right of Way Acquisition," *Right of Way*, June, 1958, pp. 33-36.

BARIBEAU, JULES, "Crossing Forest Lands In Eastern Canada," *Proceedings of the Seventh Annual National Seminar*, American Right of Way Association, Washington, D. C, 1962, pp. 71-72.

BATES, JACK B., "The Appraisal for Salvage Value," *Selected Readings*, Right of Way, Los Angeles, 1968, pp. 333-337.

BATTY, HARRY, "Capital Reinvestment Problems Created by Eminent Domain," *Right of Way*, December, 1960, pp. 35-37.

BEARDSLEY, EARLE L., "Railroad Rights of Way," *Right of Way*, June, 1956, pp. 15-18.

BEATTY, CLARENCE W. JR., "Just Compensation for or the Law on Valuation of Rights of Way," *The Appraisal Journal*, January, 1952, pp. 101-105.

BECCIA, MARTIN, "The Effect of Pipeline Easements on Subdivision Developments," *Right of Way*, August, 1960, pp. 11-16.

BEETHOVEN, EDWIN C., "Elements of Soil Engineering," *Acquisition for Right-Of-Way*, American Association of State Highway Officials, Washington, D. C, 1962, pp. 251-258.

BERRY, J.J., "There Is a Utility Alternative for Municipalities," *Public Utilities*, March 18, 1971, pp. 15-21.

BERRYMAN, GEORGE A., "The Savings Affected by Advance Right of Way Acquisition," *Right of Way*, June, 1959, pp. 15-19.

BISHOP, MAURICE F., "Legal Procedures for Acquisition," *Selected Papers of a Right of Way Conference*, University of Alabama, 1956, pp. 16-27.

BISHOP, MAURICE F., "Non-Compensable Damages In Eminent Domain Proceedings," *Selected Papers of a Right of Way Conference*, University of Alabama, 1957, pp. 16-26.

BISHOP, MAURICE F., "Opening and Closing Arguments In Eminent Domain Cases," *Right of Way*, April, 1961, pp. 13-19.

## BIBLIOGRAPHY OF APPRAISAL LITERATURE

BISHOP, MAURICE F., "Recent Developments In Eminent Domain In Alabama," *Selected Papers of a Right of Way Conference,* University of Alabama, 1961, pp. 89-109.

BISHOP, MAURICE F., PHELPS, JOSEPH D, "Enhancement In Condemnation," *Right of Way,* December, 1960, pp. 8-18.

BISSO, LOUIS, "Acquiring the Rights of Way for the Expressway Program of New Orleans," *Selected Papers of a Right of Way Conference,* University of Alabama, 1956, pp. 59-65.

BOWES, WATSON A., HART, GERALD T, "Basic Valuation Report for Highway Right of Way," *Appraisal Reporting Techniques,* American Ins. of Real Estate Appraisers, Chicago, 1951, pp. 153-189.

BRITTON, THOMAS C., "Effect In Florida of Requiring Condemnor to Pay Condemnee's Entire Litigation Expense," *Right of Way,* October, 1963, pp. 15-20.

BROOKER, HERBERT D., "A Suggested Technique for the Appraisal of a Partial Taking from an Office Building," *Right of Way,* October, 1970, pp. 34-38.

BROWN, H. H., "Utility Load Growth, the Environment, and FPC Responsibility," *Public Utilities Fortnightly,* May 7, 1970, pp. 37-40.

BROWN, MAURICE A., "Noise Pollution," *Right of Way,* June, 1970, pp. 40-41.

BRYSON, J. A., "The Use of the Appraisal In Negotiation," *Right of Way,* 1957, pp. 49-65.

BURKE, FRANK W., "Congressional Action Pertinent to Real Property Acquisition," *Right of Way,* June, 1963, pp. 7-9.

CALIFORNIA DIVISION OF HIGHWAYS, *Right of Way Manual,* California Division of Highways, Sacramento, 1955.

CAMPBELL, CHARLES W., "Preparation for the Condemnation Trial," *Right of Way,* June, 1959, pp. 35-38.

CAMPBELL, COLIN, "A Study of the Effects of Pipeline Easements on Subdivision Developments," *Right of Way,* December, 1960, pp. 23-33.

CAMPBELL, ROBERT S., JR., "The Limited Access Highway--Some Aspects of Compensation," *Right of Way,* February, 1963, pp. 29-35.

CANTERBURY, NATHAN D., "Right of Way Across Timberland," *Right of Way,* June, 1956, pp. 19-21.

CAPPS, WILLIS W., "When Is a Fixture Fixed," *Right of Way,* April, 1969.

CARLL, CLOICE D., "Valuation of a Power Line Right of Way," *The Appraisal Journal,* April, 1956, pp. 248-265.

CARLL, CLOICE D., "Valuation of Electric Transmission Line Rights of Way," *The Appraisal Journal,* July, 1958, pp. 332-348.

CARLL, CLOICE D., "Valuation of Transmission Line Rights of Way," *Condemnation Appraisal Practice,* A. I. R. E. A., Chicago, 1967, pp. 251.

CARLL, CLOICE, D., "Valuation of Water Rights," *The Appraisal Journal,* January, 1941, pp. 48-53.

CARNEY, JOHN J., "Effect of Limited Access Highways on Values of Adjoining Properties," *Assessment Administration,* IAAO.

CARTER, JAMES M., "How to Make Compensation Just," *Right of Way,* June, 1958, pp. 21-26.

CHAMBERLAIN, J. B., "Right of Way Acquisition for Oil Pipe Lines," *Appraisal Institute Magazine,* September, 1961, pp. 7-8.

CHAMBERLAIN, J. B., "Right of Way Acquisition: Pipe Line Easements," *Appraisal Institute Magazine,* Appraisal Institute of Canada, Winnipeg.

CHICHESTER, C. H. JR., "Market Data In Condemnation Appraisings," *Right of Way Conference, Selected Papers, 1961,* University, Alabama, 1961, pp. 55-59.

CHICHESTER, JOHN, "Basic Principles of Right of Way Evaluation," *Right of Way Conference, Selected Papers, 1957*, University of Alabama, University, Ala., 1957, pp. 37-38.

CLARK, GILBERT K., "Appraisal of Freeway Rights of Way Through Industrial Lands," *Valuation*, October, 1954, pp. 29-31.

CLARK, GILBERT K., "Freeway Appraising," *Right of Way*, February, 1955, pp. 5-9.

CLEVELAND, ALLEN L., "Appraisal and Right of Way Acquisition for Public Utilities," *The Appraisal Journal*, April, 1954, pp. 197-200.

CLEVELAND, ALLEN L., "Public Utility Private Rights of Way--Their Effect on Acquisition of Rights of Way for Other Uses," *Valuation*, October, 1954, pp. 61-64.

CLEVELAND, ALLEN L., "Rights of Way, Public Utility," *Technical Valuation*, American Society of Appraisers, Washington, October, 1954, pp. 61.

CLEVELAND, ALLEN L., "Sound Business Relations In Right of Way Acquisition," *Right of Way Conference*, 1959, pp. 39-43.

CLURMAN, ALBERT W., "Air Rights," *The Appraisal Journal*, July, 1964, pp. 335-338.

COATES, CULLEN W., "Encroachments On, and Permitted Use Of, Utility Rights of Way," *Right of Way*, August, 1962, pp. 29-35.

COATES, JOHN J., "Contract Right of Way Buying... How Does it Work," *Right of Way*, October, 1961, pp. 21-23.

COHN, JOSEPH D., "Role of Office of Management & Budget In Administration of Uniform Relocation Assist & Land Acquisit," *Appraisal & Valuation Manual*, Corporate Press Inc, January, 1972, pp. 338.

COOKE, A. C., "Uses of Transmission Right of Way," *Right of Way*, August, 1960, pp. 17-22.

COTTEN, ROBERT, "Types of Subdivisions," *Right of Way Conference, Selected Papers, 1962*, University of Alabama, Alabama, 1962, pp. 32-36.

COWLEY, LEONARD M., GERALD T. HART, "Appraising the Right of Flight," *The Appraisal Journal*, 1944.

CRAWFORD, CLAUDE O., "Appraisal of Rights of Way," *The Encyclopedia of Real Estate Appraising*, Edith J. Friedman, 1959, pp. 542-536.

CRAWFORD, CLAUDE O., "Appraisal of a Total Taking of a Gasoline Station," *Right of Way*, December, 1958, pp. 11-15.

CRAWFORD, CLAUDE O., "Valuation of Easement Rights," *Right of Way*, June, 1956, pp. 23-25.

CRONER, FRED, JR., "History and Nature of Eminent Domain," *Right of Way*, August, 1960, pp. 33-39.

CUNNINGHAM, F. M., "The Appraisal of Riparian Rights," *Appraisal Institute Magazine*, Appraisal Institute of Canada, Winnipeg, June 1, 1971.

CUNNYNGHAM, WILKIE, "Case of the Month," *Right of Way*, August, 1956, pp. 35-36.

CUNNYNGHAM, WILKIE, "Case of the Month," *Right of Way*, October, 1954, pp. 19-20, 28.

CUNNYNGHAM, WILKIE, RALPH BORDLEY, "Land Titles," *Acquisition for Right of Way*, American Association of Highway Officials, Washington, D. C, 1962, pp. 135-143.

DAVIDSON, THOMAS LEA, "The Planning and Organization of a Shopping Center," *Right of Way*, June, 1962, pp. 29-33.

DAVIS, JOHN W., "The Arrangement of Telephone Facilities Due to Interstate and Other Highway Work," *Right of Way*, February, 1962, pp. 17-21.

DAVIS, W. D., *The Application of Appraisal Techniques In the Acquisition of Highway Right of Way*, Colloquium on Appraisal Research, Wisconsin, 1963, pp. 18-20.

DAVIS, W. D., "Remainder Study Forms Usable by Appraisers," *Right of Way*, February, 1967, pp. 30-35.

DAVIS, W. D., "What Will the Right of Way Cost," *The Appraisal Journal*, April, 1958, pp. 242-253.

DAVIS, WILLIAM M., "The Question of Value," *Right of Way*, October, 1956, pp. 15-16.

DE VRIES, ROSCOE, "The Relationship of Drainage Easements to R-W Liaison," *Right of Way*, February, 1964, pp. 27-29.

DEFFEY, SARLE M., *The Adequate Right of Way Appraisal*, Right of Way Conference, University, Alabama, 1957, pp. 15-86.

DERBES, MAX J. JR., "The Appraisal of Easements," *Right of Way*, December, 1964, pp. 23-29.

DERBES, MAX J. JR., "So Your Property Is In the Right of Way," *The Right of Way*, August, 1958, pp. 30-34.

DERBES, MAX J. JR., "The Appraisal of Easements," *Selected Readings In Right of Way*, American Right of Way Association, Los Angeles, 1968, pp. 290-300.

DERBES, MAX J. JR. MAI, "The Tremendous Cost of Protest of Public Projects," *Right of Way*, April, 1971.

DEWEY, JOHN M., "The Missouri River Basin Development Program," *Right of Way*, October, 1954, pp. 7-9.

DIEPENBROCK, BRAM, "Equipment Values In Public Acquisition-Fact or Fiction," *Right of Way*, October, 1969, pp. 11-16.

DIERCKS, K. J., "Land Use Planning," *Right of Way*, June, 1962, pp. 43-44.

DOW, PETER, AND QUENTIN EDWARDS, *Public Rights of Way and Access to the Countryside*, Shaw, London, 1951.

DOYLE, JOHN P., "Taxation of Way," *Conference Proceedings*, National Tax Association, Columbus, 1964, pp. 482-485.

DUFFY, GEORGE C., "Damage to the Remainder--Made Simple," *Right of Way*, April, 1963, pp. 13-20.

DUNLAP, DONALD C., "Highway and Toll Road Taking," *The Appraisal Journal*, January, 1957, pp. 22-26.

DUNLAP, DONALD C., "The Appraisal of Pipeline Rights of Way," *The Appraisal Journal*, July, 1951, pp. 348-354.

EDMAN, J. J., "Lessor Has Right to Improvements," *The Appraisal Journal*, October, 1959, pp. 579-581.

EDMAN, J. J., "Loss of Indirect Access Compensable. Appraising Docket," *The Appraisal Journal*, July, 1959, pp. 412-413.

EDMAN, J. J., "Oral Agreement to Remove Minerals Is Property Right. Appraisal Docket," *The Appraisal Journal*, October, 1959, pp. 581-582.

EDMAN, J. J., "The Appraisal Docket. Expense of Moving Public Utility Facilities Occupying Public Ways," *The Appraisal Journal*, July, 1958, pp. 450-452.

EDMAN, J. J., "The Appraisal Docket. Limitations Upon Right of Access," *The Appraisal Journal*, July, 1957, pp. 445-446.

EDMAN, J. J., "The Appraisal Docket, Limitations on Right of Access," *The Appraisal Journal*, October, 1957, pp. 619-620.

EDMAN, J. J., "Unproved Oil Rights Must Be Considered. Appraisal Docket," *The Appraisal Journal*, October, 1957, pp. 623.

EHLERS, HENRY W., "An Appraiser Looks at Investment Properties," *The Right of Way*, October, 1958, pp. 7-10.

EICHHORN, VICTOR H., "Appraisal Requirements and Use by Negotiators," *Proceedings of the Seventh Annual National Seminar*, American Right of Way Association, Washington, D. C., 1961, pp. 7-8.

ELLIS, LESTER J., "Right of Way Acquisition In Massachusetts, Constitutional and Statutory Provisions," *Right of Way*, December, 1958, pp. 6-9.

ENFIELD, C. W., "Federal-State Planned Highway Construction Program, Its Effect on the Right of Way Profession," *Proceedings of the Fourth Annual National Seminar, 1958,* American Right of Way Association, Washington, D. C., 1959, pp. 23-27.

ENFIELD, CLIFTON W., AND WILLIAM A. MANSFIELD, "Fixtures Vs. Personal Property," *Right of Way,* December, 1956, pp. 10-13, 15-19, 21-23.

EVANS, BERNARD G., "Farmlands and Rights of Way," *Right of Way,* February, 1956, pp. 13-18.

EVANS, MARVIN J., "Evolution of Right of Way," *Right of Way,* June, 1957, pp. 33-36.

EVANS, MARVIN J., "Power Line Right of Way--Fee or Easement," *Right of Way,* December, 1961, pp. 27-38.

EVANS, MARVIN J., "Right of Way Relations In Electric Utilities," *Right of Way,* June, 1960, pp. 35-39.

EWING, JOSEPH NEFF, "Some Right of Way Problems As a Lawyer Sees Them," *Right of Way,* April, 1958, pp. 37-39.

EWING, WILLIAM O. JR., "Offering Prices for Pipeline Rights of Way Evaluated," *Right of Way,* February, 1968, pp. 44-47.

FABIAN, ROBERT H., "Appraising the Right of Flight," *The Appraisal Journal,* January, 1944, pp. 9-13.

FARRINGTON WILLIAM C., "The Land Developer and Rights of Way," *Right Ofway,* May, 1959, pp. P 25-28.

FEDERAL POWER COMMISSION, *P-35-Hydroelectric Power Evaluation,* Supt of Documents, U. S. Govt. Printing Office, Washington D. C, 1968.

FEDERAL POWER COMMISSION, *P-40-World Power Data,* Supt of Documents, U. S. Govt. Printing Office, Washington D. C, 1968.

FEDERAL POWER COMMISSION, *S-201-Depreciation Practices of Electric Utilites,* Supt. of Documents, U. S. Govt. Printing Office, Washington D. C, 1966.

FEDERAL POWER COMMISSION, "National Power Curve," *National Power Surve,* Federal Power Commission, December, 1964.

FENTON, HARRY R., "Appraisal of Access Rights," *Right of Way,* February, 1958, pp. 25-28.

FLETCHER, ROBERT RAY PH. D., *The Impact of Economic Development on Water Resource Use,* Oklahoma State University, 1971.

FOREST, J., "Contract, Ownership and Servitude," *Right of Way,* June, 1963, pp. 32-41.

FORNACI, CHARLES M., "Developments In the Right of Way Field," *Selected Readings In Right of Way,* 1968, pp. 192-197.

FPC, "P-36 Hydroel Power Rescs of U. S. Devel & Undevel," Supt Doc Govt Ptg Off, Wash, 1968.

FPC, "P-38 Hydroel Power Eval Supp't No 1 July 69," Supt Doc Govt Ptg Off, Wash.

FREEDLAND, FRED, "Rights of Way on and Across Department of the Army Lands," *Right of Way,* February, 1956, pp. 5-6.

FROST, JACK W., "Right of Way Problems Including Appraisal and Negotiation," *Right of Way,* December, 1960, pp. 38-42.

FULCO, ROY J., "General Summary of Remainder Studies," *Right of Way,* December, 1966, pp. 36-38.

FURMAN, ROY E., "Today's Right of Way Problems," *Right of Way,* August, 1957, pp. 15-17, 46.

GADDIS, PERCY A., "Appraising Public Utilities and Rights of Way," *National Real Estate Journal,* November 23, 1931, pp. 27-28.

GALLAGHER, JOSEPH A. SR., "The Indian's Right Returned to Indians," *Technicalities,* May, 1949, pp. 7.

GOODWIN, E. F., "The Telephone Company and Its Right of Way Problems," *Right of Way,* February, 1961, pp. 19-20.

GRAUGNARD, F. A. JR., "Rights of Way Through Sugar Cane Land," *Right of Way,* February, 1957, pp. 31-38, 62.

GRAY, LESLIE, "How to Reduce Right of Way Acquisition Cost Through the Uses of the Right of Way," *Right of Way,* October, 1959, pp. 35-38.

GREER, D. C., "Importance and Benefit of Access Controlled Highways," *Right of Way,* April, 1956, pp. 19-20.

GREGORY, R. P., "A Contractor's View of Pipeline Right of Way Problems," *Right of Way,* June, 1963, pp. 17-19.

GROSS, WILLIAM J., "Right of Way Acquisition In Ohio," *Right of Way,* February, 1962, pp. 34-39.

GURTHIE, R. R., "Value-In-Use," *Right of Way,* December, 1962, pp. 56-57.

GUSTAFSON, HAROLD M., "Pipe Lines of the Future," *American Right of Way Association,* Proceedings of the Seventh Annual National Seminar, 1961.

HAGNESTEIN, W. D., "Right of Way and Tree-Farming," *Proceedings of the Seventh Annual National Seminar,* American Right of Way Association, Washington, D. C, 1961, pp. 66-67.

HALEY, JOHN L., "Perilous Remainder Studies," *The Appraisal Journal,* October, 1966, pp. 22-24.

HALL, ARTHUR B., "Approaches to the Valuation of Air Rights," *The Appraisal Journal,* July, 1956, pp. 325-347.

HALL, CARL B., "How Title and Abstract Companies Can Assist In the Right of Way Acquisition," *Right of Way,* April, 1960, pp. 33-38.

HALL, WALTER B., "A Lawyer Talks Back," *Right of Way,* February, 1963, pp. 15-20.

HAMLEN, WILLIAM E., A. D. STANLEY, "Right of Way In the Sky," *Right of Way,* May, 1961, pp. 15-25.

HANEMANN, H. J. F., *Acquisition of Rights of Way,* Condemnation Appraisal Seminar, 1958.

HANEMANN, H. J. F., "Flood and Debris Hazards---Their Effect on Property Values," *Right of Way,* February, 1955, pp. 12-15.

HATWELL, CHARLES O., "Making the Most of Comparable Sales," *Right of Way,* February, 1971.

HAWKINS, GEORGE C., "A Study of Alabama's Eminent Domain Statutes," *Selected Papers, Right of Way Conference,* University of Alabama, 1961.

HESS, RUDOLF, "Novice or Expert," *Right of Way,* February, 1958, pp. 7-8.

HESS, RUDOLF, "Relocation of People and Homes from Freeway Rights of Way--Community Effects," *The Residential Appraiser,* April, 1962, pp. 2-10.

HESS, RUDOLF, "The Importance of Lead Time," *Right of Way,* February, 1962, pp. 7-16.

HESS, RUDOLPH, AMER RIGHT OF WAY ASSOCIATION, "Land Economic Studies In Connection with Right of Way Acquisition Panel," *Proceedings of the Sixth Annual National Seminar 1960,* American Right of Way Association, Washington, D. C., 1961, pp. 33-53.

HICKS, JAMES B., "Appraisal Methods and Techniques Applied to Public Utility Rights of Way," *Right of Way,* October, 1957, pp. 25-28.

HIGHWAY RESEARCH BOARD, *Highway Access,* Acquisition for Right-Of-Way, Washington, D. C., 1962.

HILL, AUSTIN M., "Obtaining Rights of Way Other Than by Purchase," *Right of Way,* April, 1960, pp. 11-16.

HOGAN, RICHARD A., "How the Title Company Can Help," *Proceedings of the 7th Annual Natl Seminar,* American Right of Way Association, 1961.

HOOKER, RAYMOND W., KENNETH R. POTTER, *The Impact of a New Interstate Highway on a Corridor and Input-Output Analysis,* University of Wyoming, January, 1971.

HOOPER, A. L., "Acquisition of Rights of Way," *Proceedings of the First Annual National Seminar,* ASA, Washington, D.C., 1955, pp. 23-26.

HORGAN, JOHN P., "Case of the Month," *Right of Way,* April, 1954, pp. 27-30.

HORRELL, ALBERT J., "What the Lawyer Expects from the Right of Way Man and Appraiser," *Right of Way,* February, 1958, pp. 16-18.

HOUSTON, SAM, "Case of the Month," *Right of Way,* December, 1956, pp. 47-49.

HOWARD, JACK M., "Case of the Month," *Right of Way,* February, 1954, pp. 17-18.

HOWARD, WILLIAM F., "Right-Of-Way Valuation and Acquisition," *Technical Valuation,* ASA, Washington, November, 1955, pp. 5.

HOWARD, WILLIAM F., "The Rising Cost of Right of Way and Your Responsibility," *Right of Way,* April, 1963, pp. 21-23.

HUBIN, VINCENT J., "A Suggested Technique for Valuation of Air Rights," *Right of Way,* June, 1967, pp. 32-34.

HUFFMAN, WILLIAM H., "Giving the Land Owner a Fair and Square Deal," *Right of Way,* August, 1962, pp. 7-10.

HUFFMAN, WILLIAM H., "Right of Way Acquisition - Puerto Somoza to Managua," *Right of Way,* December, 1962, pp. 9-16.

HUFFMAN, WILLIAM H., "The Aims, and Purposes of the American Rightof Way Association," *Right of Way,* October, 1959, pp. 7-10.

HUFFTS, CHRISTIAN, A. H, "Photogrammetry," *Acquisition for Right of Way,* American Association of State Highway Officials, Washington, 1962, pp. 189-207.

HUMPHREYS, LESTER W., "Real and Personal Property," *Right of Way,* February, 1958, pp. 37-40.

HUNSCHE, RALPH, "How a Title Plant May Help the Right of Way Agent," *Right of Way,* August, 1959, pp. 11-14.

HUTTS, J. MARSHALL, ALFRED RAWS, JR., "Procedure for Bringing Pipe Line Valuations Down to Date," *Technical Valuation,* May, 1945, pp. 5-13.

INTERNATIONAL COUNCIL OF APPRAISAL ORGANIZATIONS, "What Is it," *Right of Way,* October, 1963, pp. 53-54.

JACOBSON, GLENN H., "Appraisal Issues Encountered In Expressway Right-Of-Way Valuations," *Papers and Proceedings,* Wisconsin Colloquium on Appraisal Research, 1963, pp. 15-17.

JAMES, L. DOUGLAS., "The Economic Value of Real Estate Acquired Forright-Of-Way," *Land Economics,* August, 1968, pp. 363-370.

JOHNSON, CLIFFORD R., "Report on a Study of the Effects of Highway Right of Way Encroachment on Residential Property," *Right of Way,* August, 1959, pp. 21-26.

JOHNSON, HAROLD E., "Aerial Surveys Aid Land Acquisition," *Right of Way,* February, 1959, pp. 35-36.

JOHNSON, LOWELL C., "Valuation of Petroleum Mineral Rights for Ad Valorem Taxation," *The Appraisal Journal,* October, 1953, pp. 497-510.

JONES, E. P., "Photography and Mapping In Appraisal and Eminent Domain Work," *Proceedings of the Eighth Annual National Seminar, 1962,* American Right of Way Association, Washington, 1962, pp. 31-37.

JORDAN, ROBERT D., "Alabama Program and Problems of Right-Of-Way Acquisition," *Right of Way Conference, Selected Papers,* 1957, pp. 1-9.

JORDON, R. D., "The Right of Way Acquisition Problem," *Right of Way Conference,* 1956, pp. 1-8.

KAHN, SANDERS A., "The Polo Grounds and Special Purpose Property Valuation," *Right of Way,* October, 1968, pp. 10-13, 15-16.

KALTENBACH, HENRY J., "The Bureau of Public Roads, and Its Relation to Right of Way Acquisition," *Right of Way,* August, 1956, pp. 31-34.

KALTENBACH, HENRY J., "The Elastic Right — Access," *The Appraisal Journal,* January, 1967, pp. 9-16.

KAUFMAN, K. A., "Coal Exports Wont Be Cut Its Cold Shoulder for Industry," *Iron Age,* October 8, 1970, pp. 19.

KEELY, JOSEPH F., "Special Purpose Property Appraising," *Right of Way,* April, 1969, pp. 28-33.

KELLENBERGER, ALLEN N., "Special Assessment Levied Against Railroad Rights-Of-Way," *Conference Proceedings,* National Tax Association, Columbus, 1965, pp. 197-203.

KENNEDY, W. F., "Are Federal Highway Administration Appraisal Requirements Unreasonable," *Valuation,* September, 1972, pp. 44.

KILEY, EDWARD V., "The Highway Age In Transportation," *How Transportation Affects Real Estate Value,* AIREA, Chicago, March 7, 1969, pp. 12-13.

KIRK, J. E., "Accommodating Utilities Within Highway Right of Way," *Right of Way,* June, 1970, pp. 23-24 26-28.

KIRSHMAN, JOHN EMMETT, "Electric Light and Power," *Principles of Investment,* 1933, pp. 375.

KNAPP, DEWITT L., *The Market Looks at Utility Right of Way and Easements,* Proceedings of the Fourth Institute on Eminent Dom, Dallas, 1962, pp. 111-125.

KNEISS, GEORGE, "Industrial Land Development In North California," *Right of Way,* April, 1954, pp. 6-7.

KNOX, RAYMOND G., "The Impediment Vs. the Right of Way," *Right of Way,* October, 1962, pp. 53-60.

KOEPPEL, ADOLPH, "The Appraiser on the Witness Stand—The Attorney's View," *Selected Readings In Right of Way,* American Right of Way Association, 1968, pp. 532-538.

KOHL, JOHN C., "Highway As a Factor In Plant Location," *The Appraisal Journal,* January, 1959, pp. 62-68.

KOSHAL, RAJINDAR K., "Highway Investments and Externalities a Case Study of Ohio," *Bulletin of Business Research,* Ohio State University, March, 1971, pp. 4 5.

KOSINKE, CLEMENT, "Appraisers and State Right of Way Personnel," *Technical Valuation,* October, 1958, pp. 21-23.

KREVOR, HENRY H., *Legal Rules Governing Valuation of Real Property,* The American Right of Way Association, Los Angeles, 1968, pp. 170-183.

KREVOR, HENRY H., *Trends of Recent Decisions In Eminent Domain,* Right of Way Conference, 1960, pp. 27-40.

KREVOR, HENRY H., "Legislative Changes and Trends Affecting Compensation In Eminent Domain," *Right of Way,* August, 1961, pp. 23-29.

KRISTOVICH, BALDO M., "Case of the Month," *Right of Way,* October, 1955, pp. 33.

LACKEY, HARRY B., "Utility Problems Related to Controlled Access Highways," *Right of Way Conference, Selected Papers,* University of Alabama, 1957.

LACKEY, HARRY B., "Utility Problems Related to Controlled Access Highways," *Right of Way Conference, Selected Papers,* University of Alabama, 1957.

LAIDLAW, STEWARD P., "Right of Way and Land Acquisition Procedure of Central Hudson Gas and Electric Corporation," *Right of Way,* April, 1958, pp. 31-32.

LAND, DAVID E., "Acquisition of Property for Urban Renewal," *Right of Way,* December, 1963, pp. 27-32.

LAND, YATES A., "Property Damages Incident to Oil and Gas Field Operations," *Right of Way,* June, 1958, pp. 27-29.

LANDSTROM, COL. KARL S., "A Review of Appraisal Process In Granting Easements Across Federal Lands," *Selected Readings In Right of Way,* American Right of Way Association, Los Angeles, 1968, pp. 281-283.

LASKA, WALTER J., "Fee Versus Easement," *Right of Way,* February, 1967, pp. 20-23.

LATVALA, A. A., "New and Important Developments In Right-Of-Way Highways," *Proceedings of the Eighth Annual National Seminar,* Washington, D. C, 1963, pp. 23-25.

LAW, RAY E., "Preparing Exhibits for Condemnation Trials," *Right of Way,* February, 1961, pp. 21-28.

LAW, W. V., "Utility Easements and Problems," *Right of Way,* February, 1961, pp. 27-28.

LEE ADELBERT W., "Sky Values," *Right of Way,* April, 1962, pp. 47-49.

LEE, ADELBERT W., "Appraisals for Condemnation," *Selected Readings In Right of Way,* American Right of Way Association, Los Angeles, 1968, pp. 577-581.

LEE, ADELBERT W., "Right of Way Valuation," *Right of Way,* October, 1958, pp. 33-36.

LEE, ADELBERT W., "The Appraiser's Deportment In the Courtroom," *Right of Way,* October, 1963, pp. 39-44.

LEHMAN, ROBERT W, "Appraisal of a Cemetery," *Journal;Proceedings,* Am. Soc. Farm Mgrs-Rural Appraisers, Denver, November 12, 1973, pp. 48-52.

LEONARD, H. W., "Appraising Freeway Right of Way Through Commercial Area," *Valuation,* October, 1954, pp. 27-28.

LEVEL, EDWARD E., "Eminent Domain Concepts, Laws and Limitations," *Acquisition for Right of Way,* American Association of State Highway Officials, Washington, D. C, 1962, pp. 25-32.

LEVIN, DAVID R., "Appraisal Problems In Right of Way Acquisition," *Papers and Proceedings,* Wisconsin Colloquium on Appraisal Research, 1963, pp. 13-14.

LEVIN, DAVID R., "Legal Problems Surrounding the Loss of Access In Right of Way Acquisition," *Selected Papers,* Right of Way Conference, Univ of Alabama, 1961.

LEVIN, DAVID R., "Right of Way and New Highway Program," *Right of Way,* August, 1956, pp. 21-22.

LEVIN, DAVID R., "Some Aspects of Right-Of-Way Acquisition for Federal-Aid Highway Purposes," *Appraisal and Valuation Manual,* American Society of Appraisers, 1962, pp. 28-37.

LEVIN, DAVID R., "The Research Function In Right-Of-Way Acquisition," *Acquisition for Right-Of-Way,* American Association of State Highway Officials, Washington, D. C., 1962.

LEWIS, C. H. JR., "The Impact of Utility Easements on Commercial Forest Lands," *Right of Way,* June, 1963, pp. 29-31.

LEWIS, H. J., "Policy Problems of Alabama State Highway Department In Right of Way Acquisition," *Selected Papers,* Right of Way Conference, University of Alabama, 1961, pp. 138-145.

LEYDEN, J. WALLACE, "Eminent Domain," *Right of Way,* August, 1957, pp. 18-22.

LEYDEN, RICHARD J., "Appraisal of Air Rights," *Encyclopedia of Real Estate Appraising,* 1959, pp. 550-559.

LINDAS, LEONARD I., "Demeanor of the Witness," *Right of Way,* April, 1956, pp. 22-24.

LINDAS, LEONARD I., "General and Special Benefits," *Right of Way,* December, 1958, pp. 29-32.

LINDAS, LEONARD I., "Tips on Testifying," *Right of Way*, June, 1963, pp. 25-27.

LOCKYER, ALBERT W., "Appraisals of Rights-Of-Way," *The Review*, September, 1951, pp. 8-9.

LOEBBECKE, ERNEST J., "The Relationship of the Title and Abstract Company with the Right of Way Acquisition Program," *Right of Way*, April, 1959, pp. 26-33.

LORENS, EDWARD R., "Appraisal of Farm Property for Trunk Highway Right of Way In Minnesota," *Right of Way*, February, 1959, pp. 31-34.

LOWRIE, THOMAS R., "New-Jersey Turnpike Program of Acquisition of Right-Of-Way," *Right of Way*, August, 1954, pp. 5-8.

LUITEN, IRVIN H., "Enlightened Forest Management," *Right of Way*, October, 1954, pp. 15-18.

LUM, Y. T., "An Exploration of Some of the Assumptions Doctrines and Implications of Right of Way Valuations," *Selected Readings In Right of Way*, American Right of Way Association, Los Angeles, 1968, pp. 207-218.

LUM, Y. T., "Improving Methods of Right of Way Valuations," *Right of Way*, August, 1961, pp. 15-20.

LUM, Y. T., "Improving Methods of Right of Way Valuations," *Selected Readings In Right of Way*, The American Right of Way Association, Los Angeles, 1968, pp. 183-192.

LUM, Y. T., "More Exploratns of Some of Assumptns Doctns & Implicatns of Right of Way Valuations," *Selected Readings In Right of Way*, American Right of Way Association, Los Angeles, pp. 218-240.

LUM, Y. T., "Right of Way Valuations---The Meaning Comparison and Applications of Market Data," *The Real Estate Appraiser*, SREA, Chicago, January, 1965, pp. 28.

MACBRIDE, DEXTER D, "Fundamentals of R/W Acquisition: Appraising and Negotiating," *Selected Papers, R/W Conference*, University of Alabama, February 1, 1961.

MACBRIDE, DEXTER D, "Interface: Condemnation, Appraising, Right of Way, Public Works, Administration," *Valutape Audio-Library Series*, American Society of Appraisers, Washington D.C., January 1, 1973.

MACBRIDE, DEXTER D., "America's Oldest Right of Way," *Right of Way*, August, 1959, pp. 44-45.

MACBRIDE, DEXTER D., "Analysis and Report Right of Way Land Economic Studies," *Seminar, American Right of Way Association*, Denver, Colorado, November, 1958.

MACBRIDE, DEXTER D., "Comments Upon Land Economic Studies Related to Highways," *Ninth Highway Planning Conference, Western Association of State Highway Officials*, April, 1960.

MACBRIDE, DEXTER D., "Effects of Freeways on Real Estate Values," *Pacific Coast Appraisal Conference Society of Residential Appraisers*, September, 1962.

MACBRIDE, DEXTER D., "Emerging Highway Patterns, Frontage Roads, Abutting Business Properties," *Seminar, American Right of Way Association*, Portland, Oregon, November, 1958.

MACBRIDE, DEXTER D., "Fundamentals of Right of Way Acquisition, Appraising and Negotiating," *Selected Papers*, University of Alabama, 1961.

MACBRIDE, DEXTER D., "Highways & Non-User Benefits," *Right of Way*,

MACBRIDE, DEXTER D., "Right of Way Valuation Committee, Purpose, Achievements, Goals," *Proceedings of the Seventh Annual National Seminar, 1961*, American Right of Way Association, 1962.

MACBRIDE, DEXTER D., "The History and Romance of Rights of Way," *Right of Way*, October, 1955, pp. 23-27.

MACBRIDE, DEXTER D., "The Right of Way Agent and Condemnation Appraising," *Right of Way Magazine*, December, 1968.

MACDONALD, E. M., "Appraisal of Freeway Rights of Way on Rural Lands," *Technical Valuation,* October, 1954, pp. 25-26, 31-32.

MACDONALD, E. M., "Rights of Way-Freeway," *Technical Valuation,* American Society of Appraisers, October, 1954, pp. 25.

MACHEN, J. C., "Air Rights Development," *The Appraisal Journal,* April, 1966, pp. 288-294.

MAGILL, C. H., "The Origin and Function of Title Insurance," *Right of Way,* August, 1960, pp. 8-10.

MAIN, L. T., "Occupancy of Public Lands," *Proceedings of the Eighth Annual National Seminar, 1962,* Washington, D. C, 1963, pp. 60-63.

MALLARD, RAYMOND B., "My Views Concerning Condemnation and Condemnation Trials," *Right of Way,* December, 1962, pp. 50-54.

MANN, J. A., "Service Station Evaluation," *Right of Way,* October, 1954, pp. 10-14.

MANN, P. C., J. L. MIKESELL, "Electric Utility Taxes: Incidence Revisited," *Public Utilities Fortnightly,* September 24, 1970, pp. 21-25.

MANN, PATRICK C. AND JOHN L. MIKESELL, "The Public Utility: a Taxpayer or a Tax Collector," *Florida Economic Indicators,* University of Florida, 1971, pp. 4.

MARCUS, WILLIAM J., "What Is Happening In the Mortgage Market," *Right of Way,* April, 1958, pp. 7-11, 39.

MARGETIS, NICHOLAS M., "Roadside Regulations and Controls," *Acquisition for Right of Way,* American Association of State Highway Officials, Washington, D. C, 1962, pp. 603-629.

MARINER, LAWRENCE T., "Rights of Way for the Power Utility," *Proceedings of the First Annual National Seminar,* American Right of Way Association, Washington, D. C, 1956, pp. 12-14.

MARKHAM, MARION, FORNACI, CHARLES M, "Property Management and the Disposal of Improvements," *Acquisition for Right of Way,* American Association of State Highway Officials, Washington, D. C, 1962, pp. 631-640.

MCCARTHY, EARL D., "The Valuation of a Shopping Center---From the Developer's Viewpoint," *Right of Way,* October, 1964, pp. 52-54.

MCGOUGH, B. C., "Impact of Highway Improvements on Land Values As Observed In Two Florida Studies," *Right of Way,* December, 1965, pp. 37-48.

MCGOUGH, B. C., "Methodology for Highway Impact Studies," *The Appraisal Journal,* January, 1968, pp. 65-72.

MCGOUGH, BOBBY C., "A Treatise on Highway Impact," *Right of Way,* June, 1968, pp. 40-45.

MCHENRY, D. B., "Crop Damages Along Pipe Line Rights of Way," *American Right of Way Association,* 1955, pp. 26-28.

MCIVER, C. R., "Red Tape on the Right of Way," *Right of Way,* August, 1959, pp. 51-54.

MCSWEENEY, THOMAS F., "Depreciation Factors and Special Purpose Properties," *American Association of State Highway Officials,* 1962, pp. 471-494.

MCSWEENEY, THOMAS F., "Evaluation of Mineral Rights," *American Society of Appraisers,* 1960, pp. 153-160.

MENDEZ, ALFREDO, JR., "Some Aspects of Right of Way Acquisition In the Commonwealth of Puerto Rico," *Right of Way,* October, 1965, pp. P 13-17.

MEYER, EDWIN G., "Severance Damages, Fact or Fantasy," *Right of Way,* December, 1963, pp. 21022.

MEYER, HAROLD, "Practical Appraisals," *Right of Way,* October, 1958, pp. 23-26.

MILLER, C. ARC, "Estimating Basic Land Value," *Right of Way,* April, 1959, pp. 35-40.

MILLER, REX K., "Oil Pipeline Right of Way, Total Compensation and Easement for Sterling Farm," *Journal of the American Society of Farm Managers And Rural Appraisers,* October, 1961, pp. 22-28.

MOBLEY, H. H., "Roadside Merchandising Problems," American Right of Way Association, 1958, pp. 44-45.

MOEBES, CARL, "Condemnation of Mineral Rights," *Right of Way Conference,* 1960, pp. 41-46.

MOEBES, CARL G., "Condemnation of Minerals," *Right of Way,* April, 1960, pp. 7-10.

MONTGOMERY, W., "An Executive Look at the Right of Way Function," *Right of Way,* October, 1963, pp. 21-26.

MOORE, B. H., "Federal Valuation of Railroads In the U.S.," *AREA Bulletin No. 503,* American Railway Engineering Association, January 1, 1952.

MOORE, L. J., "Right of Way Procedure As Applied In the Province of British Columbia," *Right of Way,* February, 1954, pp. 13-14.

MORTIMER, J. R., "Highway Right of Way Valuation," *Journal; American Society of Farm Managers and Rural Appraisers,* April, 1959, pp. 65-68.

MOSES, ALEX I., "Contractors Problems In Obtaining Easement Grants for Extra High Voltage Transmission Lines," *Right of Way,* October, 1964, pp. 27-28.

MOSES, ALEX I., "Potestas," *Right of Way,* February, 1961, pp. 29-31.

MOSES, ALEX I., "Right of Way Acquisition," *Technical Valuation,* June, 1960, pp. 31-33.

MOSLEY, FRED M., "Rights of Way Over Navy Lands," *Right of Way,* December, 1955, pp. 13-15.

MULCAHY, JOHN V., "Fact or Fiction?. . . Transmission Line Easement," *The Real Estate Appraiser,* September, 1970, pp. 34-36.

MULCAHY, JOHN V., "Overhead Transmission Lines," *Right of Way,* April, 1959, pp. 7-16.

MURPHY, LEO A., "Reimbursement for Owner-Tenant Relocation," *Right of Way,* April, 1957, pp. 36,39.

NEALEY, MORGAN T. JR., "Acquisition of Lands for NASA'S Manned Lunar Landing Program, Cape Canaveral, Florida," *Right of Way,* October, 1963, pp. 7-12.

NELSON, EUGENE F., "Fundamentals of Acquiring Rights-Of-Way," *Selected Papers,* University of Alabama, Right of Way Conference, Alabama, 1956, pp. 33-43.

NELSON, RICHARD L., "Appraisal of Air Rights," *The Appraisal Journal,* October, 1955, pp. 495-508.

NELSON, RICHARD L., "New and Important Developments In Right-Of-Way Railroads," *Proceedings of the Eight Annual National Seminar,* American Right of Way Association, Washington, D. C, 1963, pp. 25-28.

NESS, OWEN M., "The Farmer and Rights of Way," *Right of Way,* April, 1964, pp. 21-24.

NICHOLS, FRED W., "Planning and Site Selection for Transmission Right of Way-How Why," *Right of Way,* June, 1959, pp. 7-10.

OPPERMAN, PAUL, "The Master Plan's Effect on Land and Property Development," *Right of Way,* August, 1954, pp. 20-26.

PAIGE, CLAYTON W., "Construction of De Bell Golf Course In the Cityof Burbank," *Right of Way,* April, 1958, pp. 35.

PARROTT, C. J., TVA's Appraiser Training Program," *Right of Way,* June, 1962, pp. 19-22.

PASS, HENRY, "The Negotiator," *Right of Way,* June, 1963, pp. 11-12.

PATRICK, R. W., "Need for Environmental and Aesthetic Feasibility Studies," *Right of Way,* February, 1971.

PEARSON, ALBIN S., "Courtroom Practicalities," *Right of Way,* December, 1962, pp. 23-30.

PECK, HOMER M., "Scenic Areas Along Wisconsin Highways," *Right of Way*, October, 1967, pp. 18-22.

PETERSON, CHARLES C. M., "Case of the Month," *Right of Way*, June, 1955, pp. 33-34, 40.

PETERSON, CHARLES C. M., "Injunction Vs. Condemnation," *Right of Way*, February, 1957, pp. 47-50.

PETERSON, WILLIAM H., "Case of the Month," *Right of Way*, February, 1957, pp. 19.

PHILIPS, L. A., "Problems Facing Electric Utilities In Obtaining Right of Way," *Right of Way*, August, 1959, pp. 37-39.

PHILLIPS, C. W., "Policy and Procedure," *Selected Papers, 1957*, Right of Way Conference, University of Ala., 1957, pp. 27-36.

PHILLIPS, C. W., "Right of Way Reimbursement Under Federal-Aid Procedure," *Right of Way*, October, 1960, pp. 21-28.

PILL, JOHN R., "Mineral Rights-Coal Lands," *The Appraisal Journal*, January, 1943, pp. 26.

PILMER, C. L., "The Effect of Pipelines on the Farming Operation And On Farm Land Values In Webster County, Iowa," *Right of Way*, December, 1969, pp. 33-40, 44-45.

PITT, JOHN E., "An Appraisal of Riparian Rights," *The Appraisal Journal*, January, 1954, pp. 89-94.

PITT, JOHN E., "Appraising Riparian Rights," *American Society to Appraisers Valuation Manual*, American Society of Appraisers, 1959, pp. 281.

PITTMAN, VIRGIL, "A Look at Right of Way Condemnation Proceedings," *Selected Papers, 1960*, Right of Way Conference, University of Ala., 1960.

POWERS, BENJ. M., "Leasehold Interest," *Right of Way*, August, 1955, pp. 43-44.

PRACTICAL LAND ECONOMIC STUDY PROGRAMS, *Proceedings of the Fourth Annual National Seminar, 1958*, American Right of Way Association, 1959, pp. 60-71.

PRACTICAL USE OF OUR LAND ECONOMIC STUDIES, *Proceedings of the Seventh Annual National Seminar, 1961*, American Right of Way Association, 1962, pp. 20-24.

PRYOR, FRANCIS D., "An Adequate Right of Way Appraisal," *Right of Way*, December, 1959, pp. 57-64.

RAMS, EDWIN M, "Economic Size and Value," *Right of Way*, June, 1962, pp. 48-52.

RAMS, EDWIN M., "Changing Rights-Changing Values," *The Residential Appraiser*, October, 1961, pp. 2-10.

RAMS, EDWIN M., "Market Analysis What Is it," *Right of Way*, April, 1961, pp. 27-30.

RANDALL, FRANK, "Easements," *Right of Way*, December, 1954, pp. 23-26.

RANDALL, WILLIAM J., "A Fair Compensable Award for Right-Of-Way Purposes," *Real Estate Analyst Appraisal Bulletin*, 1956, pp. 175-180.

RANKIN, DUDLEY L., "Special Problems of Pipeline Rights-Of-Way," *Right-Of-Way*, February, 1959, pp. 7-11.

RAY, RAYMOND, "Case of the Month," *Right of Way*, December, 1955, pp. 28-29.

REDEL, W. R., "Riparian Rights," *Appraisal Institute Magazine*, Appraisal Institute of Canada, Winnipeg.

REESE, LOUIE, "The Puzzle of the Power Line," *The Appraisal Journal*, October, 1967, pp. 555-560.

REZZOLLA, JOHN R. JR., "Valuation of Leased Fee and Leaseholds," *Right of Way*, April, 1960, pp. 25-30.

RHODES, RICHARD M., "Economic Effect of High Voltage Transmission Line Construction," *Right of Way*, February, 1971.

RICHTER, F. E., *The Telephone As an Economic Instrument.*

RIEMER, RICHARD L., "The Theory of Eminent Domain," *Right of Way,* April, 1971.

RIGHT OF WAY, "California Pioneers Novel Plan to House Freeway Displaces," *Right of Way,* April, 1971.

RIGHT OF WAY, "Digest of Important Appellate Court Decisions," *Right of Way,* October, 1961.

RIGHT OF WAY, "Highlights of the Electric Utility Right of Way Conference, 1957," *Right of Way,* October, 1957, pp. 51-78.

RIGHT OF WAY, "Report of Highway Research Board," *Right of Way,* June, 1969, pp. 29-30.

RIGHT OF WAY, "Right of Way In the Sky," *Right of Way,* June, 1961, pp. 15-25.

RIGHT OF WAY, "Should the Tenant Be Paid a Bonus to Move," *Right of Way,* October, 1956, pp. 5-6.

ROBERTS, JOHN A., "Appraisal of Commercial and Industrial Property," *Right of Way Conference,* 1957, pp. 100-115.

RODA, FRANK, "Legal Assumption by Appraisers," *Right of Way,* June, 1958, pp. 44-45.

ROGERS, JOHN D., "On Trial—The Attorney the Expert Witness and the Right of Way Agent," *Right of Way,* April, 1959, pp. 41-44.

ROSENCRANS, DAN, "Title Insurance Service In Right of Way Operations," *Right of Way,* February, 1962, pp. 26-28.

ROSENCRANS, DANIEL W., "Title Searches and Title Examinations for Highway Right of Ways, As Title Companies See it," *Right of Way,* April, 1954, pp. 15-19, 56-57.

SANDO, LAURENCE, "Theories of Valuation for Interim Use," *Proceedings of the Eighth Annual National Seminar,* American Right of Way Association, Washington, D. C, 1963.

SARMIENTO, EDUARDO, *Efficient Allocation of Resources In the Supply Of Water for Domestic Consumption,* University of Minnesota, 1971.

SAYRE, T. H., "Right of Way for Future Use, Encroachments, Zoning," *Proceedings of the Eighth Annual National Seminar, 1962,* American Right of Way Association, Washington, D. C, 1963.

SCHERER, L. F., "Relationship Between Engineer and Right of Way Agent In Pipeline Construction," *Right of Way,* April, 1956, pp. 7-10.

SCHMUTZ, GEORGE L., "Rights of Way and Easements," *The Appraisal Journal,* April, 1948, pp. 139-147.

SCHMUTZ, GEORGE L., "Valuation of Part Taken," *Condemnation Appraisers Handbook,* 1938, pp. 1-339.

SEARLES, SIDNEY Z., "Aesthetics In the Law," *Appraisal Digest,* 1901, pp. 1-7.

SHAW, EUGENE AIKEN, "Just Compensation In Takings Affecting Railroad Rights of Way," *Right of Way,* October, 1964, pp. 37-39.

SHELL, JOE L., "Trial of Condemnation Actions," *Right of Way,* April, 1955, pp. 26-30.

SHENKEL, WILLIAM M., "Community Benefits of an Industrial Park," *The Real Estate Appraisal,* 1911, pp. 24-36.

SIEMENS, HENRY J., "The Value of Pipeline Easements," *Appraisal Institute Magazine,* Appraisal Institute of Canada, Winnipeg.

SIMONSON, E. M., "Who Pays for the Utility Changes In Urban Renewals," *Right of Way,* October, 1963, pp. 31-38.

SINNITT, PAUL, "Case of the Month," *Right of Way,* 1956, pp. 27-29.

SMITH, FRANK A., "Right of Way Problems As They Affect the Engineer," *Right of Way,* April, 1957, pp. 25-32.

SMITH, FRANK A., "The Problems of Right of Way In Transmission of Coal by Pipeline," *Right of Way,* April, 1958, pp. 25-28.

▲ Appraisal for Special Purposes

SMITH, GILBERT A., "Acquisition of Access Rights," *Right of Way Conference, Selected Papers, 1956,* University of Alabama, University, Alabama, 1956, pp. 52-58.

SMITH, GUY V., "Significant Snare In Service Station Appraisal," *Right of Way,* August, 1970, pp. 41-53.

SMITH, J. J., "Multiple Use of Air Rights," *The Appraisal Journal,* February, 1969, pp. 53-59.

SMITH, LAMAR, "Wide Disparity In Appraised Values," *Right of Way Conference Selected Papers,* University of Alabama, University, Alabama, 1960, pp. 9-20.

SMITH, LAMAR H., "The Use of Market Data," *Right of Way Conference, Selected Papers, 1961,* University of Alabama, University, Alabama, 1961, pp. 45-48.

SMITH, LEONARD C., "The Bundle of Property Rights," *The Appraisal Journal,* October, 1956, pp. 485-489.

SNITZER, EDWARD L., "Increase or Decrease In Fair Market Value Because of a Future Condemnation," *The Real Estate Appraiser,* 1968, pp. 53-55.

SNITZER, EDWARD L., "The Navigational Servitude," *The Real Estate Appraiser,* June, 1968, pp. 49-51.

SNYDER, AREAS B., "They Can't Take My Ground!," *Right of Way,* February, 1957, pp. 23-29.

SPINDLE, JAMES A., "Underground Storage of Gas," *Right of Way,* February, 1956, pp. 7-11.

STACER, THOMAS C., "Rights of Way Through Timbered Areas," *Right of Way,* October, 1967, pp. 52-56.

STAMPER, F. A., "A Look at a Title and Abstract Plant," *Right of Way,* April, 1958, pp. 7-15.

STEWART, W. C., "Riparian and Littoral Rights," *The Appraisal Journal,* April, 1941, pp. 151-150.

STONE, ROBERT R., "The Right-Of-Way Agent In the Condemnation Trial," *American Association of State Highway Officials,* Acquisition for Right-Of-Way, Washington, D. C, 1962, pp. 103-108.

STONE, ROBERT R., "The Value of a Comparable Data Pool," *Right of Way,* October, 1959, pp. 33-34.

STORY, BEN H. JR., "Land Use Under and Adjacent to Overhead Transmission Lines," *Right of Way.*

STOVER, V. G., "A Study of Remainder Parcels Resulting from the Acquisition of Highway Rights of Way," *Dissertation Abstracts,* July, 1964, pp. 353.

STRAUB, ROBERT, "The Condemnation Law," *Right of Way Conference,* University of Alabama, 1956, pp. 9-15.

STRUKENS, H. H., "Appraisal of Rights of Way for Highway Purposes," *Technical Valuation,* pp. 25.

SYCHRAVA, L., "Some Thoughts on Feasibility Studies Occasioned by The Appraisal of Road Projects In Thailand," *Journal of Transport Economies and Policy,* September, 1968.

TAYLOR, FRANK H., "Acquiring Railroad Rights of Way," *National Real Estate Journal,* October, 1931, pp. 12-14.

TAYLOR, RICHARD., "Case of the Month," *Right of Way,* October, 1957, pp. 45.

THE AMERICAN INSTITUTE OF REAL ESTATE APPRAISERS, *Case Studies In Air Rights and Subsurface Tunnel Road Easements,* American Institute of Real Estate Appraisers, Chicago, 1900.

THE AMERICAN INSTITUTE OF REAL ESTATE APPRAISERS, *Case Studies In Air Rights and Subsurface Tunnel Road Easements,* American Institute of Real Estate Appraisers, Chicago, 1900.

THEISS, WILLIAM R., "Damages for Obstruction of Road Abutting Rural Property. Appraisal Docket," *The Appraisal Journal,* July, 1963, pp. 415-417.

# BIBLIOGRAPHY OF APPRAISAL LITERATURE

THEISS, WILLIAM R., "The Appraisal Docket. Compensation for Impairment of Access," *The Appraisal Journal*, October, 1962, pp. 547-548.

THEISS, WILLIAM R., "The Appraisal Docket. Computing Damages for Restriction of Access for Retail Use Only," *The Appraisal Journal*, October, 1964, pp. 612-613.

THIEL, FLOYD I., "A State-Federal Program of Land Economic Studies," *Right of Way*, June, 1967, pp. 28-31.

THIEL, FLOYD I., "Progress In Highway Severance Studies," *Right of Way*, April, 1966, pp. 25-29.

THOMPSON, GLENN P., "Fee Land In Lieu of Right of Way," *Right of Way*, October, 1957, pp. 39-44.

THOMPSON, GLENN P., "The Effect of Pipeline Easements on the Value of Real Estate," *Right of Way*, August, 1959, pp. 15-20.

THOMPSON, LOREN L., "Air Rights Today and Tomorrow," *Right of Way*, June, 1965, pp. 5-8.

THORNTON, W. B., "Procedure In the Acquisition of Right of Way," *Right of Way*, October, 1956, pp. 33-34.

THORNTON, W. B., "The Use and Value of Forest Land for Transmission and Pipeline Right of Way," *Right of Way*, December, 1960, pp. 19-21.

TODD, CARL L., "Air Rights-Some Valuation Points and Philosophies," *Valuation*, pp. 35-44.

TOWL, BURL A. JR., "Encroachments on Existing Rights of Way," *Right of Way*, October, 1958, pp. 17-19.

TOWL, BURL A. JR., "General Highway and Right of Way Conflicts and Problems," *Right of Way*, June, 1960, pp. 29-34.

TREADWAY, F. H. JR. M. A. I., *Impact of Electric Power Transmission Line Easements on Real Estate Values*, American Institute of Real Estate Appraisers, October, 1972.

TRENHOLM, KENNETH M., "Right of Way Agent and Appraiser Relationship In Eminent Domain Proceedings," *Technical Valuation*, February, 1961, pp. 21-23.

TRUEHEART, LAWRENCE G., "A Right of Way Engineer's Views of the New Federal Highway Program," *Right of Way*, December, 1947, pp. 17-22.

TRUEHEART, LAWRENCE G., "Mission, Buy 17, 500 Acres, Quick," *Right of Way*, August, 1956, pp. 13-19.

TURNER, HOWARD M., "The Engineering Valuation of Water Rights," *Appraisal and Valuation Manual*, 1961, pp. 137-146.

U. S. FEDERAL WORKS AGENCY, *Bibliography on Land Acquisition for Public Roads*, Public Roads Administration, Washington, 1947.

VAN BUREN, DEWITT, "Appraisal of Estates In Land Less Than the Fee," *The Appraisal Journal*, October, 1943, pp. 327-335.

VAN HORN, ALAN J., "Pipeline Problems," *The Right of Way*, February, 1971.

VANDERMARK, W. R., "Reviewing Appraisal Reports," *The Right of Way*, American Right of Way Association, Los Angeles, 1968, pp. 283-290.

VANDERPOOL, TOM, "Appraising Access or Abutter's Rights," *Journal of the American Society of Farm Managers and Rural Appraisers*, October, 1956, pp. 38-42.

VANDERPOOL, TOM, "The Appraiser Vs. the Right-Of-Way Agent," *The Valuation Manual*, 1956, pp. 147.

WAGNER, C. RAY, "Pipe Lines and Storage Tanks," *The Appraisal Journal*, July, 1967, pp. 412-416.

WAGNER, E. F., "Appraising Properties for Freeway Acquistion," *Technical Valuation*, October, 1954, pp. 23-24.

WAGNER, E. F., "Should Tenants Be Subsidezed for Cost of Moving Due to Public Improvements?," *Right of Way*, April, 1957, pp. 37-38.

WALLEY, BEN H., "Accomodation of Utilities, Compensability Requirements," *The Right of Way*, February, 1969, pp. 12-16.

WALLEY, ERSEL, "Condemnation and Appraising for Pipeline Installations," *Journal of the American Society of Farm Managers and Rural Appraisers*, April, 1957, pp. 61-68.

WALLIS, L. J., "Area Computations," *Acquisition for Right-Of-Way*, American Association of State Highway Officials, Washington, D. C., 1962, pp. 221-231.

WALSH, J. F., "Some Untechnical Thoughts on Land Titles In Right of Way Work," *Right of Way*, June, 1956, pp. 27-33.

WALTON, L. ELLIS FR., "The Interstate System a Return on Investment Analysis: Its Implications for Land Economic Studies," *Right of Way*, February, 1971.

WATTLES, GURDON H., "When Is a Line," *Right of Way*, October, 1960, pp. 51-58.

WATTLES, GURDON H., "When Is a Monument?," *Right of Way*, August, 1957, pp. 23-29.

WATTS, JOHN F., "Appraisal of the Alpaugh Irrigation Water Rights In Kern County, California," *Appraisal and Valuation Manual*.

WEBB, JOHN C., "The Comparative Approach," *Right of Way*, February, 1958, pp. 19-20.

WEHER, ROBERT H., DONA H. BAKER, JR, "Mineral Production In New Mexico In 1970," *New Mexico Business*, University of New Mexico, May, 1971, pp. 3-16.

WELLS, REX I., "Guidelines for Environmental Considerations In the Federal Highway Program," *Appraisal and Valuation Manual*, Corporate Press Incorporated, Washington, D. C, January, 1972, pp. 328.

WHITE, RAYMOND W., "Role of Private Companies In Conservation and Development of Water Resources," *Right of Way*, December, 1957, pp. 23-30.

WHITESIDE, ALBA, "Inverse Condemnation, Invasion of Air Rights," *Right of Way*, February, 1969, pp. 12-16.

WHITLEY, B. J., "Acquisition Procedure of Tennessee Gas Transmission Company," *Right of Way*, October, 1957, pp. 21-24.

WHITT, GLENN L., "Policy and Procedure on Relocation of Utility Facilities-California Division of Highways," *Right of Way*, June, 1963, pp. 13-16.

WILLIAMS, VICTOR F., "Impact of Right of Way Acquisition on the Housing Situation In Louisville, Kentucky," *Right of Way*, August, 1968, pp. 18-20.

WRIGHT, CARROLL, "Appraisal of Rural Lands for Highway Improvements," *The Appraisal Journal*, January, 1959, pp. 88-94.

WRIGHT, ROBERT R., *The Law of Airspace*, Bobbs-Merrill Company, Indianapolis, 1968, pp. 1-575.

WRIGHT, WALTER T., "Right of Way Role In Route Location," *Right of Way*, October, 1963, pp. 61-64.

YOUNG, FRANK I., "The Right of Way In the Operational Environment of Commercial Flight," *Right of Way*, December, 1969, pp. 24-29.

YOUNG, G. I. M., "Feasibility Studies," *Right of Way*, October, 1969, pp. 40-47.

YOUNG, H. J., AND R. S. THORSELL, "Environment, Economics, and Electric Utility Rights of Way," *Right of Way*, October, 1970, pp. 41-43.

ZETTEL, RICHARD M., "The Effect of Limited--Access Highways on Property and Business Values," *Right of Way*, June, 1954, pp. 9-12, 41-45.

*Case Studies In Air Rights and Subsurface Tunnel Road Easements*, American Institute of Real Estate Appraisers.

"Actual Appraisal Repts: No 17 Valuation of 1 Zone of Right of Way of a Rallroad Thru a Farming Sec.," *National Real Estate Journal*, N. R. E. J, December 7, 1931, pp. 15-18.

# BIBLIOGRAPHY OF APPRAISAL LITERATURE

"Advantages of a Practical Liasion Between Highways, Utilities and Other Affected Agencies," *Right of Way Conference Selected Papers,* University of Alabama, Alabama, 1959, pp. 31-34.

"Aerial Walkways Big Plans for the Future," *Business Week,* December 26, 1970, pp. 48-49.

"Airport-A Store Design with Entertaimment and Efficiency," *Stores,* November, 1970, pp. 4-5.

"Divergencies In Right of Way Valuations," *Appraisal Journal,* October, 1971, pp. 485-494.

"Fantasy or Fact, Do Electric Power Lines Damage Adjacent Property," *Right of Way,* June, 1967, pp. 20-23.

"The Legal Angle, Current Trends & Decisions In Emnt Domain & Rt of Way & How They Affect Real Estate," *The Appraisal Journal,* July, 1968, pp. 431.

, "Effect of High Pressure Gas Transmsn Pipelines on Real Estate Vals In N. J. Metropolitan Area," *Right of Way,* February, 1958, pp. 21, 24.

"Mut Responsbls of States & Bur of Publ Roads In Acquisitn of Rights of Way," *Right of Way Conference,* University of Alabama, 1962.

## 12-17  Revaluations

APPEL, JAMES R., "Market Analysis for a Reuse Appraisal," *The Real Estate Analyst Appraisal Bulletin,* 1957, pp. 25-28.

BEATON, J. WALLACE, "Preparing for Valuation Day," *Appraisal Institute Magazine,* Appraisal Institute of Canada, Winnipeg, March 1, 1972.

BELLANCA, ALFONSO V., "Revaluation and After the Buffalo Report," *Assesment Administration,* IAAO, Chicago, 1960, pp. 77-80.

BERNARD, BOYD T., "Problems Encountered In Re-Use Appraisal," *Technical Valuation,* 1960, pp. 62.

BROWN, G. FAIRFAX, "Supervision of Revaluation Projects," *Assessment Administration,* IAAO, Chicago, 1962, pp. 96-101.

CHAMBERLAIN, NARCISSA, *Old Rooms for New Living,* Hastings House.

CHEN, H. Y., "Valuation Under Uncertainty," *Journal of Finance and Quantitative Analysis,* September, 1967, pp. 313-326.

CLARK, HORACE F., "Bibliography," *Appraising the Home,* 1930, pp. 239-240.

CLARK, HORACE F., "Controlling the Valuation During Modernization," *Appraising the Home,* 1930, pp. 122-128.

CLARK, HORACE F., "Cubic Foot Contents," *Appraising the Home,* 1930, pp. 263-273.

CLARK, HORACE F., "Value Analysis," *Appraising the Home,* 1930.

CLEMINSHAW, J. M., "The Revaluation of Municipalities for Tax Equalization Purposes," *The Appraisal Journal,* January, 1944, pp. 52-65.

COLE, JOHN D., "The Revaluation of a City," *The Appraisal Journal,* January, 1960, pp. 47-50.

COMMITTEE FROM FIVE PRINCIPAL FEDERAL AGENCIES, *A Glossary of Housing Terms,* Washington, 1931.

COOMBE, J. P., "Maintenance of Equalized Assessments After a Revaluation Program," *Technical Valuation,* June, 1961, pp. 55-57.

DAVIS, CLAUDE J., *West Virginia State Wide Reappraisal Program,* 1900.

HART, ALAN F., "Maintaining a Revaluation Program," *New Jersey Municipalities,* February, 1961, pp. 9-12.

INTERNATIONAL ASSOCIATION OF ASSESSING OFFICERS, *Revaluation Projects, Report of the Committee on Revaluation Projects,* IAAO, Chicago, 1960.

MAJOR, E. ROWLAND, "Why Revaluation," *Technical Valuation,* June, 1957, pp. 9-13.

OLSON, LYLE H., "Reappraisals and Major Adjustments In Property Values," *National Association of Cost Accountants, Bulletin,* May 1, 1932, pp. 1155-1167.

PROCOS, DIMITRI, *Mixed Land Use Past Record and Future Prospects,* School of Architecture, Nova Scotia Canada.

RATCLIFF, WILBUR S. JR., "Revaluation of Charleston Country," *Assessment Administration,* Institute of American Assesmt Adminis Officers, Chicago, 1961, pp. 39-61.

SMITH, W. LAURENCE, AND HERBERT B. PATT, "History of a Revaluation Lease," *The Appraisal Journal,* April, 1952, pp. 225-231.

STERLING, R. R., R. E. FLAHERTY, "Role of Liquidity In Exchange Valuation," *Accounting Review,* July, 1971, pp. 441-456.

VIEIRO, RAUL OSCAR, *Revaluacion Impositiva,* 1960, pp. 10120.

WHITE, JOHN R., "Re-Use Land Appraising," *Appraisal Digest,* January, 1959, pp. 18-21.

ZEPP, EDWARD G., M.A.I., "Quotes for Re-Appraisal," *The Appraiser,* September, 1967.

# 12-18 Partial Acquisitions

ALDIS, GRAHAM, "The Valuation of Remainders," *The Appraisal Journal,* October, 1938, pp. 358-359.

ALEXANDER, WILLIAM E., "A Pitfall In Partial Taking Appraisal," *The Real Estate Appraiser,* August, 1965, pp. 38-40.

AMERICAN RIGHT OF WAY ASSOCIATION, "Just Compensation Concepts In Eminent Domain," *Proceeding of the Sixth Annual National Seminar, 1960,* Washington, D. C, 1961.

APPRAISAL JOURNAL, "Compensation In the Condemnation of Public Utilities," *The Appraisal Journal,* January, 1947, pp. 125-126.

APPRAISAL JOURNAL, "Just Compensation for a Temporary Use," *The Appraisal Journal,* April, 1945, pp. 177-181.

APPRAISAL JOURNAL, "No Severance Damages for Taking of Leasehold," The Appraisal Journal, January, 1951, pp. 129-130.

ARKANSAS LEGISLATIVE COUNCIL, *Reimbursement of Public Utlities for Relocation Facilities on State Highway Rights of Way,* Arkansas Legislative Council, Little Rock, 1958.

BAUMGARTNER, HAMPTON, JR., "Adequacy of Compensation In Federal Condemnation," *The Appraisal Journal,* January, 1963, pp. 36-47.

BERNARD, W. C., "Do Public Improvements Create Special Benefits," *The Appraisal Journal,* January, 1945, pp. 20-23.

BICKLEY, N. ALEX, "Compensable and Non-Compensable Damages," *Proceeding of the Second Institute on Eminent Domain,* Dallas, 1960, pp. 31-60.

BISHOP, MAURICE F., "Non-Compensable Damages In Eminent Domain Proceedings," *Selected Papers of a Right of Way Conference,* University of Alabama, 1957, pp. 16-26.

BLACK, LEON D., "Fair Market Value and Just Compensation," *Technical Valuation,* October, 1960, pp. 37-43.

BROOKER, HERBERT D., "A Suggested Technique for the Appraisal of a Partial Taking from an Office Building," *Right of Way,* October, 1970, pp. 34-38.

BROWNELL, KEITH W., *Partial Taking of Agricultural Land In Transition to Urban Use,* Condemnation Appraisal Seminar, 1958.

BURNS, ROBERT L., "Damages and Benefits from Constitutional Damaging and Partial Taking--Community or Special?," *Proceedings of the Third Institute on Eminent Domain 1961,* Dallas, 1961, pp. 119-138.

CAMPBELL, ROBERT S., JR., "The Limited Access Highway--Some Aspects of Compensation," *Right of Way,* February, 1963, pp. 29-35.

CARTER, JAMES M., "How to Make Compensation Just," *Right of Way,* June, 1958, pp. 21-26.

COVEY, FRANK M. JR., "Frontage Roads, to Compensate or Not to Compensate," *The Appraisal Journal,* May, 1963, pp. 236-253.

CRAWFORD, CLAUDE O., "Demonstration Appraisal of Partial Takings from Income Producing Properties," *Right of Way,* October, 1959, pp. 11-17.

CROUCH, WILLIAM H., "The Meaning of Just Compensation," *Condemnation Appraisal Practice,* A. I. R. E. A., Chicago, 1967, pp. 3-25.

CROUCH, WILLIAM H., "The Meaning of Just Compensation," *The Appraisal Journal,* April, 1960, pp. 193-208.

CROUCH, WILLIAM H., "What Does Just Compensation Mean to the Appraiser," *The Appraisal Journal,* April, 1960, pp. 193-208.

DARSEY, GLENN S., "General and Special Benefits to Remainder In Partial Takings," *Valuation Manual,* American Society of Appraisers, 1961, pp. 329.

DAVIS, W. D., "Estimation of Severance Damages In Partial Acquisition Following the Law of North Carolina," *Right of Way,* December, 1961, pp. 19-24.

DERBES, MAX J. JR., "Partial Taking Appraisal," *The Residential Appraisal,* pp. 22-24.

DOLAN, HARRY T., "Just Compensation Indemnity or Market Value," *The Appraisal Journal,* July, 1966, pp. 353-358.

DOLAN, HARRY T., "Just Compensation and the General Motors Case," *The Appraisal Journal,* July, 1945, pp. 249-255.

DOLAN, HARRY T., "Just Compensation from Government Standpoint," *Appraisal Digest,* July, 1958, pp. 1-5.

EDMAN, J. .J., "Compensation for Taking of a Camp. Appraisal Docket," *The Appraisal Journal,* July, 1957, pp. 449-450.

EDMAN, J. J., "Compensation In Taking Dams. Appraisal Docket," *The Appraisal Journal,* October, 1960, pp. 546-548.

EDMAN, J. J., "Severance Damages to One Tract for Taking of Another. Appraisal Docket," *The Appraisal Journal,* July, 1959, pp. 410.

EDMAN, J. J., "The Appraisal Docket. Water Seepage Constitutes Taking of Property," *The Appraisal Journal,* April, 1961, pp. 260-261.

ENFIELD, CLIGTON W., "The Limitations of Access In Partial Takings," *The Appraisal Journal,* January, 1959, pp. 31-40.

EVANS, JOHN M., "Practice and Procedure In Partial Takings," *Right of Way,* September, 1959, pp. 27-36.

FAVA, EDWARD, *Valuation In Condemnation - Partial Taking,* American Society of Appraisers, 1958, pp. 261-266.

FAVA, EDWARD, "Appraising Partial Taking of a Gasoline Service Center," *Appraisal and Valuation Manual,* 1961, pp. 89-95.

GARRET, H. J., "Reservoirs-Partial Taking and Easements," *Journal of the American Society of Farm Managers and Rural Appraisers*, April, 1962, pp. 121-126.

GLEAVES, MILNOR E., "Lawful Compensation In Eminent Domain," *Technicalities and Technical Valuation*, February, 1952, pp. 40-41.

HALEY, JOHN L., "Perilous Remainder Studies," *The Appraisal Journal*, October, 1966, pp. 22-24.

HALL, THOMAS H. III, BEATON, WILLIAM R, "A Partial Taking of School Grounds and the Demand for a Substitute Facility," *The Appraisal Journal*, January, 1968, pp. 73-83.

HALL, THOMAS H. III, WILLIAM, R. B, "Partial Taking of a Cemetery with a Contingent Liability," *The Appraisal Journal*, January, 1967, pp. 107-115.

HANNOCH, FRANKLIN, "A Partial Taking Appraisal," *Appraisal Reporting Techniques*, American Institute of Real Estate Appraisers, 1949, pp. 25-41.

HARRIS, EDWARD F., "Valuing the Remainder," *Right of Way*, June, 1958, pp. 46-47.

HODGES, M. B. JR., "Compensation Without Condemnation," *The Appraisal Journal*, October, 1967, pp. 581-582.

HYDER, K. LEE, ANDREW C. HAMILTON, "The Borrowing Of Private Property for Public Use," *The Appraisal Journal*, July, 1943, pp. 252-268.

JENSEN, HOWARD I, "Partial Acquisition of a Farm Property," *Valutape Audio-Library*, American Society of Appraisers, Washington D.C., January 1, 1974.

KALTENBACH, HENRY J., "Just Compenstaion," *The Appraisal Real Estate*, 1956, pp. 456.

KELLOUGH, W. R., "Analysis and Theoretical Implications of Partial Taking," *Valuation*, September, 1972, pp. 50.

KELLY, ED, "Cost to Cure, Just Compensation," *Valuation*, ASA, Washington, September, 1968, pp. 44.

KREVOR, HENRY H., "Legislative Changes and Trends Affecting Compensation In Eminent Domain," *Right of Way*, August, 1961, pp. 23-29.

LANEY, T. D., "Condominiums," *Skyscraper Management*, June, 1970, pp. 10-13.

LEWIS, HARRISON, "Damage Due to Police Power Exercised In Conjunction with a Taking," *The Appraisal Journal*, October, 1962, pp. 481-488.

LINDAS, LEONARD I., "The Measure of Compensation," *Acquisition for Right of Way*, American Association of State Highway Officials, Washington, D. C, 1962, pp. 33-39.

LUM, Y. T., "Problems In Achieving Just Compensation from the Viewpoint of he Appraiser," *Right of Way*, August, 1970.

MACBRIDE, DEXTER D., "Condemnation, Compensation and the Courts," *Proceedings*, American Bar Association National Institute, St. Louis, September, 1968.

MACBRIDE, DEXTER D., "History and Meaning of Just Compensation," *Proceedings*, Third Annual Legal Right of Way & Utility Seminar, University of Nevada, August, 1966.

MACLEOD, ROBERT R., "Adequacy of Compensation In Condemnation," *The Appraisal Journal*, October, 1963, pp. 477-482.

MCCURDY, ROBERT V., "Elements of Damage In Partial Takings," *The Real Estate Appraiser*, December, 1963, pp. 2-13.

MCGOUGH, B. C., "The Concepts and Practices for Compensation In Eminent Domain," *The Real Estate Appraiser*, March, 1969, pp. 44-47.

NUGENT, R. A. L., "Compensation for Expropriation," *Appraisal Institute Magazine*, March, 1962, pp. 27-31.

PAWLEY, ROBERT W., AND N. G. MACARTHUR, "Compensation for the Taking of Marshland Used for Hunting and Fishing," *Appraisal Institute Magazine,* May, 1959, pp. 22-24.

PINNELL, W. GEORGE, "An Alternate Approach to Highway Partial Takings," *The Appraisal Journal,* January, 1961, pp. 17-52.

RALEIGH, JAMES C., "Compensation Without Condemnation," *The Appraisal Journal,* April, 1967, pp. 256-259.

RAMS, EDWARD M., "Valuation of Partial Estates and Interests In Real Estate," *Technical Valuation,* June, 1956, pp. 16-19.

RODMAN, JAMES A. JR., "Partial Takings," *The Residential Appraiser,* December, 1957, pp. 17-18.

ROETTGER, G. J., "Just Compensation Frustration of an Owners Plans," *Appraisal Journal,* October, 1971, pp. 500-507.

ROGERS RUSSELL R., "Partial Taking," *The Appraisal Journal,* July, 1957, pp. 393-403.

SAAW, JOE S., "Adequate Compensation," *The Review,* February, 1945, pp. 15.

SHAW, EUGENE AIKEN, "Just Compensation In Takings Affecting Railroad Rights of Way," *Right of Way,* October, 1964, pp. 37-39.

STEWART, GRAEME, "Oh Is Market Value Just Compensation?," *The Appraisal Journal,* October, 1967, pp. 579.

STRUKENS, H. H., "The Economics of Partial Taking of Farm Units," *Journal of the American Society of Farm Managers and Rural Appraisers,* October, 1961, pp. 15-19.

WORSHAM, JOSEPH I., "Problems Peculiar to Partial Taking In Condemnation," *Proceedings of Fourth Institute on Emt Domain,* 1959.

## 12-19 Highest and Best Use

ABELMANN, WILLIAM W., "How to Estimate Highest and Best Use," *Real Estate Appraisal Practice,* American Institute of Real Estate Appraisers; Chicago, 1958, pp. 6-10.

ARMSTRONG, CHARLES VINCENT, "Industrial Property Records; Valuation Uses," *The Iowa State College Bulletin,* 1944.

ASHTON, MORRIS B., "Highest and Best Use," *The Appraisal Journal,* January, 1939, pp. 54-60.

ASSOC CERTIFIED & CORPORATE ACCOUNTANTS COMMITTEE, "Accounting for Inflation: Study of Techniques Under Conditions of Changing Price Levels," Gee, London, 1952.

BABCOCK, FREDERICK M., "Highest and Best Use," *Right of Way,* June, 1958, pp. 31-32.

BABCOCK, HENRY A., "On the Valuation of Land Awaiting Conversion to a Higher Use," *The American Mathematical Monthly,* March, 1933, pp. 147-153.

BONE, DAVID M., "The Concept of Highest and Best Use As Applied to Mass Appraisals," *Assessment Administration,* IAAO, Chicago, 1965, pp. 93-95.

BUREAU OF POWER, *Recreation Facility Cost and Design Use, New Release Number17581,* Federal Power Commission, Washington D. C, June 16, 1971.

CHEN, H. Y., "Valuation Under Uncertainty," *Journal of Finance and Quantitative Analysis,* September, 1967, pp. 313-326.

CHERNEY, RICHARD A., "Appraisal Principle of Highest and Best Use In Assessing Urban Vacant Land," *The Assessors Journal,* April, 1966, pp. 27-34.

CHERNEY, RICHARD A., "The Principle of Highest and Best Use," *The Real Estate Appraiser,* February, 1964, pp. 12-15.

CLICKNER, EDWIN K., "Highest Land Use As a Planning Tool," *The Appraisal Journal,* April, 1969, pp. 215-223.

CONLEE, DONALD R., "Commercial Property-Its Highest and Best Use," *The Real Estate Appraiser,* May, 1964, pp. 24-27.

CROUCH, WILLIAM H., "A Perspective Look at Highest and Best Use," *The Appraisal Journal,* April, 1966, pp. 166-176.

DARIO GONZALEZ, RUBEN, "El Concepto Del Uso Mejor Y Mas Productivo," *Boletin,* Sotave, Caracas, Venezuela, pp. 39-42.

DARK, TAYLOR, "The Rationale of Highest and Best Use," *The Real Estate Appraiser,* 1900, pp. 15.

DOLMAN, JOHN P., "A Closer Look at Highest and Best Use," *Buildings,* May, 1959, pp. 54-55.

DOLMAN, JOHN P., "Highest and Best Use," *Appraisal Digest,* January, 1960, pp. 22-24.

DRUCKER, E. R., "Review & Study of Highest & Best Use Concept," *Appraisal Institute Magazine,* Appraisal Institute of Canada, Winnipeg.

HAYES, TOM JR., "Service Station Highest and Best Use?," *The Appraisal Journal,* April, 1966, pp. 299-300.

HIGHMARK, LOUIS A., "Legal Aspects of Highest and Best Use and Value," *The Appraisal Journal,* January, 1956, pp. 33-41.

HOTELLING, HAROLD, "A General Mathematical Theory of Depreciation," *Journal American Statistical Association,* March, 1925, pp. 340-353.

INGLIS, E. R., "Site Value and Rating Procedures," *Appraisal Institute Magazine,* Appraisal Institute of Canada, Winnipeg.

JOHNSON, EARLE VINCENT, "A Problem In Location," *The Review,* September, 1955, pp. 11-14.

JOHNSON, LYLE R, SHAPIRO, ELI, OLMEARA JR, JOSEPH, "Valuation of Closely Held Stock for Federal Tax Purposes: Approach to an Objective Method," *Law Review,* University of Pennsylvania, November 1, 1951, pp. 170.

KAIN, J. F., AND QUIGLEY, J. M., "Measuring the Value of Housing Quality," *American Statistical Association Journal,* June, 1970, pp. 532-48.

KEENE, J., "Convert it to a Condominium," *House and Home,* January, 1971, pp. 106-111.

KENNEDY, DONALD A., "The Value of a Non-Conforming Use," *Technical Valuation,* February, 1960, pp. 9-10.

LOSTETTER, EARL K., "The Appraisal of Land Not Zoned to Its Highest and Best Use," *The Real Estate Appraiser,* January, 1963, pp. 36-39.

LUM Y. T., "The Highest and Best Use," *The Real Estate Appraiser,* SREA, Chicago, June, 1966, pp. 2.

MANDELLO, R., "Relationship Between Zoning and Appraisal," *Appraisal Institute Magazine,* Appraisal Institute of Canada, Winnipeg.

MATHUR, G., "The Valuation of Human Capital for Manpower Planning," *Applied Economic Papers,* September, 1964.

PENNY, A. L., "Highest and Best Use," *Appraisal Institute Magazine,* Appraisal Institute of Canada, Winnipeg.

PROCOS, DIMITRI, *Mixed Land Use Past Record and Future Prospects,* School of Architecture, Nova Scotia Canada.

RAMS, EDWIN M., "Comment on Highest and Best Use," *Technical Valuation,* February, 1957, pp. 55-56.

ROBBINS, RICHARD M., ROBERT A. JOHNSON, CRAIG HUBBARD, "Highest and Best Use," *The Appraisal Journal, Xxxvi,* April, 1968, pp. 255-261.

ROBICHEK, A. A., S. C. MYERS, "Valuation of the Firm Effects of Uncertainty In a Market Context," *The Journal of Finance,* May, 1966.

ROWLSON, JOHN F., "Highest and Best Use," *The Real Estate Appraiser,* April, 1966, pp. 8-12.

SIMMONS, MERCER W., "Testing for the Highest and Best Use," *The Residential Appraiser,* December, 1962, pp. 6-8.

STOTTLE, BURR S., "Reasonable Probability--Exception to the Rule," *The Appraisal Journal,* January, 1962, pp. 55-60.

TAYLOR, THOMAS L., "Highest and Best Use Factor In Condemnation," *Appraisal and Valuation Manual,* American Society of Appraisers, 1959, pp. 287-292.

WAGNER, PERCY E., "The Highest and Best Use of the Site," *Journal of Certified Property Managers,* June, 1940, pp. 328-338.

WALTHER, H. O., "Correlation of Data and the Value of Estimate," *Review of the Society of Residential Appraisers,* May, 1937, pp. 3-5.

WALTHER, HERMAN O., "The Principle of Highest and Best Use of Land Valuation," *Assessment Administration,* IAAO, Chicago, 1963, pp. 79-81.

WHIPPLE, R. T. M., "What Determines the Highest and Best Use?," *Appraisal Institute Magazine,* March, 1963, pp. 20-27.

WHITE, CARL, "Current Matters Affecting Public Utilities In the Valuation Concept," *Appraisal and Valuation Manual,* Corporate Press Incorporated, Washington, D. C, January, 1972, pp. 366.

WHITE, EDWARD L., "Appraising from Plans and Specifications," *The Real Estate Appraiser,* June, 1966, pp. 13-26.

YANUS, MUHAMMAD, PH. D., *Optimal Allocation of Multipurpose Reservoir Water A Dynamic Programing Model,* Vanderbilt University, 1971.

# 12-20 Expropriation

BAKER, J. ALAN, "Special Factors In Appraising for Expropriation," *Appraisal Institute Magazine,* March, 1960, pp. 17-18.

BEETH, CHANNING C., "Appraisers In Court," *The Review,* September, 1954, pp. 3-6.

BERTRAND R. MRS., "The Land Compensation Act 1973," *The Valuer,* The Incorporated Society of Valuers & Auctioneers, London, November 1, 1973, pp. 395-400.

BLAIR, D. GORDON, "Canadian Expropriation Act," *Appraisal Institute Magazine,* Appraisal Institute of Canada, Winnipeg.

COHN, WALTER W., "The Art of Testifying In Appraisal Cases," *Practical Appraising Methods,* 1940, pp. 126-128.

CORUCH, WILLIAM H., "Pretrial Conference Checklist of Factors Affecting Valuation," *The Appraisal Journal,* October, 1964, pp. 523-530.

CRAIG, R. H., "Preparation of Evidence for Presentation In Court," *Appraisal Institute Magazine,* Appraisal Institute of Canada, Winnipeg.

CRONK, E. A., "Expropriation - Powers and Procedures," *Appraisal Institute Magazine,* Appraisal Institute of Canada, Winnipeg, March 1, 1972.

▲ Appraisal for Special Purposes

DAVIS, ROBERT A., "Expropriation Appraisal Farm Lands," *Appraisal Institute Magazine,* July, 1957, pp. 10-14.

DUNN, DOMINICK R., "Some Reflections on Value In Eminent Domain Proceedings," *The Appraisal Journal,* July, 1956, pp. 415-1.

EATON, KEITH E., "Federal Expropriation Problems," *Appraisal Institute Magazine,* May, 1958, pp. 33-40.

EDMAN, J. J., "The Appraisal Docket. Sales Under Pressure Are Not Evidence of Value," *The Appraisal Journal,* October, 1957, pp. 623-624.

ELLIOTT, E. N. R., "Pitfalls of Expropriation Appraising In Canada," *The Real Estate Appraiser,* Society of Real Estate Appraisers, Chicago, July, 1964, pp. 29.

FARSTAD, E. KARL, "Market Value for Expropriation Purposes--As Seen by an Appraiser," *Appraisal Institute Magazine,* December, 1960, pp. 10-16.

FERBOS, JACQUES, *Expropriation Et Evaluation Des Biens,* Editions De L Actualite Juridique, Paris, 1965.

GLOS, HAROLD V., "Expert Appraisal Testimony Requires More Knowledge Today," *Real Estate,* February 25, 1939, pp. 10-12.

HAMILTON, ANDREW C., "Judicial Review of Appraisals," *The Appraisal Journal,* October, 1934, pp. 80-82.

HANSON, PETER, "Data Schedules," *Condemnation Appraisal Procedure,* Hanson and Pollard, pp. 259-269.

KLINCK, J. R., "Some Thoughts on Expropriation," *Appraisal Institute Magazine,* Appraisal Institute of Canada, Winnipeg.

KREVOR, HENRY H., *A Congressional Study of Just Compensation,* American Society of Appraisers, 1962, pp. 16-27.

LAMPORT, A. W., "How Do Subsequent Expropriations Affect Value," *Appraisal Institute Magazine,* September, 1963, pp. 9-10.

LAYCRAFT, J. H., "The Expropriation Procedures Act," *Appraisal Institute Magazine,* December, 1962, pp. 30-34.

LEVIT, BERT W., "The Expert Witness," *The Appraisal Journal,* July, 1939, pp. 219-226.

LIRETTE, PAUL E., "Expropriation-Louisiana Procedure," *Right of Way,* February, 1956, pp. 19-25.

MACBRIDE, DEXTER D., *Power and Process, Monograph No. 1,* American Society of Appraisers.

MORDEN, J. W., "Expropriation, Compensation, Business Damages," *Appraisal Institute Magazine,* Appraisal Institute of Canada, Winnipeg.

MORDEN, J. W., "The McCruer Report on Expropriation," *Appraisal Institute Magazine,* Appraisal Institute of Canada, Winnipeg.

NUGENT, R. A. L., "Compensation for Expropriation," *Appraisal Institute Magazine,* March, 1962, pp. 27-31.

POLLARD, W. L., "Market Value," *Condemnation Appraisal Procedure,* Hanson, Peter, and Pollard, 1934, pp. 413-434.

RAMOS MARTINEZ, JOSE A., "Naturaleza Juridica En Procedimiento Exprop," *Boletin,* Sotave, Caracas, Venezuela, pp. 17-19.

RUPERT, JOHN F., "The Appraiser Prepares for Testimony," *The Real Estate Appraiser,* November 10, 1963, pp. 32-38.

SCHMUTZ, GEORGE L., "Parallels In Canadian-U. S. Expropriation," *The Review,* April, 1953, pp. 3-6.

SNITZER, EDWARD L., "Increase or Decrease In Fair Market Value Because of a Future Condemnation," *The Real Estate Appraiser,* 1968, pp. 53-55.

STEWART, J. H., "Appraisals for Expropriation," *Appraisal Institute Magazine,* Appraisal Institute of Canada, Winnipeg.

# BIBLIOGRAPHY OF APPRAISAL LITERATURE

STEWART, J. I., "Making the Appraisal for Expropriation," *Appraisal Institute Magazine*, May, 1958, pp. 21-32.

THORSON, J. T., "Expropriation by the Crown," *Appraisal Institute Magazine*, Appraisal Institute of Canada, Winnipeg.

TODD, ERIC C. E., *The Federal Expropriation Act*, The Carswell Company, Ltd., Toronto, May, 1973.

WAGNER, PERCY E., "A Defense of the Income Approach," *Proceesings of the Third Institute on Eminent Domain*, Dallas, 1961, pp. 151-180.

WILCOX, DONALD A., "Use of Appraisals by Negotiators," *Right of Way*, 1968, pp. 447.

YOUNG, G. I. M., "Expropriation Ambiguities Under Canadian Statutes," *Appraisal Institute Magazine*, June, 1960, pp. 7-11.

YOUNG, G. I. M., "Report of the Select Commitee on Expropriation," *Appraisal Institute Magazine*, September, 1963, pp. 15-19.

## 12-21 Appraisal for Employee Transfers

ALBRIGHT, ALLEN J., "Corporate Employee Transfers: Acid Test for the Appraiser," *The Real Estate Appraiser*, July, 1964, pp. 9..

BRENNER, MARSHALL H., *Impact of Corporate Moving, Real Estate Trends of the Real Estate Broker*, University of Southern California, September, 1971.

CASEMENT, R., "Pay As You Go: Moving People In the 1970's," *The Economist*, March 27, 1971.

DOHERTY, RICHARD M., "The Growing Problem of Relocation," *The Real Estate Appraiser*, February, 1963, pp. 20-25.

ENTREKEN, HENRY C. JR., "Appraiser's Role In Employee Transfer Programs," *The Appraisal Journal*, November, 1962, pp. 2-4.

GABLER, L. R., "Population Size As a Determinant of City Expenditures and Employment Some Further Evidence," *Land Ecomomics*, May, 1971, pp. 130.

GRAYSON, HARRY, "Real Estate Problems In Transfer of Personnel," *The Real Estate Appraiser*, November, 1963, pp. 21-23.

HANFORD, HENRY S., "The Appraisal-Help or Handicap to Employee Relocation," *Appraisal Digest*, April, 1970, pp. 2-6.

HANRAHAN, DANIEL C., "Purchase of Corporate Transferee Residences," *The Real Estate Appraiser*, September, 1966, pp. 24-29.

LYON, LEE M., "Two New Facets for Employee Relocation Evaluation," *Valuation*, February, 1968, pp. 11-20.

MACEACHRON, KEITH E., "The Appraiser and Corporate Employee Transfer Plans," *The Residential Appraiser*, December, 1961, pp. 2-8, 23.

MURPHY, LEO A., "Reimbursement for Owner-Tenant Relocation," *Right of Way*, April, 1957, pp. 36,39.

NOWAK, F, J., "New Concepts In Employee Relocation Appraising," *The Real Estate Appraiser*, January, 1968, pp. 31-33.

SMITH, WALLACE F., "The Relocation Dilemma," *The Appraisal Journal*, July, 1969, pp. 424-432.

## 12-22  Site Selection

AMERICAN DRUGGIST, "Shopping Center Site: Not All Gold," *American Druggist,* June 29, 1970, pp. 61.

APPRAISAL DIGEST, "The Price of Pride," *Urban Land,* January, 1956, pp. 8-9.

AYRES, J. M., "From the Ground Up Evolution of an Office Building, Building Operation Systems," *Skyscraper Management,* December, 1970, pp. PP16 20.

BUREAU OF POWER, *Recreation Facility Cost and Design Use, New Release Number17581,* Federal Power Commission, Washington D. C, June 16, 1971.

COX, W. E. JR., E. F. COOK, "Other Dimensions Involved In Shopping Center Preference," *Journal of Marketing,* October, 1970, pp. 12-17.

DOUD, LAURENCE F., "Actual Appraisal Reports: Appraisal of Land for Future Location of Manufacturing and Holder Plant," *National Real Estate Journal,* June, 1932, pp. 55-57.

FINCH, NELSON E., "Shopping Centers As Neighbors," *The Residential Appraiser,* June, 1957, pp. 14-15.

GRIFFITH, L. B., "Case Study of Location," *The Review,* June, 1952, pp. 8-9.

JOHNSON, EARLE VINCENT, "A Problem In Location," *The Review,* September, 1955, pp. 11-14.

LAND ECONOMICS, "Value-Added Vs. Property Taxation of Business: Effects on Industrial Location," *Land Economics,* May, 1971, pp. 150-157.

MITCHELL, RICHARD E., "Industrial Site Selection Outside Urban Centers," *The Appraisal Journal,* October, 1966, pp. 597-600.

NATIONAL REAL ESTATE JOURNAL, "Actual Appraisal Reports - Small Walk-Up Apartment Building," *National Real Estate Journal,* April 13, 1931, pp. 42-44.

NATIONAL REAL ESTATE JOURNAL, "Actual Appraisal Reports - Valuation for Standard Oil Co Of New York," *National Real Estate Journal,* August 3, 1931, pp. 24-27.

NATIONAL REAL ESTATE JOURNAL, "Actual Appraisal Reports - Valuation of 25-Year Old Store," *National Real Estate Journal,* October 26, 1931, pp. 21-23.

NELSON, RICHARD LAWRENCE, *The One-Hundred Percent Location a New Concept In Motel Site Selection,* Encyclopedia of Motel Management.

PROCOS, DIMITRI, *Mixed Land Use Past Record and Future Prospects,* School of Architecture, Nova Scotia Canada.

SEYFRIED, W. R., "Location and the Centrality of Urban Land Values," *Land Economics,* August, 1970, pp. 329-333.

STARRETT, PAUL, "Location and Space Requirements of Industry," *American Institute of Real Estate Appraiser,* 1958, pp. 233-237.

VAN CLEEF, EUGENE, "Locating the Right Industry In the Right Place," *The Appraisal Journal,* April, 1958, pp. 223-226.

WALKER, J., "Levitt Town Bldr, Starts a City-Sized Community," *House & Home,* January, 1971, pp. 34.

## 12-23 Insurance Purposes

ABDOU, ELSAYED ALI PH. D., *The Concept of Equity In Life Insurance,* University of Pennsylvania, 1972.

AMERICA FIRE INSURANCE GROUP, *Casualty Claims Guide,* America Fire Insurance Group, New York, 1954.

AMERICAN APPRAISAL CO., "Reducing the Burden of Appraisal Cost to Insurance," *Clients Service Bulletin,* September 29, 1937, pp. 3..

AMERICAN SOCIETY OF APPRAISERS, "Insurance Valuations, Definitions, Derivations, and Appraisals," *Monograph,* Washington, D. C., July, 1971.

ARMSTRONG, W. Y., "Insurance Valuations the Property Owners Responsibility," *Insurance Valuations,* The American Society of Appraisers, Washington, D. C, 1971, pp. 8-18.

ASH, FRED C., "The Appraisal Docket. Actual Cash Value for Insurance Purposes," *The Appraisal Journal,* July, 1955, pp. 439-440.

BABCOCK, FREDERICK M., "The Appraisal of Properties for Mortgage Insurance," *Real Estate Record and Builders Guide,* December 8, 1934, pp. 6..

BABCOCK, FREDERICK M., "Yield Insurance Plan," *The Appraisal Journal,* October, 1942, pp. 352-356.

BELTH, J. M., "The Rate of Return on the Savings Element In Cash Value Life Insurance," *Journal of Risk and Insurance,* December, 1968.

BOLLES, W. H., "Appraising Flood Damage," *The Real Estate Appraiser,* Society of Real Estate Appraisers, Chicago, December, 1966, pp. 28.

BOLT, GEORGE K., "Insurance Adjuster and the Appraiser," *Technical Valuation,* American Society of Appraisers, Washington, November, 1952, pp. 23.

BONBRIGHT, JAMES C., "The Measurement of Fire Insurance Losses," *Appraisal Principles and Procedures,* pp. 374.

BRENNAN, J. F., "Depreciation by the Insurance Method," *The Journal of Land and Public Utility Economics,* February, 1933, pp. 16-24.

BROWN, JAMES M., "Principles Involved and Methods Used In the Establishment of Insurance Valuation," *Technical Valuation,* August, 1945, pp. 3-8.

BULKLEY, GRANT, "Depreciation--Its Importance In Insurance Appraising," *Technical Valuation,* February, 1959, pp. 29-32.

CORDIER, HENRY K., "Art Appraisals and Insurance," *Valuation,* September, 1968, pp. 37.

CHAPPELL, PAUL S., "Determining Insurable Value of Engineering Drawings," *Technical Valuation,* pp. 9.

CHO, WHEWON PH. D., *Performance In the Life Insurance Industry,* Vanderbilt University, 1971.

CLARK, PATRICK H., "Insurance Companies Look at Appraisals," *The Appraisal Journal,* February, 1939, pp. 147-151.

CRAMER, J. J., JR., W. J. SCHRADER, "Deprec Acctg & Anomalous Self-Insurance Cost," *Accounting Review,* October, 1970, pp. 698-703.

DARBY, CLEMENT H., "Depreciation for Insurance Purposes," *Technical Valuation,* October, 1958, pp. 41-42.

DE LIMA H. A., "Land Value Insurance," *National Association of Real Estate Boards,* 1926, pp. 58-87.

EDMAN, J. J., "The Appraisal Docket. Application of Insurance During Pendency of Eminent Domain Proceedings," *The Appraisal Journal*, October, 1960, pp. 124-125.

EHERT, WILLIAM C., "Appraising Fire Losses," *Appraisal and Valuation Manual*, American Society of Appraisers, 1959.

ENGLAND, WESLEY P., "On Depreciation for Insurance Purposes," *The Appraisal Journal*, July, 1936, pp. 325.

EVERTS, FRANK, "Appraising Jewelry for Insurance and Estate Purposes," *American Society of Appraisers Valuation Manual*, American Society of Appraisers, 1960, pp. 319.

FISHER, HENRY F., *Insurance Company Appraisals*, The Society of Industrial Realtors, 1953, pp. 18-28.

GALLAGHER, RUSSELL B., "Coporate Insurance Administrator," *Technicalities*, October, 1951, pp. 14-16.

GARBER, HENRY A., "Insurable Value Determination," *Technical Valuation*, September, 1966, pp. 22.

GEPHART, W. F., *Principles of Insurance*, Life, New York, 1917.

GODWIN, HOWARD S., "Casualty Deductions for Tax Purposes," *Appraisal Digest*, October, 1956, pp. 4-7.

GOLDEN, GERALD A., "An Insurance Investor In a Perplexing Market," *The Review*, July, 1949, pp. 3-8.

GOLDIN, A. J., "Appraising In Fire Insurance," *Technicalities*, October, 1951, pp. 9-12.

GORKA, FRANCIS L., "Reproductions or Replacement Costs for Insurance," *Insurance Valuations*, 1971, pp. 36-40.

GRAHAM, DAVID M., "Loss Adjustment Appraisals," *Valuation*, 1966, pp. 20-24.

GREENEBAUM, MICHAEL, "The Purchase of Real Estate by Insurance Companies," *The Appraisal Journal*, January, 1948, pp. 65-71.

GRIMM, RUDOLPH J., "Insurance Appraisals Produce Economies," *Real Estate Record*, July 20, 1940, pp. 2.

HAGENSICK, JOHN C., "The Appraisal of Sub-Standard Risks In the Adjustment of Fire Insurance Losses," *Valuation*, A. S. A, Washington, February, 1968, pp. 53-69.

HALL, ARTHUR F., "Why Life Insurance Companies Favor the Mortgage Loan," *National Real Estate Journal*, October, 1934, pp. 37-38.

HALL, FRANK D., "Appraisal Requirements of Life Insurance Companies," *Residential Appraisers Review*, August, 1935, pp. 11-12, 16.

HANEMANN, H. J. F., "Flood and Debris Hazards---Their Effect on Property Values," *Right of Way*, February, 1955, pp. 12-15.

HANSON, PETER, "Appraising for Earthquake Loans," *Condemnation Appraisal Procedure*, Hanson and Pollard, 1934, pp. 224-225, 467.

HEBB, WINSTON P, "Industrial Insurance Appraisals," *Valutape Audio-Library*, American Society of Appraisers, Washington D.C., January 1, 1974.

HOLLAND, MILTON, "Insurable Values - Fine Arts," *Technical Valuation*, ASA, Washington, 1952, pp. 41.

HORNDOHL, FRANK, "Insurance Claim Investigations, Role of the Commercial Laboratory," *Technical Evaluation*, ASA, June, 1954, pp. 62.

JURETIE, LOUIS L., "Property Valuation for Insurance Purposes," *Technical Valuation*, February, 1959, pp. 55-57.

JURETIE, LOUIS L., "What Is Insurable Value," ASA, 1956, pp. 57.

KELLOUGH, W. R., "The Appraisal of Non-Existent Property or Fire Insurance Appraisals After the Fire," *Technical Valuation*, February, 1959, pp. 59-61.

KINDER, W. J., "Effects of Disaster Cost and Availability of Property Insurance," *Technical Valuation*, 1966, pp. 53.

KOESTERS, A.F., "Appraisals for Insurance Purposes," *Technical Valuation,* February, 1958, pp. 19-20.

LEVIN, L. M., "Combination Sale of Cash Value Life Insurance and Real Estate," *National Underwriter Life and Health Insurance Edition,* January 16, 1971, pp. 20-21.

LEWBEL, CONRAD, "The Appraisal Clause In Standard Insurance Policies and Its Relation to A.S.A.," *Valuation,* October, 1958, pp. 33-35.

LICHTER, JOHN C., "Values for Insurance Purposes," *Technical Valuation,* pp. 22.

LITCHER, JOHN C., "Appraisings for Insurance Purposes," *Papers and Proceedings,* Wisconsin Colloquium on Appraisal Research, 1963, pp. 44-45.

LLOVERAS, ALBERT M., *El Catastro Territorial,* Impr. De La Universidad, Cordoba, 1951.

MACCOLLUM, DAVID V. P. E. C. S. P., "What Is the Value of a Disaster," *Valuation,* American Society of Appraisers, September, 1972, pp. 80.

MACLEOD, MORTON P., "Coinsurance---What it Is and How it Works," *Insurance Valuations, Monograph No. 4,* American Society of Appraisers, Washington, D. C, 1971, pp. 18-36.

MADDOCK, AUBREY, "Insurance Cost In the Operating Statement," *The Appraisal Journal,* January, 1939, pp. 27-29.

MAGILL, C. H., "The Origin and Function of Title Insurance," *Right of Way,* August, 1960, pp. 8-10.

MATTHEWS, MYRON L., "Insurance-Depreciation and Capital Replacement," *Technical Valuation,* American Society of Appraisers, November, 1952, pp. 4.

MCCLOY, WILLIAM M., "Actual Cash Value Equals Fair Market," *Insurance Valuations,* American Society of Appraisers, Washington, D. C, 1971, pp. 62-72.

MCCLOY, WILLIAM M., "Insurable Values," *The Review and Technical Valuation,* August, 1952, pp. 3-6.

MCCLOY, WILLIAM M., "Insurance Appraisals and the Insurance Agent," *Technicalities,* June, 1951, pp. 23-27.

MCKAY, GORDON A., "Valuation for Insurance Purposes," *Technical Valuation,* October, 1954, pp. 33-35.

MERRIAM, A. O., "Types of City Mortgages Best Suited for Life Insurance Investments," *American Life Convention Proceedings 25th Annual Meeting,* 1930, pp. 212-221.

METZ, ERIC RUDOLF, "Utility Analysis and the Selection of an Automobile Collision Insurance Deductible," *Dissertation Abstracts International,* January, 1971.

NELSON, CONRAD J., "Insurance to Value," *Technical Valuation,* June, 1957, pp. 15-18.

NOLAN, PRESTON M., "Appraising for Banks and Life Insurance Companies," *National Real Estate Journal,* June, 1925, pp. 37-38.

OLSEN, NILS ANDREAS, "Farm Credit, Farm Insurance, and Farm Taxation," *U. S. Department of Agriculture Yearbook,* 1924, pp. 185-284.

PAULY, MARK V., "Indemnity Insurance for Health Care Efficiency," *Economic and Business Bulletin,* Temple University, October, 1971, pp. 53-59.

PINK, LOUIS N., "What the Insurance Department Expects of an Appraiser," *Review of Society of Residential Appraisers,* June, 1941, pp. 4-6.

PURDON, JOHN, "Appraisal for Insurance Purposes," *Encyclopedia of Real Estate Appraising,* 1959, pp. 745-753.

PURDON, JOHN, "Appraisal for Insurance Purposes," *The Appraisal Journal,* April, 1953, pp. 234-238.

PURDON, JOHN, "Insurable Values-Legerdomain," *Insurance Valuations,* American Society of Appraisers, Washington, D.C., 1971, pp. 56-62.

PURDON, JOHN, "Problems In Appraising for Fire Insurance," *American Society of Appraisers Valuation Manual*, American Society of Appraisers, 1959, pp. 177.

PURDON, JOHN, "Special Aspects of Fire Appraising," *Technical Valuation*, June, 1958, pp. 31-33.

REED, PRENTISS B., "Insurable Values and Loss Adjustments," *Technicalities and Technical Valuation*, June, 1952, pp. 19-23.

ROBBINS, DONALD L., "Appraising Hurricane and Other Catastrophe Losses," *The Residential Appraiser*, July, 1962, pp. 17-23.

RODMAN, JOHN E., "Real Estate Appraisals Vs. Insurance Appraisals," *The Real Estate Appraiser*, January, 1900, pp. 49-51.

ROSENCRANS, DAN, "Title Insurance Service In Right of Way Operations," *Right of Way*, February, 1962, pp. 26-28.

ROSENCRANS, DAN W., "What Good Is Title Insurance?," *Technicalities*, June, 1951.

ROTHSCHILD, SIGMUND, "Fine Art and Personal Property Insurance," *Insurance Valuations*, 1971, pp. 45-56.

SARLES, KENNETH E., "The Story of Mortgage Guarantee Insurance Corporation," *The Residential Appraiser*, December, 1961, pp. 18-19.

SHEAFFER, JOHN R., "Flood Hazard Mapping-Its Uses and Limitations," *The Residential Appraiser*, February, 1962, pp. 21-24.

SMITH, DAVID H., "So You Think You Are Covered," *Technical Valuation*, February, 1954, pp. 3-6.

STARR, J. O., "Lease Guarantee Insurance," *Appraisal Journal*, April, 1972, pp. P. 175-187.

SYBRANDT, JOHN L., "Investigating Your Loss--Property Damage," *Insurance Valuations, Monograph No. 4 of the American Society of Appraisers*, Washington, D.C.

TAYLOR, GEORGE H., "Making Appraisals for Life Insurance Companies," *Proceedings 13th Annual Convention*, Mortgage Bankers Association of America, 1926, pp. 113-124.

TEBBETTS, R. S., "Appraisals for Insurance Coverage and Proof of Loss," *Technical Valuation*, December, 1946, pp. 3-6.

THOMAS, P. I., "Appraising Buildings for Insurance," *The Real Estate Appraiser*, June, 1963, pp. 23-28.

THOMPSON, R. E., "Depreciation for Insurance Purposes," *The Appraisal Journal*, April, 1936, pp. 194-196.

TRUE, WALLACE W., "Making Life Insurance Loans on Industrial Property," *National Real Estate Journal*, December, 1939, pp. 31-33.

WEAVER, W. C. JR., "Real Estate A Piece of the Action for Life Insurances," *Bests Review*, December, 1970, pp. 20.

WHITTINGTON, P. L., *Valuation for Insurance*, American Appraisal Company, Milwaukee, 1955.

WILLIS, RICHARD S., "Insurance Company Views on Real Estate Appraisal," *Appraisal Digest*, October, 1955, pp. 17-19.

WOLFF, LEWIS, "Return to Private Mortgage Insurance," *Real Estate Analyst Appraisal Bulletin*, 1960, pp. 597-600.

WURFEL, LESTER E., "Life Insurance Service and Mortgage Loans," *National Real Estate Journal*, August 9, 1926, pp. 49-53.

ZANGER, AARON, "Insuring Real Property--Actual Cash Value and Insurance," *Technical Valuation*, October, 1950, pp. 22-29.

## 12-24 Obsolescence and Depreciation

ABSUAGA, MIGUEL A., "A Practical Approach to Appraisal of Depreciable Property," *The Valuation Manual,* American Society of Appraisers, Washington, 1958, pp. 399.

ADAMS, J., "Rate-Making Status of Liberalized Depreciation," *Public Utilities Fortnightly,* February 13, 1958, pp. 260-265.

ALEXANDER, ROBERT H., "Measuring Accrued Depreciation In the Market," *The Residential Appraiser,* April, 1960, pp. 22-24.

AMERICAN HOTEL ASSOCIATION DEPRECIATION COMMITTEE, *Depreciation and Obsolescence In Hotels,* American Hotel Association, New York, 1928, pp. 24.

AMERICAN SOCIETY OF APPRAISERS, "CPA's to Consider Depreciation Based on Replacement Costs In Business Week," *American Society of Appraisers Valuation Manual,* April 5, 1958, pp. 79.

AMERICAN SOCIETY OF APPRAISERS, "Depreciation Change Urged by Machinery Dealers National Association Iron Age," *American Society of Appraisers Valuation Manual,* January 16, 1958, pp. 124.

AMERICAN SOCIETY OF APPRAISERS, "Self Help on Depreciation," *American Society of Appraisers,* Washington, D. C, November 19, 1956, pp. 99-101.

ARCHIBALD, T. R., "Stock Market Reaction to the Depreciation Switch-Back," *Accounting Review,* January, 1972, pp. 22-30.

ARSUAGA, MIGUEL A., "A Practical Approach to the Appraisal of Depreciable Property," *Appraisal and Valuation Manual,* American Society of Appraisers, Washington, D.C., 1958, pp. 399-404.

ASSOCIATED GENERAL CONTRACTORS OF AMERICA, "Depreciation Schedule Adopted," *The Constructor,* January, 1930, pp. 50-52.

AUTOMATIC CAR WASH ASSOCIATION, *Depreciation Survey,* Automatic Car Wash Association, Bellwood, 1900.

BABCOCK, FREDERICK M., "Depreciation Allowances," *The Appraisal Journal,* July, 1934, pp. 275-292.

BABCOCK, FREDERICK M., "Depreciation Obsolescence and Building Life," *Valuation of Real Estate,* 1932, pp. 401-426.

BABCOCK, FREDERICK M., "How Much Off for Depreciation," *Technical Valuation,* February, 1956, pp. 48-54.

BABCOCK, HENRY A., "Depreciation and Obsolescence," *The National Real Estate Journal,* June 24, 1929, pp. 15-18.

BACK, DENYS H., "Estimating Depreciation," *Residential Appraiser,* July, 1961, pp. 2-13.

BALLARD, J. W., "Accounting Recognition of Fact That Land Does Depreciate," *American Accountant,* March, 1931, pp. 74-75.

BEETH, CHANNING C., "Crossroads of Obsolescence," *The Review,* April, 1955, pp. 3-6.

BEETH, CHANNING C., "Do Airports Create Obsolescence," *The Real Estate Appraiser,* December, 1953, pp. 3-7.

BELL, J. N., "Shall We Take Heavier Depreciation In Early Years," *N. A. C. A. Bulletin,* November, 1955, pp. 335-342.

BEMAN, ARTHUR K., "One Quarter Century of Depreciation Change In Value," *The Appraisal Journal,* January, 1948, pp. 72-76.

BENEDICT, LOUIS, "Depreciation-What it Is and How it Is Computed," *National Association of Cost Accounts Bulletin,* New York, November 15, 1930, pp. 306-314.

BENSON, C. B., "Depreciation-Progress," *Technical Valuation,* October, 1953, pp. 41.

BENSON, C. B., "Progress In Depreciation Thinking," *Technical Valuation,* October, 1953, pp. 41-45.

BENSON, PHILIP A., NELSON L. NORTH, "Depreciation and Obsolescence," *Real Estate Principles and Practices,* 1938, pp. 286-287.

BLOXOM, ROBERT D., "Classifying Depreciation," *The Review,* April, 1956, pp. 11-14, 19.

BODFISH, MORTON, THEOBALD, A. D, "Depreciation and Obsolescence," *Real Estate Fundamentals,* 1941, pp. 13-15.

BOECKH, EVERARD HEREFORD, "Analysis of Obsolescence," *Manual of Appraisals,* 1937, pp. 310-312.

BOECKH, EVERARD HEREFORD, "Depreciation and Obsolescence," *Boeckh's Manual of Appraisals,* pp. 303.

BOECKH, EVERARD HEREFORD, "Depreciation---A Reserve for Rehabilitation," *National Real Estate Journal,* October, 1934, pp. 44.

BOEREMA, ROBERT J., "Building Design and Obsolescence In the Single Family Residence," *The Residential Appraiser,* December, 1962, pp. 9-13.

BONBRIGHT, JAMES C., "Concept of Depreciation As an Accounting Category," *Accounting Review,* June, 1930, pp. 117-119.

BONNER, JOHN T., JR., "Economic Obsolescence -- Restudied," *The Residential Appraiser,* April, 1961, pp. 9-11.

BRATTER, HERBERT, "Depreciation Under the 1954 Code, Four Methods Are Available for Computing it In Banking," *A. S. A. Valuation Manual,* The American Society of Appraisers, Washington, D. C, May, 1958, pp. 49.

BRUNDAGE, PERCIVAL F., "Depreciation an Old Subject with a New Importance," *Harvard Business Review,* 1935, pp. 334-343.

BRUNELLE, CHARLES R., "Depreciation-A Field Study," *The Review,* December, 1950, pp. 3-9.

BUCK, WALTER M. S., "The Theory of Straight Line Depreciation," *The Appraisal Journal,* July, 1948, pp. 317-320.

BULLOCK, C. L., "Depreciation Practice- an Independent Accountants Viewpoint," *Public Utility,* February 17, 1972.

BUSH, HOLLIS, "Depreciation and Obsolescence," *The Appraisal Journal,* April, 1934, pp. 250-252.

CARDOZA, LEONARD R., A. ORMSBY DONOUGH, JR., AND WALTER N. GABRIEL, "Depreciation Factors," *The Review,* February, 1950, pp. 3-6.

CHAFFE, R. S., "Physical Depreciation," *Review of Society of Residential Appraiser,* August, 1940, pp. 3-6, 16.

CHANDIAS, MARIO E., "Un Criterio De Depreciacion," *Boletin,* Sotave, Caracas, Venezuela, pp. 5-8.

CHATELAIN, LEON, JR., "Cities Will Survive," *The Residential Appraiser,* December, 1957, pp. 13-16.

CHERNEY, RICHARD A., "The Problem of Depreciation," *The Appraisal Journal,* January, 1964, pp. 87-90.

CHERNEY, RICHARD A., "The Why and How of Deterioration," *The Appraisal Journal,* July, 1957, pp. 404-408.

CHURCH, BYRON, "Let's Adopt Buyer's Terminology for Depreciation," *The Residential Appraiser,* June, 1957, pp. 3-6.

CLARK, C. D., "Economic Appraisal of Depreciation Policy," *Journal Of Business,* January, 1956, pp. 28-40.

CLARK, HORACE F., "Depreciation and Obsolescence," *Appraising the Home*, 1930, pp. 69-85.

CLARK, W. C., "Causes of Obsolescence," *National Real Estate Journal*, September 7, 1925, pp. 26-29.

CLARK, W. C., "Obsolescence," *National Assoc. of Real Estate Boards*, 1925, pp. 143-181.

CLARK, W. C., "Ways of Preventing Acceleration of Obsolescence," *National Real Estate Journal*, August 24, 1925, pp. 31-32.

CLEVELAND ASSN OF BUILDING OWNERS AND MANAGERS, "Table on Obsolescence, Depreciation & Appreciation ; Economic Life, Kinds Office Bldgs & Allowances," *Appraising Manual*, pp. 67-38.

COMISKEY, E. E., "Market Respones to Changes In Depreciation Accounting," *Accounting Review*, April, 1971, pp. 279-285.

COUGHLAN, J. D., C. D. STEINMETZ, "New Adr Rules for Depreciation," *Taxes*, December, 1971, pp. 725-737.

CRAIG, ROBERT H., "Some New Thoughts on Depreciation," *Assessment Administration*, IAAO, Chicago, 1963, pp. 81-85.

CREE, JAMES W. JR., "Economic Obsolescence," *The Appraisal Journal*, October, 1941, pp. 346-350.

CROCHERON, CLARENCE, *Control of Fixed Assets and Depreciation*, American Appraisal Co., Milwaukee, Wisc.

CROCHERON, CLARENCE, "Property and Depreciation Records for Industry," *Technicalities and Technical Valuation*, February, 1952, pp. 3-9.

DE WOLFE, P., "The Depreciation Multiplier," *Review of Economics and Statistics*, November, 1966, pp. 412-418.

DEBOOS, FRANK A., "Comments on Physical Depreciation," *The Appraisal Journal*, July, 1952, pp. 39-397.

DEBOOS, FRANK A., "Physical Depreciation Often Cause for Wide Differences," *The Appraisal Journal*, July, 1952, pp. 394-397.

DENTON JOHN H., "Depreciation Studies," Preliminary Report of the Bureau of Internal Revenue, Government Printing Office, Washington, D. C, 1931.

DENTON, JOHN H., "Depreciation," *The Appraisal Journal*, October, 1935, pp. 405-416.

DENTON, JOHN H., "Depreciation on Modern Buildings," *The Appraisal Journal*, July, 1961, pp. 406-407.

DERBES, MAX J., "Accrued Depreciation-Classical Method," *The Real Estate Appraiser*, pp. 2..

DERBES, MAX J. JR., "Accrued Depreciation-Practical Consideration," *The Real Estate Appraiser*, April, 1906, pp. 21-26.

DIERKER, GERALD J., "Accounting for Depreciation," *ASA Valuation Manual*, American Society of Appraisers, Washington, D. C., 1955, pp. 87.

DIERKER, GERALD J., "Accounting for Depreciation," *Technical Valuation*, October, 1950, pp. 18-21.

DILMORE, G., "The Estimate of Accrued Depreciation," *Appraisal Institute Magazine*, Appraisal Institute of Canada, Winnipeg.

DODDS, R. W., "Advantages and Disadvantages of Various Depreciation Methods," *Valuation Manual*, February 16, 1956, pp. 253-263.

DUBOIS, AYERS J., "Depreciation--Past and Anticipated," *The Appraisal Journal*, January, 1936, pp. 35-51.

DUNN, DOMINICK R., "Contradictions In Economic Obsolescence," *The Residential Appraiser*, September, 1957, pp. 3-4.

DWYER, JAY J., "Overcharges In Depreciation," *The Review*, January, 1946, pp. 3, 6.

EATON, J. D., "Effective Age Vs. Actual Age," *The Appraisal Journal*, July, 1966, pp. 454-458.

EDWARDS, FRANK M., "Landscaping As an Offset to Depreciation," *The Appraisal Journal*, October, 1935, pp. 4378440.

ELY, O., "Accelerated Depreciation," *Public Utilities Fortnightly*, American Society of Appraisers Valuation Manual, May 10, 1956, pp. 680-683.

F.P.C., "S-59 Depreciation Practices of Nat Gas Co," Federal Power Commission, 1961.

FEDERAL POWER COMMISSION, *S-201-Depreciation Practices of Electric Utilites*, Supt. of Documents, U. S. Govt. Printing Office, Washington D. C, 1966.

FEINSCHREIBER, R., "New Regulations Liberalize Tax Depreciation," *New York Certified Public Accountant*, September, 1971, pp. 637-640.

FIELD, RALPH V., "How to Treat Depreciation," *The Appraisal Journal*, July, 1935, pp. 369-371.

FISCHER, R. M., "Depreciation In Industrial Properties," *The Appraisal Journal*, April, 1937, pp. 143-148.

FRANKEL, EDWARD T., "Depreciation by Straight Lines and Curves," *Technicalities and Technical Valuation*, February, 1952, pp. 14-15.

FREE, VICTOR J., "Application of Depreciation Theory," *The Appraisal Journal*, April, 1939, pp. 120-127.

FREE, VICTOR J., "The Theory of Depreciation," *The Appraisal Journal*, January, 1939, pp. 46-53.

FULLERTON, PAUL, "A New Dimension In Depreciation Practice," *The Appraisal Journal*, July, 1961, pp. 319-327.

FULLERTON, PAUL, "People, Not Time, Determine Depreciation," *The Real Estate Appraiser*, February, 1963, pp. 2-3.

GALLAGHER, E. F., "Retarding Depreciation of Buildings," *Real Estate Record*, March 21, 1936, pp. 21-25.

GARRISON, BURL L., "Physical Deterioration," *The Residential Appraiser*, October, 1962, pp. 17-20.

GERRITY, HARRY, *Depreciation and Obsolescence*, National Association Building Owners and Manager, 1933, pp. 27-31.

GILLETTE, H. P., "Appraiser Outlines Method of Figuring Building Depreciation," *California Real Estate Magazine*, March, 1940, pp. 9.

GOLDSTEIN, GEORGE, "An Appraisal of Property with Improvements Fully Depreciated," *American Institute of Real Estate Appraisers*, 1949.

GOLDSTEIN, SIMEON F., "Is Depreciation Just Bookkeeping," *Technical Valuation*, 1967, pp. 26.

GORTON, JAMES, "Obsolescence and Depreciation," *Taylor Society Bulletin*, June, 1927, pp. 442-447.

GRAICHEN, R. E., "Today's Depreciation Deduction," *Valuation Manual*, A.S.A., December, 1957, pp. 27-33.

GRANT, E. L., P. T. NORTON, *Depreciation*, Ronald, New York City, 1955.

GREBLER, LEO, *Housing Market Behavior In a Declining Area*, Columbia University Press, New York, 1952.

GROGAN, JAMES J., "Depreciation," *The Appraisal Journal*, October, 1934, pp. 42-45.

GROVES, HENRY M., "How Should Depreciation Allowance Be Handled?," *System and Business Management*, October, 1934, pp. 468-469, 492-496.

GRUNSKY, ARL E., GRUNSKY, CARL E. , JR, "Appreciating and the Unearned Increment," *Valuation, Depreciation and the Rate-Base*, New York, 1917, pp. 387.

GRUNSKY, CARL E., GRUNSKY, CARL E. , JR, "Expectancy and Remaining Value," *Valuation, Depreciation, and the Rate-Base*, pp. 293-301.

GRUNSKY, CARL E., GRUNSKY, CARL E., JR., "Amortization and Depreciation Tables," *Valuation, Depreciation and the Rate-Base*, New York, 1917, pp. 387.

HANFORD, LLOYD JR., "Depreciation—Fact of Fiction," *The Real Estate Appraiser*, November, 1965, pp. 19-29.

HANLEY, E. J., "Financing Tomorrow's Steel Plant Demands Realistic Depreciation and Pricing Policy," *Valuation Manual*, A.S.A., March, 1956, pp. 338-340.

HANSON, PETER, "Overcoming Obsolescence," *National Real Estate Journal*, December 21, 1931, pp. 18.

HARTMAN, T. W., "Depreciation," *Review of Society of Residential Appraisers*, May, 1940, pp. 6-10.

HAYES, DOUGLAS A., "Inventory and Depreciation Policies-The Quantitative Appraisal," *Appraisal and Management of Securities*, pp. 207.

HAYNES, JUSTIN H., "Some Thoughts on Group Depreciation," *Technical Valuation*, February, 1956, pp. 11-21.

HEER, ROBERT R., *Depreciation Tables*, Fallon Lay Book Company, Albany, New York, 1958.

HENDRIE, ROBERT E., "Depreciation As it Relates to Appraisal Practices," *Technical Valuation*, February, 1958, pp. 27-32.

HENSON, C. B., "Progress In Depreciation Thinking," *Technical Valuation*, ASA, Washington, October, 1953, pp. 41.

HOFFMAN, ARNOLD J., "Depreciation Pitfalls for New Real Estate Owners," *Taxes*, May, 1962, pp. 399-407.

HOLECOMB, PAUL E., "Building Obsolescence and Depreciation," *Real Estate*, March 16, 1935, pp. 9-12.

HOLLEBAUGH, CLIFFORD W., "This Thing Called Depreciation," *The Residential Appraiser*, January, 1962, pp. 9-13.

HORGAN, N. J, R. P. FLOYD, JR., "MBO Approach to Prevent Technical Obsolescence," *Personnel Journal*, September, 1971, pp. 687-693.

HORNE, DONALD, "Allowance for Depreciation," *The Appraisal Journal*, July, 1941, pp. 248-252.

HORVITZ, S. A., "Tax Planning Techniques Under the New Class Life System of Depreciation," *Journal of Taxation*, June, 1972, pp. 338-348.

HOSSACK, A. B., "Development of a Sound Depreciation Policy," *Bulletin, No. 924*, American Appraisal Company, 1941, pp. 11.

HYDER, K. LEE, "Accrued Depreciation," *The Appraisal Journal*, October, 1936, pp. 353-367.

HYDER, K. LEE, "Depreciation, Obsolescence, and Lack of Utility Inresidential Property," *The Appraisal Journal*, October, 1952, pp. 544-548.

I.R.S., *Bulletin 'F' Income Tax Depreciation and Obsolescence Estimated Useful Lines and Depreciation Rate*, Government Printing Office, Washington, 1942.

INTERSTATE COMMERCE COMMISSION, "Studies Depreciable Rdwy Prop and Equip-Railroads," *Depreciation*, Interstate Commerce Comm, January 1, 1946.

JEN, F. C., R. J. HUEFNER, "Depreciation by Probability-Life," *Accounting Review*, April, 1970, pp. 290-298.

JENSEN, CARL G., "Depreciation and Obsolescence As Related to Cost of Production," *Proceedings*, International Congress on Accounting, 1929, pp. 464-478.

KAHN, SANDERS A., "Land, Does it Depreciate," *The Real Estate Appraiser*, January, 1969, pp. 28-31.

KAZDIN, S. EDWIN, "On Depreciation," *The Appraisal Journal*, April, 1936.

KEEFER, E. D., "Estimating Depreciation," *The Review*, July, 1947, pp. 15-19.

KELLOUGH, U. R., *Building Construction Cost Data 1972*, Robert Snow Means Company Inc., May, 1973.

KLEIN, JOSEPH J., "Deductions for Depreciation, Obsolescence, and Amortization, Depletion," *Federal Income Taxation*, 1929, pp. 621-683, 684-739.

KLEIN, JOSEPH J., "Depreciation and Obsolescence from the Standpoint of Federal Income Taxation," *International Congress on Accounting*, 1929, pp. 387-403.

KNOWLES, JEROME, JR., "Estimating Accrued Depreciation," *The Appraisal Journal*, January, 1967, pp. 34-43.

KOSTERS, STUART F., "An Appraisal Engineer's Review of a Much Reviewed Subject Depreciation," *Appraisal and Valuation*, 1956, pp. 111-120.

KURTZ, EDWIN B., *The Science of Valuation and Depreciation*, The Ronald Press, New York, N.Y., 1937, pp. 221.

LAMDEN, C. W., "Depreciation-A Reliability Gap," *Journal of Accountancy*, April, 1972, pp. 67-70.

LANE, B. S., "Final Regs on Depreciation and Rehabiliation of Residential Property Clarify Many Areas," *Journal of Taxation*, July, 1972, pp. 18 24.

LASSERS, WILLARD J., "The New Depreciation Regulations," *Valuation Manual*, A. S. A., November, 1956, pp. 741-745.

LEAKE, PERCY DEWE, *Depreciation and Wasting Assets and Their Treatment In Computing Annual Profit and Loss*, London, 1923.

LOUIE, CHARLES F., "Depreciation and the Cost Approach," *Appraisal Journal*, October, 1961, pp. 507-516.

LOUIE, CHARLES F., "Depreciation and the Income Approach," *The Appraisal Journal*, January, 1962, pp. 40-47.

LUNDY, VICTOR R., "Depreciation," *The Review*, June, 1953, pp. 3-4.

LUNDY, VICTOR R., "The Why of Depreciation," *The Appraisal Journal*, January, 1965, pp. 41-46.

MACHINERY AND ALLIED PRODUCTS INSTITUTE, *Equipment Replacement and Depreciation Policies and Practices*, Washington, 1956.

MACK, CURT C., "On Land Depreciation," *The Appraisal Journal*, October, 1937, pp. 377-379.

MACLEOD, MORTON P., "Allowing for Depreciation In Building Appraisals," *Appraisal and Valuation Manual*, 1958, pp. 289-300.

MACNAUGHTON, A. E., "Depreciation Under the Income Tax Act," *Appraisal Institute Magazine*, September, 1962, pp. 5-8.

MARSTON, ANSON, ROBLEY WINFREY, J. C. GEMPSTEAD, "Engineering Valuation & Depreciation," Mcgraw-Hill, New York, 1953.

MARSTON, ANSON, THOMAS R. AGG, *Depreciation Accountancy*, M, McGraw-Hill,

MARSTON, ANSON, THOMAS R. AGG, "Depreciation," *Engineering Valuation*, New York, 1936, pp. 33-136.

MARTENSON, W. J., "No Appreciation for Appreciation," *Appraisal Institute Magazine*, Appraisal Institute of Canada, Winnipeg.

MATTHEWS, MYRON L., "Insurance-Depreciation and Capital Replacement," *Technical Valuation*, American Society of Appraisers, November, 1952, pp. 4.

MAY, ARTHUR A, *The Estimate of Depreciation*, Valuation of Residential Real Estate, M.

MAY, ARTHUR A., "Return of Obsolescence," *The Review*, January, 1948, pp. 5-8, 16.

MCCORMICK, LORING O., SCHMUTZ, GEORGE L, "Depreciation and Obsolescence," *Economic Approach to Valuation Procedure*, 1933, pp. 146-182.

MCCURDY, ROBERT V., "Functional Obsolescence In Small Houses," *The Review*, March, 1956, pp. 3-7.

MCDONALD, A. M., "A Study of Depreciation In Residences," *The Appraisal Journal,* October, 1958, pp. 602-606.

MCDONALD, ADRIAN F., "Treatment of Accrued Depreciation," *Appraisal Digest,* October, 1953, pp. 1-5, 1-4.

MCMICHAEL, STANLEY L., "Depreciation," *Appraising Manual,* 1937, pp. 51-70.

MCSWEENEY, THOMAS F., "Depreciation Factors and Special Purpose Properties," *American Association of State Highway Officials,* 1962, pp. 471-494.

MELNYK, PETER F., "Improvement Assessments-Depreciation and Obsolescence," *Appraisal Institute Magazine,* December, 1962, pp. 17-20.

MILLER, DULCY B., SALLY E. KNAPP, "Obsolescence In Nursing Home Design and Construction," *The Appraiser Journal,* July, 1966, pp. 393-399.

MILLER, R. D., "Short Cut Method to Calculate Declining Balance Depreciation," *Management Accounting,* July, 1970, pp. 68-70.

MOHR, LARRY R., "Applying Depreciation In Assessments of Gas Pipelines, Railroads and Other Utilities," *Assessment Administration,* 1965, pp. 106-107.

MONTONNA, DAVID L., "Accrued Depreciation," *Appraisal Institute Magazine,* December, 1957, pp. 5-20.

MONYEK, R. H., "Asset Deprec Range Regs Adopted No Maj Changes," *Journal of Taxation,* September, 1971, pp. 150-152.

MORGAN, BELDEN, "A Problem In Obsolescence," *Residential Appraiser's Review,* November, 1935, pp. 9, 12.

MORGAN, BELDEN, "The Depreciation Controversy," *The Review,* July, 1952, pp. 12-17.

MOSER, A. W., "Depreciation Based on Unit Cost," *Journal of Accountancy,* July, 1931, pp. 25-39.

MURCHISON, KENNETH, "A Building's Life Expectancy," *Banking,* April, 1937, pp. 26-27.

NATIONAL ASSOCIATION OF BUILDING OWNERS & MANAGERS, *Obsolescence In Buildings,* 1922.

NATIONAL ASSOCIATION OF BUILDING OWNERS & MANAGERS, "Committee on Depreciation and Obsolescence," *Proceedings of Annual Convention,* Chicago.

NATIONAL ASSOCIATION OF REAL ESTATE BOARDS, *Committee on Depreciation and Obsolescence of Real Estate Improvements,* Chicago, 1929.

NATIONAL ASSOCIATION OF REAL ESTATE BOARDS, *Depreciation, Deterioration and Obsolescence In Real Estate Appraisals,* Chicago, 1931.

NATIONAL ASSOCIATION OF REAL ESTATE BOARDS, *Report by Special Committee on Depreciation and Obsolescence,* 1929.

NELSON, W. L., "Amortization and Depreciation Rates," *American Society of Appraisers.*

NEWLOVE, G. H., "Depreciation," *Journal of Accountancy,* November, 1927, pp. 432-437.

NOLAN, PRESTON M., "Building Depreciation and Obsolescence," *National Real Estate Journal,* July, 1925, pp. 39-40.

NURNBERG, H., "Observations on the Financial Reporting of Depreciation and Income Taxes," *Financial Executive,* December, 1971, pp. 39.

NURNBERG, H., "Present Val Deprec & Income Tax Allocation," *Accounting Review,* October, 1968.

OLIVER, RUSSELL H., "Depreciation Theory," *The Review,* September, 1946, pp. 18-19.

OPELKA, F. GREGORY, "Technology and Depreciation," *The Real Estate Appraiser,* January, 1964, pp. 23-29.

OSTERGREN, C. N., AND L. SZABO, AND G. G. HENTER, "Equal Life Group Method of Depreciation," *Valuation, Engineering Economist,* 1967.

PATON, WILLIAM A., "Accrued Depreciation on Seasoned Properties," *Certified Public Accountant,* July, 1927, pp. 206-210.

PELOUBET, MAURICE E., "Insufficient Depreciation What Can the Appraiser Do About it," *Appraisal and Valuation Manual,* American Soicety of Appraisers, 1959, pp. 227-234.

PELOUBET, MAURICE E., "Practical Method for Applying Current Value Depreciation," *American Society of Appraisers Manual,* January, 1958, pp. 21-25.

PERRY, HORACE B., "Depreciation-Public Utilities Properties," *Appraisal and Valuation Manual,* American Society of Appraisers, 1956, pp. 121-136.

PETERSON, CARL H., "The Depreciation Reserve," *Technical Valuation,* February, 1957, pp. 19-26.

PETERSON, CHARLES E. JR., "Appraising Obsolescence In Older Downtown Office Buildings," *Appraisal and Valuation Manual,* American Society of Appraisers, Vol. IV.

PICK, J., "Concepts of Depreciation--Business Enterprises," *New York Certified Public Accountant,* May, 1970, pp. 369-380.

PIERSALL, R. W. JR., "Depreciation and the Nonprofit Organization," *New York Certified Public Accountant,* January, 1971, pp. 57-65.

POLAK, DR. W. J., "Theories of Depreciation," *Proceedings, International Congress on Accounting, 1929,* New York, 1929, pp. 447-463.

POPE, LONNIE, "Depreciation In the Cost Approach," *The Real Estate Appraiser,* American Institute of Real Estate Appraisal, June, 1964, pp. 2.

PREINREICH, GABRIEL A., *The Theory and General Principles of Depreciation,* The Waverly Press, Inc., Baltimore, Md., 1941.

PROUTY, W. L. AND OTHERS, "Building Depreciation," *Appraisers and Assessors Manual,* 1930, pp. 67-72.

PROUTY, W. L. AND OTHERS, "Factors of City Growth Affecting Obsolescence of Buildings," *Appraisers and Assessor's Manual,* 1930, pp. 82-83.

PROUTY, W. L. AND OTHERS, "Obsolescence As Applied to Buildings," *Appraisers and Assessors Manaul,* 1930, pp. 73-90.

PROUTY, W. L. AND OTHERS, "Obsolescence Formulas," *Appraisers and Assessors Manual,* 1930, pp. 88-90.

PROUTY, W. L. AND OTHERS, "Percentage of External Obsolescence Due to Zoning," *Appraisers and Assessors Manual,* 1930, pp. 88.

PROUTY, W. L. AND OTHERS, "Physical Depreciation of Buildings," *Appraisers and Assessors Manual,* 1930, pp. 58-72.

PROUTY, W. L. AND OTHERS, "Portland, Oregon, Physical Depreciation of Buildings," *Appraisers and Assessors Manual,* 1930, pp. 116-118.

PROUTY, W. L. AND OTHERS, "St. Paul Life and Physical Depreciation of Buildings," *Appraisers and Assessors Manaul,* 1930, pp. 120.

PURDY, VICTOR M., "Market Value of Obsolete Property for Tax Assessment Purpose," *Technical Valuation,* 1965, pp. 18-20.

RANDALL, WILLIAM J., "Age, Depreciation, Future Life, and Net Condition," *Real Estate Analyst Appraisal Bulletin,* 1962, pp. 25- 2.

RASTALL, W. H., "Obsolescence, a Persistent Competitor," *Nation's Business,* September, 1930, pp. 36-38, 162-163.

REAL ESTATE ANALYST, THE, "Depreciation Frequently Incorrectly Described," *Real Estate Analyst Appraisal Bulletin,* 1950, pp. 173-176.

REAL ESTATE ANALYST, THE, "Economic Obsolescence," *Real Estate Analyst Appraisal Bulletin,* 1963, pp. 193-196.

REAL ESTATE ANALYST, THE, "Functional and Economic Obsolescence," *Real Estate Analyst Appraisal Bulletin,* 1949, pp. 177-180.

REAL ESTATE ROCORD, "New Influences Affecting Depreciation," *Real Estate Record,* February 15, 1941, pp. 6.

REAL ESTATE, ANALYST, THE, "Functional and Economic Obsolescence," *Real Estate Analyst Appraisal Bulletin,* 1949, pp. 177-180.

REEVES, CUTHBERT E., "Amortization or Depreciation Reserves," *The Appraisal Journal,* April, 1937, pp. 169-174.

REEVES, L. T., "Depreciated Incremental Cost Concept," *Appraisal Journal,* October, 1971.

REEVES, L. T. JR., "Depreciated Incremental Cost Concept," *Appraisal Journal,* October, 1971, pp. 556-560.

RENO, E. S., "Rules on Depreciation," *Appraisal and Valuation Manual,* May, 1956, pp. 59-64.

RING, ALFRED A., "Depreciation Theory and Practice In Valuation," *The Valuation of Real Estate,* 1970, pp. 184.

ROBB, JOSEPH A., "Measure of Depreciation and Obsolescence In Luxury Dwellings," *Appraisal and Valuation Manual,* 1962, pp. 188.

ROYCE, FRANK, "The High Cost of Obsolescence," *Appraisal and Valuation Manual,* 1962, pp. 181-187.

RYAN, JOHN, "Current Depreciation Allowance, an Evaluation and Criticism," *Appraisal and Valuation Manual,* 1958.

SALIERS, EARL A., *Depreciation Principles and Applications,* Ronald Press Company, New York, 1922, pp. 1-59.

SALIERS, EARL A., *Depreciation Principles and Applications,* Ronald Press, New York, 1939, pp. 482.

SARLES, KENNETH A., "Appraisers Face New Crisis Built-In Obsolescence," *The Real Estate Appraiser,* March, 1971.

SCAFF, HAROLD H., "Accounting for Economic Depreciation," *Technical Valuation,* October, 1953, pp. 7-9.

SCHARFF, M. R., "Supplemental Note on Valuation and Depreciation," *Appraisal and Valuation Manual,* February, 1957, pp. 1-11.

SCHARFF, MAURICE R., "Depreciation Studies," *Appraisal and Valuation Manual,* 1955, pp. 14.

SCHMIDT, FRITZ, "Basis of Depreciation Charges," *Harvard Business Review,* April, 1930, pp. 257-264.

SCHMUTZ, GEORGE L., "Analyzing Depreciation," *The Review,* May, 1947, pp. 12-15.

SCHMUTZ, GEORGE L., "Depreciation," *Appraisal Process,* 1941, pp. 1-229.

SCHMUTZ, GEORGE L., "Depreciation and Replacement Reserves," *California Real Estate Magazine,* October, 1936, pp. 43.

SCHUMACHER, DAVID T., "Determining Physical Depreciation, Functional and Economic Obsolescence," *Technical Valuation,* October, 1956, pp. 19-24.

SCHUMACHER, RAY J., "Depreciation Studies by the Appraiser," *Technical Valuation,* February, 1961, pp. 35-36.

SCHURAB, B., R. E. P. NICOL, "From Double Declining Balance to Sum of the Years Digits Depreciation: an Optimum Switching Rule," *Accounting Review,* April, 1969, pp. 292 296.

SHENKEL, WILLIAM M., "The Depreciation Estimate a Reconsideration," *The Real Estate Appraiser,* 1907, pp. 21-33.

SHIACH A.D., "Depreciation Recapture: How it Affects Our Client; How We Can Help Him Cope with it," ASA.

SILVERHERZ, JOSEPH D., "Computing Depreciation and Appreciation," *Real Estate Record,* Metropolitans and National Editions, October 17, 1936, pp. 11-16.

SILVERMAN, BENJAMIN, "Legal Aspects-Depreciation," *Technical Valuation,* October, 1954, pp. 38.

SILVERMAN, BENJAMIN, "Some Aspects of Depreciation," *Technical Valuation,* October, 1954, pp. 38.

SIMMONDS, H. H., "Design to Avoid Depreciation," *The Review,* January, 1949, pp. 3-5.

SMAILS, R. G. H., "Some Aspects of Depreciation," *Accounting Review,* June, 1927, pp. 101-110.

SMITH, DAVID H., "Depreciation (Cost or Replacement Value)," *Technicalities,* October, 1951, pp. 11-13.

SNYDER, BLAKE, AND RALPH W. ROBY, "Appreciation, Obsolescence, Depreciation," *Fundamentals In Real Estate,* 1927.

SODERQUIST, OSCAR, "Depreciation and Obsolescence," *The Appraisal Journal,* October, 1934, pp. 84-85.

STARRETT, PAUL, "How to Estimate Depreciation," *The Appraisal Journal,* January, 1951, pp. 85-88.

STAUB, WALTER A., "Depreciation of Appraised Values," *American Accountant,* January, 1932, pp. 6-10.

STEELE, J., "Depreciation Decimal Equivalents," *Journal of Accountancy,* June, 1972, pp. 84-85.

SULLIVAN, J. BURKE, "Reproduction Cost, Less Depreciation and Obsolescence, In Cases of Eminent Domain," *The Technical Valuation,* February, 1957, pp. 57-59, June 1957, pp. 33-35.

SWEENY, HENRY W., "Stabilized Depreciation," *Accounting Review,* September, 1931, pp. 165-178.

TANNEY, WILLIAM W., "Depreciation and Obsolescence In Theatres," *The Appraisal Journal,* April, 1939, pp. 152-158.

TAYLOR, J. J., "A Statistical Theory of Depreciation'," *Journal American Statistical Association,* December, 1923, pp. 1010-1023.

TAYLOR, JAMES R., "Depreciation Fallacies," *The Review,* April, 1949, pp. 3-4, 8.

TAYNTON, M., "Effect of Salvage Value on Depreciation Taxes," *A. S. A. Manual,* February, 1958, pp. 97-98.

TERBORGH, GEORGE, *Realistic Depreciation Policy,* Machinery and Allied Product Institute, Chicago, 1955.

THE ECONOMIST, "How Not to Depreciate," *The Economist,* April 15, 1972, pp. 68.

THOMPSON, BURTON, "On Depreciation and Obsolescence," *The Appraisal Journal,* January, 1934, pp. 142-150.

THOMSEN, C. T., "Continuous and Consistent Depreciation Formulas," *Accounting Review,* January, 1970, pp. 151-158.

TRANSOM, G. E. JR., "Current Thoughts on Depreciation," *The Real Estate Appraiser,* July, 1963, pp. 12-18.

TREASURY DEPARTMENT, *Outline for the Study of Depreciation and Maintenance,* Treasury Department, Washington, 1926, pp. 1-38.

TREDWELL, JOHN C., "On Depreciation and the Forgotten Man," *The Appraisal Journal,* October, 1937, pp. 371-373.

TROWBRIDGE, CARL R., "Deterioration," *The Appraisal Journal,* January, 1964, pp. 91-96.

TROWBRIDGE, CARL R., "The Fallacies of Depreciation," *The Real Estate Appraiser,* pp. 14.

TRUMBLE, MELVIN J., "An Obsolete Factory," *Assessment Administration,* 1957, pp. 30-45.

U. S. BUREAU OF INTERNAL REVENUE, *Depreciation Table-Buildings And Building Equipment,* April, 1931.

U. S. INTERNAL REVENUE SERVICE, "T. D. 6182 Depreciation," *American Society of Appraisers,* June 12, 1956.

WADA, S. A., "A Note on Depreciation and Growth," *Bulletin of University of Osaka Prefecture,* 1966, pp. 19-22.

WAGNER, J. J., "Standardizing Depreciation and Obsolescence," *National Real Estate Journal,* December 8, 1930.

WALES, T. J., "Estimation of an Accelerated Depreciation Learning Function," *Journal of the American Statistical Association,* December, 1966, pp. 995-1009.

WALLACE, LEW E., *Depreciation of Farm Machinery, Transamerican Society of Agriculture Engineering,* pp. 139.

WALSH, EDWARD V., "The Obsolescence Factor," *Residential Appraisers Review,* November, 1935, pp. 3-8.

WEBSTER, S. S. JR., "New Deal In Depreciation," *Certified Public Account,* August, 1934, pp. 463-467.

WECKSLER, A. N., "Capital Spending Forecast Spurred Depreciation Change," *Purchasing,* February 4, 1971, pp. 16.

WELCH, CHARLES E., "Depreciation and Obsolescence Allowances on Plant and Equipment," *Conference Proceedings,* National Tax Association, Columbus, 1962, pp. 591-595.

WENDT, PAUL F., "Depreciation and the Capitalization of Income Method," *The Appraisal Journal,* April, 1963, pp. 185-193.

WESMAN, HARVEY, "Market Evidence of Depreciation In Single-Family Homes," *The Appraisal Journal,* July, 1969, pp. 341-343.

WHELDON, GEORGE T., "Publication of Depreciation Theories," *Review of Society of Residential Appraisers,* December, 1939, pp. 3-8.

WILLIAMS, J. R., "Time and Use Depreciation," *Management Accounting,* January, 1972.

WILLIAMS, JOHN R., "Depreciation and Obsolescence As Affected by Appraisals," *Proceedings,* 1976, pp. 420-430.

WILSON, GEORGE A., *Depreciation,* Mass Society of Certified Public Accountants, Inc., December 17, 1934, pp. 5-9.

WISCONSIN PUBLIC SERVICE COMMISSION, *Depreciation, a Review of Legal and Accounting Problems,* The Commission, Madison, 1933, pp. 1-96.

WOLK, H. I., "Current Val Deprec: a Conceptual Clarification," *Accounting Review,* July, 1970, pp. 544-552.

WYCOFF, F. C., "Capital Depreciation In the Postwar Period Automobiles," *Review of Economics of Statistics,* May, 1970, pp. 168-172.

ZANGERLE, JOHN, "Depreciation and Amortization," *National Tax Association,* 1922, pp. 134-135.

ZANGERLE, JOHN, "What Is the Proper Annual Charge for Depreciation and Obsolescence," *National Real Estate Journal,* October 20, 1924, pp. 15-16.

## 12-25 Capitalization

AMERICAN INSTITUTE OF REAL ESTATE APPRAISERS, "Direct and Straight Capitalization and Valuation," *The Valuation of Real Estate,* American Institute Of Real Estate Appraisers, Chicago, 1967, pp. 278.

AMERICAN INSTITUTE OF REAL ESTATE APPRAISERS, "Rate of Capitalization of Earnings In Estimating Economic Values," *Hotel and Motel Valuation,* American Institute of Real Estate Appraisers, Chicago, 1971, pp. 16.

ARNOLD, ROBERT S., "Mortgage-Equity Capitalization and After-Tax Equity Yield," *The Appraisal Journal,* January, 1969, pp. 40-49.

ARNOLD, ROBERT S., "Mortgage-Equity Capitalization: Ellwood Method," *The Appraisal Journal,* April, 1966, pp. 196-202.

AXFORD, DR. H. M., "Capitalization of Income Property," *Appraisal Institute Magazine,* May, 1959, pp. 12-18.

BABCOCK, FREDERICK M., J. ALVIN REGISTER, "Income Distribution and Capitalization," *The Appraisal Journal,* October, 1932, pp. 31-35.

BABLER, WAYNE E., "Ad Valorem Tax Appraisals Through Capitalization of Earnings," *Conference Proceedings,* National Tax Association, Columbus, 1962, pp. 575-582.

BELTH, J. M., "The Rate of Return on the Savings Element In Cash Value Life Insurance," *Journal of Risk and Insurance,* December, 1968.

BODFISH, MORTON, THEOBALD, A. D, "Capitalization and Value," *Real Estate Fundamentals,* 1941, pp. 15-16.

BONNER, JOHN T. JR., "The Income Approach-Capitalization," *The Real Estate Appraiser,* January, 1963, pp. 2-8.

BROWN, EDWIN E., "Appraisal of Timberland Through Capitalization of the Value of Average Annual Growth," *The Assessor's Journal,* July, 1971, pp. 35-42.

BRYDEN, JOHN T., "Our Capital Investment Boom," *The Review,* July, 1952, pp. 3-6.

CHANDLER, RICHARD A., "Capitalization, Gross and Net," *Assessment Administration,* IAAO, Chicago, 1959, pp. 71-80.

CHANDLER, RICHARD A., "Use of Capitalized Income to Determine Assessed Values," *Appraisal Institute Magazine,* March, 1960, pp. 19-22.

CHILD, JOHN F. JR., AND DAVID SCRIBNER, "Analysis of Components In the Capitalization Rate Peculiar to Large-Scale FHA Housing Projects," *Appraisal and Valuation Manual,* American Society of Appraisers, 1959, pp. 139-148.

CLEVELAND, F. A, AND F. W. POWELL, "Railroad Promotion and Capitalization In the U. S," *Principles of Investment,* New York, 1909, pp. CHAPS. I, V, VI, XII, XV, VIII, XI, XVII.

COCHRAN, GAIL V., "A Short-Cut Capitalization Method for Commercialproperties," *Appraisal and Valuation Manual,* ASA, Washington, 1958, pp. 331-336.

COOK, ROBERT S., "Farmland and Capitalization of Income," *Assessment Administration,* IAAO, Chicago, 1959, pp. 67-70.

DASSO, DR. JEROME, "Understanding the Mortgage-Equity Capitalization Technique," *The Real Estate Appraiser,* September, 1968, pp. 27-32.

DONOVAN, J., "Bleak Picture The Art Market Is Feeling the Financial Pinch, Too," *Barrons,* July 6, 1970, pp. 11.

ECKERT, FRED W., "Operating and Capitalization Factors In the Valuation of Hotel Properties," *The Appraisal Journal,* April, 1946, pp. 180-186.

ELLWOOD, LEON W., "Depreciation, Capital Recovery and Capitalization," *The Appraisal Digest,* 1901, pp. 1-3.

FISCHER, R. M., "Economic Background of the Capitalization Process," *The Appraisal Journal,* October, 1937, pp. 329-342.

FISCHER, R. M., "Valuation of Capital Stock, I," *The Appraisal Journal,* April, 1944, pp. 143-153.

GIBBONS, JAMES E., "Mortgage-Equity Capitalization and After Tax Equity Yield," *The Appraisal Journal,* January, 1969, pp. 31-49.

## BIBLIOGRAPHY OF APPRAISAL LITERATURE

GOLDSTEIN, GEORGE, "Capitalization Rates In Todays Market," *The Appraisal Journal*, October, 1947, pp. 492-494.

HODGES, M. B. JR., "Income Capitalization for Investor Clients," *The Appraisal Journal*, April, 1968, pp. 175-200.

HOGARTY, T. F., "Profitability of Corporate Mergers," *Journal of Business*, July, 1970, pp. 317-327.

HOLLEBAUGH, CLIFFORD W., "The ABC's of Capitalization Tables," *The Appraisal Journal*, April, 1955, pp. 225-229.

JEAN W. H., "Terminal Value or Present Value In Capital Budgeting Programs," *Journal of Finance and Quantitative Analysis*, January, 1971.

KAZDIN, S. EDWIN, "A Fresh Look at Capitalization Methods," *The Appraisal Journal*, April, 1938, pp. 166-167.

KAZDIN, S. EDWIN, "Capitalization Rates Under Present Market Conditions," *The Appraisal Journal*, October, 1944, pp. 305-317.

KEENLEYSIDE, A., "The Theory and Use of Capitalization Tables," *Appraisal Institute Magazine*, September, 1958, pp. 12-16.

KELLOUGH, W. R., "Capitalization In the Appraisal Process," *The Real Estate Appraiser*, April, 1964, pp. 9..

KELLOUGH, W. R., "Capitalization Methods," *Technical Valuation*, pp. 27.

KNISKERN, PHILIP W., "Capitalization Rate; In Interest Tables & Their Use Etc.," *Real Estate Appraisal and Valuation*, 1933, pp. 296-490.

KNISKERN, PHILIP W., "On the Capitalization Rate Used In Max Tieger's Appraisal," *The Appraisal Journal*, April, 1933, pp. 243-244.

LAFFER, ARTHUR BETZ, PH. D., *Private Short-Term Capital Flows*, Stanford Unversity, 1972.

LEIGHLY, WILLIAM LEWIS, "Capitalization Methods," *Review of Society of Residential Appraisers*, May, 1939, pp. 8-11.

LEVY, MARK, "Establishing the Capitalization Rate," *The Appraisal Journal*, October, 1932, pp. 27-30.

LINNETT, JOHN A., "Value Through Capitalization Income," *The Appraisal Journal*, October, 1946, pp. 361-369.

MACROSSIE, WILLIAM, "Selection and Use of Capitalization Rates In the Appraisal of Motels," *The Appraisal Journal*, April, 1959, pp. 212-219.

MCCURDY, ROBERT V., "Capitalization Rates," *The Real Estate Appraiser*, Society of Real Estate Appraisers, Chicago, January, 1965, pp. 23.

MCCUTCHEON, W. B., "Figuring Risk In Capitalization," *The Review*, March, 1949, pp. 3-4.

MCELWEE, EUGENE, "New Thinking In Capitalization Techniques and Mathematics," *The Real Estate Appraiser*, Chicago, April, 1964, pp. 24.

MCMICHAEL, STANLEY L., "Capitalizing Income Into Value," *Appraising Manual*, 1937, pp. 105-114.

MERTZKE, ARTHUR J., "The Capitalization Rate of Income Property Appraisals," *Real Estate Record and Builders Guide*, January 7, 1933, pp. 3-5.

MEYER, HAROLD F., "Justifying Capitalization Rates on Farm Properties," *Journal of American Society of Farm Managers and Rural Appraisers*, October, 1965, pp. 96-103.

MONTONNA, DAVID L., "Capitalizing Amenities of Residential Property," *Review of Society of Residential Appraiser*, August, 1939, pp. 3-8.

MONTONNA, DAVID L., "Capitalizing Income Into Value," *The Appraisal Journal*, January, 1951, pp. 76-84.

MORTON, WALTER A., "The Investor Capitalization Theory of the Cost of Equity Capital," *Land Economics,* August, 1970.

PARCHER, L. A., "Capitalization Rates for Rural Properties," *The Appraisal Journal,* January, 1962, pp. 27-32.

QUIN, GEORGE ROBERT, "Capitalization Rates for Long Term Leases," *The Appraisal Journal,* January, 1935, pp. 144-148.

RAINEY, A. J., "Appraisal of Leased Property Capitalization Rate," *American Society of Appraisers,* November, 1952, pp. 31.

RATCLIFF, DR. RICHARD U., "Capitalized Income Is Not Market Value," *The Appraisal Journal,* January, 1968, pp. 33-40.

REEVES, CUTHBERT E., "On the Capitalization Rate Used In Max Tieger's Appraisal," *The Appraisal Journal,* April, 1933, pp. 238-239.

REEVES, CUTHBERT E., "The Capitalization Method In the Evaluation of Homes," *The Appraisal Journal,* January, 1934, pp. 87-92.

REIDY, MAURICE F., "An Office Building Is Worth Only a Fair Capitalization of Expected Net Income," *National Real Estate Journal,* June 10, 1929, pp. 21-24.

RING, ALFRED A., "Depreciation Expense Vs. Depreciation Rate Methods of Capitalization," *The Appraisal Journal,* July, 1962, pp. 325-332.

RING, ALFRED A., "Residual Techniques of Capitalization In Appraisal," *The Valuation of Real Estate,* 1970, pp. 283.

RING, ALFRED A., "The Direct-Ring Method of Capitalization," *The Appraisal Journal,* April, 1960, pp. 183-189.

ROSS, THURSTON H., "The Capitalization Process In Small Residential Appraisers," *Review of the Society of Residential Appraisers,* April, 1937, pp. 3-7.

SADESKY, WILLIAM V., "Relationship of the Cost of Borrowed Money To Capitalization Rates," *The Appraisal Journal,* January, 1968, pp. 9-14.

SCHARFF, MAURICE R., "Capitalization Rates In Public Utilities," *Technical Valuation,* October, 1957, pp. 7-9.

SEXAUER, GEORGE C., "Appraising Real Estate by the Capitalization Method," *National Real Estate Journal,* February, 1937, pp. 42-44.

SEXAUER, GEORGE C., "On Appraising Real Estate by the Capitalization Method," *The Appraisal Journal,* April, 1937, pp. 181-184.

SHATTUCK, CHARLES B., "Income Approach-Capitalization Process," *Real Estate Appraiser,* 1953, pp. 1060-1061.

SHWAYDER, K, "The Capital Maintenance Rule and the Net Asset Valuation Rule," *Accounting Review,* April, 1969.

SLICKTER, S. H., "Trends In Prices, Demand for Capital, and Supply of Capital," *The Appraisal Journal,* January, 1949, pp. 25-35.

SMITH, LAWRENCE E., SR., "Choosing the 'Cap Rate'," *The Residential Appraiser,* March, 1961, pp. 7-10.

SMITH, R. S., "Property Tax Capitalization In San Francisco," *National Tax Journal,* June, 1970, pp. 177-193.

THOMPSON, R. E., "Effect of Appraisal Method on Capitalization Rates," *National Real Estate Journal,* September 4, 1931, pp. 26-28.

THORNTON, J., "Estimation of Value Added and Average Returns to Capital In Soviet Industry, Cross Section Data," *The Journal of Political Economy,* University of Washington, U. S. A, December, 1965.

TREDWELL, JOHN C., "On a Suggested Approach to the Capitalization Rate," *The Appraisal Journal,* January, 1938, pp. 65-66.

WECKSLER, A. N., "Capital Spending Forecast Spurred Depreciation Change," *Purchasing,* February 4, 1971, pp. 16.

WINSOR, EDWARD H., "Tax Differential Capitalization," *The Appraisal Journal*, October, 1948, pp. 455-458.

WITTMAN, FRANK, "The Ellwood Method of Capitalization," *Appraisal Digest*, April, 1961, pp. 13-14.

WYCOFF, F. C., "Capital Depreciation In the Postwar Period Automobiles," *Review of Economics of Statistics*, May, 1970, pp. 168-172.

# 12-26 Legal Aspects of Appraisal

ADAMS, WESLEY, "The Appraiser and the Attorney In Condemnation Appraisals," *Appraisal and Valuation Manual*, American Society of Appraisers, Washington D.C., 1960.

AMERICAN INSTITUTE OF REAL ESTATE APPRAISERS, "Case Studies In Apartment House Valuation," *Case Studies In Apartment House Valuation*, American Institute of Real Estate Appraisers, Chicago, 1900.

AMERICAN INSTITUTE OF REAL ESTATE APPRAISERS, "Case Study Courses In Real Estate Appraising at the University of Chicago," *Journal American Institute of Real Estate Appraisers*, January, 1936, pp. 26-34, 166-180.

AMERICAN INSTITUTE OF REAL ESTATE APPRAISERS, "Economic Factors and Case Studies In Hotel and Motel Valuation," *Case Studies*, American Institute of Real Estate Appraisers, Chicago, 1900.

AMERICAN INSTITUTE OF REAL ESTATE APPRAISERS, "The Appraisal Docket," *Condemnation Appraisal Practice*, American Institute of Real Estate Appraisers, Chicago, 1961, pp. 153-157.

AMERICAN MUNICIPAL ASSOCIATION, *Constitutional Provisions for Tax Exemption of Publicly Owned Property In Selected States*, American Municipal Association, Washington, 1959, pp. 5.

ANDERS, DOWELL H., "The Jurys Approach to the Determination of Damages In Land Condemnation Suits," *Right of Way*, October, 1962, pp. 43-46.

APPRAISAL JOURNAL, "Just Compensation for a Temporary Use," *The Appraisal Journal*, April, 1945, pp. 177-181.

APPRAISAL JOURNAL, "Taken to the Cleaners," *The Appraisal Journal*, October, 1948, pp. 503-505.

APPRAISAL JOURNAL, "The Last of the Restrictive Covenant," *The Appraisal Journal*, October, 1953, pp. 595-597.

ARDERN, WILLIAM B., "The New Old Home," *Case Reports In Assessment Administration*, January, 1961, pp. 2-4.

ARDREY, J. HOWARD, "The System of Appraising Under the Housing Act," *National Real Estate Journal*, January, 1935, pp. 21-22.

ARNESON, HARRY R. JR., "Using Comparables In Court," *The Residential Appraiser*, October, 1957, pp. 3-6.

ARNOLD, VERN L., "Title Evidence In Washington State," *Right of Way*, 1960, pp. 47-50.

ASH, FRED C., "Denial of Jury Trial Upheld In Condemnation Case," *The Appraisal Journal*, July, 1956, pp. 429-431.

ASH, FRED C., "Power to Subpoena the Appraisal Reports of Experts," *The Appraisal Journal*, April, 1956, pp. 278-279.

ASH, FRED C., "The Appraisal Docket Actual Cash Value for Insurance Purposes," *The Appraisal Journal*, July, 1955, pp. 439-440.

ASH, FRED C., "The Appraisal Docket Expertness Not Presumed," *The Appraisal Journal*, January, 1955, pp. 117-118.

ASH, FRED C., "The Appraisal Docket No Compensation for Diversion of Traffic," *The Appraisal Journal*, January, 1957, pp. 108-109.

ASH, FRED C., "The Appraisal Docket Shopping Center Not a Nuisance," *The Appraisal Journal*, July, 1956, pp. 431-432.

ASH, FRED C., "The Appraisal Docket the Amount of Consequential Benefits Must Be Stated to Be Deducted," *The Appraisal Journal*, October, 1956, pp. 590-591.

ASH, FRED C., "The Appraisal Docket Valuation of Flowage Rights," *The Appraisal Journal*, January, 1957, pp. 109-110.

ASH, FRED C., "The Appraisal Docket: Abutting Owners' Property In Public Shade Trees," *The Appraisal Journal*, April, 1957, pp. 266.

ASHLEY, ROGER H., "Distribution and Use of Case Studies," *Right of Way*, October, 1966, pp. 32-36.

AYCOCKE, J. N., "Reconciling Conflict Between Legal Standards and Assessment Practices," *Assessment Administration*, Chicago, 1965, pp. 25-30.

BARON, GEORGE C., "Some Aspects of Expert Testimony," *Appraisal and Valuation Manual*, American Society of Appraisers, Washington, D. C, 1960, pp. 17-24.

BASSETT, EDWARD M., "Zoning: Laws, Administration, Court Decisions During the First Twenty Years," *Zoning the Laws Administration and Court Decisions During the First Twenty Years*, The Russell Sage Foundation, New York City, 1937.

BEAUDRY, PAUL, "Adequate Defense Against Appeals," *Assessment Administration*, IAAO, Chicago, 1962, pp. 54-60.

BECK, AXEL J., "Instruction to the Jury," *The Appraisal Journal*, July, 1960, pp. 332-336.

BEETH, CHANNING C., "New Clients," *The Review*, November, 1951, pp. 3-6.

BINGHAM, ROBERT F., "The Expert Witness for the Lawyer's Point of View," *Appraisal Journal*, October, 1937, pp. 343-347.

BISHOP, JESSE E., "Legal Responisbility of the Appraiser," *The Real Estate Appraiser*, SREA, Chicago, January, 1965, pp. 9.

BISHOP, MAURICE F., "The Attorney and the Appraiser," *The Real Estate Appraiser*, pp. 11.

BISHOP, MAURICE F., "The Attorney and the Appraiser (Part 1)," *The Real Estate Appraiser*, pp. 8.

BOMBRIGHT, JAMES CUMMINGS, *The Valuation of Property a Treatise on the Appraisal of Property for Different Legal Purposes*, Mcgraw-Hill Book Company Incorporated, New York and London, 1937.

BOWES, WATSON A., "Relations Between the Appraiser and His Attorney," *The Appraiser's Job In Eminent Domain Proceedings*, Univ. of Pittsburgh, Bureau of Business Research, pp. 27-36.

CARLL, CLOICE D., "Preparing to Testify—The Use of Demonstrative Evidence," *The Appraiser's Job In Eminent Domain Proceedings*, U of Pitt Bu of Bus Res In Coop with Law School, 1957, pp. 11-25.

CARLL, CLOICE D., "The Use of Demonstrative Evidence," *The Appraisal Journal*, January, 1960, pp. 24-38.

CARR, FRANCIS J., "Property Assessments Protest, Appeal, and Judicial Review," *The Journal of the State Bar of California*, November, 1964, pp. 877.

CHIRHART, EDWARD F., "Tourist Court, 1953 Decline," *Technical Valuation*, American Society of Appraisers, Washington, D. C., February, 1955, pp. 21.

CIMELY, G., "1969 Tax Reform Act Its Effect on Real Estate," *Industrial Development and Manufactures Record*, September, 1970, pp. 7-10.

## BIBLIOGRAPHY OF APPRAISAL LITERATURE

CLAY, DEANE J., "Practical Approach, Appraisal and Preparation for Trial In Condemnation Proceedings," *Technical Valuation,* June, 1959, pp. 65-68.

COCHRAN, JOHN D., "What Is Expected of the Expert Witness," *The Appraisal Journal,* October, 1959, pp. 548-553.

CONLON, CHARLES F., "Judicial Views on Tax Administration," *Western Politician Quarterly,* March, 1963, pp. 5-13.

CUNNYNGHAM, WILKIE, "Case of the Month," *Right of Way,* October, 1954, pp. 19-20, 28.

CUNNYNGHAM, WILKIE, "Case of the Month," *Right of Way,* August, 1956, pp. 35-36.

CUNNYNGHAM, WILKIE, "Case of the Month," *Right of Way,* October, 1964, pp. 19-20.

DAVIS, W. D. MAI, "Justice Department Accepts Appraisal Report Disclosure Ruling," *The Appraiser,* December, 1969.

DERBES, MAX J. JR., "The Appraiser and Court Testimony," *Right of Way,* February, 1963, pp. 21-25.

DOLAN, HARRY T., "Just Compensation and the General Motors Case," *The Appraisal Journal,* July, 1945, pp. 249-255.

DUNN, DOMINICK R., "On the Torrens Law," *Appraisal Journal,* July, 1936, pp. 323-325.

EDMAN, J. J., "Appraisal Witness Need Not Have Actually Bought and Sold Real Estate," *The Appraisal Journal,* July, 1960, pp. 381.

EDMAN, J. J., "Information Acquired by Hearsay May Be Basis of Expert Testimony. Appraisal Docket," *The Appraisal Journal,* April, 1961, pp. 258-258.

FEDERAL POWER COMMISSION, *A-78-Regulation to Govern the Preservation of Records of Natural Gas Companies,* Federal Power Commission, December 12, 1962.

FOSTER, GEORGE, JR., "What the Attorney Expects of the Appraiser," *Appraisal Digest,* January, 1961, pp. 1-6.

FOWLER, CODY, "A Lawyers View of Appraisers," *The Residential Appraiser,* August, 1958, pp. 18.

FPC, "S-184 Fed & State Comm Jurisd & Reg of Elec Gas & Telep Utils 1967," Supt Docs Govt Ptg Off, Wash.

FREE, ROBERT L., JOHN W. SPARKS, *Case Studies In Shopping Center Valuation,* American Institute of Real Estate Appraisers, Chicago, 1964.

GILL, WILLIAM L., "Corporate Security Values As Determined by the Tax Court," *A. S. A. Valuation Manual,* A. S. A, 1960, pp. 77.

GRAY, GEORGE H., "On the Residual Process In Max Tieger's Appraisal," *The Appraisal Journal,* April, 1933, pp. 251-252.

HADLEY, GEORGE C., "Legal Problems In Highway Acquisition," *The Appraisal Journal,* April, 1953, pp. 165-174.

HALE, C. W., "Impact of Federal Policy and Technological Change on Regional & Urban Planning Problems," *Land Economics,* February, 1971, pp. 24-35.

HALE, JUSTICE JOHN, "The Valuer As a Witness," *The Appraisal Journal,* April, 1961, pp. 239-245.

HAMILTON, ANDREW C., "Legal Responsibility of the Real Estate Appraiser," *The Appraisal Journal,* April, 1934, pp. 255-259.

HANDEL, MORRIS, "Legal Aspects of Appraisals and Expert Testimony In Tax Certiorari Proceedings," *Technical Valuation,* April, 1947, pp. 23-25.

HANDLER, ALAN B., "The Legal Aspects of Tax Exemptions, an Analysis Of the Second Switz Case," *New Jersey Municipalities,* January, 1963, pp. 16-20.

HANLEY, DUDLEY J., "Expert Testimony In Condemnations Trials," *The Residential Appraiser,* September, 1960, pp. 10-12.

HEPDITCH, GORDON D., "Problems In a Smaller Canadian Jurisdiction," *Assessment Administration,* IAAO, Chicago, 1961, pp. 89-92.

HIGHMARK, LOUIS A., "Legal Aspects of Highest and Best Use and Value," *The Appraisal Journal*, January, 1956, pp. 33-41.

HILL, R. D., "Keeping Electric Utilities from the Fate of Other Regulated Industries," *Commercial and Financial Chronicle*, June 18, 1970, pp. 1938-1939.

HOLZ, LEFFERT, HERMAN SCHRIER, "Real Estate Appraisals In Legal Proceedings," *The Appraisal Journal*, January, 1946, pp. 38-46.

HORGAN, JOHN P., "Case of the Month," *Right of Way*, April, 1954, pp. 27-30.

HORGAN, JOHN P., "Ten Courtroom Commandments for Appraisers," *Appraisal Journal*, January, 1960, pp. 51-56.

HORRELL, ALBERT J., "What the Lawyer Expects from the Right of Way Man and Appraiser," *Right of Way*, February, 1958, pp. 16-18.

HOUSTON, SAM, "Case of the Month," *Right of Way*, December, 1956, pp. 47-49.

HOWARD, JACK M., "Case of the Month," *Right of Way*, February, 1954, pp. 17-18.

HUBER, RICHARD G., "Courtroom Evidence and the Appraiser," *Appraisal and Valuation Manual*, 1962, pp. 150-157.

HUNNICUTT, WARREN P., "On Expert Testimony," *The Appraisal Journal*, 1938, pp. 167-170.

HURLBUTT, EDMUND C., "The Expert Witness Is a Witness," *Journal Of the American Society of Farm Managers and Rural Appraisers*, October, 1906, pp. 45-46.

HYDER, K. LEE, "A New Deal Under the Chandler Act," *The Appraisal Journal*, April, 1939, pp. 109-119.

INGRAM, DAVID, "The Role of Appraiser and Attorney In Condemnation," *Right of Way*, 1958, pp. 35-36.

INSTITUTE ON EMINENT DOMAIN, "In the Court at Law, Southwestern Legal Foundation, State Vs. Anyman, Et. Ux," *Proceedings*, 1960.

INSTITUTE'S RESEARCH COMMITTEE, "Suggested Research Topics In Real Estate Valuation," *The Appraisal Journal*, July, 1952, pp. 399-401.

JOHNSON, H. N., "Expert Testimony," *Annals of Real Estate Practice*, 1930, pp. 105-110.

JOHNSON, HENRY N., "The Expert Witness, His Personal and Professional Conduct In Litigation Involving Real Estate," *National Real Estate Journal*, July, 1930, pp. 21-23.

JONES, WALTER B., "A Judge Looks at the Expert Appraiser Witness," *The Appraiser Journal*, April, 1956, pp. 237-247.

KAHN, SANDERS A., "George Washington Bridge Approach, a Case Study," *The Appraisal Journal*, July, 1966, pp. 461-162.

KALTENBACH, HENRY J., "The Legal Angle," *The Appraisal Journal*, July, 1969, pp. 439-440.

KENNEDY, HAROLD W., "Testimony of Expert Appraisers In Condemnation Actions," *California Real Estate Magazine*, January, 1937, pp. 23.

KENNEDY, W. F., "Are Federal Highway Administration Appraisal Requirements Unreasonable," *Valuation*, September, 1972, pp. 44.

KEOGH, J. VINCENT, "The Appraiser Takes the Stand," *The Appraisal Digest*, June, 1956, pp. 1-3.

KINCAID, H. EVERT, "Legal Restrictions Which Maintain Value," *Review of Society of Residential Appraisers*, April, 1940, pp. 3-8, 13-14.

KING, BEN E., "Cases In Federal Court," *The Residential Appraiser*, October, 1958, pp. 19-23.

KLEINDIENT, RICHARD G., "Seminar Address by Deputy Attorney General Kleindienst," *The Appraiser*, March, 1970.

KOENKER, WILLIAM E., "Appropriateness of Property Taxes In an Equitable Tax Structure," *North Dakota Law Review*, May, 1965, pp. 505-529.

KOEPPEL, ADOLPH, "The Appraiser on the Witness Stand—The Attorney's View," *Selected Readings In Right of Way,* American Right of Way Association, 1968, pp. 532-538.

KRAECHE, ENNO, "Taking the Stand," *The Appraisal Journal,* April, 1954, pp. 267-269.

KRANANIEWSKI, WALTER J., "Credibility of Witnesses and Opinion Evidence," *Journal of the American Society of Farm Managers and Rural Appraisers,* October, 1961, pp. 20-21.

KREVOR, HENRY H., *Legal Rules Governing Valuation of Real Property,* The American Right of Way Association, Los Angeles, 1968, pp. 170-183.

KREVOR, HENRY H., "Legal Rules Governing Valuation of Real Property," *Right of Way,* June, 1960, pp. 7-17.

KRISTOVICH, BALDO M., "Case of the Month," *Right of Way,* October, 1955, pp. 33.

KUCERA, H. P., *The Developing Law of the Jet Airport,* Proceedgs of the 4th Inst on Eminent Domain, Dallas, 1962, pp. 171-196.

KUSWORM, SIDNEY G., "The Legal Aspect," *The Appraisal Journal,* April, 1949, pp. 232-238.

LATCHFORD, GEORGE, "Appraiser Witness In Condemnation Cases," *The Society of Industrial Realtors,* 1953, pp. 105-125.

LEE, ADELBERT W., "The Appraiser's Deportment In the Courtroom," *Right of Way,* October, 1963, pp. 39-44.

LEVIN, DAVID R., "Legal Problems Surrounding the Loss of Access In Right of Way Acquisition," *Selected Papers,* Right of Way Conference, Univ of Alabama, 1961.

LEWIN, GORDON, "Law and Municipal Ecology: Air, Water, Noise, Overpopulation," National Institute of Municipal Law Offices, Washington, D. C..

LICHT, FRANK, "What Courts Expect of Appraisers," *The Appraisal Journal,* July, 1969, pp. 325-329.

LINDAS, LEONARD I., "Demeanor of the Witness," *Right of Way,* April, 1956, pp. 22-24.

LINDAS, LEONARD I., "The Valuation Witness," *The Residential Appraiser,* June, 1960, pp. 21-23.

LINDAS, LEONARD I., "Tips on Testifying," *Right of Way,* June, 1963, pp. 25-27.

LIPPMAN, WILLIAM J., "Legal Problems of Condominiums," *The Appraisal Journal,* October, 1962, pp. 458-464.

LIRETTE, PAUL E., "Expropriation-Louisiana Procedure," *Right of Way,* February, 1956, pp. 19-25.

LOCKLEY, LAWRENCE C., "A Client's Complaint," *The Review,* September, 1952, pp. 13-16.

LOCKYER, ALBERT W., "Appraisal Testimony—The Appraiser's Viewpoint," *Appraisal Digest,* October, 1955, pp. 7-10.

LOCKYER, ALBERT W., "Too Young to Testify," *Appraisal Digest,* October, 1955, pp. 13.

LONG, JEREMIAH, M., "Basic Considerations In Cross-Examination," *The Appraisal Journal,* April, 1962, pp. 259-266.

LUM, Y. T., "Comparison and Use of Market Data In Preparation for Expert Testimony," *The Appraisal Journal,* April, 1963, pp. 178-184.

LUPARDUS, O. L., "Cross Examinations of an Expert Appraisal Witness," *Proceedings of the First Institute on Eminent Domain,* Dallas, 1959, pp. 185-197.

LYNN, ARTHUR D. JR., "Legal Problems and Obstacles In Assessing Land for Site Value Taxation," *Assessment of Land Value,* Ohio State University, 1970, pp. 143-155.

MADDOCK, AUBREY, "What the Attorney Expects of the Appraiser," *The Appraisal Journal,* April, 1939, pp. 162-164.

MARKEIM, J. WILLIAM, "Condemnation Phases, Condemnation Appraisals, Expert Testimony," *Technical Valuation,* February, 1956, pp. 25-31.

MARSTON, ANSON, THOMAS R. AGG, "Brief Summaries of 68 Important Court Valuation Decisions," *Engineering Valuation,* New York, 1936, pp. 186-252.

MARTIN, JAMES W., MILFORD ESTILL, "Valuation of Property Economic and Legal Standards," *Kentucky Law Journal,*

MARTIN, S. J., "Factors the IRS and the Courts Are Using Today In Valuing Closely Held Shares," *Journal of Taxation,* February, 1972.

MCDONALD, ADRIAN F., "The Appraiser In the Witness Box," *The Residential Appraiser,* December, 1958, pp. 13-17.

MCFADDEN, NORMAN E., "Money Markets and Real Estate Values," *American Right of Way Association,* Proceedings of the Third Annual National Seminar, Washington, D. C, 1958, pp. 9-11.

MCLEAN, W. M., "Hints to the Expert Witnees," *Appraisal Institute Magazine,* December, 1961, pp. 29-31.

MCVEAGH, J., *Land Valuation Law In New Zealand,* Butterworth, Wellington, 1952.

MELTZER, HERMAN, "Appraising and Testifying In Condemnation Proceedings," *Brooklyn Realty Magazine,* December, 1939, pp. 7.

MONTOYA, JOSEPH A., *Definition of Larger Parcel and Property Rights Acquired,* Condemnation Appraisal Seminar, 1958.

MORRIS, STEWART, LYLE W. MALEY, "Land Title and Escrow Problems," *American Right of Way Association,* Second Annual National Seminar, Washington, D. C, 1957, pp. 37-41.

NATIONAL ASSOCIATION OF COUNTY OFFICIALS, *Statement of the National Association of County Officials In Support of Payments In Lieu of Taxes,* Washington, January, 1956.

NEISWANGER, DAVID, "Experiences As a Court Appraiser In Condemnation Proceedings," *Technical Valuation,* February, 1955, pp. 13-16.

NIBLEY, ROBERT, "Legislation and Legal Decisions Affecting the Appraiser," *Technical Valuation,* October, 1961, pp. 24-30.

ORGEL, LEWIS, *Valuation Under the Law of Eminent Domain,* Michie, Charlottesville, Va., 1953.

PARTRIDGE, CHARLES, "Appraising and Court Testimony for Condemnation and Certiorari," *National Real Estate Journal,* September, 1937, pp. 36-38.

PAYNE, SILAS O., "Legal Aspects of Leasehold Appraisals," *The Appraisal Journal,* October, 1965, pp. 563-566.

PELOUBET, MAURICE E., "Depreciation Under the Revenue Act of 1934," *Journal of Accountancy,* September, 1934, pp. 169-197.

PESCHEL, J. L., "Oil and Gas Tax Planning Post-Reform Act Impact of CA-5s," *Journal of Taxation,* January, 1971, pp. 54-56.

PETERSON, CHARLES C. M., "Case of the Month," *Right of Way,* June, 1955, pp. 33-34, 40.

PHILLIPS, BARBARA ASHLEY, "The Oregon Tax Court Some Thoughts on Its First Decisions," *Oregon Law Review,* June, 1963, pp. 292-327.

PIERRE, JOHN A., "Detail on the United States Plywood-Algoma Case," *Assessment Administration,* Institute of American Assessment Officers, Chicago, 1959, pp. 129-131.

PRIESTMAN, GLYNDON, "Market Price Vs. Appraisal," *The Appraisal Journal,* October, 1942, pp. 328-334.

RANDALL, WILLIAM J., "Attorney's Condemnation Check Sheet," *The Appraisal Journal,* January, 1967, pp. 103-106.

RAY, RAYMOND, "Case of the Month," *Right of Way,* December, 1955, pp. 28-29.

RIGHT OF WAY, "Digest of Important Appellate Court Decisions," *Right of Way,* October, 1961.

## BIBLIOGRAPHY OF APPRAISAL LITERATURE

RING, ALFRED A., "Problems and Solutions In Appraisal Cases," *The Valuation of Real Estate,* 1970, pp. 485-563.

ROBERTS, JOHN A., "Eye Opener-The Appraiser In the Jury Room," *The Appraisal Journal,* July, 1963, pp. 483-488.

RODA, FRANK, "Legal Assumption by Appraisers," *Right of Way,* June, 1958, pp. 44-45.

ROGERS, "The Appraisal Docket, Offsetting Special Benefits Against Severance Damages," *The Appraisal Journal,* April, 1965, pp. 308-310.

ROGERS, JOHN D., "Case of the Month," *Right of Way,* February, 1955, pp. 27-29.

ROGERS, JOHN D., "On Trial—The Attorney the Expert Witness and the Right of Way Agent," *Right of Way,* April, 1959, pp. 41-44.

RUHE, KARL, "U. S. International Revenue Service Effect of Legislation on Real and Personal Property," *Appraisal and Valuation Manual,* Corporate Press, Incorporated, Washington, D. C, January, 1972, pp. 320.

RUSSELL, HORACE, "If Found Negligent, Appraisers Are Liable for Damages," *Appraisal Digest,* April, 1951, pp. 1-2.

RUSSELL, HORACE, "Professional Appraiser In Business and In Court," *The Residential Appraiser,* August, 1960, pp. 6-8.

SCHMUTZ, GEORGE L., *Condemnations and Court Testimony,* G. L. Schmutz, Los Angeles, February 25, 1937, pp. 1-11.

SCHMUTZ, GEORGE L., "Condemnations and Testimony In Court Procedure Related," *California Real Estate Magazine,* March, 1937, pp. 10-11.

SCHMUTZ, GEORGE L., "Court Testimony," *Condemnation Appraisers Handbook,* 1938, pp. 1-339.

SCHOFER, AUGUST, "Impact of the Highway Program from the National Viewpoint," *Right of Way,* April, 1963, pp. 53-57.

SEARLES, SIDNEY Z., "Aesthetics In the Law," *Appraisal Digest,* 1901, pp. 1-7.

SEARLES, SIDNEY Z., AND SIDNEY O. RAPHAEL, "Current Trends In the Laws of Condemnation," *The Appraisal Digest,* October, 1959, pp. 511-529.

SEWARD, D. T., "The Appraiser In Court," *Appraisal Institute Magazine,* September, 1963, pp. 6-8.

SEYMOUR, CHARLES F., "Market Value Vs Court Restrictions Against Speculative Assumptions," *The Valuation Manual,* April, 1966, pp. 296-299.

SILAS, O. PAYNE, "Legal Aspects of Leasehold Appraisals," *The Appraisal Journal,* October, 1965, pp. 563-566.

SIMMS, S. R., "Legal and Practical Aspects of Appraisal Law," *Appraisal Institute Magazine,* December, 1963, pp. 21-23.

SINNITT, PAUL, "Case of the Month," *Right of Way,* 1956, pp. 27-29.

SNITZER, EDWARD L., "The Law and Condemnation Appraisal," *The Real Estate Appraiser,* 1968, pp. 54-58.

SNITZER, EDWARD L., "The Law and Condemnation Appraisals," *The Real Estate Appraiser,* 1969, pp. 55-58.

SNITZER, EDWARD L., "The Law and Condemnation Appraising," *The Real Estate Appraiser,* March, 1970, pp. 55-57.

SPRAY, F., *Digest of Rating Valuation Case Law,* Rating and Valuation Society, London, 1965.

ST. GEORGE, JOHN F., "Certification In New York," *Assessment Administration,* Institute of American Assessment Officers, Chicago, 1961, pp. 177.

STACER, THOMAS C., "Rights of Way Through Timbered Areas," *Right of Way,* October, 1967, pp. 52-56.

SWAN, J. WILSON, "Case Studies In Depreciation," *The Review,* October, 1947, pp. 14-17.

▲ Appraisal for Special Purposes

TANNERY, FLADGER FREEMAN, "Legalistic Theories of Current Asset Val," *(m.A. Thesis)*, Austin, Texas, 1935.

TAYLOR, RICHARD., "Case of the Month," *Right of Way*, October, 1957, pp. 45.

TEXAS, COMPTROLLER'S OFFICE, *Circular to County Judges, County Attorneys, and Tax Assessors*, Austin, 1977.

THE APPRAISAL JOURNAL, "State of Washington Vs. the Mottman Mercantile Co.," *The Appraisal Journal*, January, 1959, pp. 107-117.

THEISS, WILLIAM R., "The Appraisal Docket. Applicable Law In Determining Fixtures When Market Value Not Used," *The Appraisal Journal*, April, 1963, pp. 271-273.

THEISS, WILLIAM R., "The Appraisal Docket. Apportionment of Condemnation Award Under 99-Year Lease," *The Appraisal Journal*, April, 1964, pp. 303-305.

THEISS, WILLIAM R., "The Appraisal Docket. Compensation for Changes In Traffic Patterns," *The Appraisal Journal*, January, 1962, pp. 124-125.

THEISS, WILLIAM R., "The Appraisal Docket. Compensation for Private Sewer System Installed In Public Schools," *The Appraisal Journal*, January, 1963, pp. 121-122.

THEISS, WILLIAM R., "The Appraisal Docket. Condemnation of Air Easement--Liability of County," *The Appraisal Journal*, July, 1962, pp. 415-416.

THEISS, WILLIAM R., "The Appraisal Docket. Constitutionality of Amortization Method of Eliminating Nonconforming Uses," *The Appraisal Journal*, January, 1966, pp. 123-125.

THEISS, WILLIAM R., "The Appraisal Docket. Effect of Option to Purchase In Lease--Evidence of Volume of Business," *The Appraisal Journal*, April, 1962, pp. 297-298.

THEISS, WILLIAM R., "The Appraisal Docket. Effect of Owner's Statement of Value In Tax Proceedings," *The Appraisal Journal*, October, 1962, pp. 550-551.

THEISS, WILLIAM R., "The Appraisal Docket. Effect on Value Caused by Announcement of Project," *The Appraisal Journal*, January, 1963, pp. 122-123.

THEISS, WILLIAM R., "The Appraisal Docket. Evaluating the Undeveloped Cemetery Property," *The Appraisal Journal*, April, 1962, pp. 294-295.

THEISS, WILLIAM R., "The Appraisal Docket. Inclusion of Apartment Building Furnishings In Award," *The Appraisal Journal*, April, 1962, pp. 290-297.

THEISS, WILLIAM R., "The Appraisal Docket. Increase In Value Caused by Improvement," *The Appraisal Journal*, January, 1962, pp. 126.

THEISS, WILLIAM R., "The Appraisal Docket. Offsetting Special Benefits Against Severance Damages," *The Appraisal Journal*, April, 1965, pp. 308-310.

THEISS, WILLIAM R., "The Appraisal Docket. Proper Jury Instructions In Valuating Lease," *The Appraisal Journal*, January, 1964, pp. 122-123.

THEISS, WILLIAM R., "The Appraisal Docket. Reliability of Sales--Assessment Method," *The Appraisal Journal*, January, 1964, pp. 121-122.

THEISS, WILLIAM R., "The Appraisal Docket. Right to Consequential Damages Due to Language of Interest Condemned," *The Appraisal Journal*, October, 1965, pp. 621-623.

THEISS, WILLIAM R., "The Appraisal Docket. Use by Landowners of Appraisals Prepared for the Condemning Authority," *The Appraisal Journal*, July, 1965, pp. 442-443.

THEISS, WILLIAM R., "The Appraisal Docket. Valuation of Large, Unrented and Unique Property," *The Appraisal Journal*, April, 1904, pp. 305-310.

THEISS, WILLIAM R., "The Appraisal Docket. Valuation of Underground Pipe Easement," *The Appraisal Journal*, February, 1962, pp. 416-417.

THEISS, WILLIAM R., "The Appraisal Docket, Assessed Value As Evidence of Condemnation Value," *The Appraisal Journal,* October, 1901, pp. 541-542.

THEISS, WILLIAM R., "The Appraisal Docket, Distinction Between General and Special Benefits," *The Appraisal Journal,* April, 1963, pp. 267-270.

THEISS, WILLIAM R., "The Appraisal Docket, Manner and Method of Determening Value of Fixtures," *The Appraisal Journal,* January, 1963, pp. 119-121.

THEISS, WILLIAM R., "The Appraisal Docket, Relocations As Condition Precedent to Possession by Condemning Authority," *The Appraisal Journal,* July, 1963, pp. 419-420.

THEISS, WILLIAM R., "The Appraisal Docket, Tax Assessment--Damages for Failure to Assess Equally," *The Appraisal Journal,* July, 1962, pp. 417-418.

THEISS, WILLIAM R., "The Appraisal Docket. Use of Construction Cost for Determining Assessed Value," *The Appraisal Journal,* July, 1965, pp. 440-441.

THOMPSON, BURTON, "Some Problems Confronting Appraisers In Condemnation Cases," *The Appraisal Journal,* July, 1937, pp. 270-272.

THOMPSON, GEORGE M., "The Appraiser's Requirements of the Lawyer," *The Real Estate Appraiser,* pp. 2.

THORSON, IVAN A., "Our Real Estate Tax Problem," *The Appraisal Journal,* October, 1937, pp. 357-364.

TIDEMAN, ROBERT, "Fractional Assessments--Do Our Courts Sanction Inequality?," *Hastings Law Journal,* May, 1965, pp. 573-589.

TULLEY ROBERT, "The Pros and Cons of Appraisal Legislation," *Appraisal and Valuation Manual,* 1961, pp. 231-259.

TURNER, JOHN F. C. AND ROBERT FICHTER, *Freedom to Build,* The McMillan Company, New York, May, 1973.

WALSH, JAMES L. JR., "How the Appraiser Can Aid the Attorney," *The Review,* December, 1948, pp. 6-8.

WALSH, JAMES L. JR., "Legal Liability of Appraisers," *The Review,* November, 1948, pp. 10-14.

WALTEMADE, HENRY G., "Expert Testimony In Condemnation," *Real Estate Record,* March 8, 1941, pp. 6..

WALTHER, HERMAN O., "...Truth, the Whole Truth, Nothing But the Truth," *The Appraisal Journal,* April, 1957, pp. 163-164.

WALTHER, HERMAN O., "Witness Stand Performance," *The Appraiser's Job In Eminent Domain Proceedings,* University of Pittsburgh, Pittsburgh, 1957, pp. 3705.

WEINGARTEN, EDWARD A., "Condemnation Law and Procedure," *Appraisal Digest,* October, 1959, pp. 1-7.

WHITE, JOHN R., "Significance of Governmental Intervention In the Housing Market," *The Appraisal Journal,* April, 1955, pp. 165-175.

WHITE, ROBERT B., "Case Report In Assessment Administration-Two Apartments Over a Small Store," *Special Publication,* Institute of American Assessment Officers, Chicago, April, 1971, pp. 41-47.

WILLISTON, WALTER B., "Court Testimony," *Appraisal Institute Magazine,* April, 1957, pp. 8-12.

WILSON, WILLIAM, "The Appraiser In Court," *Review of Society of Residential Appraisers,* June, 1939, pp. 14.

WOLFF, LEWIS N., "Case Study of Housing the Elderly," *Real Estate Analyst Appraisal Bulletin,* 1962, pp. 131-136.

YATES, DONALD H., "Testimony of the Expert Witness In Condemnation Proceedings," *The Appraisal Journal,* July, 1958, pp. 385-389.

▲ Appraisal for Special Purposes

## CHAPTER THREE

# Urban Property
by Philip F. Pierce, FASA, MAI, SRA.

Philip F. Pierce is recognized nationally as one of the foremost real estate investment analysts and appraisers. He was President of Pierce-Foster and Company for nearly twenty years. The firm was based in the Detroit, Michigan area. He has lectured extensively in the United States, Canada and Mexico and has published a number of articles concerning the profession.

He served in numerous capacities with the American Society of Appraisers and as their International President for two terms. He was a prime mover in supporting Licensing and Certification Legislation of Appraisers and led the Society in supporting such action. It was during his first term, as International President of the Society, that these efforts culminated in the unanimous adoption by the Board of Governors of the well-known guidelines concerning Licensing and Certification of Appraisers. Mr. Pierce was also a prime mover in encouraging universities to provide a broad base undergraduate and graduate degree programs for the multi-disciplinary profession of appraising.

He is a member of numerous other professional appraisal organizations and a member of the National Panel of Arbitrators, American Arbitration Association.

He retired at the age of forty-three and now lives in Tucson, Arizona. He is currently a Director of the Education Foundation, American Society of Appraisers.

## Urban Property

THE WEIGHT of the number of entries in this chapter of "The Bibliography of Appraisal Literature" is overwhelming. There are approximately 1,700 entries in this chapter. The range of subjects referenced demonstrates the detailed research that went into its preparation.

References were drawn from dissertations, text books, professional journals, news magazines, government bulletins and trade publications. Author input includes the full range of articles from casual observations from outside the profession to the most sophisticated in-depth study by learned appraisal professionals, educators and researchers.

Urban property appraisal has always been the most challenging professional activity within the broader field of professional practice, not because it may be the most difficult intellectually, but because of the range of types of properties involved, and the complexities inherent in the economic, social, cultural structures of our cities.

The city itself, its size, location, power resources, social influence, governmental structure, educational opportunities, economic profile and leadership influence has long been the focal point of past and present societies. From Ancient Rome to the Mayas of the Yucatan to the present metropolitan vastness of New York, Tokyo and Paris, this holds true.

A contributing factor to the wealth of any urban area is the value of its real property. The measurement of that value, whether it be in the form of a broad economic statistical profile of the community or an individual appraisal of a specific property, within the community, is often the task of professional appraisal analyses and non-professional observations alike. To facilitate that task, this compilation has been published.

Of more importance, however, is the concept of the text itself. This is "The Bibliography of Appraisal Literature" and includes reference entries from the various disciplines that constitute professional appraisal activity. Each one of us, in day-to-day activity, makes many appraisals. In the generic sense, we make many value judgments concerning the quality and quantity of tangible and intangible things. In the same fashion, the professional appraiser makes trained professional judgments concerning the quality and quantity, and/or monetary value, of tangible and intangible property. He is a trained specialist in a particular discipline (real property, machinery and equipment, personal property, public utilities, intangible property, etc). *Before becoming a trained specialist in a discipline, the appraiser must have a full understanding of the application of appraisal principles and procedures that apply to value judgments of all types of properties, whether real, personal or intangible. The underlying economic and social factors that effect value are common and apply with varying pressures, whether the property be real, personal or intangible.*

To say that one must be a generalist before one can be a specialist applies with

# BIBLIOGRAPHY OF APPRAISAL LITERATURE

equal validity, whether an individual is a professional appraiser, medical doctor, lawyer or educator. This premise is accepted by all of the recognized professions and is the cornerstone of the philosophy of the American Society of Appraisers. To this end, the American Society of Appraisers will continue to support the colleges' and universities' efforts to provide undergraduate and graduate education to those interested in the appraisal profession, and to this end, the American Society of Appraisers publishes this text, as a continuing aid to students, researchers, and educators who seek the full impact of all research data available.

# Urban Property

13-11-00  City Growth and Planning
13-12-00  Parking Facility
13-13-00  Urban Renewal
13-14-00  Central Business District Property
13-15-00  Commercial Property and Concerns
13-16-00  Housing
13-17-00  Residential Property
13-18-00  Rent and Rent Control
13-19-00  Residential Buildings
13-20-00  Commercial Buildings
13-21-00  Institutional Property and Buildings and Concerns
13-22-00  Subdivisions
13-23-00  Suburban Property

## 13-11 City Growth and Planning

ADAMS, THOMAS, LEWIS, H. M., MCCROSKY, T. T., *Population Land Values & Govt; Studies of Growth & Dist of Pop & Land Values; & of Problems of Govt*, N.Y. Regional Plan of N.Y. & Its Environs, New York, pp. 320.

ALBERT, FRANKLIN E., "Zoning and Its Effect on Land Values," *The Residential Appraiser*, December, 1962, pp. 2-5.

ALDIS, GRAHAM, "A Skeptics Note on City Planning," *The Appraisal Journal*, January, 1961, pp. 111-112.

ALEXANDER, LAURENCE A., "Problems and Potentials of Downtown," *Right of Way*, August, 1967, pp. 37-38.

AMERICAN ECONOMIC REVIEW, "Urban Growth and Development," *American Economic Review*, May, 1971, pp. 334-359.

AMERICAN INSTITUTE OF REAL ESTATE APPRAISERS, *Problems in Urban Real Estate Appraisal*, American Institute of Real Estate Appraisers, 1967.

AMERICAN SOCIETY OF PLANNING OFFICIALS, *Civic Center Planning*, Chicago, 1900.

APP, FRANK J., "Condominium Conversion In California," *The Real Estate Appraiser*, The Society of Real Estate Appraisers, Chicago Illinois, November 1, 1973, pp. 9-12.

APPEL, JAMES R., "The City's Stake In Its Downtown District," *Real Estate Analyst Appraisal Bulletin*, 1953, pp. 545-552.

APPEL, JAMES R., "Zoning Pitfalls for the Appraiser," *Real Estate Analyst Appraisal Bulletin*, 1900, pp. 251-254.

APPRAISAL DIGEST, *Values In Restricted Areas*, January, 1954, pp. 19-20.

APPRAISAL DIGEST, "Minimum Size Houses Zoning Control," *Appraisal Digest*, January, 1953, pp. 5.

APPRAISAL DIGEST, "The Price of Pride," *Urban Land*, January, 1956, pp. 8-9.

ARCHITECTURAL FORUM, "Architectural Design and Structural Requirements of Loaning Institutions," *Architectural Forum*, September, 1922, pp. 119-122.

AUGUR, TRACY B., "Decentralization Can't Wait," *The Appraisal Journal*, January, 1949, pp. 107-113.

BABCOCK, FREDERICK M., "Alley Computation-Side Alley and Dead-End Rear Alley," *The Appraisal of Real Estate*, 1924, pp. 370.

BABCOCK, FREDERICK M., "City Growth and Development," *Valuation of Real Estate*, 1932, pp. 49-78.

BABCOCK, FREDERICK M., "Corner Reflection Coefficients Frontage Equivalents Plottage Allowance," *Appraisal of Real Estate*, 1924, pp. 358-362.

BABCOCK, FREDERICK M., "Influence of Social and Racial Factors on Value," *Valuation of Real Estate*, 1932, pp. 86-92.

BABCOCK, FREDERICK M., "The Control of Neighborhoods," *The Real Estate Record*, January 16, 1937, pp. 7-15.

BABCOCK, FREDERICK M., "The Prediction of Population," *Valuation of Real Estate*, 1932, pp. 79-85.

BABCOCK, HENRY A., "An Economic Theory of Land Utilization and City Growth," *The Economist*, Chicago, June 30, 1933, pp. 4.

BABCOCK, HENRY A., "City Growth and Transportation," *The Appraisal Journal*, July, 1938, pp. 249-254.

BABCOCK, HENRY A., "Trends Affecting Urban Real Estate Values," *The Economist*, December 16, 1932, pp. 5-12.

BABCOCK, RICHARD F., JAN DRASNOW-IEKI, "Legal Aspects of Planned Unit Residential Development," *Technical Bulletin 52 of the Urban Land Institute*, 1965.

BABCOCK, WILLIAM H., "Long-Time Lease Important Factor In Growth of Cities," *National Real Estate Journal*, March 12, 1923, pp. 49-51, 53.

BACH, IRA J., "What Lies Ahead for the Inner City," *Residential Appraiser*, 1961, pp. 15-17, 22-23.

BAILEY, WILLIAM L., "Appraising Urban Communities: Techniques and Objectives," *Journal of Land and Public Utility Economics*, February, 1940, pp. 1-7.

BAILEY, WILLIAM L., "Appraising Your City: a Scientific Method of Comparing the Advantages of Different Communities," *National Real Estate Journal*, May 18, 1925, pp. 37-39.

BAILEY, WILLIAM L., "Current Census Reports and Real Estate Prospects," *Freehold*, October 1, 1940, pp. 228-231.

BAKER, O. E., "Population and City Growth," *The Real Estate Appraiser*, December 12, 1936.

BALL, CHARLES, "Zoning Code Modernization and the Appraiser," *Technical Valuation*, June, 1961, pp. 2-6.

BALLARD, WILLIAM S., "Property Damage by Public Planning," *The Appraisal Journal*, April, 1969, pp. 211-214.

BALLOU, PAUL, "Emerging Valuation Problems with Changing Patterns of Development," *The Assessors Journal*, July, 1966, pp. 9-16.

BANCO CENTRAL DE VENEZUELA, "Valor De La Construccion Privada," *Boletin*, Sotave, Caracas, Venezuela, pp. 37-43.

BARBAGELATA, JOSE, "Aranceles De Areas Urbanas De Lima," *Boletin*, Sotave, Caracas, Venezuela, pp. 37-39.

BARTHOLOMEW, HERLAND, "Preventing Disintegration of Cities," *Civil Engineering*, May, 1966, pp. 259-262.

BASHAW, FREDERICK J., "American Urbanism and the Appraisal Profession," *The Appraisal Journal*, April, 1949, pp. 183-188.

BASSETT, EDWARD M., "Zoning: Laws, Administration, Court Decisions During the First Twenty Years," *Zoning the Laws Administration and Court Decisions During the First Twenty Years*, The Russell Sage Foundation, New York City, 1937.

BEACH, D. W., "Land Costs Push Regional Centers Up and Out," *Appraisal Journal*, October, 1971, pp. 606-609.

BENNETT, SAUL Z., "The City," *A Student's Appraisal Report on a Single-Family Residence*, American Institute of Real Estate Appraisers, Chicago, 1964, pp. 2.

BERNARD, ALFRED D., "Role for Appraising of Corners," *Appraising Manual*, S. L. McMichael, 1937, pp. 383.

BLOOD, J., "Community Family Centers: Taking a Bigger Slice of Chicago Sales," *Merchandising Week*, August 23, 1971, pp. 14.

BODFISH, H. MORTON, "Changes In the Central Business District of a Growing City," *The National Real Estate Journal*, October 18, 1926, pp. 17-19.

BODFISH, H. MORTON, "Population and Peak Land Values In Business Districts," *The Journal of Land and Public Utility Economics*, August, 1930, pp. 270-277.

BODNAR, ERNEST B., "City-University Cooperative Relationships," *Management Information Service*, November, 1964.

BOECKH, EVERARD HEREFORD, "Zoning Laws," *Manual of Appraisals*, 1937, pp. 354-355.

BORCHARD, RALPH R., "Planing and Zoning Affect Almost All Uses of Land," *The Appraisal Digest*, October, 1954, pp. 1-5.

BRAUN, RICHARD L., "Freeways and Cities," *How Transportation Affects Real Estate Values*, A. I. R. E. A, Chicago, March 7, 1969, pp. 9-11.

BREMICKER, CARL T., "Area Development," *The Residential Appraiser*, February, 1957, pp. 14-16.

BRENNAN, M. L., "Community Planning Institute of Canada," *Appraisal Institute Magazine*, Appraisal Institute of Canada, Winnipeg.

BROWN, J. EVERETT, "Theory of the Urban Land Market," *Appraisal Institute Magazine*, Appraisal Institute of Canada, Winnipeg.

BROWN, LESTER G., WEIDLER, JOHN B, "The Role of the Analyst-Appraiser In Urban Problems and Urban Growth Planning," *The Real Estate Appraiser*, March, 1969.

BRUHN, JOHN A., "Zoning---Its Effect on Property Value," *The Appraisal Journal*, October, 1969, pp. 558-559.

BRUNSMAN, HOWARD G., SHYROCK, HENRY S., JR, "Population Migration---Who's Moving Where," *The Appraisal Journal*, January, 1957, pp. 74-80.

BULLINGER, CLARENCE E., *Engineering Economic Analysis*, Mcgraw-Hill, New York.

BUNKER, HENRY B., "An Appraisal of a City Block," *The Appraisal Journal*, July, 1945, pp. 275-282.

BUNKER, RAYMOND, *Town and Country or City and Region*, Melbourne University Press, May, 1973.

BURNS, JOHN C., ARTHUR J. POLLAKOWSKI, "Problems In Neighborhood Development," *Appraisal and Valuation Manual*, Corporate Press Incorporated, Washington, D. C, January, 1972, pp. 298.

BURTON, H. J., *Valuations and Depreciation of City Buildings*, Natl Assn of Bldg Owners & Mgrs, 1917.

BUSINESS WEEK, "Firmer Foundation for New Towns," *Business Week*, January 9, 1971, pp. 22.

BUTTENHEIM, HAROLD S., "How a City's Acreage Increases," *Appraising Manual*, 1937, pp. 256.

CALIFORNIA STATE OFFICE OF PLANNING, "Bibliography of Exclusive Agricultural Zoning Law," *The Journal of the American Society of Farm Managers and Rural Appraisers*, October, 1962, pp. 67-71.

CAPPER, G. C. F., "Decay, Development and Land Values," *Manchester School of Economic and Social Studies*, January, 1964, pp. 25-41.

CAPPOZZA, DENNIS, *Transportation Cost and Urban Retail Trade*, University of Southern California Working Paper 8.

CAPT, J. C., "Appraisal Significance of Census Statistics," *The Appraisal Journal*, April, 1946, pp. 125-135.

CARBERT, LESLIE E., "Property Tax Exemptions As a Tool of Planning," *Conference Proceedings*, National Tax Association, Columbus, 1965, pp. 234.

CARRUTH, E., "Big Move to New Towns," *Fortune*, 1971, pp. 94-97.

CARUSONE, PETER S., "The Shakeout In Small City CBS's," *Urban Land*, Washington, D.C., February, 1971.

CASE, FRED E., JAMES GILLISE, "Some Aspects of Land Planning--The San Fernando Valley Case," *The Appraisal Journal*, January, 1955, pp. 14-41.

CHAIN STORE AGE, "Seek Billion for New Centers," *Chain Store Age*, February, 1971, pp. 25.

CHATELAIN, LEON, JR., "Cities Will Survive," *The Residential Appraiser*, December, 1957, pp. 13-16.

CHRISTENSEN, ROBERT, "City Planning and Zoning," *The Review*, May, 1947, pp. 16-18.

CHRISTENSEN, ROBERT, "City Planning and Zoning," *The Review*, May, 1947, pp. 16-18.

CLARK, COLIN, "The Economic Functions of a City," *The Appraisal Journal*, January, 1946, pp. 69-76.

CLARK, HORACE F., "City Growth-Causes and Values," *Appraising the Home*, 1930, pp. 9-22.

CLARK, HORACE F., "Lot Appraisal," *Appraising the Home*, 1930, pp. 43-68.

CLARK, HORACE F., "Zoning," *Appraising the Home*, 1930, pp. 30-36.

CLARK, J. A., "New Proposed Valuation Taxes Will Cause Major Revisions In Estate Planning," *Journal of Taxation*, September, 1970, pp. 130-133.

CLAUS, R. JAMES, "Appraising Potential Volume of Shopping Site Sales," *Appraisal Institute Magazine*, Appraisal Institute of Canada, Winnipeg, September 1, 1971.

CLEMINSHAW, J. M., "The Revaluation of Municipalities for Tax Equalization Purposes," *The Appraisal Journal*, January, 1944, pp. 52-65.

CLICKNER, EDWIN K., "Highest Land Use As a Planning Tool," *The Appraisal Journal*, April, 1969, pp. 215-223.

CLONTS, H. A., JR., "Influence of Urbanization on Land Values at the Urban Periphery," *Land Economics*, November, 1970, pp. 489-497.

COFFIN, GEORGE H. JR., *Zoning and Property Values*, California Real Estate Association, Los Angeles, 1936.

COFFIN, GEORGE H. JR., "Appraising Property Zoned for Business," *The Appraisal Journal*, October, 1934, pp. 29-33.

COMMERCE TODAY, "Future Population Growth Seen Changing Quality of U.S. Life," *Commerce Today*, April 5, 1971, pp. 20-21.

CONVERSE, C. L., "Appraising the Corner Lot," *National Association Of Real Estate Boards, Annals of Real Estate Practice*, 1927, pp. 263-266.

COOPER K. J., "The Impact of Technology and Changing Social Patterns on Property Values," *Valuer*, The New Zealand Institute of Valuers, New Zealand, August 1, 1973, pp. 124-134.

COPELAND, HARRY E., "Appraising District Change," *Review of the Society of Residential Appraisers*, January, 1937, pp. 7-10.

COWLES, HERBERT V., *How to Assess Property In Cities and Rural Towns*, Wisconsin Tax Commission, Madison, 1914.

COWLEY, LEONARD M., "Zoning--A Source of Property Value," *The Appraisal Journal*, July, 1940, pp. 253-254.

CREEDY, JOHN A., "Navigation, Water Resources, and Patterns of Economic Growth," *How Transportation Affects Real Estate Values*, A. I. R. E. A., Chicago, March 7, 1969, pp. 37-40.

DAVIE, MAURICE R., "The Pattern of Urban Growth," *Studies In the Science of Society*, Yale University Press, New Haven, 1937.

DAVIES, DAVID G., "The Growth of Urban Governmental Spending," *Conference Proceedings*, National Tax Association, Columbus, 1965, pp. 591-599.

DE LEEUW, F., "Demand for Housing: a Review of Cross Section Evidence," *Review of Economics and Statistics*, February, 1971, pp. 1-10.

DELL, BURNHAM N., "Population," *Population, Labor and Social Form*, Little Brown and Company, Boston, 1937, pp. 54-174.

DENTON, JOHN H., "The British New Towns," *The Residential Appraiser*, December, 1959, pp. 19-23.

DES JARDINS, RICHARD J., "Zoning for Sound Neighborhoods," *The Review*, January, 1952, pp. 8-10.

DILMORE, GENE, "Corner Influence Factors from the Market," *Real Estate Appraiser*, January, 1970, pp. 27-30.

DORAU, HERBERT B., AND ALBERT G. HINMAN, *The Future of Cities,* Macmillan, New York, 1928, pp. 537-558.

DOUD, LAURENCE F., "Actual Appraisal Reports: Appraisal of Land for Future Location of Manufacturing and Holder Plant," *National Real Estate Journal,* June, 1932, pp. 55-57.

DOWNS, ANTHONY, "A Critique The Death and Life of Great American Cities," *The Appraisal Journal,* July, 1962, pp. 386-390.

DOWNS, GEORGE W., "Baltimore's Time Proven Tax Plats," *Case Reports In Assessment Administration,* September, 1961.

DOWNS, M. D., "The Coordination of Tax Assessments and Zoning," *Planners Journal,* 1935, pp. 23-24.

DOXIADIS, C. A., *Urban Renewal and the Future of the American City,* Public Administration Service, Chicago, 1966.

EDMAN, J. J., "Further Developments In Twin City Power Cases. Appraisal Docket," *The Appraisal Journal,* October, 1958, pp. 614-617.

EDMAN, J. J., "Possibility of Zoning Amendment As an Element of Value. Appraisal Docket," *The Appraisal Journal,* July, 1958, pp. 447-449.

EDMAN, J. J., "Scarcity of Land Zoned In Like Manner Pertinent. Appraisal Docket," *The Appraisal Journal,* July, 1959, pp. 413-418.

ELY, RICHARD T., "Real Estate and National Planning," *Appraisal Journal,* July, 1940, pp. 222-225.

ELY, RICHARD T., AND OTHERS, *Urban Land Economics,* B, Edwards Bros.

ENGINEERING NEWS-RECORD, "1.4 - Billion New Town Within a City Proposed," *Engineering News-Record,* June 4, 1970, pp. 14.

ERSKINE, R. C., "Anticipating the Future Value of City Real Estate," *National Real Estate Journal,* August, 1939, pp. 31-32.

FALUDI, E. G., "Urban Planning and Renewal In Canada," *Appraisal and Valuation Manual,* 1960, pp. 109-116.

FAVA, EDWARD, *Appraisal of the Value of 73-48 193rd Street,* American Society of Appraisers, pp. 103-116.

FEDERAL HOUSING ADMINISTRATION, *A Handbook on Urban Redevelopment for Cities In the United States,* Government Printing Office, Washington D. C, November, 1961, pp. 105.

FEDERAL RESERVE BANK OF CLEVELAND, "Potential Economic Growth of the United States During the Next Decade," *The Appraisal Journal,* July, 1955, pp. 413-420.

FEDERAL RESERVE BANK OF CHICAGO, "The Big City—Are Its Days Numbered," *The Appraisal Journal,* April, 1955, pp. 247-253.

FEDERAL RESERVE BANK OF CHICAGO, "The Declining Small Town," *The Appraisal Journal,* October, 1959, pp. 506-510.

FELT, JAMES, "The Changing City," *Appraisal Digest,* 1904, pp. 2-5.

FILLEY, ROBERT B., "Land Use Surveys Applied to Appraising and City Planning," *Review of Society of Residential Appraisers,* October, 1940, pp. 9-11.

FISHER, EDMOND C., "Zoning In Eminent Domain a Moral Hazard," *The Appraisal Journal,* July, 1965, pp. 331-335.

FISHER, ERNEST M., "Economics of Decentralization," *The Appraisal Journal,* April, 1942, pp. 135-142.

FOSS, GEORGE B. JR., "Interested Third Parties In Zoning," *The Appraisal Journal,* January, 1960, pp. 97-118.

FRANZEN, WILLIAM F., "Urban Property Some Disadvantages," *The Residential Appraiser,* January, 1960, pp. 12-16.

GABLER, L. R., "Population Size As a Determinant of City Expenditures and Employment Some Further Evidence," *Land Ecomomics,* May, 1971, pp. 130.

GAKENHEIMER, RALPH A., "Planning, Transportation, and the Small City," *The Appraisal Journal,* January, 1966, pp. 80-92.

GIBSON, NEVILLE E., "Project 200 - Vancouver," *Appraisal Institute Magazine,* Appraisal Institute of Canada, Winnipeg.

GIEDION, SIGFRIED, *Architecture and the Phenomena of Transition, The Three Space Conceptions In Architecture,* Oxford University Press.

GILBERT, H. M., "Asset Value of Human Organization," *Management Accounting,* July, 1970, pp. 25-28.

GITTERMAN, A. N., "On Corner Influence," *The Appraisal Journal,* April, 1933, pp. 256-258.

GLADSTONE, ROBERT M., "Does Building a City Make Economic Sense," *The Appraisal Journal,* July, 1966.

GOLDSTON, ELI, JAMES H. SCHEUER, "Zoning of Planned Residential Developments," *The Appraisal Journal,* October, 1960, pp. 449-461.

GOTTLIEB, M., "Influences on Value In Urban Land Markets, U. S. A. , 1956-1961."

GRAY, A. F. B., "Problems In Metropolitan Toronto," *Assessment Administration,* I. A. A. O, Chicago, 1961, pp. 80-82.

GREAT BRITAIN MINISTRY OF HOUSING AND LOCAL GOVERN, *Distribution of Rateable Values Between Different Classes of Property In England and Values,* H. M. Stationery Offices, London, 1956.

GREER, GUY, "The Effect of Decentralization Upon Values," *Technical Valuation,* April, 1947, pp. 26-29.

H. P. MILLER, "Population, Pollution, and Affluence," *Business Horizons,* 1971.

HAGMAN, D. G., "Open Space Planning and Property Taxation, Some Suggestions," *Wisconsin Law Review,* July, 1964, pp. 628.

HAGOOD, WAYNE D., "Feasibility Studies for Commercial Developments In Small Towns," *The Real Estate Appraiser,* August, 1967, pp. 12-16.

HAMILTON, HOWARD P., "Valuation of Improved Urban Land," *Appraisal Institute Magazine,* Appraisal Institute of Canada, Winnipeg, March 1, 1971.

HANSON, PETER, "Relation of Zoning to Appraisals," *National Real Estate Journal,* April 13, 1931, pp. 49-50.

HARMAN, GABRIEL C., "Directing the Growth of Metropolitan Areas by Cooperative Planning," *National Real Estate Journal,* December 26, 1927, pp. 26-31.

HARRIS, WILLIAM W., "Our Changing Population and the Apartment Market," *The Real Estate Appraiser,* November, 1963, pp. 24-31.

HARVEY, ROBERT O., AND W. A. V. CLARK, "Controlling Urban Growth the New Zealand and Australian Experiment," *The Appraisal Journal,* October, 1964, pp. 551-558.

HAUSER, PHILIP M., "Population Shifts," *The Appraisal Journal,* July, 1943, pp. 223-230.

HAUSER, PHILIP M., "The Challenge of Metropolitan Growth," *The Appraisal Journal,* April, 1959, pp. 220-227.

HAYES, R. W., "Man and His Car Are Not Soon Parted So Parking Layout Is a Vital Element In Development Planning," *House and Home,* September, 1971, pp. 50.

HOAGLAND, HENRY E., "City Planning and Zoning, Chapter Xxv," *Real Estate Principles,* 1940, pp. 511.

HOLDEN, ARTHUR C., "Eliminating Block Depreciation by Group Management," *Real Estate Record and Builder's Guide,* March 24, 1934, pp. 6-8.

HOYT, HOMER, *City Growth and Mortgage Risk,* Washington.

HOYT, HOMER, "City Growth and Your Building," *Real Estate,* January 16, 1937, pp. 8-9.

HOYT, HOMER, "Growth of Cities," *Skyscraper Management,* July, 1937.

HOYT, HOMER, "Urban Growth and Real Estate Values," *The Appraisal Journal,* October, 1940, pp. 332-340.

HOYT, HOMER, "Urban Growth In the Next Fifteen Years," *The Residential Appraiser,* February, 1961, pp. 2-11.

HUBIN, VINCENT J., "Pedestrian Traffic Counts," *The Appraisal Journal,* July, 1953, pp. 397-415.

HUDSON, RAY M., "Making a Town Livable, a Suggestion for Greater Stability," *National Real Estate Journal,* October 4, 1926, pp. 17-24.

HURD, RICHARD M., "Forces Creating Cities," *Principles of City Land Values,* Chapters 2-4, 1924, pp. 159.

HURD, RICHARD MELANCTHON, "Principles of City Land Values," New York, 1911.

HURTADO MARTINEZ, LUIS, ALBERTO ANGULO LOPEZ, "El Valor De Los Terrenos Para Uso Multifamiliar," *Boletin,* Sotave, Caracas, Venezuela, pp. 35-37.

IICH, S. G., "Planning In Metropolitan Winnipeg," *Appraisal Institute Magazine,* December, 1963, pp. 4-8.

INSURED MORTGAGE PORTFOLIO, *City Growth Factors,* 1936.

IOWA LAW REVIEW, "Taxation Affecting Agriculture Land Use," *Iowa Law Review,* 1965, pp. 600-618.

JENNING, JOSEPH B., "New Depreciation Provisions of the 1954 Revenue Code," *Technical Valuation,* ASA, Jamaica, June, 1955, pp. 13.

KAHN, SANDERS A., "A Look at Real Estate Planning," *The Appraisal Journal,* July, 1954, pp. 423-429.

KAPLAN, WILLIAM L., "Zoning Controls, Their Change and Modification," *The Appraisal Journal,* July, 1966, pp. 370-374.

KELLER, HARRY K., "Zoning and the Appraisers," *Appraisal Digest,* January, 1954, pp. 17-18.

KELLOUGH, W. R., "Community Planning, Its Effect on Value," *The Real Estate Appraiser,* pp. 47.

KELLOUGH, W. R., "Zoning and the Value of Real Property," *The Residential Appraiser,* October, 1960, pp. 10-11.

KENNEDY G., D. HILL, "Economic and Environmental Effects of One Way Streets In Residential Areas," *Appraisal Journal,* October, 1971, pp. 562-567.

KING, BOWDEN V., *Realtor's Guide to Architecture,* Prentice-Hall, Englwd Cliffs, N.J., 1954.

KING, PATRICK, "Effects of Establishing Restricted Industrial Zone," *Appraisal Institute Magazine,* Appraisal Institute of Canada, Winnipeg.

KINNEY, R. W., "The New Life In Small Towns," *Appraisal Institute Magazine,* Appraisal Institute of Canada, Winnipeg.

KNODELL, H. W., "The Effect of City Growth on Values," *National Real Estate Journal,* March, 1934, pp. 31-32.

KNOWLES, JEROME, JR., "City and Neighborhood Data and Analysis," *The Appraisal Journal,* April, 1967, pp. 260-268.

KOSTKA, V. J., "The Effect of Neighborhood and Community Planning on Land Values," *Appraisal Institute Magazine,* Appraisal Institute of Canada, Winnipeg.

LANGSLET, OTTO, "Cities Enter the Real Estate Business, Management of City Property," *Commonwealth Review,* May, 1937, pp. 138-139.

LARONGE, JOSEPH, "Should We Get Excited About Retail Decentralization," *National Real Estate Journal,* December, 1933, pp. 22-24, 54.

LARTITEGUI, JAVIER, "Urbanismo: Uso De La Tierra," *Boletin,* Sotave, Caracas, Venezuela, pp. 25-35.

LEANEY, D. P., "Lombard Place Development, Winnipeg," *Appraisal Institute Magazine,* Appraisal Institute of Canada, Winnipeg.

LECRAW, CHARLES S., SMITH, WILBUR S, "Zoning Applied to Parking," *The Appraisal Journal,* July, 1947, pp. 399-410.

LEE, M. W., "Absence of Zoning and Its Effect on Value," *Assessment Administration,* I.A.A.O., Chicago, 1965, pp. 96-99.

LEET, EDMUND, "Demonstration Appraisal of Property Situated at 725 South Dale Street, Denver, Colorado," *Technical Valuation,* February, 1960, pp. 33-44.

LESSINGER, JACK, "Is the Supply of Urban Land Running Out," *The Appraisal Journal,* January, 1962, pp. 61-68.

LEVIN, EARL, "Land Planning and Land Costs," *Appraisal Institute Magazine,* September, 1959, pp. 4-14.

LEVY, R., "New City In a Hurry," *Duns:,* 1971, pp. 63.

LEWIS, H. M., "Land Values, Distribution Within New York Region and Relation to Various Factors In Urban Growth," *Engineering Series, Monograph No. 3,* New York, pp. 72.

LEWIS, HAROLD M., "Relation of Assessed Value to Zoning," *Preliminary Report, No. 5,* Harold M, Lewis, Washington, 1956.

LOCKYER, ALBERT W., "Zoning and Dispersion," *Appraisal Digest,* January, 1952, pp. 11-12.

LOCKYER, ALBERT W., "Zoning As it Affects Real Estate Value," *Appraisal Digest,* April, 1958, pp. 11-12.

LOOMIS, D., "Rich Washington Suburb Rules Building Projects Must Include Units for Poor," *House and Home,* September, 1971, pp. 8..

LOVING, PHILIP L., "The Development and Application of Corner Influence and Depth Factor Tables," *Assessment Administration,* I. A. A. O, Chicago, 1960, pp. 157-162.

MALLARD, WM. F. R., "Civil Planning---Human and Other Values," *Technical Valuation,* pp. 15.

MANN, PATRICK C., "Publicly-Owned Utility Profits A Problem of Pricing," *Mississippi Valley Journal of Business and Economics,* Louisiana State University, New Orleans, 1970, pp. 45-46.

MARCANO VALLENILLA, OCTAVIO, "Breves Consideraciones Uso De La Tierra," *Boletin,* Sotave, Caracas, Venezuela, pp. 21-22.

MARFAN MONTEL, MANVEL, "Relation of Value of Four Corners of a Specific Street Intersection," *The Appraisal Journal,* April, 1955, pp. 241-246.

MARLYN, FRANK, "Metropolitan Development and District Planning," *Appraisal Institute Magazine,* September, 1960, pp. 6-8.

MARR C. R., "Study of London: Problems Associated with a Progressive Metropolis," *The Valuer,* The Commonwealth Institute of Valuers, Sydney, Australia, October 1, 1973, pp. 628-632.

MARSHALL, T., "Housing Development or Virgin Land A California Town Is Torn by Controversy," *House and Home,* August, 1970, pp. 18-19.

MAYER, L. A., "U. S. Economy In an Age of Uncertainty New Questions About the U. S. Population," *Fortune,* February, 1971, pp. 80-85.

MAYER, L. A., "U. S. Population Growth Would Slower Be Better," *Fortune,* June, 1970, pp. 80-83.

MCCOY, CHARLES R., "The Problem of a Nonconforming Use," *Real Estate Analyst Appraisal Bulletin,* 1952, pp. 57-64.

MCCUTCHEON, JAMES T., "Why Should Cities Do Their Own Assessing," *Tax Digest,* 1963, pp. 116-117.

MCDONALD, D. L., "The National Capital Commission and Its Effect on Real Estate Activities," *Appraisal Institute Magazine,* September, 1960, pp. 3-5.

MCENTIRE, DAVIS, "Population and Land Values," *The Appraisal Journal*, July, 1949, pp. 311-317.

MCGOUGH R. M., "The Impact of Town Planning on Investment Decision," *Valuer*, The New Zealand Institute of Valuers, New Zealand, August 1, 1973, pp. 91-98.

MCKEE, D. L., W. H. LEAHY, "Intra-Urban Dualism In Developing Economies," *Land Economics*, November, 1970, pp. 486-489.

MCKEEVER, J. ROSS, "Business Parks-Office Parks, Plazas and Centers," *Urban Land Institute Bulletin*, 1970.

MCMICHAEL, STANLEY, ROBERT F. BINGHAM, "City Growth Essentials," *Stanley McMichael Publishing Organization*, 1928, pp. 432.

MCMICHAEL, STANLEY L., "Alleys," *Appraising Manual*, 1937.

MCMICHAEL, STANLEY L., "Appraising Corner Lots," *Appraising Manual*, 1937.

MCMICHAEL, STANLEY L., "Types of Odd-Shaped Lots," *The Appraisal Journal*, pp. 528-529.

MCMICHAEL, STANLEY L., "Valuing Odd Shaped Lots-Appraising by Zones Merging Lot Values," *American Academy of Social and Political Science*, March, 1930, pp. 396-402.

MCMICHAEL, STANLEY L., ROBERT F. BINGHAM, "City Growth and Values," *The Stanley McMichael Publishing Organization*, 1923.

MCNAMARA, KATHERINE, *Bibliography of Planning 1928-1935*, Harvard University Press, Cambridge, 1936, pp. 232

MERCHANTS ASSOCIATION OF NEW YORK, "Report on District Population Shifts In Manhattan," *Real Estate Record and Builder's Guide*, September 26, 1931, pp. 9..

MERTZKE, ARTHUR J., "Land Values and Population," *Journal of Land and Public Utility Economics*, July, 1926, pp. 343-354.

MIELDS JR. HUGH, "Federally Assisted New Communities:New Dimensions In Urban Development," Urban Land Institute, Washington Dc, pp. 1-288.

MITCHELL, KENNETH F., "Land Planning for Residences," *The Review*, July, 1954, pp. 16-18.

MONDELLO, R., "Perspective De La Construction a Montreal," *Appraisal Institute Magazine*, Appraisal Institute of Canada, Winnipeg.

MONDELLO, ROMEO, "Relationship Between Zoning and Real Estate Appraisal," *Appraisal Institute Magazine*, June, 1961, pp. 24-27.

MONTANO, JOSEPH M., "Fundamentals of Real Property," *American Association of State Highway Officials*, 1962, pp. 7-15.

MOSS, HUNTER, "Don't Plan Downtown Without People," *The Appraisal Journal*, April, 1964, pp. 294-297.

MOURRAY, JAMES W., "Legal, Noconforming Use Appeal," *The Appraisal Journal*, October, 1966, pp. 592-595.

N. Y. TIMES INDEX, "City Plan Comm Appr Cooper Sq Urban Renew Plan Calling for 1000 Units of New Housing," *N. Y. Times Index*, January 8, 1970.

N. Y. TIMES INDEX, "Community Tensions Aroused by Heritage Village, $100-Million Condominium Developmt for Elderly South," *The N. Y. Times Index*, May 6, 1970.

N. Y. TIMES INDEX, "Ground Broken for $10-Million Co-Op Apartment House on Park Avenue," *N. Y. Times Index*, October 11, 1970.

NATIONAL ASSOCIATION OF ASSESSING OFFICERS, *Urban Land Appraisals*, Chicago, January, 1940.

NATIONAL RESOURCES COMMITTEE, URBANISM COMMITTEE, "Our Cities, Their Role In National Economy," *Our Cities, Their-role In the National Economy*, Government Printing Office, Washington, 1937.

NELSON, A. V., "Unified Standards Would Lessen Confusion In City Growth," *National Real Estate Journal*, September, 1940, pp. 10.

NEUSES, DON P., "The Rocky Road of Zoning," *The Real Estate Appraiser,* American Institute of Real Estate Appraisers, August, 1966, pp. 23.

NEUTZE, M., "Price of Land for Urban Development," *Economic Record,* September, 1970, pp. 313-328.

NICHOLS, J. C., "Planning for Permanence," *The Review,* January, 1949, pp. 15-17.

NIRENSTEIN, NATHAN, "There'll Always Be a Main Street," *The Appraisal Journal,* January, 1947, pp. 105-109.

NOLAN, JAMES J., "Small Town Appraisals," *The Real Estate Appraiser,* Society of Real Estate Appraisers Vol. Xxx, Chicago, December, 1964, pp. 17.

NORCROSS, CARL, "What Buyers Think of Reston," *Urban Land,* ULI, Washington, D.C., February, 1966.

NOWICKI JOSEPH A, "One Block...And a World Apart," *The Real Estate Appraiser,* The Society of Real Estate Appraisers, Chicago Illinois, January 1, 1974, pp. 4-8.

OAKLEAF, R. B., "Mall Treasure Trove or Trap," *Management Accounting,* June, 1970, pp. 41-43.

OLIVER, WILLIAM FREDERICK, *Planning Compensation Under the Town and Country Planning Act,* Sweet and Maxwell, London, 1954.

OPPERMAN, PAUL, "The Master Plan's Effect on Land and Property Development," *Right of Way,* August, 1954, pp. 20-26.

PAIGE, CLAYTON W., "Construction of De Bell Golf Course In the City of Burbank," *Right of Way,* April. 1958, pp. 35.

PALMER, DWIGHT, "The Location of Industry," *The Appraisal Journal,* April, 1948, pp. 125-130.

PARK, OLIVER W., "The Challenge In the Boston Predicament," *Assessment Administration,* Institute of American Assessment Officers, Chicago, 1960, pp. 23-26.

PATTERSON, SAMUEL A., "Special Assessment Problems In Totally Planned Satellite Cities," *Assessment Administration,* Institute of American Assessment Officers, Chicago, 1965, pp. 90-92.

PAXTON, KENNETH WAYNE PH. D, *Air Pollution and Property Values In Urban Areas,* The University of Tennessee, pp. 710000.

PENA GARCIA, M. A., "El Concepto De Areas Verdes," *Boletin,* Sotave, Caracas, Venezuela, pp. 21-23.

PENA GARCIA, M. A., "Valor De Areas Verdes Zonas Urbanizadas," *Boletin,* Sotave, Caracas, Venezuela, pp. 25-26.

PEREIRA, WILLIAM L., "Vistas for the Future In Planning and Architecture," *Assessment Administration,* Institute of American Assessment Officers, Chicago, pp. 28-31.

PERRY, CLARENCE ARTHUR, "Neighborhood Values In City Planning," *The Appraisal Journal,* July, 1941, pp. 253-265.

PFEFFERKORN, LAWRENCE G., "1960 Population and Housing Figures," *The Residential Appraiser,* January, 1961, pp. 21-24.

POLLAK, M. I. TAFT, "Urban Planning Ripe for Systems Analysis," *Journal Systems Management,* January, 1971, pp. 12 17.

POLLARA, F., "Trends In U. S. Population," *American Federationist,* June, 1970, pp. 9-13.

POLLARD, W. L., "Zoning In the United States," *American Academy of Political and Social Science, Annals,* May, 1931.

PROCOS, DIMITRI, *Mixed Land Use Past Record and Future Prospects,* School of Architecture, Nova Scotia Canada.

PROKOSCH, WALTHER, "Joppatowne—A Marine Oriented Community," *Urban Land,* ULI, Washington, D.C., June, 1965.

PROUTY, W. L. AND OTHERS, "Factors of City Growth Affecting Obsolescence of Buildings," *Appraisers and Assessor's Manual,* 1930, pp. 82-83.

PROUTY, W. L. AND OTHERS, "Percentage of External Obsolescence Due to Zoning," *Appraisers and Assessors Manual,* 1930, pp. 88.

PROUTY, W. L. AND OTHERS, "Population of Cities," *Appraisers and Assessors Manual,* 1930, pp. 301-303.

PRYOR, FRANCIS D., "Appraisals for Public Road Acquisition," *Technical Valuation,* June, 1960, pp. 5-10.

RAHENKAMP, J., "Zoning Scene; Regional Planning Sounds Like a Cure-All, But it Could Hurt More Than it Helps," *House and Home,* February, 1971, pp. 38.

RALEIGH, JAMES C., "Boom Town, R. I," *American Society of Appraisers Valuation Manual,* American Society of Appraisers, 1961, pp. 165.

RALEIGH, JAMES C., "What Price Zoning," The Appraisal Journal, Vol. Xxxii, J.

RAMS, EDWIN M., "Economic Analysis of Small Cities and Towns," *The Real Estate Appraiser,* March, 1962, pp. 16-21.

RAMS, EDWIN M., "The Zoning Dilemma," *The Review,* April, 1953, pp. 16-22.

RANCICH, M. T., "Land Value Changes In an Area Undergoing Urbanization," *Land Economics,* February, 1970.

RATCLIFF, RICHARD UPDEGRAFF, *Current Practices In Income Property Appraisal,* Berkeley Institute of Urban and Regional Developmt, Berkeley California, 1967.

REAL ESTATE ANALYST, THE, "Population Factors In Retail Locations," *Real Estate Analyst Appraisal Bulletin,* 1948, pp. 395-398.

REAL ESTATE ANALYST, THE, "Retail Outlets Compared with Population Changes," *Real Estate Analyst Appraisal Bulletin,* 1950, pp. 559-562.

REECE, RICHARD L., "Space-Occupying Gambits for Writers," *The Appraisal Journal,* October, 1968, pp. 599-604.

REED, VERGIL D., "Population Trends and Changes In the Next Decade," *The Appraisal Journal,* October, 1949, pp. 454-460.

RENSHAW, E. F., "Demand for Housing In the Mid-1970s," *Land Economics,* August, 1971, pp. 249-255.

RESNICK, WILLIAM C., "Social Characteristics of Cities," *The Appraisal Journal,* October, 1938, pp. 329-339.

REVIEW, THE, "Land Development In Expanding Municipalities," *The Review,* August, 1956, pp. 19-24.

RHAMSTINE, ADAM W., "Suburban Zoning," *The Review,* November, 1955, pp. 13-16, 22.

RICH, S. G., "Planning In Metropolitan Winnipeg," *Appraisal Institute Magazine,* Appraisal Institute of Canada, Winnipeg.

RING, ALFRED A., "Impact of Urban Forces Upon Property Value," *The Valuation of Real Estate,* 1970, pp. 68-78.

RING, ALFRED A., "New Technique of the Market Comparison Approach," *The Resident Appraiser,* July, 1962, pp. 2-8.

ROSEN, G. R., "U. S. Priorities: Housing Is Number One," *Duns,* October, 1970, pp. 46-47.

ROSENMAN, DOROTHY, "Shaping the Future City," *The Appraisal Journal,* January, 1943, pp. 51-55.

ROUSE, JAMES W., "Will Downtown Face Up to Its Future?," *Appraisal Digest,* January, 1958, pp. 4-7.

ROWE, LEO S., "The Political Consequences of City Growth," *Yale Review,* 1900, pp. 20-32.

ROWE, LEO S., "The Social Consequences of City Growth," *Yale Review,* 1901.

ROWLSON, JOHN F., "Zoning Vs. Alternate Value," *The Appraisal Journal,* October, 1963, pp. 513-517.

RYBECK, WALTER, "Impact of Taxation and Assessments on Urban Development," *The Real Estate Appraiser,* pp. 27.

SANFORD, GEORGE A., "Zoning and the Real Estate Appraiser," *The Residential Appraiser*, December, 1960, pp. 12-14.

SAYRE, T. H., "Right of Way for Future Use, Encroachments, Zoning," *Proceedings of the Eighth Annual National Seminar, 1962*, American Right of Way Association, Washington, D. C, 1963.

SAZAMA, G. W., "Equalization of Property Taxes for the Nation's Largest Central Cities," *National Tax Journal*, June, 1965, pp. 151-161.

SCHEUER, JAMES H., E. J GOLDSTON, WILTON S. SOGG, "Disposition of Urban Renewal Land-A Fundamental Problem In the Rebuilding of Our Cities," *The Appraisal Journal*, June, 1962, pp. 81-106.

SCHMIDT, WALTER S., "The Future of Our Cities Requires Serious Study," *National Real Estate Journal*, April, 1938, pp. 14-16.

SCHMIDT, WALTER S., "The Growing Threat of Decentralization," *Real Estate Record*, January 20, 1940, pp. 5-6.

SCHMITT, ROBERT C., "Correlates of Growth In Metropolitan Land Values," *Technical Valuation*, 1966, pp. 4..

SCHMUTZ, GEORGE L., "City Growth," *Appraisal Process*, 1941, pp. 1-229.

SEATTLE REAL ESTATE ASSOCIATION, "Reports on City Real Estate Values," The Pacific Press, Seattle, December, 1907.

SEEGER, WILLIAM R., "Supplying Water to Explosive Population Areas," *The Residential Appraiser*, November, 1962, pp. 20-23.

SEYMOUR, D. D., *Analysis of the Effects of Zoning Changes on Property Values In Two Pittsburgh Suburbs*, Dissertation Abstracts, Vol. Xxvii, No. 12, Ann Arbor, June, 1967, pp. 4442-B.

SHENEHON, HOWARD E., "Residential Growth Development In a Metropolitan Area," *The Residential Appraiser*, September, 1960, pp. 6-7.

SHENKEL, WILLIAM M., "Industrial Zoning Regulations and the Demand for Industrial Space," *The Appraisal Journal*, January, 1965, pp. 55-64.

SIEJA, EDWARD M., "Valuation According to Use Vs. Valuation According to Zoning," *Assessment Administration*, Institute of American Assessment Officers, Chicago, 1963, pp. 86-90.

SMITH, TSCHAPPAT, RACSTER, "Real Estate and Urban Development," *The Real Estate Appraiser*, Richard D Irwin, Inc., Homewood Illinois, January 1, 1973, pp. 1-481.

SMITH, KENNETH B., "Fantastic Complexes Predicted," *Appraisal Institute Magazine*, Appraisal Institute of Canada, Winnipeg.

SMITH, LARRY, "Investment Future of Central City Area," *The Appraisal Journal*, October, 1964, pp. 559-563.

SMITH, WALSTEIN, JR., "Downtownosis," *The Real Estate Appraiser*, March, 1966, pp. 19-25.

SOLOMON, R. J., "Property Values As a Structural Element of Urban Evolution," *Economic Geography*, January, 1969.

SPON, EDWARD, AND F. N. SPON LTD., *Architects and Builders Price Book*, Mcclelland and Steward, Toronto, 1958.

SQUIRE, LATHAM C., "Zoning Problems Facing the Real Estate Appraiser," *The Appraisal Journal*, January, 1949, pp. 100-106.

STEVENS, ROBERT W., "Appraisal of a Modern Municipal Incinerator," *Case Reports In Assessment Administration*, May, 1961.

SWAN, HERBERT S., "Land Values and City Growth," *Journal of Land and Public Utility Economics*, May, 1934, pp. 188-201.

SWITZER, DOROTHY, "Rural Development and Rural-Urban Balance," *Business in Nebraska, No. 326*, 1niversity of Nebraska, November, 1971, pp. 1-3.

TERON, WILLIAM, "A New Canadian Environment," *Appraisal Institute Magazine*, Appraisal Institute of Canada, Winnipeg, March 1, 1971.

THEISS, WILLIAM R., "Use of Zoning to Acquire Property at Depreciated Value. Appraisal Docket," *The Appraisal Journal*, October, 1961, pp. 544-545.

THOMPSON, PROF. WARREN S., "Effect of Population Trends on Real Estate Values," *National Real Estate Journal*, July, 1934, pp. 37-38.

THOMPSON, WARREN S., "Future Population Growth and Real Estate Values," *The Appraisal Journal*, October, 1934, pp. 31-34.

THORNDIKE, EDWARD L. AND ELLA WOODYARD, "Individual Differences In American Cities," *American Journal of Sociology*, pp. 191-224.

THORSON, IVAN A., "Los Angeles Corner Influence In Retail Business District," *Mcmichael, S. L. Appraising Manual*, 1937, pp. 380-382.

THRIFT, E. W., "Perimeter Roads and Their Functions," *Appraisal Institute Magazine*, Appraisal Institute of Canada, Winnipeg.

TIME, INC., "Instant City," *The Appraisal Journal*, July, 1967, pp. 402-403.

TINETTI, J. R. AND D. G. WARREN, "Detroit Fosters Easement Planning to Encourage Provision of Utility Easements In Early Stages of Lan," *Right of Way*, October, 1957, pp. 17-20.

TRUE, WALLACE W., "Population Analysis and Population Trends," *The Appraisal Journal*, July, 1938, pp. 207-219.

TUCKER, GILBERT M., *The Self-Supporting City*, Robert Schalkenbach Foundation, New York, 1958, pp. 1-100.

TURNER, JOHN F. C. AND ROBERT FICHTER, *Freedom to Build*, The McMillan Company, New York, May, 1973.

U. S. GOVERNMENT PRINTING OFFICE, *The City Expands, a Study of The Conversion of Land from Rural to Urban Use*, U. S. Govt. Printing Office, Washington.

URBAN LAND INSTITUTE, *New Town for California*, Urban Land Institute, Vol. Xxvi, Washington, November, 1966.

VAN LEUVEN, KARL J., "The Role of the Architect," *The Valuation Manual*, 1955, pp. 57.

WAELTI, J. J., "The Regional Impact of Public Water Storage Through Recreational Development, a Case Study," *Dissertation Abstracts*, Ann Arbor, July, 1968, pp. 30-A.

WALDRON, ROBERT F., "Deed Restrictions Vs. Zoning," *The Residential Appraiser*, June, 1959, pp. 11-13.

WALKER, J., "Levitt Town Bldr, Starts a City-Sized Community," *House & Home*, January, 1971, pp. 34.

WALL, NORBERT F., "The Township Survey System of Land Identification," *The Real Estate Appraiser*, pp. 29.

WALLACE, DAVID A., "Renaissance In Baltimore," *The Appraisal Journal*, July, 1960, pp. 365-380.

WATERSON, GEORGE T., "Decentralization's Effect on Land Values," *The Real Estate Record*, August 9, 1941, pp. 4-5.

WATSON, JOHN JAMES, "Industry and Town Planning," *The Appraisal Journal*, July, 1947, pp. 389-391.

WEAVER, ROBERT C., "The Emerging Federal Program for Cities," *The Appraisal Journal*, January, 1966, pp. 9-17.

WEBSTER, R. H., "New Towns for Old," *Appraisal Institute Magazine*, Appraisal Institute of Canada, Winnipeg, September 1, 1972.

WEEKES, R. E., "Some Salient Factors Affecting Downtown Areas," *The Appraisal Journal*, October, 1959, pp. 561-564.

WEIMER, ARTHUR M., "Population Trends and Property Values," *Review of Residential Appraisers,* May, 1938, pp. 3-7.

WEISS, E. B., "Surprise for 1980's: the Big City Population Explosion Will Fizzle," *Advertising Age,* May 4, 1970, pp. 65-66.

WENDT, PAUL F., "City Growth and Urban Land Value," *The Appraisal Journal,* April 2, 1958.

WENDT, PAUL F., "Economic Growth and Urban Land Values," *The Appraisal Journal,* July, 1958, pp. 427-443.

WENDT, PAUL F., "Lessons from the Old World for America's City Builders," *The Appraisal Journal,* July, 1961, pp. 389-398.

WENDT, PAUL F., "Urban Land Value Trends," *The Appraisal Journal,* April, 1958, pp. 254-269.

WESTEBBE, R. W., "Urbanization Problems and Prospects," *Finance and Development,* December, 1970, pp. 2-8.

WHISTON, FRANK M., "Decentralization In Chicago," *Skyscraper Management,* April, 1936, pp. 3-4, 29-30.

WHITE, JOHN R., "The Changing Internal Structure of Cities," *Appraisal Digest,* October, 1959, pp. 14-16.

WHITMORE, HENRY, "Three Hundred Years of City Growth to Be Studied In Boston," *National Real Estate Journal,* June 10, 1929, pp. 55-56.

WHITTEN, ROBERT, "Probable Effects of Changes In Population Growth," *Real Estate Record and Builders Guide,* August 25, 1934, pp. 4-5.

WHYTE, WILLIAM H., JR., "What's Wrong with City Homes," *The Residential Appraiser,* August, 1957, pp. 16-24.

WILLIAMS, HARRY G. C., "Building for the Ages," *The Appraisal Journal,* April, 1933, pp. 219-224.

WILLIAMS, LESLIE, "Prescription for Community Ailments," *The Appraisal Journal,* April, 1947, pp. 184-191.

WINTER, E. A., SMITH, W. P, "Estimating Aggregate Presidential Real Estate Values from Population-Income Data," *Appraisal and Valuation Manual,* February, 1956, pp. 89-92.

WOLFFE, LEONARD L., *New Zoning Landmarks In Planned Unit Developments,* Urban Land Institute, Washington, D. C, 1968.

WRIGHT, FRANK LLOYD, "Planning Man's Physical Environment," *The Appraisal Journal,* January, 1948, pp. 63-64.

WURSTER, CATHERINE, ET AL., "The City of 1976," *The Residential Appraiser,* January, 1957, pp. 12-24.

YOUNG, G. I. M., "Urban Land Management," *The Appraisal Journal,* April, 1969, pp. 271-278.

ZELITSKY, ALVIN, "Rehabilitations Hard-Core Problem Financing," *The Real Estate Appraiser,* pp. 24.

# 13-12 Parking Facilities

BABCOCK, FREDERICK M., "Building Cost Estimation: Investment Parking Lot," *Vauation of Real Estate,* 1932, pp. 481, 491.

BABCOCK, FREDERICK M., "Examples of Appraisal Procedure Parking Lot Property," *Valuation of Real Estate,* 1932, pp. 196-261.

BABCOCK, FREDERICK M., "Valuation of Returns Details of Valuation Procedure Parking Lots," *The Valuation of Real Estate*, Ed. 1, 1932, pp. 276-307.

BECKER, GEORGE, "Parking Lots and Garages In Central Business Districts," *The Appraisal Journal*, January, 1940, pp. 62-67.

ENGINEERING NEWS-RECORD, "Conv Cen Acknowledges Parking Is Part of Overhead," *Engineering News-Record*, June 10, 1971, pp. 31.

ENO FOUNDATION, "Rentals on Parking Lots," *Appraisal Digest*, July, 1950, pp. 8-9.

FAIR, E. W., "Parking Lot Headaches," *Banking*, September, 1970, pp. 94.

FOSTER, N. LEE, "Americas Off Street Parking Problems," *The Appraisal Journal*, January, 1955, pp. 63-76.

GOTTESMAN, JEROME, "Parking Feasibility Checklist," *Appraisal Digest*, October, 1967, pp. 7-16.

GRISELLE, SHERMAN W., "Parking Related to Residential Development," *The Appraisal Journal*, October, 1965, pp. 617-619.

HAYES, R. W., "Man and His Car Are Not Soon Parted So Parking Layout Is a Vital Element In Development Planning," *House and Home*, September, 1971, pp. 50.

HENDON, JOHN F., "Parking and Central Business District Values," *The Appraisal Journal*, July, 1954, pp. 363-374.

LAFFOON, A. L., "Demonstration Appraisal, a One Story Building and Parking Lot," *Technical Valuation*, Pueblo, Colorado, pp. 30-43.

LECRAW, CHARLES S., SMITH, WILBUR S, "Zoning Applied to Parking," *The Appraisal Journal*, July, 1947, pp. 399-410.

LIBOTT, NATHAN, "Appraisal of a Parking Lot," *Appraisal Reporting Techniques*, American Institute of Real Estate Appraisers, 1949, pp. 43-56.

LOCKYER, ALBERT W., "Parking Space Makes Value," *Appraisal Digest*, January, 1953, pp. 23-24.

MARTIN, C. VIRGIL, "Shouldn't Department Stores Invest In Human Parking Downtown," *The Appraisal Journal*, October, 1960, pp. 510-514.

MARTIN, E. KRANZ, "Parking Lots and Garages," *Technical Valuation*, October, 1959, pp. 43-46.

MARTIN, N. D., "Future of Downtown Parking," *Skyscraper Management*, November, 1970, pp. 20-23.

MCGAVIN, C. T., "The Parking Problem," *The Appraisal Journal*, April, 1941, pp. 151-159.

MCGAVIN, CHARLES T., "New Techniques In Downtown Parking Facilities," *The Appraisal Journal*, January, 1957, pp. 39053.

NATIONAL PARKING ASSOCIATION, *Parking Standards Report*, Washington, D. C..

NELSON, ROLAND D., "Appraisal of an Older Parking Garage," *The Real Estate Appraiser*, November, 1968, pp. 33-40.

ORT, ROBERT M., "Economic Aspects of Parking Spaces, Traffic Flow, Access, and Types of Traffic," *Proceedings of the Third Institute on Eminent Domain*, Dallas, 1961.

RANDALL, WILLIAM J., "Value of a Parking Space," *Real Estate Analyst Appraisal Bulletin*, 1962, pp. 173-178.

RANDALL, WILLIAM J., "Value of a Parking Space," *The Appraisal Journal*, April, 1963, pp. 207-212.

RICH, RICHARD C., *Parking Economics and Design*, Richard C. Rich and Associates, Michigan, 1968, pp. 1-47.

ROTI, RICHARD F., *Square Foot Cost Averaging Principle for Parkingstructures*, National Parking Association, Washington, D. C-.

SCHULTE, AUGUST B., "Residential District Permutations," *The Appraisal Journal*, July, 1936, pp. 283-286.

SHELGER, KURT S., "Appraisal of Parking Lots and Garages," *Encyclopedia of Real Estate Appraising*, 1959, pp. 296-316.

SNITZER, EDWARD L., "The Effect of a Reciprocal Parking Agreement In the Valuation Process," *The Real Estate Appraiser*, 1970, pp. 51.

SUSSNA, DR. STEPHEN, "Parking and Zoning a Case Study," *The Real Estate Appraiser*, November, 1967, pp. 25.

WEEKES, R. E., "Some Salient Factors Affecting Downtown Areas," *The Appraisal Journal*, October, 1959, pp. 561-564.

WELCH, KENNETH C., BRUNO FUNARO, "Parking Plans for Shopping Centers," *The Appraisal Journal*, July, 1953, pp. 424-430.

WIDEN, E. N., "Technique of Fore Casting the Growth of a Community," *National Real Estate Journal*, June 28, 1926, pp. 17-23.

## 13-13  Urban Renewal

ACHENSTEIN, ASHER, "Some Economic Characteristics of Blighted Areas," *Journal of Land and Public Utility Economics*, February, 1935, pp. 38-47.

ADELBERG, JOHN, "Achieving Design Goals In Urban Renewal," *The Appraisal Journal*, April, 1964, pp. 188-191.

ADKISSON, FLOYD, "Private Urban Renewal," *The Residential Appraiser*, October, 1959, pp. 11-12.

ALLISON, NEVILLE F., "How a Neighborhood Declines," *The Residential Appraiser*, March, 1957, pp. 18-24.

APPRAISAL JOURNAL, "Urban Renewal and Development," *The Appraisal Journal*, 1963.

APPRAISAL JOURNAL, "Valuation Problems Involving Reuse of Urban Land," *The Appraisal Journal*, 1958, pp. 569-573.

BAB, HERBERT J. G., "Property Taxes Cause Urban Decay," *The Appraisal Journal*, July, 1968, pp. 419-425.

BABCOCK, FREDERICK M., "Re-Use Analysis and Valuation," *Technical Valuation*, June, 1963, pp. 18-20.

BABCOCK, FREDERICK M., "Re-Use Analysis and Valuation," *Wisconsin Colloquium on Appraisal Research*, 1963, pp. 28-30.

BARNARD, BOYD T., "How Service Stations Can Get Back Into Renewal Areas," *The Appraisal Journal*, July, 1964, pp. 371-375.

BARNARD, BOYD T., "Problems Encountered In Reuse Appraisals," *The Appraisal Journal*, October, 1960, pp. 435-443.

BAUER, J., "The Redevelopment Program of Waterloo Ontario Downtown Area," *Appraisal Institute Magazine*, September, 1960, pp. 9-11.

BAYER, DANIEL, "The Appraiser and Urban Renewal," *Appraisal Digest*, July, 1960, pp. 1-7.

BEATTY, CLARENCE W. JR., "Market Value of Improved Land In Slums," *The Appraisal Journal*, January, 1947, pp. 87-98.

BEATTY, CLARENCE W. JR., "Market Value of Land In Slums," *The Appraisal Journal*, July, 1946, pp. 285-293.

BECK, MORRIS, "Urban Redevelopment: Influence of Property Taxation and Other Factors," *Conference Proceedings*, Columbus, 1964, pp. 239-249.

BERGER, MILES, "Assessment Techniques In Urban Renewal Areas," *Assessment Administration,* IAAO, Chicago, 1965, pp. 87-90.

BLOOM, MAX R., "Valuation Problems and Urban Redevelopment," *The Real Estate Appraiser,* SREA, Chicago, 1964, pp. 24.

BODFISH, H. MORTON, "Chart of Chicago Loop District Showing Building Replacements," *The Appraisers and Assessors Manual,* Prouty, W. L, 1930, pp. 79.

BOLLMAN, H. GORDON, "Values In Blighted Areas," *Review of Society of Residential Appraisers,* February, 1942, pp. 11-14.

BREMICKER, CARL T., "Area Development," *The Residential Appraiser,* February, 1957, pp. 14-16.

BRODSKY, H., "Residential Land and Improvement Values In a Central City," *Land Economics,* August, 1970.

BROWN, G. FAIRFAX, "Supervision of Revaluation Projects," *Assessment Administration,* IAAO, Chicago, 1962, pp. 96-101.

BROWN, LESTER G., WEIDLER, JOHN B, "The Role of the Analyst-Appraiser In Urban Problems and Urban Growth Planning," *The Real Estate Appraiser,* March, 1969.

BRUERE, HENRY, "Financial Implications of Urban Blight," *Real Estate Record,* May 6, 1940, pp. 7.

BUSINESS WEEK, "Firmer Foundation for New Towns," *Business Week,* January 9, 1971, pp. 22.

BYRNE, THOMAS A., "Urban Renewal Plans and Assessment Policy," *Assessment Administration,* Chicago, 1960, pp. 12-14.

CAPPER, G. C. F., "Decay, Development and Land Values," *Manchester School of Economic and Social Studies,* January, 1964, pp. 25-41.

CARR, ANTHONY W., "A New Look at the Underimprovement," *The Residential Appraiser,* May, 1960, pp. 11-13.

CARTER, W. PETER, "Report of the Canadian Task Force on Housing Andurban Development," *The Real Estate Appraiser,* January, 1970, pp. 44-51.

CASE, F. E., "Housing the Underhoused In the Inner City," *Journal of Finance,* May, 1971, pp. 427-444, 466-471.

COLE, JOHN D., "The Revaluation of a City," *The Appraisal Journal,* January, 1960, pp. 47-50.

COLLINS, E. R., "The Appraiser's Role In Urban Renewal," *Appraisal Institute Magazine,* Appraisal Institute of Canada, Winnipeg.

COMMERCE TODAY, "Name Changed, But Chain Stores Still Boom," *Commerce Today,* May 31, 1971, pp. 21-22.

CONNOLLY, JOHN E., "Working with Redevelopment Authorities," *The Residential Appraiser,* June, 1962, pp. 21-24.

CURRAN, DONALD J., "General Property Tax and Residential Rehabilitation," *Conference Proceedings,* National Tax Association Association, Columbus, 1964, pp. 250-258.

DOWNS, ANTHONY, "Alternative Futures for the American Ghetto," *The Appraisal Journal,* October, 1968, pp. 518-19.

DOWNS, JAMES C., "Urban Renewal Will it Influence Assessment Policy," *Assessment Administration,* IAAO, Chicago, 1960, pp. 14016.

DOXIADIS, C. A., *Urban Renewal and the Future of the American City,* Public Administration Service, Chicago, 1966.

DOYLE, B. E., "Service Station, Etc.," *Appraisal Institute Magazine,* Appraisal Institute of Canada, Winnipeg, September 1, 1971.

DUGGIN, MARSHALL E., "Improvement In Tennessee," *Assessment Administration,* Institute of American Assessment Officers, Chicago, 1961, pp. 68-76.

DUNN, DOMINICK R., "A Fallacy In Rehabilitation," *The Real Estate Appraiser,* February, 1956, pp. 13-14.

# BIBLIOGRAPHY OF APPRAISAL LITERATURE

EDMAN, J. J., "The Appraisal Docket. Slum Property Income Excluded In Determining Value," *The Appraisal Journal*, April, 1958, pp. 292-293.

FALUDI, E. G., "Urban Planning and Renewal In Canada," *Appraisal and Valvation Manual*, 1960, pp. 109-116.

FEDERAL HOUSING ADMINISTRATION, *A Handbook on Urban Redevelopment for Cities In the United States*, Government Printing Office, Washington D. C, November, 1961, pp. 105.

FERGUSON, ABNER H., "What Can We Do About Blighted Areas," *Real Estate Record*, May 24, 1941, pp. 3, 21.

FISHER, ERNEST M., *Economic Aspects of Zoning, Blighted Areas, and Rehabilitation Laws*,

GAFFNEY, M. MASON, "Property Taxes and the Frequency of Urban Renewal," *Conference Proceedings*, National Tax Association, Columbus, 1964, pp. 272-285.

GEER, M. W., *How to Profit by Rehabilitating Real Estate*, Prentice Hall, Englewood Cliffs, 1957.

GILLIES, JAMES, "Urban Renewal Bane or Blessing," *The Residential Appraiser*, April, 1960.

GRAY, ARTHUR L. JR., "Valuation Factors In Urban Renewal Projects," *Technical Valuation*, February, 1962, pp. 61-67.

GREBLER, LEO, "Land Assembly and Relocation In Urban Renewal a Study of European Methods," *The Appraisal Journal*, January, 1963, pp. 13-21.

GREY, ARTHUR, L. JR., "Valuation Factors In Urban Renewal Projects," *Technical Valuation*, February, 1962, pp. 61-67.

GROTECLOSS, EDWARD JR., "Re-Use Appraisals," *Technical Valuation*, June, 1959, pp. 51-53.

GRUEN, VICTOR, "Urban Renewal," *The Appraisal Journal*, Jan. 1956, pp. 23-29.

HALE, C. W., "Impact of Federal Policy and Technological Change on Regional & Urban Planning Problems," *Land Economics*, February, 1971, pp. 24-35.

HAMMAN, CHARLES L., "The Concept of Regional Development," *The Appraisal Journal*, October, 1957, pp. 499-504.

HANLEY, DUDLEY J., "Acquisition Appraisals In Urban Renewal," *Appraisal and Valuation Manual*, American Society of Appraisers, 1961, pp. 23-29.

HANLEY, DUDLEY J., "Acquisition Appraisals In Urban Renewal," *Appraisal Digest*, April, 1962, pp. 6 11.

HARRIS, STEPHEN M., "Some ABC's of Commercial Relocation When Urban Renewal Forces You to Move Your Business," *Valuation Manual*, A. S. A., 1964, pp. 147.

HARRIS, WILLIAM W., "Feasibility Studies In Urban Renewal Projects," *The Real Estate Appraiser*, October, 1967, pp. 21-30.

HAYES, EDWARD R., "Special Assessments for Public Improvements In Iowa," *Drake Law Review*, December, 1964, pp. 3-35.

HENDON, JOHN F., "Parking and Central Business District Values," *The Appraisal Journal*, July, 1954, pp. 363-374.

HENDRICKS, ROBERT W., "Complexities and Contrasts--Urban Renewal, 1961," *'the Residential Appraiser*, September, 1961, pp. 2-7.

HIBBEN, JAMES B., "Renewal's Riddle: the Three-Story Walk-Up," *The Appraisal Journal*, July, 1965, pp. 357.

HICKMAN, LEON E., "Alcoa Looks at Urban Redevelopment," *The Appraisal Journal*, July, 1964, pp. 363-370.

HOLDEN, ARTHUR C., "Condemnation and Urban Redevelopment," *Real Estate Record*, April 13, 1940, pp. 4-5.

HOLDEN, ARTHUR C., "Taxation As a Factor In Urban Redevelopment," *The Appraisal Journal*, April, 1947, pp. 252-260.

HOLDEN, ARTHUR C., "The Menace of Urban Blight," *The Appraisal Journal*, July, 1940, pp. 203-210.

HOLDEN, ARTHUR C., "The Significance of the Blighted Area," *The Appraisal Journal*, 1947, pp. 476-486.

HOLDEN, THOMAS S., "Urban Rehabilitation by Private Initiative," *Architectural Record*, May, 1940, pp. 86-87.

HOPKINS, ROBERT W., "Mass Appraisals In Slum Areas," *Appraisal Digest*, February, 1956, pp. 10-12.

HORAN, CHARLES J., "Appraising In the Urban Renewal Program," *Appraisal Digest*, April, 1959, pp. 1-4.

HOYT, HOMER, "Public Subsidies for Slum Clearance," *The Appraisal Journal*, October, 1945, pp. 352-361.

HOYT, HOMER, LEONARD C. SMITH, "The Valuation of Land In Urban Blighted Areas," *The Appraisal Journal*, July, 1943, pp. 199-209.

HYDER, K. LEE, "Over-Accenting the Slum Problem," *The Appraisal Journal*, April, 1945, pp. 108-109.

INTERNATIONAL ASSOCIATION OF ASSESSING OFFICERS, *Revaluation Projects, Report of the Committee on Evaluation Projects*, IAAO, Chicago, 1960.

JOHNSON, LEEVERN, "Acquisition Appraisals for Urban Renewal," *The Appraisal Journal*, April, 1961, pp. 221-228.

JOHNSON, LEEVERN, "Appraising for Urban Renewal," *The Real Estate Appraiser*, February, 1963, pp. 15-19.

JOHNSON, LEEVERN, "Land Value Write Down In Urban Renewal," *The Appraisal Journal*, April, 1962, pp. 175-180.

JOHNSON, PHILIP M., "Rehabilitation Feasibility Financing," *The Real Estate Appraiser*, January, 1970, pp. 20-27.

JOHNSON, PHILIP M., "Rehabilitation Feasibility Studies In Federally-Assisted Areas," *The Appraisal Journal*, April, 1966, pp. 183-195.

KAHN, SANDERS A., "Urban Renewal Appraising," *Valuation Manual*, 1960, pp. 117-124.

KAHN, SANDERS A., "Reuse Appraising," *Valuation Manual*, 1961, pp. 11-22.

KAHN, SANDERS A., "The Appraiser and Community Revitalization," *The Real Estate Appraiser*, pp. 13.

KIDDER, F. E., *Architects and Builders Handbook*, Wiley, New York, 1931.

KING, WILLFORD I., *The Valuation of Urban Realty for Purposes of Taxation, with Cert Secs Espec Applicable to Wisconsin*, Madison, Wisconsin, 1914.

KNIGHT, C. LOUIS, "Blighted Areas and Their Effects Upon Urban Landutilization," *American Academy of Political and Social Science*, March 30, 1930, pp. 133-138.

LANE, DAVID E., "Acquisition of Property for Urban Renewal," *Right of Way*, December, 1963, pp. 27-32.

LELACHEUR, E. B., "Halifax-An Old City Renewed," *Appraisal Institute Magazine*, Appraisal Institute of Canada, Winnipeg.

LOGGAN, HARRY B., "Planning and Executing a Reappraisal Program," *Assessors Newsletter*, April, 1960, pp. 39-45.

LOOMIS, D., "Rich Washington Suburb Rules Building Projects Must Include Units for Poor," *House and Home*, September, 1971, pp. 8..

LUM, DONALD A., "The Appraiser's Role In Urban Renewal," *Appraisal Digest*, October, 1961, pp. 10-19.

LUM, Y. T., "Reuse and Resale Values," *The Appraisal Journal*, April, 1967, pp. 226-230.

MARCKS, ALFRED R. JR., "Comparative Analysis In Reuse Appraisal," *The Appraisal Journal*, October, 1966, pp. 549-551.

MCGARRY, THOMAS F., "On the Joint Development of Urban Housing and Urban Freeways," *The Appraisal Journal,* January, 1967, pp. 119-122.

MCCORMACK, J. E., "Reuse and Value Appraisal In Urban Renewal," *Appraisal Institute Magazine,* Appraisal Institute of Canada, Winnipeg.

MCCORMACK, JAMES E., "Appraisal Limitations from the Standpoint of the Urban Renewal Agency," *Papers and Proceedings,* Wisconsin Colloquium on Appraisal Research, 1963, pp. 25027.

MCCORMACK, JAMES E., "Appraisal of Urban Renewal Property for Moderate-Income Low-Rent Public Housing," *The Appraisal Journal,* January, 1967, pp. 70-81.

MCCORMACK, JAMES E., "Reuse and Value Appraisal In Urban Renewal," *The Appraisal Journal,* October, 1958, pp. 520-530.

MCDONNELL, WILLIAM A., "Urban Replanning," *The Residential Appraiser,* June, 1959, pp. 21-24.

MCMICHAEL, STANLEY L., "Ascertaining Value In Blighted Areas," *Appraising Manual,* 1937, pp. 413-424.

MESSNER, DR. STEPHEN D., "A Benefit-Cost Analysis of Urban Redevelopment," *The Real Estate Appraiser,* 1967.

N. Y. TIMES INDEX, "City Plan Comm Appr Cooper Sq Urban Renew Plan Calling for 1000 Units of New Housing," *N. Y. Times Index,* January 8, 1970.

N. Y. TIMES INDEX, "Families Displaced by Urban Renewal Program Housed In Mobile Homes Pending Relocation," *N. Y. Times Index,* July 29, 1970.

NELSON, RICHARD L., "Commentary on Appraiser's Role In Urban Renewal," *The Appraisal Journal,* January, 1962, pp. 20-26.

NEUTZE, M., "Price of Land for Urban Development," *Economic Record,* September, 1970, pp. 313-328.

NOWICKI, JOSEPH A., "Appraising In the Ghetto," *The Real Estate Appraiser,* September, 1969, pp. 5-9.

NUTTER, C. ARMEL, "Toward Slum Eradication," *The Residential Appraiser,* July, 1959, pp. 10-11.

OBERNDORF, THEODORE W, "Idiosyncrasies of Urban Renewal Land Acquisition Program," *Valutape Audio-Library Series,* American Society of Appraisers, Washington D.C., January 1, 1973.

POOLE, J. W., "Low Cost Housing," *Appraisal Institute Magazine,* Appraisal Institute of Canada, Winnipeg, June 1, 1971.

POTTS, WALTER T. JR., "Treatment of Contract Sales In Appraisal Of Blighted Property," *The Appraisal Journal,* April, 1962, pp. 233-243.

RATCLIFF, DR. RICHARD U., *Urban Land Economics,* Mcgraw-Hill, New York.

REGISTER, J. ALVIN, "Vacant Property-Demand for Improvement Deferred," *Journal of the American Institute of Real Estate Appraisers,* October, 1932, pp. 45.

ROBBINS, IRA S., "Are Slums Inevitable," *Technical Valuation,* February, 1955, pp. 61-63.

ROE, STANLEY, "Blighted Areas," The Appraisal Journal, Vol. I, J.

ROGERS, MICHAEL H., "Neighborhood Improvement Edmonton Approach," *Appraisal Institute Magazine,* Appraisal Institute of Canada, Winnipeg.

ROSEN, G. R., "U. S. Priorities: Housing Is Number One," *Duns,* October, 1970, pp. 46-47.

RUDOLPH, MAX J., "The Appraisal of Slum Districts for Federal Housing Projects," *National Real Estate Journal,* February, 1935, pp. 39-40.

RYBECK, WALTER, "Making the Property Tax Work for Urban Development," *Property Tax Reform,* Int'l Ass'n Assessing Officers, Chicago, June 1, 1973, pp. 125-134.

SCHAAF, A. H., "Effects of Property Taxation on Slums and Renewal—A Study of Land Improvement Assessment Ratios," *Land Economics*, February, 1969, pp. 111-117.

SCHEUER, JAMES H., E. J GOLDSTON, WILTON S. SOGG, "Disposition of Urban Renewal Land-A Fundamental Problem In the Rebuilding of Our Cities," *The Appraisal Journal*, June, 1962, pp. 81-106.

SELIGMAN, DANIEL, "Present and Future of Slums," *The Residential Appraiser*, January, 1958, pp. 11-16.

SEYMOUR, CHARLES F., "A Realtor Looks at Urban Renewal," *The Appraisal*, July, 1963, pp. 319-326.

SEYMOUR, CHARLES F., "Comparison Factors In Reuse Appraising," *The Appraisal Journal*, April, 1962, pp. 165-174.

SHENKEL, WILLIAM M., "Reuse Appraisals a Critical Review," *The Apprisal Journal*, April, 1966, pp. 213-227.

SHIVELY, JOHN W., "Some Observations on Urban Renewal," *The Appraisal Journal*, July, 1962, pp. 369-372.

SIMONSON, E. M., "Who Pays for the Utility Changes In Urban Renewals," *Right of Way*, October, 1963, pp. 31-38.

SLAYTON, WILLIAM L., "Appraiser's Role In Urban Renewal," *The Appraisal Journal*, January, 1962, pp. 16-20.

SLAYTON, WILLIAM L., "Policies for Urban Renewal In the Us," *The Appraisal Journal*, October, 1969, pp. 587-594.

SLAYTON, WILLIAM L., "Protecting Values Through Urban Renewal Programs," Assessment Administration, IAAO, Chicago, 1961, pp. 27-31.

SMITH, CHARLES E., "Urban Renewal Programs from an Appraiser's Viewpoint," *The Residential Appraiser*, 1961, pp. 14-18.

SMITH, WALSTEIN, JR., "Acquisition Appraisal In Urban Renewal," *The Residential Appraiser*, March, 1961, pp. 13-17.

ST. GEORGE, JOHN F., "Urban Renewal Papraisal Series," *Appraisal And Valuation Manual*, 1961.

STARR, ROGER, "A Private Venture Into Slum Bldgs Rehabilitation," *The Appraisal Journal*, July, 1967, pp. 340-347.

STEELE, J., "Master Planning for Downtown Redevelopment," *Appraisal Institute Magazine*, Appraisal Institute of Canada, Winnipeg.

STEGMAN, MICHAEL A., "Slumlords and Public Policy," *The Appraisal Journal*, April, 1968, pp. 201-211.

SUDDERTH, WAYNE, "Appraising In Urban Renewal," *The Residential Appraiser*, May, 1961, pp. 5-8.

SURVEY OF URBAN RENWAL LAND DISPOSITION, *Real Estate Analyst Appraisal Bulletin*, 1959, pp. 559-562.

TANNEY, WILLIAM W., "Super Markets-Data Program," *The Appraisal Journal*, October, 1950, pp. 431-439.

THRIFT, ERIC W., "Urban Renewal," *Appraisal Institute Magazine*, September, 1958, pp. 7-11.

TRUE, WALLACE W., "Blighted Areas - Cause and Effect," *Review of the Society of Residential Appraisers*, February, 1937, pp. 3-5.

U. S. URBAN RENEWAL ADMINISTRATION, *Open Space Land, Planning and Taxation*, Govt. Printing Office, Washington, 1963.

U. S. URBAN RENEWAL ADMINISTRATION, *Reuse and Value Appraisals In Urban Renewal*, Urban Renewal Administration, Washington, 1958, pp. 1-10.

URBAN RENEWAL ADMINISTRATION, "Valuation Problems Involving Reuse of Urban Land," *The Appraisal Journal*, October, 1958, pp. 569-573.

VIESER, MILFORD A., "Urban Renewal- a Program for Private Enterprise," *The Appraisal Journal*, July, 1965, pp. 325-330.

WALKER, MABEL, "Property Tax Expedients In Urban Renewal," *Conference Proceedings*, National Tax Association, Columbus, 1960, pp. 44.

WALKER, MABEL, "The Assessor's Role In Urban Redevelopment," *Assessment Administration*, IAAO, Chicago, 1960, pp. 16-23.

WEEKES, R. E., "Some Salient Factors Affecting Downtown Areas," *The Appraisal Journal*, October, 1959, pp. 561-564.

WEIMER, ARTHUR M., "A Regional Bank System for Urban Renewal and Development," *The Appraisal Journal*, January, 1961, pp. 7-12.

WEISS, E. B., "Surprise for 1980's: the Big City Population Explosion Will Fizzle," *Advertising Age*, May 4, 1970, pp. 65-66.

WENGER, RALPH W., "Acquisition Appraising for Urban Renewal," *The Real Estate Appraiser*, July, 1967, pp. 22.

WHITE, JOHN R., "Re-Use Land Appraising," *Appraisal Digest*, January, 1959, pp. 18-21.

WHITE, JOHN ROBERT, "Changes In Metropolitan Areas," *The Appraisal Journal*, July, 1964, pp. 394-397.

WHYTE, WILLIAM H. JR., "Rx for Urban Sprawl," *The Residential Appraiser*, February, 1958, pp. 10-16.

WILSON, D. EARL, "The Rehabilitation Problem," *The Appraisal Journal*, July, 1944, pp. 258-260.

WILSON, WILLIAM, "Slum Clearance Legislation," *The Appraisal Journal*, July, 1941, pp. 221-228.

WINNICK, LOUIS, "Demand Factors In Urban Renewal," *Appraisal Digest*, January, 1960, pp. 16-18.

WINNICK, LOUIS, "Long-Run Changes In the Valuation of Real Estate by Gross Rents," *The Appraisal Journal*, October, 1952, pp. 484-498.

WOLFF, F. RICHARD, "Organization of an Urban Renewal Appraisal Assignment," *Appraisal Digest*, October, 1962, pp. 17-23.

WOLFF, LEWIS N., "Urban Renewal Disposition," *Real Estate Analyst Appraisal Bulletin*, 1962, pp. 517-520.

WORSEK, LEONARD, "Rehabilitation and Conservation: Urban Renewal's Ugly Ducklings," *The Appraisal Journal*, July, 1966, pp. 427-435.

YANDLE, B. JR., "Urban Renewal-The Precondition for Take-Off," *Land Economics*, November, 1970, pp. 484-486.

# 13-14 Central Business District Property

"Aerospace Resources Best Bet to Tackle Inner City Housing," *Industry Week*, March 1, 1971, pp. 14-15.

ALEXANDER, LAURENCE A., "Problems and Potentials of Downtown," *Right of Way*, August, 1967, pp. 37-38.

AMERICAN SOCIETY OF PLANNING OFFICIALS, *Sign Regulation In the Central Business District*, Chicago, 1900.

APPEL, JAMES R., "The City's Stake In Its Downtown District," *Real Estate Analyst Appraisal Bulletin*, 1953, pp. 545-552.

APPEL, JAMES R., "Valuation of Urban Land," *Real Estate Analyst Appraisal Bulletin*, 1900, pp. 193-196.

BACH, IRA J., "What Lies Ahead for the Inner City," *Residential Appraiser*, 1961, pp. 15-17, 22-23.

## ▲ Urban Property

BECKER, GEORGE, "Parking Lots and Garages In Central Business Districts," *The Appraisal Journal,* January, 1940, pp. 62-67.

BODFISH, H. MORTON, "Changes In the Central Business District of a Growing City," *The National Real Estate Journal,* October 18, 1926, pp. 17-19.

BODFISH, H. MORTON, "Chart of Chicago Loop District Showing Building Replacements," *The Appraisers and Assessors Manual,* Prouty, W. L, 1930, pp. 79.

BODFISH, H. MORTON, "Population and Peak Land Values In Business Districts," *The Journal of Land and Public Utility Economics,* August, 1930, pp. 270-277.

BODFISH, MORTON, THEOBALD, A. D, "Appraising Vacant Business Lots In Built-Up Areas," *Real Estate Fundamentals,* 1941, pp. 4-5.

BOWEN, EZRA, "The Great Downtown Debacle," *Appraisal Institute Magazine,* Appraisal Institute of Canada, Winnipeg, September 1, 1973.

BRENT, W. L., "How to Develop Central Manufacturing District," *The National Real Estate Journal,* July 12, 1926, pp. 38-41.

BRODSKY, H., "Residential Land and Improvement Values In a Central City," *Land Economics,* August, 1970.

CAPPOZZA, DENNIS, *Transportation Cost and Urban Retail Trade,* University of Southern California Working Paper 8,

CHANDIAS, MARIO E., "El Presupuesto, Esa Herramienta," *Boletin,* Sotave, Caracas, Venezuela, pp. 7-12.

COFFMAN, PAUL B., "Review and Forecast Business Conditions," *Technical Valuation,* June, 1958, pp. 3-5.

COPELAND, HARRY E., "Appraising District Change," *Review of the Society of Residential Appraisers,* January, 1937, pp. 7-10.

DAVIDSON, WILLIAM R., "Retailing: Some Significant Current Developments," *The Appraisal Journal,* January, 1957, pp. 91-98.

DAVIS, J. TAIT, "Middle Class Housing In the Central City," *The Appraisal Journal,* April, 1966, pp. 273-286.

DAVIS, W. D., "Urban Appraisals," *The Residential Appraiser,* November, 1959, pp. 5-10.

DENTON, JOHN H., WILLIAM S. KING, "Tucson Central Business District As a Changing Entity," *The Appraisal Journal,* October, 1960, pp. 515-530.

FAIR, E. W., "Parking Lot Headaches," *Banking,* September, 1970, pp. 94.

FISHER, ERNEST M., R. M. FISHER, *Urban Real Estate,* Holt, New York City, 1954.

GOODMAN, ROBERT C., HUNTER A. HOGAN JR., "Positive Principles for Downtown Redevelopment," *The Appraisal Journal,* April, 1963, pp. 255-256.

GREER, GUY, "The Effect of Decentralization Upon Values," *Technical Valuation,* April, 1947, pp. 26-29.

HALL, FRANK D., "Appraising City Real Estate," *Proceedings Fourteenth Annual Convention,* Mortgage Bankers Association of America, 1927, pp. 93-100.

HALL, JOSEPH B., "Business Districts In Motion," *The Appraisal Journal,* January, 1941, pp. 34-40.

HANCOCK, MACKLIN L., "Suburban Town Centers," *The Appraisal Journal,* April, 1965, pp. 261-272.

HANFORD, LLOYD D. SR., "The Future of the Central City," *Appraisal Institute Magazine,* June, 1960, pp. 19-22.

HEWITT, R. F., "Decentralization and the Future of Central Business Districts," *Proceedings 29th Annual Convention,* National Association of Building Owners & Managers, 1936.

HOGENSON, HARRIS O., "Downtown America-Present and Future," *Technical Valuation,* June, 1960, pp. 35-37.

HOYT, HOMER, "Urban Decentralization," *Journal of Land and Public Utility Economics,* August, 1940, pp. 270-276.

KAHN, SANDERS A., "Impact of Shopping Centers on Suburbs and Central Cities," *Valuation,* February, 1958, pp. 45-48.

KINNEY, R. W., "The Future of the Central Business District," *Appraisal Institute Magazine,* Appraisal Institute of Canada, Winnipeg.

KUEHNLE, WALTER R., "Central Business District Paradox," *The Appraisal Journal,* January, 1935, pp. 138-143.

LIVINGSTON, LAWRENCE, JR., "The Downtown Counterattack," *The Appraisal Journal,* April, 1965, pp. 249-254.

LOWDEN, J. A., "Appraisal of Shopping Centres," *Appraisal Institute Magazine,* Appraisal Institute of Canada, Winnipeg.

LUND, JOSEPH W., "Changing Pattern of Downtown Value," *The Appraisal Journal,* July, 1963, pp. 403-405.

MACBRIDE, DEXTER D., "Emerging Highway Patterns, Frontage Roads, Abutting Business Properties," *Seminar, American Right of Way Association,* Portland, Oregon, November, 1958.

MACBRIDE, DEXTER D., "Frontage Roads: a Study In Successful Planning for Major Retail Business Development," *California Highways and Public Works,* May, 1948.

MARTIN, N. D., "Future of Downtown Parking," *Skyscraper Management,* November, 1970, pp. 20-23.

MCGUINNESS, EDWARD J, MEYERS, HARRY W, "Appraising Office Buildings In the Los Angeles Market," *Valuation Magazine,* American Society of Appraisers, Washington D.C., December 1, 1973, pp. 80-93.

MCKEEVER, J. ROSS, "Business Parks-Office Parks, Plazas and Centers," *Urban Land Institute Bulletin,* 1970.

MCMAHON, THOMAS C., "Combination Pittsburgh Business, Residential and Warehouse Lots and Property," *Appraising Manual,* Mcmichael, S. L, 1937.

MCMICHAEL, STANLEY L., "Business Frontage," *Appraising Manual,* 1937, pp. 506-512.

MCMICHAEL, STANLEY L., "Land Values Per Front Foot," *Appraising Manual,* 1937, pp. 519.

MERTZKE, ARTHUR J., "Appraising Properties In Districts Shifting In Use," *National Real Estate Journal,* May 26, 1930, pp. 57-58.

MILNER, JOSEPH, "Appraisal of the Empire State Building," *American Society of Appraiser,* 1959, pp. 69-76.

MOTT, G. M., "Appraisal of Business Property," *California Real Estate Magazine,* October, 1940, pp. 9-10.

NATIONAL ASSOCIATION OF REAL ESTATE BOARDS, "Tentative Standard Form for Appraisal of Business Properties," *National Real Estate Journal,* September 5, 1927, pp. 25-28.

NELSON, RICHARD LAWRENCE, *The One-Hundred Percent Location a New Concept In Motel Site Selection,* Encyclopedia of Motel Management.

NIRENSTEIN, NATHAN, "There'll Always Be a Main Street," *The Appraisal Journal,* January, 1947, pp. 105-109.

OAKLEAF, R. B., "Mall Treasure Trove or Trap," *Management Accounting,* June, 1970, pp. 41-43.

OWEN, WILFRED, "Cities In the Motor Age," Cooper Square Publishers Inc., New York, N. Y..

PEARSON, K. G., "Big Business Discovers Real Estate," *Michigan Business Review,* March, 1971, pp. 26-32.

▲ **Urban Property**

POLIS, S. N., "Factors Which Influence Manhattan Land Values," The International Press, New York, 1933.

PROUDFOOT, MALCOLM J., "The Selection of a Business Site," *The Appraisal Journal*, January, 1939, pp. 61-72.

RAMS, EDWIN M., "Analysis of Central Business District Land Use-A New Linear Programming Method," *Appraisal and Valuation Manual*, American Society of Appraisers, 1962, pp. 67-80.

RAMS, EDWIN M., "Central Business District Land Use-Allocation," *Technical Valuation*,

RAMS, EDWIN M., "Changes In Retailing In Cent Bus Dist In U S," *Technical Valuation*, pp. 47-51.

REAL ESTATE ANALYST, THE, "Dollar Volume of Retail Stores," *Real Estate Analyst Appraisal Bulletin*, 1950, pp. 225-227.

REAL ESTATE ANALYST, THE, "Shifts of 100 Retail Locations," *Real Estate Analyst Appraisal Bulletin*, 1948, pp. 503-509.

REEVES, CUTHBERT E., "Shift In Location of a Retail District," *The Appraisal Journal*, July, 1938, pp. 267-276.

REEVES, CUTHBERT EDWARD, *The Appraisal of Urban Land and Buildings*, Municipal Administration Service, New York City, 1928.

REGIS, A. S., "Design and Use of the Property Record Card," *Assessment Administration*, Institute of American Appraisers Officers, Chicago, 1960, pp. 116-123.

RICH, RICHARD H., "Effect on Downtown Real Estate of Surburban Shopping Centers," *Skyscraper Shopping Centers*, M.

ROBINSON SIR DOVE-MEYER, "The Challenge to the Central Business District of Regional Shopping Centers," *Valuer*, The New Zealand Institute of Valuers, New Zealand, August 1, 1973, pp. 86-90.

SABIT, JULIET, HAROLD BLACK, "The Central Business District," *The Appraisal Journal*, January, 1962, pp. 69-74.

SCHACKNE, JOHN R., "On Appraising the Business District of Toledo, Ohio for Tax Purposes," *The Appraisal Journal*, January, 1938, pp. 71-73.

SOLOMON, R. J., "Property Values As a Structural Element of Urban Evolution," *Economic Geography*, January, 1969.

SOULE, N. C., "What Causes Shifting Values In Business Districts?," *National Real Estate Journal*, October 14, 1929, pp. 34-38.

STATISTICAL ABSTRACT OF THE UNITED STATES, "Metropolitan Area Statistics," Statistical Abstract of the United States, Washington, D.C., 1970.

THEISS, WILLIAM R., "The Appraisal Docket. Economic Obsolescence As Factor In Assessed Value," *The Appraisal Journal*, October, 1965, pp. 624-626.

THORSON, IVAN A., "Los Angeles Corner Influence In Retail Business District," *Mcmichael, S. L. Appraising Manual*, 1937, pp. 380-382.

UPHAM, N. J., "The Real Measure of Front Foot Values," *National Real Estate Journal*, August 6, 1928, pp. 27-29.

VAN CLEEF, EUGENE, "Saving Land Values In Central Business Districts," *The Appraisal Digest*, July, 1953, pp. 1-4.

VEGAS ROLANDO, NICOLAS, "Criterio Para Fijar Valor De Los Apartamentos," *Boletin*, Sotave, Caracas, Venezuela, pp. 3-6.

VEGAS ROLANDO, NICOLAS, "El Concepto De Valor Del Inmueble," *Boletin*, Sotave, Caracas, Venezuela, pp. 7-9.

WEEKES, R. E., "Some Salient Factors Affecting Downtown Areas," *The Appraisal Journal*, October, 1959, pp. 561-564.

WENDT, PAUL F., *Central City Property Values In San Francisco And Oakland,* Washington Highway Research Board, Washington, 1953, pp. 132-133.

WHISTON, FRANK M., "Decentralization In Chicago," *Skyscraper Management,* April, 1934, pp. 3-4, 29-30.

WOLFF, LEWIS N., "The Central Business District In Transition," *Real Estate Analyst Appraisal Bulletin,* 1963, pp. 33-36.

# 13-15 Commercial Property and Concerns

ABELMANN, WILLAM W., "Appraisal of Service Station Sites," *The Real Estate Appraiser,* Jan., Feb., 1970, pp. 31-34.

ADELSBERG, HYMAN, "New Shopping Centers," *Valuation,* February, 1954, pp. 25-26.

ADELSBERG, HYMAN, "Suburban Shopping Centers," *Technical Valuation,* February, 1954, pp. P25.

ALEXANDER, ROBERT P., "Inventory Valuation Based on Trade Levels: the Assessors Viewpoint," *Assessment Administration,* IAAO, Chicago, 1963, pp. 120-122.

ALLEN, WALTER S., "Commercial Property," *The Appraisal Journal,* October, 1960, pp. 541-542.

AMERICAN APPRAISAL CO., "Sample Appraisal of Small Commercial Property," *National Real Estate Journal,* January, 1933, pp. 30.

AMERICAN DRUGGIST, "Shopping Center Site: Not All Gold," *American Druggist,* June 29, 1970, pp. 61.

AMERICAN HOTEL ASSOCIATION DEPRECIATION COMMITTEE, *Depreciation and Obsolescence In Hotels,* American Hotel Association, New York, 1928, pp. 24.

AMERICAN INSTITUTE OF REAL ESTATE APPRAISERS, "Appraisal of a Block Front of Retail Business With Offices Above," *Demonstration Appraisal Reports,* American Institute of Real Estate Appraisers, Chicago, 1957, pp. 326-363.

AMERICAN INSTITUTE OF REAL ESTATE APPRAISERS, "Appraisal of the Place Building," *Demonstration Appraisal Reports,* American Institute of Real Estate Appraisers, Chicago, 1957, pp. 245-292.

AMERICAN INSTITUTE OF REAL ESTATE APPRAISERS, "Commercial and Industrial Functional Utility and Inutility Valuation," *The Appraisal of Real Estate,* American Institute of Real Estate Appraisers, Chicago, 1967, pp. 148.

AMERICAN INSTITUTE OF REAL ESTATE APPRAISERS, "Correlation of the Dollars & Cents of Shopping Centers,1963 with Current Appraisal Practice," *Case Studies In Shopping Center Valuation,* American Institute of Real Estate Appraisers, Chicago, 1971, pp. 23-37.

AMERICAN INSTITUTE OF REAL ESTATE APPRAISERS, "Economic Factors and Case Studies In Hotel and Motel Valuation," *Case Studies,* American Institute of Real Estate Appraisers, Chicago, 1900.

▲ Urban Property

AMERICAN INSTITUTE OF REAL ESTATE APPRAISERS, "Market Data Approach Commercial Industrial Property Valuation," *The Appraisal of Real Estate*, American Institute of Real Estate Appraisers, Chicago, 1967, pp. 351-363.

AMERICAN INSTITUTE OF REAL ESTATE APPRAISERS, "Significance of Business Trends," *Hotel and Motel Valuation*, American Institute of Real Estate Appraisers, Chicago, 1971, pp. 7.

AMERICAN INSTITUTE OF REAL ESTATE APPRAISERS, "Useful Lives of Hotels and Motels," *Hotel and Motel Valuation*, American Institute of Real Estate Appraisers, Chicago, 1971, pp. 22.

AMERICAN RIGHT OF WAY ASSOCIATION, "Roadside Merchandising Problems," *Proceedings of the Third Annual National Seminar, 1957*, Washington, D. C, 1958.

AMERICAN RIGHT OF WAY ASSOCIATION, "Title Companies and the Expanded Right of Way Problems," *Proceedings of the Third Annual National Seminar*, Washington, 1957.

AMERICAN SOCIETY OF APPRAISERS, "Shopping Center Series," *Appraisal and Valuation Manual*, pp. 51-71.

AMERICAN SOCIETY OF PLANNING OFFICIALS, *Automatic Car Washes*, Chicago, 1900.

AMERICAN SOCIETY OF PLANNING OFFICIALS, *Coin-Operated Dry Cleaning Establishments*, Chicago, 1900.

AMERICAN SOCIETY OF PLANNING OFFICIALS, *Discount Stores*, Chicago, 1900.

AMERICAN SOCIETY OF PLANNING OFFICIALS, *Highway-Oriented and Urban Arterial Commercial Areas*, Chicago, Illinois.

APPEL, JAMES R., "Commercial Land Values," *The Real Estate Analyst Appraisal Bulletin*, 1957, pp. 25-28.

APPELBAUM, WILLIAM, "Evaluating Store Sites and Determining Store Rents In Chain Store Age," *American Society of Appraisers Valuation Manual*, March, 1958, pp. 15-17.

APPRAISAL JOURNAL, "An Approach to the Appraisal of Hotel and Motel Property," *The Appraisal Journal*, April, 1958, pp. 280-288.

APPRAISAL JOURNAL, "On Picking a Location for Coin Drycleaning," *The Appraisal Journal*, October, 1962, pp. 537-540.

ARMSTRONG, ROBERT H., "A New Look at Shopping Centers," *The Appraisal Journal*, January, 1955, pp. 100-105.

ARMSTRONG, ROBERT H., "Economic Survey and Appraisal of a Retail Store Property," *Appraisal Reporting Techniques*, American Institute of Real Estate Appraisers, Chicago, 1947, pp. 37-49.

ASCHER, DAVID B., "The Building-Land Ratio and What You Can Do with it," *Technical Valuation*, October, 1953, pp. 59-60.

ASH, FRED C., "The Appraisal Docket Shopping Center Not a Nuisance," *The Appraisal Journal*, July, 1956, pp. 431-432.

ASSESSORS NEWSLETTER, "A Shopping Center Profile," *The Assessors Newsletter*, July, 1966, pp. 107.

AUTOMATIC CAR WASH ASSOCIATION, *Depreciation Survey*, Automatic Car Wash Association, Bellwood, 1900.

AXFORD, DR. H. M., "Capitalization of Income Property," *The Appraisal Institute Magazine*, May, 1959, pp. 12-18.

BABCOCK, FREDERICK M., "Appraisal of Special Use Commercial Property," *National Real Estate Journal*, August 4, 1930, pp. 20-23.

BABCOCK, FREDERICK M., "Building Cost and Investment Estimation: Hotel," *Valuation of Real Estate*, 1932, pp. 481, 492.

BABCOCK, FREDERICK M., "Earnings Revenue Expense Hotels," *Valuation of Real Estate*, 1932, pp. 244-264.

BABCOCK, FREDERICK M., "Earnings Revenue Expense Store," *Valuation of Real Estate*, 1932, pp. 243-261.

# BIBLIOGRAPHY OF APPRAISAL LITERATURE

BABCOCK, FREDERICK M., "Earnings Revenue Expense Theater," *Valuation of Real Estate*, 1932, pp. 247-266.

BABCOCK, FREDERICK M., "Examples of Appraisal Procedure Hotel Property," *Valuation of Real Estate*, 1932, pp. 196-264.

BABCOCK, FREDERICK M., "Examples of Appraisal Procedure Store Property," *Valuation of Real Estate*, 1932, pp. 190, 195-260.

BABCOCK, FREDERICK M., "Examples of Appraisal Procedure Theater Property," *Valuation of Real Estate*, 1932, pp. 202-266.

BABCOCK, FREDERICK M., "Valuation for Specific Purposes to Determine Benefits and Damages In Condemnation Store," *The Valuation of Real Estate, Ed. 1*, 1932, pp. 514.

BABCOCK, FREDERICK M., "Valuation of Returns Details of Valuation Procedure Theater," *The Valuation of Real Estate, Ed. 1*, 1932, pp. 306-380.

BABCOCK, FREDERICK M., "Valuation of Returns Details of Valuation Procedure Store," *The Valuation of Real Estate, Ed. 1*, 1932, pp. 271-393.

BABCOCK, FREDERICK M., "Valuation of Returns Details of Valuation Procedure Hotels," *The Valuation of Real Estate, Ed. 1*, 1932, pp. 280-284.

BABCOCK, HENRY A., "Appraising Income Property," *The National Real Estate Journal*, March 7, 1927, pp. 33-40.

BAKER, GEOFFREY, *Shopping Centers*, Reinhold, New York City, 1951.

BAKER, GEOFFREY B., BRUNO, FUNARO, *Motels*, Reinhold, New York City, 1955.

BAKER, LLOYD, "Valuation of a Shopping Center from the Lenders Viewpoint," *Right of Way*, December, 1964, pp. 43-45.

BALLOU, PAUL, "Modern Motel," *Assessment Administration*, Chicago, 1962, pp. 117-122.

BAPPERT JOSEPH, "Super Market Requirements," *Real Estate Analyst Appraisal Bulletin*, 1950, pp. 457-460.

BAPPERT, JOSEPH, "Charting Income Properties," *Real Estate Analyst Appraisal Bulletin*, 1956, pp. 507-510.

BAPPERT, JOSEPH, "Evolution of the Supermarket," *Appraisal Digest*, January, 1956, pp. 6-10.

BAPPERT, JOSEPH, "The Battle for the Retail Dollar," *Real Estate Analyst Appraisal Bulletin*, 1956, pp. 357-360.

BARNARD, BOYD T., "How Service Stations Can Get Back Into Renewal Areas," *The Appraisal Journal*, July, 1964, pp. 371-375.

BARR, JOHN A., "The Future of Retailing," *The Appraisal Journal*, January, 1965, pp. 88-92.

BEATON, WILLIAM R., "Commercial Leasehold Appraising," *Valuation*, January, 1967, pp. 12-26.

BECKER, GEORGE, "Appraisal of Hotels," *The Appraisal Journal*, September, 1950, pp. 328-342.

BECKET, WELTON, "Shopping Center Traffic Problems," *Appraisal Journal*, July, 1955, pp. 395-403.

BEIQUE, JEAN, "Store Rentals and Land Values," *The Appraisal Journal*, July, 1955, pp. 389-394.

BEMAN, ARTHUR K., "Appraising Legitimate Theatres," *The Appraisal Journal*, January, 1966, pp. 63-69.

BEMAN, ARTHUR K., "Appraising Shopping Centers," *The Appraisal Journal*, April, 1957, pp. 249-264.

BEMAN, ARTHUR K., "Appraising Shopping Centers," *Valuation Manual*, 1956, pp. 189.

BENNET, HAZEN, "Capitalization of Income," *Appraisal Institute Magazine*, Appraisal Institute of Canada, Winnipeg.

BENNETT, S. V., ROBERT M. MCKEY, "Appraisal of a Hotel," *Appraisal Reporting Techniques,* American Institute of Real Estate Appraisers, 1954, pp. 161-192.

BENNETT, SAUL Z., "Hotel Appraisal," *The Appraisal Journal,* July, 1954, pp. 345-352.

BEYER, BEN B., "How To Use Cost Data In the Appraisal of Retail Store Property," *Real Estate Appraisal Practice,* The American Institute of Real Estate Appraisers, 1958, pp. 189-211.

BIRNKRANT, MICHAEL, "Shopping Center Feasibility Study: Methods and Techniques," *The Journal of Property Management,* November, 1970.

BODFISH, MORTON, THEOBALD, A. D, "Appraisal of Income Property," *Real Estate Fundamentals,* 1941, pp. 10-11.

BODFISH, MORTON, THEOBALD, A. D, "Appraising Vacant Business Lots In Built-Up Areas," *Real Estate Fundamentals,* 1941, pp. 4-5.

BOECKH, EVERARD HEREFORD, "Realty, Income Analysis," *Boeckh's Manual of Appraisals,* pp. 324.

BOECKH, EVERARD HEREFORD, "Retail District Structures," *Manual of Appraisals,* pp. 183.

BOECKH, EVERARD HEREFORD, "Small Stores and Combination Stores and Apartments," *Manual of Appraisals,* pp. 128.

BOECKH, EVERARD HEREFORD, "Small Stores and Combination Stores and Apartments," *Manual of Appraisals,* pp. 128.

BOOTH, ERIC ROWLAND, "Rating Valuation of Residential and Business Premises," *The Estates Gazette,* London, 1951.

BOWEN, PERCIVAL V., "Valuation of Church Cemeteries," *The A. S. A. Valuation Manual,* American Society of Appraisers, 1964, pp. 205.

BOWES, EUGENE, "Appraisal of Retail Store Property," *The Encyclopedia of Real Estate Appraising,* 1959, pp. 258-280.

BOWES, EUGENE G., "The Appraisal of Secondary Stores," *The Appraisal Journal,* July, 1957, pp. 426-430.

BOYCE, LLOYD M., "Problems In the Valuation of Commercial Properties," *National Real Estate Journal,* June, 1932, pp. 49-50.

BRADFORD, WM. DONALD, PH. D., *Inflation, the Value of the Firm and the Cost of Capital,* The Ohio University, 1971.

BRENER, DANIEL A., "Valuation of Furniture and Fixtures In a Hotel or Motel," *A. S. A. Valuation Manual,* The American Society of Appraisers, Washington D. C, 1964, pp. 63.

BRENER, STEPHEN W., "Factors Involved In a Motels Site Survey," *Valuation,* pp. 9-16.

BRENER, STEPHEN W., "Motel Realtors Guide," *The Appraisal and Valuation Manual,* The American Society of Appraisers, Washington D. C, 1960, pp. 177-188.

BRENER, STEPHEN W., "The Motor Hotel Becomes of Age," *The Appraisal and Valuation Manual,* The American Society of Appraisers, Washington, D. C, 1962, pp. 81-92.

BRICK, J. C., "Elements of Gasoline Service-Station Value," *The Appraisal Journal,* July, 1949, pp. 338-345.

BRICK, JUSTUS C., "Gasoline Service Station Appraisal," *The Encyclopedia of Real Estate Appraising,* 1959, pp. 626-649.

BRIGHAM, EUGENE F., WESTON, J. FRED, "Evaluation of the Composite Company," *Managerial Finance,* Holt, Rinehart and Winston, New York, 1966, pp. 80.

BROTHERS, D. S., "Change In Tax Depreciation Policy and Public Regulation of Business," *Land Economics,* November, 1957, pp. 346-358.

BROWN, PAT, "Condemnation of Cemetery Land, Factors Determining Valuation," *Valuation,* October, 1957, pp. 39-43.

BROWN, ROBERT K., RAMS, EDWIN M, "Investment Articulation, Supermarkets," *Valuation Manual,* 1960, pp. 297.

BROWNLOW, G. S., *Site Value of Shops,* Estates Gazette, Ltd, London, 1956.

BRUST, KENNETH F., "Retail Location Analysis," *Valuation,* pp. 10-24.

BURKHARD, EARL E., "Appraising Supermarket Personal Property," *Case Reports In Assessment Administration,* 1960, pp. 30-32.

BURKHARD, EARL E., "Assessment Appraisals of Personal Property at a Shopping Center," *Assessors Journal,* April, 1966, pp. 47-54.

BURKHARD, EARL E., "Supermarket Equipment and Inventory Appraisal," *Technical Valuation,* October, 1960, pp. 28-32.

BURNSIDE, L. D., "Assessing a Small Shopping Center," *Case Reports In Assessment Administration,* March, 1960, pp. 9-12.

CARLSON, HAROLD J., "Appraisal of Sunnydale Plaza Shopping Center," *The Appraisal Journal,* January, 1965, pp. 115-118.

CARLSON, HAROLD J., "Problems In Appraising Commercial Properties," *The Real Estate Appraiser,* April, 1966, pp. 2-7.

CARLSON, HOWARD M., "Hotels--Replacement Costs and Rental Rates," *The Appraisal Journal,* April, 1950, pp. 185-189.

CARPER, RAYMOND E., "Assessment of Business Inventories," *Assessment Administration,* IAAO, Chicago, 1957, pp. 115-118.

CARR, FRANCIS J., "Property Assessments Protest, Appeal, and Judicial Review," *The Journal of the State Bar of California,* November, 1964, pp. 877.

CASE, FRED E., "Let's Make the FHA a Privately Controlled Business," *The Appraisal Journal,* July, 1951, pp. 370-374.

CHAIN STORE AGE, "$3.7 Billion for New, Remodeled Stores," *Chain Store Age,* January, 1971, pp. 19-21.

CHAIN STORE AGE, "$3.7 Billion for New, Remodeled Stores," *Chain Store Age,* January, 1971, pp. 19-21.

CHAIN STORE AGE, "Three-Level Centers Next Step In Malls," *Chain Store Age,* May, 1971, pp. 34-35.

CHAMBERLAIN, EDWARD, *The Theory of Monopolistic Competition Reorientation of the Theory of Value,* Harvard University, Cambridge, 1956.

CHAPMAN, FRED L., "Appraising Typical Business Properties for Loan Purposes," *The Appraisal Journal,* January, 1937, pp. 45-53.

CHARLAND, ROGER, "Shopping Center Land Value," *Assessment Administration,* IAAO, Chicago, 1961, pp. 205-211.

CHERNEY, RICHARD A., "Things We Have Noticed: Automatic Laundry Building, Reported Costs," *Case Reports In Assessment Administration,* August, 1961, pp. 30.

CHURCH, A. HAMILTON, "Manufacturing Costs and Accounts," *Engineering valuation,* Mcgraw Hill, New York, 1929, pp. 04.

CLARK, ROBERT, "The 'Total Experience' Of Super-Regional Shopping Centers," *The Real Estate Appraiser,* The Society of Real Estate Appraisers, Chicago Illinois, January 1, 1974, pp. 21-29.

CLAUS, R. JAMES, "Appraising Potential Volume of Shopping Site Sales," *Appraisal Institute Magazine,* Appraisal Institute of Canada, Winnipeg, September 1, 1971.

CLEMINSHAW, WILLIAM, "Valuation Rundamentals and Motel Appraisal," *Assessment Administration,* IAAO, Chicago, 1960, pp. 250-264.

COCHRAN, GAIL V., "A Short-Cut Capitalization Method for Commercial Properties," *Appraisal and Valuation Manual,* ASA, Washington, 1958, pp. 331-336.

COFFMAN, PAUL B., "Effect of Business Conditions Upon Value," *Technical Valuation,* February, 1956, pp. 3-6.

COFFMAN, PAUL B., "Review and Forecast Business Conditions," *Technical Valuation,* June, 1958, pp. 3-5.

▲ Urban Property

COFFMAN, PAUL B., "Valuation of Stock of Closely-Held Corporations," *Appraisal and Valuation Manual,* American Society of Appraisers, Washington, 1956, pp. 341.

COMMERCE TODAY, "Name Changed, But Chain Stores Still Boom," *Commerce Today,* May 31, 1971, pp. 21-22.

CONLEE, DONALD R., "Commercial Property-Its Highest and Best Use," *The Real Estate Appraiser,* May, 1964, pp. 24-27.

CONNAWAY, JOSEPH C., "Drive-In Theatres," *Case Reports In Assessment Administration,* September, 1958, pp. 2-3.

CONNELLY, WILLIAM F., "The Valuation of Industrial and Commercial Property for Taxation," *National Tax Association, Proceeding 20th Annual Conference,* 1927, pp. 295-308.

CONNERY, RUSSELL B., "Gasoline Service Station," *Assessment Administration,* I.A.A.O., Chicago, 1961, pp. 236-244.

COX, W. E. JR., E. F. COOK, "Other Dimensions Involved In Shopping Center Preference," *Journal of Marketing,* October, 1970, pp. 12-17.

CRAIG, ROBERT H., "Assessment and Appraisal of Seasonal Motels," *Assessors Journal,* July, 1970.

CRAWFORD, CLAUDE O., "Appraisal of a Total Taking of a Gasoline Station," *Right of Way,* December, 1958, pp. 11-15.

CROCHERON, CLARENCE, *Valuations for Corporate Mergers and Reorganizations,* American Appraisal Co., Milwaukee, Wisc., 1955.

CURTIS, S. G., "Catwalk Is Must In Urban Stores," *Chain Store Age,* May, 1970, pp. 70.

DAVIDSON, THOMAS LEA, "The Planning and Organization of a Shopping Center," *Right of Way,* June, 1962, pp. 29-33.

DAVIDSON, WILLIAM R., "Retailing: Some Significant Current Developments," *The Appraisal Journal,* January, 1957, pp. 91-98.

DEBOOS, FRANK A., "Faster, Reliable Sales Via Appraising," *The Review,* December, 1948, pp. 13-16.

DEBUTTS, CARY E., "Appraising and Leasing Retail Stores," *National Real Estate Journal,* December 22, 1930, pp. 20-22.

DERBY, LOUIS F., "Analysis of Some of the Factors Involved In Economic Valuation of Income Property," *Technicalities,* October, 1948, pp. 17-21.

DODGE, RICHARD L., "Shopping Center Appraisal Approach," *The Appraisal Journal,* January, 1962, pp. 95-108.

DOYLE, B. E., "Appraisal Report on Service Stations," *Assessors Journal,* October, 1970, pp. 47-59.

DRENNAN, GEORGE W., "Appraising Funeral Homes," *The Appraisal Journal,* April, 1948, pp. 208-209.

DRENNAN, GEORGE W., AND EDITH J. FREEDMAN., *Appraisal of a Funeral Home,* Encyclopedia of Real Estate Appraising, 1959.

DUBOIS, AYERS J., "Goldstone--Appraisal of a Business Property," *The Appraisal Journal,* January, 1933, pp. 166-167.

DUCKLIEB, BRUNO, "New Elements In Service Station Valuation," *The Appraisal Journal,* January, 1952, pp. 85-88.

ECKERT, FRED W., *Economic Factors and Case Studies In Hotel and Motel Valuation,* American Institute of Real Estate Appraisers, Chicago, 1962.

ECKERT, FRED W., "Operating and Capitalization Factors In the Valuation of Hotel Properties," *The Appraisal Journal,* April, 1946, pp. 180-186.

ECKERT, FRED W., "Operative Comparisons-The Hotel Vs. the Motel," *The Appraisal Journal,* July, 1957, pp. 356-372.

EDMAN, J. J., "The Appraisal Docket. Valuation of Cemetery Property," *The Appraisal Journal,* January, 1958, pp. 125-126.

EDMAN, J. J., "The Appraisal Docket. Valuation of Cemetery Property," *The Appraisal Journal,* July, 1957, pp. 447-449.

EDMAN, J. J., "The Appraisal Docket. Vermont Statute Recognizes Damage to Business," *The Appraisal Journal,* January, 1960, pp. 123-124.

EGGER, R. L. JR., "Liquidation and Valuation of Business Interests In Estates," *American Society of Appraisers Valuation Manual, Trusts and Estates,* February, 1956, pp. 104-107.

EICHENBERG, EUGENE, JR., "Evaluating Chain Store Locations," *Appraisal and Valuation Manual,* American Society of Appraisers, 1955, pp. 26-34.

ELLER, HERBERT D., "Appraisal of a Retail Store-Apartment Property," *Appraisal Reporting Techniques,* American Institute of Real Estate Appraisers, pp. 73-85.

ELLWOOD, LEON W., "Appraisal of a Motel," *Appraisal Reporting Techniques,* 1951, pp. 43-59.

ELLWOOD, LEON W., "Estimating Potential Volume of Proposed Shopping Centers," *The Appraisal Journal,* October, 1954, pp. 581-589.

ELLWOOD, LEON W., "Financing and Appraising New Shopping Center," *Valuation Manual Series,* American Society of Appraisers, 1955, pp. 65.

ELLWOOD, LEON W., "Shopping Center Series Financing and Appraising New Shopping Centers," *Technical Valuation,* American Society of Appraisers, June, 1954, pp. 27.

ELLWOOD, LEON W., "Shops, Stores, and Shopping Centers, Part IV," *The Appraisal Journal,* October, 1952, pp. 473-480.

ELLWOOD, LEON W., "Shops, Stores, and Shopping Centers, Part II," *The Appraisal Journal,* April, 1952, pp. 194-205.

ELLWOOD, LEON W., AND ROBERT H. ARMSTRONG, "Shops, Stores, and Shopping Centers, Part I," *The Appraisal Journal,* January, 1952, pp. 13-19.

ELLWOOD, LEON W., AND ROBERT H. ARMSTRONG, "Shops, Stores, and Shopping Centers, Part III," *The Appraisal Journal,* July, 1952, pp. 294-302.

ENGINEERING NEWS-RECORD, "Shopping Center Owners Urged to Curb Costs," *Engineering News-Record,* May 27, 1971, pp. 46.

ENTWISTLE, WALLACE E., "The Assessment of Motels and Motor Inns," *Asessment Administration,* Institute of American Assessment Officers, Chicago, 1964, pp. 182-185.

ERSKINE, R. C., "Valuing Business Subcenter Property," *The Appraisal Journal,* October, 1938, pp. 340-342.

FAVA, EDWARD, "Appraising Partial Taking of a Gasoline Service Center," *Appraisal and Valuation Manual,* 1961, pp. 89-95.

FAY, CLIFFORD T., THOMAS J. HOGAN, *Economic Factors and Case Studies In Hotel and Motel Valuation,* American Institute of Real Estate Appraisers, May, 1968.

FEDERAL RESERVE BANK OF PHILADELPHIA, "What's Behind the Discount Rumpus In Retailing," *The Appraisal Journal,* April, 1962, pp. 210-218.

FINCH, NELSON E., "Shopping Center Series: Problems of the Broker and Promoter," *Technical Valuation,* June, 1954, pp. 33.

FINCH, NELSON E., "Shopping Centers As Neighbors," *The Residential Appraiser,* June, 1957, pp. 14-15.

FINCH, NELSONE, "Shopping Center Series Problems of the Broker and Promoter," *Technical Revaluation,* June, 1954, pp. 33.

FINKEL, JULIUS, "Appraising a Cemetery Part II," *The Appraisal Journal,* October, 1951, pp. 472-478.

FINKEL, JULIUS, "Appraising a Cemetery Part III---The Valuation Process," *The Appraisal Journal,* January, 1952, pp. 64-73.

FINKEL, JULIUS, "Appraising a Cemetery: Part I--The Data Program," *The Appraisal Journal*, July, 1951, pp. 342-347.

FINKEL, JULIUS, "Condemnation Appraisal of a Cemetery," *The Appraisal Journal*, July, 1955, pp. 379-388.

FISHER, HENRY F., "Special Purpose Income Producing Properties," *The Appraisal Journal*, April, 1949, pp. 189-195.

FLEISCHMANN, LEON, "Theater Appraisals," *Journal of the American Institute of Real Estate Appraisers*, July, 1934, pp. 293-296.

FLEMING, HARRY D. JR., "Appraisal Process In the Valuation of Closely Held Corporations," *Technical Valuation*, October, 1959, pp. 23-27.

FORD, BACON, AND DAVIS, INC., "Valuation of Going Companies for Purchase on Merger Also Fair Ratio for Exchange of Securities," *Valuation Manual*, 1955, pp. 173.

FRANKLIN, R. J., "Tax and Business Considerations In Buying Property," *Taxes*, March, 1964.

FRANTZEN, HAROLD C., "The Speculative Stop-And-Shop," *The Appraisal Journal*, January, 1949, pp. 96-99.

FREE, ROBERT L., "The Market Data Approach Applied to Income Properties," *The Appraisal Journal*, pp. 504-509.

FREE, ROBERT L., JOHN W. SPPARKS, *Case Studies In Shopping Center Valuation*, American Institute of Real Estate Appraisers, Chicago, 1964.

FRIES, EUGENE H., "The Small Town Hotel," *The Appraisal Journal*, April, 1939, pp. 128-133.

FROMKES, SAUL, "Shopping Center Ruled Not a Nuisance," *Appraisal Digest*, January, 1956, pp. 21-22.

FRUIN-COLNON CONTRACTING COMPANY, *St. Louis Building Cost Index*, Fruin-Colnon Contracting Co, St. Louis, 1900.

FUNARO, BRUNO, "Planning for Better Shopping, Why, How, and Where," *Appraisal Journal*, July 1952, pp. 303-305.

GADIN, C. R., "Regional Shopping Center," *Assessment Administration*, I. A. A. O., Chicago, 1960, pp. 240-249.

GADIN, CAMILLE R., "Demonstration Appraisal a Modern Hotel," *Assessment Administration*, 1957, pp. 78-90.

GALLAGHER, RUSSELL B., "Coporate Insurance Administrator," *Technicalities*, October, 1951, pp. 14-16.

GAMMON, GEORGE W., "The Appraisal of a Small Business," *Valuation*, June, 1968, pp. 26-33.

GANNON, JAMES F. JR., "What Is the Value of a Motion Picture Theater," *The Appraisal Journal*, April, 1946, pp. 169-175.

GELMAN, M., "Financial Analyst's Approach to Valuing Stock of A Closely-Held Company," *Journal of Taxation*, June, 1972, pp. 353-354.

GEORGE, ALLAN C., "Hotel Operating Factors," *The Appraisal Journal*.

GIBSON, BLAINE C., "The Real Estate and Development Man for an Oil Company Is Looking for a Service Station Site," *Right of Way*, February, 1954, pp. 1-12.

GILL, WILLIAM L., "Corporate Security Values As Determined by the Tax Court," *A. S. A. Valuation Manual*, A. S. A, 1960, pp. 77.

GLASSBURNER, FRED R., "A Local Motel Survey," *American Society of Appraisers*, 1960, pp. 189-196.

GLOS, HAROLD V., "Valuation of a Leasehold Estate Involving a Stores Arcade and Office Buildings," *Practical Appraisal Methods*, 1940, pp. 94-97, 128.

GLOS, HAROLD V., "Valuation of a Small Store and Office Building In an Outlying Section," *Practical Appraising Methods*, 1940, pp. 82-85, 128.

# BIBLIOGRAPHY OF APPRAISAL LITERATURE

GODIN, C. R., "Demostration Appraisal of a Modern Hotel," *American Society of Appraisers,* 1959, pp. 77-88.

GOLDFARB, MORRIS, "Appraising Store Property," *National Real Estate Journal,* November, 1938, pp. 51-52.

GOLDFARB, MORRIS, "The Appraisal of Retail Store Properties," *The Appraisal Journal,* January, 1939, pp. 19-26.

GOLDING, STUART S., "Trends In Retail Leasing," *The Real Estate Appraiser,* August, 1963, pp. 26-32.

GORDON, MYRON J., "The Investment Financing and Valuation of the Corporation," *Managerial Finance,* 1962, pp. 293.

GOSSELIN, JACQUES, "Terrains Commerciaux Et Industriels," *Appraisal Institute Magazine,* Appraisal Institute of Canada, Winnipeg.

GOULD, JAY M., "Community Income and Retail Store Sales," *The Appraisal Journal,* January, 1950, pp. 9-16.

GRAASKAMP, J. A., "Dollars and Cents of Shopping Centers 1969: a Review Article," *Land Economics,* June, 1970, pp. 193-195.

GRAHAM, "Market Valuation of a Regional Shopping Center," *The Appraisal Journal,* October, 1964, pp. 589-595.

GRAHAM, D. H. JR., "Fair Market Valuation of a Regional Shopping Center," *Appraisal Digest,* October, 1964, pp. 12-18.

GRAHAM, D. H. JR., "Shopping Center Assessment," *Assessors News Letter,* March, 1963, pp. 29-32.

GRAHAM, D. H. JR., "Shopping Centers Financing Appraisal and Management," *Real Estate Appraiser,* December, 1966, pp. 15-19.

GRAHAM, DONALD H. JR., "Shopping Center Real Property Taxes," *The Appraisal Journal,* January, 1963, pp. 7-12.

GREEN, JOHN B., "On Building a Business," *The Appraisal Journal,* July, 1936, pp. 319-320.

GREENE, H. D., "Shopping Centers - Boom or Bust," *Publishers Weekly,* February 8, 1971, pp. 54-55.

GROGAN, JAMES J., "Three Concepts In Appraising a Store and Apartment Building," *Practical Appraising Methods,* 1940, pp. 188.

GRUEN, VICTOR, "Shopping Centers, Suburban and Urban," *Appraisal and Valuation Manual,* American Society of Appraisars, 1960.

GUILFORD, W. S., "Goldstone-Appraisal of a Business Property," *The Appraisal Journal,* January, 1933, pp. 167.

HAGOOD, WAYNE D., "Feasibility Studies for Commercial Developments In Small Towns," *The Real Estate Appraiser,* August, 1967, pp. 12-16.

HALL, FRANK D., "How Shopping Centers Are Financed," *The Appraisal Journal,* July, 1957, pp. 350-355.

HALL, JOSEPH P., "How to Appraise the Small Business Property," *National Real Estate Journal,* December 23, 1929, pp. 27-30.

HALL, T. H. 3RD, "Motor Hotel: Appraisals and Feasibility Studies," *Appraisal Journal,* October, 1971, pp. 568-575.

HAMBLETON, RAY W., "The Appraisal of Leased Commercial Property In Eminent Domain," *Technical Valuation,* June, 1959, pp. 35-39.

HAMILTON, ANDREW C., "Contracts for Municipal Corporations," *The Appraisal Journal,* July, 1934, pp. 341-343.

HANNOCH, FRANKLIN, "The Unpredictable Service Station," *The Appraisal Journal,* July, 1957, pp. 373-380.

HANRAHAN, DANIEL C., "Purchase of Corporate Transferee Residences," *The Real Estate Appraiser,* September, 1966, pp. 24-29.

HANSON, PETER, "Valuation of Income Property," *Annals of Real Estate Practice,* National Association of Real Estate Boards, 1929, pp. 76-80.

▲ Urban Property

HARDING, CARL G., "Appraisal of Motels," *Encyclopedia of Real Estate Appraising*, 1959, pp. 447-464.

HARDING, CARL G., "Processing Market Data In the Appraisal of Motels," *The Appraisal Journal*, January, 1958, pp. 101-110.

HARDWICK, CHARLES Z., "Roadside Merchandising Problems," *Proceedings of the Third Annual National Seminar*, American Right of Way Association, Washington, D. C., 1958, pp. 41-43.

HARRIS, KERR, FOSTER AND COMPANY; "Trends In the Hotel Business, Annual Review," *Valuation Manual, 1933-57*, ASA.

HARRIS, STEPHEN M., "Some ABC's of Commercial Relocation When Urban Renewal Forces You to Move Your Business," *Valuation Manual, A. S. A.*, 1964, pp. 147.

HARRISON, SIGMUND, "Shopping Center," *Assessment Administration*, IAAO, Chicago, 1962, pp. 113-116.

HARRISON, THOMAS, "The Advent of the Super Regional Shopping Center," *The Appraisal Journal*, January, 1968, pp. 91-97.

HAVERKORN, THOMAS W., "America's Vigorous Postwar Enterprises the Roadside Motels," *The Appraisal Journal*, July, 1958, pp. 397-406.

HAWK, R. L. D., "Some Observations on Retail Stores," *The Appraisal Journal*, October, 1955, pp. 581-586.

HAYES, TOM JR., "Service Station Highest and Best Use?," *The Appraisal Journal*, April, 1966, pp. 299-300.

HEAD, GEORGE, "How to Build a Business," *The Appraisal Journal*, April, 1936, pp. 153-158.

HEINMULLER, CARL, "Appraisal of a Water-Powered Grist Mill," *Right of Way*, April, 1962, pp. 19-24.

HELM, W. P., "Demonstration Appraisal, an Obsolete Motel," *Assessment Administration*, IAAO, Chicago, 1957, pp. 9-15.

HENDERSON AND ROSS, "Real Estate Appraisal for Standard Oil Company of New York," *Real Estate Appraising*, Henderson, New York, 1931.

HENDERSON, JAMES D., "Gasoline Service Stations," *The Appraisal Journal*, January, 1933, pp. 140-142.

HENDERSON, JAMES D., "Stores and Business Buildings," *Real Estate Appraisal*, 1931, pp. 275-309.

HOAD, WILLIAM M., "Appraising Public Recreational Projects," *The Appraisal Journal*, January, 1952, pp. 45-50.

HOGAN, LEO E., "Appraisal of a Commercial Airline," *Assessment Administration*, I. A. A. O., Chicago, 1963, pp. 218-222.

HOLLEBAUGH, CLIFFORD W., "Income Approach to Value," *Encyclopedia of Real Estate Appraising*, 1959.

HOLLINGSHEAD, WADE C., "The Fibre Box Industry, Thoughts on Value," ASA *Appraisal & Valuation Manual*, 1958, pp. 277.

HOLMES, DALE W., "Appraisal of Super Food Market," *Appraisal Digest*, October, 1960, pp. 6-10.

HOLMES, LAWRENCE G., "Furnishings In the Hotel Appraisal," *The Appraisal Journal*, April, 1942, pp. 143-152.

HORWATH, HORWORTH, "Hotel Operation Annual Studies," *Valuation Manual*, pp. 505.

HOSKINS, HENRY J. B., "Hotel Standards and Relationship," *The Appraisal Journal*, January, 1942, pp. 35-46.

HOUSE & HOME, "Very Spec Shopping Center for Very Spec Market," *House and Home*, March, 1971, pp. 88-89.

HOUSE AND HOME, "Here's a Shopping Complex That Mirrors Its Envt," *House and Home*, June, 1971, pp. 60-63.

HOYT, HOMER, "Appraisal of Shopping Centers," *Encyclopedia of Real Estate Appraising,* 1959.

HOYT, HOMER, "Classification and Significant Characteristics of Shopping Centers," *The Appraisal Journal,* April, 1958, pp. 214-222.

HOYT, HOMER, "Land Values In Shopping Centers," *The Appraisal Journal,* July, 1969, pp. 344-345.

HOYT, HOMER, "Relation of Building and Land Cost to Income or Loss In Shopping Centers," *The Appraisal Journal,* July, 1962, pp. 333-340.

HOYT, JOHN R., "Appraisal of Department Stores," *The Appraisal Journal,* October, 1939, pp. 358-361.

HUBBART, J. ROY, IRVING L. HERTZMAN, "A Formula for Building Hotel Rate Structures," *The Appraisal Journal,* July, 1948, pp. 309-316.

HUDSON, W. J., *Corporate Mergers,* New York, 1900.

HUNSCHE, RALPH, "How a Title Plant May Help the Right of Way Agent," *Right of Way,* August, 1959, pp. 11-14.

HYDER, K. LEE, "The Appraisal of Hotels," *The Appraisal Journal,* April, 1941, pp. 113-122.

HYDER, K. LEE, "The Valuation of Department Stores," *The Appraisal Journal,* October, 1944, pp. 327-333.

ILLINOIS DEPARTMENT OF REVENUE, *List of Foreign Corporations Assessed on Tangible Property In Illinois,* Illinois Department of Revenue, Springfield, 1947.

INST. OF NEWSPAPER CONTROLLERS & FINANCE OFFICERS, *Corporations - Valuation,* Inst. of Newspaper Controllers & Finance Officers, Newyork, 1957.

INTERNATIONAL ASSOCIATION OF ASSESSING OFFICERS, *Assessment and Appraisal of Shopping Centers,* Institute of American Assessment Officers, Chicago, 1957.

INTERNATIONAL ASSOCIATION OF ASSESSING OFFICERS, *Shopping Centers, Analysis and Appraisal for Assessment Purposes,* IAAO, Chicago, 1955.

INTERNATIONAL COUNCIL OF SHOPPING CENTERS, *Shopping Center Strategy,* New York.

JENSEEN, WARD J., "Booby Traps In Discount Store Site Appraisal," *The Appraisal Journal,* April, 1964, pp. 215-218.

JERRARD, W. L., "Appraisal of Cemeteries, Mausoleums and Crematories," *Appraisal and Valuation Manual,* ASA, 1958, pp. 159-187.

JOHNSON, CLIFFORD R., "Appraising Existing Successful Service Stations," *Right of Way,* December, 1969.

KAHN, SANDERS A., "Impact of Shopping Centers on Suburbs and Central Cities," *Valuation,* February, 1958, pp. 45-48.

KAHN, SANDERS A., ALVIN M. WEINTRAUB, "Real Estate and the Trucking Industry," *Valuation Manual,* 1964, pp. 189.

KAM, WILLIAM H., "Investment Analysis of Leased Commercial Land," *Real Estate Appraisal,* February, 1967, pp. 27-30.

KAMLET, MARK, "Cable TV, Its Impact on Real Property Valuations," *The Appraisal Journal,* July, 1968, pp. 426-428.

KAYLIN, S. O., "Chain Stores In New Shopping Centers," *Valuation Manual,* 1955, pp. 69.

KAYLIN, S. O., "Shopping Center Series Chain Stores In New Shopping Centers," *Technical Valuation,* June, 1954, pp. 31.

KEEFER, E. D., "Appraisal of a Two-Story Retail Store and Hotel Property," *Appraisal Reporting Techniques,* 1949, pp. 79-102.

KEEFER, E. D., "The Appraisal of Resort Hotels," *The Appraisal Journal,* January, 1946, pp. 50-58.

KELLEY, JOHN F., "Motel and Freeways," *Valuation Manual,* 1955, pp. 35.

▲ Urban Property

KELLEY, JOHN F., "Motels and Freeways," *Technical Valuation,* June, 1954, pp. 7-17.

KELLOUGH, W. R., "Appraising the Service Station Site," *The Real Estate Appraiser,* March, 1965, pp. 8-21.

KELLOUGH, W. R., "Evaluation of Operating Shopping Centers," *Valuation Manual,* 1961, pp. 121.

KELLOUGH, W. R., "The Evaluation of Operating Shopping Centers," *The Appraisal Journal,* 1961, pp. 121-136.

KISSACK, A. B., "Service Station Rent," *Real Estate Analyst Appraisal Bulletin,* 1947, pp. 161-164.

KLAFTER, MARK H., WARREN E. SHRYOCK, "A Fresh Look at the Movie Theatre Business," *The Appraisal Journal,* 1962, pp. 353-360.

KNISKERN, PHILIP W., "An Appraisal Involving a Long-Term Chain Store Lease," *Appraising Manual,* 1937, pp. 466-469.

KRAVITZ, MORRIS A., "Outlying Shopping Centers," *The Appraisal Journal,* October, 1948, pp. 478-480.

KUEHNLE, WALTER R., "Gross Income Estimates In the Valuation of Stores," *The Appraisal Journal,* October, 1939, pp. 305-325.

LAFFOON, A. L., "Demonstration Appraisal, a One Story Building and Parking Lot," *Technical Valuation,* Pueblo, Colorado, pp. 30-43.

LAURENTI, LUIGI, *Property Values and Race, Studies In Seven Cities,* University of California Press, Berkeley, L. A., 1960.

LEDERER, MARTIN W., "The Appraisal of Cemeteries I," *The Appraisal Journal,* April, 1937, pp. 107-123.

LEDERER, MARTIN W., "The Appraisal of Cemeteries II," *The Appraisal Journal,* July, 1937, pp. 225-239.

LEET, EDMUND, "Appraising Commercial Urban Land for Ad Valorem Tax Purposes," *Appraisal and Valuation Manual,* American Society of Appraisers, Washington, D. C, 1959, pp. 165-172.

LEONARD, H. W., "Appraising Freeway Right of Way Through Commercial Area," *Valuation,* October, 1954, pp. 27-28.

LESURE, JOHN D., "Hotel and Motel Valuation," *Valuation,* 1966, pp. 36-42.

LEVY, MARK, "Appraisal of a Three-Story and Full-Basement Brick Store and Apartment Building In Chicago," *Mcmichael S. I. Appraising Manual, Second Edition,* 1937, pp. 478-489.

LEVY, MARK, "How to Determine Business Rentals," *National Real Estate Journal,* November 17, 1924, pp. 41-44.

LEVY, MARK, BROTHER, "Percentage Rental Rates Based on Gross Annual Sales," *Real Estate Appraisal and Valuation,* 1933, pp. 337-338.

LEWIS, J. P., "Business Conditions Analysis," *Economic Analysis,* Mcgraw-Hill, New York, 1959, pp. 715.

LIBOTT, NATHAN, "Management," *The Appraisal Journal,* April, 1933, pp. 212-218.

LICK, JAMES E., "The Income Approach Applied to Motel Leasing," *The Real Estate Appraiser,* January, 1970, pp. 6-10.

LOSTETTER, EARL, "The Use of Cost Data In the Appraisal of Motels," *Real Estate Appraisal Practice,* American Institute of Real Estate Appraiser, 1958, pp. 387-396.

LOSTETTER, EARL K., "Analysis and Reconstruction of Motel Operating," *Real Estate Appraisal Practice,* American Institute of Real Estate Appraisers, 1958, pp. 397-409.

LOWDEN, J. A., "Factors to Be Considered In a Super-Market Site," *Appraisal Digest,* October, 1954, pp. 19-22.

LOWDEN, J. A., "Retail Store Locations," *The Appraisal Journal,* October, 1958, pp. 574-580.

LOWDEN, J. A., "Shopping Centers Challenge to the Appraiser," *The Appraisal Journal,* April, 1960, pp. 225-230.

LOWDEN, J.A., "Valuation of Shopping Centers," *The Appraisal Journal,* April, 1967, pp. 232-243.

LUCHS, FRANK J., "Commercial Property Sales," *The Appraisal Journal,* October, 1948, pp. 471-477.

LUEDDERS, DEAN R., "Obsolete Automobile Dealership Facilities," *The Appraisal Journal,* October, 1965, pp. 604-608.

MACK, CURT C., "Analysis of Comparable Sales," *The Residential Appraiser,* April, 1960, pp. 15-16.

MACLEOD, MORTON P., "The Hotel Appraisal for Ad Valorem Tax Assessment," *Appraisal and Valuation Manual,* American Society of Appraisers, 1959, pp. 89-98.

MACROSSIE, WILLIAM, "Hotels Vs. Motels," *Technicalities and Technical Valuation,* June, 1952, pp. 9-13.

MACROSSIE, WILLIAM, "Selection and Use of Capitalization Rates In the Appraisal of Motels," *The Appraisal Journal,* April, 1959, pp. 212-219.

MACROSSIE, WILLIAM, "Valuation of Motel Furnishings and Equipment," *Real Estate Appraisal Practice,* American Institute of Real Estate Appraisers, 1958, pp. 4 2-435.

MACROSSIE, WILLIAM, TREADWELL, JOHN C, "Appraisal of Sheraton Hotel, Worchester, Massachusetts," *Appraisal Reporting Techniques,* American Institute of Real Estate Appraisers, 1949, pp. 171-184.

MADDISON, PAUL, "Analysis of Service Station Sites," *The Real Estate Appraiser,* July, 1967, pp. 30-37.

MANN, J. A., "Service Station Evaluation," *Right of Way,* October, 1954, pp. 10-14.

MARCH, C. A., *Building Operation and Maintenance,* Mcgraw-Hill, New York, 1950.

MARIN, R., "Electronic Departments Getting Favored Treatment," *Merchandising Week,* October, 1970, pp. 1.

MARJASON L C, "Licensed Hotels and Liquor Shops In N.S.W.-Valuation Approach," *The Valuer,* The Commonwealth Institute of Valuers, Sydney, Australia, October 1, 1973.

MARTIN, C. VIRGIL, "Shouldn't Department Stores Invest In Human Parking Downtown," *The Appraisal Journal,* October, 1960, pp. 510-514.

MARTIN, HOWARD S., "Some Factors In Service Station Appraisals," *The Appraisal Journal,* July, 1956, pp. 393-398.

MARTIN, WENDELL H., "Automotive Shopping Center," *The Real Estate Appraiser,* September, 1970, pp. 43-46.

MASAD, RIMON NICOLA, *The Effect of Commercial Land Use on Land Value Patterns,* Austin Texas, 1958.

MAYER, L. A., "U. S. Population Growth Would Slower Be Better," *Fortune,* June, 1970, pp. 80-83.

MC MICHAEL, STANLEY L., "Avaluacion De Hoteles," *Boletin,* Sotave, Caracas, Venezuela, pp. 25-30.

MCCARTHY, EARL D., "The Valuation of a Shopping Center---From the Developer's Viewpoint," *Right of Way,* October, 1964, pp. 52-54.

MCCLOSKEY, W. D., "Modular Systems Are the Key to Ending Superflation," *Air Conditioning, Heating, and Refrigeration News,* July 20, 1970, pp. 4.

MCCORMICK, MICHAEL J., "The Effect of Discounting on Retailing," *Appraisal Institute Magazine,* December, 1961, pp. 2-7.

MCCOY, CHARLES R., "Effect of Partial Condemnation and of a Temporary Easement on the Value of a Service Stateon," *Real Estate Analyst Appraisal Bulletin,* 1954, pp. 305-311.

MCCOY, CHARLES R., "Ready-To-Wear Store Appraisal Affected by Decentralization," *Appraisal Digest,* January, 1953, pp. 14-16.

▲ Urban Property

MCCOY, CHARLES R., "The Impact of Retail Decentralization on One Downtown Appraisal," *Real Estate Analyst Appraisal Bulletin*, 1952, pp. 489-492.

MCCURDY, ROBERT V., "Discussion of Appraisal Processes for Shopping Centers," *Technical Valuation*, June, 1959, pp. 57-60.

MCKEY, ROBERT M., "Appraisal of Hotels and Resort Properties," *Encyclopedia of Real Estate Appraising*, 1959, pp. 414-446.

MCMAHON, THOMAS C., "Combination Pittsburgh Business, Residential and Warehouse Lots and Property," *Appraising Manual*, Mcmichael, S. L, 1937.

MCMICHAEL, S. L., "Appraising Gasoline Stations," *Appraising Manual*, 1937, pp. 182-198.

MCMICHAEL, STANLEY L., "Transmuting Store Rentals Into Standard-Foot Land Values," *National Real Estate Journal*, June 24, 1929, pp. 19-21.

MCREYNOLDS, TOM, "Appraising an Automobile Laundry," *Encyclopedia of Real Estate Appraising*, 1959, pp. 563-570.

MCREYNOLDS, TOM, "Frozen Custard Stands," *Real Estate Analyst Appraisal Bulletin*, 1955, pp. 225-228.

MCREYNOLDS, TOM, "Planning Suburban Shopping Centers," *Real Estate Analyst Appraisal Bulletin*, 1951, pp. 85-123.

MCREYNOLDS, TOM, WILLIAM J RANDALL, "Motel Appraising," *Real Estate Analyst Appraisal Bulletin*, 1955, pp. 257-260.

MERTZKE, ARTHUR., "Determining Capitalization Rates In Appraising Income Properties," *National Association of Real Estate Boards*, 1930, pp. 111-121.

MONTGOMERY, W. R., "Gas Station Site Selection Not Done by Set Rules," *Appraisal Digest*, April, 1954, pp. 7-10.

MONTGOMERY, W. R., "The Selection of a Service Station Site," *The Appraisal Journal*, January, 1954, pp. 67-72.

MORRELL, JOSEPH C., "Appraisal of a Super Market," *Appraisal Digest*, April, 1953, pp. 10-11.

MORRIS GUARD J., *Selection and Valuation of Service Station Sites in the Pacific Coast Area*, American, Society of Appraisers, 1964.

MORROW, R. CONRAD, "Vagaries of the Service Station Income Approach," *Real Estate Appraiser*, July, 1968, pp. 37-40.

MORSE, HARRISON H., "What the Typical Buyer Looks for In Income Property," *The Appraisal Journal*, October, 1952, pp. 535-542.

MOSS, HUNTER, "Appraisal of a Truck Terminal," *American Institute of Real Estate Appraisers*, Appraisal Reporting Techniques, 1954, pp. 1-30.

MOSS, HUNTER, "Appraising Department Stores," *The Appraisal Journal*, July, 1950, pp. 343-347.

MOTT, SEWARD H., "Recent Developments In Suburban Shopping Center," *The Appraisal Journal*, January, 1949, pp. 39-44.

MULHERN, EUGENE, "Cemetery Appraisal," *Technicalities*, October, 1959, pp. 3-8.

MURPHY, ANDREW L., "Retail Expansion-Suburban or Downtown," *Appraisal Digest*, July, 1957, pp. 7-10.

NATIONAL INSTITUTE OF REAL ESTATE BROKERS, *Guide to Commercial Property Leasing*, Chicago.

NATIONAL INSTITUTE OF REAL ESTATE BROKERS, "Feasibility Reports for Shopping Center," National Institute of Real Estate Brokers, Chicago.

NATIONAL REAL ESTATE JOURNAL, "Actual Appraisal Reports - Valuation for Standard Oil Co Of New York," *National Real Estate Journal*, August 3, 1931, pp. 24-27.

NATIONAL REAL ESTATE JOURNAL, "Actual Appraisal Reports: Appraisal of 5-Story Office and Store Building In Suburb Cleveland," *National Real Estate Journal*, May 11, 1931, pp. 25-30.

NELSON, R. L., "Outlying Shopping Centers Vs. Downtown Retail Trade," *The Appraisal Journal,* October, 1957, pp. 485-498.

NELSON, RICHARD L., *The Selection of Retail Location,* N. Y. F. W, Dodge, 1959.

NELSON, RICHARD L., "Market Analysis of Shopping Centers and Discount Houses," *The Appraisal Journal,* January, 1962, pp. 87-94.

NELSON, RICHARD LAWRENCE, *The One-Hundred Percent Location a New Concept In Motel Site Selection,* Encyclopedia of Motel Management.

NEWMAN, J. WILSON, "Does Business Have a Future," *The Appraisal Journal,* October, 1967, pp. 467.

NICHOLLS, CHARLES C. JR., "The Future of Chain Stores," *The Appraisal Journal,* July, 1943, pp. 210-215.

NOLAN, PRESTON M., "Appraising for Banks," *National Association of Real Estate Boards, Annals of Real Estate Practice,* 1925, pp. 68-91.

NORTON, FAY A., "The Appraisal of Gasoline Service-Station Properties," *The Appraisal Journal,* July, 1939, pp. 203-218.

ONEILL, JOSEPH HENRY, "Gas Station Taxes and Appraisals," *Appraisal Digest,* July, 1956, pp. 10-12.

O'CONNELL, STEPHEN C., "Ethics In Business," *The Appraisal Journal,* July, 1966, pp. 359-364.

OAKLEAF, R. B., "Mall Treasure Trove or Trap," *Management Accounting,* June, 1970, pp. 41-43.

OLSON, JAMES C., "Appraising Companies with an Eye to Rough Weather," *The Appraisal Journal.*

OMAHA BUILDING OWNERS AND MANAGERS ASSOCIATION, "Omaha Office Building Expenditures," *Appraisers and Assessors Manual,* 1930.

OPPENHEIM, JACK N., "Racing Plant Appraisal," *The Appraisal Journal,* July, 1950, pp. 11-14.

ORGEL, LEWIS, "Justice and Equity In Wherry Housing Valuation," *The Appraisal Journal,* July, 1959, pp. 298-304.

ORT, ROBERT M., "The Regional Shopping Center," *The Appraisal Journal,* February, 1964, pp. 6-11.

PEASE, R. R., "Conventions and Meetings Are Big Business for Airlines and Hotels," *Insurance,* May, 1917, pp. 18.

PENNY, ALFRED L., "A Look at Shopping Centers," *Appraisal Institute Magazine,* September, 1962, pp. 21-24.

PERLMAN, LESLIE, "Discount House Trends," *The Appraisal Journal,* July, 1963, pp. 338-342.

PETREE, NEIL, "Suburban Shopping Centers," *The Review,* June, 1952, pp. 3-5, 9.

PHILLIPS, GEORGE A., "Racial Infiltration," *The Review,* February, 1950, pp. 7-9.

PLAGER, ALFRED R., "Appraisal of Truck Terminals," *The Appraisal Journal,* April, 1961, pp. 213-220.

PLENDER JOHN, "Bankers Sue Surveyors Over Hotel Valuation," *The Valuer,* The Commonwealth Institute of Valuers, Sydney Australia, October 1, 1974, pp. 633.

PODD, GEORGE O., "Financial Analysis of Motel Operation," *The Appraisal Journal,* October, 1961, pp. 458-473.

PODD, GEORGE O., "Significant Postwar Trends In Hotel Operation," *The Appraisal Journal,* October, 1957, pp. 603-617.

PODD, GEORGE O, ., "Commerical Hotels," *The Appraisal Journal,* January, 1950, pp. 34-45.

POOD, GEORGE O., "Hotel and Motel Appraisal Data," *The Appraisal Journal,* July, 1960, pp. 318-324.

PORTER, FRANK DAVID, III, "Factors and Trends In the Service Station Industry," *The Real Estate Appraiser,* November, 1968, pp. 448.

PORTER, JOHN W., AND BENJAMIN SOLARI, "Appraisal of Large Commercial Feedlots," *Appraisal and Valuation Manual,* American Society of Appraisers, 1955.

PROUTY, W. L. AND OTHERS, "Hotel Buildings," *Appraisers and Assessors Manual,* 1930, pp. 163-168.

PROUTY, W. L. AND OTHERS, "Public Garage Construction Cost," *Appraisers and Assessors, Manual,* 1930, pp. 217-222.

PROUTY, W. L. AND OTHERS, "Service Station Construction," *Appraisers and Assessors Manual,* 1930, pp. 223-230.

QUINN, WILLIAM E., "How to Appraise the Value of a Funeral Home," *Appraisal Digest,* July, 1967, pp. 14-21.

QUINN, WILLIAM E., "Measuring the Value of Good Will In Funeral Home Appraisal," *The Appraisal Journal,* October, 1967, pp. 583.

RAAFLAUB, O. V., "Appraising the Rural Country Store," *Appraisal Institute Magazine,* June, 1964.

RAETHER, HOWARD C., *Successful Funeral Service Practice,* Prentice Hall, Englwd Cliffs, N. J..

RALEIGH, JAMES, "Appraisal of Gasoline Service Stations," *The Appraisal Journal,* January, 1966, pp. 79-82.

RAMS, EDWIN M., AND ROBERT K. BROWN, "Investment Articulation Supermarkets," *Appraisal and Valuation Manual,* 1960, pp. 279-286.

RANDALL, WILLIAM J., "Characteristics of Regional Shopping Centers," *Real Estate Analyst Appraisal Bulletin,* 1957, pp. 109-114.

RANDALL, WILLIAM J., AND TOM MCREYNOLDS, "Motel Appraising," *The Appraisal Journal,* October, 1955, pp. 529-536.

REAL ESTATE ANALYST, THE, "Coin-Operated Laundries," *Real Estate Analyst Appraisal Bulletin,* 1959, pp. 57-60.

REAL ESTATE ANALYST, THE, "Construction Costs of a One-Story Commercial Building," *Real Estate Analyst Appraisal Bulletin,* 1955, pp. 17-20.

REAL ESTATE ANALYST, THE, "Decentralization In Retail Trade," *Real Estate Analyst Appraisal Bulletin,* 1955, pp. 451-454.

REAL ESTATE ANALYST, THE, "Local Information on Retail Sales," *Real Estate Analyst Appraisal Bulletin,* 1950, pp. 279-290.

REAL ESTATE ANALYST, THE, "Population Factors In Retail Locations," *Real Estate Analyst Appraisal Bulletin,* 1948, pp. 395-398.

REAL ESTATE ANALYST, THE, "Reproduction Cost of Two-Story Frame Houses," *Real Estate Analyst Appraisal Bulletin,* 1951, pp. 513-516.

REAL ESTATE ANALYST, THE, "Residential and Commercial Construction Costs," *Real Estate Analyst Appraisal Bulletin,* 1950, pp. 525-545.

REAL ESTATE ANALYST, THE, "Retail Outlets Compared with Population Changes," *Real Estate Analyst Appraisal Bulletin,* 1950, pp. 559-562.

REAL ESTATE ANALYST, THE, "Shopping Habits and Pedestrian Traffic," *Real Estate Analyst Appraisal Bulletin,* 1948, pp. 451-457.

REAL ESTATE ANALYST, THE, "The Development of the Automobile Shopping Center," *Real Estate Analyst Appraisal,* 1949, pp. 517-520.

REAL ESTATE APPRAISER, THE, "How to Build a 496 Room Hotel In 202 Working Days," *The Real Estate Appraiser,* May, 1971, pp. 5-9.

REEVES, CUTHBERT EDWARD, *The Appraisal of Urban Land and Buildings,* Municipal Administration Service, New York City, 1928.

REGISTER, J. ALVIN, "Appraisal of a One Story Store Building," *Mcmichael, S. L. Appraising Manual*, 1937, pp. 1-652.

REVIEW OF SOCIETY OF RESIDENTIAL APPRAISERS, "Valuing Semi-Business Property," *Review of Society of Residential Appraisers*, October, 1941, pp. 12-14.

REVIEW, THE, "Architectural Preference," *The Review*, August, 1945, pp. 424-435.

RICHARD, JOHN L. JR., "Appraisal of Cemetery Lands," *The Appraisal Journal*, July, 1969, pp. 394-400.

RICK, WILLIAM B., "Planning and Developing Waterfront Property," *Urban Land Institute*, Urban Land Institute, Washington, 1964.

ROBERTS DAVID D., "Management of Shopping Centers In the USA," *The Valuer*, The Commonwealth Institute of Valuers, Sydney Australia, October 1, 1973, pp. 624-627.

ROBERTS, JOHN A., "Appraisal of Commercial and Industrial Property," *Right of Way Conference*, 1957, pp. 100-115.

ROBINSON, PETER C., "How to Appraise Commercial Properties," Prentice Hall Inc..

ROSS, THURSTON H., "The Appraisal of Major Commercial Properties," *Estate Magazine*, May, 1937, pp. 7.

RUBLOFF, ARTHUR, "Shopping Center Development and Operation," *The Appraisal Journal*, January, 1962, pp. 76-86.

SANDO, LAURENCE, "The Motel Story," *The Appraisal Journal*, July, 1952, pp. 365-372.

SAPP, ALLAN N., "Factors In Selecting the Supermarket Site," *The Real Estate Appraiser*, September, 1966, pp. 17-23.

SAXE, E. B., "The Service Station Site," *The Real Estate Appraiser*, August, 1964, pp. 14-22.

SAYER, D. D. JR., "Appraisal of a Gas Station Site," *National Real Estate Journal*, January, 1933, pp. 49-50.

SAYER, D. DAYTON, "Appraisal of a Gas Station," *California Real Estate Magazine*, August, 1940, pp. 25.

SCHIMMEL, ALFRED, "Appraising Income Properties for Mortgage Loans," *Valutape Audio-Library Series*, American Society of Appraisers, Washington D.C., January 1, 1973.

SCHMUTZ, GEORGE L., "Some Factors In the Valuation of Outlying Commercial Property," *National Real Estate Journal*, March, 1940, pp. 32-34.

SCHMUTZ, GEORGE L., "The Appraisal of Retail Store Property," *The Appraisal Journal*, January, 1940, pp. 23-29.

SCHNEIDER, JOHN S., "Analysis of Economic Background of Commercial Property," *The Appraisal Journal*, October, 1959, pp. 475-482.

SCHNELL, A. F., "Business Property Obsolescence," *Skyscraper Management*, January, 1935, pp. 8..

SCHULTZ, CARLTON, "A Modern Property Operating at a Deficit," *The Appraisal Journal*, October, 1932, pp. 46-52.

SCHULTZ, EARLE, "Effect of Age of Office Building on Income and Expense," *Appraisers and Assessors Manual, First Edition*, 1930, pp. 80.

SCHWINGLE, CLEMENT J., "Miller Salt Company," *Appraisal and Valuation Manual*, 1964, pp. 131.

SELL, R., "Tax and Business Considerations In Leasing Property," *Taxes*, March, 1964, pp. 159.

SELTZER, RICHARD J., "Where Shall I Shop," *The Appraisal Journal*, January, 1949, pp. 114-119.

SHADRAWY, BERNARD F., "Demonstration Appraisal on Commercial Property Using Income Approach," *Assessment Administration*, Institute of American Assessment Officers, Chicago, 1965, pp. 103-105.

SHEEHAN, JAMES J., *A Reappraisal of the Shopping enter Movement In the Metropolitan Cincinnati Market,* The Cincinnati Enquirer, Cincinnati, Ohio, May 15, 1961, pp. 333.

SHELGER, KURT S., "Appraisal of Parking Lots and Garages," *Encyclopedia of Real Estate Appraising,* 1959, pp. 296-316.

SHIMMON, R. E., "An Appraisal of a Commercial Condominium," *The Appraisal Journal,* July, 1964, pp. 352-357.

SHIPP, ROYAL, "How Much More Room at the Inn. . . for Net Income," *The Real Estate Appraiser,* March, 1969, pp. 15-21.

SHOWELL, BRIAN, "Public Property Corporations," *The Appraisal Journal,* April, 1963, pp. 229-235.

SISKA, FRANK J., "Inventory of a Retail Store," *Assessment Administration,* Institute of American Assessment Officers, Chicago, 1960, pp. 196-203.

SLADE, ESTER P., "Points to Consider In Appraising Shopping Centers Listed," *Appraisal Digest,* April, 1951, pp. 7-8.

SLONIM, M. J., "A Demonstration Appraisal of a One-Story Store Building," *Practical Appraising Methods,* 1940, pp. 81.

SMITH, ARNOLD R., "Feasibility Study of a Shopping Center," *Real Estate Appraiser,* July, 1967, pp. 9-15.

SMITH, GEORGE C., "Trends Affecting Commercial and Industrial Properties," *The Appraisal Journal,* July, 1939, pp. 245-251.

SMITH, GUY V., "Significant Snare In Service Station Appraisal," *Right of Way,* August, 1970, pp. 41-53.

SMITH, LARRY, "Analysis of the Earning Capacity of a Shopping Center," *The Appraisal Journal,* July, 1959, pp. 305-320.

SMITH, LARRY, "Analyzing Shopping Center Markets," *Appraisal Digest,* April, 1957, pp. 19-22.

SMITH, LARRY, "Commercial Real Estate Relationships--Downtown and Suburban," *The Appraisal Journal,* October, 1956, pp. 578-582.

SMITH, LARRY, "Economic Potential of Proposed Shopping Center," *The Appraisal Journal,* January, 1959, pp. 69-87.

SMITH, LARRY, "Market Survey of Economic Potential of a Proposed Shopping Center," *The Appraisal Journal,* January, 1959, pp. 69-87.

SMITH, LAWRENCE E., "Valuation of Neighborhood Shopping Centers," *The Appraisal Journal,* October, 1951, pp. 508-517.

SMITH, LEVIE D., "Appraising Motel Properties--A Demonstration," *The Real Estate Appraiser,* January, 1964, pp. 30-36.

SMITH, PIERCE J., "A Motel Assessment," *American Society of Appraisers Manual, 1964-1965,* 1964, pp. 67.

SMITH, WALSTEIN, JR., "Appraising the Gasoline Service Station Site," *The Real Estate Appraiser,* 1911, pp. 11-20.

SMITH, WALSTEIN, JR., "Retail Locations and Consumer Spatial Behavior," *The Real Estate Appraiser,* November, 1966, pp. 21-22.

SNORGRASS, G. VERN, "Factors to Be Considered In Hotel Evaluation by the Income Approach," *Appraisal and Valuation Manual,* American Society of Appraisers, 1958, pp. 343-354.

SOTAVE, BOLETIN, "Las Propiedades De Renta En La Tasacion," *Boletin,* Sotave, Caracas, Venezuela, pp. 19-20.

SPELMAN, E. C., "Drive-In Shopping Cener," *Technicalities and Technical Valuation,* June, 1952, pp. 4-9.

SPELMAN, EVERETT C., "Motel Appraisal," *The Appraisal Journal,* January, 1953, pp. 91-103.

STEARNS, EDWARD C., "Our Termite Problem," *The Appraisal Journal,* April, 1942, pp. 153-158.

STEELE, JOHN, "Valuation Analysis of an Automatic Car Wash Property," *The Real Estate Appraiser*, November, 1963, pp. 2-9.

STERM, JOSEPH E., "Appraisal Gasoline Station," *Technical Valuation*, October, 1959, pp. 47-50.

STEVENS, FRANCIS K., "Relation of Land Value to Office Rentals," *Real Estate Record and Builders Guide*, February 28, 1942, pp. 5-7.

STOLP, JOHN A., "On Cemetery Valuation," *The Appraisal Journal*, October, 1937, pp. 373-376.

SWAN, HERBERT S., "The Growth of Shopping Areas," *The Appraiser Journal*, July, 1945, pp. 232-240.

TANNEY, WILLIAM W., "Super Markets-Data Program," *The Appraisal Journal*, October, 1950, pp. 431-439.

TATLOW, R. H. III., "Parkington: Shopping Center Design," *The Appraisal Journal*, January, 1954, pp. 95-108.

TAYLOR, FRANK, "The Future of Hotels," *Appraisal Digest*, January, 1954, pp. 9-11.

TECHNICAL VALUATION, "Shopping Center Series," *Technical Valuation*, June, 1954, pp. 19-38.

THALHIMER, MORTON G., "Appraisal of Conventional and Drive-In Theatres," *The Appraisal Journal*, October, 1957, pp. 575-584.

THALHIMER, MORTON G., "Appraisal of Motion Picture Theatres," *Encyclopedia of Real Estate Appraising*, 1959, pp. 660-678.

THALHIMER, MORTON G., "New Influences Affecting the Appraisal of Motion Picture Theatres," *The Appraisal Journal*, October, 1951, pp. 432-442.

THEISS, WILLIAM R., "The Appraisal Docket. Effect of Option to Purchase In Lease--Evidence of Volume of Business," *The Appraisal Journal*, April, 1962, pp. 297-298.

THEISS, WILLIAM R., "The Appraisal Docket. Evaluating the Undeveloped Cemetery Property," *The Appraisal Journal*, April, 1962, pp. 294-295.

THORNE, OAKLEIGH J., "Appraising Commercial Mushroom Growing Facilities," *Valuation*, September, 1972, pp. 56.

THUDSON, F. M., "The Outlook for the Hotel Business," *The Appraisal Journal*, April, 1943, pp. 132-144.

TIEGER, MAX, "Appraisal of a Business Property," *The Appraisal Journal*, April, 1933, pp. 225-252.

TILLY, V. S., "Original or Replacement Charge for Depreciation Commercial and Financial Chronicle," *Appraisal and Valuation Manual*, February 27, 1958, pp. 947.

TOTH, LOUIS, "Hotel Statistics," *The Appraisal Journal*, October, 1941, pp. 351-362.

TOWNSEND, F. S. JR., "Evaluating Life Company Stocks; a Dilemma," *Commercial and Financial Chronicle*, September 9, 1971, pp. 741.

TREDWELL, JOHN C., "Appraisal of a One Hundred Per Cent Business Location," *Appraisal Reporting Techniques*, 1947, pp. 51-72.

TROXEL, JAY C., "No Sale Without a Purchase," *The Real Estate Appraiser*, January, 1970, pp. 51-54.

TRUE, WALLACE W., "Analysis and Reconstruction of Hotel Operating Statements," *Real Estate Appraisal Practice*, 1958, pp. 341-351.

TRUE, WALLACE W., "Appraisal of a Drive-In Theatre," *Appraisal Reporting Technique*, 1951, pp. 35-41.

TRUE, WALLACE W., "Appraising Department Stores," *The Appraisal Journal*, April, 1946, pp. 159-164.

TRUE, WALLACE W., "Significant Trends In the Motel Industry," *The Appraisal Journal*, April, 1959, pp. 228-238.

TRUE, WALLACE W., "The Appraisal of Motion Picture Theatres," *The Appraisal Journal*, July, 1942, pp. 262-270.

TULLEY, J. BENTON, "Some Problems In Connection with Shopping Center Leases," *The Appraisal Journal*, October, 1958, pp. 549-556.

TURNBULL, JAMES, "The Supermarket," *The Appraisal Journal*, October, 1939, pp. 348-353.

TURNER, ROBERT C., "Forecasting Business Activity," *The Appraisal Journal*, January, 1961, pp. 30-39.

URBAN LAND INSTITUTE, *Standard Manual of Accounting for Shopping Centers*, Urban Land Institute, Washington.

URBAN LAND INSTITUTE, *Taxation and the Shopping Center, a Statement of Policy*, Urban Land Institute, Washington, 1959, pp. 1-4.

URBAN LAND INSTITUTE, *The Dollars and Cents of Shopping Centers*, Urban Land Institute, Washington, 1966, pp. 1-191.

WAGNER, PERCY E., "The Highest and Best Use of the Site," *Journal of Certified Property Managers*, June, 1940, pp. 328-338.

WALDEN, R. R., "Demonstration Appraisal, a Modern Motel," *Assessment Administration*, IAAO, Chicago, 1957, pp. 7-9.

WALSH, DONALD, "Condemnation of a Service Station," *Right of Way*, February, 1961, pp. 9-17.

WALSH, STUART P., "Checkpoints for Downtown Malls," *Urban Land*, Urban Land Institute, Washington, D. C., October, 1966.

WALTON, WILLIAM B., "Principles of Motel Operation," *The Appraisal Journal*, October, 1961, pp. 453-458.

WARWICK, SAMUEL C., "Appraising the Cemetery In Condemnation," *The Real Estate Appraiser*, May, 1966, pp. 25-31.

WEED, KENNETH A., "Valuation of a Motel," *The Appraisal Journal*, October, 1961, pp. 473-483.

WEEKES, R. E., "Some Salient Factors Affecting Downtown Areas," *The Appraisal Journal*, October, 1959, pp. 561-564.

WEISS, E. B., "Expect One Thousand Pedestrian Shopping Malls by 1980," *Advertising Age*, September 21, 1970, pp. 50.

WELCH, KENNETH C., "The Relocation of Commercial Areas," *The Appraisal Journal*, January, 1949, pp. 45-52.

WELCH, KENNETH C., BRUNO FUNARO, "Parking Plans for Shopping Centers," *The Appraisal Journal*, July, 1953, pp. 424-430.

WENZLICK, ROY, RESEARCH CORP., "Adverse Trends In Older Shopping Districts," *The Appraisal Journal*, July, 1957, pp. 441-444.

WENZLICK, ROY, RESEARCH CORP., "Coin-Operated Laundries," *The Appraisal Journal*, July, 1959, pp. 338-340.

WHITNALL, GORDON, "Disintegrating Commercial Centers," *The Appraisal Journal*, January, 1941, pp. 9-18.

WINTER, H. ALLEN, "Selecting Hotel Sites In Recreation Areas," *The Real Estate Appraiser*, March, 1969, pp. 21-26.

WOLFF, LEWIS N., "Quick Shops," *Real Estate Analyst Appraisal Bulletin*, 1961, pp. 449-452.

WOLFSON, HENRY, "Chain Store Leasing, Appraising Locations," *Real Estate Record and Builder's Guide*, January 23, 1932, pp. 9-10.

WORSEK, LEONARD, "The Shrinkage of Cemetery Lands," *Technical Valuation*, 1966, pp. 10.

YORK, JAMES O., "The Effect of Shopping Centers on Main Street U.S.A.," *Assessment Administration*, IAAO, Chicago, 1964, pp. 97-99.

ZANGERLE, JOHN A., MCMICHAEL, STANLEY L., "Transmuting Store Rentals Into Standard Foot Land Values," *Appraising Manual*, 2nd Edition, 1937.

# BIBLIOGRAPHY OF APPRAISAL LITERATURE

ZECKENDORF, WILLIAM, "New Shopping Centers," *Appraisal Digest,* October, 1950, pp. 22.

ZUCKER, R. P., "Stores Urged to Back Joint Shopping Center Promotions," *Merchandising Week,* May 24, 1971, pp. 7.

*Appraisal of Motel Furniture, Fixtures, M-E,* American Society of Appraisers, Washington.

*Case Studies In Shopping Center Salvation,* American Institute of Real Estate Appraisers, 1964.

*Economic Factors and Case Studies In Hotel and Motel Valuation,* American Institute of Real Estate Appraisers, 1968.

"Actual Appraisal Reports: Demonstration Appraisal of 3-Story Store," *National Real Estate Journal,* May 25, 1931, pp. 28-31.

"Actual Appraisal Reports: No. 3 Demonstration Appraisal of Small Store and Office Building," *National Real Estate Journal,* February 16, 1931, pp. 26-31.

"Airport-A Store Design with Entertaimment and Efficiency," *Stores,* November, 1970, pp. 4-5.

"Boutiques a Way Out of a Dilemma," *American Druggist.*

"Building a Mall In a Clay Pit," *Chain Store Age,* May, 1970, pp. 50.

"Carpeted Malls Give Feeling of Intimacy," *Chain Store Age,* May, 1970, pp. 39.

"Census of Retail Stores Shows an 0.8% Drop In 1970," *Advertising Age,* October 12, 1970, pp. 27.

"Chain Fleets Leased or Owned," *Chain Store Age,* January, 1970, pp. 36.

"Chain Stores Go Vertical," *Chain Store Age,* June, 1970, pp. 18-19.

"Coast Shopping Center Boom: Quieter But Still Strong," *Merchandising Week,* 1971, pp. 6.

"Designing Your Store to Sell More," *Merchandising Week,* September 14, 1970, pp. 4.

"Expect Upswing In New Stores," *Chain Store Age,* May, 1971, pp. 30-33.

"Garages Sprouting As Limbs of Centers," *Chain Store Age,* March, 1971, pp. 42.

"Hometown Store Takes to the Road," *Business Week,* June 20, 1970, pp. 118-120.

"Hotel and Restaurant Chains Are Good Performers," *Magazine of Wall Street,* April 10, 1971, pp. 18-20.

"Is Your Company Ready to Profit from an Annual Appraisal," *Business Management,* June, 1970, pp. 21-22.

"Major Retailers Affirming Their Faith In Downtown," *Publishers Weekly,* May 31, 1971, pp. 119-120.

"Malls Within Malls Generate Excitement," *Chain Store Age,* January, 1971, pp. 32.

"Minie-Mall Challenges Big Center," *Chain Store Age,* 1970, pp. 62.

"Motel Room at Bargain Rates," *Business Week,* August 22, 1970, pp. 20.

"Number of Drug Stores Still Dropping," *American Druggist,* October 5, 1970, pp. 84.

"Partnership with Center Shops Urged," *Edition and Publisher,* February 27, 1971, pp. 37.

"Planning Multi-Level Malls," *Chain Store Age,* June, 1970, pp. 13200.

"Precast Concrete Offers Stores and Malls One Modular Path," *Chain Store Age,* August, 1971, pp. 18-21.

"Pressure Grows for Better Landscaping," *Chain Store Age,* September, 1970, pp. 48-50.

"Regional Shopping Center Is Dissected," *American Druggist,* February 8, 1971, pp. 72.

"Remodels Add Light and Color," *Chain Store Age,* September, 1970, pp. 24-27.

"Retailers Advised to Keep Stores Flexible," *American Druggist,* September 7, 1970, pp. 81.

"Shopping Center Growth Hinges on Merchant Landlord Ties," *Merchandising Week,* January 18, 1971, pp. 3..

"Shopping Center Sales Show Enormous Gain," *Commerce Today,* December 14, 1970, pp. 26.

"Shopping Centers Grow Into Shopping Cities," *Business Week,* September 4, 1971, pp. 34-38.

"Showcase Stairway Adds to Sales Area," *Chain Store Age,* September, 1970, pp. 70.

"Shutdowns Stalk Big-City Stores," *Business Week,* October 10, 1970, pp. 28.

"Tallest Concrete Building Sets Place In High Rise Boom," *Engineering News-Record,* July 9, 1970, pp. 20.

"Tie Center Industry to Economy," *Chain Store Age,* July, 1970, pp. 30 32.

"Wall Street Turns Its Eyes to Shop Centers," *American Druggist,* March 8, 1971, pp. 63.

"Will Modular Units Find a Place In the Non-Residential Market?," *House and Home,* May, 1970, pp. 94-97.

"Winston Plans Malls of 200, 000 Sq. Ft," *Chain Store Age,* July, 1970, pp. 27.

"World-Wide Boom In Jet-Age Hotels," *Business Week,* August 8, 1970, pp. 32-34.

"7 Keys to Making it In a Tough Market," *House and Home,* September, 1970, pp. 62-67.

# 13-16 Housing

APPRAISAL DIGEST, "The Potential Housing Demand," *Business Bulletin of the Cleveland Trust Company,* October, 1950, pp. 1-3.

APPRAISAL DIGEST, "Trend of the Times There's a Set of New Buyers," *Business Week,* April, 1955, pp. 1-3.

APPRAISAL INSTITUTE MAGAZINE, "A New Era In Housing," *Appraisal Institute Magazine,* December, 1959, pp. 23-27.

APPRAISAL INSTITUTE MAGAZINE, "Check List for Habitability," *Appraisal Institute Magazine,* September, 1961, pp. 34-36.

ARCHITECTURAL FORUM, "Room Values," *Architectural Forum,* November, 1939, pp. 4.

ARDREY, J. HOWARD, "The System of Appraising Under the Housing Act," *National Real Estate Journal,* January, 1935, pp. 21-22.

ATKINSON, L. J., "Factors Affecting the Purchase Value of New Houses," *Survey of Current Business,* August, 1966.

AUSLANDER, ELYSE, "No Economic Analysis In Dispersal of Low Income Housing," *The Appraiser,* April, 1971.

BATCHELOR, HARRY H., "Inspection Problems," *The Residential Appraiser,* October, 1956, pp. 20-24.

BEHMAN, B., D. CODELLA, "Wage Rates and Housing Prices," *Industrial Relations,* February, 1971, pp. 86-104.

BEMAN, ARTHUR K., "Appraising the Large-Scale Housing Project," *Encyclopedia of Real Estate Appraising,* 1959, pp. 214-233.

BENNETT, K. W., "Modular Homes: Now Is the Hour," *Iron Age,* February 18, 1971, pp. 39-40.

BLOOD, J., "Community Family Centers: Taking a Bigger Slice of Chicago Sales," *Merchandising Week,* August 23, 1971, pp. 14.

BODFISH, MORTON, HOYT, HOMER, "**The Housing Demand Source,**" *The Review,* January, 1949, pp. 14.

BODFISH, MORTON, WITTAUCSH, WILLIAM, "**The Consumer's Housing Dollar,**" *The Residential Appraiser,* June, 1957, pp. 16-18.

BOWERS, RAYMOND A., "**Home Planning Trends,** *The Review,* September, 1945, pp. 8-12.

BRANDT, L., POPLE, HARRY E, "Chart for Computing Cubic Foot Value of Homes," *The National Real Estate Journal,* June, 1932, pp. 31-34.

BROWN, LESTER C., WEIDLER, JOHN B, "**1966 Housing Purchases In Great Britain,**" *The Real Estate Appraiser,* pp. 19.

BRUEGGEMAN, WILLIAM BERNARD-PH. D., *The Impact of Private Construction and Government Housing Programs In a Local Housing Market,* Ohio State University, 1970.

C.M.H.C., "Check List for Habitability," *Appraisal Institute Magazine,* Appraisal Institute of Canada, Winnipeg.

CANNON, DOUGLAS V., "**Inventory of Speculative Home Building,**" *The Appraisal Journal,* April, 1955, pp. 230-240.

CARTER, W. P., "**Task Force on Housing,**" *Appraisal Institute Magazine,* Appraisal Institute of Canada, Winnipeg.

CARTER, W. PETER, "**Report of the Canadian Task Force on Housing Andurban Development,**" *The Real Estate Appraiser,* January, 1970, pp. 44-51.

CASE, F. E., "**Housing the Underhoused In the Inner City,**" *Journal of Finance,* May, 1971, pp. 427-444, 466-471.

CASE, FRED E., "**Let's Make the FHA a Privately Controlled Business,**" *The Appraisal Journal,* July, 1951, pp. 370-374.

CHAMBERS, M. M., "**Tax Exemption of Faculty Housing,**" *School and Society,* March, 1960, pp. 113-115.

CHEN, Y. P., "**Present State and Fiscal Significance of Property Tax Exemptions for the Aged,**" *National Tax Journal,* June, 1965, pp. 162-174.

CHEN, Y. P., "**Taxation of the Aged: Some Issues and Possible Solution,**" *Conference Proceeding,* National Tax Association, Columbus, 1965, pp. 206-225.

CHILD, JOHN F. JR., AND DAVID SCRIBNER, "**Analysis of Components In the Capitalization Rate Peculiar to Large-Scale FHA Housing Projects,**" *Appraisal and Valuation Manual,* American Society of Appraisers, 1959, pp. 139-148.

CHURCH, BYRON, "**A Case History of Housing,**" *The Appraisal Journal,* April, 1960, pp. 209-212.

CLARK, FOREST F., *Appraising the Home,* Prentice Hall, New York, 1930.

CLARK, HORACE F., "**Appraising the Newly Finished House,**" *Appraising the Home,* 1930, pp. 129-151.

COHEN, MORRIS, "**That Coming Boom In Housing,**" *The Real Estate Appraiser,* September, 1967, pp. 3.

COLLINS, E. R., "**The Cost of Land for Public Housing,**" *Appraisal Institute Magazine,* Appraisal Institute of Canada, Winnipeg.

COLLINS, G. ROWLAND, "**Financial Factors In the Demand for Housing,**" *The Residential Appraiser,* May, 1960, pp. 3-10.

DANAHEY, THOMAS P., "**Survey of Housing Facilities In Detroit Indicates Need of Home Building,**" *The Appraisal Journal,* October, 1935, pp. 471-474.

DAVIS, J. TAIT, "**Middle Class Housing In the Central City,**" *The Appraisal Journal,* April, 1966, pp. 273-286.

DAY, J. EDWARD, "Changes In the Housing Economy," *The Residential Appraiser,* September, 1957, pp. 5-10.

DE LEEUW, F., "Demand for Housing: a Review of Cross Section Evidence," *Review of Economics and Statistics,* February, 1971, pp. 1-10.

DORAU, HERBERT B., "How Completely Will Housing Be Socialized," *Thereview,* July, 1949, pp. 9-12.

DUBOIS, AYERS J., "The Valuation and Mortgage Risk Rating Systems of the Federal Housing Administration," *Appraisal Journal,* July, 1935, pp. 324-334.

DUFFY, G., "HUD Supports Air Conditioning of 46,000 Public Housing Units for Elderly," *Air Conditioning, Heating and Refrigeration News,* August 3, 1970. pp. 2.

EBERHARDT, DUANE O., "Real Estate Price Escalation In Selected Residential Areas of Flagstaff, Arizona," *Arizona Business Journal,* Northern Arizona University, 1971, pp. 21-22.

ECKERSBERG, ALFRED K., "Housing for the Elderly," *The Appraisal Journal,* October, 1962, pp. 523-534.

ECKLEY, ROBERT S., "The Demand for New Housing," *The Appraisal Journal,* July, 1953, pp. 367-376.

EICHEN, C., "Color In Your Model Houses Can Sell or Kill a Sale, it Depends on How You Use it," *House and Home,* April, 1971, pp. 38.

ERNST, E. CHARLES, "Appraising the Project House," *Technical Valuation,* February, 1960, pp. 23-24.

FEDERAL RESERVE BANK OF CHICAGO, "The Economic Consequences of the Baby Boom," *The Appraisal Journal,* April, 1956, pp. 208-212.

FEDERAL RESERVE BANK OF PHILADELPHIA, "The Amazing Demand for Housing," *The Appraisal Journal,* October, 1955, pp. 537-540.

FEDERAL TAX ADMINISTRATION, *State and Local Tax Status of Military Housing Programs,* Federation of Tax Administrators, Chicago, 1956.

FISHER, ERNEST M., LEO GREBLER, "A Stocktaking of Housing In the United States," *The Appraisal Journal,* July, 1951, pp. 295-303.

FISHER, ROBERT M., *Twenty Years of Public Housing,* Harper and Brothers, New York City, 1959, pp. 62.

FORD, JAMES, "Bibliography of Housing Bibliographies," *Slums and Housing,* Harvard University Press, Cambridge, 1936, pp. 1000-1002.

FULLER, ROBERT S., "Changing Characteristics of Dwellings," *Appraisal Journal,* October, 1953, pp. 555-559.

GALLAGHER, JOSEPH A. SR., "The House Is Larger Than the Desk," *Technical Valuation,* A. S. A, June, 1954, pp. 3.

GALUSH, ROBERT J., "Types of Factory-Built Homes In the Midwest," *The Real Estate Appraiser,* November, 1970, pp. 21-25.

GELFARD, J. E., "Mortgage Credit & Low Mid Income Housing Demand," *Land Economics,* May, 1970, pp. 163-170.

GELLER, CARL, "Home Building In Europe," *The Review,* October, 1949, pp. 1 3-6.

GOLDBLATT, ABRAHAM, "The Census of Housing and the Appraiser," *The Residential Appraiser,* January, 1962, pp. 2-4.

GOLDEN, GERALD A., "Government Participation In Housing," *The Review,* May, 1954, pp. 12-18.

GRACE, THOMAS G., "Elements Considered In FHA Appraisals," *Real Estate Record and Builders Guide,* April 23, 1941, pp. 3-4.

GRANFIELD, MICHAEL EDWARD PH. D., "An Econometric Model of Residential Location," 1970.

GREAT BRITAIN MINISTRY OF HOUSING AND LOCAL GOVERN, *Distribution of Rateable Values Between Different Classes of Property In England and Values,* H. M. Stationery Offices, London, 1956.

GREBLER, LEO, "New Indicators of the Housing Market," *The Appraisal Journal,* January, 1950, pp. 54-62.

GREER, GUY, "Housing Prosperity's Only Laggard," *The Appraisal Journal,* October, 1948, pp. 424-428.

GUTHRIE, R. R., "Housing---Shortage?," *The Review,* January, 1949, pp. 7-8.

HAEGER, LEONARD G., "Sensible Housing Standards," *The Residential Appraiser,* November, 1959, pp. 17-22.

HALEY, HARRY B., "The Clock Ticks Nowhere As it Does at Home," *The Appraisal Journal,* January, 1953, pp. 67-78.

HANSBERGER, R. V., "Big Business In the Big Housing Market of the 70'S," *The Real Estate Appraiser,* May, 1970, pp. 43-47.

HARDY, NEAL J., **"Program of FHA,"** *The Residential Appraiser,* November, 1961, pp. 15-17.

HARRISON, DAVID C., "Housing Rehabilitation and the Pittsburgh Graded Property Tax," *Duquesne University Law Review,* 1964, pp. 213-243.

HART, L. C., "The Outlook for Building Material Production," *The Appraisal Journal,* January, 1947, pp. 99-104.

HATFIELD, SAMUEL M., *An Evaluation of Land Use and Dwelling Unit Data Derived from Aerial Photography,* Division of Highways, Urban Research Section, Chicago, September, 1962.

HEILBTUN, JAMES, "Real Estate Taxes and Urban Housing," *Real Estate Taxes an Urban Housing,* Columbia University Press, New York, 1966.

HOEFER, ROLAND G., **"FHA Rating Vs. Breakdown Depreciation,"** *The Residential Appraiser,* July, 1958, pp. 10-15.

HOLDEN, THOMAS S., "Present Supply and Demand Factors In the Housing Field," *The Appraisal Journal,* October, 1951, pp. 468-471.

HOUSE AND HOME, "Modular House Draws Crowds to New York City Museum," *House and Home,* November, 1970, pp. 26.

HOUSING AND REDEVELOPMENT BOARD, 'How Turnover Multiplies Impact of New Housing," *The Appraisal Journal,* New York, October, 1966, pp. 596-597.

HURTADO MARTINEZ, LUIS, "Metodo De Avaluo Para Vivienda Unifamiliar," *Boletin,* Sotave, Caracas, Venezuela, pp. 9-12.

HURTADO MARTINEZ, LUIS, ALBERTO ANGULO LOPEZ, "El Valor De Los Terrenos Para Uso Multifamiliar," *Boletin,* Sotave, Caracas, Venezuela, pp. 35-37.

JARCHON, ALFRED W., "F. H. A.'s Appraisal Concepts," *ASA Valuation Manual,* ASA, 1959, pp. 131.

JARCHOW, ALFRED W., "Current F. H. A. Appraiser Concepts," *The Residential Appraiser,* November, 1957, pp. 12-18.

JARCHOW, ALFRED W., "F.H.A.'s Appraisal Concepts," *Appraisal and Valuation Manual,* ASA, 1959, pp. 131-138.

JOHNSON, RALPH J., "Homes for Aging Buyers," *The Review,* January, 1954, pp. 14-16.

KAIN, J. F., AND QUIGLEY, J. M., "Measuring the Value of Housing Quality," *American Statistical Association Journal,* June, 1970, pp. 532-48.

KARPE, ELMER F., "Housing In Northern Europe," *The Review,* March, 1952, pp. 17-19.

KEEZER, DR. DEXTER M, "The Relative Position of Housing In Competition for the Consumer Dollar," *The Appraisal Journal,* January, 1949, pp. 9-14.

KEITH, N.S., "An Assessment of National Housing Needs," *Law and Contemporary Problems,* April, 1967, pp. 209-219.

KELLEY, WILLIAM T., "Marketing Research and House Design," *The Appraisal Journal*, April, 1960, pp. 235-241.

KELLOUGH, W. R., "The Metropolitan Toronto Housing Market," *Technical Valuation*, 1966, pp. 24.

KELLY, BURNHAM, "The Emerging Housing Industry," *The Residential Appraiser*, May, 1958, pp. 3-7, 12.

KINGSBURY, LAURA MABEL, *The Economics of Housing As Presented by Economists, Appraisers and Other Evaluating Groups*, Kings Crown Press, New York, 1946.

KKAIN, J. F., J. M. ZUIGLEY, "Measuring the Value of Housing Quality," *American Statistical Association Journal*, June, 1970, pp. 532-548.

KLAMDN, S. B., "Economic Outlook The Outlook for Housing and Mortage Markets," *Commercial and Financial Chronicle*, May 7, 1970, pp. 17.

KNIGHT, C., "Military Launches Housing Attack-First Modulars Move In with General Electric In Command," *House and Home*, February, 1971, pp. 20.

KNISKERN, P. W., "Symbols for Recording Room Counts," *Real Estate Appraisal and Valuation*, 1933, pp. 334.

L. ALBRECHT, "Priority Decoration In the Home," *Supervisory Management*, August, 1970, pp. 22-24.

LALLI, F., "Modular Housing: the Phantom That Parades As an Industry," *House and Home*, June, 1970, pp. 64-75.

LINDSLEY, J. C., "A Paraplegic's Residence," *The Review*, March, 1950, pp. 10-12.

LOCKWOOD, WARREN J., "Housing Market Analysis In the F.H.A.," *The Appraisal Journal*, July, 1949, pp. 367-371.

MACK, CURT C., "F.H.A. Cost Range," *The Review*, June, 1953, pp. 3-5.

MACNAUGHTON, D., "Obstacles to Housing Progress," *The Review*, September, 1953, pp. 19-21.

MARSHALL, T., "Housing Development or Virgin Land A California Town Is Torn by Controversy," *House and Home*, August, 1970, pp. 18-19.

MARTIN, WILLIAM MCCHESNEY, "Housing and Mortgage Finance," *Appraisal Digest*, July, 1957, pp. 1-3.

MCCLOY, H. F., "Corporations and Their Transferee Problems," *The Real Estate Appraiser*, May, 1966, pp. 13-17.

MCDONALD, A. M., "A Study of Depreciation In Residences," *The Appraisal Journal*, October, 1958, pp. 602-606.

MENDEZ, ALFREDO, JR., "Some Aspects of Right of Way Acquisition In the Commonwealth of Puerto Rico," *Right of Way*, October, 1965, pp. P 13-17.

MOBILE HOMES MANUFACTURERS ASSOCIATION, *Formula for Determining the Feasibility of Mobile Housing Developments*, Chicago.

MOBILE HOMES MANUFACTURERS ASSOCIATION, *Formula for Financing Mobile Housing Developments*, Chicago.

MOSS, HUNTER, "Appraising Motor Courts," *The Appraisal Journal*, pp. 235-242.

MOSS, HUNTER, "Special Knowledge Required In Appraising Motor Courts," *Appraisal Digest*, October, 1952, pp. 14-16.

N. Y. TIMES INDEX, "Architects G. Valk & T. Amenta Design for Year Round Homes at Price Less Than $30000," *N. Y. Times Index*, May 24, 1970.

N. Y. TIMES INDEX, "City Plan Comm Appr Cooper Sq Urban Renew Plan Calling for 1000 Units of New Housing," *N. Y. Times Index*, January 8, 1970.

N. Y. TIMES INDEX, "City Planning Community Approves Plans for 1000 Apts In Wash Heights for People of Low & Mid Income," *N. Y. Times Index*, January 22, 1970.

N. Y. TIMES INDEX, "Community Tensions Aroused by Heritage Village, $100-Million Condominium Developmt for Elderly South," *The N. Y. Times Index*, May 6, 1970.

N. Y. TIMES INDEX, "Kittay House Bronx 12-Story $5.7-Million Complex at 2550 Webb Av Catering to Elderly Residents," *N. Y. Times Index*, January 3, 1970.

NELSON, WALTER C., "Housing Economics," *The Residential Appraiser*, November, 1958, pp. 13-16.

NELSON, WALTER C., "How Budget Balancing Can Strengthen the Housing Market," *The Residential Appraiser*, April, 1959, pp. 15-18.

NEWMAN, D. K., "The Low-Cost Housing Market," *Monthly Labor Review*, December, 1966, pp. 1362-68.

NOLAN, FRAND W. SR., "Neighborhood Research," *The Residential Appraiser*, November, 1958, pp. 7-9.

NORCROSS DR.CARL, "Townhouses and Condominiums:Residents' Likes and Dislikes," Urban Land Institute, Washington D.C..

NOWICKI, JOSEPH A., "Common Mistakes In Home Design," *The Review*, July, 1955, pp. 3-9.

OSENBAUGH, CHARLES L., "Integrated Housing and Value," *The Appraisal Journal*, January, 1967, pp. 17-20.

OWENS-CORNING FIBERGLAS, "The Tenant's Point of View," *Urban Land*, February, 1970.

PAPAGEORGIOU, GEORGE J. AND EMILIO CASETTI, *Journal of Regional Science*, University of Pennsylvania, December, 1971, pp. 385-389.

PARKINSON, G., "Here's a Builder Who Uses the Apartment Buyers Money to Build the Apartments," *House and Home*, January, 1971, pp. 20.

PLEETER, SAUL PH. D., *The Effects of Public Housing on Neighboring Property Values and Rents In Buffalo, New York*, St. University of New York, Buffalo, 1971.

PRATT, ROBERT J. A., "Demand for Housing-1963," *The Residential Appraiser*, November, 1962, pp. 8-12, 16.

PRINCE, W. H., "On Landscaping," *The Appraisal Journal*, September, 1936, pp. 77-78.

RALEIGH, JAMES C., "Boom Town, R. I," *American Society of Appraisers Valuation Manual*, American Society of Appraisers, 1961, pp. 165.

RANDALL, ROLAND R., "On Planning and Building for Retirement," *The Appraisal Journal*, October, 1965, pp. 615-616.

RATHBUN, DANIEL B., "The Veterans Home-Loan Program Success or Failure," *The Appraisal Journal*, July, 1954, pp. 400-408.

REAL ESTATE ANALYST, THE, "Cubic Costs," *Real Estate Analyst Series on Old Style Two-Family Building*, 1949, pp. 93-96.

REAL ESTATE ANALYST, THE, "Cubic Foot Costs," *Real Estate Analyst Series on Brick Bungalow*, Vl. Xxiv, No. 7, 1955, pp. 57-60.

REAL ESTATE ANALYST, THE, "Cubic Foot Costs," *Real Estate Analyst Series on Six-Room California Bungalow*, 1950, pp. 169-172.

REAL ESTATE ANALYST, THE, "Estimating Livable Space and Cubic Content," *Real Estate Analyst Appraisal Bulletin*, 1948, pp. 269-272.

REAL ESTATE ANALYST, THE, "Reproduction Cost of Two-Story Frame Houses," *Real Estate Analyst Appraisal Bulletin*, 1951, pp. 513-516.

REEVES, CUTHBERT E., "Appraising Residential Property," *Appraising Residential Property--Methods Cost Data & Instr Espec Helpful to Appraisers for Underwrit*, Cuthbert E. Reeves, Buffalo, 1934.

RENSHAW, E. F., "**Demand for Housing In the Mid-1970S**," *Land Economics,* August, 1971, pp. 249-255.

RESIDENTIAL APPRAISER, "**Credit for Home Building**," *The Residential Appraiser,* April, 1959, pp. 12-14.

REVIEW, THE, "**California Voters Defeat State Public Housing**," *The Review,* April, 1949, pp. 21.

REVIEW, THE, "**Housing Report for 1951**," *The Review,* January, 1952, pp. 15.

REVIEW, THE, "**Rental Housing Shortage or Surplus**," *The Review,* October, 1951, pp. 15-16.

RIEMER, SVEND, "**Livability-A New Factor In Home Value**," *The Appraisal Journal,* April, 1946, pp. 148-158.

RITLEY, ROGER D., "**Measurement of Effective Demand for Multifamily Housing**," *Appraisal and Valuation Manual,* pp. 73-88.

ROBINS, PHILIP KENNETH, PH. D., "**A Theory and Test of Housing Market Behavior**," *A Theory and Test of Housing Market Behavior,* University of Wisconsin, 1972, pp. 162.

RODWIN, LLOYD, "**The Paradox of Boston's Middle Income Housing Progress**," *The Appraisal Journal,* January, 1951, pp. 42-55.

ROSEN, G. R., "**U. S. Priorities: Housing Is Number One**," *Duns,* October, 1970, pp. 46-47.

ROULAC STEPHEN E, QUICK PERRY D, "**The Housing Crises and Public Policy**," *The Real Estate Appraiser,* The Society of Real Estate Appraisers, Chicago Illinois, January 1, 1974, pp. 14-20.

RUDOLPH, MAX J., "**The Appraisal of Slum Districts for Federal Housing Projects**," *National Real Estate Journal,* February, 1935, pp. 39-40.

SCHEICK, WILLIAM H., "**News In Housing Research**," *The Review,* June, 1954, pp. 3-6.

SCHIEFFELIN, WILLIAM JAY, "**Housing and Taxation**," *Architectural Forum,* March, 1939, pp. 206.

SCHUMACHER, ERNEST P., "**VA-FHA Value Concepts**," *The Review,* 1954, pp. 14-15.

SHOWELL, BRIAN, "**Public Property Corporations**," *The Appraisal Journal,* April, 1963, pp. 229-235.

SMITH, G. A., "**Who's Building the Modulars**," *House & Home,* June, 1971, pp. 46-59.

SMITH, WALLACE F., "**Housing for the Elderly, and Evaluation of Existing and Proposed Programs**," *The Appraisal Journal,* April, 1964, pp. 177-185.

SMITH, WALLACE F., "**The Housing Preferences of Elderly People**," *The Appraisal Journal,* October, 1962, pp. 515-522.

SPARKMAN, JOHN J., "**Features of the New Housing Act**," *The Residential Appraiser,* October, 1961, pp. 11-16.

STONE, MAJOR EDWARD, "**Solving the Housing Dilemma**," *The Review,* February, 1948, pp. 18-24.

SUSNIR, JOHN, "**Industrialized Housing**," *The Real Estate Appraiser,* March, 1970, pp. 38-41.

SWAN, HERBERT S., "**The Demand for Housing**," *The Appraiser Journal,* January, 1945, pp. 62-74.

TERBORGH, GEORGE, "**Fluctuations In Housing Construction**," *The Appraisal Journal,* January, 1938, pp. 50-56.

U. . S FEDERAL HOUSING ADMINISTRATION, *Uniform System of Accounts for Large Scale Housing Projects,* Govt. Printing Office, Washington, 1936.

U. S. FEDERAL HOUSING ADMINISTRATION, *Structure and Growth of Residential Neighborhoods,* Govt. Printing Office, Washington, 1939.

U. S. FEDERAL HOUSING ADMINISTRATION, *Underwriting Manual,* Govt. Printing Office, Washington, 1936.

# BIBLIOGRAPHY OF APPRAISAL LITERATURE

U. S. GOVERNMENT PRINTING OFFICE, "FHA Techniques of Housing Market Analysis," Supt of Docs, U. S. Govt Ptg Office, Washington, D.C., 1900.

VAUGHAN, G. A., "Inadequate Wiring In Canadian Homes," *Appraisal Institute Magazine*, Appraisal Institute of Canada, Winnipeg.

WALLACE, JOHN C., "Appraisal of a Modern Nursing Home," *Assessor Journal*, International Association of Assessing Officers, Chicago, Illinois, April, 1969.

WEENEY, JAMES LEE, *A Dynamic Theory of the Housing Market*, Stanford University, 1971.

WENDT, PAUL F., "Analysis of Housing Demand In the San Francisco Metropolitan Area," *The Appraisal Journal*, July, 1948, pp. 346-355.

WENDT, PAUL F., "Estimating California's Housing Demand, 1954 to 1965," *The Appraisal Journal*, October, 1954, pp. 561-572.

WENZLICK, ROY, "The Tremendous Demand for Housing In the Next Few Decades," *The Appraisal Journal*, January, 1964, pp. 97-107.

WHYTE, WILLIAM H., JR., "What's Wrong with City Homes," *The Residential Appraiser*, August, 1957, pp. 16-24.

WOLF, ARTHUR L., "Homes Veterans Can Own," *The Review*, May, 1946, pp. 10-12.

WOLFF, LEWIS N., "Case Study of Housing the Elderly," *Real Estate Analyst Appraisal Bulletin*, 1962, pp. 131-136.

WOLITZER, P., "Co-Operative Housing Corporation-Development, Accounting, and Taxation," *New York Certified Public Accountant*, June, 1970, pp. 463-474.

WOOD, RAMSAY, "Housing Needs and the Housing Market," *The Appraisal Journal* October, 1946, pp. 380-388.

WOOD, RAMSAY, "The Setting for a Housing Program," *The Appraisal Journal*, January, 1947, pp. 110-118.

WRIGHT, CHARLES G., "Housing Potential for 1954," *The Review*, December, 1953, pp. 9-11.

YANDLE, B. JR., "Urban Renewal-The Precondition for Take-Off," *Land Economics*, November, 1970, pp. 484-486.

ZIMMERMAN, EARL M., "Demonstration Appraisal of a Nursing Home," *Assessment Administration*, Chicago, 1964, pp. 185-190.

*A Students Appraisal Report on an Apartment House*, American Institute of Real Estate Appraisers, 1966.

*Econometric Model of Residential Location*, Duke University, 1970.

"Baltimore Will Cool Housing for Elderly; Lorain Wants it," *Air Conditioning Heating and Refrigeration News*, July 27, 1970, pp. 1.

"Banker-Builder Team Proves That Private Enterprise Can Meet Housing Needs of Renewal-Area Residents," *House and Home*, June, 1970, pp. 42.

"Builder Says Standard Materials Make His Modulars Look Like Stick-Built Houses," *House and Home*, July, 1970, pp. 27.

"California Housing Starts," *Wall Street Journal*, pp. 36.

"California; Under the Glitter, a Growing Sense of the Market," *House and Market*, May, 1971, pp. 74-92.

"Can Technology Solve the Housing Problem," *Industry Week*, January 18, 1971, pp. 6-27.

"Capitalization Rates for Apartment Properties, a Symposium," *The Appraisal Journal*, October, 1942, pp. 357-367.

"Contemporary Hilltop House That's Selling Well to Young Working Couples," *House and Home,* 1971, pp. 44.

"Contemporary Ideas for the Built-For-Sale House," *House and Home*, September, 1970, pp. 82-87.

▲ **Urban Property**

"Credit Ease Help for Housing," *Financial World,* August 12, 1970, pp. 3.

"Detached Townhouses Add an Extra Dimension to Narrow Waterfront Lots," *House and Home,* December, 1970, pp. 42.

"Effects of Alternative Real Estate Taxes on Maintenance & Rehabilitation of Urban Rental Housing," *Dissertation Abstracts,* Ann Arbor, November, 1964, pp. 2808.

"Factory-Built Housing Rolls by Road and Rail," *Engineering News-Record,* July 23, 1970, pp. 21.

"Ford Decides to Get Out of Modular Housing," *Engineering News-Record,* September 3, 1970, pp. 41.

"Four Special Projects for Special Multi-Family Markets," *House and Home,* January, 1971, pp. 112-119.

"Here's Design That Hits the Market, and Cuts Costs Too," *House and Home,* March, 1971, pp. 68-73.

"High Money Cost May Stall Housing Recovery," *Engineering News-Record,* December 3, 1970, pp. 42.

"Housing Partnership Makes First Investment," *Engineering News Record,* October 22, 1970.

"Housing 20 Pickup," *Chemical Week,* November 25, 1970, pp. 16.

"Housing: Set for Take-Off In 71," *Chemical Week,* September 23, 1970, pp. 19.

"Low Income Housing Project Builds In the Round," *Engineering News- Record,* August 6, 1970, pp. 40.

"Mobile Modular," *House and Home,* June, 1970, pp. 56-63.

"Modular Housing: No Shell Game," *Financial World,* January 6, 1971, pp. 6..

"New Yorks Urban Housing Program Displays Its Innovative Plans," *Houe,* House & Home, November, 1970, pp. 28.

"Recipe for Housing," *Chemical Week,* August 11, 1971, pp. 11.

"Score One for the Tenants: They Win a Standard Lease for Public Housing," *House and Home,* April, 1971, pp. 26.

"Space Revolution In Multilevel House," *House and Home,* Modular House Draws, pp. M.

"Split Plan Transforms a Problem Area Into a Plus Feature," *House and Home,* June, 1971, pp. 36.

"This Turnkey Public Housing Capitalizes on a Skinny, Quarter-Acre Site," *House and Home,* January, 1971, pp. 78.

"Three Townhouse Projects That Sell Environment," *House and Home,* November, 1970, pp. 58-63.

"Two on One Triplexes Save Open Space on a Tight Suburban Site," *House and Home,* November, 1970, pp. 321.

"U. S. Housing Growing In Numbers, Conveniences and Valuations," *Commerce Today,* March 22, 1971, pp. 23.

"Vacation Condominiums That Fit Into Their Heavily-Wooded Surroundings," *House and Home,* June, 1970, pp. 36.

"What Happens When California-Style Package Like This Hits a Market That's Used to Housing Like This?," *House and Home,* pp. 42-49.

"8 Projects That Set a Standard for Government-Subsidy Housing," *House and Home,* December, 1970, pp. 66-78.

"Some Implications of Variable Interest Rate Mortgages for the Small Saver & the House Owner," *Business and Economic Review,* University of South Carolina.

## 13-17 Residential Property

ABRAMS, CHARLES, "The New Gresham's Law of Neighborhoods--Fact or Fiction," *The Appraisal Journal,* 1951, pp. 324-337.

ADKINS, WILLIAM G., "Dallas Expressway Study," *The Residential Appraiser,* April, 1958, pp. 16-24.

ADKISSON, FLOYD, "Private Urban Renewal," *The Residential Appraiser,* October, 1959, pp. 11-12.

AINSWORTH, LAWRENCE G., "Large Glass Areas In Homes - How and Why Used," *The Review,* November, 1949, pp. 17-19.

ALBERT, FRANKLIN E., "Zoning and Its Effect on Land Values," *The Residential Appraiser,* December, 1962, pp. 2-5.

ALBERT, STERLING H., "Neighborhood Factors Affecting Residential Values," *The Appraisal Journal,* January, 1960, pp. 81-89.

ALLINGHAM, A. P., "Appraisal of a Residence In Vicinity of Buffalo, New York," *Appraising Manual,* S. L. McMichael, 1937, pp. 492-495.

ALLISON, NEVILLE F., "A Study of Severance Damages," *The Residential Appraiser,* February, 1959, pp. 18-22.

ALLISON, NEVILLE F., "How a Neighborhood Declines," *The Residential Appraiser,* March, 1957, pp. 18-24.

AMERICAN INSTITUTE OF PLANNERS JOURNAL, "Model of Residential Land Values," *American Institute of Planners Journal,* May, 1965, pp. 172.

AMERICAN INSTITUTE OF REAL ESTATE APPRAISERS, "Neighborhood Analysis," *Acquisition for Right-Of-Way,* American Association of State Highway Officials, Washington, 1962, pp. 315-327.

ANDERSON, ROBERT E., "Appraising As a Sales Tool," *The Residential Appraiser,* December, 1956, pp. 18-21.

ANDERSON, ROBERT E., "The Comparison Approach In Appraising Residential Properties," *The Appraisal Journal,* April, 1960, pp. 177-181.

APP, FRANK J., "Condominium Conversion In California," *The Real Estate Appraiser,* The Society of Real Estate Appraisers, Chicago Illinois, November 1, 1973, pp. 9-12.

ARCHITECHTURAL FORUM, "Estimating the Selling Price of a Suburban Residence," *Architectural Forum,* April, 1920, pp. 165.

ARMSTRONG, ROBERT H., "Neighborhood Analysis," *The Appraisal Journal,* April, 1938, pp. 155-160.

ARNESON, HARRY R. JR., "Using Comparables In Court," *The Residential Appraiser,* October, 1957, pp. 3-6.

AUBLE, TALMAGE D., "Residential Appraisal In the Postwar Period," *The Appraisal Journal,* January, 1944, pp. 42-49.

AUMACK, HARRY F., "Neighborhood Yardsticks," *The Review,* August, 1953, pp. 12-16.

BABCOCK, FREDERICK M., "The Appraisal System of the FHA," *Review of the Society of Residential Appraisers,* December, 1936, pp. 3-5.

BABCOCK, FREDERICK M., "The Selection of Mortgages," *The Residential Appraisers Review,* September, 1935, pp. 5-7.

BABCOCK, FREDERICK M., MAURICE R. MASSEY, JR, WALTER L. GREENE, "Techniques of Residential Location Rating," *The Appraisal Journal,* April, 1938, pp. 133-140.

BABCOCK, RICHARD F., JAN DRASNOW-IEKI, "Legal Aspects of Planned Unit Residential Development," *Technical Bulletin 52 of the Urban Land Institute,* 1965.

BADGLEY, L. DURWARD, "Implications of the Current Residential Mortgage Pattern," *The Appraisal Journal,* July, 1948, pp. 326-329.

BALL, WILLIAM H., "Residences In Russia," *The Residential Appraiser,* April, 1959, pp. 9-11.

BARETTE, L. A., "Opposite Sides of the Tracks," *The Residential Appraiser,* July, 1957, pp. 6-8.

BAUER, FRANK, VERLE N. FRYE, "Residential Cost Analysis a Simplified Service to Appraisers," *Technicalities and Technical Valuation,* June, 1952, pp. 31-33.

BAYER, DANIEL, "Appraisal of Sites Designated for Middle-Income Housing," *The Appraisal Journal,* January, 1965, pp. 48-54.

BAZAN, HORACE B., "Activity Report of F. H. A. Fee Appraisals," *Technical Valuation,* October, 1958, pp. 20, 24.

BEEHLER, GEORGE W. JR., "Colored Occupancy Raises Values," *The Review,* September, 1945, pp. 3-6.

BEETH, CHANNING C., "Influence of Airports on Residential Values," *The Real Estate Appraiser,* July, 1956, pp. 6-10.

BEMAN, ARTHUR K., "Appraising the Large-Scale Housing Project," *Encyclopedia of Real Estate Appraising,* 1959, pp. 214-233.

BENEDICT, JARED W., "A Report on Fees," *The Residential Appraiser,* December, 1959, pp. 15-18.

BENNETT, EDWARD P. JR., "The Appraisal Report and the Review Appraiser," *The Residential Appraiser,* October, 1960, pp. 13-14.

BENNETT, K. W., "Modular Homes: Now Is the Hour," *Iron Age,* February 18, 1971, pp. 39-40.

BENNETT, S. Z., "Acquisition Philosophies and Experiences," *The Residential Appraiser,* April, 1957, pp. 14-23.

BENNETT, SAUL Z., "Appraiser's Certificates," *A Student's Appraisal Report on Single-Family Residences,* American Institute of Real Estate Appraisers, Chicago, 1964, pp. 22.

BENNETT, SAUL Z., "Description of the Improvements," *A Student's Appraisal Report on Single-Family Residences,* American Institute of Real Estate Appraisers, Chicago, pp. 9.

BENNETT, SAUL Z., "Description the Property," *Student's Appraisal Report on an Apt House,* American Institute of Real Estate Appraisers, Chicago, 1966, pp. 13.

BENNETT, SAUL Z., "Neighborhood Data," *A Student's Report on an Apartment House,* American Institute of Real Estate Appraisers, Chicago, 1966, pp. 12.

BENNETT, SAUL Z., "Site Analysis," *A Student's Appraisal Report on Single-Family Residences,* American Institute of Real Estate Appraisers, Chicago, pp. 5.

BENNETT, SAUL Z., "The Neighborhood," *A Student's Appraisal Report on an Apartment House,* America Institute of Real Estate Appraisers, Chicago, 1966, pp. 3.

BENSON, CHARLES A., "A Test of Transition Theories," *The Residential Appraiser,* August, 1958, pp. 3-8.

BENTON, PHILIP H, "Soil Mechanics-An Important Factor In Residential Property Evaluation," *The Real Estate Appraiser,* April, 1963, pp. 17-22.

BLAIR, W. EDWIN, "How to Make Rental Appraisals," *The National Real Estate Journal,* July 14, 1924, pp. 25-27.

BLOOD, J., "Community Family Centers: Taking a Bigger Slice of Chicago Sales," *Merchandising Week,* August 23, 1971, pp. 14.

BLUE, JESSE B., "Shall We Lead or Follow," *The Review of the Society of Residential Appraisers,* September, 1937, pp. 9-11.

BLUMBERG, AARON, MELNICOFF, STERN, OSCAR I, "Philadelphia Survey of New Home Sales," *The Appraisal Journal*, April, 1951, pp. 243-245.

BOATRIGHT, RONALD OLAN, *The Appraisal of Urban Residential Property A Theoretical and Empirical Model of Price Determination*, The University of Florida, 1971.

BODFISH, MORTON, HOYT, HOMER, "The Housing Demand Source," *The Review*, January, 1949, pp. 14.

BODFISH, MORTON, THEOBALD, A. D, "Appraising a Single-Family Residence," *Real Estate Fundamentals*, 1941, pp. 7-9.

BOECKH, EVERARD HEREFORD, "Residential Lot Widths, Etc," *Manual of Appraisals*, 1937, pp. 347-352.

BOEREMA, ROBERT J., "Building Design and Obsolescence In the Single Family Residence," *The Residential Appraiser*, December, 1962, pp. 9-13.

BOHANNON, DAVID D., "Industries As Neighbors," *The Residential Appraiser*, June, 1957, pp. 7-9.

BONBRIGHT, JAMES CUMMINGS, "The Valuation of Property," Mcgraw-Hill Book Co., Inc., N.Y. and London, 1937.

BONNER, JOHN T. JR., "The Operator's Premium," *The Residential Appraiser*, November, 1958, pp. 10.

BOOTH, ERIC ROWLAND, "Rating Valuation of Residential and Business Premises," *The Estates Gazette*, London, 1951.

BOURLAND, FREDERICK B., "Value of Residential Property," *News Release from the Society of Appraisers*, May 3, 1941.

BRIARD, S. E., "Grid Rating Residences," *The Review*, December, 1946, pp. 7-10.

BRODSKY, H., "Residential Land and Improvement Values In a Central City," *Land Economics*, August, 1970.

BRODSKY, HAROLD, "Residential Land and Improvement Values In a Central City," *Land Economics*, August, 1970.

BROWN, ROBERT K., RAMS, EDWIN M, "The Role of Buyer Motivation In Neighborhood Analysis," *Valuation Manual*, 1959, pp. 253.

BURGHOFF, J. R., "Gross Rent Multiplier In Residential Appraising," *The Real Estate Appraiser*, pp. 2.

BURNS, FRITZ B., "Building Communities," *The Review*, October, 1948, pp. 3-5.

BURNS, LELAND S., AND FRANK G. MITTELBACH, "Location-Fourth Determinant of Residential Value," *The Appraisal Journal*, April, 1964, pp. 237-346.

BURROWS, R. D., "Price Changes of Residential Property," *The Appraisal Journal*, April, 1945, pp. 167-176.

CANNON, DOUGLAS V., "Inventory of Speculative Home Building," *The Appraisal Journal*, April, 1955, pp. 230-240.

CARR, FRANCIS J., "Property Assessments Protest, Appeal, and Judicial Review," *The Journal of the State Bar of California*, November, 1964, pp. 877.

CARTER, J. H., "Problems In the Regulation and Taxation of Mobile Homes," *The Iowa Law Review*, pp. 16-58.

CHESLER, E. R., "Residential Swimming Pool Costs," *The Residential Appraiser*, November, 1961, pp. 13-14.

CHESSMAN, MARK, "The Important Fundamental of Residential Appraising," *National Real Estate Journal*, March, 1936, pp. 55-56.

CHESSMAN, MARK, "Valuation of a Small Residential Property In a Newer District," *Practical Appraising Methods*, 1940, pp. 36-38.

CHIRHART, EDWARD F., "Tourist Court, 1953 Decline," *Technical Valuation*, American Society of Appraisers, Washington, D. C., February, 1955, pp. 21.

CHURCH, BYRON, "Residential Neighborhood Trends In the 50's and 60's," *The Residential Appraiser*, May, 1963, pp. 20-23.

CHURCH, BYRON, "The Crystal Ball Gazer," *The Residential Appraiser*, January, 1960, pp. 23-24.

CLARK, FOREST F., *Appraising the Home*, Prentice Hall, New York, 1930.

CLAY, GRADY, "The Good Address," *The Review*, November, 1954, pp. 6-10.

COCHRANE, D. H., "The Method of Analyzing Residential Areas," *Appraisal Institute Magazine*, March, 1963, pp. 15-19.

COHEN, B. I., "Another Theory of Residential Segregation," *Land Economics*, August, 1971, pp. P. 314-315.

COPELAND, HARRY E., "Appraising District Change," *Review of the Society of Residential Appraisers*, January, 1937, pp. 7-10.

CORDIER, HENRY K., *The Appraisal of Fine Arts and Residential Contents*, American Society of Appraisers, January, 1972.

COTTON, W. OWEN, "Extending Substitution," *The Residential Appraiser*, February, 1958, pp. 8-9.

CRAIG, R. H., "Some Aspects of the Residential Real Estate Market In the Halifax-Dartmouth Area of Nova Scotia," *The Appraisal Institute Magazine*, March, 1962, pp. 7-13.

CURRAN, DONALD J., "General Property Tax and Residential Rehabilitation," *Conference Proceedings*, National Tax Association Association, Columbus, 1964, pp. 250-258.

DAIL, CHARLES C., "The Sewer Utility," *The Residential Appraiser*, May, 1959, pp. 19-21.

DANAHEY, THOMAS P., "Survey of Housing Facilities In Detroit Indicates Need of Home Building," *The Appraisal Journal*, October, 1935, pp. 471-474.

DANNIEL, W. S., "Appraising Residential Property," *Review of Society of Residential Appraisers*, May, 1941, pp. 6-10.

DECKER, ORVILLE, "Trailer Parks Are Here to Stay," *American Society of Appraisers*, 1961, pp. 69-88.

DERBES, MAX J. JR., "Reliability of Comparable Sales," *The Residential Appraiser*, March, 1961, pp. 20-22.

DES JARDINS, RICHARD J., "Zoning for Sound Neighborhoods," *The Review*, January, 1952, pp. 8-10.

DRUMN, EDWARD P., "An Introduction to FHA Methods," *The Residential Appraiser*, May, 1958, pp. 3-11.

DUBOIS, AYERS J., "Pitfalls In Residential Appraising," *Review of Society of Residential Appraisers*, December, 1939, pp. 15-16.

DUBOIS, AYERS J., "Valuation of Residential Properties In Small Towns," *Review of Society of Residential Appraisers*, October, 1939, pp. 3-9.

DUBOIS, AYERS J., "Valuation of Residential Properties Under War Conditions," *The Appraisal Journal*, October, 1944, pp. 349-358.

DUKE, RICHARD D., "Mobility----A New Aspect of Community Life," *Appraisal Digest*, October, 1953, pp. 22-23.

EAGLE, GORDON E., "Residential Appraisal for Mortgage Purposes," *Appraisal Institute Magazine*, Appraisal Institute of Canada, Winnipeg.

EDMAN, J. J., "Homeowner Is Entitled to Recover for Negligence In FHA Appraisal. Appraisal Docket," *The Appraisal Journal*, April, 1961, pp. 257-258.

EIKMEYER, LEO J., "Analysing the High Rise Apartment," *Appraisal Institute Magazine*, Appraisal Institute of Canada, Winnipeg.

ENEMARK, FRED, "Effect on Residential Property Values of Industrial Development," *The Residential Appraiser*, November, 1960, pp. 2-4.

EXPRESS PUBLISHING CO., *San Antonio, Texas Average Value of Dwelling Units for Block Areas, by Blocks, 1950,* Express Publishing Co., San Antonio, 1952.

FARM AND LAND REALTOR, "The Developing Mobile Home Community Industry," *National Institute of Farm and Land Brokers,* Chicago Ill. 60611, January, 1971.

FEDERAL HOME LOAN BANK REVIEW, *Neighborhood Standards As They Affect Investment Risk,* 1935.

FEDERAL HOUSING ADMINISTRATION, "FHA Analysis of Residential Properties Near Airports," *The Appraisal Journal,* October, 1961, pp. 538-540.

FEDERAL RESERVE BANK OF CHICAGO, "Mobile Homes, a Maturing Industry," *The Appraisal Journal,* April, 1961, pp. 246-250.

FEDERAL RESERVE BANK OF CLEVELAND, "Urban Real Estate Finance," *The Appraisal Journal,* April, 1947, pp. 202-210.

FERGUSON, HILL, "Are One Hundred Percent Residence Loans Again Being Made," *The Appraisal Journal,* July, 1935, pp. 371-372.

FIREY, WALTER, "Residential Sectors Re-Examined," *The Appraisal Journal,* October, 1950, pp. 451-453.

FITZGERALD, WILLIAM F., "U. S. Act May Extend Maryland Law for Same Size Home Awards," *The Appraiser,* September, 1968.

FLICKINGER, LOWELL D., "Trends In the Mobile Home Park Industry," *The Appraisal Journal,* July, 1965, pp. 344-345.

FRIEDMAN, ALBERT L., "Depreciation and Neighborhood Value," *Appraisal Digest,* October, 1961, pp. 5-9.

FULLER, ROBERT, "Residential Land Values In the 1960's," *The Residential Appraiser,* September, 1960, pp. 19-21.

FULLER, ROBERT S., "Changing Characteristics of Dwellings," *Appraisal Journal,* October, 1953, pp. 555-559.

GADE, GEORGE, "Economics of Operating a Mobile Home Park," *The Appraisal Journal,* July, 1965, pp. 351-357.

GAY, L. W., *The Cubic Foot Method of Determining the Value of Residence Property,* National Association of Real Estate Boards, 1926, pp. 363-367.

GILMORE, FRANK V., "Inspection During Construction," *Residential Appraisers Review,* February, 1936, pp. 3-6.

GOLDSTON, ELI, JAMES H. SCHEUER, "Zoning of Planned Residential Developments," *The Appraisal Journal,* October, 1960, pp. 449-461.

GRAHAM, J. W., "Reproduction Value Vs Reproduction Cost of Residences," *The Appraisal Journal,* October, 1934, pp. 61-64.

GRANFIELD, MICHAEL EDWARD PH. D., "An Econometric Model of Residential Location," 1970.

GRISELLE, SHERMAN W., "Parking Related to Residential Development," *The Appraisal Journal,* October, 1965, pp. 617-619.

GRUELICH, RICHARD H. JR., *Property Valuation,* Austin, Texas.

HAGOOD, WAYNE D., "Units Of Comparison," *The Residential Appraiser,* September, 1962, pp. 17-24.

HALL, JAMES R., "Inflation---The Home Owner---The Investor," *Technical Valuation,* February, 1960, pp. 45-48.

HALL, JOSEPH B., "What a Residential Appraisal Manual Should Include," *The Appraisal Journal,* October, 1933, pp. 22-31.

HAMILIN, BEN W., "Fourth Dimension Approach to Valuation of Residential Subdivision Land," *Technical Valuation,* June, 1961, pp. 51-54.

HANRAHAN, DANIEL C., "Purchase of Corporate Transferee Residences," *The Real Estate Appraiser,* September, 1966, pp. 24-29.

HANSON, A. E., "Residential Appraisals-Never a Precise Answer," *Appraisal Institute Magazine*, Appraisal Institute of Canada, Winnipeg.

HARDING, CARL G., "Appraisal of a Trailer Park Under Condemnation," *Appraisal Reporting Techniques*, American Institute of Real Estate Appraisers, 1954, pp. 85-122.

HARRISON, LOUIS A., "Valuation of Land In Built-Up Residential Areas," *Review of Society of Residential Appraisers*, pp. 13-41.

HARTMAN, FRANKLIN L., "Statistics of Neighborhood Analysis," *The Appraisal Journal*, July, 1961, pp. 352-358.

HARTNETT, EDGAR C., "Effect of a Highway on the Market Values of Adjoining Residential Property," *Real Estate Analyst Appraisal Bulletin*, 1961, pp. 73-80.

HARVEY, ROBERT O., "Residential Construction In 1963," *The Appraisal Journal*, July, 1963, pp. 327-332.

HATHAWAY, PAUL L., "Land Values In Older Neighborhoods," *The Review*, 1945, pp. 3-6.

HATHAWAY, PAUL L., "Transportation-A Factor In Residential Values," *Residential Appraisers Review*, August, 1935, pp. 3-5, 16.

HELD, HARRY, "The Fundamentals of Appraising Residential Real Estate," *Appraisal Digest*, July, 1952.

HENDRICKS, ROBERT W., "Residential Amenities Along Freeways," *The Resendential Appraiser*, June, 1960, pp. 2-10.

HERRMAN, CYRIL C., "Society Foundation Manuscript Competition," *The Real Estate Appraiser*, March, 1970, pp. 26-27.

HOLDEN, ARTHUR C., "Checking Neighborhood Obsolescence," *Real Estate Record*, February 15, 1936, pp. 18-25.

HOLLEBAUGH, CLIFFORD W., "Judging Older Neighborhoods," *The Review*, 1953, pp. 15-19.

HOLLEBAUGH, CLIFFORD W., "Physical Condition — Its Impact on Real Estate Values," *The Real Estate Appraiser*, January, 1963, pp. 9-13.

HOLLEBAUGH, CLIFFORD W., "Residential Amenities," *The Residential Appraiser*, March, 1960, pp. 3-8.

HOLLEBAUGH, CLIFFORD W., "The Income Approach In Residential Appraising," *The Residential Appraiser*, May, 1961, pp. 12-14.

HORN, RONALD R., "Mobile Home Parks: on Site Costs," *The Real Estate Appraiser*, September, 1970, pp. 24-31.

HOTCKISS, L. M., "Residential Contents Appraising," *Valuation Manual*, ASA, 1956, pp. 239.

HOUSE AND HOME, "Modular House Draws Crowds to New York City Museum," *House and Home*, November, 1970, pp. 26.

HOWARD, JEROME L., "Where Do We Go from Here," *The Residential Appraiser*, November, 1960, pp. 16-20.

HOYLE, FRED W., "Over-Improvement and Under-Improvement," *Residential Appraiser*, February, 1961, pp. 15-18.

HOYT, HOMER, "Residential Sectors Revisited," *The Appraisal Journal*, October, 1950, pp. 445-450.

HUGHES, JOHN D., "Trends In Residential Design," *The Appraisal Journal*, July, 1949, pp. 360-366.

HUNTLEY, GENE, "The Community Benefit of By-Pass Highways," *Right of Way*, June, 1957, pp. 29-32.

HURLEY, W. B., "Industry As a Residential Barometer," *The Review*, September, 1954, pp. 7-9.

HURTADO MARTINEZ, LUIS, ALBERTO ANGULO LOPEZ, "El Valor De Los Terrenos Para Uso Multifamiliar," *Boletin*, Sotave, Caracas, Venezuela, pp. 35-37.

HYDER, K. LEE, "Depreciation, Obsolescence, and Lack of Utility In Residential Property," *The Appraisal Journal,* October, 1952, pp. 544-548.

HYDER, K. LEE, "Residential Appraising," *Building Loan Journal,* January, 1940, pp. 14.

INMAN, PETER L., "Appraisal of Mobile Home Parks," *The Real Estate Appraiser,* September, 1970.

INNARD, WILLIAM N., *Transmission Line Right's of Way and Residential Values,* 1965.

INSTITUTE OF REAL ESTATE MANAGEMENT, *Study of Mobile Homes and Management,* Chicago, Illinois.

JACOBSON, CHARLES E., "The Development of a Mobile Home Park," *The Appraisal Journal,* July, 1965, pp. 347-350.

JAMES, M. H., *Residential Appraising,* April, 1938, pp. 196-197.

JARCHOW, ALFRED W, "Measuring Trends In Home Prices," *Valuation Magazine,* American Society of Appraisers, Washington D C, December 1, 1973, pp. 102-109.

JOHNSON, CLIFFORD R., "Report on a Study of the Effects of Highway Right of Way Encroachment on Residential Property," *Right of Way,* August, 1959, pp. 21-26.

KAHN, SANDERS A., "The Appraiser and Community Revitalization," *The Real Estate Appraiser,* pp. 13.

KAIN, JOHN F., *The Journey -To-Work As a Determinent of Residential Location,* Land Corporation, December, 1961, pp. 1-41.

KANE, C. V., *Motor Courts - from Planning to Profits,* Ahrens Publishing Co., New York, 1954.

KEDZIERSKI, S. L., "Relation of Owner-Occupied Residential Property Value to Family Income," *The Appraisal Journal,* April, 1937, pp. 155-168.

KELLOUGH, W. R., "Community Planning, Its Effect on Value," *The Real Estate Appraiser,* pp. 47.

KERN, JAMES M., "Why Quality Counts," *The Residential Appraiser,* January, 1957, pp. 7-8.

KINNARD, WILLIAM N. JR., "Tower Lines and Residential Property Values," *The Appraisal Journal,* April, 1967, pp. 269-284.

KISSACK, A. B., "Capacity and Utility," *Real Estate Analyst Appraisal Bulletin,* 1948, pp. 29-32.

KISSACK, A. B., "Lost Accessibility," *Real Estate Analyst Appraisal Bulletin,* 1948, pp. 127-130.

KISSACK, A. B., "Placing the Risk," *Real Estate Analyst Appraisal Bulletin,* 1947, pp. 519-522.

KLUTZNICK, PHILIP M., "Neighborhood Development," *The Appraisal Journal,* July, 1947, pp. 583-586.

KNISKERN, PHILIP W., "Some Value Factors In Residential Property," *The Appraisal Journal,* October, 1933, pp. 6-10.

KNISKERN, PHILIP W., "The Market Value of a Home," *The Appraisal Journal,* April, 1945, pp. 124-134.

KNOWLES, JEROME, JR., *Residential Costs Manual, Basic House Approach,* Knowles, Jerome Jr. , and Associates, Northeast Harbor Me., 1954.

KNOWLES, JEROME, JR., "City and Neighborhood Data and Analysis," *The Appraisal Journal,* April, 1967, pp. 260-268.

KNOWLES, JEROME, JR., "New Points In Eminent Domain," *The Residential Appraiser,* November, 1956, pp. 11-15.

KOENIG, JOHN JR., "Housing to Fit Budgets," *The Review,* September, 1949, pp. 16-17, 23.

KRUGER, RUDOLPH, "Valuation of Potential Business Sites," *Review Of The Society of Residential Appraisers,* November, 1939, pp. 12-14.

LALLI, F., "Modular Housing: the Phantom That Parades As an Industry," *House and Home,* June, 1970, pp. 64-75.

▲ Urban Property

LAMBTON, ANN KATHERINE SWYNFORD, *Landlord and Peasant In Persia,* Oxford University Press, New York, 1953.

LANE, B. S., "Final Regs on Depreciation and Rehabiliation of Residential Property Clarify Many Areas," *Journal of Taxation,* July, 1972, pp. 18 24.

LAUNER, E. J., "Residential Quantity Survey Cost Estimates," *Appraisal Digest,* January, 1959, pp. 14-15.

LAUREN, SIDNEY, "Problem with Paints," *The Residential Appraiser,* Chicago, February, 1959, pp. 5.

LAURENTI, LUIGI, *Property Values and Race, Studies In Seven Cities,* University of California Press, Berkeley, L. A., 1960.

LAYDEN, ARTHUR L., "Appraisal Reports," *Residential Appraisers Review,* February, 1936, pp. 7-9, 13.

LEE, ADELBERT W., "Appraising Residential Properties," *Technical Valuation,* pp. 3.

LEIGHLY, WILLIAM LEWIS, "Capitalization Methods," *Review of Society of Residential Appraisers,* May, 1939, pp. 8-11.

LEISK, HERBERT N., "The Appraiser and the Public," *The Residential Appraiser,* October, 1956, pp. 16-18.

LEWE, JOHN C. JR., "Winter Inspections," *The Residential Appraiser,* February, 1959, pp. 3-4.

LEWIS, CHARLES F., "Neighborhood Development and Protection," *Real Estate Record,* July 18, 1936, pp. 9-11.

LIBOTT, NATHAN, "Pitfalls In Residential Appraising," *The Appraisal Journal,* April, 1935, pp. 259-263.

LITTERER, OSCAR F., "Drop In Residential Prices Only Moderate," *The Appraisal Journal,* January, 1950, pp. 46-53.

LOCKYER, A. W., "Residential Property Trends," *The Appraisal Journal,* January, 1950, pp. 97-102.

LOSTETTER, EARL K., "Income Residential Properties," *The Residential Appraiser,* March, 1961, pp. 2-6.

LOWDEN, J. A., "Analysis of Apartment Block Operating Statements," *Appraisal Institute Magazine,* Appraisal Institute of Canada, Winnipeg.

LUDLOW, WILLIAM H., "Neighborhood Planning Committee Suggests Novel Real-Estate Development," *American City,* September, 1937, pp. 77-78.

LUTSCH, MARTIN G., "The Appraiser In the Role of Stabilizer," *Review of the Society of Residential Appraisers,* June, 1937, pp. 3-4.

LYON, LEE M., "Toward Eliminating Schizophrenia from Residential Evaluation," *The Real Estate Appraiser,* pp. 670800.

MARKEIM, J. WILLIAM, "Neighborhood and Market Analysis," *Journal of Property Management,* June, 1941, pp. 3 9-331.

MASON, W. BEVERLEY, JR., "A Perspective of FHA," *The Residential Appraiser,* October, 1958, pp. 6-9.

MAY, ARHUR, "Appraising the Home Part I," *The Appraisal Journal,* January, 1951.

MAY, ARTHUR A., *The Valuation of Residentail Real Estate,* Prentice-Hall Incorporated, New York, 1942.

MAY, ARTHUR A., *The Valuation of Residential Real Estate,* 1968.

MCDONALD, ADRIAN F., "Practical Applications of Appraisal Fundamentals," *The Residential Appraiser,* February, 1960, pp. 3-8.

MCMAHON, THOMAS C., "Combination Pittsburgh Business, Residential and Warehouse Lots and Property," *Appraising Manual,* Mcmichael, S. L, 1937.

MCMICHAEL, STANLEY L., "Influence of Governmental Activities on Home Valuation Technique," *Appraising Manual,* 1937, pp. 330-345.

MEREDITY, L. DOUGLAS, "Financing the House That Jack Built," *The Appraisal Journal,* April, 1948, pp. 215-221.

MERTZKE, A. J., "Valuation Principles As Applied to Residential Property," *The Appraisal Journal,* October, 1933, pp. 2-3.

MEYER, EDWIN G., "Partial Taking Negotiations," *The Residential Appraiser,* April, 1961, pp. 22-24.

MOBILE HOMES MANUFACTURERS ASSOCIATION, *Formula for Determining the Feasibility of Mobile Housing Developments,* Chicago.

MONTONNA, DAVID L., "Capitalizing Amenities of Residential Property," *Review of Society of Residential Appraiser,* August, 1939, pp. 3-8.

MONTONNA, DAVID L., "Rental-Sales Ration for Residences," *The Review,* March, 1951, pp. 3-6.

MORGAN, BELDEN, *Technique of Unit Cost Compilation for Residential Appraising,* Society of Residential Appraisers.

MORGAN, JAMES V., "FHA's Opportunities," *The Residential Appraiser,* April, 1958, pp. 3-6.

MORRELL, JOSEPH C., "How Do You Cube a House?," *Appraisal Digest,* October, 1950, pp. 6-8.

MORROW, R. CONRAD, "Interim Residential Improvements," *The Appraisal Journal,* April, 1969, pp. 243-246.

MOTT, SEWARD H., "The Benefits of Controlled Neighborhood Planning," *Architectural Record,* November, 1940, pp. 36-37.

MUELLER, EVA, BEORGE DATONA, "Consumer Optimism Weakening," *The Residential Appraiser,* November, 1957, pp. 9-11.

MURRAY, HENRY T., "A Random Sample of Market Data As the Basic of Comparison," *The Residential Appraiser,* March, 1962, pp. 11-13.

N. Y. TIMES INDEX, "Families Displaced by Urban Renewal Program Housed In Mobile Homes Pending Relocation," *N. Y. Times Index,* July 29, 1970.

NASH, W. W., M. L. COLEAN, *Residential Rehabilitation,* Mc Graw-Hill, New York, 1959.

NATIONAL REAL ESTATE JOURNAL, "Actual Appraisal Report -Valuation of Property on Typical Old Dwelling," *National Real Estate Journal,* September 28, 1931, pp. 22-24.

NAYLOR, R. VELDON, *Mobile Home Park Appraisals,* American Society of Appraisers, January, 1972.

NESSER, RICHARD S., "Depreciation Formulated for Ad Valorem Appraisals-Residential Property," *Appraisal and Valuation Manual,* American Society of Appraisers, 1962, pp. 195-206.

NEWCOMB, ROBINSON, "Mobile Home Parks an Analysis of Characteristics," *Urban Land Institute Technical Bulletin,* 65, Urban Land Institute.

NUTTER, C. ARMEL, "Financing: Key to Residential Market Trends," *The Review,* May, 1953, pp. 3-6.

O'BRIEN, W. H., "Appraising Lumber In Home Construction," *Review of the Society of Residential Appraisers,* February, 1937, pp. 9-11.

OELAND, L. L., "Appraising Residential Property," *National Real Estate Journal,* April 20, 1925, pp. 38-39.

OGBURN, WILLIAM F., "The Changing Family," *The Appraisal Journal,* October, 1936, pp. 400-407.

OSENBAUGH, CHARLES L., "Integrated Housing and Value," *The Appraisal Journal,* January, 1967, pp. 17-20.

PERRY, CLARENCE ARTHUR, "Neighborhood Values In City Planning," *The Appraisal Journal,* July, 1941, pp. 253-265.

PHILLIPS, GEORGE A., "Racial Infiltration," *The Review,* February, 1950, pp. 7-9.

PICKARD, W. C., "Conversations with Occupants," *The Residential Appraiser,* October, 1959, pp. 3-4, 8.

RAMS, EDWIN M., "Airports In Residential Areas," *The Review,* October, 1952, pp. 18-22.

RAMS, EDWIN M., "Comparative Study of Neighborhoods by Scale Analysis," *The Real Estate Appraiser,* November, 1963, pp. 13-20.

RAMS, EDWIN M., "Cost Adjustments," *The Residential Appraiser,* April, 1957, pp. 3-6.

RAMS, EDWIN M., "Cost Parameters-Single Family Dwellings," *The Residential Appraiser,* December, 1960, pp. 7-10.

RAMS, EDWIN M., "Residential Rehabilitation-Value Concepts and Valuations," *The Residentail Appraiser,* June, 1962, pp. 7-14.

RANDALL, WILLIAM J., "Appraisal Guide for Mobile Home Parks," *Mobile Homes Manufacturers Association,*

RANDALL, WILLIAM J., "Land Value As a Percentage of Total Sales Price of Residences," *Real Estate Analyst Appraisal Bulletin,* 1962, pp. 251-254.

RANDALL, WILLIAM J., "Mobile Home Subdivisions," *The Appraisal Journal,* July, 1967, pp. 360-373.

RANDALL, WILLIAM J., "The Misconception of the Value of Rooming Houses," *The Appraisal Journal,* April, 1958, pp. 275-279.

RANDALL, WILLIAM J., AND C. W. MCGREADY, "The Appraisal of Trailer Courts," *Real Estate Analyst Appraisal Bulletin,* 1958, pp. 441-448.

REAL ESTATE ANALYST, THE, "Estimating Livable Space and Cubic Content," *Real Estate Analyst Appraisal Bulletin,* 1948, pp. 269-272.

REAL ESTATE ANALYST, THE, "Factors In Appraising a Tourist Court," *Real Estate Analyst Appraisal Bulletin,* 1951, pp. 231-234.

REAL ESTATE ANALYST, THE, "Notes on the A. P. H. A. Methods of Neighborhood Appraising," *Real Estate Analyst Appraisal Bulletin,* 1951, pp. 461-468.

REAL ESTATE ANALYST, THE, "Reproduction Cost of One-Story Brick Veneer Houses," *Real Estate Analyst Appraisal Bulletin,* 1952, pp. 195-198.

REAL ESTATE ANALYST, THE, "Residential Construction Costs," *Real Estate Analyst Appraisal Bulletin,* 1950, pp. 337-354.

REAL ESTATE ANALYST, THE, "The Probable Life of Single-Family Residences," *Real Estate Analyst Appraisal Bulletin,* 1953, pp. 17-20.

REAL ESTATE RECORD, "Neighborhood Appraisals As a Guide for Investors," *Real Estate Record,* September 7, 1935, pp. 6-7.

REEVES, CUTHBERT E., "Valuation of Land," *Appraising Residential Property,* Buffalo, pp. 10-21.

REEVES, CUTHBERT EDWARD, *Appraising Residential Property Methods Cost Data and Instructions,* Holling Press, Buffalo, 1934.

RENNE, ROLAND R., *Residential Appraisal Manual,* Roy Wenzlick and Company, St. Louis, 1958.

RESIDENTIAL APPRAISER, "Airport Studies," *The Residential Appraiser,* March, 1957, pp. 13-14.

RESIDENTIAL APPRAISER, "Credit for Home Building," *The Residential Appraiser,* April, 1959, pp. 12-14.

RESIDENTIAL APPRAISER, "Proximity Study No. 3," *The Residential Appraiser,* January, 1962, pp. 16-20.

REVIEW OF SOCIETY OF RESIDENTIAL APPRAISERS, "Code of Ethics of the Society of Residential Appraisers," *Review of Society of Residential Appraisers,* June, 1940, pp. 15-61.

REVIEW OF SOCIETY OF RESIDENTIAL APPRAISERS, "Valuing Semi-Business Property," *Review of Society of Residential Appraisers*, October, 1941, pp. 12-14.

REVIEW, THE, "Architectural Preference," *The Review*, August, 1945, pp. 424-435.

REVIEW, THE, "Commerical Uses Enter a Residential Area," *The Review*, January, 1950, pp. 14-16.

REVIEW, THE, "Cost and Utiltiy In the Basementless House," *The Review*, September, 1949, pp. 18-23.

REVIEW, THE, "Neighborhood Transition," *The Review*, July, 1946, pp. 15-21.

REVIEW, THE, "Rental Housing Shortage or Surplus," *The Review*, October, 1951, pp. 15-16.

REVIEW, THE, "Sales Trend In Los Angeles," *The Review*, 1949, pp. 22.

REVIEW, THE, "The Society of Residential Appraisers, Los Angeles Chapter, Charting Costs," *The Review*, January, 1947, pp. 18-22.

REYNOLDS, KIRK, "Five Types of Costly Appraisal Mistakes," *Review of Society of Residential Appraisers*, January, 1938, pp. 11-13.

RICHARDS, RALPH H., "What of the Coming Real Estate Boom," *Review of Society of Residential Appraisers*, November, 1939, pp. 7-11.

RICKS, ROBERT, "Appraisal of Residences In the Panhandle of Texas," *Residential Appraisers Review*, September, 1935, pp. 13-14.

RIGHT OF WAY, "Should the Tenant Be Paid a Bonus to Move," *Right of Way*, October, 1956, pp. 5-6.

RING, ALFRED A., "Value Analysis of Neighborhood Characteristics," *The Valuation of Real Estate*, 1970, pp. 78-93.

RING, ALFRED A., "What's Behind Your Cost Estimate," *The Residential Appraiser*, December, 1956, pp. 6-9, 12.

RAMS, EDWIN M., AND ROBERT K. BROWN, "The Role of Buyer Motivation In Neighborhood Analysis," *Appraisal and Valuation Manual*, 1959, pp. 253-260.

RODDER, NORMAN J., "Appraising Residential Heating Equipment," *Review of the Society of Residential Appraisers*, September, 1936, pp. 5-8.

RODMAN, JAMES A. JR., "Partial Takings," *The Residential Appraiser*, December, 1957, pp. 17-18.

RODWIN, LLOYD, "The Theory of Residential Growth and Structure," *The Appraisal Journal*, July, 1950, pp. 295-317.

ROSS, THORSTON, "Tables of Additions and Deductions of Influences Affecting Residential Lots," *Appraising Manual*, 1937, pp. 329-330.

ROSS, THURSTON H., "Market Significance of Declining Neighborhoods," *The Appraisal Journal*, April, 1955, pp. 203-211.

ROSS, THURSTON H., "The Capitalization Process In Small Residential Appraisers," *Review of the Society of Residential Appraisers*, April, 1937, pp. 3-7.

ROWLANDS, DAVID T., "Sound Judgement In Appraising," *Review of the Society of Residential Appraisers*, August, 1936, pp. 9-11.

RUSSELL, HORACE, "FHA Appraisals and Negligence," *The Residential Appraiser*, June, 1961, pp. 23-24.

SANDERS, CURTIS A., "The Reasonable Range of Value," *The Residential Appraiser*, May, 1962, pp. 10-12.

SAUCIER, JOHN W., "Reactions of Negro Buyers," *The Residential Appraiser*, May, 1959, pp. 3-11.

SCHAAF, A. H., "Effect of Federal Mortgage Underwriting on Residential Construction," *The Appraisal Journal*, January, 1967, pp. 54-69.

SCHIETINGER, E. F., "Race and Residential Market Values In Chicago," *Land Economics*, November, 1954, pp. 301-308.

▲ Urban Property

SCHLEGEL, W. J., "Appraising the Plumbing," *Review of the Society of Residential Appraisers*, June, 1936, pp. 1-6.

SCHMUTZ, GEORGE L., "Depreciation In Luxury Homes," *The Appraisal Journal*, April, 1943, pp. 125-131.

SCHMUTZ, GEORGE L., "Leasehold Damage," *Condemnation Appraiser's Handbook*, 1938, pp. 1-339.

SCHMUTZ, GEORGE L., "The Neighborhood," *Appraisal Process*, 1941, pp. 1-229.

SCHNITMAN, L. SETH, "Sociological Changes Effecting New Residential Construction," *Real Estate Record and Builders Guide*, September 12, 1931, pp. 10-11.

SCHULTE, AUGUST B., "Information Plant for Real Estate Appraising," *Society of Residential Appraisers Research Bulletin*, No. 2, March, 1937, pp. 1-38.

SCHUMACHER, ERNEST P., "Residential Lot Analysis," *The Review*, September, 1947, pp. 14-18.

SCOTT, ROBERT V., "Residential Value," *The Appraisal Journal*, July, 1952, pp. 353-356.

SELIGMAN, DANIEL, "Present and Future of Slums," *The Residential Appraiser*, January, 1958, pp. 11-16.

SELLERS, RANDOLPH F., "Real Estate Values and Appraisal of Residence Property," *National Real Estate Journal*, June 27, 1927, pp. 46-47.

SEYFRIED, WARREN R., "Predicting the Economic Growth Potential of the Community," *The Appraisal Journal*, January, 1958, pp. 54-60.

SHATTUCK, CHARLES B., *Residential Appraising*, California Real Estate Association, Los Angeles, 1936, pp. 1-86.

SHELGER, KURT S., "Technique of Analyzing Residential Areas," *The Appraisal Journal*, October, 1957, pp. 566-574.

SHENEHON, HOWARD E., "Residential Growth Development In a Metropolitan Area," *The Residential Appraiser*, September, 1960, pp. 6-7.

SLATER, RONALD W., MARVIN A. MCGONIGAL, "Mobile Home Park Development," *Appraisal Institute Magazine*, Appraisal Institute of Canada, Winnipeg.

SMETHURST, R. G., "When Why, What, Where How of Condominiums," *Appraisal Institute Magazine*, Appraisal Institute of Canada, Winnipeg.

SMITH, FRED E., "A Demonstration Appraisal of a Residence Property," *National Real Estate Journal*, March, 1935, pp. 46-49.

SMITH, FRED E., "A Demonstration Appraisal of a Resident Property," *Practical Appraising Methods*, 1940, pp. 32-35.

SMITH, G. A., "Who's Building the Modulars," *House & Home*, June, 1971, pp. 46-59.

SOCIETY OF REAL ESTATE APPRAISERS, *A Guide to Appraising Residences*, Society of Real Estate Appraiser, Chicago, 1904.

SOCIETY OF RESIDENTIAL APPRAISERS, *Review of the Society of Residential Appraisers*, The Valuation of Residential Real Estate, Chicago, Ill..

SOCIETY OF RESIDENTIAL APPRAISERS, "Appraisers Handbook," *Society of Residential Appraisers*, October, 1938.

SPILLER, ROBERT J., "Review of Older Developments--Today," *The Residential Appraiser*, May, 1962, pp. 19-22.

SPRING, TERRENCE, "Daily Public Relations," *The Residential Appraiser*, January, 1989, pp. 13.

STEAD, WILLIAM H., "Long-Term Analysis of Residential Property," *The Review*, October, 1948, pp. 12-16.

STEAD, WILLIAM H., "The Short-Run Outlook for Residential Property," *Appraisal Digest*, April, 1951, pp. 9..

STEARNS, EDWARD C., "Our Termite Problem," *The Appraisal Journal,* April, 1942, pp. 153-158.

STERLING, H. ALBERT, "Neighboring Factors Affecting Residential Values," *The Appraisal Journal,* January, 1960, pp. 81-89.

STERN, OSCAR I., "Long Range Effect of Colored Occupancy," *The Review,* January, 1946, pp. 4-6.

SURVEY RESEARCH CENTER, UNIVERSITY OF MICHIGAN, "Buyer Preferences Surveyed," *The Review,* Housing and Home Finance Agency, February, 1953, pp. 7.

TANNENBAUM, A. A., "New Techniques In Residential Construction."

THOMSON, ROBERT H., "A Dependable Cost Short-Cut," *The Residential Appraiser,* February, 1957, pp. 3-8.

THORSON, IVAN A., "Residential Property," *The Appraisal Journal,* October, 1933, pp. 14-21.

TRUE, WALLACE W., "Neighborhood Analysis In Appraising," *National Real Estate Journal,* November, 1937, pp. 38-40.

TUCKER, HAROLD J., "The Correlation of the Three Approaches In Residential Appraising," *Technical Valuation,* February, 1961, pp. 46-48.

U. S. FEDERAL HOUSING ADMINISTRATION, *Structure and Growth of Residential Neighborhoods,* Govt. Printing Office, Washington, 1939.

VAN CLEEF, EUGENE, "Let's Begin to Tear Down," *The Appraisal Journal,* October, 1954, pp. 573-575.

VAN RASSEL, A. JOHN, "Residential Land Valuation," *Appraisal Institute Magazine,* Appraisal Institute of Canada, Winnipeg.

WAGNER, E. F., "Should Tenants Be Subsidized for Cost of Moving Due to Public Improvements?," *Right of Way,* April, 1957, pp. 37-38.

WAGNER, PERCY E., "On Neighborhood Income," *The Appraisal Journal,* April, 1936, pp. 197-198.

WALL, NORBERT F., "Planning the Housing Market Analysis," *The Appraisal Journal,* January, 1968, pp. 98-101.

WALSH, EDWARD V., "Amenities and How to Appraise Them," *National Real Estate Journal,* February, 1941, pp. 18-20.

WALSH, JAMES A., "Small Homes Described As Assets to Communities," *The Appraisal Digest,* July, 1953, pp. 14.

WALTHER, H. O., "Appraising Residential Property-From Application to Loan Disbursement," *Residential Appraisers Review,* December, 1935, pp. 3-5, 11.

WALTHER, H. O., "Correlation of Data and the Value of Estimate," *Review of the Society of Residential Appraisers,* May, 1937, pp. 3-5.

WEAVER, HOWARD SILAS, *City Residential Appraising,* Weaver School of Real Estate, Kansas City Missouri, 1962.

WEBSTER, JOHN K., "Rental Analysis for Residences," *The Review,* April, 1953, pp. 9-11.

WEED, KENNETH A., "How to Analyze Apartment Building Neighborhoods and Develop Rent Schedules," *Real Estate Appraisal Practice,* 1958, pp. 105-116.

WENZLICK, ROY, RESEARCH CORP., *Residential Appraisal Manual,* Roy Wenzlick Research Corp., St. Louis, 1958.

WICKENS, DAVID L., *Residential Real Estate,* National Bureau of Economic Research, New York, 1941, pp. 300.

WILLIAMS, JAY, "Detail Cost of Residences," *Appraisers and Assessors Manual,* 1930, pp. 1-500.

WILSON, JOHN W., "Residential Demand for Electricity," *Quarterly Review of Economics and Business,* University of Illinois, April, 1971, pp. 7-19.

WINTER, E. A., SMITH, W. P, "Estimating Aggregate Residential Real Estate Values from Population-Income Data," *Appraisal and Valuation Manual,* February, 1956, pp. 89-92.

WINTERHALT, J. H., "So You Want to Buy a House," *Appraisal Institute Magazine,* Appraisal Institute of Canada, Winnipeg.

WOLTZ, SETH P., "Analyzing Residential Neighborhoods," *The Residential Appraiser,* August, 1960, pp. 2-5.

WOLTZ, SETH P., "FHA Program Gets Setback," *The Residential Appraiser,* September, 1960, pp. 8, 21.

WORTH, WILLARD J., "New Materials for Housebuilding," *The Residential Appraiser,* pp. 8.

*A Students Appraisal Report on a Single-Family Residence,* American Institute of Real Estate Appraisers.

*Econometric Model of Residential Location,* Duke University, 1970.

*Mobile Home Park Appraisals,* American Society of Appraisers, Washington.

*Review of Project Proposal for the Development of a Mobile Home Park,* Mobile Homes Manufacturers Association, Chicago.

"Actual Appraisal Reports: No. 4 Demonstration Appraisal of Building," *National Real Estate Journal,* March 2, 1931, pp. 30-34.

"Authentic Spanish Styling Appeals to Renters In a Southwestern Market," *House and Home,* 1970.

"Mobile Modular," *House and Home,* June, 1970, pp. 56-63.

"Modular Housing: No Shell Game," *Financial World,* January 6, 1971, pp. 6..

"Motel Room at Bargain Rates," *Business Week,* August 22, 1970, pp. 20.

"Old Mansion Now Has Biggest Backyard Pool In Beverly Hills," *Engineering News-Record,* September 24, 1970, pp. 26-27.

"Scientists Build a House," *Industry Research,* November, 1970, pp. 48-51.

"Single-Family Residential Appraisal Manual," American Institute of Real Estate Appraisers.

"Actual Appraisal Reports: Valuation of New House of Med Size Located In Baltimore Residential Subdiv," *National Real Estate Journal,* July 6, 1931, pp. 32-35.

# 13-18 Rent and Rent Control

AARON, H., "Rent Controls & Urban Developmt: a Case Study of Mexico City," *Social & Economic Studies,* December, 1966, pp. 314-328.

APPELBAUM, WILLIAM, "Evaluating Store Sites and Determining Store Rents In Chain Store Age," *American Society of Appraisers Valuation Manual,* March, 1958, pp. 15-17.

ARNESON, HARRY R., "Establishing Rentals on Real Estate," *Appraisal Institute Magazine,* December, 1963, pp. 32-33.

ARNOLD, PHILIP N., HENRY A. BABCOCK, "Rent Reserved In Lease Above Rental Value," *The Appraisal Journal,* October, 1932, pp. 36-44.

# BIBLIOGRAPHY OF APPRAISAL LITERATURE

AYRES, J. M., "From the Ground Up Evolution of an Office Building, Building Operation Systems," *Skyscraper Management,* December, 1970, pp. PP16 20.

BABCOCK, FREDERICK M., "Computing Rents for Fractional Part of Any Month by Days," *Appraisal of Real Estate,* 1924, pp. 339.

BACKMAN, JULES, "Impact of Rent Control Upon Income," *The Appraisal Journal,* January, 1951, pp. 9-17.

BEIQUE, JEAN, "Store Rentals and Land Values," *The Appraisal Journal,* July, 1955, pp. 389-394.

BENSON, PHILIP A., NELSON L. NORTH, "Actual or Potential Rent As a Measure of Value," *Real Estate Principles and Practices,* 1938, pp. 287-288.

BENSON, PHILIP A., NORTH NELSON L, "Value Computed from Rentals," *Real Estate Principles and Practices,* 1938, pp. 299-300.

BIGLER, S. H., "Office Rental Rates of Tomorrow," *The Appraisal Journal,* April, 1948, pp. 210-214.

BLAIR, W. EDWIN, "How to Make Rental Appraisals," *The National Real Estate Journal,* July 14, 1924, pp. 25-27.

BLDG OWNERS & MGRS ASSN OF SEATTLE, "Ground Floor Rental Committee," *Skyscraper Management,* September, 1932, pp. 13-14.

BODFISH, MORTON, A. D. THEOBALD, "Stabilizing of Rentals," *Real Estate Fundamentals,* 1941, pp. 11-12.

BOND, F. A., "The Relation of Rents to Value," *The Residential Appraisers Review,* September, 1935, pp. 10, 11, 15.

BRINDLEY, WILLIS, "Retail Rentals As a Guide to Real Estate Values," *National Real Estate Journal,* August 17, 1931, pp. 19-20.

BURGHOFF, J. R., "Gross Rent Multiplier In Residential Appraising," *The Real Estate Appraiser,* pp. 2.

CARLSON, HOWARD M., "Hotels--Replacement Costs and Rental Rates," *The Appraisal Journal,* April, 1950, pp. 185-189.

CHAPMAN, FRED L., "Developing Rent Schedules," *The Appraisal Journal,* January, 1942, pp. 26-35.

CLARK, HORACE F., "Rents As an Index of Values," *Appraising the Home,* 1930, pp. 86-95.

COHEN, J. SOLIS, "Landlord and Tenant, Partners," *Saturday Evening Post,* December 27, 1930.

CORNYN, JOHN E., "Accounting for Rent Control," *The Appraisal Journal,* July, 1942, pp. 215-227.

CRAFT, D. JAMES, MARJORIE A. BILLINGS, "Apartment Rents Is Yours In Line," *Utah Economic and Business Review,* University of Utah, November, 1971, pp. 1-3, 6.

DANAHEY, THOMAS P., "Survey of Housing Facilities In Detroit Indicates Need of Home Building," *The Appraisal Journal,* October, 1935, pp. 471-474.

DE SALES PEREZ, FRANCISCO, "El Tribunal Inquilinato," *Boletin,* Sotave, Caracas, Venezuela, pp. 4-5.

DE SALVO, J. S., "Effects of the Property Tax on Operating and Investment Decisions of Rental Property Owners," *National Tax Journal,* March, 1971, pp. 45-50.

DERBES, MAX J. JR., "Determining Fair Rental Value," *The Appraisal Journal,* April, 1953, pp. 267-268.

DESALVO, J. S., "Effects of the Property Tax on Operating and Investment Decisions," *National Tax Journal,* March, 1971, pp. 45 50.

FIELD, SAMUEL, "Rental Income Analysis In Appraisals," *Real Estate Record,* September 14, 1940, pp. 7.

FOWLER, G., "Property Owners on Resort Areas Find it Incr Difficult to Rent Their Summer Homes," *N. Y. Times Index,* July 5, 1970.

▲ Urban Property

GAGE, DANIEL D., "Appraisal Methods In Wartime Rent Control," *The Appraisal Journal,* July, 1946, pp. 250-258.

GLAZE, BERT T., "Relationship of Market Value and Rent a Market Sample of Single Family Houses," *The Appraisal Journal,* October, 1966, pp. 574-580.

GRANT, ROSS, "The Los Angeles Plan for Determinining Office Rental Values," *Skyscraper Management,* June, 1934, pp. 14-15.

HAMILTON, H. P., "Apartment Development Trends In Canada," *Appraisal Institute Magazine,* Appraisal Institute of Canada, Winnipeg.

HOYT, HOMER, "Effect of Rents Opertg Expenses & Constr Costs Upon New Income of Regional Shopping Centers," *The Appraisal Journal,* January, 1963, pp. 65-70.

HOYT, HOMER, "Effects of National Defense Program on Rents and Values," *Review of Society of Residential Appraisers,* October, 1940, pp. 5-8.

JANSSEN, M. R., F. H. ATKINSON, M. P. KELSEY, "Is Field Renting Good Or Bad," *Journal of the American Society of Farm Managers and Rural Appraisers,* October, 1960, pp. 84-91.

JERRETT, HERMAN D., "Urban Land Rent," *Theory of Real Property Valuation,* Chapter Xi, 1938.

KNISKERN, P. W., "Theoretical Conversion of Traffic Into Rental Value, Formula and Comment," *Real Estate Appraisal and Valuation,* 1933, pp. 342-343.

KNISKERN, PHILIP W., "Rent Analysis Tables and Comment," *Real Estate Appraisal and Valuation,* 1933, pp. 331-334.

LEVY, MARK, "How to Determine Business Rentals," *National Real Estate Journal,* November 17, 1924, pp. 41-44.

LEVY, MARK, BROTHER, "Percentage Rental Rates Based on Gross Annual Sales," *Real Estate Appraisal and Valuation,* 1933, pp. 337-338.

MACROSSIE, WILLIAM, "Treatment of Excess Rentals on Commercial Properties," *Appraisal Digest,* July, 1950, pp. 14-16.

MAISEL, SHERMAN J., "Have We Underestimated Increases In Rents and Shelter Expenditures," *The Journal of Political Economy,* April, 1949, pp. 106-117.

MATTHEWS, STEWART B., "The Effect of Rent Control on Real Estate Values," *The Appraisal Journal,* October, 1942, pp. 323-327.

MCMICHAEL, STANLEY L., "Rentals Formula for Determining a Reasonable Rental," *Appraising Manual,* 1937, pp. 513-516.

MCMICHAEL, STANLEY L., "Transmuting Store Rentals Into Standard-Foot Land Values," *National Real Estate Journal,* June 24, 1929, pp. 19-21.

MONTONNA DAVID L., "Recognition and Treatment of Excess Rentals In Appraising," *The Appraisal Journal,* January, 1950, pp. 81-90.

MONTONNA, DAVID L., "Rental-Sales Ration for Residences," *The Review,* March, 1951, pp. 3-6.

MORGAN, BELDEN, "Can You Qualify As a Building Inspector?," *The Review,* April, 1956, pp. 3-6.

NAZARIO, LUIS A., "Como Estimar La Renta," *Boletin,* Sotave, Caracas, Venezuela, pp. 23-32.

OGUR, DAVID JONATHAN, PH. D., *The Impact of Colleges and Universities on Local Rental Housing Markets,* Cornell University, 1970.

PARKINSON, G., "Here's a Builder Who Uses the Apartment Buyers Money to Build the Apartments," *House and Home,* January, 1971, pp. 20.

PEARSON, F. A., W. I. MYERS, J. H. LORIE, "Rents, Building Activity, and Full Employment," *The Appraisal Journal,* January, 1946, pp. 19-22.

PEARSON, F. A., W. I. MYERS, J. H. LORIE, "Rents, Building Activity, And Full Employment," *The Appraisal Journal*, January, 1946, pp. 19-22.

PLEETER, SAUL PH. D., *The Effects of Public Housing on Neighboring Property Values and Rents In Buffalo, New York*, St. University of New York, Buffalo, 1971.

PRATT, LOUIS M., "Percentage of Sales Paid for Rent," *The Appraisal Journal*, October, 1934, pp. 83-84.

PRIMM, H. M., "A Suggestion for Determining Cash Rental on Illinois Farms," *Journal of the American Society of Farm Managers and Rural Appraisers*, October, 1952, pp. 114-116.

REDMOND, JOHN T., "Appraisals and Rental Rates," *Skyscraper Management*, October, 1931, pp. 5-7.

REEVES, CUTHBERT E., "Deriving Land Value from Rental Data," *The Appraisal Journal*, January, 1939, pp. 37-45.

REEVES, CUTHBERT E., "On Net Rentals of Taxpayer Properties," *The Appraisal Journal*, January, 1937, pp. 69-72.

REGISTER, J. ALVIN, "Las Propiedades De Renta En La Tasacion," *Boletin*, Sotave, Caracas, Venezuela, pp. 22.

REVIEW OF SOCIETY OF RESIDENTIAL APPRAISERS, "Relationship of Rents to Value," *Review of Society of Residential Appraisers*, September, 1941, pp. 2-5.

ROETTGER, G. J., "Just Compensation Frustration of an Owners Plans," *Appraisal Journal*, 1971.

SANDERS, CURTIS A., "Rent Multipliers," *The Residential Appraiser*, pp. 9..

SCALF, RICHARD L., "Rental Surveys and the Appraiser," *Technical Valuation*, December, 1967, pp. 3..

SCHMUTZ, GEORGE L., "Setting Comparable Rentals," *The Review*, December, 1946, pp. 14-17.

SCHMUTZ, GEORGE L., "The Influence of Rents and Commodity Prices," *The Appraisal Journal*, July, 1934, pp. 322-328.

SCHORR, PHILIP, "Only As Much As the Rents Will Bear," *The Appraisal Journal*, July, 1967, pp. 348-354.

SCHWULST, EARL B., "Impact of Present Economy Upon Rental and Price Structure," *The Appraisal Journal*, July, 1947, pp. 317-325.

SHERIDAN, LEO J., "The Sheridan-Karkow Formula for Determining Rental Value of Office Space," *Skyscraper Management*, 'April, 1934, pp. 12-18, 12-14.

SHERIDAN, LEO J., "Trends of Office Space, Rentals, and Occupancy," *The Appraisal Journal*, April, 1940, pp. 111-120.

SOMERVILLE, EDWIN L., "Rental Appraisal In Class A Buildings," *Skyscraper Management*, December, 1934, pp. 8-9.

SOTAVE, BOLETIN, "Las Propiedades De Renta En La Tasacion," *Boletin*, Sotave, Caracas, Venezuela, pp. 19-20.

STEVENS, FRANCIS K., "Relation of Land Value to Office Rentals," *Real Estate Record and Builders Guide*, February 28, 1942, pp. 5-7.

STROUSE, BENJAMIN A., "Regional Shopping Center, Tenancy, Leasing, and Financing," *Technical Valuation*, October, 1957, pp. 31-33.

THALER, D., "You Can Make Money In Low Income Rural Housing," *House And Home*, June, 1970, pp. 84-88.

THORSON, IVAN A., "Appraising Properties Involving Both Contract Rent and Economic Rents--Reversion Rights," *Technicalities*, February, 1950, pp. 23-25.

THORSON, IVAN A., "Contract Vs. Economic Rent: I,," *The Appraisal Journal*, April, 1940, pp. 121-139.

THORSON, IVAN A., "The Inapplicability of the Ricardian Rent Theory to Present Day Conditions," *The Appraisal Journal*, July, 1935, pp. 360-365.

WEBSTER, JOHN K., "Rental Analysis for Residences," *The Review*, April, 1953, pp. 9-11.

WEED, KENNETH A., "How to Analyze Apartment Building Neighborhoods and Develop Rent Schedules," *Real Estate Appraisal Practice*, 1958, pp. 105-116.

WELLS. H. C., "Apartment Management Is a Misnomer the Term Should Be Apartment Marketing," *House and Home*, December, 1970, pp. 44.

WENDT, PAUL F., "Effects of Federal Rent Control," *The Appraisal Journal*, January, 1950, pp. 17-28.

WENZLICK, DELBERT S., "What About Rents," *The Appraisal Journal*, January, 1933, pp. 95-103.

WHITNEY, RAMEY C., *The Valuation of Rental Housing*, Omaha and Lincoln, Nebraska, University of Nebraska, Lincoln, 1953.

WICKSELL, KNUT, VALUCE, *Capital and Rent*, Rinehart, New York, 1954.

"Building Management, Uses Human In Tenant Relations Program," *Skyscraper Management*, July, 1970, pp. 17-18.

"Rentals or Condominiums," *House and Home*, April, 1972, pp. 82 87.

"Score One for the Tenants: They Win a Standard Lease for Public Housing," *House and Home*, April, 1971, pp. 26.

"Trends In Homeownership and Rental Costs," *Monthly Labor Review*, July, 1970, pp. 26-31.

"Washington Suburbs Fight Plan to Rescue Townhouse Project by Renting it to the Poor," *House and Home*, May, 1971, pp. 20.

"Wrestling with Rent," *Economist*,

# 13-19 Residential Buildings

ABRAMS, CHARLES, "The New Greshan's Law of Neighborhoods--Fact or Fiction," *The Appraisal Journal*, 1951, pp. 324-337.

ACOLIA, GEORGE R., "Garden Apartment Site," *Case Reports In Assessment Administration*, December, 1960, pp. 46-47.

ADAMS, LEWIS W., "Good Vs. Poor Design In Landscape Architecture," *The Residential Appraiser*, July, 1961, pp. 18-20, 24.

ADDINGTON, WENDELL G., "Mutual Ownership of Residential Cooperatives and Condominiums," *Valuation*, December, 1967, pp. 46-56.

ADKINS, WILLIAM G., "Dallas Expressway Study," *The Residential Appraiser*, April, 1958, pp. 16-24.

ADKISSON, FLOYD, "Private Urban Renewal," *The Residential Appraiser*, October, 1959, pp. 11-12.

AINSWORTH, LAWRENCE G., "Large Glass Areas In Homes - How and Why Used," *The Review*, November, 1949, pp. 17-19.

ALBERT, FRANKLIN E., "Zoning and Its Effect on Land Values," *The Residential Appraiser*, December, 1962, pp. 2-5.

ALBERT, STERLING H., "Neighborhood Factors Affecting Residential Values," *The Appraisal Journal*, January, 1960, pp. 81-89.

ALLINGHAM, A. P., "Appraisal of a Residence In Vicinity of Buffalo, New York," *Appraising Manual*, S. L. McMichael, 1937, pp. 492-495.

# BIBLIOGRAPHY OF APPRAISAL LITERATURE

ALLISON, NEVILLE F., "A Study of Severance Damages," *The Residential Appraiser,* February, 1959, pp. 18-22.

AMER INSTITUTE OF REAL ESTATE APPRAISERS, "**Student's Appraisal Rept on Apt House,**" American Institute of Real Estate Appraisers.

AMERICAN INSTITUTE OF REAL ESTATE APPRAISERS, "**Appraisal of the Catherine Apartments, an 8-Family Apartment Block,**" *Demonstration Appraisal Reports,* American Society of Real Estate Appraisers, Chicago, 1957, pp. 158-205.

AMERICAN INSTITUTE OF REAL ESTATE APPRAISERS, "**Appraisal of the Elevator Apartment Property,**" *Demonstration Appraisal Reports,* American Institute of Real Estate Appraisers, Chicago, 1957, pp. 206-241.

AMERICAN INSTITUTE OF REAL ESTATE APPRAISERS, "**Appraisal of the Value of a Single-Family Dwelling, Cambridge, Massachusetts,**" *Demonstration Appraisal Reports,* American Institute of Real Estate Appraisers, Chicago, 1957, pp. 84-116.

AMERICAN INSTITUTE OF REAL ESTATE APPRAISERS, "**Case Studies In Apartment House Valuation,**" *Case Studies In Apartment House Valuation,* American Institute of Real Estate Appraisers, Chicago, 1900.

AMERICAN INSTITUTE OF REAL ESTATE APPRAISERS, "**Fair Market Value Appraisal of Apartment House,**" *Demonstration Appraisal Reports,* American Institute of Real Estate Appraisers, Chicago, 1957, pp. 119-157.

AMERICAN INSTITUTE OF REAL ESTATE APPRAISERS, "**Residential Styles and Functional Utility Valuation,**" *The Appraisal of Real Estate,* American Institute of Real Estate Appraisers, Chicago, 1967, pp. 131.

AMERICAN SOCIETY OF PLANNING OFFICIALS, *Apartments In the Suburbs,* Chicago, 1900.

ANDERSON, ROBERT E., "**Appraising As a Sales Tool,**" *The Residential Appraiser,* December, 1956, pp. 18-21.

ANDERSON, SENECA B., "**Cooperatives and Condominiums,**" *The Residential. Apraiser,* August, 1962, pp. 2-6.

ANDREWS, JAMES, "**Assessment Problems of Condominium Ownership,**" *Urban Land,* November, 1963, pp. 1-3.

APPRAISAL DIGEST, "**How About the Old House,**" *Real Estate Analyst Appraisal Bulletin,* October, 1956, pp. 17-20.

APPRAISAL DIGEST, "**How Much Is Your House Worth? Don't Trust Your Own Judgment; Rather, Hire an Appraiser,**" *Changing Times,* April, 1952, pp. 3-5.

APPRAISAL DIGEST, "**Minimum Size Houses Zoning Control,**" *Appraisal Digest,* January, 1953, pp. 5.

APPRAISAL DIGEST, "**More Prefabricated Houses, But Stiffer Competition,**" *House and Home,* December, 1955, pp. 22-24.

APPRAISAL INSTITUTE MAGAZINE, "**Check List for Habitability,**" *Appraisal Institute Magazine,* September, 1961, pp. 34-36.

APPRAISAL JOURNAL, "**$25-Million Colony House, 30-Story Apartment Building Being Erected In Fort Lee,**" *Appraisal Journal,* August 2, 1971.

APPRAISAL JOURNAL, "**40-Million-Dollar Condominium Complex Consisting of Two 40-Story Bldgs Starts to Rise In Honolulu,**" *Appraisal Journal,* May 31, 1971.

ARCHITECTURAL FORUM, "**Three Jinx In New Apartments,**" *Architectural Forum,* September, 1940, pp. 210-212.

ARDERN, WILLIAM B., "**The New Old Home,**" *Case Reports In Assessment Administration,* January, 1961, pp. 2-4.

ARDOUIN, LOUIS, "**Certification of Appraisers,**" *The Review,* Society of Residential Appraisers, January, 1938, pp. 6-8.

▲ **Urban Property**

ARMSTRONG, W. Y., "Insurance Valuations the Property Owners Responsibility," *Insurance Valuations,* The American Society of Appraisers, Washington, D. C, 1971, pp. 8-18.

ARNESON, HARRY R. JR., "Using Comparables In Court," *The Residential Appraiser,* October, 1957, pp. 3-6.

ATKINSON HARRY GRANT, "The Process of Appraising Single-Family Homes," *The Appraisal Journal,* April, 1936, pp. 146-152.

BABCOCK, FREDERICK M., "Building Cost and Investment Estimation: House," *Valuation of Real Estate,* 1932, pp. 482, 495.

BABCOCK, FREDERICK M., "Examples of Appraisal Procedure House Property," *Valuation of Real Estate,* 1932, pp. 213-218.

BABCOCK, FREDERICK M., "On Appraisal of Old Houses," *Appraisal of Real Estate,* New York City, 1924, pp. 207-212.

BABCOCK, FREDERICK M., "The Appraisal System of the FHA," *Review of the Society of Residential Appraisers,* December, 1936, pp. 3-5.

BABCOCK, FREDERICK M., "The Selection of Mortgages," *The Residential Appraisers Review,* September, 1935, pp. 5-7.

BABCOCK, FREDERICK M., "Valuation of Returns Details of Valuation Pocedure Houses," *The Valuation of Real Estate, Ed. 1,* 1932, pp. 320-395.

BAIRD, JOHN W., "National Apartment House Market Outlook," *The Appraisal Journal,* April, 1964, pp. 209-213.

BALDWIN, H. G., "Appraising Buildings by the Cubic Foot Method," *Building Management and Maintenance,* August, 1926, pp. 30-32.

BALDWIN, H. G., "Comparative Methods In Establishing the Value of Buildings," *Proceedings 15th Annual Convention,* Mortgage Bankers Association of America, 1928, pp. 127-137.

BALL, WILLIAM H., "Residences In Russia," *The Residential Appraiser,* April, 1959, pp. 9-11.

BALLARD, WILLIAM S., "Appraising the Single House from Three Approaches," *Appraisal Digest,* October, 1955, pp. 22-24.

BANK OF AMERICA APPRAISAL DEPARTMENT, "Cost Data Single Family Residence," *Technical Valuation,* June, 1961, pp. 7-25.

BAPPERT, JOSEPH, "Appraisal of a Split Level House," *Real Estate Analyst Appraisal Bulletin,* 1958, pp. 351-356.

BARETTE, L. A., "Opposite Sides of the Tracks," *The Residential Appraiser,* July, 1957, pp. 6-8.

BARNARD, BOYD T., *Background for Appraising Old Homes,* Freehold, December, 1939, pp. 414-416.

BARNARD, BOYD T., "The Appraisal of Old Homes," *The Appraisal Journal,* January, 1940, pp. 42-49.

BASCH, JACOB, *Manual of Reproduction Cost Data of Residential Buildings,* Oak Glen, 1933.

BAZAN, HORACE B., "Activity Report of F. H. A. Fee Appraisals," *Technical Valuation,* October, 1958, pp. 20, 24.

BEARDEN, THOMAS H., "Multi-Family Dwellings," *The Real Estate Appraiser,* October, 1965, pp. 27-34.

BEARDEN, THOMAS H., "The Income Approach In Appraising Apartments," *The Real Estate Appraiser,* October, 1963, pp. 15-23.

BEATON, WILLIAM R., "The Detached House Condominium," ULI, Washington, D. C., March, 1970.

BECHERER, RICHARD W, "How to Determine the Feasibility of an Apartment Project," *Valutapes Audio-Library Series,* American Society of Appraisers, Washington D.C., January 1, 1973.

BECK, FRITZ W., "Appraisal of an Elevator Apartment Property," American Institute of Real Estate Appraisers, *Appraisal Reporting Techniques,* 1947, pp. 86-104.

## BIBLIOGRAPHY OF APPRAISAL LITERATURE

BECKER, ALVIN G. AND ARTHUR E. WARNER, "**Condominium,**" *A. S. A. Valuation Manual,* American Society of Appraisers, 1964.

BEEHLER, GEORGE W. JR., "**Colored Occupancy Raises Values,**" *The Review,* September, 1945, pp. 3-6.

BEILHARZ, ALFRED J., "**Appraising an Apartment House,**" *Practical Appraising Methods,* 1940, pp. 53-54.

BELL, FRED A., "**Insulation,**" *The Review,* November, 1947, pp. 14-18.

BEMAN, ARTHUR K., "**Economic Analysis of Apartment House Construction,**" *Appraisal Journal,* April, 1900, pp. 176-179.

BENNETT, K. W., "**Modular Homes: Now Is the Hour,**" *Iron Age,* February 18, 1971, pp. 39-40.

BENNETT, SAUL Z., "**A Student's Appraisal Report on an Apartment House,**" *A Student's Appraisal Report on an Apartment House,* American Institute of Real Estate Appraisers, Chicago, 1966.

BENNETT, SAUL Z., "**Correlation and Value Conclusion,**" *A Student's Report on an Apartment House,* American Institute of Real Estate Appraisers, Chicago, 1966, pp. 19.

BENNETT, SAUL Z., "**Cost Approach,**" *A Student's Appraisal Report on an Apartment House,* American Institute of Real Estate Appraisers, Chicago, 1966, pp. 15.

BENNETT, SAUL Z., "**Description the Property,**" *A Student's Appraisal Report on an Apt House,* American Institute of Real Estate Appraisers, Chicago, 1966, pp. 13.

BENNETT, SAUL Z., "**Market Data Approach,**" *A Student's Report on an Apartment House,* American Institute of Real Estate Appraisers, Chicago, 1966, pp. 31.

BENNETT, SAUL Z., "**Record Data,**" *A Student's Report on an Apt House,* American Institute of Real Estate Appraisers, Chicago, 1966, pp. P-9.

BENNETT, SAUL Z., "**The Neighborhood,**" *A Student's Appraisal Report on an Apartment House,* America Institute of Real Estate Appraisers, Chicago, 1966, pp. 3.

BENNETT, SAUL Z., "**Qualifications of the Appraiser,**" *A Student's Report on an Apartment House,* American Institute of Real Estate Appraisers, Chicago, 1966, pp. 23.

BLOOD, J., "**Community Family Centers: Taking a Bigger Slice of Chicago Sales,**" *Merchandising Week,* August 23, 1971, pp. 14.

BLUM, MAYER I., "**Privately-Built Apartment Buildings,**" *The Appraisal Journal,* April, 1950, pp. 231-236.

BLUMBERG, AARON, MELNICOFF, STERN, OSCAR I, "**Philadelphia Survey of New Home Sales,**" *The Appraisal Journal,* April, 1951, pp. 243-245.

BODFISH, MORTON, HOYT, HOMER, "**The Housing Demand Source,**" *The Review,* January, 1949, pp. 14.

BODFISH, MORTON, THEOBALD, A. D, "**Appraising the Duplex or Double House, Two-Flat and Three-Flat,**" *Real Estate Fundamentals,* 1941, pp. 9-10.

BOECKH, EVERARD HEREFORD, "**Costs-Apartment Buildings,**" *Boeckh's Manual of Appraisals,* pp. 147.

BOECKH, EVERARD HEREFORD, "**Costs-Institutional Buildings,**" *Manual of Appraisals,* pp. 49.

BOECKH, EVERARD HEREFORD, "**Costs/Residences,**" *Manual of Appraisals,* pp. 49.

BOECKH, EVERARD HEREFORD, "**Small Stores and Combination Stores and Apartments,**" *Manual of Appraisals,* pp. 128.

BOECKH, EVERARD HEREFORD, "**Valuation of Large Old-Style House Under New Analytic System of Measurement,**" *Practical Appraising Methods,* 1940, pp. 39-44.

## Urban Property

BOECKH, EVERARD HEREFORD, "What Is the True Value of the Apartment-Garage Combination," *American Building Association News,* June, 1937, pp. 344-345.

BONTJES, JOHN H., "Factory-Built Houses," *The Real Estate Appraiser,* February, 1947, pp. 3-8.

BOURLAND, FREDERICK B., "How Long Do Houses Live," *The Review of the Society of Residential Appraisers,* January, 1939, pp. 3-8.

BRODNAX, A. CARROLL, "Apartment Planning and Design," *The Real Estate Appraiser,* November, 1962, pp. 5-7.

BROERSMA, WILLIAM T., "Guide to Small Home Specs," *The Review,* January, 1953, pp. 10-13.

BROERSMA, WILLIAM T., "Planning Larger Homes," *The Review,* December, 1953, pp. 14-15.

BRUEGGEMAN, WILLIAM BERNARD-PH. D., *The Impact of Private Construction and Government Housing Programs In a Local Housing Market,* Ohio State University, 1970.

BUCKLEY, ROBERT, DON M. SOULE, "Effects of Work and Residence Locations on Family Tax Burdens In Kentucky," University of Kentucky, 1971, pp. 22.

BUSINESS WEEK, "Pumping Money Into Housing," *Business Week,* September 26, 1970, pp. 66-67.

BYERS, JOHN, R. B., "Relationship Between the Value of the House and the Lot," *Residential Appraisers Review,* 1935, pp. 3-5, 15.

CAMPBELL, GEORGE L., "Prefabs Valued by Income," *The Review,* November, 1946, pp. 15-17.

CHANDLER, RICHARD A., "Condominiums," *Assessment Administration,* IAAO, Chicago, 1962, pp. 108-112.

CHAPMAN, GORDON J., "Public Acceptance of Prefabricated Housing," *The Appraisal Journal,* January, 1954, pp. 57-66.

CHURCH, BYRON, "The Crystal Ball Gazer," *The Residential Appraiser,* January, 1960, pp. 23-24.

CHURCH, BYRON M., "Special Consideration In Appraising Duplex Residences," *The Residential Appraiser,* October, 1957, pp. 19-20.

CLARK, HORACE F., "Appraising the Newly Finished House," *Appraising the Home,* 1930, pp. 129-151.

CLARK, HORACE F., "Appraising the Old House," *Appraising the Home,* 1930, pp. 105-121.

CLARK, HORACE F., "Method of Computing Depreciation of a Single-Family Frame Dwelling," *Appraising the Home,* 1930, pp. 375.

CLARK, HORACE F., "Practical Methods of Appraising Houses," *Appraising the Home,* 1930, pp. 96-104.

CLARK, LOUIS M., "The Real Estate Condominium, Its Tax Problems Andimplications," *The Appraisal Journal,* October, 1967, pp. 481-486, 490-492.

CLURMAN, DAVID, "The Condominium Program," *Appraisal Digest,* March, 1965, pp. 18-23.

COHEN, B. I., "Another Theory of Residential Segregation," *Land Economics,* August, 1971, pp. P. 314-315.

COHN, ALEXANDER, "Condominiums In Israel," *The Appraisal Journal,* January, 1967, pp. 88-101.

COTTON, W. OWEN, "Extending Substitution," *The Residential Appraiser,* February, 1958, pp. 8-9.

COWARD, WILLIAM, *Old American Houses—1700-1850,* McCann.

CRAFT, D. JAMES, MARJORIE A. BILLINGS, "Apartment Rents Is Yours In Line," *Utah Economic and Business Review,* University of Utah, November, 1971, pp. 1-3, 6.

DALGETY, GEORGE S., "Appraising Luxury Homes," *The Appraisal Journal*, October, 1950, pp. 526-529.

DALGETY, GEORGE S., "Mortgage Appraisals of Single Family Residences," *The Appraisal Journal*, July, 1952, pp. 382-387.

DANAHEY, THOMAS P., "Survey of Housing Facilities In Detroit Indicates Need of Home Building," *The Appraisal Journal*, October, 1935, pp. 471-474.

DAVIDSON, JAMES R., C. D. DAVIDSON, "Appraisal of a 13-Flat Building," *The Appraisal Journal*, July, 1934, pp. 344-354.

DAVIS, D. B., "A Method of Valuing Homesites," *National Real Estate Journal*, January 6, 1930, pp. 45-46.

DAVIS, IRWIN, STANLEY HAMILTON, "Condominiums: a Comparative Analysis," *Appraisal Institute Magazine*, January, 1969, pp. 53-57.

DAVIS, J. TAIT, "Middle Class Housing In the Central City," *The Appraisal Journal*, April, 1966, pp. 273-286.

DERBES, MAX J. FR., "Return Requirements of the Apartment Investment," *The Real Estate Appraiser*, August, 1963, pp. 16-25.

DERBES, MAX J. JR., "Gross Income Multiple of the Apartment," *The Real Estate Appraiser*, October, 1963, pp. 29-30.

DERBES, MAX J. JR., "Reliability of Comparable Sales," *The Residential Appraiser*, March, 1961, pp. 20-22.

DITCHY, CLAIR W., "Modern Residential Design," *The Review*, May, 1947, pp. 3-5.

DOELGER, WILLIAM E. P., "Planning a New Apartment House," *Appraisal Digest*, July, 1958, pp. 21-24.

DOHERTY, RICHARD M., "The Growing Problem of Relocation," *The Real Estate Appraiser*, February, 1963, pp. 20-25.

DOLAN, THOMAS A., "The Case History of an Apartment House," *The Appraisal Journal*, October, 1947, pp. 487-491.

DRISCOLL, T. LORIN, "Judging Prefab Market Value," *Appraisal Digest*, 1957, pp. 10-11.

DUBOIS, AYERS J., "Severance Damage to an Apartment Site," *The Appraisal Journal*, January, 1933, pp. 153-166.

DUBOIS, AYERS J., "The Long-Term Lease As an Instrument of Home Finance," *The Appraisal Journal*, October, 1943, pp. 354-366.

DUNCAN, KENNETH, "Can You Read Blue Prints... Ability to Do So Tells What the House Will Be Like," *Appraisal Digest*, January, 1952, pp. 15-17.

DUNHAM, HOWARD W. JR., "Gross Income Estimate of the Apartment," *The Real Estate Appraiser*, 1963, pp. 2-11.

DUNN, DOMINICK R., "Our Glass Houses," *The Real Estate Appraiser*, 1970, pp. 39-41.

DUNN, DOMINICK R., "The Miracle House," *The Residential Appraiser*, January, 1962, pp. 8, 13.

DYKE, JOHN B., "Assessment of Condominiums," *Assessment Administration*, Institute of American Assessment Officers, Chicago, 1963, pp. 239-281.

EBERHARDT, DUANE O., "Real Estate Price Escalation In Selected Residential Areas of Flagstaff, Arizona," *Arizona Business Journal*, Northern Arizona University, 1971, pp. 21-22.

EDDINS, ROBERT E., "Appraisal of a Walk-Up Apartment Property," *Appraisal Reporting Techniques*, American Institute of Real Estate Appraisers, 1947, pp. 105-118.

EIKMEYER, LEO J., "Analyzing the High-Rise Apartment," *The Appraisal Journal*, July, 1966, pp. 444-448.

ELLER, HERBERT D., "Appraisal of a Retail Store-Apartment Property," *Appraisal Reporting Techniques*, American Institute of Real Estate Appraisers, pp. 73-85.

▲ Urban Property

ELLWOOD, L. W., "Analysis and Reconstruction of Operating Statements of Elevator Apartments," *Real Estate Appraisal Practice*, American Institute of Real Estate Appraisers, pp. 125-130.

ELLWOOD, L. W., "Analysis and Reconstruction of Operating Statements of Walk-Up Apartments," *The Appraisal Journal*, October, 1957, pp. 521-526.

ELLWOOD, LEON W., "Apartment Earning Experience," *The Appraisal Journal*, April, 1949, pp. 246-251.

EMERSON, DONALD M., "Typical Operating Expenses for Apartments," *Technical Valuation,* July, 1968, pp. 47-58.

EMERSON, F. C., "Valuation of Residential Amenities: an Econometric Approach," *Appraisal Journal*, April, 1972, pp. 268-277.

ENTREKEN, HENRY C. JR., "A Short Commentary on Apartment Appraisals," *The Real Estate Appraiser*, November, 1962, pp. 2-4.

ENTREKEN, HENRY C. JR., "Appraising Apartments for Mortgage Lenders," *The Appraisal Journal*, October, 1965, pp. 531-536.

EVANS, DONALD D., "Condominiums," *The Appraisal Journal*, July, 1964, pp. 339-344.

EXPRESS PUBLISHING CO., *San Antonio, Texas Average Value of Dwelling Units for Block Areas, by Blocks, 1950*, Express Publishing Co., San Antonio, 1952.

FIELD, RALPH V., *What Price Home*, Freehold, September 1, 1937, pp. 158-159.

FISHER, ERNEST M., "Appraisal of Old Houses," *Principles of Real Estate Practice*, 1923, pp. 116-130.

FISK, KENNETH, "A Tale of Lands and Buildings," *The Appraisal Journal*, February, 1956, pp. 16-22.

FORD, JAMES, "Appraising for Multi-Family Housing Projects Appraising for Condemnation," *Slums and Housing*, Harvard University Press, Cambridge, 1936, pp. 529-540.

FORD, JAMES, "Bibliography of Housing Bibliographies," *Slums and Housing*, Harvard University Press, Cambridge, 1936, pp. 1000-1002.

FOSSLER, DUANE M., "Apartment Construction and Cost," *The Appraisal Journal*, June, 1962, pp. 11-12.

FOWLER, G., "Property Owners on Resort Areas Find it Very Difficult to Rent Their Summer Homes," *N.Y. Times Index*, July 5, 1970.

FRANTZEN, HAROLD G., "Appraising the Old House," *Appraisal Digest*, July, 1954, pp. 14-16.

FREEBRUG, CHARLES H., "Prefab Progress," *The Review*, April, 1955, pp. 8-11.

FULLERTON, PAUL, "Depreciation In Residential Buildings," *Real Estate Analyst Appraisal Bulletin*, 1957, pp. 335-338.

GALLAGHER, JOSEPH A. SR., "The House Is Larger Than the Desk," *Technical Valuation*, A. S. A, June, 1954, pp. 3.

GALUSH, ROBERT J., "Types of Factory-Built Homes In the Midwest," *The Real Estate Appraiser*, November, 1970, pp. 21-25.

GELBAND, J. F., "Sale of a Cooperative Apartment," *Magazine of Wall Street*, May 22, 1971, pp. 34.

GELLER, CARL, "Home Building In Europe," *The Review*, October, 1949, pp. 1 3-6.

GENNACO, FRANK, "Demonstration Appraisal an Old Dwelling," *Assessment Administration*, I. A. A. O, Chicago, 1957, pp. 22-23.

GIBBONS, J. E., "Feasibility Study-Apartments," *Appraisal Institute Magazine*, Appraisal Institute of Canada, Winnipeg.

GIBBONS, JAMES E., "Apartment Feasibility Studies," *The Appraisal Journal*, July, 1968, pp. 331-332.

GILL, WILLIAM J., "Dwelling Depreciation," *The Residential Appraiser*, December, 1961, pp. 9-11.

# BIBLIOGRAPHY OF APPRAISAL LITERATURE

GLOS, HAROLD V., "Valuation of a 38-Unit Apartment Building In a Well-Developed District," *Practical Appraising Methods*, 1940, pp. 82-85, 128.

GODFREY, RICHARD G., "Duplexes Triplexes Quadruplexes a Sound Real Estate Investment," *Residential Appraiser*, May, 1960, pp. 8-10.

GOLDMAN, ARTHUR SWORN, "The Economics of Quality Homes," *The Residential Appraiser*, July, 1959, pp. 16-24.

GOLDMAN, THEORDORE M., "Apartment Construction Quality Versus Costs," *The Appraisal Journal*, July, 1969, pp. 330-336.

GOOD, FREDERICK H., ROBERT J. DUNHAM, "The Demand for Apartments In Mature Communities," *The Appraisal Journal*, April, 1964, pp. 230-236.

GORDON, G. W. E., "The Impact of Prefabrication on the Canadian Home Industry," *Appraisal Institute Magazine*, December, 1960, pp. 24-27.

GOTTLIEB, M., "New Measures of Value of Nonfarm Building U.S.A. Annually, 1850-1939," *The Review of Economics and Statistics*, University of Wisconsin, U. S. A, November, 1965.

GRANFIELD, MICHAEL EDWARD PH. D., "An Econometric Model of Residential Location," 1970.

GREENE, ALFRED J. JR., "High Rise Apartment House," *Assessment Administration*, I. A. A. O, Chicago, 1961, pp. 212-219.

GROGAN, JAMES J., "Three Concepts In Appraising a Store and Apartment Building," *Practical Appraising Methods*, 1940, pp. 188.

GROVES, RICHARD N., "Appraising the Split-Level House," *Appraisal Digest*, October, 1954, pp. 6-7.

GRUNDMEIER, HAROLD H., "Appraisal of a Custom-Built Home," *Assessment Administration*, I. A. A. O, Chicago, 1963, pp. 208-217.

GRUNERT, HAROLD F., "The Ultra-Modern Home," *Appraisal Digest*, January, 1955, pp. 1-3.

GUINEY, JOSEPH, "Case Report on Walk-Up Apartments," *Assessment Administration*, Chicago, 1964, pp. 174-178.

HACKETT, F. HUNTER, "The Market Trend for Luxury Homes," *The Review*, January, 1951, pp. 3-7.

HAGOOD, WAYNE D., "Units Of Comparison," *The Residential Appraiser*, September, 1962, pp. 17-24.

HALEY, HARRY B., "The Clock Ticks Nowhere As it Does at Home," *The Appraisal Journal*, January, 1953, pp. 67-78.

HAMILTON, RAYMOND WARREN, *The Public Housing Program In the United States: an Analysis and Evaluation*, University of Maryland, 1971.

HANFORD, LLOYD D., "Apartment Building Income and Expense Analysis," *The Appraisal Journal*, January, 1964, pp. 35-37.

HANFORD, LLOYD D. SR., "Condominium Feasibility Study, Planning from the Ground Up," *Journal of Property Management*, Institute of Real Estate Management, Chicago, May, 1969.

HARRIS, WILLIAM W., "Our Changing Population and the Apartment Market," *The Real Estate Appraiser*, November, 1963, pp. 24-31.

HARTMAN, T. W., "Valuation of Luxury Homes," *A Study In Depreciation*, Office of County Assessor, Los Angeles, 1941.

HATFIELD, SAMUEL M., *An Evaluation of Land Use and Dwelling Unit Data Derived from Aerial Photography*, Division of Highways, Urban Research Section, Chicago, September, 1962.

HENDRICKS, ROBERT W., "The Saga of the Split-Level," *The Residential Appraiser*, August, 1957, pp. 3-9.

HEUCK, ROBERT, "Cincinnati Method of Establishing Reconstruction Costs of Dwellings," *The Appraisal Journal,* July, 1934, pp. 303-308.

HIBBEN, JAMES B., "Renewal's Riddle: the Three-Story Walk-Up," *The Appraisal Journal,* July, 1965, pp. 357.

HILTON, HOLLAND, "The Appraisal of Condominiums," *The Real Estate Appraiser,* July, 1967, pp. 2-8.

HO, CHIN, "Cooperative Apartments and Condominiums," *The Appraisal Journal,* October, 1961, pp. 529-531.

HOLLEBAUGH, CLIFFORD W., "The Appraisal of a Mansion," *The Residential Appraiser,* June, 1962, pp. 15-18.

HOME OWNER'S LOAN CORPORATION, "Effect on Home Values of Appraisals by the Home Owner's Loan Corporation," *Federal Home Loan Bank Review,* January, 1935, pp. 119-123.

HOPKINS, ROBERT W., "Old Houses Present Problems," *Appraisal Digest,* July, 1951, pp. 19-20.

HORTON, GEORGE S., "Valuation of a Typical 6-Story Elevator Apartment House In Brooklyn," *Practical Appraising Methods,* 1940, pp. 55-56.

HOUSE & HOME, "There Are No Inside St In This 17-Acre Condominium," *House & Home,* September, 1971, pp. 40.

HOUSE AND HOME, "Modular House Draws Crowds to New York City Museum," *House and Home,* November, 1970, pp. 26.

HOYT, HOMER, "Expressways and Apartment Sites," *The Appraisal Journal,* January, 1959, pp. 103-106.

HUGHES, R. G., "Home Builders Plea," *The Review,* October, 1953, pp. 3-6.

HYNES, G. DEWEY, "Appraising and Financing Home Today," *The Review,* September, 1948, pp. 21-24.

INTERNATIONAL ASSOCIATION OF ASSESSING OFFICERS, *Appraisal of a Garden Apartment,* Chicago, Illinois.

INTERNATIONAL ASSOCIATION OF ASSESSING OFFICERS, *Guidelines for Appraising Condominiums,* Chicago, Illinois.

JACKSON, FREDERICK W., "Buyer's Choice of Down Payments," *The Residential Appraiser,* February, 1959, pp. 23-24.

JACOBSEN, NORMAN, "Computerized Apartment House Appraisal," *California Real Estate Magazine,* California Real Estate Board, California, January, 1970.

JENNETT, C. B., "The Valuation of Farm Homes," *Appraisal Journal,* January, 1934, pp. 108-111.

JOHNSON, LEEVERN, "The Appraisal of Homes," *The Appraisal Journal,* October, 1956, pp. 511-517.

JOHNSON, RALPH J., "Research and Home Building," *The Real Estate Appraiser,* February, 1964, pp. 26-31.

JOHNSTON, GEORGE C. JR., "How to Appraise an Old House," *Long Island Realty Magazine,* August, 1941, pp. 4, 9.

JOHNSTONE, W. GORDON, "What's Happening to the Value of Mansions," *Appraisal Digest,* January, 1951, pp. 23-24.

KAZDIN, S. EDWIN, "The Six-Story Elevator Apartment Building," *The Appraisal Journal,* October, 1935, pp. 433-436.

KEEFER, E. D., "Risk Rating Homes," *Review of Society of Residential Appraisers,* January, 1938, pp. 3-5.

KEEGAN, NORMAN J., "The Home Owner Vs. the Condemner Appraiser," *The Residential Appraiser,* January, 1962, pp. 21-23.

KEENE, J., "Convert it to a Condominium," *House and Home,* January, 1971, pp. 106-111.

KELLER, HARRY K., "The Appraisal of the Garden Type Apartment," *Valuation,* April, 1950, pp. 6-10.

KELLEY, JOHN F., "Residences and Freeways," *The Appraisal Journal,* October, 1957, pp. 505-520.

KELLEY, WILLIAM T., "How Buyers Shop for a New Home," *The Appraisal Journal,* April, 1957, pp. 209-214.

KELLY, W. T., "Marketing Research and House Design," *The Appraisal Journal,* April, 1960, pp. 235-241.

KENDALL, LEON T., NORMAN W. STRUNK, "Home Buying Patterns," *The Residential Appraiser,* January, 1959, pp. 22-24.

KENNEDY, DAVID O D., "Two-Story House Described As Most Economical," *Appraisal Digest,* October, 1953, pp. 14-16.

KENNEDY, JOHN P., "Appraisal of Old Houses," *Basis of Real Estate Values,* 1925, pp. 39-54.

KERN, JAMES M., "Why Quality Counts," *The Residential Appraiser,* January, 1957, pp. 7-8.

KINNARD, DR. WILLIAM N. JR. , SRA, MAI, *A Guide to Appraising Apartments,* Society of Real Estate Appraisers, Chicago, April, 1966.

KINNARD, WILLIAM N. JR., "The Peculiarities of Apartment Appraisals," *Valuation,* September, 1966, pp. 5-12.

KISSACK, A. B., "A Single-Family Dwelling," *Real Estate Analyst Appraisal Bulletin,* 1948, pp. 89-92.

KNIGHT, C., "Military Launches Housing Attack-First Modulars Move In with General Electric In Command," *House and Home,* February, 1971, pp. 20.

KNISKERN, PHILIP W., "Practical Suggestions for Appraising Homes," *National Association of Real Estate Boards,* 1927, pp. 186-223.

KNISKERN, PHILIP W., "The Field of the Real Estate Counselor," *The Residential Appraiser,* pp. 14.

KNOWLES, JEROME, *Single Family Residential Appraisal Manual,* AIREA, Chicago, 1967.

KOENIG, JOHN JR., "Housing to Fit Budgets," *The Review,* September, 1949, pp. 16-17, 23.

KUEHNLE, WALTER R., "Appraisal of a Single Family Residence," *Appraisal Reporting Techniques,* 1947, pp. 9-14.

KUEHNLE, WALTER R., "Valuation of Vacant Lot Suitable at Future Date for Multi-Story Apartment Development," *Practical Appraising Methods,* 1940, pp. 70-74.

LAFFOON, A. L., "Demonstration Appraisal, a One Story Building and Parking Lot," *Technical Valuation,* Pueblo, Colorado, pp. 30-43.

LALLI, F., "Modular Housing: the Phantom That Parades As an Industry," *House and Home,* June, 1970, pp. 64-75.

LANE, JOHN W., "New Treatment of Private Dwelling Depreciation," *Appraisal Digest,* April, 1961, pp. 10-11.

LANEY, T. D., "Condominiums," *Skyscraper Management,* June, 1970, pp. 10-13.

LARONGE, JOSEPH, "Valuation of a 20-Unit Apartment Building with Attached Garage In a Suburban District," *Practical Appraising Methods,* 1940, pp. 59-62.

LAUNER, E. J., "Cost Breakdown-Dwelling, Garage and Porch," *Technical Valuation,* A. S. A, November, 1952, pp. 40.

LAUNER, E. J., "Cost Breakdown-Medium Dwelling," *Technical Evaluation,* A. S. A, Washington, February, 1952, pp. 43.

LAURENTI, LUIGI, "Effects of Nonwhite Purchases on Market Prices of Residences," *The Appraisal Journal,* July, 1952, pp. 314-329.

LEGAS, FRANCES K., "Small Apartments In Seattle," *The Real Estate Appraiser,* February, 1960, pp. 16-20.

LEMON, RALPH B., "Cost Approach for Apartment Buildings," *The Real Estate Appraiser,* November, 1965, pp. PP, 2-13.

▲ Urban Property

LEVY, MARK, "Appraisal of a Three-Story and Full-Basement Brick Store and Apartment Building In Chicago," *Mcmichael S. I. Appraising Manual, Second Edition,* 1937, pp. 478-489.

LEWE, JOHN C. JR., "Winter Inspections," *The Residential Appraiser,* February, 1959, pp. 3-4.

LIPMAN, M. RONALD, "The Market Approach In the Appraisal of Garden Apartments," *The Real Estate Appraiser,* July, 1963, pp. 36-39.

LIPPMAN, WILLIAM J., "Legal Problems of Condominiums," *The Appraisal Journal,* October, 1962, pp. 458-464.

LIVINGSTON, MAXINE, "Living In a Contemporary House," *The Residential Appraiser,* November, 1957, pp. 3-8.

LOCKWOOD, A. N., "Appraising a Single-Family Home," *The Appraisal Journal,* October, 1950, pp. 493-497.

LOCKYER, ALBERT W., "Appraisal of Luxury Dwellings," *The Appraisal Journal,* April, 1958, pp. 181-185.

LUEDTKE, WALDEMAR W., "An Appraisal of a Mansion-Type Home," *Assessment Administration,* I. A. A. O, Chicago, 1964, pp. 168-173.

LUEDTKE, WALDEMAR W., "The Modern Mansion--Big Value, Small Market," *Case Reports In Assessment Administration,* February, 1960.

LUM, T. T., "Feasibility Analysis of Condominiums," *Appraisal Journal,* April, 1972, pp. 246 252.

LYON, ROBERT L., "A New Home on the Fringe of an Older Area," *The Review,* February, 1946, pp. 3-6.

LYON, ROBERT L., "Analyze New Homes for Future Sales Appeal," *The Review,* August, 1945, pp. 6-9.

MACEACHRON, KEITH E., "The Appraiser and Corporate Employee Transfer Plans," *The Residential Appraiser,* December, 1961, pp. 2-8, 23.

MACLEOD, R. J., "The Condominium In Canada," *The Real Estate Appraiser,* May, 1971, pp. 29-35.

MACROSSIE, WILLIAM, "Appraising Cooperative Apartments," *Appraisal Digest,* 1953, pp. 5-8.

MAISEL, SHERMAN J., "Have We Underestimated Increases In Rents and Shelter Expenditures," *The Journal of Political Economy,* April, 1949, pp. 106-117.

MANFIELD, W. S., "Model Apartment Appraisal," *National Real Estate Journal,* July 21, 1930, pp. 46-49.

MANN, WINSTON S., "Valuation of Homes In Later Stages of Economic Life," *The Real Estate Appraiser,* American Institute of Real Estate Appraisers, Chicago, May, 1964, pp. 34.

MARCUM, VINCENT L., "Demonstration Appraisal of a Ninety-Eight Unit Apartment Project," *Technical Valuation,* October, 1959, pp. 13-22.

MARSHALL, J. W., "Residence Costs-An Approach," *Technicalities,* June, 1951, pp. 10-11.

MARTIN, T. MAXMILLIAN, "The Valuation of Converted Apartment Buildings," *The Real Estate Appraiser,* April, 1960, pp. 12-14.

MATTER, J. AUBREY, "Appraisal of a Restored Home," *Assessment Administration,* Institute of American Assessment Officers, Chicago, 1963, pp. 190-207.

MAY, ARTHUR A, *The Valuation of Residential Real Estate,* Prentice-Hall, Inc, New York, 1953, pp. 3.

MAY, ARTHUR A, "Appraising the Home," *The Appraisal Journal,* October, 1951, pp. 498-502.

MAY, ARTHUR A, "Appraising the Home," *The Appraisal Journal,* July, 1951, pp. 314-323.

MAY, ARTHUR A, "Appraising the Home," *The Appraisal Journal,* January, 1951.

MAY, ARTHUR A, "Appraising the Home, II," *The Appraisal Journal,* April, 1951, pp. 225-232.

MAY, ARTHUR A, "Let's Look at Appraisals," *Review of Society of Residential Appraisers,* June, 1940, pp. 2-5.

MAY, ARTHUR A., "Streamlining the Appraisal Business," *Review of the Society of Residential Appraisers,* March, 1937, pp. 6-9.

MAY, ARTHUR A., "The Appraisal Report," *Valuation of Residential Real Estate,* 1942.

MAYER, GEORGE E., "The Market Approach In Residential Appraising," *Appraisal Digest,* April, 1961, pp. 23-24.

MAYHEW, ROBERT R., "Amenity Factors In Establishing a Cap Rate," *The Residential Appraiser,* September, 1960, pp. 13-14.

MCCALLUM, ANGUS, "The Architect's View of the Responsibilities of the Appraiser," *Residential Appraiser,* February, 1961, pp. 18-22.

MCCARTHY, CHARLES R., "New Store Building Attached to Old Farm Building and Three Apartment Dwelling," *Assessment Administration,* Institute of American Assessment Officers, Chicago, 1961, pp. 220-226.

MCCORMICK, LORING O., *Factors Affecting Apartment House Valuation,* Los Angeles, January 28, 1937.

MCCROSKY, T. T., "Today's Subdivision Problems," *Review of Society of Fesidential Appraisers,* November, 1941, pp. 7-10.

MCCURDY, ROBERT V., "Estimating the Cost of Residential Construction," *Technical Valuation,* June, 1962, pp. 5-10.

MCCURDY, ROBERT V., "Functional Obsolescence In Small Houses," *The Review,* March, 1956, pp. 3-7.

MCCUTCHEON, W. B., "Beyond the Serviced Suburbs," *The Residential Appraiser,* September, 1957, pp. 22-24.

MCDONALD, A. M., "Appraising Residential Property," *The Appraisal Journal,* April, 1953, pp. 258-266.

MCDONALD, ADRIAN F., "Practical Applications of Appraisal Fundamentals," *The Residential Appraiser,* February, 1960, pp. 3-8.

MCDONALD, ADRIAN F., "Principles of Land Use," *The Residential Appraiser,* April, 1959, pp. 3-7, 11.

MCDONALD, ADRIAN F., "Rules In Condemnation," *The Residential Appraiser,* January, 1958, pp. 3-7.

MCDONALD, ADRIAN F., "The Appraiser In the Witness Box," *The Residential Appraiser,* December, 1958, pp. 13-17.

MCGOVERN, JOHN E., "Appraisal of Large-Scale Suburban Projects," *The Appraisal Journal,* April, 1940, pp. 140-146.

MCGUINESS, EDWARD J., "Assessing Luxury Homes In Beverly Hills," *Assessors Journal,* October, 1968.

MCINTOSH, KENNETH W., "Coaching the Expert," *The Residential Appraiser,* September, 1958, pp. 13-17.

MCKAY, E. O., "Apartment Building Management," *Appraisal Institute Magazine,* Appraisal Institute of Canada, Winnipeg.

MCKELDIN, THEODORE R., "Ethical Valuations for Effective State Government," *The Residential Appraiser,* January, 1958, pp. 9-10.

MCKIBBIN, FRANK B., "Appraising for Lending Institutions," *Residential Appraiser's Review,* October, 1935, pp. 6-15.

MCLAUGHLIN, FRANK, "On Severance Damages to an Apartment Site by Dubois," *The Appraisal Journal,* April, 1933, pp. 254-255.

MCMICHAEL, STANLEY L., "Appraising Furnished Apartment Houses," *Appraising Manual,* 1937, pp. 151-159.

MCMICHAEL, STANLEY L., "Appraising Homes," *Appraising Manual,* 1937, pp. 317-330.

MCNULTY, CHARLES S., "The Appraisal of Super-Adequate Residences," *Assessors Journal,* January, 1969.

MELAMED, ANSHEL, "High-Rent Apartments In the Suburbs," *The Appraisal Journal*, April, 1962, pp. 279-289.

MERTZKE, ARTHUR J., "Appraising the Market Value of a House," *National Real Estate Journal*, October 27, 1930, pp. 34-37.

MERTZKE, ARTHUR J., "On Appraisal of Old Houses," *Real Estate Appraising a Ten-Lesson Course, Chapter Xi*, 1927.

MILLER, KENNETH C. JR., "Built In Traffic Controls---Master Key to Livable House," *The Residential Appraiser*, September, 1962, pp. 14-16.

MITCHELL, KENNETH F., "Land Planning for Residences," *The Review*, July, 1954, pp. 16-18.

MORGAN, BELDEN, "A Demonstration Appraisal," *Residential Appraiser's Review*, March, 1936, pp. 7-9.

MORRELL, JOSEPH C., "Method of Appraising Garden Apartment Is Illustrated," *Appraisal Digest*, July, 1951, pp. 5-6.

MOSBY, WILLIAM E., "Appraising Single Family Residences," *Appraisal Journal*, April, 1935, pp. 253-258.

MOSBY, WILLIAM E., "Methods of Appraising Single Family Residence," *Residential Appraisers Review*, June, 1935, pp. 6-7. 12.

MULLENIX, C. A., "Reviving the Profit of Old Buildings," *National Real Estate Journal*, March, 1934, pp. 33-34.

MURRAY, WILLIAM H., "Used Houses," *The Review*, December, 1955, pp. 3-6. 10.

N. Y. TIMES INDEX, "Community Tensions Aroused by Heritage Village, $100-Million Condominium Developmt for Elderly South," *The N. Y. Times Index*, May 6, 1970.

N. Y. TIMES INDEX, "Ground Broken for $10-Million Co-Op Apartment House on Park Avenue," *N. Y. Times Index*, October 11, 1970.

N. Y. TIMES INDEX, "Yale Univ Architectural Students' Conversion 1-Rm Apt Over Garage Into Spacious Living Quarters," *N. Y. Times Index*, January 25, 1970, pp. 71.

NATIONAL ASSOCIATION OF REAL ESTATE BOARDS, "Life Expectancy Table of Three Classes of Dwelling by Types of Construction," Clard, H. F., *Appraising the Home*, 1930.

NATIONAL REAL ESTATE JOURNAL, *How the HOLC Is Valuing Homes*, January, 1934, pp. 21-22.

NATIONAL REAL ESTATE JOURNAL, "Actual Appraisal Reports - Small Walk-Up Apartment Building," *National Real Estate Journal*, April 13, 1931, pp. 42-44.

NATIONAL REAL ESTATE JOURNAL, "Actual Appraisal Reports - Valuation of 25-Year Old Store," *National Real Estate Journal*, Octobr 26, 1931, pp. 21-23.

NATIONAL REAL ESTATE JOURNAL, "Actual Appraisal Reports: Valuation for Reorganization Purposes of 7-Story Kitchenette Apartments," *National Real Estate Journal*, April, 1933, pp. 29-30.

NEISWANGER, DAVID, "Appraising Residential Real Estate In 1947," *The Appraisal Journal*, January, 1947, pp. 79-86.

NEISWANGER, DAVID, "Appraising Single-Family Homes," *National Real Estate Journal*, November, 1937, pp. 41-42.

NEISWANGER, DAVID, "Appraising the Small Home," *The Appraisal Journal*, April, 1937, pp. 124-129.

NELSON, HENRY PH. D., *The Theory of Residential Location*, Princeton University, 1971.

NELSON, R. L., "FHA Operating Expense Data In 608 Housing," *The Appraisal Journal*, January, 1957, pp. 8-21.

NELSON, ROBERT V., "The Heat Pump In a Home," *The Review*, April, 1950, pp. 3-6.

NORTH, E. G., "The One-Family House-A Perennial Appraisal Headache," *The Appraisal Journal*, April, 1954, pp. 163-167.

NORTH, E. G., "Multifamily Housing-Appraising Today's Cliff Dwellings," *The Appraisal Journal,* January, 1955, pp. 7-13.

NORTH, E. G., "Multifamily Housing-Appraising Today's Cliff Dwellings," *The Appraisal Journal,* April, 1955, pp. 190-195.

NORTH, E. G., "The One-Family House-A Perennial Appraisal Headache," *The Appraisal Journal,* July, 1954, pp. 330-335.

NORTH, E. G., "The One-Family House-A Perennial Appraisal Headache," *The Appraisal Journal,* October, 1954, pp. 525-530.

NORTH, E. G., "The One-Family House-A Perennial Appraisal Headache," *The Appraisal Journal,* January, 1962, pp. 7-15.

NORTH, E. G., "The One-Family House-A Perennial Appraisal Headache," *The Appraisal Journal,* January, 1954, pp. 7-14.

NORTH, E. G., "The One-Family House-A Perennial Appraisal Headache," *The Appraisal Journal,* July, 1962, pp. 373-379.

NORTH, E. G., "The One-Family House-A Perrenial Appraisal Headache," *The Appraisal Journal,* October, 1962, pp. 509-514.

NORTH, E. G., "The One-Family House-A Perrennial Appraisal Headache," *The Appraisal Journal,* April, 1962, pp. 225-232.

NOWICKI, JOSEPH A., "Dangers In Apartment Appraisals," *The Real Estate Appraiser,* January, 1964, pp. 5-12.

NYE, JAMES L., "Counseling an Owner," *The Review,* August, 1952, pp. 10-15.

OKEEFE, RAYMOND T., "Financial Aspects of Condominiums," *The Appraisal Journal,* October, 1962, pp. 465-469.

OGBURN, WILLIAM F., "The Changing Family," *The Appraisal Journal,* October, 1936, pp. 400-407.

OGUR, DAVID JONATHAN, PH. D., *The Impact of Colleges and Universities on Local Rental Housing Markets,* Cornell University, 1970.

OLAVE, OSCAR A., "Valuacion De Condominios," *Boletin,* Sotave, Caracas, Venezuela, pp. 17.

OPELKA, F. GREGORY, "Apartment Appraising Needs Income Approach," *The Real Estate Appraiser,* December, 1967, pp. 13-19.

OPELKA, F. GREGORY, "Appraising Condominiums," *The Real Estate Appraiser,* March, 1970, pp. 15-25.

OPELKA, F. GREGORY, "Condominium Value Does Not Equal Sales Price," *Real Estate Appraiser,* March, April, 1971, pp. 43-44.

OPELKA, F. GREGORY, "Home Loan Appraisal Problems," *Wisconsin Colloquium on Appraisal Research, Papers and Proceedings,* 1963, pp. 33-37.

OPELKA, F. GREGORY, "Market Data Approach on Apartments," *The Real Estate Appraiser,* September, 1963, pp. 19-22.

OSBORN, FRANK K., "Don't Underestimate the Single Family Residence," *The Real Estate Appraiser,* SREA, Chicago, July, 1964, pp. 17.

OSBORN, FRANK K., "The Income Approach In Appraising Apartments," *The Real Estate Appraiser,* June, 1965, pp. 9-18.

OWEN, THORNTON W., "Points to Investigate for Apartment Appraisals," *The Review,* June, 1946, pp. 22-24.

OWEN, WILFRED, "Cities In the Motor Age," Cooper Square Publishers Inc., New York, N. Y..

OWENS-CORNING FIBERGLAS, "The Tenant's Point of View," *Urban Land,* February, 1970.

▲ Urban Property

PAGANO, WILLIAM B., "The Big Weakness In Factory Made Houses," *Appraisal Digest*, October, 1954, pp. 8-9.

PALMER, ALFRED W., "Valuation of a 50-Unit Apartment Building In Anoutlying District," *Practical Appraising Methods,* 1940, pp. 66-67.

PAPAGEORGIOU, GEORGE J. AND EMILIO CASETTI, *Journal of Regional Science,* University of Pennsylvania, December, 1971, pp. 385-389.

PARKER, W. C., "Residential Improvements on Commercial Property," *Appraisal Institute Magazine,* Appraisal Institute of Canada, Winnipeg.

PAUL, SAMUEL, "Apartments Their Design and Development," *The Real Estate Appraiser,* January, 1969, pp. 48-49.

PEACOCK, GEORGE R., "The Appraisal Processes and the Condominium," *The Appraisal Journal,* July, 1964, pp. 345-351.

PINTO, EDWIN, *How to Buy a House,* San Jose State College, August 6, 1971.

PODELL, BERTRAM L., AND S. HERBERT, "Valuation of Condominiums for Real Estate Tax Purposes," *Real Estate Forum,* November, 1969.

POLLEY, JOSEPH H., "Anatomy of a House," *The Real Estate Appraiser,* November, 1968, pp. 40-45.

POLLEY, JOSEPH H., "Loss-Of-Setback Tables for Residential Buildings," *The Real Estate Appraiser,* Society of Real Estate Appraisers, Chicago, October, 1966, pp. 13.

PRATT, DOROTHY AND RICHARD, *A Guide to Early American Homes - South,* Mcgraw-Hill.

PRATT, LOUIS M., "Appraising Fractional Parts of Residential Property," *Review of the Society of Residential Appraisers,* March, 1937, pp. 10-13.

PRATT, LOUIS M., "Racial Restrictions and Their Effect on Valuation," *Review of Society of Residential Appraisers,* April, 1939, pp. 13-51.

PRENTICE, PERRY, "The Power to Appraise," *The Residential Appraiser,* May, 1960.

PRENTICE, PERRY F., "Home of Tomorrow," *The Residential Appraiser,* pp. 18.

PRESSLEY, LESTER N., "Demonstration Appraisal A 1956 Residence," *Assessment Administration,* Institute of American Assessment Officers, Chicago, 1957, pp. 15-21.

PRICE, JAMES R., "Typical Prefab Buyers," *The Review,* April, 1956, pp. 8-9.

PROUTY, W. L. AND OTHERS, "Analysis of Cost, Apartment Buildings," *Appraisers and Assessors Manual,* 1930, pp. 30.

PROUTY, W. L. AND OTHERS, "Apartment Houses," *Appraisers and Assessors Manual,* 1930, pp. 150-161.

PROUTY, W. L. AND OTHERS, "Residence Buildings," *Appraisers and Assessors Manaul,* 1930, pp. 104-109.

R. G. RIDKER, G. A. HENNING, "Determinants of Residential Property Values with Special Reference to Air Pollution," *Review of Economics and Statistics,* May, 1967, pp. 246-257.

RAMS, EDWIN M., "Investment Dynamics-Multi-Family Units," *Appraisal and Valuation Manual,* American Society of Appraisers, 1961, pp. P 111-120.

RANDELL, MURRAY E., "Why I Would Build an All-Electric Building," *The Appraisal Journal,* October, 1966, pp. 552-561.

REAL ESTATE ANALYST, THE, "A Better Method for Finding Reproduction Cost of Typical Residences," *Real Estate Analyst Appraisal Bulletin,* pp. 361-368.

REAL ESTATE ANALYST, THE, "A. P. H. A. Method of Appraising Housing Structures," *Real Estate Analyst Appraisal Bulletin,* 1951, pp. 443-448.

REAL ESTATE ANALYST, THE, "Construction Costs on an 8-Family Garden-Type Apartment," *Real Estate Analyst Bulletin,* 1961, pp. 557-562.

REAL ESTATE ANALYST, THE, "Estimating the Value of Porches," *Real Estate Analyst Appraisal Bulletin,* 1953, pp. 461-464.

REAL ESTATE ANALYST, THE, "Measuring Quality of Housing and Environment," *Real Estate Analyst Appraisal Bulletin,* 1951, pp. 363-366.

REAL ESTATE ANALYST, THE, "Reproduction Cost of a Standard Brick Ranch House," *Real Estate Analyst Appraisal Bulletin,* 1952, pp. 441-444.

REAL ESTATE ANALYST, THE, "Residential Construction Costs," *Real Estate Analyst Appraisal Bulletin,* 1950, pp. 337-354.

REAL ESTATE APPRAISER, "A Demonstration of the Three Approaches to Value of a Low-Rise Apartment Building," *The Real Estate Appraiser,* July, 1970, pp. 18-28.

REEVES, CUTHBERT E., "Appraising Residential Property," *Appraising Residential Property--Methods Cost Data & Instr Espec Helpful to Appraisers for Underwrit,* Cuthbert E. Reeves, Buffalo, 1934.

REGISTER, J. ALVIN, "Appraisal of a One Story Store Building," *Mcmichael, S. L. Appraising Manual,* 1937, pp. 1-652.

RESIDENTIAL APPRAISER, "Proximity Study No. 3," *The Residential Appraiser,* January, 1962, pp. 16-20.

REVIEW, THE, "Commerical Uses Enter a Residential Area," *The Review,* January, 1950, pp. 14-16.

REYNOLDS, FRANK G., "Appraisal of a Three-Flat," *The Review,* May, 1946, pp. 17-22.

REYNOLDS, KIRK, "Five Types of Costly Appraisal Mistakes," *Review of Society of Residential Appraisers,* January, 1938, pp. 11-13.

RITLEY, ROGER D., "Measurement of Effective Demand for Multifamily Housing," *Appraisal and Valuation Manual,* pp. 73-88.

ROBB, JOSEPH A., "Measure of Depreciation and Obsolescence In Luxury Dwellings," *Appraisal and Valuation Manual,* 1962, pp. 188.

ROESCH, RICHARD R., "A Discussion of Condominium Legislation with Particular Reference to the Michigan Act," *Assessment Administration,* Instituteof American Assessment Officers, Chicago, 1963, pp. 143-152.

ROWLSON, JOHN F., "Mobile Home Parks-Techniques and Procedures," *The Real Estate Appraiser,* July, 1965, pp. 25-31.

SARLES, KENNETH E., "How to Use Market Data In the Appraisal of Apartment Buildings," *Real Estate Appraisal Practice,* 1958, pp. 131-138.

SATHER, KENT N., "Analyzing Apartment Market Characteristics," *Journal of Property Management,* September, 1970.

SCHLITT, CARL D., "History of Condominiums," *The Appraisal Journal,* October, 1962, pp. 453-457.

SCHNEIDER, GEORGE A., "On Appraisal of Old Houses," *California Real Estate Principles and Practices,* 1927, pp. 487-489.

SHATTUCK, CHARLES B., "Appraising Single-Family Homes," *The Appraisal Journal,* January, 1935, pp. 118-129.

SHATTUCK, CHARLES B., "What Price the American Home," *The Appraisal Journal,* October, 1933, pp. 34-41.

SHELGER, KURT S., "Motivation of Four-Units Buyers," *The Residential Appraiser,* September, 1957, pp. 13-18, 21.

SHENKEL, WILLIAM M., "Cash Flow and Multiple Regression Techniques; Comparative Anal of Apt Properties," *Journal of Property Management,* November, 1969.

SHIMMON, R. E., "An Appraisal of a Commercial Condominium," *The Appraisal Journal,* July, 1964, pp. 352-357.

SIMMONS, MERCER W., "Testing for the Highest and Best Use," *The Residential Appraiser,* December, 1962, pp. 6-8.

SLADE, LESTER P., *Appraisal of Old Homes,* New York State Society of Real Estate Appraisers, Albany, 1940.

SMETHURST, R. G., "The When, Why, What, Where and How of Condominiums," *Appraisal Institute Magazine,* pp. 2-7.

SMITH, G. A., "Who's Building the Modulars," *House & Home,* June, 1971, pp. 46-59.

SMITH, LEVIE D. JR., "Property Analysis and Functional Utility In Appraisal of the Single Family Home," *The Residentail Appraiser,* April, 1961, pp. 2-5.

SMITH, WILLIAM B., "Appraisal of Condominiums," *The Real Estate Appraiser,* September, 1964, pp. 2-12.

SOCIETY OF REAL ESTATE APPRAISERS, *A Guide to Appraising Residences,* Society of Real Estate Appraiser, Chicago, 1904.

SOCIETY OF RESIDENTIAL APPRAISERS, *Review of the Society of Residential Appraisers,* The Valuation of Residential Real Estate, Chicago, Ill..

SPRING, TERRENCE, "Daily Public Relations," *The Residential Appraiser,* January, 1989, pp. 13.

STERLING, H. ALBERT, "Neighboring Factors Affecting Residential Values," *The Appraisal Journal,* January, 1960, pp. 81-89.

STEWART, W. C., "Apartment Management," *The Real Estate Appraiser,* November, 1962, pp. 13-16.

STUDDARD, KENNETH E., "Tax Aspects of Apartment Ownership," *The Residential Appraiser,* July, 1962, pp. 13-16.

SURVEY RESEARCH CENTER, UNIVERSITY OF MICHIGAN, "Buyer Prefeerences Surveyed," *The Review,* Housing and Home Finance Agency, February, 1953, pp. 7.

SWENSSON, EARL S., "A Fresh Look at Apartment Design," *The Real Estate Appraiser,* January, 1961, pp. 13-18.

TECHNICAL BULLETIN, "Apartment Communities--The Next Big Market," *Technical Bulletin,* Urban Land Institute, Washington, D. C, pp. 61.

THALER, D., "Built for Sale Apartments: a Threat to You," *House and Home,* September, 1970, pp. 68-73.

THALER, D., "You Can Make Money In Low Income Rural Housing," *House And Home,* June, 1970, pp. 84-88.

THEISS, WILLIAM R., "The Appraisal Docket. Inclusion of Apartment Building Furnishings In Award," *The Appraisal Journal,* April, 1962, pp. 290-297.

THEOBALD, A. D., "The Small House Is Good Security," *The Review,* October, 1950, pp. 9-11.

THERA, JOHN M., "The Uninformed Buyer," *The Residential Appraiser,* March, 1959, pp. 3-5, 10.

THOMAS, C. L., "Fundamental Considerations In Appraising Homes," *Review of Society of Residential Appraisers,* January, 1941, pp. 9-13.

THULMAN, ROBERT K., "The Floor Furnace In Small Homes," *The Review,* February, 1950, pp. 10-12.

TOURTELOT, ROBERT H., "Separate Assessment of Condominiums," *Hastings Law Journal,* February, 1963, pp. 289-301.

URBAN LAND INSTITUTE, *New York's First School-Apartment House,* Urban Land Institute, Washington, July, 1967.

WAGNER, J. J., "Appraising Used Homes for Listing Purposes," *National Real Estate Journal,* December 8, 1930, pp. 16-20.

WAGNER, PERCY E., "Appraisal of Small Multifamily Apartments," *The Appraisal Journal,* July, 1958, pp. 379-384.

WAGNER, PERCY E., "Condominiums," *The Appraisal Journal,* January, 1964, pp. 7-20.

WAGNER, PERCY E., "Living In the Sky, Condominium Homes," *Appraisal Institute Magazine,* 1970, pp. 25-31, 38.

WALTHER, H. O., "Appraising Single and Two-Family Residences," *National Real Estate Journal,* December, 1937, pp. 33-35.

WALTHER, HERMAN O., "Appraisal of a Single-Family Residence," *Appraisal Reporting Techniques,* 1954, pp. 239-256.

WAYTAS, R. E., "Factory Built Housing," *The Real Estate Appraiser,* November, 1970, pp. 19-20.

WEAVER, HOWARD SILAS, *City Residential Appraising,* Weaver School of Real Estate, Kansas City Missouri, 1962.

WEED, KENNETH A., "How to Analyze Apartment Building Neighborhoodsand Develop Rent Schedules," *Real Estate Appraisal Practice,* 1958, pp. 105-116.

WEED, KENNETH A., "How to Use Cost Data In the Appraisal of Apartment Buildings," *Real Estate Appraisal Practice,* 1958, pp. 139-151.

WEIMER, ARTHUR M., "Current Appraisal Economics," *The Residential Appraiser,* July, 1959, pp. 3-5.

WEIMER, ARTHUR M., "Location and Cycle Factors In Mortgage Risk," *Review of Society of Residential Appraisers,* February, 1938.

WELLS. H. C., "Apartment Management Is a Misnomer the Term Should Be Apartment Marketing," *House and Home,* December, 1970, pp. 44.

WELLS, H. C., "Insurance Companies Are Getting Some Great Apartment Deals at the Housing Industrys Expense," *House and Home,* September, 1970, pp. 46.

WENDT, PAUL F., SUI N. WONG, "Investment Performance, Common Stocks Versus Apartment Houses," *Journal of Finance,* December, 1965, pp. 633-646.

WENZLICK, ROY, "The Tremendous Demand for Housing In the Next Few Decades," *The Appraisal Journal,* January, 1964, pp. 97-107.

WESMAN, HARVEY, "Market Evidence of Depreciation In Single-Family Homes," *The Appraisal Journal,* July, 1969, pp. 341-343.

WHITE, JOHN R., "Significance of Governmental Intervention In the Housing Market," *The Appraisal Journal,* April, 1955, pp. 165-176.

WHITE, JOHN ROBERT, "Apartment Living on the Wane," *The Appraisal Journal,* January, 1956, pp. 20-22.

WHITE, ROBERT B., "Case Report In Assessment Administration-Two Apartments Over a Small Store," *Special Publication,* Institute of American Assessment Officers, Chicago, April, 1971, pp. 41-47.

WHYTE, WILLIAM H. JR., "Rx for Urban Sprawl," *The Residential Appraiser,* February, 1958, pp. 10-16.

WHYTE, WILLIAM H., JR., "What's Wrong with City Homes," *The Residential Appraiser,* August, 1957, pp. 16-24.

WILLIAMS, ROBERT M., "An Index of Asking Prices for Single Family Dwellings," *The Appraisal Journal,* January, 1954, pp. 33-38.

WILLIAMS, ROBERT M., "Fluctuations In Residential Building In the United States and Six Cities, 1918-1934," *The Appraisal Journal,* April, 1956, pp. 195-207.

YALE LAW JOURNAL, "Toward an Equitable and Workable Program of Mobile Home Taxation," *Yale Law Journal,* March, 1962, pp. 702-719.

YELLOTT, JOHN I., "Solar Heating for Homes," *The Residential Appraiser,* September, 1958, pp. 18-22.

ZANGERLE, JOHN A., "On Appraisal of Old Houses," *Principles of Real Estate Appraising*, Cleveland, 1924.

*A Guide to Appraising Apartments,* Society of Real Estate Appraisers, 1965.

*A Students Appraisal Report on a Single-Family Residence,* American Institue of Real Estate Appraisers, 1964.

*Appraising Apartment Buildings,* California Real Estate Association, 1966.

*Case Studies In Apartment House Valuation,* American Institute of Real Estate Appraisers, 1969.

*Condominiums In Connecticut A Survey of Residential Condominium Developments,* University of Connecticut, October, 1971.

*Econometric Model of Residential Location,* Duke University, 1970.

*Trends of Office Building Design and Comparative Operating Studies of New and Old Buildings,* American Institute of Real Estate Appraisers.

"Actual Appraisal Reports: No. 1 Valuation of Small Store, Apartment and Office Property," *National Real Estate Journal,* January 19, 1931, pp. 12-16.

"Actual Appraisal Reports: No. 16 Valuation of Vacant Lot," *National Real Estate Journal,* November 9, 1931, pp. 24-28.

"Atmosphere-Coronado Cays, a Waterfront Community with Carribbean Character," *House and Home,* May, 1971, pp. 92-95.

"Building Management, Uses Human In Tenant Relations Program," *Skyscraper Management,* July, 1970, pp. 17-18.

"Buildings Under Sonic Boom," *The Residential Appraiser,* November, 1958, pp. 18-21.

"Contemporary Hilltop House That's Selling Well to Young Working Couples," *House and Home,* 1971, pp. 44.

"Contemporary Ideas for the Built-For-Sale House," *House and Home,* September, 1970, pp. 82-87.

"Crash Program From Ground Breaking to Model Apartments In Ten Weeks," *House and Homes,* September, 1971, pp. 36-3.

"Design for Privacy: it Rents These Apartments Faster Than They Can Be Built," *House and Home,* January, 1971, pp. 84.

"Detached Townhouses Add an Extra Dimension to Narrow Waterfront Lots," *House and Home,* December, 1970, pp. 42.

"Family Apartments," *House and Home,* November, 1970, pp. 68-72.

"Ford Decides to Get Out of Modular Housing," *Engineering News-Record,* September 3, 1970, pp. 41.

"Four-Story Apartment Building That Saves Its Glamour for an Interior Court," *House and Home,* July, 1970, pp. 34.

"Housing Partnership Makes First Investment," *Engineering News Record,* October 22, 1970.

"How to Avoid a Uniform Look In a Row of Almost Uniform Duplex Houses," *House and Home,* January, 1971, pp. 82.

"How to Put Life Into Flat Apartment Sites," *House and Home,* June, 1970, pp. 76-83.

"Lightweight Steel Framing Breaks the Three Story Barrier for These Apartments," *House and Home,* January, 1971, pp. 70.

"Mobile Modular," *House and Home,* June, 1970, pp. 56-63.

"Modular Housing: No Shell Game," *Financial World,* January 6, 1971, pp. 6..

"Modular Plan Cuts Cost on These Beach Front Apartments In California," *House and Home,* June, 1970, pp. 40.

"Nations Largest Pre-Fabber Proposes a Modular High Rise System," *House and Home,* June, 1970, pp. 38.

## BIBLIOGRAPHY OF APPRAISAL LITERATURE

"New Modular High-Rise System That Goes Up on Jacks a Story at a Time," *House and Home,* January, 1971, pp. 58.

"Patio Villas Are First Part of a New Resort Community at Hilton Head Island," *House and Home,*

"Perini Corp to Erect Condominium Apts on Land it Owns In Chamberslanding on Lake Tahoe," *The New York Times Index,* February 1, 1900.

"Prebuilt Homes Come a Long Way," *Business Week,* July 18, 1970, pp. 27.

"Precast Concrete Panel System Cuts Condominium Construction Time In Half," *House and Home,* October, 1970, pp. 34.

"Rentals or Condominiums," *House and Home,* April, 1972, pp. 82 87.

"Single-Family Residential Appraisal Manual," American Institute of Real Estate Appraisers.

"This Leisure-Oriented Apartment Project Draws on an Upper-Income Market," *House and Home,* September, 1970, pp. 44.

"To Get the Facts on Aluminum Framing, Ryan Homes Puts Up a Prototype House," *House and Home,* September, 1970, pp. 34.

"Washington Suburbs Fight Plan to Rescue Townhouse Project by Renting it to the Poor," *House and Home,* May, 1971, pp. 20.

"7 Keys to Making it In a Tough Market," *House and Home,* September, 1970, pp. 62-67.

"8 Projects That Set a Standard for Government-Subsidy Housing," *House and Home,* December, 1970, pp. 66-78.

"Actual Appraisal Reports: Valuation of New House of Med Size Located In Baltimore Residential Subdiv," *National Real Estate Journal,* July 6, 1931, pp. 32-35.

## 13-20 Commercial Buildings

ABERTHAW CO., *Cost of Industrial Building Index,* Aberthaw Co., Construction Managers, Boston.

ALDIS, GRAHAM, "Income Factors In the Appraisal of Office Building," *Real Estate Appraisal Practices,* American Institute of Real Estate Appraisers, Chicago, 1958, pp. 259-272.

ALDIS, GRAHAM, "Rating the Office Building," *The Appraisal Journal,* October, 1940, pp. 325-331.

ALDIS, GRAHAM, "Some Fresh Facts About Office Building Operations," *The Appraisal Journal,* January, 1957, pp. 89-90.

ALDIS, GRAHAM, "Statistical Tools for the Office Building Appraiser," *The Appraisal Journal,* April, 1952, pp. 243-246.

ALDIS, GRAHAM, "The Appraiser and the Office Building," *The Appraisal Journal,* January, 1950, pp. 91-96.

ALLINGHAM ALLISON P., "The Appraisal of Warehouses," *The Appraisal Journal,* October, 1938, pp. 354-357.

AMERICAN APPRAISAL CO., "Mill Building Detail Cost Brick Mill Building Table," *Appraisers and Assessors Manual,* W. L. Prouty and Others, 1930.

AMERICAN INSTITUTE OF REAL ESTATE APPRAISERS, *Trends In Office Building Design and Comparative Operating Studies of New and Old Building,* American Institute of Real Estate Appraisers, Chicago, 1900.

AMERICAN INSTITUTE OF REAL ESTATE APPRAISERS, "Appraisal of a Block Front of Retail Business With Offices Above," *Demonstration Appraisal Reports,* American Institute of Real Estate Appraisers, Chicago, 1957, pp. 326-363.

AMERICAN INSTITUTE OF REAL ESTATE APPRAISERS, "Appraisal of the Place Building," *Demonstration Appraisal Reports,* American Institute of Real Estate Appraisers, Chicago, 1957, pp. 245-292.

AMERICAN SOCIETY OF PLANNING OFFICIALS, *Civic Center Planning,* Chicago, 1900.

ARMSTRONG, ROBERT H., "An Approach to Office Building Valuation," *The Apraisal Journal,* January, 1940, pp. 9-22.

AYRES, J. M., "From the Ground Up Evolution of an Office Building, Building Operation Systems," *Skyscraper Management,* December, 1970, pp. PP16 20.

BABCOCK, FREDERICK M., "Earnings Revenue Expense Theater," *Valuation of Real Estate,* 1932, pp. 247-266.

BABCOCK, FREDERICK M., "Valuation of Returns Details of Valuation Procedure Theater," *The Valuation of Real Estate, Ed. 1,* 1932, pp. 306-380.

BABCOCK, HENRY A., "Appraising Income Property," *The National Real Estate Journal,* March 7, 1927, pp. 33-40.

BAILEY, GEORGE R., "Estimation of Accrued Depreciation In the Appraisal of Office Buildings," *The Appraisal Journal,* April, 1958, pp. 270-274.

BAILEY, GEORGE R., "Functional Design of Office Buildings," *The Appraisal Journal,* April, 1956, pp. 173-186.

BALDWIN, H. G., "Appraising Buildings by the Cubic Foot Method," *Building Management and Maintenance,* August, 1926, pp. 30-32.

BALDWIN, H. G., "Comparative Methods In Establishing the Value of Buildings," *Proceedings 15th Annual Convention,* Mortgage Bankers Association of America, 1928, pp. 127-137.

BALL, THOMAS B., "Buildings," *Church Valuation,* Church Valuation Consultants, 1968, pp. 15.

BAPPERT, JOSEPH, "Charting Income Properties," *Real Estate Analyst Appraisal Bulletin,* 1956, pp. 507-510.

BARTLETT, CHARLES R., "Demonstration Appraisal a Modern Office Building," *Assessment Administration,* IAAO, Chicago, 1957, pp. 47-67.

BECKER, GEORGE, "Valuation of Office Buildings," *The Appraisal Journal,* October, 1967, pp. 496-506.

BELL, FRED A., "Insulation," *The Review,* November, 1947, pp. 14-18.

BIGLER, S. H., "Office Rental Rates of Tomorrow," *The Appraisal Journal,* April, 1948, pp. 210-214.

BLDG MGRS & OWNERS ASSN OF NEW YORK, INC, "Taxation Committee, Survey of Depreciation of Office Structures In New York City,,' *Real Estate Record and Builders Guide,* June 30, 1928, pp. 8.

BOLER, F. C., "What Makes an Office Building Click," *The Appraisal Journal,* July, 1952, pp. 357-364.

BOUCHA, MARVIN E., "Demonstration Appraisals, a Fifty-Year-Old Office Building," *Assessment Administration,* IAAO, Chicago, 1957, pp. 69-77.

BRAVER, WILLIAM, WAGNER, ARTHUR R, "New Trends In Medical Facilities," *The Journal of Property Management,* March, 1971.

BROOKER, HERBERT D., "A Suggested Technique for the Appraisal of a Partial Taking from an Office Building," *Right of Way*, October, 1970, pp. 34-38.

BROWN, NORBERT, "Economic Life of Structural and Mechanical Parts of Office Buildings," *Real Estate Record and Builders Guide*, March 5, 1932, pp. 5-8.

BURCHFIELD, B. C., "The Appraisal of Warehouses," *The Appraisal Journal*, October, 1935, pp. 441-445.

BURTON, H. J., *Valuations and Depreciation of City Buildings*, Natl Assn of Bldg Owners & Mgrs, 1917.

CHURCH, EUGENE B., "The Effects of Variable Office Depth," *Real Estate Record and Builder's Guide,* January 23, 1923, pp. 5-8.

CLARK, ROBERT M., "Civic Tax Exemptions--The Edmonton Civic Center Plan," *The Appraisal Journal*, May, 1951, pp. 172-184.

CLAUS, R. JAMES, "Appraising Potential Volume of Shopping Site Sales," *Appraisal Institute Magazine*, Appraisal Institute of Canada, Winnipeg, September 1, 1971.

CLEVELAND ASSN OF BUILDING OWNERS AND MANAGERS, "Table on Obsolescence, Depreciation & Appreciation ; Economic Life, Kinds Office Bldgs & Allowances," *Appraising Manual*, pp. 67-38.

COBLEIGH, I. U., "Office Building Shares," *Commercial and Financial Chronicle*, January 14, 1971, pp. 123.

COFFIN, GEORGE H. JR., "Appraisal of a Commercial Building," *Appraising Manual*, S. L. McMichael, 1937, pp. 469-478.

COURTNEY, ALBERT J., "Operating Expenses of Office Buildings," *The Appraisal Journal*, October, 1956, pp. 527-534.

COWLEY, LEONARD M., "Appraisal of a Loft Building," *Appraisal Reporting Techniques*, American Institute of Real Estate Appraisers, 1951, pp. 125-151.

CRAWFORD, EDWARD J. JR., "Office Building Appraisals," *The Appraisal Digest*, October, 1952, pp. 21-22.

DAVIDSON, JAMES R., C. D. DAVIDSON, "Appraisal of a 13-Flat Building," *The Appraisal Journal,* July, 1934, pp. 344-354.

DAVIS, J. C., "More Market Orientation Asked for Office Building Appraisals," *Skyscraper Management,* March, 1971, pp. 18-19.

DRENNAN, SHELDON L., "Appraisal of a One-Story Factory Property," *Appraisal Reporting Techniques*, 1951, pp. 61-70.

EDMAN, J. J., "Valuation of Land Improved with Factory Buildings. Appraisal Docket," *The Appraisal Journal*, October, 1957, pp. 620-622.

EDMONDS, M. G., "Twin, Quad and Six-Plex No Longer Palaces, Movie Theaters Sport the Profitable Now Look," *Barrons,* June 28, 1971, pp. 11.

ENGINEERING NEWS-RECORD, "Conv Cen Acknowledges Parking Is Part of Overhead," *Engineering News-Record,* June 10, 1971, pp. 31.

EVERS, CECIL C., *The Commercial Problems In Buildings,* Record and Guide Co., New York, 1914.

FEATHERMAN, B. E., "Consider the Total Warehouses Concept for Maximum Profit, Efficiency," *Industrial Development and Manufactures Record,* July, 1970, pp. 14-16.

FISHER, ROBERT MOORE, "The Boom In Office Buildings," *Technical Bulletin 58 of the Urban Land Institute,* 1900.

FISK, KENNETH, "A Tale of Lands and Buildings," *The Appraisal Journal,* February, 1956, pp. 16-22.

FRANCOIS, WALDO E., "On Medical Clinics," *The Appraisal Journal,* April, 1965, pp. 296-298.

FREE, ROBERT L., *Demonstration Appraisal Multi-Story Factory,* The Society of Industrial Realtors, 1953, pp. 57-70.

▲ **Urban Property**

FREE, ROBERT L., "Appraisal of Medical Buildings," *The Appraisal Journal,* January, 1958, pp. 81-86.

GLOS, HAROLD V., "Valuation of a Leasehold Estate Involving a Stores Arcade and Office Buildings," *Practical Appraisal Methods,* 1940, pp. 94-97, 128.

GLOS, HAROLD V., "Valuation of a Small Store and Office Building In an Outlying Section," *Practical Appraising Methods,* 1940, pp. 82-85, 128.

GOTTLIEB, M., "New Measures of Value of Nonfarm Building U.S.A. Annually, 1850-1939," *The Review of Economics and Statistics,* University of Wisconsin, U. S. A, November, 1965.

GOULD, J. P., "Market Value and the Theory of Investment of the Firm," *American Economic Review,* February, 1967, pp. 42-49.

GRANT, ROSS, "The Los Angeles Plan for Determinining Office Rental Values," *Skyscraper Management,* June, 1934, pp. 14-15.

GRIFFITH, C. R., "Office Building Feasibility Study for Medium Size Metropolitan Areas," *Journal of Property Management,* November, 1969.

HART, GERALD T., "Analysis of Economic Background of Office Buildings," *Real Estate Appraisal Practice,* American Institute of Real Estate Appraisers, 1958, pp. 245-248.

HART, GERALD T., "Design, Materials, and Construction Cost Factors In the Appraisal of Office Buildings," *Real Estate Appraisal Practice,* American Institute of Real Estate Appraisers, 1958.

HART, GERALD T., "Economic Background of Office Building," *The Appraisal Journal,* April, 1961, pp. 207-212.

HASKETT, JACK, "Building Appraisal for Municipal Offices," *Municipal South,* January, 1965, pp. 15-16.

HENDERSON, JAMES D., "Office Buildings," *Real Estate Appraising,* 1931, pp. 225-249.

HERD, JOHN J., "A Broker's Observation on Office Buildings," *The Appraisal Journal,* July, 1961, pp. 328-332.

HERTEL, HENRY, *Banker's Scientific Appraisal System for Land and Buildings,* Bankers Appraisal Company, Cleveland, 1919.

HYDER, K. LEE, "Valuation of Modern 10-Story Office Building," *Practical Appraising Methods,* 1940, pp. 86-93.

JENNINGS, CHRISTOPHER R., "Predicting Demand for Office Space," *The Appraisal Journal,* July, 1965, pp. 377-382.

KEESLER, WILLIAM F., "Appraising Old Multi-Storied Industrial Properties," *The Appraisal Journal,* October, 1950, pp. 498-502.

KERLER, ROBERT G., "Appraisal of the Midway Theatre," *Appraisal Reporting Techniques,* 1949, pp. 103-120.

KERLER, ROBERT G., "Theatre Appraisals Involve Many Unusual Factors," *Appraisal Digest,* April, 1951, pp. 14-16.

KING, C. A., T. G. GRANT, "Office Building Appraisal," *Appraisal Reporting Techniques,* 1949, pp. 121-153.

KIRK, THOMAS W., "Unit Construction Costs for Commercial and Industrial Buildings," *Real Estate Analyst Appraisal Bulletin,* pp. 409-416.

KIRK, THOMAS W., "Unit Construction Costs for Commercial and Industrial Buildings," *Real Estate Analyst Appraisal Bulletin,* pp. 409-416.

KOBER, CHARLES A. JR., "Appraising an Office Building," *The Appraisal Journal,* October, 1950, pp. 487-492.

KRIEGER, LAWRENCE W., "Cost Vs. Value In a Monumental Office Building," *Assessment Administration,* Institute of American Appraisers Officers, Chicago, 1964, pp. 194-202.

KRUGER, RUDOLPH, "Valuation of Potential Business Sites," *Review Of the Society of Residential Appraisers,* November, 1939, pp. 12-14.

KUHN, GEORGE A., "Analysis of Office Building Expense," *The Appraisal Journal*, January, 1935, pp. 169-172.

LARONGE, JOSEPH, "Office-Building Income and Investment Relationships," *The Appraisal Journal*, July, 1940, pp. 211-221.

LAURIE, ALEX, KIPLINGER, D. C, NELSON, KENNARD S., "Commercial Flower Forcing, Cost of Production," *Ther Appraisal Jornal*, October, 1965, pp. 537-540.

LEVY, MARK, "Valuation of a Six-Story Office Building In a Small City," *Practical Appraising Methods*, 1940, pp. 98-101.

MACROSSIE, WILLIAM, "Appraisal of Income Property-Office Buildings," *Encyclopedia of Real Estate Appraising*, Friedman, Edith J, 1959, pp. 234-257.

MACROSSIE, WILLIAM, "Treatment of Excess Rentals on Commercial Properties," *Appraisal Digest*, July, 1950, pp. 14-16.

MATTHEWS, MYRON L., "Dow Building Cost Calculation and Valuation Guide," F. W. Dodge Corporation, New York, April, 1959.

MCELWEE, EUGENE, "Appraisal of an Office Building," *The Real Estate Appraiser*, May, 1965, pp. 14-22.

MCKAY, CHARLES WATSON, *Valuing Industrial Properties*, New York, 1922.

MCMICHAEL, STANLEY L., "Appraising an Office Building," *Appraising Manual*, 1937, pp. 133-150.

MCMICHAEL, STANLEY L., "Industrial and Warehouse Property Appraisals," *Appraisers Manual*, 1937, pp. 160-172.

MILNER, JOSEPH, "Appraisal of the Empire State Building," *American Society of Appraiser*, 1959, pp. 69-76.

NATIONAL REAL ESTATE JOURNAL, "Actual Appraisal Reports: Appraisal of 5-Story Office and Store Building In Suburb Cleveland," *National Real Estate Journal*, May 11, 1931, pp. 25-30.

NELSON, ROLAND D., "An Appraisal Guide to Appraising New and Older Office Buildings," *Technical Valuation*, December, 1967, pp. 42-45.

NESSER, RICHARD S., "Appraisal of a Warehouse," *Assessor's Journal*, January, 1969.

NESSER, RICHARD S., "Reorganization of New Haven Office," *Assessment Administration*, Institute of American Assessment Officers, Chicago, 1961, pp. 63-67.

PETERSON, CHARLES E. JR., "Valuation of Older Downtown Medical Office Bldgs," *Appraisal and Valuation Manual*, American Society of Appraisers, 1961, pp. 103-109.

PROUTY, W. L. AND OTHERS, "Life of Office Buildings," *Appraisers and Assessors Manual*, 1930, pp. 81.

PROUTY, W. L. AND OTHERS, "Store Buildings," *Appraisers and Assessors Manual*, 1930.

PROUTY, W. L. AND OTHERS, "Theater Building Construction," *Appraisers and Assessors Manual*, 1930, pp. 199-201.

PROUTY, W. L. AND OTHERS, "Warehouse Building Construction," *Appraisers and Assessors Manual*, 1930, pp. 211-216.

RANDALL, WILLIAM J., "Variations In Drug Store Rentals," *Real Estate Analyst Appraisal Bulletin*, 1957, pp. 443-446.

RANDELL, MURRAY E., "Trends In Office-Building Management," *The Appraisal Journal*, January, 1941, pp. 19-28.

RANDELL, MURRAY E., "Why I Would Build an All-Electric Building," *The Appraisal Journal*, October, 1966, pp. 552-561.

REAL ESTATE ANALYST, THE, "Constructions Costs on a Small Office Building," *Real Estate Analyst Appraisal Bulletin*, 1956, pp. 33-38.

REAL ESTATE ANALYST, THE, "How Much Are Vacant Theaters Worth," *Real Estate Analyst Bulletin*, 1959, pp. 411-414.

▲ Urban Property

REAL ESTATE ANALYST, THE, "Theaters for Rent or for Sale," *Real Estate Analyst Appraisal Bulletin,* 1952, pp. 163-170.

REIDY, MAURICE F., "An Office Building Is Worth Only a Fair Capitalization of Expected Net Income," *National Real Estate Journal,* June 10, 1929, pp. 21-24.

REVIEW, THE, "The Clinic," *The Review,* June, 1950, pp. 19-20.

RIVAROLA, CARLOS H., "Metodo Tasacion Por Pisos Y Departamentos," *Boletin,* Sotave, Caracas, Venezuela, pp. 5-10.

SARMA, L. V. L. N., K. S. H. RAO, "Leverage and the Value of the Firm," *Journal of Finance,* September, 1969, pp. 673-677.

SCHNEIDER, JOHN S., "Appraisal of Warehouses," *The Appraisal Journal,* January, 1961, pp. 41-46.

SELIGMAN, DANIEL, "The Future of the Office Building Boom," *The Real Estate Appraiser,* October, 1963, pp. 24-28.

SHERIDAN, LEO J., "Commercial and Office Buildings," *The Appraisal Journal,* February, 1947, pp. 367-374.

SHERIDAN, LEO J., "The Sheridan-Karkow Formula for Determining Rental Value of Office Space," *Skyscraper Management,* April, 1934, pp. 12-18, 12-14.

SHERIDAN, LEO J., "Trends of Office Space, Rentals, and Occupancy," *The Appraisal Journal,* April, 1940, pp. 111-120.

SHERIDAN, LEO J., "Valuing Office Building Space by the Formula Method," *The Economist,* July 14, 1933, pp. 11-12.

SOLIS-COHEN, J. JR., "New Considerations In Appraising Moving Picture Theatres," *The Appraisal Journal,* April, 1950, pp. 223-226.

STEVENS, FRANCIS K., "Relation of Land Value to Office Rentals," *Real Estate Record and Builders Guide,* February 28, 1942, pp. 5-7.

URBAN LAND INSTITUTE, *The Oakland Alameda County Coliseum Complex,* Urban Land Institute, Washington, January, 1965.

WALLACE, J. WAGNER, "Industrial Plant," *Assessment Administration,* IAAO, Chicago, 1961, pp. 194-204.

WEBB, A. JAY, "The Case for Old Industrial Buildings," *The Appraisal Journal,* July, 1963, pp. 408-411.

WEEKES, R. E., "Some Salient Factors Affecting Downtown Areas," *The Appraisal Journal,* October, 1959, pp. 561-564.

WELCH, KENNETH C., "The Relocation of Commercial Areas," *The Appraisal Journal,* January, 1949, pp. 45-52.

WOOD, J. D., "Industrialized Housing," *Appraisal Institute Magazine,* Appraisal Institute of Canada, Winnipeg, June 1, 1971.

*Trends of Office Building Design and Comparative Operating Studies of New and Old Buildings,* American Institute of Real Estate Appraisers.

"Actual Appraisal Reports: Demonstration Appraisal of 3-Story Store," *National Real Estate Journal,* May 25, 1931, pp. 28-31.

"Actual Appraisal Reports: No. 1 Valuation of Small Store, Apartment and Office Property," *National Real Estate Journal,* January 19, 1931, pp. 12-16.

"Actual Appraisal Reports: No. 4 Demonstration Appraisal of Building," *National Real Estate Journal,* March 2, 1931, pp. 30-34.

"Actual Appraisal Repts: Valuation of Phila Hotel & Apartment Propty for Purposes of Secrg Tax Reduct," *National Real Estate Journal,* National Realty Valuation Corporation, December, 1933.

"Buildings Under Sonic Boom," *The Residential Appraiser,* November, 1958, pp. 18-21.

"Enlarged Bus Terminal to Carry Office Tower," *Engineering News Record,* August 6, 1970, pp. 37.

## BIBLIOGRAPHY OF APPRAISAL LITERATURE

"Gas In Newest Sports Arena," *Public Utilities Fortnightly,* October 22, 1970, pp. 110.

"Medical Building, Design, Development, Management," *Institute of Real Estate Management,* Chicago, Illinois.

"Multipurpose Stadium Sports 680 Feet Dia Dome," *Engineering News Record,* April 1, 1971, pp. 13.

"New Modular High-Rise System That Goes Up on Jacks a Story at a Time," *House and Home,* January, 1971, pp. 58.

"Offices Can Rent Modern Art," *Office,* June, 1970, pp. 69-70.

"Offices In a Former Warehouse," *Administrative Management,* December, 1970, pp. 80-81.

"Offices of the Year for 1970 Landscaped Administration Building Wins First Award," *Administrative Management,* April, 1971, pp. 18-84.

"Planning Multi-Level Malls," *Chain Store Age,* June, 1970, pp. 13200.

"Systems Design Forestalls Buildings Obsolescence," *Engineering Newsrecord,* July 16, 1970, pp. 32.

# 13-21 Institutional Property, Buildings and Concerns

ALEXANDERSON, K. W., "Bank Branch Location Feasibility Analysis," *The Real Estate Appraiser,* July, 1969, pp. 43-48.

ALLINGHAM, ALLISON P., "Special Purpose Properties-Banking," *The Appraisal Journal,* October, 1932, pp. 78-79.

AMERICAN INSTITUTE OF REAL ESTATE APPRAISERS, "Case Study Courses In Real Estate Appraising at the University of Chicago," *Journal American Institute of Real Estate Appraisers,* January, 1936, pp. 26-34, 166-180.

AMERICAN SOCIETY OF PLANNING OFFICIALS, *Sign Regulation In the Central Business District,* Chicago, 1900.

ARMSTRONG, ROBERT H., "Observations on Branch Banking," *The Appraisal Journal,* April, 1956, pp. 223-236.

ASTROLENK B., "The Economics of Branch Banking," *Principles of Investments,* New York, 1930.

BABCOCK, FREDERICK M., "Examples of Appraisal Procedure Library," *Valuation of Real Estate,* 1932, pp. 218-222.

BABCOCK, FREDERICK M., "Public Buildings Valuation of Returns," *Valuation of Real Estate,* 1932, pp. 319-330.

BAINUM, ROBERT, "Nursing Home Appraisals," *The Appraisal Journal,* July, 1966, pp. 380-392.

BALDWIN, H. G., "Ethics of an Institutional Appraiser," *The Real Estate Appraiser,* 1900, pp. 6.

BALL, THOMAS B., "Art Glass Windows," *Church Valuation,* Church Valuation Consultants, 1968, pp. 169.

BALL, THOMAS B., "Bells," *Church Valuation,* Church Valuation Consultants, 1968, pp. 189.

▲ Urban Property

BALL, THOMAS B., "Church Terms," *Church Valuation*, Church Valuation Consultants, 1968, pp. 253.

BALL, THOMAS B., "Depreciation Guide," *Church Valuation*, Church Valuation Consultants, 1968, pp. 239.

BALL, THOMAS B., "How to Use the Manual," *Church Valuation*, Church Valuation Consultants, 1968, pp. 5.

BALL, THOMAS B., "Pipe Organ," *Church Valuation*, Church Valuation Consultants, 1968, pp. 185.

BALL, THOMAS B., "Symbolism," *Church Valuation*, Church Valuation Consultants, 1968, pp. 239.

BALL, THOMAS L., *Church Valuation*, Church Valuation Consultants, 1968.

BALL, THOMAS L., "Buildings," *Church Valuation*, Church Valuation Consultants, Hales Corner, 1968, pp. 15-148.

BALL, THOMAS L., "Construction Adjustment Factors," *Church Valuation*, Church Valuation Consultants, Hales Corners, 1968, pp. 11.

BALL, THOMAS L., "Pipe Organ," *Church Valuation*, Church Valuation Consultants, Hales Corners, 1968, pp. 185.

BANK ADMINISTRATION INSTITUTE LIBRARY, *Site Selection for New Bank Buildings*, Band Administration Institute Library, Park Ridge, 1900.

BAPPERT, JOSEPH, "The Cost and Value of Stained Glass Windows," *Real Estate Analyst Appraisal Bulletin*, 1959, pp. 531-534.

BARTLETT, CHARLES R., "Property Taxes In Texas School Districts," *Governor's Committee on Public School Education Mittee on Public School Education*, Dallas, 1969.

BELL, FRED A., "Insulation," *The Review*, November, 1947, pp. 14-18.

BELL, THOMAS L., "Art Glass Windows Considered In Valuation," *Church Valuation*, Church Valuation Consultants, Hales Corners, 1968, pp. 169-175.

BEMAN, ARTHUR K., "Appraising Hospitals," *The Appraisal Journal*, April, 1949, pp. 204-208.

BERG, G. H., "Evaluation of a Hospital As a Long-Term Borrower," *Financial Analysts Journal*, March, 1971, pp. 23-32.

BERRERA, STEPHEN F., "Appraising for Savings Banks," *Appraisal Digest*, April, 1950, pp. 16.

BODNAR, ERNEST B., "City-University Cooperative Relationships," *Management Information Service*, November, 1964.

BONBRIGHT, JAMES CUMMINGS, "The Valuation of Property," Mcgraw-Hill Book Co., Inc., N.Y. and London, 1937.

BOUCHA, MARVIN E., "Skilled Nursing Home Evaluation," *The Appraisal Journal*, January, 1966, pp. 45-47.

BOWEN, PERCIVAL V., "Valuation of Church Cemeteries," *The A. S. A. Valuation Manual*, American Society of Appraisers, 1964, pp. 205.

BOYESEN, LOUIS K., "A Bank's Real Estate Loan Department," *The National Real Estate Journal*, November 11, 1929, pp. 26-29.

CASTELLANOS, JOSE N., "Catastro Y Hacienda Publica," *Boletin*, Sotave, Caracas, Venezuela, pp. 17-19.

CLAWSON, MARION, "Should Public Lands Pay Taxes," *American Forests*, March, 1965, pp. 11-13.

CRAWFORD, LOTTIE L., VICTOR R. LUNDY, "The Valuation of Hospitals," *The Appraisal Journal*, October, 1939, pp. 326-333.

DAVIS, W. D., "Appraisal of the Value of a Church," *Appraisal Reporting Techniques*, Amer Inst of Real Estate Appraisers, Vol. IV, 1954, pp. 31-60.

DOLMAN, JOHN P., "Market Data In Church Appraisal," *The Appraisal Journal,* January, 1961, pp. 13-18.

DONOGH, A. ORMSBY, "What Constitutes a Good Appraisal Library," *The Residential Appraiser,* August, 1962, pp. 18-24.

DRAKE LAW REVIEW, "Taxation-Exemption of Charitable, Religious and Educational Institutions from Property Taxes," *Drake Law Review,* December, 1962, pp. 87-91.

DUFFY, G., "Systems Building Proves Less Expensive for School Construction-Ashrae-Panel," *Air Conditioning, Heating and Refrigeration News,* July 20, 1970, pp. 15.

EDMAN, J. J., "Valuation of School Property. Appraisal Docket," *The Appraisal Journal,* October, 1958, pp. 613.

FEDERAL RESERVE BANK OF PHILADELPHIA, "The Heat Pump," *The Appraisal Journal,* October, 1956, pp. 535-542.

FEDERAL RESERVE BANK OF PHILADELPHIA, "What's Behind the Discount Rumpus In Retailing," *The Appraisal Journal,* April, 1962, pp. 210-218.

FIELD, WAYNE, "Checkpoints for Building a Nursing Home," *The Appraisal Journal,* July, 1966, pp. 400-406.

FISK, KENNETH, "A Tale of Lands and Buildings," *The Appraisal Journal,* February, 1956, pp. 16-22.

FLESHMAN, ROBERT M., "On Nursing Homes," *The Appraisal Journal,* October, 1962, pp. 542-544.

FREDRICKSON, R., H. A. HAMRE, R. E. WAYTAS, "Appraising Nursing Homes," *The Real Estate Appraiser,* July, 1970, pp. 10-17.

GAGE, DANIEL D., DONALD L. WOODWARD, "Evaluating Special Purpose Property of Nonprofit Institutions," *The Appraisal Journal,* October, 1940, pp. 341-347.

GATES, PHILIP B., "Obsolescence In Church and School Properties," *American Society of Appraisers,* 1961, pp. 97-102.

GILL, WILLIAM J., "Making Mortgages on Proprietary Hospitals," *The Real Estate Appraiser,* July, 1963, pp. 20-22.

GILL, WILLIAM J., "The Mortgage Murder Case," *The Appraisal Journal,* October, 1964, pp. 547-550.

GIMMY, ARTHUR E., "Appraising General Hospitals," *The Appraisal Journal,* April, 1966, pp. 234-244.

GIMMY, ARTHUR E., "California Chapter Studies Convalescent Hospital Appraisals," *The Appraiser,* April, 1968.

GRUELICH, RICHARD H. JR., *Property Valuation,* Austin, Texas.

HAINES, HOWARD, "Does Your Banker Know You?," *Valuation Manual,* A. S. A, 1958, pp. 87.

HALL, THOMAS H. III, BEATON, WILLIAM R, "A Partial Taking of School Grounds and the Demand for a Substitute Facility," *The Appraisal Journal,* January, 1968, pp. 73-83.

HALL, THOMAS H. III, WILLIAM R. BEATON, "Appraisal Analysis of Branch Bank Sites," *The Appraisal Journal,* July, 1965, pp. 336-343.

HANNAH, FREDERICK J., "Appraisal of the Value of a Y. M. C. A.," *Appraisal Reporting Techniques,* American Institute of Real Estate Appraisers, 1954, pp. 61-84.

HELMBERGER, JOHN D., *State and Local Taxation of Banks P. H. D. Thesis,* University of Minnesota, 1960.

HYDER, K. LEE, "The Appraisal of Bank Properties," *The Appraisal Journal,* January, 1943, pp. 39-50.

JOHNSTONE, PAULINE, *Byzantine Tradition In Church Embroidery,* Alectiranti, London.

KAHN, SANDERS A., "Real Estate Makes the College Team," *The Appraisal Journal,* April, 1951, pp. 233-238.

KELLEHER, PAUL E., "Leased Postal Facilities In New England," *Valuation Manual*, 1964, pp. 113.

KELLY, FRANCIS J., "Need for Hospital Appraisals," *Valuation Manual*, ASA, 1956-57.

KINNARD, WILLIAM N., "Educating Tomorrow's Appraiser," *The Real Estate Appraiser*, pp. 2..

KINNARD, WILLIAM N., "The Approaching Crisis In Appraisal Education," *The Appraisal Journal*, April, 1968, pp. 166-174.

KNISKERN, P. W., "Better Appraisal Standards Urged," *Savings Bank Journal*, March, 1932, pp. 38-39, 44.

LAMSON, J. E., "Factors That Will Substantiate the Valuation of a Closely Held Corporation," *Journal of Taxation*, April, 1971, pp. 226-229.

LARSON, MARTIN A., "You, the Church and Tax Exempt Wealth," *Assessors Journal*, April, 1966, pp. 10-16.

LEVY, MARK, "Institutional Purchases of Real Estate," *The Appraisal Journal*, July, 1949, pp. 296-310.

LINDQUIST, H. C., "Importance of Appraisals to Lending Institutions," *The Appraisal Journal*, April, 1947, pp. 237-241.

MARTIN, JAMES M., "Obsolescence and the Assessment of Public Service Properties," *Conference Proceedings*, National Tax Association, Columbus, 1960, pp. 410-426.

MCKIBBIN, CLIFFORD W., "Is the Public School a Nuisance," *The Appraisal Journal*, July, 1940, pp. 260-263.

NELSON, FORREST S., "A Banker's Appraisal," *The Review*, January, 1948, pp. 3-4.

NOLAN, PRESTON M., "Appraising for Banks and Life Insurance Companies," *National Real Estate Journal*, June, 1925, pp. 37-38.

OGUR, DAVID JONATHAN, PH. D., *The Impact of Colleges and Universities on Local Rental Housing Markets*, Cornell University, 1970.

PARDUE, MORRIS HAYWARD PH. D., *An Econometric Investigation of the Supply and Demand for Bank Loans 1954-1965*, Tulane University, 1971.

PLANNING DEPARTMENT, *University Payments for Municipal Services*, June, 1958.

PRAVER, STANLEY, "The Economics of Modern Nursing Homes," *35-39*, April, 1965.

PROUTY, W. L. AND OTHERS, "Bank Building Construction," *Appraisers and Assessors Manual*, 1930, pp. 197-199.

REAL ESTATE ANALYST, THE, "Construction Cost of Churches," *Real Estate Analyst Appraisal Bulletin*, 1949, pp. 41-44.

REAL ESTATE ANALYST, THE, "Construction Cost of Churches," *Real Estate Analyst Appraisal Bulletin*, 1953, pp. 385-388.

REAL ESTATE ANALYST, THE, "Construction Costs on a Small Bank Building," *Real Estate Analyst Appraisal Bulletin*, 1956, pp. 217-222.

REIDY, MAURICE F., DREW, ARTHUR W, "Church Property," *The Appraisal Journal*, October, 1932, pp. 71-75.

REITLINGER, *Italian Schools 14th Century Up, Review of Market Prices*, New York.

REVIEW, THE, "The Clinic," *The Review*, June, 1950, pp. 19-20.

RICHTER, F. E., A. STANDISH, *Investments of Banks and Insurance Company*, Harvard Business Review, July, 1925.

ROSS, WALTER W., "British Vs. American Banking In War Time," *The Appraisal Journal*, July, 1942, pp. 248-258.

SARMA, L. V. L. N., K. S. H. RAO, "Leverage and the Value of the Firm," *Journal of Finance*, September, 1969, pp. 673-677.

SINCLAIR, GEORGE D., "Church Valuations," *Technical Valuations*, June, 1957, pp. 45-49.

SMITH, LEVIE D., "Valuation of Modern Church Properties," *The Appraisal Journal*, April, 1966, pp. 203-212.

SOTAK, ANDREW, "Appraising Nursing Homes," *The Appraisal Journal*, April, 1962, pp. 190-199.

STEVENS, ROBERT W., "Appraisal of a Modern Municipal Incinerator," *Case Reports In Assessment Administration*, May, 1961.

THEISS, WILLIAM R., "The Appraisal Docket. Compensation for Private Sewer System Installed In Public Schools," *The Appraisal Journal*, January, 1963, pp. 121-122.

TILGHMAN-MAYER COMPANY, *Index of Construction Cost of Bank Buildings*, Tilghman-Mayer Company, Allentown, Pa.

TRUE, WALLACE, "The Appraisal of Special Purpose Properties for Lending Purposes," *Valuation*, March, 1945, pp. 3-6.

U. S. GOVERNMENT PRINTING OFFICE, *Survey of FHA-Assisted Nursing Homes*, Superintendent of Doc,U.S. Govt Printing Off, Washington, D. C..

VIZARD, RICHARD, "The Economic Impact of a Small College," *The Appraisal Journal*, April, 1968, pp. 287-290.

WALDO, FRANCOIS, "An Institutional Investor Evaluates the Appraisal Reports," *The Appraisal Journal*, October, 1967, pp. 550-554.

WEEKS, E. W., "A Library In Action," *The Residential Appraiser*, March, 1958, pp. 21-24.

WELLS, GEORGE E., "Financing Nursing Homes," *The Appraisal Journal*, July, 1965, pp. 391-432.

ZANGERLE, JOHN A., *The Principles of Land and Building Appraisals As Scientifically Applied In Cuyahoga County*, 1931.

Natl Elec Rate Bk Rate Scheds for Elec Serv In Communities of 2500 Pop or More Residtl Commercial an, Federal Power Comission, Washington, D. C., September, 1970.

"Banker-Builder Team Proves That Private Enterprise Can Meet Housing Needs of Renewal-Area Residents," *House and Home*, June, 1970, pp. 42.

"Building Boom Continues for Nations Banks," *Burroughs Clearing House*, April, 1971, pp. 16.

"Community Center Is Doomed," *American Druggist*, February 22, 1971, pp. 54.

"Cruciform Library Costs Less Than One of Rectangular Shape," *Engineering News-Record*, May 21, 1970, pp. 48-49.

"Effects of Real Prop Assesmt on Amt of Local Initiative In School Districts of Mississippi," *Dissertation Abstracts*, September, 1964, pp. 1693.

"Library Construction," *Special Libraries*, December, 1970, pp. 574.

"Management Contracting Brings Dividends on a California Campus," *Engineering News Record*, April 29, 1971, pp. 17.

"Prop Tax-Hospitals & Nursg Homes-Facilts Reasonably Necessary for Hosp Purposes Held Within Stat Exem," *Rutgers Law Review*, 1962, pp. 614-618.

"Triple-Use Design Saves Money on Campus Arena," *Engineering News Record*, January 28, 1971, pp. 13.

# 13-22 Subdivisions

AARON, JOSEPH, "Economics of Residential Subdivision," *Technical Valuation,* ASA.

ANGELL, STEPHEN LEROY, "Appraisal of Subdivisions," *Encyclopedia of Real Estate Appraising,* Edith J. Friedman, 1959.

BAKER, HARRISON R., *How to Appraise Land Suitable for Land Subdivision,* 1900.

BAKER, HARRISON R., "The Appraisal of Subdivision Acreage New Factors Old Principles," *The Appraisal Journal,* April, 1965, pp. 25-34.

BARWICK, H. G., "Subdivision Valuation Compared," *Appraisal Institute Magazine,* Appraisal Institute of Canada, Winnipeg.

BODFISH, MORTON, THEOBALD, A. D, "Appraising Vacant Lots In Subdivisions," *Real Estate Fundamentals,* 1941, pp. 6-7.

BOHANNON, DAVID D., "Converting Farms to Subdivisions," *The Appraisal Journal,* October, 1945, pp. 362-364.

CAMPBELL, COLIN, "A Study of the Effects of Pipeline Easements on Subdivision Developments," *Right of Way,* December, 1960, pp. 23-33.

CARR, ANTHONY W., "Appraising Within Subdivisions," *The Real Estate Appraiser,* May, 1963, pp. 26-29.

COLEMAN, DAN, "Trends In Subdivision and Hillside Development," *The Appraisal Journal,* October, 1965, pp. 575-586.

COLLINS, E. R., "Subdivision Planning In Relation to Appraisal Problems," *Appraisal Institute Magazine,* January, 1959, pp. 6-11.

COTTEN, ROBERT, "Types of Subdivisions," *Right of Way Conference, Selected Papers, 1962,* University of Alabama, Alabama, 1962, pp. 32-36.

DAVIS, E. G., "Appraisal of Land for Subdivisions," *Appraisal Institute Magazine,* May, 1958, pp. 14-20.

DERBES, MAX J. JR., "The Effect of an Electric Transmission Line Through a Subdivision," *Right of Way,* April, 1968, pp. 28-38.

EDMAN, J. J., "Determining Cost of Subdivision and Improvement of Land. Appraisal Docket," *The Appraisal Journal,* July, 1958, pp. 449-450.

EDMAN, J. J., "The Appraisal Docket. Determining Cost of Subdivision and Improvement of Land," *The Appraisal Journal,* July, 1958, pp. 449-452.

FEDERAL RESERVE BANK OF CHICAGO, "The Economic Consequences of the Baby Boom," *The Appraisal Journal,* April, 1956, pp. 208-212.

FULLER, ROBERT S., "Hillside Subdivisions," *The Review,* July, 1953, pp. 3-5.

GERKIN, LEONARD, "The Economics of Hillside Subdivisions," *Technical Valuation,* February, 1961, pp. 2-7.

GOTTLIEB, M., "Influences on Value In Urban Land Markets, U. S. A., 1956-1961."

HAALAND ARNE W., "Backward Valuation of Potential Subdivisions," *Appraisal and Valuation Manual,* American Society of Appraisers, 1959, pp. 211-214.

HAGOOD, WAYNE D., "Lot Valuations In Tract Subdivision," *The Residential Appraiser,* June, 1961, pp. 9-13.

HALEY, BYRON R., "Outdoor Recreation Subdivisions," *The Real Estate Appraiser,* October, 1971, pp. 14-18.

HAMILIN, BEN W., "Fourth Dimension Approach to Valuation of Residential Subdivision Land," *Technical Valuation,* June, 1961, pp. 51-54.

HATCH, CHESTER W., "Effects of Transmission Lines on Subdivision Properties," *Technical Valuation,* February, 1953, pp. 17-20, 23.

KOELBEL, WALTER A., "The Land Developer and a Golf Course Subdivision," *Urban Land,* Urban Land Institute, Washington, D. C, 1964.

LANGER, H. P., "The Valuation of Lands Suitable for Subdivision," *Appraisal Institute Magazine,* Appraisal Institute of Canada, Winnipeg.

LESSINGER, JACK, "Is the Supply of Urban Land Running Out," *The Appraisal Journal,* January, 1962, pp. 61-68.

MASHKE, D. K., "The Cost of Subdividing," *The Appraisal Institute Magazine,* September, 1963, pp. 11-14.

MCCROSKY, T. T., "Today's Subdivision Problems," *Review of Society of Residential Appraisers,* November, 1941, pp. 7-10.

MCDIARMID, M. C., "Net Value Loss, Potential Subdivision Acreage," *Appraisal Institute,* 1970, pp. 15-17.

MCMICHAEL, STANLEY L., *Real Estate Subdivisions,* Prentice-Hall, New York, 1949.

OROURRK, GERALD A., "Appraising Acreage for Subdivision," *The Appraisal Journal,* July, 1952, pp. 373-381.

PETRY, ELDON H., "The Valuation of Raw Land with Subdivision Potential," *Appraisal Institute Magazine,* September, 1964.

RUSSELL, HUGH H., "New Subdivision Trends," *The Review,* May, 1946, pp. 6-9.

SACHS, EARL, "An Apparently Harmless Easement Smashes Subdivision Plans," *The Appraisal Journal,* January, 1966, pp. 117-118.

SCHLAGENHAUF, PAUL, "The Appraisal of Vacant Subdivision Lots for Taxation Purposes," *The Appraisal Journal,* January, 1934, pp. 93-97.

SOLOMON, R. J., "Property Values As a Structural Element of Urban Evolution," *Economic Geography,* January, 1969.

THEISS, WILLIAM R., "The Appraisal Docket. FHA Approval As a Factor In Value of Subdivision Property," *The Appraisal Journal,* Octobr, 1961, pp. 543.

THEOBALD, A. E., *Financial Aspects of Subdivision Development,* Research Institute for Economic Research, Chicago & New York, 1930.

WAGNER, PERCY E., "Subdivision Costs," *The Residential Appraiser,* May, 1957, pp. 12-14.

▲ Urban Property

# 13-23  Suburban Property

AMERICAN SOCIETY OF PLANNING OFFICIALS, *Apartments In the Suburbs,* Chicago, 1900.

ARCHITECHTURAL FORUM, "Estimating the Selling Price of a Suburban Residence," *Architectural Forum,* April, 1920, pp. 165.

BARBAGELATA, JOSE, "Tasacion De Terrenos Pre-Urbanos," *Boletin,* Sotave, Caracas, Venezuela, pp. 11-17.

BAUER, PAUL, "New Incentives to the Suburban Trend," *The Review,* March, 1946, pp. 18-20.

BLAIR, W. EDWIN, "How to Make Rental Appraisals," *The National Real Estate Journal,* July 14, 1924, pp. 25-27.

BONBRIGHT, JAMES CUMMINGS, "The Valuation of Property," Mcgraw-Hill Book Co., Inc., N.Y. and London, 1937.

BUNKER, RAYMOND, *Town and Country or City and Region,* Melbourne University Press, May, 1973.

CHANDIAS, MARIO E., "Valoracion De Grandes Fracciones Preurbanas," *Boletin,* Sotave, Caracas, Venezuela, pp. 5-7.

DAVIS, W. D., "Rurban Appraisals," *Appraisal Institute Magazine,* Appraisal Institute of Canada, Winnipeg.

DAVIS, WILLIAM D. SR., "Land Appraisals In the Urban Fringe," *The Real Estate Appraiser,* September, 1965, pp. 29-32.

DEVELOPMENT VALUE, "Town and Country," *Development Value,* April, 1971, pp. 176.

EGERTON, J. W., "The Problem of Rurban Properties," *Appraisal Institute Magazine,* Appraisal Institute of Canada, Winnipeg, June 1, 1973.

FEDERAL RESERVE BANK OF CHICAGO, "The Economic Consequences of the Baby Boom," *The Appraisal Journal,* April, 1956, pp. 208-212.

FISHER, ERNEST M., "Speculation In Suburban Lands," *The Appraisal Journal,* October, 1933.

GADDIS, PORTER L., "The Appraisal of Suburban Properties," *Journal of the American Society of Farm Managers and Rural Appraisal,* April, 1948, pp. 28-41.

GRUELICH, RICHARD H. JR., *Property Valuation,* Austin, Texas.

GRUEN, VICTOR, "Shopping Centers, Suburban and Urban," *Appraisal and Valuation Manual,* American Society of Appraisars, 1960.

HANCOCK, MACKLIN L., "Suburban Town Centers," *The Appraisal Journal,* April, 1965, pp. 261-272.

HOUSE, PETER, "Farm Land Assessment In Rural-Urban Fringe," *The Appraisal Journal,* January, 1961, pp. 57-62.

HOUSE, PETER, "Partial Tax Exemption for Farmland Properties In the Rural-Urban Fringe," *The Appraisal Journal,* July, 1968, pp. 393-407.

HULSE, FRED E., *Property Tax Problems In Rural - Urban Fringe Areas,* Dept of Agriculture, College Park, Md., 1952.

KAHN, SANDERS A., "Impact of Shopping Centers on Suburbs and Central Cities," *Valuation,* February, 1958, pp. 45-48.

LARONGE, JOSEPH, "Valuation of a 20-Unit Apartment Building with Attached Garage In a Suburban District," *Practical Appraising Methods,* 1940, pp. 59-62.

LAURENTI, LUIGI, *Property Values and Race, Studies In Seven Cities,* University of California Press, Berkeley, L. A., 1960.

LOOMIS, D., "Rich Washington Suburb Rules Building Projects Must Include Units for Poor," *House and Home,* September, 1971, pp. 8..

MCCUTCHEON, W. B., "Beyond the Serviced Suburbs," *The Residential Appraiser,* September, 1957, pp. 22-24.

MCGOVERN, JOHN E., "Appraisal of Large-Scale Suburban Projects," *The Appraisal Journal,* April, 1940, pp. 140-146.

MCREYNOLDS, TOM, "Planning Suburban Shopping Centers," *Real Estate Analyst Appraisal Bulletin,* 1951, pp. 85-123.

MELAMED, ANSHEL, "High-Rent Apartments In the Suburbs," *The Appraisal Journal,* April, 1962, pp. 279-289.

MORGAN, BELDEN, "Values In Transition Areas Some New Concepts," *The Review,* March, 1952, pp. 5-10.

MOTT, SEWARD H., "Recent Developments In Suburban Shopping Center," *The Appraisal Journal,* January, 1949, pp. 39-44.

NATIONAL REAL ESTATE JOURNAL, "Actual Appraisal Reports: Appraisal of 5-Story Office and Store Building In Suburb Cleveland," *National Real Estate Journal,* May 11, 1931, pp. 25-30.

OLAVE, OSCAR A., "Tasacion De Una Gran Superficie," *Boletin,* Sotave, Caracas, Venezuela, pp. 8-9.

PARROT, ALFRED F., "The Return from the Suburbs," *Appraisal Digest,* October, 1960, pp. 15-18.

PAULSEN, R. G., "Central City Land Use and Suburban Financial Support," *Land Economics,* November, 1970, pp. 497-502.

PETREE, NEIL, "Suburban Shopping Centers," *The Review,* June, 1952, pp. 3-5, 9.

PORTER, STEPHEN, "Effect of Business In the Suburbs," *The Review,* August, 1951, pp. 8-10.

PORTER, STEPHEN L., "Decentralization Seen Revising Suburban Property Values," *The Appraisal Digest,* April, 1951, pp. 10-11.

REAL ESTATE RECORD AND BUILDERS GUIDE, "Ten-Year Movement to Suburbs Measured," *Real Estate Record and Builders Guide,* September 20, 1941, pp. 6-7.

RHAMSTINE, ADAM W., "Suburban Zoning," *The Review,* November, 1955, pp. 13-16, 22.

RICH, RICHARD H., "Effect on Downtown Real Estate of Surburban Shopping Centers," *Skyscraper Shopping Centers.*

SCHUMACHER, ARNOLD C., "From Suburbia to Interurbia," *The Appraisal Journal,* July, 1963, pp. 369-373.

SIMPSON, HERBERT D., AND JOHN E. BURTON, *The Valuation of Vacant Land In Suburban Areas, Chicago Areas,* Institute for Economic Research Northwestern Univ., Chicago, 1931, pp. 1-56.

SIMPSON, HERBERT DOWNS, "The Valuation for Vacant Land In Suburban Areas," The Institute of Economic Research, Chicago, 1931.

SINGLETON, C. G. JR., AND SCOFIELD, W. H., "Land Syndication In the Rural-Urban Fringe," *The Appraisal Journal,* October, 1962, pp. 494-500.

SMITH, LARRY, "Commercial Real Estate Relationships--Downtown and Suburban," *The Appraisal Journal,* October, 1956, pp. 578-582.

STILES, LYNN A., "Financing Government In the Suburbs: the Role of the Property Tax," *Conference Proceedings,* National Tax Association, Colombus, 1960, pp. 52.

▲ Urban Property

STUART, DARWIN G., AND ROBERT B. TESKA, *"Who Pays for What: a Cost-Revenue Analysis of Suburban Land Use Alternatives."*

SWEET, GILBERT N., "**On Thoughts Regarding Idle Suburban Land**," *The Appraisal Journal,* January, 1938, pp. 66-69.

U. S. GOVERNMENT PRINTING OFFICE, *The City Expands, a Study of Theconversion of Land from Rural to Urban Use,* U. S. Govt. Printing Office, Washington.

WOODLAND PIERCE CO., "**Appraisal, Rate, and Service Investigation of the Surburban Water Company**," *Engineering Valuation,* 1931.

*An Analysis of Relationship Between N. J. Suburban Shopping Centers & Home Values In Adjacent Nabord,* New York University, 1972.

"**New Assault on Suburban Zoning**," *Business Week,* February 16, 1971, pp. 30.

"**Two on One Triplexes Save Open Space on a Tight Suburban Site**," *House and Home,* November, 1970, pp. 321.

BIBLIOGRAPHY OF APPRAISAL LITERATURE

## CHAPTER FOUR

# Rural Property

by James H. Trees, ASA, MAI.

Mr. Trees is a Farm and Ranch specialist with an extensive appraisal practice centered in Chandler, Arizona. He is a member of the American Institute of Real Estate Appraisers, American Society of Appraisers, American Society of Farm Managers and Rural Appraisers, American Society of Range Management, Mesa-Chandler-Tempe Board of Realtors and the National Association of Realtors.

Offices held by Mr. Trees include Presidential terms for Arizona Chapter of the American Society of Appraisers, the Arizona Association of Realtors, and the Mesa-Chandler-Tempe Board of Realtors

Mr. Trees received a BA degree from the University of Illinois, and an MA degree from the University of Iowa. He has served as Guest Lecturer on behalf of the College of Business Adminstration, Arizona State University, and the American Society of Farm Managers and Rural Appraisers.

## Rural Property

THE RELATIVE significance of Rural Property Appraising within the scope of the multi-disciplinary concept of appraising held by the American Society of Appraisers is best exemplified by the simple fact that there are more acres of rural property in these United States than any other category of Real Property.

However, the general basic concept utilized in the appraisal of Rural Property demands a complete understanding of approved appraisal practices and principles that are employed in all other categories of property.

Under Rural Property Classification may fall the appraisal of irrigated land, dry farm land, land in rain belts, cattle ranches, sheep ranches, swine farms, Federal and State grazing leases, allotments and permits, pen feeding cattle operations, cotton gins, alfalfa dehydration plants, farm machinery and equipment, fruit orchards, citrus groves, nut groves, vineyards, growing crops, livestock, lessor's interest, lessee's interest, irrigation wells, etc.

William G. Murray, Ph.D., Professor of Economics, Iowa State University, in his text entitled, FARM APPRAISAL AND VALUATION, defines a competent farm appraisal as follows: "Farm appraisal is a systematic process of identifying, classification, and evaluating the characteristics of a farm in order to make a well reasoned judgement of its value. The making of a farm appraisal involves two major parts, the first devoted to the identification and classification, and second to valuation—the placing of a value of the property identified and classified in the first part."

This well conceived, all inclusive, approach to value is equally pertinent in the appraisal of all types of rural property. A competent, well disciplined rural appraiser is fully cognizant of the fact that in his special field there are certain factors contributing to value that are not necessarily valid evidence of value in other classes of property. A complete understanding of the Society's Aims and Objectives will serve the appraiser well in making these considered judgements. The genesis of all economic or aesthetic returns from any use is generated by the land.

Land value may arise from full ownership, fractional ownership, and/or as allottee, permittee, lessor's interest, lessee's interest, mortgagor's or mortgagee's interests, easement interest, and others.

*In the field of rural appraisal, the prime and initial value to be extracted is the value of the land.* Building improvements constructed on the land and/or special uses of the land may increase or decrease land values.

Modern agri-technology has provided many new methods of land manipulation that influence economic returns. Some of these changes can be construed as unconventional practices when placed in juxtaposition with past techniques of operation. Well informed rural appraisers are abreast of the most modern practices employed in agriculture, thus are able to value the new processes in relation to their degree of success as measured by the adaptability and acceptability by potential users. The hallmark of a competent appraiser is to be capable of seeking out a proper balance between the past, present, and probable future trends in land use changes. Change, for the sake of change alone, has seldom proven beneficial to man. However, there is a close correlation between the ageless history of land development and the improvements in the life style of mankind.

The practitioner of rural appraising must constantly bear in mind the ultimate goal of agriculture within its many facets of operations that constitute agricultural activities. Simply stated, that goal is to provide people with better lives. This goal is achieved by providing food, fiber, and shelter in greater quantities with higher qualities for the benefit of generations yet to come.

A study of the preterhuman development of the land that sustains all existing life gives the rural appraiser an appreciation of the magnitude of his responsibilities. "Under all is the land. Upon its wise utilization and widely allocated ownership depends the survival and growth of free institutions and of our civilization." (Preamble, THE CODE OF ETHICS, National Association of Realtors).

The earth surface area approximates 196 million square miles. Geographers estimate that 50 million square miles of land is above sea level. The remainder of the land supports lakes, seas and oceans of the world. Land is found 36,000 feet below sea level, the world's deepest ocean floor, at the bottom of the Pacific Ocean's Mariana Trench. Under Siberia's Lake Baikal, the world's deepest inland lake at 5,000 feet, lies the land. At 29,000 feet above sea level on the top of Mount Everest, the world's highest point, there lies land. In the Antarctic buried under thousands of feet of ice pack on Vinson Massif Mountain, at 16,000 feet above sea level, lies the land. Under ALL is the land.

Land is timeless. The fertile soils found on the earth's surface, that currently sustain man, originated through eons of time wherein rock formations disintegrated by sun, wind, and water into sand crystals and then finally into soil. Many of the primeval species of fauna were not sufficiently mobile or able to adapt to nature's incessant changing climate, forage, and topography, and thus became extinct.

Paleontologists, paleobotanists, and anthropologists find that throughout this incalculable period of time, mankind has been the most successful of all species of life in adapting to the whims of nature because of his power to reason and learn.

Land is an adversary of man. Man is an adversary of land.

Land knows no superior entity other than the sun, the genesis of life on earth. Energy, furnished by the sun, controls the rain, snow fall, seasonal climates, and the winds in relation to where and when each of the elements of weather shall effect land. Land in turn controls where man and his allied amenities of food, fiber, shelter, and comfort shall thrive and prosper. Land holds no high regard for man when he violates nature's plans.

Modern man has exhibited little respect for land in the last century. In the United States, destruction of vast native forests by man-made fires and uncontrolled timber harvesting has upset the natural rate of water runoff into streams, lakes, and rivers. This has resulted in severe erosion of fertile soils being washed down to sediment rivers and flow into the oceans. That irreplacable commodity, soil, has been lost forever to man. There is no less land coverage on the earth but man is denied the benefits of the fertility of that lost top soil.

In America, our progenitors found ample land along the Atlantic Coast that was suitable for and capable of supporting their needs. Ignorant of good land management, the emigrants tilled their land tracts until all native fertility was extracted. Then they moved westward where nature had provided millions of acres of fertile glacial soils lying nearly flat and easily made tillable. Continued population increases brought forth demands for increased food and fiber resulting in further westward expansion of agricultural developments into marginal, sandy, silted soils that had heretofore been natural grazing areas for native animals and domestic cattle and sheep.

In the mid 1930's, nature struck back at the developers of this marginal land with extreme drouth and devastating winds that carried the light surface soils in tremendous dust clouds which had never before been encountered by the residents of the abused areas. Blowing dust not only completely eroded plowed fields of all top soil but added to the devastation by dropping the dust accumulation on undisturbed grazing land, burying and killing native grasses that were annually consumed by range animals and wild life.

Rural land is constantly subjected to hazards not noticeably effecting urban property. Planted crops must risk hazards of drouth, rain storms, hail, killing frosts, insects, soil depletion, and floods before harvest times. Cattle and sheep ranches suffer from extreme periods of drouth, from blizzards that cover range feed, from cattle starvation, from death losses of new born animals in the cold and rainy periods, and from uncontrolled predators.

Modern agri—technology has found methods of partially controlling insect infestation and soil depletion. Soil depletion is the more devastating.

Mr. Charles E. Kellog, United States Department of Agriculture, in the 1957 annual publication entitled SOIL, best summarized man's efforts to cooperate with nature in the matter of soil conservation. In Mr. Kellog's paper entitled WE SEEK TO LEARN, he states "Two hundred generations of men and women have given us what is in our minds about soils and soil fertility—the arts and skills and organized body of knowledge that we now call science."

Modern man has an opportunity, through the ownership and operation of rural land within the scope of modern agri-science, to retract his adversary attitude toward the primary souce of his existence, i.e., the land. Even if he does effect improvement in the land, nature still reserves the right to quickly erase all such improvements by earthquakes, volcanic eruptions, hurricanes, and floods.

Man has created a new threat to his own comfortable existence in the United States; this is known as the population explosion. The burden of supplying the need of feeding, clothing, and sheltering this multitude rests on rural property. To house and employ the growing population, towns and cities are expanding beyond the recognized urban boundaries, deep into rural areas for the construction of residential subdivisions and for commercial and industrial uses. Each acre of agricultural land taken by this type of encroachment reduces, proportionately, the acreage needed to feed, clothe, and house the increased population.

Further diminution of agricultural land acreage has occurred in the southwestern semi-arid states where irrigation is mandatory to grow crops. To supplement the Nation's needs for food and fiber during World War II, many acres of marginal land were plowed up and farmed by deep well irrigation outside of organized irrigation districts. The marginal desert land had precious little native fertility and required excessive amounts of fertilizer and water to produce crops. The large volume of underground water pumped, in those areas, soon lowered the static water level to a depth that nearly exhausted the water supply. The high cost of pumping the water, from extreme depths for the growing crops, created an economic deficit from the operation. In one single county, over 75,000 acreas of marginal farm land has been abandoned and allowed to revert to its native desert growth.

In 1950, there were an estimated 3,000,000 farms and ranches in the United States. In the past two decades, that number has been reduced about 40 percent. The United States Department of Agriculture records show that 60 percent of all rural land sales during that interim period were for farm and ranch enlargements. Declining net returns per unit of measurement necessitated increasing the number of units of production to offset the increased costs of operation. During the twenty-year period, farm land prices increased 13 percent while grazing land prices increased 60 percent in the forty-eight contiguous states. Experienced rural appraisers are able to measure these changes by the fundamental laws of supply and demand.

Inexperienced rural appraisers might well be advised that current open market sales of rural property must be carefully studied and analyzed. No longer can the appraiser assume that the purchase of a farm or ranch was for its continued use as a farm or ranch. *Experienced, competent rural appraisers know, with ever increasing evidence available, that the prime factor to ascertain, relating to farm or ranch land sales, is the INTENDED USE of the land by the buyer.* Astute and financially capable entrepreneurs, in the modern market, know they must pay more for rural land than farmers or ranchers can afford to pay for land to cultivate or graze. Residential, commercial, and industrial land purchasers are willing to pay more for land having the proper location, total area needed, available public utilities, adequate zoning regulations, and convenient access to the property. This class of purchaser needs the legal rights to the property as well as the value of the tangible and intangible amenities.

It behooves the modern appraiser to catalogue and index sales into categories of proposed land uses by the purchasers, i.e., cultivated land, range land, industrial sites, commercial uses, gasoline service stations, hydroponic gardening, recreation, schools, universities, governmental agency uses, small acreages for residential ranchettes, etc. Over a period of time, price trends will develop in each category. Compared index sales become worthy of being truly comparable sales only within the limits of proper divisions of uses.

An extensive library of texts prepared by prominent rural appraisers, copies of periodic appraisal publications, and a ready reference source of information in a Bibliography File, are of utmost importance to the competent appraiser of rural property.

Under ALL is the land, the most precious of all commodities available to mankind. Rural appraisers will do well to value land with an appreciation of the complexity of the process and an understanding of the importance of land to the future of man.

# Rural Property

14-11   General Agriculture
14-12   Crop Allotment
14-13   Soils
14-14   Irrigated Land
14-15   Dry Farm Land
14-16   Dairy Farms
14-17   Groves and Orchards
14-18   Ranches and Grazing Land

## 14-11 General Agriculture

ABDEL-BADDIE F E, "An Econometric Analysis of Factors Affecting Land Values In Western Oklahoma," *Dissertation Abstracts,* June, 1968, pp. 4780-A.

ADAMS, R. L., "Basic Cost of Producing Farm Products," *Technical Valuation,* November, 1952, pp. 12-17.

ALBERS, M. H., "The Income Approach to Value - Rural Real Estate," *The Appraisal Institute Magazine,* April, 1968, pp. 41-47.

ALBERS, M. H., "The Income Approach to Value-Rural Real Estate," *Appraisal Institute Magazine,* Appraisal Institute of Canada, Winnipeg.

AMER SOC OF FARM MGRS & RURAL APPRAISERS JOUR OF, "American Rural Appraisal System," *Journal of the American Society of Farm Managers and Rural Appraisers,* A.S.F.M.R.A., October, 1946, pp. 84-99.

AMERICAN INSTITUTE OF REAL ESTATE APPRAISERS, *Problems In Rural Real Estate Appraisal,* American Institute of Real Estate Appraisers, 1968.

AMERICAN INSTITUTE OF REAL ESTATE APPRAISERS, *101 Rural Appraisal Problems with Suggested Solutions,* American Institute of Real Estate Appraisers, Chicago, 1958.

AMERICAN SOCIETY OF APPRAISERS, WASHINGTON, "Market to Basic Rural Appraisal," American Society of Appraisers, Washington.

AMERICAN SOCIETY OF FARM MANAGERS AND RURAL APPRAISERS, "Professional Advancement Means More Income," *Journal of the American Society of Farm Managers & Rural Appraisers,* April, 1956, pp. 8-9.

ANDAL, M. E., "Economic Trends Affecting Agricultural Values," *Appraisal Institute Magazine,* Appraisal Institute of Canada, Winnipeg, March 1, 1971.

ARNOLD, MAX P, "Impact of Property Taxes As a Fixed Charge Against Agricultural Land," *Journal; Proceedings,* Am. Soc. Farm Mgrs-Rural Appraisers, Denver, November 27, 1973, pp. 74-80.

ARNOLD, MAX P., "A Rural Land Appraisal for Ad Valorem Tax Purposes," *The Valuation Manual,* American Society of Appraisers, Washington, 1958, pp. 385-398.

AUMELL, R. G., "Income Approach to Value for Farm Properties," *Appraisal Institute Magazine,* Appraisal Institute of Canada, Winnipeg, March 1, 1971.

BARTLETT, ROLAND W., "Interdependence of Urban and Rural Economies," *The Appraisal Journal,* January, 1950, pp. 63-71.

BASHAW, FREDERICK J., "Value In a Dynamic Land Economy," *The Review,* 1900, pp. 16-22.

BEAUDOIN, FERNAND, "Income Approach In Appraising of Farms," *Appraisal Institute Magazine,* Appraisal Institute of Canada, Winnipeg.

BECKER, MANNING H, "Farm/Ranch Leases--Looking Ahead," *Journal; Proceedings,* Am. Soc. Farm Mgrs-Rural Appraisers, Denver, November 27, 1973, pp. 33-35.

BELL, RICHARD E, "American Agriculture In the World Economy," *Journal; Proceedings,* Am. Soc. Farm Mgrs-Rural Appraisers, Denver, November 27, 1973, pp. 94-100.

BERWICK, A. J., "Evaluating Farm Buildings As a Part of the Modern Farm Appraisal," *The Journal of the American Society of Farm Managers and Rural Appraisers,* October, 1962, pp. 31-35.

BOWEN, JOHN R., "Appraising Specialty Farms," *The Journal of the American Society of Farm Managers and Rural Appraisers,* April, 1945, pp. 49-54.

BOWMAN, J. D., "An Economic Analysis of Midwest Farm Land Values and Farm Land Income--1860,1900," *Yale Economic Essay,* October, 1965.

BRADFORD, C. R., "The Use of Soils and Crop Data In Farm Appraising," *Appraisal Institute Magazine,* Appraisal Institute of Canada, Winnipeg.

BRESNAHAN, C. A., "The Agricultural Situation and Outlook," *The Appraisal Journal,* January, 1956, pp. 30-32.

BUREAU OF AGRICULTURAL ECONOMICS, *Land Settlement,* Department of Agriculture, Washington, 1934.

BUREAU OF AGRICULTURAL ENGINEERING, *Agricultural Engineering,* Department of Agriculture, Washington, 1937.

BUREAU OF AGRICULTURAL ENGINEERING, *Land Drainage,* Department of Agriculture, Washington, 1936.

BURNEY, WILLARD W, "Feedlot Appraisal Problems," *Journal; Proceedings,* Am. Soc. Farm Mgrs-Rural Appraisers, Denver, November 27, 1973, pp. 43-47.

BURR, HUDSON, "A New Approach to Rural Appraising," *The Appraisal Journal,* January, 1935, pp. 155-164.

CALIFORNIA STATE OFFICE OF PLANNING, "Bibliography of Exclusive Agricultural Zoning Law," *The Journal of the American Society of Farm Managers and Rural Appraisers,* October, 1962, pp. 67-71.

CARDON, BARTLEY P, "Nutrient Recycling--Modern Energy Management," *Journal; Proceedings,* Am. Soc. Farm Mgrs-Rural Appraisers, Denver, November 27, 1973, pp. 81-93.

CHAPMAN, ROBERT L, "Appraisal Problems," *Journal; Proceedings,* Am. Soc. Farm Mgrs-Rural Appraisers, Denver, November 27, 1973.

CHERRY, RUSSELL C., AND ALVIN B. WOOTEN, "Comparative Investment Yields Agricultural Land Vs. Selected Securities," *Journal of American Society of Farm Management and Rural Appraisers,* October, 1966, pp. 53-59.

CLARK, RALPH E., "A Prosperous Farm," *Assessment Administration,* IAAO, Chicago, 1957, pp. 93-102.

COLWELL, R. N., *Aerial and Space Photographs As Aids to Land Evaluation,* pp. 324.

CONGDON, WALTER B., "Livestock and Crop Appraisals," *Technical Evaluation,* American Society of Appraisers, June, 1954, pp. 45.

CONNOLLY, DANIEL E., "Farm Appraising Is Described As Field for Specialists," *Appraisal Digest,* October, 1951, pp. 6-7.

COOK, ROBERT S., "Farmland and Capitalization of Income," *Assessment Administration,* IAAO, Chicago, 1959, pp. 67-70.

COOPER K. J., "The Impact of Technology and Changing Social Patterns on Property Values," *Valuer,* The New Zealand Institute of Valuers, New Zealand, August 1, 1973, pp. 124-134.

CORMAN, R. R., "Problems Encountered In Rural Appraising," *Appraisal Institute Magazine,* Appraisal Institute of Canada, Winnipeg.

CROUSE, EARL F., AND CHARLES H. EVERETT, *Rural Appraisals,* Prentice-Hall, Inc., Englwd Cliffs, N. J., 1956.

CROUSE, EARL F., CHARLES H. EVERETT, "Appraisal of Rural Property," *The Encyclopedia of Real Estate Appraising,* 1959, pp. 368-413.

CROWLEY, WILLIAM DAVID JR., "Influence, Net Real Estate Income on Prices of Agricultural Properties," Oregon State University, 1972.

CUNNINGHAM, J. B., "Adjusting Appraisals to Changing Conditions," *Journal of the American Society of Farm Managers and Rural Appraisers,* October, 1956, pp. 43-51.

DAVIDSON, J. B., "Life, Service and Cost of Service of Farm Machinery," *Iowa Engineering Experiment Station Bulletin 103,* 1900.

DAVIES, C. M., "Soil Productivity and Agricultural Land Value," *Appraisal Institute Magazine,* Appraisal Institute of Canada, Winnipeg.

DAVIS, IRVING F. JR., *A Statistical Approach to Real Estate Value with Applications to Farm Appraisal,* January, 1965.

DAVIS, W. D., "Basic Value In Farm Appraising," *The Appraisal Journal,* October, 1944, pp. 340-344.

DAVIS, W. D., "Rural Appraisal Procedures," *The Appraisal Journal,* October, 1946, pp. 349-360.

DAVIS, W. D., "Rural Appraisal Requirements In Federal Condemnation," *American Society of Farm Managers and Rural Appraisers,* October, 1963, pp. 58-73.

DAVIS, W. D., "The Analysis of Comparable States," *Journal of the American Society of Farm Managers and Rural Appraisals,* April, 1962, pp. 113-115.

DAVIS, W. D., "The Appraisal of Farms," *The Appraisal Journal,* January, 1951, pp. 11-119.

DIESSLIN, HOWARD G., "Effects of Improving Technology on Land Values," *Journal of the American Society of Farm Managers and Rural Appraisers,* April, 1956, pp. 38-42.

DILL, ORVAL, MELTON, JAMES O, SIGARTY, MYRON W, "Mortgage Lenders' View of Rural Land Values," *Journal; Proceedings,* Am. Soc. Farm Mgrs-Rural Appraisers, Denver, November 27, 1973, pp. 101-109.

DOANE, D. HOWARD, "Rural Appraising," *The Appraisal Journal,* October, 1934, pp. 46-50.

DOANE, D. HOWARD, "Twenty Five Years of Progress," *The Journal of the American Society of Farm and Rural Appraisers,* April, 1955, pp. 10-14.

DONETH, JOHN G., "Farm Management and Machine Accounting," *Journal of the American Society of Farm Managers and Rural Appraisers,* April, 1963, pp. 61-69.

DOWELL, JESSE M, HUTCHINSON, JIM, "Management Reports: 'So You Think You're Writing A Good Report!,'" *Journal; Proceedings,* Am. Soc. Farm Mgrs-Rural Appraisers, Denver, November 27, 1973, pp. 113-120.

DUERR, MICHAEL G., "Can Agriculture Adjust to the Common Market," *The Appraisal Journal,* October, 1962, pp. 501-502.

DURHAM, WILLIAM K., "Social Security," *Journal of the American Society of Farm Managers and Rural Appraisers,* April, 1963, pp. 31-32.

DUVALL, GARNER W., "Appraisal of Farm Land In an Urbanized Area," *Assessors News Letter,* June, 1964, pp. 67-68.

EDMAN, J. J., "Tenant's Rights to Compensation for Growing Corps. Appraisal Docket," *The Appraisal Journal,* October, 1958, pp. 613-614.

EISGRUGER, LUDWIG M., "The Human Factor In Farm Management," *Journal of the American Society of Farm Managers and Rural Appraisers,* April, 1962, pp. 07-73.

ELLIOTT, F. E., "Place of Professional Farm Management and Rural Appraisal In American Agriculture," *Journal of the American Society of Farm Managers and Rural Appraisers,* April, 1949, pp. 6-9.

ENGLEHORN, V. A., "Preview 1952 Appraisal," *Journal of the American Society of Farm Managers and Rural Appraisers,* October, 1952, pp. 149-152.

ENGLEHORN, V. A., "The American Society Approach to Various Kinds of Value," *Journal of the American Society of Farm Managers and Rural Appraisers,* April, 1960, pp. 4-8.

## Rural Property

EVANS, BERNARD G., "Farmlands and Rights of Way," *Right of Way,* February, 1956, pp. 13-18.

FARM AND RANCH BROKERS MANUAL, *National Institute of Farm and Land Brokers.*

FEDEEAL RESERVE BANK OF KANSAS CITY, "Farm Finance In This Modern Era," *The Appraisal Journal,* Federal Reserve Bank of Kansas City, January, 1960, pp. 90-96.

FEDERAL RESERVE BANK OF CLEVELAND, "Airplanes In Agriculture," *The Appraisal Journal,* October, 1959, pp. 572-577.

FEDERAL RESERVE BANK OF CLEVELAND, "Liquidity In the Agriculture Sector," *The Appraisal Journal,* July, 1963, pp. 396-401.

FEDERAL RESERVE BANK OF CLEVELAND, "The Surge In Farm Income," *The Appraisal Journal,* April, 1959, pp. 239-243.

FEDERAL RESERVE BANK OF RICHMOND, "Farm Real Estate-A Complicated Price Program," *The Appraisal Journal,* January, 1955, pp. 96-99.

FIELD, RALPH V., "Farm Land Appraisal Standards," *The Appraisal Journal,* January, 1938, pp. 40-49.

FINOL, VINCENCIO BAEZ, *El Impuesto Predial Rural Su Institucion En Venenzuela,* Consejo De Bienestar Rural, Caracas, 1961.

FLEET, C. J., "Use of Linear Programming In Farm Planning," *Journal of the American Society of Farm Managers and Rural Appraisers,* April, 1963, pp. 55-60.

FORREST C. HOLVECK, "Farm Personal Property Discovery and Valuation," *Assessment Administration,* Institute of American Appraisers Officers, Chicago, 1965, pp. 135-133.

FORSBERG, WINIFIELD, "Trends In Cost Allocation on Rented Farms," *Journal of the American Society of Farm Managers and Rural Appraisers,* April, 1963, pp. 38-46.

FRANZEN, WILLIAM F., "Appraising Rural Property In Todays Market," *The Appraisal Journal,* January, 1953, pp. 58-66.

FRUIN, E. G., "Yardstick for Farm Earning Comparisons," *Journal of the American Society of Farm Managers and Rural Appraisers,* October, 1948, pp. 196-197.

GADDIS, P. L., "Some Fundamentals of Farm Appraisal," *The Appraisal Journal,* April, 1946, pp. 143.

GAMBLE, W. P., "Current Appraisal Problems," *Journal of the American Society of Farm Managers and Rural Appraisers,* October, 1949, pp. 109-115.

GARCIA PAREDES, JENARO, "Metodologia Evaluacion De Fincas Rusticas," *Boletin,* Sotave, Caracas, Venezuela, pp. 45-50.

GARRISON CHARLES B., "New Industry In Rural Areas The Local Economic Import," *Tennessee Survey of Business,* University of Tennessee, April, 1971, pp. 3-6, 15-16.

GOTSCH, C. H., C. P. A. TIMMER, "A Consistent Estimate of the Value of Animal Products In West Pakistan," *Pakistan Development Review,* 1967, pp. 485-803.

GRAF, WAYNE J., "The Importance of Farm Managers and Rural Appraisers," *Journal of the American Society of Farm Managers and Rural Appraisers,* October, 1956, pp. 51-56.

GROETSCH, FOREST L., "Evaluation Fields Cut Up by Highways," *Journal of the American Society of Farm Managers and Rural Appraisers,* October, 1949, pp. 142-144.

GUERRERO, DANTE, "Formula Aprovechamiento De Los Terrenos," *Boletin,* Sotave, Caracas, Venezuela, pp. 20-33.

GUERRERO, SAULO E., "Importancia Reglamentacion De La Ley Agraria," *Boletin,* Sotave, Caracas, Venezuela, pp. 3-4.

GUILFORD, W. S, "Appraising Berry Farms," *The Appraisal Journal,* July, 1938, pp. 262-266.

HAMMAR, CONRAD H., "Land Classification to Aid the Appraiser," *Journal of Land and Public Utility Economics*, August, 1939, pp. 277-286.

HANNAH, H. W., "Procedures Ordinarily Involved In Buying a Farm," *Journal of the American Society of Farm Managers and Rural Appraisers*, April, 1947, pp. 50-52.

HARDIN, LOWELL S., "The Impact of Technological Changes on Farm Management," *Journal of the American Society of Farm Managers and Rural Appraisers*, April, 1957, pp. 8-10.

HEDGE, A M, KLINGEBIEL, A A, "The Use of Soil Maps," *1957 Year Book*, U.S. Government Printing Office, Washington, D.C., January 1, 1957, pp. 400-411.

HELLER, ROGER, "Looking Ahead--Farm/Ranch Leases," *Journal; Proceedings*, Am. Soc. Farm Mgrs-Rural Appraisers, Denver, November 27, 1973, pp. 36-37.

HENINGTON, CHARLES R., "Reconciling Different Indications of Farm Land Values," *Assessment Administration*, IAAO, Chicago, 1965, pp. 82-87.

HENRY, ERNEST E., "Appraising Farm Lands," *The Appraisal Journal*, January, 1946, pp. 33-37.

HENRY, ROSS F., "A Modern Farm," *Assessment Administration*, IAAO, Chicago, 1960, pp. 212-219.

HESTE, W. F., "Demonstration Appraisal--A Run Down Farm," *Assessment Administration*, I. A. A. O., Chicago, 1957, pp. 102-112.

HOBBS, W. E., "Accounting for Buildings In Farm Property Valuation," *The Appraisal Journal*, July, 1937, pp. 262-269.

HOLCOMB, J. M., "An Academic Approach to Professional Management," *Journal of the American Society of Farm Managers and Rural Appraisers*, October, 1963, pp. 25-27.

HOLCOMB, J. M., "What Are the Possibilities of Low Cost Farm Appraisals," *Journal of the American Society of Farm Managers and Rural Appraisers*, April, 1963, pp. 80-83.

HOUSE, PETER, *Preferential Assessment of Farmland In the Rural-Urban Fringe of Maryland*, U. S. Dept of Agriculture Economic Research Servic, Washington, 1961, pp. 20.

HOYT, HOMER, "Appraisal of Different Types of Real Property," *The Appraisal Journal*, July, 1964, pp. 383-393.

HUBBARD, DAVID F., "Research for Farm Appraisals," *Journal of the American Society of Farm Managers and Rural Appraisers*, October, 1959, pp. 8-11.

IGNATYEV, G. M., "Classification of Cultural and Natural Vegetation Sites As a Basis for Land Evaluation," *Land Evaluation*, pp. 104.

INSTITUTO AGRARIO NACIONAL (VZLA.), "Manual De Procedimientos Para Avaluo De Fincas," *Boletin*, Sotave, Caracas, Venezuela, pp. 35-42.

JENKINS, W. A., "Farm Credit In Canada," *Appraisal Institute Magazine*, Appraisal Institute of Canada, Winnipeg.

JENSEN, HOWARD I, "Market Approach to Basic Rural Appraisal," *Valutape Audio-Library Series*, American Society of Appraisers, Washington D.C., January 1, 1973.

JENSEN, HOWARD I, "Partial Acquisition of a Farm Property," *Valutape Audio-Library*, American Society of Appraisers, Washington D.C., January 1, 1974.

JOHNSON, BARRY E, "Appraisal of Leasehold Interests," *Journal; Proceedings*, Am. Soc. Farm Mgrs-Rural Appraisers, Denver, November 27, 1973, pp. 38-42.

JOHNSON, DONAL, "Research As an Input In Agricultural Production," *Journal; Proceedings*, Am. Soc Farm Mgrs-Rural Appraisers, Denver, November 27, 1973, pp. 69-70.

JOHNSON, RUSSELL BRUCE, PH. D., *Agricultural Loan Evaluation with Discriminant Analysis*, University of Missouri, 1971.

JOUR OF AMER SOC OF FARM MGRS & RURAL APPRAISERS, "California Society of Farm Managers and Rural Appraisers Suggested Appraisal Outline," *Journal of the American Society of Farm Managers and Rural Appraisers*, October, 1962, pp. 29-30.

JOUR OF AMER SOC OF FARM MGRS & RURAL APPRAISERS, "Minimum Provisions for an Act to Certify Real Property Appraisers," *Journal of the American Society of Farm Managers and Rural Appraisers*, October, 1962, pp. 62-66.

JOUR OF AMER SOC OF FARM MGRS & RURAL APPRAISERS, "The American Rural Appraisal System," *Journal of the American Society of Farm Managers and Rural Appraisers*, October, 1946, pp. 84-99.

JUDSON, A. R., "Appraising Under Virgin or Changing Conditions," *Journal of the American Society of Farm Managers and Rural Appraisers*, April, 1950, pp. 51-59.

KELLOG, CHARLES E, "We Seek to Learn," *1957 Yearbook U.S. Dept. of Agriculture*, United States Government Printing Office, Washington, D.C., January 1, 1957, pp. 1-11.

KELLOUGH, W. R., "Agricultural Economics and Appraisal Sources," *Appraisal Institute Magazine*, Appraisal Institute of Canada, Winnipeg.

KELLOUGH, W. R., "Agriculture Economics and Appraisal Sources," *AIREA*, July, 1967, pp. 17-20.

KELLOUGH, W. R., "Income Approach on a Muck Farm," *Appraisal Institute Magazine*, Appraisal Institute of Canada, Winnipeg.

KIREBSTEIN, RONALD GARY PH. D., *Temporal Production Interdependency In Agriculture Arising from Water Quality*, University of Washington, 1971.

KLEMME, A. W., "New Developments In Fertilizer Use," *Journal of the American Society of Farm Managers and Rural Appraisers*, April, 1951, pp. 59-64.

KNISKERN, PHILIP W., "Land," *Real Estate Appraisal and Valuation*, 1933, pp. 267-290.

KNOWLES, JEROME, JR., "Appraisal of Seasonal Country Property," *Appraisal Reporting Techniques*, 1951, pp. 1-34.

KOENINGS, ROMAN, "Federal Programs for Outdoor Recreation As They Stand," *Journal of American Society of Farmers and Managers of Rural Appraisers*,

KRAUSZ, N. G. P. AND FREDERICK G. PINK, "Agricultural Assessing Practices: Legislative Action to Control Rural Land Assessing In Areas Subject," *County Officer*, April, 1963, pp. 151-158.

LASSITER, ROY ., MCPHERSON, W. K, *Agricultural Land Prices In Palm Beach County, Florida, 1940-1955*, Florida Agricultural Experiment Station, Gainesville, 1959.

LASSITER, ROY L., "Subsidence and Land Values of Organic Soils," *The Appraisal Journal*, October, 1958, pp. 542-548.

LAWRENCE, DAVID M., MAY, HAROLD G, REES, W. H, *Modern Methods of Valuation of Land, Housing, and Buildings*, The Estates Gazette, London, 1949, pp. 2.

LAWRENCE, DAVID M., REES, W. H, *Modern Methods of Land, Houses, and Buildings*, Estates Gazette, London, 1956.

LESSINGER, JACK, "Exclusive Agricluture Zoning, an Appraisal," *Land Economics*, May, 1958.

MAHAFFY, A. W., "Price Vs. Value and the Theory of Rural Appraisal," *The Appraisal Institute Magazine*, December, 1961, pp. 20-25.

MANZUR PACHECO, RUBEN, "Consideraciones La Forma Geometrica," *Boletin*, Sotave, Caracas, Venezuela, pp. 31-34.

MATSON, ARTUR J., NORMAN E. ZISCHKE, "Estimating Market Value of Farmland on Basis of Soil Ratings In Brookings County, South Dakora," *Journal of the American Society of Farm Managers and Rural Appraisers*, October, 1963, pp. 49-57.

MCDONALD, ADRIAN F., "The Meaning of Value," *Encyclopedia of Real Estate Appraising*, Friedman, Edith J, 1959, pp. 15-36.

# BIBLIOGRAPHY OF APPRAISAL LITERATURE

MCDONALD, D. L., "The National Capital Commission and Its Effect on Real Estate Activities," *Appraisal Institute Magazine,* September, 1960, pp. 3-5.

MCFARLEN, T. A., "The Rural Appraisal Report," *Appraisal Institute Magazine,* January, 1957, pp. 16-17.

MCLAUGHLIN, WALTER W., "A Comparison of Landlord and Tenant Earnings on 50-50 Livestock Lease and Crop Share Lease," *Journal of the American Society of Farm Managers and Rural Appraisers,* October, 1947, pp. 86-89.

MCMAHEN, D. H., "Effect of Improving Technology on Land Values In the Mountain States," *Journal of the American Society of Farm Managers and Rural Appraisers,* April, 1956, pp. 52-56.

MEENEN, H. J., "The Impact of Technology and Government Programs Upon Value," *Journal of the American Society of Farm Manager and Rural Appraisers,* April, 1957, pp. 76-81.

MONTANO, JOSEPH M., "Fundamentals of Real Property," *American Association of State Highway Officials,* 1962, pp. 7-15.

MORGAN, BELDEN, "Values In Transition Areas Some New Concepts," *The Review,* March, 1952, pp. 5-10.

MORRISON, E. R., "Bench Marks In Finding Value," *Journal American Society of Farm Managers and Rural Appraisers,* April, 1960, pp. 16-21.

MORSE, TRUE D., "Practical Aspects of Rural Appraising," *The Appraisal Journal,* July, 1940, pp. 230-235.

MORSE, TRUE D., "The American Rural Appraisal System," *The Appraisal Journal,* July, 1940, pp. 23--235.

MORSE, TRUE D., "The Gyroscope of Rural Appraisals," *The Appraisal Journal,* July, 1937, pp. 219-224.

MORSY, NASHAAT, "Valuation of Agricultural Land In Egypt After the Agrarian Reform Law," *Technical Valuation,* February, 1956, pp. 7-10, 25-29, 35-39, 13-15.

MURRAY, WILLIAM G, "What Is a Farm Appraisal?," *Farm Appraisal and Valuation,* Iowa State University Press, Ames Iowa, January 1, 1961, pp. 3-11.

N. Y. TIMES INDEX, "Indian Community Threatened by Land Boom," *N. Y. Times Index,* October 18, 1970.

NOLAN, JAMES J., "Appraisal of Acreage Property," *The Real Estate Appraiser,* November, 1969, pp. 39-42.

NORE, KENNETH C., "Use of Airphoto Interpretation In Agricultural Land Economics Research," *Land Economics,* November, 1961, pp. 321-326.

ONTARIO DEPT OF AGRICULTURE, "Considerations In Buying a Farm," *Appraisal Institute Magazine,* Appraisal Institute of Canada, Winnipeg.

OWEN, GEORGE, "Farm Land Value and Farm Credit," *Appraisal Institute Magazine,* Appraisal Institute of Canada, Winnipeg.

OWEN, GEORGE, "Mortgage Lending In the Agricultural Industry," *Appraisal Institute Magazine,* Appraisal Institute of Canada, Winnipeg.

PADDOCK, JAMES C., "California Orchard and Vineyard Appraisals," *The Appraisal Journal,* October, 1968, pp. 576-592.

PAWLEY, R. W., "Rural Appraising-A Prescription," *Appraisal Institute Magazine,* Appraisal Institute of Canada, Winnipeg.

PAWLEY, R. W., "The Appraisal of a Farm Business," *Appraisal Institute Magazine,* Appraisal Institute of Canada, Winnipeg.

PEARSON, NORMAN, "Effect of Urbanization on Agricultural Land," *Appraisal Institute Magazine,* Appraisal Institute of Canada, Winnipeg, September 1, 1972.

▲ Rural Property

PENA GARCIA, M. A., "El Metodo Residual En La Practica Del Avaluo Rural," *Boletin*, Sotave, Caracas, Venezuela, pp. 5-6.

PENA GARCIA, M. A., "Un Mercado En Recesion Para La Tierra," *Boletin*, Sotave, Caracas, Venezuela, pp. 21.

PETERSON, T. A., "Credit As a Factor of Production In Agriculture," *Appraisal Institute Magazine*, 1969, pp. 39-51.

PORTER, JOHN W., "Appraisal of Hopyards," *Technical Valuation*, February, 1963, pp. 28-30.

PRIMM, HAROLD M., "A New Look at Basis for Charging Farm Management Fees- Pros and Cons," *Journal of the American Society of Farm Managers and Rural Appraisers*, October, 1962, pp. 58-59.

PROUTY, W. L. AND OTHERS, "Greenhouses, Barns, Sheds and Miscellaneous Buildings," *Appraisers and Assessors Manual*, 1930, pp. 231-236.

PROUTY, W. L. AND OTHERS, "The Appraisal of Merchandise, Fixtures, Equipment, Furniture, Household Goods, Livestock," *Appraisers, and Assessors Manual*, 1930, pp. 421-460.

RAAFLAUB, O. V., "Appraising the Rural Country Store," *Appraisal Institute Magazine*, Appraisal Institute of Canada, Winnipeg.

REHNBERG, REX D., "Agicultural Land Values," *Technical Valuation*, October, 1957, pp. 17-21.

ROE, G. P., "Valuation of Rural Properties-The Effects of Management," *Appraisal Institute Magazine*, September, 1969, pp. 17-23.

ROGERS, C. N., "The Comparative Method of Appraisal," *Jour of Amer Soc of Farm Mgs & Rural Appraisers*, October, 1946, pp. 117-122.

ROGERS, JOHN V., "Why Does the Land In the Inner Blue Grass Sell Higher Than Other Land?," *Journal of the Amer Soc of Farm Mgrs & Rural Appraisers*, October, 1953, pp. 138-141.

RUSSELL, BRUCE, "Buildings for Tenant-Operated Farms," *Journal of the American Society of Farm Managers and Rural Appraisers*, April, 1946, pp. 49-51.

RYAN, JOHN L., "Government Regulations Affecting the Value of Agricultural Properties," *The Appraisal Journal*, July, 1956, pp. 399-407.

SARGENT, FREDERIC O., "Land Market and Price, Analysis In an Agro-Industrial Economy," *The Appraisal Journal*, July, 1959, pp. 259-264.

SCOFIELD, WILLIAM H., "Federal Programs and Policies Affecting Farmland Values," *Assessment Administration*, Institute of American Assessment Officers, Chicago, 1965, pp. 119-123.

SCOFIELD, WILLIAM H., "Land Prices and Farm Earnings," *The Appraisal Journal*, January, 1965, pp. 100-113.

SCOTT, JOHN T. JR., "Economic Impact of Industrialization on Traditional Rural Areas," *Journal of the Society of American Farm Managers and Rural Appraisers*, October, 1968, pp. 8-13.

SHAPIRO, H., "Assessment and Taxation of Tangible Personal Property on Farms," *National Tax Journal*, March, 1965, pp. 25.

SHAPIRO, HARVEY, *Taxation of Tangible Personal Property Used In Agriculture*, U. S. Dept of Agriculture Economic Research Servic, Washington, 1962, pp. 1-45.

SIMON, ROBERT E., "The Effect of Concepts on the Value of Land," *Appraisal and Valuation Manual*, 1964, pp. 107.

SIMONETT, D. S., "Land Evaluation Studies with Remote Sensors In the Infrared and Radar Regions," *Land Evaluation*, pp. 349.

SOLBERG, ERLING D., "Countryside, USA," *The Residential Appraiser*, October, 1959, pp. 14-24.

STEWARD, CHARLES L., "The Non-Immunity of Farm Land to Atomic Developments," *The Appraisal Journal*, October, 1947, pp. 464-470.

STEWARD, CHARLES L., "The Place of Buildings In Appraising Illinois Farms," *The Appraisal Journal*, April, 1935, pp. 248-252.

STEWART, CHARLES L., "Buying a Farm," *The Appraisal Journal*, April, 1942, pp. 125-131.

STEWART, CHARLES L., "Factors Influencing Price of Farm Land," *The Appraisal Journal*, July, 1949, pp. 351-359.

STEWART, CHARLES L., "Gross Earnings As a Guide In Farm Appraisals," *The Appraisal Journal*, July, 1939, pp. 230-239.

STRUNG, J., "Farm Appraising," *Appraisal Institute Magazine*, September, 1963, pp. 21-22.

SUTER, ROBERT C, *The Appraisal of Farm Real Estate (Book)*, Interstate Printers and Publishers Inc, Lafayette Indiana, January 1, 1974.

SUTER, ROBERT C., "The Management Process," *Journal of the American Society of Farm Managers and Rural Appraisers*, October, 1963, pp. 5-18.

SWANEY, FRED, "Developing Land for Recreational Use," *Farm and Land Realtor*, January, 1971.

SWANSON, EARL R., "Crop Intensity and Income Stability," *Jour of Amer Soc of Farm Mgrs & Rural Appraisers*, October, 1962, pp. 45-48.

SWANSON, EARL R., "Tenant's Labor Contribution and Highest Return Farming Systems," *Journal of the American Society of Farm Managers and Rural Appraisers*, April, 1961, pp. 79-85.

SWITZER, DOROTHY, "Rural Development and Rural-Urban Balance," *Business In Nebraska, No. 326*, University of Nebraska, November, 1971, pp. 1-3.

THEISS, WILLIAM R., "Damages for Obstruction of Road Abutting Rural Property. Appraisal Docket," *The Appraisal Journal*, July, 1963, pp. 415-417.

THOMAS, BERY E., "Assessment of Farm Personal Property," *Assessment Administration*, IAAO, Chicago, 1957, pp. 159-161.

THOMSON, F. L., *Agricultural Prices*, Mcgraw-Hill Book Company, 1936.

THORKELSON, GERALD F., "Rural Appraisals to Meet Users Needs," *Jour of Amer Soc of Farm Mgrs & Rural Appraisers*, April, 1961, pp. 63-76.

THOS, D. WOODS, E. J. MCCORMICK R. E. BLANCHARD, "Farm Tenant Selection - an Objective Method," *Jour of Amer Soc of Farm Mgrs & Rural Appraisers*, October, 1958, pp. 38-46.

THRUN, FRED MARTIN, *A Local Farm Real Estate Price Index*, E. Lansing, Michigan, 1929.

TIDEMANN, ARTHUR R, KLEMMEDSON, JAMES O, "Effect of Mesquite on Physical and Chemical Properties of the Soil," *Journal of Range Management Vol 26 No.1*, Society of Range Management, Denver Colorado, pp. 27-29.

TOLCOTT, M., H. E. HENNEFRUND, N. G. LACY, "Valuation of Real Estate with Special Reference to Farm Real Estate," *Agriculture Economics Bibliography*,

TOWNSEND, T. L., "A Vision of Rural Appraising," *Appraisal Institute Magazine*, Appraisal Institute of Canada, Winnipeg.

TOWNSEND, T. L., "Changing Concepts In Rural Appraising," *Appraisal Institute Magazine*, Appraisal Institute of Canada, Winnipeg.

TOWNSEND, T. L., "The Changing Concepts In Rural Appraising Since the Thirties," *Appraisal Institute Magazine*, March, 1964.

TOWNSEND, T. L., "The Income Approach to Valuing Farm Lands," *Appraisal Institute Magazine*, Appraisal Institute of Canada, Winnipeg.

TRENT, I. J., "Valuation of Rural Lands-Cleared Acre Basis," *Appraisal Institute Magazine*, September, 1965, pp. 44-46.

▲ Rural Property

TURPIE, A., "Rural Appraisal Principles - Town and Farm," *Appraisal Institute Magazine*, January, 1957, pp. 13-15.

TURPIE, A., "Rural Appraisal Principles-Town and Farm," *Appraisal Institute Magazine*, Appraisal Institute of Canada, Winnipeg.

U. S. DEPARTMENT OF AGRICULTURE, *Yearbook of Agriculture, 1943-1947, Science of Farming*, Govt. Printing Office, Washington, 1949.

U. S. GOVERNMENT PRINTING OFFICE, *The City Expands, a Study of The Conversion of Land from Rural to Urban Use*, U. S. Govt. Printing Office, Washington.

VAN VUUREN, W., *Agricultural Land Prices and Returns In an Advanced Urban and Industrial Economy*, Dissertation Abstracts, Ann Arbor, March, 1969, pp. 2863-A.

VERHAGEN, A. M., F. HIRST, A. G. LLOYD, "Expected Values of Cost and Revenuesdependent on Drought," *Australian Journal of Agricultural Economics*, December, 1968.

VINCENT, G., "L'Evaluation Des Bien-Fonds Agricoles," *Appraisal Institute Magazine*, Appraisal Institute of Canada, Winnipeg.

WALD, HASKELL P., *Taxation of Agricultural Land In Underdeveloped Economies; a Survey and Guide to Policy*, University Press, Cambridge, 1959, pp. 1-231.

WALLACE, JAMES J., "How to Maximize Farm Profits In the Next Few Years," *Journal of the American Society of Farm Managers and Rural Appraiser*, October, 1951, pp. 151-156.

WALLACE, JAMES J., "Medium Farm," *Journal of the American Society of Farm Managers and Rural Appraisers*, April, 1957, pp. 23.

WALLACE, LEW E., *Depreciation of Farm Machinery*, Transamerican Society of Agriculture Engineering, pp. 139.

WEEKS, DAVID, "The Impact on Farm Land Values of Increased Population," *The Appraisal Journal*, October, 1951, pp. 479-497.

WESTBY, R. L., ALFRED, A. H, SAYNWITTGENSTEIN, L, "The Potential of Large-Scale Air Photographs and Radar Alimetry In Land Evaluation," *Land Valuation*, pp. 376.

WHITELAW, ROBERT, "Supervised Woodlots," *Appraisal Institute Magazine*, Appraisal Institute of Canada, Winnipeg.

WILLNETTE, MCDONNELL, WOLCOTT, EDUCATION COMMITTEE, "Allotment Valuation," *Problems In Rural Real Estate Appraisal*, pp. 23.

WILNETTE, MCDONNELL, WOLCOTT, "Basic Principles and Procedures," *Problems In Rural Real Estate Appraisal*, pp. 1.

WILNETTE, MCDONNELL, WOLCOTT, "Farm Operating Statements," *Problems In Rural Real Estate Appraisal*, pp. 10.

ZANGERLE, J. A., "Table for Comparing Allotment Property Adjoining Acreage Property," *Appraising Manual, 2nd Edition*, 1937.

"American Institute of Real Estate Appraisers," *Rural Appraisal Problems with Suggested Solutions*,

*Effects of Upstream Watershed Developmt Upon Prices & Values of Affected Farmland In Selected Areas*, Dissertation Abstracts, Vol. Xxvii, No. 1, Ann Arbor, July, 1966, pp. 15-A.

*Study of Certain Aspects of Agricultl Land Taxation In State of Punjab, India Vol. Xxvii-A, No. 1.*, Dissertation Abstracts, Ann Arbor, July, 1966.

*Economic Appraisal of Role of Government In Agricultural Utilization Research & Product Development*, University of Georgia, 1971.

## 14-12 Crop Allotment

ADAMS, RICHARD L., *Farm Management Crop Manual,* University of California, Berkeley California, 1953.

BRADFORD, C. R., "Making Use of Soils and Crops Data In the Valuation of Farm Property," *The Appraisal Institute Magazine,* June, 1960, pp. 14-18.

CONGDON, WALTER B., "Livestock and Crop Appraisals," *Technical Valuation,* American Society of Appraisers, June, 1954, pp. 45.

ELKIN, A. DAVIS, "The Effects on Rural Appraisal Values of Government Acreage Allotments and Price Controls," *Journal of the American Society of Farm Managers and Rural Appraisers, Vol. Xix,* April, 1955, pp. 22-26.

GALE, JOHN F., "How Much Is a Crop Allotment Worth," *The Appraisal Journal,* July, 1965, pp. 370-376.

ROBINSON, E. B., "Factors Which Affect the Appraisal of Field Crop Farms In California," *Journal of the American Society of Farm Managers and Rural Appraisers,* October, 1953, pp. 113-120.

SWANSON, EARL R., "Crop Intensity and Income Stability," *Jour of Amer Soc of Farm Mgrs & Rural Appraisers,* October, 1962, pp. 45-48.

TRASK, ELWOOD E., "Farm Appraisal - Acreage and Crops," *Technical Valuation,* June, 1955, pp. 53-57.

WALLACE, JAMES J., "How to Maximize Farm Profits In the Next Few Years," *Journal of the American Society of Farm Managers and Rural Appraiser,* October, 1951, pp. 151-156.

WILLNETTE, MCDONNELL, WOLCOTT, EDUCATION COMMITTEE, "Allotment Valuation," *Problems In Rural Real Estate Appraisal,* pp. 23.

## 14-13 Soils

BAILEY, REX R., "How Much Increased Yields Shall Be Recognized from New Soil Treatments In Permanent Productivity," *Journal, American Society of Farm Mgrs and Rural Appraisers,* April, 1951, pp. 40-43.

BEETHOVEN, EDWIN C., "Elements of Soil Engineering," *Acquisition for Right-Of-Way,* American Association of State Highway Officials, Washington, D. C, 1962, pp. 251-258.

## Rural Property

BERTRAMSON, B. R., "Soil Aeration In Relation to Fertility," *The Journal of the American Society of Farm Managers and Rural Appraisers*, October, 1948, pp. 31-35.

BRADFORD, C. R., "Soils In Relation to Rural Appraising," *The Appraisal Institute Magazine*, December, 1957, pp. 21-31.

DILLE, J. M., "Reclamation In Its Practical Aspects," *Journal of The American Society of Farm Managers and Rural Appraisers*, October, 1949, pp. 145-151.

DOWELL, J. M., "Practical Soil Conservation," *Journal of the American Society of Farm Managers and Rural Appraisers*, October, 1947, pp. 107-113.

GIFFORD, GERALD F, SHAW, CONNER B, "Soil Moisture Patterns on Two Chained Pinyon-Juniper Sites In Utah," *Range Management*, Society of Range Management, Denver Colorado, November 1, 1973, pp. 436-440.

HALL, A. A., "Use of Soil Classification In Determining Farm Land Values," *Assessment Administration*, I. A. A. O, Chicago, 1957, pp. 187-191.

HEDGE, A M, KLINGEBIEL, A A, "The Use of Soil Maps," *1957 Year Book*, U.S. Government Printing Office, Washington, D.C., January 1, 1957, pp. 400-411.

JACOBS, JAMES PH. D., *Exemplified by Specific Pollutants In Agricultural Runoff*.

KLEMME, A. W., "New Developments In Fertilizer Use," *Journal of the American Society of Farm Managers and Rural Appraisers*, April, 1951, pp. 59-64.

LASSITER, ROY L., "Subsidence and Land Values of Organic Soils," *The Appraisal Journal*, October, 1958, pp. 542-548.

LYON AND BUCKMAN, "The Nature and Properties of Soils," *A.S.A. Valuation Manual*, Macmillan, New York, 1951.

MATSON, ARTUR J., NORMAN E. ZISCHKE, "Estimating Market Value of Farmland on Basis of Soil Ratings In Brookings County, South Dakota," *Journal of the American Society of Farm Managers and Rural Appraisers*, October, 1963, pp. 49-57.

MISCHKE, ARTHUR, "Getting Scientific with Soils and Sales," *Assessment Administration*, 1960, pp. 50-52.

MORRISON, E. R., "Know Your Soils to Become a Rural Appraiser," *Journal of the American Society of Farm Managers and Rural Appraisers*, April, 1963, pp. 70-74.

MURRAY, WILLIAM G., "Use of Soil Classification In Determining Farm Values," *Assessment Administration*, IAAO, Chicago, 1957, pp. 180-185.

NELSON, ALBERT H., "Use of Soil Classification In Determining Farm Land Values," *Assessment Administration*, Institute of American Assessment Officers, Chicago, 1957, pp. 185-187.

ODELL, R. T., "Characteristics of Some Important Illinois Soils," *Journal of the American Society of Farm Managers and Rural Appraisers*, October, 1954, pp. 10-17.

ODELL, RUSSELL T., "The Effect of Physical Properties of Soils on Productivity," *Journal of the American Society of Farm Managers and Rural Appraisers*, April, 1948, pp. 42-47.

PARTAIN, LLOYD E., "The Profit Aspects of Soil Conservation," *Journal of the American Society of Farm Managers and Rural Appraisers*, April, 1948, pp. 60-69.

U. S. AGRICULTURAL RESEARCH SERVICE, *Farm Real Estate Taxes, Recent Trends and Developments*, U. S. Agricultural Research Service, Washington, 1960, pp. 1-14.

WEAVER, HOWARD S., *Real Estate Appraising: Farm Land Division*, Weaver Real Estate Appraisal Traning Services, 1940.

WEITZELL, E. C., "Credit for Financing Soil Conservation," *The Appraisal Journal*, April, 1948, pp. 189-199.

WHITE, RAYMOND W., "Role of Private Companies In Conservation and Development of Water Resources," *Right of Way,* December, 1957, pp. 23-30.

WILNETT, MCDONNELL, WOLCOTT, "Soils," *Problems In Rural Real Estate Appraisal,* pp. 7.

## 14-14   Irrigated Land

AKIN, WAYNE M., "A Supplement for Use In Appraising Irrigated Farms by the American Rural Appraisal System," *Journal of the American Society of Farm Managers and Rural Appraisers,* April, 1949, pp. 53-55.

BRESNAHAN, C. A., "Development of Irrigation Water Rights," *Appraisal and Valuation Manual,* The American Society of Appraisers, Washington, D. C, 1956, pp. 227-237.

BRESNAHAN, C. A., "Irrigation Water," *Appraisal Journal,* July, 1948, pp. 336-345.

COLLINS, H. G., "Security Value of Irrigation Farms," *Appraisal Institute Magazine,* March, 1961, pp. 14-18.

DORAN, SAMUEL M, "The Economic Feasibility of Irrigation Development," *Journal; Proceedings,* Am. Soc. Farm Mgrs-Rural Appraisers, Denver, November 27, 1973, pp. 5-15.

GILBERT, DEWAYNE E., "Climatic In Rural Irrigation Conditions Factors In Rural Land Valuation," *Assessment Administration,* I. A. A. O, Chicago, 1964, pp. 137-140.

KNOBEL, FRED, "Irrigated Pastures of California and Appraisal Factors Involved," *Journal of the American Society of Farm Managers and Rural Appraisers,* October, 1953, pp. 129-137.

O'CONNOR, JAMES G, "Appraisal of Irrigation Projects," *Journal; Proceedings,* Am. Soc. Farm Mgrs-Rural Appraisers, Denver, November 27, 1973, pp. 17-21.

SHAFFER, FORD G., "Appraisal of Irrigated Land," *The Appraisal Journal,* October, 1950, pp. 512-518.

WATTS, JOHN F., "Appraisal of the Alpaugh Irrigation Water Rights In Kern County, California," *Appraisal and Valuation Manual,*

WOOD, IVAN D., "Physical Essentials for Irrigation," *Jour of Amer Soc of Farm Mgrs & Rural Appraisers,* April, 1955, pp. 56-58.

WORLEY DON, "Efficient Use of Irrigation Water," *Journal; Proceedings,* American Society Farm Mgrs-Rural Appraisers, Denver, November 27, 1973, pp. 1-5.

## 14-15  Dry Farm Land

ABEL, HAROLD, "Effect of Expanding Western Population on Livestock Marketing and Range Value," *The Appraisal Journal*, April, 1953, pp. 239-243.

ADAMS, RICHARD L., *Farm Management Crop Manual*, University of California, Berkeley California, 1953.

AHMEN, M.M. A., "An Economic Evaluation of Farmland for Tax Assessment, Tulsa County, Oklahoma," *Dissertation Abstracts*, September, 1965, pp. 1384.

BAILEY, REX R., "Appraisals for Tax Assessment," *Journal of the American Society of Farm Managers and Rural Appraisers*, April, 1949, pp. 36-42.

BAILEY, REX R., "How Much Increased Yields Shall Be Recognized from New Soil Treatments In Permanent Productivity," *Journal, American Society of Farm Mgrs and Rural Appraisers*, April, 1951, pp. 40-43.

BAILEY, REX R., "The Appraisal of a Farm Operated Under the Missouri Balanced Farming Program," *Journal of the American Society of Farm Managers and Rural Appraisers*, October, 1948, pp. 141-146.

BAKER, VERNE, "Farm Appraising," *Right of Way*, December, 1954, pp. 13-16.

BARTLETT, CHARLES R., "Appraisal In Relation to Assessment of Farm Land," *The Residential Appraiser*, October, 1960, pp. 7-9.

BEAUDOIN FERNAND J., "The Application of Income Approach to Value In Appraising of Farms for Agricultural Purposes," *Appraisal Institute Magazine*, 1968, pp. 9-16.

BEAUDOIN, FERNAND J., "Bench-Mark Appraisals In Farm Valuation," *Appraisal Institute Magazine*, January, 1970, pp. 17-26.

BERWICK, A. J., "Comments on Paper by W. N. Thompson and James O. Melton," *The Journal of the American Society of Farm Manager and Rural Appraisers*, October, 1962, pp. 60-61.

BOHANNON, DAVID D., "Converting Farms to Subdivisions," *The Appraisal Journal*, October, 1945, pp. 362-364.

BRADFORD, C. R., "Making Use of Soils and Crops Data In the Valuation of Farm Property," *The Appraisal Institute Magazine*, June, 1960, pp. 14-18.

BROWN OLIVER S., "Appraisal and Management Adjustments Under Controls and Changing Production," *Journal of the American Society of Farm Managers and Rural Appraisers*, May, 1950, pp. 49-50.

BUREAU OF AGRICULTURAL ECONOMICS, *Land Settlement*, Department of Agriculture, Washington, 1934.

BUZZARD, GLENN W., "Trends In Appraising Farms for Loans," *Journal of the American Society of Farm Managers and Rural Appraisers*, April, 1963, pp. 75-79.

CARMAN, H. F., J. G. POLSON, "Tax Shifts Occurring As a Result of Differential Assessment of Farmland California 1968-1969," *National Tax Journal*, December, 1971.

CASE, H. C. M., "Value of Illinois Farm Land," *The Appraisal Journal*, July, 1934, pp. 336-340.

COOMBS, WHITNEY, *Taxation of Farm Property*, U. S. Printing Office, Washington, 1930.

COOPER, J. ROBERT, *Alternative Methods and Techniques for the Assessment of Farm Real Estate*, Clemson Agricultural College, Clemson, So. Carolina, 1957.

CUNNINGHAM, J. B., "Farm Lease," *Journal of the American Society of Farm Managers and Rural Appraisers*, October, 1952, pp. 119-120.

DAVIS, ROBERT A., "Expropriation Appraisal Farm Lands," *Appraisal Institute Magazine*, July, 1957, pp. 10-14.

DAVIS, W. D., "Farm Values Under War Conditions," *The Appraisal Journal*, July, 1942, pp. 228-236.

DAVIS, W. D., "How to Appraise Grain Farms," *The Appraisal Journal*, October, 1957, pp. 583-597.

DILLE, J. M., "Reclamation In Its Practical Aspects," *Journal of The American Society of Farm Managers and Rural Appraisers*, October, 1949, pp. 145-151.

DUNN, DOMINICK R., "Valuation of Farm Acreage," *The Appraisal Journal*, October, 1958, pp. 597-598.

EDMAN, J. J., "Severance Damages for Division of Farms. Appraisal Docket," *The Appraisal Journal*, April, 1959, pp. 268-269.

ELLIOTT, RALPH A., "Grass Farming," *Journal of the American Society of Farm Managers and Rural Appraisers*, April, 1951, pp. 48-50.

ENGLEHORN, V. A., "Problems of Appraisal Under a Grassland Farming System," *Journal of the American Society of Farm Managers and Rural Appraisers*, October, 1950, pp. 98-102.

EVERETTE, C. H., "The Farm Manager's Responsibility on Property Taxes," *Journal of the American Society of Farm Managers and Rural Appraisers*, October, 1955, pp. 33-37.

FARM APPRAISAL WORK AT COLLEGE LEVEL, *Journal of the American Society of Farm Managers and Rural Appraisers*, October, 1950, pp. 112-127.

FEDERAL RESERVE BANK OF CHICAGO, "Something New In Farm Land Values," *The Appraisal Journal*, January, 1958, pp. 111-117.

FEDERAL RESERVE BANK OF ST. LOUIS, "Farm Land Values," *The Appraisal Journal*, October, 1960, pp. 542-543.

FERGUSON, FRANCIS E, *Wisconsin Colloquium on Appraisal Research*, Wisc Colloq on Apprsl Resch, Papers & Proceedings, 1963, pp. 31-32.

FICK, H. G. E., "Appraisal of Farm Land," *Assessment Administration*, Institute of American Assessment Officers, Chicago, 1962, pp. 21-36.

FIELD, RALPH V., "Farm Land Appraisal Standards," *The Appraisal Journal*, January, 1938, pp. 40-49.

FIELD, RALPH V., "What Is Farm," *The Appraisal Journal*, April, 1944, pp. 133-142.

GAHR, EDMOND W., "Approved Method of Farm Assessments," *Technical Valuation*, February, 1960, pp. 51-53.

GOOD, WILLIAM CHARLES, *Production and Taxation In Canada from the Farmers Standpoint*, Garden City Press, Toronto, 1919.

GUTSCHENRITTER, FRANK, "Changing Techniques and Procedures Used In Appraising Farms," *Technical Valuation*, June, 1962, pp. 17-20.

HALL, A. A., "Use of Soil Classification In Determining Farm Land Values," *Assessment Administration*, I. A. A. O, Chicago, 1957, pp. 187-191.

HALL, HENRY C., "Farm Real Estate Values," *Journal of the American Society of Farm Managers and Rural Appraisers*, October, 1959, pp. 12-15.

HARTER, HUGH I., "Use of Sales Data In Making Farm Appraisals," *Journal of the American Society of Farm Managers and Rural Appraisers*, April, 1954, pp. 35-39.

▲ **Rural Property**

HARVEY, WILLIAM A., "Weed Control and Farm Land Valuatuon," *The Appraisal Journal,* October, 1951, pp. 526-529.

HENEBERRY, WILLIAM H., *Assessment of Farm Real Estate for Property Taxes,* Michigan State University, East Lansing, 1960.

HOUSE, PETER, "Partial Tax Exemption for Farmland Properties In the Rural-Urban Fringe," *The Appraisal Journal,* July, 1968, pp. 393-407.

HUDELSON, ROBERT R., "The American System of Farm Appraisal In Theory and Practice," *Journal of the American Society of Farm Management In Rural Appraisers,* April, 1945, pp. 44-48.

HUGHES, EARL M., "The Large Farm," *Journal of the American Societyof Farm Managers and Rural Appraisers,* April, 1957, pp. 24-28.

HULSE, FRED E., *Improving Farm Building Assessment Techniques,* College Park Department of Agriculture, College Park, Md., 1952.

HURLBURT, VIRGIL L., "Technology and Farmland Values," *Journal of the American Society of Farm Managers and Rural Appraisers,* October, 1960, pp. 75-83.

HUTCHINSON, R. M., "Appraisal of a Farm Property," *Appraisal Reporting Techniques,* AIREA, 1947, pp. 15-36.

JENNETT, C. B., "The Valuation of Farm Homes," *Appraisal Journal,* January, 1934, pp. 108-111.

JESNESS, O. B., "Factors Affecting Farm Land Prices," *ASA Valuation Manual,* December, 1957, pp. 84-85.

JOHNSON, E. C., "The Farm Real Estate Situation," *The Appraisal Journal,* January, 1947, pp. 51-56.

JUNDT, DWIGHT W., "Farm Land Prices, Future and Long-Range Outlook," *Journal of A. S. F. M. R. A.,* October, 1966, pp. 91-97.

L, AUSTIN, A., "Effect of Size of Farm on Investmt In Land Bldgs & Implements & Machinery In the Corn Belt," *Journal of the American Society of Farm Managers and Rural Appraisers,* October, 1945, pp. 93-97.

LEISTRITZ, FREDERICK LARRY, *Simulation Analysis of the Farm Real Estate Market and Farm Enlargement In Southwest Nebraska,* University of Nebraska, 1970.

LEROHL, M. L., "Farm Capital and Farm Taxation," *Appraisal Institute Magazine,* 1967, pp. 2-15.

LOCKWOOD, A. N., "The Dilemma of the Farm Appraiser," *Appraisal Digest,* January, 1961, pp. 7-9.

LORENS, EDWARD R., "Appraisal of Farm Property for Trunk Highway Right of Way In Minnesota," *Right of Way,* February, 1959, pp. 31-34.

MATTHEWS, WILLIAM P., "Farm Management and Rural Appraisal, Service and Charges," *Journal of the American Society of Farm Managers and Rural Appraisers,* April, 1956, pp. 10-16.

MAUCH, ARTHUR, "How Alternate Farm Programs Affect the Economy," *The Appraisal Journal,* October, 1956, pp. 573-577.

MAYER, LESTER B., "Farm Appraisals In a Period of Declining Prices," *Journal of the American Society of Farm Managers and Rural Appraisers,* April, 1949, pp. 24-27.

MCANELLY, E. E., "What Essentials Are Desired In an Appraisal by the Appraiser," *Journal of the American Society of Farm Managers and Rural Appraisers,* April, 1948, pp. 88092.

MCCARTHY, CHARLES R., "New Store Building Attached to Old Farm Building and Three Apartment Dwelling," *Assessment Administration,* Institute of American Assessment Officers, Chicago, 1961, pp. 220-226.

MCGOUGH R. M., "The Impact of Town Planning on Investment Decision," *Valuer,* The New Zealand Institute of Valuers, New Zealand, August 1, 1973, pp. 91-98.

MEHREN, GEORGE L., "Support and Control In the Farm Economy," *The Appraisal Journal*, October, 1949, pp. 423-430.

MELLOR, ROSS, "Farm Appraisal Problems," *The Appraisal Journal*, April, 1970, pp. 34-36.

MILLER, J. EARL, "Bulk Appraisals of Farm Lands," *The Appraisal Journal*, April, 1943, pp. 115-124.

MITCHELL, JACK, "Grassland Farming In Operation," *Journal of the American Society of Farm Manager and Rural Appraisers*, April, 1951, pp. 51-52.

MORSE, TRUE D., "Estimating the Value of Farm Lands," *The Appraisal Journal*, April, 1936, pp. 159-165.

MORSE, TRUE D., "The Influence of Special Assessments on Farm Values," *The Appraisal Journal*, July, 1935, pp. 335-341.

MOSHER, M. L., "Farms Are Growing Large-What of It?," *Journal of The American Society of Farm Managers and Rural Appraisers*, April, 1957, pp. 11-20.

MURRAY, HENRY T., "Appraisal of Farms and Ranches," *The Appraisal Journal*, April, 1954, pp. 250-255.

MURRAY, W. G., "A Preview of the Farm Appraisal Panel Meeting," *Journal of the American Society of Farm Managers and Rural Appraisers*, April, 1952, pp. 42-49.

MURRAY, WILLIAM G., *Farm Appraisal and Valuation*, Iowa State University Press, Ames, 1961, pp. 433.

MURRAY, WILLIAM G., *Farm Appraisal and Valuation*, 1969.

MURRAY, WILLIAM G., "Farm Appraisals," *The Valuation of Real Estate*, Iowa State College, Ames, Iowa, 1940.

MURRAY, WILLIAM G., "Use of Soil Classification In Determining Farm Values," *Assessment Administration*, IAAO, Chicago, 1957, pp. 180-185.

NELSON, ALBERT H., "Use of Soil Classification In Determining Farm Land Values," *Assessment Administration*, Institute of American Assessment Officers, Chicago, 1957, pp. 185-187.

NESS, OWEN M., "The Farmer and Rights of Way," *Right of Way*, April, 1964, pp. 21-24.

NIKOLITCH, RADOJE, "The Adequate Family Farm Mainstay of the Farm Economy," *The Appraisal Journal*, January, 1966, pp. 97-104.

NORTON, L. F., "Recent Developments Affecting the Appraisal of Farms," *Journal of the American Society of Farm Managers and Rural Appraisers*, pp. 28-33.

NOWELL, R. I, "The Farm Mortgage Outlook," *The Appraisal Journal*, January, 1949, pp. 53-60.

OLCOTT, MARGARET, HELEN E. HENNERFRUND, *Valuation of Real Estate with Special Reference to Farm Real Estate*, U. S. Bureau of Agricultural Economics, Washington, D. C., December, 1935.

OLSEN, NILS ANDREAS, "Farm Credit, Farm Insurance, and Farm Taxation," *U. S. Department of Agriculture Yearbook*, 1924, pp. 185-284.

OREGON STATE TAX COMMISSION, *Cost Factors for Farm Buildings*, Oregon State Tax Commission, Salem, Oregon, 1960.

OWEN, GEORGE, "Mortgage Lending In the Agricultural Industry," *Appraisal Institute Magazine*, 1969, pp. 12-22.

PAARLBERG, DON, "Farm Real Estate Prices," *Journal of the American Ssociety of Farm Mangers and Rural Appraisers*, October, 1950, pp. 103-106.

PATT, H. B., AND DAVIS, "Appraising of Damages to Farm by Power Line Easements," *The Appraisal Journal*, July, 1947, pp. 330-338.

PATTEN, JOHN W., "Valuation of a Breeding Farm Lump Sum Purchase," *American Society of Appraisers Valuation Manual*, American Society of Appraisers, pp. 303.

▲ Rural Property

PAWLEY, ROBERT W., "Rural Appraising-A Prescription for Sound Farm Financing," *Appraisal Institute Magazine*, June, 1961, pp. 17-23.

PAWLEY, ROBERT W., "The Appraisal of a Farm Business," *Appraisal Institute Magazine*, September, 1960, pp. 20-29.

PIKE, HERBERT, "An Appraisal Method for Corn-Belt Farms," *The Appraisal Journal*, January, 1941, pp. 54-68.

PILMER, C. L., "The Effect of Pipelines on the Farming Operation And on Farm Land Values In Webster County, Iowa," *Right of Way*, December, 1969, pp. 33-40, 44-45.

POS, JACOB, "Farm Buildings Appraisal, Old and New Construction," *Appraisal and Valuation Manual*, 1960, pp. 259-278.

RAWLINGS, BROWN R., "Farm Price Stability In 1952," *The Appraisal Journal*, July, 1952, pp. 337-342.

REAL ESTATE ANALYST, THE, "Construction Cost of a Frame Ranch House," *Real Estate Analyst Appraisal Bulletin*, 1953, pp. 57-64.

REISS, FRANKLIN J., "Is $900 Per Acre Too Much for Farmland?," *Journal of the American Society of Farm Managers and Rural Appraisers*, October, 1969, pp. 3-9.

REYNOLDS, J. E., "An Economic Investigation of Farmland Values In the U. S," *Dissertation Abstracts*, May, 1967, pp. 3673-A.

ROBINSON, E. B., "Factors Which Affect the Appraisal of Field Crop Farms In California," *Journal of the American Society of Farm Managers and Rural Appraisers*, October, 1953, pp. 113-120.

ROSS, WILL H., "Unit Acre Method In Farm Appraising," *The Appraisal Journal*, January, 1943, pp. 57-63.

ROSSMILLER, G. E., "Farm Real Estate Value Patterns In the U. S, 1930-1662," *Dissertation Abstracts*, Ann Arbor, September, 1966, pp. 566-A.

RUSH, DONALD R., "Appraising Farms and Ranches," *Technicalities*, May, 1949, pp. 9-12.

RUSH, DONALD R., "Historical Appraisals of Farm Lands," *Journal of the American Society of Farm Managers and Rural Appraisers*, April, 1948, pp. 93-98.

RUSSELL, BRUCE, "Buildings for Tenant-Operated Farms," *Journal of the American Society of Farm Managers and Rural Appraisers*, April, 1946, pp. 49-51.

SANDLIN, H. J., "Market for Farm Appraisal," *The Appraisal Journal*, January, 1960, pp. 119-121.

SCHARN, WILLIAM H. JR., "Farm Appraisals Search the Market," *The Real Estate Appraiser*, January, 1969, pp. 52-55.

SCOFIELD, WILLIAM H., "Land Prices and Farm Earnings," *The Appraisal Journal*, January, 1965, pp. 100-113.

SEARS, G. E., "Finance for Farming," *Journal of the American Society of Farm Managers and Rural Appraisers*, April, 1961, pp. 25-31.

SHATTOCK, CHARLES B., "Economic Aspect of Farm Land Valuation," *The Appraisal Journal*, October, 1948, pp. 451-454.

SHEPPARD, D. W., "Assessment of Farm Personal Property," *Assessment Administration*, Institute of American Assessment Officers, Chicago, 1957, pp. 154-158.

SMITH, GLENN C., "Appraisal of Farms," *The Appraisal Journal*, October, 1950, pp. 503-511.

SMITH, W. J., "Facts Supporting Farm Appraisals," *Journal of American Society of Farm Managers and Rural Appraiser*, October, 1945, pp. 127-133.

SMITH, W. J., "Farm Appraisals In Canada," *Journal of the American Society of Farm Managers and Rural Appraisers*, October, 1953, pp. 121-123.

# BIBLIOGRAPHY OF APPRAISAL LITERATURE

SOMERFIELD, H. B., "To What Extent Should Appraisal Value of Farm Land Fluctuate with Price Levels," *Journal of the American Society of Farm Managers and Rural Appraisers,* October, 1947, pp. 98-101.

SORTOR, CHARLES H., "Physical Analysis of Soils As a Factor In Farm Land Evaluation," *Appraisal and Valuation Manual,* 1961, pp. 155-164.

SPEEDY SQUIRE L., "Criteria for Property Investment," *Valuer,* The New Zealand Institute of Valuers, New Zealand, August 1, 1973, pp. 110-117.

STALCUP, H. E., "Farm Buildings In Rural Appraising," *The Appraisal Journal,* January, 1959, pp. 483-490.

STEWARD, CHARLES L., "Factors Influencing Price of Farm Land," *The Appraisal Journal,* July, 1949, pp. 351-359.

STEWARD, CHARLES L., "Farm Land Value Problems," *The Appraisal Journal,* October, 1950, pp. 458-466.

STEWARD, CHARLES L., "Farm Realty Values," *The Appraisal Journal,* January, 1944, pp. 14-30.

STEWARD, CHARLES L., "Point-Of-History Land Appraisals," *Journal of the American Society of Farm Managers and Rural Appraisers,* April, 1954, pp. 40-44.

STEWART, C. L., "Farm Appraisals In European Countries," *Journal of the American Society of Farm Managers and Rural Appraisers,* October, 1949, pp. 127-133.

STEWART, CLYDE E., "The Concept of Normal Value In Farm Land Appraisal," *Journal of the American Society of Farm Managers and Rural Appraisers,* October, 1947, pp. 117-118.

STOLINSKI, JOSEPH C., "Assessment of Farm Personal Property," *Assessment Administration,* IAAO, Chicago, 1957, pp. 158-159.

THOMPSON, W. N. AND JAMES O. MELTON, "A New Look at Bases for Charging Professional Farm Management Fees," *Jour. of Amer. Soc. of Farm Mgrs. & Rural Appraisers,* October, 1962, pp. 49-57.

U. S. AGRICULTURAL RESEARCH SERVICE, *Taxes Levied on Farm Property in the United States and Methods of Estimating Them,* Government Printing Office, Washington, August, 1956, pp. 1-47.

U. S. AGRICULTURAL RESEARCH SERVICE, *Taxes Levied on Farm Real Estate In 1958,* U. S. Agricultural Reaearch Service, Washington, 1959, pp. 1-11.

VANVUUREN, W., "An Evaluation of Ontario's Farm Assessment Proposals for Property Taxation," *Canadian Journal of Agricultural Economics,* July, 1970.

VERHAGEN, A. M., F. HIRST, A. G. LLOYD, "Expected Values of Cost and Revenues dependent on Drought," *Australian Journal of Agricultural Economics,* December, 1968.

WAGNER, J. J., "Valuation of Farm Land," *The Appraisal Journal,* October, 1947, pp. 544-557.

WATKINS, O. R., "Future Living Patterns and Their Impact on Farm Real Estate Values," *Assessment Administration,* IAAO, Chicago, 1965, pp. 124-126.

WEBER, GUIDO L., "Appraisal of Farms," *The Real Estate Appraiser,* April, 1964, pp. 24-28.

WEBER, GUIDO L., "How to Appraise Farm Buildings," *The Appraisal and Valuation Manual,* 1959, pp. 309-316.

WHIPP, DONALD V. JR., "Application of Weighted Average to Farmland," *Technical Valuation,* June, 1962, pp. 25-28.

WILCOX, WALTER W., "Current Factors Affecting Farm Earnings," *Jour of Amer Soc of Farm Mgrs & Rural Appraisers,* April, 1947, pp. 43-49.

WILLS, J. E., "Economics of Farm Buildings," *Journal of the Society of American Farm Managers and Rural Appraisers,* April, 1964, pp. 27-32.

WOOLEY, J. C., R. P. BEASLEY, *The Appraisal of Farm Buildings,* October, 1941.

## 14-16   Dairy Farms

"Actual Appraisal Reports: Valuation of 97-Acre Wisconsin Dairy Farm," *National Real Estate Journal.*

ARNOLD, P. T. DIX, "Valuation of Purebred Dairy Cattle," *Appraisal and Valuation,* American Society of Appraisers, Washington, D.C., 1960, pp. 169-176.

BURNEY, WILLARD W, "Feedlot Appraisal Problems," *Journal; Proceedings,* Am. Soc. Farm Mgrs-Rural Appraisers, Denver, November 27, 1973, pp. 43-47.

DAVIS, W. D., "How to Appraise Dairy Farms," *The Appraisal Journal,* July, 1958, pp. 415-425.

DAVIS, W. D. SR., "Cow Farm U.S.A.," *The Real Estate Appraiser,* October, 1964, pp. 2-10.

FIEDLER, A. C., "Appraisal of Dairy Farms," *Journal of the Society of American Farm Managers and Rural Appraisers,* April, 1945, pp. 55-61.

LOCKWOOD, A. N., "Appraisal of a Dairy Farm," *Appraisal Reporting Techniques,* American Institute of Real Estate Appraiser, pp. 89-124.

MORSE, TRUE D., "The Data Program for the Appraisal of Dairy Farms," *The Appraisal Journal,* 1937, pp. 9-16.

MURRAY, WILLIAM G., *Farm Appraisal and Valuation,* 1969.

MURRAY, WILLIAM G., "Farm Appraisal and Valuation," *Appraisal Institute Magazine,* Appraisal Institute of Canada, Winnipeg.

## 14-17   Groves and Orchards

BAKER, VERNE A., "Appraising Citrus Groves," *Valuation,* June, 1956, pp. 22-23.

BEATON, WILLIAM R., THOMAS H. HALL, III, "The Valuation of a Pecan Grove and the Effect of the Water Table," *The Real Estate Appraiser,* June, 1968, pp. 35-46.

BLANCH, GRANT E., "Valuing an Orchard," *Valuation,* June, 1956, pp. 10-13.

BOICE, LLOYD J., "Appraising a Fruit Farm," *Appraisal Digest,* April, 1954, pp. 22-24.

CARTER, A. C., "The New Look In Orchards," *Appraisal Institute Magazine,* Appraisal Institute of Canada, Winnipeg, June 1, 1971.

CHESTNUT, LOUIS C., AND LYLE W. HEFFRON, "Factors Affecting Value of Deciduous Orchards," *The Appraisal Journal,* January, 1958, pp. 61-66.

GUILFORD, W. S., "The Appraisal of a Prune Orchard," *The Appraisal Journal,* July, 1934, pp. 329-335.

JEWETT APPRAISAL SERVICE, "Actual Appraisal Reports: No. 19 Valuation of 12 yr. Old Florida Citrus Grove," *National Real Estate Journal,* Jewett Appraisal Service, Vero Beach, Florida, January, 1932, pp. 53-54.

LLOYD, J. W., "Appraising Fruit and Truck Lands," *The Appraisal Journal,* July, 1934, pp. 356.

MURRAY, WILLIAM G., *Farm Appraisal and Valuation,* 1969.

NANNEY, L. C., "Appraisal of Citrus Lands," *The Appraisal Journal,* January, 1935, pp. 149-154.

PADDOCK, JAMES C., "California Orchard and Vineyard Appraisals," *The Appraisal Journal,* October, 1968, pp. 576-592.

PARCHER, L. A., "Evaluation of Pecan Trees," *The Appraisal Journal,* July, 1962, pp. 361-368.

SHULTIS, ARTHUR, AND B. B. BURLINGAME, "Appraising Damages In Fruit Tree Destruction," *Journal of the Society of American Farm Managers and Rural Appraisers,* April, 1949, pp. 56-62.

STUART, WILLIAM N., "Demonstration Appraisal on Citrus Property," *Assessment Administration,* IAAO, Chicago, 1964, pp. 141-145.

TRASK, ELWOOD E., "Appraising Avocado Groves," *Valuation,* October, 1954, pp. 57-58.

WESTGATE, TEVIS T., "Appraising Citrus Groves," *Appraisal and Valuation Manual,* 1956, pp. 359-364.

WHITE, JOHN B., "Citrus Groves," *Assessment Administration,* Institute of American Assessment Officers, Chicago, 1956, pp. 70-71.

WISTRAND, GLEN L., WOOTEN, ALVIN B, "Use of the Income Approach for the Appraisal of Pecan Orchards," *Journal of the Society of American Farm Managers and Rural Appraisers,* October, 1968, pp. 40-44.

## 14-18 Ranches and Grazing Land

ABEL, HAROLD, "Effect of Expanding Western Population on Livestock Marketing and Range Value," *The Appraisal Journal,* April, 1953, pp. 239-243.

AXLUND, DONALD L., "The Major Forage Group Method of Range Evaluation," *Valuation,* December, 1967, pp. 23-25.

BAILEY, GEORGE J., "Economic Problems of the Western Range Livestock Industry," *Journal of the America Society of Farm Managers and Rural Appraisers,* October, 1949, pp. 134-138.

BOWES, WATSON A., "Appraisal of Four Million Acres of Western Land," *The Appraisal Journal,* American Society of Appraisers, Washington, D. C, January, 1948, pp. 19-26.

BOX, THADIS W., "Biological Factors and the Productive Value of Rangelands," *The Appraisal Journal,* July, 1966, pp. 458-460.

COOK, C WAYNE, "Public Lands and Grazing Fees," *Journal; Proceedings,* Am. Soc. Farm Mgrs-Rural Appraisers, Denver, November 27, 1973, pp. 58-60.

COWLEY, LEONARD M., "The Appraisal of a Western Ranch," *The Appraisal Journal,* July, 1947, pp. 339-356.

ENGLEHORN, V. A., "Western Ranch Appraisal," *Journal of the American Society of Farm Managers and Rural Appraisers,* 1960, pp. 47-56.

▲ Rural Property

FARR JR, WILLIAM, "The Cattle Industry- a Look at the Future," *Journal; Proceedings,* Am. Soc. Farm Mgrs-Rural Appraisers, Denver, November 27, 1973, pp. 71-73.

HAY, GEORGE C., "The Valuation of Grazing and Ranch Lands In British Columbia," *Appraisal Institute Magazine,* September, 1964.

HOWELL, DONALD E, "Federal Grazing Fees," *Journal; Proceedings,* Am. Soc. Farm Mgrs-Rural Appraisers, Denver, November 27, 1973, pp. 61-65.

KEENLEYSIDE, A., "Cattle Ranching In British Columbia," *Appraisal Institute Magazine,* Appraisal Institute of Canada, Winnipeg.

LOVE, R. MERTON, "Range Management Standards," *The Appraisal Journal,* July, 1954, pp. 409-414.

MORRISON, E. R., "Development of American Society Approach to Range Appraisals," *Journal of the American Society of Farm Managers and Rural Appraisers,* pp. 63-65.

MORSE, ROBERT R, "The Professional Takes a Look at Grazing Fees," *Journal; Proceedings,* Am. So. Farm Mgrs-Rural Appraisers, Denver, November 27, 1973, pp. 66-68.

MORSE, TRUE D., "Ranch Appraising," *The Appraisal Journal,* October, 1937, pp. 348-356.

MURRAY, HENRY T., "Appraisal of Farms and Ranches," *The Appraisal Journal,* April, 1954, pp. 250-255.

NANNEY, L. C., "The Appraisal of Alfalfa Lands In Semiarid Regions," *The Appraisal Journal,* October, 1940, pp. 348-354.

NATL REAL ESTATE JOUR, ACTUAL APPRAISAL REPORTS, "Valuation of a 183.5 Acre California Citrus Ranch," *National Real Estate Journal,*

NESIUS, ERNEST J., "The Worth of an Acre of Pasture," *Journal of the American Society of Farm Managers and Rural Appraisers,* October, 1952, pp. 153-156.

RANGE APPRAISAL COMMISSION, "Ranch Appraisals," *Jour of Amer Soc of Farm Man & Rural Appraisers,* April, 1951, pp. 136-148.

ROBBINS, PAUL, "What Is the Market Price of Pasture," *Journal of the American Society of Farm Managers and Rural Appraisers,* October, 1950, pp. 116-118.

RUSH, DONALD R., "Appraising Farms and Ranches," *Technicalities,* May, 1949, pp. 9-12.

SALVAGE, WILLIAM L., "Ranch Appraisal," *Technical Valuation,* 1965, pp. 7-10.

SCHMUTZ, GEORGE L., "Cattle Ranch Appraising," *The Appraisal Journal,* January, 1953, pp. 88-90.

SPARHAWK, HOWARD E., "On Appraising Western Cattle Ranches," *The Appraisal Journal,* January 2, 1967, pp. 44-53.

VANDERPOOL, TOM, "Ranch Appraising," *The Valuation Manual,* 1959, pp. 317.

WASSER, CLINTON H., "Developments and Trends In Range Managements," *The Appraisal Journal,* July, 1953, pp. 377-384.

WELSH, THOMAS M., "How to Appraise Ranch and Grazing Lands," *Real Estate Appraisal Practice,* 1958, pp. 544-562.

WILNETTE, MCDONNELL, WOLCOTT, "Problems In Cattle Ranch Value," *Problems In Rural Real Estate Appraisal,* 1968, pp. 27.

WRIGHT, CARROLL, "Factors Involved In the Appraisal of a Livestock Ranch In the Western States," *Appraisal and Valuation Manual,* February, 1959, pp. 23-28.

"Actual Appraisal Reports: Valuation of a 180. 5 Acre California Citrus Ranch," *National Real Estate Journal,*

## CHAPTER FIVE

# Recreational Property

by Charles N. MacNear, Jr., FASA.

Mr. Charles N. MacNear, Jr., a member of the College of Fellows, American Society of Appraisers, has served the Society in numerous offices, including the Presidency of San Francisco Chapter, International Educational Conference Chairman (1966 and 1974), Regional Governor, International President (1972—73).

He has assisted the American Institute of Banking as an Instructor in Agriculture Credit, and instructed Advanced Real Estate Appraisal courses at the University of California (Ext.). Mr. MacNear received a BS degree from the University of Massachusetts, and is presently associated with the Bank of America, as Assistant Vice President, Appraisal Department.

## ▲ Recreational Property

RECREATIONAL Property encompasses a wide range of the Appraisal Disciplines . . . from Real Property (Urban, Rural, and Natural Resources); Personal Popery (chattels); to Machinery and equipment (Special Service). Appraisal of Recreational Property generally requires considerable special knowledge and expertise on the part of the appraiser.

Recreational Property is defined as any property, personal or real, that is utilized by people in their leisure time. This can range from very complex properties such as ski resorts to simple properties such as a single camp site in the wilderness. Their use may change with the season, an example being the gondola lift that carries skiers in the winter and sight-seers in the summer. In broad terms they would be classified as Whole Investment Properties as they would be expected to produce benefits in the form of direct monetary returns. They would also be marketable, however, in many cases it would be a limited market.

Often, Recreational Properties will have a portion of the whole property that is irreplaceable or be of such nature that replacement by purchase of an identical or equivalent property is severly limited. This would cause added elements of value. Such a situation may exist when the recreational use is dependent upon a natural resource such as a lake, water front, ski slope, etc.

The intangible elements can be as important as the tangible in the whole property appraisal.

The appraisal may encompass the three classes of appraisal practice operations, depending on the purpose of the appraisal:

1. The estimation of the cost of producing or replacing the physical property.

2. The forecasting of the monetary earning power of the whole property.

3. The valuation or determination of the worth of the whole property.

The forecasting of the monetary earning power of the property can often be very difficult because of the type of property under appraisal. Most incomes and cash flows depend upon both leisure time and money being available in addition to all the normal economic factors affecting income-producing properties. Many are very dependent upon factors over which there is little or no control, such as the weather to supply snow.

## The Appraisal Report:

The property must be fully described in the report including the value characteristics, physical condition and the legal rights and restrictions encompassed in the ownership where these are not obvious.

The legal rights and restrictions may be a problem with Recreational Property when their function is dependent upon a natural resource such as a lake, waterway or mountain slope which may be utilized by other ownerships. This may be especially so when those uses may not be compatible with the use under appraisal.

The objective of the appraisal must be clearly stated, e.g. to estimate cost, to determine value, or to forecast earning power.

Recreational Properties are special purpose properties that require special knowledge to perform the work necessary to determine value. The sources of information and/or data must be summarized and stated in full in the Appraisal Report, so that verification desired by any user of the Report may be accompiished.

# Recreational Property

15-11   Bowling Alleys
15-12   Camps
15-13   Country Clubs
15-14   Golf Course
15-15   Resort Property
15-16   Lake Property
15-17   Marina
15-18   Aquarium
15-19   Yacht Harbor
15-20   Parks
15-21   Amusement Parks
15-22   Hunting Property
15-23   Swimming Pool
15-24   Skiing Area
15-25   Tourist Industry

▲ Recreational Property

## 15-11 Bowling Alleys

BEMAN, ARTHUR K., "Appraising Bowling Centers," *Appraisal Journal*, April, 1962, pp. 247-254.

COATES, THOMAS, "Lease and Income Factors In the Bowling Industry," *The Appraisal Journal*, July, 1963, pp. 383-386.

GOLOBIC, REX, "Income Factors of Bowling Alleys," *The Appraisal Journal*, October, 1963, pp. 502-511.

GROSSO, ANTHONY P., "Appraisal of a Bowling Alley," *Assessment Administration*, I. A. A. O, Chicago, 1963, pp. 180-189.

HOLBROOK, M. JEFFREY, "How to Appraise a Bowling Alley," *The Appraisal Journal*, October, 1957, pp. 544-550.

MAGA, P. J., "Bowling and Equipment Costs for Bowling Centers," *The Appraisal Journal*, April, 1964, pp. 299-302.

MCREYNOLDS, TOM, "Bowling Alleys As Long Term Investments," *Real Estate Analyst Appraisal Bulletin*, 1956, pp. 83-86.

MCREYNOLDS, TOM, "Bowling-Big Business, and Getting Bigger," *Real Estate Analyst Appraisal Bulletin*, 1955, pp. 581-584.

REAL ESTATE ANALYST, THE, "An Analysis of a 36-Lane Bowling Alley," *Real Estate Analyst Appraisal Bulletin*, 1960, pp. 155-160.

ROYAL, PEYTON K., ARTHUR K. BEMAN, "Bowling Alleys," *The Appraisal Journal*, April, 1962, pp. 245-258.

## 15-12 Camps

EDMAN, J. J., "Compensation for Taking of a Camp. Appraisal Docket," *The Appraisal Journal*, July, 1957, pp. 449-450.

KOENINGS, ROMAN, "Federal Programs for Outdoor Recreation As They Stand," *Journal of American Society of Farmers and Managers of Rural Appraisers,*

## 15-13 Country Clubs

ALMER, ZALMER, "Old Orchard Country Club: a Study of Open Land Planning," *Urban Land*, April, 1964.

AMERICAN INSTITUTE OF REAL ESTATE APPRAISERS, *Guide to the Analysis of Golf Courses and Country Clubs*, American Institute of Real Estate Appraisers, Chicago, 1900.

CARB, MEREDITH R., "Appraisal of a Country Club," *The Encyclopedia of Real Estate Appraising,* Prentice-Hall, Inc., Englwd Cliffs, N. J., 1959.

HARRIS, KERR, FORESTER AND COMPANY, *Clubs In Town and Country,* Harris, Forster and Company, New York, 1967.

HORWATH AND HORWATH, "Country Club Operation In 1966," *The Horwath Accountant,* Horwath and Horwath, New York, 1967.

KAMLET, MARK, "Valuation Factors for Country Club Developments," *The Appraisal Journal,* October, 1965, pp. 587-589.

SOUTHERN CALIFORNIA GOLF ASSOCIATION, *Annual Studies of Operations,* Los Angeles.

*Guide to the Analysis of Golf Courses and Country Clubs,* American Institute of Real Estate Appraisers, 1969.

## 15-14  Golf Courses

AMERICAN INSTITUTE OF REAL ESTATE APPRAISERS, *Guide to the Analysis of Golf Courses and Country Clubs,* American Institute of Real Estate Appraisers, Chicago, 1900.

APPRAISAL JOURNAL, "Country Club Appraisal," *The Appraisal Journal,* October, 1960, pp. 544.

CLIFFER, HAROLD J., *Planning the Golf Clubhouse,* National Golf Foundation, Inc., Chicago, 1956.

COOK, WALTER L., "A Light on Golf," *Parks and Recreation,* National Golf Foundation, Inc., Chicago, September, 1963.

CORNISH, GEOFFREY S., "How to Build and Maintain a Putting Green," *National Golf Foundation Information Sheet,* National Golf Foundation Inc., Chicago.

CROUCH, WILLIAM H., "Acreage Valuation of Land for a Golf Course," *The Appraisal Journal,* October, 1964.

ECKHOFF, HARRY C., "Golf Club Planning," *Urban Land,* Urban Land Institute, Washington, D. C., September, 1963.

ECKHOFF, HARRY C., "What's Happening In Golf Course Development," *Urban Land,* Washington, D. C., February, 1965.

GEMEINHARDT, ROBERT J., *Golf Course Clubhouses,* The American Appraisal Company, Wisconsin, 1966.

HINES, JIMMY, "Golf Course Planning and Development," *Urban Land,* Urban Land Institute, Washington, D. C..

IRWINE, ALFRED G., "For Golf Courses, Existing and Proposed," *Valuation,* ASA, Washington, D. C, June, 1966.

KOELBEL, WALTER A., "The Land Developer and a Golf Course Subdivision," *Urban Land,* Urban Land Institute, Washington, D. C, 1964.

LOCKYER, ALBERT W., "Appraising a Golf Club," *Appraisal Digest,* July, 1953, pp. 11-12.

NATIONAL GOLF FOUNDATION, INC., *Municipal Golf Course Organizing and Operating Guide,* Chicago, 1955.

PAIGE, CLAYTON W., "Construction of De Bell Golf Course In the City of Burbank," *Right of Way,* April, 1958, pp. 35.

REAL ESTATE APPRAISER, THE, "Building a Golf Course? What Should it Really Cost You?," *The Real Estate Appraiser,* March, 1971, pp. 27-30.

REAL ESTATE INVESTMENT LETTER, "Golf Courses As Real Estate Investments," Institute for Business Planning Inc, New York, June 15, 1960.

RILEY, WILLIAM H., "Privately Owned Golf Course," *Assessment Administration*, Institute of American Assessment Officers, Chicago, 1961, pp. 227-235.

SOUTHERN CALIFORNIA GOLF ASSOCIATION, *Annual Studies of Operations*, Los Angeles.

WELD, WALLACE W., "Floodlighting for the Golf Course," *National Golf Foundation Information Sheet*, Chicago: National Golf Foundation, Inc,

*Annual Catalog*, Witteck Golf Range Supply Company, Chicago.

*Guide to the Analysis of Golf Courses and Country Clubs*, American Institute of Real Estate Appraisers, 1969.

"These Golf Course Condominiums Have Strong Appeal to the Investment Buyer," *House and Home*, June, 1970, pp. 34.

## 15-15 Resort Property

"Vacation Condominiums That Fit Into Their Heavily-Wooded Surroundings," *House and Home*, June, 1970, pp. 36.

BUREAU OF POWER, *Recreation Facility Costs and Design Use*, Federal Power Commission, Washington, December, 1970.

DEGLER, GEORGE FREDERICK, PH. D., *The Dynamics of the Commercial Outdoor Recreation Industry In Southern Indiana*, Purdue University, 1971.

DINGER, JULIUS J., "Recreational Real Estate," *The Real Estate Appraiser*, November 12, 1970, pp. 26-36.

FOWLER, G., "Property Owners on Resort Areas Find it Incr Difficult to Rent Their Summer Homes," *N. Y. Times Index*, July 5, 1970.

HOAD, WILLIAM M., "Appraising Public Recreational Projects," *The Appraisal Journal*, January, 1952, pp. 45-50.

KEEFER, E. D., "The Appraisal of Resort Hotels," *The Appraisal Journal*, January, 1946, pp. 50-58.

MOLONEY, J. L., "Value of Recreational Lands," *Appraisal Institute Magazine*, Appraisal Institute of Canada, Winnipeg, March 1, 1973.

NIEHAUS, T. B., "Merchantable Timber Values In Recreational Developments," *The Appraisal Journal*, October, 1968, pp. 570-575.

ROBINSON, W. ALFRED, "Summer Resort Property Appraisals," *The Appraisal Digest*, April, 1954, pp. 5-6.

SWANEY, FRED, "Developing Land for Recreational Use," *Farm and Land Realtor*, January, 1971.

VIELE, G. ROBERT, "Appraisal of Lake and Recreational Property," *The Real Estate Appraiser*, September, 1971, pp. PP-5-13.

## 15-16 Lake Property

LEAVITT, ROBERT W., "Appraisal of Adirondack Lakeshore Properties," *Appraisal Digest*, July, 1947, pp. 21-22.

THEISS, WILLEAM R., "The Appraisal Docket, Damages for Loss of Private Use of Lake," *The Appraisal Journal*, October, 1962, pp. 548.

VIELE, G. ROBERT, "Appraisal of Lake and Recreational Property," *The Real Estate Appraiser*, September, 1971, pp. PP-5-13.

WAELTI, J. J., "The Regional Impact of Public Water Storage Through Recreational Development, a Case Study," *Dissertation Abstracts*, Ann Arbor, July, 1968, pp. 30-A.

WISCONSIN BUREAU OF RECLAMATION, *Recreation Site Evaluation*, Madison, 1968, pp. 1-50.

## 15-17 Marina

HUNTER, JENEL L., "Appraisal of Marinas, Field Data to Be Obtained, Format of Report," *Valuation*, February, 1964, pp. 10-13.

LANDON, RICHARD R., "Marina Management," *Appraisal Institute Magazine*, Appraisal Institute of Canada, Winnipeg.

PROKOSCH, WALTHER, "Joppatowne-A Marine Oriented Community," *Urban Land*, ULI, Washington, D. C., June, 1965.

REED, ROBERT D., DUNN, PAULA, "Valuation of the Cedar Point Marina," *The Appraisal Journal*, April, 1967, pp. 206-222.

WILSON, PETER M., "Marinas, Development and Economic Factors," *The Appraisal Journal*, April, 1967, pp. 119-205.

YORSHIS, STANLEY H., "Oceanfront Appraisals," *The Appraisal Journal*, July, 1968, pp. 353-359.

## 15-18 Aquarium

BROPHY, JAMES C., "Aquarium Appraisal," *Valuation*, pp. 48-51.

## 15-19 Yacht Harbor

PILLSBURY H WATTS, PORTER JOHN W, "Appraising Yacht Harbors," *Appraisal and Valuation Manual Series,* American Society of Appraisers, Washington, D.C., January 1, 1956, pp. 248-257.

## 15-20 Parks

DEGLER, GEORGE FREDERICK, PH. D., *The Dynamics of the Commercial Outdoor Recreation Industry In Southern Indiana,* Purdue University, 1971.

JOHNSTOME, W. GORDON, "Appraising the Baseball Park," *The Appraisal Journal,* pp. 209-215.

JONES, CARRIE MAUDE, *How to Appraise a Ball Park,* August 1, 1937.

KITCHEN, J. W., HENDERSON, W. S., "Land Values Adjacent to an Urban Neighborhood Park," *Land Economics,* August, 1967.

MUNCY, DOROTHY A., "Planning Guidelines for Industrial Park Development," *Urban Land,* December, 1970.

NAYLOR, VELDON R, "Mobile Home Park Appraisals," *Valutape Audio-Library Series,* American Society of Appraisers, Washington D.C., January 1, 1973.

## 15-21 Amusement Parks

ROGERS, RUSSELL R., "The Appraisal of an Amusemant Park," *The Appraisal Journal,* April, 1951, pp. 218-244.

## 15-22 Hunting Property

KOENINGS, ROMAN, "Federal Programs for Outdoor Recreation As They Stand," *Journal of American Society of Farmers and Managers of Rural Appraisers,*

## 15-23 Swimming Pool

"Old Mansion Now Has Biggest Backyard Pool In Beverly Hills," *Engineering News-Record,* September 24, 1970, pp. 26-27.

CHESLER, E. R., "Residential Swimming Pool Costs," *The Residential Appraiser,* November, 1961, pp. 13-14.

HASTINGS, BYRON, "Swimming Pool Bonanza," *Real Estate Analyst Appraisal Bulletin,* 1958, pp. 249-282.

WHITE, WALLACE E., "Assessment of Swimming Pools," *Assessors Topics,* August, 1961, pp. 104.

## 15-24 Skiing Area

SIMERAL WILLIAM B, "A Guide to the Appraisal of Ski Areas," *Appraisal and Valuation Manual Series,* American Society of Appraisers, Washington, D.C., January 1, 1972, pp. 16-33.

## 15-25 Tourist Industry

DAVIS, H. D., "Investing In Tourism," *Finance and Development,* March, 1967, pp. 1-8.

## CHAPTER SIX

# Public Utilities

by Carl White, CPA.

Carl White is a recently retired Partner, Chairman of the Public Utility Committee and firm Director of Services to Public Utilities of an International Firm of Certified Public Accountants.

He holds an M.B.A. issued by the University of Michigan. His undergraduate work was in general engineering.

He has been a member of all of the national and several state professional accounting associations and substantially all public utility industry associations. For these he has been a committeeman, panelist moderator and contributor of papers and articles.

He has planned and participated in all phases, except legal, of numerous rate and other regulatory matters and testified as an expert witness before many federal, state and local regulatory agencies, also courts. He has independently represented regulatory agencies.

His experience also includes public utility organizational and operating programs, including electronic system programs in both the corporate and publicly owned sectors of the industry. The latter includes multi-purpose dam and water supply projects.

His substantial financial experience includes a long history of revenue bond and corporate debt and equity programming.

▲ Public Utilities

PRINCIPLES of Appraisal Practice are pertinent to all business and their properties; to public utilities (energy utilities; electric, gas and water when used as an energy-health utilities; water and sanitary sewage disposal — and communication utilities; telephone, telegraph and other communication systems) as to any other property or going business concern. However, *there is a major and different force present for public utilities and their properties. That force is regulation and one of its principal components, rates and rate–making*. Such differences of application principally affect the appraisal of earnings of public utilities.

This discussion of application of principles of appraisal practice deals only with regulated public utilities and their used and useful public utility properties devoted to serving the public in their separate jurisdictional service areas. Hereinafter in this section the use of the term "public utility" or "public utility property" will refer only to regulated public utilities.

## Other Properties Operated by Regulated Public Utilities

Many public utilities operate other nonregulated properties that have separate earning power or have earning power which depends upon the operation of the public utility properties. These other properties are not public utility properties because they are not regulated and, with rare exceptions, their prices are not subject to the rate making concepts of regulation; therefore, they are not covered in this section of the Bibliography. Appraisal of other unregulated businesses or properties operated by a regulated public utility enterprise is subject to application of principles of appraisal practices on the same basis as any other unregulated industry, business or property, subject only to appreciation or limitations that may be inherent in its attachment to a regulated public utility.

## Physical Public Utility Property

When appraisal of physical public utility property on other than an original cost basis is required, the regulatory agency generally has the power to set guide lines as to whether such appraisals are to be on the basis of trended reproduction cost new less depreciation, value of existing property, or on the basis of replacement with new and technologically current property. Regulation further has the power of determining the basis of sound value or trended reproduction cost new less depreciation value, of determining the basis of arriving at depreciation deducted therein; that is, on the basis of a ratio of accumulated depreciation after any appropriate adjustment thereof or on the basis of observed depreciation.

In arriving at decisions relating to physical property, regulatory agencies may question the basis of the application of principles of appraisal practices used. Nevertheless, after considering those above guidelines generally used in practice by the regulatory agency having jurisdiction, the fundamental principles of appraisal practices applied to other unregulated properties, discussed in other sections of this Bibliography, govern the appraiser in arriving at value for physical public utility property.

In addition to the power of determining the value of public utility properties, individually and combined, devoted to public utility service, regulation also makes the determination as to whether such assets are chargeable to consumers; and if so, when, at the time of acquisition or through depreciation or amortization chargeable to operating expenses.

### Earnings and Rates of Public Utilities

An important factor in the determination of value for public utilities is earning power, both present and future. Earnings are directly related to the rates a public utility charges its customers. Therefore, rate making, the setting of such rates, governs earnings and is one of the most important powers of regulation.

Rates are the unit prices which a public utility charges its customers. These rates are set by the regulatory agency having jurisdiction over the public utility after public hearings or other means of communication involving all interested parties. They are, for a public utility, the same as the prices set individually by organizations in other industries serving the public on a non-regulated competitive basis. In using its rate making power, regulation substantially takes the place of competition.

A main factor in rate making is the responsibility (which is generally governed by competition in other industries) of attempting to match costs or expenses and revenues of regulated public utilities. The proper matching of costs and revenues is basic to the determination of public utility rates and therefore is basic to the determination of earnings and value.

## Regulation and Regulatory Agencies' Powers

To determine what property is regulated public utility property and to determine the effect of regulation on it, regulation and the applicable regulatory agency's statutes, practices and procedures must be examined and their impact understood.

Also in consideration of public utilities and regulation it must be remembered that each public utility is a separately regulated entity and may have a number of separately regulated areas. Applicable rate and other regulatory programs must be applied to each such area as a separate regulatory entity.

Each public utility generally began as a public utility service to a separately populated area. It then enlarged and grew with the area; therefore, each public utility has a different age and has different construction costs for its long-life property devoted to public utility service. Costs differed in the different periods of time during the construction of the public utility property in service. Also, the economy of the area and growth factors of the area served may have changed materially during the service life of the public utility. Further, public utilities may or may not control their source of supply or generation, which programs must be considered as a part of their individual asset value or operating cost problems. These, together with the impact of regulation and of the rate and regulatory programs and practices of the applicable regulatory agencies require not only investigation of regulation generally but of the specific regulatory programs applicable to the public utility properties being appraised.

The orders issued and the files of the respective regulatory agencies provide decisions made for each public utility and each of its regulatory areas. These must be analyzed; their impact is final, subject only to review by the courts.

The Bibliography lists the reportings of the major orders of all regulatory agencies and furnishes appropriate reference to the orders and other regulatory material of federal regulatory agencies. It indicates that because of the differences of philosophy and constant changes in state and local regulatory agencies, reference should be made to the respective agency for applicable orders and regulatory material.

Regulation concepts and processes encompass the following factors for public utilities;

Regulation of rates charged for services rendered, to insure that such rates are reasonable to the consumers and provide a fair return to the investor on the value of the used and useful public utility property devoted to rendering service to the public. Such regulation equally protects both the consumer and the investor.

Definition of cost, cost elements, bases of cost allocations, and the bases of costing and valuing public utility plant and related assets used and useful in service to the public.

Approval of bases of providing depreciation or amortization.

Approval of financing, including capital stock and short term and long term indebtedness, to determine that the financing proposed is for purposes that will not burden the consumer and will fairly compensate the investor.

Approval of major extensions and betterments of public utility plant from the viewpoint of cost of service.

Review of acquisitions, mergers and consolidations to determine the effect on the consumers.

Establishment of Uniform Systems of Accounts and prescription of specific accounts and the manner in which such accounts are to be kept.

Definition of form and content of reports to be filed periodically by the public utility with the applicable regulatory agency for use by that agency and by the public, both investing and non-investing.

Establishment of areas to be served by the public utility.

Establishment of public utility service regulations to insure that proper service will be rendered the consumers.

Licensing of projects using waterways for generation of power.

Holding hearings and accepting testimony of witnesses.

Carrying out duties under the above powers.

The above have been a part of regulation for many years. The following programs have also been a part of such regulation but have assumed great and costly importance in the last few years:

Safety, particularly in pipelines
Pollution control
Ecology

Reference to the statutes, regulations and procedures referred to under the regulatory agencies indexed in the Bibliography will indicate the numerous variations as between Commissions. Such numerous variations require that an appraiser have full knowledge of the Commission having jurisdiction over the public utility under appraisal.

## Regulatory Agencies Having Jurisdiction Over Public Utilities

As to their *interstate* operations, all public utilities except water and sewerage public utilities are regulated by one of the following federal regulatory agencies:

Federal Power Commission, as to gas and electricity

Federal Power Commission, as to licensed power projects using waterways for power generation

Federal Communications Commission, as to telephone and communication systems

Rural Electrification Administration, as to electric and telephone cooperatives and other borrowers of R.E.A. funds

U.S. Department of Health, Education and Welfare, as to certain water and sewerage programs

U.S. Department of Transportation, as to gas pipeline safety

Securities and Exchange Commission, as to public financing of public utility corporations and regulatory control of gas and electric public utility holding companies.

All *intrastate* operations of gas, electric, communication and water and sewerage public utilities are regulated by their respective state, territory or local regulatory agencies. All states and territories have public utility regulatory agencies and within some states there are local regulatory agencies for some political subdivisions, such as counties and cities.

A few states do not regulate certain segments of the public utility industry. Among others, Minnesota and South Dakota do not regulate the gas and electric segments; Texas does not regulate the electric and telephone segments. Regulation for such segments in these states is initiated at the political governing body level with unresolved differences being decided by the Courts.

Dual regulation often occurs and gives rise to much conflict and at times, differing regulatory decisions in the same case, since, for the same public utility the jurisdictional federal agency has interstate transmission jurisdiction and frequently generation and supply jurisdiction and state agencies have domestic and intrastate jurisdiction. Also, state and regional or local regulatory agencies often differ in their practices and procedures. Further, each regulatory agency generally has different rate and regulatory philosophies. Within the same jurisdiction the facts in each case govern, which tends to upset overall patterns of regulation.

The foregoing is true of capital stock corporations. Also, seven states fully regulate municipally owned and other publically owned utilities at the state level; several others have varying degrees of regulation. Several other states have introduced legislation leading to full regulation. Even when the latter are not subject to regulatory agency jurisdiction, they are regulated by their political governing body. The Supreme Court has upheld the rate and regulatory powers of such political governing bodies. (The Bibliography has reference to a publication, Federal and State Commission Jurisdiction and Regulation of Electric, Gas and Telephone Companies, prepared jointly by federal regulatory commission and N.A.R.U.C. the association of all regulators).

Control, similar to regulatory control, is provided by revenue bond counsel and by investment bankers when financing is provided to publicly owned utilities. The financing contracts generally specify that the utility will be operated and accounted for on the basis of utility practices followed by formally regulated public utilities, and very often the contracts specifically prescribe the use of Uniform System of Accounts used by such regulated utilities.

Further, with respect to regulation, it is pertinent to note that all regulatory agency decisions are subject to court review. In many areas, major regulatory agencies have contributed leading uncontested decisions. However, many regulatory decisions are contested and either upheld or changed by decision of the United States Supreme Court, by a Court of Appeals where the Supreme Court has decided not to review the decision, or by State courts. Such decisions generally become precedent for other regulatory matters. (The Bibliography contains references to the reporting of all important decisions).

## Rates and Rate Making

While all factors in public utility regulation are important and have impact on the appraisal of a public utility or its properties, rate making and its impact on earnings is probably the most important factor.

Costing and valuation of long-life public utility property, return on funds invested in such property and the expenses of operating the properties are the important components of the rate making factor.

The cost of value factors in rate making are as follows:

*Rate Base,* which is the public utility plant

▲ **Public Utilities**

and working capital used and useful in serving the customers, costed or valued on the basis used by the regulatory agency having jurisdiction.

*Cost of Service*, which includes two factors:

*Return* and related *Rate of Return* to be earned by the investors (debt and equity investors) on their investment in the value of public utility assets devoted to public utility service.

*Operating Expenses* which include income taxes applicable to public utility operations. For public utilities income taxes applicable to public utility operations are included in Operating Expenses; such taxes are computed after deducting interest on the debt invested in public utility assets devoted to public service.

*Rate Base*,, representing the value of the public utility assets on which investors are entitled to earn a Return, is valued on one of three generally accepted valuation bases used in the regulation of public utilities, although there are variations used by several regulatory agencies. The three bases are:

    Original cost, less depreciation
    Fair value
    Reproduction cost new, less depreciation

The following are brief descriptions of the three bases:

*Original cost,* less depreciation, is the cost of the public utility assets at the date first devoted to public service by the person then devoting them to public service. Original cost lives through acquisitions, mergers, or sales and furnishes a major basis for consideration of whether rates should change on the acquisition of public utility property by others. Depreciation is generally the accumulated depreciation which has been paid by the customer through rates.

Original cost, less depreciation, is prescribed for rate making purposes by all but about 20 state regulatory agencies, and in practically all cases by federal regulatory agencies.

*Fair value* has been defined by the United States Supreme Court as the value arrived at after judging the factors of original cost, less depreciation; reproduction cost new, less depreciation (in some cases this depreciation is observed depreciation, rather than a ratio of accumulated depreciation); and the earning ability of the public utility. About 20 states' regulatory agencies use fair value for rate making.

*Reproduction cost new,* less depreciation, as the sole basis of valuation of the public utility rate base, is used only by the State of Ohio.

Among the major variations to the foregoing bases are the following:

Several state Supreme Court decisions have allowed statutory fair value regulatory commissions to use original cost as the only element of fair value that need be considered in arriving at fair value. Therefore, these states (considered fair value jurisdictions above) could, for practical purposes, be considered original cost states.

Sometimes original cost rate making is augmented by recognition of acquisition adjustment (cost in addition to original cost) and substantially becomes one form of fair value rate making.

Acquisition adjustments arise in an acquisition of a public utility by another public utility. The purchasing utility is required to record the original cost of the public utility assets acquired and the acquisition adjustment. Acquisition adjustments generally represent acquisition costs in addition to original costs but not greater than reproduction cost new, less depreciation. Any other additional costs generally represent intangible adjustments.

The amortization of such acquisition adjustment could represent a charge to operating expenses the same as depreciation, to the extent that this acquisition furnished the public utility's customers, among other things, with operations at reduced cost, with better management, with better engineering, with a better credit rating and with greater financing power. In these cases, some, but not all, regulatory commissions allow all or a portion of the amortization of the acquisition adjustment to operating expenses for rate purposes.

Among the minor variations, a "prudent investment" philosophy has arisen, although this basis is substantially original cost.

*Return* is the amount which customers must repay the investors in a public utility for the use of their capital investment in the Rate Base used and useful and devoted to public utility service. It represents a cost to the public utility and its customers the same as salaries and wages are costs. Return includes the cost of all components of capital invested in public utility assets:

> Debt, both long and short term
> Preferred stock
> Common equity, including common stock, capital or paid-in surplus and earnings retained in the business as surplus.

*Return* is a matter of judgement considering several factors. The cost of money factor is a computation in which annual cost values are assigned to the separate elements of the capital structure. Generally speaking, except for extraordinary situations, the imbedded interest cost of debt and dividend cost of preferred stock are used for these two components of capital. The return to the common equity investors in a public utility is arrived at after judging the many economic risks, the management and other factors to allow the public utility to maintain a strong status in all financial and management areas. Likewise it cannot be overly adequate or would be too costly to the consumers of a particular public utility.

This points up an interesting phenomena of Return available to investors in public utilities and its related affect on earnings. Because regulation only provides rates to pay actual Operating Expenses and a reasonable return on the investment in Rate Base devoted to public service, there are only four important avenues which a utility can use to increase the return to its equity holders:

> It can trade on its equity by financing a greater amount of investments in Rate Base through debt; although this should not make the debt-equity capitalization ratio out of line with generally accepted limits for debt of 40% to 60% of capitalization.
>
> It can reinvest internally-generated funds; although it should maintain a stable and a growing dividend policy to maintain strength in its equity securities
>
> It can institute cost reduction programs; although such cost reduction programs must not endanger service to the customers.
>
> It can institute growth programs; although the growth programs must be to customers in the area in which it has a certificate from regulatory authorities to operate; also, the utility cannot discriminate between customers.

Needless to say, public utilities can issue more equity securities, the proceeds of which when invested in public utility operating property will form the basis for returning a greater amount of money to the equity holders as a group; however, such amount generally does not increase the Rate of Return.

The *Rate of Return* earned by utilities is the subject of additional possible limitations. Generally, regulatory agencies constantly survey and review the Rate of Return earned by utilities under their jurisdiction. When such return does not fall with a zone of reasonableness, the regulatory agency has a rate conference with the public utility with respect to possible changes in such rates. The results of the rate conference could either change the rates on an informal basis or be the starting point for a formal rate hearing.

The zone of reasonableness varies, but for discussion it could be considered to be within one-half of one percent of the rate of return allowed in the last rate case of the particular utility.

*Operating Expenses* are comprised of the actual operation, maintenance, tax depreciation and general administrative expenses of the public utility during a selected test year (the most recent year or 12 months for which financial and cost information is available) adjusted for known contractual, economic and operating changes in the utility, Such Operating Expenses, which the public utility is entitled to recover intact from its customers, will reflect known experience adjusted so as to be applicable to near future periods when the rates being set will be in effect.

The application of principles of appraisal practices in analyzing and projecting Operating Expenses takes adequate recognition of the cost of fuel, wages and salaries, materials and supplies, taxes and depreciation. It should be noted that to electric public utilities fuel cost is a major factor for those generating their own source of supply and, similarly the cost of purchased power is major for those not generating their own supply. The cost of gas is a very substantial part of natural gas public utility Operating Expenses. With the ever changing energy supply and the emergence of nuclear fuel for electric utilities, fuel factors are becoming more cost important.

## Characteristics of Public Utilities

There is a significant difference in characteristics, as between public utilities and other industries. Public utilities are generally franchised for construction purposes by the political body governing the cities or incorporated areas served. For outlying areas and for many incorporated areas, certificates of public convenience and necessity are obtained from the regulatory agency having jurisdiction.

Public utilities have the right of eminent domain.

Public utilities have the responsibility of serving any applicant for service in the territory they serve.

For public utilities, the substantial investment in Rate Base makes public utility plant their most significant asset. Inventories of materials and supplies are held for minor construction and repairs and are not a material factor, although some utilities may have large inventories of generating fuel, and some may have inventories of saleable products as a part of other non-regulated operations. In industrial companies furnishing products to the public, inventories are the saleable product and usually are more significant than other assets. Plant, property and equipment in other industries is generally not significant with the possible exception of the cement and metal production industries, and is not generally the basis of earning power.

For example, the net investment in utility plant per dollar of annual revenues ranges from approximately $4.00 to $9.00 for electric utilities, depending upon whether power supply is generated or purchased. The dollars of plant investment in major segments of public utilities is compared to each dollar of annual revenues as follows:

| | |
|---|---|
| Water | — about $3.50 to $4.50 |
| Telephone | — about $3.50 to $4.00 for the independents |
| | — about $2.50 to $3.00 for the Bell System |
| Natural gas pipelines | —about $2.00 to $2.50 |
| Natural gas distribution | —about $4.00 to $5.00 |
| Electric generating | —about $5.00 to $9.00 |
| Electric distribution | —about $4.00 to $5.00 |

These compare with 30¢ to 35¢ investment in operating plant when compared with each dollar of annual sales for industries furnishing products to others, with a greater ratio for the cement and metal production industries and a far less ratio for the service industries.

A current trend that may reduce future investment in public utilities with some offsetting effects in operating expenses is the trend toward leasing of equipment. Transportation equipment and general building leasing has been prevalent in the public utility industry for a number of years. With the recent growth in generation requirements, there has been a trend from ownership to leasing for stand-by and peaking generating equipment, such as gas turbine and diesel generation engines. These leased assets do not presently represent a material amount of the value of serving customers of the utility although it is not exactly known to what extent this trend will grow.

The fuel cores for nuclear generating plants represent a very substantial investment for a public utility. The trend for these is toward leasing. Most of such leasing in the long run represents substantially the same cost to the consumer as does ownership by the public utility; however, there are exceptions. One state has a state agency which purchases nuclear fuel for leasing to the utilities at interest rates enjoyed by political subdivisions of a state which are less than the rates public utility or other profit oriented organization would pay.

Among characteristics of utilities which differ from other industries are the differences in accounting because of the large investment in public utility operating plant. These include the following, of which an appraiser should make general note:

Capitalization of overheads, including general and administrative expenses and supervision expenses, together with interest on borrowed funds, and Return on equity and other funds during the period these funds are used in construction. These overheads represent credits to operating expenses for general and supervision expenses capitalized and credits to other income or income deductions for interest and Return capitalized and charged to public utility plant. These overheads will be returned by customers through depreciation included in rates over the life of the plant after operations commence.

Other industries do not generally capitalize such expenses because they believe they do not have a large amount of construction, except in isolated instances, and that their personnel is not generally responsible for construction. In public utilities administrative and supervisory employees are generally versed in, and administer, the construction programs.

Contributions and advances in aid of construction are paid to the public utility by individual customers when revenues received will not return to the public utility a full rate of return on the investment in assets serving them. These are deducted from the Rate Base when determining Return. Generally this allows for a reduction in depreciation expenses charged to public utility Operating Expenses when such contributions are material in amount.

Inventories such as natural gas in storage and natural gas in pipelines (the packing of the pipeline) are included in fixed assets.

Inventories of meters, transformers, and related measuring and control equipment whether in or out of service and spare or insurance parts for generating and similar equipment are included in utility plant; depreciation is provided on these.

Conversion costs of public utilities, when conversion from one type of equipment or type of energy to another is made, such as the conversion to dial-type telephones from the magnetotype telephones and the conversion from manufactured to natural gas, are deferred and amortized over a reasonable period of time based on projected savings or on additional benefits to customers.

Requirements by governmental authorities affect the valuation of all business property; however, to public utilities in many cases they represent greatly increased costs and increased capital requirements. Governmental authorities require the replacement of, or at least the moving of, public utility lines or plants for roadway and other community developments. There are many governmental authorities which do not reimburse the utilities for such costs

Rates provide only for return of Operating Expenses actually incurred or programmed; therefore, energy distribution public utilities generally have a fuel adjustment clause in their rates to reflect fuel cost changes in current public utility billings. Otherwise, these changes in fuel costs must be borne by or flow through to the equity investors. In a period of substantially rising fuel prices, such recovery must be immediate. A rise in fuel cost or a decrease in fuel cost generally triggers a fuel adjustment clause within a month after the change.

There are also some reporting characteristics which are different for public utilities. Among these are the following:

The arrangement of the balance sheet placing Utility Plant, the major asset, at the top of the asset statement; also, the placement of all Capitalization components at the top of the liability statement.

The arrangement of the income statement to include public utility Operating Revenues and public utility Operating Expenses at the beginning of the statement so as to show the Net Operating Income from public utility operations before other income and interest and

▲ Public Utilities

other deductions. This is the Net Operating Income that should represent Return on the Rate Base devoted to public service, although to be helpful the basis of valuing the Rate Base must be known.

Unfortunately, such Net Operating Income is quite often applied to the Rate Base by analysts without sufficient knowledge of the basis of Rate Base valuation used by the regulatory agency having jurisdiction in the determination of rates and, therefore, the earnings of the utility.

The inclusion in Operating Expenses of income taxes applicable to public utility operations and the basis of computation of such taxes. While interest is a cost of capital and not an operating expense for public utilities, nevertheless, interest cost, applicable to public utility Rate Base, available for deduction for income tax purposes, is deducted in computing income taxes included in operating expenses for rate and financial reporting purposes.

EDITOR'S NOTE: *Perhaps the most substantive factor which emerges from any serious consideration of the structure, practice and procedure of the Appraisal of Public Utilities in the United States is that of* **Regulation.** *Whether by utility case decision or administrative fiat,* **Regulation** *demands paramount attention. Because of this factor, an outline of key data sources and regulatory bodies is printed below.*

## Publications and Services

(Issued by Public Utilities Reports, Inc.; 1828 L Street, N. W., Washington D. C. 20036)

- Public Utility Reports
- Advance Sheets, Public Utility Reports
- PUR Digest
- Public Utilities Fortnightly
- PUR Executive Information Service
- PUR Question Sheets
- FURA — Current Service — FPC
- PUR Guide Program
- PURVIEW
- Cases and Text on Public Utility Regulation (Rev.) by Francis X. Welch
    - Preparing For the Utility Rate Case (1954)
    - Conduct of the Utility Rate Case (1955)
- Ruling Principles of Utility Regulation — Rate of Return and Supplement A (1974) by Ellsworth Nichols and Francis X. Welch
- Trends and Topics in Utility Recognition (1969) by George E. Turner
- Federal Utility Regulation Annotated, Vol. 2, with Supplemental Volumes A, B, C, and D

## National Association of Regulatory Utility Commissioners: Major Informational Sources

"Federal and State Commission Jurisdiction and Regulation of Electric, Gas and Telephone Utilities"

(Prepared in cooperation with NARUC and the Federal Communications Commission. Source: Superintendent of Documents, U.S. Government Printing Office, Washington, D. C. 20402).

"NARUC Publication List"

(Issued annually, in December. Source: NARUC, 3327 ICC Building, P. O. Box 684, Washington, D. C. 20044)

- "Proceedings"
- "Depreciation Practices"
- "Blue Bulletin Service"
- Various Accounting Reports, Lists
- Annual Report Forms
- Motor and Air Carrier Data
- Railroad Reports, Rates, Manuals
- NARUC Convention Addresses
- NARUC Committee Reports
- Separations Manuals
- Report, Committee on Secretarial Offices
- History, NARUC, by R. E. Kreeger

## Federal Power Commission

A Mailing Service, maintained by the FPC, and serviced from: FPC, Washington, D. C. 20426, includes:

- RU — all orders in rule-making dockets
- RO — all opinions
- FPC News (weekly)

The following publications are issued by the Superintendent of Documents, U.S. Government Printing Office, Washington, D. C. 20402:

Publications List:
General Information
Reports
Electric Power
Natural Gas
Special Reports
Statutes
Maps
List of Units of Property
(for use in connection with Uniform System of Accounts)

## Federal Communications Commission

The publications below-noted are sold in volume units by the Superintendent of Documents, U.S. Government Printing Office, Washington, D. C. 20402:

"Rules and Regulations"
(grouped into 10 volumes: price of volume entitles purchaser to receive amended pages for an indefinite period).

## United States Department of Agriculture Rural Electrification Administration

Publications listed below may be obtained from the Superintendent of Documents, U.S. Government Printing Office, Washington, D. C. 20402:

*REA Electric Borrowers*
REA Bulletins (additions, revisions, deletions)
Alphabetic Index (REA bulletins, contract forms, specifications)
Numerical List (REA Bulletins for the electrification program)
Electrification Program (Bulletins, contract forms, miscellaneous publications)
Uniform System of Accounts

*REA Telephone Borrowers*
REA Bulletins (additions, revisions, deletions)
Alphabetic Index (REA Bulletins, TE&CM and TOM Manuals, REA Contract Forms, specifications)
Numerical List (REA Bulletins, telephone program)
Telephone Program (Bulletins, forms, miscellaneous publications).

## United States Department of Health, Education, Welfare

Documents Source: Environmental Health Service, Bureau of Solid Waste Management, Washington, D. C.:

"An Accounting System for Incinerator Operations" (Report SW-17 ts; Eric R. Zausner)

"An Accounting System for Sanitary Landfill Operations"
(Report SW-15 ts; Eric R. Zausner)

"An Accounting System for Solid Waste Collection"
(Report SW-27 ts; Eric R. Zausner)

## Water Pollution Control Federation

Documents Source: WPCF, 3900 Wisconsin Avenue, Washington, D. C. 20016

"Uniform System of Accounts for Wastewater Utilities"
(Manual of Practice No. 10).

## Securities and Exchange Commission

Documents Source: SEC, Washington, D.C.

Applicable to Security transactions, financing of all business, including Public Utilities:
Securities Act, 1933
Securities Act, 1934

Applicable to Electric, Gas, Public Utility

Holding Companies and their Subsidiaries only:

    Securities Act, 1935
    Uniform System of Accounts:
        Holding Companies
        Service Companies

## State, Regional, Local Regulatory Commissions

Each Commission operates under its own Regulatory Statute, and prescribes its own rules, regulations, procedures, uniform systems of accounts, within its jurisdiction. This structure of Regulation is subject to constant change. Current information must be secured from the apposite Regulatory Commission.

Because the Uniform System of Accounts prescribed by the several commissions generally follows a national system, there is listed below State Regulatory Commissions and the Uniform Systems of Accounts prescribed by each in the categories of Electric, Gas, Telephone, Water:

## State Regulatory Commissions — Uniform Systems of Accounts

| State | Electric | Gas | Telephone | Water |
|---|---|---|---|---|
| Alabama | NARUC | NARUC | FCC | NARUC |
| Alaska | | Under Consideration | | |
| Arizona | NARUC | NARUC | NONE | NARUC |
| Arkansas | FPC | FPC | FCC (Modified) | |
| California | FPC | FPC | FCC | OWN |
| Colorado | NARUC | NARUC | FCC | NARUC |
| Connecticut | (NARUC) | (NARUC) | FCC | OWN |
| Delaware | FPC | FPC | FCC | NARUC |
| District of Columbia | FPC | FPC | FCC | NARUC |
| Florida | NARUC | NARUC | FCC | NARUC |
| Georgia | NARUC | NARUC | FCC | NARUC |
| Hawaii | NARUC | NARUC | FCC | NARUC |
| Idaho | NARUC | NARUC | FCC | NARUC |
| Illinois | | | | OWN |
| Indiana | NARUC | NARUC | FCC | NARUC |
| Iowa | NARUC (Modified) | NARUC (Modified) | FCC (Modified) | NARUC |
| Kansas | FPC | FPC | FCC | NARUC |
| Kentucky | FPC | FPC | FCC | NARUC |
| Louisiana | FPC (Modified) | FPC (Modified) | FCC | |
| Maine | | NARUC | | OWN |
| Maryland | FPC | FPC | FCC | NARUC |
| Massachusetts | FPC (Modified) | FPC (Modified) | FCC | NARUC |
| Michigan | NARUC | NARUC | FCC | NARUC |
| Minnesota | No State Regulation | No State Regulation | FCC | No State Regulation |
| Mississippi | NONE | NONE | NONE | NONE |
| Missouri | FPC | FPC | FCC | NARUC |
| Montana | FPC | FPC | FCC | OWN |
| Nebraska | No State Regulation | No State Regulation | FCC | No State Regulation |
| Nevada | FPC | FPC | FCC | |
| New Hampshire | | | | OWN |

# BIBLIOGRAPHY OF APPRAISAL LITERATURE

| | | | | |
|---|---|---|---|---|
| New Jersey | NARUC (Modified) | NARUC (Modified) | FCC | NARUC |
| New Mexico | NARUC or FPC | NARUC or FPC | FCC | NARUC |
| New York | OWN | OWN | OWN | OWN |
| North Carolina | NARUC | NARUC | FCC | NARUC |
| North Dakota | NARUC | NARUC | FCC | NARUC |
| Ohio | FPC | FPC | FCC | NARUC |
| Oklahoma | NARUC | NARUC | FCC | NARUC |
| Oregon | NARUC | NARUC | FCC | NARUC |
| Pennsylvania | FPC | FPC | FCC | NARUC |
| Puerto Rico | NONE | NARUC | FCC | NARUC |
| Rhode Island | NARUC (Modified) | NARUC (Modified) | NONE | NARUC |
| South Carolina | NARUC | FPC | FCC | NARUC |
| South Dakota | No State Regulation | No State Regulation | FCC | No State Regulation |
| Tennessee | NARUC | NARUC | FCC | NARUC |
| Texas | No State Regulation | Secondary State Regulation | No State Regulation | |
| Utah | NARUC | NARUC | FCC | NARUC |
| Vermont | FPC | NARUC | FCC | NARUC |
| Virginia | NARUC | NARUC | OWN | NARUC |
| Virgin Islands | Owned by Gov. | Only Bottled Gas | FCC | Owned by Gov. |
| Washington | NARUC | NARUC | FCC | NARUC |
| West Virginia | NARUC | FPC | FCC | NARUC |
| Wisconsin | NARUC (Modified) | NARUC (Modified) | FCC (Modified) | NARUC |
| Wyoming | FPC | FPC | FCC | NARUC |

## Public Utility Industry Associations, Major Publications

American Gas Association
   Founded 1918 (AGA)
     *AGA* — Monthly
American Public Gas Association
   Founded 1961
     *Gas Facts* — Newsletter—Monthly
American Public Power Association
   Founded 1940
     *Public Power* — Monthly
American Waterworks Association
   Founded 1881
     *AWA Journal* — Monthly
Municipal Finance Officers Association
   Founded 1906
     *Municipal Finance* — Quarterly
National Cable Television Association
     *Membership Bulletin* — Weekly
Northwest Public Power Association
     *Northwest Public Power Bulletin* — Monthly

Southern Gas Association
     *Progress* — Quarterly
U.S. Independent Telephone Association
   Founded 1915
Edison Electric Institute (EEI)
   Founded 1933
     *EEI Bulletin* — Monthly
Independent Natural Gas Association
   Founded 1944
     *Membership Bulletin* — Weekly
National Association of Regulatory Utilities Commissioners
   Founded 1889
     *Bulletin* — Semi-Monthly
National Rural Electric Cooperative Association
   Founded 1942
     *Rural Electrification* — Monthly
Tennessee Valley Public Power Association
   Founded 1947
     *TVPPA News* — Monthly

▲ Public Utilities

National Association of Water Companies
   Founded 1963
      *Conference* — Quarterly

## Public Utility Industry Directories

Brown's Directory of North American Gas Companies
(Harcourt Brace Jovanovich Publications)

McGraw-Hill Directory of Electric Utilities
(McGraw-Hill Publishing Company)

Telephony's Directory of the Telephone Industry
(R.R. Donnelly Directories)

Investor Owner Water Companies
(National Association of Water Companies)

Publicly Owned Electric Utilities
(American Public Power Association)

Publicly Owned Gas Utilities
(American Public Gas Association)

## Public Utility Industry Glossaries

Glossary of Important Power and Rate Terms; Abbreviations and Units of Measurement (Federal Power Commission)

Glossary of Electric Utility Terms; Financial and Technical with Nuclear (Edison Electric Institute)

Glossary of Terms — Manufactured and Mixed Gas (American Gas Association)

Glossary of Oil and Gas Terms (Howard R. Williams and Charles J. Myers; Banks and Company and Matthew Bender & Company)

Glossary of Water and Wastewater Control Engineering (American Society of Civil Engineers)

---

# Public Utilities

16-11   General Value
16-12   Electric
16-13   Gas
16-14   Water
16-15   Communications Systems
16-16   Sanitary Sewer

## 16-11  General Value

ABBOT, ACTOR T. JR., "Joint Utility Corridors," *Right of Way,* June, 1970, pp. 47-50.

ADAMS, J., "Rate-Making Status of Liberalized Depreciation," *Public Utilities Fortnightly,* February 13, 1958, pp. 260-265.

ALYEA, PAUL E., *Assessment of Public Utilities In Alabama,* University of Alabama, Montgomery, 1952.

ARKANSAS LEGISLATIVE COUNCIL, *Reimbursement of Public Utlities for Relocation Facilities on State Highway Rights of Way,* Arkansas Legislative Council, Little Rock, 1958.

BAGGE, CARL E., *Utilities-Presidents Council on Recreation and Natural Beauty,* Federal Power Commission, Washington D. C, December 27, 1968.

BARTON, STANLEY B., "The Organization and Functions of a Public Utility Company Land Department," *Right of Way,* October, 1957, pp. 11-16.

BAUER, JOHN, NATHANIEL GOLD, *Public Utility Valuation for Purpose of Rate Control,* Macmillan, New York City, 1934.

BECKLEY, J. H., "Capital and Maintenance Expenditures In Public Utility Accounting," *Principles of Investment,* Journal of Land and Public Utility Economics, February, 1928.

BEHMAN, B., D. CODELLA, "Wage Rates and Housing Prices," *Industrial Relations,* February, 1971, pp. 86-104.

BERRY, J. J., "There Is a Utility Alternative for Municipalities," *Public Utilities,* March 18, 1971, pp. 15-21.

BIGRAS, ROLAND, "Real Estate Values Unaffected by High Tension Power Lines," *Right of Way,* April, 1964.

BLANCHARD, C. F., "Publicly Owned Electric Business," *Public Utilities Fortnightly,* June 18, 1970, pp. 43-45.

BOGGS, JOHN I., "Appraisal of a Utility Property for a Prospective Purchaser," *American Society of Appraisers Valuation Manual,* 1958, pp. 197.

BOGGS, JOHN I., "Depreciation of Public Utility Property," *Technical Valuation,* October, 1962, pp. 18-22.

BOGGS, JOHN I., "Measurement of Profitability of Public Utility Operations," *Technical Valuation,* pp. 3.

BONBRIGHT, JAMES C., "Valuation of Public Utilities and Other Enterprises for Tax Purposes," *The Valuation of Property,* 1937.

BOOTH, ERNEST, *Valuations for Rating,* Butterworth and Co, London, 1932.

BOOTH, ERIC ROWLAND, "Rating Valuation of Residential and Business Premises," *The Estates Gazette,* London, 1951.

BOSLAND, CHELCIE C., "The Valuation of Public Utility Enterprises by the Securities and Exchange Commission," *The Journal of Finance,* March, 1964, pp. 96-106.

BROWN, H. H., "Utility Load Growth, the Environment, and FPC Responsibility," *Public Utilities Fortnightly,* May 7, 1970, pp. 37-40.

BRUCH, ALBERT P., "Special Utility Valuation Problems," *Technical Valuation,* American Society of Appraisers, Washington, November, 1955, pp. 45.

BRYANT, JOHN M., HERRMAN, R. R, *Elements of Utility Rate Determination,* Mcgraw-Hill, New York, 1940.

BUREAU OF POWER, *Recreation Facility Costs and Design Use,* Federal Power Commission, Washington, December, 1970.

▲ **Public Utilities**

BYRNE, WILLIAM H., "Rate Making for Public Utilities," *Technical Valuation,* October, 1953, pp. 51-53.

CABOT, PHILIP, D. W. MALLOT, *Problems In Public Utility Management,* New York, Shaw, 1927.

CARPENTER, MAURICE P., "Assessment of Public Utility Properties," *Assessment Administration,* IAAO, Chicago, 1957, pp. 161-166.

CHANDLER, MARVIN, "How Public Utilities Look to the Investor," *A. S. A. Valuation Manual,* American Society of Appraisers, Washington, D. C., 1955, pp. 145.

CHAPMAN, CHARLES M., "Reliability of the Stock and Debt Approach Inthe Appraisal of Utility Property," *Conference Proceedings,* National Tax Association, Columbus, 1962, pp. 583-587.

COLORADO LEGISLATIVE COUNCIL, *Report to the Colorado General Assembly Public Utility Assessments,* Denver, December, 1959.

CUMMINGS, JOHN S., "The Role of the Engineer In the Preparation of a Utility Rate Case," *The A. S. A. Valuation Manual,* 1959, pp. 47.

DAHLSTROM, B. P., "Original Cost Valuation and Other Current Factors Affecting Utility Rates," *Appraisal and Valuation Manual,* American Society of Appraisers, 1955, pp. 159-166.

DARRACH, CHARLES GOBRECHT, *Valuation of the Properties of Public Utility Corporations,* The Bradford Press, Philadelphia, 1913.

DIERKER, GERALD J., "Importance of Utility Company Records," *ASA Valuation Manual,* American Society of Appraiser, Washington, D. C., 1956, pp. 63.

DORAU, HERBERT B., "Currency Debasement and Public Utility Valuations," *Technical Valuations,* April, 1950, pp. 20-33.

DUBIELZIG, R. C., "Development of Capitalization Rates for Public Utility Valuation," *Assessment Administration,* IAAO, Chicago, 1963, pp. 131-139.

DUFFY, G., "HUD Supports Air Conditioning of 46,000 Public Housing Units for Elderly," *Air Conditioning, Heating and Refrigeration News,* August 3, 1970, pp. 2.

EAST CENTRAL REGIONAL ADVISORY COMMITTEE, *Electric Power In the East Central Region 1970-1980-1990,* Federal Power Commission, Washington D. C, December, 1969.

EATHERLY, BILLY J., "The Role of Economic Theory In Public Util Reg," *Mississippi Business Review,* Mississippi State University, January, 1971.

EDMAN, J. J., "Further Developments In Twin City Power Cases. Appraisal Docket," *The Appraisal Journal,* October, 1958, pp. 614-617.

EDMAN, J. J., "The Appraisal Docket. Expense of Moving Public Utility Facilities Occupying Public Ways," *The Appraisal Journal,* July, 1958, pp. 450-452.

EDMAN, J. J., "Use of Reproduction Cost In Valuation of Public Utility Property. Appraisal Docket," *The Appraisal Journal,* April, 1958, pp. 294-296.

ELY, O., "Accelerated Depreciation," *Public Utilities Fortnightly, American Society of Appraisers Valuation Manual,* May 10, 1956, pp. 680-683.

ELY, O., "Accelerated Depreciation and Share Earnings," *Public Utilities Fortnightly, American Society of Appraisers Valuation Manual,* December 20, 1956, pp. 992-995.

ETTEMAN, DAVID K., "Utility Tax Valuation from Common Stock Prices," *Public Utilities Fortnightly,* May, 1964, pp. 19-31.

FEC, *S-200-Statistics of Publicly Owned Electric Utilities,* Supt. of Documents, U. S. Govt. Printing Office, Washington D. C, 1968.

FEDERAL POWER COMMISSION, *R-16-National Electric Rate Book,* Supt of Documents, U. S. Govt. Printing Office, Washington D. C.

FEDERAL POWER COMMISSION, *R-16-National Electric Rate Book,* Supt of Documents, U. S. Govt. Printing Office, Washington D.C.

FEDERAL POWER COMMISSION, *A-77-Regulation to Govern the Preservation of Records of Public Utilities and Licensees,* Supt. of Documents, U. S. Govt. Printing Office, Washing D. C, December 12, 1962.

FEDERAL POWER COMMISSION, *P-40-World Power Data,* Supt of Documents, U. S. Govt. Printing Office, Washington D. C, 1968.

FEDERAL POWER COMMISSION, *S 17 Electric Power Statistics,* Supt. of Documents, U. S. Govt. Printing Office, Superintendent of Documents.

FEDERAL POWER COMMISSION, "National Power Curve," *National Power Surve,* Federal Power Commission, December, 1964.

FISHER, WILLIAM C., "Developments of Maps for Outside Public Utility Plant," *Technical Valuation,* October, 1954, pp. 49-50.

FLOY, HENRY, *Valuation of Public Utility Properties,* Mcgraw-Hill, New York City, 1912.

FOSTER, HORATIO A., *Engineering Valuation of Public Utilities and Factories,* Van Nostrand, New York City, 1913.

FPC, "A-106 Uniform System of Acctg Prescr for Pub Utils & Licences 1-1-70," Supt Docs Govt Ptg Off, Wash.

FPC, "Evaluation Report, Lower Tule Development," Power Staff Report, FPC, Washington D.C., 1968.

GARFIELD, PAUL J, LOVEJOY, WALLACE F, *Public Utility Economics,* Prentice-Hall Inc, Englewood Cliffs N J, January 1, 1964.

GLAESER, MARTIN G., *Outlines of Public Utility Economics,* Macmillan, New York City, 1927.

GRAHAM, WILLARD J., *Public Utility Valuation,* University of Chicago Press, Chicago, 1934.

GREENBAUM, IRVING PHD, "Return on Investment In Elec Util Ind & Pub Util Comm Rate Base Det: Orig Cost Fair Val Reprod Cost," The Ohio State University, 1970.

GREENBAUM, MICHAEL, "Appraisals, Appraisers, and the Regulatory Bodies," *Appraisal and Valuation Manual,* Washington, D. C., January, 1972, pp. 10.

GREENEBAUM, MICHAEL, "Appraisals, Appraisers, and the Regulatory Bodies," *Technical Valuation,* A. S. A, Washington, September, 1966.

GRONINGER, TAYLOR E., *Public Utility Rate-Making,* Bobbs-Merrill, Indianapolis, 1928.

GRUNSKY, CARL E., GRUNSKY, CARL E., JR, "Appreciating and the Unearned Increment," *Valuation, Depreciation and the Rate-Base,* New York, 1917, pp. 387.

GRUNSKY, CARL E., GRUNSKY, CARL E., JR, "Expectancy and Remaining Value," *Valuation, Depreciation, and the Rate-Base,* pp. 293-301.

GURNEE, MARK S., "Utility Relocations and the U. S. Army Corps of Engineers," *Right of Way,* December, 1963, pp. 17-20.

HAYES, H. V., *Public Utilities, Their Fair Present Values and Return,* Van Nostrand, New York.

HAZEN, ALLEN, *Meter Rates for Water Works,* Wiley, New York, 1918.

HECKMAN, J. W., "A Realistic Approach to Utility Property, Valuation for Tax Purposes," *Valuation,* October, 1964, pp. 7-13.

HEILMAN, R. E., "Customer Ownership of Public Utilities," *Journal of Land and Public Utility Economics,* January, 1925.

HICKS, JOHN RICHARD, *The Incidence of Local Rates In Great Britain,* The University Press, Cambridge, 1945.

▲ **Public Utilities**

HICKS, JOHN RICHARD, *The Problem of Valuation for Rating*, The University Press, Cambridge, 1944.

HUTCHINSON, IRA K., "Appraisal of Utility Easements In the State of Hawaii," *Appraisal and Valuation Manual*, Corporate Press, Incorporated, Washington, D. C, January, 1972, pp. 314.

JAFFEE, BRUCE LEWIS PH. D., *Aspects of the Regulated Public Utility: Misallocation, Marginal Cost Pricing, and Depreciation*, The John Hopkins University, 1971.

KAUFMAN, K. A., "Pollution Rules Could Choke Industry to Death," *Iron Age*, February 11, 1971, pp. 21.

KINNARD, WILLIAM N. JR., "Tower Lines and Residential Property Values," *The Appraisal Journal*, April, 1967, pp. 269-284.

KIRSHMAN, JOHN EMMETT, "The Principle of Competitive Cost In Public Utility Regulation," *Yale Law Journal*, 1926.

KOSTER, STUART F., "An Approach to Fair Return for Public Utilities," *Valuation*, February, 1968, pp. 38-41.

KOSTERS, STUART F., "Regulations of the Public Utility Rate Base," *Valuation Manual*, 1955, pp. 81.

KREBS, WILLIAM SAMUEL, "Types of Util Rate Bases Under Deprec Res Acctg," *Social and Philosophical Sciences*, St Louis, 1946.

KUEHNLE, W. R., "Public Utility Valuation," *Appraisal Journal*, April, 1972, pp. 195-237.

LYNDON, LAMAR, *Rate-Making for Public Utilities*, Mcgraw-Hill, New York, 1923.

MACRAE, CAMERON F., "The Role of Counsel for the Utility Company In Rate Proceedings," *American Society of Appraisers Valuation Manual*, American Society of Appraisers, 1956, pp. 75.

MALONE, CLARENCE J, "Valuation of Public Utilities for Ad Valorem Tax," *Valutape Audio-Library Series*, American Society of Appraisers, Washington, D.C., January 1, 1973.

MALTBIE, W H, "Theory and Practice of Public Utility Valuation," Mcgraw-Hill, New York, January 1, 1924.

MANN, PATRICK C., "Publicly-Owned Utility Profits A Problem of Pricing," *Mississippi Valley Journal of Business and Economics*, Louisiana State University, New Orleans, 1970, pp. 45-46.

MOHR, LARRY R., "Applying Depreciation In Assessments of Gas Pipelines, Railroads and Other Utilities," *Assessment Administration*, 1965, pp. 106-107.

MULLENDORE, WALTER E., ARTHUR L. ELHOLM, *Electric and Gas Utilities, Procedures and Analysis of Inputs by Region, Texas-Input-Output Project*, University of Texas at Arlington, 1971.

NEILSON, CHARLESWORTH K., "Inflation and Utility Earnings," *Technical Valuation*, October, 1962, pp. 26-30.

NIEHANS, J., "Interest Rates, Forced Saving, and Prices In the Long Run," *Review of Economic Studies*, October, 1965.

OCHS, HARRY T. JR., "Property Allocation Problems In Utility Rate Cases," *Appraisal and Valuation Manual*, American Society of Appraisers, 1960, pp. 41-48.

OLMSTEAD, HAROLD M., "The Role of the Hearing Examiner In Rate Proceedings," *American Society of Appraisers Manual*, 1956, pp. 81.

PERRY, H. B., "Public Utility Fixed Charges," *Technical Valuation*, American Society of Appraisers, June, 1956, pp. 29.

PERRY, HORACE B., "Depreciation-Public Utilities Properties," *Appraisal and Valuation Manual*, American Society of Appraisers, 1956, pp. 121-136.

POND, O. L., *Public Utilities*, Bobbs-Merrill, Indianapolis, Ind., 1932.

# BIBLIOGRAPHY OF APPRAISAL LITERATURE

PORTER, GEORGE D., "Index Numbers and Trending In Public Utility Valuation," *American Society of Appraisers Valuation Manual,* American Society of Appraisers, 1958, pp. 227.

PROUTY, FRANK H., "Valuation and Rate Base of Public Utilities," *American Society of Appraisers Valuation Manual,* 1956, pp. 101-109.

RANDALL, FRANK, "Valuations of Easements for Public Utility Purposes," *Technical Valuation,* November, 1955, pp. 9.

REID, WILLIAM L., "Utility Relocations In New Highway Construction," *Right of Way,* June, 1969, pp. 36-37, 40-41.

REILLY, JOHN J., "Expectancy of Public Utility Property," *Appraisal and Valuation Manual,* 1958, pp. 219-226.

RETF, W. E., "Marketing Plan for Utility Companies," *Public Utilities,* December 23, 1971.

SCAARFF, MAURICE R., F. J. LEERBURGER, JOSEPH JENNING, *Depreciation Ofpublic Utility Property,* Burstein and Chappe, New York, 1940.

SCHARFF, MAURICE R., "Evaluation and Trends In Public Utilities," *Technical Valuation,* June, 1959, pp. 61-63.

SCHARFF, MAURICE R., "Valuation and Rate Regulation Overseas," *Technical Valuation,* June, 1963, pp. 4-6.

SEIDMAN, M. I., "Depreciation and Retirement Problems of Utilities," *Journal of Accountancy,* June, 1932, pp. 452-460.

SHAW AND SONS LTD., *Shaw's Practical Guide to Valuation for Rating,* Shaw and Sons, Ltd., London, 1959.

SILVERMAN, BENJAMIN, "Fundamental Concepts of Regulation," *Appraisal and Valuation Manual,* pp. 59.

STOWE, THOMAS C., "What Constitutes Utility Investigation," *The Real Estate Appraiser,* July, 1966, pp. 35-37.

TRAVIS, BROLEY E., "Reliability of the Stock and Debt Indicator Utility Property," *Technical Valuation,* pp. 5..

TRAVIS, BROLEY, E., "Appraisal of Public Utility Property," *Valuation,* October, 1958, pp. 13-19.

TREBING, HARRY M., "Essays on Public Utility Pricing and Regulation," *Public Utilities Studies,* Michigan State University, 1971, pp. 465.

TROWBRIDGE, CARL R., "Establishing Equitable Charges for Utility Company Franchises," *The Real Estate Appraiser,* January, 1970, pp. 35-37.

UNITED STATES BUREAU OF CENSUS, *Assessed Valuation of Property And Amounts and Rates of Levy 1860-1912,* Washington, 1915.

WAILS, CHARLES E., "Assessment of Public Utility Properties," *Assessment Administration,* IAAO, Chicago, 1957, pp. 169-171.

WALLACE, W. H., "Valuation of Public-Service Properties for Assessment Purposes," *The Appraisal Journal,* October, 1940, pp. 309-319.

WEDGEWOOD, JOSIAH C., *The Land Question, Taxation and Rating of Land Values,* The Labour Party, London, 1920, pp. 11.

WELCH, FRANCIS Y., *Conduct of the Utility Rate Case,* Public Utilities Reports, Inc., Washington, 1955.

WELCH, FRANCIS Y., *Preparing for the Utility Rate Case,* Public Utilities Reports, Inc., Washington, 1954.

WHITE, CARL, "Current Matters Affecting Public Utilities In the Valuation Concept," *Appraisal and Valuation Manual,* Corporate Press Incorporated, Washington, D. C, January, 1972, pp. 366.

WHITTEN, WILCOX, *Valuation of Public Utilities,* The Banks Law Publishing Company, New York, 1928, pp. 189, 196.

WHITTEN, R H, "Valuation of Public Service Corporations," *Bank Law Publications,* January 1, 1914.

WOLFF, WILLIAM R., "Rate Making Procedures," *Appraisal and Valuation Manual,* 1956, pp. 71.

WOOD, HARVEY, E., *Public Utility Law, State and Federal,* Vernon Law Book Company, Kansas City, Mo, 1926.

WORKING COMMITTEE ON UTILITIES, *Report to the Vice President and to the President's Council on Recreation and Natural Beauty,* Government Printing Office, Washington, D. C., December 7, 1968.

WYER, SAMUEL S., *Regulation,* The Sears and Simpson Company, Columbus, Ohio, 1913, pp. 1-313.

"Baltimore Will Cool Housing for Elderly; Lorain Wants it," *Air Conditioning Heating and Refrigeration News,* July 27, 1970, pp. 1.

"Budget and the Utilities," *Public Utilities,* February 17, 1972.

"Future Reserves Tied to Market Prices," *Oil and Gas Journal.*

"Return on Investmt In Elec Util Ind & Pub Util Comm Rate Base Determination Orig Cost Fair Value," *Dissertation Abstracts International, the Humanities and Social Sciences,* 1971.

"Selected Papers Derived at the Workshop on the Valuation of Public Utilities," *National Tax Journal,* Selected Papers Derived at the Workshop on the Val, National Tax Journal.

"Storage Area Uses Unusually Heavy Wall-Thickness Pipe," *Oil and Gas Journal,* August 3, 1970, pp. 89.

"Treasury Adopts Depreciation Plan," *Public Utilities Fortnightly,* July 8, 1971, pp. 50-51.

"Utilities Get In on the Write-Off Bill," *Business Week,* February 27, 1971, pp. 41.

"Utilities Throw Cold Water on Thermal Pollution Report," *Engineering News-Record,* October 8, 1970, pp. 14.

GRUNSKY, CARL E. , JR, "Probable Useful Life of Var Artcls of Character Most Frequently Encntrd In Pub Util Valuations," *Valuation, Depreciation and the Rate-Base,* pp. 270-287.

"Interest During Construction-Accounting or Rate-Making Requirement," *Public Utilities,* February 17, 1972.

# 16-12 Electric

ALDERFER, EVAN B., "Electric Utilities Go Nuclear," *The Appraisal Journal,* July, 1967, pp. 404-410.

BAGGE, C. E., "Electric Power: an Industry In Crisis and Transition," *Public Utilities Fortnightly,* June 4, 1970, pp. 55-56.

BELL, FRED A., "Insulation," *The Review,* November, 1947, pp. 14-18.

BLANCHARD, C. F., "Publicly Owned Electric Business," *Public Utilities Fortnightly,* June 18, 1970, pp. 43-45.

BUREAU OF POWER, "Electric System Planning and Operation Study--1960-69," *Staff Report, Bureau of Power,* June, 1967.

CAYWOOD, RUSSELL E., *Electric Utility Economics,* Mcgraw-Hill Co, New York, January 1, 1956.

CHRISIAN, VIRGIL L., CLAUDE M.VAUGHAN,Electric Power As a Leading Industry In the TVA Region," *Mississippi Valley Journal of Business and Economics,* April, 1971, pp. 32-42.

## BIBLIOGRAPHY OF APPRAISAL LITERATURE

COOK, D. C., "Capability of Electric Utilities to Fulfill Future Needs," Public Utilities for, Public Utilities Fortnightly, Vol. Lxxxvi, P.

DERBES, MAX J. JR., "The Effect of an Electric Transmission Line Through a Subdivision," *Right of Way*, April, 1968, pp. 28-38.

EAST CENTRAL REGIONAL ADVISORY COMMITTEE, *Electric Power In the East Central Region 1970-1980-1990*, Federal Power Commission, Washington D. C, December, 1969.

EVANS, MARVIN J., "Right of Way Relations In Electric Utilities," *Right of Way*, June, 1960, pp. 35-39.

FEC, *S-200-Statistics of Publicly Owned Electric Utilities*, Supt. of Documents, U. S. Govt. Printing Office, Washington D. C, 1968.

FEDERAL POWER COMMISSION, *R-16-National Electric Rate Book*, Supt of Documents, U. S. Govt. Printing Office, Washington D. C.

FEDERAL POWER COMISSION, *Hydroelectric Power Evaluation, Supplement I*, Federal Power Comission, Washington, D. C, November, 1969.

FEDERAL POWER COMISSION, *Statistics of Publicly Owned Electric Utilities In the United States 1968*, Federal Power Comission, Washington, D. C., 1968.

FEDERAL POWER COMMISSION, *S 204 Hydroelectric Plant Construction Cost and Annual Production Expenses*, Supt. of Documents, U. S. Govt. Printing Office, Washington, D. C., 1968.

FEDERAL POWER COMMISSION STAFF REPORT, *Air Pollution and the Regulated Electric Power and Natural Gas Industries*, Federal Power Commission, Washington, D. C., September, 1968.

FEDERAL POWER COMMISSION, *Development of Electrically Powered Vehicles*, Bureau of Power, Federal Power Commission, Washington, D.C., February, 1967.

FEDERAL POWER COMMISSION, *Electric Power Statistics*, Federal Power Comission, Washington, D. C, December, 1970.

FEDERAL POWER COMMISSION, *Electric Utility Depreciation Practices Classes A and B Privately Owned Companies*, U. S. Government Printing Office, Washington, D. C., January, 1970.

FEDERAL POWER COMMISSION, *Hydroelectric Power Valuation*, Federal Power Commission, Washington, D. C., March, 1968.

FEDERAL POWER COMMISSION, *Manpower for Elec. Power Ind. Rept. on Conf. Spons. by Fed. Power Commission*, Federal Power Commission, Washington, D. C., May 6, 1968.

FEDERAL POWER COMMISSION, *P-35-Hydroelectric Power Evaluation*, Supt of Documents, U. S. Govt. Printing Office, Washington D. C, 1968.

FEDERAL POWER COMMISSION, *S-201-Depreciation Practices of Electric Utilites*, Supt. of Documents, U. S. Govt. Printing Office, Washington D. C, 1966.

FEDERAL POWER COMMISSION, *Water Resources Appraisal for Hydroelectric Licensing, Wisconsin River Basin, Wisconsin*, Federal Power Commission, Washington, D. C, 1969.

FEDERAL POWER COMMISSION, *Water Resources Appraisal for Hydroelectric Licensing Weber River Basin-Utah-Wyoming*, Federal Power Commission, 1971.

FEDERAL POWER COMMISSION, "Electric Load Supply Situation 1971," *Electric Load Supply Situation 1971 Summer Loads*, Federal Power Commission, Washington, D. C., May 6, 1971.

FPC, "Air Pollu In Reg Elec Power & Nat Gas Industries," FPC, Wash D.C., September, 1968.

FPC, "Fed Reg of Elec Power Ind Under Pts 11 & 111 of Fed Power Act," FPC, Wash, July, 1967.

FPC, "Manpower for Elec Power Rept on Conf Spons by FPC," FPC, Wash, D.C., May 6, 1968.

FPC, "P-36 Hydroel Power Rescs of U. S. Devel & Undevel," Supt Doc Govt Ptg Off, Wash, 1968.

▲ Public Utilities

FPC, "P-38 Hydroel Power Eval Supp't No 1 July 69," Supt Doc Govt Ptg Off, Wash.

FPC, "S-184 Fed & State Comm Jurisd & Reg of Elec Gas & Telep Utils 1967," Supt Docs Govt Ptg Off, Wash.

GREENBAUM, IRVING PHD, "Return on Investment In Elec Util Ind & Pub Util Comm Rate Base Det: Orig Cost Fair Val Reprod Cost," The Ohio State University, 1970.

HATCH, CHESTER W., "Effects of Transmission Lines on Subdivision Properties," *Technical Valuation,* February, 1953, pp. 17-20, 23.

HILL, R. D., "Keeping Electric Utilities from the Fate of Other Regulated Industries," *Commercial and Financial Chronicle,* June 18, 1970, pp. 1938-1939.

JENSEN, DANIEL LYLE, "Cost Allocation for Rate Making In Electric Utilities--A Study of Alternative Methods," *Dissertation Abstracts International- A, the Humanities and Social Sciences,* April, 1971.

KNIGHT, C., "Military Launches Housing Attack-First Modulars Move In with General Electric In Command," *House and Home,* February, 1971, pp. 20.

MANN, P. C., J. L. MIKESELL, "Electric Utility Taxes: Incidence Revisited," *Public Utilities Fortnightly,* September 24, 1970, pp. 21-25.

MAYNARD, E. L., "Property Taxation of Electric and Gas Utilities," *Conference Proceedings,* National Tax Association, Columbus, 1959, pp. 248-251.

MCCALLUM, J. E., "Electrification of Steam Railroads," *Harvard Business Review,* January, 1930.

MELICHER, R. W, "Financing Electric Utilities The Value of Common Stock Warrants," *Public Utilities Fortnightly,* July 16, 1970, pp. 33-37.

MISFELDT, DOUGLAS E., "Electric Utility Property," *Assessment Administration,* 1961, pp. 245-247.

MULLENDORE, WALTER E., ARTHUR L. ELHOLM, *Electric and Gas Utilities, Procedures and Analysis of Inputs by Region, Texas-Input-Output Project,* University of Texas at Arlington, 1971.

PHILIPS, L. A., "Problems Facing Electric Utilities In Obtaining Right of Way," *Right of Way,* August, 1959, pp. 37-39.

RANDELL, MURRAY E., "Why I Would Build an All-Electric Building," *The Appraisal Journal,* October, 1966, pp. 552-561.

RIGHT OF WAY, "Highlights of the Electric Utility Right of Way Conference, 1957," *Right of Way,* October, 1957, pp. 51-78.

SILVERMAN, BENJAMIN, "Fundamental Concepts of Regulation," *Appraisal and Valuation Manual,* pp. 59.

SOUTHWEST REGIONAL ADVISORY COMMITTEE, *Electric Power In the Southwest,* Federal Power Commission, Washington D. C, April, 1969.

THE WEST CENTRAL REGIONAL ADVISORY COMMITTEE, *Electric Power In West Central, U. S,* Federal Power Commission, Washington D. S, June, 1969.

VENNARD, EDWIN, *The Electric Power Business,* Mcgraw-Hill Co, New York, January 1, 1962.

YOUNG, H. J., AND R. S. THORSELL, "Environment, Economics, and Electric Utility Rights of Way," *Right of Way,* October, 1970, pp. 41-43.

*S-206-Statistics of Privately Owned Electric Utilities In the United States,* Supt. of Documents, U. S. Govt. Printing Office, Washington D. C, 1969.

*Water Rescs Apprsl for Hydroelec Lic'g Conn River Basin Vt N. H. Mass--Conn,* Federal Power Commission, Washington, D. C, 1966.

*Water Rescs Apprsl for Hydroelec Lic'g Swan Falls Devel, Snake River Idaho Proj 503 Ownd by I. P. Cm,* Federal Power Commission, Washington, D. C., 1968.

*Water Resources Appraisal for Hydroelec Licensing So Fork Amer River Basin Calif New Release N 17531,* Federal Power Commission, May 24, 1971.

*Water Resources Appraisal for Hydroelectric Licensing, Oneida Development, Bear River, Idaho,* Federal Power Commission, Washington, D. C, 1968.

"Making the Future Brighter with Electric Energy," *Public Utilities Fortnightly,* June 10, 1971, pp. 45-48.

"Problems In Use of Stock & Debt & Income Factors In Assessment of Telephone & Electric Utilities," *Conference Proceedings,* National Tax Association, Columbus, 1960, pp. 390-400.

"Return on Investmt In Elec Util Ind & Pub Util Comm Rate Base Determination Orig Cost Fair Value," *Dissertation Abstracts International, the Humanities and Social Sciences,* 1971.

"Utilities Can Ease Energy Shortage by Curbing Market Expansion Programs," *Air Conditioning Heating and Refrigeration News,* November 16, 1970, pp. 7.

"Utilities Throw Cold Water on Thermal Pollution Report," *Engineering News-Record,* October 8, 1970, pp. 14.

# 16-13   Gas

"Economics of the Gas Industry," *Proceedings Southwest Legal Foundation--1962,* Matthew Bender Co, San Francisco Calif, January 1, 1962.

"Fuel Gas Engineering Practices," *Gas Engineers Handbook,* The Industrial Press, New York, January 1, 1965.

"Gas In Newest Sports Arena," *Public Utilities Fortnightly,* October 22, 1970, pp. 110.

"Gas Ups Stationary Market Share," *Oil and Gas Journal,* December 28, 1970, pp. 79.

"Utilities Can Ease Energy Shortage by Curbing Market Expansion Programs," *Air Conditioning Heating and Refrigeration News,* November 16, 1970, pp. 7.

"Utilities Throw Cold Water on Thermal Pollution Report," *Engineering News-Record,* October 8, 1970, pp. 14.

"Effect of High Pressure Gas Transmsn Pipelines on Real Estate Vals In N. J. Metropolitan Area," *Right of Way,* February, 1958, pp. 21, 24.

F.P.C., "S-59 Depreciation Practices of Nat Gas Co," Federal Power Commission, 1961.

FEDERAL POWER COMISSION, *A Staff Report on National Gas Supply and Demand,* Bureau of National Gas, Washington, D. C, September, 1969.

FEDERAL POWER COMISSION, *Statistics of Interstate Natural Gas Pipeline Companies, 1969,* Federal Power Comission, Washington, D. C., 1969.

FEDERAL POWER COMMISSION, *Records of Natural Gas Companies,* Federal Power Commission, December 12, 1962.

FEDERAL POWER COMMISSION, *Cost of Pipeline & Compressor Sta. Constr. Under Nonbudget Type Certif. Authoriza. As Reptd by Pipe,* Federal Power Commission, Washington, D. C., 1970.

FEDERAL POWER COMMISSION, *S-205-Statistics for Interstate Natural Gas Pipeline Companies,* Supt. of Documents, U. S. Govt. Printing Office, Washington D. C, 1969.

▲ Public Utilities

FEDERAL POWER COMMISSION, *United States Imports and Exports of Natural Gas--1965*, Federal Power Commission, Washington, D.C., 1965.

FPC, "S-184 Fed & State Comm Jurisd & Reg of Elec Gas & Telep Utils 1967," Supt Docs Govt Ptg Off, Wash.

KIRSHMAN, JOHN EMMETT, "Gas Industry," *Principles of Investment*, 1933, pp. 403.

MAYNARD, E. L., "Property Taxation of Electric and Gas Utilities," *Conference Proceedings*, National Tax Association, Columbus, 1959, pp. 248-251.

MULLENDORE, WALTER E., ARTHUR L. ELHOLM, *Electric and Gas Utilities, Procedures and Analysis of Inputs by Region, Texas-Input-Output Project*, University of Texas at Arlington, 1971.

PAIGE, C. E., "Gas Industry In America," *American Gas Assoication Monthly*, July, 1931.

SILVERMAN, BENJAMIN, "Fundamental Concepts of Regulation," *Appraisal and Valuation Manual*, pp. 59.

WEDEMEYER, KARL ERIC PH. D., *Interstate Natural Gas Supply and Intrastate Market Behavior*, University of Southern California, 1972.

# 16-14  Water

AMERICAN WATER WORKS ASSOCIATION, "Survival and Retirement of Water Works Facilities," *The Association*, New York City, 1947.

BRAMS, MARVIN, "Pricing Policies of the Water Industry A Case Study of Northern New Castle County, Delaware," *Economic and Business Bulletin*, Temple University, April, 1971, pp. 37-42.

COSGROVE, MICHAEL HENRY PH. D., "Cost and Quality of Water Service In Ohio Cities," *Cost and Quality of Water Service In Ohio Cities*, Ohio State University, 1971.

FEDERAL POWER COMISSION, *Water Resources Appraisal for Hydroelectric Licensing, Weber River Basin, Utah-Wyoming*, Federal Power Commission, Washington, D. C..

FEDERAL POWER COMMISSION, *Hydroelectric Power Valuation*, Federal Power Commission, Washington, D. C., March, 1968.

FEDERAL POWER COMMISSION, *Upper White River Basin Water Appraisal*, Federal Power Commission, Washington D. C, July, 1966.

FEDERAL POWER COMMISSION, *Water Resources Appraisal for Hydroelectric Licensing, South Fork American River Basin, California*, Federal Power Commission, Washington, D. C, 1971.

FEDERAL POWER COMMISSION, *Water Resources Appraisal for Hydroelectric Licensing, Wisconsin River Basin, Wisconsin*, Federal Power Commission, Washington, D. C, 1969.

FEDERAL POWER COMMISSION, *Water Resources Appraisal for Hydroelectric Licensing, Feather River Basin, California*, Federal Power Commission, Washington, D. C., 1967.

FEDERAL POWER COMMISSION, *Water Resources Appraisal for Hydroelectric Licensing Weber River Basin-Utah-Wyoming*, Federal Power Commission, 1971.

GILLETTE, H P, "Valuation of Water Power Rights," *Engineering and Contracting Magazine*, January 1, 1912, pp. Vol. 38.

GOURLWY, H. J. F., *Water Supply*, Encyclopedia Britanica, 1900.

HAY, LEON E, GRINNELL, D J, *Water Utility Accounting,* Municipal Finance Officers Assn, Am. Water Wks Asn, Ann Arbor Mich, January 1, 1970.

HAZEN, ALLEN, *Meter Rates for Water Works,* Wiley, New York, 1918.

KIREBSTEIN, RONALD GARY PH. D., *Temporal Production Interdependency In Agriculture Arising from Water Quality,* University of Washington, 1971.

KIRSHMAN, JOHN EMMETT, "Water Works," *Principles of Investment,* 1933, pp. 426.

LEWIN, GORDON, "Law and Municipal Ecology: Air, Water, Noise, Overpopulation," National Institute of Municipal Law Offices, Washington, D. C..

MONCUR, JAMES E. T. PH. D., *A Programming Approach to the Valuation of Water In Alternative Uses,* Washington State University, 1971.

SCHARFF, MAURICE R., "Revenue Requirements and Rates of Municipal Water Utilities," *Technical Valuation,* 1966, pp. 17.

SILVERMAN, BENJAMIN, "Fundamental Concepts of Regulation," *Appraisal and Valuation Manual,* pp. 59.

SORTOR, CHARLES H., "Evaluation of Deep Water Wells," *Appraisal and Valuation Manual,* American Society of Appraisers, 1959, pp. 327-336.

TODD, DAVID KEITH (EDITOR), "A Compendium of Useful Information on Water Resources," *The Water Encyclopedia,* Water Information Center, Port Wasington N.Y., January 1, 1970.

TURNEAURE, F. E., "Valuation of the Davenport, Iowa, Water Company," *Engineering Valuation.*

TURNER, HOWARD M., "The Engineering Valuation of Water Rights," *Appraisal and Valuation Manual,* 1961, pp. 137-146.

TURNEURE, F. E., H. L. RUSSEL, *Public Water Supplies,* New York, 1908.

VOSKUIL, W. N., *The Economics of Water Power Development,* Chicago, 1928.

WATSON, LESLIE J., "The Valuation of Water In Hawaii," *Appraisal and Valuation Manual,* 1962, pp. 117-126.

WILLIS, REED WESTON PH. D., "Political Economics of Colorado's Ground Water Development and Use," Colorado State University, 1970.

WOODLAND PIERCE CO., "Appraisal, Rate, and Service Investigation of the Surburban Water Company," *Engineering Valuation,* 1931.

YANUS, MUHAMMAD, PH. D., *Optimal Allocation of Multipurpose Reservoir Water A Dynamic Programing Model,* Vanderbilt University, 1971.

*Water Rescs Apprsl for Hydroelec Lic'g Swan River Basin Vt N. H. Mass--Conn,* Federal Power Commission, Washington, D. C, 1966.

*Water Rescs Apprsl for Hydroelec Lic'g Swan Falls Devel, Snake River Idaho Proj 503 Ownd by I. P. Cm,* Federal Power Commission, Washington, D. C., 1968.

*Water Resources Appraisal for Hydroelec Licensing So Fork Amer River Basin Calif New Release N 17531,* Federal Power Commission, May 24, 1971.

*Water Resources Appraisal for Hydroelectric Licensing, Oneida Development, Bear River, Idaho,* Federal Power Commission, Washington, D. C, 1968.

"Largest Underground Reservoir to Hold 100 Million Gallons of Water," *Engineering News-Record,* December 3, 1970, pp. 20-21.

"Survival and Retirement Experience with Water Works Facilities," *Committee Report,* Lancaster Press Inc, Lancaster Pa, January 1, 1947.

"Utilities Can Ease Energy Shortage by Curbing Market Expansion Programs,'' *Air Conditioning Heating and Refrigeration News,* November 16, 1970, pp. 7.

"Utilities Throw Cold Water on Thermal Pollution Report," *Engineering News-Record,* October 8, 1970, pp. 14.

## 16-15 Communications Systems

BARRAN, A. J., "The General Telephone Story," *Right of Way,* June, 1955, pp. 11-16.

CONNORS, JOHN E., "Purchase of Real Estate-Telephone Co," *Right of Way,* April, 1958, pp. 19-21.

CRUNDEN, ALLAN B., D DONALD R. BELCHER, "The Straight-Line Depreciation Accounting Practice of Telephone Companies In the U. S," *Proceedings of the International Congress of Accounting,* New York, 1929, pp. 351-386.

DAGGETT, S., "Telephone Consolidation Under the Act of 1921," *The Journal of Land and Public Utility Economics,* February, 1931.

DANNER, E. H., "Property Taxation of Telephone Company Property," *Conference Proceedings,* National Tax Association, Columbus, 1959, pp. 241-247.

DAVIS, JOHN W., "The Arrangement of Telephone Facilities Due to Interstate and Other Highway Work," *Right of Way,* February, 1962, pp. 17-21.

FPC, "S-184 Fed & State Comm Jurisd & Reg of Elec Gas & Telep Utils 1967," Supt Docs Govt Ptg Off, Wash.

GOODWIN, E. F., "The Telephone Company and Its Right of Way Problems," *Right of Way,* February, 1961, pp. 19-20.

KIRSHMAN, JOHN EMMETT, "The Telegraph," *Principles of Investment,* 1933, pp. 436.

KIRSHMAN, JOHN EMMETT, "The Telephone," *Principles of Investment,* 1933, pp. 474.

PARKER, D. W., "A Realistic Approach to the Problems of Telephone Utility Assessment," *Technical Valuation,* October, 1962, pp. 34-36.

SILVERMAN, BENJAMIN, "Fundamental Concepts of Regulation," *Appraisal and Valuation Manual,* pp. 59.

## 16-16 Sanitary Sewer

ALPER, ZALMAN Y., "The Septic Tank System of Sewage Disposal," *The Appraisal Journal,* April, 1957, pp. 189-192.

BUBBIS, N. S., "Sewage and Drainage Problems In Greater Winnipeg," *Appraisal Institute Magazine,* Appraisal Institute of Canada, Winnipeg.

## BIBLIOGRAPHY OF APPRAISAL LITERATURE

DAIL, CHARLES C., "The Sewer Utility," *The Residential Appraiser*, May, 1959, pp. 19-21.

ENGINEERING NEWS-RECORD, "Sewerage and Dam Construction Costs Jump 9 to 10%," *Engineering News-Record*, March 18, 1971, pp. 106-108.

GIBSON, HOWARD L., "The Septic-Tank System," *The Review*, June, 1949, pp. 11-16.

HAMILTON, H. P., "An Appraisal Education," *Appraisal Institute Magazine*, Appraisal Institute of Canada, Winnipeg.

SILVERMAN, BENJAMIN, "Fundamental Concepts of Regulation," *Appraisal and Valuation Manual*, pp. 59.

THEISS, WILLIAM R., "The Appraisal Docket. Compensation for Private Sewer System Installed In Public Schools," *The Appraisal Journal*, January, 1963, pp. 121-122.

TOWNSEND, T. L., "Sewage Lagoons," *The Appraisal Journal*, April, 1964, pp. 253-257.

WEIL, ANDREW L., KENT MAY WATSMAL, RON N., "Unsettled, Settled Law of Sewer Assessments Simon Appeal," *University of Pittsburgh Law Review*, June, 1964, pp. 653-681.

## CHAPTER SEVEN

# Natural Resources

by Clement J. Schwingle, FASA

Mr. Clement J. Schwingle was Chairman of The American Appraisal Company, Inc., the world's largest valuation organization, from 1967 through 1972, following nine years as President; he was a member of its Board of Directors for 24 years, having been associated with the company since 1922.

He is a nationally-known authority on tax depreciation, capital stock valuation, and industrial appraisal matters and has been the author of numerous technical articles for professional journals. For many years, he directed the company's activities in the international field. Mr. Schwingle is a Registered Professional Engineer in the State of Wisconsin and is associated with a number of professional organizations, including the American Society of Appraisers and the Wisconsin Society of Professional Engineers.

Mr. Schwingle received his education at Loras College in Dubuque, Iowa, and thereafter at Marquette University; he attended the 25th Advanced Management Program at Harvard University.

▲ Natural Resources

NATURAL TREASURES—hidden away by nature over the span of time, sometimes far below the surface of fertile farm lands, sometimes in out-cropping strata on inaccessible mountain sides, or again near or on the surface where men observe them with the naked eye—comprise an amazing part of our national wealth.

Search for new sources is carried on unceasingly and methodically, and only by the services of government, prospectors, promoters, scientists, and investors are they located and converted to commercial utility and value. Others, such as forests, can readily be viewed.

When a resource is to be exploited and bankers and investors are called upon to furnish the development capital, the given technical facts must be verified and interpreted in terms of prospective commercial value. It falls to the appraiser, necessarily equipped with a substantial background of experience and knowledge of the field and reflecting unbiased judgment, to assume that responsibility.

The basic factors, subject to the appraiser's consideration and investigation, include:

Location, quality, and indicated extent of reserves commercially recoverable.

Distance from market.

Cost of development to a point of profitable operation.

Prospective rate, trend, and period of recovery of reserves.

Estimated cost of recovery to the point of conversion or shipment.

Estimated cost of conversion and marketing.

Income and severance taxes.

Recorded sales and offering prices of comparable reserves or units of product.

Prevailing royalties paid by lessees for the exploitation of similar reserves.

From careful study of these and other relevant factors, the utility or value of the reserves may be estimated or reported upon on the basis of one or more of the following generally accepted methods of procedure:

Comparison with actual or proposed exchanges of comparable reserves at arms-length transactions.

On a royalty basis where there is evidence of the terms and conditions of prevailing leases and methods of exploitation.

On the basis of the present worth of prospective earning power of the reserves to a point of conversion of marketability, allowing a rate of return that is reasonable and consistent with the hazard of realization on the justified capital.

Reversion value of the land after exploitation of the resource.

The references which follow offer the appraiser an in-depth range of source material helpful not only in valuation techniques but which is also informative as to the property and economic characteristics of the various resources.

# Natural Resources

17-11   Coal
17-12   Timber and Timberland
17-13   Trees and Shrubs
17-14   Minerals
17-15   Oil and Gas
17-16   Water and Reservoirs
17-17   Fisheries and Marine Deposits

## 17-11 Coal

"Big Coal Crisis Burns Itself Out," *Business Week,* December 5, 1970.

"Coal A New Look at an Old Industry," *Financial World,* September 30, 1970, pp. 7.

"Coal Chemicals In the Eighties Seen Reviving As a Major Force After Turmoil During Seventies," *Oil Paint and Drug Reporter,* March 1, 1971, pp. 7.

"Coal Controls," *The Economist,* October 3, 1970, pp. 54.

"Coal Shortage Chills Chemical Profit Hopes," *Chemical Week,* October 21, 1970, pp. 21-22.

BRETEY, P. R., "Coal-The Giant Revived," *Financial Analysts Journal,* January, 1971, pp. 54-58.

BREWER, T., "Earth Resources," *Datamation,* August 15, 1970, pp. 25-28.

KAUFMAN, K. A., "Coal Exports Won't Be Cut Its Cold Shoulder for Industry," *Iron Age,* October 8, 1970, pp. 19.

MCMNUS, G. J., R., K. A. KAUFMAN, "Coal Crisis Goes Critical," *Coal Crisis Goes Critical.*

PILL, JOHN R., "Mineral Rights-Coal Lands," *The Appraisal Journal,* January, 1943, pp. 26.

## 17-12 Timber and Timberland

ALASKA REVIEW OF BUSINESS AND ECONOMIC CONDITIONS, "Alaska's Lumber Markets," *Alaska Review of Business and Economic Conditions,* University of Alaska, October, 1971, pp. 1-28.

ALEXANDER, L. B., "Timberland Appraisal," *Appraisal Institute Magazine,* Appraisal Institute of Canada, Winnipeg, June 1, 1971.

BANGO, HENRY L., "A Timbermans Look at Right of Way Acquisition," *Right of Way,* June, 1958, pp. 33-36.

BANZHAF, GEORGE, "Appraisal of Timberlands," *The Appraisal Journal,* June, 1962, pp. 29-32.

BARIBEAU, JULES, "Crossing Forest Lands In Eastern Canada," *Proceedings of the Seventh Annual National Seminar,* American Right of Way Association, Washington, D. C, 1962, pp. 71-72.

BEUTER, J. H., "New Look In Appraisal of Timber Value," *Forest Industries,* February, 1971, pp. 26 28.

BRATTON, ALLEN W., "Assessment of Timberlands," *Valuation,* June, 1955, pp. 33-36.

BROWN, EDWIN E., "Appraisal of Timberland Through Capitalization of the Value of Average Annual Growth," *The Assessor's Journal,* July, 1971, pp. 35-42.

## BIBLIOGRAPHY OF APPRAISAL LITERATURE

BROWN, WILBUR L., "Technical Aspects of Timber Valuation," *Assessment Administration,* IAAO, Chicago, 1964, pp. 89-94.

BUYS, A. A., "Appraisal of Forest Land In Canada," *Appraisal Institute Magazine,* March, 1961, pp. 6-10.

CAIN, STATLEY A., "Natural Resources Related to Real Estate Problems," Vol. Xxiii.

CAMERON, J. A., "Utility Forestry and Land Management," *Right of Way,* April, 1962, pp. 16-17.

CANTERBURY, NATHAN D., "Right of Way Across Timberland," *Right of Way,* June, 1956, pp. 19-21.

CHAPMAN, H. H., W. H. MEYER, *Forest Valuation,* Mcgraw-Hill, New York, 1947.

CLARK, EDWARD L., "Property Tax Aspects of Forest Resource Development In the Rocky Mountain Area," *Assessment Administration,* IAAO, Chicago, 1960, pp. 112-115.

COLE, F. M., "Condemnation Appraisal of Woodlands," *Technical Valuations,* 1967, pp. 62.

DUERR, WILLIAM A., *Fundamentals of Forestry Economics,* Mcgraw-Hill, New York, 1960.

ELLIS, ROSS M., "Methods and Practices In Appraising Timber for Eminent Domain," *The Appraisal Journal,* July, 1960, pp. 301-317.

ELLIS, ROSS M., "Methods In Appraising Timber," *Condemnation Appraisal Practice,* American Institute of Real Estate Appraisers, Chicago, 1967, pp. 318.

FEDERAL RESERVE BANK OF SAN FRANCISCO, "Lumber Out on a Limb," *The Appraisal Journal,* April, 1965, pp. 298-304.

FISK, KENNETH, "Tree Loss for Tax Reports," *The Review,* November, 1951, pp. 14-16.

HALL, THOMAS H. III, "An Approach to Timberland Appraisal," *The Appraisal Journal,* April, 1962, pp. 292-293.

HARDIN, C. M., "Outlook for Timber Supply Is Good," *Paper Trade Journal,* April, 1971, pp. 48-49.

JOHNSON, ERNEST H., "Timber Taxation In Maine," *Assessment Administration,* IAAO, Chicago, 1961, pp. 114-115.

JOHNSON, RALPH S., "Forest Taxation Alternatives," *Assessment Administration,* IAAO, Chicago, 1961, pp. 98-110.

LEHMAN, H. O., "The Effects of Trees and Planting on Property Values," *Appraisal and Valuation Manual,* 1959, pp. 173-176.

LEWIS, GORDON D., *A Possible Approach to Forest Land Taxation,* Forest & Consvn Expermt Sta University of Montana, Missoula, September, 1962, pp. 15.

LEWIS, HENRY W., "Assessing Forest Land and Timber for Property Taxes," *Popular Government,* May, 1956, pp. 3-7.

LUITEN, IRVIN H., "Enlightened Forest Management," *Right of Way,* October, 1954, pp. 15-18.

MACDONALD, KENNETH M., "The Valuation of Standing Timber," *Appraisal and Valuation Manual,* American Society of Appraisers, Vol. Vii, p. 153.

MAIN, ALDEN CHESTER PH. D., *The Impact of Forestry and Forest-Related Industries on a Local Economy, Baldwin County, Alabama,* Auburn University, 1971.

MEAD, WALTER J., "Effect of Capital Gains Taxation on Timber Resource Allocation," *Conference Proceedings,* 1965, pp. 342-359.

MEADOW, BEN, "Evaluation of Standing Timber," *The Appraisal Journal,* April, 1967, pp. 251-255.

MINISTERIO DE AGRICULTURA Y CRIA DE VZLA., "Anotaciones Sobre Valoraciones Forestales," *Boletin,* Sotave, Caracas, Venezuela, pp. 31-35.

MINOR, CHARLES, D., "Forestors Approach to the Value of Forest Products," *The Appraisal Journal,* October, 1956, pp. 523-526.

MOAK, JAMES E., "Forest Appraisals for Assessment of Ad Valorem Taxes," *Journal of the American Society of Farm Managers and Rural Appraisers,* October, 1966, pp. 60-66.

NIEHAUS, T. B., "Merchantable Timber Values In Recreational Developments," *The Appraisal Journal,* October, 1968, pp. 570-575.

PENNSYLVANIA STATE CHAMBER OF COMMERCE, "Special State Taxes; Exemptions on Forest Products and Forest Crop Lands," *Special State Taxes % of Exemptions Forest Products and Forest Crop Lands,* Pennsylvania State Chamber of Commerce, Harrisburg, Pennsylv, July, 1960.

RODRIGUEZ, LOUIS J., "Louisianas Natural Resources How Strong an Economic Development Asset," *Louisiana Business Review,* Louisiana State University, Baton Rouge, 1971, pp. 6.

SCHMUTZ, GEORGE L., EDWIN E. LUNSTEAD, FEDERIC W. WILHELMI, "Redwood Forest Property-Rating and Valuation," *The Appraisal Journal,* April, 1950, pp. 209-214.

SCUSSEL, GEORGE P., "The Income Approach and Forestry Valuation," *Valuation,* August, 1967, pp. 51-57.

SOMBERG, SEYMOUR L., AND EDWARD STUART, JR., "The Fair Market of Standing Timber," *Technical Valuation,* October, 1963, pp. 12-16.

STACER, THOMAS C., "Rights of Way Through Timbered Areas," *Right of Way,* October, 1967, pp. 52-56.

STUART, EDWARD, JR., "Special Factors to Be Considered In Appraising Timberlands," *American Society of Appraisers,* Vol. V, p. 205.

SUTHERLAND, CHARLES F., AND ELLIS T. WILLIAMS, "Timberland and Taxes In Maine: Property and Federal Income Taxes," *Maine Law Review,* 1965, pp. 227-251.

THORNTON, W. B., "The Use and Value of Forest Land for Transmission and Pipeline Right of Way," *Right of Way,* December, 1960, pp. 19-21.

VERMONT TAX DEPARTMENT, *Timberland Appraisal Guide,* Vermont Tax Department, Montpelier, Vermont, May, 1960, pp. 1-13.

WEYERHAEUSER COMPANY, *Plain Talk About Trees and Taxes,* Weyerhaeuser Company, Tacoma.

WILLIAMS, ELLIS T., *State Guides for Assessing Forest Land and Timber,* U. S. Forest Service, Washington, 1956, pp. 1-52.

WILLIAMS, ELLIS T., "Forest Tax Alternatives and Trends," *Assessment Administration,* Institute of American Assessment Officers, Chicago, 1960, pp. 97-102.

WILLIAMS, ELLIS T., "Some Aspects of Forest Taxation Under the Forest Crop Law and Under the General Property Tax In Wis," *Land Economics,* February, 1960, pp. 65-78.

WILLIAMS, ELLIS T., "Trends In Forest Taxation," *National Tax Journal,* June, 1961, pp. 113-114.

WILLIAMS, ELLIS T., "What Lies Ahead In Forest Assessment?," *Assessment Administration,* Institute of American Assessment Officers, Chicago, 1958, pp. 43-57.

ZETTLEMOYER, CHARLES L., AND MICHAEL ADES, "Timberlands Taxation In Kentucky," *Timberlands Taxation In Kentucky,* Legislative Research Commission, Frankfort, Kentucky, 1963.

*Forestry Tenures & Taxes In Can. Economic Effects of Taxatn & of Regltg of Crown Forests by Province,* Canadian Tax Foundation, Toronto, 1957.

"Loggers Double Annual Production," *Forest Industries,* June, 1970.

"Lumber Prices Fail to Catch Fire," *Business Week,* June 5, 1971, pp. 40.

## 17-13 Trees and Shrubs

"Court Case: Tree Preservation Orders," *The Valuer*, The Incorporated Society of Valuers & Auctioneers, London, December 1, 1973, pp. 428.

ASH, FRED C., "The Appraisal Docket: Abutting Owners' Property In Public Shade Trees," *The Appraisal Journal*, April, 1957, pp. 266.

CONNELL, E. A., "Trees As Definite Factors In Real Estate Appraising," *National Real Estate Journal*, December 9, 1929, pp. 53.

HAGNESTEIN, W. D., "Right of Way and Tree-Farming," *Proceedings of the Seventh Annual National Seminar*, American Right of Way Association, Washington, D. C, 1961, pp. 66-67.

KAMLET, MARK, "Legal Factors In Evaluating Land with Tree Growths," *The Appraisal Journal*, January, 1968, pp. 108-109.

MAIN, ALDEN CHESTER PH. D., *The Impact of Forestry and Forest-Related Industries on a Local Economy, Baldwin County, Alabama*, Auburn University, 1971.

MCMICHAEL, STANLEY L., "What Are Trees Worth?," *Appraising Manual*, 1937, pp. 432-437.

PETRIE, JOSEPH A., "Appraising a Tree," *Technicalities*, May, 1949, pp. 39.

SPICER, O. W., "The Valuation of Trees," *Appraisal Digest*, July, 1953, pp. 18-20.

WEBER, WALTER W., "How to Appraise Trees," *National Real Estate Journal*, September 2, 1929, pp. 33.

WEYERHAEUSER COMPANY, *Plain Talk About Trees and Taxes*, Weyerhaeuser Company, Tacoma.

## 17-14 Minerals

AMENDOLAGINE, EMANUEL, "Valuation of Assaying Cutting & Ore Picking of Lenticular Uranium Ore," *Appraisal and Valuation Manual*, American Society of Appraisers, Washington, 1958, pp. 191-196.

AMERICAN SOCIETY OF PLANNING OFFICIALS, "Land Use Controls In the Surface Extraction of Minerals," Chicago.

BAXTER, C. H., R. D. PARKS, *Examination and Valuation of Mineral Property*, Addison Wesley, Cambridge, 1957.

BAYNE, BROWNRIDGE, *Petrographic Analysis of Determining Quality of Coarse Aggregates*, Canadian Good Roads Association, 1958.

BEIZER, J., K. A. KAUFMAN, "Minings Public Land Prospects Soar," *Iron Age*, June 25, 1970, pp. 49-54.

BREWER, T., "Earth Resources," *Datamation*, August 15, 1970, pp. 25-28.

BROADBENT, LORIN J., "Eminent Domain Valuation of Land Containing Minerals," *The Appraisal Journal*, January, 1961, pp. 63-77.

## ▲ Natural Resources

CAIN, STATLEY A., "Natural Resources Related to Real Estate Problems," Vol. Xxiii.

COFFIN, GEORGE H. JR., *The Appraisal of Rock, Sand, and Gravel Deposits*, California Real Estate Association, Los Angeles, 1937.

DIX, W. B., "Some Aspects of Mine Taxation In Ontario," *Canadian Tax Journal*, July, 1957, pp. 263-270.

DOWNING, W. C., "Appraisal of a Gravel Pit," *Appraisal Institute Magazine*, January, 1959, pp. 16-18.

EDMAN, J. J., "Oral Agreement to Remove Minerals Is Property Right. Appraisal Docket," *The Appraisal Journal*, October, 1959, pp. 581-582.

EDMAN, J. J., "Unconsidered Mineral Rights May Be of Real Value. Appraisal Docket," *The Appraisal Journal*, October, 1958, pp. 613-614.

EDMAN, J. J., "Valuation of Gravel Properties. Appraisal Docket," *The Appraisal Journal*, January, 1961, pp. 127-129.

EDMAN, J. J., "Valuation of Sand & Gravel Which May Be Removed Without Destroying Value of Land Appraisal Docket," *The Appraisal Journal*, April, 1959, pp. 266-268.

GREAT BRITAIN MINISTRY OF HOUSING & LOCAL GOVT, "Valuation of Land with Underlying Natural Resources," *The Appraisal Journal*, April, 1935, pp. 236-241.

HAMILTON, HOWARD D., "Taxes and Taconite, Iron Ore Tax Legislation In the Lake Superior Region," *National Tax Journal*, December, 1964, pp. 324-354.

HEPDITCH, G. D., "The Appraisal of Sand and Gravel Deposits," *Appraisal and Valuation Manual*, American Society of Appraiser, 1959, pp. 149-158.

HOOVER, HERBERT C., *Principles of Mining*, Mcgraw-Hill, New York, 1909.

INDUSTRIAL RESEARCH, "Mud to Build with," *Industrial Research*, May, 1971, pp. 23.

JOHNSON, LOWELL C., "Valuation of Petroleum Mineral Rights for Ad Valorem Taxation," *The Appraisal Journal*, October, 1953, pp. 497-510.

LANE, J. F., "Recent Developments In the Field of Percentage Depletion, Abstract In Rock Products," *Valuation Manual*, A. S. A, April, 1956, pp. 126.

LEMON, J. D., "Problems In Mine Evaluation," *Management Accounting*, September, 1971, pp. 46-48.

LUSE, JAY D, "Appraisal of Gravel Lands," *Journal; Proceedings*, Am. Soc. Farm Mgrs-Rural Appraisers, Denver, November 27, 1973, pp. 53-57.

MCSWEENEY, THOMAS F., "Evaluation of Mineral Rights," *American Society of Appraisers*, 1960, pp. 153-160.

MILLMAN, DEANE A., *A Brief History of Iron Ore Mining and Taxation In Minnesota*, Department of Taxation, St. Paul, 1964, pp. 15 PAGES.

MOEBES, CARL G., "Condemnation of Minerals," *Right of Way*, April, 1960, pp. 7-10.

OBERBILLIG, ERNEST, "Appraisal of Mineral Lands," *The Appraisal Journal*, October, 1964, pp. 485-521.

PARK, R. D., *Examination and Valuation of Mineral Property*, Addison-Wesley, Cambridge, Mass., 1952.

RANDALL, WILLIAM J., "Problems In Lead Mining Appraisals," *Real Estate Analyst Appraisal Bulletin*, 1960, pp. 93-100.

RECK, ROBERT OTTO, *The Regional Economic and Enviromental Impacts of the Uranium Mining and Milling Industry*, University of Maryland, 1971.

ROMANOVA, M. A., "Spectral Laminance of Sand Deposits As a Tool In Land Evaluation," *Land Evaluation*, pp. 342.

SCHMUTZ, GEORGE L., "Rock, Sand and Gravel Deposits," *Condemnation Appraisers Handbook*, 1938, pp. 1-339.

SCHMUTZ, GEORGE L., "The Valuation of Rock Sand and Gravel Deposits," *The Appraisal Journal*, April, 1948, pp. 174-17.

THEISS, WILLIAM R., "The Appraisal Docket. Valuation of Mineral Rights," *The Appraisal Journal*, January, 1905, pp. 129-132.

U. S. GOVERNMENT PRINTING OFFICE, *Dictionary of Mining, Mineral and Related Terms*, U. S. Government Printing Office, Washington, D. C..

WEHER, ROBERT H., DONA H. BAKER, JR, "Mineral Production In New Mexico In 1970," *New Mexico Business*, University of New Mexico, May, 1971, pp. 3-16.

WHEELER, BLEEKER L., "The Valuation of Mineral Properties," *Appraisal and Valuation Manual*, 1958, pp. 185-190.

*Geological Survey Professional Paper #820 Stock #2401-00307*, US Dept of Interior, Washington, D.C., January 1, 1973.

*Valuation of Mines and Quarries*, California State Board of Equalization, Sacramento Calif, January 1, 1973.

"Mine Valuation by the Hoskold Formula," *Appraisal and Valuation Manual*, Washington, D. C, January, 1972, pp. 34.

"Mining In Georgia Big Business with a Bigger Future," *Atlanta Economic Review*, Georgia State University, July, 1971, pp. 1 78.

## 17-15   Oil and Gas

APPRAISAL JOURNAL, "The Appraisal of a Natural Gas Pipeland," *The Appraisal Journal*, January, 1951, pp. 56-75.

BARBEAU, JACQUES, *Oil and Gas Production and Taxes*, Canadian Tax Foundation, Toronto, March, 1963.

BREWER, T., "Earth Resources," *Datamation*, August 15, 1970, pp. 25-28.

BURT, O. R., R. G. CUMMINGS, "Production and Investment In Natural Resource Industries," *American Economics Review*, September, 1970, pp. 576-590.

CAMPBELL, JOHN M, *Oil Property Valuation*, Prentice-Hall, Inc., New Jersey, 1959.

CARB, MEREDITH R., AND A. HELBING, JR., "Appraisal of an Oil Works," *The Appraisal and Valuation Manual*, 1956, pp. 257-270.

CHAMBERLAIN, J. B., "Right of Way Acquisition for Oil Pipe Lines," *Appraisal Institute Magazine*, September, 1961, pp. 7-8.

DONOGHUE, DAVID, "The Data Program In the Appraisal of a Producing Oil and Gas Property," *The Appraisal Journal*, October, 1942, pp. 347-351.

DRISCOLL, ROBERT L., "Condemnation of Underground Reservoirs for Storage of Natural Gas," *The Appraisal Journal*, January, 1965, pp. 67-72.

EDMAN, J. J., "Unproved Oil Rights Must Be Considered. Appraisal Docket," *The Appraisal Journal*, October, 1957, pp. 623.

EVANS, LOUIS H., "Our Diminishing Oil Reserves," *The Appraisal Journal*, April, 1949.

FEDERAL POWER COMISSION, *A Staff Report on National Gas Supply and Demand*, Bureau of National Gas, Washington, D. C, September, 1969.

FEDERAL POWER COMISSION, *Statistics of Interstate Natural Gas Pipeline Companies, 1969*, Federal Power Comission, Washington, D. C., 1969.

▲ **Natural Resources**

FEDERAL POWER COMMISSION STAFF REPORT, *Air Pollution and the Regulated Electric Power and Natural Gas Industries,* Federal Power Commission, Washington, D. C., September, 1968.

FEDERAL POWER COMMISSION, *Depreciation Practices of Natural Gas Companies, 1901,* Federal Power Comission, Washington, D. C, 1961.

FEDERAL POWER COMMISSION, *National Gas Supply and Demands,* Federal Power Commission, Washington D. C, October 1, 1969.

FPC, "Air Pollu In Reg Elec Power & Nat Gas Industries," FPC, Wash D.C., September, 1968.

GIBSON, BLAINE C., "The Real Estate and Development Man for an Oil Company Is Looking for a Service Station Site," *Right of Way,* February, 1954, pp. 1-12.

GREAT BRITAIN MINISTRY OF HOUSING & LOCAL GOVT, "Valuation of Land with Underlying Natural Resources," *The Appraisal Journal,* April, 1935, pp. 236-241.

HARTMAN, J. W., "The Appraisal of Oil Properties for Assessment Purposes," *Bulletin,* National Tax Association, 1929, pp. 18-21.

HENDERSON, JAMES D., "Gasoline," *Real Estate Appraising,* 1931, pp. 311-324.

HURLEY, JAMES J., "Estimates Actual Depreciation of Underground Mains," *Appraisal and Valuation Manual,* ASA, 1958, pp. 301-310.

JENSEN, JAMES E., "The Continental Shelf - a Petroleum Frontier," *The Appraisal Journal,* October, 1958, pp. 589-596.

JOHNSON, LOWELL C., "Valuation of Petroleum Mineral Rights for Ad Valorem Taxation," *The Appraisal Journal,* October, 1953, pp. 497-510.

JOHNSON, ROBERT T., "An Alternative Approach to Price Determination of Natural Gas," *Dissertation Abstracts International-A, the Humanities and Social Sciences,* April, 1971.

KANSAS LEGISLATIVE COUNCIL, *Ad Valorem Taxation of Oil and Gas Property, 78 Kansas Counties 1958,* Kansas Legislative Council Research Department, Topeka, Kansas, 1959.

KASSAK, PETER J., "Gas—Total Energy System In Building Operations," *The Appraisal Journal,* October, 1966, pp. 562-573.

LAND, YATES A., "Property Damages Incident to Oil and Gas Field Operations," *Right of Way,* June, 1958, pp. 27-29.

LUNSFORD, C. R., "Valuing a Petroleum Refinery for Ad Valorem Tax Purposes," *Assessment Administration,* I. A. A. O, Chicago, 1965, pp. 112-118.

MCDANIEL, G. A., "How to Quickly Evaluate Exploration Projects," *World Oil,* July, 1970, pp. 131.

MCDONALD, J., "Oil & the Environment, the View from Maine," *Fortune,*

MILLER, ALTEN S., *Valuation of Gas Properties for Rate-Making,* 1917.

MILLER, REX K., "Oil Pipeline Right of Way, Total Compensation and Easement for Sterling Farm," *Journal of the American Society of Farm Managers Andrural Appraisers,* October, 1961, pp. 22-28.

MISFELDT, DOUGLAS E., "Appraisal of a Natural Gas Transmission Pipeline," *Assessment Administration,* 1963, pp. 223-225.

MISFELDT, DOUGLAS E., "Natural Gas Pipe Line," *Assessment Administration,* 1962, pp. 123-127.

NATIONAL REAL ESTATE JOURNAL, "Actual Appraisal Reports - Valuation for Standard Oil Co Of New York," *National Real Estate Journal,* August 3, 1931, pp. 24-27.

PAINE, PAUL, *Oil Property Valuation,* Wiley, New York, 1942.

PESCHEL, J. L., "Oil and Gas Tax Planning Post-Reform Act Impact of CA-5s," *Journal of Taxation,* January, 1971, pp. 54-56.

QUINLAN, H. F., "Inspection and Valuation of Oil Rigs," *American Society of Appraisers Valuation Manual,*

REYES, N. C., *Financial and Operating Ratios of the Gas Industry,* New York, 1927.

RODRIGUEZ, LOUIS J., "Louisiana's Natural Resources How Strong an Economic Development Asset," *Louisiana Business Review,* Louisiana State University, Baton Rouge, 1971, pp. 6.

ROSAN, R. A., "Some Do & Some Don't Take Accelerated Depreciation In American Gas Association Proceedings," *Appraisal and Valuation Manual,* 1955.

SMITH, ARTHUR A., "Changes Proposed In Oil and Gas Depletion Allowance," *Public Affairs Comment,* May, 1963.

SOUTH DAKOTA LEGISLATIVE RESEARCH COUNCIL, *Oil and Gas Taxation Practices In Selected States,* South Dakota Legislative Research Council, Ltd., Pierre, S. D., 1960.

SPINDLE, JAMES A., "Underground Storage of Gas," *Right of Way,* February, 1956, pp. 7-11.

STARRETT, PAUL, "Demonstration Appraisal: Oil Company Bulk Plant, on Leased Ground," *Society of Industrial Realtors,* Evaluating Industrial Real Estate, 1953, pp. 29-56.

THORNTON, WILLIAM W., *Law of Oil and Gas,* Anderson, Fifth Edition, Cincinnati, Ohio, 1932.

VAN FLEET, J. B., "The Taxation and Valuation of Oil and Gas Resources," *Assessment Administration,* IAAO, Chicago, 1963, pp. 125-131.

WANENMACHER, J. M., "Oil and Gas Appraisals," *The Appraisal Journal,* July, 1946, pp. 264-275.

WARD, STANLEY, "Some Comments on the Valuation of a Federally Regulated Natural Gas Pipeline," *Conference Proceedings,* National Tax Association, Columbus, 1961, pp. 86.

WELCH, RONALD B., "Ad Valorem Taxation of Petroleum Producing Properties," *Assessors News Letter,* February, 1964, pp. 15-17.

"Fuel Stocks Shrink to the Danger Point," *Business Week,* August 29, 1970, pp. 20.

"Industry Acts to Curb Oil Spills," *Industry Week,* May 11, 1970, pp. 19.

"New Undersea Oil-Storge Method to Get Test," *Oil and Gas Journal,* May 10, 1971, pp. 42.

"Offshore Oil Leases Add Fuel to Energy Vs. Environment Clash," *Industry Week,* May 10, 1971, pp. 24-25.

"Oil Spills Who Pays," *Chemical Week,* March 3, 1971, pp. 20.

"Pollution Heating the Oil," *The Economist,* July 25, 1970, pp. 70.

"San Jose Oils Rich But Risky Boomtown," *National Petroleum News,* January, 1971, pp. 52-54.

"Sinking Platform Links Undersea Oil Storage Tank with Surface," *Engineering News-Record,* May 21, 1970, pp. 46.

"War on Pollution," *Oil and Gas Journal,* June 1, 1970, pp. 91-113.

## 17-16   Water and Reservoirs

ASH, FRED C., "Value As a Potential Power Site," *The Appraisal Journal*, April, 1955, pp. 278-279.

CARHART, ARTHUR H., *Water--Or Your Life*, Lippincott, Philadelphia, 1959.

CLYDE, GEORGE D., "Water Resources, Their Development and Utilization from a National Point of View," *Journal of the American Society of Farm Managers and Rural Appraisers*,

CREEDY, JOHN A., "Navigation, Water Resources, and Patterns of Economic Growth," *How Transportation Affects Real Estate Values*, A. I. R. E. A., Chicago, March 7, 1969, pp. 37-40.

DEWEY, JOHN M., "The Missouri River Basin Development Program," *Right of Way*, October, 1954, pp. 7-9.

EDMAN, J. J., "Compensation In Taking Dams. Appraisal Docket," *The Appraisal Journal*, October, 1960, pp. 546-548.

ENGINEERING NEWS-RECORD, "Atkinson Group Bids Low on Lower Granite Dam," *Engineering News-Record*, May 7, 1970, pp. 20.

ENGINEERING NEWS-RECORD, "Atkinson Scores In Solo Bid on Cochiti Dam," *Engineering News-Record*, May 21, 1970, pp. 40.

ENGINEERING NEWS-RECORD, "Sewerage and Dam Construction Costs Jump 9 to 10%," *Engineering News-Record*, March 18, 1971, pp. 106-108.

FEDERAL POWER COMMISSION, *Bear River Basin Report-Staff Evaluation of Water Resources Appraisal for Hydroelectric Licensing*, Oneida and Logan Development, January 2, 1969.

FEDERAL POWER COMMISSION, *Evaluation Report, Mystic Lake Development*, Federal Power Commission, Washington D. C, 1968.

FEDERAL POWER COMMISSION, *Evaluation Report, Swan Falls Development*, Federal Power Commission, Washington D. C, 1968.

FEDERAL POWER COMMISSION, "Feather River Basin Water Appraisal Report," Federal Power Commission, Washington, D. C., October, 1967.

FLETCHER, ROBERT RAY PH. D., *The Impact of Economic Development on Water Resource Use*, Oklahoma State University, 1971.

FPC, "Evaluation Report, Lower Tule Development," Power Staff Report, FPC, Washington D.C., 1968.

GILLETTE, H P, "Valuation of Water Power Rights," *Engineering and Contracting Magazine*, January 1, 1912, pp. Vol. 38.

GOOD, H. A., A. R. PURCHASE, C. E. JOSLYN, "Acquisition of Property for the Red River Floodway In Manitoba," *The Appraisal Institute Magazine*, December, 1963, pp. 24-28.

HAVEMAN, ROBERT H., "An Expost Eval of Water Rescs Investmts," Baltimore and London.

KNETSCH, JACK L., C.' JENNINGS PARROTT, "Estimating the Influence of Large Reservoirs on Land Values," *The Appraisal Journal*, October, 1964, pp. 537-546.

MANN, W. PERLE, MANN, JACK K, "Analysis of the Influence of the Pearl River Reservoir on Land Prices In the Area," *The Appraisal Journal*, January, 1968, pp. 42-45.

MELLOR, PHILLIP, "Selected Problems of Procedure and Compensation Encountered In Federal Reservoir Condemnation," *Proceedings of the Fourth Institute on Eminent Domain*, 1962, pp. 49-66.

MORSEY, NASHAAT, "The Long-Term Storage Policy of Nile Water In Egypt," *Technical Valuation*, November, 1955, pp. 31.

POTTER, W. E., "The Missouri Basin Plan In Operation," *The Appraisal Journal*, October, 1955, pp. 547-559.

RODRIGUEZ, LOUIS J., "Louisiana's Natural Resources How Strong an Economic Development Asset," *Louisiana Business Review*, Louisiana State University, Baton Rouge, 1971, pp. 6.

WAELTI, J. J., "The Regional Impact of Public Water Storage Through Recreational Development, a Case Study," *Dissertation Abstracts*, Ann Arbor, July, 1968, pp. 30-A.

WIEBE, JACOB EDWIN PHD, "Effects of Investments In Water Resources on Regional Income and Employment," The University of Tennessee, 1970.

YANUS, MUHAMMAD, PH. D., *Optimal Allocation of Multipurpose Reservoir Water A Dynamic Programing Model*, Vanderbilt University, 1971.

"Corps to Construct Dam In Existing Reservoir," *Engineering News Record*, September 24, 1970, pp. 12.

"Largest Underground Reservoir to Hold 100 Million Gallons of Water," *Engineering News-Record*, December 3, 1970, pp. 20-21.

*Water Resources Appraisal for Hydroelec Licensing Merrimack R. Basin N. H.-Mass. Bureau of Power*, Federal Power Commission, Washington, D.C., August, 1968.

"Study of Timing of Construction of Impounding Dam to Augment Raw Water Supply of Water Supply Firms," *A Study of the Timing of Construction of an Impounding Dam to Augment the Raw Water Supply of Water S*, L. Lehigh University.

## 17-17 Fisheries, Marine Deposits

BREWER, T., "Earth Resources," *Datamation*, August 15, 1970, pp. 25-28.

CARLSON, ERNEST WILLIAM PH. D., *Theoretical and Empirical Explorations In the Economics of Marine Resources*, Boston College, 1972.

CHAPMAN, W. M., "Aquabusiness the Harvest from the Sea," *Journal of World Business*,

CRUTCHFIELD, JAMES A., "Valuation of Fishery Resources," *Land Economics*, May, 1962, pp. 145-154.

"Metals from the Sea," *Chemical Week*, May 12, 1971, pp. 37.

"Offshore Oil Leases Add Fuel to Energy Vs. Environment Clash," *Industry Week*, May 10, 1971, pp. 24-25.

"Pumping Money Out of the Sea," *Business Week*, July 11, 1970, pp. 54-55.

## CHAPTER EIGHT

# Fine Arts, Objects of Value, Collectors Items

by Henry K. Cordier, ASA

Mr. Henry Cordier, a Senior Member of the American Society of Appraisers, is an art appraiser and consultant, art broker, and owner of a West Coast art restoration facility. He is a Founding Member of the Valuers' Consortium, an Appraisal Resources Panel Member of the American Arbitration Association, and a State Licensed independent insurance adjustor.

In addition to membership on the ASA International Publications Committee, Mr. Cordier is a member of the Society's International Board of Examiners, and the ASA Educational Foundation; he is also Chairman of the Special Publications Awards Committee.

▲ Fine Arts

ONE DAY in the recent past, I was ushered into the office of a well known corporation attorney. As I approached his massive desk, he rose, looked me over carefully, and as we were shaking hands, he said: "You know, you are the first art appraiser I have ever met face to face. Where do you fellows keep yourselves? What do you do for a living?"

I could have told him that he would have seen more art appraisers if he would specialize in insurance or divorce matters, but instead, I told him that he should not be too concerned because the judge in the case probably would harbor the same questions. My task was to provide him with the foundation for the value in his case, and one which would stand up under cross-examination.

This attorney does not stand alone in his quizzical attitude. The history of professional appraising in the United States is rather short. The original appraisers were "technical appraisers", introducing professionally the valuations of Real Estate and Business Enterprises. The Machinery and Equipment Appraisers were considered to be in the minor league, the Art Appraisers as somewhat nebulous strangers who appeared to speak a different language, and the appraisers of Intangibles were considered to be a mixture of Professor Einstein and the Wall Street Journal. Not only did some of the "Old Guard" discourage an active membership drive for the Fine Arts field, but some established art appraisers, always anxious to be lone wolves, did the same.

Today, this situation has changed. All ASA Members, regardless of their specialty, have noticed that the multi-disciplinary approach of the Society is not only a drawing card, adding prestige, but that all tentacles of the appraisal field have the same direction and purpose, namely: the establishment of value, according to the needs of an assignment. In fact, the Society is the only nationwide testing-certifying organization for ALL classifications of the total appraisal field, including art appraisal. I attribute this to the recognition that all appraisal skills should be gathered under one banner, just as there are surgeons, internists, psychiatrists, etc., in the field of medicine, or trial attorneys, government lawyers, judges, and many other sub-categories in the field of law. The recognition is firm and sincere. After two successful national art seminars in the past, I was asked to organize a Fine Arts Appraisal Seminar in Los Angeles. When I suggested that such a Seminar should be oriented to the art-interested public, there was enthusiastic support at all levels of the Society and, with the active support and cooperation of the University of California Extension, Arts and Humanities Division, an elegant seminar at the Beverly Hilton Hotel in Beverly Hills was presented in February, 1974. Non-art oriented appraisers purchased the first tickets. The respect and understanding of both the Society and their individual members is most gratifying.

Let us go back now to the attorney of whom I spoke in the beginning of this introduction. After concluding our talk, he was anxious to know more about my work, and again wondered in general about the need for art appraisers. My answer to him, in capsule form, would read like this:

*"Your bank is advising you monthly of the exact state of your bank account, and you can find the values of your stock or bond investments in your newspaper daily. But do you know the value of your art objects or collectibles? Some of these may have been inherited, others purchased many years ago. What if you lose them by accident, fire or theft? What if you donate them? What if you sell them, or use them as security? Think of the limited edition crystal plate which you bought in 1965 for $35.00 and which may sell for forty times this today. Or the Picasso drawing which you picked up in Paris in 1950. Or the Louis XV gilt chair which belonged to your grandparents. The early silver dollar which you found when their home was razed for a new freeway . . . or of the old family Bible or the flintlock gun which Grandpa would not part with. Do you know whether the Moreland painting in your possession is authentic? And do you realize the importance of having solid identification and reliable proof? I do not have to stress the importance of these questions – this is evident. Art objects and collectibles should be watched, depending on their nature and importance. Fashion categories, such as modern abstracts or art nouveau, should be checked as often as strong market conditions indicate, upward or downward. It is always up to the owner to be aware of reasons for urgency, and he should demand experience, responsibility and professionalism from the person or firm to which he turns for advice. In his turn, the art valuer should strive for excellence, and be more than a mere giver of figures. He should advise, recommend, question, think, and be sincere and loyal in his dealings with his principal. He should consider vital facts, such as the history of the article, condition, the wishes and sometimes the special needs of the owner.*

*In short, in a civilized society, with a goodly percentage of the population having a valid stake in the huge field and variety of art objects and collectibles, the importance of maintaining up-to-date valuations contributes to the assessment of the wealth of a nation."*

The next question of my attorney friend was: "How do you become an art appraiser?" My answer, again in capsule form, was: "You must have a basic knowledge of the field of art, of general pricing, of retail sales, auction receipts, the art world, of insurance, a smattering of law, or anything else which your assignment demands. The most basic background is the trade in art or collector's items, but you might also have been a collector or purchaser, or a professor or teacher of art. You must read text books, magazines, auction news, the art gossip papers, and last but not least, the magazine advertisements which give you a good clue as to what is most in demand. You learn as you practice, and even Bernard Berenson, the original famous arbiter of the art field, was still studying and learning in his early nineties."

Next question: "Why don't the owners of art get this information from museums?" Answer: "Many of the hundreds of museums in this country have excellent experts in the respective fields, but they are interested in other things than value and are operating on a non-profit basis. This means that their interest centers upon the acquisition of works of art per se (normally not for value's sake) and in the proper administration, conservation and publicity of their institutions. In fact, they come to appraisers when they receive donations for which they need a neutral valuation, normally paid for by the donor. I enjoy these assignments because of the sometimes rare and unusual articles donated and the valuation problems connected with these."

Next question by my host: "What valuation problems could you have - don't they always want fair market value?" My response: "First of all, we are subject to different valuation requirements as the case may demand. Most of the time, our clients need fair market valuation, which generally is the highest price, in terms of money, which would be achieved between knowledgeable buyers and sellers, neither under pressure to buy or sell, with a reasonable exposure to the market and to time, under due consideration of the status and location of the seller and the anticipated nature of the buyer. While this concept generally coincides with principal court decisions, I am hedging a bit already because who in the world ever gets the highest price in terms of money when he wants to sell something? Even the choicest piece of real estate, of art, of literary property, etc., probably will actually sell for less than the highest proven figure. Anyway, fair market value is only one valuation pillar which we may have to establish." (Other value questions will be discussed later in this introduction).

In discussing art appraisal, it should be understood that it represents a sub-classification of the Personal Property discipline which is not discussed separately in this Bibliography. Although I do not believe that there will ever be a perfect list of categories, I would suggest that Personal Property appraisers classify themselves as follows:

**a. Personal Property, General.** These are appraisers who are willing and able to undertake the appraisal of all general property which may or may not include individual sub-categories, or for which no specialty appraiser can be located. Example: While there are a number of craftsmen engaged in the manufacture or sale of Spanish Style Silver Saddles, none were willing or able (in a recent instance which confronted me) to supply a desired appraisal for Estate or Insurance purposes. After a thorough indoctrination to the peculiarities of this rather limited field, I supplied appraisals to the satisfaction of the Trustee and the Insurance Underwriter.

**b. Personal Property, Special.** These appraisers, mostly by their own volition and training, purposely limit themselves to such fields as: Gems and Jewelry, Stamps, Musical Instruments, all types of other collector's items, General Residential Contents, Furs and Fur Garments, Chattels, etc.

**c. Fine Arts, General.** The writer will regularly undertake the appraisal of Fine Arts articles, including General Residential or Institutional Contents. Such appraisal will often include valuable sterling silver flatware, chinaware, pianos and other articles only remotely connected with the Fine Arts field. Since too many varieties of art works or collector's items exist, often within the same assignment, it would be impractical to engage several specialty appraisers for the same assignment.

**d. Fine Arts, Special.** These appraisers are normally experts in a special field, such as Paintings and Sculpture (sometimes for only one type, artist or school), Graphics, Oriental Art, Modern Art, etc. Many of these persons are actively engaged in their respective occupation (Dealers, Researchers, Museum or College representatives), and therefore, render invaluable services both in the establishment of an appraisal and serving as expert witnesses. Their specialized knowledge gives them decisive influence in the outcome of claims or litigation.

When leafing the pages of this Bibliography, the immense width and scope of the Fine Arts and other Personal Property field becomes very evident. As varied as the subjects enumerated and the type and personalities of the appraisers themselves, are the demands which are directed at them. Strangely enough, in spite of the importance and impact of the appraisers work, his services are not as yet demanded to the extent of other professions, e.g., Accounting, which also involves itself primarily with dollar figures. While every businessman or business organization takes the need for the accountant for granted, both for statistics and for consultations, the appraisal profession, only about fifty years old as an organized system, is only lately gaining the acceptance it deserves.

Who then will call on Personal Property appraisers and for what reasons? I am always amazed at the diversity of assignments. It may be an appraisal for insurance purposes (the most common demand), for the valuation or dissolution of estate contents, for sale or disposal, for arbitration, for donation or divorce purposes, for the settlement or investigation of an insurance claim, for the questions of gain or loss of value, for the owner's personal edification as to what he owns, what he may leave to children or in what ratio to distribute it. Quite frequently, the appraiser also acts as a consultant, much more so in the Fine Arts field than in others where the general facts or identity of the appraised articles are basically well known. While every owner of Real Estate or Machinery normally knows what he owns, the owner of Fine Art articles frequently does not, especially when an article was received as a gift or inheritance. The Fine Arts appraiser will identify, research, coordinate, advise. Quite often, the value is of secondary importance and the stress lies in identification, authentication, purchase or sale arrangements, insurance recommendations (such as the differentiations between residential furnishings, Fine Arts articles, Fine Arts breakable articles in the same appraisal), maintenance and preservation questions, storage advice, etc.

It, therefore, becomes evident that many Fine Arts appraisers are specialists in their respective fields. Most of them will be available for such general work as the establishment of an insurance schedule, but when an attorney needs appraisal assistance in a litigation matter, he often will put the emphasis on the appraiser's specialized knowledge and appraisal expertise.

# Fine Arts, Objects of Value, Collector's Items

18-11　Paintings
18-12　Graphic Art
18-13　Sculpture
18-14　Crafts
18-15　Collector's Items
18-16　Antiques
18-17　Gems and Jewelry
18-18　Furniture
18-19　Furs and Fur Garments

# 18-11  Painting

ALPATOV, M. W., *Art Treasures of Russia*, Thames and Hudson, 1968.

ANDRADE, J. M. PITA, *Treasures of Spain from Altamira to the Catholickings*, Skira, 1967.

ARCHER, W. G., *Paintings of the Sikhs*, Her Majesty's Stationery Office for Vic & Al Mus., London.

ART DIGEST, "Prices on the European Art Mart," *Art Digest*, May 15, 1944.

AUBOYER, JANINE, *The Art of Afghanistan*, Hamlyn, London.

AVERMAETE, ROGER, *Rubens and His Times*, George Allen and Unain, 1968.

BALLO, GUIDO, R. H. BOOTHROYD, *The Critical Eye a New Approach to Art Appreciation*, Hacker Art Books Incorporated, London, 1966.

BARNETT, DOUGLAS, BASIT GRAY, "Painting of India," Skira Inc., pp. 214.

BASKETT, JOHN, *Constable Oil Sketches*, Barrie and Rockliff.

BATAILLE, GEORGES, *Manet*, Skira.

BATLIN, MARTIN, *Watercolours from the Turner Bequest 1819 1845*, Tate Gallery.

BATSFORD, B. T., *Water-Colour Painting In Britain*, Jonathan Mayne and Basil Taylor.

BAYOR, HERBERT, *Painter Designer Architect*, Hacker Art Books Incorporated, New York.

BAZIN, GERMAIN, *The Baroque: Principles, Styles, Modes & Themes*, Thames & Hudson.

BEASLEY, J. D., B. ASHMORE, *Greek Sculpture and Paintings*, Cambridge University Press, London.

BEAZLEY, J. D., BERNARD ASHMOLE, *Greek Sculpture and Painting*, Cambridge University Press, 1966.

BELBUI, GIAM GUIDO, *Iranian Art*, Pall Mall Press, London.

BELLONI, GIAN GUIDO AND LILIANE FEDI DALL-ASEN, *Iranian Art*, Pall Mall Press.

BENESCH, OTTO, *German Painting from Durer to Holbein*, Skira Art Books Incorporated, 1966.

BENTLEY, NICHOLAS, *The Victorian Scene*, Weidenfeld and Nicholson, London.

BERENSON, BERNARD, *Homeless Paintings of the Renaissance*, Thames and Hudson, London.

BERENSON, BERNARD, *Italian Pictures of the Renaissance*,

BERENSON, BERNARD, *Suing and Knowing*, Evelyn Adams and Mackay, London.

BERRY-HILL HENRY AND SIDNEY, *Ernest Lawson, American Impressionist*, F. Lewis Publishers Lt. ., London.

BLAGBROUGH, ELIZABETH M, "The Appraising of American Paintings," *Valutapes Audio-Library Series*, American Society of Appraisers, Washington D.C., January 1, 1973.

BLUNT, ANTHONY, PHOEBE POAL, *Picasso the Formative Years*, Hacker Artbooks Incorporated, Greenwich, 1962.

BOGER, LOUISE ADE, BOGER, H. BATTERSON, *Decorative Arts*, Scribners Publishers.

BOINNE, ALBERT, *The Academy and French Paintings In the 19th Century*, Phaidon Press, 1971.

# BIBLIOGRAPHY OF APPRAISAL LITERATURE

BOLOGNA, FERDINANDO, *Early Italian Painting Romanesque and Early Medieval Art*, London.

BOSKOVITS, MIKLOS, *Tuscan Paintings of the Early Renaissance*, Corvina Press, N. P.

BOSWELL, PEYTON, JR., *Modern American Paintings*, Dodd-Mead and Co.

BOTARI, STEFANO, *Antonello Da Messina*, Hacker Art Books Incorporated, Greenwich, 1955.

BOUDAILLE, GEORGES, *Courbet*, Hacker Art Books Incorporated, Greenwich, 1969.

BREDIUS, ABRAHAM, *The Paintings of Rembrant*, Phaidon.

BRON, EDITH DE, *The Price of Three Cezannes*, Chapman and Hall Ltd, London.

BROPHY, JOHN, *The Face In Western Art*, Hacker Art Books Inc., London, 1963.

BROWNESS, ALAN, *Recent British Paintings*, Lund Humphrives.

BUSSAGLI, MARIO, *Painting of Central Asia*, Skira.

BUSSAGLI, MARIO, CALEMBUS SIVARAMAMURTI, *5000 Years of the Art of India*, Hacker Art Books Incorporated, New York, 1971.

CABANNE, PIERRE, *Picasso*, George G. Harrap, London.

CABANNE, PIERRE, *Rubens*, Thames and Hudson.

CAIX, PIERRE, GEORGES BOUDAILLE, "Picasso: the Blue and Rose Periods," *Picasso the Blue and Rose Periods*, Hacker Art Books Incorporated, Breenwich, 1966.

CAKE, VAN DEREN, *The Painter and the Photograph from Delacroix to Warhol*, University of New Mexico, Albuquerque.

CHAMOUX, FRANCOIS, *Greek Art*, Barrie and Rockliff, 1966.

CHIARELLI, RENZO, *European Painting In the Fifteenth Century*, Viking Press, New York, 1961.

CLARK, KENNETH, *The Drawings of Leonardo Da Vinci In the Royal Collection*,

CLARK, SIR KENNETH, *Rembrandt and the Italian Renaissance*, Hacker Art Books Incorporated, London, 1966.

CLAVEL, BERNARD, *Leonard De Vinci*, George G. Harrap, London.

CLEMENS, ROBERT J., *Michelangelos Theory of Art*, Hacker Art Books Incorporated, New York, 1961.

CLEMENTS, ROBERT J., *Michelangelo a Self Portrait*, University of London, London.

CLIFFORD, DEREK, *Art and Understanding*, Hugh Evelyn, London.

CLIFFORD, DEREK, *The Paintings of P. A. De Laszlo*, Literary Services and Production, 1969.

CLIFFORD, DEREK, *Watercolours of the Norwich School*, Cory, Adams and Mackay.

COCKE, RICHARD, *Pier Francesco Mola*, Clarendon Press-Oxford University Press, London.

COCKE, RICHARD, *The Complete Paintings of Raphael*, Weidenfeld and Nicolson, London.

COOMBS, DAVID, *Churchill His Paintings*, Hamish Hamilton.

COOPER, DAVID, *Picasso Theatre*, Hacker Art Books Incorporated, New York, 1968.

COOPER, DOUGLAS, *Picasso Theatre*, Herbert Jenkins, London.

COTTE, SABINE, *Claude Lorrain*, Hacker Art Books Incorporated, New York, 1970.

COURTHION, PIERRE, *Romanticism*, Skira.

COX, WARREN E., "The Intrinsic Value of Art," *The A. S. A. Valuation Manual*, American Society of Appraisers, 1956, pp. 179.

▲ Fine Arts

CRIVELLATO, VALENTINE, "Tiepolo," Hacker Art Books Inc., London, 1963, pp. 98.

CROUEN, THOMAS, *A Treasury of Art Masterpieces*, Simon and Schuster.

CZOBOR, AGNES, *Rembrandt and His Circle*, Clematis Press, Ltd., London.

DAULTE, FRANCOIS, *French Watercolors of the Nineteenth Century*,

DAVIES, MARTIN, *The National Gallery, London, Volume III*, Brussels, 1970.

DAWNES, KERRY, *Hawksmoor*, Thames and Hudson.

DAWSONS OF PALL MALL, *Art Prices Current*, Wm. Dawson and Sons Ltd, Cannon Hse Kent, Eng.

DEMUS, OTTO, *Romanesque Mural Painting*, Hacker Art Books Incorporated, New York, 1971.

DESCHARNES, ROBERT, *The World of Salvador Dali*, Macmillan, London.

DIAMOND, MAURICE, *Indian Miniature Paintings*, The Uffici Series.

DOBIE, J. FRANK, TOM LEA, *A Portfolio of Six Paintings*, University of Texas Press, 1968.

DONOVAN, J., "Bleak Picture The Art Market Is Feeling the Financial Pinch, Too," *Barrons*, July 6, 1970, pp. 11.

DUBY, GEORGES, *The Europe of the Cathedral 1140-1280*, Skira Art Books Incorporated, 1966.

DUBY, GEORGES, *The Making of the Christian West*, Skira Art Books Incorporated, 1967.

DUPIN, JACQUES, *Miro*, Hacker Art Books Incorporated, New York, 1962.

DUSSLER, LUITPOLD, *Raphel: a Critical Catalogue of His Pictures, Wall-Paintings and Tapestries*, Phaidon.

ELIOT, ALXANDER, *Three-Hundred Years of American Painting*, Hackerart Books Incorporated, New York, 1957.

ENGGASS, ROBERT, *The Painting of Baciccio*, Pennsylvania State University Press.

EPPINK, NORMAN, *The History and Techniques of Printmaking*, University of Oklahoma Press.

ERNANDEZ, JUSTINO, *Guide to Mexican Art*, The University of Chicago Press, Chicago, 1968.

ETTLINGER, L. D., *The Complete Paintings of Leonardo*, Weidenfeld & Nicolson, London.

FANIEL, STEPHONE, FRANCAIS-HACHETTE, *Collection Connaissance Des Arts*, Le Dix-Huitieme Siecle, Le Dix-Huitteme Siec.

FELD, CHARLES, *Picasso His Recent Drawings 1966-1968*, Hacker Art Books Incorporated, New York, 1970.

FLETCHER, JENNIFER, *Rubens*, Phaidon Press, London, October, 1968.

FLEXNER, JAMES THOMAS, *Nineteenth Century American Painting*, Hacker Art Books Incorporated, New York, 1970.

FLIETZE, HANS, *Treasures of the Great National Galleries*, Garden City Books, 1900.

FRANZERO, CARLO MARIA, *Leonardo*, W. H. Allen.

FRASNAY, ANIEL, *The Artists World*, J. M. Dent, London.

FRIEDLAINDER, WALTER, *Mannerism and Anti Mannerism In Italian Painting*, Columbia University Press, New York.

FRIEDLANDER, MAX J., *From Van Eych to Bruegel*, Phaidon Press, London.

FURST, H., "Christies Since 1942 a Discourse on Values," *Apollo*, February, 1945, pp. 35.

# BIBLIOGRAPHY OF APPRAISAL LITERATURE

GARAS, KLARA, "Eighteenth Century Venetian Paintings," *Eighteenth Century Venetian Paintings*, Corvina Press, 1968.

GASSIER, PIERRE, *Goya*, Skira.

GELDZAHLER, HENRY, *New York & Sculpture 1940-1970*, Pall Mall Press, London.

GERMAIN, EDGAR H., *Degas*, Abram, 1900.

GERSON, DR. H., *The Paintings of Rembrandt*, The Phaidon Press, London.

GOLDING, JOHN, *Cubism A History and an Analysis 1907-1914*, Faber and Faber, 1969.

GOLDSCHEIDER, LUDWIG, *Michelangelo Drawings*, Phaidon Press, London.

GOLDSCHEIDER, LUDWIG, *Vermeer Paintings*, Phaidon Press, London.

GOULD, CECIL, PIETRO ZAMPETTI, *The Complete Paintings of Giorgione*, Weidenfeld and Nicolson.

GRAY, BASIL, *Persian Painting*, Skira, 1961.

GUTFELD, LUDWIG, *Jewish Art from the Bible to Chagall*, W. H. Allen, London.

HACK, B., *Rembrandt - His Life Work and Times*, Thames and Hudson, London.

HACKER ART BOOKS, "Masterpcs of Asian Art In Amer Colls II," Hacker Art Books, New York, 1970, pp. 150.

HACKER ART BOOKS INC., **Mantle Fielding's Dictionary of Amer Painters, Sculptors & Engravers**," Hacker Art Books Inc., New York, 1965, pp. 592.

HAGES, COLIN, *Renoir*, The Colour Library of Art, 1969.

HAIDIE, MARTIN, *Water Colour Painting In Britain*,

HALLADE, MADELEIN, *The Gandhara Style*, Thames and Hudson, London.

HALLADE, MADELEINE, *Gandharan Art of North India*, Hacker Art Books Incorporated, New York, 1968.

HAMMACHER, A. M., *Genius and Disaster the Ten Creative Years of Vincent Van Gogh*, Hacker Art Books Incorporated, New York, 1969.

HAMPTON, CHRISTOPHER, *The Etruscans and the Survival of Etruria*.

HARDIE, MARTIN, *Water Colour Painting In Britain*,

HARDIE, MARTIN, *Water-Colour Painting In Britain II, the Romantic Period*, Batsford.

HARRIS, ENRIQUETA, *Goya*, Phaidon Press Ltd., London.

HARRIS, J. R., *Egyptian Art*, Spring Books, London.

HARTT, FREDERICK, *The Drawings of Michelangelo*, Thames and Huds On, London.

HAYNES, DENYS, *Fifty Masterpieces of Classical Art In the British Museum*, British Museum, 1970.

HELD, JULIUS S., *Rembrandts Aristotle and Other Rembrandt Studies*, Oxford University Press, London.

HENDY, PHILLIP, *Piero Della Francesca and the Early Renaissance*, Weidenfeld and Nicolson, London.

HENRY FRANCHOISE, *Irish Art In the Romanesque Period 1020 1170 A. D*, Methuen and Company, London.

HERBERT, ROBERT L., *Neo Impressionism*, *Guggenheim Museum*, New York, 1968.

HERTLEIN, G. C., "Artist Views Discovery Through Computerized Graphics," *Computers and Automation*, August, 1970, pp. 25-26.

HIDESLEY, C. HUGH, "The Appraisal of Fine Arts," *Valuation*, American Society of Appraisers, September, 1972, pp. 12.

HILLIER, BEVIS, *Art Deco,* Studio Vista, London.

HILTON, TIMOTHY, *The Pre-Raphaelites,* Thames and Hudson.

HINE, ROBERT V., "Bartlett's West: Drawing the Mexican Border," *Bartlett's West: Drawing the Mexican Border,* Yale University, Fort Worth, 1968.

HISLOP, RICHARD, "The Annual Art Sales Index," Art Sales Ltd, Weybridge England, January 1, 1973, pp. 934.

HODIN, J. P., *Ruszbowshi, Life and Work,* Cory, Adams and Machay, 1966.

HOFMANN, WERNER, *Expressionist Watercolors,* Hacker Art Brooks Incorporated, New York, 1967.

HOLME, BRYON, *Masterpieces In Color,* New York.

HUGHES, ROBERT, *Heaven or Hell In Western Art,* Weidenfeld and Nicolson, London.

HURWITT, S., "Sputter-Etching A Dual Purpose Tool," *Industrial Research,* September, 1970, pp. 60-62.

HUYGHE, RENE, *Watteau,* Hacker Art Books Incorporated, New York, 1970.

HYAM, LESLIE A., "Appraisal of Fine Arts," *Technical Valuation,* ASA, Washington, October, 1953, pp. 11.

HYAM, LESLIE A., "Fine Arts - Liquidations," *Technical Valuation,* ASA, October, 1953, pp. 11.

INTERART PUBLISHERS INC., *International Art Market,* New York, March, 1961.

IRWIN, DAVID, *Neo-Classical Art,* Faver and Faber, London.

JACKSON, RILLA EVELYN, *American Arts,* Rand-Mcnotty and Company, 1927.

JOSEPH, MICHAEL, *The Sculpture of David Wynne,* London.

KAGANOVICH, A. L., *The Arts of Russia 17th and 18th Centuries,* The Cresset Press, London.

KELDER, DIANE, *The French Impressionists and Their Century,* Pall Mall Press.

KELLEY, JOHN F., "Fine Arts Appraisals," *Technical Valuation,* June, 1954, pp. 41.

KELP, JOHN P., "Value Trends from Recent Auction Sales of Modern European Paintings," *Appraisal and Valuation Manual,* Corporate Press Incorporated, Washington, D. C, January, 1972, pp. 256.

KENNETH, CLARK, *Rembrandt-And the Italian Renaissance,* John Murray, London.

KENT, FRANK, "Icons of the Community," *Monograph No. Three,* American Society of Appraisers, Washington D.C., January 1, 1970.

KENT, FRANK W., "Introduction to the Sections," *Icons of the Community, Monograph No. 3,* ASA, Washington, D.C., 1970, pp. 7-15.

KENT, FRANK W., "Paintings," *Icons of the Community, Monograph, No. 3,* ASA, Washington, D. C, pp. 21-31.

KITSON, MICHAEL, *The Complete Paintings of Caravaggio,* Weidenfeld and Nicolson, London.

KORNILOVICH, KIRA, *The Arts of Russia from the Origins to the End of the 16th Century,* The Cresset Press, London.

LAMARRE, JOHN H., "Fine Arts Appraisals," *Technical Valuation,* A. S. A., October, 1954, pp. 41.

LAMARRE, JOHN H., "Probable Future of Fine Arts Appraisal," *Technical Valuation,* A. S. A, Washington, November, 1954, pp. 41.

LANDOLT, HANSPETER, *German Painting the Late Middle Ages 1350-1500,* Skira Art Books Incorporated, 1968.

LANDRY, JUDITH, *Miro,* Faber and Faber, London.

# BIBLIOGRAPHY OF APPRAISAL LITERATURE

LANGE, KURT, MAX HIRMER, *Egypt Architecture, Sculpture, Paintings,* 4th Edition, Phaidon, London.

LASSAIGN, JACQUES, *Dufy,* Skira, Switzerland.

LASSAIGNE, JACQUES, *Flemish Painting the Century of Van Eyck,* Skira, 1957.

LASSAIGNE, JACQUES, "Part Four, Expression of Architecture In Space," *History of Modern Painting,* Albert Skira, Geneve, 1950, pp. 149-157.

LAZARE, VICTOR, *Old Russian Murals from the Xi to the Xvi Century,* Phaidon Press, London.

LEACH, BERNARD, *Kenzin and His Tradition,* Faber and Faber, London.

LEIRIES, MICHEL AND JACQUELINE DELANGE, *African Art,* Thames and Hudson, 1968.

LEWIS, JOHN, EDWIN SMITH, *The Graphic Reproduction and Photography Of Works of Arts,* Faber and Faber, London.

LEYMAIRE, J., H. READ, W. S. LIEBERMAN, *Henri Matisse,* University of California Press.

LEYMARIE, JEAN, *Impressionist Drawings,* Skira.

LEYMARIE, JEAN, *Picasso Drawings,* Skira.

LISTER, RAYMOND, *Victorian Narrative Paintings,* Museum Press Ltd, London.

LOVRET, FREDERICK I, "Oil Paintings and Their Worth," *Valuation,* American Society of Appraisers, September, 1972, pp. 70-78.

LUNDY, VICTOR R., "New Developments In Building Material and Design," *The Appraisal Journal,* January, 1958, pp. 27-33.

MALLAR, OLIVER, *Later Georgian Pictures In the Royal Collection,* Phaidon, London.

MAORTGAT, ANTON, *The Art of Ancient Mesopotamia,*

MAIURE, AMEDEO, *Roman Painting,* Skira.

MALRAUX, ANDRE, *Flowering of the Italian Renaissance,* Hacker Art Books Incorporated, New York, 1965.

MANHEIM, FRANK, *A Garland of Weights,* The Bodley Head, London.

MARTINDALE, ANDREW, *The Complete Paintings of Giotto,* Weidenfeld and Nicolson, London.

MARX, CLAUDE ROGER, *Rembrandt,* Hacker Art Books Incorporated, Paris, 1960.

MEER, F. VAN DER, *Early Christian Art,* Faber and Faber, London.

MEISS, MILLARD, *The Great Age of Fresco,* Hacker Art Books Incorporated, New York, 1970.

MICHALOWSKI, KAZIMIERZ, *Art of Ancient Egypt,* Hacker Art Books Incorporated, New York, 1968.

MILLER, D. C., W. S. LIEBERMAN, *The New Japanese Painting and Sculpture,* Doubleday and Co. Inc, 1966.

MILLER, HENRY, ROLAND PENROSE, *Picasso and Company Brassia,* Thames and Hudson.

MIYAGAUA TORAS, *Modern Japanese Painting,* Waid Lock and Company and Kodansha International, 1967.

MOIXER, MIKLOS, *Dutch Painting,* Clematic Press, London.

MONTGOMERY, CHARLES F., *American Furniture: the Federal Period 1788-1825 In the Henry Francis Du Pont Winterthur Museum,* Thames and Hudson, 1967.

MORASSI, ANTONIO, *Titian,* Hacker Art Books Incorporated, Greenwich, 1967.

MULLINS, EDWIN, *Josif Herman, Paintings and Drawings,* Evelyn, Adams and Mackay.

NEATHY, NIGEL, *The Saltram Collection*, National Trust Publication, London.

NEUMANN, JAROMIR, *The Picture Gallery of Prague Castle*, London.

NEW YORK METROPOLITAN MUSEUM OF ART, *Decorative Art from the Samuel H. Kress Collection*, Phaidon Press, London, 1964.

NICOLL, JOHN, *The Pre-Raphaelites*, The Studio Vista.

NIKI, TAMON, *Fifty Painters of Japan*, The Japan Fine Arts Dealers Association, 1966.

OLDEROGGE, DMITRY, *Negro Art*, Institute of Ethnography, Leningerad, 1969.

OMAN, CHARLES, *English Domestic Silver*, Adam, Charles Black, London.

OPPE, A. P., *Raphael*, Elek Books, 1970.

PALLOTTINO, MASSIMO, *Etruscan Painting*, Skira.

PASSEION, ROGER, *French Prints of the Twentieth Century*, Pall Mallpress.

PENROSE, ROLAND, *The Sculpture of Picasso*, The Museum of Modern Art.

PIANKOFF, ALEXANDER, *The Pyramid of Unas*, Oxford University Press, London, 1969.

PICARD, GILBERT, *Roman Painting*, Hacker Art Books Incorporated, 1970.

PICARD, GILBERT, *Roman Paintings*, Elek Books, 1968.

PIGNATTI, TERISIO, *Pietro Longhi*, Phaidon Press Ltd., London.

POPE-HENNESSY, JOHN, *Raphael*, Phaidon, 1970.

PRIEST, ALAN, *Aspects of Chinese Paintings*, Macmillan, New York, 1954.

PRIEST, ALAN, *The Sculpture of Joseph Coletti*, Collier-Macmillan.

RAUSCHENBUSCH, DR. H., *International Directory of Arts*, 1958.

RAWSON, P. S., *The Indian Sword*, The Arms and Armour Series, 1968.

RAYNAL, MAURICE, *History of Modern Painting from Picasso to Surrealism*, Albert Skira, Geneva, Switzerland, 1950.

RAYNAL, MAURICE, *Modern Painting*, Albert Skira, Geneva, 1953.

RAYNAL, MAURICE, "Part One-Sidetracks of Post-Impressionism and Fauvism," *History of Modern Painting*, Albert Skira, Geneva, 1950, pp. 15-38.

RAYNAL, MAURICE, "Part Three After Cubism," *History of Modern Painting*, Albert Skira, Geneva, 1950, pp. 131-144.

RAYNAL, MAURICE, "Part Two-From Visual Forms to Absolute Form-Cubism," *History of Modern Painting*, Albert Skira, Geneva, 1950, pp. 39-66.

RAYNAL, MAURICE, "Part Two: Reactions to Cubism," *History of Modern Painting*, Albert Skira, Geneva, 1950, pp. 69-134.

READE, BRAIN, *Ballet Designs and Illustrations 1581 - 1940*, Her Majesty's Stationery Office, 1967.

REITLINGER, *Edovard Vuilliard 1868-1940*, Review of Market Values, New York.

REITLINGER, *Esteban Murillo 1617-1682*, Review of Market Values, New York.

REITLINGER, *Filippino Lippi 1460-1505*; Review of Market Prices, New York.

REITLINGER, *Flemish Primitives Pre-1540*, Market Price Review,

REITLINGER, *Flemish School 1600-1800*, Review of Market Price.

REITLINGER, *Ford Maddox Brown, 1821-1893*, Review of Market Prices, Holt, Rinehart and Winston, New York, 1961.

## BIBLIOGRAPHY OF APPRAISAL LITERATURE

REITLINGER, *Francesco Francia 1450-1517, Review of Market Prices,* Holt, Rinehart and Winston, New York.

REITLINGER, *Francesco Guardi 1712-1793, Review of Market Prices,* New York.

REITLINGER, *Francis Cotes 1725-1770, a Review of Market Prices.*

REITLINGER, *Francois Boucher, 1704-1770, Review of Market Prices,* Holt, Rinehart and Winston, New York, 1961.

REITLINGER, *Frans Hals 1584-1666, Review of Market Prices,* New York.

REITLINGER, *Frans Van Mieris 1635-1681; Review of Market Prices,* New York.

REITLINGER, *Fred Walker 1840-1875; Review of Market Values,* New York.

REITLINGER, *French Primitives Before 1500; a Review of Market Prices,* New York.

REITLINGER, *Gabriel Metsu 1615-1661, Review of Market Value,* Holt, Rinehart and Winston, New York.

REITLINGER, *George Frederick Watts 1817-1904, Review of Market Values,* New York.

REITLINGER, *George Morland 1763-1804, Review of Market Values,* New York.

REITLINGER, *George Romney 1734-1802, Review of Market Values,* New York.

REITLINGER, *George Stubbs 1724-1806, Review of Market Values,* New York.

REITLINGER, *Georges Braque 1881, Review of Market Prices,* Holt, Rinehart and Winston, New York, 1961.

REITLINGER, *Georges Pierre Seurat 1859-1891, Review of Market Values,* New York.

REITLINGER, *Georges Rouault 1871-1958, Review of Market Values,* New York.

REITLINGER, *Gerard Dow 1613-1675, Review of Market Prices,* New York.

REITLINGER, *Gerard Terborch 1617-1681, Review of Market Values,* New York.

REITLINGER, *German Primitives Before 1530, Review of Market Values,* New York.

REITLINGER, *Giambattista Moroni 1525-1578, Review of Market Values,* New York.

REITLINGER, *Giambattista Tiepolo 1693-1770, Review of Market Values,* New York.

REITLINGER, *Giandomenicho Tiepolo 1727-1804, Review of Market Values,* New York.

REITLINGER, *Giorgione 1477-1510, Review of Market Prices,* Holt, Rinehart and Winston, New York.

REITLINGER, *Goustau Courbett 1819-1877, a Review of Market Prices,* New York.

REITLINGER, *Goya 1746-1828, Review of Market Prices,* New York.

REITLINGER, *Guido Reni 1575-1642; Review of Market Values,* New York.

REITLINGER, *Hans Holbin 1497-1543, Review of Market Prices,* New York.

REITLINGER, *Hans Memling 1430-1494; Review of Market Prices,* New York.

REITLINGER, *Henri Fantin-Latour 1836-1904, Review of Market Prices,* New York.

REITLINGER, *Henri Matisse 1869-1954, Review of Market Prices,* New York.

REITLINGER, *Honore Daumier 1808-1879, Review of Market Prices,* New York.

REITLINGER, *Hubert Robert 1733-1808, Review of Market Values,* New York.

REITLINGER, *Il Parmegianino 1504-1540, Review of Market Values,* New York.

REITLINGER, *Il Tintoretto 1518-1599, Reveiw of Market Values*, New York.

REITLINGER, *Il Veronese 1528-1588, Review of Market Values*, New York.

REITLINGER, *Italian Schools 14th Century Up, Review of Market Prices*, New York.

REITLINGER, *Jacob Van Ruysdael 1628-1682, Review of Market Values*, New York.

REITLINGER, *Jacques Louis David 1748-1825, Review of Market Prices,*

REITLINGER, *James A. McNeil Whistler 1834-1903, a Review of Market Values*, New York.

REITLINGER, *James Tissot 1836-1902, Review of Market Prices*, New York.

REITLINGER, *James Ward 1767-1859, Review of Market Values*, New York.

REITLINGER, *Jan Brueghel 1568-1625, Review of Market Prices*, Holt, Rinehart and Winston, New York, 1961.

REITLINGER, *Jan Josefsz Van Goyen 1596-1675, Review of Market Prices*, New York.

REITLINGER, *Jan Steen 1626-1679, Review of Market Values*, New York.

REITLINGER, *Jan Van Eyck 1385-1441; Review of Market Prices,*

REITLINGER, *Jan Van Huysum 1682-1749, Review of Market Prices*, New York.

REITLINGER, *Jan Vermeer 1632-1675, Review of Market Values*, New York.

REITLINGER, *Jean Baptiste Chardin 1699-1775, Review of Market Prices*, New York.

REITLINGER, *Jean Baptiste Corot 1796-1875, Review of Prices*, New York.

REITLINGER, *Jean Baptiste Greuze 1725-1805, Review of Market Prices*, New York.

REITLINGER, *Jean Baptiste Pater 1696-1736, Review of Market Values*, New York.

REITLINGER, *Jean Bastien Lepage 1849-1885, Review of Market Prices*, New York.

REITLINGER, *Jean Dominique Ingres 1780-1867, Review of Market Prices*, New York.

REITLINGER, *Jean Francois Millet 1814-1875, Review of Market Values*, New York.

REITLINGER, *Jean Honore Fragonard 1732-1806, Review of Market Prices*, Holt, Rinehart and Winston, New York.

REITLINGER, *Jean Louis Gericault 1791-1824, Review of Market Prices*, New York.

REITLINGER, *Jean Marc Nattier 1685-1766, Review of Market Values*, New York.

REITLINGER, *Johann Zoffany 1733-1810, Review of Market Prices*, New York.

REITLINGER, *John Constable 1776-1837, Review of Market Prices,*

REITLINGER, *John Crome 1769-1821, Review of Market Prices,*

REITLINGER, *John Ferneley 1781-1861, Review of Market Price*, New York.

REITLINGER, *John Hoppner 1759-1810, Review of Market Prices*, New York.

REITLINGER, *John Linnell Sr. , 1792-1882, Review of Market Prices*, New York.

REITLINGER, *John Martin 1789-1854, Review of Market Prices*, New York.

REITLINGER, *John Sell Cotman 1782-1842, Review of Market Prices*, New York.

REITLINGER, *John Singer Sargent 1856-1925, Review of Market Values*, New York.

REITLINGER, *Joseph Israels 1824-1911, Review of Market Prices*, New York.

REITLINGER, *Joseph Mallord William Turner 1775-1851, Review of Market Values*, New York.

REITLINGER, *Joshua Reynolds 1723-1792, Review of Market Values*, New York.

## BIBLIOGRAPHY OF APPRAISAL LITERATURE

REITLINGER, *Jules Breton 1827-1906, Review of Market Prices*, Holt, Rinehart and Winston, New York, 1961.

REITLINGER, *Karl Fabritius 1624-1654, Review of Market Prices*, New York.

REITLINGER, *Le Nain Brothers 1568-1677, Review of Market Prices*, New York.

REITLINGER, *Lord Leighton 1830-1896, Review of Market Prices*, New York.

REITLINGER, *Lorenzo Lotto 1480-1556, Review of Market Prices*, New York.

REITLINGER, *Luca Signorelli 1441-1523, Review of Market Values*, New York.

REITLINGER, *Luca Signorelli 1441-1523, Review of Market Prices*, New York.

REITLINGER, *Ludonvico Carraci 1555-1619, Review of Market Prices*, Holt, Rinehart and Winston, New York, 1961.

REITLINGER, *Mabuse 1470-1532, Review of Market Prices*, New York.

REITLINGER, *Marc Chagall 1887, Review of Market Prices*, Holt, Rinehart and Winston, New York, 1961.

REITLINGER, *Maurice Quentin De Latour 1704-1788, Review of Market Prices*, New York.

REITLINGER, *Maurice Utrillo 1883-1955, Review of Market Prices*, New York.

REITLINGER, *Meindert Hobbema 1638-1709, Review of Market Prices*, New York.

REITLINGER, *Michelangelo Buonarotti 1475-1564, Review of Market Values*, New York.

REITLINGER, *Myles Birket Foster 1825-1899, Review of Market Prices*, New York.

REITLINGER, *Nicolas Lancret 1690-1743, Review of Market Prices*, New York.

REITLINGER, *Nicolas Maes 1632-1698, Review of Market Prices*, New York.

REITLINGER, *Nicolas Poussin 1594-1665, Review of Market Values*, New York.

REITLINGER, *Paul Cezanne 1839-1906, a Review of Market Prices*, Holt, Rinehart and Winston, New York, 1961.

REITLINGER, *Piero Della Francesca 1416-1492, a Review of Market Prices*, Holt, Rinehart and Winston, New York.

REITLINGER, *Pierre Bonnard 1867-1947, Review of Market Prices*, Holt, Rinehart and Winston, New York, 1961.

REITLINGER, *Pieter Breughel 1525-1569; Review of Market Prices*, Holt, Rinehart and Winston, New York, 1961.

REITLINGER, *Pietro Perugino 1446-1524, Review of Market Values*, New York.

REITLINGER, G. R., "**Economics of Taste, the Rise and Fall of Objects D Art Prices Since 1750**," *Apollo*, December, 1963, pp. 528.

REITLINGER, GERALD, *The Economics of Taste*, Holt, Rinehart and Winston, New York, 1961.

REITLINGER, GERALD, "**A. V. Copey-Fielding 1787-1855, Review of Market Price**," *The Economics of Taste*, pp. 309.

REITLINGER, GERALD, "**Adriaen Van De Velde 1635-1672, Review of Market Values**," *The Economics of Taste*, New York, pp. 473.

REITLINGER, GERALD, "**Albrecht Durer 1471-1528, Review of Market Prices**," *The Economics of Taste*, pp. 303.

REITLINGER, GERALD, "**Alessandro Botticell 1444-1510, Review of Market Prices**," *The Economics of Taste*, Holt, Rinehart and Wiston, New York, 1961, pp. 254.

REITLINGER, GERALD, "**Alfred Sisley 1840-1899, a Review Of Market**," *The Economics of Taste*, New York, pp. 452.

REITLINGER, GERALD, "**Amadeo Modigliani 1884-1920, Review of Market Values**," *The Economics of Taste*, New York, pp. 393.

▲ Fine Arts

REITLINGER, GERALD, "Andrea Del Sarto 1487-1531, Review of Market Values," 2The Economics of Taste, New York.

REITLINGER, GERALD, "Andrea Del Verrochio 1435-1488, Review of Market Values," *The Economics of Taste*, New York, pp. 86.

REITLINGER, GERALD, "Andrea Mantegna 1431-1506, a Review of Market Prices," *The Economics of Taste*, New York, pp. 378.

REITLINGER, GERALD, "Annibale Carracci 1560-1609, Review of Market Prices," *The Economics of Taste*, New York, 1961, pp. 268.

REITLINGER, GERALD, "Antoine Wattequ 1684-1721; Review of Market Values," *The Economics of Taste*, New York, pp. 490.

REITLINGER, GERALD, "Antonio Canaletto 1697-1768, Review of Market Prices," *The Economics of Taste*, New York, 1961, pp. 265.

REITLINGER, GERALD, "Antonio Pollaruolo 1432-1498, Review of Market Prices," *The Economics of Taste*, New York, pp. 412.

REITLINGER, GERALD, "Antonis Mor 1512-1576, Review of Market Values," *The Economics of Taste*, New York, pp. 395.

REITLINGER, GERALD, "Arthur Devis the Elder 1708-1787," *The Economics of Taste*, pp. 298.

REITLINGER, GERALD, "Ben Marshall 1766-1835, Review of Market Prices," *The Economics of Taste*, New York, pp. 380.

REITLINGER, GERALD, "Benjamin West 1738-1820, Review of Market Values," *The Economics of Taste*, New York, pp. 493.

REITLINGER, GERALD, "Bronzina Angelo 1502-1572, Review of Market Prices," *The Economics of Taste*, 1961, pp. 262.

REITLINGER, GERALD, "Camille Pissaro 1831-1903, Review of Market Prices," *The Economics of Taste*, New York, pp. 411.

REITLINGER, GERALD, "Carlo Crivecci 1435-1495, Review of Market Prices," *The Economics of Taste*, pp. 289.

REITLINGER, GERALD, "Carlo Solci 1616-1686, Review of Market Prices," *The Economics of Taste*, pp. 299.

REITLINGER, GERALD, "Chaim Soutine 1894-1944, Review of Market Values," *The Economics of Taste*, New York, pp. 453.

REITLINGER, GERALD, "Charles Francis Daubigny 1817-1878, Review of Market Prices," *The Economics of Taste*, pp. 292.

REITLINGER, GERALD, "Charles Robert Leslie 1794-1859, Review of Market Prices," *The Economics of Taste*, New York, pp. 368.

REITLINGER, GERALD, "Cima Di Conneguano 1460-1517, Review of Market Prices," *The Economics of Taste*, 1961, pp. 273.

REITLINGER, GERALD, "Clarkson Stanfield 1793-1867, Review of Market Values," *The Economics of Taste*, New York, pp. 455.

REITLINGER, GERALD, "Claude Le Lorrain 1600-1682; Review of Market Prices," *The Economics of Taste*, pp. 275.

REITLINGER, GERALD, "Claude Monet 1840-1926, Review of Market Values," *The Economics of Taste*, New York, pp. 394.

REITLINGER, GERALD, "Corregio 1494-1534, Review of Market Prices," *The Economics of Taste*, pp. 282.

REITLINGER, GERALD, "Daniel Maclise 1811-1870, Review of Market Prices," *The Economics of Taste*, New York, pp. 375.

REITLINGER, GERALD, "Dante G. Rosetti 1828-1882, Review of Market Values," *The Economics of Taste*, New York, pp. 438.

REITLINGER, GERALD, "David Cox 1783-1859, Review of Market Prices," *The Economics of Taste*, pp. 287.

REITLINGER, GERALD, "David Teniers 1610-1674; Review of Market Values," *The Economics of Taste*, New York, pp. 458.

REITLINGER, GERALD, "David Wilkie 1785-1841, Review of Market Values," *The Economics of Taste*, New York, pp. 496.

## BIBLIOGRAPHY OF APPRAISAL LITERATURE

REITLINGER, GERALD, "Diego Velasquez 1599-1660, Review of Market Values," *The Economics of Taste*, New York, pp. 477.

REITLINGER, GERALD, "Domeico Del Ghirlandajo 1449-1494, Review of Market Prices," *The Economics of Taste*, New York, pp. 327.

REITLINGER, GERALD, "Dominichino 1581-1641, Review of Market Prices," *The Economics of Taste*, pp. 300.

REITLINGER, GERALD, "Edgar Degas 1839-1917, Review of Market Prices," *The Economics of Taste*, pp. 295.

REITLINGER, GERALD, "Edouard Manet 1832-1883, Review of Market Prices," *The Economics of Taste*, New York, pp. 377.

REITLINGER, GERALD, "Edwin Long 1829-1891, Review of Market Prices," *The Economics of Taste*, New York, pp. 373.

REITLINGER, GERALD, "El Greco 1548-1614, Review of Market Prices," *The Economics of Taste*, New York, pp. 333.

REITLINGER, GERALD, "Ernest Meissonier 1815-1891, Review of Market Prices," *The Economics of Taste*, New York, pp. 383.

REITLINGER, GERALD, "Eugene Boudin 1824-1898, Review of Market Prices," *The Economics of Taste*, New York, pp. 258.

REITLINGER, GERALD, "Eugene Delacroix 1798-1863, Review of Market Prices," *The Economics of Taste*, pp. 297.

REITLINGER, GERALD, "Pablo Picasso 1881, Review of Market Values," *The Economics of Taste*, pp. 410.

REITLINGER, GERALD, "Patrick Nasmyth 1786-1831, Review of Market Values," *The Economics of Taste*, pp. 402.

REITLINGER, GERALD, "Paul Gauguin 1848-1903, Review of Market Prices," *The Economics of Taste*, pp. 324.

REITLINGER, GERALD, "Paul Potter 1625-1659, Review of Market Value," *The Economics of Taste*, pp. 413.

REITLINGER, GERALD, "Paul Signac 1863-1935, Review of Market Values," *The Economics of Taste*, pp. 451.

REITLINGER, GERALD, "Pelbert Cvyp 1620-1691, Review of Market Prices," *The Economics of Taste*, pp. 291.

REITLINGER, GERALD, "Philips Wooverman 1614-1688, Review of Market Values," *The Economics of Taste*, pp. 498.

REITLINGER, GERALD, "Pierre A. Renoir 1841-1919, Review of Market Values," *The Economics of Taste*, pp. 427.

REITLINGER, GERALD, "Pieter De Hooch 1629-1683, Review of Market Prices," *The Economics of Taste*, pp. 343.

REITLINGER, GERALD, "Quentin Matsys 1466-1530, Review of Market Prices," *The Economics of Taste*, pp. 383.

REITLINGER, GERALD, "Raoul Duffy 1880-1953, Review of Market Price," *The Economics of Taste*, pp. 303.

REITLINGER, GERALD, "Raphael 1483-1520, Review of Market Value," *The Economics of Taste*, pp. 417.

REITLINGER, GERALD, "Rembrandt 1606-1669, Review of Market Value," *The Economics of Taste*, pp. 421.

REITLINGER, GERALD, "Richard Wilson 1714-1782, Review of Market Values," *The Economics of Taste*, pp. 497.

REITLINGER, GERALD, "Roger Van Der Weyden 1400-64; Review of Market Values," *The Economics of Taste*, pp. 493.

REITLINGER, GERALD, "Salomon Van Ruysdael 1600-1670, Review of Market Values," *The Economics of Taste*, pp. 447.

REITLINGER, GERALD, "Salvatore Rosa 1615-1673, Review of Market Values," *The Economics of Taste*, pp. 437.

REITLINGER, GERALD, "Sebastiano Del Prombo 1485-1547, Review of Market Values," *The Economics of Taste*, pp. 409.

▲ Fine Arts

REITLINGER, GERALD, "Sir Anthony Van Dyck 1599-1641, Review of Market Values," *The Economics of Taste*, pp. 474.

REITLINGER, GERALD, "Sir Augustus John 1879, Review of Market Values," *The Economics of Taste*, pp. 357.

REITLINGER, GERALD, "Sir Edward Burnes-Jones 1833-1898, Review of Market Prices," *The Economics of Taste*, pp. 264.

REITLINGER, GERALD, "Sir Edwin Landser 1802-1873, Review of Market Prices," *The Economics of Taste*, pp. 406.

REITLINGER, GERALD, "Sir Edwin Landser 1802-1873, Review of Market Prices," *The Economics of Taste*, pp. 358.

REITLINGER, GERALD, "Sir Henry Raeburn 1756-1823, Review of Market Values," *The Economics of Taste*, pp. 416.

REITLINGER, GERALD, "Sir Peter Rubens 1577-1640, Review of Market Values," *The Economics of Taste*, pp. 441.

REITLINGER, GERALD, "Sir William Quiller Orchardson 1835-1910, Review of Market Values," *The Economics of Taste*, pp. 403.

REITLINGER, GERALD, "Sporting Pictures, Review of Market Values," *The Economics of Taste*, pp. 453.

REITLINGER, GERALD, "Theodore Rousseau 1812-1867, Review of Market Values," *The Economics of Taste*, pp. 440.

REITLINGER, GERALD, "Thomas Gainsborough 1727-1788, Review of Market Prices," *The Economics of Taste*, pp. 320.

REITLINGER, GERALD, "Thomas-Girtin 1775-1802, Review of Market Prices," *The Economics of Taste*, pp. 329.

REITLINGER, GERALD, "Titian 1480-1576, Review of Market Prices," *The Economics of Taste*, pp. 464.

REITLINGER, GERALD, "Toulouse-Lautrec 1864-1901 Review of Market Prices," *The Economics of Taste*, pp. 361.

REITLINGER, GERALD, "Venetian School 15th and 16th Centuries, Review of Market Values," *The Economics of Taste*, pp. 479.

REITLINGER, GERALD, "Vigee-Lebrun 1755-1842; Review of Market Values," *The Economics of Taste*, pp. 486.

REITLINGER, GERALD, "Willem Van De Velde 1633-1707, Review of Market Values," *The Economics of Taste*, pp. 473.

REITLINGER, GERALD, "Willem Van Mieris 1662-1747, Review of Market Values," *The Economics of Taste*, pp. 388.

REITLINGER, GERALD, "William Collins 1788-1847, Review of Prices," *The Economics of Taste*, pp. 277.

REITLINGER, GERALD, "William Etty 1787-1849, Review of Market Prices," *The Economics of Taste*, pp. 305.

REITLINGER, GERALD, "William Frith 1824-1909, Review of Market Prices," *The Economics of Taste*, pp. 319.

REITLINGER, GERALD, "William Hogarth 1697-1764, Review of Market Prices," *The Economics of Taste*, pp. 340.

REITLINGER, GERALD, "William Holman Hunt 1827-1910, Review of Market Prices," *The Economics of Taste*, pp. 346.

REITLINGER, GERALD, "William Muller 1812-1845; Review of Market Values," *The Economics of Taste*, pp. 398.

REITTLINGER, GERALD, "Giovanni Bellini, 1427-1516, Market Prices," *The Economics of Taste*, pp. 247.

RICE, DAVID TALBOT, TAMARA TALBOT RICE, *Icons the Natasha Allen Collection*, The National Gallery of Ireland.

RICHTER, G. M. A., *Korai Archaic Greek Maidens a Study In the Development of the Kore Type In Greek Sculpture*, Phaidon, London, January, 1969.

RIDLEY, MICHAEL, "Oriental Art," *Oriental Art*, John Gifford Ltd, London.

# BIBLIOGRAPHY OF APPRAISAL LITERATURE

RIGBY, DOUGLAS, ELIZABETH RIGBY, *Lock, Stock and Barrell, the Story of Collecting,*

ROBERTSON, GILES, *Giovanni Bellini,* Oxford University Press, London.

ROBERTSON, MARTIN, *Greek Painting,* Skira, 1959.

ROGER-MARX, CLAUDE, SABINE COTTE, *Delacroix,* Hacker Art Books Incorporated, New York, 1970.

ROTHCHILD, SIGMUND, "Appraisal of Contempory Art," *Appraisal and Valuation Manual,* Corporate Press Incorporated, Washington, D. C, January, 1972, pp. 402.

ROTHSCHILD, SIGMUND, "A Methodology of Art Appraisal," *Appraisal and Valuation Manual,* 1955, pp. 185.

ROTHSCHILD, SIGMUND, "Appraisal of Contemporary Art," *Valutape Audio-Library Series,* American Society of Appraisers, Washington, D.C., January 1, 1973.

ROTHSCHILD, SIGMUND, "Fine Arts Valuations," *Technical Valuation,* October, 1954, pp. 59.

ROTHSCHILD, SIGMUND, "Methodology for Statistical Comparison of Value As Applied to a Contemporary Artist," *Technical Valuation,* January, 1967, pp. 45.

ROTHSCHILD, SIGMUND, "Pointers In Fine Art Valuation," *Technical Valuation,* October, 1954, pp. 59.

ROWLAND, BENJAMIN, *The Art and Architecture of India,* Penguin Books Books.

RUBIN, WILLIAM S, *Dada, Surrealism and Their Heritage,* Museum of Modern Art, New York.

RUBIN, WILLIAM S., *Dada and Surrealist Art,* Thames and Hudson, 1970.

SATIE, JEAN PAUL, *Essays In Aesthetics,* Peter Owen, 1964.

SAVAGE, G., "Market for Modern Art," *Studio,* March, 1964, pp. 130-131.

SEILERN, COUNT, *Flemish Paintings and Drawings at 56 Princes Gate London, 1969,* Maggs Bros, London.

SELZ, JEAN, *Drawings and Watercolours 19th Century,* Clematis Press Ltd.

SERULLAZ, MAURICE, *The French Drawings,* Cassell.

SHAPLEY, FEIN RUSK, *Paintings from the Samuel U. Kress Collection Italion Schools, Xiii-Xv Century,*

SHAW, G. B., "Comments on Prices for Works of Art," *Art News,* 1929, pp. 23.

SHAW, J. BYAM, *Paintings by Old Masters at Christ Church Oxford,* Phaidon.

SILVERMAN, BENJAMIN, "Considerations of Authenticity," *Technical Valuation,* February, 1955, pp. 57.

SINGLETON, CHARLES S., *Art, Science and History In the Renaissance,* John Hopkins Press, London.

SMITH, BERNARD, *Australian Painting 1788-1970,* Oxford University Press, London.

SMYTH, W. A., "Putting Values on Fine Arts," *Technical Valuation,* October, 1953, pp. 35.

SOTHEBY, *Sotheby's Annual Review,* Sotheby, London, 1961.

SPECTOR, JACK L., *Murals of Delacroix at St. Sulpice,* Hacker Art Books Incorporated, New York, 1967.

STAFF OF THE FRICK COLLECTION, *The Frick Collection, the Painting,* Princeton University, USA.

STECHOU, W., *Northern Renaissance Art 1400-1600,* Prentice-Hall, Inc, 1966.

STENICO, ARTURO, *Roman and Etruscan Painting,* Viking Press, New York, 1963.

SUMOWSKI, WERNER, *Casper David Friedrich: Studien*, Franz Steinervarlag, Wiesbaden, 1970.

SURTEES, VIRGINIA, *The Paintings and Drawings of Dante Gabriel Rossetti*, Oxford University Press.

SWEET, FREDERICK A., *Miss Mary Cassatt, Impressionist from Pennsylvania*, University of Oklahoma Press, 1966.

SYDNEY, EARL OF PEMBROKE, *Paintings and Drawings at Wilton House*, Phaidon.

TAIT, STUART C., **"The Specific Principles In Appraising Fine Art,"** *Technical Valuation*, A. S. A., Washington, February, 1952, pp. 16.

URBACH, ZSUZSA, *Early Netherlandish Paintings*, The Clematis Press Ltd., Chelsea, S. W.

VAN DYKE, JOHN C., *A History of Painting*, College Histories of Art, October, 1902.

VERDIER, PHILIPPE, *The Walters Art Gallery Catalogue of the Painted Enamels of the Renaissance*, Altimore, 1967.

VERZONE, PAOLO, *From Theodoric to Charlemagne*, Methuen, London.

VRIESEN, GUSTAV, MAX IMAHL, *Robert Delaunay Light and Color*, Hacker Art Books Incorporated, New York, 1969.

WADLEY, NICHOLAS, *Manet*, The Coloue Library of Art, 1969.

WALHU, R. A., *The Best of Beardsley*, Spring Books, London.

WATERHOUSE, ELLIS, *Gainsborough*, Paul Hamlyn, London.

WATERHOUSE, ELLIS, *Italian Baroque Painting*, Phaidon Press Ltd., London.

WELLER, ALLEN S., *Contemporary American Painting and Sculpture*, University of Illinois Press, Urbana, 1967.

WHINNEY, MARGARET, *Early Flemish Painting*, Faber and Faber, 1968.

WHITE, JAMES, *The National Gallery of Ireland*, Thames and Hudson, London.

WHITE, JON MANCHIP, *Diego Velezquez Painter and Courtier*,

WOJTUSIAK, J, **"Arts New Patterns for Giving and Getting,"** *Conference Board Record*, June, 1970, pp. 32-34.

ZUBOU, V. P., *Leonardo Da Vinci*, Oxford University Press, London.

*From Romantic to Post Impressinnism*, Clematis Press, London.

*Master Drawings 19th, 20th Century*, Clematis Press, London.

*The Bowes Museum, Barnard Castle Catalogue of Spanish and Italian Paintings*, County Council of Durham, 1970.

*The Complete Work of Michelangelo*, Macdonald, London.

*Treasures of Louvre V I Fr 4th Millenium to Dawn of Renaissance V 11 Fr Renaissance & Impressionist*, Weidenfeld and Nicolson, London.

*Unfamiliar Masterpieces of Painting*, Peter Owen Ltd, London.

*US of America. the National Gallery of Art A Twenty-Five Year Report*, National Gallery of Art, Washington D. C.

*Watercolours of the Norwich School*, Cory Adams and Mackay.

**"Bull Market In Western Art,"** *Business Week*, June 13, 1970, pp. 92-93.

**"Chemicals and Art They Seem to Go Well Together,"** *Oil Paint and Drug Reporter*, January 25, 1971, pp. 5.

**"Companies Lend Their Expertise to the Arts,"** *Business Week*, May 15, 1971, pp. 102.

**"Estate Assets Art In Decedents Estates Trust Company Gallery Join In Program,"** *Trusts and Estates*, March, 1971, pp. 223-225.

## BIBLIOGRAPHY OF APPRAISAL LITERATURE

"Modern Masters at Auctions," *Arts,* March, 1965, pp. 36-37.

"Modernist Prices," *Art Digest,* February 1, 1935, pp. 12.

"Old Master Prices," *Art Digest,* April 15, 1931, pp. 18.

"Revised Values Seen In Sale of the Lewis Collection of Paintings," *Art News,* March 29, 1930, pp. 16.

"Saint Louis First Rembrandt a $130,000 Buy," *Art Digest,* November 1, 1950, pp. 9.

"Velasquez Over Priced, Over Prized," *The Economist,* February 6, 1971, pp. 24.

"Will the Real Picasso Please Stand Out," *Industry Week,* December 21, 1970, pp. 35.

# 18-12  Graphic Art

ACKERMAN, JAMES S., *Palladios Villas,* Institute of Fine Arts, New York University.

AMAYA, MARIO, *Pop As Art,* Studio Vista, 1965.

ANTAL, FREDERICK, *Classicism and Romanticism with Other Studies In Art History,* Routledge and Kegan Paul Ltd, London.

ARNASON, H. H., *A History of Modern Art,* Thames and Hudson, London.

ART DIGEST, "$10,000 for a Print," *Art Digest,* April 15, 1936.

ART DIGEST, "Prices on the European Art Mart," *Art Digest,* May 15, 1944.

BACOU, ROSELINE, *The Italian Drawings,* Cassell.

BACOU, ROSELINE, "The German, Flemish and Dutch Drawings," *The German, Flemish and Dutch, Drawings,* Cassell.

BALLO, GUIDO, R. H. BOOTHROYD, *The Critical Eye a New Approach to Art Appreciation,* Hacker Art Books Incorporated, London, 1966.

BARO, GENE, *Claes Oldenburg Drawings and Prints,* Hacker Art Books Incorporated, New York, 1969.

BERENSON, BERNARD, *Italian Pictures of the Renaissance,*

BOGER, LOUISE ADE, BOGER, H. BATTERSON, *Decorative Arts,* Scribners Publishers.

BOLOGNA, FERDINANDO, *Early Italian Painting Romanesque and Early Medieval Art,* London.

BOSKOVITS, MIKLOS, *Tuscan Paintings of the Early Renaissance,* Corvina Press, N. P.

BOYLE, T., "Ap Operator Transmit Christmas Season Art," *Editor and Publisher,* December 26, 1970, pp. 14.

BURKE, JOSEPH, COLIN CADWELL, *Hogarth the Complete Engravings,* Hacker Art Books Incorporated, New York, 1969.

CARTER, JOHN, PERRY MUIR, *Printing and the Mind of Man,* Hacker Art Books Incorporated, New York, 1967.

CLARK, KENNETH, *Leonardo Da Vinci Drawings,* Phaidon, London.

CLARK, KENNETH, *The Drawings of Leonardo Da Vinci In the Royal Collection,*

CLARK, KENNETH, "Leonardo the Anatomist Drawings of Leonardo at Windsor Vol 111 Anatomical Drawings," Phaidon Press, 1969.

▲ Fine Arts

CLAVEL, BERNARD, *Leonard De Vinci,* George G. Harrap, London.

CLIFFORD, DEREK, *Collecting English Drawings,*

COX, WARREN E., "The Intrinsic Value of Art," *The A. S. A. Valuation Manual,* American Society of Appraisers, 1956, pp. 179.

DAWSONS OF PALL MALL, *Art Prices Current,* Wm. Dawson and Sons Ltd, Cannon Hse Kent, Eng.

DIEHL, PROF. CONRAD, "Diehl's Anatomy for Artist and Students," Hacker Art Books Inc., New York, 1988.

DOCKSTADER, FREDERICK J., *South America Indian Art,* Studio Vista, London.

DODD, EDWARD, *Polynesian Art,* R. Hale and Co, London.

DODGSON, CAMPBELL, *Durer Engravings and Etchings,* Da Capo Press, New York, 1967.

EPPINK, NORMAN, *The History and Techniques of Printmaking,* University of Oklahoma Press.

ERNANDEZ, JUSTINO, *Guide to Mexican Art,* The University of Chicago Press, Chicago, 1968.

ETHERIDGE, KEN, *Collecting Drawings,* Bell.

FERRARI, ENRIQUE LAFUENTE, *Joya His Complete Etchings Aquatints And Lithographs,* Hacker Art Books Incorporated, New York, 1963.

FLIETZE, HANS, *Treasures of the Great National Galleries,* Garden City Books, 1900.

FOSTER, JOSEPH K., *Posters of Picasso,* W. H. Allen, London.

FRENVO, IVAN, *North Italian Drawings In the Budapest Museum of Finearts,* The Clematis Press, Ltd., London.

FURST, H., "Christies Since 1942 a Discourse on Values," *Apollo,* February, 1945, pp. 35.

GOHM. D. C., *Maps and Prints,* John Fifford Ltd, London.

GRABAR, ANDRE, *The Beginning of Christian Art 200 - 395 A.D.,* Thames and Hudson, London.

GRAND, P. M., *Art Prehistorique,* La Bibliothequedes Arts, Paris.

HACKER ART BOOKS, "Masterpcs of Asian Art In Amer Colls II," Hacker Art Books, New York, 1970, pp. 150.

HARRIS, J. R., *Egyptian Art,* Spring Books, London.

HERTLEIN, G. C., "Artist Views Discovery Through Computerized Graphics," *Computers and Automation,* August, 1970, pp. 25-26.

HIDESLEY, C. HUGH, "The Appraisal of Fine Arts," *Valuation,* American Society of Appraisers, September, 1972, pp. 12.

HILLER, J., *Hokusai Drawings,* Phaidon, 1966.

HIND, ARTHUR M., *A Catalogue of Rembrandts Etchings,* Da Capo Press, New York, 1967.

HINE, ROBERT V., "Bartlett's West: Drawing the Mexican Border," *Bartlett's West: Drawing the Mexican Border,* Yale University, Fort Worth, 1968.

HIRMER, MAX, PEDRO DE PALOL, *Early Medieval Art In Spain,* Thames and Hudson, London.

HOPKINS, JON H., *Orozco, a Catalogue of His Graphic Work,* Northern Arizona University, Flagstaff, 1967.

HURWITT, S., "Sputter-Etching A Dual Purpose Tool," *Industrial Research,* September, 1970, pp. 60-62.

HYAM, LESLIE A., "Appraisal of Fine Arts," *Technical Valuation,* ASA, Washington, October, 1953, pp. 11.

HYAM, LESLIE A., "Fine Arts - Liquidations," *Technical Evaluation,* ASA, October, 1953, pp. 11.

## BIBLIOGRAPHY OF APPRAISAL LITERATURE

INTERART PUBLISHERS INC., *International Art Market*, New York, March, 1961.

INTERNATIONAL COMMERCE, "Australian Printing, Graphic Arts Industry Offering U. S. Firms Export Opportunities," *International Commerce*, October 5, 1970, pp. 20.

JACKSON, RILLA EVELYN, *American Arts*, Rand-Mcnotty and Company, 1927.

JOHNSTONE, PAULINE, *Byzantine Tradition In Church Embroidery*, Alectiranti, London.

KAGANOVICH, A. L., *The Arts of Russia 17th and 18th Centuries*, The Cresset Press, London.

KAINEN, JACOB, *The Etchings of Canaletto*, The Smithsonian, 1967.

KELLEY, JOHN F., "Fine Arts Appraisals," *Technical Valuation*, June, 1954, pp. 41.

KELLY, ROB ROY, *American Wood Type 1828-1900*, Hacker Art Books Incorporated, New York, 1969.

KENT, FRANK, "Icons of the Community," *Monograph No. Three*, American Society of Appraisers, Washington D.C., January 1, 1970.

KENT, FRANK W., "Drawings," *Icons of the Community, Monograph, No. 3*, ASA Washington, D.C., 1970, pp. 63-67.

KENT, FRANK W., "Introduction to the Sections," *Icons of the Community, Monograph No. 3*, ASA, Washington, D.C., 1970, pp. 7-15.

KORNILOVICH, KIRA, *The Arts of Russia from the Origins to the End of the 16th Century*, The Cresset Press, London.

LAMARRE, JOHN H., "Fine Arts Appraisals," *Technical Valuation*, A. S. A., October, 1954, pp. 41.

LEONHARD, KURT, *Picasso His Graphic Works*, Thames and Hudson, London.

LEONHARD, KURT, *Picasso: Graphic Work*, Thames and Hudson, 1967.

LEVY, MICHAEL, *A History of Western Art*, Thames and Hudson.

LEWIS, JOHN, EDWIN SMITH, *The Graphic Reproduction and Photography Of Works of Arts*, Faber and Faber, London.

LEYMAIRE, J., H. READ, W. S. LIEBERMAN, *Henri Matisse*, University of California Press.

LION GOLDSCHMIDT, DAISY, *Chinese Art Bronze, Jade, Sculpture, Ceramics*, Studio Books, 1960.

LUCAS, LOUISE, *Art Book*, Hugh Evelyn, London.

LUST, HERBERT, *Jiacomette the Complete Graphics*, Hacker Art Books Incorporated, New York, 1970.

MASTER, ROBERT E. L. AND JEAN HOUSTON, *Psychedelic Art*, Weidenfeld and Nicolson, London.

MEER, F. VAN DER, *Early Christian Art*, Faber and Faber, London.

MELOT, MICHEL, *The Graphic Works of the Impressionists Manet, Pissarro, Renoir, Cezanne, Sisley*, Thames and Hudson, London.

MORSE, PETER, *John Sloans Prints*, Yale University Press, London.

PAL, PRATAPADITYA, *The Art of Tibet*, New York Graphic Society.

PAULSON, RONALD, *Hogarth's Graphic Works*, Yale University Press, London.

POPPER, FRANK, *Origins and Developments of Kinetic Art*,

PRATAPADITYA, PAL, *The Art of Tibet*, New York Graphic Society.

RACZ, ISTUAN, *Treasures of Medieval Finland*,

RADEMACHER, HELLMUT, *Masters of German Poster Art*, Hacker Art Books Incorporated, New York, 1966.

RAUSCHENBUSCH, DR. H., *International Directory of Arts*, 1958.

REITLINGER, G. R., "Economics of Taste, the Rise and Fall of Objects D Art Prices Since 1750," *Apollo,* December, 1963, pp. 528.

RICHTER, GISELA, *A Handbook of Greek Art,* Phaidon Press Ltd., London.

ROSENBERG, JAKOB, *On Quality In Art,* Phaidon.

ROSENBLUM, ROBERT, *Cubism and Twentieth Century Art,* Hacker Art Books Incorporated, New York, 1966.

ROTHCHILD, SIGMUND, "Appraisal of Contempory Art," *Appraisal and Valuation Manual,* Corporate Press Incorporated, Washington, D. C, January, 1972, pp. 402.

ROTHSCHILD, SIGMUND, "A Methodology of Art Appraisal," *Appraisal and Valuation Manual,* 1955, pp. 185.

ROTHSCHILD, SIGMUND, "Fine Arts Valuations," *Technical Valuation,* October, 1954, pp. 59.

ROTHSCHILD, SIGMUND, "Methodology for Statistical Comparison of Value As Applied to a Contemporary Artist," *Technical Valuation,* January, 1967, pp. 45.

ROTHSCHILD, SIGMUND, "Pointers In Fine Art Valuation," *Technical Valuation,* October, 1954, pp. 59.

RUHMER, EBERHARD, *Grunewald Drawings,* Phaidon Press, London.

RUSSOLI, FRANCO, *Modigliani Drawings and Sketches.*

SAVAGE, G., "Market for Modern Art," *Studio,* March, 1964, pp. 130-131.

SAVAGE, GEORGE, *French Decorative Art 1638-1793,* The Penguin Press, 1969.

SCHMIED, WIELAND, *Alfred Kubin,* Pall Mall Press, London.

SCRANTON, ROBERT L., *Aesthetic Aspects of Ancient Art,* University of Chicago Press.

SHAW, G. B., "Comments on Prices for Works of Art," *Art News,* 1929, pp. 23.

SILVERMAN, BENJAMIN, "Considerations of Authenticity," *Technical Valuation,* February, 1955, pp. 57.

SINGH, MADANJEET, *Himalayan Art,* Unesco Art Books, Macmillia, London.

SINGLETON, CHARLES S., *Art, Science and History In the Renaissance,* John Hopkinspress, London.

SMITH, ROBERT C., *The Art of Portugal,* Weidenfeld and Nicolson, London.

SMYTH, W. A., "Putting Values on Fine Arts," *Technical Valuations,* October, 1953, pp. 35.

SOTHEBY, *Sotheby's Annual Review,* Sotheby, London, 1961.

SPECTOR, JACK L., *Murals of Delacroix at St. Sulpice,* Hacker Art Books Incorporated, New York, 1967.

STERN, HENRI, *L'Art Byzantin,* Presses Universitaires De France.

SWEET, FREDERICK A., *Miss Mary Cassatt, Impressionist from Pennsylvania,* University of Oklahoma Press, 1966.

TAIT, STUART C., "The Specific Principles In Appraising Fine Art," *Technical Valuation,* A. S. A., Washington, February, 1952, pp. 16.

TIMM, WERNER, *The Graphic Art of Edvard Munch,* Studio Vista, 1969.

VERZONE, PAOLO, *From Theodoric to Charlemagne,* Methuen, London.

WALFFLIN, HEINRICH, *The Art of Albrecht Durer,* Phaidon Press, 1980, pp. R. W. LUFF.

WADLEY, NICHOLAS, *The Drawings of Van Gogh,* Paul Hamlyn, London.

WALDMAN, DIANE, *Roy Lichtenstein Drawings and Prints,* Hacker Art Books Incorporated, New York, 1970.

WARK, ROBERT R.,, *Early Brit Drawings In Huntington Coll 1600-1750,* Huntington Library, 1969.

WECHSLER, HERMAN J., *Great Prints and Printmakers,* Thames and Hudson, London.

WOJTUSIAK, J, "Arts New Patterns for Giving and Getting," *Conference Board Record,* June, 1970, pp. 32-34.

*A Guide to Mexican Art,* University of Chicago, USA.

*Chinese Art,* The Pall Mall Press, London.

*From Romantic to Post Impressionism,* Clematis Press, London.

*One Hundred Unpublished Drawings of Henry De Toulouse-Lautrec,* Hacker Art Books Incorporated, Boston, 1965.

"Graphics Exhibition In Mexico Projects Sales of 9. 1 Million," *International Commerce,* July 27, 1970, pp. 37.

"Survey of Grafic Arts Cameras," *Graphic Arts Monthly,* December, 1970, pp. 24-09.

"Velasquez Over Priced, Over Prized," *The Economist,* February 6, 1971, pp. 24.

"Will the Real Picasso Please Stand Out," *Industry Week,* December 21, 1970, pp. 35.

# 18-13  Sculpture

AINASON, H. H., *Jacques Lipchitz Sketches In Bronze,* Pall Mall Press, London.

AUBOYER, JANINE, *The Art of Afghanistan,* Hamlyn, London.

AVERY, CHARLES, *Florentine Renaissance Sculpture,* John Murray, 1970.

BALLO, GUIDO, R. H. BOOTHROYD, *The Critical Eye a New Approach to Art Appreciation,* Hacker Art Books Incorporated, London, 1966.

BEASLEY, J. D., B. ASHMORE, *Greek Sculpture and Paintings,* Cambridge University Press, London.

BOGER, LOUISE ADE, BOGER, H. BATTERSON, *Decorative Arts,* Scribners Publishers.

BOWNESS, ALAN, *Modern Sculpture,* Dulton Vista Pictureback, 1965.

CHARLESTON, R. J., JOHN AYERS, *The James A. De Rothschild Collection at Waddesdon Manor,* The National Trust Office Du Livee, Fribourg.

CLEMENTS, ROBERT J., *Michelangelo a Self Portrait,* University of London, London.

CLIFFORD, DEREK, *Art and Understanding,* Hugh Evelyn, London.

COOPER, DOUGLAS, *Picasso Theatre,* Herbert Jenkins, London.

COX, WARREN E., "The Intrinsic Value of Art," *The A. S. A. Valuation Manual,* American Society of Appraisers, 1956, pp. 179.

DAVIE, GIBSON A., DONALD B. GOODALL, *Charles Umlauf, Sculptor,* University Art Museum, London, 1967.

DAVIES, MARTIN, *The National Gallery, Oondon, Volume III,* Brussels, 1970.

DAWNES, KERRY, *Hawksmoor,* Thames and Hudson.

DAWSONS OF PALL MALL, *Art Prices Current,* Wm. Dawson and Sons Ltd, Cannon Hse Kent, Eng.

▲ Fine Arts

FLIETZE, HANS, *Treasures of the Great National Galleries*, Garden City Books, 1900.

FURST, H., "Christies Since 1942 a Discourse on Values," *Apollo*, February, 1945, pp. 35.

GELDZAHLER, HENRY, *New York & Sculpture 1940-1970*, Pall Mall Press, London.

HACKER ART BOOKS INC, "Mantle Fielding's Dictionary of Amer Painters, Sculptors & Engravers," Hacker Art Books Inc, New York, 1965, pp. 592.

HALLADE, MADELEIN, *The Gandhara Style*, Thames and Hudson, London.

HAMMACHER, A. M., *Modern English Sculpture*, Thames and Hudson, London.

HAMMACHER, A. M., *The Evolution of Modern Sculpture*, Hacker Art Books Incorporated, New York, 1969.

HANFMANN, GEORGE M. A., *Classical Sculpture*, Hacker Art Books Incorporated, Greenwich, 1967.

HART, FREDERICK, *Michelangelo the Complete Sculpture*, Thames and Hudson, 1970.

HELD, JULIUS S., *Rembrandts Aristotle and Other Rembrandt Studies*, Oxford University Press, London.

HENDY, PHILLIP, *Piero Della Francesca and the Early Renaissance*, Weidenfeld and Nicolson, London.

HERTLEIN, G. C., "Artist Views Discovery Through Computerized Graphics," *Computers and Automation*, August, 1970, pp. 25-26.

HIDESLEY, C. HUGH, "The Appraisal of Fine Arts," *Valuation*, American Society of Appraisers, September, 1972, pp. 12.

HILLIER, BEVIS, *Art Deco*, Studio Vista, London.

HYAM, LESLIE A., "Appraisal of Fine Arts," *Technical Valuation*, ASA, Washington, October, 1953, pp. 11.

HYAM, LESLIE A., "Fine Arts - Liquidations," *Technical Valuation*, ASA, October, 1953, pp. 11.

INTERART PUBLISHERS INC., *International Art Market*, New York, March, 1961.

JACKSON, RILLA EVELYN, *American Arts*, Rand-Mcnotty and Company, 1927.

JAMES, PHILIP, ED., *Henry Moore on Sculpture*, Macdonald and Co.

JOSEPH, MICHAEL, *The Sculpture of David Wynne*, London.

KELLEY, JOHN F., "Fine Arts Appraisals," *Technical Valuation*, June, 1954, pp. 41.

KENT, FRANK, "Icons of the Community," Monograph No. Three, American Society of Appraisers, Washington D.C., January 1, 1970.

KENT, FRANK W., "Introduction to the Sections," *Icons of the Community*, Monograph No. 3, ASA, Washington, D. C., 1970, pp. 7-15.

KENT, FRANK W., "Sculpture," *Icons of the Community*, Monograph No. 3, ASA, Washington, D.C., 1970, pp. 31-39.

KEUTNER, HERBERT, *Sculpture Renaissance to Rococo*, Hacker Art Books Incorporated, Greenwich, 1967.

KIRKPATRICK, DIANE, *Eduardo Paolozzi*, Hacker Art Books Incorporated, Greenwich, 1971.

KOEPF, DR. HANS, PROFESSOR, ED. J. E.SCHUL, *Masterpieces of Sculpture, from the Greeks to Modern Times*, Macdonald and Co. Ltd, London.

LACY, A. D., *Greek Pottery In the Bronze Age*, Methuen, London.

LAMARRE, JOHN H., "Fine Arts Appraisals," *Technical Evaluation*, A. S. A, October, 1954, pp. 41.

LANGE, KURT, MAX HIRMER, *Egypt Architecture, Sculpture, Paintings, 4th Edition*, Phaidon, London.

# BIBLIOGRAPHY OF APPRAISAL LITERATURE

LICHT, FRED, *Sculpture Nineteenth and Twentieth Centuries,* Hacker Art Books Incorporated, Greenwich, 1967.

LION GOLDSCHMIDT, DAISY, *Chinese Art Bronze, Jade, Sculpture, Ceramics,* Studio Books, 1960.

MARTIN, J. R., *Rubens: the Antwerp Altarpieces,* Thames and Hudson, 1969.

MARYON, *Metalwork and Enameling,* Chapman and Hall.

MEAUZE, PIERRE, *African Art Sculpture,* Weidenfeld and Nicolson, 1968.

MEILACH, DONA, DON SEIDON, *Direct Metal Sculpture,* George Allen and Unwin, London.

MILLER, D. C., W. S. LIEBERMAN, *The New Japanese Painting and Sculpture,* Doubleday and Co. Inc, 1966.

MILLER, D. C., W. S. LIEHERMANN, *The New Japanese Paintings and Sculpturers,* Doubleday and Company Incorporated, 1966.

OVERDEN, DENNIS, *African Art - the Colour Library of Art,* Paul Hamlyn, 1968.

PENROSE, ROLAND, *The Sculpture of Picasso,* The Museum of Modern Art.

PRIEST, ALAN, *The Sculpture of Joseph Coletti,* Collier-Macmillan.

RAUSCHENBUSCH, DR. H., *International Directory of Arts,* 1958.

RAY, ANTHONY, *English Delftware Pottery,* Faber and Faber, London.

READE, BRAIN, *Ballet Designs and Illustrations 1581 - 1940,* Her Majesty's Stationery Office, 1967.

REITLINGER, G. R., "**Economics of Taste, the Rise and Fall of Objects D Art Prices Since 1750,**" *Apollo,* December, 1963, pp. 528.

RICHMOND, SIR IAN, *Roman Archaeology and Art,* Farber, 1969.

RICHTER, G. M. A., *Korai Archaic Greek Maidens a Study In the Development of the Kore Type In Greek Sculpture,* Phaidon, London, January, 1969.

RICHTER, GISELA M. A., *Perspective In Greek and Roman Art,* Phaidon Press, 1970.

ROBERTSON, D. S., *Greek and Roman Architecture,* Cambridge University Press, 1969.

ROBERTSON, GILES, *Giovanni Bellini,* Oxford University Press, London.

ROTHCHILD, SIGMUND, "**Appraisal of Contempory Art,**" *Appraisal and Valuation Manual,* Corporate Press Incorporated, Washington, D. C, January, 1972, pp. 402.

ROTHSCHILD, SIGMUND, "**Pointers In Fine Art Valuation,**" *Technical Valuation,* October, 1954, pp. 59.

SALVINI, ROBERTO, *Medieval Sculpture,* Hacker Art Books Incorporated, Greenwich, 1967.

SAVAGE, G., "**Market for Modern Art,**" *Studio,* March, 1964, pp. 130-131.

SAVAGE, GEORGE, *18th Century German Porcelain,* Spring Books, 1967.

SEMENZATO, CAMILLO, *La Scultura Del Seicento E Del Settecento,* Alfieri, 1967.

SHAW, G. B., "**Comments on Prices for Works of Art,**" *Art News,* 1929, pp. 23.

SILVERMAN, BENJAMIN, "**Considerations of Authenticity,**" *Technical Valuation,* February, 1955, pp. 57.

SMYTH, W. A., "**Putting Values on Fine Arts,**" *Technical Valuation,* October, 1953, pp. 35.

SOTHEBY, *Sotheby's Annual Review,* Sotheby, London, 1961.

STOLL, R. T., *Architecture and Sculpture In Early Britain Celtic Saxon Norman,* Thames and Hudson, London.

▲ Fine Arts

TAIT, STUART C., "The Specific Principles In Appraising Fine Art," *Technical Valuation*, A. S. A., Washington, February, 1952, pp. 16.

TROWELL, MARGARET, *Classical African Sculpture*, Faber and Faber, 1970.

WEBSTER, T. B. L., *Hellenistic Art*, Art of the World Series, Methuen, 1966.

WELLER, ALLEN S., *Contemporary American Painting and Sculpture*, University of Illinois Press, Urbana, 1967.

WERNER, ALFRED, *Modigliani Sculpture*, Hacker Art Books Incorporated, Switzerland, 1962.

*The Mediaeval Architect*, Wayland Publishers, London.

*The Praeger Encyclopedia of Ancient Greek Civilization*, Hacker Art Books Incorporated, New York.

"500, 000 for a Sculpture by Desiderio Da Settignano," *Art Digest*, December 1, 1931, pp. 5.

DONALD SEIDEN, *Direct Metal Sculpture*, George Allen A.

MAN, DAVID, *European Sculpture*, Studio Vista, 1970.

# 18-14 Crafts

ASIA HOUSE GALLERY PUBLICATIONS, *The Art of the Korean Potter, Silla, Koryo, Yi*, Asia House Gallery Publications.

BALL, THOMAS L, "**Valuation Considerations for Art Glass Windows**," *Valutapes Audio-Library Series*, American Society of Appraisers, Washington D.C., January 1, 1973.

BALL, THOMAS L., *Valuation Considerations for Art Glass Windows*, American Society of Appraisers.

BALLO, GUIDO, R. H. BOOTHROYD, *The Critical Eye a New Approach to Art Appreciation*, Hacker Art Books Incorporated, London, 1966.

BARRETT, FRANKLIN S., *Worcester Porcelain and Lund's Bristol*, Faber and Faber, London, December, 1966.

BERGES, RUTH, *Collectors Choice of Porcelain and Faience*, Thomas Yoseloff, London.

BLUM, SHIRLEY NEILSON, *Early Netherlandish Triptychs, a Study In Patronage*, University of California, 1969.

BLUNT, WILFRED, *Isfahan-Pearl of Persia*, Eleh Books Ltd, London.

BOGER, LOUISE ADE, BOGER, H. BATTERSON, *Decorative Arts*, Scribners Publishers.

BOUQUET, A. C., *European Brasses*,

BROOKSHAW, DOREEN, *Pottery Craft*, Frederick Warne, London.

CALATCHI, ROBERT DE, *Oriental Carpets*, Charles E. Tuttle Company, 1968.

CESCINSKY, HERBUT, MALCOLM R. WEBSTER, *English Domestic Clocks*, Hamlyn Group, London.

CHAFFERS, WILLIAM, *Collectors Handbook of Marks and Monograms on Pottery and Porcelain,*

CHARLES, ROLLO, "**Continental Porcelain of the 18 Century**," Hacker Art Books Inc., London, 1964, pp. 198.

CHARLESTON, R. J., *English Porcelain 1745-1850*, Hacker Art Books, London, 1965.

# BIBLIOGRAPHY OF APPRAISAL LITERATURE

CHARLESTON, R. J., *German Glass,*

CHARLESTON, R. J., *World Ceramics,* Paul Hamlyn, 1968.

CHARLESTON, R. J., JOHN AYERS, *The James A. De Rothschild Collection at Waddesdon Manor,* The National Trust Office Du Livee, Fribourg.

CHARLESTON, ROBERT J., *World Ceramics,* Hacker Art Books Incorporated, London, 1968.

CHARPENTRAT, PIERRE, *L' Art Baisque,* Presses Universitaires De France.

CHEMICAL WEEK, "New Impressions on Ceramic Tile," *Chemical Week,* August 25, 1971.

COLDSTREAM, J. N., *Greek Geometric Pottery, a Local Survey of Ten Local Styles and Their Chronology.*

COLLARD, ELIZABETH, *Nineteenth Century Pottery and Porcelain In Canada,* Mcgill University Press, Montreal, 1967.

COOK, R. M., *Greek Painting Pottery,* Methuen, London.

COX, WARREN E., "How to Look at a Pot," *A. S. A. Valuation Manual,* American Society of Appraisers, 1961, pp. 174.

CRIPPS, WILFRED JOSEPH, *Old English Plate,* Paul Hamlyn, London.

CUSHION, JOHN P., *Animals In Pottery and Porcelain,* Cory, Adams Andmackay, London, 1966.

DAVIS, DEREK C., KEITH MIDDLEMAS, "Coloured Glass," *Coloured Glass,* The Cressent Press, Barrie and Rocklift.

DAWSONS OF PALL MALL, *Art Prices Current,* Wm. Dawson and Sons Ltd, Cannon Hse Kent, Eng.

DE JONGE, C. H., *Delft Ceramics,* Pall Mall Press.

DELIEB, ERIC, *Silver Boxes,* The Cresset Press, Barrie and Rocklift.

DUTTON, *Americas Arts and Skills,* Editors of Life.

ERNANDEZ, JUSTINO, *Guide to Mexican Art,* The University of Chicago Press, Chicago, 1968.

FAGG, WILLIAM, *Miniature Wood Carving In Africa,* Hacker Art Books Incoporated, New York, 1970.

FISHER, STANLEY, *English Ceramics,* Ward Lock and Company, London.

FLETCHER, H. MORLEY, *Investing In Pottery and Porcelain,*

FLIETZE, HANS, *Treasures of the Great National Galleries,* Garden City Books, 1900.

FURST, H., "Christies Since 1942 a Discourse on Values," *Apollo,* February, 1945, pp. 35.

GODDEN, GEOFFREY, *Masons Patent Ironstone China,* Barrie and Jenkins, London.

GODDEN, GEOFFREY, "Handbook of British Pottery and Porcelain Marks," *The Handbook of British Pottery and Porcelain Marks,* Herbert Jenkins, London.

GODDEN, GEOFFREY A., *Caughley and Worcester Porcelains 1775-1800,* Herbert Jenkins, London.

GRANDJEAN, BREDO L., *Dansk Ostindisk Porcelain,* Thaning and Appelsforalag, Copenhagen.

HAAS, DR. ROBERT BARLETT, "All About Collecting and the Adult Learner," *Appraisal and Valuation Manual,* Corporate Press Incorporated, Washington, D. C, January, 1972, pp. 416.

HAEDAHE, HANS ULRICH, *Metalwork,* Weidenfeld and Nicolson, London.

HARDEN, D. B., K. S. PAINTER, R. H. PINDER, *Masterpieces of Glass,*

## Fine Arts

HELFTS, JACQUES, *French Master Goldsmiths and Silversmiths from The Seventeenth to the Nineteenth Century,* Hacker Art Books Incorporated, New Yor, 1966.

HERTLEIN, G. C., "**Artist Views Discovery Through Computerized Graphics,**" *Computers and Automation,* August, 1970, pp. 25-26.

HILLIER, BEVIS, *Pottery and Porcelain 1700-1914,* Weidenfeld and Nicolson, London.

HONEY, W. B., *English Pottery and Porcelain,* Adam and Charas.

HUGHES, G. BERNARD, *Victorian Pottery and Porcelain,* Spring Books, London.

HUGHES, THIRLE AND BERNARD, *English Painted Enamels,* Spring Books, 1967.

HYAM, LESLIE A., "**Appraisal of Fine Arts,**" *Technical Valuation,* ASA, Washington, October, 1953, pp. 11.

INTERART PUBLISHERS INC., *International Art Market,* New York, March, 1961.

JACKSON, RILLA EVELYN, *American Arts,* Rand-Mcnotty and Company, 1927.

KELLEY, JOHN F., "**Fine Arts Appraisals,**" *Technical Valuation,* June, 1954, pp. 41.

KENT, FRANK, "**Icons of the Community,**" *Monograph No. Three,* American Society of Appraisers, Washington D.C., January 1, 1970.

KENT, FRANK W., "**Crafts,**" *Icons of the Community, Monograph No. 3,* 1970, pp. 67-81.

KENT, FRANK W., "**Introduction to the Sections,**" *Icons of the Community, Monograph No. 3,* ASA, Washington, D.C., 1970, pp. 7-15.

LACY, A. D., *Greek Pottery In the Bronze Age,* Methuen, London.

LAMARRE, JOHN H., "**Fine Arts Appraisals,**" *Technical Valuation,* A. S. A., October, 1954, pp. 41.

LAND, ARTHUR, *Greek Pottery-Third Edition,* Faber.

LEE, RUTH WEBB, *Nineteenth Century Art Glass,*

LEVINE, GEORGE J., *Inscribed Lowestaft Porcelain,* English Porcelain Circle, 1968.

LION GOLDSCHMIDT, DAISY, *Chinese Art Bronze, Jade, Sculpture, Ceramics,* Studio Books, 1960.

LISTER, RAYMOND, *Eleven Engravings by Edward Calout,* Golden Head.

LLOYD, WARD, *Investing In Georgian Glass,* Barrie and Jenkins, London.

LOCSIN, LEANDRO, "**Oriental Ceramics Discovered In the Philippines,**" *Oriental Ceramics Discovered In the Philippines,* Charles E. Tuttle Company, 1967.

MAN, FELIX H., *Artists Lithographs,* Hacker Art Books Incorporated, New York, 1970.

MARYON, *Metalwork and Enameling,* Chapman and Hall.

MEISSNER, KURT, *Japanese Woodblack Prints In Miniature: the Genre of Surimono,* Kegan Paul, 1970.

MORLEY FLETCHER, H., *Investing In Pottery and Porcelain,*

O'DONNELL, GEORGENE, *Miniaturia,* Hobbies-Lightner Publishing Company.

PINTON, EDWARD AND EVA PINTO, *Tunbridge & Scottish Souvenir Woodware,* Bell.

PIPER, JOHN, *Stained Glass Art or Anti-Art,* Studio Vista, London.

RAUSCHENBUSCH, DR. H., *International Directory of Arts,* 1958.

RAY, ANTHONY, *English Delftware Pottery,* Faber and Faber, London.

REITLINGER, G. R., "**Economics of Taste, the Rise and Fall of Objects D' Art Prices Since 1750,**" *Apollo,* December, 1963, pp. 528.

RICE, DENNIS G., *Rockingham Pottery and Procelain,* Barrie and Jenkins, London.

RIDGWAY, MAURICE H., *Chester Goldsmiths from Earily Time to 1726,* John Sherratt and Sone Ltd, Cheshire.

ROSE, MURIEL, *Artist Potters In England,* Faber and Faber, 1970.

ROTH, H. LING, *Oriental Silverwork: Malay and Chinese,* Oxford University Press, 1966.

SANDON, HENRY, *British Pottery and Procelain,* John Gifford Ltd, London.

SAVAGE, GEORGE, *18th Century German Porcelain,* Spring Books, 1967.

SCHURMANN, ULRICH, *Central Asian Rugs,* London.

SHAW, G. B., "Comments on Prices for Works of Art," *Art News,* 1929, pp. 23.

SILVERMAN, BENJAMIN, "Considerations of Authenticity," *Technical Valuation,* February, 1955, pp. 57.

SKELLEY, LELOISE DAVIS, *Modern Fine Glass,*

SMYTH, W. A., "Putting Values on Fine Arts," *Technical Valuation,* October, 1953, pp. 35.

STAZZI, FRANCESCO, *Italian Porcelain,* Weidenfeld and Nicolson.

TAYLOR, LUCY B., *Know Your Fabrics,* John Wiley and Son, New York.

TREWICK, HENRY, *The Craft and Design of Monumental Brass,* Human Ities Press, London.

UNTRACHT, OPPI, *Metal Techniques for Craftsmen,* Robert Hale and Co, London.

WATERER, JOHN W., *A Guide to the Conservation and Restoration of Objects Made Wholly or In Part of Leather,* G. Bell and Sons Lts, London.

WATKINS, LURA WOODSIDE, *Early New England Potters and Their Wares,* Archon Books, London.

WENHORN, EDWARD, *The Practical Book of American Silver,* Lippencott.

WILLS, GEOFFREY, *The Pottery of Old England,*

WILSON, DAVID, OLE-KLINDT-JENSEN, *Viking Art,* Allen and Unwin, London.

WINGATE, ISABEL, *Textile Fabrics,* Prentice-Hall.

# 18-15 Collectors' Items

ALEXANDER, J. J. G., A. C. DE LA MARE, *The Italian Manuscripts In the Library of Majir,* J. R. Abbey.

ALLEN, BRYAN, *Print Collecting,* Muller, 1970.

ALLEN, BRYAN, *Print Collecting,* Muller, 1970.

ALPATOV, M. W., *Art Treasures of Russia,* Thames and Hudson, 1968.

AMERICAN GEM SOCIETY, "Jewelry and Jewelers: Booklet for Future Reference," American Gem Society, Los Angeles, 1939.

ANTON, FERDINAND, *Ancient Mexican Art,* Hacker Art Books Incorporated, New York, 1969.

ART NEWS, "Art Prices In U.S.," *Art News,* November, 1957, pp. 161.

ART NEWS, "Art Values Vindicated," *Art News,* December 13, 1930, pp. 14.

▲ Fine Arts

AUBOYER, JANINE, *The Art of Afghanistan,* Hamlyn, London.

BAILLIE, G. H., C. CLUTTON, ILBERT, C. A., "Britten's Old Clocks and Watches and Their Makers," *Brittens Old Clocks and Watches and Their Makers,* Eyre and Spottiswoode, London.

BAINES, ANTHONY, *European and American Musical Instruments,* B. T. Batsford Ltd, London.

BALLO, GUIDO, R. H. BOOTHROYD, *The Critical Eye a New Approach to Art Appreciation,* Hacker Art Books Incorporated, London, 1966.

BANDINELLI, RANUCCIO BIANCHI, *The Buried City Excavations at Leptismagna,* Weidenfeld and Nicholson, London.

BANK, HERMAN, "Precious Stones and Minerals," *Precious Stones and Minerals Warne,* 1970.

BAZIN, GERMAIN, *The Baroque: Principles, Styles, Modes & Themes,* Thames & Hudson.

BEAFORD, JOHN, *Collectors Prices 9-English Crystal Glass, Collectorsprices 10. Old Worcester China,*

BEAN, JACOB, FELICE STUMPELE, *Drawings from New York Collections I. the Italion Renaissance Ii. the 17th Century In Italy,* New York Graphic Society, Greenwich, Conn..

BEDFORD, JOHN, *Collectors Pieces No. 17 Jade and Other Hardstone Carvings, No. 18. Chinese and Japanese Lacquer,* Cassell and Co., London.

BEDFORD, JOHN, DEREK AUSTIN, *Old Sheffield Plate,* Cassell, London.

BELLONI, GIAN GUIDO AND LILIANE FEDI DALL-ASEN, *Iranian Art,* Pall Mall Press.

BENTLEY, NICHOLAS, *The Victorian Scene,* Weidenfeld and Nicholson, London.

BERENSON, BERNARD, *Suing and Knowing,* Evelyn Adams and Mackay, London.

BLAIR, CLAUDE, *European Armour Circa 1066 to Circa 1700,* Batsford, Loncon.

BLAIR, CLAUDE, *Pistols of the World,* B. T. Batsford Ltd, London.

BLUNT, ANTHONY, *Studies In Renaissance and Baroque Art,* Phaidon, London.

BOESEN, BOJE, *Old Danish Silver,* Hassing Publisher.

BOSWELL, P., "Going, Going, Gone," *Art Digest,* December 1, 1940, pp. 3.

BOUQUET, A. C., *European Brasses,*

BRADLEY, VON ALLEN, *Gold In Your Attic,* Leet.

BREDIUS, ABRAHAM, *The Paintings of Rembrant,* Phaidon.

BRIGHAM, CLARENCE S., "Paul Revere's Engravings," *Paul Revere's Engravings,* Atheneum, New York, 1969.

BRUNNER, HERBERT, *Old Table Silver,* Faber and Faber, London.

BRUTON, ERIC, *Clocks and Watches,* Paul Hamyln, London.

CAKE, VAN DEREN, *The Painter and the Photograph from Delacroix to Warhol,* University of New Mexico, Albuquerque.

CALATCHI, ROBERT DE, *Oriental Carpets,* Charles E. Tuttle Company, 1968.

CAMEHL, ADA WALKER, *Blue China Book,* Tudor.

CARLE, DONALD DE, *Clocks and Their Value,* Nag Press, London.

CASASSA, E. A. J., "Discovery and Loss of a Korean Masterpiece," *Technical Valuation,* pp. 14.

CESCINSKY, HERBUT, MALCOLM R. WEBSTER, *English Domestic Clocks,* Hamlyn Group, London.

CHAMOUX, FRANCOIS, *Greek Art,* Barrie and Rockliff, 1966.

## BIBLIOGRAPHY OF APPRAISAL LITERATURE

CLARK, KENNETH, *Leonardo Da Vinci Drawings*, Phaidon, London.

CLARK, KENNETH, *The Drawings of Leonardo Da Vinci In the Royal Collection,*

CLARK, KENNETH, "**Leonardo the Anatomist Drawings of Leonardo at Windsor Vol 111 Anatomical Drawings**," Phaidon Press, 1969.

CLEMENS, ROBERT J., *Michelangelos Theory of Art*, Hacker Art Books Incorporated, New York, 1961.

CLEMENTS, ROBERT J., *Michelangelo a Self Portrait,* University of London, London.

CLIFFORD, DEREK, *Art and Understanding,* Hugh Evelyn, London.

CLIFFORD, DEREK, *Collecting English Drawings,*

COBB, J, "New Look In Manuscripts," *Special Libraries,* November, 1970, pp. 483-485.

COCKE, RICHARD, *Pier Francesco Mola,* Clarendon Press-Oxford University Press, London.

COCKE, RICHARD, *The Complete Paintings of Raphael,* Weidenfeld and Nicolson, London.

COCKERELL, SYDNEY C., *Old Testament Miniatures, Introduction and Legends,* Phaidon Press, 1970.

COLE, ANN KILBORN, *The Golden Guide to American Antiques,* Golden Press, 1968.

COLLARD, ELIZABETH, *Nineteenth Century Pottery and Porcelain In Canada,* Mcgill University Press, Montreal, 1967.

COMSTOCK, HELEN, *The Looking Glass In America,* The Viking Press, New York.

CONNELLY, C., "Stalking the Back Roads In Search of Rare Books," *Publishers Weekly,* February 22, 1971, pp. 133.

COOPER, DOUGLAS, *Picasso Theatre,* Herbert Jenkins, London.

CORDIER, HENRY K, "**The Appraisal of Fine Arts and Residential Contents**," *Valutape Audio-Library Series,* American Society of Appraisers, Washington D.C., January 1, 1973.

CORDIER, HENRY K, "**Valuation Problems and the Client**," *Valutape Audio-Library Series,* American Society of Appraisers, Washington D.C., January 1, 1973.

COX, WARREN E., "**Marks-An Assistance In Dating Chinese Objects of Art**," *The A. S. A. Valuation Manual,* American Society of Appraisers, 1962, pp. 158.

CRIPPS, WILFRED JOSEPH, *Old English Plate,* Paul Hamlyn, London.

CUSHION, J. P., *English China Collecting for Amateurs,* Frederick Muller, 1967.

DAMASE, JACQUES, *Carriages,* Weidenfeld and Nicolson, London.

DANCE, PETER S., *Rare Shells,* Faber and Faber, London.

DAULTE, FRANCOIS, *French Watercolors of the Nineteenth Century,*

DAVIES, DEREK C., *Coloured Glass,* Herbert Jenkins, London.

DAVIES, MARTIN, *The National Gallery, London, Volume III,* Brussels, 1970.

DAVIS, DEREK C., KEITH MIDDLEMAS, "**Coloured Glass**," *Coloured Glass,* The Cressent Press, Barrie and Rocklift.

DAVIS, DEREK C. AND KEITH MIDDLEMAS, *Coloured Glass,* Herbert Jenkins, London.

DAWNES, KERRY, *Hawksmoor,* Thames and Hudson.

DAWSONS OF PALL MALL, *Art Prices Current,* Wm. Dawson and Sons Ltd, Cannon Hse Kent, Eng.

DE JONGE, C. H., *Delft Ceramics,* Pall Mall Rress.

▲ Fine Arts

DEEBLES, V. A., "How to Appraise Coins for an Estate," *Numismatist*, March, 1957, pp. 271-273.

DELIEB, ERIC, *Silver Boxes*, The Cresset Press, Barrie and Rocklift.

DELIEB, ERIC, *Silver Boxes*, The Cresset Press, Barrie and Rocklift.

DEMICK, A., "Value of Art," *Arts*, September, 1972, pp. 25.

DOBIE, J. FRANK, TOM LEA, *A Portfolio of Six Paintings*, University of Texas Press, 1968.

DOCKSTADER, FREDERICK J., *South America Indian Art*, Studio Vista, London.

DODD, EDWARD, *Polynesian Art*, R. Hale and Co, London.

DONNELLY, P. J., *Blanc De Chine*, Faber and Faber Ltd, 1969.

DOWLE, ANTHONY, PATRICK FINN, *Coins*, John Gifford Ltd, London.

DUSSLER, LUITPOLD, *Raphel: a Critical Catalogue of His Pictures, Wall-Paintings and Tapestries*, Phaidon.

EDEY, WINTHROP, *French Clocks*, Studio Vista.

ENGGASS, ROBERT, *The Painting of Baciccio*, Pennsylvania State University Press.

EPPINK, NORMAN, *The History and Techniques of Printmaking*, University of Oklahoma Press.

ERNANDEZ, JUSTINO, *Guide to Mexican Art*, The University of Chicago Press, Chicago, 1968.

ETHERIDGE, KEN, *Collecting Drawings*, Bell.

ETTLINGER, L. D., *The Complete Paintings of Leonardo*, Weidenfeld & Nicolson, London.

ETTLINGER, L. D., *The Complete Paintings of Michelangelo*, Weidenfeld and Neiolson, London.

FERNIER, ROBERT, *Gustan Courbet*, Pall Mall Press, London.

FERRERO, MDRCEDES VIALE, *Rare Carpets from East and West*, Orbis Books-The Bodley Head, London.

FISHER, STANLEY W., *China Collectors Guide*, F. R. S. A, 1900.

FLIETZE, HANS, *Treasures of the Great National Galleries*, Garden City Books, 1900.

FOSTER, JOSEPH K., *Posters of Picasso*, W. H. Allen, London.

FRANSES, JACK, *European and Oriental Rugs*, John Gifford Ltd, London.

FRANZERO, CARLO MARIA, *Leonardo*, W. H. Allen.

FRASNAY, DANIEL, *The Artists World*, J. M. Dent, London.

FURST, H., "Christies Since 1942 a Discourse on Values," *Apollo*, February, 1945, pp. 35.

GELDZAHLER, HENRY, *New York & Sculpture 1940-1970*, Pall Mall Press, London.

GODDEN, A. GEOFFREY, *Minton Pottery and Porcelain of the First Period 1793 - 1950*, The Cresset Press, Barrie and Rockeiff.

GODDEN, GEOFFREY, *Masons Patent Ironstone China*, Barrie and Jenkins, London.

GODDEN, GEOFFREY, "Handbook of British Pottery and Porcelain Marks," *The Handbook of British Pottery and Porcelain Marks*, Herbert Jenkins, London.

GODDEN, GEOFFREY A., *Antique China and Glass Under F5*, Arthurtbacker.

GOLDSCHEIDER, LUDWIG, *Michelangelo Drawings*, Phaidon Press, London.

# BIBLIOGRAPHY OF APPRAISAL LITERATURE

GRATE, PONTUS, CARL NORDENFALK, "Treasures of Swedish Art," *Treasures of Swedish Are,* Kaye and Ward, London.

GROS-GALLINER, GABRIELLA, "Glass: a Guide for Collectors," *Glass: a Guide for Collectors,* Muller, 1970.

GURDIS, REYNAL AND COMPANY, *Late Georgian, the Connoisseur Period,*

GUTFELD, LUDWIG, *Jewish Art from the Bible to Chagall,* W. H. Allen, London.

HAAS, DR. ROBERT BARLETT, "All About Collecting and the Adult Learner," *Appraisal and Valuation Manual,* Corporate Press Incorporated, Washington, D. C, January, 1972, pp. 416.

HACKER ART BOOKS INC, "Mantle Fielding's Dictionary of Amer Painters, Sculptors & Engravers," Hacker Art Books Inc, New York, 1965, pp. 592.

HAEDAHE, HANS ULRICH, *Metalwork,* Weidenfeld and Nicolson, London.

HAGES, COLIN, *Renoir,* The Colour Library of Art, 1969.

HALLADE, MADELEIN, *The Gandhara Style,* Thames and Hudson, London.

HANSEN, HENRY H., "Costume and Styles," Hacker Art Books Inc., New York, 1956, pp. 160.

HARDEN, D. B., K. S. PAINTER, R. H. PINDER, *Masterpieces of Glass,*

HARRIS, ENRIQUETA, *Goya,* Phaidon Press Ltd., London.

HASTINGS, MACDONALD, *English Sporting Guns,* Ward Lock, London.

HAYDEN, ARTHUR, *Chats on Old Furniture a Practical Guide for Collectors,* F. A. Stokes Company, New York.

HAYES, JOHN, *Gainsborough As Printmaker,* A. Zwemmer, London.

HELD, JULIUS S., *Rembrandts Aristotle and Other Rembrandt Studies,* Oxford University Press, London.

HENDY, PHILLIP, *Piero Della Francesca and the Early Renaissance,* Weidenfeld and Nicolson, London.

HENRY FRANCHOISE, *Irish Art In the Romanesque Period 1020 1170 A. D,* Methuen and Company, London.

HERST JR, HERMAN, "Philately and the Appraisal of Postage Stamps," *Valutape Audio-Library,* American Society of Appraisers, Washington D.C., January 1, 1974.

HIDESLEY, C. HUGH, "The Appraisal of Fine Arts," *Valuation,* American Society of Appraisers, September, 1972, pp. 12.

HILLIER, BEVIS, *Art Deco,* Studio Vista, London.

HILLIER, BEVIS, *Pottery and Porcelain 1700-1914,* Weidenfeld and Nicolson, London.

HIRMER, MAX, PEDRO DE PALOL, *Early Medieval Art In Spain,* Thames Andhudson, London.

HOBSON, A. R. A., *The Art of the Bookbinder,*

HORNUNG, CLARENCE PEARSON, "Source Book of Antiques & Jewelry Designs Cont Over 3800 Engravings of Vict Amer Incl Jewelry Silver," G. Braziller, New York, 1968.

HOSFORD, WANDA, "Chinese Antiquities--Ivory," *Appraisal & Valuation Manual,* Corporate Press Incorporated, Washington, D.C.

HUGHES, G. BERNARD, *Antique Sheffield Plate,* Batsford, London.

HUGHES, GRAHAM, *Modern Silver Throughout the World 1880-1967,* Studio Vista.

HUNTER, FREDERICK W., *Stiegel Glass,*

INTERART PUBLISHERS INC., *International Art Market,* New York, March, 1961.

JACKSON, CHARLES J., *English Goldsmiths and Thui Marks,* Dover Publications Incorporated, New York, 1964.

JACKSON, RILLA EVELYN, *American Arts,* Rand-Mcnotty and Company, 1927.

JACOBS, FLOR GILL, *A History of Doll Houses,* Charles Scribners.

JAFFE, L. C., *The World of the Impressionists the Artists Who Painted with Delight In Being Alive,* Hammond Inc, London.

JAMES, PHILIP, ED., *Henry Moore on Sculpture,* Macdonald and Co.

JENYNS, SOAMES, "Later Chinese Porcelain—The Chaing Dynasty: 1644-1912," *Later Chinese Porcelain the Chaing Dynasty: 1644-1912,* Faber and Faber, London.

JEUDWINE, W. R., "Prices and Values," *Apollo,* December, 1955, pp. 227.

JOSEPH, MICHAEL, *The Sculpture of David Wynne,* London.

KATES, G. M., *Chinese Household Furniture,* Dover Publications, 1962.

KENT, FRANK, "Icons of the Community," *Monograph No. Three,* American Society of Appraisers, Washington D.C., January 1, 1970.

KENT, FRANK W., "Introduction to the Sections," *Icons of the Community, Monograph No. 3,* ASA, Washington, D. C., 1970, pp. 7-15.

KENT, FRANK W., "The Print," *Icons of the Community, Monograph No. 3,* ASA, Washington, D. C., 1970, pp. 39-63.

KESSLER, CHARLES S., *Max Beckmanns Triptychs,* The Belknap Press Of Harvard University Press, Cambridge, Mass., 1970.

KRESS, SAMUEL H., *Renaissance Medals,* Phaison Press, London.

KUZEL, VLADISLAV, "A Book of Jewelry," Wingate, London, 1963.

L ORANGE, H. P., P. J. NODHAGEN, *Mosaics from Antiquity to the Early Middle Ages,* Methuen and Co. Ltd, London.

LACY, A. D., *Greek Pottery In the Bronze Age,*

LAING, LLOYD R., *Coins and Archaelogy,* Weidenfeld and Nicolson, London.

LAMARRE, JOHN H., "Fine Arts Appraisals," *Technical Valuation,* A. S. A., October, 1954, pp. 41.

LARKMAN, BRIAN, *Metalwork Designs of Today,* John Murray, London.

LARSON, KNUT, *Rugs and Carpets of the Orient,* Bedford, London.

LAUGHTON, BRUCE, *Philip Wilson Steer,* Clarendon Press/Oxford University Press, London.

LAVIN, IRVING, *Bernini and the Crossing of St. Peter,* New York University Press, 1969.

LEE, RUTH WEBB, *Nineteenth Century Art Glass,*

LEIRIES, MICHEL AND JACQUELINE DELANGE, *African Art,* Thames and Hudson, 1968.

LEROI-GOURHAN, ANDRE, *Treasures of Prehistoric Art,* Hacker Art Books Incorporated, New York, 1967.

LEVY, M., "Attributions and Valuations," *Studio,* January, 1962, pp. 20.

LEYMAIRE, J., H. READ, W. S. LIEBERMAN, *Henri Matisse,* University of California Press.

LISTER, RAYMOND, *College Stamps of Oxford and Cambridge,* The Colden Press.

LITTLE, W. L., *Staffordshire Blue: Underglaze Blue Transfer Printed Earthenware,* Batsford, London.

# BIBLIOGRAPHY OF APPRAISAL LITERATURE

LOBER, G. J., "Art As a Financial Investment," *Art Digest,* October 1, 1939, pp. 33.

LOPEZ, REY JOSE, *Velazquez Work and World,* Faber and Faber.

LUCAS, E. LOUISE, *Art Books a Basic Bibliography of the Fine Arts,* Hacker Art Books Incorporated, Greenwich, 1968.

LUPPINO, RECCO, **Currier and Ives Prints and Early American Pewter,"** *A. S. A. Valuation Manual,* A. S. A., 1959, pp. 199.

LUPPINO, RECCO, "Early Colt Firearms and The Pennsylvania Long Rifle," *A. S. A. Valuation Manual,* A. S. A., 1960, pp. 125.

MAORTGAT, ANTON, *The Art of Ancient Mesopotamia,*

MACHLUP, F., "The Book Value of Monetary Gold," *Banca Nazionale Del Lavoro Quarterly Review, No. Xcix,* December, 1971.

MACKET-BEESON, A. E. J., *Chessmen,* Weidenfeld and Nicolson, London.

MANHEIM, FRANK, *A Garland of Weights,* The Bodley Head, London.

MARCUSE, SYBIL, *Musical Instruments: a Comprehensive Dictionary,* County Life, London.

MARTIN, J. R., *Rubens: the Antwerp Altarpieces,* Thames and Hudson, 1969.

MARTINDALE, ANDREW, *The Complete Paintings of Giotto,* Weidenfeld and Nicolson, London.

MASSIN, *Letter and Image,* Hacker Art Books Incorporated, London, 1970.

MAYER, CHRISTA C., *Masterpieces of Western Textiles from the Art Institute of Chicago,* Art Institute of Chicage Publications Department, 1969.

MCCAWLEY, PATRICIA K., *Antique Glass Paperweights,* Spink and Son, London.

MCCLELLAN, ELISABETH, *History of American Costume,* Hacker Art Books Incorporated, New York, 1969.

MCINNES, N., "Striking it Rich In Gold Coins the Biggest Pay-Off Goes To the Mint," *Barrons,* May 31, 1971, pp. 9-13.

MEISSNER, KURT, *Japanese Woodblack Prints In Miniature: the Genre Of Surimono,* Kegan Paul, 1970.

MELOT, MICHEL, *The Graphic Works of the Impressionists Manet, Pissarro, Renoir, Cezanne, Sisley,* Thames and Hudson, London.

MIDDLEMAS, KEITH, ERIC DELIEB, *Silver Boxes,* Herbert Jenkins, London.

MITTEN, DAVID GORDON, SUZANNAH F. DOESINGER, *Master Bronzes from the Classical World,* Graphic Society, London.

MOORE, HANNAH HUDSON, "The Collector's Manual," Tudor Publishing Company, New York. 1935.

MOORE, N. HUDSON, *Old Glass-European and American,* B.

MOORE, N. HUDSON, *The Old China Book.*

MORTON, PHILIP, *Contemporary Jewelry a Studio Handbook,* Holt, Rinehart and Winston, New York, 1970.

MOSORIAK, *The Curious History of Music Boxes.*

MULLER, PRISICILLA E., *Jewels In Spain 1500-1800,* The Hispanic Society of America, New York.

MURRAY, JOHN, *Old English Plate,* W. J. Cripps.

NARKISS, BEZALEL, *Hebrew Illuminated Manuscripts,* Hacker Art Books Incorporated, Jerusalem, 1969.

NEGUS, ARTHUR, MAX ROBERTSON, *Going for a Song English Furniture,* B. B. C. Publications, London.

NEUMANN, JAROMIR, *The Picture Gallery of Prague Castle*, London.

NIKI, TAMON, *Fifty Painters of Japan*, The Japan Fine Arts Dealers Association, 1966.

O'DONNELL, GEORGENE, *Miniaturia*, Hobbies-Lightner Publishing Company.

OMAN, CHARLES, *Caroline Silver 1625-1688*, Faber and Faber, 1971.

OMAN, CHARLES, *English Domestic Silver*, Adam, Charles Black, London.

OMAN, CHARLES, *The Golden Age of Hispanic Silver 1440 - 1665*, Her Majestys Stationery Office, London.

OTTO, ALEXANDER, *Illum Ms In Bodleian Liby Oxford German Dutch Flemish French & Spanish Schools*, Clarendon Press, Oxford Univ. Press.

OVERDEN, DENNIS, *African Art - the Colour Library of Art*, Paul Hamlyn, 1968.

OWEN, PAT, *The Story of Royal Copenhagen Plates*, Viking Import House.

PALMER, BROOKS, *A Treasury of American Clocks*, Collier Macmillan.

PASSEION, ROGER, *French Prints of the Twentieth Century*, Pall Mall Press.

PENROSE, ROLAND, *The Sculpture of Picasso*, The Museum of Modern Art.

PIANKOFF, ALEXANDER, *The Pyramid of Unas*, Oxford University Press, London, 1969.

PIPER, JOHN, *Stained Glass Art or Anti-Art*, Studio Vista, London.

PIPER, JOHN, *Stained Glass Art or Anti-Art*, Studio Vista, 1968.

POPE-HENNESSY, JOHN, *Paolo Uccello*, Phaidon, London.

PRAZ, MARIO, "*Mnemosyne, the Parallel Bet Lit and Visual Arts*, Oxford University Press.

PRIEST, ALAN, *The Sculpture of Joseph Coletti*, Collier-Macmillan.

PUBLISHERS WEEKLY, "Bazaar Bookshop In an Empty Nest Community," *Publishers Weekly*, January 25, 1971, pp. 246-248.

RADCLIFFE, ANTHONY, *European Bronze Statuettes*, 1966.

RAUSCHENBUSCH, DR. H., *International Directory of Arts*, 1958.

RAWSON, P. S., *The Indian Sword*, The Arms and Armour Series, 1968.

READ, SIR HERBERT, JEAN CASSOU, JOHN SMITH, *Jan Le Witt*, Routledge And Kegan Paul.

REED, STANLEY, *Oriental Rugs and Carpets*, Weidenfeld and Nicolson, London.

REITLINGER, G. R., "Economics of Taste, the Rise and Fall of Objects D' Art Prices Since 1750," Apollo, December, 1963, pp. 528.

RICHTER, G. M. A., *Korai Archaic Greek Maidens a Study In the Development of the Kore Type In Greek Sculpture*, Phaidon, London, January, 1969.

RICHTER, GISELA, *A Handbook of Greek Art*, Phaidon Press Ltd., London.

RIDGWAY, MAURICE H., *Chester Goldsmiths from Early Time to 1726*, John Sherratt and Sone Ltd., Cheshire.

RIEFSTAHL, ELIZABETH, *Ancient Egyptian Glass and Glazes In the Brooklyn Museum*, Brooklyn Museum, New Hork.

ROBERTSON, GILES, *Giovanni Bellini*, Oxford University Press, London.

ROSEMARY, FREEMAN, *English Emblem Books*, Chatto and Windus, London.

ROSENBERG, JAKOB, *On Quality In Art*, Phaidon.

ROTH, H. LING, *Oriental Silverwork: Malay and Chinese*, Oxford University Press, 1966.

# BIBLIOGRAPHY OF APPRAISAL LITERATURE

ROTHE, EDITH, *Mediaeval Book Illumination In Europe*, Thames and Hudson, London.

SABBADINI, ALEX, "Estate Appraiser: Fine Art, Personal Property; Important Role In the Community," *Valutape Audio-Library Series*, American Society of Appraisers, Washington D.C., January 1, 1973.

SANDON, HENRY, *British Pottery and Procelain*, John Gifford Ltd, London.

SATIE, JEAN PAUL, *Essays In Aesthetics*, Peter Owen, 1964.

SAVAGE, G., "Art for Investment," *Studio*, 1961, pp. 30.

SCHMIED, WIELAND, *Alfred Kubin*, Pall Mall Press, London.

SCHURMANN, ULRICH, *Central Asian Rugs*, London.

SEABY, H. A., *Greek Coins and Their Values*, B. A. Seaby Ltd, London.

SHAW, G. B., "Comments on Prices for Works of Art," *Art News*, 1929, pp. 23.

SILVERMAN, BENJAMIN, "Considerations of Authenticity," *Technical Valuation*, February, 1955, pp. 57.

SKELLEY, LELOISE DAVIS, *Modern Fine Glass*,

SMYTH, W. A., "Putting Values on Fine Arts," *Technical Valuation*, October, 1953, pp. 35.

SNOWMAN, A. KENNETH, *Eighteenth Century Gold Boxes of Europe*, Faber and Faber Ltd, London.

SOTHEBY, *Sotheby's Annual Review*, Sotheby, London, 1961.

STAFF OF THE FRICK COLLECTION, *The Frick Collection, the Painting*, Princeton University, USA.

STAZZI, FRANCESCO, *Italian Porcelain*, Weidenfeld and Nicolson.

STEINGRABER, ERICH, *Royal Treasures*, Weidenfeld and Nicolson, London.

STERN, HENRI, *L'Art Byzantin*, Presses Universitaires De France.

STRONG, D. E., *Greek and Roman Gold and Silver Plate*, Methuen and Company, London.

SURTEES, VIRGINIA, *The Paintings and Drawings of Dante Gabriel Rossetti*, Oxford University Press.

SUTHERLAND, C. H. V., *Gold*, Hacker Art Books Incorporated, London, 1960.

SYBILLE, HAYNES, *Etruscan Bronze Utensil*, The British Museum, 1965.

THORNTON, PETER, *Baroque and Rococo Silks*, Faber and Faber, London.

TREWICK, HENRY, *The Craft and Design of Monumental Brass*, Humanities Press, London.

UNTERKIRCHER, FIANZ, *European Illuminated Manuscripts*, Thames and Hudson, London.

VAN BRAAN, FRED A., *World Collector's Annuary*, Delft Bower Nethlnds, 1946.

WARDLE, PATRICIA, *Victorian Lace*, Herbert Jenkins, London.

WARK, ROBERT R.,, *Early Brit Drawings In Huntington Coll 1600-1750*, Huntington Library, 1969.

WARREN, ISABELLA C., "Experiences on the Distaff Side of A.S.A.," *Valutape Audio-Library Series*, American Society of Appraisers, Washington, D.C., January 1, 1973.

WATERHOUSE, ELLIS, *Gainsborough*, Paul Hamlyn, London.

WATERHOUSE, ELLIS, *Italian Baroque Painting*, Phaidon Press Ltd., London.

WATSON, F., "Price of Art," *Magazine of Art*, November, 1943, pp. 605.

▲ Fine Arts

WEBSTER, T. B. L., *Hellenistic Art,* Art of the World Series, Methuen, 1966.

WERNER, ALFRED, *Degas Pastels,* Barrie and Rockliff, London.

WHINNEY, MARGARET, *Early Flemish Painting,* Faber and Faber, 1968.

WHITE, JAMES, *The National Gallery of Ireland,* Thames and Hudson, London.

WILKINSON, F., *Flintlock Pistols,* Arms and Armour Press, London.

WILKINSON, FREDERICK, *Edged Weapon,* Guiness Superlatives, London.

WILKINSON, O. N., *Old Glass,* Ernest Benn Ltd, London.

WILLS, GEOFFREY, *Silver,* John Gifford Lts, London.

WILLS, GEOFFREY, *Silver for Pleasure and Investment, a Guide to Eighteenth-Century English Silver,* John Gifford, 1969.

WILLS, GEOFFREY, *The Pottery of Old England,*

WINNING, HASSO VON, *Precolumbian Art of Mexico and Central America,* Thames and Hudson, London.

WITZLEBEN, ELIZABETH VON., *French Stained Glass,* Thames and Hudson, London.

WOODHOUSE, C. PLATTEN, *The Victoriana Collectors Handbook,* Bell.

*US of America. the National Gallery of Art A Twenty-Five Year Report,* National Gallery of Art, Washington, D.C.

*World Collector's Annuary,* Minerva Publishing Co., Amsterdam.

"Beauty and Other Forms of Value," *Glasgow Art Review,* No. 3, 1946, pp. 23.

"High Prices In Butterworth Auction," *Art News,* November, 1954, pp. 7.

"Lesson In Value Collection at Christies," *Art News,* January, 1957, pp. 15.

"Oppenheimer Sale with List of Prices," *Connoisseur,* September, 1936, pp. 179-181.

"Stamps Not Such a Good Business," *The Economist,* April 10, 1971, pp. 87.

"Values Then and Now Dispersal of the John Watkins Brett Collection, 1864," *Antiques,* November, 1932, pp. 167-168.

"Vanderbilt Prices," *Art News,* May 1, 1945, pp. 9.

"What Price Art Old Master Market," *Art Digest,* October 1, 1938, pp. 26.

## 18-16 Antiques

AKEHURST, RICHARD, *Antique Weapons,* John Gifford Ltd., London.

BALLO, GUIDO, R. H. BOOTHROYD, *The Critical Eye a New Approach to Art Appreciation,* Hacker Art Books Incorporated, London, 1966.

BARRIE AND ROCKLIFFE, *French Furniture and Interior Decoration of the 18th Century,*

BEAFORD, JOHN, *Collectors Prices 9-English Crystal Glass, Collectors Prices 10. Old Worcester China.*

# BIBLIOGRAPHY OF APPRAISAL LITERATURE

BLUM, SHIRLEY NEILSON, *Early Netherlandish Triptychs, a Study In Patronage*, University of California, 1969.

BLUNT, ANTHONY, *Studies In Renaissance and Baroque Art*, Phaidon, London.

BOND, HAROLD LEWIS, *An Encyclopedia of Antiques*, Tudor Publishing.

CARDUCCI, CARLO, *Italian Gold and Silver*, Oldbourne Press, 1964.

CHAMOUX, FRANCOIS, *Greek Art*, Barrie and Rockliff, 1966.

COLE, ANN KILBORN, *The Golden Guide to American Antiques*, Golden Press, 1968.

COLE, ANNE KILBORN, *Antiques*, Mccay.

COLE, ANNE KILBORN, *The Beginning Antique Collector's Handbook and Guide to 1000 Items to Collect.*

COLERIDGE, ANTHONY, *Chippendale Furniture*, Faber and Faber, London.

CONNOISSEUR, *Concise Encyclopedia of Antiques*, Hawthorn Books.

COWARD, WILLIAM, *Old American Houses---1700-1850*, Mccann.

COWIE, DONALD, *The Antiques Yearbook*, The Fanting Press, 1960.

CROOK, J. MORDAUNT, *Victorian Architecture. a Visual Anthology*, Johnson Reprint Co, London.

DE CANN, C. G. L., *Adventures In Antiques*, Buller, 1965.

DENISION, TONY, *Antiques In Britain Series,*

DOMENECH, RAFAEL, LUIS PEREZ BUENO, *Antique Spanish Furniture*, The Archive Press, New York.

DREPPARD, CARL W., *A Dictionary of American Antiques*, Doubleday, 1952.

EDEY, WINTHROP, *French Clocks*, Studio Vista.

ELLIS, C. G., *Antique Rugs from the Near East*, Bell.

FALKINER, RICHARD, *Investing In Antique Jewellery*, The Cresset Press, Barrie and Rocklift.

FLIETZE, HANS, *Treasures of the Great National Galleries*, Garden City Books, 1900.

FURST, H., "Christies Since 1942 a Discourse on Values," *Apollo*, February, 1945, pp. 35.

GLOAG, JOHN, *Short Dictionary of Furniture*, Allen and Unwin, London.

GODDEN, GEOFFREY A., *Antique China and Glass Under F5*, Arthurtbacker.

GRAND, P. M., *Art Prehistorique*, La Bibliothequedes Arts, Paris.

GROS-GALLINER, GABRIELLA, "Class: a Guide for Collectors," *Glass: a Guide For Collectors*, Muller, 1970.

HAAS, DR. ROBERT BARLETT, "All About Collecting and the Adult Learner," *Appraisal and Valuation Manual*, Corporate Press Incorporated, Washington, D. C, January, 1972, pp. 416.

HAMPTON, CHRISTOPHER, *The Etruscans and the Survival of Etruria.*

HAYDEN, ARTHUR, *Chats on Old Furniture a Practical Guide for Collectors*, F. A. Stokes Company, New York.

HAYDEN, ARTHUR, *Chats on Old Furniture a Practical Guide for Collectors*, F. A. Stokes Company, New York.

HEINZ, DORA, *Medieval Tapestries*, Methuen, London.

HENRY FRANCHOISE, *Irish Art In the Romanesque Period 1020 1170 A. D*, Methuen and Company, London.

HER MAJESTYS STATIONERY OFFICE, *English Desks and Bureaux,* Her Majesty's Stationery Office.

HIGGINS, REYNOLD, *Greek Terracottas,* Barnes and Noble, New York, 1969.

HINCKLEY, F. LEWIS, *A Directory of Antique Furniture,* Crown Publishers, New York, 1953.

HIRMER, MAX, PEDRO DE PALOL, *Early Medieval Art In Spain,* Thames And Hudson, London.

HOFFMAN, HERBERT, *Greek Gold Jewelery from Age of Alexander,* 1965.

HORNUNG, CLARENCE PEARSON, "Source Book of Antiques & Jewelry Designs Cont Over 3800 Engravings of Vict Amer Incl Jewelry Silver," G. Braziller, New York, 1968.

HOSFORD, WANDA, "Chinese Antiquities--Ivory," *Appraisal & Valuation Manual,* Corporate Press Incorporated, Washington, D. C..

HUGHES, G. BERNARD, *Antique Sheffield Plate,* Batsford, London.

HUGHES, THERLE, "Cottage Antiques," *Cottate Antiques,* Lutterworth Press.

JACKSON, RILLA EVELYN, *American Arts,* Rand-Mcnotty and Company, 1927.

JENYNS, SOAMES, "Later Chinese Porcelain--The Chaing Dynasty: 1644-1912," *Later Chinese Porlelain the Chaing Dynasty: 1644-1912,* Faber and Faber, London.

KENT, FRANK, "Icons of the Community," *Monograph No. Three,* American Society of Appraisers, Washington D.C., January 1, 1970.

KENT, FRANK W., "Antiquities," *Icons of the Community, Monograph, No. 3,* ASA, Washington, D. C., pp. 1521.

KENT, FRANK W., "Introduction to the Sections," *Icons of the Community, Monograph No. 3,* ASA, Washington, D.C., 1970, pp. 7-15.

L ORANGE, H. P., P. J. NODHAGEN, *Mosaics from Antiquity to the Early Middle Ages,* Methuen and Co. Ltd, London.

LAMARRE, JOHN H., "Fine Arts Appraisals," *Technical Valuation,* A.S.A., October, 1954, pp. 41.

LARSON, KNUT, *Rugs and Carpets of the Orient,* Bedford, London.

LINGLETON, ESTHER, *The Furniture of Our Forefathers,* Garden City, 1913.

LLOYD, WARD, *Investing In Georgian Glass,* Barrie and Jenkins, London.

LOCKWOOD, LUKE VINCENT, *Colonial Furniture In America,*

LOCSIN, LEANDRO, "Orienta Ceramics Discovered In the Philippines," *Oriental Ceramics Discovered In the Philipines,* Charles E. Tuttle Company, 1967.

MACDONALD TAYLOR, MARGARET, *English Furniture From the Middle Ages and Modern Times,* Evans Brothers Ltd., 1965.

MACKAY, JAMES, *An Introduction to Small Antiques,* Garnstone Press, 1970.

MARCUSE, SYBIL, *Musical Instruments: a Comprehensive Dictionary,* County Life, London.

MARGON, LESTER, *World Furniture Treasures,* Reinhold.

MARSH, MORITON, *The Easy Expert In Collecting and Restoring American Antiques,*

MAYER, CHRISTA C., *Masterpieces of Western Textiles from the Art Institute of Chicago,* Art Institute of Chicage Publications Department, 1969.

MCCAWLEY, PATRICIA K., *Antique Glass Paperweights,* Spink and Son, London.

## BIBLIOGRAPHY OF APPRAISAL LITERATURE

MCCLINTON, KATHERINE MORRISON, "Antiques In Miniature," *1972 July -- Conrioisseur,* Barrie and Jenkins, London.

MCCLURE, EBERLEIN, *The Practical Book of American Antiques,* Garden City, 1926.

MERCER, ERIC, *Furniture 700-1700,* Weidenfeld and Nicolson, 1969.

MEYRICK, SIR SAMMUEL RUSH, *Specimens of Ancient Furniture Drawn from Existing Authorities,* W. Pickering, London.

MIDDLEMAS, KEITH, ERIC DELIEB, *Silver Boxes,* Herbert Jenkins, London.

MOORE, N. HUDSON, *Old Glass-European and American.*

MURRAY, JOHN, *The Lure of Antiques.*

NEGUS, ARTHUR, MAX ROBERTSON, *Going for a Song English Furniture,* B. B. C. Publications, London.

NEVEROV, O., *Antique Cameos In the Hermitage Collection,* Collets, Wellington.

ORMSBEE, THOMAS H., *Early American Furniture Makers,* Archer House.

PALMER, BROOKS, *A Treasury of American Clocks,* Collier Macmillan.

PATINA PRESS, *The Antique Dealer and Collector's Guide,* Patina Press, London.

PIPER, JOHN, *Stained Glass Art or Anti-Art,* Studio Vista, 1968.

PUGIN, AUGUSTUS WELBY N., *Gothic Furniture Fifthteenth Century Style,* Ackerman and Company, London.

RAMSEY, L. G. G., "The Connoisseur: New Guide to Antiques," *The Connoisseur New Guide to Antique,* Ramsey, L. G. G., Dutton and Company.

RAMSEY, LIG. G., "Unusual Piece of Furniture by Leleu," *Connoisseur,* June, 1964, pp. 134-406.

RAWSON, P. S., *The Indian Sword,* The Arms and Armour Series, 1968.

REED, STANLEY, *Oriental Rugs and Carpets,* Weidenfeld and Nicolson, London.

RHOADES, ORILLE BOURASSA, *The World of Antique Arts,* Lightner Publishing Company.

RICE, DENNIS G., *Rockingham Pottery and Procelain,* Barrie and Jenkins, London.

ROTH, H. LINY, *Oriental Silverwork: Malay and Chinese,* Oxford University Press, 1966.

RUSH, RICHARD H., *Antiques As an Investment,* Prentice-Hall, Englewood Cliffs, 1968.

SANDON, HENRY, *British Pottery and Procelain,* John Gifford Ltd, London.

SATIE, JEAN PAUL, *Essays In Aesthetics,* Peter Owen, 1964.

SCOTT, AMORET, CHRISTOPHER SCOTT, *Antiques As an Investment,* Oldbourne, London.

SEMENZATO, CAMILLO, *La Scultura Del Seicento E Del Settecento,* Alfieri, 1967.

SINGLETON, ESTHER, *Collecting of Antiques,* Macmillan, New York.

SOTHEBY, *Sotheby's Annual Review,* Sotheby, London, 1961.

SPEARS, NATHANIEL, *The Antique Dealer,* New York City.

*SPECK, G. E., E. SUTHERLAND, English Antiques,* Wardlock, London.

STEINGRABER, ERICH, *Antique Jewelry,* F. A. Praeger, New York, 1957.

STENICO, ARTURO, *Roman and Etruscan Painting,* Viking Press, New York, 1963.

▲ Fine Arts

THOMPSON, ARTHUR P., "The Specific Appraisal of a Classic Piece of Georgian Furniture of Antique Value," *Technical Valuation*, ASA, Washington, June, 1952, pp. 26.

TOLLER, JANE, *Antique Minature Furniture In Great Britain and America*, G. Bell and Sons, London.

TRENDALL, A. D., *Greek Vases In the Felton Collection*, O. U. P. Melbourne, 1968.

VERLET, PIERRE, *French Cabinetmakers of the Eighteenth Century*, Hacker Art Books ted, New York, 1965.

WARDLE, PATRICIA, *Victorian Lace*, Herbert Jenkins, London.

WARMAN, EDWIN G., *Fifth & Sixth Antiques and Current Prices*,

WAY, R. P., "The Antique Dealer."

WILLIAMS, L., "Spirited Bidding Top-Grade Antiques Continue to Command Lofty Prices," *Barrons*, February 1, 1971, pp. 9.

WILLS, GEOFFREY, *Antique Glass*, John Gifford Ltd, London.

WINCHESTER, EDITH, *The Antiques Treasury*,

WITZLEBEN, ELIZABETH VON., *French Stained Glass*, Thames and Hudson, London.

WOLSEY, S. W., AND R. W. P. LUFF, *Furniture In England: the Age of the Joiner*, Arthur Barker, London.

WOODHOUSE, CHARLES PLATTEN, *Investment In Antiques and Art What, Where and How to Buy*, Bell, London, 1963.

# 18-17  Gems and Jewelry

AMERICAN GEM SOCIETY, "Jewelry and Jewelers: Booklet for Future Reference," American Gem Society, Los Angeles, 1939.

BANK, HERMAN, "Precious Stones and Minerals," *Precious Stones and Minerals Warne*, 1970.

BEDFORD, JOHN, *Collectors Pieces No. 17 Jade and Other Hardstone Carvings, No. 18, Chinese and Japanese Lacquer*, Cassell and Co., London.

BOARDMAN, JOHN, *Archaic Greek Gems*, Thames and Hudson, London.

BOARDMAN, JOHN, *Greek Gems and Finger Rings*, Hacker Art Books Inc. Art Books Incorporated, London, 1966.

BOARDMAN, JOHN, "Engraved Gems: the Ionides Collections," *Engraved Gems The Ionides Collection*, Thames and Hudson, London.

BOARDMAN, JOHN, "Island Gems: a Study of Greek Seals In the Geometric and Early Archaic Periods," *Island Gems a Study of Greek Seals In the Geometric and Early Archaic Periods*, Society for the Promotion of Hellenic Studies, 1963.

BOUTROSS, JAMES, "Fine Arts, Pearls," *Technical Valuation*, American Society of Appraisers, October, 1954, pp. 19.

BOUTROSS, JAMES J., "Cultured Pearls," *A. S. A. Valuation Manual*, American Society of Appraisers, 1961, pp. 219.

BRADFORD, ERNIE, *Four Centuries of European Jewelery*, Spring Books.

BRADFORD, ERNIE, *English Victorian Jewelery*, Spring Books, 1968.

# BIBLIOGRAPHY OF APPRAISAL LITERATURE

CARDUCCI, CARLO, *Italian Gold and Silver*, Oldbourne Press, 1964.

CLIFFORD, ANN, *Cut-Steel and Berlin Iron Jewellery*, Adams and Dart, Bath.

COX, WARREN E., "Diamonds and Pearls Vs Works of Art for Solid Investments," *A. S. A. Valuation Manual*, American Society of Appraisers, 1958.

CROWNINGSHIELD, ROBERT, "Gem Testing Instruments and the Progressive Appraiser," *The A. S. A. Valuation Manual*, American Society of Appraisers, pp. 203.

EVERTS, FRANK, "Appraising Jewelry for Insurance and Estate Purposes," *American Society of Appraisers Valuation Manual*, American Society of Appraisers, 1960, pp. 319.

FALKINER, RICHARD, *Investing In Antique Jewellery*, The Cresset Press, Barrie and Rocklift.

FREEMAN, SEYMOUR, "Quality Analysis of Diamonds and Its Relationship to Value," *Valutape Audio-Library Series*, American Society of Appraisers, Washington D.C., January 1, 1973.

GERE, CHARLOTTE, *Victorian Jewellery Design*, William Kimber, London.

GREGORIETTI, GUIDO, *Jewelry Through the Ages*, Hacker Art Books Incorporated, New York, 1969.

HARTMAN, JOAN M., *Chinese Jade of Five Centuries*, London.

HERZ, WALTER, "Cultured Pearl," *Technical Valuation*, A. S. A., November, 1952, pp. 10.

HIGGINS, REYNOLD, *Jewellery from Classical Lands*, The British Museeum, 1965.

HIGGINS, REYNOLD ALLEYNE, *Greek and Roman Jewellery*, Metheun, London, 1961.

HOFFMAN, HERBERT, *Greek Gold Jewellery from Age of Alexander*, 1965.

HORNUNG, CLARENCE PEARSON, "Source Book of Antiques & Jewelry Designs Cont Over 3800 Engravings of Vict Amer Incl Jewelry Silver," G. Braziller, New York, 1968.

HUGHES, GRAHAM, *Jewellery*, Studio Vista, London.

JELENSKI, CONSTANTINE, *Leonor Fini*, Hacker Art Books Incorporated, London, 1968.

KORNITZER, LOUIS, *Gem Trader*, New York, 1939.

KRANER, M. R., "Cover 70 A Very Quiet Show Has Gems of 1920s Style Design," *Publishers Weekly*, November 16, 1970, pp. 62-66.

KRAUS, EDWARD H., C. B. SLAWSON, *Gem and Gem Materials*, Mcgraw-Hill, New York, 1947.

KRESS, SAMUEL H., *Renaissance Medals*, Phaison Press, London.

KUZEL, VLADISLAV, "A Book of Jewelry," Wingate, London, 1963.

LEWIS, M. D. S., *Antique Paste Jewellery*, Faber, 1970.

MALIM, T. H., "Who Says Diamonds Are Expensive," *Iron Age*, July 23, 1970, pp. 58-59.

MCDONALD, LUCILLE S., *Jewels and Gems*, Crowell, New York, 1940.

MORTON, PHILIP, *Contemporary Jewelry a Studio Handbook*, Holt, Rinehart and Winston, New York, 1970.

MULLER, PRISICILLA E., *Jewels In Spain 1500-1800*, The Hispanic Society of America, New York.

NEVEROV, O., *Antique Cameos In the Hermitage Collection*, Collets, Wellington.

RACZ, ISTUAN, *Treasures of Medieval Finland*,

RICHTER, GISELA M. A., *Engraved Gems of the Romans, the Engraved Gemsof the Greeks, Etruscans and Romans, Part II*, Phaidon Press, 1971.

ROGERS, GRANCES, ALICE BEARD, *5000 Years of Gems and Jewelry,* Lippencott, Philadelphia, 1947.

ROLLAND, L. G., "**Diamonds Resources,**" *Financial World,* December 23, 1970, pp. 21.

SAVAGE, GEORGE, *Chinese Jade,* Cory, Adams and Mackay, 1965.

SELWYN, A., *The Retail Jewellers Handbook and Merchandise Manual for Sales Personnel,* Heywood and Company Limited, London, 1946.

SMITH, GRACE HOWARD AND EUGENE RANDOLPH SMITH, *Watch Keys As Jewelry,* Syracuse University Press, Syracuse, New York, 1967.

STEINGRABER, ERICH, *Antique Jewelry,* F. A. Praeger, New York, 1957.

STRASBURG, MAX, "**Diamond Appraisals,**" *American Society of Appraisers Valuation Manual,* 1958, pp. 83.

STRASBURG, MAX, "**Fine Arts, Diamonds,**" *American Society of Appraisers Valuation Manual,* November, 1952, pp. 8..

U. S. BUREAU OF FOREIGN AND DOMESTIC COMMERCE, *Jewelry Distribution by Retail Jewelers,* U. S. Goverment Printing Office, Washington, 1931.

WHITLOCK, HERBERT PERCY, "Jade and the Antique Use of Gems," The American Museum of Natural History, 1934.

WILLATT, N., "**Rough on Diamonds: De Beers Will Drink to the End of the U. S. Recession,**" *Barrons,* April 19, 1971, pp. 9.

WILLS, GEOFFREY, *Silver,* John Gifford Ltd., London.

"**Bear Market In Diamonds,**" *Business Week,* May 23, 1970, pp. 55.

"**How to Buy a Diamond,**" *The Readers Digest,* Readers Digest Assn, Pleasantville, N.Y., May 1, 1970.

"**Reappraisal Is Recommended As Inflation Hits Jewelry Values,**" *National Underwriter Property and Casualty Insurance,* October 9, 1970, pp. 61.

# 18-18  Furniture

AKSTON, J. J., "**Editorial to Sell or Not to Sell,**" *Art,* May, 1972, pp. 29.

BARRIE AND ROCKLIFFE, *French Furniture and Interior Decoration of the 18th Century,*

BOLENDER, LEE, LEE, *Fashions In Furnishings,* Mcgraw-Hill.

BURNS, RUTH N., "**Wedgewood--What Is It?,**" *Appraisal and Valuation Manual,* Corporate Press Incorporated, Washington, D. C, January, 1972, pp. 396.

BURR, GRACE HARDENDORFF, *Hispanic Furniture,* The Archive, New York.

CESCINSKY, HERBERT, *English Furniture from Gothic to Sherton,* Aover Publications, 1969.

CORDIER, HENRY K, "**The Appraisal of Fine Arts and Residential Contents,**" *Valutape Audio-Library Series,* American Society of Appraisers, Washington D.C., January 1, 1973.

DE BELLAIGUE, G., "**18th Century French Furniture,**" *Apollo,* January, 1963, pp. 16-23.

FACK, ALBERT, *Fine Point of Furniture,* Albert Fack.

FITZGERALD, DESMOND, *Georgian Furniture,* 1969.

GLOAG, JOHN, *Short Dictionary of Furniture,* Allen and Unwin, London.

GOTTSHALL, FRANKLIN H., *Heirloom Furniture,* Bruce Publishing Company, 1900.

GRANDJEAN, SERGE, *Empire Furniture,* Faber and Faber, London.

HAAS, DR. ROBERT BARLETT, "All About Collecting and the Adult Learner," *Appraisal and Valuation Manual,* Corporate Press Incorporated, Washington, D. C, January, 1972, pp. 416.

HOLLOWAY, E. S., *The Practical Book of American Furniture and Decoration,*

HONOUR, HUGH, *Cabinetmakers and Furniture Designers,* Hacker Art Books Incorporated, London, 1969.

JARRY, MADELEINE, *World Tapestry,* Hacker Art Books Incorporated, New York, 1969.

KATES, G. M., *Chinese Household Furniture,* Dover Publications, 1962.

LES PUBLICATIONS DE FRANCAIS, "Muebles Et Ensembles," *Styles of France,*

LUTTON, WILLIAM R., "Some Remarks on How to Identify Describe & Appraise Elusive French Regency Style of Furnishing," *Appraisal and Valuation Manual,* Washington, D. C., January, 1972.

MACDONALD TAYLOR, MARGARET, *English Furniture Form the Middle Ages and Modern Times,* Evans Brothers Ltd, 1965.

MCCLURE, EBERLEIN, *The Practical Book of American Antiques,* Garden City, 1926.

MEYRICK, SIR SAMMUEL RUSH, *Specimens of Ancient Furniture Drawn from Existing Authorities,* W. Pickering, London.

MONTGOMERY, CHARLES F., *American Furniture: the Federal Period 1788-1825 In the Henry Francis Du Pont Winterthur Museum,* Thames and Hudson, 1967.

ODOM, WILLIAM M., *Italian Furniture,* The Archive Press, New York.

PUGIN, AUGUSTUS WELBY N., *Gothic Furniture Fifteenth Century Style,* Ackerman and Company, London.

WANSCHER, OLE, *The Art of Furniture,* Allen and Unwin, 1968.

WOLDEY, S. W., R. W. P. LUFF, *Furniture In England, the Age of the Joines,* B, Arthur Baiker.

WOLSEY, S. W., AND R. W. P. LUFF, *Furniture In England: the Age of the Joiner,* Arthur Barker, London.

YOUNG, GARY, "The Appraisal of Furnishings," *The Appraisal Journal,* January, 1938, pp. 11-21.

# 18-19  Furs and Fur Garments

MCCLELLAN, ELISABETH, *History of American Costume,* Hacker Art Books Incorporated, New York, 1969.

## CHAPTER NINE

# Intangible Property

by John G. Russell, ASA, PE.

Mr. John Russell is a Senior Member of the American Society of Appraisers and a Registered Professional Engineer in the States of Wisconsin and Missouri.

Since 1963, he has been employed by The American Appraisal Company, Inc. in the Financial Valuation Division, where he has been engaged almost entirely in the valuation of business enterprise, closely held corporate stock, and intangibles of all types, as well as continuing his involvement in public utility work and technical valuation.

A native of Missouri, Mr. Russell was graduated from the University of Missouri with an M. E. degree.

▲ Intangible Property

THE American Society of Appraisers, in establishing Intangible Property as one of the seven major appraisal disciplines, has recognized the significance of this asset classification to the appraisal profession. The valuation of intangibles may be required for a variety of purposes, including estate and gift tax, federal income tax, basis for depreciation, ad valorem taxation, allocation of purchase price to establish basis for sale, purchase or merger, investment, condemnation, interruption of income or business, financing and funding, authentication, identification, liquidation.

Intangible assets associated with a business enterprise first came under intensive analysis in the latter part of the 19th and the early 20th centuries. In connection with public utility rate making, there were numerous court cases in this early period and later which laid the foundation for the recognition and evaluation of intangibles, particularly with respect to goodwill and going concern value. The courts have recognized "that there is an element of value in an assembled and established plant, doing business and earning money, over one not thus advanced", and that this element of value is "a property right" which should be considered in determining the value of the property on which the owner has a right to make a fair return. The going value thus recognized is not to be confused with goodwill, in the sense of that "element of value which inheres in the fixed and favorable consideration of customers arising from an established and well-known and well-conducted business," ... "U.S. Supreme Court in Los Angeles Gas and Elect. Corp. vs. Railroad Commission, 289 U.S. 287, 313, (1933)". The next greatest impetus to the need for appraisal of intangibles, as well as tangible assets, was created by the enactment of the 1913 Revenue Act, requiring the establishment of bases for depreciation for income tax purposes. The adoption of the 1954 Internal Revenue Code, coupled with the increasing number of business acquisitions, mergers and consolidations, which reached a peak in the late 1960's, gave rise to the increasing need for the recognition of the importance and the appraisal of intangible assets.

The American Society of Appraisers subdivides Intangible Property into equities, futue potentials and personal subjectives. In a discussion of the appraisal of intangibles and the literature relating thereto, however, it is more convenient to think of intangibles as of two general types. *The first category comprises intangible assets or rights which have an existence separate and apart from other intangibles, or from a business enterprise, and which can be identified and valued individually and separably.* In this classification are included mortgages, leaseholds, leases, securities, bonds, preferred and common stocks, license agreements, contracts, covenants, trademarks and trade names, copyrights. Such intangible property is generally evidenced by some form of legal document or written agreement which serves to identify the asset, define the legal rights and restrictions relating thereto, and describe other characteristics, all of which must be considered in their valuation. It should be noted that the first three intangibles listed above—mortgages, leaseholds, and leases—relate to real or other tangible property, while the rest are normally connected with some form of business enterprise. The distinction is important in the evaluation of appraisal literature relating to Intangible Property.

*The second category of intangibles are those which are inseparably related to the "on going" business aspect of a business enterprise, and which, perhaps unfortunately, are sometimes referred to by the collective terms "goodwill" and/or "going concern value".* They include such intangible elements as the company name and reputation, management and assemblage of personnel, sales and distribution organization, market penetration and technical know-how. These intangibles do not lend themselves to individual valuation, and are generally valued collectively in conjunction with an evaluation of the entire enterprise. Also included under this general category is the valuation of the entire business enterprise, or the valuation of all or part of the capital stock of a closely held corporation.

With respect to an operating business enterprise, intangible assets are an essential element which, together with working capital and tangible fixed assets (land, buildings, machinery and equipment) combine to produce the operating and profitable enterprise. Thus, in appraising tangible property for continued use in an operating business, it is essential to consider the property within the context of the entire enterprise. If not, the entire appraisal may be open to attack as a fractional appraisal, and the conclusions may be considered invalid.

The intangible elements of a successful business enterprise transform what might otherwise be idle, dormant, tangible property—the plants, inventory, and machinery and equipment—into an operating, viable business, capable of development, production and marketing of products or services which provide earnings sufficient for a fair return on an investment in the total business enterprise, including both tangible and intangible elements. These intangibles are the very life blood of an enterprise, and without them an idle facility may truly be a "dead plant".

The appraiser of intangibles should have intimate working knowledge of economic, financial, accounting, tax, operating and technical aspects of business in general, and of the particular industry in which the subject of the appraisal is engaged. Evaluation of intangibles or an entire enterprise requires consideration of many factors, including long range objectives, prior operating performance, the nature of the business enterprise, its financial condition, reputation and standing in the industry, economic and earnings potential, as well as the capacity, condition and efficiency of plant property and equipment. In the final analysis, prime consideration is given to future earnings potential and the translation of this future potential into present value through appropriate capitalization rates or discount factors. The valuation of intangibles requires the exercise of informed judgement and experience, and leans heavily on intuition, as well as upon technical and analytical ability.

The importance of the appraisal discipline—Intangible Property—to the multidisciplinary concept of appraising is belied by the comparative lack of appraisal literature relating to the field, except for those intangibles closely related to real property—as mortgages, leases and leaseholds. There are between 450 and 500 references included under Intangible Property, less than 5% of the total listings in this appraisal bibliography, which are concerned with intangibles or related fields. Of these, about 75% are related to real property rights, and these are divided about equally among those dealing with mortgages, leases and leaseholds; and income and investment property appraisals.

Mortgages and leases, within the context of most of the appraisal literature referenced, are classified as intangibles in the sense that they convey the *right* to use the property, rather than the property itself. There are two ways to acquire exclusive rights to use real estate—purchase or leases. A leasehold is simply an interest in property less than a fee. Leases, particularly net leases, may sometimes be regarded as financing devices and sale–leasebacks may be alternatives to fee purchase and mortgage financing.

Some of the articles discuss the appraisal of the property under mortgage or lease, rather than the intangible itself. A mortgage is the instrument given to secure some act on the part of the borrower—usually his repayment of a loan made by the mortgagor. The mortgage is generally accompanied by a bond or note, which evidences the obligation of the debtor to repay the loan which is secured by the mortgage. The intangible subject to appraisal is the right to the future stream of income required by the note, comprised of principal and interest payments. The appraisal requires consideration of the security for the loan, which may entail an appraisal of the property under mortgage, and knowledge of current mortgage financing markets, interest rates, and discounting procedures.

The appraisal of a leasehold or the evaluation of a lease requires intimate knowledge on the part of the appraiser of the current real estate and rental market, prevailing economic rentals for the type of property leased, and current interest rates and financing trends. Obviously the appraisal of such intangibles is closely related to the real property appraisal discipline.

The bibliography references include articles relating to appraising for mortgage loan purposes, articles relating to mortgages, credit, portfolio analysis; mortgage–equity capitalization methods, leases, appraisal of sale–leasebacks; investment property valuation, income property appraisal; income models and forecasting.

The remaining articles referenced, comprising approximately 25% of the total references under Intangible Property, relate to the other types of intangible property and rights discussed. The relative scarcity of the appraisal literature concerning such intangibles is apparent. The references listed include articles about financing, appraising intangibles, valuation of capital stock, security analysis, valuation of goodwill and patent valuation. Several references are more general and relate to capital investment, inflation, cost of capital, capital budgeting, money and banking, principles of investment, growth forecasting, and cash flow analysis. It will be noted that many of the articles do not specifically cover the appraisal of intangible assets but present information about specialties involved. For example, several references are included which are intended to acquaint the appraiser with the nature of patents and inventions, but which do not deal with the valuation of patents.

It is noted that many of the articles referenced have been written by attorneys, accountants, educators and financial writers. This is not unusual considering that one of the principal reasons for the valuation of intangibles is tax related—income, estate and gift tax.

The appraiser of intangibles must also keep himself informed on current tax and financial trends. Sources not listed here include reports of tax Court cases, Revenue Rulings of the Internal Revenue Service; and write-ups which may be found in the several Federal Tax Services available, including *Commerce Clearing House, Prentice-Hall, Tax Management, Inc.* and others.

# BIBLIOGRAPHY OF APPRAISAL LITERATURE

The appraiser of intangibles must be familiar with the various financial services and publications, notably *Moody's* and *Standard & Poor's* and other sources of financial information. The tax services mentioned above present periodic listings of accounting, Business law and tax articles, many of which relate to intangibles.

It is to be hoped that the body of literature relating to the appraisal of intangible property will continue to expand, and that, in time, the status of the appraisal literature on Intangible Property will match the importance of this discipline to the appraisal profession.

# Intangible Property

19-11  Loans

19-12  Mortgages and Equities

19-13  Leases

19-14  Capital Formation

19-15  Investments

NOTE: The reference units contained in this section describe, in addition to publications and articles specifically devoted to Investment appraisal process and procedure, numerous commentaries on Investment resource areas (such as Paintings, Collectibles, Jewelry). This additional reference/research material has been included because of the current interest in Personal Property as a major alternative to investment in Real Estate. Investment patterns have caused major retrenchment in the market for Stocks; Real Property investment activity has reflected re-analysis and caution. In consequence, the Personal Property investment emphasis, so dominant today, requires a complete orientation in the investor's attitudes, background information, experience and expertise.

19-16  Stocks and Bonds

19-17  Cash Flow Analysis

19-18  Securities and Registration of Securities

19-19  Good Will

19-20  Patents

19-21  Copyrights

19-22  Trademarks

## 19-11 Loans

BAKER, LLOYD, "Valuation of a Shopping Center from the Lenders Viewpoint," *Right of Way*, December, 1964, pp. 43-45.

BEETH, CHANNING C., "How to Spot a Sour Loan," *The Review*, July, 1954, pp. 21-24.

BERG, G. H., "Evaluation of a Hospital As a Long-Term Borrower," *Financial Analysts Journal*, March, 1971, pp. 23-32.

BILLINGS, VIOLA C., "Special Notes for the Lender," *The Review*, August, 1950, pp. 23-24.

BILLINGS, VIOLA C., "What the Lender Wants In an Appraisal," *The Appraisal Digest*, October, 1950, pp. 14-16.

BLISS, GEORGE L., "Appraisal Protection for Borrowers," *The Review*, September, 1948, pp. 11-12.

BLUE, JESSE B., "Give the Borrower a Break," *The Appraisal Journal*, April, 1941, pp. 173-179.

BOECKH, EVERARD HEREFORD, "New Analytic System for Measuring Loan Values," *National Real Estate Journal*, December 21, 1931, pp. 25-27.

BOWEN, DELBERT, "Relation of Financing to Market Value," *The Residential Appraiser*, December, 1961, pp. 12-16.

BOYESEN, LOUIS K., "A Bank's Real Estate Loan Department," *The National Real Estate Journal*, November 11, 1929, pp. 26-29.

BURNETT, T. S., "The Dangers of Inflationary Costs Warn Lenders to Keep Behind the Market," *The Mortgage Banker*, November 15, 1941, pp. 1, 8.

BUTTERWORTH, ROBERT M., "The Lender's Appraisal Requirements," *The Real Estate Appraiser*, May, 1964, pp. 2.

BUZZARD, GLENN W., "Trends In Appraising Farms for Loans," *Journal of the American Society of Farm Managers and Rural Appraisers*, April, 1963, pp. 75-79.

CADY, R. E., "Appraising In a Saturated Market: the Lender's Viewpoint," *The Appraisal Journal*, January, 1966, pp. 27-31.

CAMERON, C. C., "Appraising In a Time of Ample Credit," *The Appraisal Journal*, April, 1965, pp. 176-180.

CARTWRIGHT, FRANK P., "Construction Qualities Needed for Good Loans," *The National Real Estate Journal*, October 18, 1926, pp. 35-37.

CHAPMAN, FRED L., "Appraising Typical Business Properties for Loan Purposes," *The Appraisal Journal*, January, 1937, pp. 45-53.

COGHLAN, THOMAS J., "Mortgage Lending on a National Scale," *Appraisal and Valuation Manual*, American Society of Appraisers, 1960, pp. 343-352.

CRAMER, FLOYD, "A Lender's Appraisal Policy," *The Review*, March, 1952, pp. 12-15.

DODGE, JOSEPH W., "Real Estate Loans, Values, and Appraisals," *The Appraisal Journal*, April, 1940, pp. 105-110.

ELLWOOD, LEON W., "Appraisal for Mortgage Loan Purposes," *Encyclopedia of Real Estate Appraising*, Friedman, 1959, pp. 681-227.

FERGUSON, HILL, "Are One Hundred Percent Residence Loans Again Being Made," *The Appraisal Journal*, July, 1935, pp. 371-372.

FITZPATRICK, JOHN S., "Appraising Practice and Procedure In Savings and Loan Associations," *Review of the Society of Residential Appraisers,* February, 1937, pp. 3-6.

FREY, HERBERT O., "Looking at Appraisals from a Bank's Point of View," *Philadelphia Real Estate Magazine,* November, 1940, pp. 29, 66-67.

GILL, WILLIAM J., "The Appraisers Approach to Specialty Loans," *The Real Estate Appraiser,* July, 1964, pp. 26-28.

HAIGHT, JAMES R., "Some Factors Determining Future Values," *National Real Estate Journal,* January, 1940, pp. 34-37.

HALL, ARTHUR F., "Why Life Insurance Companies Favor the Mortgage Loan," *National Real Estate Journal,* October, 1934, pp. 37-38.

HALL, FRANK D., "Appraisals for Mortgage Loan Purposes," *The Appraisal Journal,* January, 1947, pp. 37-41.

HALL, FRANK D., "Appraising for Mortgage Loan Purposes," *National Real Estate Journal,* February, 1938, pp. 40-42.

HALL, HENRY C., "What Does a Loan Committee Want In an Appraisal Report," *Journal of the American Society of Farm Managers and Rural Appraisers,* October, 1947, pp. 94-97.

HANSBERGER, R. V., "Big Business In the Big Housing Market of the 70's," *The Real Estate Appraiser,* May, 1970, pp. 43-47.

HANSON, PETER, "Appraising for Earthquake Loans," *Condemnation Appraisal Procedure,* Hanson and Pollard, 1934, pp. 224-225, 467.

HARRIS, W. G., "Basic Concepts of Lenders Appraisals," *The Review,* February, 1948, pp. 12-15.

HOF, FREDERICK B., "What a Lender Looks for In a Mortgage Investment of an Appraisal," *Technical Valuation,* February, 1963, pp. 22-23.

HOLDEN, THOMAS S., "Real Estate Loans—Values and Appraisals," *Review of Residential Appraisers,* September, 1938, pp.

HOME OWNER'S LOAN CORPORATION, "Effect on Home Values of Appraisals by the Home Owner's Loan Corporation," *Federal Home Loan Bank Review,* January, 1935, pp. 119-123.

HOPKINS, CHARLES I., "Revisions In the GI Loan Program," *Residential Appraiser,* November, 1956, pp. 23-24.

HOWARD, JEROME L., "Mortgage Loan Appraisals-Use and Misuse," *The Real Estate Appraiser,* SREA, Chicago, November, 1964, pp. 14.

HOYT, HOMER, "Critical Tests of the Soundness of Current Real Estate Loans," *The Appraisal Journal,* January, 1947, pp. 73-78.

JOHNSON, RUSSELL BRUCE, PH. D., *Agricultural Loan Evaluation with Discriminant Analysis,* University of Missouri, 1971.

KAZDIN, S. EDWIN, *Limitations of Appraisal As a Guide In Lending on Income Properties,* Colloquium on Appraisal Research, Wisconsin, 1963, pp. 38-40.

KERN, JAMES M., "Why the Lender's Appraiser Should Be a Salaried Officer," *The Review,* June, 1950, pp. 11-13.

KNISKERN, PHILIP W., "Assuring Accuracy In Valuation for Federal Home Loans," *Real Estate Record and Builders Guide,* May 5, 1934, pp. 6..

KNISKERN, PHILIP W., "Making Appraisals for Loans," *National Real Estate Journal,* July 14, 1924, pp. 27-30.

KNISKERN, PHILIP W., "Mortgage Loan Appraisal Method and Procedure," *National Real Estate Journal,* July 7, 1930, pp. 46-49.

LANGUM, JOHN K., "Fiscal and Credit Aspects of the War Economy," *The Appraisal Journal,* April, 1951, pp. 202-207.

LAUNER, E. J., "Motel and Tourist Court Appraising for Loan and Investment Purposes," *Technicalities and Technical Valuation*, June, 1952, pp. 33-39.

LINDQUIST, HARRY C., "Appraising Under the Wyatt Program," *The Review*, November, 1946, pp. 7-10.

MAGA, P. J., "Construction Inspections--The Lender's Viewpoint," *The Real Estate Appraiser*, pp. 35.

MCLEAN, E. E., "Farm Real Estate and Loan Outlook," *Journal of the American Society of Farm Managers and Rural Appraisers*, October, 1948, pp. 184-191.

MEREDITY, L. DOUGLAS, "Loaning for Tomorrow," *The Appraisal Journal*, April, 1948, pp. 215-221.

MILLER, HENRY S., "Appraising for Loans," *Journal American Institute Real Estate Appraiser*, October, 1934, pp. 85-86.

MOULTON, HAROLD G., "Economic Potentials and Requirement," *The Appraisal Journal*, January, 1950, pp. 29-34.

NATIONAL ASSOCIATION OF REAL ESTATE BOARDS, "Special Committee Recommends Appraisal Basis for Building and Loan Associations," *National Real Estate Journal*, January 24, 1927, pp. 48.

NELSON, R. D., A. J. J. POLLAKOWSKI, "Effect of Financing on Value," *Appraisal Journal*, April, 1970, pp. 279-285.

NETZER, DICK, "New York City's Finances," *Conference Proceedings*, National Tax Association, Columbus, 1965, pp. 579-590.

NIELSON, HOWARD N., "The Commercial Mortgage Loan Application," *The Appraisal Journal*, April, 1950, pp. 237-242.

OPELKA, F. GREGORY, "Home Loan Appraisal Problems," *Wisconsin Colloquium on Appraisal Research, Papers and Proceedings*, 1963, pp. 33-37.

OWEN, GEORGE, "Mortgage Lending In the Agricultural Industry," *Appraisal Institute Magazine*, 1969, pp. 12-22.

PAPE, LEROY F., "Appraising for Mortgage Loan Purposes," *Practical Appraising Methods*, pp. 20-21.

PARDUE, MORRIS HAYWARD PH. D., *An Econometric Investigation of the Supply and Demand for Bank Loans 1954-1965*, Tulane University, 1971.

RATHBUN, DANIEL B., "The Veterns Home-Loan Program Success or Failure," *The Appraisal Journal*, July, 1954, pp. 400-408.

REILLY, JOHN A., "Restricted Lending Program," *The Review*, February, 1952, pp. 3-6.

RICHARD, F. DONALD, "The Importance of the Appraiser to the Lender," *The Appraisal Journal*, July, 1948, pp. 289-294.

ROBINSON, J. NATTS, *Robinsonian Building and Loan Interest Tables*, Brookline, Mass.

RUSSELL, HORACE, "Appraising for Long Term Mortgage Loans," *The Appraisal Journal*, April, 1935, pp. 264-266.

RUSSELL, HORACE, "Cautions on Lender's Appraisal of GI Security," *The Review*, September, 1946, pp. 3-4.

RUSSELL, HORACE, "Relation of Appraisal to Long Term Mortgage Loans," *Real Estate Record and Builders Guide*, December 29, 1934, pp. 6-7.

SANFORD, RALPH S., "Determining the Value of a Promotional Idea," *Appraisal and Valuation Manual*, pp. 243.

SNORGRASS, VERN G., "Evaluating a Small Going Business," *American Society of Appraisers Valuation Manual*, 1959, pp. 261.

SOCIETY OF RESIDENTIAL APPRAISERS, *Construction Loan Procedure*, The Society, July, 1938.

STUNARD, EUGENE W., "Capitalization Approach and Financing," *Real Estate Appraiser*, May, 1967, pp. 31-36.

THOMAS, HARRY F., "Report to a Loan Committee," *The Review*, February, 1946, pp. 17-21.

THOMSON, W. F., "Appraiser and Mortgage Lender," *Appraisal Institute Magazine*, Appraisal Institute of Canada, Winnipeg.

TRUE, WALLACE, "The Appraisal of Special Purpose Properties for Lending Purposes," *Valuation*, March, 1945, pp. 3-6.

TRUE, WALLACE W., "Making Life Insurance Loans on Industrial Property," *National Real Estate Journal*, December, 1939, pp. 31-33.

TUCKER, J. WALTER, JR., "Lenders Rules," *The Review*, January, 1955, pp. 19-20.

VAUGHAN, J. L. JR., "Appraising Intangibles," *The Valuation Manual*, 1955, pp. 135.

WATKINS, PHILIP L., "Appraisal Facts for Mortgage Loans," *Savings Bank Journal*, March, 1928, pp. 12-13, 76.

WILKEN, ARNOLD A., "The Effect of the GI Guaranty Loan Program," *The Appraisal Journal*, January, 1956, pp. 48-56.

WURFEL, LESTER E., "Life Insurance Service and Mortgage Loans," *National Real Estate Journal*, August 9, 1926, pp. 49-53.

## 19-12 Mortgages and Equities

AKIN, PAUL, "The Mortgage Market and FNMA," *The Appraisal Journal*, July, 1955, pp. 421-426.

ALLEN, FRED H., "Applying a Mortgage Portfolio Analysis," *Real Estate Record*, October, 1940, pp. 4, 8, 22.

AMERICAN BANKERS ASSOCIATION, *Home Mortgage Manual*, The Association, New York, 1943.

APPRAISAL DIGEST, "Institutional Presidents Panel on Mortgage Lending and Appraising Problems," *Appraisal Digest*, April, 1958, pp. 21-24.

ARDITTI, F. D., "Risk and the Required Return on Equity," *Journal of Finance*, March, 1967.

ARNOLD, ROBERT S., "Mortgage-Equity Capitalization and After-Tax Equity Yield," *The Appraisal Journal*, January, 1969, pp. 40-49.

ARNOLD, ROBERT S., "Mortgage-Equity Capitalization: Ellwood Method," *The Appraisal Journal*, April, 1966, pp. 196-202.

BABCOCK, FREDERICK M., "Determination of Mortgage Risk," *The Appraisal Journal*, October, 1952, pp. 584-591.

BABCOCK, FREDERICK M., "The Appraisal of Properties for Mortgage Insurance," *Real Estate Record and Builders Guide*, December 8, 1934, pp. 6..

BABCOCK, FREDERICK M., "The Selection of Mortgages," *The Residential Appraisers Review*, September, 1935, pp. 5-7.

BADGLEY, L. DURWARD, "Implications of the Current Residential Mortgage Pattern," *The Appraisal Journal*, July, 1948, pp. 326-329.

BADGLEY, L. DURWARD, "The Long Term Outlook for Construction Real Estate and Mortgage Investments," *The Appraisal Journal*, January, 1946, pp. 23-31.

BEMAN, ARTHUR K., "Mortgage and Real Property Rating Proceedings," *The Appraisal Journal*, October, 1946, pp. 409-414.

BODFISH, MORTON, THEOBALD, A. D, "Appraisal of Lease Equities," *Real Estate Fundamentals*, 1941, pp. 18-19.

▲ **Intangible Property**

BOTTS, RALPH R., "Rate of Return on Mortgages Purchased at a Discount," *The Appraisal Journal*, July, 1953, pp. 341-345.

BROOKE, RUSSELL J., "Chattel Mortgage List," *Technical Valuation*, pp. 11.

BROWN, FREDERICK J., "Industrial Property Appraisal for Mortgage Purposes," *Appraisal Digest*, October, 1951, pp. 17-18.

BROWN, PAT, "Mortgage Investment Evaluation-California Trust Deeds," *Technical Valuation*, October, 1956, pp. 35-39.

BRUNEAU, A. R., "Valuation of Equities," *Appraisal Institute Magazine*, Appraisal Institute of Canada, Winnipeg.

BUSSING, IRVIN, "Some Effects of the Emergency on Mortgages and Real Estate," *Real Estate Record and Builders Guide*, October 25, 1941, pp. 5-7.

BYRD, H. O., "Future Trends In Mortgage Foreclosures," *The Appraisal Journal*, October, 1944, pp. 359-362.

CAMP, EHNEY A., JR., "Mortgage Crossroads," *The Review*, June, 1954, pp. 7-10.

CHANDLER, RICHARD A., "Market Value and Equity Every Year," *Assessment Administration*, IAAO, Chicago, 1960, pp. 64-71.

CHURCH, BYRON, "Mortgage Value-Wrong Then and Wrong Now," *The Real Estate Appraiser*, March, 1963, pp. 23-25.

COES, HAROLD V., "Appraisals and Property Accounting," *National Association of Cost Accountants Bulletin*, May 1, 1932, pp. 1168-1174.

COGHLAN, THOMAS J., "Mortgage Lending on a National Scale," *Appraisal and Valuation Manual*, American Society of Appraisers, 1960, pp. 343-352.

COLLINS, G. ROWLAND, "Availability of Mortgage Money for Home Construction," *The Residential Appraiser*, October, 1956, pp. 3-9.

COPPARD CHARLES, "A Look at Low-Start Mortgages," *Valuer*, The Incorporated Society of Valuers & Auctioneers, London, November 1, 1973, pp. 381.

DALGETY, GEORGE S., "Mortgage Appraisals of Single Family Residences," *The Appraisal Journal*, July, 1952, pp. 382-387.

DASSO, DR. JEROME, "Understanding the Mortgage-Equity Capitalization Technique," *The Real Estate Appraiser*, September, 1968, pp. 27-32.

DAVIS, W. D., "The Analysis of Equity Returns," *Appraisal Institute Magazine*, 1968, pp. 27-31.

DILL, ORVAL, MELTON, JAMES O, SIGARTY, MYRON W, "Mortgage Lenders' View of Rural Land Values," *Journal; Proceedings*, Am. Soc. Farm Mgrs-Rural Appraisers, Denver, November 27, 1973, pp. 101-109.

DOERING, WARNER W., "The Use of Statistical Techniques In Equity Determinations," *Conference Proceedings*, National Tax Association, Columbus, 1964, pp. 390-398.

DOLAN, THOMAS A., "Principles of Mortgage Investments," *The Appraisal Journal*, April, 1954, pp. 193-196.

DUBOIS, AYERS J., "The Valuation and Mortgage Risk Rating Systems of the Federal Housing Administration," *Appraisal Journal*, July, 1935, pp. 324-334.

EDMONDS, E. C., "The Mortgage Market," *The Appraisal Journal*, April, 1957, pp. 215-222.

ELLWOOD, L. W., "Depreciation and Appreciation," *The Appraisal Journal*, July, 1956, pp. 351-360.

ELLWOOD, L. W., "Emphasis on Equity," *Appraisal Institute Magazine*, Appraisal Institute of Canada, Winnipeg.

ELLWOOD, L. W., "Emphasis on Equity," *The Appraisal Journal*, July, 1964, pp. 332-334.

ELLWOOD, L. W., "Estimating Prospects for Equity Yield," *Appraisal Institute Magazine*, Appraisal Institute of Canada, Winnipeg.

ELLWOOD, L. W., "Wherry Condemnation Spotlights Problem of Equity Valuation," *The Appraisal Journal*, April, 1960, pp. 165-176.

ELLWOOD, LEON W., "Appraisal for Mortgage Loan Purposes," *Encyclopedia of Real Estate Appraising*, Friedman, 1959, pp. 681-227.

ELLWOOD, LEON W., "Appraisals for the Mortgage Investor," *The Appraisal Journal*, January, 1943, pp. 23-25.

ELLWOOD, LEON W., "Influence of the Available Mortgage on Value," *The Appraisal Journal*, October, 1949, pp. 446-453.

ELLWOOD, LEON W., "More About the Appraisal of Mortgage Security," *The Real Estate Appraiser*, Society of Real Estate Appraisers, June, 1964, pp. 11.

ELLWOOD, LEON W., "Value Concepts In Appraising Mortgage Security," *The Appraisal Journal*, October, 1953, pp. 581-585.

ENTREREN, HENRY C. JR., "Appraising Apartments for Mortgage Lenders," *The Appraisal Journal*, October, 1965, pp. 531-536.

FENWICK, D. R., "After Tax Equity Yields," *Appraisal Institute Magazine*, Appraisal Institute of Canada, Winnipeg, June 1, 1973.

FISCHER, ERNEST M., "Real Estate Prices and Mortgage Financing," *The Appraisal Journal*, January, 1948, pp. 10-14.

FISCHER, ERNEST M., "Real Estate Prices and Mortgate Financing," *The Appraisal Journal*, January, 1948, pp. 10-14.

FISHER, ROBERT MOORE, "Variable Rate Mortgages," *The Appraisal Journal*, July, 1967, pp. 325-332.

FRANTZEN, HAROLD C., "Mortgage Credit and the Real Estate Market," *Appraisal Digest*, April, 1957, pp. 17-18.

FRANTZEN, HAROLD C., "The Appraiser and the Mortgage Officer," *The Appraiser Journal*, October, 1952, pp. 499-503.

FRANTZEN, HAROLD G., "Appraiser and Mortgage Officer Work Closely Together," *Appraisal*, January, 1953, pp. 9-12.

FREY, HERBERT O., "Looking at Appraisals from a Bank's Point of View," *Philadelphia Real Estate Magazine*, November, 1940, pp. 29, 66-67.

FROMKES, SAUL, OTTO FROMKES, "Total Mortgage Debt," *The Review*, May, 1955, pp. 12-14.

GALLAGHER, PAUL W., "A Mortgage Officer's Appraisal of the Appraiser," *Appraisal Digest*, October, 1960, pp. 19-22.

GELFAND, J. E., MORTGAGE, CONSTRUCTION, A, "Mortgage, Construction, and Real Estate Markets," *Federal Reserve Bulletin*, March, 1971, pp. 167.

GELFARD, J. E., "Mortgage Credit & Low Mid Income Housing Demand," *Land Economics*, May, 1970, pp. 163-170.

GIBBONS, JAMES E., "Appraising for the Mortgage," *The Residential Appraiser*, December, 1957, pp. 6-8.

GIBBONS, JAMES E., "Mortgage-Equity Capitalization and After Tax Equity Yield," *The Appraisal Journal*, January, 1969, pp. 31-49.

GILL, WILLIAM J., "Making Mortgages on Proprietary Hospitals," *The Real Estate Appraiser*, July, 1963, pp. 20-22.

GOLDEN, G. A., "The Pulse of the Mortgage Market," *The Review*, April, 1952, pp. 3-6.

GREENE, FRED T., "Competition for Mortgages," *The Review*, March, 1954, pp. 14-19.

GRUNSKY, CARL E., GRUNSKY, CARL E., JR, "Amount Of an Annuity," *Valuation, Depreciation and the Rate-Base*, New York, 1917, pp. 387.

GRUNSKY, CARL E., GRUNSKY, CARL E., JR, "Annuity Which I Will Purchase," *Valuation, Depreciation, and the Rate-Base*, pp. 340-342.

## ▲ Intangible Property

HALL, ARTHUR F., "Why Life Insurance Companies Favor the Mortgage Loan," *National Real Estate Journal*, October, 1934, pp. 37-38.

HALL, FRANK D., "Appraisals for Mortgage Loan Purposes," *The Appraisal Journal*, January, 1947, pp. 37-41.

HALL, FRANK D., "Appraising for Mortgage Loan Purposes," *National Real Estate Journal*, February, 1938, pp. 40-42.

HAYES, THOMAS J., "Mortgage Situation Affects All Property Appraisals," *Appraisal Digest*, January, 1952, pp. 20-21.

HENDERSON AND ROSS, "Real Estate Appraisal for Investors Mortgage Company," *Henderson, J. D.*, pp. 199-224.

HODGES, M. B. JR., "Ellwood Plus-Or Equity Yield After Taxes," *Real Estate Appraiser*, September, 1969, pp. 11-22.

HOF, FREDERICK B., "What a Lender Looks for In a Mortgage Investment of an Appraisal," *Technical Valuation*, February, 1963, pp. 22-23.

HOLTON, JAMES L., "Safety Factors In the Mortgage Picture," *Appraisal Digest*, July, 1950, pp. 21-22.

HOWARD, JEROME L., "Mortgage Loan Appraisals-Use and Misuse," *The Real Estate Appraiser*, SREA, Chicago, November, 1964, pp. 14.

HOYT, HOMER, *City Growth and Mortgage Risk*, Washington.

JAMIESON, J. B., "Equity Participation," *Appraisal Institute Magazine*, Appraisal Institute of Canada, Winnipeg.

JARCHOW, ALFRED, WALDSMAR WEICHBROTT, "Carpeting and Permanent Floors, Effect on Mortgage and Risk," *The Real Estate Appraiser*, September, 1968, pp. 40-47.

JOHNSON, IRVING E., *The Instant Mortgage-Equity Technique*, May, 1973.

KAZDIN, S. EDWIN, "Appraising Credit Worth for a Mortgage Loan," *National Real Estate Journal*, September, 1934, pp. 25-26.

KAZDIN, S. EDWIN, "The Appraisal and the Mortgage Banker," *The Appraisal Journal*, October, 1947, pp. 471-475.

KAZDIN, S. EDWIN, "The Valuation of Guaranteed Mortgages," *The Appraisal Journal*, January, 1937, pp. 17-22.

KLAMDN, S. B., "Economic Outlook The Outlook for Housing and Mortage Markets," *Commercial and Financial Chronicle*, May 7, 1970, pp. 17.

KNISKERN, PHILIP W., "Capitalization Rate; In Interest Tables & Their Use Etc.," *Real Estate Appraisal and Valuation*, 1933, pp. 296-490.

KNISKERN, PHILIP W., "Mortgage Loan Appraisal Method and Procedure," *National Real Estate Journal*, July 7, 1930, pp. 46-49.

KNISKERN, PHILIP W., "Value Factors That Affect Mortgage Appraisals," *National Real Estate Journal*, June 23, 1930, pp. 34-36.

KUHNLE DR. JOHN H, "The Federal National Mortgage Association Conventional Mortgage Program," *The Real Estate Appraiser*, The Society of Real Estate Appraisers, Chicago Illinois, November 1, 1973, pp. 14-19.

LAUNER, E. J., "Appraising for Mortgage Purposes," *Appraisal and Valuation Manual*, American Society of Appraisers, 1955, pp. 91-101.

MARCUS, WILLIAM J., "Current Influence of Mortgage Credit Upon Real Estate and Prices," *The Appraisal Journal*, October, 1948, pp. 487-494.

MARCUS, WILLIAM J., "What Is Happening In the Mortgage Market," *Right of Way*, April, 1958, pp. 7-11, 39.

MARTIN, WILLIAM MCCHESNEY, "Housing and Mortgage Finance," *Appraisal Digest*, July, 1957, pp. 1-3.

MARTZKE, ARTHUR J., "Is Interest on Mortgage a Factor In Appraising," *National Real Estate Journal,* February 17, 1930, pp. 54-55.

MEREDITY, L. DOUGLAS, "New Concepts for Mortgage Appraisals," *The Residential Appraiser,* August, 1960, pp. 20-24.

MERRIAM, A. O., "Types of City Mortgages Best Suited for Life Insurance Investments," *American Life Convention Proceedings 25th Annual Meeting,* 1930, pp. 212-221.

MOLLAN, WILLIAM W., "Appraisal of 608 Equities," *The Appraisal Journal,* January, 1950, pp. 72-80.

MOORE, ROBERT C., "The Dynamics of Mortgage Interest," *The Appraisal Journal,* January, 1968, pp. 25-32.

MOWLL, WILLIAM L., "An Architect Speaks for Regulation of the Mortgage Investments of Lending Institution," *Architectural Forum,* November, 1933, pp. 23-26.

NATIONAL APPRAISAL FORUM, *Joint Committee on Appraisal and Mortgage Analysis,* National Appraisal Forum, Washington, D. C, November 19, 1937.

NATIONAL ASSOCIATION OF MUTUAL SAVINGS BANKS, "Mortgage Committee," *Real Estate Record and Builders Guide,* May 19, 1934, pp. 8-9.

NEWCOMBE, DEWEY, "How to Appraise Percentage Leases," *The Appraisal Journal,* April, 1964, pp. 247-252.

NIELSON, HOWARD N., "The Commercial Mortgage Loan Application," *The Appraisal Journal,* April, 1950, pp. 237-242.

NOWELL, R. I, "The Farm Mortgage Outlook," *The Appraisal Journal,* January, 1949, pp. 53-60.

OKEEFE, PAUL T., "The Changing Mortgage Outlook," *Appraisal Digest,* January, 1955, pp. 8-11.

OLEARY, J. J., "Outlook for Mortgages on Income Properties," *Commercial And Financial Chronicle,* January 29, 1970, pp. 298.

OWEN, GEORGE, "Mortgage Lending In the Agricultural Industry," *Appraisal Institute Magazine,* 1969, pp. 12-22.

PAPE, LEROY F., "Appraising for Mortgage Loan Purposes," *Practical Appraising Methods,* pp. 20-21.

PARKINSON, THOMAS I., "Inflation Stalks the Mortgage," *The Review,* November, 1950, pp. 3-4.

QUINN, THOMAS, "The 30-Year Guaranteed Mortgage," *Appraisal Digest,* October, 1954, pp. 22-24.

RATHJE, FRANK C., "A Present Approach to Mortgage Financing," *The Appraisal Journal,* October, 1948, pp. 466-470.

REAL ESTATE RECORD, "Technique for Evaluating Mortgage Risks," *Real Estate Record,* August, 10, 1940, pp. 3-4.

RING, ALFRED A., "Equity Appraising and Financing," *The Valuation of Real Estate,* 1970, pp. 315-330.

RIVARD, L., "Second Mortgages," *Appraisal Institute Magazine,* Appraisal Institute of Canada, Winnipeg, March 1, 1971.

ROSS, THURSTON H., "Effect of Mortgage Financing on Real Estate Values," *The Appraisal Journal,* April, 1953, pp. 203-210.

ROUSE, JAMES W., "The Mortgage Man's Role In G. I. Financing," *The Appraisal Journal,* July, 1946, pp. 299-303.

RUSSELL, HORACE, "Appraisal Data and Control of Mortgage Lending Policy," *National Appraisal Forum,* 1937, pp. 14-22.

RUSSELL, HORACE, "Appraising for Long Term Mortgage Loans," *The Appraisal Journal,* April, 1935, pp. 264-266.

RUSSELL, HORACE, "Cautions on Lender's Appraisal of GI Security," *The Review,* September, 1946, pp. 3-4.

RUSSELL, HORACE, "Relation of Appraisal to Long Term Mortgage Loans," *Real Estate Record and Builders Guide*, December 29, 1934, pp. 6-7.

RUTAN, HAROLD, "The Future of Mortgage Financing," *The Appraisal Journal*, January, 1946, pp. 59-61.

SARLES, KENNETH E., "The Story of Mortgage Guarantee Insurance Corporation," *The Residential Appraiser*, December, 1961, pp. 18-19.

SCANLAN, E. L., "Streamlining the Mortgage," *The Appraisal Journal*, January, 1940, pp. 59-61.

SCHAAF, A. H., "Effect of Federal Mortgage Underwriting on Residential Construction," *The Appraisal Journal*, January, 1967, pp. 54-69.

SCHELLING, CLINTON W., "Mortgage Appraising and the Money Market," *Technical Valuation*, October, 1953, pp. 47.

SMITH, ALAN H., "Equalization of the Property Tax and Equity," *Conference Proceedings*, National Tax Association, Columbus, 1963, pp. 611.

SMITH, LEE THOMPSON, "The Menace Arising from Issue of Real Estate Mortgage Bonds Based Upon Excessive Appraisals," *Trust Companies*, July, 1925, pp. 49-51.

SULLIVAN, RICHARD B., "The Appraisal Plant and the Mortgage Industry," *The Residential Appraiser*, June, 1960, pp. 16-20.

THAYER, DONALD C., "A Mortgage Analysis," *The Appraisal Journal*, January, 1936, pp. 67-70.

THOMSON, W. F., "Appraiser and Mortgage Lender," *Appraisal Institute Magazine*, Appraisal Institute of Canada, Winnipeg.

WAGNER, PERCY E., "Appraising and Mortgage Lending," *The Appraisal Journal*, January, 1960, pp. 69-73.

WENZLICK, ROY, "Most One Hundred Percent Mortgages Are Now Safe," *Real Estate Analyst Appraisal Bulletin*, 1951, pp. 45-48.

WHITE, JOHN R., "Charges In the Equity Real Estate Market," *The Appraisal Journal*, October, 1964, pp. 576-578.

WINSTON, CAREY, "Mortgage Financing of Industrial Construction," *The Appraisal Journal*, October, 1965, pp. 609-614.

WINSTON, CAREY, "The Appraisal and Changes In Mortgage Banking," *The Appraisal Journal*, April, 1964, pp. 167-171.

YARMON, E. N., "Changing Views on Equity Investment," *Appraisal Institute Magazine*, Appraisal Institute of Canada, Winnipeg.

ZOCK, RICHARD, *Equities and Private Pensions Plans*, University of Colorado, 1971.

# 19-13 Leases

AAMODT, OTARM, T T MCCROSKY, "Sale and Leaseback," *Government Studies of Growth and Distribution of Land Values, J*, January, 1966, pp. WINTER.

ADELSBERG, HYMAN, "Sale-Leasebacks," *Valuation and Appraisal Manual*, American Society of Appraisers, Washington, 1959, pp. 37-46.

ALBRIGHT, CLAUDE D, "Government Lease Restoration Settlement-Appraisal Problems," *Valuation Magazine*, American Society of Appraisers, Washington D C, December 1, 1973, pp. 52-65.

ALLSOPP, ERNEST S., "Industrial Financing by Purchase Lease," *The Appraisal Journal*, April, 1948, pp. 156-164.

## BIBLIOGRAPHY OF APPRAISAL LITERATURE

AMERICAN INSTITUTE OF REAL ESTATE APPRAISERS, "The Appraisal of Lease Interests," *The Appraisal of Real Estate*, American Institute of Real Estate Appraisers, Chicago, 1967, pp. 339-423.

APPRAISAL JOURNAL, "No Severance Damages for Taking of Leasehold," The Appraisal Journal, January, 1951, pp. 129-130.

APPRAISAL JOURNAL, "On Percentage Leases," *The Appraisal Journal*, July, 1947, pp. 416-417.

APPRAISAL JOURNAL, "Valuation of Fee Encumbered with Leasehold," *The Appraisal Journal*, July, 1949, pp. 383-384.

ARNOLD, PHILIP N., HENRY A. BABCOCK, "Rent Reserved In Lease Above Rental Value," *The Appraisal Journal*, October, 1932, pp. 36-44.

BABCOCK, WILLIAM H., "Long-Time Lease Important Factor In Growth of Cities," *National Real Estate Journal*, March 12, 1923, pp. 49-51, 53.

BEATON, WILLIAM R., "Commercial Leasehold Appraising," *Valuation*, January, 1967, pp. 12-26.

BECKER, MANNING H, "Farm/Ranch Leases--Looking Ahead," *Journal; Proceedings*, Am. Soc. Farm Mgrs-Rural Appraisers, Denver, November 27, 1973, pp. 33-35.

BEMAN, ARTHUR K., "Long-Term Lease Appraisal a Challenging Assignment," *Appraisal Digest*, October, 1951, pp. 8-9.

BENNETT, MYRON, "Cash Leases--Equitable Sharing," *Journal; Proceedings*, Am. Soc. Farm Mgrs-Rural Appraisers, Denver, November 27, 1973, pp. 29-32.

BOARD COMMISSION RATES IN CITIES OF OVER 100,000, "Digest of Schedules on Appraisals, Sales Leases, Etc., In Cities of 100,000 Population and Over," *The National Real Estate Journal*, April 20, 1937, pp. 84-93.

BODFISH, MORTON, THEOBALD, A. D, "Appraisal of Lease Equities," *Real Estate Fundamentals*, 1941, pp. 18-19.

BONNER, JOHN T. JR., "Appraisal of Short-Term Leaseholds In Condemnation Cases," *The Appraisal Journal*, January, 1955, pp. 59-62.

BOYER, RALPH F., AND JOHN P. WILCOX, "An Economic Appraisal of Leasehold Valuation In Condemnation Proceedings," *The University of Miami Law Review*, April, 1963, pp. 245-275.

BROWN, ROBERT KEVIN, "Tax Considerations In Sale-Leaseback Transactions," *The Appraisal Journal*, October, 1969, pp. 564-568.

BRUNIE, CHARLES H., "Sale-Leaseback Rates of Return," *The Appraisal Journal*, October, 1960, pp. 501-504.

CAMPBELL, HARRY S., JR., "Percentage Leases In Today's Market," *The National Real Estate Journal*, May, 1934, pp. 30-32.

CLARK, LOUIS M., "Changing Considerations In Sales and Leaseback Transactions," *The Appraisal Journal*, May, 1965, pp. 232-242.

COATES, THOMAS, "Lease and Income Factors In the Bowling Industry," *The Appraisal Journal*, July, 1963, pp. 383-386.

COOPER, JAMES, "Lease Interest Valuations," *Appraisal and Valuation Manual*, ASA, 1960, pp. 71-76.

CUNNINGHAM, J. B., "Farm Lease," *Journal of the American Society of Farm Managers and Rural Appraisers*, October, 1952, pp. 119-120.

DALGETY, GEORGE S., "Security In Long Term Leases," *The Appraisal Journal*, July, 1940, pp. 255-259.

DALGETY, GEORGE S., "The Appraisal of Long Term Leaseholds," *The Appraisal Journal*, April, 1948, pp. 165-173.

DASSO, JEROME J., WILLIAM N. KINNARD, STEPHEN D. MESSNER, "Lender Participation Financing," *The Real Estate Appraiser*, March, 1971, pp. 13-19, 11-25, 33-40.

DEBOOS, FRANK A., "Leasehold Interests Fair Market Value," *The Appraisal Journal*, April, 1953, pp. 244-246.

DEBUTTS, CARY E., "Appraising and Leasing Retail Stores," *National Real Estate Journal,* December 22, 1930, pp. 20-22.

DUBOIS, AYERS J., "The Long-Term Lease As an Instrument of Home Finance," *The Appraisal Journal,* October, 1943, pp. 354-366.

EDMAN, J. J., "Lessor Has Right to Improvements," *The Appraisal Journal,* October, 1959, pp. 579-581.

ERBACH, GEORGE H., "Assessing Leased Equipment," *Assessors News Letter,* August, 1958, pp. 92-93., 103-105.

FEDERAL HOME LOAN BANK REVIEW, *Centralized Appraisals As a Lending Safeguard,* October, 1941, pp. 15-18.

FLANAGAN, CHARLES P., "Financing of Leasehold Estates," *The Appraisal Journal,* July, 1968, pp. 387-388.

FOGLESONG, CHARLES W., "The Computations of Yields on Sale Leaseback Transactions," *The Appraisal Journal,* January, 1964, pp. 39-49.

FREE, ROBERT L., "The Appraisal of Sandwich Leases," *The Appraisal Journal,* June, 1958, pp. 354-359.

FRIBOURG, ALBERT W., "Reappraisal and Improvement Clauses In Long-Term Leases," *Building Investment and Maintenance,* November, 1926, pp. 32-34.

FRIEDMAN, A. R., "Percentage Leases," *Skyscraper Management,* January, 1936, pp. 12-13.

GAZTAMBIDE, DR. JUAN B., "Valuation of Leasehold In Puerto Rico for Inheritance Tax Purpose," *Appraisal & Valuation Manual,* Corporate Press Inc, Wash D. C., January, 1972, pp. 232.

GIBBONS, JAMES E., "Leases and Their Effect on Value," *The Real Estate Appraiser,* August, 1970, pp. 29-33.

GINGRICH, LAVERNE, "Lease Bargaining," *Journal of the American Society of Farm Managers and Rural Appraisers,* October, 1962, pp. 36-40.

GLOS, HAROLD V., "Valuation of a Leasehold Estate Involving a Stores Arcade and Office Buildings," *Practical Appraisal Methods,* 1940, pp. 94-97, 128.

GOLDEN, GERALD A., "Absentee Lenders Appraisals," *The Review,* September, 1953, pp. 8-11.

GOWLAND, RUSSELL W., "Leasing Problems Resulting from New Technologies and Suggestions for Their Solution," *Journal of the American Society of Farm Managers and Rural Appraisers,* October, 1950, pp. 107-109.

GRACER, GENE, "New Techniques for Estimating Leaseholds," *Technical Valuation,* 1900, pp. 4.

GRONER, ORVILLE, "Real Estate Investments Under Liquidating Leases," *The Appraisal Journal,* April, 1949, pp. 252-256.

HAMBLETON, RAY W., "The Appraisal of Leased Commercial Property In Eminent Domain," *Technical Valuation,* June, 1959, pp. 35-39.

HELLER, ROGER, "Looking Ahead--Farm/Ranch Leases," *Journal; Proceedings,* Am. Soc. Farm Mgrs-Rural Appraisers, Denver, November 27, 1973, pp. 36-37.

HENDERSON, JAMES D., "The Percentage Lease," *Real Estate Appraising,* 1931, pp. 298-301.

HENDERSON, PHILIP A., "The Role of Bargaining In the Development of Leasing Arrangements," *Journal of the American Society of Farm Managers and Rural Appraisers,* April, 1962, pp. 105-112.

HITCHINGS, T. C. JR., "The Valuation of Leasehold Interests and Some Elements of Damage Thereto," *Proceedings of the Second Institute on Eminent Domain,* Dallas, 1960, pp. 61-75.

HOLBROOK, MILLARD C., "Why the Percentage Lease," *National Real Estate Journal*, April 1, 1929, pp. 48-50.

HURLBURT, VIRGIL L., "Adjusting Leases to Cope with Changing Technology," *Journal of the American Society of Farm Managers and Rural Appraisers*, April, 1957, pp. 42-53.

HYDER, K. LEE, "Actual Appraisal Reports-Valuation of Theater, Store, Office, and Recreation Building," *National Real Estate Journal*, August 31, 1931, pp. 12-20.

HYDER, K. LEE, "Fundamentals of Leasehold Valuation," *Building Investment and Maintenance*, December, 1925, pp. 37-38, 58.

HYDER, K. LEE, "Percentage Lease Rates," *The Appraisal Journal*, April, 1934, pp. 205-215.

HYDER, K. LEE, "What's Wrong with Percentage Leases," *Real Estate Record and Builders Guide,* February 16, 1935, pp. 24-26.

INTERNATIONAL ASSOCIATION OF ASSESSING OFFICERS, *Leased Equipment*, Chicago.

INTERNATIONAL ASSOCIATION OF ASSESSING OFFICERS, *The Assessment of Leased Equipment*, Institute of American Assessment Officers, Chicago, 1959.

JOHNSON, BARRY E, "Appraisal of Leasehold Interests," *Journal; Proceedings*, Am. Soc. Farm Mgrs-Rural Appraisers, Denver, November 27, 1973, pp. 38-42.

KEESLING, FRANK M., "Property Taxation of Leased and Other Limited Interests," *California Law Review*, August, 1959, pp. 470-490.

KELLEHER, PAUL E., "Leased Postal Facilties In New England," *Valuation Manual*, 1964, pp. 113.

KIZER, JOHN O., "Valuation of Leasehold Estates In Eminent Domain," *West Virginia Law Review*, February, 1965, pp. 101-115.

KNISKERN, PHILIP W., "Capitalization Rate; In Interest Tables & Their Use Etc.," *Real Estate Appraisal and Valuation*, 1933, pp. 296-490.

KOBER, CHARLES A. JR., "How to Analyze and Interpret Percentage Lease Income," *The Appraisal Journal*, April, 1958, pp. 360-364.

LARONGE, JOSEPH, "Valuation of the Fee Under a Reappraisal Lease," *Journal of the American Institute of Real Estate Appraisers*, October, 1937, pp. 331-324.

LARONGE, JOSEPH, "Valuation of the Fee Under a Reappraisal Lease," *The Appraisal Journal*, October, 1937, pp. 311-324.

LEDBETTER, HOWARD, "Valuation of Leased Equipment for Ad Valorem Tax Purposes," *Assessment Administration*, I. A. A. O, Chicago, 1963, pp. 90-93.

LEVY, MARK, "Valuation of a Leasehold," *National Real Estate Journal*, July 8, 1929, pp. 23-26.

LICK, JAMES E., "The Income Approach Applied to Motel Leasing," *The Real Estate Appraiser*, January, 1970, pp. 6-10.

LUM, Y. T., "Values Leaseholds and the Appraising of Leaseholds by the Residuals," *The Real Estate Appraiser*, February, 1963, pp. 4-11.

MANN, J. F., "Valuation of Air Lease , Condemned by Eminent Domain," *Buildings and Building Management*, February 10, 1930, pp. 63-64.

MATHENY, EDWARD T., "Leasehold Interests," *The Appraisal Journal*, July, 1959, pp. 375-385.

MCCASLIN, A. A., "Appraising the Estates In a 99-Year Lease," *National Real Estate Journal*, February, 1932, pp. 27-30.

MCCOY, CHARLES R., "Improvements on Leased Ground," *Real Estate Analyst Appraisal Bulletin*, 1953, pp. 121-124.

## ▲ Intangible Property

MCMICHAEL, STANLEY L., *Leases, Percentage, Short and Long Term,* Prentice-Hall, New York, 1947.

MCMICHAEL, STANLEY L., *Long Term Land Leaseholds,* Cleveland, Ohio, 1921.

MCMICHAEL, STANLEY L., "**Appraising Interest In Percentage Leases**," *Appraising Manual,* 1937, pp. 258-263.

MCMICHAEL, STANLEY L., "**Appraising Leasehold Estates**," *The Appraisal Journal,* October, 1947, pp. 495-503.

MCMICHAEL, STANLEY L., "**Appraising Leasehold Estates**," *The Appraisal Journal,* October, 1947, pp. 495-503.

MCMICHAEL, STANLEY L., "**Leasehold Appraisals**," *Appraising Manual,* 1937, pp. 243-257.

MCMICHAEL, STANLEY L., PAUL O KEEFE, *Leases, Percentage, and Long Term,* Prentice-Hall, Englwd Cliffs, N. J., 1959.

MERTZKE, ARTHUR J., "**Appraising a Lease Hold**," *National Real Estate Journal,* 1929, pp. 1-4.

MORROW, R. CONRAD, "**Leasee Improvements and Condemnation**," *The Appraisal Journal,* September, 1966, pp. 15-16.

MOSER, LEROY C., "**Leases**," *American Association of State Highway Officials,* Acquisition for Right of Way, Washington, D. C, 1962, pp. 371-403.

MOSER, LEROY C., "**Rights of Lessor and Lessee In Eminent Domain Cases**," *American Association of State Highway Officials,* Acquisition for Right Of Way, Washington, D.C., 1962, pp. 419-444.

MROTER, RAYMOND D., "**Aspects of Possessory Interest Valuation In California**," *The Appraisal Journal,* July, 1965, pp. 383-390.

NATIONAL INSTITUTE OF REAL ESTATE BROKERS, *Guide to Commercial Property Leasing,* Chicago.

*NATIONAL REAL ESTATE JOURNAL,* "**Valuation of Lessor's Interest In Leasehold Estate**," *National Real Estate Journal,* March 16, 1931, pp. 22-23.

OKEEFE, PAUL T., "**Valuation of Leaseholds**," *Appraisal Digest,* October, 1958, pp. 1-3.

PAYNE, SILAS O., "**Legal Aspects of Leasehold Appraisals**," *The Appraisal Journal,* October, 1965, pp. 563-566.

PEARCE, C. J., "**Percentage Leases**," *The Appraisal Journal,* April, 1935, pp. 242-247.

PEDERSON, B. E., "**Leasing of Farm Equipment**," *Journal of the American Society of Farm Managers and Rural Appraisers,* October, 1962, pp. 41-44.

PETERSON, RONALD S., "**Assessment of Leasehold Interests In Tax-Exempt Realty In California**," *California Law Review,* December, 1960, pp. 806-815.

PURNELL, CHARLES G., "**The Valuation of the Leasehold Estate**," *Proceedings of the First Institute on Eminent Domain, 1959,* Dallas, 1959, pp. 79-99.

QUIN, GEORGE ROBERT, "**Capitalization Rates for Long Term Leases**," *The Appraisal Journal,* January, 1935, pp. 144-148.

RAINEY, A. J., "**Appraisal of Leased Property Capitalization Rate**," *American Society of Appraisers,* November, 1952, pp. 31.

RAINEY, ARTHUR J., "**Appraising a Leased Property**," *Technicalities and Technical Valuation,* February, 1952, pp. 10-13.

REAL ESTATE ANALYST, THE, "**How Good an Investment Is a Leaseback?**," *Real Estate Analyst Appraisal Bulletin,* 1953, pp. 325-328.

REGISTER, J. ALVIN, "**Valuation of Lessor's Interest In Leasehold Estate Made for Purpose of Federal Estate Tax**," *Practical Appraising Methods,* 1940, pp. 1-128.

REZZOLLA, JOHN R. JR., "**Valuation of Leased Fee and Leaseholds**," *Right of Way,* April, 1960, pp. 25-30.

RICKS, R. BRUCE, "Valuation of Lessor and Lessee Interests In a Physical Asset," *The Appraisal Journal*, April, 1966, pp. 268-272.

RING, ALFRED A., "Leasehold Estates and Leased Fee Appraising," *The Valuation of Real Estate*, 1970, pp. 299-315.

ROBERTS, CHARLES A., "Depreciation Allowances to Lessess," *National Income Tax Magazine*, June, 1929, pp. 221-223.

ROE, STANLEY, "Appraising Property Under Percentage Lease," The Appraisal Journal, Vol. II.

ROE, STANLEY, "Leasehold Interests," The Appraisal Journal, October 1958.

SACKMAN, JULIUS L., "Compensation Upon the Partial Taking of a Leasehold Interest," *Proceedings of the Third Institute on Eminent Domain*, 1961.

SADESKY, WILLIAM V., "Appraising Lease Terms and Conditions," *The Appraisal Journal*, January, 1964, pp. 71-78.

SANDO, LAURENCE, "Appraisal of Leasehold Interests," *Proceedings Of The Third Institute on Eminent Domain*, 1961.

SCHMUTZ, GEORGE L., "Leasehold Valuation Graphs," *Appraising Manual*, pp. 256-257.

SCHMUTZ, GEORGE L., "Leases," *Condemnation Appraiser Handbook*, 1938, pp. 1-339.

SELL, R., "Tax and Business Considerations In Leasing Property," *Taxes*, March, 1964, pp. 159.

SHAPIRO, IRVING D., "Investment Implications of the Salelease Transaction," *The Appraisal Journal*, April, 1958, pp. 186200.

SHAPIRO, IRVING D., "The Flexibility of Long-Term Leases," *The Appraisal Journal*, April, 1957, pp. 166-181.

SHENKEL, WILLIAM M., "Net Ground Lease Analysis for Decision-Making Purposes," *Journal of Property Management*, 1903.

SILAS, O. PAYNE, "Legal Aspects of Leasehold Appraisals," *The Appraisal Journal*, October, 1965, pp. 563-566.

SKEER, DAVID, "A Lessee's Interest In Condemnation," *The Appraisal Journal*, April, 1959, pp. 166-174.

SKYSCRAPER MANAGEMENT, *Chicago's Percentage Lease Study*, April, 1937, pp. 12-13.

SLOSSON, FRANK S., "Percentage Leases," *Skyscraper Management*, February, 1937.

SMITH, W. LAURENCE, AND HERBERT B. PATT, "History of a Revaluation Lease," *The Appraisal Journal*, April, 1952, pp. 225-231.

SOLIS-COHEN, J. JR., "Appraisal of Leaseholds," *Encyclopedia of Real Estate Appraising*, 1959, pp. 465-482.

SOLIS-COHEN, J. JR., "Valuation of Leaseholds," *The Appraisal Journal*, April, 1956, pp. 266-269.

SPROULL, EDWARD I., "Standardizing Leased Equipment Values and Auditing Duplicate Reportings," *Assessment Administration*, IAAO, Chicago, 1965, pp. 55-58.

STARR, J. O., "Lease Guarantee Insurance," *Appraisal Journal*, April, 1972, pp. P. 175-187.

STARRETT, PAUL, "Demonstration Appraisal: Oil Company Bulk Plant, on Leased Ground," *Society of Industrial Realtors*, Evaluating Industrial Real Estate, 1953, pp. 29-56.

STEINER, J. JEFFERSON F., "Appraisal of Leasehold Interests," *Right of Way Conference, Selected Papers*, University of Alabama, 1957, pp. 87-99.

STREVKENS, HERBERT H., "Measuring the Leasehold Interests," *The Real Estate Appraiser*, August, 1964, pp. 2-13.

STROUSE, BENJAMIN A., "Regional Shopping Center, Tenancy, Leasing, and Financing," *Technical Valuation*, October, 1957, pp. 31-33.

THALER, D., "Built for Sale Apartments: a Threat to You," *House and Home*, September, 1970, pp. 68-73.

THEISS, WILLIAM R., "The Appraisal Docket. Effect of Option to Purchase In Lease--Evidence of Volume of Business," *The Appraisal Journal,* April, 1962, pp. 297-298.

THEISS, WILLIAM R., "The Appraisal Docket. Leasehold Interest In Wherry Project," *The Appraisal Journal,* July, 1964, pp. 435-436.

THEISS, WILLIAM R., "The Appraisal Docket. Proper Jury Instructions In Valuating Lease," *The Appraisal Journal,* January, 1964, pp. 122-123.

THORSON, IVAN A., "Is This the Right Way to Appraise Leased Properties," *Technicalities,* June, 1951, pp. 6-9.

THORSON, IVAN A., "Lease Adjustments," *The Appraisal Journal,* October, 1949, pp. 497-500.

THORSON, IVAN A., "Leasehold Percentages Which Are Paid on Gross Sales of Various Kinds of Business In California," *San Francisco Real Estate Board Yearbook,* 1936, pp. 31.

TORREY, WILLIAM W., "What Price Sale-Leasebacks," *The Appraisal Journal,* April, 1954, pp. 174-182.

TOWNSEND, T. L., "The Rights of Leasing," *Appraisal Institute Magazine,* Appraisal Institute of Canada, Winnipeg.

TULLEY, J. BENTON, "Some Problems In Connection with Shopping Center Leases," *The Appraisal Journal,* October, 1958, pp. 549-556.

WARWICK, SAMUEL C., "Effect of Lease Options on Values," *The Appraisal Journal,* April, 1967, pp. 244-248.

WARWICK, SAMUEL C., "Evaluating the Lessee's Interest," *Appraisal and Valuation Manual,* 1962, pp. 218-225.

WARWICK, SAMUEL C., "Leasehold Interest Paradox," *The Real Estate Appraiser,* April, 1966, pp. 30-33.

WEBB, JAMES A., "Methods of Appraising Leaseholds and Various Leasehold Interests," *National Real Estate Journal,* March 12, 1923, pp. 21.

WEISS, H. K., "Valuation of Land Under Long Term Leases," *Appraisal Journal,* October, 1971, pp. 520-525.

WEISS, HAROLD G., "The Negotiation of Commercial Leases," *Appraisal and Valuation Manual,* 1956, pp. 331.

WILCOX, JOHN P., "Valuation of Leasehold Interest Under Law of Eminent Domain," *The Appraisal Journal,* October, 1963, pp. 453-471.

WILLIAMSON, J. PETER, BOWER, R. S, "Lease Negotiation Using a Time-Sharing Computer," *Appraisal Institute Magazine,* March, 1967, pp. 41-49.

WILNETT, MCDONNELL, WOLCOTT, "Leasehold Problems," *Problems In Rural Real Estate Appraisal,* 1968, pp. 19.

WOLFSON, HENRY, "The Modern Percentage Lease," *The Appraisal Journal,* April, 1933, pp. 194-199.

WOLTMAN, FREDERICK, "Leasehold Securities As Investments," *The Appraisal Journal,* January, 1936, pp. 71-72.

WON, PHILIP W., "Appraisal of Residential Leasehold Interests," *The Residential Appraiser,* July, 1960, pp. 10-15.

WON, PHILIP W., "Simplifying the Leasehold Appraisal," *The Real Estate Appraiser,* June, 1963, pp. 16-22.

WON, PHILIP W., "The Different Approaches to Valuing Residential Leaseholds," *The Real Estate Appraiser,* July, 1971, pp. 23-29.

WOODRUFF, WAYNE O., "Legal Damages In the Partial Taking of a Leasehold Interest," *Proceedings of the Fourth Interest,*

YARMON, ELLIOTT N., "Net Leases," *Appraisal Institute Magazine,* Appraisal Institute of Canada, Winnipeg.

"Chain Fleets Leased or Owned," *Chain Store Age,* January, 1970, pp. 36.

"Depreciation on Leased Building," *Journal of Taxation,* January, 1971, pp. 24.

# BIBLIOGRAPHY OF APPRAISAL LITERATURE

"Offshore Oil Leases Add Fuel to Energy Vs. Environment Clash," *Industry Week,* May 10, 1971, pp. 24-25.

"Score One for the Tenants: They Win a Standard Lease for Public Housing," *House and Home,* April, 1971, pp. 26.

"The Appraisal of Lease Interests," *The Appraisal of Real Estate 5th Edition,* American Institute of Real Estate Appraisers.

"18th Ann Study of Shop Center Trends Abstracts of Late Leases Projns of Fut Goals Trends Problems," *Chain Store Age,* May, 1970.

## 19-14 Capital Formation

AKSTON, J. J., "Editorial to Sell or Not to Sell," *Art,* May, 1972, pp. 29.

ALLINGHAM, A. P., "Commodity Dollars," *The Appraisal Journal,* April, 1943, pp. 247-248.

BABCOCK, FREDERICK M., "Business Conditions Stress Importance of Appraisals," *Real Estate Record and Builders Guide,*

BANKS, W. E., "Present Value and the Close Corporation," *Taxes,* January, 1971, pp. 33-44.

BASS, BOYLSTON B., "Tight Money Again," *The Residential Appraiser,* October, 1958, pp. 3-5.

BATEMAN, R. H., "Appraising the Going Concern," *Appraisal Journal,* October, 1971.

BEATON, WALLACE, "The Measurement of Corporate Wealth," *The Technical Valuation,* American Society of Appraisers, Vol. Xv, No. 2, Washington, D. C, January, 1967, pp. 27.

BING, RALPH A, "Avoiding the Pitfalls of Equity Valuation Methods," *Commercial and Financial Chronicle,* December 16, 1965.

BRADFORD, WM. DONALD, PH. D., *Inflation, the Value of the Firm and the Cost of Capital,* The Ohio University, 1971.

BRIGHAM, EUGENE F., WESTON, J. FRED, *Managerial Finance,* Holt, Rinehart, and Winston, New York, 1966.

BRIGHAM, EUGENE F., WESTON, J. FRED, "Valuation and the Cost of Capital," *Managerial Finance,* Holt, Rinehart, and Winston, New York, 1966, pp. 275.

BRUERE, HENRY, "Financial Implications of Urban Blight," *Real Estate Record,* May 6, 1940, pp. 7.

BRYDEN, JOHN T., "Our Capital Investment Boom," *The Review,* July, 1952, pp. 3-6.

BUSINESS WEEK, "Pumping Money Into Housing," *Business Week,* September 26, 1970, pp. 66-67.

CAMERON, C. C., "Appraising In a Time of Ample Credit," *The Appraisal Journal,* April, 1965, pp. 176-180.

CLEVELAND, F. A., AND F. W. POWELL, "Railroad Promotion and Capitalization In the U. S.," *Principles of Investment,* New York, 1909, CHAPS. I, V, VI, XII, XV, VIII, XI, XVII.

CRAGIN, RAYMOND T., "Appraiser's Part Important In Figuring Assets of Companies," *Eastern Underwriter,* June 12, 1936, pp. 6.

CROCHERON, CLARENCE, *Valuations for Corporate Mergers and Reorganizations,* American Appraisal Co., Milwaukee, Wisc., 1955.

DAVID, MARTIN, "Evaluating Structural Changes In Capital Gains Taxation," *Conference Proceedings,* National Tax Association, Columbus, 1965, pp. 644-652.

## Intangible Property

DEAN, J., "Four Ways to Write Off Capital Investment Management Should Have a Wider Tax Choice," *Journal of Business*, April, 1956, pp. 79-89.

ENGINEERING NEWS-RECORD, "1.4 - Billion New Town Within a City Proposed," *Engineering News-Record*, June 4, 1970, pp. 14.

ENGLE, NATHANIEL, "Business Research In the Appraisal Field," *The Appraisal Journal*, October, 1950, pp. 425-430.

FISCHER, R. M., "Economic Background of the Capitalization Process," *The Appraisal Journal*, October, 1937, pp. 329-342.

GIBBONS, JAMES E., "Capitalization Rates and the Money Market," *Appraisal Digest*, October, 1961, pp. 22-24.

HEATH, J. JR., "Valuation Factors, Techniques In Mergers and Acquisitions," *Financial Executive*, April, 1972, pp. 34-36.

JEAN W. H., "Terminal Value or Present Value In Capital Budgeting Programs," *Journal of Finance and Quantitative Analysis*, January, 1971.

JEWETT, JOHN G., "A New Approach to Industrial Financing," *The Appraisal Journal*, April, 1947, pp. 235-236.

KASCLE, E, "Valuation of Closely Held Corporations," *Taxes (Magazine)*, July 1, 1965, pp. 454-463.

KELLY, PILSON W., "The Recovery of Capital, on the Basis of Value," *Technical Valuation*, January, 1949, pp. 3-9.

KILBORNE, R. D., "Principles of Money and Banking," *Principles of Investment*, Chapters Xviii, Xix, Xxvii, 1932.

KNISKERN, PHILIP W., "Expenses, Capital Charges, and Other Deductions," *Real Estate Appraisal and Valuation*, 1933, pp. 380-396.

KUMAR, P., "Market Power, Growth, Leverage, and the Valuation of the Firm," *Journal of Finance*,

LAFFER, ARTHUR BETZ, PH. D., *Private Short-Term Capital Flows*, Stanford Unversity, 1972.

LERNER, EUGENE M., CARLETON, WILLARD T., "Integration of Capital Budgeting," *American Economic Review*, September, 1964, pp. 683-702.

LEROHL, M. L., "Farm Capital and Farm Taxation," *Appraisal Institute Magazine*, 1967, pp. 2-15.

MARSTON, ANSON, THOMAS R. AGG, "The Intangible Values Known As Preliminary Expense and Going Value," *Engineering Valuation*, Mcgraw-Hill, New York, 1936, pp. 335.

MATHUR, G., "The Valuation of Human Capital for Manpower Planning," *Applied Economic Papers*, September, 1964.

MATTHEWS, MYRON L., "Insurance-Depreciation and Capital Replacement," *Technical Valuation*, American Society of Appraisers, November, 1952, pp. 4.

MCLEAN, J. G., "How to Evaluate New Capital Investment," *Economic Analysis*, Harvard Business Review, November, 1958, pp. 56-69.

MEAD, WALTER J., "Effect of Capital Gains Taxation on Timber Resource Allocation," *Conference Proceedings*, 1965, pp. 342-359.

MERRILL, EUGENE S., "Determination of Profit of a New Mining Enterprise As a Basis for Attracting Capital," American Society of Appraisers, 1956, pp. 169-178.

MORONEY, ROBERT E, "Most Courts Overvalue Closely Held Stocks," *Taxes (Magazine)*, March 1, 1973.

MORRISON, D. G., "Cash Flow Valuation and Yield Valuation," *Appraisal Journal*, January, 1972.

NETZER, DICK, "New York City's Finances," *Conference Proceedings*, National Tax Association, Columbus, 1965, pp. 579-590.

NORGAARD, RICHARD L., "Evaluating Intercorporate Risk, Returns, and Trends," *Journal of Financial and Quantitive Analysis,* University of Washington, September, 1971, pp. 1069-1082.

PAGE, GEORGE A. JR., "Massachusetts Real Estate Syndication Tax and Other Pitfalls," *Boston University Law Review,* 1963, pp. 491-521.

PERRY, H. B., "The Appraisal Engineer In Financing," *American Society of Appraisers Manual,* American Society of Appraisers, 1958, pp. 97.

PLANT, PETER B, DOLIN, ARMIN H, "Agency Mergers and Acquisitions," National Underwriter Co., Cincinnatti, January 1, 1969.

SCHARF, CHARLES A, "Determining the Purchase Price," pp. 43-58.

SCHARFF, MAURICE R., "Rate, Regulation and Capital Formation," *Appraisal and Valuation Manual,* 1960, pp. 147.

SHWAYDER, K, "The Capital Maintenance Rule and the Net Asset Valuation Rule," *Accounting Review,* April, 1969.

SNORGRASS, VERN G., "Evaluating a Small Going Business," *American Society of Appraisers Valuation Manual,* 1959, pp. 261.

SONNENSCHIEN, FRANK E., "Effect of Life Estimates on Capital Value," *The Appraisal Journal,* January, 1946, pp. 62-68.

STAPLETON, R. C., "Stock Valuation and Capital Budgeting Decision Rules for Risky Projects," *Journal of Finance,* March, 1971.

STUNARD, EUGENE W., "Capitalization Approach and Financing," *Real Estate Appraiser,* May, 1967, pp. 31-36.

VASS, DANIEL T., "Factors Presently Being Emphasized In Valuing Closely Held Corporations," *Journal of Taxation (Journal),* June 1, 1973.

VAUGHAN, J. L. JR., "Appraising Intangibles," *The Valuation Manual,* 1955, pp. 135.

"Expect Upswing In New Stores," *Chain Store Age,* May, 1971, pp. 30-33.

"Portfolio Analysis Stock Valuation and Capital Budgeting," *Journal of Finance,* March, 1971, pp. 95-117.

"Taxation of Income from Capital," *Journal of Business,* April, 1971, pp. 175-179.

"The Future Partnerships," *The Valuer,* The Incorporated Society of Valuers & Auctioneers, London, November 1, 1973, pp. 374-375.

"This Turnkey Public Housing Capitalizes on a Skinny, Quarter-Acre Site," *House and Home,* January, 1971, pp. 78.

"Wall Street Turns Its Eyes to Shop Centers," *American Druggist,* March 8, 1971, pp. 63.

"Statistical Criteria for Asset Valuation by Specific Price Index," *Accounting Review,* January, 1969.

## 19-15 Investments

NOTE: The reference units contained in this section describe, in addition to publications and articles specifically devoted to Investment appraisal process and procedure, numerous commentaries on Investment resource areas (such as Paintings, Collectibles, Jewelry). This additional reference/research material has been included because of the current interest in Personal Property as a major alternative to investment in Real Estate. Investment patterns have caused major retrenchment in the market for Stocks; Real Property investment activity has reflected re-analysis and caution. In consequence, the Personal Property investment emphasis, so dominant today, requires a complete orientation in the investor's attitudes, background information, experience and expertise.

▲ **Intangible Property**

ABELMANN, W. W., *Market Data Approach,* Condemnation Appraisal Seminar, 1958.

ABSUAGA, MIGUEL A., "A Practical Approach to Appraisal of Depreciable Property," *The Valuation Manual,* American Society of Appraisers, Washington, 1958, pp. 399.

ADIKES, JOHN, "Appraising the Economic Outlook," *Appraisal Digest,* October, 1953, pp. 10-11.

AHEARN, D. S., "1970s-More Rewarding Decade for Bond Investors," *Commercial and Financial Chronicle,* May 7, 1970, pp. 1453.

AIN, S. N., "How to Value Common Stocks Pensions Trust Investments, Trusts and Estates," *Trusts and Estates,* pp. 1073-1075.

AMERICAN ECONOMIC ASSOCIATION, *Reading In Price Theory,* R. D. Irwin, Chicago, 1952.

APPRAISAL JOURNAL, "$25-Million Colony House, 30-Story Apartment Building Being Erected In Fort Lee," *Appraisal Journal,* August 2, 1971.

APPRAISAL JOURNAL, "40-Million-Dollar Condominium Complex Consisting of Two 40-Story Bldgs Starts to Rise In Honolulu," *Appraisal Journal,* May 31, 1971.

ARCHER, W. G., *Paintings of the Sikhs,* Her Majesty's Stationery Office for Vic & Al Mus., London.

ARMSTRONG, ROBERT H., "The Post-War Investment Market," *The Appraisal Journal,* July, 1942, pp. 241-247.

ARNDT, ROBERT E, "Return on Investment, Earnings Growth Rates and P/E Growth Theory In Merger Planning," *Mergers and Acquisitions,* March 1, 1973, pp. 43-58.

ARSUAGA, MIGUEL A., "A Practical Approach to the Appraisal of Depreciable Property," *Appraisal and Valuation Manual,* American Society of Appraisers, Washington, D.C., 1958, pp. 399-404

ASCHER, DAVID B., "How to Sell Property for Life Annuities," *The Appraisal Journal,* January, 1953, pp. 79-82.

ASSOCIATION OF CERTIFIED AND PUBLIC ACCOUNTANTS, *Accounting for Inflation: a Study of Techniques Under Conditions of Changing Price Levels,* Gee, London, 1952.

ASTROLENK B., "The Economics of Branch Banking," *Principles of Investments,* New York, 1930.

AUCKLAND UNIVERSITY, "The Valuation of Investment Property," *Valuer,* The New Zealand Institute of Valuers, New Zealand, June 17, 1973, pp. 84.

BABCOCK, FREDERICK M., "Building Cost and Investment Estimation: Hotel," *Valuation of Real Estate,* 1932, pp. 481, 492.

BABCOCK, FREDERICK M., "Building Cost and Investment Estimation: House," *Valuation of Real Estate,* 1932, pp. 482, 495.

BABCOCK, FREDERICK M., "Building Cost Estimation Investment Exclusive of Land: Factory," *Valuation of Real Estate,* 1932, pp. 482, 494.

BABCOCK, FREDERICK M., "Building Cost Estimation: Investment Parking Lot," *Vauation of Real Estate,* 1932, pp. 481, 491.

BABCOCK, FREDERICK M., "Building Cost, Furnitute and Equipment Investment Estimation: Theater," *Valuation of Real Estate,* 1932, pp. 482, 484, 493.

BABCOCK, FREDERICK M., "Cost Estimation 1-Buildings; 2-Investment Exclusive of Land," *Valuation of Real Estate,* pp. 477-495.

BABCOCK, FREDERICK M., "Earnings Revenue Expense Theater," *Valuation of Real Estate,* 1932, pp. 247-266.

BABCOCK, FREDERICK M., "Earnings Revenue Expense: Parking Lot," *Valuation of Real Estate,* 1932, pp. 244-261.

BABCOCK, FREDERICK M., "Earnings, Revenue, Expense," *Valuation of Real Estate,* 1932, pp. 225-266.

# BIBLIOGRAPHY OF APPRAISAL LITERATURE

BABCOCK, FREDERICK M., "On the Annuity System," *Appraisal Journal,* October, 1936, pp. 437.

BABCOCK, HENRY A., "Definition of 'Appraisal' 'Valuation' 'Cost Estimation' and 'Earning Forecast'," *Appraisal Principles and Procedures,* Irwin Company, Homewood Illinois, January 1, 1968, pp. 3-11.

BACOU, ROSELINE, *The Italian Drawings,* Cassell.

BACOU, ROSELINE, "The German, Flemish and Dutch Drawings," *The German, Flemish and Dutch, Drawings,* Cassell.

BADGER, E. E., "Investment Principles and Practices," *Principles of Investment,* New York City, 1928, pp. 117.

BAILEY, E. NORMAN, "Real Estate Investment Trusts: an Appraisal," *The Appraisal Journal,* 1966, pp. 486-499.

BARNETT, DOUGLAS, BASIT GRAY, "Painting of India," Skira Inc., pp. 214.

BARO, GENE, *Claes Oldenburg Drawings and Prints,* Hacker Art Books Incorporated, New York, 1969.

BARRON'S, "More Bond Buyers: by Year-End, Says Sidney Homer, Interest Rates Will Be Lower," Barron's, September 14, 1970, pp. 3.

BASKETT, JOHN, *Constable Oil Sketches,* Barrie and Rockliff.

BATAILLE, GEORGES, *Manet,* Skira.

BATEMAN, R. H., "Appraising the Going Concern," *Appraisal Journal,* October, 1971.

BATTY, HARRY, "Capital Reinvestment Problems Created by Eminent Domain," *Right of Way,* December, 1960, pp. 35-37.

BEAN, JACOB, FELICE STUMPELE, *Drawings from New York Collections I. the Italion Renaissance II. the 17th Century In Italy,* New York Graphic Society, Greenwich, Conn.

BEASLEY, J. D., B. ASHMORE, *Greek Sculpture and Paintings,* Cambridge University Press, London.

BEATON, J. WALLACE, "Sun of Valuation Day," *Valuation,* American Society of Appraisers, September, 1972, pp. 84.

BEATON, WALLACE, "The Measurement of Corporate Wealth," *Appraisal and Valuation Manual,* Washington, D. C, January, 1972, pp. 44.

BEAUCHAMP, J. LYLE, "Appraisal Issues In Pre-Loss & Post-Loss Situations," *Papers and Proceedings,* Wisconsin Colloquium on Appraisal Research, 1963, pp. 46-53.

BENEDICT, LOUIS, "Depreciation-What it Is and How it Is Computed," *National Association of Cost Accounts Bulletin,* New York, November 15, 1930, pp. 306-314.

BENESCH, OTTO, *German Painting from Durer to Holbein,* Skira Art Books Incorporated, 1966.

BENGE, ROLAND, A., "Appraising Economic Trends," *The Review,* February, 1948, pp. 3-8.

BENTLEY, NICHOLAS, *The Victorian Scene,* Weidenfeld and Nicholson, London.

BERENSON, BERNARD, *Homeless Paintings of the Renaissance,* Thames and Hudson, London.

BERENSON, BERNARD, *Italian Pictures of the Renaissance,*

BERGES, RUTH, *Collectors Choice of Porcelain and Faience,* Thomas Yoseloff, London.

BERLAND, ABEL E., "A Proposed Equity Investment Program In a Competitive Market," *Appraisal Journal,* October, 1964, pp. 531-536.

BLAIR, CLAUDE, *European Armour Circa 1066 to Circa 1700,* Batsford, Loncon.

BLUME, E., "On the Assessment of Risk," *Journal of Finance,* March, 1971.

BOARDMAN, JOHN, *Greek Gems and Finger Rings,* Hacker Art Books Inc., London, 1966.

BOARDMAN, JOHN, "Engraved Gems: the Ionides Collection," *Engraved Gems The Ionides Collection,* Thames and Hudson, London.

BOARDMAN, JOHN, "Island Gems: a Study of Greek Seals In the Geometric and Early Archaic Periods," *Island Gems a Study of Greek Seals In the Geometricand Early Archaic Periods,* Society for the Promotion of Hellenic Studies, 1963.

BODFISH, MORTON, THEOBALD, A. D, "The Rate of Capitalization," *Real Estate Fundamentals,* 1941, pp. 16-71.

BONBRIGHT, JAMES C., "Depreciation As Deduction from Replacement Cost New," *The Valuation of Property,* 1937.

BOTARI, STEFANO, *Antonello Da Messina,* Hacker Art Books Incorporated, Greenwich, 1955.

BOUDAILLE, GEORGES, *Courbet,* Hacker Art Books Incorporated, Greenwich, 1969.

BOUQUET, A. C., *European Brasses.*

BOURNEUF, HENRI, "Techniques In Analyzing Current Investment Offerings," *The Appraisal Digest,* January, 1964, pp. 14-18.

BOWEN, DELBERT, "Relation of Financing to Market Value," *The Residential Appraiser,* December, 1961, pp. 12-16.

BOWNESS, ALAN, *Modern Sculpture,* Dulton Vista Pictureback, 1965.

BRADFORD, ERNIE, *Four Centuries of European Jewelery,* Spring Books.

BREDIUS, ABRAHAM, *The Paintings of Rembrant,* Phaidon.

BRON, EDITH DE, *The Price of Three Cezannes,* Chapman and Hall Ltd, London.

BROWN, PAT, "Mortgage Investment Evaluation-California Trust Deeds," *Technical Valuation,* October, 1956, pp. 35-39.

BROWNELL, KEITH W., *Partial Taking of Agricultural Land In Transition to Urban Use,* Condemnation Appraisal Seminar, 1958.

BROWNESS, ALAN, *Recent British Paintings,* Lund Humphrives.

BRUNNER, HERBERT, *Old Table Silver,* Faber and Faber, London.

BRYDEN, JOHN T., "Our Capital Investment Boom," *The Review,* July, 1952, pp. 3-6.

BUILDING INVESTMENT, "Building Cost Index," *Appraisal and Valuation,* 1933, pp. 303.

BURKE, JOSEPH, COLIN CADWELL, *Hogarth the Complete Engravings,* Hacker Art Books Incorporated, New York, 1969.

BURNETT, T. S., "The Dangers of Inflationary Costs Warn Lenders to Keep Behind the Market," *The Mortgage Banker,* November 15, 1941, pp. 1, 8.

BURT, O. R., R. G. CUMMINGS, "Production and Investment In Natural Resource Industries," *American Economics Review,* September, 1970, pp. 576-590.

BUTTS, WILLIAM W., "Regaining Confidence of American Investors," *The Appraisal Journal,* July, 1933, pp. 319-323.

CABANNE, PIERRE, *Rubens,* Thames and Hudson.

CAIX, PIERRE, GEORGES BOUDAILLE, "Picasso: the Blue and Rose Periods," *Picasso the &Lue and Rose Periods,* Hacker Art Books Incorporated, Breenwich, 1966.

CALATCHI, ROBERT DE, *Oriental Carpets,* Charles E. Tuttle Company, 1968.

CALVERT, GEOFFREY N., "Land and Real Estate As a Field of Investment for Pension Funds," *The Appraisal Journal,* April, 1969, pp. 257-270.

CARDUCCI, CARLO, *Italian Gold and Silver,* Oldbourne Press, 1964.

CARLE, DONALD DE, *Clocks and Their Value,* Nag Press, London.

CARMICHAEL, D. R., MAYNARD, R. M., "Auditing and Reporting for Security Valuations," *Journal of Accounting,* April, 1971, pp. 67-68.

CASE, FRED E., "Comparative Real Estate Investment Experience," *The Appraisal Journal,* June, 1960, pp. 337-344.

CHANDLER, MARVIN, "How Public Utilities Look to the Investor," *A. S. A. Valuation Manual,* American Society of Appraisers, Washington, D. C., 1955, pp. 145.

CHARLES, ROLLO, "Continental Porcelain of the 18 Century," Hacker Art Books Inc., London, 1964, pp. 198.

CHARLESTON, R. J., *English Porcelain 1745-1850,* Hacker Art Books, London, 1965.

CHARLESTON, R. J., *German Glass.*

CHARLESTON, ROBERT J., *World Ceramics,* Hacker Art Books Incorporated, London, 1968.

CHERRY, RUSSELL C., AND ALVIN B. WOOTEN, "Comparative Investment Yields Agricultural Land Vs. Selected Securities," *Journal of American Society of Farm Management and Rural Appraisers,* October, 1966, pp. 53-59.

CHRISTIANSEN W. K. S., "The Financing of Property Investments," *Valuer,* The New Zealand Institute of Valuers, New Zealand, August 1, 1973, pp. 99-109.

CLARK, KENNETH, *The Drawings of Leonardo Da Vinci In the Royal Collection.*

CLARK, SIR KENNETH, *Rembrandt and the Italian Renaissance,* Hacker Art Books Incorporated, London, 1966.

CLARK, W. C., "Appraisal of a New Construction Project," *Building Investment and Maintenance,* October, 1926, pp. 10, 32, 36, 40, 42, 46, 48, 50.

CLIFFORD, DEREK, *Collecting English Drawings,*

CLIFFORD, DEREK, *Watercolours of the Norwich School,* Cory, Adams and Mackay.

CLURMAN, DAVID, "Appraisal and Investment Factors In Public Realty Entities," *The Appraisal Journal,* July, 1963, pp. PP, 293-300.

COBLEIGH, I. U., "Office Building Shares," *Commercial and Financial Chronicle,* January 14, 1971, pp. 123.

COBLEIGH, I. U., "Views on Market Turbulence and Attractiveness of Bonds," *Commercial and Financial Chronicle,* June 4, 1970, pp. 1781.

COFFMAN, PAUL B., "Review and Forecast Business Conditions," *Technical Valuation,* June, 1958, pp. 3-5.

COLERIDGE, ANTHONY, *Chippendale Furniture,* Faber and Faber, London.

COLLARD, ELIZABETH, *Nineteenth Century Pottery and Porcelain In Canada,* Mcgill University Press, Montreal, 1967.

COOK, R. M., *Greek Painting Pottery,* Methuen, London.

COOMBS, DAVID, *Churchill His Paintings,* Hamish Hamilton.

COOPER, ARTHUR PH. D., *An Appraisal of the Forecasting Performance of the Council of Economic Advisers,* Nichols, Georgia St. University, 1971.

CORDIER, HENRY K., *The Appraisal of Fine Arts and Residential Contents,* American Society of Appraisers, January, 1972.

CORDIER, HENRY K., "Introductory Presentation and Welcome to Fine Arts Appraisers," *Appraisal and Valuation Manual,* Corporate Press Incorporated, Washington, D.C., January, 1972, pp. 386.

COTTE, SABINE, *Claude Lorrain,* Hacker Art Books Incorporated, New York, 1970.

COX, WARREN E., "The Intrinsic Value of Art," *The A. S. A. Valuation Manual*, American Society of Appraisers, 1956, pp. 179.

CRAGIN, RAYMOND T., "Appraiser's Part Important In Figuring Assets of Companies," *Eastern Underwriter*, June 12, 1936, pp. 6.

CRIPPS, WILFRED JOSEPH, *Old English Plate*, Paul Hamlyn, London.

CRIVELLATO, VALENTINE, "Tiepolo," Hacker Art Books Inc., London, 1963, pp. 98.

CROCHERON, CLARENCE, "Appraisal As a Business Tool," *Commerce and Finance*, May, 1928, pp. 1023-1024.

D.C. STORUD, "Land Values," *Town Planning Review*, April, 1966, pp. 69-70.

DAULTE, FRANCOIS, *French Watercolors of the Nineteenth Century*,

DAVIES, DEREK C., *Coloured Glass*, Herbert Jenkins, London.

DAVIS, DEREK C. AND KEITH MIDDLEMAS, *Coloured Glass*, Herbert Jenkins, London.

DAVIS, H. D., "Investing In Tourism," *Finance and Development*, March, 1967, pp. 1-8.

DE BELLAIGUE, G., "18th Century French Furniture," *Apollo*, January, 1963, pp. 16-23.

DE SALVO, J. S., "Effects of the Property Tax on Operating and Investment Decisions of Rental Property Owners," *National Tax Journal*, March, 1971, pp. 45-50.

DEAN, J., "Four Ways to Write Off Capital Investment Management Should Have a Wider Tax Choice," *Journal of Business*, April, 1956, pp. 79-89.

DELIEB, ERIC, *Investing In Silver*, Barrie and Rockcliffe, London.

DENISION, TONY, *Antiques In Britain Series*,

DERBES, MAX J. FR., "Return Requirements of the Apartment Investment," *The Real Estate Appraiser*, August, 1963, pp. 16-25.

DESALVO, J. S., "Effects of the Property Tax on Operating and Investment Decisions," *National Tax Journal*, March, 1971, pp. 45 50.

DIETZ, P. O., G. P. WILLIAMS, "Influence of Pension Fund Asset Valuations on Rate of Return," *Financial Executive*, May, 1970, pp. 32-35.

DILMORE, G., "Monetizing the Entrepreneurial Factor," *Appraisal Institute Magazine*, Appraisal Institute of Canada, Winnipeg.

DOCKSTADER, FREDERICK J., *South America Indian Art*, Studio Vista, London.

DODD, EDWARD, *Polynesian Art*, R. Hale and Co, London.

DODGSON, CAMPBELL, *Durer Engravings and Etchings*, Da Capo Press, New York, 1967.

DOLAN, THOMAS A., "Principles of Mortgage Investments," *The Appraisal Journal*, April, 1954, pp. 193-196.

DOMENECH, RAFAEL, LUIS PEREZ BUENO, *Antique Spanish Furniture*, The Archive Press, New York.

DUNCAN, KENNETH, "Equipment Obligations," *Principles of Investment*, 1924.

DUPIN, JACQUES, *Miro*, Hacker Art Books Incorporated, New York, 1962.

DYESS, WILLIAM B., AND GILMORE R. O., *Mathematics of Business and Finance, Including Rent Compound Interest and Annuity Tables*, Mcgraw-Hill, New York, 1942.

EDMAN, J. J., "Value of a Franchise Illusive Where it Can Be Cancelled at Will. Appraisal Docket," *The Appraisal Journal*, July, 1956, pp. 449.

EHLERS, HENRY W., "An Appraiser Looks at Investment Properties," *The Right of Way*, October, 1958, pp. 7-10.

ELIOT, ALEXANDER, *Three-Hundred Years of American Painting*, Hacker Art Books Incorporated, New York, 1957.

ELLWOOD, L. W., "Estimating Prospects for Equity Yield," *Appraisal Institute Magazine*, Appraisal Institute of Canada, Winnipeg.

ENGGASS, ROBERT, *The Painting of Baciccio*, Pennsylvania State University Press.

ENGLE, NATHANIEL, "Business Research In the Appraisal Field," *The Appriasal Journal*, October, 1950, pp. 425-430.

F.P.C., "S-59 Depreciation Practices of Nat Gas Co," Federal Power Commission, 1961.

FALKINER, RICHARD, *Investing In Antique Jewelry*, December, 1968.

FARRELL, PAUL B. JR., "Computer-Aided Financial Risk Simulation," *The Appraisal Journal*, January, 1969, pp. 58-73.

FEC, *S-200-Statistics of Publicly Owned Electric Utilities*, Supt. of Documents, U. S. Govt. Printing Office, Washington D. C, 1968.

FEDERAL HOME LOAN BANK REVIEW, *Neighborhood Standards As They Affect Investment Risk*, 1935.

FEDERAL POWER COMMISSION, *S-201-Depreciation Practices of Electricutilites*, Supt. of Documents, U. S. Govt. Printing Office, Washington D. C, 1966.

FEDERAL POWER COMMISSION, *S-205-Statistics for Interstate Natural Gas Pipeline Companies*, Supt. of Documents, U. S. Govt. Printing Office, Washington D. C, 1969.

FEDERAL POWER COMMISSION, *United States Imports and Exports of Natural Gas--1965*, Federal Power Commission, Washington D. C., 1965.

FEDERAL POWER COMMISSION, *Upper White River Basin Water Appraisal*, Federal Power Commission, Washington D. C, July, 1966.

FEDERAL POWER COMMISSION, *Water Resources Appraisal for Hydroelectric Licensing Santee River Basin South and North Carolina*, Federal Power Commission, Washington D. C, 1970.

FEDERAL POWER COMMISSION, *Water Resources Appraisal for Hydroelectric Licensing Green Island Development Hudson River*, Federal Power Commission, Washington D. C, April 7, 1971.

FEDERAL POWER COMMISSION, *Water Resources Appraisal for Hydroelectric Licensing Weber River Basin-Utah-Wyoming*, Federal Power Commission, 1971.

FEDERAL RESERVE BANK OF CLEVELAND, "Liquidity and Economic Stability," *The Appraisal Journal*, July, 1963, pp. 387-395.

FEDERAL RESERVE BANK OF CLEVELAND, "Potential Economic Growth of the United States During the Next Decade," *The Appraisal Journal*, July, 1955, pp. 413-420.

FEDERAL RESERVE BANK OF CHICAGO, "The Economic Consequences of the Baby Boom," *The Appraisal Journal*, April, 1956, pp. 208-212.

FELD, CHARLES, *Picasso His Recent Drawings 1966-1968*, Hacker Art Books Incorporated, New York, 1970.

FERRARI, ENRIQUE LAFUENTE, *Joya His Complete Etchings Aquatints And Lithographs*, Hacker Art Books Incorporated, New York, 1963.

FINANCIAL WORLD, "Investors Discover Bond Pitfalls," *Financial World*, July 22, 1970, pp. 6.

FINANCIAL WORLD, "Stocks Vs. Bonds In a New Business Climate," *Financial World*, September 23, 1970, pp. 7.

FINBURGH, BERT J., "Using a Form Appraisal for an Out of Town Investor," *The Residential Appraiser*, October, 1960, pp. 15-21.

FINNEGAN, G T, "Valuation of Business Interests," *Trusts and Estates Lxviii*, April 1, 1939, pp. 473.

FISHER, E. M., *Advanced Principles of Real Estate Practice*, Principles of Investment, New York City, 1930.

FISHER, R. M., "The Accuracy of Forecasts," *Technical Valuation,* June, 1955, pp. 17.

FISHER, STANLEY, *English Ceramics,* Ward Lock and Company, London.

FLEMING, HARRY D. JR., "Appraisal Process In the Valuation of Closely Held Corporations," *Technical Valuation,* October, 1959, pp. 23-27.

FLETCHER, H. MORLEY, *Investing In Pottery and Porcelain.*

FLETCHER, JENNIFER, *Rubens,* Phaidon Press, London, October, 1968.

FLEXNER, JAMES THOMAS, *Nineteenth Century American Painting,* Hacker Art Books Incorporated, New York, 1970.

FORBES, "Money-Men The Consumer and the Investor Are the Same Guy," *Forbes,* September 1, 1970, pp. 43-44.

FRANCOIS, WALDO, "An Institutional Investor Evaluates the Appraisal Report," *The Appraisal Journal,* October, 1967, pp. 550-554.

FRANCOIS, WALDO E., "What the Investor Wants and Needs from the Appraiser," *Real Estate Appraiser,* December, 1964, pp. 13-16.

FROST, F. DANIELS, LEES, CHARLES R., LINK, RICHARD M., *2th Tax Institute Proceedings Univ So. California,* Matthew Bender and Co., January 1, 1960, pp. 438.

FRYXELL, CARL A., "Should Appreciation Be Brought Into the Account," *Accounting Review,* June, 1930, pp. 157-158.

GAMMON, GEORGE W., "Capital Recovery with Changing Price Levels," *Valuation A.S.A.,* September, 1968, pp. 25.

GARAS, KLARA, *Eighteenth Century Venetian Painting,* The Clematis Press, Ltd, London.

GASSIER, PIERRE, *Goya,* Skira.

GAUMNITZ, J. E., "Appraising Performance of Investment Portfolios," *The Journal of Finance,* June, 1970.

GELBAND, J. F., "Investing In Bonds," *Magazine of Wall Street,* June 6, 1970, pp. 34.

GELDZAHLER, HENRY, *New York & Sculpture 1940-1970,* Pall Mall Press, London.

GIBBONS, JAMES E., "The Money Market," *Real Estate Appraiser,* September, 1971, pp. 24-29.

GODFREY, RICHARD G., "Duplexes Triplexes Quadruplexes a Sound Real Estate Investment," *Residential Appraiser,* May, 1960, pp. 8-10.

GOLDEN, G. A., "Counteracting the Dollar's Fluctuations," *The Review,* August, 1951, pp. 3-6.

GOLDEN, GERALD A., "An Insurance Investor In a Perplexing Market," *The Review,* July, 1949, pp. 3-8.

GOLDFARB, MORRIS, "On Entrepreneur's Increment," *The Appraisal Journal,* January, 1936, pp. 82-84.

GOLDSCHEIDER, LUDWIG, *Michelangelo Drawings,* Phaidon Press, London.

GOLDSCHEIDER, LUDWIG, *Vermeer Paintings,* Phaidon Press, London.

GOOD, SHELDON F., "An Approach to Creating Value In the Marketing of Investment Property," *The Appraisal Journal,* July, 1968, pp. 15-17.

GORDON, MYRON J., "The Investment Financing and Valuation of the Corporation," *Managerial Finance,* 1962, pp. 293.

GOSS, R. O., "Towards an Economic Appraisal of Port Investments," *Journal of Transport Economics and Policy,* September, 1967.

GOTTLIEB, J. R., "Trust Policy and Real Estate As a Quality Investment, II," *The Appraisal Journal,* July, 1954, pp. 377-399.

GOTTLIEB, J. R., "Trust Policy and Real Estate Asa a Quality Investment, I," *The Appraisal Journal,* April, 1954, pp. 263-249.

GOULD, J. P., "Market Value and the Theory of Investment of the Firm," *American Economic Review,* February, 1967, pp. 42-49.

GRAASKAMP, JAMES, *A Guide to Feasibility Analysis,* Society of Real Estate Appraisers, Chicago, 1900.

GRAHAM, BENJAMIN, "The Intelligent Investor," Harper & Brothers, New York, January 1, 1954, pp. 163-164.

GRAHAM, DONALD H. JR., "Owner's Analysis of Yields on Major Real Estate Investment," *Appraisal Journal,* October, 1965, pp. 541-548.

GRAICHEN, R. E., "Today's Depreciation Deduction," *Valuation Manual,* A. S. A., December, 1957, pp. 27-33.

GRANDJEAN, SERGE, *Empire Furniture,* Faber and Faber, London.

GRAY, BASIL, *Persian Painting,* Skira, 1961.

GREENBAUM, IRVING PHD, "Return on Investment In Elec Util Ind & Pub Util Comm Rate Base Det: Orig Cost Fair Val Reprod Cost," The Ohio State University, 1970.

GRONER, ORVILLE, "Real Estate Investments Under Liquidating Leases," *The Appraisal Journal,* April, 1949, pp. 252-256.

GUTHMAN, H. G., "Actuarial Versus Sinking Fund Type Formula for Valuation," *Accounting Review,* September, 1930, pp. 226-230.

HACK, B., *Rembrandt - His Life Work and Times,* Thames and Hudson, London.

HACKER ART BOOKS, "Masterpcs of Asian Art In Amer Colls II," Hacker Art Books, New York, 1970, pp. 150.

HACKER ART BOOKS INC., "Mantle Fielding's Dictionary of Amer Painters, Sculptors & Engravers," Hacker Art Books Inc., New York, 1965, pp. 592.

HAIGHT, JAMES R., "Money---The Measuring Stick of Values," *The Appraisal Journal,* October, 1942, pp. 340-346.

HAIGHT, JAMES R., "Some Factors Determining Future Values," *National Real Estate Journal,* January, 1940, pp. 34-37.

HALL, JAMES R., "Inflation---The Home Owner---The Investor," *Technical Valuation,* February, 1960, pp. 45-48.

HAMMACHER, A. M., *Modern English Sculpture,* Thames and Hudson, London.

HANAO, YOCHIO, "Operating Statement - Income and Expenses," *The Real Estate Appraiser,* July, 1966, pp. 2-14.

HANEMANN, H. J. F., *Acquisition of Rights of Way,* Condemnation Appraisal Seminar, 1958.

HANFMANN, GEORGE M. A., *Classical Sculpture,* Hacker Art Books Incorporated, Greenwich, 1967.

HANFORD, LLOYD D. SR., "The Market Data Approach and Investment Property Appraisal," *The Real Estate Appraiser,* Chicago, December, 1966, pp. 2-10.

HANLEY, E. J., "Financing Tomorrow's Steel Plant Demands Realistic Depreciation and Pricing Policy," *Valuation Manual,* A. S. A., March, 1956, pp. 338-340.

HANSBERGER, R. V., "Big Business In the Big Housing Market of the 70's," *The Real Estate Appraiser,* May, 1970, pp. 43-47.

HARDEN, D. B., K. S. PAINTER, R. H. PINDER, *Masterpieces of Glass.*

HARRISS, C LOWELL, "Estate Taxes and the Family Owned Business," *California Law Review Xxxviii,* March 1, 1950, pp. 119-128.

HARTMAN, H. H., "Fair Value," *Principles of Investment,* Boston, 1920.

HARTMAN, JOAN M., *Chinese Jade of Five Centuries,* London.

HAWK STEPHEN L, KRONCKE CHARLES O, "Some Refinements In the Real Estate Investment Decision Process," *The Real Estate Appraiser,* The Society of Real Estate Appraisers, Chicago Illinois, January 1, 1974, pp. 13.

HAYES, DOUGLAS A., "Techniques for Estimating Earning Power-Determination of Investment Standards and Values," *Appraisal and Management of Securities,* pp. 279.

HAYES, K., "How Investors In America Have Fared Lately In Banking," *Valuation Manual,* ASA, April, 1956, pp. 66-67.

HAYES, SAMUEL L. III, AND LEONARD M. HARLAN, "Real Estate As a Corporate Investment," *The Appraisal Journal,* July, 1968, pp. 361-382.

HEINZ, DORA, *Medieval Tapestries,* Methuen, London.

HELFTS, JACQUES, *French Master Goldsmiths and Silversmiths from The Seventeenth to the Nineteenth Century,* Hacker Art Books Incorporated, New York, 1966.

HEMMER, EDGAR HAROLD, PH.D., *A-Valuation Model for Investments In Real Estate,* Purdue University, 1972.

HENDY, PHILLIP, *Piero Della Francesca and the Early Renaissance,* Weidenfeld and Nicolson, London.

HIGGINS, REYNOLD, *Jewellery from Classical Lands,* The British Museum, 1965.

HIMMELBLAU, DAVID, "Annuity Method of Depreciation," *International Congress of Accounting,* New York, 1929, pp. 335-350.

HIND, ARTHUR M., *A Catalogue of Rembrandts Etchings,* Da Capo Press, New York, 1967.

HIRMER, MAX, PEDRO DE PALOL, *Early Medieva Art In Spain,* Thames And Hudson, London.

HODGES, M. B. JR., "Income Capitalization for Investor Clients," *The Appraisal Journal,* April, 1968, pp. 175-200.

HOF, FREDERICK B., "What a Lender Looks for In a Mortgage Investment of an Appraisal," *Technical Valuation,* February, 1963, pp. 22-23.

HOGARTY, T. F., "Profitability of Corporate Mergers," *Journal of Business,* July, 1970, pp. 317-327.

HOMER, S., "Individual Savings Flow Into Bond Market," *Burroughs Clearing House,* December, 1970, pp. 15.

HOMES, S., "Bond Market In a Changing World," *Commercial and Financial Chronicle,* May 3, 1971, pp. 1447.

HONAD, YOSHIO, "Operating Statement - Income and Expenses," *Real Estate Appraiser,* SREA, Chicago, July, 1966, pp. 2.

HOSSACK, J. E., *Fixed Asset Accounting,* American Appraisal Company, Milwaukee, Wisconsin, 1955.

HUBIN, VINCENT J., "Tax Advantages of Realty Investments," *Appraisal Digest,* March, 1959, pp. 16-17.

HUGHES, GRAHAM, *Jewellery,* Studio Vista, London.

HUGHES, GRAHAM, *Modern Silver Throughout the World 1880-1967,* Studio Vista.

HUGHES, THIRLE AND BERNARD, *English Painted Enamels,* Spring Books, 1967.

HUYGHE, RENE, *Watteau,* Hacker Art Books Incorporated, New York, 1970.

HYAM, LESLIE A., "Fine Arts - Liquidations," *Technical Evaluation,* ASA, October, 1953, pp. 11.

INDUSTRY WEEK, "Discount Bonds Merit Place In Young Mgrs Portfolio," *Industry Week,* April 26, 1971, pp. 35.

INNOCENTI, R. E., "Are Bonds Currently Reasonable Investments for Pension Funds," *Trusts and Estates,* October, 1970, pp. 865-868.

JACKSON, CHARLES J., *English Goldsmiths and Thui Marks,* Dover Publications Incorporated, New York, 1964.

JARCHOW, ALFRED, WALDSMAR WEICHBROTT, "Carpeting and Permanent Floors, Effect on Mortgage and Risk," *The Real Estate Appraiser,* September, 1968, pp. 40-47.

JARRY, MADELEINE, *World Tapestry,* Hacker Art Books Incorporated, New York, 1969.

JELENSKI, CONSTANTINE, *Leonor Fini,* Hacker Art Books Incorporated, London, 1968.

JEWETT, JOHN G., "A New Approach to Industrial Financing," *The Appraisal Journal,* April, 1947, pp. 235-236.

JOHNSON, LYLE R, SHAPIRO, ELI, OLMEARA JR, JOSEPH, "Valuation of Closely Held Stock for Federal Tax Purposes: Approach to an Objective Method," *Law Review,* University of Pennsylvania, November 1, 1951, pp. 170.

JOHNSON, R W, "Financial Management 4th Ed. Part 6," *Valuing of Business Enterprises,* pp. 501-561.

JONES, E., "Principles of Railway Transportation," *Principles of Investment,* New York, 1924.

JONES, E., L. C. BIGHAM, "Principles of Public Utilities," *Principles of Investment,* New York, 1931, pp. 29-44.

JOSEPH, MICHAEL, *The Sculpture of David Wynne,* London.

KAHN, CASE-SCHIMMEL, *Real Estate Appraisal and Investment,* 1963.

KAHN, SANDERS A., FREDERICK CASE, ALFRED SCHIMMEL, *Real Estate and Investment,* Ronald Press, New York, 1963, pp. 468.

KAINEN, JACOB, *The Etchings of Canaletto,* The Smithsonian, 1967.

KAM, WILLIAM H., "Investment Analysis of Leased Commercial Land," *Real Estate Appraisal,* February, 1967, pp. 27-30.

KAPLAN, R. S., R. RALL, "Investor Evaluation of Accounting Information Some Empirical Evidence," *Journal of Business,* April, 1972, pp. 225-257.

KAPLAN, R. S., R. RALL, "Investor Evaluation of Accounting Information Some Empirical Evidence," *Journal of Business,* April, 1972, pp. 225-257.

KAPROW, ALAN, *Assemblage Environments and Happenings,* Hacker Art Books Incorporated, New York, 1965.

KAUFMAN, H., "Bond and Interest Rate Outlook In the Context of a Non-Boom Economy," *Commercial and Financial Chronicle,* February 25, 1971, pp. 615.

KAZDIN, S. EDWIN, "Investment Property Valuation," *Appraisal Digest,* 1911, pp. 13.

KELLOUGH, W. R., "Analysis and Theoretical Implications of Partial Taking," *Valuation,* September, 1972, pp. 50.

KENNETH, CLARK, *Rembrandt-And the Italian Renaissance,* John Murray, London.

KERN, JAMES M., "Why Quality Counts," *The Residential Appraiser,* January, 1957, pp. 7-8.

KEUTNER, HERBERT, *Sculpture Renaissance to Rococo,* Hacker Art Books Incorporated, Greenwich, 1967.

KILBORNE, R. D., "Principles of Money and Banking," *Principles of Investment,* Chapters Xviii, Xix, Xxvii, 1932.

KING, WILLFORD I., "If I Had a Million Dollars to Invest," *The Appraisal Journal,* July, 1944, pp. 223-231.

KINNARD, WILLIAM N. JR., "The Financial Logic of Investment Property Appraising," *Real Estate Appraiser,* May, 1969, pp. 13-21.

KIRKPATRICK, DIANE, *Eduardo Paolozzi,* Hacker Art Books Incorporated, Greenwich, 1971.

KIRSHMAN, JOHN EMMETT, *Principles of Investment*, Mcgraw-Hill Book Co., New York, 1933.

KIRSHMAN, JOHN EMMETT, "Financial Analysis of Railroads," *Principles of Investment*, 1933, pp. 309.

KIRSHMAN, JOHN EMMETT, "Gas Industry," *Principles of Investment*, 1933, pp. 403.

KIRSHMAN, JOHN EMMETT, "Regulation of Public Utilities," *Principles of Investment*, 1933, pp. 345.

KIRSHMAN, JOHN EMMETT, "Stock Prices," *Principles of Investment*, 1933, pp. 734.

KIRSHMAN, JOHN EMMETT, "The Asset Element of Credit," *Principles of Investment*, 1933, pp. 158.

KIRSHMAN, JOHN EMMETT, "The Telegraph," *Principles of Investment*, 1933, pp. 436.

KIRSHMAN, JOHN EMMETT, "The Telephone," *Principles of Investment*, 1933, pp. 474.

KIRSHMAN, JOHN EMMETT, "Value, Price and Yield," *Principles of Investment*, 1933, pp. 108.

KIRSHMAN, JOHN EMMETT, "Water Works," *Principles of Investment*, 1933, pp. 426.

KLAMDN, S. B., "Economic Outlook The Outlook for Housing and Mortage Markets," *Commercial and Financial Chronicle*, May 7, 1970, pp. 17.

KOEPF, DR. HANS, PROFESSOR, ED. J. E. SCHUL, *Masterpieces of Sculpture, from the Greeks to Modern Times*, Macdonald and Co. Ltd., London.

KRAFT, K., L. STARKWEATHER, "Analysis of Industrial Securities," *Principles of Investment*, New York, 1929.

KUMAR, P., "Market Power, Growth, Leverage, and the Valuation of the Firm," *Journal of Finance*.

LACY, A. D., *Greek Pottery In the Bronze Age*.

LAING, LLOYD R., *Coins and Archaelogy*, Weidenfeld and Nicolson, London.

LANDAUER, JAMES D., "Real Estate As an Investment," *The Appraisal Journal*, October, 1960, pp. 426-434.

LANDOLT, HANSPETER, *German Painting the Late Middle Ages 1350-1500*, Skira Art Books Incorporated, 1968.

LANDRY, JUDITH, *Miro*, Faber and Faber, London.

LARSON, KNUT, *Rugs and Carpets of the Orient*, Bedford, London.

LASSAIGN, JACQUES, *Dufy*, Skira, Switzerland.

LASSAIGNE, JACQUES, *Flemish Painting the Century of Van Eyck*, Skira, 1957.

LAUNER, E. J., "Motel and Tourist Court Appraising for Loan and Investment Purposes," *Technicalities and Technical Valuation*, June, 1952, pp. 33-39.

LAVIN, IRVING, *Bernini and the Crossing of St. Peter*, New York University Press, 1969.

LEONHARD, KURT, *Picasso His Graphic Works*, Thames and Hudson, London.

LEROI-GOURHAN, ANDRE, *Treasures of Prehistoric Art*, Hacker Art Books Incorporated, New York, 1967.

LEUTHOLD, S. C., "Spotting Tops and Bottoms Multiples of Normalized Earnings Book Values Are Useful Guides," *Barrons*, June 19, 1972, pp. 5.

LEVIN, L. M., "Combination Sale of Cash Value Life Insurance and Real Estate," *National Underwriter Life and Health Insurance Edition*, January 16, 1971, pp. 20-21.

LEVY, R., "Money In Mini Theaters," *Duns*, October, 1970, pp. 63 64.

# BIBLIOGRAPHY OF APPRAISAL LITERATURE

LEWIN, GORDON, "Law and Municipal Ecology: Air, Water, Noise, Overpopulation," National Institute of Municipal Law Offices, Washington, D. C..

LEYMAIRE, J., H. READ, W. S. LIEBERMAN, *Henri Matisse,* University of California Press.

LEYMARIE, JEAN, *Impressionist Drawings,* Skira.

LEYMARIE, JEAN, *Picasso Drawings,* Skira.

LICHT, FRED, *Sculpture Nineteenth and Twentieth Centuries,* Hacker Art Books Incorporated, Greenwich, 1967.

LION GOLDSCHMIDT, DAISY, *Chinese Art Bronze, Jade, Sculpture, Ceramics,* Studio Books, 1960.

LISTER, RAYMOND, *College Stamps of Oxford and Cambridge,* The Colden Press.

LOCKYER, ALBERT W., "Investment Property Trends," *Appraisal Digest,* January, 1954, pp. 14-16.

LOCSIN, LEANDRO, "Oriental Ceramics Discovered In the Philippines," *Oriental Ceramics Discovered In the Philipines,* Charles E. Tuttle Company, 1967.

LONG, CLARENCE D. JR., *Building Cycles and the Theory of Investment,* Princeton University Press, Princeton, 1940.

LONG, H. A., "Closed-End Bond Fund Sponsored by John Hancock," *Trusts and Estates,* January, 1971, pp. 47.

LOPEZ, REY JOSE, *Velazquez Work and World,* Faber and Faber.

LOUIS F. KORING, JR., "Patent Valuations an Increasingly Important Apraisal Function," *Appraisal and Valuation Manual,* Corporate Press, Incorporated, Washington, D. C, January, 1972, pp. 218.

LOVE, HAROLD C., "Risk and Uncertainty Factors," *Appraisal Institute Magazine,* Appraisal Institute of Canada, Winnipeg.

LOVRET, FREDERICK I, "Oil Paintings and Their Worth," *Valuation,* American Society of Appraisers, September, 1972, pp. 70-78.

LUCAS, E. LOUISE, *Art Books a Basic Bibliography of the Fine Arts,* Hacker Art Books Incorporated, Greenwich, 1968.

LUKENS, C. JR. M. A. I., *The Appraiser and Real Estate Feasibility Studies,* American Institute of Real Estate Appraisers, August, 1972.

LUST, HERBERT, *Jiacomette the Complete Graphics,* Hacker Art Books Incorporated, New York, 1970.

MAAS, JEREMY, *Victorian Painters,* Hacker Books Incorporated, New York.

MACDONALD TAYLOR, MARGARET, *English Furniture Form the Middle Ages and Modern Times,* Evans Brothers Ltd, 1965.

MACRAE, R. M., "Short Term Discount Bonds for a Prosperous 1970," *Financial Chronicle,* January 2, 1970, pp. 69.

MAKELA, BENJAMIN R, "How to Use and Invest In Letter Stock," Presidents' Publishing House Inc, January 1, 1970.

MALKIEL, B. G., J. G. CRAGG, "Expectations and the Structure of Share Prices," *American Economic Review,* September, 1970, pp. 601-617.

MALONE, CLARENCE J., "Valuation of Public Utilities for Ad Valorem Tax" *Valutape Audio-Library Series,* American Society of Appraisers, Washington, D.C., January, 1973.

MALRAUX, ANDRE, *Flowering of the Italian Renaissance,* Hacker Art Books Incorporated, New York, 1965.

MAN, FELIX H., *Artists Lithographs,* Hacker Art Books Incorporated, New York, 1970.

MARCUSE, SYBIL, *Musical Instruments: a Comprehensive Dictionary,* County Life, London.

MARSHALL, W. & YOUNG, A., "Controlling Shareholders Servicing Costs," *Harvard Business Review*, January, 1971, pp. 71-78.

MARTIN, JAMES W., MILFORD ESTILL, "Valuation of Property Economic and Legal Standards," *Kentucky Law Journal*.

MARX, CLAUDE ROGER, *Rembrandt*, Hacker Art Books Incorporated, Paris, 1960.

MAY, M., "Investment Opportunities Stock Valuation Model Based on Growth Patterns of Equity," *Journal of Finance*, September, 1971, pp. 993-994.

MCCAWLEY, PATRICIA K., *Antique Glass Paperweights*, Spink and Son, London.

MCCLINTON, KATHERINE MORRISON, "Antiques In Miniature," *1972 July -- Connoisseur*, Barrie and Jenkins, London.

MCDONALD, ADRIAN F., "Long-Term Investment Value, a Fiction," *The Review*, September, 1951, pp. 19-23.

MCKEOWN, J. C., "Additivity of Net Realizable Values," *Accounting Review*, July, 1972, pp. 527-532.

MCLEAN, J. G., "How to Evaluate New Capital Investment," *Economic Analysis*, Harvard Business Review, November, 1958, pp. 56-69.

MCMICHAEL. S. L., "Band of Investment Theory," *Real Estate Today*, April, 1971.

MCMICHAEL, JAMES M., *Real Estate Investment Analysis and Programming*, L. A. Exchg Division California Real Estate Assocn, 1968.

MCREYNOLDS, TOM, "Bowling Alleys As Long Term Investments," *Real Estate Analyst Appraisal Bulletin*, 1956, pp. 83-86.

MELICHER, R. W, "Financing Electric Utilities The Value of Common Stock Warrants," *Public Utilities Fortnightly*, July 16, 1970, pp. 33-37.

MILLER, D. C., W. S. LIEHERMANN, *The New Japanese Paintings and Sculpturers*, Doubleday and Company Incorporated, 1966.

MIYAGAUA TORAS, *Modern Japanese Painting*, Waid Lock and Company and Kodansha International, 1967.

MOIXER, MIKLOS, *Dutch Painting*, Clematic Press, London.

MOLINARI, GEORGE, "Capitalization Rates and Incentive Financing," *The Appraisal Journal*, July, 1969, pp. 337-340.

MONTONNA, D. L., "Gross Income and Expenses," *Appraisal Institute Magazine*, Appraisal Institute of Canada, Winnipeg.

MONTONNA, DAVID L., "Analysis of Operating Statement," *Appraisal Institute Magazine*, February, 1958, pp. 9-16.

MONTONNA, DAVID L., "How I Met an Appraisal Problem Involving an Investment Property," *The Appraisal Journal*, July, 1949, pp. 346-350.

MOORE, WILLIS, "The American Association of Museums," *Proceedings: International Appraisal Conference*, American Society of Appraisers (Unpublished Ms), Toronto, June 28, 1973.

MORASSI, ANTONIO, *Titian*, Hacker Art Books Incorporated, Greenwich, 1967.

MORLEY FLETCHER, H., *Investing In Pottery and Porcelain*.

MORRIS, STEWART, LYLE W. MALEY, "Land Title and Escrow Problems," *American Right of Way Association*, Second Annual Iational Seminar, Washington, D. C, 1957, pp. 37-41.

MORSE, HARRISON H., "What the Typical Buyer Looks for In Income Property," *The Appraisal Journal*, October, 1952, pp. 535-542.

MORTON, WALTER A., "The Investor Capitalization Theory of the Cost of Equity Capital," *Land Economics*, August, 1970.

MOSS, DAVID S., "Equity Yields on Real Estate Investments," *The Appraisal Journal*, pp. 412-423.

MULLINS, EDWIN, *Josif Herman, Paintings and Drawings*, Evelyn, Adams and Mackay.

MUNDY, F. W., "**Earning Power of Railroads,**" *Principles of Investment,* New York, pp. 325.

MURRAY, JOHN, *Antiques.*

MURRAY, JOHN, *The Lure of Antiques.*

MURRAY, R. F., "**Investing for Assured Monthly Income,**" *Magazine of Wall Street,* August 29, 1970, pp. 12-14.

MURRAY, R. F., "**Probabilities Favor Stock Market Rise In Next Few Years,**" *Commercial and Financial Chronicle,* January 14, 1971, pp. 123.

MURRAY, R. F., "**Stock Market Needs a Bond Market Recovery,**" *Commercial and Financial Chronicle,* January 29, 1970, pp. 292-293.

MURRAY, T. G., "**Signal: Land Is Big Money,**" *Dun's,* July, 1970, pp. 58-60.

NEATHY, NIGEL, *The Saltram Collection,* National Trust Publication, London.

NEGUS, ARTHUR, MAX ROBERTSON, *Going for a Song English Furniture,* B. B. C. Publications, London.

NELSON, R. D., A. J. J. POLLAKOWSKI, "**Effect of Financing on Value,**" *Appraisal Journal,* April, 1970, pp. 279-285.

NELSON, RICHARD LAWRENCE, *The One-Hundred Percent Location a New Concept In Motel Site Selection,* Encyclopedia of Motel Management.

NELSON, ROLAND D., "**Overall Rate-Band of Investment Style,**" *The Appraisal Journal,* January, 1969, pp. 25-30.

NESSER, RICHARD S., "**The Variable Annuity Premise,**" *Appraisal and Valuation Manual,* American Society of Appraisers, 1961, pp. 281-290.

NEUMANN, JAROMIR, *The Picture Gallery of Prague Castle,* London.

NEWCOMB, ROBINSON, *Mobile Home Parks Part I an Analysis of Characteristics,* Urban Land Institute.

NICHOLIN, JORGE, "**A Few Aspects of Property Investment In Mexico,**" *The Appraisal Journal,* July, 1967, pp. 386-401.

NORGAARD, RICHARD L., "**Evaluating Intercorporate Risk, Returns, and Treds,**" *Journal of Financial and Quantitative Analysis,* University of Washington, September, 1971, pp. 1069-1082.

NURNBERG, H., "**Observations on the Financial Reporting of Depreciation and Income Taxes,**" *Financial Executive,* December, 1971, pp. 39.

OLEARY, J. J., "**Outlook for Mortgages on Income Properties,**" *Commercialand Financial Chronicle,* January 29, 1970, pp. 298.

ODOM, WILLIAM M., *Italian Furniture,* The Archive Press, New York.

OLSON, IRVING J, "**Valuation of a Closely Held Corporation,**" *Journal of Accountancy,* August 1, 1969.

OLSON, LYLE H., "**Appraising As an Economic Factor,**" *The Appraisal Journal,* July, 1935, pp. 310-315.

OLSON, OLOF W, "**Valuation of a Going Concern,**" *Valuation Magazine,* American Society of Appraisers, Washington D.C., December 1, 1973, pp. 118-125.

OMAN, CHARLES, *English Domestic Silver,* Adam, Charles Black, London.

OTTO, ALEXANDER, *Illum Ms In Bodleian Liby Oxford German Dutch Flemish French & Spanish Schools,* Clarendon Press, Oxford Univ. Press.

OWEN, WILFRED, "**Cities In the Motor Age,**" Cooper Square Publishers Inc., New York, N. Y..

PACEY, M. D., "**Can You Top This, Towering Bond Yields Are Attracting Investors and Savers Alike,**" *Barrons,* January 6, 1970, pp. 9.

PARKINSON, G., "Here's a Builder Who Uses the Apartment Buyers Money to Build the Apartments," *House and Home,* January, 1971, pp. 20.

PARVIN, ROBERT G., "Asset Valuation," *The Appraisal Journal,* October, 1954, pp. 550-560.

PASSEION, ROGER, *French Prints of the Twentieth Century,* Pall Mallpress.

PATTBERG, E. J., "American Bond Market-Sound and Attractive," *Commercial and Financial Chronicle,* May 28, 1970, pp. 1701.

PEARSON, K. G., "Big Business Discovers Real Estate," *Michigan Business Review,* March, 1971, pp. 26-32.

PEATMAN, JOHN GREY, "The Psychology of Real Estate Investments," *The Appraisal Journal,* October, 1942, pp. 335-339.

PETERS, W., "Deduction for Depreciation Before Acquisition of the Asset," *American Society of Appraisers Manual,* January, 1958, pp. 55-57.

PETERSON, CARL H., "The Depreciation Reserve," *Technical Valuation,* February, 1957, pp. 19-26.

PIGNATTI, TERISTO, *Museo Correr,* Hacker Art Books Incorporated, Bergamo, 1958.

PLUM, LESTER, HUMPHREY, JOSEPH H, *Investment Analysis and Management,* Richard D Irwin Inc, Chicago, January 1, 1951.

POTTER, J., "Is the Recovery In Stocks Too Fast Two Investment Counselors Examine the Market," *Insurance,* April 1, 1971, pp. 40.

POTTER, J. C., "Investment Counselor Looks for Rising Stock Prices Says Time to Buy Is Now," *Insurance,* July 1, 1970, pp. 31-34.

PRIEST, ALAN, *The Sculpture of Joseph Coletti,* Collier-Macmillan.

QUIGLEY IAN H., "Profit and Risk Factor-A Modern Approach," *The Valuer,* The Commonwealth Institute of Valuers, Sydney Austrailia, October 1, 1973, pp. 588-601.

R. WRAIGHT, "Record Season In the London Salerooms," *Studio,* October, 1964, pp. 158-163.

RADCLIFFE, ANTHONY, *European Bronze Statuettes,* 1966.

RAMS, EDWIN M., "Investment Dynamics-Multi-Family Units," *Appraisal and Valuation Manaul,* American Society of Appraisers, 1961, pp. P 111-120.

RAMS, EDWIN M., AND ROBERT K. BROWN, "Investment Articulation Supermarkets," *Appraisal and Valuation Manual,* 1960, pp. 279-286.

RANDALL, WILLIAM J., "Age, Depreciation, Future Life, and Net Condition," *Real Estate Analyst Appraisal Bulletin,* 1962, pp. 25- 2.

RANDALL, WILLIAM J., "An Appraisal Vs an Investment Analysis, or How to Double Your Real Estate Investment In 5 Years," *Real Estate Analyst Bulletin,* 1961, pp. 603-614.

RAPKIN, CHESTER, "Role of Real Estate Taxes In the Investment Experience of Real Property," *The Appraisal Journal,* October, 1954, pp. 486-496.

REAL ESTATE ANALYST, THE, "How Good an Investment Is a Leaseback?," *Real Estate Analyst Appraisal Bulletin,* 1953, pp. 325-328.

REAL ESTATE INVESTMENT LETTER, "Golf Courses As Real Estate Investments," Institute for Business Planning Inc, New York, June 15, 1960.

REAL ESTATE RECORD, "Neighborhood Appraisals As a Guide for Investors," *Real Estate Rcord,* September 7, 1935, pp. 6-7.

REILLEY, FRANK K, "What Determines the Ratio of Exchange In Corporate Mergers," *Financial Analysts Journal,* December 1, 1962, pp. 47-50.

REVIEW, THE, "New Shelter-Income Ratio," *The Review,* March, 1953, pp. 21.

REYNOLDS, GRAHAM, *Victorian Paintings.*

RICE, DAVID TALBOT, TAMARA TALBOT RICE, *Icons the Natasha Allen Collection,* The National Gallery of Ireland.

RICHTER, F. E., A. STANDISH, *Investments of Banks and Insurance Company,* Harvard Business Review, July, 1925.

RICHTER, GISELA M. A., *The Engraved Gems of the Greeks and the Etrauscans,*

RICKS, R. BRUCE, "Tax Shelter and Annual Cash Flow In Investment Real Estate," *The Appraisal Journal,* April, 1966, pp. 300-303.

RICKS, R. BRUCE, "Valuation of Lessor and Lessee Interests In a Physical Asset," *The Appraisal Journal,* April, 1966, pp. 268-272.

RIESTERER LLOYD V, "The Investment Decision - Yes or No," *Valuer,* The New Zealand Institute of Valuers, New Zealand, August 1, 1973, pp. 118-123.

RING, A. A., "The Earnings Approach to Value," *Appraisal Institute Magazine,* Appraisal Institute of Canada, Winnipeg.

ROBERTSON, GILES, *Giovanni Bellini,* Oxford University Press, London.

ROBERTSON, M., "At the Sales London," *Oriental Art,* pp. 160-164.

RODEN, P. F., "Overlooked Factors Which Make the Outlook for Bonds Bleak," *Commercial and Financial Chronicle,* December 31, 1970, pp. 1891.

RODEWALD, G. E. JR., C. B. BAKER, "Interim Period Asset Valuation A Method for Making Investment Decisions," *Agricultural Economics Research,* April, 1969.

ROGER-MARX, CLAUDE, SABINE COTTE, *Delacroix,* Hacker Art Books Incorporated, New York, 1970.

ROLL, R., "Investment Diversification and Bond Maturity," *Journal of Finance,* March, 1971, pp. 51-66.

ROSENBLUM, ROBERT, *Cubism and Twentieth Century Art,* Hacker Art Books Incorporated, New York, 1966.

ROSS, BYRON F., "Use of Appraisals In Accounting, Investments and Taxes," *The Real Estate Appraiser,* November, 1968, pp. 25-29.

ROSS, THURSTON H., "Real Estate As an Investment," *The Appraisal Journal,* January, 1948, pp. 49-56.

ROTH, H. LINY, *Oriental Silverwork: Malay and Chinese,* Oxford University Press, 1966.

ROWLSON, JOHN F., "Investment Property An Analysis of Motivation," *The Real Estate Appraiser,* May, 1957, pp. 2-9.

RUSH, RICHARD H., *Antiques As an Investment,* Prentice-Hall, Englewood Cliffs, 1968.

RUSSOLI, FRANCO, *Modigliani Drawings and Sketches,*

SALVINI, ROBERTO, *Medieval Sculpture,* Hacker Art Books Incorporated, Greenwich, 1967.

SAVAGE, GEORGE, *Chinese Jade,* Cory, Adams and Mackay, 1965.

SAVAGE, GEORGE, *18th Century German Porcelain,* Spring Books, 1967.

SCHALL, I. D., "Asset Valuation and Firm Investment," *Journal of Business,* January, 1972.

SCHALL, L. D., "Asset Valuation, Firm Investment, and Firm Diversification," *Journal of Business,* 1972, pp. JOURNAL OF BUSINESS, VOL. XLV.

SCHEEFLY, J E, "The Sale of the Family Business: Income and Estate Planning Implications," *Taxes (Magazine),* February 1, 1968, pp. 85-91.

SCHIACH, A D, "Valuation Factors and Techniques In Mergers and Acquisitions," *Valutape Audio-Library,* American Society of Appraisers, Washington D C, January 1, 1974.

SCHMUTZ, GEORGE L., "Some Annuity Computations," *The Appraisal Journal,* January, 1936, pp. 52-61.

SCHMUTZ, GEORGE L., "Valuation of Intangible Property," *The Appraisal Journal*, October, 1953, pp. 533-537.

SCHNEIDER, JOHN S., "Appraisal of Warehouse," *The Appraisal Journal*, January, 1961.

SCHOEN, HARRY, "Evaluation and Financing of Real Estate Specialties," *Appraisal and Valuations Manual*, 1961, pp. 59-67.

SCHURMANN, ULRICH, *Central Asian Rugs*, London.

SCHWINGLE, C J, "Valuation of a Family Business," *12th Annual Tulane Institute Proceedings*, Hansen Press, January 1, 1963.

SCOTT, AMORET, CHRISTOPHER SCOTT, *Antiques As an Investment*, Oldbourne, London.

SEABY, H. A., *Greek Coins and Their Values*, B. A. Seaby Ltd, London.

SELDIN, MAURY, "Real Estate Investment Policy Based on Forecast," M.

SERULLAZ, MAURICE, *The French Drawings*, Cassell.

SHAPIRO, IRVING D., "Investment Implications of the Salelease Transaction," *The Appraisal Journal*, April, 1958, pp. 166-181.

SHAPLEY, FEIN RUSK, *Paintings from the Samuel U. Kress Collection Italian Schools, Xiii-Xv Century,*

SHAW, J. BYAM, *Paintings by Old Masters at Christ Church Oxford*, Phaidon.

SHERMER, MALCOLM, "Bonded Debt In Appraisals," *National Real Estate Journal*, August, 1941, pp. 27-28.

SHIACH A. D., "Depreciation Recapture: How it Affects Our Client; How We Can Help Him Cope with it," ASA, Valutape Series.

SHIPLEY, ROBERT C. JR., "Property Valuation and the Internal Revenue Code," *Valuation*, September, 1972, pp. 32.

SIBERLING, NORMAN J., *Dynamics of Business*, Mcgraw Hill, New York, 1940.

SINGLETON, C. G. JR., AND SCOFIELD, W. H., "Land Syndication In the Rural-Urban Fringe," *The Appraisal Journal*, October, 1962, pp. 494-500.

SMITH, BERNARD, *Australian Painting 1788-1970*, Oxford University Press, London.

SMITH, GUY V., "Significant Snares In Service Stations Appraisal," *Right of Way*, August, 1970.

SMITH, GUY-HAROLD, *Conservation of Natural Resources*, John Wiley and Sons Incorporated, New York.

SMITH, HALBERT C., "Investment Analysis In Appraising," *Real Estate Appraiser*, September, 1967, pp. 19-25.

SMITH, LARRY, "Investment Future of Central City Area," *The Appraisal Journal*, October, 1964, pp. 559-563.

SMITH, LARRY, "Problems of Real Estate Investment Analysis of Large Projects," *Wisconsin Colloquim on Appraisal Research, Papers and Proceedings*, 1963, pp. 41-43.

SNORGRASS, VERN G., "Evaluating a Small Going Business," *American Society of Appraisers Valuation Manual*, 1959, pp. 261.

SPRINKEL, BERLY W., "The Economic Picture--Now and Tomorrow," *The Appraisal Journal*, October, 1962, pp. 471-480.

SREA COMMITTEE PAPER, "Corporate Real Estate Transfer Program: the Appraiser's Viewpoint," *The Real Estate Appraiser*, 1968.

STAFF OF THE FRICK COLLECTION, *The Frick Collection, the Painting*, Princeton University, USA.

STAFFORD, L. D., "Depreciation As a Business Expense," *Manufactures News*, August, 1929, pp. 9-10, 65-67.

STAHL, SHELDON W., "On Economic Forecasting," *The Appraisal Journal*, April, 1968, pp. 291-298.

## BIBLIOGRAPHY OF APPRAISAL LITERATURE

STANLEY, A. L., "Evaluating Intangibles for Executive Decision," *Economic Analysis*, September, 1955, pp. 781.

STAPLETON, R. C., "Stock Valuation and Capital Budgeting Decision Rules for Risky Projects," *Journal of Finance*, March, 1971.

STATISTICAL ABSTRACT OF THE UNITED STATES, "Metropolitan Area Statistics," Statistical Abstract of the United States, Washington, D.C., 1970.

STEINGRABER, ERICH, *Royal Treasures*, Weidenfeld and Nicolson, London.

STEVENS, ROGER L., "What I Look for In a Real Estate Investment," *The Appraisal Journal*, October, 1961, pp. 491-500.

STRONG, D. E., *Greek and Roman Gold and Silver Plate*, Methuen and Company, London.

SUTHERLAND, C. H. V., *Gold*, Hacker Art Books Incorporated, London, 1960.

SVOBODA, ALBERT C., "Real Estate for Endownent Fund Investment," *The Appraisal Journal*, January, 1954, pp. 43-47.

SWAN, CLIFFORD L., "Appraising a Going Business," *American Society of Appraisers Valuation Manual*, 1957, pp. 43.

SWEET, FREDERICK A., *Miss Mary Cassatt, Impressionist from Pennsylvania*, University of Oklahoma Press, 1966.

SYBILLE, HAYNES, *Etruscan Bronze Utensil*, The British Museum, 1965.

TAYLOR, JAMES R., "Accruals for Depreciation," *The Review*, May, 1949, pp. 3-4, 14.

THE APPRAISAL JOURNAL, "Inflation and Your Income," *The Appraisal Journal*, July, 1936, pp. 330.

THOMPSON, R. E., "On Entrepeneur's Increment," *The Appraisal Journal*, January, 1936, pp. 82.

THORSON, IVAN A., "Appraising Properties Involving Both Contract Rent and Economic Rents--Reversion Rights," *Technicalities*, February, 1950, pp. 23-25.

TISHMAN, DAVID, "Investing In Real Estate," *Appraisal Digest*, April, 1958, pp. 18-20.

TOLLER, JANE, *Antique Minature Furniture In Great Britain and America*, G. Bell and Sons, London.

TROXELL, D CHASE, "Corporate Acquisitions- Basis," *Tax Management 196 Tm*,

TRUE, WALLACE W., "Appraising for Investment Purposes," *The Appraisal Journal*, October, 1943, pp. 346-353.

TURNER, ROBERT C., "Economic Vulnerability, the Lesson of 1957-1958," *The Appraisal Journal*, January, 1959, pp. 8-14.

UNTERKIRCHER, FIANZ, *European Illuminated Manuscripts*, Thames and Hudson, London.

VANCIL, RICHARD F, "Intangible Assets," *Accounting for Business Combinations and Goodwill*, pp. 1047-1060.

VAUGHAN JR, JOHN L, "Appraising Intangibles," *Valutape Audio-Library Series*, American Society of Appraisers, Washington D.C., January 1, 1973.

VAUGHAN, J. L. JR., "Appraising Intangibles," *The Valuation Manual*, 1955, pp. 135.

WADLEY, NICHOLAS, *Manet*, The Coloue Library of Art, 1969.

WADLEY, NICHOLAS, *The Drawings of Van Gogh*, Paul Hamlyn, London.

WALDMAN, DIANE, *Roy Lichtenstein Drawings and Prints*, Hacker Art Books Incorporated, New York, 1970.

WALDO, FRANCOIS, "An Institutional Investor Evaluates the Appraisal Reports," *The Appraisal Journal*, October, 1967, pp. 550-554.

## ▲ Intangible Property

WALL, WILLIAM J, "The Appraiser and the Real Estate Tax Shelter," *Valuation Magazine*, American Society of Appraisers, Washington D C, December 1, 1973, pp. 94-101.

WALLICH, H. C., "Traditional Vs. Performance Stock Valuation Analysis," *Commercial and Financial Chronicle*, February 18, 1971, pp. 547.

WANSCHER, OLE, *The Art of Furniture*, Allen and Unwin, 1968.

WARREN, G. F., F. A. PEARSON, *Gold and Prices*, John Wiley and Sons, Inc., New York, 1935.

WATERHOUSE, ELLIS, *Gainsborough*, Paul Hamlyn, London.

WEAVER, W. C. JR., "Real Estate A Piece of the Action for Life Insurances," *Bests Review*, December, 1970, pp. 20.

WECHSLER, HERMAN J., *Great Prints and Printmakers*, Thames and Hudson, London.

WEISS, E. B., "Expect One Thousand Pedestrian Shopping Malls by 1980," *Advertising Age*, September 21, 1970, pp. 50.

WELSCH, G. A., "A Fundamental Appraisal of Profit Planning and Control," *Managemt Acctg*, April, 1969.

WENDT, P. F., A. R. CERF, "Appraisers Bookshelf, Real Estate Investment Analysis and Taxation," *The Real Estate Appraiser*, March, 1970, pp. 61-62.

WENDT, PAUL F., SUI N. WONG, "Investment Performance, Common Stocks Versus Apartment Houses," *Journal of Finance*, December, 1965, pp. 633-646.

WERNER, ALFRED, *Modigliani Sculpture*, Hacker Art Books Incorporated, Switzerland, 1962.

WESSEL, R. H., "Economic and Stock Market Forecast for 1970," *Commercial and Financial Chronicle*, January 22, 1970, pp. 212.

WHITE, CARL, "Current Matters Affecting Public Utilities In the Valuation Concept," *Appraisal and Valuation Manual*, Corporate Press Incorporated, Washington, D. C, January, 1972, pp. 366.

WIEBE, JACOB EDWIN PHD, "Effects of Investments In Water Resources on Regional Income and Employment," The University of Tennessee, 1970.

WILFRED R., "Statistical Analysis of Industrial Property Retirements," *Engineering Valuation*, 1936.

WILLIAMS, JOHN B., *The Theory of Investment Value*, North-Holland Publishing Company, Amsterdam, 1956.

WILLIAMS, W., "Valuation of Closely-Held Corporations," *Trusts and Estates*, March, 1971, pp. 184-188.

WILLIAMSON, J. P., "Computerized Approaches to Bond Switching," *Financial Analysts Journal*, January, 1970, pp. 65-72.

WILLIS, H. P., BOGAN, J. I, *Investment Banking*, New York, 1929.

WINFREY, ROBLEY, "Statistical Analyses of Industrial Property Retirement," *Iowa Engineering Experiment Station Bulletin No. 125*, Iowa State College of Agriculture & Mechanic Arts, Ames, December 11, 1935, pp. 1-176.

WOLK, H. I., "The Relevant Costing Approach to Asset Valuation and Income Determination, a Critique," *Dissertation Abstracts*, April, 1969, pp. 3265-A.

WOODHOUSE, CHARLES PLATTEN, *Investment In Antiques and Art What, Where and How to Buy*, Bell, London, 1963.

WRIGHT, J. W., "Aggressive Approach to Bond Investment," *Trusts and Estates*, May, 1970, pp. 409-411.

YARMON, ELLIOT H., "Changing Views on Equity Investment," *Appraisal Institute Magazine*.

# BIBLIOGRAPHY OF APPRAISAL LITERATURE

"Building Profits Slip," *Chemical Week,* June 16, 1971, pp. 13.

"Companies Lend Their Expertise to the Arts," *Business Week,* May 15, 1971, pp. 102.

"Device for Measrg Sensitivity of Internal Economy of an Economic Base--Subst for Input-Output Anal.," *Valuation,* 1965, pp. 18-24.

"Effect of Rate of Return Reguln on Investmt Critra of Firm Its Impact on Grwth Study of Elec Utility," *Dissertation Abstracts International,* June, 1971.

"Floating Bonds Tax Chink," *The Economist,* October 24, 1973, pp. 93.

"Fuel Stocks Shrink to the Danger Point," *Business Week,* August 29, 1970, pp. 20.

"Gas Ups Stationary Market Share," *Oil and Gas Journal,* December 28, 1970, pp. 79.

"High Money Cost May Stall Housing Recovery," *Engineering News-Record,* December 3, 1970, pp. 42.

"Hot Sales In Property Shares," *Business Week,* November 28, 1970, pp. 34-36.

"Housing Partnership Makes First Investment," *Engineering News Record,* October 22, 1970.

"Industrys Hidden Dividends," *Nations Business,* October, 1970, pp. 74-77.

"Investment Corner Mortgage Your Home to the Roof," *Industry Week,* March 22, 1971, pp. 33.

"Investment Sting In the Budgets Tail," *The Economist,* April 8, 1972, pp. 72.

"Land Sales A Lower Key," *Business Week,* January 23, 1971, pp. 84.

"Life Insurance for Holders of Stock Options," *Insurance,* April, 1971, pp. 26.

"Mass Mutual Life Exchanges Properties In 5 Cities for Site Near Los Angeles Airport," *Insurance,* August 15, 1970, pp. 8.

"Money and Bond Markets," *Federal Reserve Bank of New York, Monthly Review,* pp. 98-103.

"New Depreciation Rule Detailed: Change Will Aid Businessmen In 70s," *Commerce Today,* February 22, 1971, pp. 16-18.

"Oil Growth to Zoom Fifty Percent Over Forecast," *Oil and Gas Journal,* August 24, 1970, pp. 25.

"Our Way of Life Depends on the Bond Markets Future," *Commercial & Financial Chronicle,* November 27, 1969, pp. 1696-1697.

"Pollution Does Find a Friend at the Bank," *Business Week.*

"Portfolio Analysis Stock Valuation and Capital Budgeting," *Journal of Finance,* March, 1971, pp. 95-117.

"Protecting Virgin Islands Ecology Is Good Business," *Engineering News-Record,* May 6, 1971, pp. 22.

"Pumping Money Out of the Sea," *Business Week,* July 11, 1970, pp. 54-55.

"Retirement Annuity Bonds 14 Per Cent," *The Economist,* December 5, 1970, pp. 95-96.

"Short-Term High Coupon Corporate Bonds Revisited," *Magazine of Wallstreet,* May 9, 1970, pp. 20-22.

"Some Theoretical Considerations for Future Trading In Commodts Reqrg Transformation Services," *Dissertation Abstracts International-A. the Humanities and Social Sciences,* April, 1971.

"These Golf Course Condominiums Have Strong Appeal to the Investment Buyer," *House and Home,* June, 1970, pp. 34.

"Tight Money Speeds Up Changes," *Chain Store Age,* May, 1970.

"Value Theory and User Participation," *Architectural Design*, May, 1972, pp. 319.

"Zero Population Growth What Effect on Business," *Industry Week*, March 15, 1971, pp. 26.

"500 Biggest Corporations by Market Value," *Forbes*, May 15, 1970.

"Statistical Criteria for Asset Valuation by Specific Price Index," *Accounting Review*, January, 1969.

"Some Implications of Variable Interest Rate Mortgages for the Small Saver & the House Owner," *Business and Economic Review*, University of South Carolina.

## 19-16 Stocks and Bonds

AHEARN, D. S., "1970s-More Rewarding Decade for Bond Investors," *Commercial and Financial Chronicle*, May 7, 1970, pp. 1453.

AIN, S. N., "How to Value Common Stocks Pensions Trust Investments, Trusts and Estates," *Trusts and Estates*, pp. 1073-1075.

ARCHIBALD, T. R., "Stock Market Reaction to the Depreciation Switch-Back," *Accounting Review*, January, 1972, pp. 22-30.

BARRON'S, "More Bond Buyers: by Year-End, Says Sidney Homer, Interest Rates Will Be Lower," *Barron's*, September 14, 1970, pp. 3.

BERANEK, WILLIAM, "The Effect of Leverage on the Market Value of Common Stock," *Managerial Finance*, University of Wisconsin, Madison, 1965, pp. 292.

BERNARD, ARNOLD, *Evaluation of Common Stocks*, Simon and Schuster, New York, 1959.

BIERMAN, H. JR., "The Valuation of Stock Options," *Journal of Finance and Quantitative Analysis*, 1967, pp. 327-34.

BING, R. A., "Can We Improve Methods of Appraising Growth Stocks," *ASA Valuation Manual*, September, 1956, pp. 1069.

BING, R. A., "Survey of Practioners Stock Evaluation Methods," *Financial Analysts Journal*, May, 1971, pp. 55-60.

BOWER, D. H., R. S. BOWER, *Test of a Stock Valuation Model*, May, 1970.

BRENNAN, M., "Note on Dividend Irrelevance and the Gordon Valuation Model," *Journal of Finance*, November, 1971.

CHAPMAN, CHARLES M., "Reliability of the Stock and Debt Approach Inthe Appraisal of Utility Property," *Conference Proceedings*, National Tax Association, Columbus, 1962, pp. 583-587.

CLENDENIN, J. C., AND M. VAN CLEAVE, "Growth and Common Stock Values," *Journal of Finance*, December, 1954, pp. 365-377.

CLENDENIN, S. C., "Dividend Growth As Determinant of Common Stock Values," *Trusts and Estates*, February, 1957, pp. 104-106.

COBLEIGH, I. U., "Office Building Shares," *Commercial and Financial Chronicle*, January 14, 1971, pp. 123.

COBLEIGH, I. U., "Views on Market Turbulence and Attractiveness of Bonds," *Commercial and Financial Chronicle*, June 4, 1970, pp. 1781.

COFFMAN, PAUL B., "Valuation of Stock of Closely-Held Corporations," *Appraisal and Valuation Manual*, American Society of Appraisers, Washington, 1956, pp. 341.

CRAGIN, RAYMOND T., "Appraiser's Part Important In Figuring Assets of Companies," *Eastern Underwriter*, June 12, 1936, pp. 6.

CRETIEN, P. D. JR., "Convertible Bond Debt Values Criticized," *Commercial and Financial Chronicle*, December 16, 1971, pp. 4.

CROCKETT, J., I. FRIEND, "The Integration of Capital Budgeting and Stock Valuation," *American Economic Review,* March, 1967.

DODD, DAVID LE FEVRE, *Stock Watering The Judical Valuation of Property for Stock-Issue Purposes,* Columbia University Press, New York, 1930.

ETTEMAN, DAVID K., "Utility Tax Valuation from Common Stock Prices," *Public Utilities Portnightly,* May, 1964, pp. 19-31.

FINANCIAL WORLD, "Investors Discover Bond Pitfalls," *Financial World,* July 22, 1970, pp. 6.

FINANCIAL WORLD, "Stocks Vs. Bonds In a New Business Climate," *Financial World,* September 23, 1970, pp. 7.

FISCHER, R. M., "Valuation of Capital Stock, I," *The Appraisal Journal,* April, 1944, pp. 143-153.

FISCHER, R. M., "Valuation of Stock In a Going Concern," *American Society of Appraisers Valuation Manual,* 1955, pp. 72.

FISHER, DONALD M., "The Western States Study of the Stock and Debt Approach to Railroad and Utility Valuations," *Assessment Administration,* Institute of American Appraisers Officers, Chicago, 1964, pp. 80-90.

GATES, W., "Timely Appraising of 100 Leading Stocks Looking to the Year Ahead," *A. S. A. Valuation Manual,* December 22, 1956, pp. 320-322.

GELBAND, J. F., "Investing In Bonds," *Magazine of Wall Street,* June 6, 1970, pp. 34.

GELMAN, M., "Financial Analyst's Approach to Valuing Stock of Closely-Held Company," *Journal of Taxation,* June, 1972, pp. 353-354.

GLUNT, DAVID, *Valuation of Closely Held Corporate Stocks,* American Appraisal Company, Milwaukee, 1956.

GLUNT, DAVID, "Valuations of Closely Held Corporate Stock," *Valuation,* April, 1968, pp. 220-232.

GRUNEWALD, ADOLPH E, "Stock Valuation In Federal Taxation," *Graduate School Business Administration, Michigan State University,* E Lansing, January 1, 1961.

GRUNEWALD, ADOLPH E, "Stock Valuation In Federal Taxation," *Occasional Paper #4,* Michigan State University, January 1, 1961.

HOGARTY, T. F., "Profitability of Corporate Mergers," *Journal of Business,* July, 1970, pp. 317-327.

HOLLANDER, LOUIS H., "Public Auction of Stocks and Bonds," *Valuation Manual,* ASA, 1958, pp. 129.

HOMER, S., "Individual Savings Flow Into Bond Market," *Burroughs Clearing House,* December, 1970, pp. 15.

HOMES, S., "Bond Market In a Changing World," *Commercial and Financial Chronicle,* May 3, 1971, pp. 1447.

INNOCENTI, R. E., "Are Bonds Currently Reasonable Investments for Pension Funds," *Trusts and Estates,* October, 1970, pp. 865-868.

KAUFMAN, H., "Bond and Interest Rate Outlook In the Context of a Non-Boom Economy," *Commercial and Financial Chronicle,* February 25, 1971, pp. 615.

KIRSHMAN, JOHN EMMETT, "Stock Prices," *Principles of Investment,* 1933, pp. 734.

KIST, R. T., "Appraising Is the Broker's Business," *The Appraisal Journal,* July, 1961, pp. 337-344.

LAWINGER, E. G., "Appraising Close-Held Stock-Val Methods & Concepts," *Trusts and Estates,* October, 1971, pp. 816-819.

LOGUE, DENNIS EMBARDT PH. D., *An Empirical Appraisal of the Efficiency of the Market for First Public Offerings of Common Stock,* Cornell University, 1971.

LONG, H. A., "Closed-End Bond Fund Sponsored by John Hancock," *Trusts and Estates,* January, 1971, pp. 47.

MACRAE, R. M., "Short Term Discount Bonds for a Prosperous 1970," *Financial Chronicle,* January 2, 1970, pp. 69.

MALKIEL, B. G., J. G. CRAGG, "Expectations and the Structure of Share Prices," *American Economic Review,* September, 1970, pp. 601-617.

MARSHALL, W. & YOUNG, A., "Controlling Shareholders Servicing Costs," *Harvard Business Review,* January, 1971, pp. 71-78.

MARTIN, S. J., "Factors the IRS and the Courts Are Using Today In Valuing Closely Held Shares," *Journal of Taxation,* February, 1972.

MAY, M., "Investment Opportunities Stock Valuation Model Based on Growth Patterns of Equity," *Journal of Finance,* September, 1971, pp. 993-994.

MERRILL, EUGENE S., "Effects of Market Pressure and Distribution of Listed Common Stocks," *ASA Valuation Manual,* American Society of Appraisers, 1958, pp. 147.

MEYERS, ROBERT M, "Valuation of Preferred Stocks of Closely Owned Businesses," *Valuation Magazine,* American Society of Appraisers, Washington D.C., December 1, 1973, pp. 22-33.

MORONEY, ROBERT E, "Most Courts Overvalue Closely Held Stocks," *Taxes (Magazine),* March 1, 1973.

MURRAY, R. F., "Probabilities Favor Stock Market Rise In Next Few Years," *Commercial and Financial Chronicle,* January 14, 1971, pp. 123.

MURRAY, R. F., "Stock Market Needs a Bond Market Recovery," *Commercial and Financial Chronicle,* January 29, 1970, pp. 292-293.

NEW ZEALAND SOCIETY OF ACCOUNTANTS, *Report on Valuation of Unquoted Shares,* New Zealand,

NICHOLS, PHILIP, "Tax Valuation of Stocks: Factors In Determining Market Value for Estate, Income Taxes," *Trusts and Estates Lxxx,* January 1, 1945, pp. 93.

PATTBERG, E. J., "American Bond Market-Sound and Attractive," *Commercial Intangible Property and Financial Chronicle,* May 28, 1970, pp. 1701.

PEARSON, F. A., W. I. MEYERS, E. E. VIDAL, "Stock Market," *The Appraisal Journal,* January, 1951, pp. 95-105.

POTTER, J., "Is the Recovery In Stocks Too Fast Two Investment Counselors Examine the Market," *Insurance,* April 1, 1971, pp. 40.

POTTER, J. C., "Investment Counselor Looks for Rising Stock Prices Says Time to Buy Is Now," *Insurance,* July 1, 1970, pp. 31-34.

RICE, RALPH S, "The Valuation of Close Held Stocks: a Lottery In Federal Taxation," *Law Review Xcvii,* University of Pennsylvania, December 1, 1950, pp. 385-388.

RODEN, P. F., "Overlooked Factors Which Make the Outlook for Bonds Bleak," *Commercial and Financial Chronicle,* December 31, 1970, pp. 1891.

ROLL, R., "Investment Diversification and Bond Maturity," *Journal of Finance,* March, 1971, pp. 51-66.

ROTH, LOVIS, "Bases of Common Stock Valuation," *The Appraisal Journal,* January, 1947, pp. 119-123.

ROTH, LOVIS, "Bases of Preferred Stock Valuation," *The Appraisal Journal,* October, 1947, pp. 528-534.

SCHMIDT, H. E., *Stocks of Closely Held Corporations,* M, November, 1952, pp. 17.

SEVERSON, HARRY L., "Government Bonds and Construction Expenditure Projections," *The Appriasal Journal,* July, 1962, pp. 413-414.

SHELTON, J. P., "The Value Line Contest A Test of the Predictability of Stock-Price Changes," *Journal of Business of the University of Chicago,* July, 1967, pp. 251-269.

SHERMER, MALCOLM, "Bonded Debt In Appraisals," *National Real Estate Journal,* August, 1941, pp. 27-28.

SHIACH, ALEXANDER D., "Valuation of Closely Held Stock," *Valutape Audio-Library Series,* American Society of Appraisers, Washington D.C., January 1, 1973.

STONE, J. E, "Valuation of Closely Held Stocks In Trusts and Estates," *American Society of Appraisers Valuation Manual,* February, 1956, pp. 116-118.

TANNEY, WILLIAM W., "Demonstration Appraisal: Small Plant, Value Company's Capital Stock," *Evaluating Industrial Real Estate,* The Society of Industrial Realtors, 1953, pp. 71-104.

TOWNSEND, F. S., "Evaluating Life Company Stocks a Dilemma," *Commercial and Financial Chronicle,* September 9, 1971, pp. 741.

TRAVIS, BROLEY E., "Reliability of the Stock and Debt Indicator Utility Property," *Technical Valuation,* pp. 5..

WALLICH, H. C., "Traditional Vs. Performance Stock Valuation Analysis," *Commercial and Financial Chronicle,* February 18, 1971, pp. 547.

WENDT, PAUL F., SUI N. WONG, "Investment Performance, Common Stocks Versus Apartment Houses," *Journal of Finance,* December, 1965, pp. 633-646.

WESSEL, R. H., "Economic and Stock Market Forecast for 1970," *Commercial and Financial Chronicle,* January 22, 1970, pp. 212.

WILLIAMSON, J. P., "Computerized Approaches to Bond Switching," *Financial Analysts Journal,* January, 1970, pp. 65-72.

WOLFE, HENRY D, "Valuation of Securities and Organized Exchanges," *Thesis,* University of Wisconsin, January 1, 1938.

WRIGHT, J. W., "Aggressive Approach to Bond Investment," *Trusts and Estates,* May, 1970, pp. 409-411.

*Spec Provns of Pers Prop Tax Laws of 31 States In Reln to Stock In Trade Aspects of Pers Prop Taxatn,* American Municipal Association, Chicago, 1959.

"Attractive Bonds at Discount Prices," *Financial World,* June 3, 1970, pp. 4.

"Bond Market A Patch of Blue," *Business Week,* July 11, 1970, pp. 15-16.

"Bond Market Faces Crucial Turning Point," *Commercial and Financial Chronicle,* July 2, 1970, pp. 2077.

"Bonds Good Buys if You Can Get Them," *Financial World,* October 14, 1970, pp. 13.

"Bonds Are Where the Money Is," *The Economist,* July 25, 1970, pp. 47.

"Bonds for Investment Backlogs," *Financial World,* September 2, 1970, pp. &94.

"Bonds-Bull Market at Last," *Financial World,* December 30, 1970, pp. 10.

"Can Stocks Shake the Liquidity Jitter," *Business Week,* June 27, 1970, pp. 42.

"Estate and Gift Tax Valuation of Closely Held Holding Company Stock," *Virginia Law Review Vol. 50,* pp. 337-352.

"Floating Bonds Tax Chink," *The Economist,* October 24, 1973, pp. 93.

"Fuel Stocks Shrink to the Danger Point," *Business Week,* August 29, 1970, pp. 20.

"Gas Ups Stationary Market Share," *Oil and Gas Journal,* December 28, 1970, pp. 79.

"Hot Sales In Property Shares," *Business Week,* November 28, 1970, pp. 34-36.

"Life Insurance for Holders of Stock Options," *Insurance,* April, 1971, pp. 26.

"Money and Bond Markets," *Federal Reserve Bank of New York, Monthly Review,* pp. 98-103.

"More Bond Buyers by Year-End, Says Sidney Homer, Interest Rates Will Be Lower," *Barrons,* May, 1970.

"Our Way of Life Depends on the Bond Markets Future," *Commercial & Financial Chronicle,* November 27, 1969, pp. 1696-1697.

"Portfolio Analysis Stock Valuation and Capital Budgeting," *Journal of Finance,* March, 1971, pp. 95-117.

"Retirement Annuity Bonds 14 Per Cent," *The Economist,* December 5, 1970, pp. 95-96.

"Short-Term High Coupon Corporate Bonds Revisited," *Magazine of Wall Street,* May 9, 1970, pp. 20-22.

# 19-17 Cash Flow Analysis

BAILEY, C. DOUGLAS, "The General Rate," *Ratings and Valuation Society,* 1967.

BARISH, NORMAN N., "Evaluating Intangibles," *Economics Analysis for Engineer Managerial Decision Making,* New York City, 1962.

BATEMAN, R. H., "Appraising the Going Concern," *Appraisal Journal,* October, 1971.

BLUME, E., "On the Assessment of Risk," *Journal of Finance,* March, 1971.

BUSHAM, K. J., "Valuation of Close Corporation Securities," *Trusts and Estates Xc,* Matthew Bender Co., Inc., New York, April 1, 1951, pp. 152.

COMISKEY, E. E., "Market Responses to Changes In Depreciation Accounting," *Accounting Review,* April, 1971, pp. 279-285.

CRAGIN, RAYMOND T., "Appraiser's Part Important In Figuring Assets of Companies," *Eastern Underwriter,* June 12, 1936, pp. 6.

DEMARA, CYRIL R., "On Forecasting Income," *The Appraisal Journal,* July, 1933, pp. 362.

DIETZ, P. O., G. P. WILLIAMS, "Influence of Pension Fund Asset Valuations on Rate of Return," *Financial Executive,* May, 1970, pp. 32-35.

GLADSTONE, WILLIAM F, "Tax Aspects of Allocation of Purchase Price of a Business," , October 1, 1966, pp. 36-44.

GROVES, HENRY M., "How Should Depreciation Allowance Be Handled?," *System and Business Management,* October, 1934, pp. 468-469, 492-496.

HANFORD, JR LLOYD D, "The Use of Discount Cash Flow Analysis," *The Real Estate Appraiser,* The Society of Real Estate Appraisers, Chicago Illinois, November 1, 1973, pp. 31-37.

HARTWIG, JOSEPH D, "Valuation Problems Before the IRS and the Tax Court," *13th Annual Institute on Federal Taxation,* Matthew Bender and Co, New York, January 1, 1955, pp. 1-143.

HYSOM, JOHN, CHARLES JUENGLING, "Computerized Cash Flow Analysis, a New Way to Evaluate Cash Project Feasibility," *Urban Land,* October, 1970.

JOHNSON, LYLE R, SHAPIRO, ELI, OLMEARA JR, JOSEPH, "Valuation of Closely Held Stock for Federal Tax Purposes: Approach to an Objective Method," *Law Review,* University of Pennsylvania, November 1, 1951, pp. 170.

KASCLE, E, "Valuation of Closely Held Corporations," *Taxes (Magazine),* July 1, 1965, pp. 454-463.

KUMAR, P., "Market Power, Growth, Leverage, and the Valuation of the Firm," *Journal of Finance,*

# BIBLIOGRAPHY OF APPRAISAL LITERATURE

LAFFER, ARTHUR BETZ, PH. D., *Private Short-Term Capital Flows*, Stanford Unversity, 1972.

LERNER, EUGENE M., CARLETON, WILLARD T., "Integration of Capital Budgeting," *American Economic Review*, September, 1964, pp. 683-702.

LEUTHOLD, S. C., "Spotting Tops and Bottoms Multiples of Normalized Earnings Book Values Are Useful Guides," *Barrons*, June 19, 1972, pp. 5.

MCCARTHY, GEORGE D, HEALY, ROBERT E, *Valuing a Company*, Roland Press, New York, January 1, 1971, pp. 1-521.

MONTONNA, DAVID L., "Analysis of Operating Statement," *Appraisal Institute Magazine*, February, 1958, pp. 9-16.

NORGAARD, RICHARD L., "Evaluating Intercorporate Risk, Returns, and Trends," *Journal of Financial and Quantitive Analysis*, University of Washington, September, 1971, pp. 1069-1082.

POWELL, ROGER K, "Valuation Cases: Practical Utility of Listed Comparatives Under Recent Decisions," *Proceedings Sixth Annual Institute on Federal Taxation*, Matthew Bender and Co Inc, New York, January 1, 1948, pp. 173.

RICKS, R. BRUCE, "Tax Shelter and Annual Cash Flow In Investment Real Estate," *The Appraisal Journal*, April, 1966, pp. 300-303.

RIGGE, ALBERT G., "Corporate Appraisers," *The Appraisal Journal*, July, 1960, pp. 299-300.

RING, ALFRED A., "Income Forecasting and Analysis In Valuation," *The Valuation of Real Estate*, 1970, pp. 205.

RING, ALFRED A., "Income Forecasting and Income Conversion," *The Appraisal Journal*, October, 1950, pp. 481-486.

RING, ALFRED A., "Operating Expense Forecasting and Analysis," *The Valuation of Real Estate*, 1970, pp. 219.

SCHARF, CHARLES A, "Determining the Purchase Price," pp. 43-58.

SCHEEFLY, J E, "The Sale of the Family Business: Income and Estate Planning Implications," *Taxes (Magazine)*, February 1, 1968, pp. 85-91.

SHENKEL, WILLIAM M., "Cash Flow Analysis: an Application of Conversational Computer Programming," *Journal of Property Management*, July, 1969.

SHENKEL, WILLIAM M., "Cash Flow and Multiple Regression Techniques; Comparative Anal of Apt Properties," *Journal of Property Management*, November, 1969.

STUETZER JR, HERMAN, "Valuing Business Interests of a Decedent," *The Implication of Revenue Ruling 59-60*, Matthew Bender Co Inc, New York, January 1, 1960, pp. 1196.

SWAN, CLIFFORD L., "Appraising a Going Business," *American Society of Appraisers Valuation Manual*, 1957, pp. 43.

TAYLOR, JAMES R., "Accruals for Depreciation," *The Review*, May, 1949, pp. 3-4, 14.

THORNE, O. J., "Industrial Park Cash Flow Analysis," *Industrial Development and Manufactures Record*, February 30, 1971, pp. 2-9.

VATTER, W. J., "Income Models, Book Yields, and Rate of Return," *Accounting Review*, October, 1966, pp. 681-698.

VAUGHAN JR, JOHN L, "Appraising Intangibles," *Valutape Audio-Library Series*, American Society of Appraisers, Washington D.C., January 1, 1973.

VAUGHAN, J. L. JR., "Appraising Intangibles," *The Valuation Manual*, 1955, pp. 135.

## 19-18 Securities and Registration of Securities

BADGER, R. E., "Valuation of Industrial Securities," *Principles of Investment,* New York City, 1925.

BADGER, RALPH, "Valuation of Closely Held Securities," *The Technical Valuation,* 1900, pp. 13.

BADGER, RALPH E, *Valuation of Industrial Securities,* Prentice-Hall Inc, New York, January 1, 1925.

BAUMOL, W. J., B. G. MALKIEL, R. E. QUANDT, "The Valuation of Convertible Securities," *The Quarterly Journal of Economics,* February, 1966.

BOGEN, J., "Analysis of Railroad Securities," *Principles of Investment,* New York, 1928, pp. 325.

BOSLAND, CHELCIE C., "The Valuation of Public Utility Enterprises by the Securities and Exchange Commission," *The Journal of Finance,* March, 1964, pp. 96-106.

CARMICHAEL, D. R., MAYNARD, R. M., "Auditing and Reporting for Security Valuations," *Journal of Accounting,* April, 1971, pp. 67-68.

CLIFFORD, ARTHUR M., *The Evaluation of Corporate Securities, Including the Determination of Fair Market Value,* Los Angeles, Calif., 1938.

COX, WARREN E., "Securities Vs. Works of Art for Investment Purposes," *The A. S. A. Valuation Manual,* American Society of Appraisers, 1960, pp. 87.

DALGETY, GEORGE S., "Security In Long Term Leases," *The Appraisal Journal,* July, 1940, pp. 255-259.

ELLWOOD, LEON W., "Value Concepts In Appraising Mortgage Security," *The Appraisal Journal,* October, 1953, pp. 581-585.

FINEHAUM, M. L., "Disposal & Land Valuation of Restricted Securities," *Trusts and Estates,* October, 1971, pp. 840-843.

FORD, BACON, AND DAVIS, INC., "Valuation of Going Companies for Purchase on Merger Also Fair Ratio for Exchange of Securities," *Valuation Manual,* 1955, pp. 173.

GILL, WILLIAM L., "Corporate Security Values As Determined by the Tax Court," *A. S. A. Valuation Manual,* A. S. A, 1960, pp. 77.

GRAHAM, DODD, COTTLE, "Security Analysis: Principles and Technique," *Security Analysis,* Mcgraw Hill, January 1, 1962.

GRAHAM, BENJAMIN, D. L. DODD, *Security Analysis,* Mcgraw-Hill, New York City, 1951.

HAYNES, JOHN L., "Real Estate Appraisals Under the Securities Act," *Real Estate Record and Builders Guide,* October 27, 1934, pp. 5-6.

HENDERSON, JAMES DOUGALD, *Real Estate Appraising a Practical Work on Appraising and Appraisal Methods,* Banker and Tradesman Publishing Company, Cambridge, Mass., 1931.

KIRSHMAN, JOHN EMMETT, "Real-Estate Securities," *Principles of Investment,* 1933, pp. 571.

KOSHAL, RAJINDAR K., "Highway Investments and Externalities a Case Study of Ohio," *Bulletin of Business Research,* Ohio State University, March, 1971, pp. 4 5.

LOSS, LOUIS, *Securities Regulations,* Little, Boston, 1951.

MCCLELLAN, W A, "Valuation of Closely Held Securities: Accounting Know-How Is the Key," *The Journal of Accounting,* March 1, 1966, pp. 47-55.

STANLEY, A. L., "Evaluating Intangibles for Executive Decision," *Economic Analysis,* September, 1955, pp. 781.

WOLTMAN, FREDERICK, "Leasehold Securities As Investments," *The Appraisal Journal,* January, 1936, pp. 71-72.

## 19-19 Good Will

BARISH, NORMAN N., "Evaluating Intangibles," *Economics Analysis for Engineer Managerial Decision Making,* New York City, 1962.

BATEMAN, R. H., "Appraising the Going Concern," *Appraisal Journal,* October, 1971.

HERD, JOHN J., "On the Valuation of Good Will," *The Appraisal Journal,* July, 1963, pp. 407-408.

MARSTON, ANSON, THOMAS R. AGG, "The Intangible Values Known As Preliminary Expense and Going Value," *Engineering Valuation,* Mcgraw-Hill, New York, 1936, pp. 335.

MARSTON, WINFREY, HEMPSTEAD, "Appraisal of Intangible Property," *Engineering Valuation and Depreciation,*

PINE, VANDERLYN R., "Measurement Procedures for Estimating Goodwill," *American Funeral Director,* National Funeral Directors Association, Milwaukee, Wisconsin.

RUHE, KARL, "The IRS Position on Allocation of Intangibles In Business Acquisitions," September 1, 1965, pp. 50-54.

SCHMUTZ, GEORGE L., "Valuation of Intangible Property," *The Appraisal Journal,* October, 1953, pp. 533-537.

SILVERMAN, BENJAMIN, "Corporate Franchises," *Appraisal and Valuation Manual,* pp. 215.

SKINNER, ROBERT G, "How the IRS Carries on Its Unrelenting Search for Purchases of Goodwill," November 1, 1968, pp. 288-291.

SNORGRASS, VERN G., "Evaluating a Small Going Business," *American Society of Appraisers Valuation Manual,* 1959, pp. 261.

STANLEY, A. L., "Evaluating Intangibles for Executive Decision," *Economic Analysis,* September, 1955, pp. 781.

STAPLETON, THOMAS M, "Intangible Assets In the Television Industry," *Taxes,* October 1, 1970, pp. 685-690.

SWAN, CLIFFORD L., "Appraising a Going Business," *American Society of Appraisers Valuation Manual,* 1957, pp. 43.

VANCIL, RICHARD F, "Intangible Assets," *Accounting for Business Combinations and Goodwill,* pp. 1047-1060.

VAUGHAN, J. L. JR., "Appraising Intangibles," *The Valuation Manual,* 1955, pp. 135.

VAUGHAN, JOHN L. JR., *Appraising Intangibles,* American Society of Appraisers, January, 1972.

*Accounting for Goodwill; Research Study #10,* American Institute of Certified Public Accountants, January 1, 1968.

"**Intangible Assets; APB Opinion #17**," *The Journal of Accountancy,* American Institute of Accountants, September 1, 1970, pp. 85-89.

# 19-20  Patents

BARISH, NORMAN N., "**Evaluating Intangibles**," *Economics Analysis for Engineer Managerial Decision Making,* New York City, 1962.

BATEMAN, R. H., "**Appraising the Going Concern**," *Appraisal Journal,* October, 1971.

LOUIS F. KORING, JR., "**Patent Valuations an Increasingly Important Apraisal Function**," *Appraisal and Valuation Manual,* Corporate Press, Incorporated, Washington, D. C, January, 1972, pp. 218.

PENMAN, S. H., "**What Net Value?--An Extension of a Familiar Debate**," *Accounting Review,* April, 1970, pp. 333-346.

SCHMUTZ, GEORGE L., "**Valuation of Intangible Property**," *The Appraisal Journal,* October, 1953, pp. 533-537.

SEIDEL, A H, "**What the General Practitioner Shoud Know About Patent Law and Practice**," American Law Institute, September 1, 1956.

SILVERMAN, BENJAMIN, "**Corporate Franchises**," *Appraisal and Valuation Manual,* pp. 215.

STANLEY, A. L., "**Evaluating Intangibles for Executive Decision**," *Economic Analysis,* September, 1955, pp. 781.

SWAN, CLIFFORD L., "**Appraising a Going Business**," *American Society of Appraisers Valuation Manual,* 1957, pp. 43.

TUSKA, C D, *An Introduction to Patents for Inventors and Engineers,* Dover Publications, January 1, 1964.

VAUGHAN, J. L. JR., "**Appraising Intangibles**," *The Valuation Manual,* 1955, pp. 135.

WOODLING, GEORGE V, "**Inventions and Their Protection**," Clark Boardman Co Ltd, New York, January 1, 1964.

*Encyclopaedia of Patent Practice (Robert Calvert, Editor),* Reinhold Publisher, New York.

*Patent, Trademark and Copyright Tax Guide,* Patent Law Association of Chicago.

*Tax Angles In Patents, Trademarks, Copyrights,* Tax Analysis, January 1, 1968.

# 19-21  Copyrights

BARISH, NORMAN N., "**Evaluating Intangibles**," *Economics Analysis for Engineer Managerial Decision Making,* New York City, 1962.

BATEMAN, R. H., "**Appraising the Going Concern**," *Appraisal Journal,* October, 1971.

SCHMUTZ, GEORGE L., "**Valuation of Intangible Property**," *The Appraisal Journal,* October, 1953, pp. 533-537.

SEIDEL, A H, "**What the General Practitioner Shoud Know About Patent Law and Practice**," American Law Institute, September 1, 1956.

SILVERMAN, BENJAMIN, "Corporate Franchises," *Appraisal and Valuation Manual*, pp. 215.

STANLEY, A. L., "Evaluating Intangibles for Executive Decision," *Economic Analysis*, September, 1955, pp. 781.

SWAN, CLIFFORD L., "Appraising a Going Business," *American Society of Appraisers Valuation Manual*, 1957, pp. 43.

*Patent, Trademark and Copyright Tax Guide*, Patent Law Association of Chicago.

*Tax Angles In Patents, Trademarks, Copyrights*, Tax Analysis, January 1, 1968.

"Aerial Walkways Big Plans for the Future," *Business Week*, December 26, 1970, pp. 48-49.

## 19-22 Trademarks

BARISH, NORMAN N., "Evaluating Intangibles," *Economics Analysis for Engineer Managerial Decision Making*, New York City, 1962.

SEIDEL, A H, "What the General Practitioner Shoud Know About Patent Law and Practice," American Law Institute, September 1, 1956.

SILVERMAN, BENJAMIN, "Corporate Franchises," *Appraisal and Valuation Manual*, pp. 215.

SWAN, CLIFFORD L., "Appraising a Going Business," *American Society of Appraisers Valuation Manual*, 1957, pp. 43.

*Patent, Trademark and Copyright Tax Guide*, Patent Law Association of Chicago.

*Tax Angles In Patents, Trademarks, Copyrights*, Tax Analysis, January 1, 1968.

# CHAPTER TEN

# Machinery and Equipment

Part I
by George D. Sinclair, ASA, MAI, SR/WA.
Part II
by John Alico, ASA, PE.

PART I

President of Keystone Appraisal Company of Philadelphia, Mr. Sinclair is Senior International Vice President of the American Society of Appraisers and Past President of the Philadelphia Chapter, A.S.A.

President of Chapter 9, American Right of Way Association for 1973, he is a member of the American Institute of Real Estate Appraisers, Property Consultants Society of England, and Philadelphia Board of Realtors

Mr. Sinclair served as Instructor in the Value of Machinery and Equipment course given by the American Society of Appraisers at various universities throughout the country.

His appraisal work has included Federal, State and local assignments, as well as many of the nation's larger industrial corporations, banks and insurance companies.

## Machinery and Equipment

MACHINERY and Equipment is a term that often has been misused and misunderstood within and without the appraisal profession for many years. The machinery and equipment appraisal discipline, as defined in the appraisal disciplines of the American Society of Appraisers, is "home" to appraisers of all the various categories of machinery and equipment. This bibliography offers machinery and equipment appraisers and those with like interest, an insight into the many complex facets of this challenging field of endeavor.

Machinery and equipment in the broad sense comprises all items that are not appraised as real property. In general, machinery and equipment is classed as a marketable property; however, there are certain classes of equipment that are nonmarketable. Items of machinery and equipment are purchased for a use, or with intent to produce a product. As a general rule, machinery and equipment is not purchased as an investment property, that is, with intent to produce an income stream similar to that resulting from an investment apartment house or commercial property.

The uses of machinery and equipment appraisals and the purposes they serve are summarized in the following analysis.

The concept of machinery and equipment appraisals had its start before the turn of the century. The first major use of machinery and equipment appraisals was by the insurance industry. Appraisals of machinery and equipment made for insurance purposes should serve two main purposes. First, they should establish proper value in accordance with the terms of the policy in force. Secondly, they must serve as a reliable proof of loss in event of a disaster.

The next major increase in the number of machinery and equipment appraisals occurred with the enactment of the income tax and other federal tax laws. Depreciation then became an item of concern to all industries and businesses. The recent growth of mergers and acquisitions has increased the demand for professional machinery and equipment appraisal. The allocation of a gross purchase price to the several items purchased is a task that requires currency, i.e. keeping abreast with the times.

The use of machinery and equipment appraisals by public utilities also has played an important role in the machinery and equipment field. The present day problems of all utilities makes this field most challenging. Recently designed and developed equipment in the atomic energy field is but one example. The problems of ecology and environmental controls and their place in the valuation process also add new dimensions to machinery and equipment appraisals.

Many of our states are now including personal property in their *ad valorem* tax assessments. The "mass tax appraisal" concept presents many unique problems to the machinery and equipment appraiser that are not found elsewhere. The complex procedure required to determine market value, where a detailed analysis is not possible, is but one of the challenges of this type of work.

The sale, purchase, and/or leasing of machinery and equipment has been a growing field ever since the end of World War II. This field demands not only a knowledge of the market place, but also requires a complete understanding of the value concept. Machinery and equipment may have more than one market value; i.e., a market value in-place as part of a total operating unit, or a market value for off-site use. Machinery and Equipment may have a liquidation value under forced sale conditions, or as part of an orderly sale.

Needless to say, these values may vary and the appraiser must be aware of all factors that change or affect the difference.

The condemnation of private property for public use has involved greater use of machinery and equipment appraisals than any other activity. The acquisition of private property by our Highway Departments, Redevelopment Authorities and other governmental agencies has created a demand for qualified machinery and equipment appraisers unheard of prior to 1950. The acquisition of real estate or real property, as a general rule, follows a standard form. Most condemning authorities, as well as condemnees, view the valuation of real estate in accordance with the accepted standard. However, there is no standard format when machinery and equipment is being acquired. The formats and requirements may vary from agency to agency, area to area, but the concept of value in a machinery and equipment report must remain constant.

The field of machinery and equipment has a limited amount of published literature. The articles that are incorporated in this bibliography nevertheless offer the greatest source data available. It is important to realize that no appraiser can limit his appraisal vision to one restricted field. The valuation of machinery and equipment for any given purpose must reflect the considerations of the entire scope of valuation. A complete understanding of the machinery and equipment valuation concept can be achieved only when it is based on a foundation of the "total value" concept.

A machinery and equipment appraiser does not, of necessity, have to be a real estate expert. However, a qualified machinery and equipment appraiser must have an understanding of the real estate valuation process.

All of the various purposes of appraisals we have discussed require an understanding of what is properly to be included as either machinery and equipment or as real property. An understanding of other disciplines is thus required of the machinery and equipment appraiser. He is not required to appraise Personal Property, Intangible Property or prepare a Technical Valuation, but he must be understand and be familiar with the concepts of each.

The strength of the American Society of Appraisers lies in this concept. The full utility of this bibliography will be achieved only when all of us understand this concept and make it a part of our day-by-day professional activity.

# PART II

John Alico is President of Alico Engineers and Appraisers, Incorporated, a firm of consulting engineers and industrial appraisers, headquartered in Southfield, Michigan. He is a mechanical engineer (Columbia University) and a Registered Professional Engineer in the states of Michigan, New York, Wisconsin and Connecticut.

His experience includes approximately 21 years Consulting Engineer-Industrial Appraiser, plus responsibilities as Director of Metals Processing and Fabrication-Copper mining operations, General Manager-aluminum extrusion and forging plant, and Director of Research and Development of a magnesium fabrication company.

Mr. Alico is a Senior member of the American Society of Appraisers, American Society of Mechanical Engineers, American Institute of Mining, Metallurgical and Petroleum Engineers, American Society of Metals, National Society of Professional Engineers, Engineering Society of Detroit, and the Columbia Engineering School Alumni Association. He has served these organizations in a number of capacities including those of officer and director.

Qualified as an Industrial Appraiser and expert witness for the U.S. Department of Justice and other Governmental agencies, Mr. Alico is also qualified as an International Consultant on metals processing for the United Nations.

He is the author of approximately 60 technical papers on metals production and processing and machinery and equipment valuation. He has instructed regular courses in machinery and equipment appraisal at Oakland University as well as seminars sponsored by ASA in a number of colleges and universities in the United States.

### ▲ Machinery and Equipment

THE MACHINERY and equipment appraisal discipline is growing in recognition and becoming increasingly important as an art. There are no definitive formulas which could be used to appraise machinery and equipment and, hence, the discipline cannot be described as a science. The fact that it is an art makes "The Bibliography of Appraisal Literature" an important research reference.

*The three classic approaches cannot be applied to the appraisal of machinery and equipment and correlated to determine the correct set of values.* Depending upon the characteristics of the appraisal problem, it may be possible to use the Market Data Approach or the Cost Data Approach. As machinery and equipment is generally bought to be used, by itself or in conjunction with other items, to produce a part or a product which is to be sold at a profit, it is not possible to derive a basis for using the Income Approach.

The Market Data Approach is applicable in appraisal problems where machinery and equipment is to be sold for liquidation purposes, either in a Voluntary or Involuntary (such as a creditor's auction) process. The Cost Data Approach takes the reproduction, or replacement, cost new plus the installation cost and from this total subtracts the combined depreciation and obsolescence considerations to arrive at a value in place. Given the right set of circumstances it is possible for these values to be widely different for the item being appraised.

The Bibliography of Appraisal Literature provides a ready background of published information which gives to the already experienced Appraiser source material to use in better understanding the appraisal problem. A better understanding of the problem should result in a more thorough analysis with a correspondingly improved statement of data which will make the report as nearly scientific as is possible.

The Appraiser may be given an unusual assignment in that the appraisal problem involves possible uses other than the highest and best use for a given machine or group of machines. By referring to the Bibliography he may find an approach to the solution of the problem through another appraiser's published experience. The Bibliography of Appraisal Literature is an invaluable collection of individual examples which will provide a vital and useful background to the M/E Appraiser.

# Machinery and Equipment

| | |
|---|---|
| 20-11 | Furnishings and Fixtures |
| 20-12 | Construction Equipment |
| 20-13 | Environmental Control Equipment |
| 20-14 | Fabrication Process |
| 20-15 | Industrial Machinery |

## 20-11  Furnishings and Fixtures

ADAMS, JOHN C. JR., "Determination of Service Life of Mass Plant Items," *Valuation Manual,* American Society of Appraisers, Washington, D.C., 1964, pp. 73.

ALICO, JOHN, "The Appraisal of Machinery and Equipment," *Valutape Audio-Library Series,* American Society of Appraisers, Washington D.C., January 1, 1973.

AMERICAN SOCIETY OF APPRAISERS, WASHINGTON, "Appraisal of Machinery and Equipment," American Society of Appraisers, Washington.

ASH, FRED C., "Trade Fixtures of Land Owner," *The Appraisal Journal,* October, 1955, pp. 600.

BABCOCK, FREDERICK M., "Building Cost, Furnitute and Equipment Investment Estimation: Theater," *Valuation of Real Estate,* 1932, pp. 482, 484, 493.

BALL, THOMAS B., "Fixed Furniture and Equipment," *Church Valuation,* Church Valuation Consultants, 1968, pp. 195.

BRENER, DANIEL A., "Valuation of Furniture and Fixtures In a Hotel or Motel," *A. S. A. Valuation Manual,* The American Society of Appraisers, Washington D. C, 1964, pp. 63.

BROOKE, R. J., "Appraisal Methods," *The Appraisal of Machinery and Equipment,* pp. 17.

CAPPS, WILLIS W., "When Is a Fixture Fixed," *Right of Way,* April, 1969.

COHEN, SAMUEL H., "Fixture Appraisal," *Appraisal and Valuation Manual,* American Society of Appraisers, Washington, 1961, pp. 31.

DAVIS, N. L., "The Appraisers Training and Education," *Appraisal of Machinery and Equipment,* 1969, pp. 99.

DIEPENBROCK, BRAM, "Equipment Values In Public Acquisition-Fact or Fiction," *Right of Way,* October, 1969, pp. 11-16.

DIX, S. M., "The Problem with Value-In-Place Less Salvage In Determining Fixture Damage," *Right of Way,* April, 1969, pp. 34-36.

DIX, SAMUEL M, "Eminent Domain: Principles of Fixture Appraisal," *Valutape Audio-Library Series,* American Society of Appraisers, Washington D.C., January 1, 1973.

DIX, SAMUEL M., "Fixture Qualification and Valuation for Condemnation of the Major Industrial Complex," *The Appraisal Journal,* April, 1966, pp. 245-257.

DIX, SAMUEL M., "Fixture Qualification In Eminent Domain," *The Appraisal Journal,* April, 1969, pp. 235-238.

DOLAN, HARRY T., "Trade Fixtures In Condemnation. Confusion," *The Appraisal Journal,* April, 1968, pp. 263-265, 268-269.

DOLAN, HARRY T., "Trade Fixtures In Federal Condemnation," *The Appraisal Journal,* October, 1965, pp. 499-507.

ENFIELD, CLIFTON W., AND WILLIAM A. MANSFIELD, "Fixtures Vs. Personal Property," *Right of Way,* December, 1956, pp. 10-13, 15-19, 21-23.

FLEMING, KENNETH W, "The Appraisal of Motel Furniture, Fixtures, M/E," *Valutape Audio-Library Series,* American Society of Appraisers, Washington D.C., January 1, 1973.

HIGHWAY RESEARCH BOARD, *Valuation and Condemnation Problems Involving Trade Fixtures,* NCHRP Report 94, Washington, D.C.

HOLMES, LAWRENCE G., **"Furnishings In the Hotel Appraisal,"** *The Appraisal Journal,* April, 1942, pp. 143-152.

MACHINERY & ALLIED PRODUCTS INSTITUTE, *MAPI Replacement Manual,* Machinery & Allied Products Institute, Washington, 1950.

MACHINERY AND ALLIED PRODUCTS INSTITUTE, *An Introduction to Equipment on Analysis,* Washington, 1956.

MACHINERY AND ALLIED PRODUCTS INSTITUTE, *Company Procedural Manual on Equipment Analysis,* Washington, 1951.

MACHINERY AND ALLIED PRODUCTS INSTITUTE, *Equipment Replacement and Depreciation Policies and Practices,* Washington, 1956.

MACHINERY AND ALLIED PRODUCTS INSTITUTE, *MAPI Business Investment Manual,* Washington, 1957.

PAILET, GUSTAVE, **"Forced Sale and Liquidation Values of M/E,"** *Valutape Audio-Library Series,* American Society of Appraisers, Washington D.C., January 1, 1973.

PROUTY, W. L. AND OTHERS, **"The Appraisal of Merchandise, Fixtures, Equipment, Furniture, Household Goods, Livestock,"** *Appraisers, and Assessors Manual,* 1930, pp. 421-460.

ROITMAN, SOL, **"Education, Training Needed When You Receive an Assignment for Fixture and M/E Appraisal,"** American Society of Appraisers, Washington, D.C., January 1, 1973.

SCHAFF, ARTHUR, **"The Appraisal of Trade Fixtures,"** *Appraisal Digest,* April, 1963, pp. 10.

TERBORGH, GEORGE, *Realistic Depreciation Policy,* Machinery and Allied Product Institute, Chicago, 1955.

THEISS, WILLIAM R., **"The Appraisal Docket, Manner and Method of Determening Value of Fixtures,"** *The Appraisal Journal,* January, 1963, pp. 119-121.

THULMAN, ROBERT K., **"The Floor Furnace In Small Homes,"** *The Review,* February, 1950, pp. 10-12.

WILSON, WILLIAM, **"The Law of Fixtures,"** *The Appraisal Journal,* October, 1938, pp. 307-315.

*Building Construction Cost Data 32nd Edition,* Means Co. Inc., Duxbury Mass., January 1, 1974, pp. 292.

"Reflective Glass Is Hot Item Taking Architecture by Storm," *Industry Week,* February 1, 1971, pp. 61-62.

## 20-12 Construction Equipment

AMERICAN SOCIETY OF APPRAISERS, WASHINGTON, **"Appraisal of Machinery and Equipment,"** American Society of Appraisers, Washington.

BLACK, I. G., **"Metals Pick Up Speed In Building Materials Race,"** *Iron Age,* April 29, 1971, pp. 37.

BROOKE, R. J., **"Apparisal Methods,"** *The Appraisal of Machinery and Equipment,* pp. 17, ASA Monograph.

DAVIS, N. L., **"The Appraisers Training and Education,"** *Appraisal of Machinery and Equipment, Monograph,* ASA, 1969, pp. 99.

▲ **Machinery and Equipment**

ENGINEERING NEWS-RECORD, "Atkinson Scores In Solo Bid on Cochiti Dam," *Engineering News-Record,* May 21, 1970, pp. 40.

GIVENS, HARRY, "Construction Equipment and the Significant Approach," *Technical Valuation,* A. S. A, Washington, D. C, September, 1966, pp. 17.

MACHINERY AND ALLIED PRODUCTS INSTITUTE, *Equipment Replacement and Depreciation Policies and Practices,* Washington, 1956.

MILLER MARTIN D., "New Ideas and Materials In Construction," *The Appraisal Journal,* April, 1962, pp. 267-278.

NELSON, W. L., *Petroleum Refinery Engineering,* Mcgraw-Hill, New York, 1958.

NELSON, W. L., "Replacement Value," *American Society of Appraisers Valuation Manual,* June 2, 1952, pp. 111.

PAILET, GUSTAVE, *Forced Sale and Liquidation Values of Machinery and Equipment,* American Society of Appraisers, January, 1972.

PLETZ, C. L., "Putting a Value on Used Construction Machinery," *Technical Valuation,* pp. 4-9.

PULVER, HARRY E., *Construction Estimates and Costs,* Mcgraw-Hill, New York, 1947.

SCHROPP, T. L., "Appraisal Identification," *The Appraisal of Machinery and Equipment,* ASA, Monograph, 1969, pp. 31.

TERBORGH, GEORGE, *Realistic Depreciation Policy,* Machinery and Allied Product Institute, Chicago, 1955.

## 20-13  Environmental Control Equipment

AMERICAN SOCIETY OF APPRAISERS, WASHINGTON, "Appraisal of Machinery and Equipment," American Society of Appraisers, Washington.

CARRIER, W. H., "Appraising Air Conditioning and Cooling Equipment," *The Review of the Society of Residential Appraisers,* November, 1936, pp. 4-6.

DAVIS, N. L., "The Appraisers Training and Education," *Appraisal of Machinery. and Equipment,* ASA Monograph, 1969, pp. 99.

DUFFY, G., "HUD Supports Air Conditioning of 46,000 Public Housing Units for Elderly," *Air Conditioning, Heating and Refrigeration News,* August 3, 1970, pp. 2.

FPC, "Air Pollu In Reg Elec Power & Nat Gas Industries," FPC, Wash., D. C., Spetember, 1968.

INTERNATIONAL ASSOCIATION OF ASSESSING OFFICERS, *Environmental Control Facilities,* Chicago, Illinois.

JAROS, ALFRED L. JR., "Air Conditioning Costs," *Technical Valuation,* ASA, February, 1955, pp. 64.

JOACHIM, HARRY J., "New Innovations In Environmental Control, What Effect on Values," *The Real Estate Appraiser,* January, 1968, pp. 20-22.

KAUFMAN, K. A., "Pollution Rules Could Choke Industry to Death," *Iron Age,* February 11, 1971, pp. 21.

LAROS, ALFRED L., "What Does Air Conditioning Cost," *Technical Valuation,* A. S. A, Washington, February, 1954, pp. 64.

LEGGE, HAROLD, "The Influence of Air Conditioning on Value of Dwellings," *The Appraisal Journal,* October, 1955, pp. 560-563.

MACHINERY AND ALLIED PRODUCTS INSTITUTE, *Equipment Replacement and Depreciation Policies and Practices,* Washington, 1956.

MCMICHAEL, STANLEY L., "**Appraising Air-Conditioning Equipment,**" *Appraising Manual,* 1937.

MCNULTY, J. W., "**Amortization of Pollution Control Facilities How the New Election Works,**" *Journal of Taxation,* April, 1971, pp. 211-214.

MILLS, DOREMUS L., "**Radiant Heating Explained for the Appraiser,**" *Appraisal Digest,* October, 1950, pp. 19-21.

PAILET, GUSTAVE, *Forced Sale and Liquidation Values of Machinery and Equipment,* American Society of Appraisers, January, 1972.

WILLIAMS, D. N., "**Pay-As-You-Pollute Plan No Limits Just Cash,**" *Iron Age,* January 14, 1971, pp. 45.

"Pollution Does Find a Friend at the Bank," *Business Week,*

"Sulfur Tax Pollutants Standards Are Urged In the Clean Air Fight," *Oil, Paint, and Drug Reporter,* February 8, 1971, pp. 4.

## 20-14  Fabrication Process

AMERICAN SOCIETY OF APPRAISERS, WASHINGTON, "**Appraisal of Machinery and Equipment,**" American Society of Appraisers, Washington.

BOLZ, R W, "Production Processes," Penton, Cleveland, January 1, 1961.

BROOKE, R. J., "**Appraisal Methods,**" *The Appraisal of Machinery and Equipment,* pp. 17.

DAVIS, N. L., "**The Appraisers Training and Education,**" *Appraisal of Machinery and Equipment,* 1969, pp. 99.

DEBOOS, FRANK A., "A New Steel Prefab," *The Review,* November, 1950, pp. 14-15.

GARBER, L. L., "Concerning Prestressed Concrete," *Technical Valuation,* February, 1958, pp. 55-60.

MACHINERY AND ALLIED PRODUCTS INSTITUTE, *Equipment Replacement and Depreciation Policies and Practices,* Washington, 1956.

PAILET, GUSTAVE, *Forced Sale and Liquidation Values of Machinery and Equipment,* American Society of Appraisers, January, 1972.

TERBORGH, GEORGE, *Realistic Depreciation Policy,* Machinery and Allied Product Institute, Chicago, 1955.

## 20-15 Industrial Machinery

ALICO, JOHN, "The Appraisal of Machinery and Equipment," *Valutape Audio-Library Series*, American Society of Appraisers, Washington D.C., January 1, 1973.

ALICO, JOHN, "The Valuation of Hydraulic Extrusion Presses," *Valuation*, pp. 63-73.

AMERICAN SOCIETY OF APPRAISERS, WASHINGTON, "Appraisal of Machinery and Equipment," American Society of Appraisers, Washington.

BOLZ, R W, "Production Processes," Penton, Cleveland, January 1, 1961.

BROOKE, R. J., "Appraisal Methods," *The Appraisal of Machinery and Equipment*, ASA Monograph, pp. 17.

BURNELL, WILLIAM U., "Machinery and Equipment-Going Concern Values," *Technical Valuation Manual*, American Society of Appraisers, October, 1953, pp. 33.

DANA, RICHARD TURNER, *Handbook of Construction Equipment Its Cost and Use*, Mcgraw Hill Book Company, New York, 1926.

DAVIS, N. L., "The Appraisers Training and Education," *Appraisal of Machinery and Equipment*, ASA Monograph, 1969, pp. 99.

DIEPENBROCK, BRAM, "Equipment Values In Public Acquisition-Fact or Fiction," *Right of Way*, October, 1969, pp. 11-16.

HARDS, I BLAIR, "Approach to Value: Electronic Mfg and Testing Equipment," *Valuation Magazine*, American Society of Appraisers, Washington D C, December 1, 1973, pp. 76-79.

KAWAHITO, KIYOSHI PHD, "The Steel Import Problem of the United States and the Japanese Steel Industry," University of Maryland, 1971.

KIPERS, R F, "Manufacturing Analysis," Mcgraw-Hill, New York, January 1, 1949.

MACHINERY AND ALLIED PRODUCTS INSTITUTE, *Equipment Replacement and Depreciation Policies and Practices*, Washington, 1956.

MCKAY, CHARLES WATSON, *Valuing Industrial Properties*, New York, 1922.

OSTENDORF, E. L., "Appraisal of an Industrial Plant," *Appraisal Reporting Techniques*, A. I. R. E. A., 1947, pp. 119-161.

OWEN, LEROY D., "Appraisal Points Industrial Executives Expect to Find," *California Real Estate Magazine*, November, 1935, pp. 30-32.

PAILET, GUSTAVE, *Forced Sale and Liquidation Values of Machinery and Equipment*, American Society of Appraisers, January, 1972.

PAILET, GUSTAVE, "Forced Sale and Liquidation Values of M/E," *Valutape Audio-Library Series*, American Society of Appraisers, Washington D.C., January 1, 1973.

PARSONS, C. W. S., "Estimating Machining Costs," *American Society of Appraisers Valuation Manual*, Mcgraw-Hill, New York, 1957.

POTTER, EDWARD, "Industrial Appraisals Pertaining to Liquidating Values," *Technical Valuation*, 1966, pp. 9-13.

RALEIGH, JAMES C., "Appraisal of a Tank Farm," *The Real Estate Appraiser*, November, 1970, pp. 36-38.

RUSINOFF S E, "Forging and Forming Metals," American Technical Society, Chicago, January 1, 1952.

SCHROPP, T. L., "Appraisal Identification," *The Appraisal of Machinery and Equipment*, ASA Monograph, 1969, pp. 31.

## BIBLIOGRAPHY OF APPRAISAL LITERATURE

SINCLAIR, G. D., "Appraisal Concepts," *The Appraisal of Machinery and Equipment,* ASA Monograph, pp. 7.

TERBORGH, GEORGE, *Realistic Depreciation Policy,* Machinery and Allied Product Institute, Chicago, 1955.

WALLACE, LEW E., *Depreciation of Farm Machinery, Transamerican Society of Agriculture Engineering,* pp. 139.

"Huge Press Speeds Casting of Building Panels," *Engineering News-Record,* December 17, 1970, pp. 73.

"Machinery and Equipment Guide," *Guidebook,* Construction Publishing Co, New York, January 1, 1973.

"Plan for Value: Tools and Equipment," *Purchasing,* 1970.

BIBLIOGRAPHY OF APPRAISAL LITERATURE

# CHAPTER ELEVEN

# Costs
by Frank C. Swift, ASA.

Mr. Frank Swift, a Senior Member of the American Society of Appraisers, is currently managing partner of the Marshall and Swift Publishing Company.

For approximately twenty years, Mr. Swift has been associated with a publication which publishes manuals on Building Costs; he has experience as a General Contractor and Cost Estimator for five years. He holds a BA degree in Mathematics from the University of Redlands, California.

# ▲ Costs

OF THE SEVEN major appraisal classifications, that of Cost Estimation falls under Technical Valuations. While the determination of costs may be a part of some of the other disciplines, there are a number of appraisal assignments which require the services of one who is competent in estimating costs of producing or replacing physical property.

*Just as the appropriate method for appraising an investment property (for example, an apartment house), is the investment analysis method; and the appropriate method of appraising a marketable non-investment property (for example, a single family residence), is the sales analysis method; the cost summation method is appropriate when appraising a non-investment, non-marketable, property (for example, a church).* Non-marketable does not mean that this type of property is never bought and sold, but that sales are so rare that the value cannot be determined by the sales analysis method.

Any report of a cost estimate should clearly state that it is a cost appraisal and not a determination of investment value or market value. More detailed description of the physical property is required for some purposes than others, but the report should always contain the proper data to identify the property and describe at least the major cost-important considerations.

Cost appraisals are required in the following instances:

Arriving at a reasonable amount of fire insurance to carry on buildings. Replacement cost insurance with a co-insurance penalty requires an accurate up-to-date cost estimate. Also, when adjusting a loss, a detailed cost estimate must be made.

In *ad valorem* tax jurisdictions which require separate assessed values on the land and improvements, the cost of the improvements must be determined.

When a piece of improved investment real estate is purchased, the cost of the improvements must be known in order to allocate a portion of the purchase price to the depreciable items.

To determine the feasibility of a proposed income-producing property, two appraisals are required, an appraisal of value, and an appraisal of the required investment (cost).

When the depreciated reproduction cost of a building is needed, not only must the estimator arrive at the total improvement cost, but the cost to cure the worn components must sometimes be estimated and many cost appraisers must develop an expertise in estimating physical depreciation.

Determining the production cost of investment property is important to regulatory bodies to guard against overpricing of a stock based on a fictitiously high earning forecast.

Retrospective cost estimates are often required in rate making for public utilities.

Special cost knowledge is required for estimating engineering construction such as bridges, highways, dams, etc.

The cost appraiser not only needs to have a thorough knowledge and understanding of current costs, but should also understand the use of cost trend indexes which are useful in updating original costs or making retrospective appraisals.

The cost appraiser may work exclusively in his discipline; for example, if his assignment is an insurance appraisal. Or, he may work as a team with another appraisal discipline; for example, in the case of a feasibility study. Frequently an appraiser qualified in some other discipline, such as real estate, might also be qualified as a cost appraiser.

The literature in the field of cost estimates falls generally into the following groups:

*Texts* which furnish detailed instructions on how to build-up the cost of a structure listing what must be included, how to measure and determine quantities, and guides to estimating installation costs.

*Publications* which list costs of various structures and/or their components. They range from costs of completed buildings based on total area or volume, to detailed unit-in-place costs for the various components of the structure.

*Articles* on changes in building costs for various periods, and articles on the cost estimating of specific items from structures to timber.

*Texts* on appraisal practices which describe the role of the cost estimator in the broad field of appraising.

# Costs

| | |
|---|---|
| 21-11 | Economic Theory |
| 21-12 | Replacement |
| 21-13 | Building |
| 21-14 | Rising Costs |
| 21-15 | Cost Surveys |
| 21-16 | Engineering Construction |
| 21-17 | Historical |
| 21-18 | Forecasting |
| 21-19 | Summation |
| 21-20 | Indexes |
| 21-21 | Cost to Cure |

## 21-11 Economic Theory

ABEL, VICTOR D, "A Study of Rising Costs," *The Review,* March, 1946, pp. 7-8.

AMERICAN ECONOMIC ASSOCIATION, *Reading In Price Theory,* R. D. IRWIN, Chicago, 1952.

AMERICAN INSTITUTE OF ARCHITECTS, "Cubic Contents of Buildings," American Institute of Architects, May, 1928.

ARENA, JOHN J., "Is the United States Pricing Itself Out of World Markets," *The Appraisal Journal,* January, 1966, pp. 58-62.

ARMSTRONG, LOU, "Cost Today and Value Tomorrow," *Technicalities,* May, 1949, pp. 31-36.

ARMSTRONG, WILLIAM Y., "Is the Cost Approach Necessary," *The Appraisal Journal,* January, 1963, pp. 71-80.

BABCOCK, FREDERICK M., "Distinction Between Value and Cost," *Appraisal Principles and Procedures,* 1900.

BABCOCK, HENRY A., "Definition of 'Appraisal' 'Valuation' 'Cost Estimation' and 'Earning Forecast'," *Appraisal Principles and Procedures,* Irwin Company, Homewood Illinois, January 1, 1968, pp. 3-11.

BALL, THOMAS B., "Construction Adjustment Factors," *Church Valuation,* Church Valuation Consultants, 1968, pp. 11.

BALL, THOMAS L, "Cost Manuals and Cost Data," *Valutape Audio-Library Series,* American Society of Appraisers, Washington D.C., January 1, 1973.

BALL, THOMAS L., *Cost Manuals and Cost Data,* American Society of Appraisers, January, 1972.

BALLARD, W. H., "Expense As a Factor In Appraising," *National Association of Real Estate Boards,* 1929, pp. 81-84.

BEATTIE, R. D., J. E. VIVIAN, "When Making Cost Estimates Watch Your Language," *Chemical Engineering,* January, 1953, pp. 172.

BEETH, CHANNING C., "Today's Appraisal Digest Must Reflect Today's Cost," *Appraisal Digest,* January, 1954, pp. 4-6.

BOHANNON, DAVID D., "Building Trends," *The Review,* September, 1948, pp. 3-6.

BONNER, JOHN T. JR., "Inaccuracies of Costs," *Appraisal Digest,* October, 1958, pp. 11-12.

BOWEN, PERCIVAL V., "Role of Operating Costs In Future Valuation," *Appraisal Journal,* July, 1950, pp. 370-373.

BRUNDAGE, PERCIVAL F., "Depreciation an Old Subject with a New Importance," *Harvard Business Review,* 1935, pp. 334-343.

BURNS, WARREN W., "Salvage by Foreclosure," *The Review,* July, 1948, pp. 12-15.

CHAFFE, R. S., "Physical Depreciation," *Review of Society of Residential Appraiser,* August, 1940, pp. 3-6, 16.

CHALMERS, T. G., "Comments on No Appreciation for Appreciation," *Appraisal Institute Magazine,* Appraisal Institute of Canada, Winnipeg.

CHANDAK, MADHUSUDAN LAL, *Law of Costs Valuation and Accounts,* Law Book Company, Allahabad, 1968.

CHANDIAS, MARIO E., "Amortizacion E Intereses De Capital," *Boletin,* Sotave, Caracas, Venezuela, pp. 7-11.

CLEVELAND HOUSING CO., "Tabular Analysis of the Division of the Building Dollar," *Appraising Manual*, S. L. McMichael, 1937.

CLURMAN, ALBERT W., "Land Costs Vs. Land Allowance," *The Appraisal Journal*, October, 1964, pp. 604-605.

CROCHERON, CLARENCE, "Property and Depreciation Records for Industry," *Technicalities and Technical Valuation*, February, 1952, pp. 3-9.

CUNLIFFE, H. L., "Cost Vs Appraised Value," *The Review*, September, 1951, pp. 3-5, 18.

DAVIDSON, J. B., "Life, Service and Cost of Service of Farm Machinery," *Iowa Engineering Experiment Station Bulletin 103*, 1900.

DAVIS, WILLIAM D., *The Cost Approach*, American Association of State Highway Officials, Washington, D. C., 1962, pp. 337-345.

DENTON JOHN H., "Depreciation Studies," *Preliminary Report of the Bureau of Internal Revenue*, Government Printing Office, Washington, D. C, 1931.

DETROIT REAL ESTATE BOARD, "Schedule of Unit Costs Based on Cubical Contents of Buildings In Effect In Detroit," *Mcmichael, S. L. Appraising Manual*, 1937, pp. 299.

DONETH, JOHN G., "Farm Management and Machine Accounting," *Journal of the American Society of Farm Managers and Rural Appraisers*, April, 1963, pp. 61-69.

DUNN, DOMINICK R., "Construction Data for the Appraisers," *Review of Society of Residential Appraisers*, August, 1939, pp. 11-13, 10-12,PP.10-12.

DWYER, JAY J., "Overcharges In Depreciation," *The Review*, January, 1946, pp. 3, 6.

ELLWOOD, L. W., "Valuing by Cost of Ownership," *The Review*, September, 1948, pp. 8-10. 12.

ELLWOOD, LEON W., "Cost Trends," *The Appraisal Journal*, January, 1947, pp. 32-36.

FISCHER, R. M., "Depreciation In Industrial Properties," *The Appraisal Journal*, April, 1937, pp. 143-148.

FISH, JOHN C. L., *Engineering Economics*, Mcgraw Hill, New York City, 1923.

GOLDSTEIN, GEORGE, "An Appraisal of Property with Improvements Fully Depreciated," *American Institute of Real Estate Appraisers*, 1949.

GOLDSTEIN, SIMEON F., "Is Depreciation Just Bookkeeping," *Technical Valuation*, 1967, pp. 26.

HARVEY, ROBERT O., "Observations on the Cost Approach," *The Appraisal Journal*, October, 1953, pp. 514-518.

HORTON, E. B. JR., "How to Use Cost Estimates," *The Appraisal Journal*, October, 1958, pp. 513-519.

HURD, RICHARD M., "Observations on Building Obsolescence," *Real Estate Record*, April 12, 1940, pp. 5-7.

JOHNSON, E. HOLLAND, "Cost Data In Appraising," *The Appraisal Journal*, July, 1941, pp. 24-247.

JUSTUS, FRED E. JR., "A Primer on Costs," *Journal of the American Society of Farm Managers and Rural Appraisers*, October, 1963, pp. 19-24.

KELLOUGH, W. R., "The Unit In Place Reproduction Cost System," *Technical Valuation*, October, 1958, pp. 37-39.

KIRSHMAN, JOHN EMMETT, "The Principle of Competitive Cost In Public Utility Regulation," *Yale Law Journal*, 1926.

KNOWLES JR., JEROME, "Estimacion Del Monto De La Depreciacion," *Boletin*, Sotave, Caracas, Venezuela, pp. 29-36.

LEMLEY, B. W., "Value of Appraisals to the Cost Accountant," *Bulletin*, National Association of Cost Accountants, May, 1932, pp. 1175-1181.

▲ Costs

LOUIE, CHARLES F., "**Depreciation and the Cost Approach,**" *Appraisal Journal,* October, 1961, pp. 507-516.

MANN, PATRICK C. AND JOHN L. MIKESELL, "**The Public Utility: a Taxpayer or a Tax Collector,**" *Florida Economic Indicators,* University of Florida, 1971, pp. 4.

MARSTON, ANSON, THOMAS R. AGG, "**Depreciation,**" *Engineering Valuation,* New York, 1936, pp. 33-136.

MARTLING, W. LOCKWOOD, JR., "**Curing Obsolescence,**" *The Review,* April, 1951, pp. 3-7, 18.

MASHKE, D. K., "**The Costs of Subdividing,**" *Appraisal Institute Magazine,* Appraisal Institute of Canada, Wnnipeg.

MATTHEWS, MYRON L., "**Construction Costs In Canada,**" *Appraisal Institute Magazine,* Appraisal Institute of Canada, Winnipeg.

MATTHEWS, MYRON L., "**The Cost Cycle,**" *The Review,* January, 1947, pp. 8-11.

MATTHEWS, MYRON L., "**The Enigmas of Estimating Construction Costs,**" *Appraisal Institute Magazine,* Appraisal Institute of Canada, Winnipeg.

MC MICHAEL, STANLEY L., "**Depreciacion,**" *Boletin,* Sotave, Caracas, Venezuela, pp. 37-42.

MCANLY, H. T., "**Recognizing the Deficiency of Depreciation Provisions Based Upon Historical Costs,**" *N. A. A. Bulletin,* American Society of Appraisers, February, 1958, pp. 5-15.

MEENEN, H. J., "**The Impact of Technology and Government Programs Upon Value,**" *Journal of the American Society of Farm Manager and Rural Appraisers,* April, 1957, pp. 76-81.

MONTONNA, D. L., "**Accrued Depreciation,**" *Appraisal Institute Magazine,* Winnipeg.

MURCHISON, KENNETH, "**A Building's Life Expectancy,**" *Banking,* April, 1937, pp. 26-27.

NEWMAN, D. K., "**The Low-Cost Housing Market,**" *Monthly Labor Review,* December, 1966, pp. 1362-68.

NOLAN, JAMES J, "**Cost Is Not Always Value,**" *Valutape Audio-Library Series,* American Society of Appraisers, Washington D.C., January 1, 1973.

NOLAN, PRESTON M., "**Determining Cost and Capitalization Rate,**" *National Real Estate Journal,* July, 1925, pp. 33-35.

NUETZMAN, R. A., "**Cost, Income, Market,**" *The Real Estate Appraiser,* pp. 23.

O'FLAHERTY, JOHN D., "**An Appraiser's Dilemma: the Cost Approach to Value,**" *The Real Estate Appraiser,* January, 1969, pp. 5-16.

PARSON, G. E., "**Construction Costs Report,**" *Appraisal Institute Magazine,* Appraisal Institute of Canada, Winnipeg.

PARSONS, C. W. S., "**Estimating Machining Costs,**" *American Society of Appraisers Valuation Manual,* Mcgraw-Hill, New York, 1957.

POTTER, EDWARD, "**Industrial Appraisals Pertaining to Liquidating Values,**" *Technical Valuation,* 1966, pp. 9-13.

PROUTY, W. L., "**Costs of Loft Buildings,**" *Appraisers and Assessors Manual,* 1930.

PROUTY, W. L. AND OTHERS, "**Determining Building and Labor Costs Over a Period of Years,**" *Appraisers and Assessors Manual,* 1930, pp. 15-34.

PROUTY, W. L. AND OTHERS, "**Union Wage Scales,**" *Appraisers and Assessors Manual,* 1930, pp. 33.

RANDALL, WILLIAM J., "**Treatment of Demolition Costs In the Appraisal Process,**" *Real Estate Analyst Appraisal Bulletin,* October, 1959, pp. 439 -42.

REAL ESTATE ANALYST, THE, "**Cubic Content and Reproduction Cost,**" *Real Estate Analyst Appraisal Bulletin,* 1948, pp. 227-230.

REAL ESTATE ANALYST, THE, "**Cubic Costs,**" *Real Estate Analyst Series on Old Style Two-Family Building,* 1949, pp. 93-96.

REAL ESTATE ANALYST, THE, "Reproduction Cost of a Brick Ranch House," *Real Estate Analyst Appraisal Bulletin,* 1954, pp. 85-88.

REAL ESTATE ANALYST, THE, "Reproduction Cost of California-Type Bungalow," *Real Estate Analyst Appraisal Bulletin,* 1952, pp. 337-340.

REAL ESTATE ANALYST, THE, "Reproduction Cost of One-Story Brick Veneer Houses," *Real Estate Analyst Appraisal Bulletin,* 1952, pp. 195-198.

REEVES, L. T. JR., "Depreciated Incremental Cost Concept," *Appraisal Journal,* October, 1971, pp. 556-560.

RICHARDS, JOHN L. JR., "The Principle of Substitution," *Technical Valuation,* February, 1958, pp. 21-22.

RING, A. A., "Problems and Pitfalls of Cost Approach," *Appraisal Institute Magazine,* Appraisal Institute of Canada, Winnipeg.

RING, ALFRED A., "Cost Pitfalls," *The Review,* May, 1956, pp. 3-4, 6.

RING, ALFRED A., "Gastos De Depreciacion," *Boletin,* Sotave, Caracas, Venezuela, pp. 39-44.

ROYAL, PEYTON K., "Market Data, Cost, and Income Analysis," *The Appraisal Journal,* April, 1962, pp. 245-247.

RYAN, JAMES A., "Improving the Engineering Load Factor of Property Records," *The Appraisal and Valuation Manual,* 1955, pp. 119-126.

SHURBERG, MERWIN, "Economic Factors In Property Valuations," *Appraisal and Valuation Manual,* p. 65.

SKOGSTAD, TOR, "Use of Published Trends and Costs Data In Appraisals of Real Estate Improvements," *Appraisal and Valuation Manual,* 1964, pp. 79.

SMITH, LEONARD C., *Economic Life,* August 1, 1938.

THORN, BURTON R., "Life of Building Components," *The Review,* September, 1950, pp. 16.

TOWERS, ALBERT G. JR., "Cost Methods Now In Use," *The Review,* September, 1953, pp. 22-24.

TOWNSEND, GILBERT, *How to Estimate,* American Technical Society, Chicago, 1939.

TROXEL, JAY C., "Purchaser's Cost Is Value Ceiling," *The Review,* September, 1945, pp. 14-15.

WALSH, H. VANDERVOORT, "Finding Reproduction Cost," *The Appraisal Journal,* April, 1934, pp. 228-231.

WELCH, HIRAM, U., "Unit Cost Factors," *The Appraisal Journal,* April, 1934, pp. 194-198.

WILFRED R., "Statistical Analysis of Industrial Property Retirements," *Engineering Valuation,* 1936.

WINFREY, ROBLEY, "Statistical Analyses of Industrial Property Retirement," *Iowa Engineering Experiment Station Bulletin No. 125,* Iowa State College of Agriculture & Mechanic Arts, Ames, December 11, 1935, pp. 1-176.

WOLK, H. I., "The Relevant Costing Approach to Asset Valuation and Income Determination, a Critique," *Dissertation Abstracts,* April, 1969, pp. 3265-A.

## 21-12  Replacement

AMERICAN SOCIETY OF APPRAISERS, "CPA's to Consider Depreciation Based on Replacement Costs In Business Week," *American Society of Appraisers Valuation Manual,* April 5, 1958, pp. 79.

BONBRIGHT, JAMES C., "Depreciation As Deduction from Replacement Cost New," *The Valuation of Property,* 1937.

BONBRIGHT, JAMES C., "Replacement Cost As a Measure of Value," *Appraisal Principles & Procedures,* pp. 145.

CARLSON, HOWARD M., "Hotels--Replacement Costs and Rental Rates," *The Appraisal Journal,* April, 1950, pp. 185-189.

DERBES, MAX J. SR., "Market Value Vs. Replacement Value," *The Residential Appraiser,* November, 1960, pp. 21-22.

DUNN, DOMINICK R., "Construction Data for the Appraisers," *Review of Society of Residential Appraisers,* August, 1939, pp. 11-13, 10-12,PP.10-12.

EDMAN, J. J., "Admissibility of Reproduction Cost As Evidence of Value. Appraisal Docket," *The Appraisal Journal,* July, 1960, pp. 384-386.

EDMAN, J. J., "The Appraisal Docket. Use of Reproduction Cost Method Inappropriate for Wherry Housing," *The Appraisal Journal,* July, 1961, pp. 413-415.

GODTHWAITE, G. E., "Reproduction Cost and Falling Price Levels," *National Municipal Review,* July, 1932, pp. 427-433.

GORKA, FRANCIS L., "Reproductions or Replacement Costs for Insurance," *Insurance Valuations,* ASA Monograph, 1971, pp. 36-40.

GOSSELIN, JACQUES, "Methodes D'Estimer Le Cout De Reproduction Ou De Remplacement," *Appraisal Institute Magazine,* Appraisal Institute of Canada, Winnipeg.

GRAHAM, J. W., "Reproduction Value Vs Reproduction Cost of Residences," *The Appraisal Journal,* October, 1934, pp. 61-64.

GRUNSKY, CARL E., GRUNSKY, CARL E., JR, "Depreciation, Amortization and the Replacement Requirement," *Valuation, Depreciation and the Rate-Base,* pp. 84-103.

HERRICK, ANSON, "Shall Depreciation Be Computed Upon Reproduction Cost?," *Bulletin,* National Association of Cost Accountants, New York, November 15, 1928, pp. 320-325.

HEUCK, ROBERT, "Cincinnati Method of Establishing Reconstruction Costs of Dwellings," *The Appraisal Journal,* July, 1934, pp. 303-308.

JEMING, JOSEPH B., "Depreciation on a Replacement Cost Basis for Public Utilities," *Technical Valuation,* February, 1954, pp. 13-14.

KELLOUGH, W. R., "The Unit In Place Reproduction Cost System," *Technical Valuation,* October, 1958, pp. 37-39.

MARSHALL, J. W., "Replacement Cost and Condemnation," *Technical Valuation,* February, 1961, pp. 49-51.

PAULSON, PHILIP A., "Replacement Cost No Ceiling on Condemnation Award," *Technical Valuation,* February, 1957, pp. 69-70.

POPE, L. E., "Replacement Cost Fits Standard New Home," *The Review,* April, 1950, pp. 20-21.

REAL ESTATE ANALYST, THE, "Estimating Replacement Cost," *Real Estate Analyst Appraisal Bulletin*, 1955, pp. 391-394.

SCHMIDT, FRITZ, "Importance of Replacement Value," *Accounting Review*, September, 1930, pp. 235-242.

SCHUMACHER, DAVID T., "Replacement Cost Is Not Replacement Value," *Technical Valuation*, June, 1956, pp. 14-15.

SHAY, HERBERT K., "Reproduction Cost Less Depreciation-An Important Tool In Assessing Real Property," *Assessors News Letter*, January, 1957, pp. 3-6.

STEINBERGER, E. A., "Original Cost Depreciation Vs. Replacement Cost--From a Stockholders Viewpoint," *Technicalities and Technical Valuation*, February, 1952, pp. 22-25.

TOWERS, ALBERT G. JR., "Cost Methods Now In Use," *The Review*, September, 1953, pp. 22-24.

WENZLICK, ROY, RESEARCH CORP., "Estimating Replacement Cost," *The Appraisal Journal*, October, 1956, pp. 507-510.

WILLIAMS, WALTER, "The Replacement Cost Concept," *Land Economics*, August, 1961, pp. 279-281.

# 21-13 Building Costs

ABERTHAW CO., *Cost of Industrial Building Index,* Aberthaw Co., Construction Managers, Boston.

AMERICAN APPRAISAL CO., *Building Cost Index,* American Appraisal Co., Milwaukee.

AMERICAN APPRAISAL CO., "Construction Costs for Industrial Buildings Compared with 1913 Costs," *Real Estate Appraisal and Valuation,* P. W. Kniskern, 1933, pp. 301.

AMERICAN APPRAISAL CO., "Mill Building Detail Cost Brick Mill Building Table," *Appraisers and Assessors Manual,* W. L. Prouty and Others, 1930.

AMERICAN INSTITUTE OF REAL ESTATE APPRAISERS, "Building Cost Estimates," *The Appraisal of Real Estate,* American Institute of Real Estate Appraisers, Chicago, 1967, pp. 180.

ARTHUR, WILLIAM, *Estimating Building Costs,* Scientific Book Corp., New York, 1928.

ARTHUR, WILLIAM, *New Building Estimators Handbook.*

ARTHUR, WILLIAM, "Detail Cost, 5-Story Loft Building," *Appraisers' and Adjusters' Handbook,* Appraisers and Assessors Manual, 1930.

BABCOCK FREDERICK M., FREDERICK M., *Building Cost and Investment Estimation: Library.* Valuation of Real Estate, 1932.

BABCOCK, FREDERICK M., "Building Cost and Investment Estimation: Hotel," *Valuation of Real Estate,* 1932, pp. 481, 492.

BABCOCK, FREDERICK M., "Building Cost and Investment Estimation: House," *Valuation of Real Estate,* 1932, pp. 482, 495.

BABCOCK, FREDERICK M., "Building Cost Estimation Investment Exclusive of Land: Factory," *Valuation of Real Estate,* 1932, pp. 482, 494.

BABCOCK, FREDERICK M., "Building Cost Estimation: Investment Parking Lot," *Vauation of Real Estate,* 1932, pp. 481, 491.

BABCOCK, FREDERICK M., "Building Cost, Furnitute and Equipment Investment Estimation: Theater," *Valuation of Real Estate,* 1932, pp. 482, 484, 493.

BABCOCK, FREDERICK M., "Cost Estimation 1 Buildings; 2 Investment Exclusive of Land," *Valuation of Real Estate*, pp. 477-495.

BALL, TOM, "New Building Products and Structural Systems Challenge the Appraiser," *Valuation*, December, 1967, pp. 57-61.

BANK OF AMERICA APPRAISAL DEPARTMENT, "Cost Data Single Family Residence," *Technical Valuation*, June, 1961, pp. 7-25.

BARNES, FRANK E., *Estimating Building Costs*, Mcgraw Hill Book Company, New York City, 1931, pp. 656.

BLACK, ALEX G., "Artificial Elements In Current Building Costs," *The Review*, May, 1946, pp. 13-14.

BLACK, I. G., "Metals Pick Up Speed In Building Materials Race," *Iron Age*, April 29, 1971, pp. 37.

BOECKH, EVERARD HEREFORD, "Building Cost Index Numbers," *Manual of Appraisals*, 1937, pp. 22-28.

BOECKH, EVERARD HEREFORD, "Costs-Farm Building," *Boeckh's Manual of Appraisals*, pp. 246.

BOECKH, EVERARD HEREFORD, "Costs-Farm Building," *Boeckh's Manual of Appraisals*, pp. 246.

BOECKH, EVERARD HEREFORD, "Costs-Industrial Buildings," *Boeckh's Manual of Appraisals*, pp. 205.

BOECKH, EVERARD HEREFORD, "Costs-Institutional Buildings," *Manual of Appraisals*, pp. 49.

BOECKH, EVERARD HEREFORD, "Costs-Miscellaneous Buildings," *Manual of Appraisals*, pp. 281.

BUILDING INVESTMENT, "Building Cost Index," *Appraisal and Valuation*, 1933, pp. 303.

CLARK, HORACE F., "Cost Factors In Building," *Appraising the Home*, 1930, pp. 152-164.

DINGMAN, CHARLES F., *Estimating Building Costs*, Mcgraw-Hill Book Company, Inc., New York, 1931.

DINGMAN, CHARLES F., *Estimating Building Costs*, 3rd Edition, Mcgraw-Hill Book Company, New York, 1944.

DODGE, F. W. CORP., *Dow Building Cost Calculation and Valuation Guide*, F. W. Dodge, New York, April 6, 1959, pp. 504-505.

DRISCOLL, FRED S., "The Changing Cost Structure of the Building Industry," *The Appraisal Journal*, October, 1948, pp. 459-405.

DUFFY, G., "Systems Building Proves Less Expensive for School Construction-Ashrae-Panel," *Air Conditioning, Heating and Refrigeration News*, July 20, 1970, pp. 15.

DUNN, DOMINICK R., "Construction Data for the Appraisers," *Review of Society of Residential Appraisers*, August, 1939, pp. 11-13, 10-12,PP.10-12.

EDGERTON, W. H., "Building Costs and Cost Approach," *Appraisal Institute Magazine*, Appraisal Institute of Canada, Winnipeg.

EDGERTON, W. H., "Construction Costs In Canada," *Appraisal Institute Magazine*, Appraisal Institute of Canada, Winnipeg.

EDGERTON, WILLIAM H., "Building Costs and Trends," *Appraisal Journal*, January, 1967.

EDGERTON, WILLIAM H., "Building Costs and Trends," *Appraisal Journal*, October, 1969, pp. 613-616.

EDWARDES, CYRIL R., "Building Costs--Future Indicative," *The Appraisal Journal*, July, 1945, pp. 271-274.

ENGINEERING NEW RECORD, "Schedule of Costs, Story Loft Building, 1927," *Appraisers and Assessors Manual*, 1930.

ENGINEERING NEWS RECORD, "Cost Elements on Five Actual Buildings Constructed In 1926," *Appraisers and Assessors Manual*, 1930, pp. 24-35.

# BIBLIOGRAPHY OF APPRAISAL LITERATURE

FAVELA, NORVEL F., "How Roofing Values Are Determined," *The Real Estate Appraisers*, September 20, 1966, pp. 30.

FAVELA, NORVEL F., "Roofing In Hurricane Areas," *The Residential Appraiser*, February, 1962, pp. 13-24.

FOSSLER, DUANE M., "Apartment Construction and Cost," *The Appraisal Journal*, June, 1962, pp. 11-12.

FRUIN-COLNON CONTRACTING COMPANY, *St. Louis Building Cost Index*, Fruin-Colnon Contracting Co, St. Louis, 1900.

GOBLE, EMERSON, "What Lies Ahead for Building Costs," *Architectural Record*, September, 1941, pp. 39-40, 102, 104.

HOYT, HOMER, "Relation of Building and Land Cost to Income or Loss In Shopping Centers," *The Appraisal Journal*, July, 1962, pp. 333-340.

JAROS, ALFRED L. JR., "Air Conditioning Costs," *Technical Valuation*, ASA, February, 1955, pp. 64.

KELLOUGH, U. R., *Building Construction Cost Data 1972*, Robert Snow Means Company Inc., May, 1973.

LEVITT, CHARLES H., *Law of the Construction Industry In New York State*, Northeastern Retail Lumbermen's Association, Rochester, 1943.

LOWNDES, WILLIAM S., *Estimating Building Costs*, International Textbook Company, Scranton Penna., 1927.

LUNDY, VICTOR R., "New Developments In Building Material and Design," *The Appraisal Journal*, January, 1958, pp. 27-33.

MATTHEWS, M. L., "Construction Costs In Canada," *Appraisal Institute Magazine*, Appraisal Institute of Canada, Winnipeg.

MATTHEWS, MYRON L., "Building Construction Costs," *Technical Valuation*, February, 1957, pp. 61-66.

MATTHEWS, MYRON L., "Building Cost Dip," *The Review*, March, 1949, pp. 5.

MATTHEWS, MYRON L., "Building Costs Continue Upward Climb," *Appraisal Digest*, October, 1958, pp. 4-5.

MATTHEWS, MYRON L., "Construction Costs In Canada," *Appraisal Institute Magazine*, Appraisal Institute of Canada, Winnipeg.

MATTHEWS, MYRON L., "Dow Building Cost Calculation and Valuation Guide," F. W. Dodge Corporation, New York, April, 1959.

MEANS, ROBERT S., *Building Construction Cost Data*, Robert S Means, Buxbury, Mass., 1950.

MORGAN, BELDEN, "Can You Qualify As a Building Inspector?," *The Review*, April, 1956, pp. 3-6.

N. Y. TIMES INDEX, "Architects G. Valk & T. Amenta Design for Year Round Homes at Price Less Than $30000," *N. Y. Times Index*, May 24, 1970.

N. Y. TIMES INDEX, "City Plan Comm Appr Cooper Sq Urban Renew Plan Calling for 1000 Units of New Housing," *N. Y. Times Index*, January 8, 1970.

N. Y. TIMES INDEX, "City Planning Community Approves Plans for 1000 Apts In Wash Heights for People of Low & Mid Income," *N. Y. Times Index*, January 22, 1970.

N. Y. TIMES INDEX, "Ground Broken for $10-Million Co-Op Apartment House on Park Avenue," *N. Y. Times Index*, October 11, 1970.

O'BRIEN, W. H., "Appraising Lumber In Home Construction," *Review of the Society of Residential Appraisers*, February, 1937, pp. 9-11.

PEURIFY, *Estimating Construction Costs*, Mcgraw-Hill, 1958.

PROUTY, W. L., "Costs of Loft Buildings," *Appraisers and Assessors Manual*, 1930.

PROUTY, W. L. AND OHTERS, "Determining Building and Labor Costs Over a Period of Years," *Appraisers and Assessors Manual,* 1930, pp. 15-34.

PROUTY, W. L. AND OTHERS, "Building Cost Details," *Appraisers and Assessors,* 1930, pp. 237-252.

PROUTY, W. L. AND OTHERS, "Building Cost Methods," *Appraisers and Assessors Manual,* 1930, pp. 91-103.

PROUTY, W. L. AND OTHERS, "Building Depreciation," *Appraisers and Assessors Manual,* 1930, pp. 67-72.

PROUTY, W. L. AND OTHERS, "Denver Building Cost Chart," *Appraisers and Assessors Manual,* 1930, pp. 19.

PROUTY, W. L. AND OTHERS, "Denver System, Cost of Residence, Store Building, Office Building," *Appraisers and Assessors Manual,* 1930, pp. 102-103.

PROUTY, W. L. AND OTHERS, "Factory Building Construction," *Appraisers and Assessors Manual,* 1930, pp. 205-211.

PROUTY, W. L. AND OTHERS, "Fraternal Building Construction," *Appraisers and Assessors Manual,* 1930, pp. 194-196.

PROUTY, W. L. AND OTHERS, "Life of Buildings," *Appraisers and Assessors Manual,* 1930, pp. 40-57.

PULVER, HARRY E., *Construction Estimates and Costs,* Mcgraw-Hill, New York, 1947.

REAL ESTATE ANALYST, THE, "Building Cost-Market Price Relationship," *Real Estate Analyst Appraisal Bulletin,* 1957, pp. 57-60.

REAL ESTATE ANALYST, THE, "Reproduction Cost of a Standard Brick Ranch House," *Real Estate Analyst Appraisal Bulletin,* 1952, pp. 441-444.

REEVES, CUTHBERT E., "The Basis of Building Costs for Assessment Purposes," *Appraisal Digest,* January, 1955, pp. 4-7.

REVIEW, THE, "Cost and Utility In the Basementless House," *The Review,* September, 1949, pp. 18-23.

REYNOLDS, C. W., "Building Inventory," *Commonwealth Review,* M, pp. 370500.

SCHEIDT, JOHN, "Building Appraisals," *Appraisal and Valuation Manual,* 1964, pp. 271.

SHUTE, CLYDE, "Compiler Current Trends of Building Costs," *Architectural Record,*

SKOGSTAD, TOR, "Use of Published Trends and Costs Data In Appraisals of Real Estate Improvements," *Appraisal and Valuation Manual,* 1964, pp. 79.

TERBORGH, GEORGE, "Fluctuations In Housing Construction," *The Appraisal Journal,* January, 1938, pp. 50-56.

THORN, BURTON R., "Life of Building Components," *The Review,* September, 1950, pp. 16.

TOWERS, ALBERT G. JR., "Cost Methods Now In Use," *The Review,* September, 1953, pp. 22-24.

TURNER CONSTRUCTION COMPANY, *Building Cost Index,* Turner Construction Company, New York.

WALKER, J., "Levitt Town Bldr, Starts a City-Sized Community," *House & Home,* January, 1971, pp. 34.

WEED, KENNETH A., "How to Use Cost Data In the Appraisal of Apartment Buildings," *Real Estate Appraisal Practice,* 1958, pp. 139-151.

"Building Cost-Market Price Relationship," *Real Estate Analyst Appraisal Bulletin,* 1957, pp. 57-60.

"Construction Costs Soar," *Chain Store Age,* pp. 28-30.

"Crash Program From Ground Breaking to Model Apartments In Ten Weeks," *House and Homes,* September, 1971, pp. 36-3.

"Heres Design That Hits the Market, and Cuts Costs Too," *House and Home,* March, 1971, pp. 68-73.

"Library Construction," *Special Libraries,* December, 1970, pp. 574.

"Lightweight Steel Framing Breaks the Three Story Barrier for These Apartments," *House and Home,* January, 1971, pp. 70.

"Modular Plan Cuts Cost on These Beach Front Apartments In California," *House and Home,* June, 1970, pp. 40.

"Nations Largest Pre-Fabber Proposes a Modular High Rise System," *House and Home,* June, 1970, pp. 38.

"Plan for Value: Materials," *Purchasing,* June 25, 1970, pp. 71-74.

"Precast Concrete Panel System Cuts Condominium Construction Time In Half," *House and Home,* October, 1970, pp. 34.

"Reflective Glass Is Hot Item Taking Architecture by Storm," *Industry Week,* February 1, 1971, pp. 61-62.

"To Get the Facts on Aluminum Framing, Ryan Homes Puts Up a Prototype House," *House and Home,* September, 1970, pp. 34.

"Utilization of Appropriate Data from Market to Support Land Value & Construction Cost In Cost Aprch," *Selected Papers, 1961,* Right of Way Conference, University of Ala., 1961.

## 21-14 Rising Costs

ABEL, VICTOR D, "A Study of Rising Costs," *The Review,* March, 1946, pp. 7-8.

ASSOC CERTIFIED & CORPORATE ACCOUNTANTS COMMITTEE, "Accounting for Inflation: Study of Techniques Under Conditions of Changing Price Levels," Gee, London, 1952.

DUNN, DOMINICK R., "Construction Data for the Appraisers," *Review of Society of Residential Appraisers,* August, 1939, pp. 11-13, 10-12,PP.10-12.

HOLDEN, ARTHUR C., "Present and Future Trends In the Battle to Reduce Costs," *The Appraisal Journal,* January, 1949, pp. 86-92.

HOWARD, WILLIAM F., "The Rising Cost of Right of Way and Your Responsibility," *Right of Way,* April, 1963, pp. 21-23.

MCCLOSKEY, W. D., "Modular Systems Are the Key to Ending Superflation," *Air Conditioning, Heating, and Refrigeration News,* July 20, 1970, pp. 4.

TERBORGH, GEORGE, "Fluctuations In Housing Construction," *The Appraisal Journal,* January, 1938, pp. 50-56.

THRUN, FRED MARTIN, *A Local Farm Real Estate Price Index,* E. Lansing, Michigan, 1929.

TOWERS, ALBERT G. JR., "Cost Methods Now In Use," *The Review,* September, 1953, pp. 22-24.

WALSH, EDWARD V., "Recent Price Trends," *The Review,* March, 1951, pp. 8-9.

WEISS, E. B., "What Zero Population Growth Will Mean to Marketers," *Advertising Age,* June 15, 1970, pp. 80.

WEISS, W. B., "Is Free Mass Transportation In Down-Town's Future," *Stores,* April, 1971, pp. 51-52.

## 21-15 Cost Surveys

BEATTIE, R. D., J. E. VIVIAN, "When Making Cost Estimates Watch Your Language," *Chemical Engineering,* January, 1953, pp. 172.

BEETH, CHANNING C., "An Inspection Routine," *The Review,* April, 1951, pp. 14-16.

CRANSTONE, J. G., "Comparative Costs Survey," *Appraisal Institute Magazine,* Appraisal Institute of Canada, Winnipeg.

LAUNER, E. J., "**Residential Quantity Survey Cost Estimates**," *Appraisal Digest,* January, 1959, pp. 14-15.

LEVIN, EARL, "**Land Planning and Land Costs**," *Appraisal Institute Magazine,* September, 1959, pp. 4-14.

MARSHALL AND STEVENS PUBLICATION COMPANY, *Marshall Valuation Service Rapid Method of Computing Building Costs,* Marshall and Stevens, Los Angeles, Inc., 1962.

MATTHEWS, MYRON L., "**Dow Building Cost Calculation and Valuation Guide**," F. W. Dodge Corporation, New York, April, 1959.

PARSONS, C. W. S., "**Estimating Machining Costs**," *American Society of Appraisers Valuation Manual,* Mcgraw-Hill, New York, 1957.

SURVEY RESEARCH CENTER, UNIVERSITY OF MICHIGAN, "**Buyer Preferences Surveyed**," *The Review,* Housing and Home Finance Agency, February, 1953, pp. 7.

TOWERS, ALBERT G. JR., "**Cost Methods Now In Use**," *The Review,* September, 1953, pp. 22-24.

UNDERWOOD, GEORGE, *Construction Costs,* Mcgraw-Hill, Newyork, 1950.

UNDERWOOD, GEORGE, *Estimating Construction Costs,* Mcgraw-Hill, New York, 1930.

WEISS, E. B., "**What Zero Population Growth Will Mean to Marketers**," *Advertising Age,* June 15, 1970, pp. 80.

WOODWORTH, LEO D., "**Industrial Appraisers Vs. Mechanical Surveys**," *National Real Estate Journal,* June 13, 1927, pp. 24-26.

## 21-16 Engineering Construction

AMERICAN INSTITUTE OF ARCHITECTS, "**Cubic Contents of Buildings**," American Institute of Architects, May, 1928.

ASSOCIATED GENERAL CONTRACTORS, *Trend of Construction Cost,* The Constructor, 1900.

BALL, THOMAS B., "**Construction Adjustment Factors**," *Church Valuation,* Church Valuation Consultants, 1968, pp. 11.

BINGHAM, JOHN, "**Construction Costs**," *The Appraisal Journal,* January, 1946, pp. 47-49.

## BIBLIOGRAPHY OF APPRAISAL LITERATURE

BOECKH, EVERARD HEREFORD, "Changing Construction Costs," *Residential Appraiser's Review*, September, 1935, pp. 3-4, 7, 15.

BOECKH, EVERARD HEREFORD AND ASSOCIATES, "Index Numbers of Construction Costs," *Boeckh and Associates, Inc.*,

BRUEGGEMAN, WILLIAM BERNARD-PH. D., *The Impact of Private Construction and Government Housing Programs In a Local Housing Market*, Ohio State University, 1970.

COLEAN, MILES, "Mechanized Construction Methods Are on the March," *Appraisal Digest*, October, 1954, pp. 9-11.

CONDON, JOHN A., "Construction Cost Planning," *Appraisal and Valuation Manual*, Corporate Press Incorporated, Washington, D.C, January, 1972, pp. 226.

COOPER, GEORGE H., *Building Construction Estimating*, Mcgraw-Hill, New York, 1945.

COOPER, GEORGE H., *Building Construction Estimating*, Mcgraw-Hill, New York, 1959.

DALLAVIA, L., "Estimating General Construction Costs," *Valuation Manual*, American Society of Appraisers, New York City, 1957.

DUFFY, G., "Systems Building Proves Less Expensive for School Construction-Ashrae-Panel," *Air Conditioning, Heating and Refrigeration News*, July 20, 1970, pp. 15.

ELLWOOD, L. W., "Figuring Construction Costs," *The Review*, June, 1946, pp. 15-20.

ENGINEERING NEWS-RECORD, "Atkinson Scores In Solo Bid on Cochiti Dam," *Engineering News-Record*, May 21, 1970, pp. 40.

ENGINEERING NEWS-RECORD, "Sewerage and Dam Construction Costs Jump 9 to 10%," *Engineering News-Record*, March 18, 1971, pp. 106-108.

FAULKNER, P. G., "Understanding Basic Principles and Terms of Building Construction," *The Appraisal Journal*, January, 1964, pp. 79-85.

FEDERAL POWER COMMISSION, *S 204 Hydroelectric Plant Construction Cost and Annual Production Expenses*, Supt. of Documents, U. S. Govt. Printing Office, Washington D. C., 1968.

FEDERAL POWER COMMISSION, *Cost of Pipeline & Compressor Sta. Constr. Under Nonbudget Type Certif. Authoriza. As Reptd by Pipe*, Federal Power Commission, Washington, D. C., 1970.

FISH, JOHN C. L., *Engineering Economics*, Mcgraw Hill, New York City, 1923.

FISH, JOHN C. L., "Engineering Method," *Technical Valuation*, 1950.

GLUNT, DAVID, "Construction Cost Indexes," *American Society of Appraisers*, 1958, pp. 323-330.

HERTZMAN, IRVING L., "Construction Cost Indexes," *The Appraisal Journal*, January, 1950, pp. 109-104.

HOLDEN, THOMAS S., "Postwar Construction Costs," *The Review*, February, 1945, pp. 12-14.

HOYT, HOMER, "Effect of Rents Opertg Expenses & Constr Costs Upon New Income of Regional Shopping Centers," *The Appraisal Journal*, January, 1963, pp. 65-70.

JACKS, MORRIS, "Estimating Structural Value, Vol. IV," *Appraisal and Valuation Manual*, ASA, 1959, pp. 99-112.

JAROS, ALFRED L. JR., "Air Conditioning Costs," *Technical Valuation*, ASA, February, 1955, pp. 64.

KELLOUGH, U. R., *Building Construction Cost Data 1972*, Robert Snow Means Company Inc., May, 1973.

LAROS, ALFRED L., "What Does Air Conditioning Cost," *Technical Valuation*, A. S. A, Washington, February, 1954, pp. 64.

LUNDY, VICTOR R., "New Developments In Building Material and Design," *The Appraisal Journal*, January, 1958, pp. 27-33.

▲ Costs

LYON, ROBERT L., "Inspecting New Construction," *The Review,* November, 1945, pp. 7-10.

MARSHALL AND STEVENS PUBLICATION COMPANY, *Marshall Valuation Service Rapid Method of Computing Building Costs,* Marshall and Stevens, Los Angeles, Inc., 1962.

MARSTON, ANSON, ROBLEY WINFREY, J. C. GEMPSTEAD, "Engineering Valuation & Depreciation," Mcgraw-Hill, New York, 1953.

MARSTON, ANSON, THOMAS R. AGG, "Depreciation," *Engineering Valuation,* New York, 1936, pp. 33-136.

MARSTON, ANSON, THOMAS R. AGG, "Wage and Price Trends, Construction-Cost Indexes," *Engineering Valuation,* New York, 1936, pp. 253-294.

MATTHEWS, MYRON L., "Construction Costs and Trends," *Technical Valuation,* American Society of Appraisers, February, 1956, pp. 34.

MATTHEWS, MYRON L., "Construction Costs for Valuation Purposes," *American Society of Appraisers Valuation Manual,* American Society of Appraisers, 1960, pp. 229.

MATTHEWS, MYRON L., "The Construction Cost Approach to Value," *Appraisal Digest,* October, 1959, pp. 8-12.

MATTHEWS, MYRON L., "The Enigma of Estimating Construction Costs," *Appraisal Institute Magazine,* June, 1961, pp. 7-13.

MATTHEWS, MYRON L., "What's Happening to Construction Costs," *American Society of Appraisers Valuation Manual,* American Society of Appraisers, 1956, pp. 277.

MATTHEWS, MYRON L., "1955 Construction Cost Survey," *American Society of Appraisers Valuation Manual,* American Society of Appraisers, 1955, pp. 275.

MCCURDY, ROBERT V., "Estimating the Cost of Residential Construction," *Technical Valuation,* June, 1962, pp. 5-10.

MILLER MARTIN D., "New Ideas and Materials In Construction," *The Appraisal Journal,* April, 1962, pp. 267-278.

PARSON, G. E., "Construction Costs Report," *Appraisal Institute Magazine,* Appraisal Institute of Canada, Winnipeg.

PROUTY, W. L., "Classifying and Determining Cubic Foot Costs," *Residential Appraiser's Review,* March, 1936, pp. 3-6.

PROUTY, W. L. AND OHTERS, "Determining Building and Labor Costs Over a Period of Years," *Appraisers and Assessors Manual,* 1930, pp. 15-34.

REAL ESTATE ANALYST, THE, "Construction Cost of a Frame Ranch House," *Real Estate Analyst Appraisal Bulletin,* 1953, pp. 57-64.

REAL ESTATE ANALYST, THE, "Construction Cost of Churches," *Real Estate Analyst Appraisal Bulletin,* 1953, pp. 385-388.

REAL ESTATE ANALYST, THE, "Construction Cost of Churches," *Real Estate Analyst Appraisal Bulletin,* 1949, pp. 41-44.

REAL ESTATE ANALYST, THE, "Construction Costs of a Colonial Style Savings and Loan Office Building," *Real Estate Analyst Appraisal Bulletin,* 1957, pp. 211-216.

REAL ESTATE ANALYST, THE, "Construction Costs of a One-Story Commercial Building," *Real Estate Analyst Appraisal Bulletin,* 1955, pp. 17-20.

REAL ESTATE ANALYST, THE, "Construction Costs on a Small Bank Building," *Real Estate Analyst Appraisal Bulletin,* 1956, pp. 217-222.

REAL ESTATE ANALYST, THE, "Construction Costs on an 8-Family Garden-Type Apartment," *Real Estate Analyst Appraisal Bulletin,* 1961, pp. 557-562.

REAL ESTATE ANALYST, THE, "Constructions Costs on a Small Office Building," *Real Estate Analyst Appraisal Bulletin,* 1956, pp. 33-38.

REAL ESTATE ANALYST, THE, "Residential Construction Costs," *Real Estate Analyst Appraisal Bulletin,* 1950, pp. 405-420.

REAL ESTATE ANALYST, THE, "Residential Construction Costs," *Real Estate Analyst Appraisal Bulletin,* 1950, pp. 337-354.

REVIEW, THE, "Construction Costs Composition," *The Review,* March, 1952, pp. 10.

RHODES, RICHARD M., "Economic Effect of High Voltage Transmission Line Construction," *Right of Way,* February, 1971.

SACLES, KENNETH E., "Appraiser's Responsibility In Reporting Substandard New Construction," *The Real Estate Appraiser,* November, 1964, pp. 22.

SEVERSON, HARRY L., "Government Bonds and Construction Expenditure Projections," *The Appraisal Journal,* July, 1962, pp. 413-414.

THALER, D., "Built for Sale Apartments: a Threat to You," *House and Home,* September, 1970, pp. 68-73.

THEISS, WILLIAM R., "The Appraisal Docket. Use of Construction Cost for Determining Assessed Value," *The Appraisal Journal,* July, 1965, pp. 440-441.

TILGHMAN-MAYER COMPANY, *Index of Construction Cost of Bank Buildings,* Tilghman-Mayer Company, Allentown, Pa.

TOWERS, ALBERT G. JR., "Cost Methods Now In Use," *The Review,* September, 1953, pp. 22-24.

"Banker-Builder Team Proves That Private Enterprise Can Meet Housing Needs of Renewal-Area Residents," *House and Home,* June, 1970, pp. 42.

"Construction Costs Soar," *Chain Store Age,* pp. 28-30.

"Corps to Construct Dam In Existing Reservoir," *Engineering News Record,* September 24, 1970, pp. 12.

"Heres a New High Rise System That Mixes Light and Heavy Construction," *House and Home,* August, 1970, pp. 26.

"Library Construction," *Special Libraries,* December, 1970, pp. 574.

"Waterways Buildup Off In 70, But Still Big," *Chemical Week,* March 24, 1971, pp. 14.

## 21-17 Historical Costs

BUCHANAN, ROBERT R., "Is There a Special Value for Antique Buildings?," *Appraisal Institute Magazine,* 1968, pp. 37-42.

MCANLY, H. T., "Recognizing the Deficiency of Depreciation Provisions Based Upon Historical Costs," *N. A. A. Bulletin,* American Society of Appraisers, February, 1958, pp. 5-15.

## 21-18 Forecasting

ARIES, R. S., R. D. NEWTON, *Chemical Engineering Cost Estimation,* Mcgraw-Hill, New York City, 1955.

BEATTIE, R. D., J. E. VIVIAN, "When Making Cost Estimates Watch Your Language," *Chemical Engineering,* January, 1953, pp. 172.

▲ Costs

BOWEN, PERCIVAL V., "Role of Operating Costs In Future Valuation," *Appraisal Journal*, July, 1950, pp. 370-373.

DAVIS, NOBLE L., "Machinery and Equipment Cost Trends--How Are They Used," *Valuation*, 1900, pp. 64-72.

DEWEY, EDWARD R., E. F. DAKIN, "Cycles, the Science of Prediction, with 1950 Postscript," Holt, New York, 1949.

EDMAN, J. J., "Determining Cost of Subdivision and Improvement of Land Appraisal Docket," *The Appraisal Journal*, July, 1958, pp. 449-450.

EDMAN, J. J., "The Appraisal Docket Determining Cost of Subdivision and Improvement of Land," *The Appraisal Journal*, July, 1958, pp. 449-452.

FISCHER, R. M., "The Accuracy of Forecasts," *Technical Valuation*, June, 1955, pp. 17.

FISCHER, R. M., "The Future of Prices," *The Appraisal Journal*, January, 1944, pp. 66-72.

GIBBONS, JAMES E., "Income Forecast," *The Appraisal Journal*, October, 1960, pp. 505-509.

HAIGHT, JAMES R., "Some Factors Determining Future Values," *National Real Estate Journal*, January, 1940, pp. 34-37.

HALL, FRANK D., "Appraising the Future," *National Real Estate Journal*, July, 1941, pp. 25-26.

HULTEM, JOHN J., "Minimum Facts for Cost Estimates," *The Review*, September, 1950, pp. 17-22.

LYON, ROBERT L., "Background for Cost Estimating," *The Review*, October, 1945, pp. 12-14.

MALM, WILLIAM E., "A Sound Method of Cost Calculation," *Skyscraper Management*, March, 1935, pp. 6-7, 31-32.

MARTINEZ R., NESTOR, "Fluctuaciones Costo Tierra Motivadas," *Boletin*, Sotave, Caracas, Venezuela, pp. 7-9.

MATTHEWS, MYRON L., "Cost Trend Forecast," *The Review*, August, 1953, pp. 17-20.

NUTTER, C. ARMEL, "The Market Ahead," *The Residential Appraiser*, November, 1959, pp. 23-24.

RING, ALFRED A., "Operating Expense Forecasting and Analysis," *The Valuation of Real Estate*, 1970, pp. 219.

STAHL, SHELDON W., "On Economic Forecasting," *The Appraisal Journal*, April, 1968, pp. 291-298.

STANFORD, MELVIN J., "Forecasting Future Land Values," *Appraisal Institute Magazine*, Appraisal Institute of Canada, Winnipeg, September 1, 1973.

THOMSON, ROBERT H., "A Dependable Cost Short-Cut," *The Residential Appraiser*, February, 1957, pp. 3-8.

TOWERS, ALBERT G. JR., "Simplicity Cost Estimating," *The Appraisal Journal*, January, 1952, pp. 89-93.

## 21-19 Summation

FISH, JOHN C. L., *Engineering Economics*, Mcgraw Hill, New York City, 1923.

FISH, JOHN C. L., "Engineering Method," *Technical Valuation*, 1950.

GLASS, EDWARD F., "**Common Errors in Appraising**". *Review,* December, 1949, pp. 3-6, 10.

MATTHEWS, MYRON L. "**The Construction Cost Approach to Value**". *Appraisal Digest,* October, November, December, 1959, p. 8-12.

OCHS, HARRY T., JR. "**Application of Price Indexes in Appraisals**". *Appraisal and Valuation Manual,* Vol. 3, 1958, pp. 311-322.

O'FLAHERTY, JOHN D. "**An Appraiser's Dilemma: The Cost Approach to Value**". *Real Estate Appraiser,* January, February, 1969, pp. 5-15.

## 21-20 Indexes

BOECKH, EVERARD HEREFORD, "**Individual Costs Section,**" *Manual of Appraisals,* pp. 287.

BOECKH, EVERARD HEREFORD, "**Use of Cost Indexes,**" *The Review,* July, 1953, pp. 19-20.

MARSHALL AND STEVENS PUBLICATION COMPANY, *Marshall Valuation Service Rapid Method of Computing Building Costs,* Marshall and Stevens, Los Angeles, Inc., 1962.

MATTHEWS, MYRON L., "**Dow Building Cost Calculation and Valuation Guide,**" F. W. Dodge Corporation, New York, April, 1959.

MCKEE-BERGER-MANSUETO, *Building Cost File,* Construction Publishing Co., Inc.

MOSELLE-, PAXTON, *National Construction Estimator,* Craftsman Book Company.

PAVITT, *Dodge Manual for Building Construction,* Mcgraw Hill Information Systems Co..

WILLIAMS, ROBERT M., "**An Index of Asking Prices for Single Family Dwellings,**" *The Appraisal Journal,* January, 1954, pp. 33-38.

*Commercial-Industrial Construction Estimating and Engineering,* International Estimating Services; Richardson.

## 21-21 Cost to Cure

KELLY, ED, "**Cost to Cure, Just Compensation,**" *Valuation,* ASA, Washington, September, 1968, pp. 44.

## CHAPTER TWELVE

# Land

by Edwin M. Rams, BS, JD, LL.M.

Edwin M. Rams, urban economist and real estate appraiser, is Director, Urban Research Associates, Economic & Real Estate Consultants, Washington, D.C. Author of three books and numerous articles and research papers published in the United States and foreign professional journals. Recipient of the Arthur A. May Memorial Award for 1966 from the American Institute of Real Estate Appraisers for contributions to appraisal theory and practice as reflected in the Condemnation Appraisal Handbook (1963). Member of the Washington Society of Investment Analysts, American Institute of Real Estate Appraisers, and Lambda Alpha, honorary land economics society (International President, 1965-67).

▲ Land

*Rich man – poor man, scholar and workman, socialite or peasant, all sharing a common bondage and heritage – land.*

*Land, like the atmosphere and the bodies of water that divide it, is one of the common denominators for all human activity. Through the ages, it has been and is a motivator for human progress and also a detonator for conflict among men and nations.*

*Land – the universal constant of mankind – not subject to creation or destruction; it pervades the minds of all men because from birth through life and on to the final hour, land has been the silent partner of man – the entrance, stage, and passageway for all of the human race.*

THE USE and benefits derived from land by society form an ever changing trilogy encompassing the aesthetic, functional, and economic aspects. The value parameters assigned by individual generations to each of these areas differ because the fabric of society forms a mosaic of problems, issues, and perspectives prevailing over a given time continuum.

Manifestly, the advantages bestowed by land are of two dimensions, i.e., tangible and intangible. These service characteristics traverse a range of benefits from the esoteric to mundane realities involving food and materials for shelter. It is within this broad context that the triad of aesthetics, function, and economics must be viewed and examined. This is profiled against the basic attributes of land, to wit, immobility, indestructibility, and environmental bias.

## Aesthetic Benefits

The measure of a benefits is to imagine and portray a situation, condition, or environment in absence of that which is or could be classed as an appendant in a given scenario. This would be a modified scenario with the absence of all vegetation, hills and valleys — a surface with no variations in contour, essentially a smooth moon-like earth environment.

The differences in the two scenarios represent the aesthetic benefits of land in our environment. The resultant spatial relationships, variations, and panorama of colors provide a backdrop which because of its obvious and continuing presence is taken for granted—a too frequently unrecognized gift.

Recent societal concern about the environment has generated a resurgence of interest in the aesthetic as a by-product of land. The detriments imposed by an advanced industrialized society on land, and the vital appurtenances of air and water — comprising an environmental trinity—have drawn elements of society into groups exhibiting profound concern. The defenders of the environment make one central plea, i.e., retention and preservation of an inseparable part of mankind, which is the environment with land as its central foundation.

A disregard of the crushing effect of destroying and/or crippling of the environment due to the advanced industrialized state could bring about two levels of human existence. One engulfed in a morass and jungle of a ravaged landscape; the other living a laboratory-like full life cycle in a completely fabricated brick-mortar-plastic circumscribed plenum.

A disposable society mentality, which is a post WW II reflex of an industrial state, may regretably view the environment as one more replaceable item. Perhaps the threshold point of irreversability of environmental pollution and damage has not been reached. Only the fortune of time and the catalysm of an ecological self-correcting and curing process may prevail to forestall mankind's reaching of this crucial threshold level.

Portents of contemporary economic man suggest one unlearned lesson, that is, that which is explicitly free today, may tomorrow bear implicitly high costs.

A sagacious adage for the amorphous citizenry concerned with the environment might read, "The needs of the moment dictate action" (Sait).

## Functional — Economic Benefits

It was eight decades ago when John R. Commons (1893) elicited the following in capturing the essence of the functional benefits of land when he said, "Land is valuable primarily because it furnishes only room and situation".

The function of land can be divided into four major categories.
- A. Classes of Land
    1. Agricultural
    2. Forest
    3. Recreational
    4. Urban and non-urban
- B. Water Resources
- C. Sub-surface use
- D. Super-surface use

Because of the interdependence of function and economic value, the two notions become inseparable when considered in the context of land. Any consideration of the economic benefits of land is a study of spatial economics; the allocation of land, whether for recreational, agricultural, or urban use has implicit spatial connotations of economic activity. Manifestly, time and spatial dimensions take on important economic significance in relationship to the use, allocation, and value of land.

Spatial differentiation of economic activity is traceable to one of several fundamental relationships and underlying forces prevailing in a given setting. One involves the internal economy of an area, say a city, and its dependence or independence to the external economies of a state or region. These factual parameters give recognition to the reality that economic activity is spatially distributed. Some functions are not divisible — say a large industrial plant providing a number of jobs to the local labor force. Other activities, like retail trade, are vulnerable to market segmentation.

The second aspect relates to land inputs and requirements for the various economic activities agglomorated into an urban form. These vary over time and quantity-quality dimensions.

Finally, underscoring the above two factors are transport costs which signal the competitive position of an urban area in terms of markets, accessability, etc. for the localized goods and services.

These contravening forces, one for concentration and the other for dispersion (the spatial dimension) result in an interplay of transport costs which can be crucial to the future growth and development of an area. The derivatives *via* a translation of these collective forces represent a hierarchy of urban land uses and functions. It is an ever changing hierarchy based on altered transport networks, complementary and compatible adjacent and market domain use, and market segmentation due to competing central place activities. Factor changes, and their relative strength, result in new and emerging spatial configurations.

Contemporary thinking and practice concerning the commercial influence of activities in an urban land context are accountable to the early work of Fetter a half century ago. He formulated "The Economic Law of Market Areas" which is as follows:

"The boundary line between the territories tributary to two geographically competing markets for like goods is a hyperbolic curve. At each point on this line the difference between freights from the two markets is just equal to the difference between the market prices, whereas on either side of this line the freight difference and the price difference are unequal. The relation of prices in the two markets determines the location of the boundary line: the lower the relative price the larger the tributary area". (Frank A. Fetter, The Economic Law of Market Areas, The Quarterly Journal of Economics, 1924, p. 520).

Subsequent extensions and refinements, in a similar and broader frame of reference are indicated in the efforts of Reilly (The Law of Retail Trade Movement), Christaller and Lösch (Central Place Theory), and Berry (Range of a Good); much of present day location theory, urban market structures, and hierarchies of cities-urban centers rests on the research of these students and scholars of the urban scene.

On the intraurban scene, Edward Chamberlin's theory of spatial monopoly (1933) i.e., "that control over supply which is the seller's by virtue of his location" developed the intrigue of the 100% locations for one of many urban functions.

The totality of current day thinking concerning land utilization, which is the function and economy of land, rests on three important precepts. They are: *space, time,* and *technique*. Therein are the keys to "economic space", whether concerning vertical use (height of buildings) or expansion (succession to a higher land use), since all rests squarely and is dependent on land.

## Land Valuation, In Retrospect and Prospect

It was nearly two and one-half thousand years ago that Aristotle was concerned with the value of property *vis-a-vis* assessments and the function and needs of government.

As to the change produced in oligarchies and constitutional governments by the alteration of the qualification. When this arises, not out of any variation in the qualification, but only out of the increase of money, it is well to compare the general valuation of property with that of past years; annually in those cities in which the census is taken annually and in larger cities every third or fifth year[1].

Three centuries later, in 58 B.C., Cicero having been banished from Rome and his house and villas burned, the Consuls ascertained the indemnity due to the damage. Cicero was quite unhappy with the findings and in a letter, in 57 B.C., to Atticus stated:

But the fact is, my dear Pomponius, those very same men — you know quite well whom I mean — who cut my wings, do not wish them to grow again. But I hope they are growing[2].

Judicial valuation including charges to the jury were of particular interest to the people concerning war assessment levies in England in 1083. The following are questions presented to the jurors by the Domesday Commissioners[3].

What is the name of the mansion?
Who held it in the time of King Edward?
Who now holds it?
How many hides are there?
How many teams — in demesne — of the tenants?
How many villeins — cottars — slaves?
How many freeman — sokeman?
How much wood — meadow — pasture?
How many mills? How many fisheries?
How much has been added or taken away?
How much was the whole worth?
How much is it worth now?
How much has or had each freeman or sokeman there?
And if more can be had than is had?

Note the very explicit concern about retrospective value, current value, prospective value, before and after value, leasehold interests, etc.

Capitalization, rent and capital value, was clearly understood in England in 1450. In a letter written at London, the fifteenth day of October in the 29th year of King Henry VI, the writer suggested ".... for if the widow will sell it after fourteen year or fifteen year that it may be lett"[4]. The Years Purchase concept (which still prevails) indicates a capitalization rate between 6½% to 7%.

Speculation in land with escalating rents resulted from the sale of Abbey lands by Henry VIII in 1536. As one writer has reported:

".... Rack renting, evictions, and the conversion of arable land to pasture were the natural result, for surveyors wrote up values at each transfer, and unless the last purchaser squeezed his tenants, the transaction would not pay[5].

Contemporary land and property appraisal practice reflects the advances in the state of the art, its evolutionary process, and the prevailing socioeconomic environment and related investment climate.

In a complex and highly urbanized society, land has become more crucial in its important role as a basic vehicle and ingredient in providing the various facilities on the urban landscape. Advances in technology make possible super-structures — literally cities under one roof. Accordingly, locational aspects and concentration of activities have heightened enormously the importance and pivotal character of principal sites in contrast to adjacent and intervening land; land which serves as a connecting link and on the economic scale of value, must be assigned a secondary or tertiary position.

Whereas a half century ago, the concept of a 100% location derived from a singular use, department or variety store, current indexes suggest that multi-use giant complexes have superseded the singular use in generating prime and monopolistic locations and corresponding values. These developments, once established, will not be as vulnerable to displacement (locationwise) as in previous eras involving a single and principally retail use.

What appears to be emerging is not a substitute *per se* of the 100% location of yesteryear, but a number of prime developments scattered over the urbanized area in the frame of reference of a megalopolis.

Within this prevailing context the author has formulated an anchor index of relative investment quality which is plausible and applicable predicated on the domain and influence of competing facilities. The concept is a *de-facto riskless rate* which is taken to be that net rate of return (on equity or overall) imputed to prime large and complex urban investment properties. Implicit in the riskless rate are market position and dominance of the complex within its market area, the location of the development, the quality of development (materials-design-aesthetics) and tenancies (kind, financial credit, prestige-share of market in terms of services/products). Accordingly, all other competing and related investments have inputed capitalization parameters at levels higher than the *de-facto* riskless rate — which in essence concerns the quantity, durability, quality, and continuity of net income. In the street language of the real estate investment community, its the best and safest real estate deal in town. Correspondingly, where the risk is higher, a higher rate of return is mandated. This places all real estate investments along a risk/rate-of-return continuum, profiled over time. It is merely a recognition and a paralleling of market behavior, investment thinking, and corresponding investment decision-making of the real estate marketplace. Subsequently, as locations change or new competitive facilities increase the economic stress on current inventory, with emerging and increasing functional risk, a re-arrangement of properties along the risk/rate-of-return continuum would result.

In summary then, the components for analysis to ascertain and identify the *de-facto* riskless rate are:

1. Quality of location
2. Scale of development
3. Quality of development
4. Quantity and quality of income

These techniques, plus other advances in the analysis of equity yield-capital structure of investment properties, might suggest a three or four tier investment market in larger urban centers. Two, three, or four properties might be categorized as prime; the second tier might include a dozen properties, the third several dozen, and finally the balance would fall into the fourth class.

*Underscoring all land use and development is the classic notion and market reality of maximizing land utilization, i.e., the highest and best use.* To properly integrate the notion of a *de-facto* riskless rate, plus other important elements, a reformulation of the definition of highest and best use has been facilitated as follows.

*Highest and Best Use:* A legal and perceived most profitable use, based on forecast market demand and associated risk, producing the maximum net benefits, monetary and/or other, for the longest forseeable period of time

It should be noted that the primary target is a use which is both legal and most profitable. This is basic and fundamental and represents the identity part of the definition. The three key elements which follow are the measures part of the concept, i.e., the existence of a market underscored by parameters of risk concerned with market entry of the new development (if this be the case), the production of net benefits (which can be money and/or other forms of amenities, etc.), and finally, the longest foreseeable (predicted) period of time.

Two basic attributes prevail in implementing the concept of highest and best use; they include: (1) its subjective nature, and (2) its futuristic quality. Both elements are inextricably united — simple because both possess a high degree of uncertainty.

The inclusion of market demand and risk (both requiring a forecast) gives recognition to several important, and at times overlooked, facets of highest and best use. First, a forecast concerns the future; it is different than a projection simply because it recognizes *turning points,* i.e., changes in demand and corresponding risk in the future; simply the potential vulnerability of an investment over time. The second matter, of equal importance, is that demand is a key element of feasibility — which is the primacy of any highest and best use analysis (in particular a proposed development). The inclusion of risk is simply a recognition of reality — all matters undertaken in contemplation and based on the future involve risk. The very nature of the definition of value, i.e., present worth of future benefits, implies (1) the future, and (2) an element of risk due to future potential changes in value.

Further development of valuation techniques encompassing analysis regarding cash flow, capital structure, in-depth studies of supply and demand of real estate facilities, absorption rates, urban dynamics-economics, etc. suggests a new level of professional competence, public acceptance, and changing function of the real estate appraiser. Concomitantly, the changing image will generate an independence, of scholarship and practice, thus attracting new talent which over time, will provide a new foundation for professionalism.

Much of current date real property appraisal activity had its genesis in the Magna Charta (1215), a forerunner of the U.S. Constitution. The Fifth and Fourteenth Amendments, plus the evolving concepts of the Ninth Amendment, all give status and probity to real property possessed by citizens of the Republic. This has and continues to be the forum for participation in the constantly expanding measure in the good life, as well as liberty to pursue the good life.

Some ideas and concepts contained herein were gleaned from the author's new books nearing completion, "Real Estate Appraising Handbook", Prentice-Hall).

## References

1. Aristotle, "Politics", Book V, Ch. VI
2. Cicero, Letter to Atticus, Rome, Oct. B.C. 57
3. Round, Feudal England
4. Paston Letters, 15 Oct. 1450
5. R. H. Tawney, Religion and the Rise of Capitalism, Penguin Ed. p. 114

# Land

| | |
|---|---|
| 22-11 | Vacant |
| 22-12 | Underwater |
| 22-13 | Tideland |
| 22-14 | Indian |
| 22-15 | Hillside |
| 22-16 | Acquisition |
| 22-17 | Subdivision |
| 22-18 | Raw Land |

*NOTE: This sub-section has been employed to reflect, in addition to specific reference sources for data on Raw Land, the broad concept of Land as the major resource for economic activity and the chief predication for all Real Property appraisal activity. Generic material has been included, to provide student, researcher and practitioner an information basis which will adequately environ the concept of Land.*

| | |
|---|---|
| 22-19 | Urban Land Value |
| 22-20 | Rural Land Value |
| 22-21 | Utilization |
| 22-22 | Lots |
| 22-23 | Marshland |
| 22-24 | Waterfront Property |

## 22-11 Vacant

BADEN, POWELL, BADEN, HENRY, *The Land Systems of British India,* Clarendon Press, Oxford, 1892.

BASHAW, FREDERICK J., "Value In a Dynamic Land Economy," *The Review,* 1900, pp. 16-22.

BECKETT, P. H. T., "Method and Scale of Land Resource Surveys In Relation to Precision and Cost," *Land Evaluation,* 1900, pp. 53.

BENNETT, H. H., "The Coming Technological Revolution on the Land," *The Appraisal Journal,* January, 1947, pp. 16-21.

BODFISH, MORTON, THEOBALD, A. D, "Appraising Vacant Business Lots In Built-Up Areas," *Real Estate Fundamentals,* 1941, pp. 4-5.

BODFISH, MORTON, THEOBALD, A. D, "Appraising Vacant Lots In Subdivisions," *Real Estate Fundamentals,* 1941, pp. 6-7.

BODFISH, MORTON, THEOBALD, A. D, "Appraising Vacant Property," *Real Estate Fundamentals,* 1941, pp. 3-4.

CHASE, PRENTICE T., "Land," *The Appraisal Journal,* July, 1940, pp. P&. 245-252.

CHERNEY, RICHARD A., "Appraisal Principle of Highest and Best Use In Assessing Urban Vacant Land," *The Assessors Journal,* April, 1966, pp. 27-34.

CLURMAN, ALBERT W., "Land Costs Vs. Land Allowance," *The Appraisal Journal,* October, 1964, pp. 604-605.

COLE, LEE W., "Appraisal of Vacant Land," *Appraisal Reporting Techniques,* American Institute of Real Estate Appraisers, 1951, pp. 71-88.

COLWELL, R. N., *Aerial and Space Photographs As Aids to Land Evaluation,* pp. 324.

COSTA RICA, *Laws, Statutes, Etc. . . Reglamento De La Ley General De Terrenos Baldios,* Imprenta Nacional, San Jose, Costa Rica, 1940.

DEBOOS, FRANK A., "Application of Depth Tables to Vacant Lots," *The Appraisal Journal,* October, 1949, pp. 467-470.

EDMAN, J. J., "Capitalization of Income Inappropriate for Vacant Land "Appraisal Docket," *The Appraisal Journal,* July, 1961, pp. 415.

ELY, RICHARD T., AND G. S. WEHRWEIN, *Land Economics,* Macmillan.

FOGARTY, F., "Land a New Kind of Boom," *Architectural Forum,* February, 1957, pp. 100-105, 134-136, 148-151.

FULLERTON, PAUL, "Development Analysis for the Valuation of Vacant Land," *The Appraisal Journal,* April, 1965, pp. 211-225.

GONZALEZ, CONCHA J., *Tierra Y Valorizacion,* La Reforma Tributaria Municipal, Antares, 1956.

GOODSPEED, M. J., "Sampling Considerations In Land Evaluation," *Land Evaluation,* 1900, pp. 40.

HAMMAR, CONRAD H., "Land Classification to Aid the Appraiser," *Journal of Land and Public Utility Economics,* August, 1939, pp. 277-286.

KAHN, SANDERS A., "Land, Does it Depreciate," *The Real Estate Appraiser,* January, 1969, pp. 28-31.

KAZDIN, S. EDWIN, "On Land," *The Appraisal Journal,* April, 1938, pp. 166-167.

KNISKERN, PHILIP W., "Land," *Real Estate Appraisal and Valuation,* 1933, pp. 267-290.

MACBRIDE, DEXTER D, "The Value of Land," *The Real Estate Appraiser*, Society of Real Estate Appraisers, Chicago, March 1, 1968.

MARSELE, PETER R. AND ALFRED CALABRESE, "Taxation of Open Spaces: Its Pros and Cons," *Assessors News Letter*, January, 1965, pp. 3-7.

MAYER, EDWIN, "Land Appraisal Pitfalls," *American Society of Appraisers Valuation Manual*, American Society of Appraisers, 1956, pp. 221.

MERTZKE, ARTHUR J., "Appraising Business Vacant Sites," *National Real Estate Journal*, 1928, pp. ART. 1-4.

ROBINSON, WILLIAM W., *Land In California*, University of California, Berkeley, Calif, 1948.

SCHLAGENHAUF, PAUL, "The Appraisal of Vacant Subdivision Lots for Taxation Purposes," *The Appraisal Journal*, January, 1934, pp. 93-97.

SCHMIDT, WALTER S., "On Valuation of Vacant Land," *The Appraisal Journal*, April, 1933, pp. 255-256.

SOLOMON, R. J., "Property Values As a Structural Element of Urban Evolution," *Economic Geography*, January, 1969.

STEINER, RICHARD L., "Pricing a New Commodity: Cleared Land," *The Appraisal Journal*, January, 1959, pp. 49-53.

SWAFFORD, EMMETT, "Demonstration Appraisal of the Effect of an Interstate Highway on Rural Land Value," *Assessment Administration*, IAAO, Chicago, 1965, pp. 126-130.

THEISS, WILLIAM R., "The Appraisal Docket. Valuation of Large, Unrented and Unique Property," *The Appraisal Journal*, April, 1904, pp. 305-310.

WESTGATE, TEVIS T., "A Hole In the Ground Is Worth More Than the Land Itself," *Appraisal and Valuation Manual*, 1958, pp. 405.

## 22-12 Underwater

CUNNINGHAM, F. M., "Valuation of Industrial Submerged Land," *Appraisal Institute Magazine*, 1967, pp. 22-30.

ROTHSTEIN, A. J., "Deep Ocean Mining Today and Tomorrow," *Columbia Journal of World Business*, January, 1971.

SNITZER, EDWARD L., "Some Valuation Problems of Underwater Lands," *Real Estate Appraiser*, 1969, pp. 55-57.

## 22-13 Tideland

LEFEAVER, JAMES H., "The Appraisal of Tidelands," *Appraisal and Valuation Manual*, American Society of Appraisers, 1959, pp. 191-198.

## 22-14 Indian Land

BARNEY, RALPH A., *Indians Claims Appraisals*, International Fraternity of Lambda Alpha, July, 1962.

BARNEY, RALPH A., "Indian Claims or the Historical Appraisal," *The Appraisal Journal*, April, 1963, pp. 169-177.

COSTA RICA, *Laws, Statutes, Etc. . . Reglamento De La Ley General De Terrenos Baldios*, Imprenta Nacional, San Jose, Costa Rica, 1940.

EDMAN, J. J., "The Appraisal Docket. Right to Condemn Indian Lands," *The Appraisal Journal*, April, 1959, pp. 265-266.

GALLAGHER, JOSEPH A. SR., "The Indian's Right Returned to Indians," *Technicalities*, May, 1949, pp. 7.

HOWELL, BEN R., "Relations and Problems In Dealing with Navajo Indians," *Right of Way*, December, 1958, pp. 17-21.

STARRETT, PAUL, "Appraisal of Land In Indian Claims," *Encyclopedia of Real Estate Appraising*, 1959, pp. 510-523.

## 22-15 Hillside

COLEMAN, DAN, "Trends In Subdivision and Hillside Development," *The Appraisal Journal*, October, 1965, pp. 575-586.

GERKIN, LEONARD, "The Economics of Hillside Subdivisions," *Technical Valuation*, February, 1961, pp. 2-7.

INDERBITZEN, ANTON L., "Inherent Hazards of Hillside Property," *The Appraisal Journal*, January, 1961, pp. 83-86.

MORGAN, BELDEN, "The Valuation of Hillside Properties," *Review of Society of Residential Appraisers*, March, 1939, pp. 12-14.

STONE, ROBERT, "Geology and Hillside Appraisal," *The Residential Appraiser*, January, 1961, pp. 9-11.

## 22-16 Acquisition

AMERICAN RIGHT OF WAY ASSOCIATION, "Co-Ordination of Engineering, Right of Way Acquisition and Construction," *Proceedings of the Second National Seminar, 1956*, Washington, D. C, 1957.

AMERICAN RIGHT OF WAY ASSOCIATION, "Modern Techniques In Public Land Acquistion," *Proceedings of the Sixth Annual National Association, 1960*, Washington, D. C, 1961.

▲ Land

BENNETT, H. H., "The Coming Technological Revolution on the Land," *The Appraisal Journal,* January, 1947, pp. 16-21.

BENNETT, S. Z., "Acquisition Philosophies and Experiences," *The Residential Appraiser,* April, 1957, pp. 14-23.

BISHOP, MAURICE F., "Legal Procedures for Acquisition," *Selected Papers of a Right of Way Conference,* University of Alabama, 1956, pp. 16-27.

BURKE, FRANK W., "Congressional Action Pertinent to Real Property Acquisition," *Right of Way,* June, 1963, pp. 7-9.

BUTTENHEIM, HAROLD S., "How a City's Acreage Increases," *Appraising Manual,* 1937, pp. 256.

CUNNYNGHAM, WILKIE, RALPH BORDLEY, "Land Titles," *Acquisition for Right of Way,* American Association of Highway Officials, Washington, D. C, 1962, pp. 135-143.

DAVIDSON, ROBERT C., "Excess Property Acquisitions," *Technical Valuation,* 1900, pp. 17.

DEZEEUW, J. W., "Land Requisition In Manitoba," *Appraisal Institute Magazine,* Appraisal Institute of Canada, Winnipeg.

EASTBURN, WALTER N., "Some Aspects of Property Acquisition and Ownership by Railroads," *Technical Valuation,* January, 1949, pp. 10-16, 23-24.

FITZGERALD, WILLIAM F., "Federal Land Acquisition and Appraisal Conference Created," *The Appraiser,* February, 1969.

FORNACI, CHARLES M., "Land Acquisitions," *Valuation Manual,* 1964, pp. 85.

FRANKLIN, R. J., "Tax and Business Considerations In Buying Property," *Taxes,* March, 1964.

GOLDSTINE, HARRY, "Acquirement of Property by Condemnation," *National Real Estate Journal,* November 19, 1923, pp. 24-26.

GOOD, H. A., A. R. PURCHASE, C. E. JOSLYN, "Acquisition of Property for the Red River Floodway In Manitoba," *The Appraisal Institute Magazine,* December, 1963, pp. 24-28.

GOODRICH, HAROLD S., "Appraising for Army Land Acquisition," *The Appraisal Journal,* July, 1951, pp. 355-364.

GREENEBAUM, MICHAEL, "The Purchase of Real Estate by Insurance Companies," *The Appraisal Journal,* January, 1948, pp. 65-71.

GROSS, WILLIAM J., "Acquisitions for Future Use," *American Association of State Highway Officials,* Washington D. C, 1962.

GROSS, WILLIAM J., "Right of Way Acquisition In Ohio," *Right of Way,* February, 1962, pp. 34-39.

HADLEY, GEORGE C., "Legal Problems In Highway Acquisition," *The Appraisal Journal,* April, 1953, pp. 165-174.

HAINES, C. GRODON, "Tax Consequences to Owners As a Result of Public Acquisition," *Proceedings of the Sixth Annual National Seminar,* American Right of Way Association, Washington, D. C, 1961.

HALL, CARL B., "How Title and Abstract Companies Can Assist In the Right of Way Acquisition," *Right of Way,* April, 1960, pp. 33-38.

HANLEY, DUDLEY J., "Acquisition Appraisals In Urban Renewal," *Appraisal and Valuation Manual,* American Society of Appraisers, 1961, pp. 23-29.

HANLEY, DUDLEY J., "Acquisition Appraisals In Urban Renewal," *Appraisal Digest,* April, 1962, pp. 6 11.

HENDERER, EDMOND, "Appraisal and Acquisition Problems--Pennsylvania Yard," *Right of Way,* February, 1964, pp. 35-36. 49-52.

HESS, RUDOLF, "Excess Lands-California's Concept and Conduct of Marginal Land Acquisition," *Right of Way,* December, 1962, pp. 31-46.

HESS, RUDOLPH, AMER RIGHT OF WAY ASSOCIATION, "Land Economic Studies In Connection with Right of Way Acquisition Panel," *Proceedings of the Sixth Annual National Seminar 1960,* American Right of Way Association, Washington, D. C., 1961, pp. 33-53.

HOWARD, WILLIAM F., "Right-Of-Way Valuation and Acquisition," *Technical Valuation,* ASA, Washington, November, 1955, pp. 5.

HUFFTS, CHRISTIAN, A. H, "Photogrammetry," *Acquisition for Right of Way,* American Association of State Highway Officials, Washington, 1962, pp. 189-207.

JOHNSON, HAROLD E., "Aerial Surveys Aid Land Acquisition," *Right of Way,* February, 1959, pp. 35-36.

JOHNSON, LEEVERN, "Acquisition Appraisals for Urban Renewal," *The Appraisal Journal,* April, 1961, pp. 221-228.

JORDAN, ROBERT D., "Alabama Program and Problems of Right-Of-Way Acquisition," *Right of Way Conference, Selected Papers,* 1957, pp. 1-9.

JORDON, R. D., "The Right of Way Acquisition Problem," *Right of Way Conference,* 1956, pp. 1-8.

LAIDLAW, STEWARD P., "Right of Way and Land Acquisition Procedure of Central Hudson Gas and Electric Corporation," *Right of Way,* April, 1958, pp. 31-32.

LAND, DAVID E., "Acquisition of Property for Urban Renewal," *Right of Way,* December, 1963, pp. 27-32.

LEVIN, DAVID R., "The Research Function In Right-Of-Way Acquisition," *Acquisition for Right-Of-Way,* American Association of State Highway Officials, Washington, D. C., 1962.

LEVY, MARK, "Institutional Purchases of Real Estate," *The Appraisal Journal,* July, 1949, pp. 296-310.

LOEBBECKE, ERNEST J., "The Relationship of the Title and Abstract Company with the Right of Way Acquisition Program," *Right of Way,* April, 1959, pp. 26-33.

LOWRIE, THOMAS R., "New-Jersey Turnpike Program of Acquisition of Right-Of-Way," *Right of Way,* August, 1954, pp. 5-8.

MCKAY, R. J., "Tax Considerations In the Acquisition and Ownership of Real Estate," *Appraisal Institute Magazine,*

NEALEY, MORGAN T. JR., "Acquisition of Lands for NASA's Manned Lunar Landing Program, Cape Canaveral, Florida," *Right of Way,* October, 1963, pp. 7-12.

PETERS, W., "Deduction for Depreciation Before Acquisition of the Asset," *American Society of Appraisers Manual,* January, 1958, pp. 55-57.

PHILLIPS, C. W., "An Effective Acquisition Program," *The Residential Appraiser,* September, 1961, pp. 18-19.

PRYOR, FRANCIS D., "Appraisals for Public Road Acquisition," *Technical Valuation,* June, 1960, pp. 5-10.

SANDO, LAURENCE, "Highway Land Acquisition In the United States," *The Appraisal Journal,* April, 1969, pp. 165-176.

SMITH, GILBERT A., "Acquisition of Access Rights," *Right of Way Conference, Selected Papers, 1956,* University of Alabama, University, Alabama, 1956, pp. 52-58.

SMITH, WALSTEIN, JR., "Acquisition Appraisal In Urban Renewal," *The Residential Appraiser,* March, 1961, pp. 13-17.

STOVER, V. G., "A Study of Remainder Parcels Resulting from the Acquisition of Highway Rights of Way," *Dissertation Abstracts,* July, 1964, pp. 353.

THEISS, WILLIAM R., "Use of Zoning to Acquire Property at Depreciated Value. Appraisal Docket," *The Appraisal Journal,* October, 1961, pp. 544-545.

▲ Land

U. S. FEDERAL WORKS AGENCY, *Bibliography on Land Acquisition for Public Roads,* Public Roads Administration, Washington, 1947.

WALL, NORBERT F., "Acquisition Cost Analysis of Large Tracts of Land Intended for Governmental and Related Uses," *The Real Estate Appraiser,* November, 1968, pp. 25-28.

WENGER, RALPH W., "Acquisition Appraising for Urban Renewal," *The Real Estate Appraiser,* July, 1967, pp. 22.

WHEELER, MORGAN, "Acquisition of Land Interests for Nation's First Minutemen Missile Installation In Montana," *R. O. W,* October, 1964, pp. 9-15.

# 22-17  Subdivision

BECCIA, MARTIN, "The Effect of Pipeline Easements on Subdivision Developments," *Right of Way,* August, 1960, pp. 11-16.

BODFISH, MORTON, THEOBALD, A. D, "Appraising Vacant Lots In Subdivisions," *Real Estate Fundamentals,* 1941, pp. 6-7.

BOHANNON, DAVID D., "Converting Farms to Subdivisions," *The Appraisal Journal,* October, 1945, pp. 362-364.

CARR, ANTHONY W., "Appraising Within Subdivisions," *The Real Estate Appraiser,* May, 1963, pp. 26-29.

COLLINS, E. R., "Subdivision Planning In Relation to Appraisal Problems," *Appraisal Institute Magazine,* January, 1959, pp. 6-11.

COTTEN, ROBERT, "Types of Subdivisions," *Right of Way Conference, Selected Papers, 1962,* University of Alabama, Alabama, 1962, pp. 32-36.

DAVIS, E. G., "Appraisal of Land for Subdivisions," *Appraisal Institute Magazine,* May, 1958, pp. 14-20.

DAVIS, W. D., *The Application of Appraisal Techniques In the Acquisition of Highway Right of Way,* Colloquium on Appraisal Research, Wisconsin, 1963, pp. 18-20.

DERBES, MAX J. JR., "The Effect of an Electric Transmission Line Through a Subdivision," *Right of Way,* April, 1968, pp. 28-38.

DILMORE, GENE, *The New Approach to Real Estate Appraising,* Prentice-Hall, 1971, pp. 214.

FULLER, ROBERT S., "Hillside Subdivisions," *The Review,* July, 1953, pp. 3-5.

HAALAND ARNE W., "Backward Valuation of Potential Subdivisions," *Appraisal and Valuation Manual,* American Society of Appraisers, 1959, pp. 211-214.

HAGOOD, WAYNE D., "Lot Valuations In Tract Subdivision," *The Residential Appraiser,* June, 1961, pp. 9-13.

HALEY, BYRON R., "Outdoor Recreation Subdivisions," *The Real Estate Appraiser,* October, 1971, pp. 14-18.

HORNE, ARCHIE J., "Valuation of Land for Subdividing," *Review of Society of Residential Appraisers,* January, 1940, pp. 12-13.

JERRETT, HERMAN DANIEL, "The Theory of Real Property Valuation," Keystone, Press, Sacramento, 1938.

MASHKE, D. K., "The Cost of Subdividing," *The Appraisal Institute Magazine,* September, 1963, pp. 11-14.

MCDIARMID, M. C., "Net Value Loss, Potential Subdivision Acreage," *Appraisal Institute Magazine,* Appraisal Institute of Canada, Winnipeg.

OROURRK, GERALD A., "Appraising Acreage for Subdivision," *The Appraisal Journal*, July, 1952, pp. 373-381.

RANDALL, WILLIAM J., "Mobile Home Subdivisions," *The Appraisal Journal*, July, 1967, pp. 360-373.

RUSSELL, HUGH H., "New Subdivision Trends," *The Review*, May, 1946, pp. 6-9.

SACHS, EARL, "An Apparently Harmless Easement Smashes Subdivision Plans," *The Appraisal Journal*, January, 1966, pp. 117-118.

THEISS, WILLIAM R., "The Appraisal Docket. FHA Approval As a Factor In Value of Subdivision Property," *The Appraisal Journal*, October, 1961, pp. 543.

THEOBALD, A. E., *Financial Aspects of Subdivision Development*, Research Institute for Economic Research, Chicago & New York, 1930.

WAGNER, PERCY E., "Subdivision Costs," *The Residential Appraiser*, May, 1957, pp. 12-14.

## 22-18  Raw Land

*NOTE: This sub-section has been employed to reflect, in addition to specific reference sources for data on Raw Land, the broad concept of Land as the major resource for economic activity and the chief predication for all Real Property appraisal activity. Generic material has been included, to provide student, researcher and practitioner an information basis which will adequately environ the concept of Land.*

ABELMANN, WILLIAM W., "How to Estimate Highest and Best Use," *Real Estate Appraisal Practice*, American Institute of Real Estate Appraisers, Chicago, 1958, pp. 6-10.

AITCHISON, G. D., K. GRANT, "Terrain, Evaluation for Engineering," *Land Evaluation*, 1900, pp. 125.

AMER INSTITUTE OF REAL ESTATE APPRAISERS, "The Appraisal of Real Estate Revised," *Amer Institute of Real Estate Appraisers*, 1967.

AMERICAN INSTITUTE OF REAL ESTATE APPRAISERS, *Appraising of Real Estate*, American Institute of Real Estate Appraisers, 1960.

AMERICAN INSTITUTE OF REAL ESTATE APPRAISERS, *How Transportation Affects Real Estate Values*, American Institute of Real Estate Appraisers, Chicago, 1900.

AMERICAN INSTITUTE OF REAL ESTATE APPRAISERS, *The Appraisal of Real Estate*, Education Committee, Chicago, 1951.

AMERICAN INSTITUTE OF REAL ESTATE APPRAISERS, "Case Study Courses In Real Estate Appraising at the University of Chicago," *Journal American Institute of Real Estate Appraisers*, January, 1936, pp. 26-34, 166-180.

AMERICAN INSTITUTE OF REAL ESTATE APPRAISERS, "Economic Trends," *The Appraisal of Real Estate*, The American Institute of Real Estate Appraisers, Chicago, 1967, pp. 68.

AMERICAN INSTITUTE OF REAL ESTATE APPRAISERS, "The Appraisal Docket," *Condemnation Appraisal Practice*, American Institute of Real Estate Appraisers, Chicago, 1961, pp. 153-157.

ANDERSON, ARNOLD C., "The Effect of Transportation on Values," *How Transportation Affects Real Estate Values*, A.I.R.E.A., Chicago, March 7, 1969, pp. 14-18.

ANGELL, STEPHEN LEROY, "Appraisal of Subdivisions," *Encyclopedia of Real Estate Appraising*, Edith J. Friedman, 1959.

APPRAISAL DIGEST, "New Patterns of Land Value," *The Appraisal Digest,* July, 1954, pp. 23-24.

ARKANSAS DIVISION OF ASSESSMENT COORDINATION, *Legal Section, Real Estate and Personal Property Assessment Manual,* Arkansas Division of Assessment Coordination, Little Rock, 1956.

ARMSTRONG, ROBERT H., "Continued Decline Shown In Real Estate Values," *Appraisal Digest,* October, 1951, pp. 4-5.

ARMSTRONG, ROBERT H., "Economics and Appraising," *National Real Estate Journal,* December, 1940, pp. 18.

ARMSTRONG, ROBERT H., "Real Estate Markets," *The Appraisal Journal,* October, 1941, pp. 363-374.

ASCHER, DAVID B., "How to Sell Property for Life Annuities," *The Appraisal Journal,* January, 1953, pp. 79-82.

ASSESSORS NEWSLETTER, "Real Estate Transfer Tax," *Assessors Newsletter,* July, 1966, pp. 103.

ATKINS GEORGE, "Building a Clientele In the Appraisal Business," *National Real Estate Journal,* April, 1932, pp. 28-30.

ATLAS MARTIN, *Tax Aspects of Real Estate Transactions,* Bureau of National Affairs, Washington, D. C, 1955.

BABCOCK, F. MORRISON, *Real Estate Valuation,* Bureau of Business, U of Mich Ann Arbor, 1932.

BABCOCK, FREDERICK M., "Approaches to Real Estate Valuation," *Real Estate Appraiser,* pp. 29.

BABCOCK, FREDERICK M., "The Valuation Data," *The Valuation of Real Estate, Ed. 1,* 1932, pp. 41-48.

BABCOCK, FREDERICK MORRISON, *The Appraisal of Real Estate,* The Macmillan Company, New York, 1924.

BACKMAN, JULES, "The Real Estate Market and the General Economy," *The Appraisal Journal,* January, 1964, pp. 21-28.

BALDWIN, ROGER S., "Market Value As Related to Real Estate," *The Appraisal Journal,* October, 1947, pp. 535-539.

BARNARD, BOYD T., "Pitfalls Appraising Real Estate," *Real Estate Magazine,* September, 1941, pp. 3, 16-17.

BEATON, W. R., ERNEST MCCLOSKEY, PHILIP PICKENS, "Appraisal and Acquisition of Borrow Pits," *The Real Estate Appraiser,* October, 1969, pp. 29-38.

BEDFORD, E. W., "Why Buy Real Estate," *The Appraisal Journal,* May, 1945, pp. 135-137.

BELL, STOUGHTON, "The Cambridge, Mass., System of Real Estate Assessment," National Tax Association, August, 1917, pp. 196-198.

BENKERT, WILLIAM C., "Public Need for Real Estate Board Appraisal Service," *National Real Estate Journal,* September, 1927, pp. 49.

BENSON, PHILIP A., "Real Estate Appraisals and Values," *Savings Bank Journal,* November, 1931, pp. 9-10.

BENSON, PHILIP A., NORTH, NELSON L, *Real Estate Principles and Practices,* Prentice-Hall, New York, 1954.

BENSON, PHILIP A., NORTH, NELSON L, "Assessed Valuations," *Real Estate Principles and Practices,* 1938, pp. 30-32.

BENSON, PHILIP A., NORTH, NELSON L, "General Rules for Determining Land Values," *Real Estate Principles and Practices,* 1938, pp. 290-292.

BENSON, PHILIP A., NORTH, NELSON L, "The Valuation of Real Estate," *Real Estate Principles and Practices,* 1938, pp. 281-300.

BERNARD, ALFRED D., *Some Principles and Problems of Real Estate Valuation,* U. S. Fidelity and Guaranty Co, Baltimore, 1913.

BICKNELL, F. B., "Appraisal Committee Procedure," *The Annals of Real Estate Practice*, National Association of Real Estate Boards, 1925, pp. 109-121.

BIGELOW, WALTER S., "Importance of the Appraisal Committee," *The National Real Estate Journal*, July 2, 1923, pp. 47-48.

BISHOP, JESSE E., "Legal Responsibility of the Appraiser," *The Real Estate Appraiser*, SREA, Chicago, January, 1965, pp. 9.

BISHOP, MAURICE F., "The Attorney and the Appraiser," *The Real Estate Appraiser*, pp. 11.

BISHOP, MAURICE F., "The Attorney and the Appraiser (Part 1)," *The Real Estate Appraiser*, pp. 8.

BLASE, M. G., W. G. STAUB, "Real Property Taxes In the Rural Urban Fringe," *Land Economics*, May, 1971, pp. 168 174.

BLISS, GEORGE M., "Cost of Developing Raw Land Into Building Lots," *Technical Valuation*, October, 1957, pp. 23-25.

BLOOM, MAX R., "Valuation Problems and Urban Redevelopment," *The Real Estate Appraiser*, SREA, Chicago, 1964, pp. 24.

BOECKH, EVERARD HEREFORD, "Land Valuation," *Manual of Appraisals*, 1937.

BOLTON, REGINALD P., *Building for Profit, Principles Governing the Economic Improvement of Real Estate*, Devinne Press, New York, 1911.

BORSAK, GEORGE, "The Influence of Airport Operations on Value of Adjacent Real Estate," *Assessment Administration*, IAAO, Chicago, 1961, pp. 20-26.

BOWES, WATSON A., "Appraisal of Four Million Acres of Western Land," *The Appraisal Journal*, American Society of Appraisers, Washington, D. C, January, 1948, pp. 19-26.

BOYESEN, LOUIS K., "A Bank's Real Estate Loan Department," *The National Real Estate Journal*, November 11, 1929, pp. 26-29.

BOYKIN, JAMES H., "Severances Studies, Their Future Role In Remainder Property Appraisals," *The Real Estate Appraiser*, January, 1970, pp. 10-16.

BOYLAND, WILLIAM E., "Assessing—New York Real Estate Taxes," *Technical Valuation*, American Society of Appraisers, Washington, D. C, October, 1953, pp. 17.

BOYLAND, WILLIAM E., "Real Estate Tax Assessing In New York City," *Technical Valuation*, October, 1953, pp. 17-20.

BRANSCOMB, HARVIE JR., "Postponing Income Taxes on Real Estate Transactions," *The Appraisal Journal*, October, 1957, pp. 598-602.

BRENT, W. L., "Valuing Industrial Real Estate," *The National Real Estate Journal*, June 30, 1924, pp. 27-30.

BRINDLEY, WILLIS, "Retail Rentals As a Guide to Real Estate Values," *National Real Estate Journal*, August 17, 1931, pp. 19-20.

BROWN, ROBERT K., "Who Is the Typical Buyer?," *The Real Estate Appraiser*, May, 1963, pp. 29-31.

BRUNK, LLOYD S., "Appraisal Formula for Close-In Acreage," *The Appraisal Journal*, July, 1965, pp. 363-369.

BURGESS, GEORGE W., "Airports In the Balance Sheet of Real Estate Values," *The Appraisal Journal*, January, 1948, pp. 27-34.

BURKE, WILLIAM J., "The Listing & Valuation of Real Estate In the City of Buffalo, N. Y.," *Proceedings of 17th Annual Conference*, National Tax Association, 1924, pp. 212-217.

BURNELL, WILLIAM U., "A Program for Lower Taxes In Real Estate Improvements," *Valuation Manual*, American Society of Appraisers, 1959, pp. 29.

BURNELL, WILLIAM V., "Are New Laws Necessary for Real Estate Taxation," *Appraisal and Valuation Manual*, American Society of Appraisers, 1961, pp. 261-266.

BURNELL, WILLIAM V., "The Real Estate Tax Burden Versus Property Value," *Appraisal and Valuation Manual,* 1960.

BURTON, JOHN E., "Modifying and Supplementing General Property Tax a Base for Real Estate Taxes," *National Tax Association-Proceedings 27th Annual Conference,* 1934, pp. 55-74.

BUSSING, IRVIN, "Some Effects of the Emergency on Mortgages and Real Estate," *Real Estate Record and Builders Guide,* October 25, 1941, pp. 5-7.

BUTZ, ROBERT, "A Wider Real Estate Market," *The Review,* April, 1948, pp. 11-12.

CADWALLADER, CLYDE T., *How to Deal In Real Estate,* Prentice-Hall, New York, 1955, pp. 362.

CALDWELL, BERNARD L., "Tax Factors Which Affect Real Estate Values," *The Appraisal Journal,* October, 1964, pp. 564-575.

CALIFORNIA REAL ESTATE ASSOCIATION, *California Real Estate Magazine,* California Real Estate Association, Los Angeles, 1920.

CALVERT, GEOFFREY N., "Land and Real Estate As a Field of Investment for Pension Funds," *The Appraisal Journal,* April, 1969, pp. 257-270.

CAMERON, J. A., "Utility Forestry and Land Management," *Right of Way,* April, 1962, pp. 16-17.

CARLSON, DAVID M., BEN H. STORY JR., "Computers In Real Estate Appraising," *The Real Estate Appraiser,* October, 1966, pp. 2.

CASE, FRED E., "Comparative Real Estate Investment Experience," *The Appraisal Journal,* June, 1960, pp. 337-344.

CASEY, JAMES, J., "Cambridge System of Real Estate Valuation," *Bulletin,* National Tax Association, pp. 184-187.

CASEY, W. J., *Tax Shelter In Real Estate,* Institute for Business Planning, Inc., New York, 1957.

CHAMPNEY, ALBERT E., "Taxing Private Uses for Profit of Exempt Real Property," *Assessors News Letter,* January, 1960, pp. 4-9.

CHARLAND, ROGER, "The Basic Principles of Real Property Value," *Appraisal Valuation Manual,* American Society of Appraisers, 1960, pp. 57-70.

CHERNEY, RICHARD A., "Use of Sales-Assessment Ratios In Assessing Real Property," *The Appraisal Journal,* October, 1955, pp. 516-528.

CIMELY, G., "1969 Tax Reform Act Its Effect on Real Estate," *Industrial Development and Manufactures Record,* September, 1970, pp. 7-10.

CLARK, J. A., "New Proposed Valuation Taxes Will Cause Major Revisions In Estate Planning," *Journal of Taxation,* September, 1970, pp. 130-133.

CLARK, JOHN G., "The Real Estate Cycle In San Diego, California 1900-1932," *The Appraisal Journal,* May, 1933, pp. 207-211.

CLOVER, VERNON T., *Trego County Real Estate Assessment Plan,* State Printer, Topeka, Kansas.

CLURMAN, DAVID, "Appraisal and Investment Factors In Public Realty Entities," *The Appraisal Journal,* July, 1963, pp. PP, 293-300.

COLEAN, MILES, *Impact of Govt on Real Estate Finance In the U. S.,* Princeton University, Princeton, 1950.

CONNORS, JOHN E., "Purchase of Real Estate-Telephone Co," *Right of Way,* April, 1958, pp. 19-21.

COOPER, J. ROBERT, *Alternative Methods and Techniques for the Assessment of Farm Real Estate,* Clemson Agricultural College, Clemson, So. Carolna, 1957.

COSTA RICA, *Laws, Statutes, Etc. . . Reglamento De La Ley General De Terrenos Baldios,* Imprenta Nacional, San Jose, Costa Rica, 1940.

CRAWFORD, EDWARD J., "Personal Element In Realty Appraising," *Real Estate Record and Builders Guide,* December 31, 1941, pp. 5-6.

D.C. STORUD, "Land Values," *Town Planning Review,* April, 1966, pp. 69-70.

DAVIES, WILLIAM E., "Technical Information for Real Estate Experts," *Real Estate Board of New York, Diary and Manual,* 1915.

DAVIS, W. D., "Should a Charge Be Made for Buildings In Appraising Unimproved Land," *Journal of the American Society of Farm Managers and Rural Appraisers,* October, 1947, pp. 102-104.

DAVIS, W. D. SR., "Using Remainder Studies In an Appraisal," *The Real Estate Appraiser,* February, 1963, pp. 26-40.

DAY, JOSEPH P., "Appraisal of Real Estate by Sales Method," *Building Investment and Maintenance,* October, 1926, pp. 9-10.

DEBOOS, FRANK A., "Appraisal of Major Assistance In Real Estate Transactions," *The Appraisal Journal,* January, 1952, pp. 110-113.

DENTON, JOHN H., "Market Theory In Real Estate Appraising," *The Real Estate Appraiser,* September, 1963, pp. 2-13.

DERBES, MAX J. JR., "Use, Development, or Speculation of Real Estate," *Appraisal Journal,* April, 1964, pp. 219-229.

DILMORE, GENE, "Estimate of Accrued Depreciation," *The Real Estate Appraiser,* pp. 31.

DINGER, JULIUS J., "Recreational Real Estate," *The Real Estate Appraiser,* November 12, 1970, pp. 26-36.

DODGE, JOSEPH W., "Real Estate Loans, Values, and Appraisals," *The Appraisal Journal,* April, 1940, pp. 105-110.

DONOGH, A. ORMSBY, "What's Wrong with Real Estate Valuation," *The Residential Appraiser,* August, 1961, pp. 9-11.

DOWLING, J. W. F., "Land Evaluation for Engineering Purposes In Northern Nigeria," *Land Evaluation,* pp. 147.

DOWLING, ROBERT E., "Real Estate-The Walls Fell Down," *Technical Valuation,* October, 1954, pp. IU.

DUHAMEL, L. A., "Land Tenure In Alberta," *Appraisal Institute Magazine,* Appraisal Institute of Canada, Winnipeg.

DUNN, CECIL L., "Inflation As a Factor In Real Estate Appraisal," *The Appraisal Journal,* October, 1946, pp. 389-394.

DUNN, CECIL L., "Inflation In Real Estate," *The Review,* April, 1947, pp. 12-13.

DUNN, DOMINICK R., "Can Real Estate Have More Than One Value," *The Appraisal Journal,* April, 1937, pp. 175-179.

DUVALL, LOY CLEVELAND LEE, *The Taxation and Equalization of City, Town and County Real Estate,* W. M. Warlick, Dallas, Texas, 1901.

EDMAN, J. J., "The Appraisal Docket. Valuation of Real Estate Subject to Deed Restrictions on Use," *The Appraisal Journal,* January, 1961, pp. 123-125.

EDWARDS, EDWARD E., "Real Estate Economics. a Return to Fundamentals," *The Appraisal Journal,* April, 1949, pp. 239-242.

ELLWOOD, LEON W., *Ellwood Tables for Real Estate Appraising and Financing,* Ellwood, Leon W., Ridgewook, N. Y., 1959.

ELLWOOD, LEON, W., *Ellwood Tables for Real Estate Appraising and Financing,* American Institute of Real Estate Appraisers, Chicago, 1967.

FEDERAL HOME LOAN BANK REVIEW, *Real Estate Recovery Parallels Defense Boom,* February, 1942, pp. 155-157.

FINEHAUM, M. L., "Disposal & Land Valuation of Restricted Securities," *Trusts and Estates,* October, 1971, pp. 840-843.

FINNIS, FREDERIC H., *Real Property Assessment In Canada,* Canadian Tax Foundation, Toronto, 1962.

FISCHER, ERNEST M., "Real Estate Prices and Mortgage Financing," *The Appraisal Journal,* January, 1948, pp. 10-14.

FISHER, ERNEST M., "Appraisal Problems Inherent In Real Estate Market Behavior Professional Concepts," *Valuation Manual,* 1964, pp. 181.

FISHER, ERNEST M., "Real Estate Appraisals," *National Real Estate Journal,* August, 1935, pp. 49.

FISHER, ERNEST M., "Real Estate Value," *Advanced Principles of Real Estate Practice,* 1930, pp. 148-175.

FISHER, ERNEST M., "Research and Real Estate Appraisals," *The Appraisal Journal,* April, 1950, pp. 205-208.

FISHER, ERNEST M., "The Nature of the Urban Real Estate Market," *The Appraisal Journal,* January, 1952, pp. 51-55.

FISHER, ERNEST M., "The Role of Credit In the Real Estate Market," *The Appraisal Journal,* April, 1947, pp. 221-230.

FREEMAN, RAOUL J., "Real Estate Assessment and Electronic Computers," *The Appraisal Journal,* April, 1959, pp. 182-184.

FRIDEMAN, EDITH J., *Encyclopedia of Real Estate Appraising,* 1968.

FRIEDMAN, EDITH JUDITY, *Encyclopedia of Real Estate Appraising,* Prentice-Hall, Englwd Cliffs, N. J., 1965.

GEBHART, J. C., *Prohibition and Real Estate Values,* Amer Acad of Polit & Soc Sci Annals Vol Clxiii, September, 1932, pp. 105-112.

GEORGE, ERNEST, "Real Estate Exchange and Taxation," *The Residential Appraiser,* December, 1962, pp. 17-23.

GITTERMAN, A. N., *Real Estate Data Its Filing and Use by the Appraiser,* Real Estate Record and Builders Guide, July 7, 1934, pp. 8-9.

GOODSPEED, M. J., "Sampling Considerations In Land Evaluation," *Land Evaluation,* 1900, pp. 40.

GOODYEAR, J. LEO, "Unincorporated Areas Offer Many Unusual Challenges," *Appraisal Digest,* April, 1954, pp. 20-22.

GOTTLIEB, J. R., "Trust Policy and Real Estate Asa a Quality Investment, I," *The Appraisal Journal,* April, 1954, pp. 263-249.

GRAHAM, DONALD H. JR., "Owner's Analysis of Yields on Major Real Estate Investment," *Appraisal Journal,* October, 1965, pp. 541-548.

GRAVES, H. WALTER, "Tomorrow's Real Estate Market," *The Review,* July, 1956, pp. 12-16.

GRONER, ORVILLE, "Real Estate Investments Under Liquidating Leases," *The Appraisal Journal,* April, 1949, pp. 252-256.

HAGGSTROM, ROBERT J., "A Human Relations Approach to Real Estate Management," *The Appraisal Journal,* January, 1955, pp. 87-95.

HALL, FRANK D., "Can Real Estate Value Be Stabilized?," *Review of Society of Residential Appraisers,* November, 1939, pp. 306.

HALL, FRANK D., "Seven Keys to Real Estate Values," *Address Given at the Regional Conference of the National Association of Real Estate Boards,* Richmond, Virginia, May, 1938.

HALL, HENRY C., "Farm Real Estate Values," *Journal of the American Society of Farm Managers and Rural Appraisers,* October, 1959, pp. 12-15.

HAMMAR, CONRAD H., "Land Classification to Aid the Appraiser," *Journal of Land and Public Utility Economics,* August, 1939, pp. 277-286.

HANAO, YOSHIO, "Real Estate Appraising In Japan," *The Real Estate Appraiser,* April, 1963, pp. 10-16.

HANFORD, LLOYD JR., "Forecasting Real Estate Taxes," *The Real Estate Appraisal,* pp. 47.

HARTWIG, J. D., "Tax Considerations In Real Estate Transactions," *Michigan State Bar Journal,* October, 1961, pp. 14-23.

HAYES, SAMUEL L. III, AND LEONARD M. HARLAN, "Real Estate As a Corporate Investment," *The Appraisal Journal*, July, 1968, pp. 361-382.

HAYNES, JOHN L., "Real Estate Appraisals Under the Securities Act," *Real Estate Record and Builders Guide*, October 27, 1934, pp. 5-6.

HECHT, LEE I., "Appraising for Taxation of Real Estate," *Annals of Real Estate Practice*, National Association of Real Estate Boards, 1928, pp. 143-153.

HEFTI, WILMA C., *How to Keep Real Estate Office Records*, Prenticehall, Incorporated, New York, 1954.

HEILBRUN, JAMES, "Real Estate Taxes and Urban Housing N.J.," Columbia University Press, 1966.

HEILBTUN, JAMES, "Real Estate Taxes and Urban Housing," *Real Estate Taxes an Urban Housing*, Columbia University Press, New York, 1966.

HEMMER, EDGAR HAROLD, PH.D., *A-Valuation Model for Investments In Real Estate*, Purdue University, 1972.

HENDERSON AND ROSS, "Real Estate Appraisal for Investors Mortgage Company," *Henderson, J. D.*, pp. 199-224.

HENDERSON, JAMES D., *Pocket Manual for Appraising Real Estate*, Baner and Tradesman Publishing Company, Cambridge, Mass., 1932.

HENDERSON, JAMES D., *Real Estate Appraising*, Banker & Tradesman Publishing Company, 1931.

HEWEN, LORING M., "Comprehensive Rules Governing Realty Appraisals Needed," *Real Estate Record and Builders Guide*, May 14, 1932, pp. 7.

HIGGINS, WARREN J., *Impact of Federal Taxation on Real Estate Decisions*, University of Connecticut, Real Estate Repts No 11, 1971.

HOGAN, HOWARD T., "Judicial Review of Real Estate Tax Assessments," *New York State Bar Journal*, February, 1963, pp. 51-57.

HOGUET, ROBERT L., "Real Estate Appraisals In the Post-Depression Era," *Real Estate Record and Builders Guide*, December 22, 1934, pp. 5-6.

HOLDEN, THOMAS S., "Postwar Trends In Real Estate and Construction," *The Appraisal Journal*, July, 1946, pp. 276-284.

HOLLAND, DANIEL M., "The Taxation of Unimproved Value In Jamaica," *Conference Proceedings*, National Tax Association, Columbus, 1965, pp. 442-470.

HOLMES, LAWRENCE G., "Appraising Real Estate for Tax Purposes, The Income Method," *Journal of Land and Public Utility Economics*, November, 1938.

HOLMES, LAWRENCE G., "Our Real Estate Tax Economcy Shouldcome of Age," *The Appraisal Journal*, October, 1943, pp. 315-326.

HOOT, WELDON, "The Distinction Between Value and Valuation and Its Application to Real Estate," *American Academy of Political and Social Science*, March, 1930, pp. 61-66.

HOPKINS, ED W., "Changing Aspects of Real Estate Appraising," *The Appraisal Journal*, January, 1934, pp. 104-107.

HOWARD, T. HOGAN, "Judicial Review of Real Estate Tax Assessments," *The Real Estate Appraiser*, January, 1963, pp. 28-33.

HOWORTH, PHILIP H., "Site Value Taxation, a Solution to Allocation Problems In the Taxation of Real Estate," *Massachusetts Law Quarterly*, March, 1962, pp. 28-36.

HOYT, HOMER, "Critical Tests of the Soundness of Current Real Estate Loans," *The Appraisal Journal*, January, 1947, pp. 73-78.

HOYT, HOMER, "Effect of Cyclical Fluctuations Upon Real Estate Finance," *The Appraisal Journal*, April, 1947, pp. 211-217.

HUBIN, VINCENT J., "Tax Advantages of Realty Investments," *Appraisal Digest*, March, 1959, pp. 16-17.

HUSBAND, WILLIAM H., FRANK RAY ANDERSON, *Real Estate Analysis,* Irwin, Chicago, 1948, pp. 410.

ILLINOIS DEPARTMENT OF REVENUE, *Real Property Assessment Manual,* Illinois Department of Revenue, Springfield, 1952.

INSTITUTE OF REAL ESTATE MANAGEMENT, *Journal of Real Estate Management,* Chicago, May, 1935.

INSTITUTE OF REAL ESTATE MANAGEMENT, "**Feasibility Study Techniques,**" *Institute of Real Estate Management,* Chicago, Illinois.

INSTITUTE'S RESEARCH COMMITTEE, "**Suggested Research Topics In Real Estate Valuation,**" *The Appraisal Journal,* July, 1952, pp. 399-401.

INWOOD, WILLIAM, *Tables of Interest and Mortality for the Purchasing of Estates and Valuation of Properties,* Lockwood and Son, London, 1930.

IOWA PROPERTY TAX DIVISION, *Summary of Real Estate Assessment Ratio Study,* Iowa Property Tax Division, Des Moines, 1962.

JACOBS, J. L., "**Systematic Real Property Appraisal and Assessment Equalization,**" *Assessors News Letter,* January, 1964, pp. 3-5.

JEFFERY, RICHARD, "**Realtors, Builders and Appraisers,**" *The Review,* November, 1947, pp. 8-11.

JERRETT, HERMAN D., *The Theory of Real Property Valuation,* Keystone Press, Sacramento, Calif., 1938.

KAHN, CASE-SCHIMMEL, *Real Estate Appraisal and Investment,* 1963.

KAHN, SANDERS A., "**A Look at Real Estate Planning,**" *The Appraisal Journal,* July, 1954, pp. 423-429.

KAHN, SANDERS A., "**Real Estate Makes the College Team,**" *The Appraisal Journal,* April, 1951, pp. 233-238.

KAHN, SANDERS A., ALVIN M. WEINTRAUB, "**Real Estate and the Trucking Industry,**" *Valuation Manual,* 1964, pp. 189.

KAHN, SANDERS A., FREDERICK CASE, ALFRED SCHIMMEL, *Real Estate and Investment,* Ronald Press, New York, 1963, pp. 468.

KALTENBACH, HENRY J., "**Just Compenstaion,**" *The Appraisal Real Estate,* 1956, pp. 456.

KAMLET, MARK, "**Cable TV, Its Impact on Real Property Valuations,**" *The Appraisal Journal,* July, 1968, pp. 426-428.

KANSAS AGRICULTURAL EXPERIMENT STATION MANHATTAN, *The Trend of Real Estate Taxation In Kansas from 1910 to 1923,* Kansas State Printing Plant, Topeka, 1925.

KENTUCKY DEPARTMENT OF REVENUE, *Kentucky Real Property Assessment Manual,* Kentucky Department of Revenue, Frankfort, 1950.

KERN, JAMES M., "**The Valuation of Real Estate,**" *The Appraisal Journal,* October, 1947, pp. 540-543.

KIBBEY, GERALD S., "**Second Trust Deed-Friend or Foe,**" *The Real Estate Appraiser,* October, 1964, pp. 29.

KILEY, EDWARD V., "**The Highway Age In Transportation,**" *How Transportation Affects Real Estate Value,* AIREA, Chicago, March 7, 1969, pp. 12-13.

KILMORE, GENE, "**The New Approach to Real Estate Appraising,**" *The New Approach to Real Estate Appraising,* Prentice Hall, Englwd Cliffs, N.J., 1971.

KING, WILLFORD I., *The Valuation of Urban Realty for Purposes of Taxation, with Cert Secs Espec Applicable to Wisconsin,* Madison, Wisconsin, 1914.

KINNARD, DR. WILLIAM N., "**Reducing Uncertainty In Real Estate Decisions,**" *The Real Estate Appraiser,* November, 1968, pp. 10-17.

KINNARD, WILLIAM N., STEPHEN D. MESSNER, *Industrial Real Estate,* Society of Industrial Realtors, Washington, D. C..

KINNARD, WILLIAM N. JR., "New Thinking In Appraisal Theory," *The Real Estate Appraisal,* August, 1966, pp. 2-13.

KIRSHMAN, JOHN EMMETT, "Real-Estate Securities," *Principles of Investment,* 1933, pp. 571.

KISSACK, A. B., "A Single-Family Dwelling," *Real Estate Analyst Appraisal Bulletin,* 1948, pp. 89-92.

KISSACK, A. B., "Capacity and Utility," *Real Estate Analyst Appraisal Bulletin,* 1948, pp. 29-32.

KISSACK, A. B., "Conclusion of a Single Value," *Real Estate Analyst Appraisal Bulletin,* pp. 35-38.

KISSACK, A. B., "Placing the Risk," *Real Estate Analyst Appraisal Bulletin,* 1947, pp. 519-522.

KIZER, JOHN O., "Valuation of Leasehold Estates In Eminent Domain," *West Virginia Law Review,* February, 1965, pp. 101-115.

KNIGHT, C. LOUIS, "Blighted Areas and Their Effects Upon Urban Land Utilization,"*American Academy of Political and Social Science,* March 30, 1930, pp. 133-138.

KNISKERN, P. W., "Aberdeen Gardens Appraisal Certificate, Facsimile," *Real Estate Appraisal and Valuation,* 1933, pp. 491-497.

KNISKERN, P. W., "Theoretical Conversion of Traffic Into Rental Value, Formula and Comment," *Real Estate Appraisal and Valuation,* 1933, pp. 342-343.

KNISKERN, PHILIP W., *Real Estate Appraisal and Valuation,* Ronald Press Co., New York, 1933.

KNISKERN, PHILIP W., "Assuring Accuracy In Valuation for Federal Home Loans," *Real Estate Record and Builders Guide,* May 5, 1934, pp. 6..

KNISKERN, PHILIP W., "Capitalization Rate; In Interest Tables & Their Use Etc.," *Real Estate Appraisal and Valuation,* 1933, pp. 296-490.

KNISKERN, PHILIP W., "Determining Values In Real Estate," *Savings Bank Journal,* January, 1930, pp. 46-49.

KNISKERN, PHILIP W., "Making Appraisals for Loans," *National Real Estate Journal,* July 14, 1924, pp. 27-30.

KNISKERN, PHILIP W., "Mortgage Loan Appraisal Method and Procedure," *National Real Estate Journal,* July 7, 1930, pp. 46-49.

KNISKERN, PHILIP W., "Practical Method for Approximating Land Values," *Real Estate Appraisal and Valuation,* 1933, pp. 282-283.

KNISKERN, PHILIP W., "Practical Suggestions for Appraising Homes," *National Association of Real Estate Boards,* 1927, pp. 186-223.

KNISKERN, PHILIP W., "Rent Analysis Tables and Comment," *Real Estate Appraisal and Valuation,* 1933, pp. 331-334.

KNISKERN, PHILIP W., "The Field of the Real Estate Counselor," *The Residential Appraiser,* pp. 14.

KNISKERN, PHILIP W., "The Valuation Process, Income Valuation, Physical Valuation," *Real Estate Appraisal,* 1933, pp. 235-266.

KNISKERN, PHILIP W., "Value," *Real Estate Appraisal and Valuation,* 1933, pp. 3-107.

KNISKERN, PHILIP W., "Value Factors That Affect Mortgage Appraisals," *National Real Estate Journal,* June 23, 1930, pp. 34-36.

KNISKERN, PHILIP WHEELER, *Real Estate Appraisal and Valuation,* Theronald Press Company, New York, 1933.

KNODELL, H. W., "The Effect of City Growth on Values," *National Real Estate Journal,* March, 1934, pp. 31-32.

KNOWLES, JEROME, JR., JOHN E. PERVEAR, *Real Estate Appraisal Manual,* Jerome Knowles Jr., Northeast Harbor Me., 1965.

KOBER, CHARLES A. JR., *The Education and Ethics of the American Institute of Real Estate Appraisers*, Right of Way Conference, Selected Papers, University of Ala., 1961, pp. 40-44.

KOHLER, RICHARD E., "Estimating the Values of Landscaping," *Real Estate Analyst Appraisal Bulletin*, 1960, pp. 237-240.

KRATOVIL, ROBERT, *Real Estate Law*, Prentice-Hall, 1958.

KRAUSZ, DR. N. G. P., "Estate Planning," *Journal of the American Society of Farm Managers and Rural Appraisers*, April, 1961, pp. 40-45.

KREVOR, HENRY H., "Legal Rules Governing Valuation of Real Property," *Right of Way*, June, 1960, pp. 7-17.

KUEHNLE, WALTER R., "The Trend of Real Estate Prices," *The Appraisal Journal*, January, 1947, pp. 57-65.

KUEHNLE, WALTER R., "Valuation of Real Estate for Ad Valorem Tax Purposes," *The Appraisal Journal*, January, 1953, pp. 26-34.

KUNKLE, J. D., "Developing Industrial Appraisal Business," *National Real Estate Journal*, August 23, 1926, pp. 54-55.

KUNKLE, J. D., "The Appraisal of Industrial Waterfront Lands," *National Association of Real Estate Boards*, 1928, pp. 728-732.

KUNKLE, J. D., "Units of Industrial Property Values," *National Real Estate Journal*, April 19, 1926, pp. 45-47.

KURNOW, ERNEST, "Trends In Property Value," *The Appraisal Journal*, April, 1961, pp. 186-199.

LAIDLAW, J. B., "Statutory Authority Whereunder Real Property Is Assessed In Alberta," *Appraisal Institute Magazine*, December, 1962, pp. 5-8.

LAMBRECHT, RICHARD G., "The Basis of Real Estate Values," *National Real Estate Journal*, April 4, 1927, pp. 37-43.

LAMULLE, L. X., "Wholesale Value Vs. Retail Value," *The Real Estate Appraiser*, November, 1960, pp. 22-23.

LANDAUER, JAMES D., "Real Estate As an Investment," *The Appraisal Journal*, October, 1960, pp. 426-434.

LANGSLET, OTTO, "Cities Enter the Real Estate Business, Management of City Property," *Commonwealth Review*, May, 1937, pp. 138-139.

LARONGE, JOSEPH, "Valuation of the Fee Under a Reappraisal Lease," *Journal of the American Institute of Real Estate Appraisers*, October, 1937, pp. 331-324.

LASSER, J. K., CASEY, WILLIAM J., "Impact of Taxes on Real Estate Values," *The Appraisal Journal*, January, 1952, pp. 94-100.

LAWRENCE, EDWARD R., "Meaning of the Term Comparables In Pennsylvania Real Estate Assessment," *University of Pittsburgh Law Review*, October, 1965, pp. 126-136.

LEE, DONALD E., "Appraisals-A Management Tool In Government Operations," *The Real Estate Appraiser*, SREA, Chicago, December, 1964, pp. 8.

LEE, M. W., "Zoning, Myth or Magic," *The Real Estate Appraiser*, SREA, April, 1964, pp. 2.

LEISK, HERBERT N., "Formula for Irregular Lots," *The Real Estate Appraiser*, March, 1954, pp. 7-11, 20.

LEISK, HERBERT N., "How to Get Appraisal Business," *Encyclopedia of Real Estate Appraising*, Edith Friedman, Editor, 1959, pp. 788-805.

LEISTRITZ, FREDERICK LARRY, *Simulation Analysis of the Farm Real Estate Market and Farm Enlargement In Southwest Nebraska*, University of Nebraska, 1970.

LEUBBERT, RAFAEL C., "Disposal Holding Formula Applied to Real Estate Valuation," *The Real Estate Appraiser*, SREA, Chicago, October, 1967, pp. 27.

LEVIN, EARL, "Land Planning and Land Costs," *Appraisal Institute Magazine,* September, 1959, pp. 4-14.

LEVIN, L. M., "Combination Sale of Cash Value Life Insurance and Real Estate," *National Underwriter Life and Health Insurance Edition,* January 16, 1971, pp. 20-21.

LEVY, MARK, "How to Determine Business Rentals," *National Real Estate Journal,* November 17, 1924, pp. 41-44.

LILLY, JOSEPH, "Considerations In Real Estate Assessments," *Real Estate Record and Builders Guide,* February 28, 1942, pp. 3-5.

LINDBURG, WALLACE A., "For We Must Think Young," *The Real Estate Appraiser,* SREA, Chicago, October, 1964, pp. 32.

LINDOP, JOHN CUMMINGS, "The Effect of Motor Traffic on Real Estate Values," *National Real Estate Journal,* October, 1937, pp. 40-41.

LIPMAN, M. RONALD, "The Market Approach In the Appraisal of Garden Apartments," *The Real Estate Appraiser,* July, 1963, pp. 36-39.

LOUIS, CHARLES F., "Depreciation and Real Estate Appraisals," *The Appraisal Journal,* October, 1961.

LOVE, HAROLD C., "Risk and Uncertainty Factors In Real Estate Appraisal," *The Assessors Journal,* July, 1966, pp. 17-25.

LOVE, T. L., "Modular Housings Impact Upon Real Estate Appraisal," *Appraisal Journal,* April, 1972, pp. 208-216.

LUDLOW, WILLIAM H., "Neighborhood Planning Committee Suggests Novel Real-Estate Development," *American City,* September, 1937, pp. 77-78.

LUEBBERT, RAFAEL C., "An Analytical Study of Physical Depreciation," *The Real Estate Appraiser,* September, 1968, pp. 13-21.

LUEBBERT, RAFAEL C., "Disposal-Holding Formulae Applied to Real Estate Valuation," *The Real Estate Appraiser,* September, 1967, pp. 27-32.

LUM Y. T., "The Highest and Best Use," *The Real Estate Appraiser,* SREA, Chicago, June, 1966, pp. 2.

LUTZ, H. L., "The Somers System of Realty Valuation," *Quarterly Journal of Economics,* 1910, pp. PP, 172-181.

MACBRIDE, DEXTER D., "Effects of Freeways on Real Estate Values," *Pacific Coast Appraisal Conference Society of Residential Appraisers,* September, 1962.

MACLEOD, R. J., "The Condominium In Canada," *The Real Estate Appraiser,* May, 1971, pp. 29-35.

MACROSSIE, WILLIAM, "Appraisal of Income Property-Office Buildings," *Encyclopedia of Real Estate Appraising,* Friedman, Edith J, 1959, pp. 234-257.

MACROSSIE, WILLIAM, "Approach to Real Estate Value," *Appraisal and Valuation Manual,* American Society of Appraisers, 1955, pp. 242-243.

MACROSSIE, WILLIAM, "Valuation of Motel Furnishings and Equipment," *Real Estate Appraisal Practice,* American Institute of Real Estate Appraisers, 1958, pp. 4 2-435.

MAIR, GEORGE, "Elementary Real Estate Appraisal, a Programmed Text," *Elementary Real Estate Appraisal, a Programed Text,* W. C. Brown Co, Dubuque, 1966.

MAISEL, SHERMAN J., SCHAFF, ALBERT H, "The Business of Real Estate Brokerage---Current Performance and Future Potential," *The Appraisal Journal,* July, 1957, pp. 337-34.

MALEY, LYLE W., "Legal Descriptions of Real Estate," *The Appraisal Journal,* January, 1954, pp. 13-88.

MALOTT, J. O., "Collegiate Courses In Realty, 1932," *U. S. Office of Education, No. 101,* Washington, D. C, May 4, 1933, pp. 3.

MANUFACTURERS APPRAISAL CO., *The Somers System of Realty Valuation,* Cleveland, 1909.

MAO, J. C. T., *Cases In Real Estate Finance,* Univ of Michigan, Bureau of Business Research, Ann Arbor, Michigan, 1959.

MARCUS, WILLIAM J., "Current Influence of Mortgage Credit Upon Real Estate and Prices," *The Appraisal Journal,* October, 1948, pp. 487-494.

MARTIN, PRESTON, *Real Estate Principles and Practices,* Macmillan, New York, 1959.

MARTIN, W. H., "Aviation-Economic Impact on Real Estate," *Appraisal Journal,* April, 1972, pp. 231-234.

MARTIN, WENDELL H., "Remote Land-Development or Exploitation," *Urban Land,* February, 1971.

MARTZKE, ARTHUR J., "Is Interest on Mortgage a Factor In Appraising," *National Real Estate Journal,* February 17, 1930, pp. 54-55.

MARX, LEONARD, "Real Estate Economic Outlook," *The Appraisal Journal,* July, 1950, pp. 363-369.

MASON, TOM, "Appraisal of Waterfront Properties," *California Real Estate Magazine,* July, 1937, pp. 38-40.

MATTER, J. AUBREY, "Exemption of Institutional Real Estate," *Assessment Administration,* Institute of American Assessment Officers, Chicago, 1957, pp. 145-153.

MATTHEWS, STEWART B., "The Effect of Rent Control on Real Estate Values," *The Appraisal Journal,* October, 1942, pp. 323-327.

MAUCH, ARTHUR, "Agricultural Problems Affecting Future Real Estate Markets," *The Appraisal Journal,* October, 1954, pp. 576-580.

MAY, ARTHUR A, *The Valuation of Residential Real Estate,* Prentice-Hall, Inc, New York, 1953, pp. 3.

MAY, ARTHUR A., *The Valuation of Residentail Real Estate,* Prentice-Hall Incorporated, New York, 1942.

MAY, ARTHUR A., *The Valuation of Residential Real Estate,* 1968.

MAYER, HAROLD M., "Current and Prospective Population Trends-Some Real Estate Implications," *The Appraisal Journal,* April, 1955, pp. 212-224.

MCCASLIN, A. A., "Appraising the Estates In a 99-Year Lease," *National Real Estate Journal,* February, 1932, pp. 27-30.

MCCLELLAND, HARRY, "Current Trends Affecting Real Estate," *The Appraisal Journal,* January, 1948, pp. 35-39.

MCCLOY, HOWARD F., *Managing Corporate Real Estate,* American Management Association, New York, 1967.

MCCORMACK, JAMES E., "Valuation Perplexities In Pricing Cleared Land," *The Appraisal Journal,* January, 1959, pp. 41-48.

MCCORMICK, LORING O., SCHMUTZ, GEORGE L, "Economic Approach to Valuation Procedure," *Journal of the American Institute of Real Estate Appraisers,* July, 1933.

MCCOY, CHARLES R., "The Impact of Retail Decentralization on One Downtown Appraisal," *Real Estate Analyst Appraisal Bulletin,* 1952, pp. 489-492.

MCCURDY, ROBERT V., "Capitalization Rates," *The Real Estate Appraiser,* SREA, Chicago, January, 1965, pp. 23.

MCCURDY, ROBERT V., "Elements of Damage In Partial Takings," *The Real Estate Appraiser,* December, 1963, pp. 2-13.

MCDONALD, ADRIAN F., "Expressways and Real Estate Values," *The Review,* February, 1953, pp. 10-16, 14-20.

MCDONALD, ADRIAN F., "Fundamentals of Real Estate Appraising," *The Appraisal Journal,* January, 1952, pp. 56-63.

MCFADDEN, NORMAN E., "Money Markets and Real Estate Values," *American Right of Way Association,* Proceedings of the Third Annual National Seminar, Washington, D. C, 1958, pp. 9-11.

MCGARRY, D. F., "Appraisal-Valuation of Real Estate," *Realty Blue Book of California,* Keystone Pub. Co, Los Angeles, 1924.

MCGOUGH, B. C., "The Concepts and Practices for Compensation In Eminent Domain," *The Real Estate Appraiser,* March, 1969, pp. 44-47.

MCGRATH, GEORGE W., "Emphasis on Depreciation Allowances," *Real Estate Record,* June 20, 1936, pp. 13-16.

MCGUIRE, JOSEPH, WINTER, E. P, "Method of Measuring Change In Real Estate Values," *The Appraisal Journal,* July, 1955, pp. 404-412.

MCKAY, R. J., "Tax Considerations In the Acquisition and Ownership of Real Estate," *Appraisal Institute Magazine,*

MCKEY, ROBERT M., "Appraisal of Hotels and Resort Properties," *Encyclopedia of Real Estate Appraising,* 1959, pp. 414-446.

MCLAUGHLIN, CHARLES J., "Taxation of Real Estate," *The Appraisal Journal,* April, 1940, pp. 153-155.

MCLEAN, E. E., "Farm Real Estate and Loan Outlook," *Journal of the American Society of Farm Managers and Rural Appraisers,* October, 1948, pp. 184-191.

MCMICHAEL, STANLEY L., *Real Estate Subdivisions,* Prentice-Hall, New York, 1949.

MCMICHAEL, STANLEY L., "The Influence of the Automobile on Real Estate," *National Association of Real Estate Boards, Annals,* 1928, pp. 204-219.

MCMICHAEL, STANLEY L., "Trends In Urban Real Estate Values Past And Future," *American Academy of Social and Political Science,* March, 1930, pp. 170-176.

MCPHERSON, L. V., "Initial Effects of the Seaway on Real Estate Values In Cornwall," *Appraisal Institute Magazine,* July, 1957, pp. 26-28.

MCSPADDEN, FRANK J, "Guidelines for a Narrative Real Estate Appraisal," *The Real Estate Appraiser,* November, 1967, pp. 21.

MERTZKE, ARTHUR J., "Annuity and Present Worth Tables- Their Use In Appraising Real Estate," *National Real Estate Journal,* May 27, 1929, pp. 36-37.

MERTZKE, ARTHUR J., "Real Estate Appraisal Practices," *The Appraisal Journal,* July, 1933, pp. 298-309.

MERTZKE, ARTHUR J., "What Items Do Appraiser Include Under Expenses," *National Real Estate Journal,* February 3, 1930, pp. 22-24.

MILLER, WILLIAM STANLEY, "Valuation of Real Estate for Taxation," *The Appraisal Journal,* April, 1941, pp. 123-130.

MONDELLO, ROMEO, "Relationship Between Zoning and Real Estate Appraisal," *Appraisal Institute Magazine,* June, 1961, pp. 24-27.

MORRELL, JOSEPH C., "The Real Estate Consultant," *Appraisal Digest,* July, 1956, pp. 14-17.

MORRIS, VICTOR P., "The Economic Position of Real Estate," *The Appraiser Journal,* July, 1939, pp. 258-262.

MOSS, DAVID S., "Equity Yields on Real Estate Investments," *The Appraisal Journal,* pp. 412-423.

MULLENIX, C. A., "Reviving the Profit of Old Buildings," *National Real Estate Journal,* March, 1934, pp. 33-34.

MURPHY, J. W., "Scientific Evaluation of Real Estate," *National Real Estate Journal,* July 11, 1900, pp. 27-31.

MURRAY, T. G., "Signal: Land Is Big Money," Dun's, July, 1970, pp. 58-60.

MURRAY, WILLIAM G., "Challenge Facing Real Estate Appraisers Today," *Journal of the American Society of Farm Managers and Rural Appraisers,* April, 1961, pp. 55-58.

N. Y. TIMES INDEX, "Indian Community Threatened by Land Boom," *N. Y. Times Index,* October 18, 1970.

NATIONAL ASSOCIATION OF MUTUAL SAVINGS BANKS, "Mortgage Committee," *Real Estate Record and Builders Guide*, May 19, 1934, pp. 8-9.

NATIONAL ASSOCIATION OF REAL ESTATE BOARDS, December 12, 1927, pp. 29.

NATIONAL ASSOCIATION OF REAL ESTATE BOARDS, *Committee on Depreciation and Obsolescence of Real Estate Improvements*, Chicago, 1929.

NATIONAL ASSOCIATION OF REAL ESTATE BOARDS, *Depreciation, Deterioration and Obsolescence In Real Estate Appraisals*, Chicago, 1931.

NATIONAL ASSOCIATION OF REAL ESTATE BOARDS, *Real Estate Appraisals*, Chicago, 1931.

NATIONAL ASSOCIATION OF REAL ESTATE BOARDS, "Committee on Appraisal Methods-Answers to Appraisal Questions," *National Real Estate Journal*, July 21, 1930, pp. 53-54.

NATIONAL ASSOCIATION OF REAL ESTATE BOARDS, "Glossary Terms," *Standards of Appraisal Practice*, April, 1929.

NATIONAL ASSOCIATION OF REAL ESTATE BOARDS, "Real Estate Appraisal Form," *National Real Estate Journal*, March 4, 1929, pp. 64.

NATIONAL ASSOCIATION OF REAL ESTATE BOARDS, "Report on Survey of Committee Work," *National Real Estate Journal*, January 11, 1926, pp. 53-54.

NATIONAL INSTITUTE OF REAL ESTATE BROKERS, *Corporate Employee Relocation*.

NATIONAL INSTITUTE OF REAL ESTATE BROKERS, *Guide to Commercial Property Leasing*, Chicago.

NATIONAL REAL ESTATE JOURNAL, *Appraisal Committees Win Fame for Real Estate Boards*, June 11, 1928, pp. 37.

NEISWANGER, DAVID, "Appraising Residential Real Estate In 1947," *The Appraisal Journal*, January, 1947, pp. 79-86.

NELSON, H. V., "Bibliography on Real Estate Subjects-Appraisals," *The Administration of Real Estate Boards*, Macmillian, New York, 1936, pp. 199-200.

NELSON, H. V., "Board Appraisals," *The Administration of Real Estate Boards*, Macmillan, New York, 1925, pp. 144-166.

NELSON, H. V., "Education for Realtors," *National Real Estate Journal*, December 1, 1924, pp. 25-30.

NELSON, ROLAND D., "Real Estate Taxes and Value," *The Appraisal Journal*, January, 1966, pp. 41-43.

NICOLLS, J. P., "Real Estate Values In Vancouver a Reminiscence," *Appraisal Institute Magazine*, March, 1963.

NOLAN, JAMES J., "Appraisal of Integrated Real Estate," *Technical Valuation*, December, 1968, pp. 34-39.

OKEEFE, PAUL T., "A Letter About Real Estate Appraisers," *Appraisal Digest*, October, 1955, pp. 1-2.

OMARA, LAURENCE, "Acquisition of Real Estate," *The Review*, July, 1953, pp. 13-15.

O'BRIEN, GENERAL JOHN J., "The Arm Takes the Land," *The Appraisal Journal*, pp. 116-123.

OLCOTT, MARGARET, HELEN E. HENNERFRUND, *Valuation of Real Estate with Special Reference to Farm Real Estate*, U. S. Bureau of Agricultural Economics, Washington, D. C., December, 1935.

OWEN, LEROY D., *Industrial Real Estate*, Los Angeles, 1936, pp. 24.

PAARLBERG, DON, "Farm Real Estate Prices," *Journal of the American Society of Farm Mangers and Rural Appraisers*, October, 1950, pp. 103-106.

PARKE, FENTON M., "Appraisal of Industrial Real Estate," *Annals of Real Estate Practice*, National Association of Real Estate Boards Vol. Vi, 1925, pp. 57-79.

PARTRIDGE, CHARLES, "Appraising Waterfront and Industrial Property," *National Real Estate Journal*, March, 1938, pp. 54-57.

PEARSON, F. A., AND R. G. KING, "The Real Estate Cycle," *The Appraisal Journal*, October, 1940, pp. 301-308.

PEARSON, K. G., "Big Business Discovers Real Estate," *Michigan Business Review*, March, 1971, pp. 26-32.

PEATMAN, JOHN GREY, "The Psychology of Real Estate Investment," *The Appraisal Journal*, October, 1942, pp. 335-339.

PETRY, ELDON H., "The Valuation of Raw Land," *Appraisal Institute Magazine*, Appraisal Institute of Canada, Winnipeg.

PETRY, ELDON H., "The Valuation of Raw Land with Subdivision Potential," *Appraisal Institute Magazine*, September, 1964.

PIAZZA, COSMO C., "Value In the Equilibrium Stage," *The Real Estate Appraiser*, pp. 34.

PITMAN, HAYDEN W., "Exemption of Institutional Real Estate," *Assessment Administration*, Institute of American Assessments Officers, Chicago, pp. 137-141.

PORTER, LESTER W., "Importance of Market Experience," *Evaluating Industrial Real Estate*, The Society of Industrial Realtors, 1953, pp. 132-136.

PORTER, LESTER W., "The Technique of Appraising Industrial Real Estate," *Annals of Real Estate Practice*, 1928, pp. 706-721.

PULIS, ARTHUR G. JR., "Appraising Raw Acreage for Residential Development," *The Review*, January, 1946, pp. 14-19.

PURDY, LAWSON, *The Assessment of Real Estate*, National Municipal League, Philadelphia.

RAGLEY, MAX, "Physical Value Comes First In Real Estate Appraising," *National Real Estate Appraising*.

RALYA, DON L., "Planned Unit Developments-The F. H. A. Program," *The Real Estate Appraiser*, February, 1967, pp. 2-10.

RANDALL, WILLIAM J., "A Fair Compensable Award for Right-Of-Way Purposes," *Real Estate Analyst Appraisal Bulletin*, 1956, pp. 175-180.

RANDALL, WILLIAM J., "An Appraisal Vs an Investment Analysis, or How to Double Your Real Estate Investment In 5 Years," *Real Estate Analyst Bulletin*, 1961, pp. 603-614.

RANDALL, WILLIAM J., "Appraisal of Damages to Real Estate Caused by Its Proximity to an Airport Serving Jet Transports," *Real Estate Analyst Appraisal Bulletin*, 1953, pp. 233-236.

RANDALL, WILLIAM J., "Characteristics of Regional Shopping Centers," *Real Estate Analyst Appraisal Bulletin*, 1957, pp. 109-114.

RANDALL, WILLIAM J., "Value of a Parking Space," *Real Estate Analyst Appraisal Bulletin*, 1962, pp. 173-178.

RAPKIN, CHESTER, "Role of Real Estate Taxes In the Investment Experience of Real Property," *The Appraisal Journal*, October, 1954, pp. 486-496.

RATCLIFF, DR. RICHARD U., *Real Estate Valuation and Highway Condemnation Awards*, University of Wisconsin, Madison, 1966.

RATCLIFF, DR. RICHARD U., "Modern Real Estate Valuation, Theory and Application," *The Real Estate Appraiser*, 1965.

RATCLIFF, DR. RICHARD U., "The Price and Rewards of Professionalism," *The Real Estate Appraiser*, August, 1967, pp. 3.

RATCLIFF, RICHARD UPDEGRAFF, *Real Estate Analysis*, McGraw Hill, New York, 1949.

RATCLIFF, RICHARD UPDEGRAFF, *Real Estate Valuation and Highway Condemnation Awards,* Univ of Wisconsin, Graduate School of Business, Madison, 1966.

RATCLIFF, RICHARD UPDEGRAFF, *Real Property,* 1906.

RAUBER, EARLE L., "Economic Trends Affecting Real Estate," *The Appraisal Journal,* October, 1949, pp. 503-508.

REAL ESTATE ANALYST APPRAISAL BULLETIN, "Census Data to Aid the Appraiser," *Real Estate Analyst Appraisal Bulletin,* 1951, pp. 295-298.

REAL ESTATE ANALYST, THE, "Construction Costs of a One-Story Commercial Building," *Real Estate Analyst Appraisal Bulletin,* 1955, pp. 17-20.

REAL ESTATE ANALYST, THE, "Factors In Appraising a Tourist Court," *Real Estate Analyst Appraisal Bulletin,* 1951, pp. 231-234.

REAL ESTATE ANALYST, THE, "Land Appraising," *Real Estate Analyst Appraisal Bulletin,* pp. 233-236.

REAL ESTATE ANALYST, THE, "Land of Limited Useful Life," *Real Estate Analyst Appraisal Bulletin,* 1951, pp. 145-148.

REAL ESTATE ANALYST, THE, "Local Information on Retail Sales," *Real Estate Analyst Appraisal Bulletin,* 1950, pp. 279-290.

REAL ESTATE ANALYST, THE, "Replacement Cost, Worth and Market Price," *Real Estate Analyst Appraisal Bulletin,* 1949, pp. 33-40.

REAL ESTATE ANALYST, THE, "Reproduction Cost of California-Type Bungalow," *Real Estate Analyst Appraisal Bulletin,* 1952, pp. 337-340.

REAL ESTATE ANALYST, THE, "Residential Construction Costs," *Real Estate Analyst Appraisal Bulletin,* 1950, pp. 405-420.

REAL ESTATE ANALYST, THE, "Rule of Thumb," *Real Estate Analyst Appraisal Bulletin,* 1949, pp. 273-276.

REAL ESTATE ANALYST, THE, "The Planned Industrial Development from the Appraiser's Viewpoint," *Real Estate Analyst Appraisal Bulletin,* 1956, pp. 409-412.

REAL ESTATE ANALYST, THE, "The Probable Life of Single-Family Residences," *Real Estate Analyst Appraisal Bulletin,* 1953, pp. 17-20.

REAL ESTATE ANALYST, THE, "Three Values," *Real Estate Analyst Appraisal Bulletin,* 1948, pp. 303-309.

REAL ESTATE INVESTMENT LETTER, "Golf Courses As Real Estate Investments," Institute for Business Planning Inc, New York, June 15, 1960.

REAL ESTATE RECORD AND BUILDERS GUIDE, "Ten-Year Movement to Suburbs Measured," *Real Estate Record and Builders Guide,* September 20, 1941, pp. 6-7.

REAL ESTATE, ANALYST, THE, "Functional and Economic Obsolescence," *Real Estate Analyst Appraisal Bulletin,* 1949, pp. 177-180.

REALTY BLUE BOOK OF CALIFORNIA, "Dictionary of Real Estate Terms," Keystone Publishing Co, Los Angeles, 1924, pp. 348-364.

REED, DONNELL D., "Real Estate Analysis and Value," *The Appraisal Journal,* July, 1945, pp. 256-262.

REED, HENRY E., "The True Value of Real Estate," *The Appraisal Journal,* July, 1935, pp. 342-350.

REEVES, CUTHBERT E., "Deriving Land Value from Rental Data," *The Appraisal Journal,* January, 1939, pp. 37-45.

REEVES, CUTHBERT E., "Valuation of Land," *Appraising Residential Property,* Buffalo, pp. 10-21.

REEVIS, CUTHBERT E., "Real Estate Value Index," *The Appraisal Journal,* July, 1944, pp. 232-236.

## BIBLIOGRAPHY OF APPRAISAL LITERATURE

REGISTER, J. ALVIN, "Vacant Property-Demand for Improvement Deferred," *Journal of the American Institute of Real Estate Appraisers,* October, 1932, pp. 45.

REGISTER, NORMAN, "Influence of Airports on Value of Adjacent Real Estate," *Assessment Administration,* Institute of American Appraisers Officers, Chicago, 1959, pp. 96-97.

REIDY, MAURICE F., "Real Estate In Ancient Times," *The Appraisal Journal,* April, 1936, pp. 117-122.

REINMUTH, J. E., WEIDLER, J. B, "Decision-Making, to List or Not to List, That Is the Question," *The Real Estate Appraiser,* March, 1970, pp. 36-38.

RENO, RICHARD R., *Profitable Real Estate Exchanging,* Prentice-Hall, Englwd Cliffs, N. J., 1956.

REVIEW, THE, "Sales Trend In Los Angeles," *The Review,* 1949, pp. 22.

REYNOLDS, TEMPLE A., "Creation of Recreation Areas," *The Real Estate Appraiser,* September, 1969, pp. 43-47.

RICHARDS, RALPH H., "What of the Coming Real Estate Boom," *Review of Society of Residential Appraisers,* November, 1939, pp. 7-11.

RICKS, R. BRUCE, "Tax Shelter and Annual Cash Flow In Investment Real Estate," *The Appraisal Journal,* April, 1966, pp. 300-303.

RING, ALFRED A., *The Valuation of Real Estate,* Prentice-Hall, Englwd Cliffs, N. J., 1963.

RING, ALFRED A., "Appraisal Factors and Considerations In Site Analysis," *The Valuation of Real Estate,* 1970, pp. 95.

RING, ALFRED A., "Demonstration Appraisal," *The Valuation of Real Estate,* 1970, pp. 375-457.

RING, ALFRED A., "Equity Appraising and Financing," *The Valuation of Real Estate,* 1970, pp. 315-330.

RING, ALFRED A., "Fundamentals of Land Valuation," *The Valuation of Real Estate,* 1970, pp. 114-131.

RING, ALFRED A., "History and Importance of Value Thought," *The Valuation of Real Estate,* 1970, pp. 13-27.

RING, ALFRED A., "Impact of Political, Social and Economic Forces on Valuation," *The Valuation of Real Estate,* 1970, pp. 55.

RING, ALFRED A., "Leasehold Estates and Leased Fee Appraising," *The Valuation of Real Estate,* 1970, pp. 299-315.

RING, ALFRED A., "Mathematics of Property Valuation," *The Valuation of Real Estate,* 1970, pp. 247-266.

RING, ALFRED A., "Nature and Principles of Property Valuation," *The Valuation of Real Estate,* 1970, pp. 27-43.

RING, ALFRED A., "Professional Standards and Responsibilities of Appraisal," *The Valuation of Real Estate,* 1970, pp. 359.

RING, ALFRED A., "Residual Techniques of Capitalization In Appraisal," *The Valuation of Real Estate,* 1970, pp. 283.

RING, DR. AA., "Streamlining the Income Approach to Value," *The Real Estate Appraiser,* January, 1969, pp. 38-43.

RING, DR. AA., N. L. NORTH, "Real Estate Principles and Practices Questions and Problems," *The Real Estate Appraiser,* 1967, pp. 62.

ROBINSON, WILLIAM W., *Land In California,* University of California, Berkeley, Calif, 1948.

RODGERS, RAYMOND, "Impact of Inflation on Real Estate Value," *Appraisal Digest,* April, 1959, pp. 9-12.

ROSS, THURSTON H., "Effect of Mortgage Financing on Real Estate Values," *The Appraisal Journal,* April, 1953, pp. 203-210.

ROSS, THURSTON H., "Real Estate As an Investment," *The Appraisal Journal,* January, 1948, pp. 49-56.

ROTHSCHILD, VAL J., "Board Appraisals and the Secretary's Opportunity," *Annals of Real Estate Practice,* National Association of Real Estate Boards, 1925, pp. 95-107.

ROWLANDS, DAVID T., "Certification of Real Estate Appraisers by Public Authority," *The Appraisal Journal,* October, 1936, pp. 349-352.

ROWLANDS, DAVID T., "Commonly Accepted Evidences of Real Estate Value for Purposes of Taxation," *American Academy of Political and Social Science Annals,* March, 1930, pp. 88-96.

ROWLSON, JOHN F., "Highest and Best Use," *The Real Estate Appraiser1,* April, 1966, pp. 8-12.

ROWLSON, JOHN F., "Investment Property An Analysis of Motivation," *The Real Estate Appraiser,* May, 1957, pp. 2-9.

ROWLSON, JOHN F., "Land Utilization and Marketability An Application of Feasibility Study," *The Real Estate Appraiser,* pp. 52.

RUCH, PAUL E., "Effects of Climate and Weather on Real Estate Values," *The Appraisal Journal,* October, 1954, pp. 531-549.

RUHE, KARL, "U. S. International Revenue Service Effect of Legislation on Real and Personal Property," *Appraisal and Valuation Manual,* Corporate Press, Incorporated, Washington, D. C, January, 1972, pp. 320.

SAAW, EUGENE A., "Rail Transportation's Effect Upon Real Estate Values," *The Appraisal Journal,* October, 1969, pp. 532-537.

SAMMON, JOHN P., "Data Processing In the Preparation of Real Estate Appraisals," *Technical Valuation,* pp. 34.

SANDISON, R. W., C. O. LIVINGSTON, "The Tax Reform Act of 1969 As it Affects Estate," *The Real Estate Appraiser,* March, 1970, pp. 5-15.

SANFORD, GEORGE A., "Zoning and the Real Estate Appraiser," *The Residential Appraiser,* December, 1960, pp. 12-14.

SAPP, ALLAN N., "Factors In Selecting the Supermarket Site," *The Real Estate Appraiser,* September, 1966, pp. 17-23.

SAXE, E. B., "The Service Station Site," *The Real Estate Appraiser,* August, 1964, pp. 14-22.

SCHARN, WILLIAM H. JR., "Farm Appraisals Search the Market," *The Real Estate Appraiser,* January, 1969, pp. 52-55.

SCHIMMEL, ALFRED, "Some Standards for the Appraisal of Real Estate for Tax Assessment Purposes," *Appraisal and Valuation Manual,* pp. 232.

SCHMIDT, EDWARD BENJAMIN, "A Case Study of Scientific Assessment For Tax Purposes," *The 1946 Reappraisal of Real Estate In York Nebraska,* University of Nebraska, Lincoln, Nebraska, 1948, pp. 1-59.

SCHMIDT, WALTER S., "Real Estate Outlook for 1935," *The Appraisal Journal,* April, 1935, pp. 270-272.

SCHMUTZ, GEORGE L., "Appraising In Our Times," *National Real Estate Journal,* December, 1940, pp. 31.

SCHMUTZ, GEORGE L., "Legislation and Real Estate Values," *The Appraisal Journal,* October, 1934, pp. 65-73.

SCHMUTZ, GEORGE L., LORING O. MCCORMICK, "The Influence of Real Estate Taxes on Values," *The Appraisal Journal,* January, 1933, pp. 128-131.

SCHNEIDER, GEORGE A., *California Real Estate Principles and Practices,* Prentice-Hall, Inc., New York, 1927, pp. 1-921.

SCHNEIDER, GEORGE A., "On Appraisal of Old Houses," *California Real Estate Principles and Practices,* 1927, pp. 487-489.

SCHULTE, AUGUST B., "Information Plant for Real Estate Appraising," *Society of Residential Appraisers Research Bulletin,* No. 2, March, 1937, pp. 1-38.

SCHULTZ, CARLTON, "The Commodity Price Level and Real Estate Values," *The Appraisal Journal,* July, 1934, pp. 355-356.

SCHULTZ, MORTIMER L., "Real Estate Syndication," *The Residential Appraiser,* December, 1962, pp. 14-16.

SCHWARTZ, JAY, "The Appraiser and Condemnation," *The Real Estate Appraiser,* April, 1963, pp. 25-27.

SEAVER, GUY J., "Finding the Facts to Determine Values," *National Real Estate Journal,* May, 1932, pp. 38-40.

SELDIN, MAURY, "Real Estate Investment Policy Based on Forecast." ASA Valuation Manual, 1964-65, pp. 199-204.

SELIGMAN, DANIEL, "The Future of the Office Building Boom," *The Real Estate Appraiser,* October, 1963, pp. 24-28.

SEYMOUR, CHARLES F., "A Realtor Looks at Urban Renewal," *The Appraisal,* July, 1963, pp. 319-326.

SHANNON, WILLIAM, "Cooperating with the Federal Real Estate Board," *National Real Estate Journal,* April 23, 1923, pp. 39-40.

SHEFFER, H. FRAZIER, "Real Estate Appraising a Profession," *Technical Valuation,* pp. 31.

SHENKEL, WILLIAM M., "Regional Analysis," *The Real Estate Appraiser,* January, 1967, pp. 18-28.

SHOPLIN, AUGUST, *A Study of Relationships Between Assessments and Selling Price of Real Estate In Wyoming 1957-58,* U. of Wyoming Div of Business & Economic Research, Laramie, 1959.

SHUGRUE, FRANK R., "The Nature of Real Estate Appraisal," *Encyclopedia of Real Estate Appraising,* 1959, pp. 3-14.

SMITH, FRED E., "A Demonstration Appraisal of a Residence Property," *National Real Estate Journal,* March, 1935, pp. 46-49.

SMITH, HALBERT C., AND CARL J. TSCHAPPAT, "Monetary Policy and Real Estate Values," *The Appraisal Journal,* January, 1966, pp. 18-26.

SMITH, LARRY, "Problems of Real Estate Investment Analysis of Large Projects," *Wisconsin Colloquim on Appraisal Research, Papers and Proceedings,* 1963, pp. 41-43.

SMITH, WALSTEIN, JR., "The Appraiser and the Real Estate Cycle," *The Real Estate Appraiser,* pp. 2.

SOCIETY OF INDUSTRIAL REALTORS, *Industrial Parks: Their Growth and Impact on the Industrial Real Estate Market,* Washington, D. C..

SQUIRE, LATHAM C., "Zoning Problems Facing the Real Estate Appraiser," *The Appraisal Journal,* January, 1949, pp. 100-106.

STANTON, WOLCOTT P., "Appraisal Troubles In the Desert," *The Appraisal Journal,* July, 1944, pp. 217-222.

STEINER, RICHARD L., "Pricing a New Commodity: Cleared Land," *The Appraisal Journal,* January, 1959, pp. 49-53.

STEUER, AARON, "The Building Residual Method In Real Estate Appraising," *The Appraisal Journal,* July, 1947, pp. 357-360.

STEVENS, ROGER L., "What I Look for In a Real Estate Investment," *The Appraisal Journal,* October, 1961, pp. 491-500.

SVOBODA, ALBERT C., "Real Estate for Endowment Fund Investment," *The Appraisal Journal,* January, 1954, pp. 43-47.

TAYLOR, DINSMORE, "Judicial Decisions on the Value of Real Estate," *The Appraisal Journal,* April, 1938, pp. 113-119.

THE UNIVERSITY OF UTAH, *Real Estate Activities In Salt Lake, Davis, Weber and Utah Counties,* University of Utah Parts 1-2, 1971.

THOMAS, EDMUND E., "Real Estate Financing In Today's Market," *Appraisal Digest,* January, 1960, pp. 14-15.

▲ Land

THOMPSON, GLENN P., "The Effect of Pipeline Easements on the Value of Real Estate," *Right of Way*, August, 1959, pp. 15-20.

THOMPSON, PELL, "How to Appraise Real Estate," *Savings Bank Journal*, July, 1933, pp. 26.

THOMPSON, PROF. WARREN S., "Effect of Population Trends on Real Estate Values," *National Real Estate Journal*, July, 1934, pp. 37-38.

THOMPSON, R. E., "On Real Estate Having More Than One Value," *The Appraisal Journal*, July, 1937, pp. 278-280.

THOMPSON, STEPHEN G., "What's Ahead In 1955 for Real Estate," *Technical Valuation*, June, 1955, pp. 47.

THORSON, IVAN A., "Our Real Estate Tax Problem," *The Appraisal Journal*, October, 1937, pp. 357-364.

THORSON, IVAN A., "The Use of Tables and Formulas in Real Estate Appraisal-II," *The Appraisal Journal*, April, 1934, pp. 232-237.

THORSON, IVAN A., "Use of Tables & Formulas In Real Estate Appraisals," *The Appraisal Journal*, January, 1934, pp. 112-124.

TISHMAN, DAVID, "Investing In Real Estate," *Appraisal Digest*, April, 1958, pp. 18-20.

UNGER, MAURICE A., *Real Estate Principles and Practices*, Southwestern Publishing Company, 1968.

VAN SCHAICK, GEORGE S., *Ascertaining Real Estate Facts*, Eastern Underwriters, Vol. XXXVII, No. 40, September, 1936, pp. 26, 134.

VANDERLIP, FRANK A., "Professional Status of Real Estate Appraising," *The Appraisal Journal*, April, 1935, pp. 269-270.

WADE, G., "Land Clearing," *Appraisal Institute Magazine*, Appraisal Institute of Canada, Winnipeg.

WALKER, JOAN MANOR, "Analyst's Tools Air Developer's Decisions," *Real Estate Appraiser*, September, 1970, pp. 55-57.

WALKER, MABEL, "Unsettled Questions In Real Estate Taxation," *Tax Policy*, June, 1960.

WATKINS, O. R., "Future Living Patterns and Their Impact on Farm Real Estate Values," *Assessment Administration, IAAO*, Chicago, 1965, pp. 124-126.

WEAVER, W. C. JR., "Real Estate A Piece of the Action for Life Insurances," *Bests Review*, December, 1970, pp. 20.

WEBB, JAMES A., "Basic Factors In Making Appraisals," *National Real Estate Journal*, February 26, 1923, pp. 23-26.

WEBB, JAMES A., "Eleven Books on the Subject of Appraisals," *National Real Estate Journal*, March 26, 1923, pp. 29.

WEED, KENNETH A., "How to Analyze Apartment Building Neighborhoods and Develop Rent Schedules," *Real Estate Appraisal Practice*, 1958, pp. 105-116.

WEILER, ROBERT J., "Is Downtown Really Overtaxed?," *The Real Estate Appraiser*, March, 1969, pp. 12-15.

WEIMER, ARTHUR M., "Economic Opportunity, Population Trends and Real Estate Value," *Review of Society of Residential Appraisers*, December, 1938, pp. 7-10.

WEIMER, ARTHUR M., "Real Estate Outlook for 1952," *The Appraisal Journal*, January, 1952, pp. 80-84.

WEIMER, ARTHUR M., "The Market Principle Approach to Real Estate Analysis," *The Appraisal Digest*, April, 1952, pp. 18-21.

WENDT, P. F., A. R. CERF, "Appraisers Bookshelf, Real Estate Investment Analysis and Taxation," *The Real Estate Appraiser*, March, 1970, pp. 61-62.

WENDT, PAUL F., *Real Estate Appraisal*, Henry Holt and Company, Inc., New York, 1956.

WENDT, PAUL F., "The University and Real Estate Research," *The Appraisal Journal*, January, 1949, pp. 93-95.

WENZLICK, ROY, "The Future of Raw Land," *Assessors News Letter,* July, 1961, pp. 79-81.

WESTERFIELD, RAY B., "The Effects of Inflation on Savings and Real Estate Values," *The Appraisal Journal,* October, 1951, pp. 459-467.

WHITE, JOHN R., "Charges In the Equity Real Estate Market," *The Appraisal Journal,* October, 1964, pp. 576-578.

WHITE, JOHN R., "Relationship of Real Estate Cost and Value," *The Appraisal,* April, 1950, pp. 243-251.

WHITMORE, HENRY, "Three Hundred Years of City Growth to Be Studied In Boston," *National Real Estate Journal,* June 10, 1929, pp. 55-56.

WICKENS, DAVID L., *Residential Real Estate,* National Bureau of Economic Research, New York, 1941, pp. 300.

WILLIS, RICHARD S., "Insurance Company Views on Real Estate Appraisal," *Appraisal Digest,* October, 1955, pp. 17-19.

WILNETTE, MCDONNELL, WOLCOTT, "Problems In Rural Real Estate Appraisal," *American Institute of Real Estate Appraisers,*

WILSON, P. M., "Economic Trends and Real Estate," *Appraisal Institute Magazine,* June, 1963, pp. 21-27.

WOLFF, LEWIS, "Current Practice In Real Estate Syndication," *Real Estate Analyst Appraisal Bulletin,* 1959, pp. 347-350.

WOLFF, LEWIS, "Real Estate Aspects of the Current Tax Structure," *Real Estate Analyst Appraisal Bulletin,* 1960, pp. 451-454.

YARMON, ELLIOT N., "The Effect of Syndication and Real Estate Investment Trust on Value," *Appraisal Institute Magazine,* June, 1963, pp. 28-31.

ZANGERIE, JOHN A., *Principles of Real Estate Appraising,* The Stanley McMichael Pub. Co, Cleveland, Ohio, 1924.

ZAVIN, LOUIS B., "Tax Opportunities In Real Estate," *Appraisal and Valuation Manual,* American Society of Appraisers, 1960, pp. 309-318.

## 22-19 Urban Land Value

ABRAHAMS, BASIL GEORGE, "Fictitious Land Values," *The Appraisal Journal.*

ADAMS, THOMAS, LEWIS, H. M., MCCROSKY, T. T., *Population Land Values & Govt; Studies of Growth & Dist of Pop & Land Values; & of Problems of Govt,* NY Regional Plan of NY & Its Environs, New York, pp. 320.

ADKINS, WILLIAM G., *Effects of the Dallas Central Expressway on Land Values and Land Use,* Texas Transportation Institute, College Station, Tex, 1957.

ALLISON, NEVILLE F., AND MEREDITH H. JAMES, SR., "Land Value Patterns," *The Residential Appraiser,* October, 1955, pp. 10-21.

AMERICAN INSTITUTE OF REAL ESTATE APPRAISERS, *How Transportation Affects Real Estate Values,* American Institute of Real Estate Appraisers, Chicago, 1900.

APPRAISAL JOURNAL, "Valuation Problems Involving Reuse of Urban Land," *The Appraisal Journal,* 1958, pp. 569-573.

ARMSTRONG, ROBERT H., "Future Urban Land Valuation," *The Appraisal Journal,* January, 1945, pp. 24-36.

ARNOLD, MAX P., C. N. BLOOMFIELD, JACK HULL, "Urban Land Valuation for Taxation Purposes," *Technicalities and Technical Valuation,* February, 1962, pp. 18-19.

BABCOCK, FREDERICK M., "The Character of Land Value," *Valuation of Real Estate*, 1932, pp. 26-33.

BABCOCK, HENRY A., "The Maximum Value of Urban Land Converted to Diverse Uses." *Econometrica*, April, 1935, pp. 147-169.

BEMAN, ARTHUR K., "Mortgage and Real Property Rating Proceedings," *The Appraisal Journal*, October, 1946, pp. 409-414.

BENSON, W. A., "Canada Land Inventory," *Appraisal Institute Magazine*, Appraisal Institute of Canada, Winnipeg, June 1, 1971.

BLASE, M. G., W. G. STAUB, "Real Property Taxes In the Rural Urban Fringe," *Land Economics*, May, 1971, pp. 168 174.

BODFISH, MORTON, THEOBALD, A. D, "Computing Land Value by the Income Approach," *Real Estate Fundamentals*, 1941, pp. 17-18.

BOECKH, EVERARD HEREFORD, "Land Valuation," *Manual of Appraisals*, 1937.

BOWEN, JOHN R., "Land Prices Vs. Land Values," *The Journal of the American Society of Farm Managers and Rural Appraisers*, April, 1947, pp. 31-34.

BOYKIN, JAMES H., "Severances Studies, Their Future Role In Remainder Property Appraisals," *The Real Estate Appraiser*, January, 1970, pp. 10-16.

BROWN, HARRY GUNNISON, *Land-Value Taxation Around the World*, Robert Schalkenbach Foundation, New York City, 1955.

BROWNELL, KEITH W., *Partial Taking of Agricultural Land In Transition to Urban Use*, Condemnation Appraisal Seminar, 1958.

BRUHN, JOHN A., "Zoning---Its Effect on Property Value," *The Appraisal Journal*, October, 1969, pp. 558-559.

BUNKER, RAYMOND, *Town and Country or City and Region*, Melbourne University Press, May, 1973.

BURKE, WILLIAM J., "The Listing & Valuation of Real Estate In the City of Buffalo, N. Y.," *Proceedings of 17th Annual Conference*, National Tax Association, 1924, pp. 212-217.

BURNELL, WILLIAM V., "The Real Estate Tax Burden Versus Property Value," *Appraisal and Valuation Manual*, 1960.

BURTON, JOHN E., "Changing Land and Building Values In the Chicago Wholesale District," *Skyscraper Management*, January, 1933, pp. 10-14.

BURTON, JOHN E., "Disparities In Land Values," *Journal of Land and Puplic Utility Economics*, May, 1938, pp. 201-203.

BUTTENHEIM, HAROLD S., "Some Modifications of Urban Land Policies In America," *Journal of Land and Public Utility Economics*, 1935, pp. 154-163.

CASETTI, E., "Equilibrium Land Values and Population Densities In an Urban Setting," *Economic Geography*, January, 1971.

CHERRY, RUSSELL C., AND ALVIN B. WOOTEN, "Comparative Investment Yields Agricultural Land Vs. Selected Securities," *Journal of American Society of Farm Management and Rural Appraisers*, October, 1966, pp. 53-59.

COE, R. K., "The Impact of New Industrial Nucleus on Surrounding Land Values," *Dissertation Abstracts*, January, 1965, pp. 3903.

COLOAN, H. BRONSON, "The History of Site Valuation Taxation Used for Municipal Purposes," *Assessment Administration*, IAAO, Chicago, 1961, pp. 12-19.

CORNICK, PHILIP H., "The Going Value of Real Estate," *American Academy of Social and Political Science, Annals*, March, 1930, pp. 177.

CRAIGIE, EDWARD JOHN, *Municipal Justice, the Case for Land Value Rating*, Edward J. Craigie, Adelaide, Australia, 1952.

CROUSE, EARL F., "Effect of Improving Technology on Land Values with Special Emphasis for the South," *The Journal of the American Society of Farm Managers and Rural Appraisers*, April, 1956, pp. 43-47.

CUMMINGS, LAWRENCE B., "Real Estate Record and Guide," *The Real Estate Record and Guide*, February 25, 1933, pp. 3-4.

DE LIMA H. A., "Land Value Insurance," *National Association of Real Estate Boards*, 1926, pp. 58-87.

DEBOOS, FRANK A., "Are You Familiar with Basics of Land Value," *Appraisal Digest*, January, 1955, pp. 19-21.

DORAU, HERBERT B., "Urbanism and the Future of Land Values," *The Appraisal Journal*, January, 1949, pp. 15-24.

DORAU, HERBERT B., AND ALBERT G. HINMAN, *Urban Land Economics*, Macmillian Company, New York, 1928, pp. 570.

DUHAMEL, L. A., "Land Tenure In Alberta," *Appraisal Institute Magazine*, Appraisal Institute of Canada, Winnipeg.

ELDER, HERBERT W., "Land Value Along the Gulf Freeway In Houston, Texas," *The Appraisal Journal*, April, 1953, pp. 223-230.

FEDERAL RESERVE BANK OF CLEVELAND, "Urban Real Estate Finance," *The Appraisal Journal*, April, 1947, pp. 202-210.

FINEHAUM, M. L., "Disposal & Land Valuation of Restricted Securities," *Trusts and Estates*, October, 1971, pp. 840-843.

FISHER, OSCAR, "Application of Relative Factor Ratings In Land Evaluation," *Real Estate Record and Builders Guide*, July 28, 1934, pp. 6-10.

FULLER, ROBERT, "Residential Land Values In the 1960'S," *The Residential Appraiser*, September, 1960, pp. 19-21.

FULLER, ROBERT S., "How High Can Land Prices Go," *The Residential Appraiser*, February, 1957, pp. 9-11.

GARRISON, BURL L., "Land Has No Value," *Valuation*, 1900, pp. 56-71.

GARRISON, WILLIAM L., M. MERTZ, *Influence of Highway Improvements on Urban Land*, U of Wash., Dept of Geography Vol. V, Seattle, 1958.

GATES, NILES, "Let's Give Industry a Break on Land Prices," *Valuation*, 1965, pp. 2-10.

GIBBONS, F. R., J. N. ROWAN, R. C. DOWNES, "The Role of Humans In Land Evaluation," *Land Evaluation*, 1900, pp. 231.

GILLIES, JAMES, "Urban Land Trends," *Technical Valuation*, October, 1961, pp. 31-34.

GLOVER, CHARLES P., *A Technique of Appraisals of City Land Values*, Florida Association of Real Estate Boards, Jacksonville, 1925, pp. 64.

GOLDEN, JAY S., *Land Values In Chicago Before and After Express-Way Construction*, Chicago Area Transportation Study, Chicago, October, 1968, pp. 65.

GOODSPEED, M. J., "Sampling Considerations In Land Evaluation," *Land Evaluation*, 1900, pp. 40.

GREENE, ALFRED J., "Developing Land Value Maps," *Assessment Administration*, 1960, pp. 151-154.

GREENE, ALFRED J. JR., "Correlation of Land and Building Values and the Relative Effort Required to Assess Each," *Assessment Administration*, I. A. A. O, Chicago, 1964, pp. 95-96.

GUNNING, WALTER E., "Gross Estimate of Value for Large Land Areas," *The Appraisal Journal*, October, 1963, pp. 489-492.

HALL, PETER GEOFFREY, *Land Values, the Report of the Proceedings of a Colloquium Held In London*, London, 1965.

HAMMAR, CONRAD H., "Land Classification to Aid the Appraiser," *Journal of Land and Public Utility Economics*, August, 1939, pp. 277-286.

HARRISON, LOUIS A., "Valuation of Land In Built-Up Residential Areas," *Review of Society of Residential Appraisers*, pp. 13-41.

HATHAWAY, PAUL L., "Land Values In Older Neighborhoods," *The Review*, 1945, pp. 3-6.

HIGGS, GERALD B., "Non Urban Land Appraisal and the Development Unit Chart," *Technical Valuation*, A. S. A., Washington, January, 1967, pp. 49.

HOAGLAND, HENRY E., "Real Estate Value, Chapter Xii," *Real Estate Principles*, 1940, pp. 511.

HOLBROOK, JEFFREY, "Economic Factors Affecting Real Estate Values," *Right of Way*, June, 1955, pp. 17-19.

HOOKER, JOHN P., "Financial History of a Chicago Property," *The Appraisal Journal*, July, 1933, pp. 346-355.

HOYT, *Dynamic Factors In Land Values*, Urban Land Institute, Washington, March, 1960, pp. 16.

HOYT, HOMER, "Changing Patterns of Land Values," *Land Economics*, May, 1960, pp. 109-111.

HOYT, HOMER, "Land Values In Shopping Centers," *The Appraisal Journal*, July, 1969, pp. 344-345.

HOYT, HOMER, "The Future Trend of Ruban Land Values," *The Appraisal Journal*, April, 1944, pp. 121-126.

HOYT, HOMER, "Urban Growth and Real Estate Values," *The Appraisal Journal*, October, 1940, pp. 332-340.

HOYT, HOMER, "What Causes Peak Land Values," *National Real Estate Journal*, May, 1934, pp. 29.

HOYT, HOMER, LEONARD C. SMITH, "The Valuation of Land In Urban Blighted Areas," *The Appraisal Journal*, July, 1943, pp. 199-209.

HURD, RICHARD M., *Principles of City Land Values*, New York, 1903.

HURD, RICHARD M., "Distribution of Urban Land Values," *Yale Review*, August, 1902, pp. 99. 124-145.

IRWIM, S. C., *The Mensuration of Land Values and the Cubing Priceof Buildings*, Irwin, S. C., Glendale, Calif., 1930.

JERRARD, L. P., "The Valuation of Land," *Transactions of the American Society of Civil Engineers*, 1919, pp. 582-644.

JERRETT, HERMAN D., "The Basic Value of Urban Land," *Theory of Real Property Valuation*, Chapter Viii, 1938.

JERRETT, HERMAN D., "Urban Land Rent," *Theory of Real Property Valuation*, Chapter Xi, 1938.

JERRETT, HERMAN D., "Urban Land Valuation," *Theory of Real Property Valuation*, Chapter V, 1938.

JOHNSON, LEEVERN, "Land Value Write Down In Urban Renewal," *The Appraisal Journal*, April, 1962, pp. 175-180.

KAHN, SANDERS A., "Valuation of Urban Land," *Valuation Manual*, 1959, pp. 159-164.

KAM, WILLIAM H., "Investment Analysis of Leased Commercial Land," *Real Estate Appraisal*, February, 1967, pp. 27-30.

KELLOUGH, W. R., "Zoning and the Value of Real Property," *The Residential Appraiser*, October, 1960, pp. 10-11.

KOELBEL, WALTER A., "The Land Developer and a Golf Course Subdivision," *Urban Land*, Urban Land Institute, Washington, D. C, 1964.

KRISTOL, IRVING, "Common Sense About the Urban Crisis," *The Appraisal Journal*, April, 1968, pp. 281-285.

KUEHNLE, WALTER R., "A New Approach to Urban Land Valuations," *The Appraisal Journal*, April, 1933, pp. 189-193.

LAIDLAW, J. B., "Statutory Authority Whereunder Real Property Is Assessed In Alberta," *Appraisal Institute Magazine*, December, 1962, pp. 5-8.

LEHIGH UNIVERSITY, *An Analysis of the Potential Effects of a Movement Toward a Land Value Based Property Tax*, Economic Education League, Institute of Research, Albany, 1958.

LEHMAN, H. O., "The Effects of Trees and Planting on Property Values," *Appraisal and Valuation Manual*, 1959, pp. 173-176.

LEMLY, J. H., *Expressway Influence on Land Use and Value, Atlanta 1941-1956*, Georgia State College of Business Administration, Atlanta, Ga., 1958.

LESSINGER, JACK, "Is the Supply of Urban Land Running Out," *The Appraisal Journal*, January, 1962, pp. 61-68.

LEVIN, EARL, "Land Planning and Land Costs," *Appraisal Institute Magazine*, September, 1959, pp. 4-14.

LEVY, MARK, "Transportation-A Fundamental of Land Values," *Electric Railway Journal*, November, 1931, pp. 624-626.

LEWIS, H. M., "Land Values, Distribution Within New York Region and Relation to Various Factors In Urban Growth," *Engineering Series, Monograph No. 3*, New York, pp. 72.

LINDER, THOMAS, "Property Valuations and the Tax Assessor," *Bulletin, National Tax Association*, 1923, pp. 271-275.

MARSTON, ANSON, THOMAS R. AGG, "Valuation of Land," *Engineering Valuatiion*, New York, 1936, pp. 387-401.

MILLER C. ARC, "Estimating Basic Land Value," *Right of Way*, April, 1959, pp. 35-40.

MURPHY, J. W., "Valuation of War Surplus Real Property," *The Appraisal Journal*, October, 1947, pp. 521-527.

NESSER, RICHARD S., "How to Find Urban Land Value," *American Society of Appraiser Valuation Manual*, American Society of Appraisers, 1964, pp. 93.

NEUTZE, M., "Price of Land for Urban Development," *Economic Record*, September, 1970, pp. 313-328.

NEWCOMB, ROBINSON, "Are Urban Land Pressures Easing," *Appraisal Digest*, August, 1958, pp. 10-12.

NEWCOMB, ROBINSON, "Urban Land Use Shifts to Low Gear," *The Appraisal Journal*, July, 1964, pp. 376-382.

OHNO, K., "Rising Trend of Urban Land Values In Japan 1955-1969," *The Kokumin-Keizai Zasshi*, March, 1970.

ORR, JOHN, *Taxation of Land Values As it Affects Landowners and Others*, P. S. King and Son, London, 1912.

OXFORD AND ASQUITH, *The Land Values Taxes*, The Liberal Publication Department, London, 1909.

PAGE, ALFRED N., "Race and Property Values," *The Appraisal Journal*, July, 1968, pp. 334-341.

REEVES, CUTHBERT E., *The Appraisal of Urban Land and Buildings*, Municipal Administration Service, New York, 1928, pp. 1-160.

ROBERTSON, JOHN MACKINNON, *The Great Budget: a Justification Explanation & Examination of the Taxes on Land Values*, The Liberal Publication Department, London, 1910, pp. 1-64.

ROBINSON, WILLIAM W., *Land In California*, University of California, Berkeley, Calif, 1948.

SCHEFTEL, YETTA, "A Study of Certain Discriminatory Taxes on Land, Boston and New York," *The Taxation of Land Value*, Houghton Mifflin Company, 1916, pp. 1-489.

SELLERS, RANDOLPH F., "Real Estate Values and Appraisal of Residence Property," *National Real Estate Journal*, June 27, 1927, pp. 46-47.

SEYFRIED, WARREN R., "The Centrality of Urban Land Values," *Land Economics*, September, 1963, pp. 275-284.

STEINER, RICHARD L., "Pricing a New Commodity: Cleared Land," *The Appraisal Journal*, January, 1959, pp. 49-53.

U. S. GOVERNMENT PRINTING OFFICE, *The City Expands, a Study of The Conversion of Land from Rural to Urban Use,* U. S. Govt. Printing Office, Washington.

WENDT, PAUL F., *Influence of Transportation Changes on Urban Land Uses and Values,* Institute of Business and Economic Research, Berkeley U of Calif., 1960, pp. 1-13.

WENDT, PAUL F., "**Urban Land Value Trends,**" *The Appraisal Journal,* April, 1958, pp. 254-269.

WILLIAMS, ROBERT M., "**Measuring Fluctuations In Asking Prices for Land In Los Angeles,**" *The Appraisal Journal,* April, 1962, pp. 181-189.

*Graphic Summary of Munic Imprvmt & Finan As Affctd by Untaxing of Imprvmts & Taxation of Land Value,* Harper and Bros., New York, 1958.

*100 Yrs of Land Values In Chicago the Relationship of Growth of Chicago to the Rise In Its Land Vals,* University of Chicago Press, Chicago, 1933, pp. 519.

## 22-20 Rural Land Value

ALLISON, NEVILLE F., AND MEREDITH H. JAMES, SR., "**Land Value Patterns,**" *The Residential Appraiser,* October, 1955, pp. 10-21.

AMERICAN INSTITUTE OF REAL ESTATE APPRAISERS, *How Transportation Affects Real Estate Values,* American Institute of Real Estate Appraisers, Chicago, 1900.

APPEL, JAMES R., "**Commercial Land Values,**" *The Real Estate Analyst Appraisal Bulletin,* 1957, pp. 25-28.

BABCOCK, FREDERICK M., "**The Character of Land Value,**" *Valuation of Real Estate,* 1932, pp. 26-33.

BECKER, R. J., "**Land Valued As a Commodity,**" *Journal of the American Society of Farm Mgrs & Rural Appraisers,* October, 1958, pp. 32-37.

BEMAN, ARTHUR K., "Mortgage and Real **Property Rating Proceedings,**" *The Appraisal Journal,* October, 1946, pp. 409-414.

BENSON, W. A., "**Canada Land Inventory,**" *Appraisal Institute Magazine,* Appraisal Institute of Canada, Winnipeg, June 1, 1971.

BLASE, M. G., W. G. STAUB, "**Real Property Taxes In the Rural Urban Fringe,**" *Land Economics,* May, 1971, pp. 168 174.

BOECKH, EVERARD HEREFORD, "**Land Valuation,**" *Manual of Appraisals,* 1937.

BOWEN, JOHN R., "**Land Prices Vs. Land Values,**" *The Journal of the American Society of Farm Managers and Rural Appraisers,* April, 1947, pp. 31-34.

BOYKIN, JAMES H., "**Severances Studies, Their Future Role In Remainder Property Appraisals,**" *The Real Estate Appraiser,* January, 1970, pp. 10-16.

BROWN, HARRY GUNNISON, *Value Taxation Around the World,* Robert Schalkenbach Foundation, New York City, 1955.

BROWNELL, KEITH W., *Partial Taking of Agricultural Land In Transition to Urban Use,* Condemnation Appraisal Seminar, 1958.

BRUHN, JOHN A., "**Zoning---Its Effect on Property Value,**" *The Appraisal Journal,* October, 1969, pp. 558-559.

BUNKER, RAYMOND, *Town and Country or City and Region,* Melbourne University Press, May, 1973.

BURTON, JOHN E., "**Disparities In Land Values,**" *Journal of Land and Puplic Utility Economics,* May, 1938, pp. 201-203.

CASE, H. C. M., "Value of Illinois Farm Land," *The Appraisal Journal*, July, 1934, pp. 336-340.

CHERRY, RUSSELL C., AND ALVIN B. WOOTEN, "Comparative Investment Yields Agricultural Land Vs. Selected Securities," *Journal of American Society of Farm Management and Rural Appraisers*, October, 1966, pp. 53-59.

COE, R. K., "The Impact of New Industrial Nucleus on Surrounding Land Values," *Dissertation Abstracts*, January, 1965, pp. 3903.

CORNICK, PHILIP H., "The Going Value of Real Estate," *American Academy of Social and Political Science, Annals*, March, 1930, pp. 177.

CROUSE, EARL F., "Effect of Improving Technology on Land Values with Special Emphasis for the South," *The Journal of the American Society of Farm Managers and Rural Appraisers*, April, 1956, pp. 43-47.

CUMMINGS, LAWRENCE B., "Real Estate Record and Guide," *The Real Estate Record and Guide*, February 25, 1933, pp. 3-4.

DE LIMA H. A., "Land Value Insurance," *National Association of Real Estate Boards*, 1926, pp. 58-87.

DEBOOS, FRANK A., "Are You Familiar with Basics of Land Value," *Appraisal Digest*, January, 1955, pp. 19-21.

DEPARTMENT OF AGRICULTURE, *Land Valuation*, Department Of Agriculture, Washington, 1935, pp. 126.

DUHAMEL, L. A., "Land Tenure In Alberta," *Appraisal Institute Magazine*, Appraisal Institute of Canada, Winnipeg.

EDMAN, J. J., "Valuation of Sand & Gravel Wh May Be Removed Without Destroying Value of Land Appraisal Docket," *The Appraisal Journal*, April, 1959, pp. 266-268.

ELDER, HERBERT W., "Land Value Along the Gulf Freeway In Houston, Texas," *The Appraisal Journal*, April, 1953, pp. 223-230.

FEDERAL RESERVE BANK OF CHICAGO, "Something New In Farm Land Values," *The Appraisal Journal*, January, 1958, pp. 111-117.

FEDERAL RESERVE BANK OF ST. LOUIS, "Farm Land Values," *The Appraisal Journal*, October, 1960, pp. 542-543.

FINEHAUM, M. L., "Disposal & Land Valuation of Restricted Securities," *Trusts and Estates*, October, 1971, pp. 840-843.

FISHER, OSCAR, "Application of Relative Factor Ratings In Land Evaluation," *Real Estate Record and Builders Guide*, July 28, 1934, pp. 6-10.

FULLER, ROBERT S., "How High Can Land Prices Go," *The Residential Appraiser*, February, 1957, pp. 9-11.

GARRISON, BURL L., "Land Has No Value," *Valuation*, 1900, pp. 56-71.

GATES, NILES, "Let's Give Industry a Break on Land Prices," *Valuation*, 1965, pp. 2-10.

GIBBONS, F. R., J. N. ROWAN, R. C. DOWNES, "The Role of Humans In Land Evaluation," *Land Evaluation*, 1900, pp. 231.

GOODSPEED, M. J., "Sampling Considerations In Land Evaluation," *Land Evaluation*, 1900, pp. 40.

GREENE, ALFRED J., "Developing Land Value Maps," *Assessment Administration*, 1960, pp. 151-154.

GREENE, ALFRED J. JR., "Correlation of Land and Building Values and the Relative Effort Required to Assess Each," *Assessment Administration*, I. A. A. O, Chicago, 1964, pp. 95-96.

GUNNING, WALTER E., "Gross Estimate of Value for Large Land Areas," *The Appraisal Journal*, October, 1963, pp. 489-492.

HALL, A. A., "Use of Soil Classification In Determining Farm Land Values," *Assessment Administration*, I. A. A. O, Chicago, 1957, pp. 187-191.

▲ Land

HALL, PETER GEOFFREY, *Land Values, the Report of the Proceedings of a Colloquium Held In London*, London, 1965.

HAMMAR, CONRAD H., "Land Classification to Aid the Appraiser," *Journal of Land and Public Utility Economics*, August, 1939, pp. 277-286.

HERTZ, CARL F., "Effect of Improving Technology on Land Values, In the Corn Belt," *Journal of the American Society of Farm Managers and Rural Appraisers*, April, 1956, pp. 48-51.

HIGGS, GERALD B., "Non Urban Land Appraisal and the Development Unit Chart," *Technical Valuation*, A. S. A., Washington, January, 1967, pp. 49.

HOAGLAND, HENRY E., "Real Estate Value, Chapter Xii," *Real Estate Principles*, 1940, pp. 511.

HOLBROOK, JEFFREY, "Economic Factors Affecting Real Estate Values," *Right of Way*, June, 1955, pp. 17-19.

HOYT, HOMER, "Changing Patterns of Land Values," *Land Economics*, May, 1960, pp. 109-111.

HOYT, HOMER, "What Causes Peak Land Values," *National Real Estate Journal*, May, 1934, pp. 29.

HURLBURT, VIRGIL L., "Technology and Farmland Values," *Journal of the American Society of Farm Managers and Rural Appraisers*, October, 1960, pp. 75-83.

IGNATYEV, G. M., "Classification of Cultural and Natural Vegetation Sites As a Basis for Land Evaluation," *Land Evaluation*, pp. 104.

IOWA LAW REVIEW, "Taxation Affecting Agriculture Land Use," *Iowa Law Review*, 1965, pp. 600-618.

IRWIM, S. C., *The Mensuration of Land Values and the Cubing Priceof Buildings*, Irwin, S. C., Glendale, Calif., 1930.

JERRARD, L. P., "The Valuation of Land," *Transactions of the American Society of Civil Engineers*, 1919, pp. 582-644.

JESNESS, O. B., "Factors Affecting Farm Land Prices," *Asa Valuation Manual*, December, 1957, pp. 84-85.

KELLOUGH, W. R., "Zoning and the Value of Real Property," *The Residential Appraiser*, October, 1960, pp. 10-11.

KRAUSZ, N. G. P., "Legal Liability of Farm Managers and Rural Appraisers," *Journal of the American Society of Farm Managers and Rural Appraisers*, April, 1963, pp. 33-37.

KRAUSZ, N. G. P. AND FREDERICK G. PINK, "Agricultural Assessing Practices: Legislative Action to Control Rural Land Assessing In Areas Subject," *County Officer*, April, 1963, pp. 151-158.

LAIDLAW, J. B., "Statutory Authority Whereunder Real Property Is Assessed In Alberta," *Appraisal Institute Magazine*, December, 1962, pp. 5-8.

LEHIGH UNIVERSITY, *An Analysis of the Potential Effects of a Movement Toward a Land Value Based Property Tax*, Economic Education League, Institute of Research, Albany, 1958.

LEHMAN, H. O., "The Effects of Trees and Planting on Property Values," *Appraisal and Valuation Manual*, 1959, pp. 173-176.

LEMLY, J. H., *Expressway Influence on Land Use and Value, Atlanta 1941-1956*, Georgia State College of Business Administration, Atlanta, Ga., 1958.

LEVY, MARK, "Transportation-A Fundamental of Land Values," *Electric Railway Journal*, November, 1931, pp. 624-626.

LINDER, THOMAS, "Property Valuations and the Tax Assessor," *Bulletin, National Tax Association*, 1923, pp. 271-275.

MARSTON, ANSON, THOMAS R. AGG, "Valuatiion of Land," *Engineering Valuatiion*, New York, 1936, pp. 387-401.

METCALFE, C. B., "Rural Land Values In Southern Rhodesia," *Journal of the American Society of Farm Managers and Rural Appraisers,* October, 1959, pp. 16-21.

MILLER C. ARC, "Estimating Basic Land Value," *Right of Way,* April, 1959, pp. 35-40.

MITCHELL, RICHARD E., "Industrial Site Selection Outside Urban Centers," *The Appraisals Journal,* October, 1966, pp. 597-600.

MURPHY, J. W., "Valuation of War Surplus Real Property," *The Appraisal Journal,* October, 1947, pp. 521-527.

ORR, JOHN, *Taxation of Land Values As it Affects Landowners and Others,* P. S. King and Son, London, 1912.

OXFORD AND ASQUITH, *The Land Values Taxes,* The Liberal Publication Department, London, 1909.

PAGE, ALFRED N., "Race and Property Values," *The Appraisal Journal,* July, 1968, pp. 334-341.

PAWLEY, R. W., "The Appraisal of a Farm Business," *Appraisal Institute Magazine,* Appraisal Institute of Canada, Winnipeg.

REISS, FRANKLIN J., "Economic Environment of Rural Appraisals or Some Characteristics of Current Farmland Market," *Journal of the American Society of Farm Managers and Rural Appraisers,* April, 1966, pp. 57-61.

ROBINSON, WILLIAM W., *Land In California,* University of California, Berkeley, Calif, 1948.

ROGERS, JOHN V., "Why Does the Land In the Inner Blue Grass Sell Higher Than Other Land?," *Journal of the Amer Soc of Farm Mgrs & Rural Appraisers,* October, 1953, pp. 138-141.

SELLERS, RANDOLPH F., "Real Estate Values and Appraisal of Residence Property," *National Real Estate Journal,* June 27, 1927, pp. 46-47.

SOLARI, VIRGILIO S, "Costos Produccion En La Agricultura," *Boletin,* Sotave, Caracas, Venezuela, pp. 51-60.

STEINER, RICHARD L., "Pricing a New Commodity: Cleared Land," *The Appraisal Journal,*

TRENT, I. J., "Valuation of Rural Lands-Cleared Acre Basis," *Appraisal Institute Magazine,* September, 1965, pp. 44-46.

U. S. GOVERNMENT PRINTING OFFICE, *The City Expands, a Study of Theconversion of Land from Rural to Urban Use,* U. S. Govt. Printing Office, Washington.

WARREN, S. W., "Farm Land Values," *The Journal of the American Society of Farm Managers and Rural Appraisers,* October, 1951, pp. 157-164.

WARREN, STANLEY W., "The Small Farm," *The Journal of the American Society of Farm Managers and Rural Appraisers,* April, 1957, pp. 21-22.

WEAVER, HOWARD S., *Real Estate Appraising: Farm Land Division,* Weaver Real Estate Appraisal Traning Services, 1940.

WEBER, GUIDO L., "Appraisal of Farms," *The Real Estate Appraiser,* April, 1964, pp. 24-28.

WEEKS, DAVID, "The Impact on Farm Land Values of Increased Population," *The Appraisal Journal,* October, 1951, pp. 479-497.

"Ad Valorem Taxation & Its Relation to Agricltl Land Taxation Problems In Fla Greenbelt Law Interptns," *University of Florida Law Review,* 1964, pp. 521-539.

"How Transport's Affects Real Est Vals Papers Pres At Appraisal Institute Seminar for Fed Govt Apprs," American Institute of Real Estate Appraisers, Chicago, March, 1969.

## 22-21 Utilization

ABRAMS, CHARLES, "New Social Trends In Land Utilization," *The Appraisal Journal*, October, 1941, pp. 331-345.

ADKINS, WILLIAM G., *Effects of the Dallas Central Expressway on Land Values and Land Use*, Texas Transportation Institute, College Station, Tex, 1957.

ALMER, ZALMER, "Old Orchard Country Club: a Study of Open Land Planning," *Urban Land*, April, 1964.

ATKINSON, HARRY GRANT, "Some Principles of Land Utilization," *The Appraisal Journal*, October, 1936, pp. 425-431.

BABCOCK, HENRY A., "An Economic Theory of Land Utilization and City Growth," *The Economist*, Chicago, June 30, 1933, pp. 4.

BABCOCK, HENRY A., "The Maximum Value of Urban Land Converted to Diverse Uses," *Econometrica*, April, 1935, pp. 147-169.

BADEN, POWELL, BADEN, HENRY, *The Land Systems of British India*, Clarendon Press, Oxford, 1992.

BASHAW, FREDERICK J., "Value In a Dynamic Land Economy," *The Review*, 1900, pp. 16-22.

BECKETT, P. H. T., "Method and Scale of Land Resource Surveys In Relation to Precision and Cost," *Land Evaluation*, 1900, pp. 53.

BENN, B. O., W. E. GRABAW, "Terrain Evaluation As a Function of User Requirements," *Land Evaluation*, 1900, pp. 64.

BENNETT, H. H., "The Coming Technological Revolution on the Land," *The Appraisal Journal*, January, 1947, pp. 16-21.

BENSON, W. A., "Canada Land Inventory," *Appraisal Institute Magazine*, Appraisal Institute of Canada, Winnipeg, June 1, 1971.

BOECKH, EVERARD HEREFORD, "Land Improvements," *Manual of Appraisals*, pp. 364.

BORCHARD, RALPH R., "Planing and Zoning Affect Almost All Uses of Land," *The Appraisal Digest*, October, 1954, pp. 1-5.

BOYCE, BYRL N., "The Impending Problem of Land Use at the Interstate Interchange," *Right of Way*, June, 1969, pp. 31-35.

BREMICKER, CARL T., "Area Development," *The Residential Appraiser*, February, 1957, pp. 14-16.

BUREAU OF AGRICULTURAL ECONOMICS, *Land Settlement*, Department of Agriculture, Washington, 1934.

BURNELL, WILLIAM U., "A Program for Lower Taxes In Real Estate Improvements," *Valuation Manual*, American Society of Appraisers, 1959, pp. 29.

DERBES, MAX J., "Mathematics of the Land Development Prospectus," *The Real Estate Appraiser*, March, 1969, pp. 38-44.

DEWEY, JOHN M., "The Missouri River Basin Development Program," *Right of Way*, October, 1954, pp. 7-9.

DIERCKS, K. J., "Land Use Planning," *Right of Way*, June, 1962, pp. 43-44.

EDMAN, J. J., "Determining Cost of Subdivision and Improvement of Land. Appraisal Docket," *The Appraisal Journal*, July, 1958, pp. 449-450.

EDMAN, J. J., "Valuation of Land Improved with Factory Buildings. Appraisal Docket," *The Appraisal Journal*, October, 1957, pp. 620-622.

FARRINGTON WILLIAM C., "The Land Developer and Rights of Way," *Right Of Way*, May, 1959, pp. P 25-28.

FILLEY, ROBERT B., "Land Use Surveys Applied to Appraising and City Planning," *Review of Society of Residential Appraisers*, October, 1940, pp. 9-11.

FLOODWAY COMMITTEE, "Acquisition of Property for Red River Floodway," *Appraisal Institute Magazine*, Appraisal Institute of Canada, Winnipeg.

HATFIELD, SAMUEL M., *An Evaluation of Land Use and Dwelling Unit Data Derived from Aerial Photography*, Division of Highways, Urban Research Section, Chicago, September, 1962.

HEATH, SPENCER, "Why Does Valuable Land Lie Idle," *The Appraisal Journal*, July, 1939, pp. 227-229.

HECHT, LESTER S., "Benefit to the Property Owner As Affecting Assessments for Improvements to Real Estate," *Pennsylvania Bar Association Quarterly*, June, 1965, pp. 399-409.

HEENAN, G. WARREN, "The Economic Effect of Rapid Transit on Real Estate Development," *The Appraisal Journal*, April, 1968, pp. 212-224.

HERRMANN, CYRIL C., "The Outlook for Industrial Land Use In American," *The Real Estate Appraiser*, March, 1970, pp. 26-27.

HOAGLAND, HENRY E., "Urban Land Utilization," *Real Estate Utilization*.

HOYLE, FRED W., "Over-Improvement and Under-Improvement," *Residential Appraiser*, February, 1961, pp. 15-18.

HUCK, ROBERT, "The Use of Real Estate," *Assessment Administration*, IAAO, Chicago, 1964, pp. 103-109.

INDUSTRIAL RESEARCH, "Mud to Build with," *Industrial Research*, May, 1971, pp. 23.

JAMES, L. DOUGLAS, "The Economic Value of Real Estate Acquired For Right-Of-Way," *Land Economics*, August, 1968, pp. 325-336.

KNISKERN, PHILIP W., "Re-Use Land Utilization Studies and Advisory Consultation," *The Appraisal Journal*, July, 1957, pp. 325-336.

LEMLY, J. H., *Expressway Influence on Land Use and Value, Atlanta 1941-1956*, Georgia State College of Business Administration, Atlanta, Ga., 1958.

MARKHAM, MARION, FORNACI, CHARLES M, "Property Management and the Disposal of Improvements," *Acquisition for Right of Way*, American Association of State Highway Officials, Washington, D. C, 1962, pp. 631-640.

MARTIN, WENDELL H., "Remote Land-Development or Exploitation," *Urbanland*, February, 1971.

MICKLE, D. GRANT, "Effect of Traffic and Parking on Land Use and Value," *Assesment Administration*, IAAO, Chicago, 1956, pp. 6-11.

RAMS, EDWIN M., "Central Business District Land Use-Allocation," *Technical Valuation*.

REGISTER, J. ALVIN, "Vacant Property-Demand for Improvement Deferred," *Journal of the American Institute of Real Estate Appraisers*, October, 1932, pp. 45.

ROWLSON, JOHN F., "Land Utilization and Marketability An Application of Feasibility Study," *The Real Estate Appraiser*, pp. 52.

SHENKEL, WILLIAM M., "The Valuation of Industrial Land," *The Real Estate Appraiser*, January, 1965, pp. 14-22.

SIEJA, EDWARD M., "Valuation According to Use Vs. Valuation According to Zoning," *Assessment Administration*, Institute of American Assessment Officers, Chicago, 1963, pp. 86-90.

STARRETT, PAUL, "Location and Space Requirements of Industry," *American Institute of Real Estate Appraiser*, 1958, pp. 233-237.

STEWART, PHILIP O., "Impact of Recreational Use on Land Values," *The Real Estate Appraiser*, June, 1967, pp. 2-22.

THEISS, WILLIAM R., "The Appraisal Docket. Probable Future Use of Condemned Property," *The Appraisal Journal*, October, 1961, pp. 543-545.

TRUEHEART, LAWRENCE G., "Mission, Buy 17, 500 Acres, Quick," *Right of Way*, August, 1956, pp. 13-19.

WEDGEWOOD, JOSIAH C., *The Land Question, Taxation and Rating of Land Values*, The Labour Party, London, 1920, pp. 11.

WHITE, JOHN R., "Re-Use Land Appraising," *Appraisal Digest*, January, 1959, pp. 18-21.

WOOLEY, R. J., "Value to the Owner-The Canso Causeway Case," *Appraisal Institute Magazine*, Appraisal Institute of Canada, Winnipeg.

"Sierra Club Mounts a New Crusade," *Business Week*, May 23, 1970, pp. 64-65.

## 22-22 Lots

"Actual Appraisal Reports: No. 16 Valuation of Vacant Lot," *National Real Estate Journal*, November 9, 1931, pp. 24-28.

ARCHITECTURAL FORUM, "Appraising the Value of Lots of Unusual Dimensions," *Architectural Forum*, March, 1920, pp. 131-132.

BERNARD, ALFRED D., "Irregular Shaped Inside Lots," *Some Principles and Problems of Real Estate Valuation*, Baltimore, 1913.

BLISS, GEORGE M., "Cost of Developing Raw Land Into Building Lots," *Technical Valuation*, October, 1957, pp. 23-25.

BODFISH, MORTON, THEOBALD, A. D, "Appraising Vacant Business Lots In Built-Up Areas," *Real Estate Fundamentals*, 1941, pp. 4-5.

BODFISH, MORTON, THEOBALD, A. D, "Appraising Vacant Lots In Subdivisions," *Real Estate Fundamentals*, 1941, pp. 6-7.

BOECKH, EVERARD HEREFORD, "Residential Lot Widths, Etc.," *Manual of Appraisals*, 1937, pp. 347-352.

BYERS, JOHN, R. B., "Relationship Between the Value of the House and the Lot," *Residential Appraisers Review*, 1935, pp. 3-5, 15.

CLARK, HORACE F., "Lot Appraisal," *Appraising the Home*, 1930, pp. 43-68.

DEBOOS, FRANK A., "Application of Depth Tables to Vacant Lots," *The Appraisal Journal*, October, 1949, pp. 467-470.

EDMAN, J. J., "The Appraisal Docket Shrinkage of Lot Is Compensible Damage," *The Appraisal Journal*, January, 1959, pp. 122-123.

EDMAN, J. J., "Valuation of Adjoining Lots In One Ownership. Appraisal Docket," *The Appraisal Journal*, April, 1958, pp. 291-292.

GARZON, JULIAN, "Techniques for the Appraisal of Irregular Lots," *Assessment Administration*, I. A. A. O, Chicago, 1960, pp. 155-156.

JERSEY CITY, NEW JERSEY BUREAU OF ASSESSMENT, "Formula Used to Determine Value Per Front Foot When Lot Value Is Given," *Appraising Manual*, Mcmichael, A. L., 1937, pp. 520-521.

KRANZ, MARTIN E., "Parking Lots and Garages," *Technical Valuation*, October, 1959, pp. 43-46.

LEISK, HERBERT N., "Formula for Irregular Lots," *The Real Estate Appraiser*, March, 1954, pp. 7-11, 20.

MCMICHAEL, STANLEY L., "Triangular Lots," *American Academy of Social and Poltical Science*, March, 1930, pp. 386-394.

MCMICHAEL, STANLEY L., "Types of Odd-Shaped Lots," *The Appraisal Journal*, pp. 528-529.

MCMICHAEL, STANLEY L., "Valuing Odd Shaped Lots-Appraising by Zones Merging Lot Values," *American Academy of Social and Political Science*, March, 1930, pp. 396-402.

MCPHERSON, L. D., "Inaccuracies of Appraisals Based on Lot Tables," *National Real Estate Journal*, September 2, 1929, pp. 34-35.

REAL ESTATE ANALYST, THE, "Estimating Values of Unusual Lots," *Real Estate Analyst Appraisal Bulletin*, 1949, pp. 465-468.

REAL ESTATE BOARD OF NEW YORK, "Corner Lot Rules," *Diary and Manual*, 1937, pp. 278.

SARLES, KENNETH E., "Limitations of Single Lots," *The Review*, September, 1953, pp. 3-6.

SCHUMACHER, ERNEST P., "Residential Lot Analysis," *The Review*, September, 1947, pp. 14-18.

## 22-23 Marshland

PAWLEY, R. W., N. G. MACARTHUR, "Compensation for the Taking of Marshland," *Appraisal Institute Magazine*, Appraisal Institute of Canada, Winnipeg.

PAWLEY, ROBERT W., AND N. G. MACARTHUR, "Compensation for the Taking of Marshland Used for Hunting and Fishing," *Appraisal Institute Magazine*, May, 1959, pp. 22-24.

## 22-24 Waterfront Property

ANTON, SHICKREY, "Real Estate Practices of the Port of New York Authority," *Right of Way*, February, 1962, pp. 51-53.

APPRAISAL JOURNAL, "Compensable Deprivation of Riparian Rights," *The Appraisal Journal*, October, 1954, pp. 603.

BALDWIN, FLETCHER N. JR., "The Impact of the Commerce Clause on the Riparian Rights Doctrine," *The Appraisal Journal*, July, 1964, pp. 398-434.

BERIAULT, RAYMOND J., "Effect of the St. Lawrence Seaway on Land Values," *Appraisal Institute Magazine*, January, 1959, pp. 22-24.

DAVIES, C. M., "Classification and Grading of Beach Property," *Appraisal Institute Magazine*, Appraisal Institute of Canada, Winnipeg, June 1, 1971.

GOSS, R. O., "Towards an Economic Appraisal of Port Investments," *Journal of Transport Economics and Policy*, September, 1967.

JOHNSON, RICHARD B., "A Waterfront Title Problem In Massachusetts," *Appraisal and Valuation Manual*, ASA, 1962, pp. 146-149.

KUNKLE, J. D., "The Appraisal of Industrial Waterfront Lands," *National Association of Real Estate Boards*, 1928, pp. 728-732.

MASON, TOM, "Appraisal of Waterfront Properties," *California Real Estate Magazine*, July, 1937, pp. 38-40.

MCMICHAEL, STANLEY L., "Harbor and Waterfront Property Appraisal," *Appraising Manual*, 1937, pp. 172-181.

MORRISON, CHARLES W., "Manhatten's Water-Front Problem," *The Appraisal Journal*, July, 1942, pp. 259-261.

MORSEY, NASHAAT, "The Long-Term Storage Policy of Nile Water In Egypt," *Technical Valuation*, November, 1955, pp. 31.

PARTRIDGE, CHARLES, "Appraising Waterfront and Industrial Property," *National Real Estate Journal*, March, 1938, pp. 54-57.

PETERSON, CHARLES E. JR., "Valuation of River Frontage for Industrial Use," *Appraisal and Valuation Manual*, American Society of Appraisers, 1960, pp. 295-302.

PITT, JOHN E., "An Appraisal of Riparian Rights," *The Appraisal Journal*, January, 1954, pp. 89-94.

REDEL, W. R., "Riparian Rights," *Appraisal Institute Magazine*, Appraisal Institute of Canada, Winnipeg.

RICK, WILLIAM B., "Planning and Developing Waterfront Property," *Urban Land Institute*, Urban Land Institute, Washington, 1964.

STEWART, W. C., "Appraisal of Water-Front Property," *The Appraisal Journal*, October, 1941, pp. 375-384.

STEWART, W. C., "Riparian and Littoral Rights," *The Appraisal Journal*, April, 1941, pp. 151-150.

THEISS, WILLEAM R., "The Appraisal Docket, Damages for Loss of Private Use of Lake," *The Appraisal Journal*, October, 1962, pp. 548.

THOMPSON, R. E., "Actual Appraisal Reports-Valuation of Water Front Pier Property," *National Real Estate Journal*, November, 1933, pp. 45-47.

THOMPSON, R. E., "Appraisal of Water-Front Real Estate," *The Appraisal Journal*, July, 1936, pp. 293-300.

TIEGER, MAX, "Riparian Valuation Land," *The Appraisal Journal*, October, 1949, pp. 431-440.

WILSON, D. EARL, "Actual Appraisal Reports Series 11: No 1 Industrial Riverfront Valuation for Tax Reduction Purposes," *National Real Estate Journal*, April, 1934, pp. 40-42.

"Atmosphere-Coronado Cays, a Waterfront Community with Carribbean Character," *House and Home*, May, 1971, pp. 92-95.

"Detached Townhouses Add an Extra Dimension to Narrow Waterfront Lots," *House and Home*, December, 1970, pp. 42.

"Modular Plan Cuts Cost on These Beach Front Apartments In California," *House and Home*, June, 1970, pp. 40.

"Waterways Buildup Off In 70, But Still Big," *Chemical Week*, March 24, 1971, pp. 14.

BIBLIOGRAPHY OF APPRAISAL LITERATURE

# CHAPTER THIRTEEN

# Industry

by A. D. Shiach, ASA.

Mr. A. D. Shiach is President of Marshall and Stevens, Incorporated and Chairman of the Board of Directors of Cooper Appraisals Limited, a Canadian affiliate of Marshall and Stevens, Incorporated.

Mr. Shiach has been actively engaged in the appraisal profession since 1946. He has prepared, or supervised, appraisals covering the major categories of land, buildings, intangibles, machinery and equipment in industrial, commercial, governmental, residential and farm uses. Appraisals prepared by Mr. Shiach were used for purposes of sale/purchase, insurance, rental, financing, income tax, ad valorem tax, condemnation (including urban renewal projects), allocation of purchase price, property records, stock and business valuations. He has also prepared, or supervised, economic feasibility, depreciation, construction cost estimates, land use and casualty loss studies. He is the author of the internally used "Property Records Manual," and a number of articles published in technical and financial magazines.

Mr. Shiach is a Senior Member of the American Society of Appraisers and is a National Panel Member, American Arbitration Association. He is also a Fellow of the Incorporated Society of Valuers and Auctioneers, a European society. He received a B.A. degree at De Pauw University, where he majored in Business Administration; supplementary studies were completed at Ohio State University. Mr. Shiach has testified as an expert witness in the Superior Court, State of California, and the Federal District Court.

## Industry

THE TERM "Industry" to many of us brings to mind immediately the picture of steel mills with their massive blast furnaces, molten pig iron and huge fabrication buildings. To others the first image is the complex, erector-set appearance of a major refinery. It depends upon where we were brought up. If it was Toledo — it could be the refinery, if it was Pittsburgh — the steel mill, if it was Crawley, Louisiana — it would be a rice mill. In Stevens Point, Wisconsin, it would be a paper mill. If it was on the River Clyde in Scotland — it would be a shipyard. It is also the 10 man machine shop across the street from the steel mill. The variety and complexity connoted by the term "Industry" is almost endless.

Industry, as used in this bibliography and defined by Webster is:
 a. any particular branch of productive, especially manufacturing, enterprise (the paper industry);
 b. any large scale business activity (the motion picture industry);
 c. manufacturing productive enterprises collectively, especially as distinguished from agriculture.

*The valuation of an industrial enterprise can involve every discipline in the appraisal profession.* While a number of appraisal societies are basically restricted to one discipline such as real property, the professional requirements and disciplines involved in the appraisal of an industrial enterprise can include all of the multi-discipline specialists of the American Society of Appraisers. For example, the valuation of the ABC Manufacturing Company included the following tangible and intangible assets, which, in turn, required utilization of most of the appraisal disciplines.

| Tangible Assets | Appraisal Discipline |
|---|---|
| Land | Real Property — Urban |
| Buildings | Real Property — Urban |
| Leaseholders Interests in Real Estate | Real Property — Urban |
| Machinery and Equipment | Machinery and Equipment (Basic Industry) |
| Automotive Equipment | Machinery and Equipment (Basic Industry) |
| Dies, Jigs, Fixtures | Machinery and Equipment (Basic Industry) |
| Molds, Patterns | Machinery and Equipment (Basic Industry) |
| Fine Arts (President's office and Board Room) | Personal Property (Fine Arts) |
| **Intangible Assets** | |
| Patents | Intangible Property |
| Franchise Agreements | Intangible Property |
| Goodwill | Intangible Property |

In addition to basic property characteristics of the assets appraised, a number of special value factors must be considered by the appraiser. These include: What are the general economics of the basic industry of which the ABC Manufacturing Company is a part? What is the competitive picture of the basic industry relative to other industries? What is the competitive position of the ABC Manufacturing Company within its industry? Does the machinery and equipment have excessive functional obsolescence? Do the plant facilities reflect a good maintenance program? Has the financial data as submitted been audited? Do the remaining calendar lives of the patents exceed their economic lives? Do the income projections attributed to these patents appear reasonable in view of industry norms? What are some of the other valuation factors that should be reviewed and considered in the appraisal of an industrial enterprise such as the ABC Manufacturing Company? It is to help those who need to know get answers to these kinds of questions, readily and authoritatively, that the Industry Bibliography section was included.

Considering the broad scope of the category, "Industry," it is difficult to precisely classify literature relating to valuation. The "Industry" bibliography as presented here by the American Society of Appraisers does reflect the depth of the subject.

For example, the references in the bibliography have published dates from the year 1911 forward, and subject matter relates to:

Industry wide background material,
Specific "how to" articles,
Economics of particular geographical areas,
A special bibliography on industrial real estate,
Industrial site selection both in and outside urban areas,
Bulk power and environmental pollution,
Special valuation articles on what executives expect to have covered in an appraisal,
Long term trends in industry,
Planned industrial development from the appraisers' point of view,
Industrial real estate,
Economics of industrial housing,
Service life of industrial property units,
Industrial plant trends,
Valuation of industrial securities, mining valuation,
Considerations affecting value of an industrial atomic energy enterprise.

This spectrum of material on the category "Industry" is just the beginning of the assistance this bibliography provides the professional or lay person seeking practical, quick and authoritative information on industrial valuation problems. The researcher or user of the "industry" category should review other pertinent categories. Each of the other 15 categories is capable of contributing to specific valuation problems within the multi-discipline requirements of most industrial appraisals.

Probably no other category is better served by the total bibliography than the category of "Industry." Valuation problems relating to industry have the potential to require more appraisal disciplines, techniques and general background than any other category. The breadth and depth of this bibliography added to the American Society of Appraisers' basic concept of multiple appraisal disciplines serves this requirement well.

# Industry

23-11   Industrial Property
23-12   Industrial Park
23-13   Technology
23-14   Heavy Industry
23-15   Light Industry
23-16   Raw Material Processing
23-17   Dairy Products Processing Plant
23-18   Atomic Energy Plant
23-19   Shipyard

## 23-11 Industrial Property

AGTHE, DONALD E., "The Economics of North Florida Industrial Parks," *The Economics of North Florida Industrial Parks,* Florida State University, 1970.

ALLSOPP, ERNEST S., "Industrial Financing by Purchase Lease," *The Appraisal Journal,* April, 1948, pp. 156-164.

AMERICAN APPRAISAL CO., "Construction Costs for Industrial Buildings Compared with 1913 Costs," *Real Estate Appraisal and Valuation,* P. W. Kniskern, 1933, pp. 301.

AMERICAN INSTITUTE OF REAL ESTATE APPRAISERS, "Commercial and Industrial Functional Utility and Inutility Valuation," *The Appraisal of Real Estate,* American Institute of Real Estate Appraisers, Chicago, 1967, pp. 148.

AMERICAN INSTITUTE OF REAL ESTATE APPRAISERS, "Pertinent Sales Reports on Large Industrial Properties," *Case Studies,* September, 1969.

ARMSTRONG, CHARLES VINCENT, "Industrial Property Records; Valuation Uses," *The Iowa State College Bulletin,* 1944.

ARMSTRONG, ROBERT H., "The Valuation of Industrial Real Estate," *The Appraisal Journal,* April, 1943, pp. 145-155.

ARMSTRONG, ROBERT H., "Valuation of Industrial Property Part IV," *The Apraisal Journal,* October, 1953, pp. 519-528.

ARMSTRONG, ROBERT H., "Valuation of Industrial Property, Part I," *The Appraisal Journal,* January, 1953, pp. 35-46.

ARMSTRONG, ROBERT H., "Valuation of Industrial Property, Part II," *The Appraisal Journal,* April, 1953, pp. 211-216.

ARMSTRONG, ROBERT H., "Valuation of Industrial Property, Part III," *The Appraisal Journal,* July, 1953, pp. 385-393.

BABCOCK, FREDERICK M., "Examples of Appraisal Procedure Factory Property," *Valuation of Real Estate,* 1932, pp. 209-213.

BABCOCK, FREDERICK M., "Valuation of Returns Factory Details of Valuation Procedure," *The Valuation of Real Estate,* Ed. 1, 1932, pp. 318-329.

BADGER, R. E., "Valuation of Industrial Securities," *Principles of Investment,* New York City, 1925.

BAKER, DONALD M., "Market Value of an Engineering Specialty," *Technicalities,* January, 1948, pp. 5-7, 20-26.

BALLOU, PAUL, "The Appraisal of an Industrial Facility," *Assessment Administration,* IAAO, Chicago, 1964, pp. 146-154.

BEARSLEE, LOUIS B., "The Relation of the Switch Track to Industrial Property," *The Appraisal Journal,* October, 1934, pp. 55-60.

BEATON, WILLIAM R., "Appraisal Analysis of Land Allocation for Industrial Use," *Valuation,* December, 1967, pp. 11-12.

BOBLETT, ROBERT P., "Factors In Industrial Location," *The Appraisal Journal,* October, 1967, pp. 523-526.

BOECKH, EVERARD HEREFORD, "Costs-Industrial Buildings," *Boeckh's Manual of Appraisals,* pp. 205.

BOERKE, E. M., "Industrial Appraisal," *The Appraisal Journal,* October, 1946, pp. 401-408.

BOHANNON, DAVID D., "Industries As Neighbors," *The Residential Appraiser,* June, 1957, pp. 7-9.

▲ Industry

BOLAND, C. T., "New Law Sets Rules for Depreciation by Regulated Industries," *Journal of Taxation,* July, 1970, pp. 48-49.

BRAZER, HARVEY E., "The Value of Industrial Property As a Subject of Taxation," *Canadian Public Administration,* June, 1961, pp. 137-147.

BRENT, W. L., "Valuing Industrial Real Estate," *The National Real Estate Journal,* June 30, 1924, pp. 27-30.

BROWN, FREDERICK J., "Industrial Property Appraisal for Mortgage Purposes," *Appraisal Digest,* October, 1951, pp. 17-18.

BURCHFIELD, W. G., "Industrial Property," *The Appraisal Journal,* January, 1933, pp. 132-137.

BURNELL, WILLIAM U., "Valuation of Cargo Vessels," *Valuation Manual,* 1956, pp. 153.

CALLAN, PROF. JOHN G., "Industrial Location," *The National Real Estate Journal,* November 25, 1929, pp. 20-25.

CLARK, GILBERT K., "Appraisal of Freeway Rights of Way Through Industrial Lands," *Valuation,* October, 1954, pp. 29-31.

CLAY, WILLIAM, *An Analysis of the Speculative Construction of Factory Buildings In Industrial Development,* Mississippi State University, 1971.

CONNELLY, WILLIAM F., "The Valuation of Industrial and Commercial Property for Taxation," National Tax Association, *Proceeding 20th Annual Conference,* 1927, pp. 295-308.

COOPER K. J., "The Impact of Technology and Changing Social Patterns on Property Values," *Valuer,* The New Zealand Institute of Valuers, New Zealand, August 1, 1973, pp. 124-134.

CROCHERON, CLARENCE, "Property and Depreciation Records for Industry," *Technicalities and Technical Valuation,* February, 1952, pp. 3-9.

CUNNINGHAM, F. M., "Valuation of Industrial Submerged Land," *Appraisal Institute Magazine,* 1967, pp. 22-30.

DARM, ADAM EUGENE, *Graduate Appraisal of the Industrial Technology Program at California State College,* University of California, 1971.

DEGRAFF, HERRELL, "The Land Foundation for Industrial Society," *The Appraisal Journal,* July, 1947, pp. 301-309.

DERBES, JR., MAX J., "Elementos De Valor Inmobiliario Industrial," *Boletin,* Sotave, Caracas, Venezuela, pp. 27-35.

DRENNAN, GEORGE W., "Industrial Plant Trends," *The Appraisal Journal,* January, 1949, pp. 83-85.

ELY, O., "Accelerated Depreciation," *Public Utilities Fortnightly,* American Society of Appraisers *Valuation Manual,* May 10, 1956, pp. 680-683.

ELY, O., "Accelerated Depreciation and Share Earnings," *Public Utilities Fortnightly,* American Society of Appraisers *Valuation Manual,* December 20, 1956, pp. 992-995.

EMERY, HAZEN C., "Personal Property of Manufacturers," *Assessment Administration,* American Assessment Officers, Chicago, 1961, pp. 83.

FISCHER, R. M., "Depreciation In Industrial Properties," *The Appraisal Journal,* April, 1937, pp. 143-148.

FISKE, W. P., J. E. BECKETT, *Industrial Accountants Handbook,* Prentice-Hall, Englwood, Cliffs, 1957.

FOSTER, HORATIO A., *Engineering Valuation of Public Utilities and Factories,* Van Nostrand, New York City, 1913.

FREEMAN, E. STEWART, "Valuation Problems In Industrial Accounting," *The Appraisal Journal,* October, 1951, pp. 451-458.

FULLERTON, PAUL, *Appraisal of Industrial Property,* Encyclopedia of Real Estate Appraising, 1959, pp. 317-367.

FULLERTON, PAUL, "Determinining Industrial Land Values from a Net-Net Lease," *Real Estate Aanlyst Appraisal Bulletin,* 1957, pp. 537-540.

FULLERTON, PAUL, "The Planned Industrial Development from the Appraisers Viewpoint," *The Appraisal Journal*, April, 1957, pp. 244-248.

GADDIS, PERCY A., "A Check-List for Appraising Industrial Property," *National Real Estate Journal*, July, 1933, pp. 33.

GADDIS, PERCY A., "Industrial Property," *The Appraisal Journal*, October, 1933, pp. 63-66.

GAILLARD, WILLIAM E. G., "Preferential Treatment of Industrial Realty," *The Appraisal Journal*, July, 1936, pp. 289-292.

GARRISON CHARLES B., "New Industry In Rural Areas The Local Economic Import," *Tennessee Survey of Business*, University of Tennessee, April, 1971, pp. 3-6, 15-16.

GATES, NILES S., "Speculators-Please Don't Play with Industrial Land," *Technical Valuation*, A.S.A. Conference, Washington, 1966, pp. 60.

GIBSON, K., "Impact Oil and Gas Industry on Canadian Economy," *Appraisal Institute Magazine*, Appraisal Institute of Canada, Winnipeg.

GRAY, RICHARD J., "Current Union Policies," *The Review*, October, 1945, pp. 1, 10.

GREEN, WILLIAM H., "The Textile Industry--Its Dilemma and Solution," *Journal of Business*, 1971, pp. 2-5.

GREGORY, E. SANFORD, "Trends and Valuation of Industrial Real Estate," *Valuation*, November, 1955, pp. 12-15.

GRUELICH, RICHARD H. JR., *Property Valuation*, Austin, Texas.

HALL, H. B., "The Appraisal of Industrial Properties," *National Real Estate Journal*, July, 1923, pp. 28-30.

HANLEY, E. J., "Financing Tomorrow's Steel Plant Demands Realistic Depreciation and Pricing Policy," *Valuation Manual*, A. S. A., March, 1956, pp. 338-340.

HARRIS, CHAUNCY D., "The Market As a Factor In the Location of Industry In the United States," *The Appraisal Journal*, January, 1956, pp. 57-86.

HEBB, WINSTON P, "Industrial Insurance Appraisals," *Valutape Audio-Library*, American Society of Appraisers, Washington D.C., January 1, 1974.

HERRMANN, CYRIL C., "The Outlook for Industrial Land Use In America," *The Real Estate Appraiser*, March, 1970, pp. 26-27.

HINSHAW, ANDREW J., "Functional and Economic Obsolescence of Industrial Installations," *Technical Valuation*, June, 1963, pp. 12-17.

HOGAN, HUNTER A. JR., "The Technique of Industrial Property Valuation," *The Appraisal Journal*, January, 1951, pp. 89-94.

HOLDEN, THOMAS S., "Trends In Industrial Construction," *The Appraisal Journal*, April, 1947, pp. 167-172.

HUDSEN, H. R., "Appraisal of Industrial Property," *The Appraisal Journal*, October, 1950, pp. 472-480.

HUDSEN, H. R., "Industrial Property and Its Development," *Right Of Way*, February, 1964, pp. 21-26.

HYDER, K. LEE, "The Appraisal of Industrial Property," *The Appraisal Journal*, October, 1934, pp. 19-28.

HYDER, LEE K., "Actual Appraisal Reports - Valuation of the Real Estate In Industrial Property," *National Real Estate Journal*, January, 1932, pp. 22-26.

JEWETT, JOHN G., "A New Approach to Industrial Financing," *The Appraisal Journal*, April, 1947, pp. 235-236.

JOPLIN, A. F., "Industrial Parks," *Appraisal Institute Magazine*, Appraisal Institute of Canada, Winnipeg.

KAUFMAN, K. A., "Pollution Rules Could Choke Industry to Death," *Iron Age*, February 11, 1971, pp. 21.

KLEMME, RANDALL T., "Community Development As Forerunner of Industrial Development," *The Appraisal Journal*, October, 1960, pp. 444-448.

KNEISS, GEORGE, "Industrial Land Development In North California," *Right of Way*, April, 1954, pp. 6-7.

KRAFT, K., L. STARKWEATHER, "Analysis of Industrial Securities," *Principles of Investment*, New York, 1929.

KUEHNLE, WALTER R., "Fundamental Approaches," *The Society of Industrial Realtors*, 1953, pp. 5-17.

KUNKLE, J. D., "Developing Industrial Appraisal Business," *National Real Estate Journal*, August 23, 1926, pp. 54-55.

KUNKLE, J. D., "Industrial Plant Values," *National Real Estate Journal*, August 4, 1930, pp. 41-43.

KUNKLE, J. D., "The Appraisal of Industrial Waterfront Lands," *National Association of Real Estate Boards*, 1928, pp. 728-732.

KUNKLE, J. D., "Units of Industrial Property Values," *National Real Estate Journal*, April 19, 1926, pp. 45-47.

LAYDEN, ARTHOR L., "Considerations In Appraising Industrial Property," *The Appraisal Journal*, April, 1934, pp. 249-227.

LOEWENSTEIN, LOUIS K., DAVID BRADWELL, "What Makes Desirable Industrial Property," *The Appraisal Journal*, April, 1966, pp. 263-267.

MARSTON, ANSON, THOMAS R. AGG, "Average Service Life of Industrial-Property Units," *Engineering Valuation*, New York, 1936, pp. 497-514.

MARSTON, ANSON, THOMAS R. AGG, "Industrial-Property Mortality Type Curves," *Engineering Valuation*, New York, 1936, pp. 515-534.

MARSTON, ANSON, THOMAS R. AGG, "Valuation of Private Industrial Property," *Engineering Valuation*, New York, 1936, pp. 420-454.

MAYER, HAROLD M., "Some Current Trends Effecting the Value of Industrial Property," *The Appraisal Journal*, January, 1958, pp. 87-96.

MC MICHAEL, STANLEY L., "Tasacion De Propiedades Industriales," *Boletin*, Sotave, Caracas, Venezuela, pp. 41-46.

MCCORMACK, JAMES E., "Appraisal of Industrial Property," *The Appraisal Journal*, January, 1947, pp. 23-31.

MCGUIRE, D. C., "Factors In Industrial Location," *The Appraisal Journal*, April, 1942, pp. 120-124.

MCKAY, CHARLES WATSON, *Valuing Industrial Properties*, Industrial Extension Institute, New York, 1922.

MCLAUGHLIN, GLEEN E., "Criteria In the Selection of Cities for Industrial Location," *The Appraisal Journal*, April, 1949, pp. 168-172.

MCMICHAEL, STANLEY L., "Industrial and Warehouse Property Appraisals," *Appraisers Manual*, 1937, pp. 160-172.

MCMURRY, ROBERT N., "Mental Illness In Industry," *The Appraisal Journal*, April, 1960, pp. 251-260.

MITCHELL, RICHARD E., "Industrial Site Selection Outside Urban Centers," *The Appraisals Journal*, October, 1966, pp. 597-600.

MONRAD, OSCAR, "Use of Market Data In Appraising Industrial Property," *The Appraisal Journal*, April, 1956, pp. 187-194.

MORRISON, CHARLES W., "The Postwar Industrial Plant," *The Appraisal Journal*, January, 1944, pp. 31-37.

MUNCY, DOROTHY A., "Planning Guidelines for Industrial Park Development," *Urban Land*, December, 1970.

NATIONAL ASSOCIATION OF REAL ESTATE BOARDS, *Standard Appraisal Work-Sheet-Industrial Property,* 1929.

NATIONAL ASSOCIATION OF REAL ESTATE BOARDS, "How to Appraise Industrial Property," *National Real Estate Journal,* February 7, 1927, pp. 26-28.

NATIONAL ASSOCIATION OF REAL ESTATE BOARDS, "Industrial Property Division," *Annals of Real Estate Practice,* 1927, pp. 183-190.

NATIONAL ASSOCIATION OF REAL ESTATE BOARDS, "Standard Appraisal Form for Industrial Property," *Appraising Manual,* 1937, pp. 537-540.

NATIONAL REAL ESTATE JOURNAL, *Industrial Decentralization,* November, 1938, pp. 41.

NELSON, R. D., A. J. POLLAKOWSKI, L. SABROSKY, "Appraisal of an Industrial Warehouse Property," *The Real Estate Appraisers,* March, 1970, pp. 41-51.

OHMAN, ROBERT E., "Demonstration Appraisal of an Industrial Property," *Technical Valuation,* June, 1963, pp. 24-41, 44-54.

OSTENDORF, E. L., "Appraisal of an Industrial Plant," *Appraisal Reporting Techniques,* A. I. R. E. A., 1947, pp. 119-161.

OWEN, LEROY D., *Industrial Real Estate,* Los Angeles, 1936, pp. 24.

OWEN, LEROY D., "Appraisal Points Industrial Executives Expect to Find," *California Real Estate Magazine,* November, 1935, pp. 30-32.

PAPER INDUSTRY, W. W., "Difference Between Appraisal and Inventory," *The Paper Industry,* October, 1922, pp. 923-924.

PARKE, FENTON M., "Appraisal of Industrial Real Estate," *Annals of Real Estate Practice,* National Association of Real Estate Boards Vol. Vi, 1925, pp. 57-79.

PARTRIDGE, CHARLES, "Appraising Waterfront and Industrial Property," *National Real Estate Journal,* March, 1938, pp. 54-57.

POTTER, EDWARD, "Industrial Appraisals Pertaining to Liquidating Values," *Technical Valuation,* 1966, pp. 9-13.

POTTER, GEORGE S., "Industrial Property Appraisals," *Appraisal Digest,* October, 1955, pp. 1 19-21.

PROUTY, FRANK H., "What Is the Value Today of an Industrial Property," *National Real Estate Journal,* September, 1932, pp. 37-39.

PROUTY, W. L. AND OTHERS, "Assessors Valuation of Industrial Plants," *Appraisers and Assessors Manual,* 1930, pp. 352-419.

PROUTY, W. L. AND OTHERS, "Factory Building Construction," *Appraisers and Assessors Manual,* 1930, pp. 205-211.

RALEIGH, JAMES C., "Appraisal of a Tank Farm," *The Real Estate Appraiser,* November, 1970, pp. 36-38.

REVIEW, THE, "New Products for Builders," *The Review,* February, 1952, pp. 7-9.

RICHARDSON, WILLIAM A. JR., "The Impact of Industrial Parks," *Valuation,* December, 1968, pp. 44-50.

ROBERTS, FRANK B., "Appraisal of a Sawmill and Appurtenances 1663," *The Appraisal Journal, Xxxv,* January, 1967, pp. 126-127.

ROBERTS, JOHN A., "Appraisal of Commercial and Industrial Property," *Right of Way Conference,* 1957, pp. 100-115.

ROE, STANLEY, "Appraisal of an Industrial Property," *Appraisal Reporting Technique,* Vol. IV.

ROSS, CHARLES M., "Appraisal of Cold Storage Plants," *Encyclopedia of Real Estate Appraising,* 1959, pp. 602-613.

ROSS, CHARLES M., AND JOHN PORTER, "Economic Appraisal of Cold Storage Plants," *Apprsisal and Valuation Manual,* 1956, pp. 299-308.

ROYCRAFT, D. F., *Industrial Building Details,* F. W. Dodge, New York, 1959.

▲ Industry

SARGENT, FREDERIC O., "Land Market and Price, Analysis In an Agro-Industrial Economy," *The Appraisal Journal,* July, 1959, pp. 259-264.

SCHWINGLE, C. J., "The Developing Challenge of Industrial Valuations," *Technical Valuation,* October, 1960, pp. 6-10.

SCOTT, JOHN T. JR., "Economic Impact of Industrialization on Traditional Rural Areas," *Journal of the Society of American Farm Managers and Rural Appraisers,* October, 1968, pp. 8-13.

SHENKEL, WILLIAM M., *A Guide to Appraising Industrial Property,* Society of Real Estate Appraisers, Chicago.

SHENKEL, WILLIAM M., "The Valuation of Industrial Land," *Assessors News Letter,* June, 1965, pp. 83-89.

SHENKEL, WILLIAM M., "The Valuation of Industrial Land," *The Real Estate Appraiser,* January, 1965, pp. 14-22.

SHENREL, WILLIAM M., "Estimating the Demand for Industrial Real Estate," *The Real Estate Appraiser,* September, 1965, pp. 13-22.

SHENREL, WILLIAM M., "The Valuation of Industrial Land," *The Real Estate Appraiser,* January, 1965, pp. 16.

SMITH, GEORGE C., "Trends Affecting Commercial and Industrial Properties," *The Appraisal Journal,* July, 1939, pp. 245-251.

SMITH, LELAND F., "Inner City Industrial Districts," *Urban Land,* May, 1971.

STARRETT, PAUL, "How to Appraise Industrial Properties," *The Appraisal Journal,* January, 1959, pp. 54-61.

STARRETT, PAUL, "Location and Space Requirements of Industry," *American Institute of Real Estate Appraiser,* 1958, pp. 233-237.

TROXEL JAY C, "Functional Analysis of Industrial Property:Relationship to Economic Principles," *The Real Estate Appraiser,* The Society of Real Estate Appraisers, Chicago Illinois, January 1, 1974, pp. 30-35.

TRUE, WALLACE W., "Financing Industrial Real Estate," *The Appraisal Journal,* January, 1939, pp. 30-36.

TRUMBLE, MELVIN J., "An Obsolete Factory," *Assessment Administration,* 1957, pp. 30-45.

VAN CLEEF, EUGENE, "Locating the Right Industry In the Right Place," *The Appraisal Journal,* April, 1958, pp. 223-226.

VAN NOY, C. W., *Guide for Making Costs Estimates for Chemical-Type Operations,* U. S. Bureau of Mines, Washington, 1949.

VARTY, LEO G., "The Appraisal of an Industrial Loft Building," *Annals of Real Estate Practice,* 1928, pp. PP, 722-727.

WAGNER, C. RAY, "Appraisal of Industrial Property," *Assessors Topics,* May, 1957.

WALDRON, ROBERT, "Appraising Industrial Property," *Appraisal Digest,* November, 1960, pp. 23-24.

WILFRED R., "Statistical Analysis of Industrial Property Retirements," *Engineering Valuation,* 1936.

WILLIAMS, D. N., "Pay-As-You-Pollute Plan No Limits Just Cash," *Iron Age,* January 14, 1971, pp. 45.

WILSON, D. EARL, "Actual Appraisal Reports Series 11: No 1 Industrial Riverfront Valuation for Tax Reduction Purposes," *National Real Estate Journal,* April, 1934, pp. 40-42.

WINFREY, ROBLEY, "Statistical Analyses of Industrial Property Retirement," *Iowa Engineering Experiment Station Bulletin No. 125,* Iowa State College of Agriculture & Mechanic Arts, Ames, December 11, 1935, pp. 1-176.

WOOD, CHARLES P., "The Location of Industry," *The Appraisal Journal,* October, 1945, pp. 339-347.

WOODWARD, DONALD B., "Long Term Trends In Industry," *The Appraisal Journal,* April, 1948, pp. 148-155.

WOODWORTH, LEO D., "Industrial Appraisers Vs. Mechanical Surveys," *National Real Estate Journal,* June 13, 1927, pp. 24-26.

WORCHESTER, THOMAS, "Plant Design for Long-Term Value," *The Appraisal Journal,* October, 1951, pp. 503-507.

"Coal A New Look at an Old Industry," *Financial World,* September 30, 1970, pp. 7.

"CPI Rides High In Building Boom," *Chemical Week,* March 17, 1971, pp. 10-11.

"Industrial Waste a New Source of Low Cost Bricks and Blocks," *House and Home,* September, 1971, pp. 48.

"Industry Depreciates Nader' Challenge," *Iron Age,* June 3, 1971, pp. 47.

"Industrys Hidden Dividends," *Nations Business,* October, 1970, pp. 74-77.

*Industrial Profitability Growth & Size Long Term Firm Level Study of Cost Behavior In Steel Industry,* University of Wisconsin Milwaukee, 1971.

"Industrial Managers Speak Out In Pollution Survey," *Modern Manufacturing,* September, 1970, pp. 167-168.

## 23-12 Industrial Park

BOLEY, ROBERT E., "Effects of Industrial Parks on the Community," *The Appraisal Journal,* October, 1959, pp. 554-560.

BOLEY, ROBERT E., "Rx for Successful Industrial Park," *Urban Land,* July, 1967.

FISHER, LEIGH, "Aiport Industrial Parks," *Urban Land,* ULI, Washington, D.C., 1966.

RICHARDSON, WILLIAM A. JR., "The Impact of Industrial Parks," *Valuation,* December, 1968, pp. 44-50.

SHENKEL, WILLIAM M., "Community Benefits of an Industrial Park," *The Real Estate Appraisal,* 1911, pp. 24-36.

## 23-13 Technology

BRYANT, W. D., "Industrial Trends Affecting Real Estate Markets," *The Appraisal Journal,* July, 1949, pp. 321-337.

CARESTIO, R. M. JR., "Land Absorption In Industrial Parks," *Industrial Development and Manufacturers Record,* January, 1971, pp. 18-21.

COLEAN, MILES, "Mechanized Construction Methods Are on the March," *Appraisal Digest,* October, 1954, pp. 9-11.

COOPER K. J., "The Impact of Technology and Changing Social Patterns on Property Values," *Valuer,* The New Zealand Institute of Valuers, New Zealand, August 1, 1973, pp. 124-134.

ENEMARK, FRED, "Effect on Residential Property Values of Industrial Development," *The Residential Appraiser,* November, 1960, pp. 2-4.

FUNKE, JOHN H., "Impact of Containerization," *How Transportation Affects Real Estate Values,* American Institute of Real Estate Appraisers, Chicago, March 7, 1969, pp. 41-43.

GARBER, H. A., "Trends of Industry," *The Appraisal of Machinery and Equipment Monograph*, A.S.A., 1969, pp. 53.

GEORGE, E. O., FRANK ROBY, CLYDE CLARK, "Wiring Advances," *The Residential Appraiser*, May, 1958, pp. 17.

GREEN, WILLIAM H., "The Textile Industry--Its Dilemma and Solution," *Journal of Business*, 1971, pp. 2-5.

HALE, C. W., "Impact of Federal Policy and Technological Change on Regional & Urban Planning Problems," *Land Economics*, February, 1971, pp. 24-35.

HART, LARRY C., "Building Materials Today," *The Review*, November, 1946, pp. 23-24.

HORGAN, N. J, R. P. FLOYD, JR., "MBO Approach to Prevent Technical Obsolescence," *Personnel Journal*, September, 1971, pp. 687-693.

HURD, RICHARD M., "Forces Creating Cities," *Principles of City Land Values*, Chapters 2-4, 1924, pp. 159.

LENDRUM, JAMES T., "Heating Research," *The Review*, March, 1948, pp. 11-14.

LETCHFIELD, F. T., "Impact of Engineering Upon Our Economy," *The Appraisal Journal*, October, 1953, pp. 487-496.

LUND, JOSEPH W., "Present Industrial Trends--Shape of Things to Come," *The Appraisal Journal*, July, 1955, pp. 356-362.

MCMAHEN, D. H., "Effect of Improving Technology on Land Values In the Mountain States," *Journal of the American Society of Farm Managers and Rural Appraisers*, April, 1956, pp. 52-56.

MEENEN, H. J., "The Impact of Technology and Government Programs Upon Value," *Journal of the American Society of Farm Manager and Rural Appraisers*, April, 1957, pp. 76-81.

RAMS, EDWIN M., "Technology Innovation and Value Perspectives," *Technical Valuation*, pp. 5.

ROSE, C. W., D. A. THOMAS, "Remote Sensing of Land Surface Temperature and Some Applications," *Land Evaluation*, pp. 367.

VERMILYA, SHERWOOD S., "Appraisal of a Modern Industrial Plant," *Assessment Administration*, IAAO, Chicago, 1963, pp. 120-160.

"Can Technology Solve the Housing Problem," *Industry Week*, January 18, 1971, pp. 26-27.

"Industry Depreciates Nader Challenge," *Iron Age*, June 3, 1971, pp. 47.

# 23-14 Heavy Industry

BACKMAN, JULES, *The Economics of the Chemical Industry*, Manufacturing Chemists Association, Washington D. C, 1900.

BLACK, I. G., "Metals Pick Up Speed In Building Materials Race," *Iron Age*, April 29, 1971, pp. 37.

CROOK, HOWARD W., "Appraisal of Portland Cement Plants," *Valuation*, February, 1968, pp. 21-37.

DOFSTEDT, CARL J., "Factors In the Appraisal or Evaluation of a Portland Cement Plant," *Appraisal and Valuation Manual*, American Society of Appraisers, 1958, pp. 267-276.

HYDER, K. LEE, "Fair Value of Industrial Plants," *The Appraisal Journal*, July, 1945, pp. 241-248.

LINN, HAROLD, "A Modern Industrial Planet," *Assessment Administration*, I.A.A.O., Chicago, 1957, pp. 23-29.

LINN, HAROLD, "Demonstration Appraisal, a Modern Industrial Plant, *Assessment Administration*, I.A.A.O., Chicago, 1957, pp. 23-30.

LUNSFORD, C. R., "Valuing a Petroleum Refinery for Ad Valorem Tax Purposes," *Assessment Administration*, I. A. A. O, Chicago, 1965, pp. 112-118.

NELSON, W. L., *Petroleum Refinery Engineering*, Mcgraw-Hill, New York, 1958.

NELSON, W. L., "Refinery Depreciation Rates," *American Society of Appraisers*, April 23, 1952, pp. 141.

PETERSON, CHARLES E. JR., "Valuation of Cement Manufacturing Plant," *Appraisal and Valuation Manual*, American Society of Appraisers, Vol. Vii, 1962, pp. 93-102.

PETROLEUM REFINERY ENGINEERING, *Petroleum Refinery Engineering*, Mcgraw-Hill, New York, 1949.

RALEIGH, JAMES C., "Appraisal of a Tank Farm," *The Real Estate Appraiser*, November, 1970, pp. 36-38.

REDDING, E. D., "An Approach to a Method of Evaluating Chemical Plants and Refineries," *Appraisal and Valuation Manual*, American Society of Appraisers, 1959, pp. 267-280.

SAUNDERS, G. A., *Estimating Structural Steel*, Mcgraw-Hill, New York, 1959.

WEAVER, J. R., "Appraisal of Chemical Plants," *The Appraisal Journal*, April, 1962, pp. 219-224.

"Heres a New High Rise System That Mixes Light and Heavy Construction," *House and Home*, August, 1970, pp. 26.

"Smoke Cited As Killer," *Engineering New Record*, January 21, 1971, pp. 12.

## 23-15 Light Industry

"Heres a New High Rise System That Mixes Light and Heavy Construction," *House and Home*, August, 1970, pp. 26.

VAUGHAN, J. L. JR., "Valuation of Simple Industrial Properties," *Technical Valuation*, February, 1953, pp. 45-46, 56.

## 23-16 Raw Material Processing

ALLINGHAM, ALLISON P., "Appraising Grain Elevators," *Annals of Real Estate Practice*, National Association of Real Estate Boards, 1927, 1934, pp. 309-321.

AMENDOLAGINE, EMANUEL, "Valuation of Assaying Cutting & Ore Picking of Lenticular Uranium Ore," *Appraisal and Valuation Manual*, American Society of Appraisers, Washington, 1958, pp. 191-196.

AMERICAN SOCIETY OF PLANNING OFFICIALS, "Land Use Controls In the Surface Extraction of Minerals," Chicago.

GREEN, WILLIAM H., "The Textile Industry--Its Dilemma and Solution," *Journal of Business*, 1971, pp. 2-5.

## 23-17 Dairy Products Processing Plant

JOHNSTON, RICHARD STANLEY PH. D., *The Growth of Firms In Some Food Marketing and Processing Industries*, North Carolina State University, 1970.

## 23-18 Atomic Energy Plant

MCMANUS, G. J., "Every Pinch Releases Its Grip," *Iron Age*, May 27, 1971, pp. 63-64.

SILVERMAN, BENJAMIN, "Considerations Affecting Value In an Industrial Atomic Energy Enterprise," *Appraisal and Valuation Manual*, pp. 30.

STEWARD, CHARLES L., "The Non-Immunity of Farm Land to Atomic Developments," *The Appraisal Journal*, October, 1947, pp. 464-470.

## CHAPTER FOURTEEN

# Transportation

by Norman E. Carlson, ASA, PE.

Mr. Carlson is a partner of Coverdale & Colpitts, Consulting Engineers, and Senior Vice President of URS/Coverdale & Colpitts, Inc., Transportation and Industrial Consultants. He is responsible for valuation studies of transportation and industry and for technical and economic studies of all modes of land transport.

A graduate of University of Minnesota in Mechanical Engineering, Mr. Carlson is a Registered Professional Engineer in several states and a member of the American Society of Mechanical Engineers, the American Society of Appraisers (Senior Member), and Panel of Arbitration of the American Arbitration Association. He has testified on valuations of transport property before Federal and State Courts and Interstate Commerce hearings.

▲ Transportation

THE DETERMINATION of value in the area generally classified as "transportation" requires competence in two, and in some cases three, different disciplines of the appraisal profession. This results from the need of value determinations of different types of property for different purposes.

In general, the property is of two types: (1) real estate being acquired by a governmental agency for a transportation facility, and (2) the property of a transportation company. Included in the latter are both real estate and other property. The appraisal or valuation of each of these is discussed subsequently.

## Real Estate for Transportation Facility

The principal need for appraisals for this purpose is to establish the value of real estate for the construction or improvement of highways, mass transit rights of way and airports. This involves the appraisal of land, improvements to land and, in some instances, evaluation of the damage to adjoining property. The appraisal of real estate for roads is also an area in which competence in the appraisal of partial acquisitions is often of primary importance.

The development of generally acceptable practices for appraisal of land for highway right-of-way has been accelerated and made more consistent since World War II as a result of the huge highway expansion and airport programs. The guidelines promulgated by the various Federal departments and the case law resulting from condemnation hearings in Federal and State courts provide the philosophy and the general methods with which the appraisal of land for right-of-way and airport purposes should be treated.

The evaluation of the effect, if any, of new construction, or improvements to highways or airports which will result in increased traffic, on the abutting and neighboring property is also in the province of the experienced real estate specialist. This may require more skill than that of the appraisal of the land to be acquired because this evaluation frequently must be made in an atmosphere of intense feeling that individuals' rights are being violated.

With the increased concern of the public in the environment, and the resulting activity of the Federal and State government departments, a new field of evaluation work is developing in which persons skilled in real estate appraisal for transportation purposes may play a significant role. The National Environmental Policy Act of 1969 (NEPA) requires that an environmental impact statement be prepared as a part of the decision-making process for, among other Federal actions, any program of highway or airport construction. Numerous states are now adopting similar requirements for projects under their jurisdiction.

Among the requirements for an acceptable statement is an assessment of the effect of the proposed project on present and future land use of the actual land under consideration and the adjoining land as well.

## Property of Transportation Companies

Appraisals or valuation studies are frequently needed of one category of transportation company property or for the entire physical property; and, in some instances, the value of certain intangible assets.

The transportation enterprises for which studies may be made are:

| | |
|---|---|
| Railroads | Airlines |
| Bus companies | Airport service companies |
| Trucking companies | Ferry operations |
| Water shipping companies | Pipelines |

The purpose for which a study is needed may be for use in one of the following:

| | |
|---|---|
| Sale of Property | Equipment leasing |
| Purchase of property | Financing |
| Condemnation | Insurance |
| Mergers | Taxation |
| Allocation of assets | Depreciation schedules |
| Confirmation of values | Rate making |

The property may include the real estate for terminal and maintenance facilities or, in the case of a railroad, the right-of-way land.

The appraisal of land is in the province of a real estate appraiser; in the case of a railway study, one with understanding of the appraisal of right-of-way land.

The other physical property of a transportation company may consist of such categories as buildings; track, bridges and tunnels (railroads); shop machinery and equipment; locomotives and cars, buses, aircraft or vessels; furniture and office equipment; inventories; and others, depending on the type of operation. The segregation of the items of property for a regulated transportation company among the various categories is defined in published documents by Federal and regulatory agencies, or by industry associations, a number of which are included in this bibliography.

The philosophy and methodology of the valuation of various categories of transportation property generally follows those which are appropriate for the valuation of machinery and equipment.

As is the case in the valuation of any physical property, it is imperative to have a thorough understanding of the characteristics of the element of property and the manner in which it operates in the particular enterprise.

The literature devoted specifically to the appraisal and valuation of the property of transportation companies is very limited; however, much of the general valuation literature and that included in the "Machinery and Equipment" section contain much which is helpful in the valuation of transportation property. In recent years there have been numerous court cases and hearings by regulatory agencies in which values of transportation company property have been adjudicated. This has been particularly true of urban transit companies of which many have been acquired by public agencies. In some of these, the value of certain intangible assets have been included in the total value at which ownership is transferred. Generally, the values of these assets are determined on bases similar to those used in the evaluation of intangible assets as discussed elsewhere in this volume.

The valuation of transportation property is not an esoteric field, but, as with the other disciplines of the appraisal profession, it requires the understanding of the basic principles of appraisal, a knowledge of the various methods of determining value for the different purposes and knowledge of the several types of property used in the industry.

# Transportation

24-11 Impact of Transportation
24-12 Traffic
24-13 Airport
24-14 Railroads
24-15 Highways
24-16 Highway Beautification
24-17 Automobiles
24-18 Bridges
24-19 Rapid Transit
24-20 Truck Terminal

## 24-11 Impact of Transportation

ADKINS, WILLIAM G., *Effects of the Dallas Central Expressway on Land Values and Land Use*, Texas Transportation Institute, College Station, Tex, 1957.

ADKINS, WILLIAM G., "Dallas Expressway Study," *The Residential Appraiser*, April, 1958, pp. 16-24.

ALEXANDER, ROBERT H., "Interviewing for Freeway Reactions," *The Residential Appraiser*, March, 1958, pp. 3-6.

AMERICAN INSTITUTE OF PLANNERS JOURNAL, "Effects of Public Investments on Urban Land Values," *American Institute of Planners Journal*, July, 1966, pp. 204.

AMERICAN INSTITUTE OF REAL ESTATE APPRAISERS, *How Transportation Affects Real Estate Values*, American Institute of Real Estate Appraisers, Chicago, 1900.

AMERICAN RIGHT OF WAY ASSOCIATION, "The Federal Highway Program and Its Impact," *Proceedings of the Second Annual National Seminar, 1956*, Washington, D. C, 1957.

AMERICAN TRANSIT ASSOCIATION, "Classification of Accounts for Bus Operating Companies," *Transit Bulletin*, American Transit Association.

ANDERSON, ARNOLD C., "The Effect of Transportation on Values," *How Transportation Affects Real Estate Values*, A.I.R.E.A., Chicago, March 7, 1969, pp. 14-18.

ATHERTON E B, "Appraising Noise Damages on Federal-Aid Highway Projects," *The Real Estate Appraiser*, The Society of Real Estate Appraisers, Chicago Illinois, November 1, 1973, pp. 4-8.

ATHERTON, EDWARD B, "Appraising Noise Damages on Federal-Aid Highway Projects," *Valuation Magazine*, American Society of Appraisers, Washington D.C., December 1, 1973, pp. 44-51.

AUTOMATIC CAR WASH ASSOCIATION, "Cost of Doing Business--Manual," *Cost of Doing Business Manual*, Automatic Car Wash Association, Bellwood, 1900.

BABCOCK, HENRY A., "City Growth and Transportation," *The Appraisal Journal*, July, 1938, pp. 249-254.

BALFOUR, FRANK C., "America's Highway Problems and Their Likely Effect on Real Estate Markets," *The Appraisal Journal*, October, 1954, pp. 497-524.

BALFOUR, FRANK C., "Land Economic Studies: Result of Interchanges on Limited Access Highways, Effect of Traffic Changes," *Right of Way Conference Selected Papers*, University of Alabama, 1959.

BECK, MORRIS, "Interstate Variations In the Finance of Shared Functions of State and Local Government," *Conference Proceedings*, National Tax Association, Columbus, 1965, pp. 614-627.

BRADLEY, CARL H. H., "The Effect of New Roads on Values," *Right of Way*, February, 1961, pp. 41-48.

BRINTON, JOHN H., *Effect of Highway Landscape Development on Nearby Property*, Highway Research Board National Research Council, Washington, 1969.

BUILDING INVESTMENT AND MAINTENANCE, "Problem of Obsolescence," *Building Investment and Maintenance*, October, 1925, pp. 35-36.

▲ Transportation

CAPPOZZA, DENNIS, *Transportation Cost and Urban Retail Trade*, University of Southern California Working Paper 8.

CREEDY, JOHN A., "Navigation, Water Resources, and Patterns of Economic Growth," *How Transportation Affects Real Estate Values*, A. I. R. E. A., Chicago, March 7, 1969, pp. 37-40.

FAIR, E. W., "Parking Lot Headaches," *Banking*, September, 1970, pp. 94.

GAKENHEIMER, RALPH A., "Planning, Transportation, and the Small City," *The Appraisal Journal*, January, 1966, pp. 80-92.

GARRISON, WILLIAM L., M. MERTZ, *Influence of Highway Improvements on Urban Land*, U of Wash., Dept of Geography Vol. V, Seattle, 1958.

GOLBERG, M. A., "Transportation, Urban Land Values, and Rents A Synthesis," *Land Economics*, May, 1970, pp. 153-162.

GROSS, WILLIAM J., "Acquisitions for Future Use," *American Association of State Highway Officials*, Washington D. C, 1962.

HATHAWAY, PAUL L., "Transportation-A Factor In Residential Values," *Residential Appraisers Review*, August, 1935, pp. 3-5, 16.

HERRING, FRANK W., "Transportation and Property Values," *Technical Valuation*, July, 1950, pp. 25-31.

HESS, RUDOLF, "The Effect of Access Controlled Highways on Abutting and Adjacent Properties," *Selected Papers*, Right of Way Conference, University of Ala., 1957.

HESS, RUDOLF, "The Influence of Modern Transportation on Values—Freeways," *The Assessors Journal*, December, 1965, pp. 26-32.

HIGHWAY RESEARCH BOARD, *Scenic Easements--Legal Administrative and Valuation Problems and Procedures*, Washington, D. C..

HOOKER, RAYMOND W., KENNETH R. POTTER, *The Impact of a New Interstatehighway on a Corridor and Input-Output Analysis*, University of Wyoming, January, 1971.

HOYT, HOMER, "Expressways and Apartment Sites," *The Appraisal Journal*, January, 1959, pp. 103-106.

HULLEY, ROBERT B., "People Injuriously Affected by Pub Wks Construct'n," *Appraisal Institute Magazine*, Appraisal Institute of Canada, Winnipeg.

HURD, RICHARD M., "Forces Creating Cities," *Principles of City Land Values*, Chapters 2-4, 1924, pp. 159.

HURD, RICHARD MELANCTHON, "Principles of City Land Values," New York, 1911.

INDUSTRY WEEK, "Mass Transit Becomes Tool Solving Urban Probs," *Industry Week*, June 8, 1970, pp. 14-16.

INTERSTATE COMMERCE COMMISSION, "Uniform System Accounts Class I Class II Common and Contract Motor Carriers of Property," *Carriers of Property*, Interstate Commerce Commission.

JOHNSON, B. D. L., "Super-Port In Perspective," *Appraisal Institute Magazine*, Appraisal Institute of Canada, Winnipeg.

KALTENBACH, HENRY J., "The Federal Highway Program and Its Significance to Real Estate," *The Appraisal Journal*, July, 1956, pp. 377-384.

KENNEDY, FRANCIS H., "Noise Progress -- Street Cars to Jets, and Beyond," *Assessment Administration*, IAAO, Chicago, 1959, pp. 106-110.

KILEY, EDWARD V., "The Highway Age In Transportation," *How Transportation Affects Real Estate Value*, AIREA, Chicago, March 7, 1969, pp. 12-13.

LANIER, R. S., "Buildings and the Sonic Boom," *The Appraisal Journal*, April, 1968, pp. 251-254.

LEMLY, J. H., *Expressway Influence on Land Use and Value, Atlanta 1941-1956*, Georgia State College of Business Administration, Atlanta, Ga., 1958.

LEVIN, DAVID R, "Highway Transportation Effects on Values," *How Transportation Affects Real Estate Values*, A. I. R. E. A, Chicago, March 7, 1969, pp. 4-8.

LINDOP, JOHN CUMMINGS, "The Effect of Motor Traffic on Real Estate Values," *National Real Estate Journal*, October, 1937, pp. 40-41.

LVIN, C., BELAND, R. DALE, "Outdoor Noise & Metro Environmt Case Study of L. A. with Spec Ref to Aircraft," Los Angeles Dept. of City Planning, Los Angeles, 1970.

MACBRIDE, DEXTER D, "Effects of Freeways on Real Estate Values," *Proceedings Pacific Coast Conference*, Society of Real Estate Appraisers, September 1, 1962.

MACBRIDE, DEXTER D, "Frontage Roads: a Study In Successful Planning for Major Retail Business Development," *Highways and Public Works*, State of California, May 1, 1948.

MARTIN, N. D., "Future of Downtown Parking," *Skyscraper Management*, November, 1970, pp. 20-23.

MARTIN, NORENE DAN, "The Traffic Crunch," *Appraisal Institute Magazine*, Appraisal Institute of Canada, Winnipeg, June 1, 1973.

MARTIN, W. H., "Aviation-Economic Impact on Real Estate," *Appraisal Journal*, April, 1972, pp. 231-234.

MILLER, M. D., "Wings Over the Post-War World," *The Appraisal Journal*, July, 1942, pp. 209, 214.

NUTTING, WALLACE, "Pennsylvania Beautiful," *Pennsylvania Beautiful*, Garden City Publisher, 1935.

OHARE, ROBERT J. M., "Suburban Transportation, Its Impact on Persons and Property," *The Real Estate Appraiser*, December, 1967, pp. 3-11.

PAXTON, KENNETH WAYNE PH. D, *Air Pollution and Property Values In Urban Areas*, The University of Tennessee.

R. G. RIDKER, G. A. HENNING, "Determinants of Residential Property Values with Special Reference to Air Pollution," *Review of Economics and Statistics*, May, 1967, pp. 246-257.

REAL ESTATE ANALYST, THE, "The Development of the Automobile Shopping Center," *Real Estate Analyst Appraisal*, 1949, pp. 517-520.

RENAUD, CLEMENT, "Dommages Aux Residus, Routes Sans Acces," *Appraisal Institute Magazine*, Appraisal Institute of Canada, Winnipeg.

RIGHT OF WAY, "California Pioneers Novel Plan to House Freeway Displaces," *Right of Way*, April, 1971.

SARLES, KENNETH E., "Flexibility of Depreciation," *The Real Estate Appraiser*, January, 1963, pp. 14-18.

SCOTT, JOHN T. JR., "Economic Impact of Industrialization on Traditional Rural Areas," *Journal of the Society of American Farm Managers and Rural Appraisers*, October, 1968, pp. 8-13.

STAPLES, JACK D., "Uniform Relocation Assistance & Real Property Acquisition Policies Act of 1970 P. L. 91-646," *Appraisal & Valuation Manual*, Corporate Press Inc, Wash D. C., January, 1972, pp. 334.

SUTTE, DONALD T. JR. M. A. I., *Appraisal of Roadside Advertising Signs*, American Institute of Real Estate Appraisers, June, 1972.

SWAFFORD, EMMETT, "Demonstration Appraisal of the Effect of an Interstate Highway on Rural Land Vlaue," *Assessment Administration*, IAAO, Chicago, 1965, pp. 126-130.

SWICK, E. H., "The National Interstate and Defense Highway Program," *Right of Way*, August, 1963, pp. 5-8.

TONTI, D. LOUIS, "The Garden State Parkway, Economic Impact In New Jersey," *The Appraisal Journal*, October, 1959, pp. 537-542.

TROAST, PAUL L., "The Effect of Freeways on Property Values," *The Review*, January, 1952, pp. 11, 16-17.

U. S. FEDERAL WORKS AGENCY, *Bibliography on Land Acquisition for Public Roads*, Public Roads Administration, Washington, 1947.

VAN CLEEF, EUGENE, "Locating the Right Industry In the Right Place," *The Appraisal Journal*, April, 1958, pp. 223-226.

WALLACE, DAVID A., "Renaissance In Baltimore," *The Appraisal Journal*, July, 1960, pp. 365-380.

WALTER, K. W., "Community Motor Fuel Needs," *Appraisal Institute Magazine*, Appraisal Institute of Canada, Winnipeg.

WALTON, L. ELLIS FR., "The Interstate System a Return on Investment Analysis: Its Implications for Land Economic Studies," *Right of Way*, February, 1971.

WATERS, L. LESLIE, JOSEPH R. HARTLEY, "The St. Lawrence Seaway-A New Erie Canal?," *The Appraisal Journal*, April, 1957, pp. 223-235.

WELLS, R. L., *Economics of Motor Freight Transportation*, Harvard Business Review,

WENDT, PAUL F., *Influence of Transportation Changes on Urban Landuses and Values*, Institute of Business and Economic Research, Berkeley U of Calif., 1960, pp. 1-13.

WILLIAMS, D. N., "Pay-As-You-Pollute Plan No Limits Just Cash," *Iron Age*, January 14, 1971, pp. 45.

YOUNG, G., "Transportation Industry Converges on the Marketing Man," *Industrial Marketing*, June, 1970, pp. 36-39.

*Automobile Red Book Monthly*, National Market Reports Inc, Chicago Illinois.

*N.A.D.A. Official Used Car Guide Monthly*, National Automobile Dealers Association, Washington Dc.

"How Top Executives View Transportation Industrys Outlook," *Commercial and Financial Chronicle*, September 17, 1970, pp. 787.

"How Transport'n Affects Real Est Vals Papers Pres At Appraisal Institute Seminar for Fed Govt Apprs," American Institute of Real Estate Appraisers, Chicago, March, 1969.

"National Environmental Act of 1969," U S Government Printing Office, Washington Dc, January 1, 1969.

"Noise Abatement and Control, Highway Research Record No. 448," *Highway Research Board, National Research Council*, National Acadamy of Sciences, Washington D.C.

"Transcorp Could Aid Transportation Industry," *Industry Week*, May 25, 1970, pp. 27.

"Zero Population Growth What Effect on Business," *Industry Week*, March 15, 1971, pp. 26.

## 24-12 Traffic

ADKINS, WILLIAM G., "Dallas Expressway Study," *The Residential Appraiser*, April, 1958, pp. 16-24.

ASH, FRED C., "The Appraisal Docket No Compensation for Diversion of Traffic," *The Appraisal Journal*, January, 1957, pp. 108-109.

ATWATER R. B., "Traffic: the Market Indicator," *The Appraisal Journal*, October, 1958, pp. 561-568.

BECKET, WELTON, "Shopping Center Traffic Problems," *Appraisal Journal*, July, 1955, pp. 395-403.

## BIBLIOGRAPHY OF APPRAISAL LITERATURE

BROWN, MAURICE A., "Noise Pollution," *Right of Way,* June, 1970, pp. 40-41.

CAPPOZZA, DENNIS, *Transportation Cost and Urban Retail Trade,* University of Southern California Working Paper 8.

CREEDY, JOHN A., "Navigation, Water Resources, and Patterns of Economic Growth," *How Transportation Affects Real Estate Values,* A. I. R. E. A., Chicago, March 7, 1969, pp. 37-40.

FAIR, E. W., "Parking Lot Headaches," *Banking,* September, 1970, pp. 94.

INDUSTRY WEEK, "Mass Transit Becomes Tool Solving Urban Probs," *Industry Week,* June 8, 1970, pp. 14-16.

LARONGE, JOSEPH, "Traffic Counts," *The Appraisal Journal,* April, 1938, pp. 146-154.

MARTIN, N. D., "Future of Downtown Parking," *Skyscraper Management,* November, 1970, pp. 20-23.

MCNULTY, J. W., "Utility Aspects of Antipollution Taxes," *Public Utilities Fortnightly,* September 10, 1970, pp. 21 24.

MICKLE, D. GRANT, "Effect of Traffic and Parking on Land Use and Value," *Assesment Administration,* IAAO, Chicago, 1956, pp. 6-11.

MILLER, KENNETH C. JR., "Built In Traffic Controls---Master Key to Livable House," *The Residential Appraiser,* September, 1962, pp. 14-16.

ROYAL BANK, "Our Highways and Our Traffic," *Appraisal Institute Magazine,* Appraisal Institute of Canada, Winnipeg.

SUMMER, J. D., "An Analysis of Mississippi River Traffic," *Journal of Land and Public Utility Economics,* November, 1931.

THEISS, WILLIAM R., "The Appraisal Docket. Compensation for Changes In Traffic Patterns," *The Appraisal Journal,* January, 1962, pp. 124-125.

THRIFT, E. W., "Perimeter Roads and Their Functions," *Appraisal Institute Magazine,* Appraisal Institute of Canada, Winnipeg.

WATERS, L. LESLIE, "Free Transit, a Way Out of Traffic Jams," *The Appraisal Journal,* January, 1960, pp. 63-68.

WEISS, W. B., "Is Free Mass Transportation In Down-Town's Future," *Stores,* April, 1971, pp. 51-52.

WENZLICK, ALBERT, "Pedestrian Traffic Chart," *The Real Estate Appraisal,* 1931, pp. 455.

WIEAND, KENNETH FRANKLIN JR. PH. D., *Property Values and Air Pollution A Cross-Section Analysis of the St. Louis Urban Area,* Washington University, 1970.

WILLIAMS, LESLIE, "Appraising Postwar Traffic," *The Appraisal Journal,* October, 1944, pp. 318-326.

WILLIAMS, LESLIE, "Traffic and Housing," *The Appraisal Journal,* October, 1948, pp. 495-500.

"Building Designers Join War on Air Pollution," *Engineering-News Record,* August 19, 1971, pp. 21.

"Federal Tax Incentive for Pollution Control," *New York Certified Public Accountant,* October, 1970, pp. 803-808.

"How Top Executives View Transportation Industrys Outlook," *Commercial and Financial Chronicle,* September 17, 1970, pp. 787.

"Task Force Recommends Tax Relief In Pollution Fight," *Industry Week,* December 14, 1970, pp. 13-14.

## 24-13 Airport

ARMSTRONG, ROBERT H., "The Airport Valuation Problem," *The Appraisal Journal*, October, 1943, pp. 336-345.

BEETH, CHANNING C., "Do Airports Create Obsolescence," *The Real Estate Appraiser*, December, 1953, pp. 3-7.

BEETH, CHANNING C., "Influence of Airports on Residential Values," *The Real Estate Appraiser*, July, 1956, pp. 6-10.

BIBY, JOHN E. JR., "Problems of Airport Expansion," *The Real Estate Appraiser*, September, 1956, pp. 18-21.

BORSAK, GEORGE, "The Influence of Airport Operations on Value of Adjacent Real Estate," *Assessment Administration*, IAAO, Chicago, 1961, pp. 20-26.

BUCK, A. A., "The Airplane Company and the Jet Age," *The Appraisal Journal*, October, 1959, pp. 455-460.

BURGESS, GEORGE W., "Airports In the Balance Sheet of Real Estate Values," *The Appraisal Journal*, January, 1948, pp. 27-34.

CIVIL AERONAUTICS BOARD, "Uniform System of Accounts and Reports for Certificated Route Air Carriers," Civic Aeronautics Board, Washington Dc.

COWLEY, LEONARD M., "Appraising Highways of the Sky," *The Appraisal Journal*, July, 1943, pp. 250-251.

COWLEY, LEONARD M., "The Appraiser Looks at Aviation," *The Appraisal Journal*, January, 1945, pp. 57-61.

EDMAN, J. J., "Airport Owner Not Liable for Low Flying Planes. Appraisal Docket," *The Appraisal Journal*, July, 1961, pp. 410-412.

FEDERAL HOUSING ADMINISTRATION, "FHA Analysis of Residential Properties Near Airports," *The Appraisal Journal*, October, 1961, pp. 538-540.

FEDERAL RESERVE BANK OF CLEVELAND, "Airplanes In Agriculture," *The Appraisal Journal*, October, 1959, pp. 572-577.

FISHER, LEIGH, "Airport Industrial Parks," *Urban Land*, ULI, Washington, D.C., 1966.

FOSTER, JOSEPH A., "The Aiport a Community Asset," *How Transportation Affects Real Estate Values*, Chicago, March 7, 1969, pp. 24-27.

GRICE, ALEXANDER P., "The Effects of Airports on Value," *Valuation*, October, 1962, pp. 10-13.

HAAR, CHARLES M., "Airport Noise and the Urban Dweller: a Proposed Solution," *The Real Estate Appraiser*, pp. 21-26.

HOGAN, LEO E., "Appraisal of a Commercial Airline," *Assessment Administration*, I. A. A. O., Chicago, 1963, pp. 218-222.

HOOVER, I. H., "The Aircraft Noise Problem," *How Transportation Affects Real Estate Values*, AIREA, Chicago, March 7, 1969, pp. 287-331.

INGERMAN, SIDNEY HERBERT, PH. D, *Industrial Growth and Wage Structure formation In the California Peninsula Aerospace Industry*, University of California, Berkely, California, 1970.

KRAECHE, ENNO, "Appraisal of the Value of McDonnell Aircraft Corporation Plant," *Appraisal Reporting Techniques*, 1954, pp. 123-160.

KUCERA, H. P., *The Developing Law of the Jet Airport,* Proceedgs of the 4th Inst on Eminent Domain, Dallas, 1962, pp. 171-196.

LANIER, R. S., "Buildings and the Sonic Boom," *The Appraisal Journal,* April, 1968, pp. 251-254.

LEWIN, GORDON, "Law and Municipal Ecology: Air, Water, Noise, Overpopulation," National Institute of Municipal Law Offices, Washington, D. C..

LVIN, C., BELAND, R. DALE, "Outdoor Noise & Metro Environmt Case Study of L. A. with Spec Ref to Aircraft," Los Angeles Dept. of City Planning, Los Angeles, 1970.

MACDONALD, RICHARD A., "The Airline Company and the Jet Age," *The Appraisal Journal,* October, 1959, pp. 461-464.

MARTIN, W. H., "Aviation-Economic Impact on Real Estate," *Appraisal Journal,* April, 1972, pp. 231-234.

NEISWANGER, DAVID, AND C. L. THOMAS, "Sample Airport Appraisal," *Review of Society of Residential Appraisers,* June, 1941, pp. 7-10.

OCONNOR, THOMAS A., "Airports and Adjacent Realty In the Miami Area," *Assessment Administration,* IAAO, Chicago, 1959, pp. 101-106.

RAMS, EDWIN M., "Airport Buffer Plan," *The Review,* July, 1953, pp. 8-9.

RAMS, EDWIN M., "Airports In Residential Areas," *The Real Estate Appraiser,* October, 1952, pp. 18-22.

RAMS, EDWIN M., "Airports In Residential Areas," *The Review,* October, 1952, pp. 18-22.

RANDALL, WILLIAM J., "Appraisal of Damages to Real Estate Caused by Its Proximity to an Airport Serving Jet Transports," *Real Estate Analyst Appraisal Bulletin,* 1953, pp. 233-236.

REGISTER, NORMAN, "Influence of Airports on Value of Adjacent Real Estate," *Assessment Administration,* Institute of American Appraisers Officers, Chicago, 1959, pp. 96-97.

RESIDENTIAL APPRAISER, "Airport Studies," *The Residential Appraiser,* March, 1957, pp. 13-14.

RIGHT OF WAY, "Right of Way In the Sky," *Right of Way,* June, 1961, pp. 15-25.

SCHMUTZ, GEORGE L., "Valuation of Avigation Easements," *The Appraisal Journal,* October, 1952, pp. 465-472.

SIEJA, EDWARD M., "Airports, Noise and Property," *Assessment Administration,* Institute of American Assessment Officers, Chicago, 1959, pp. 97-101.

STRUNCK, JAMES E., "Avigational Easements--Case Studies," *The Appraisal Journal,* April, 1963, pp. 194-206.

WADLINGTON, I. L., "How to Appraise Airports," *The Appraisal Journal,* July, 1957, pp. 381-390.

WALTHER, H. O., *A Study of the Impact of Airports on the Market Value of Real Estate In Adjacent Areas,* Chicago, 1960.

WALTHER, HERMAN O., "Effect of Jet Airports on Market Value of Vicinage Real Estate," *The Appraisal Journal,* October, 1959, pp. 465-468.

WALTHER, HERMAN O., "Effect of Jet Airports on the Value of Vicinal Real Estate," *Proceedings of the Fourth Institute on Eminent Domain,* 1962, pp. 149-170.

WALTHER, HERMAN O., "Land Values Near Airports," *How Transportation Affects Real Estate Values,* AIREA, Chicago, April 7, 1969, pp. 32-36.

WALTHER, HERMAN O., "Land Values Near Airports," *How Transportation Affects Real Estate Values,* AIREA, Chicago, April 7, 1969, pp. 32-36.

WILLIAMS, CHARLES H., "The Effect of Jet Noise on Residential Areas," *The Residential Appraiser,* August, 1962, pp. 16-18, 24.

"Airport-A Store Design with Entertainment and Efficiency," *Stores,* November, 1970, pp. 4-5.

"How Top Executives View Transportation Industry's Outlook," *Commercial and Financial Chronicle,* September 17, 1970, pp. 787.

"Mass Mutual Life Exchanges Properties In 5 Cities for Site Near Los Angeles Airport," *Insurance,* August 15, 1970, pp. 8.

"Welfare Costs of Monoptimal Airport Utilization," University of Minnesota, 1970.

FEDERAL ACCOUNTING OFFICE, "FAA Rept Rev of Fed Participation in Cost of Airport Projs Involving Donated Lands," *The Real Estate Appraiser,* Federal Accounting Office, November, 1967, pp. 31-38.

## 24-14 Railroads

AMERICAN RIGHT OF WAY ASSOCIATION, "Joint Occupancy of Railroad Right of Way," *Proceedings of the Seventh Annual National Seminar,* Washington, 1961.

BOGEN, J., "Analysis of Railroad Securities," *Principles of Investment,* New York, 1928, pp. 325.

BREWER, HOMER T., "Allocation Problems In Railroad Assessment," *Conference Proceedings,* National Tax Association, Columbus, 1965, pp. 171-178.

CARR, JAMES E., "Inequitable Property Tax Treatment of Railroads," *Conference Proceedings,* National Tax Association, Columbus, 1964, pp. 471-480.

CHAPMAN, CHARLES M., "Property Taxation of Railroad Properties," *Conference Proceedings,* National Tax Association, Columbus, 1959, pp. 252-265.

CLEVELAND, F. A, AND F. W. POWELL, "Railroad Promotion and Capitalization In the U. S," *Principles of Investment,* New York, 1909, CHAPS. I, V, VI, XII, XV, VIII, XI, XVII.

COHEN, LEO, "Recent Railroad Tax Litigations and the Valuation of Railroads," *Conference Proceedings,* National Tax Association, Columbus, 1965, pp. 179-195.

EASTBURN, WALTER N., "Some Aspects of Property Acquisition and Ownership by Railroads," *Technical Valuation,* January, 1949, pp. 10-16, 23-24.

FISHER, DONALD M., "The Western States Study of the Stock and Debt Approach to Railroad and Utility Valuations," *Assessment Administration,* Institute of American Appraisers Officers, Chicago, 1964, pp. 80-90.

FREDERICKS, A. A., "The Plight of the Railroads," *Assessment Administration,* Institute of American Appraisers Officers, Chicago, 1963, pp. 140-142.

INTERSTATE COMMERCE COMMISSION, "Studies Depreciable Rdwy Prop and Equip-Railroads," *Depreciation,* Interstate Commerce Comm, January 1, 1946.

INTERSTATE COMMERCE COMMISSION, "Uniform System of Accounts for Railroad Companies," *System of Accounts,* Interstate Commerce Commission, Washington DC.

JONES, E., "Principles of Railway Transportation," *Principles of Investment,* New York, 1924.

KELLENBERGER, ALLEN N., "Special Assessment Levied Against Railroad Rights-Of-Way," *Conference Proceedings,* National Tax Association, Columbus, 1965, pp. 197-203.

KENNEDY, JAMES C., "Railroad Ad Valorem Taxation -- a Current Appraisal," *Conference Proceedings,* National Tax Association, Columbus, 1963, pp. 602-610.

KIRSHMAN, JOHN EMMETT, "Economics of Railroad Transportation," *Principles of Investment,* 1933, pp. 259.

KIRSHMAN, JOHN EMMETT, "Financial Analysis of Railroads," *Principles of Investment*, 1933, pp. 309.

KONCEL, EDWARD F., "Railroad Operating Property," *Assessment Administration*, IAAO, Chicago, 1961, pp. 248-256.

LAHNER, W. F., "Report of the National Association of Railway Tax Commissions," Pennsylvania Railroad Company, Philadelphia, 1963.

LASSITER, ROY L., "Reproduction Cost As a Basis for Ad Valorem Railroad Taxation," *Public Fortnightly*, October, 1961, pp. 667-672.

MARKS, R. E., "The Railroads and the Super Highways," *Right of Way*, December, 1957, pp. 11-15.

MARTIN, JAMES W., "Progress Toward More Accurate Valuation of Railroads for Taxation," *The Appraisal Journal*, January, 1955, pp. 77-86.

MCCALLUM, J. E., "Electrification of Steam Railroads," *Harvard Business Review*, January, 1930.

MOORE, B. H., "Federal Valuation of Railroads In the U.S.," *Area Bulletin No.503*, American Railway Engineering Association, January 1, 1952.

MUNDY, F. W., "Earning Power of Railroads," *Principles of Investment*, New York, pp. 325.

NATIONAL ASSOCIATION OF TAX ADMINISTRATORS, *Appraisal of Railroadand Other Public Utility Property for Ad Valorem Tax Purposes*, Chicago, 1954.

NELSON, RICHARD L., "New and Important Developments In Right-Of-Way Railroads," *Proceedings of the Eight Annual National Seminar*, American Right of Way Association, Washington, D.C., 1963, pp. 25-28.

NEW JERSEY COMMISSION ON STATE TAX POLICY, *The Railroad Tax Problem*, New Jersey Commission on State Tax Policy, Trenton, New Jersey, May, 1964.

OESTERLE, HARRIS, "Railroad Property," *Assessment Administration*, IAAO, Chicago, 1962, pp. 132-136.

OGDEN, JAMES N., "Railroads Deserve Tax Equality," *Conference Proceedings*, National Tax Association, Columbus, 1960, pp. 377-388.

RALEIGH, JAMES C., "Evaluation of Railroad Siding Availability," *Real Estate Appraiser*, June, 1966, pp. 28-30.

ROBINSON, M. E., "The Evolution of Steam Railroad Electrification," *The Journal of Land and Public Utility Economics*, February, 1932.

SAAW, EUGENE Ea., "Rail Transportation's Effect Upon Real Estate Values," *The Appraisal Journal*, October, 1969, pp. 532-537.

SHEEDAN, DENNIS D., "The Valuation of a Major Railroad," *Case Reports In Assessment Administration*, Institute of American Assessment Officers, Chicago, October, 1959, pp. 54-55.

SHERRINGTON C. E. M., *The Economics of Rail Transportation In Great Britain*, New York, 1928.

SWAIN, H. H., "Economic Aspects of Railroad Receivership," *Principles of Investment*, pp. P, 70.

TAYLOR, FRANK H., "Acquiring Railroad Rights of Way," *National Real Estate Journal*, October, 1931, pp. 12-14.

"Actual Appraisal Repts: No 17 Valuation of 1 Zone of Right of Way of a Rallroad Thru a Farming Sec.," *National Real Estate Journal*, N. R. E. J, December 7, 1931, pp. 15-18.

"How Top Executives View Transportation Industry's Outlook," *Commercial and Financial Chronicle*, September 17, 1970, pp. 787.

"Super Railroads No Supertransportation," *Railway Age*, May 10, 1971, pp. 15.

## 24-15 Highways

ADKINS, WILLIAM G., "Dallas Expressway Study," *The Residential Appraiser,* April, 1958, pp. 16-24.

ADKINS, WILLIAM G., "Effects of the Dallas Central Expressway on Land Values and Land Use," Texas Transportation Institute, College Station, Tex, 1957.

ALEXANDER, ROBERT H., "Interviewing for Freeway Reactions," *The Residential Appraiser,* March, 1958, pp. 3-6.

AMERICAN ASSOCIATION OF STATE HIGHWAY OFFICIALS, *Acquisition for Right of Way,* The Association, Washington, 1962.

AMERICAN INSTITUTE OF ARCHITECTS, "The Highway Isn't Always Right," *The Appraisal Journal,* April, 1966, pp. 295-296.

AMERICAN INSTITUTE OF REAL ESTATE APPRAISERS, "Appraisal of 20 X Road East Lansing Michigan," *Demonstration Appraisal Reports,* American Institute of Real Estate Appraisers, Chicago, 1957, pp. 1-46.

AMERICAN RIGHT OF WAY ASSOCIATION, "Roadside Merchandising Problems," *Proceedings of the Third Annual National Seminar, 1957,* Washington, D. C, 1958.

AMERICAN RIGHT OF WAY ASSOCIATION, "The Appraiser and the Frontage Road," *Proceedings of the First Annual National Seminar, 1955,* Washington, D. C, 1956.

AMERICAN RIGHT OF WAY ASSOCIATION, "The Federal Highway Program and Its Impact," *Proceedings of the Second Annual National Seminar, 1956,* Washington, D. C, 1957.

AMERICAN SOCIETY OF PLANNING OFFICIALS, *Highway-Oriented and Urban Arterial Commercial Areas,* Chicago, Illinois.

ANDERSON JAMES A., "The New Highway Program," *Right of Way,* December, 1956, pp. 34-36.

APPRAISAL DIGEST, "New York State Thruway," *Appraisal Digest,* July, 1955.

ASH, FRED C., "The Appraisal Docket, Right of Access to Limited Access Highway," *The Appraisal Journal,* 1956, pp. 589-590.

ATHERTON E B, "Appraising Noise Damages on Federal-Aid Highway Projects," *The Real Estate Appraiser,* The Society of Real Estate Appraisers, Chicago Illinois, November 1, 1973, pp. 4-8.

ATHERTON, EDWARD B, "Appraising Noise Damages on Federal-Aid Highway Projects," *Valuation Magazine,* American Society of Appraisers, Washington D.C., December 1, 1973, pp. 44-51.

BALDWIN, H. G., "Acquisition of Rights of Way for the New York State Thruway," *Right of Way,* June, 1955, pp. 6-10.

BALFOUR, FRANK C., "America's Highway Problems and Their Likely Effect on Real Estate Markets," *The Appraisal Journal,* October, 1954, pp. 497-524.

BALL, CHARLES, MICHAEL TEITZ, "Expressway and Industrial Location," *The Appraisal Journal,* April, 1959, pp. 203-211.

BEATON, WILLIAM R., THOMAS H. , III, "Service Site Considerations on the Interstate Highway," *The Appraisal Journal,* October, 1968, pp. 559-567.

BISSO, LOUIS, "Acquiring the Rights of Way for the Expressway Program of New Orleans," *Selected Papers of a Right of Way Conference,* University of Alabama, 1956, pp. 59-65.

BRADLEY, CARL H. H., "The Effect of New Roads on Values," *Right of Way,* February, 1961, pp. 41-48.

# BIBLIOGRAPHY OF APPRAISAL LITERATURE

BRAUN, RICHARD L., "Freeways and Cities," *How Transportation Affects Real Estate Values*, A. I. R. E. A, Chicago, March 7, 1969, pp. 9-11.

BROWN, G. FAIRFAX, "Effect of Limited Access Highways on Values of Adjoining Properties," *Assessment Administration*, IAAO, Chicago, 1957, pp. 177-179.

BUFFINGTON, JESSE L., *Case Studies of 25 Remainder Parcels Along Interstate Loop 820 Fort Worth, Texas*, Texas Transportation Interstate, College Station, 1961.

CAMPBELL, ROBERT S., JR., "The Limited Access Highway--Some Aspects of Compensation," *Right of Way*, February, 1963, pp. 29-35.

CARTER, HOUSTON, "The Property Owners Viewpoint on the Road Program," *Right of Way*, April, 1961, pp. 41-43.

CASS, F. M., "Ontario Highway Development Program," *The Appraisal Institute Magazine*, June, 1960, pp. 12-13.

CHAMPION, ROBERT E., "Highway Utility Problems," *Right of Way*, February, 1969, pp. 32-35.

CHRISTIAN, A. H., "Texas Style Freeways and the Closed Corridor Freeways," *Right of Way*, December, 1957, pp. 31-34.

CLARK, GILBERT K., "Appraisal of Freeway Rights of Way Through Industrial Lands," *Valuation*, October, 1954, pp. 29-31.

CLARK, GILBERT K., "Freeway Appraising," *Right of Way*, February, 1955, pp. 5-9.

COHN, JOSEPH D., "Role of Office of Management & Budget In Administration of Uniform Relocation Assist & Land Acquisit," *Appraisal & Valuation Manual*, Corporate Press Inc, January, 1972, pp. 338.

COVEY, FRANK M. JR., "Frontage Roads, to Compensate or Not to Compensate," *The Appraisal Journal*, May, 1963, pp. 236-253.

DAVIS, JERRY C., "The Highway Scandals Four Years Later," *The Real Estate Appraiser*, 1965, pp. 5.

DAVIS, W. D., "9-Point Remainder Study 'Standards'," *Appraisal Institute Magazine*, Appraisal Institute of Canada, Winnipeg.

DAVIS, WILLIAM D., *Site Valuation*, American Association of State Highway Officials, Washington, D. C, 1962, pp. 329-336.

DUKE, RICHARD DE LA BARRE, "The Effect of a Depressed Expressway—A Detroit Case Study," *The Appraisal Journal*, October, 1958, pp. 487-507.

DUNLAP, DONALD C., "Highway and Toll Road Taking," *The Appraisal Journal*, January, 1957, pp. 22-26.

ELDER, HERBERT W., "Land Value Along the Gulf Freeway In Houston, Texas," *The Appraisal Journal*, April, 1953, pp. 223-230.

ELLIS, LESTER J., "The New Federal-Aid Highway Program," *Right of Way*, February, 1957, pp. 39-42.

ENFIELD, C. W., "Federal-State Planned Highway Construction Program, Its Effect on the Right of Way Profession," *Proceedings of the Fourth Annual National Seminar, 1958*, American Right of Way Association, Washington, D. C., 1959, pp. 23-27.

ENFIELD, CLIFTON W., "Highway Appraisal Problems," *The Residential Appraiser*, July, 1960, pp. 3-8.

FICK, H. G. E., "The Roads Are Wider," *Journal of the American Society of Farm Managers and Rural Appraisers*, October, 1956, pp. 32-37.

FLORIDA STATE ROAD DEPARTMENT, "Severance Study Interstate 95," *Valuation*, 1900, pp. 11-21.

FREE, ROBERT L., "Highway Highlights," *The Review*, August, 1953, pp. 3-7.

GOLDEN, JAY S., *Land Values In Chicago Before and After Express-Way Construction*, Chicago Area Transportation Study, Chicago, October, 1968, pp. 65.

GREER, D. C., "Importance and Bebefit of Access Controlled Highways," *Right of Way*, April, 1956, pp. 19-20.

GROETSCH, FOREST L., "Evaluation Fields Cut Up by Highways," *Journal of the American Society of Farm Managers and Rural Appraisers*, October, 1949, pp. 142-144.

GROTECLOSS, EDWARD JR., "Roads and Value," *Technical Valuation*, October, 1958, pp. 29-32.

HADLEY, GEORGE C., "Legal Problems In Highway Acquisition," *The Appraisal Journal*, April, 1953, pp. 165-174.

HADLEY, GEORGE C., "Preparation and Conduct of Highway Condemnation Proceedings," *The Appraisal Journal*, July, 1953, pp. 416-423.

HARTNETT, EDGAR C., "Effect of a Highway on the Market Values of Adjoining Residential Property," *Real Estate Analyst Appraisal Bulletin*, 1961, pp. 73-80.

HARVEY, REESE, "Relation of the State Highway Department to Local Government Units," *Selected Papers*, University of Alabama.

HEANEY, DONALD L., "Valuation of Property for Highways Under Eminent Domain," Automotive Safety Foundation, Washington, 1960.

HELSTAD, ORRIN L., "Appraisal Issues In Highway Condemnation Litigation," *Papers and Proceedings*, Wisconsin Colloquium on Appraisal Research, 1963, pp. 7-12.

HENDRICKS, ROBERT W., "Residential Amenities Along Freeways," *The Resendential Appraiser*, June, 1960, pp. 2-10.

HESS, RUDOLF, "Excess Lands-California's Concept and Conduct of Marginal Land Acquisition," *Right of Way*, December, 1962, pp. 31-46.

HESS, RUDOLF, "Land Economic Studies," *Proceedings of the Fifth Annual National Seminar*, American Right of Way Association, Washington, D. C., 1960.

HESS, RUDOLF, "Relocation of People and Homes from Freeway Rights of Way--Community Effects," *The Residential Appraiser*, April, 1962, pp. 2-10.

HESS, RUDOLF, "The Effect of Access Controlled Highways on Abutting and Adjacent Properties," *Selected Papers*, Right of Way Conference, University of Ala., 1957.

HIGHWAY RESEARCH BOARD, *Highway Access*, Acquisition for Right-Of-Way, Washington, D. C., 1962.

HIGHWAY RESEARCH BOARD, *Scenic Easements--Legal Administrative and Valuation Problems and Procedures*, Washington, D. C..

HIGHWAY RESEARCH BOARD, NATIONAL ACADEMY OF SCIENCE, "The Highwayman Isn't All Bad," National Academy of Science, pp. 670100.

HOOKER, RAYMOND W., KENNETH R. POTTER, *The Impact of a New Interstate Highway on a Corridor and Input-Output Analysis*, University of Wyoming, January, 1971.

HOOVER, RICHARD I., "Appraisal for a Highway Department," *The Appraisal Journal*, July, 1960, pp. 359-363.

HUNTLEY, GENE, "The Community Benefit of By-Pass Highways," *Right of Way*, June, 1957, pp. 29-32.

JEFFERSON, GEORGE T., "A History of Highways," *The Residential Appraisers*, March, 1959, pp. 16-19.

KALTENBACH, HENRY J., "The Bureau of Public Roads, and Its Relation to Right of Way Acquisition," *Right of Way*, August, 1956, pp. 31-34.

KALTENBACH, HENRY J., "The Federal Highway Program and Its Significance to Real Estate," *The Appraisal Journal*, July, 1956, pp. 377-384.

KELLEY, JOHN F., "Motel and Freeways," *Valuation Manual*, 1955, pp. 35.

KELLEY, JOHN F., "Motels and Freeways," *Technical Valuation*, June, 1954, pp. 7-17.

KELLEY, JOHN F., "Residences and Freeways," *The Appraisal Journal*, October, 1957, pp. 505-520.

KOSHAL, RAJINDAR K., "Highway Investments and Externalities a Case Study of Ohio," *Bulletin of Business Research,* Ohio State University, March, 1971, pp. 4 5.

LEMLY, J. H., *Expressway Influence on Land Use and Value, Atlanta 1941-1956,* Georgia State College of Business Administration, Atlanta, Ga., 1958.

LEVIN, DAVID R, "Highway Transportation Effects on Values," *How Transportation Affects Real Estate Values,* A. I. R. E. A, Chicago, March 7, 1969, pp. 4-8.

LEVIN, DAVID R., "Highway Interchange Areas," *Right of Way,* June, 1962, pp. 13-18.

LEVIN, DAVID R., "Report on the Scenic Roads and Parkways Study," *Right of Way,* February, 1968, pp. 25-29.

LEVIN, DAVID R., "Some Aspects of Right-Of-Way Acquisition for Federal-Aid Highway Purposes," *Appraisal and Valuation Manual,* American Society of Appraisers, 1962, pp. 28-37.

LEVIN, DAVID R., "The Joint Use Concept and Urban Freeway Development," *The Appraisal Journal,* July, 1968, pp. 409-411.

LEWIS, H. J., "Policy Problems of Alabama State Highway Department In Right of Way Acquisition," *Selected Papers,* Right of Way Conference, University of Alabama, 1961, pp. 138-145.

LORENS, EDWARD R., "Appraisal of Farm Property for Trunk Highway Right of Way In Minnesota," *Right of Way,* February, 1959, pp. 31-34.

LORENS, EDWARD R., "Requirements of Highway Department Appraisals," *Journal of the American Society of Farm Managers and Rural Appraisers,* April, 1961, pp. 59-62.

LOWRIE, THOMAS R., "New-Jersey Turnpike Program of Acquisition of Right-Of-Way," *Right of Way,* August, 1954, pp. 5-8.

MACBRIDE, DEXTER D, "Effects of Freeways on Real Estate Values," *Proceedings Pacific Coast Conference,* Society of Real Estate Appraisers, September 1, 1962.

MACBRIDE, DEXTER D, "Frontage Roads: a Study In Successful Planning for Major Retail Business Development," *Highways and Public Works,* State of California, May 1, 1948.

MACBRIDE, DEXTER D, "Highways and Non-User Benefits," *Right of Way Magazine,* American Right of Way Assn, Los Angeles, April 1, 1960.

MACBRIDE, DEXTER D, "Interface: Condemnation, Appraising, Right of Way, Public Works, Administration," *Valutape Audio-Library Series,* American Society of Appraisers, Washington D.C., January 1, 1973.

MACDONALD, E. M., "Rights of Way-Freeway," *Technical Evaluation,* American Society of Appraisers, October, 1954, pp. 25.

MARGETIS, NICHOLAS M., "Roadside Regulations and Controls," *Acquisition for Right of Way,* American Association of State Highway Officials, Washington, D. C, 1962, pp. 603-629.

MARKS, R. E., "The Railroads and the Super Highways," *Right of Way,* December, 1957, pp. 11-15.

MAXWELL, GEORGE I., "Severance Damages In Highway Appraisals," *Journal of the American Society of Farm Managers and Rural Appraisers,* October, 1958, pp. 23-26.

MACGARRY, THOMAS F., "On the Joint Development of Urban Housing and Urban Freeways," *The Appraisal Journal,* January, 1967, pp. 119-122.

MCDONALD, ADRIAN F., "Expressways and Real Estate Values," *The Review,* February, 1953, pp. 10-16, 14-20.

MCGOUGH, B. C., "Impact of Highway Improvements on Land Values As Observed In Two Florida Studies," *Right of Way,* December, 1965, pp. 37-48.

MCGOUGH, B. C., "Methodology for Highway Impact Studies," *The Appraisal Journal,* January, 1968, pp. 65-72.

MCGOUGH, BOBBY C., "A Treatise on Highway Impact," *Right of Way,* June, 1968, pp. 40-45.

MOBLEY, H. H., "Roadside Merchandising Problems," American Right of Way Association, 1958, pp. 44-45.

MORTIMER, J. R., "Highway Right of Way Valuation," *Journal; American Society of Farm Managers and Rural Appraisers,* April, 1959, pp. 65-68.

MOSS, HUNTER, "Appraising Motor Courts," *The Appraisal Journal,* pp. 235-242.

MOSS, HUNTER, "Special Knowledge Required In Appraising Motor Courts," *Appraisal Digest,* October, 1952, pp. 14-16.

NUSBAUM, ROGER F., "Highway Beautification Program," *Right of Way,* August, 1966, pp. 36-40.

NUTTER, C. ARMEL, "The Highway System and Appraisers," *The Residential Appraiser,* May, 1961, pp. 18-21.

NUTTING, WALLACE, "Pennsylvania Beautiful," *Pennsylvania Beautiful,* Garden City Publisher, 1935.

PECK, HOMER M., "Scenic Areas Along Wisconsin Highways," *Right of Way,* October, 1967, pp. 18-22.

PHILLIPS, C. W., "Relation of the Bureau of Public Roads to the State Highway Department," *Selected Papers, 1956,* Right of Way Conference, Alabama, 1956.

PINNELL, W. GEORGE, "An Alternate Approach to Highway Partial Takings," *The Appraisal Journal,* January, 1961, pp. 17-52.

PRYOR, FRANCIS D., "Appraisals for Public Road Acquisition," *Technical Valuation,* June, 1960, pp. 5-10.

RATCLIFF, RICHARD UPDEGRAFF, *Real Estate Valuation and Highway Condemnation Awards,* Univ of Wisconsin, Graduate School of Business, Madison, 1966.

REID, WILLIAM L., "Utility Relocations In New Highway Construction," *Right of Way,* June, 1969, pp. 36-37, 40-41.

RIGHT OF WAY, "California Pioneers Novel Plan to House Freeway Displaces," *Right of Way,* April, 1971.

RIGHT OF WAY, "Report of Highway Research Board," *Right of Way,* June, 1969, pp. 29-30.

ROBERTS, AUSTIN, L. JR., "The Impact of the Highway Program on Utilities," *Right of Way,* October, 1957, pp. 29-33.

ROSENCRANS, DANIEL W., "Title Searches and Title Examinations for Highway Right of Ways, As Title Companies See it," *Right of Way,* April, 1954, pp. 15-19, 56-57.

SANDO, LAURENCE, "Highway Land Acquisition In the United States," *The Appraisal Journal,* April, 1969, pp. 165-176.

SCHOFER, AUGUST, "Impact of the Highway Program from the National Viewpoint," *Right of Way,* April, 1963, pp. 53-57.

SMITH, CARL S., "Effect of Limited Access Highway on Values of Adjoining Properties," *Assessment Administration,* IAAO, Chicago, 1957, pp. 176-177.

SMITH, LAMAR H., "After Value Support for Highway Taking Remainders," *The Appraisal Journal,* January, 1965, pp. 93-99.

SMITH, LAMAR H., "Appraisal for Highway Acquisitions," *The Appraisal Journal,* April, 1964, pp. 203-208.

STANTON, BEN E., "Economic Impact Studies of Highway Construction," *The Appraisal Journal,* July, 1962, pp. 339-404.

STAPLES, JACK D., "Uniform Relocation Assistance & Real Property Acquisition Policies Act of 1970 P. L. 91-646," *Appraisal & Valuation Manual,* Corporate Press Inc, Wash D. C., January, 1972, pp. 334.

SUTTE, DONALD T. JR. *Appraisal of Roadside Advertising Signs,* American Institute of Real Estate Appraisers, June, 1972.

SUTTE, DONALD T. JR., *Appraisal of Roadside Advertising Signs,* American Institute of Real Estate Appraisers, June, 1972.

SWAFFORD, EMMETT, "Demonstration Appraisal of the Effect of an Interstate Highway on Rural Land Value," *Assessment Administration,* IAAO, Chicago, 1965, pp. 126-130.

SWICK, E. H., "The National Interstate and Defense Highway Program," *Right of Way,* August, 1963, pp. 5-8.

SYCHRAVA, L., "Some Thoughts on Feasibility Studies Occasioned by The Appraisal of Road Projects In Thailand," *Journal of Transport Economies and Policy,* September, 1968.

TAYLOR, RICHARD H., "Advantages of a Practical Liason Between Highways, Utilities and Other Affected Agencies," *Selected Papers, Right of Way Conference,* University of Alabama, 1959, pp. 35-38.

THIEL, FLOYD I., "Progress In Highway Severance Studies," *Right of Way,* April, 1966, pp. 25-29.

THRIFT, ERIC W., "Perimeter Roads and Their Functions," *Appraisal Institute Magazine,* January, 1959, pp. 12-18.

TROAST, PAUL L., "The Effect of Freeways on Property Values," *The Review,* January, 1952, pp. 11, 16-17.

U. S. FEDERAL WORKS AGENCY, *Bibliography on Land Acquisition for Public Roads,* Public Roads Administration, Washington, 1947.

VAN DEUSEN, FRANCIS B., "Expressway Experience," *The Review,* May, 1954, pp. 3-5.

VANDERPOOL, TOM, "Appraising Access or Abutter's Rights," *Journal of the American Society of Farm Managers and Rural Appraisers,* October, 1956, pp. 38-42.

VANDERPOOL, TOM, "Highways and Buy-Ways," *The Appraisal and Valuation Manual,* 1958, pp. 337-342.

WAGNER, E. F., "Appraising Properties for Freeway Acquistion," *Technical Valuation,* October, 1954, pp. 23-24.

WELLS, REX I., "Guidelines for Environmental Considerations In the Federal Highway Program," *Appraisal and Valuation Manual,* Corporate Press Incorporated, Washington, D. C, January, 1972, pp. 328.

WHITT, GLENN L., "Policy and Procedure on Relocation of Utility Facilities-California Division of Highways," *Right of Way,* June, 1963, pp. 13-16.

WOLDEN, RUSSELL L., "The Impact of Freeways and Redevelopments on the Assessments Roll," *Technical Valuation,* October, 1959, pp. 35-37.

WRIGHT, CARROLL, "Appraisal of Rural Lands for Highway Improvements," *The Appraisal Journal,* January, 1959, pp. 88-94.

ZETTEL, RICHARD M., "The Effect of Limited--Access Highways on Property and Business Values," *Right of Way,* June, 1954, pp. 9-12, 41-45.

"Advantages of a Practical Liasion Between Highways, Utilities and Other Affected Agencies," *Right of Way Conference Selected Papers,* University of Alabama, Alabama, 1959, pp. 31-34.

## 24-16 Beautification

GARRISON, WILLIAM L., M. MERTZ, *Influence of Highway Improvements on Urban Land*, U of Wash., Dept of Geography Vol. V, Seattle, 1958.

KALTENBACH, HENRY J., "The Bureau of Public Roads, and Its Relation to Right of Way Acquisition," *Right of Way*, August, 1956, pp. 31-34.

KOSHAL, RAJINDAR K., "Highway Investments and Externalities a Case Study of Ohio," *Bulletin of Business Research*, Ohio State University, March, 1971, pp. 4 5.

LORENS, E. R., "The Highway Beautification Act of 1965," *The Real Estate Appraiser*, November, 1966, pp. 2-13.

PATRICK, R. W., "Need for Environmental and Aesthetic Feasibility Studies," *Right of Way*, February, 1971.

PECK, HOMER M., "Scenic Areas Along Wisconsin Highways," *Right of Way*, October, 1967, pp. 18-22.

## 24-17 Automobiles

AMERICAN TRANSIT ASSOCIATION, "Classification of Accounts for Bus Operating Companies," *Transit Bulletin*, American Transit Association.

CAPPOZZA, DENNIS, *Transportation Cost and Urban Retail Trade*, University of Southern California Working Paper 8.

FAIR, E. W., "Parking Lot Headaches," *Banking*, September, 1970, pp. 94.

HAYES, R. W., "Man and His Car Are Not Soon Parted So Parking Layout Is a Vital Element In Development Planning," *House and Home*, September, 1971, pp. 50.

MCMICHAEL, STANLEY L., "The Influence of the Automobile on Real Estate," *National Association of Real Estate Boards, Annals*, 1928, pp. 204-219.

MCREYNOLDS, TOM, "Appraising an Automobile Laundry," *Encyclopedia of Real Estate Appraising*, 1959, pp. 563-570.

METZ, ERIC RUDOLF, "Utility Analysis and the Selection of an Automobile Collision Insurance Deductible," *Dissertation Abstracts International*, January, 1971.

REVIEW, THE, "Automobile Facilities for Modern Subdivisions," *The Review*, April, 1951, pp. 8-10.

WYCOFF, F. C., "Capital Depreciation In the Postwar Period Automobiles," *Review of Economics of Statistics*, May, 1970, pp. 168-172.

*N.A.D.A. Official Used Car Guide Monthly*, National Automobile Dealers Association, Washington Dc.

## 24-18 Bridges

KAHN, SANDERS A., "George Washington Bridge Approach, a Case Study," *The Appraisal Journal*, July, 1966, pp. 461-162.

WHITE, JOHN ROBERT, "George Washington Bridge Approach, a Case Study," *The Appraisal Journal*, January, 1966, pp. 32-40.

## 24-19 Rapid Transit

AMERICAN TRANSIT ASSOCIATION, "Classification of Accounts for Bus Operating Companies," *Transit Bulletin*, American Transit Association.

HEENAN, G. WARREN, "The Economic Effect of Rapid Transit on Real Estate Development," *The Appraisal Journal*, April, 1968, pp. 212-224.

MACDONALD, E. M., "Rights of Way-Freeway," *Technical Valuation*, American Society of Appraisers, October, 1954, pp. 25.

MULDOON, JOSEPH, "Valuation Challenges of a New Rapid Transit System," *How Transportation Affects Real Estate Values*, A.I.R.E.A., Chicago, March 7, 1969, pp. 19-20.

SMITH, R. GILMAN, "Is Public Transit Expendable," *The Appraisal Journal*, July, 1958, pp. 341-344.

SPENGLER, E. H., *Land Valued In New York In Relation to Transit Facilities*, Columbia University Press, New York, 1930.

WELLS, R. L., *Economics of Motor Freight Transportation*, Harvard Business Review,

## 24-20 Truck Terminal

WOEHLER, ELMER C., "Over the Road to Truck Terminal Appraising," *The Appraisal Journal*, January, 1963, pp. 107-114.

## CHAPTER FIFTEEN

# Government Property and Concerns
by Norman E. Lauer, ASA, MAI, MBA.

Norman E. Lauer, graduated cum laude from Gonzaga University, Spokane, Washington, with a degree of Bachelor of Business Administration; he has received a Master of Business Administration Degree from the Wharton School of Finance, University of Pennsylvania, and has college majors in economics, accounting, philosophy, and banking and finance.

He began his real estate career with The Penn Mutual Life Insurance Company as a real estate analyst, specializing in purchase-leaseback transactions in the mortgage loan department. In 1958, he accepted an assignment with the General Services Administration in Washington, D.C., as real estate appraiser, where he advanced to Deputy Chief Appraiser, Public Buildings Service and, finally, in 1963, to Chief Appraiser, Region III, General Services Administration, Washington, D.C. Moving to the Department of Justice, he became Chief Appraiser for the Department in 1972.

Mr. Lauer obtained his MAI designation in 1962 and became a Senior Member of the American Society of Appraisers in 1971. He is a member of the faculty of American University School of Business Administration, and is an instructor for the American Institute of Real Estate Appraisers.

▲ **Government Property**

THE PURPOSE of this introduction is not to extol the many virtues of the American Society of Appraisers or this valuable book which has resulted from the Society's efforts. Rather, an attempt will be made to show the magnitude and diversity of the real estate function in the Federal sector and to define the role of the staff appraiser and the part he plays in managing these assets for the common good. A parallel spectrum of projects, functions and responsibilities exists in State, Regional, City, County governments; while this commentary examines but one of the strata, the importance and interdependence of each level are patent and must be understood if the total concept of "Government Property and Concerns" is to be fully recognized.

The General Services Administration has compiled some revealing and exciting statistics relative to the quantity and cost of real estate owned and leased by the Federal Government. A summary is presented below.

## Summary
### Real Estate Owned As Of June 30, 1972

| Item | Inside United States | Outlying Areas of United States | Foreign countries | Total |
| --- | ---: | ---: | ---: | ---: |
| Number of installations[1] | 20,643 | 199 | 328 | 21,170 |
| Total acres | 760,676,388 | 553,510 | 5,720 | 761,235,618 |
| Number of buildings[2] | 403,323 | 4,297 | 2,786 | 410,406 |
| Building floor area[2] (thousands of square feet) | 2,483,667 | 16,841 | 19,703 | 2,520,211 |
| Total cost (thousands of dollars) | 75,408,203 | 2,501,131 | 4,757,554 | 82,666,888 |

[1] Excludes Department of Defense (military functions) in Alaska, Hawaii, outlying areas of the United States and foreign countries.
[2] Excludes Department of Defense (military functions) in outlying areas of the United States and foreign countries.

## Summary
Real Estate Leased as of June 30, 1972

| Item | Inside United States | Outlying areas of United States | Foreign countries | Total |
|---|---:|---:|---:|---:|
| Number of leases[1] | 61,317 | 325 | 6,884 | 68,526 |
| Total acres | 1,370,948 | 11,830 | 307,681 | 1,690,459 |
| Number of building locations[1] | 48,910 | 283 | 10,008 | 59,201 |
| Building floor area[1] | 179,834,470 | 872,747 | 19,493,087 | 200,200,304 |
| Annual rental | $463,840,060 | $2,452,562 | $61,912,312 | $528,204,934 |

[1] Excludes Department of Defense (military functions) in outlying areas of the United States and in foreign countries.

These figuress are without comparative orientation, since similar statistics on the private sector are not presented. However, they do show, with only a moment's thought and contemplation, that the real property function of the Federal Government takes on monumental proportion. How is this vast workload divided?

The Bureau of Land Management, through the Department of the Interior, administers 539,165,803.2 acres of the total land owned by the United States. Of this amount, 471,631,492 acres represent public domain land, the balance having been acquired by purchase, donation, etc. Much of this land is used by cattle ranchers throughout the west for grazing and recreation through lease and permits from BLM. BLM, by far, administers the greatest proportion of Federal land.

Several of the Government agencies, such as Forest Service, through the Department of Agriculture, Fish and Wildlife Service and the National Park Service, through the Department of the Interior, and the Department of Defense, also administer large areas of the public domain. However, these agencies have also acquired large holdings by direct purchase as a result of carrying out their assigned functions. The Corps of Engineers, for example, has several large public works programs going forward at all times and these projects, involving flood control, improvement of navigation, harbor improvement, etc., require the purchase of thousand of acres of land and improvements each year. The types of property purchased are unbelievable but schools, cemeteries, railroads, grain elevators, gas stations, stores, hot dog stands, curio stands, amusement parks, commercial fish farms, cold storage plants, mining properties, sand and gravel deposits, and oil wells are among them. The acquisition of these properties is often complicated by existing leases, life estates, divided interests, missing or unknown heirs, inadequate legal description and the special purpose nature of the property itself.

One of the functions of the General Services Administration is the acquisition of sites for Federal office buildings. These usually involve urban property and can range in size from a few thousand square feet to several acres. Since these sites are often located on the fringe of the downtown central area, assemblage again usually involves a number of different type improvements which seldom develops the property to its highest and best use.

General Services Administration also conducts one of the largest leasing operations in the Government and is exceeded only by the United States Postal Service in this regard. As of June 30, 1972, GSA was managing 7,795 leases involving annual rental of approximately 246 million dollars.

Although the Department of Defense disposes of much of its surplus property which originates overseas, GSA has predominate responsibility in the states for the sale of both real and related surplus personal government property. Much of the real property involves special purpose manufacturing plants or military facilities which are excess to the needs of the service or which are technologically obsolete. The related personal property ranges from bulldozers to cotter pins; from automobiles to ambulances.

The foregoing discussion points out some of the agencies which handle much of the in-house real estate activity for the Government. In addition, there are several agencies which perform real estate activities not directly related to the Government's ownership or leasing of property. Reference is made to the Federal Housing Administration and the Veterans Administration which, over their years of existence, have insured and guaranteed millions of dollars of mortgage credit. The Small Business Administration, as the name implies, makes direct loans to small businessmen who as yet do not have a sufficient credit rating or size to go directly to the private capital markets of the country.

The Internal Revenue Service, in the processing of income tax returns, is often confronted with the valuation of stocks and bonds, good will and other intangibles, objects d'art, gifts of all kinds to nonprofit organizations, and many other items of real and personal property. These problems often arise because of a dispute between the Revenue Service and the taxpayer as to the value of an item claimed as a tax deduction.

This brief summary of a part of the activities of some of the agencies of the Federal Government is sufficient to show that the property involved covers the full spectrum and, if spoken of in terms of valuation, the property involved covers all of the major appraisal disciplines.

The management of this workload requires thousands of Federal employees with many specialties and, among these specialties is the professional appraiser — numbering approximately 3,000. The workload and responsibility of these men is very large for virtually all actions taken in regard to the purchase, sale, leasing or any other action pertaining to real or personal property which involves monies of the Federal Treasury, are supported by approved appraisal reports.

It is the responsibility of the staff appraisers and their supervisors to prepare appraisal reports which truly reflect the apposite kind of value or estimated cost information requested by their organizational superiors.

In those instances where appraisal contracts are let with appraisers outside the Government, it is the responsibility of the supervising appraiser to see that the fee for the assignment is reasonable and that the submitted appraisal report fully and factually supports the estimated value.

In order to insure that the public, as well as the Government, is properly protected in matters of valuation, the selection of appraisers is based on a thorough investigation of the prospective appraiser's character, education, background, and experience. A college education, as well as several years' experience is generally required for the minimum grade of journeyman staff appraiser.

It is noted with pride that some of the officials of the Federal Government have set the pace for excellence of workmanship in the profession of appraising, and the acquisition of real property. In-house training seminars are regularly scheduled, and most

Federal appraisers are given the advantage of attending the outstanding appraisal courses offered by the American Society of Appraisers (ASA), The American Institute of Real Estate Appraisers (MAI), and the Society of Real Estate Appraisers (SREA).

Moreover, at least some of the chief appraisers in the Government encourage their staff appraisers to achieve professional status by actively working towards membership in one or more of the above appraisal societies. It is unfortunate that there are still those who, through ignorance or ineptness, do not see the advantage of working towards professional excellence, or assisting the individuals on their staff in achieving their highest potential.

In addition to training programs and appraisal courses, two recent Government publications have been widely accepted as guides to improving the appraisal process and the acquisition of real property. They are the *Uniform Appraisal Standards for Federal Land Acquisitions*, and *A Procedural Guide for the Acquisition of Real Property by Governmental Agencies*.

Finally, the staff appraisers throughout the country must cope with what some have termed a 'quiet revolution' in land use in the switch from private control to greater public control of this resource. Many private entrepreneurs are giving greater thought to the social and environmental impact of their developments voluntarily, while others are being forced to cooperate by public laws and public opinion. This new "land ethic" has implications that reach far beyond land itself.

It is already affecting millions of people — what they can do with their property, where they can build or buy new homes, how close they will be living to industry, power plants and shopping centers.

It involves the development of new governmental mechanisms; altered local-state and state-federal relationships; and above all concerned public consideration of how people want the country to look and function in years to come.

Hundreds of articles and books have been written about these problems, and it is the obligation of the appraiser to sift through them and find those that will assist him in the solution of his appraisal problems. With the writing so widespread, it has become an almost impossible task to know what has been written and where to find it. With the typical shortage of personnel on the appraisal staffs throughout the Government, time is of the essence. This new Bibliography of Appraisal Literature will be of great and lasting benefit to the appraiser, as well as the other disciplines which are a part of the valuation function and profession throughout the country.

# Government Property

25-11  Military Installations and Facilities
25-12  Military Reservations
25-13  Firing Range
25-14  Missile Site
25-15  Naval Yard

## 25-11 Military Installations and Facilities

CLARK, RAMSEY, "The Appraiser's Role In Federal Lands," *The Real Estate Appraiser,* The Real Estate Appraiser.

DAVIS, W. D., "A Critical Analysis of Government Appraising," *The Residential Appraiser,* January, 1961, pp. 3-5.

FEDERAL RESERVE BANK OF BOSTON, "Economic Impact of a Military Base," *The Appraisal Journal,* October, 1961, pp. 535-538.

FEDERAL RESERVE BANK OF ST. LOUIS, "Trends In Government Expenditures," *The Appraisal Journal,* January, 1961, pp. 115-119.

FEDERAL TAX ADMINISTRATION, *State and Local Tax Status of Military Housing Programs,* Federation of Tax Administrators, Chicago, 1956.

FEDERATION OF TAX ADMINISTRATORS, *Federal Property Reservations and State and Local Property Taxes,* Federation of Tax Administrators, Chicago, 1960.

FLICK, JOHN E., "State Tax Liability of Servicemen and Their Dependents," *Washington and Lee Law Review,* 1964, pp. 22-47.

FREEDLAND, FRED, "Rights of Way on and Across Department of the Army Lands," *Right of Way,* February, 1956, pp. 5-6.

GOODRICH, HAROLD S., "Appraising for Army Land Acquisition," *The Appraisal Journal,* July, 1951, pp. 355-364.

GURNEE, MARK S., "Utility Relocations and the U. S. Army Corps of Engineers," *Right of Way,* December, 1963, pp. 17-20.

KNIGHT, C., "Military Launches Housing Attack-First Modulars Move In with General Electric In Command," *House and Home,* February, 1971, pp. 20.

LITTELL, NORMAN M., "Lands for War Purposes," *The Appraisal Journal,* January, 1943, pp. 15-22.

MARPLES, RICHARD A, "Appraisal Practices In the U.S. Army Corps of Engineers," *Valutape Audio-Library Series,* American Society of Appraisers, Washington D.C., January 1, 1973.

PARRY, J. F., J. A. HEGINBOTTOM, W. R. COWAN, "Terrain Evaluation In Mobility Studies for Military Vehicles," *Land Evaluation,* pp. 160.

PORTER, PAUL W., "Navy Planning In San Diego Reviewed by Engineering Chief," *Right of Way,* August, 1955, pp. 25-26.

U. S. ARMY CORPS OF ENGINEERS, *Real Property Appraiser's Handbook,* U. S. Army Corps of Engineers, Washington, 1956.

"Corps to Construct Dam In Existing Reservoir," *Engineering News Record,* September 24, 1970, pp. 12.

"Date Processing Serves Many Government Needs," *Modern Government,* September, 1964, pp. 43-51.

"G. I. Appraisal Service," *The Review,* July, 1945, pp. 11-12.

"Government Accounting, Auditing, and Financial Reporting," *Governmental Accounting,* Municipal Finance Officers Association, Ann Arbor Mich., January 1, 1968.

▲ Government Property

## 25-12 Military Reservations

CLARK, RAMSEY, "The Appraiser's Role In Federal Lands," *The Real Estate Appraiser,* The Real Estate Appraiser.

DAVIS, W. D., "A Critical Analysis of Government Appraising," *The Residential Appraiser,* January, 1961, pp. 3-5.

FEDERAL RESERVE BANK OF ST. LOUIS, "Trends In Government Expenditures," *The Appraisal Journal,* January, 1961, pp. 115-119.

FREEDLAND, FRED, "Rights of Way on and Across Department of the Army Lands," *Right of Way,* February, 1956, pp. 5-6.

KNIGHT, C., "Military Launches Housing Attack-First Modulars Move In with General Electric In Command," *House and Home,* February, 1971, pp. 20.

MARPLES, RICHARD A, "Appraisal Practices In the U.S. Army Corps of Engineers," *Valutape Audio-Library Series,* American Society of Appraisers, Washington D.C., January 1, 1973.

PARRY, J. F., J. A. HEGINBOTTOM, W. R. COWAN, "Terrain Evaluation In Mobility Studies for Military Vehicles," *Land Evaluation,* pp. 160.

RANDALL, WILLIAM J., "The Appraisal of Privately Owned Housing on Military Reservations," *Real Estate Analyst Appraisal Bulletin,* 1956, pp. 327-332.

U. S. ARMY CORPS OF ENGINEERS, *Real Property Appraiser's Handbook,* U. S. Army Corps of Engineers, Washington, 1956.

## 25-13 Firing Range

CLARK, RAMSEY, "The Appraiser's Role In Federal Lands," *The Real Estate Appraiser,* The Real Estate Appraiser.

DAVIS, W. D., "A Critical Analysis of Government Appraising," *The Residential Appraiser,* January, 1961, pp. 3-5.

## 25-14 Missile Site

CLARK, RAMSEY, "The Appraiser's Role In Federal Lands," *The Real Estate Appraiser,* The Real Estate Appraiser.

DAVIS, W. D., "A Critical Analysis of Government Appraising," *The Residential Appraiser,* January, 1961, pp. 3-5.

FEDERAL RESERVE BANK OF ST. LOUIS, "Trends In Government Expenditures," *The Appraisal Journal,* January, 1961, pp. 115-119.

NEALEY, MORGAN T. JR., "Acquisition of Lands for NASA's Manned Lunar Landing Program, Cape Canaveral, Florida," *Right of Way,* October, 1963, pp. 7-12.

WHEELER, MORGAN, "Acquisition of Land Interests for Nation's First Minutemen Missile Installation In Montana," *R. O.W.,* October, 1964, pp. 9-15.

## 25-15 Naval Yard

CLARK, RAMSEY, "The Appraiser's Role In Federal Lands," *The Real Estate Appraiser*, The Real Estate Appraiser.

FEDERAL RESERVE BANK OF ST. LOUIS, "Trends In Government Expenditures," *The Appraisal Journal*, January, 1961, pp. 115-119.

PORTER, PAUL W., "Navy Planning In San Diego Reviewed by Engineering Chief," *Right of Way*, August, 1955, pp. 25-26.

# Index of Authors

# Index of Authors

AAMODT, OTARM, 19-13.
AARON, H., 12-11, 13-11, 13-18.
AARON, JOSEPH, 13-22.
ABBOT, ACTOR T. JR., 12-16, 16-11.
ABBOUD, SAMIR, 11-11, 11-14, 11-19.
ABDEL-BADDIE F E, 11-11, 11-14, 14-11.
ABDOU, ELSAYED ALI PH. D., 12-23.
ABEL, HAROLD, 13-11, 14-15, 14-18, 14-21.
ABEL, VICTOR D., 21-11, 21-14.
ABELMANN, W. W., 19-15.
ABELMANN, WILLAM W., 13-15.
ABELMANN, WILLIAM W., 11-11, 11-19, 12-19, 22-18.
ABERTHAW CO., 13-20, 21-13.
ABRAHAMS, BASIL GEORGE, 22-19.
ABRAMS, CHARLES, 12-11, 12-13, 13-17, 13-19, 22-21.
ABSUAGA, MIGUEL A., 11-11, 12-24, 19-15.
ACCREDITED RURAL APPRAISERS, 12-14.
ACHENSTEIN, ASHER, 13-13.
ACKERMAN, ALAN L., 12-14.
ACKERMAN, JAMES S., 18-12.
ACKROYD, P. H., 11-11, 11-19.
ACOLIA, GEORGE R., 12-13, 13-19.
ADAMS, J., 12-24, 16-11.
ADAMS, JOHN C. JR., 20-11.
ADAMS, JOHN F. JR., 11-11, 11-19.
ADAMS, LEWIS W., 13-19.
ADAMS, PAUL, 11-11, 11-19, 12-11.
ADAMS, R. L., 14-11.
ADAMS, RICHARD L., 14-12, 14-15.
ADAMS, THOMAS, 13-11, 22-19.
ADAMS, THOMAS S., 12-11.
ADAMS, WESLEY, 12-14, 12-26.
ADDINGTON, WENDELL G., 13-19.
ADELBERG, JOHN, 13-13.
ADELSBERG, HYMAN, 11-11, 11-12, 11-14, 11-18, 12-11, 12-14, 13-15.
ADELSBERG, HYMAN, 19-13.
ADIKES, JOHN, 11-11, 19-15.
ADKINS, WILLIAM G., 13-17, 13-19, 22-19, 22-21, 24-11, 24-12, 24-15.
ADKISSON, FLOYD, 13-13, 13-17, 13-19.
ADLER, M., 11-11, 11-14.
AGTHE, DONALD E., 23-11.
AGUAYO, RAMON CARLOS, 11-11, 11-14, 11-18.
AHEARN, D. S., 19-15, 19-16.
AHMEN, M.M. A., 12-11, 14-15.
AIN, S. N., 19-15, 19-16.
AINASON, H. H., 18-13, 19-15.
AINSWORTH, LAWRENCE G., 13-17, 13-19.
AITCHISON, G. D., 22-18.
AKEHURST, RICHARD, 18-16.
AKIN, PAUL, 19-12.
AKIN, WAYNE M., 14-14.
AKRON REAL ESTATE BOARD, 11-13, 11-14, 11-16.
AKSTON, J. J., 11-18, 18-18, 19-14.
ALAND, ROBERT HARRIS, 12-11, 12-12.
ALASKA REVIEW OF BUSINESS AND ECONOMIC CONDITIONS, 17-12.
ALBERS, M. H., 14-11.
ALBERT, FRANKLIN E., 13-11, 13-17, 13-19.
ALBERT, STERLING H., 13-17, 13-19.
ALBRIGHT, ALLEN J., 12-21.
ALBRIGHT, CLAUDE D, 19-13.
ALDERFER, EVAN B., 11-11, 11-18, 16-12.
ALDIS, GRAHAM, 11-11, 11-13, 12-15, 12-18, 13-11, 13-20.
ALEXANDER, J. J. G., 18-15, 19-15.
ALEXANDER, L. B., 17-12.
ALEXANDER, LAURENCE A., 12-16, 13-11, 13-14.
ALEXANDER, ROBERT H., 11-11, 11-12, 11-13, 11-14, 12-24, 24-11, 24-15.
ALEXANDER, ROBERT P., 12-13, 13-15.
ALEXANDER, WILLIAM E., 12-18.
ALEXANDERSON, K. W., 13-21.
ALICO, JOHN, 12-24, 20-11, 20-15.
ALLAN, BRITT H., 11-14, 11-16.
ALLARD, JOSEPH L., 12-14.
ALLEN, ALBERT E., 12-13.
ALLEN, BRYAN, 18-15.
ALLEN, EDWIN G., 12-11.
ALLEN, ELLIS S., 11-11, 11-13.
ALLEN, FRED H., 19-12.
ALLEN, WALTER S., 13-15.
ALLES, WAYNE, 11-11, 11-13.
ALLIN, B. C., 11-11, 11-12, 11-18.
ALLINGHAM ALLISON P., 13-20.
ALLINGHAM, A. P., 11-11, 11-14, 11-16, 13-17, 13-19, 19-14.
ALLINGHAM, ALLISON P., 13-21, 23-16.
ALLISON, NEVILLE F., 11-11, 11-13, 11-14, 11-19, 12-14, 13-13, 13-17, 13-19.
ALLISON, NEVILLE F., AND MEREDITH H. JAMES, SR., 22-19, 22-20.
ALLISON, VEVILLE F., 11-11, 11-18.
ALLPHIN, ROBERT, 12-13.
ALLSOPP, ERNEST S., 19-13, 23-11.
ALMER, ZALMER, 15-13, 22-21.
ALPATOV, M. W., 18-11, 18-15.
ALPER, ZALMAN Y., 16-16.
ALVERT, EUGENE, 11-11, 11-13, 11-16.
ALYEA, PAUL E., 12-13, 16-11.
AMAYA, MARIO, 18-12, 19-15.
AMENDOLAGINE, EMANUEL, 17-14, 23-16.
AMER INSTITUTE OF REAL ESTATE APPRAISERS, 11-11, 11-14, 11-15, 11-16, 13-16, 13-19, 22-18.
AMER SOC OF FARM MGRS & RURAL APPRAISERS JOUR OF, 14-11.
AMERICA FIRE INSURANCE GROUP, 12-23.
AMERICAN APPRAISAL CO., 21-13.
AMERICAN APPRAISAL CO., 12-23, 13-15, 13-20, 21-13, 23-11.
AMERICAN ASSOCIATION OF STATE HIGHWAY OFFICIALS, 12-16, 24-15.
AMERICAN BANKERS ASSOCIATION, 19-12.
AMERICAN DRUGGIST, 12-22, 13-15.
AMERICAN ECONOMIC ASSOCIATION, 11-11, 19-15, 21-11.

# BIBLIOGRAPHY OF APPRAISAL LITERATURE

AMERICAN ECONOMIC REVIEW, 13-11.
AMERICAN GEM SOCIETY, 18-15, 18-17.
AMERICAN HOTEL ASSOCIATION DEPRECIATION COMMITTEE, 12-24, 13-15.
AMERICAN INSTITUTE OF ARCHITECTS, 21-11, 21-16, 24-15.
AMERICAN INSTITUTE OF PLANNERS JOURNAL, 13-17, 24-11.
AMERICAN INSTITUTE OF REAL ESTATE APPRAISAL, 11-11, 11-14, 13-11.
AMERICAN INSTITUTE OF REAL ESTATE APPRAISERS, 11-11, 11-12, 11-13, 11-14, 11-15, 11-16, 11-18, 11-19, 12-11, 12-14, 12-16, 12-25, 12-26, 13-15, 13-17, 13-19, 13-20, 13-21, 14-11, 15-13, 15-14, 19-13, 21-13, 22-18, 22-19, 22-20, 23-11, 24-11, 24-15.
AMERICAN MUNICIPAL ASSOCIATION, 12-11, 12-26.
AMERICAN RIGHT OF WAY ASSOCIATION, 12-14, 12-15, 12-16, 12-18, 13-15, 22-16, 24-11, 24-14, 24-15.
AMERICAN SOCIETY OF APPRAISERS, 11-11, 11-12, 11-13, 11-15, 12-11, 12-13, 12-14, 12-15, 12-23, 12-24, 13-15, 21-12.
AMERICAN SOCIETY OF APPRAISERS, WASHINGTON, 14-11, 20-11, 20-12, 20-13, 20-14, 20-15.
AMERICAN SOCIETY OF FARM MANAGERS AND RURAL APPRAI, 11-11, 14-11.
AMERICAN SOCIETY OF PLANNING OFFICIALS, 12-15, 12-16, 13-11, 13-14, 13-15, 13-19, 13-20, 13-21, 13-23, 17-14, 23-11, 23-16, 24-15.
AMERICAN TRANSIT ASSOCIATION, 24-11, 24-17, 24-19.
AMERICAN WATER WORKS ASSOCIATION, 16-14.
ANDAL, M. E., 14-11.
ANDERS, DOWELL H., 12-14, 12-26.
ANDERSON JAMES A., 12-16, 24-15.
ANDERSON, BENJAMIN MCALESTER, 11-11, 11-18.
ANDERSON, LYN FOSTER, 12-11.
ANDERSON, LYNN FOSTER, 12-11.
ANDERSON, MEL, 11-14.
ANDERSON, ROBERT E., 13-17, 13-19.
ANDERSON, SENECA B., 13-19.
ANDERSON, ARNOLD C., 22-18, 24-11.
ANDRADE, J. M. PITA, 18-11, 19-15.
ANDREWS, JAMES, 12-13, 13-19.
ANDREWS, R. B., 12-11.
ANGEL, CARLOS JULIO, 12-16.
ANGELL, STEPHEN, 12-11, 12-13.
ANGELL, STEPHEN LEROY, 13-22, 22-18.
ANGERS, A. G., 12-16, 20-11.
ANGULO LOPEZ, ALBERTO, 11-11, 11-17, 11-19.
ANON., 11-18.
ANSON, JOHN B., 12-14.
ANTAL, FREDERICK, 18-12.
ANTON, FERDINAND, 18-15.
ANTON, SHICKREY, 22-24.
ANTONMATTEI, JOSE E., 11-11, 11-19.
APP FRANK J, 13-11, 13-17.
APPEL JAMES R., 11-14, 11-16.
APPEL, JAMES R., 11-11, 12-14, 12-16, 12-17, 13-11, 13-14, 13-15, 22-20.
APPELBAUM, WILLIAM, 13-15, 13-18.
APPELSON, WALLACE B., 12-11, 12-13.
APPRAAISAL DIGEST, 12-14.
APPRAISAL DIGEST, 11-11, 11-12, 11-13, 11-14, 11-16, 11-17, 11-18, 12-14, 12-22, 13-11, 13-16, 13-19, 19-11, 19-12, 22-18, 24-15.

APPRAISAL INSTITUTE MAGAZINE, 11-11, 11-13, 13-16, 13-19.
APPRAISAL JOURNAL, 11-11, 11-12, 11-13, 11-16, 11-18, 12-14, 12-16, 12-18, 12-26, 13-13, 13-15, 13-19, 15-14, 17-15, 19-13, 19-15, 22-19, 22-24.
ARCHER, W. G., 18-11, 19-15.
ARCHIBALD, T. R., 12-24, 19-16.
ARCHITECHTURAL FORUM, 13-17, 13-23.
ARCHITECTURAL FORUM, 11-11, 11-18, 13-11, 13-16, 13-19, 19-11, 22-22.
ARDERN, WILLIAM B., 12-26, 13-19.
ARDISSONO, ROBERT J., 11-13, 11-14, 11-17.
ARDITTI, F. D., 19-12.
ARDOUIN, LOUIS, 13-17, 13-19.
ARDREY, J. HOWARD, 12-26, 13-16.
ARENA, JOHN J., 11-11, 11-18, 21-11.
ARGENTINE REPUBLIC, 11-18, 11-19.
ARIES, R. S., 21-18.
ARKANSAS DIVISION OF ASSESSMENT COORDINATION, 12-13, 22-18.
ARKANSAS LEGISLATIVE COUNCIL, 12-11, 12-16, 12-18, 16-11.
ARKANSAS RAILROAD COMMISSION, TAX DIVISION, 12-11, 12-13.
ARMSTRONG, CHARLES VINCENT, 12-19, 23-11.
ARMSTRONG, EDWIN F., 11-11, 11-12.
ARMSTRONG, LOU, 21-11.
ARMSTRONG, ROBERT H., 11-11, 11-13, 11-16, 11-17, 11-18, 11-19, 12-11, 13-15, 13-17, 13-20, 13-21, 19-15, 22-18, 22-19, 23-11, 24-13.
ARMSTRONG, W. Y., 12-11, 12-23, 13-19.
ARMSTRONG, WILLIAM Y., 11-11, 21-11.
ARNASON, H. H., 18-12, 19-15.
ARNDT, ROBERT E, 19-15.
ARNESON JR, H. R., 11-12.
ARNESON JR, HARRY R., 11-18.
ARNESON, HARRY R., 13-18, 22-18.
ARNESON, HARRY R. JR., 11-11, 11-12, 12-14, 12-26, 13-17, 13-19.
ARNOLD, JAMES A. JR., 12-11.
ARNOLD, MAX P, 12-11, 14-11.
ARNOLD, MAX P., 11-11, 11-13, 12-11, 12-12, 12-13, 14-11, 22-19.
ARNOLD, MAX, C. N. BLOOMFIELD, AND JACK HULL, 12-11, 22-19.
ARNOLD, P. T. DIX, 14-16, 14-21.
ARNOLD, PHILIP N., 13-18, 19-13.
ARNOLD, ROBERT S., 11-11, 11-14, 12-11, 12-25, 19-12.
ARNOLD, RONALD S., 11-11, 11-14.
ARNOLD, VERN L., 12-16, 12-26.
ARROW, KENNETH JOSEPH, 11-11, 11-18.
ARSUAGA, MIGUEL A., 11-11, 12-24, 19-15.
ART DIGEST, 11-19, 18-11, 18-12.
ART NEWS, 18-15.
ARTHAND, CLAUDE, 11-18.
ARTHUR, JOHN, 12-13.
ARTHUR, WILLIAM, 21-13.
ARTILES, SEBASTIAN, 11-11, 11-18.
ASCHER, DAVID B., 11-11, 11-14, 11-16, 11-18, 13-15, 19-15, 22-18.
ASCHMAN, FREDERICK T., 11-18.
ASH, FRED C., 11-11, 11-13, 11-14, 12-11, 12-14, 12-15, 12-16, 12-23, 12-26, 13-15, 17-13, 17-16, 20-11, 24-12, 24-15.
ASHLEY, ROGER H., 12-16, 12-26.
ASHTON, MORRIS B., 12-19.

▲ Index of Authors

ASHTON, R. E., 12-11, 12-13.
ASIA HOUSE GALLERY PUBLICATIONS, 18-14, 19-15.
ASSESSING OFFICIALS OF CONNECTICUT, 12-13.
ASSESSORS NEWSLETTER, 11-12, 12-11, 12-13, 12-16, 13-15, 22-18.
ASSOC CERTIFIED & CORPORATE ACCOUNTANTS COMMITTEE, 12-19, 21-14.
ASSOCIATED GENERAL CONTRACTORS, 21-16.
ASSOCIATED GENERAL CONTRACTORS OF AMERICA, 12-24.
ASSOCIATION OF APPRAISAL EXECUTIVES, 11-11, 11-12, 11-13, 11-14.
ASSOCIATION OF CERTIFIED AND PUBLIC ACCOUNTANTS, 11-19, 19-15.
ASTROLENK B., 13-21, 19-15.
ATHERTON E B, 12-14, 24-11, 24-15.
ATHERTON E. B., 12-15.
ATHERTON, E. B., 12-14, 12-15.
ATHERTON, EDWARD B, 12-15, 24-11, 24-15.
ATKINS GEORGE, 22-18.
ATKINS, DAVID, 11-11, 11-19.
ATKINSON HARRY GRANT, 11-11, 11-12, 11-14, 11-16, 11-17, 11-19, 13-19.
ATKINSON, H. G., 11-14, 11-19.
ATKINSON, L. J., 13-16.
ATLAS MARTIN, 12-11, 22-18.
ATWATER R. B., 24-12.
AUBLE TALMAGE D., 13-17.
AUBOYER, JANINE, 18-11, 18-13, 18-15, 19-15.
AUCKLAND UNIVERSITY, 19-15.
AUGUR, TRACY B., 13-11.
AUMACK, HARRY F., 13-17.
AUMELL, R. G., 14-11.
AUSLANDER, ELYSE, 13-16.
AUSTIN, PECK, 12-11, 12-14.
AUTOMATIC CAR WASH ASSOCIATION, 11-15, 12-24, 13-15, 24-11.
AVERMAETE, ROGER, 18-11, 19-15.
AVERY, CHARLES, 18-13.
AXFORD, DR. H. M., 11-14, 12-25, 13-15, 13-17.
AXKROYD, PETER H., 11-11, 11-18.
AXLUND, DONALD L., 14-18.
AYCOCKE, J. N., 12-13, 12-26.
AYRES, J. M., 12-22, 13-18, 13-20.
AYRES, LEONARD P., 11-18, 11-19.


BAB, HERBERT J. G., 12-11, 13-13.
BABCOCK, DR. HENRY A., 11-11, 11-12, 11-13, 11-16.
BABCOCK, FREDERICK M., 11-11, 11-13, 11-14, 11-16, 11-17, 11-18, 11-19, 12-11, 12-14, 12-16, 12-19, 12-23, 12-24, 12-25, 13-11, 13-12, 13-13, 13-15, 13-17, 13-18, 13-19, 13-20, 13-21, 19-12, 19-14, 19-15, 20-11, 21-11, 21-13, 22-18, 22-19, 22-20, 23-11.
BABCOCK, HENRY A, 11-13, 19-15, 21-11.
BABCOCK, HENRY A., 11-11, 11-12, 11-13, 11-16, 11-17, 11-19, 12-11, 12-19, 12-24, 13-11, 13-15, 13-20, 22-19, 22-21, 24-11.
BABCOCK, RICHARD F., 13-11, 13-17, 18-26.
BABCOCK, WILLIAM H., 11-11, 11-12, 11-18, 13-11, 19-13.
BABLER, WAYNE E., 12-11, 12-25.
BABY, RENE, 11-11, 11-19.
BACH, IRA J., 13-11, 13-14.
BACK, DENYS H., 11-11, 11-18, 12-24.

BACKMAN, JULES, 13-18, 22-18, 23-14.
BACOU, ROSELINE, 18-12, 19-15.
BADEN, POWELL, 11-11, 11-18, 12-11, 22-11, 22-21.
BADGER, E. E., 19-15.
BADGER, R. E., 12-11, 19-18, 23-11.
BADGER, RALPH, 12-11, 19-18.
BADGER, RALPH E, 19-18, 20-15.
BADGLEY, L. DURWARD, 13-17, 19-12.
BAGBY, JOHN JR., 11-12.
BAGGE, C. E., 16-12.
BAGGE, CARL E., 16-11.
BAGLEY, ELEANOR S., 11-11, 11-16.
BAILEY, C. DOUGLAS, 11-11, 19-17.
BAILEY, E. NORMAN, 19-15.
BAILEY, GEORGE J., 14-18, 14-21.
BAILEY, GEORGE R., 13-20.
BAILEY, HOP, JR., 11-11, 11-13, 11-17.
BAILEY, REX R., 12-11, 12-13, 14-13, 14-15.
BAILEY, WILLIAM L., 13-11.
BAILLIE, G. H., 18-15, 19-15.
BAINES, ANTHONY, 18-15.
BAINUM, ROBERT, 13-21.
BAIRD, JOHN W., 13-19.
BAKER, DONALD M., 23-11.
BAKER, GEOFFREY, 13-15.
BAKER, GEOFFREY B., 13-15.
BAKER, HARRISON R., 13-22.
BAKER, J. ALAN, 12-20.
BAKER, JAMERS S., 11-14, 11-19.
BAKER, LLOYD, 11-11, 11-13, 11-19, 12-11, 13-15, 19-11.
BAKER, O. E., 13-11.
BAKER, VERNE, 12-16, 14-15.
BAKER, VERNE A., 12-11, 14-17.
BALDERSTON, C. CANBY, 11-11, 11-19.
BALDWIN, FLETCHER N. JR., 22-24.
BALDWIN, H. G., 11-12, 11-14, 11-16, 12-16, 13-19, 13-20, 13-21, 24-15, 24-19.
BALDWIN, HARRY, 11-11, 11-19.
BALDWIN, ROGER S., 22-18.
BALDWIN, ROSALIND G., 12-12.
BALFOUR, FRANK C., 12-14, 12-16, 24-11, 24-15.
BALL, CHARLES, 13-11, 24-15.
BALL, JOHN, 11-14, 11-16.
BALL, THOMAS B., 11-17, 13-09, 13-20, 13-21, 20-11, 21-11, 21-16.
BALL, THOMAS L, 18-14, 21-11.
BALL, THOMAS L., 11-15, 12-11, 12-13, 13-21, 18-14, 21-11.

BALL, TOM, 21-13.
BALL, WILLIAM H., 13-17, 13-19.
BALLAINE, WESLEY C., 12-11.
BALLARD, E. D., 12-11, 12-13.
BALLARD, J. W., 11-19, 12-24.
BALLARD, W. H., 11-11, 11-19, 12-14, 21-11.
BALLARD, WILLIAM S., 11-11, 11-12, 13-11, 13-19.
BALLIM, FRED A., 11-11.
BALLO, GUIDO, 18-11, 18-12, 18-13, 18-14, 18-15, 18-16.
BALLOU, PAUL, 11-11, 11-16, 12-13, 13-11, 13-15, 23-11.
BALLOU, PAUL H., 12-12, 12-13.
BANCO CENTRAL DE VENEZUELA, 13-11.
BANCROFT, D. A., 12-11, 12-13.
BANDINELLI, RANUCCIO BIANCHI, 18-15, 18-16, 19-15.
BANGO, HENRY L., 12-16, 17-12.
BANK ADMINISTRATION INSTITUTE LIBRARY, 13-21.

BANK OF AMERICA APPRAISAL DEPARTMENT, 13-19, 21-13.
BANK, HERMAN, 18-15, 18-17.
BANKS, W. E., 19-14.
BANZHAF, GEORGE, 17-12.
BAPPERT JOSEPH, 13-15.
BAPPERT, JOSEPH, 11-14, 13-15, 13-19, 13-20, 13-21, 22-18.
BARAN, EDWARD S., 12-13.
BARBAGELATA, JOSE, 13-11, 13-23.
BARBEAU, JACQUES, 12-11, 17-15.
BARBOUR, SIR DAVID MILLER, 11-11, 11-13, 11-17.
BARETTE, L. A., 13-17, 13-19.
BARIBEAU, JULES, 12-16, 17-12.
BARISH, NORMAN N., 11-11, 11-13, 11-14, 11-16, 11-19, 19-17, 19-19, 19-20, 19-21, 19-22.
BARNARD, BERNARD L., 12-11, 12-13.
BARNARD, BOYD T., 11-11, 11-12, 11-13, 11-14, 11-16, 11-17, 11-18, 13-13, 13-15, 13-19, 22-18.
BARNES, FRANK E., 21-13.
BARNES, JOHN W., 12-11.
BARNETT, DOUGLAS, 18-11, 19-15.
BARNEY, RALPH A., 22-14.
BARO, GENE, 18-12, 19-15.
BARON, GEORGE C., 12-26.
BARONE, RAY R., 11-11, 11-12, 11-16.
BARR, GERALD R., 12-13.
BARR, JOHN A., 13-15.
BARRAN, A. J., 16-15.
BARRETT, FRANKLIN S., 18-14, 19-15.
BARRIE AND ROCKLIFFE, 18-16, 18-18, 19-15.
BARRON'S, 19-15, 19-16.
BARRY, DAVID N., 12-14, 12-15.
BARTHOLOMEW, HERLAND, 13-11.
BARTLETT, CHARLES R., 12-11, 12-13, 13-20, 13-21, 14-15.
BARTLETT, ROLAND W., 11-11, 11-16, 14-11.
BARTON, STANLEY B., 16-11.
BARWICK, H. G., 13-22.
BASCH, JACOB, 13-19.
BASHAW, FREDERICK J., 11-11, 13-11, 14-11, 22-11, 22-21.
BASKETT, JOHN, 18-11, 19-15.
BASS, BOYLSTON B., 11-11, 11-13, 19-14.
BASSETT, EDWARD M., 12-26, 13-11.
BATAILLE, GEORGES, 18-11, 19-15.
BATCHELOR, HARRY H., 11-11, 11-12, 11-13, 11-16, 13-16.
BATEMAN, R. H., 19-14, 19-15, 19-17, 19-19, 19-20, 19-21.
BATES, JACK B., 12-16.
BATLIN, MARTIN, 18-11.
BATSFORD, B. T., 18-11, 19-15.
BATTLE, THOMAS G., 12-13.
BATTY, HARRY, 12-15, 12-16, 19-15.
BAUER, FRANK, 13-17.
BAUER, J., 13-13.
BAUER, JOHN, 16-11.
BAUER, M. H., 11-11, 11-13.
BAUER, PAUL, 13-23.
BAUMGARTNER, HAMPTON, JR., 12-14, 12-18.
BAUMOL, W. J., 19-18.
BAXTER, C. H., 17-14.
BAYER, DANIEL, 13-13, 13-17.
BAYLOR, DR. ALLEN O., 11-11, 11-13, 11-14, 11-16, 11-17.
BAYNE, 17-14.
BAYNTON-WILLIAMS, 11-14, 11-16.
BAYOR, HERBERT, 18-11, 19-15.
BAZAN, HORACE B., 13-17, 13-19.
BAZIN, GERMAIN, 18-11, 18-15, 19-15.
BDADFORD, ERNLE, 18-17.
BEACH, D. W., 13-11.
BEACH, DONALD R., 12-13.
BEAFORD, JOHN, 18-15, 18-16.
BEAN, JACOB, 18-15, 19-15.
BEAN, PHILIP R., 11-11, 11-13.
BEARDEN, THOMAS H., 13-19.
BEARDSLEY, EARLE L., 12-16.
BEARSLEE, LOUIS B., 23-11.
BEASLEY, J. D., 18-11, 18-13, 19-15.
BEATON, J WALLACE, 11-11, 11-13, 11-18.
BEATON, J. WALLACE, 12-17, 19-15.
BEATON, W. R., 22-18.
BEATON, WALLACE, 19-14, 19-15.
BEATON, WILLIAM R., 12-11, 13-15, 13-19, 14-17, 19-13, 23-11, 24-15.
BEATTIE, R. D., 21-11, 21-15, 21-18.
BEATTY, CLARENCE W. JR., 12-14, 12-16, 13-13.
BEAUBIER, DAVID W., 11-11, 11-18.
BEAUCHAMP, J. LYLE, 11-11, 11-16, 19-15.
BEAUDOIN FERNAND J., 14-15.
BEAUDOIN, FERNAND, 14-11.
BEAUDOIN, FERNAND J., 14-15.
BEAUDRY, PAUL, 12-13, 12-26.
BEAZLEY, J. D., 18-11.
BECCIA, MARTIN, 12-15, 12-16, 22-17.
BECHERER, RICHARD W, 13-19, 13-60.
BECK, AXEL J., 12-26.
BECK, F. W., 11-13, 12-14.
BECK, FRITZ W., 13-19.
BECK, MORRIS, 12-11, 13-13, 24-11.
BECKER, ALVIN G. AND ARTHUR E. WARNER, 13-19.
BECKER, GEORGE, 11-14, 11-17, 12-11, 13-12, 13-14, 13-15, 13-20.
BECKER, MANNING H, 14-11, 19-13.
BECKER, R. J., 22-20.
BECKET, WELTON, 13-15, 24-12.
BECKETT, P. H. T., 11-14, 22-11, 22-21.
BECKLEY, J. H., 16-11.
BEDFORD, E. W., 22-18.
BEDFORD, JOHN, 18-15, 18-17.
BEECROFT, ERIC, 12-11.
BEEHLER, GEORGE W. JR., 13-17, 13-19.
BEETH, CHANNING C., 11-11, 11-13, 11-14, 11-16, 11-17, 12-14, 12-20, 12-24, 12-26, 13-17, 19-11, 21-11, 21-15, 24-13.
BEETHOVEN, EDWIN C., 12-16, 14-13.
BEGGS, D. WENDELL, 22-18.
BEHMAN, B., 13-16, 16-11.
BEILHARZ, ALFRED J., 13-19.
BEIQUE, JEAN, 13-15, 13-18.
BEIZER, J., 17-14.
BELBUI, GIAM GUIDO, 18-11, 19-15.
BELL, FRED A., 13-19, 13-20, 13-21, 16-12.
BELL, J. N., 12-24.
BELL, RICHARD E, 14-11.
BELL, SPURGEON E., 12-15.
BELL, STOUGHTON, 12-13, 22-18.
BELL, THOMAS L., 13-21.
BELLANCA, ALFONSO V., 12-13, 12-17.
BELLONI, GIANGUIDO AND LILIANE FEDI DALL-ASEN, 18-11, 18-15.

BELLS, ZURA E., 12-12.
BELTH, J. M., 12-23, 12-25.
BEMAN, ARTHUR K., 11-11, 11-14, 11-16, 11-18, 11-19, 12-24, 13-15, 13-16, 13-17, 13-19, 13-21, 15-11, 19-12, 19-13, 22-19, 22-20.
BENEDICT, JARED W., 13-17.
BENEDICT, LOUIS, 12-24, 19-15.
BENESCH, OTTO, 18-11, 19-15.
BENGE, ROLAND, A., 11-16, 11-19, 19-15.
BENKERT, WILLIAM C., 22-18.
BENN, B. O., 22-21.
BENNET, HAZEN, 11-14, 11-19, 13-15.
BENNETT, EDWARD P. JR., 13-17.
BENNETT, H. H., 11-11, 22-11, 22-16, 22-21.
BENNETT, K. W., 13-16, 13-17, 13-19.
BENNETT, MYRON, 19-13.
BENNETT, PHILIP E., 11-13, 12-14.
BENNETT, S. V., 13-15.
BENNETT, S. Z., 11-11, 11-12, 11-13, 13-17, 22-16.
BENNETT, SAUL Z., 11-11, 11-14, 11-16, 11-19, 12-14, 12-15, 13-11, 13-15, 13-17, 13-19.
BENNTT, SAUL Z., 13-19.
BENSON, C. B., 12-24.
BENSON, CHARLES A., 13-17.
BENSON, GEORGE C. AND OTHERS, 12-11.
BENSON, PHILIP A., 11-11, 11-13, 11-14, 12-13, 12-14, 12-24, 13-18, 22-18.
BENSON, W. A., 11-11, 22-19, 22-20, 22-21.
BENTLEY, HOWARD H., 11-14, 11-19.
BENTLEY, NICHOLAS, 18-11, 18-15, 19-15.
BENTON, PHILIP H, 13-17.
BERANEK, WILLIAM, 19-16.
BERENSON, BERNARD, 18-11, 18-12, 18-15, 19-15.
BERG, G. H., 13-21, 19-11.
BERGER, MILES, 11-11, 11-12, 12-13, 13-13.
BERGER, THEODORE, 12-11.
BERGES, RUTH, 18-12, 18-14, 19-15.
BERGREN, ARTHUR L., 12-13.
BERHOFF, WILLIAM EARL, 11-11, 11-17.
BERIAULT, RAYMOND J., 22-24.
BERLAND, ABEL E., 19-15.
BERMAN, W. I., 11-11, 11-16.
BERNARD, ALFRED D., 11-11, 11-16, 11-19, 13-11, 22-18, 22-22.
BERNARD, ARNOLD, 19-16.
BERNARD, BOYD T., 11-14, 11-16, 12-17.
BERNARD, W. C., 11-11, 12-14, 12-18.
BEROES, MARIANO, 11-11, 11-13, 11-17.
BERRERA, STEPHEN F., 13-21.
BERRY-HILL HENRY AND SIDNEY, 18-11.
BERRY, J. J., 12-16, 16-11.
BERRYMAN, GEORGE A., 12-16.
BERTRAMSON, B. R., 14-13.
BERTRAND R. MRS., 12-20.
BERWICK, A. J., 14-11, 14-15.
BEUTER, J. H., 17-12.
BEYER, BEN B., 13-15.
BIBY, JOHN E. JR., 24-13.
BICKLEY, N. ALEX, 12-15, 12-18.
BICKNELL, F. B., 22-18.
BIERMAN, H. JR., 19-16.
BIGELOW, WALTER S., 22-18.
BIGLER, S. H., 13-18, 13-20.
BIGRAS, ROLAND, 16-11.
BILLINGS, VIOLA C., 11-14, 11-19, 19-11.

BING, R. A., 19-16.
BING, RALPH A, 19-14.
BINGHAM, JOHN, 21-16.
BINGHAM, ROBERT F., 12-26.
BINTLIFF, BENNETT B., 11-14, 11-16.
BIRCK, LAURITS VILHELM, 11-11, 11-17.
BIRD, F., 11-11, 11-14.
BIRD, RICHARD M., 12-11.
BIRNHOLZ, JACK, 11-13, 11-14.
BIRNKRANT, MICHAEL, 13-15.
BISHOP, JESSE E., 11-11, 11-12, 12-26, 22-18.
BISHOP, MAURICE F., 12-14, 12-15, 12-16, 12-18, 12-26, 22-16, 22-18.
BISHOP, SAMUEL M., 12-13.
BISSO, LOUIS, 12-16, 24-15.
BLACK, ALEX G., 21-13.
BLACK, I. G., 20-12, 21-13, 23-14.
BLACK, LEON D., 12-18.
BLAGBROUGH, ELIZABETH M, 18-11.
BLAIR, CLAUDE, 18-15, 19-15.
BLAIR, D. GORDON, 12-20.
BLAIR, W. EDWIN, 13-17, 13-18, 13-23.
BLAKELY, A. P., 11-11, 11-12.
BLANCH, GRANT E., 14-17.
BLANCHARD, C. F., 12-15, 16-11, 16-12.
BLASE, M. G., 12-11, 22-18, 22-19, 22-20.
BLDG MGRS & OWNERS ASSN OF NEW YORK, INC, 12-11, 13-20.
BLDG OWNERS & MGRS ASSN OF SEATTLE, 13-18.
BLETTNER, ROBERT A., 11-14, 11-16.
BLISS, GEORGE L., 11-11, 11-16, 19-11.
BLISS, GEORGE M., 22-18, 22-22.
BLOCK, ALEXANDER, 11-18, 11-19.
BLOOD, J., 11-19, 13-11, 13-15, 13-16, 13-17, 13-19.
BLOOM, GEORGE, 11-11, 11-14, 11-16.
BLOOM, GEORGE F., 11-14, 11-16.
BLOOM, MAX R., 13-13, 22-18.
BLOUGH, J. ROY, 12-12.
BLOXOM, ROBERT D., 12-24.
BLUE, JESSE B., 13-17, 19-11.
BLUM, MAYER I., 13-19.
BLUM, SHIRLEY NEILSON, 18-14, 18-16.
BLUMBERG, AARON, 13-17, 13-19.
BLUMBERG, AARON J., 11-11, 11-13.
BLUME, , . E., 11-11, 19-15, 19-17.
BLUNT, ANTHONY, 18-11, 18-15, 18-16, 19-15.
BLUNT, WILFRED, 18-14.
BOARD COMMISSION RATES IN CITIES OF OVER 100, 000, 19-13.
BOARDMAN, JOHN, 18-16, 18-17, 19-15.
BOATRIGHT, RONALD OLAN, 13-17.
BOBLETT, ROBERT P., 23-11.
BODFISH, H. MORTON, 13-11, 13-13, 13-14, 14-13.
BODFISH, MORTON, 11-11, 11-12, 11-14, 11-16, 11-17, 11-18, 11-19, 12-24, 12-25, 13-14, 13-15, 13-16, 13-17, 13-18, 13-19, 13-22, 19-12, 19-13, 19-15, 22-11, 22-17, 22-19, 22-22.
BODNAR, ERNEST B., 13-11, 13-21.
BOECKH, E. H., 11-15.
BOECKH, EVERARD HEREFORD, 11-11, 11-13, 11-14, 11-15, 11-16, 11-17, 11-19, 12-24, 13-11, 13-15, 13-17, 13-19, 14-15, 19-11, 21-13, 21-16, 21-20, 22-18, 22-19, 22-20, 22-21, 22-22, 23-11.
BOECKH, EVERARD HEREFORD AND ASSOCIATES, 21-16.
BOEREMA, ROBERT J., 12-24, 13-17.

BOERKE, E. M., 23-11.
BOESEN, 18-15.
BOETTCHER, LLOYD D., 12-15.
BOGEN, J., 19-18, 24-14.
BOGER, LOUISE ADE, 18-11, 18-12, 18-13, 18-14.
BOGGS, JOHN I., 16-11.
BOHANNON, DAVID D., 11-11, 13-17, 13-22, 14-15, 21-11, 22-17, 23-11.
BOICE, LLOYD J., 14-17.
BOINNE, ALBERT, 18-11.
BOLAND, C. T., 23-11.
BOLENDER, LEE, 18-18.
BOLER, F. C., 13-20.
BOLEY, BERTRAM S., 12-11.
BOLEY, ROBERT E., 23-12.
BOLLES, W. H., 12-23.
BOLLMAN, H. GORDON, 13-13.
BOLOGNA, FERDINANDO, 18-11, 18-12, 19-15.
BOLT, GEORGE K., 12-23.
BOLTON, REGINALD P., 22-18.
BOLZ, R W, 20-14, 20-15.
BOMBRIGHT, JAMES CUMMINGS, 12-26.
BONBRIGHT, JAMES C., 11-11, 11-14, 11-16, 11-17, 12-11, 12-13, 12-14, 12-15, 12-23, 12-24, 16-11, 19-15, 21-12.
BONBRIGHT, JAMES CUMMINGS, 13-17, 13-21, 13-23.
BOND, F. A., 11-19, 13-18.
BOND, HAROLD LEWIS, 18-16.
BONE, DAVID M., 12-13, 12-19.
BONNER, JOHN, 11-11, 11-14.
BONNER, JOHN T. JR., 11-11, 11-13, 12-14, 12-25, 13-17, 19-13, 21-11.
BONNER, JOHN T., JR., 12-24.
BONTJES, JOHN H., 11-11, 11-14, 13-19.
BOOT, HARRY E., 12-11.
BOOTH, ERIC ROWLAND, 12-11, 13-15, 13-17, 16-11.
BOOTH, ERNEST, 12-11, 16-11.
BORCHARD, RALPH R., 13-11, 22-21.
BORDLEY, R. C., 12-14.
BORSAK, GEORGE, 12-13, 22-18, 24-13.
BORST, A., 12-11.
BOSKOVITS, MIKLOS, 18-11, 18-12.
BOSLAND, CHELCIE C., 12-11, 16-11, 19-18.
BOSWELL, P., 18-15.
BOSWELL, PEYTON, JR., 18-11.
BOTARI, STEFANO, 18-11, 19-15.
BOTTS, RALPH R., 19-12.
BOUCHA, MARVIN E., 12-13, 13-20, 13-21.
BOUCK, ROLLAND, 12-13.
BOUDAILLE, GEORGES, 18-11, 19-15.
BOUQUET, A. C., 18-14, 18-15, 19-15.
BOURLAND, FREDERICK B., 13-17, 13-19.
BOURNEUF, HENRI, 19-15.
BOUTROSS, JAMES, 18-17.
BOUTROSS, JAMES J., 18-17.
BOWEN, DELBERT, 11-17, 19-11, 19-15.
BOWEN, EZRA, 13-14.
BOWEN, JOHN R., 14-11, 22-19, 22-20.
BOWEN, PERCIVAL V., 11-11, 11-13, 11-16, 12-11, 12-14, 13-15, 13-21, 21-11, 21-18.
BOWER, D. H., 19-16.
BOWERS, RAYMOND A., 11-18, 13-16.
BOWES, EUGENE, 13-15.
BOWES, EUGENE G., 11-14, 11-16, 13-15.
BOWES, W. A., 11-14, 11-17.
BOWES, WATSON A., 11-11, 11-12, 11-19, 12-14, 12-15, 12-16, 12-26, 14-18, 22-18.
BOWMAN, J. D., 14-11.
BOWMAN, W. J., 11-11, 11-13, 11-16.
BOWMAN, WILLIAM J., 11-11, 11-16.
BOWNESS, ALAN, 18-13, 19-15.
BOX, THADIS W., 14-18.
BOYCE BYRL N, 12-11.
BOYCE, BYRL N., 22-21.
BOYCE, LLOYD M., 12-11, 13-15.
BOYD, JOHN T. JR, 11-11, 11-14.
BOYD, THOMAS G., 12-13.
BOYER, RALPH F., AND JOHN P. WILCOX, 12-14, 19-13.
BOYESEN, LOUIS K., 13-21, 19-11, 22-18.
BOYKIN, JAMES H., 11-11, 11-16, 22-18, 22-19, 22-20.
BOYLAND, WILLIAM E., 12-11, 12-13, 22-18.
BOYLE, ROBERT P., 12-15.
BOYLE, T., 18-12.
BRABENT, DAVIS, 11-11, 11-14, 11-18.
BRACELAND, JOSEPH J., 11-18.
BRACHMAN, H. J., 11-11, 11-14, 11-16.
BRADEY, A. I., 12-15.
BRADFORD, C. R., 11-11, 11-14, 14-11, 14-12, 14-13, 14-15.
BRADFORD, ERNIE, 18-17, 19-15.
BRADFORD, WM. DONALD, PH. D., 13-15, 19-14.
BRADLEY, CARL H. H., 24-11, 24-15.
BRADLEY, VINCENT P., 11-11, 11-14, 11-18.
BRADLEY, VON ALLEN, 18-15.
BRADY, HOBART C., 11-11, 11-12.
BRAMS, M. R., 12-11, 12-13.
BRAMS, MARVIN, 16-14.
BRANDT, L., 11-14, 13-16.
BRANSCOMB, HARVIE JR., 12-11, 22-18.
BRASSELL, ROSELYN S., 12-13.
BRATTER, HERBERT, 12-24.
BRATTON, ALLEN W., 12-13, 17-12.
BRAUN, RICHARD L., 13-11, 24-15.
BRAVER, WILLIAM, 13-20.
BRAY, JOHN W., 11-11, 11-14, 11-19.
BRAZER, HARVEY E., 12-11, 23-11.
BREDIUS, ABRAHAM, 18-11, 18-15, 19-15.
BREMICKER, CARL T., 13-11, 13-13, 22-21.
BRENER, DANIEL A., 13-15, 20-11.
BRENER, STEPHEN W., 13-15.
BRENNAN, J. F., 12-23.
BRENNAN, M., 19-16.
BRENNAN, M. J., 12-11.
BRENNAN, M. L., 13-11.
BRENNER, MARSHALL H., 11-18, 12-21.
BRENT, W. L., 13-14, 22-18, 23-11.
BRESNAHAN, C. A., 12-15, 14-11, 14-14.
BRETEY, P. R., 17-11.
BREWER, HOMER T., 12-13, 24-14.
BREWER, T., 11-11, 17-11, 17-14, 17-15, 17-17.
BRIARD, S. E., 13-17.
BRICK, J. C., 13-15.
BRICK, JUSTUS C., 13-15.
BRICKMAN, RICHARD I., 12-15.
BRIDGES, BENJAMIN, JR., 12-11.
BRIERLY, HENRY CHARLES, 12-11.
BRIGGS, J., 11-11, 11-13, 12-14.
BRIGHAM, CLARENCE S., 18-15.
BRIGHAM, E. F. P., 12-15.
BRIGHAM, EUGENE F., 11-14, 11-19, 12-11, 13-15, 19-14.
BRINDLEY, WILLIS, 13-18, 22-18.

## Index of Authors

BRINSMADE, ROBERT BRUCE, 11-11, 11-13, 11-18.
BRINTON, JOHN H., 24-11.
BRITTON, THOMAS C., 12-14, 12-16.
BROADBENT, LORIN J., 12-15, 17-14.
BRODNAX, A. CARROLL, 13-19.
BRODSKY, H., 13-13, 13-14, 13-17.
BRODSKY, HAROLD, 13-14, 13-17.
BROEMMEL, BERT W., 12-11.
BROERSMA, WILLIAM T., 13-19.
BRON, EDITH DE, 18-11, 19-15.
BROOKE, R. J., 11-11, 11-16, 20-11, 20-12, 20-14, 20-15.
BROOKE, RUSSELL J., 19-12.
BROOKER, HERBERT D., 12-16, 12-18, 13-20.
BROOKS, J. H., 12-14.
BROOKS, ROBERT B. JR., 11-11, 11-18.
BROOKS, ROBERT PRESTON, 12-11.
BROOKSHAW, DOREEN, 18-14, 19-15.
BROPHY, JAMES C., 15-18.
BROPHY, JOHN, 18-11, 19-15.
BROTHERS, D. S., 12-11, 13-15.
BROUGHTON, A. G. S., 12-11.
BROWN GEORGE D., 11-14, 11-16.
BROWN OLIVER S., 14-15.
BROWN, C. V., 12-13.
BROWN, E. CAREY, 12-11.
BROWN, E. R., 12-11.
BROWN, EDWIN E., 12-25, 17-12.
BROWN, FREDERICK J., 19-12, 23-11.
BROWN, G. FAIRFAX, 12-13, 12-17, 13-13, 24-15.
BROWN, GEORGE D., 11-11.
BROWN, H. H., 12-16, 16-11.
BROWN, HARRY GUNNISON, 12-11, 22-19, 22-20.
BROWN, J. BRUCE, 11-11, 11-13.
BROWN, J. EVERETT, 13-11.
BROWN, JAMES M., 12-23.
BROWN, JOHN P., 12-11.
BROWN, JUANITA C, 11-11, 11-12.
BROWN, LESTER C., 13-16.
BROWN, LESTER G., 13-11, 13-13.
BROWN, LONDO H., 12-11.
BROWN, MAURICE A., 12-16, 24-12.
BROWN, NORBERT, 13-20.
BROWN, PAT, 12-14, 13-15, 19-12, 19-15.
BROWN, R. K., 11-11, 11-12.
BROWN, R.O., 11-14, 11-16.
BROWN, ROBERT K, 11-11, 11-12.
BROWN, ROBERT K., 13-15, 13-17, 22-18.
BROWN, ROBERT KEVIN, 12-11, 19-13.
BROWN, ROBERT L, 11-11, 11-12.
BROWN, UDELL C., 12-12, 12-13.
BROWN, WILBUR L., 12-13, 17-12.
BROWN, WYLIE W., 12-13.
BROWNELL, KEITH U., 12-15, 12-18, 19-15, 22-19, 22-20.
BROWNER, VINCENT, 11-11, 11-12.
BROWNESS, ALAN, 18-11, 19-15.
BROWNLOW, G. S., 13-15.
BROWNSTEIN, PHILIP N., 11-16, 11-18.
BROZEN YALE, 11-11.
BRUCH, ALBERT P., 16-11.
BRUCHE, ALBERT, 11-11, 11-16, 12-14.
BRUEGGEMAN, WILLIAM BERNARD-PH. D., 13-16, 13-19, 21-16.
BRUERE, HENRY, 13-13, 19-14.
BRUHN, JOHN A., 13-11, 22-19, 22-20.
BRUNDAGE, PERCIVAL F., 11-13, 12-24, 21-11.
BRUNEAU, A. R., 19-12.
BRUNELLE, CHARLES R., 12-24.
BRUNIE, CHARLES H., 19-13.
BRUNK, LLOYD S., 11-14, 11-16, 22-18.
BRUNNER, HERBERT, 18-15, 19-15.
BRUNSMAN, HOWARD G., 13-11.
BRUNSON, THEO R., 11-11, 11-12, 11-18.
BRUST, KENNETH F., 13-15.
BRUTON, ERIC, 18-15, 19-15.
BRYANT, JOHN M., 16-11.
BRYANT, W. D., 23-13.
BRYDEN, JOHN T., 12-25, 19-14, 19-15.
BRYSON, J. A., 12-16.
BRYSON, LYMAN, 11-11, 11-16.
BUBBIS, N. S., 16-16.
BUCHANAN, ROBERT R., 11-13, 18-16, 21-17.
BUCK, A. A., 24-13.
BUCK, WALTER M. S., 11-11, 11-14, 11-16, 12-24.
BUCKLEY, ROBERT, 12-11, 13-19.
BUECHLER, ALFRED G., 12-11.
BUFFINGTON, JESSE L., 24-15.
BUILDING INVESTMENT, 19-15, 21-13.
BUILDING INVESTMENT AND MAINTENANCE, 11-11, 24-11.
BULKLEY, GRANT, 12-23.
BULLINGER, CLARENCE E., 13-11.
BULLOCK, C. L., 11-16, 12-24.
BUNKER, HENRY B., 13-11.
BUNKER, RAYMOND, 13-11, 13-23, 22-19, 22-20.
BUNTING, GEORGE R., 11-14, 11-16.
BURBANK, DANIEL E., 12-11.
BURCHFIELD, B. C., 13-20.
BURCHFIELD, W. G., 23-11.
BUREAU OF AGRICULTURAL ECONOMICS, 14-11, 14-15, 22-21.
BUREAU OF AGRICULTURAL ENGINEERING, 12-15, 14-11.
BUREAU OF BUSINESS AND ECONOMIC RESEARCH, 12-11.
BUREAU OF POWER, 12-19, 12-22, 15-15, 16-11, 16-12.
BUREAU OF TAXATION, 12-11, 12-13.
BURGESS, GEORGE V. T., 11-11, 11-18, 11-19.
BURGESS, GEORGE W., 22-18, 24-13.
BURGHOFF, J. R., 13-17, 13-18.
BURKE, FRANK W., 12-16, 22-16.
BURKE, JOSEPH, 18-12, 19-15.
BURKE, WILLIAM J., 12-11, 22-18, 22-19.
BURKEY, MACK G., 11-14, 11-19.
BURKHARD, EARL E., 11-14, 11-15, 12-11, 12-13, 13-15.
BURKHEIMER, WILLIAM D., 11-11, 11-14.
BURLAKE, J. M., 11-12.
BURNELL, W. V., 11-11, 11-14, 11-19.
BURNELL, WILLIAM U., 11-11, 11-14, 11-18, 11-19, 12-11, 20-15, 22-18, 22-21, 23-11.
BURNELL, WILLIAM V., 12-11, 22-18, 22-19.
BURNETT, T. S., 19-11, 19-15.
BURNEY, WILLARD W, 14-11, 14-16.
BURNS, E. J., 11-14, 11-19.
BURNS, FRITZ B., 13-17.
BURNS, JOHN C., 13-11.
BURNS, JOSEPH P., 12-13.
BURNS, LELAND S., 13-17.
BURNS, ROBERT L., 12-14, 12-15, 12-18.
BURNS, RUTH N., 18-18.
BURNS, WARREN W., 11-14, 11-19, 21-11.

BURNSIDE, L. D., 12-13, 13-15.
BURR, GRACE HARDENDORFF, 18-18, 19-15.
BURR, HUDSON, 14-11.
BURROUGHS ADDING MACHINE CO., 12-11.
BURROUGHS, ROY J., 11-11, 11-12, 11-14, 11-19.
BURROWS, R. D., 13-17.
BURROWS, R. DOUGLAS, 11-11, 11-12.
BURT, F. P., 11-11, 11-12.
BURT, O. R., 17-15, 19-15.
BURTCH, THOMAS, 11-11, 11-14, 11-16.
BURTON, H. J., 13-11, 13-20.
BURTON, JOHN E., 12-11, 12-13, 22-18, 22-19, 22-20.
BUSH, HOLLIS, 12-24.
BUSHAM, K J, 12-11, 19-17.
BUSINESS WEEK, 13-11, 13-13, 13-19, 19-14.
BUSSAGLI, MARIO, 18-11, 19-15.
BUSSING, IRVIN, 19-12, 22-18.
BUTLER, GORDON, 11-14, 11-16.
BUTTENHEIM, HAROLD S., 13-11, 22-16, 22-19.
BUTTERWORTH, ROBERT M., 19-11.
BUTTS, WILLIAM W., 19-15.
BUTZ, ROBERT, 22-18.
BUYS, A. A., 17-12.
BUZZARD, GLENN W., 14-15, 19-11.
BYERS, EUGENE, 12-11.
BYERS, JOHN, R. B., 13-19, 22-22.
BYRD, H. O., 19-12.
BYRNE, THOMAS A., 12-13, 13-13.
BYRNE, WILLIAM H., 16-11.

C.M.H.C., 13-16.
CAKE, VAN DEREN, 18-11, 18-15.
CABANNE, PIERRE, 18-11, 19-15.
CABOT, PHILIP, 16-11.
CADENHEAD, G. M., 11-11, 11-13.
CADWALLADER, CLYDE T., 22-18.
CADY, R. E., 19-11.
CAHILL, FRANK P., 12-11, 12-14.
CAIN, STATLEY A., 17-12, 17-14.
CAIX, PIERRE, 18-11, 19-15.
CALATCHI, ROBERT DE, 18-14, 18-15, 19-15.
CALDWELL, BERNARD L., 12-11, 22-18.
CALIF STATE BOARD OF EDUCATION DIV OF ASSMT STDRDS, 12-13.
CALIFORNIA BUILDING-LOAN LEAGUE, 11-14, 11-16.
CALIFORNIA DIVISION OF HIGHWAYS, 12-16.
CALIFORNIA OFFICE OF STATE CONTROLLER, 12-11, 12-13.
CALIFORNIA REAL ESTATE ASSOCIATION, 11-11, 11-12, 11-13, 11-14, 22-18.
CALIFORNIA STATE OFFICE OF PLANNING, 13-11, 14-11.
CALLAN, PROF. JOHN G., 23-11.
CALLAWAY, SAM, 12-13.
CALUSEN, DON H., 11-11, 11-12.
CALVERT, GEOFFREY N., 19-15, 22-18.
CALVIN, BRENDA, 11-11, 11-18.
CAMEHL, ADA WALKER, 18-15.
CAMERON, C. C., 11-11, 19-11, 19-14.
CAMERON, J. A., 17-12, 22-18.
CAMP, EHNEY A., JR., 19-12.
CAMPBELL, BERT, 11-14, 11-16.

CAMPBELL, CHARLES W., 12-14, 12-16.
CAMPBELL, COLIN, 12-14, 12-15, 12-16, 13-22.
CAMPBELL, GEORGE L., 13-19.
CAMPBELL, HARRY S., JR., 19-13.
CAMPBELL, JOHN M, 17-15.
CAMPBELL, ROBERT S., JR., 12-16, 12-18, 24-15.
CAMPBELL, S. J., 11-14, 11-19.
CAMPNEY, ALBERT E., 11-16, 12-11, 12-12, 12-13.
CANNON, DOUGLAS V., 13-16, 13-17.
CANNON, FERMOR S., 11-11, 11-16.
CANTERBURY, NATHAN D., 12-16, 17-12.
CANTWELL, ROBERT C. III, 11-11, 11-14, 11-16, 11-19.
CAPLAN, BENEDICTO, 12-11.
CAPPER, G. C. F., 11-11, 13-11, 13-13.
CAPPOZZA, DENNIS, 13-11, 13-14, 24-11, 24-12, 24-17.
CAPPS, WILLIS W., 12-16, 20-11.
CAPT, J. C., 11-14, 13-11.
CARB, MEREDITH R., 15-13, 17-15.
CARBERT, LESLIE E., 12-11, 13-11.
CARDON, BARTLEY P, 14-11.
CARDOZA, LEONARD R., 11-14, 11-16, 11-19, 12-24.
CARDUCCI, CARLO, 18-16, 18-17, 19-15.
CARESTIO, R. M. JR., 23-13.
CAREW, JOHN F., 11-14, 11-16.
CARHART, ARTHUR H., 17-16.
CARLE, DONALD DE, 18-15, 19-15.
CARLL, C. E., 12-15.
CARLL, CLOICE D., 12-14, 12-15, 12-16, 12-26.
CARLL, CLOICE, D., 12-16.
CARLSON, ALFRED E., 12-11, 12-13.
CARLSON, DAVID M., 22-18.
CARLSON, ERNEST WILLIAM PH. D., 17-17.
CARLSON, HAROLD J., 13-15.
CARLSON, HOWARD M., 13-15, 13-18, 21-12.
CARMAN, H. F., 12-11, 12-13, 14-15.
CARMAN, LEWIS A., 11-11, 11-14.
CARMICHAEL, D. R., 11-11, 19-15, 19-18.
CARMICHAEL, JAMES J., 11-14, 11-16.
CARNEY, JOHN J., 11-11, 11-14, 11-19, 12-16.
CARPENTER, MAURICE P., 12-13, 16-11.
CARPENTER, P. E., 12-15.
CARPER, RAYMOND E., 12-13, 13-15.
CARR, ANTHONY W., 11-11, 11-16, 12-12, 12-13, 13-13, 13-22, 22-17.
CARR, FRANCIS J., 12-13, 12-26, 13-15, 13-17.
CARR, JAMES E., 12-11, 24-14.
CARR, WAGGONER, 12-13.
CARRIER, W. H., 20-13.
CARROLL, WESLEY C., 11-11, 11-12.
CARRUTH, E., 13-11.
CARRUTHERS, G. R., 11-14, 11-16.
CARTER, A. C., 14-17.
CARTER, HOUSTON, 24-15.
CARTER, J. H., 12-11, 13-17.
CARTER, JAMES M., 12-16, 12-18.
CARTER, JOHN, 18-12.
CARTER, LOCH, 12-11.
CARTER, W. P., 13-16.
CARTER, W. PETER, 13-13, 13-16.
CARTWRIGHT, FRANK P., 19-11.
CARUSONE, PETER S., 13-11.
CASASSA, E. A. J., 18-15.
CASE, F. E., 13-13, 13-16.
CASE, FRED E., 11-11, 11-13, 11-14, 11-16, 11-18, 12-14, 13-11, 13-15, 13-16, 19-15, 22-18.

CASE, H. C. M., 14-15, 22-20.
CASEMENT, R., 11-18, 12-21.
CASETTI, E., 12-12, 22-19.
CASEY, JAMES, J., 12-11, 22-18.
CASEY, W. J., 12-11, 22-18.
CASS, F. M., 24-15.
CASTELLANOS, JOSE N., 13-21.
CASTENHOLZ, WILLIAM B., 11-11, 11-14, 11-19.
CATO, C. JACK, 12-11.
CAWTHRA, CHARLES E., 11-11, 11-16.
CAYWOOD, RUSSELL E, 16-12.
CESCINSKY, HERBERT, 18-18.
CESCINSKY, HERBUT, 18-14, 18-15, 19-15.
CHADEAYNE, ROBERT O., 11-11, 11-12, 11-18.
CHAFFE, R. S., 11-11, 12-24, 21-11.
CHAFFERS, WILLIAM, 18-14.
CHAIN STORE AGE, 13-11, 13-15.
CHALMERS, T. G., 11-11, 11-17, 21-11.
CHAMBERLAIN, EDWARD, 11-11, 11-16, 13-15.
CHAMBERLAIN, J. B., 12-16, 17-15.
CHAMBERLAIN, NARCISSA, 11-18, 12-17.
CHAMBERS, M. M., 13-16.
CHAMBERS, R. J., 11-11, 11-13.
CHAMOUX, FRANCOIS, 18-11, 18-15, 18-16, 19-15.
CHAMPION, ROBERT E., 24-15.
CHAMPNEY, ALBERT E., 12-11, 12-13, 22-18.
CHANDAK, MADHUSUDAN LAL, 21-11.
CHANDIAS, MARIO A., 11-11, 11-16.
CHANDIAS, MARIO E., 11-11, 11-12, 11-13, 11-14, 11-16,
    11-18, 11-19, 12-24, 13-14, 13-23, 21-11.
CHANDLER, JAMES K., 11-14.
CHANDLER, K. WILLIAM, 11-11, 11-16.
CHANDLER, MARVIN, 16-11, 19-15.
CHANDLER, RICHARD A., 12-13, 12-25, 13-19, 19-12.
CHAPMAN, CHARLES M., 12-11, 16-11, 19-16, 24-14.
CHAPMAN, FRED L., 13-15, 13-18, 19-11.
CHAPMAN, GORDON J., 13-19.
CHAPMAN, H. H., 17-12.
CHAPMAN, ROBERT L, 14-11.
CHAPMAN, W. M., 17-17.
CHAPPELL, PAUL S., 12-23.
CHARBEAU, JULES, 12-11.
CHARLAND, ROGER, 12-11, 13-15, 22-18.
CHARLES, ROLLO, 18-14, 19-15.
CHARLESTON, R. J., 18-13, 18-14, 19-15.
CHARLESTON, ROBERT J., 18-14, 19-15.
CHARPENTRAT, PIERRE, 18-14, 19-15.
CHASE, PRENTICE T., 22-11.
CHATELAIN, LEON, JR., 12-14, 12-24, 13-11.
CHATTERS, CARL H., 11-11, 11-19.
CHEMICAL WEEK, 18-14, 19-15.
CHEN, H. Y., 12-17, 12-19.
CHEN, Y. P., 12-11, 13-16.
CHENEY, SHELDON, 11-14.
CHENG, P. L., 12-13.
CHENG, PAO L., 12-11.
CHERNEY, RICHARD A., 11-11, 11-12, 11-14, 11-16, 11-19,
    12-13, 12-19, 12-24, 13-15, 22-11, 22-18.
CHERRY, RUSSELL C., 14-11, 19-15, 22-19, 22-20.
CHESLER, E. R., 13-17, 15-23.
CHESSMAN, MARK, 11-11, 11-12, 11-18, 13-17.
CHESTNUT, LOUIS C., 14-17.
CHIARELLI, RENZO, 18-11.
CHICAGO REAL ESTAE BOARD, 11-14.
CHICAGO REAL ESTATE BOARD, 11-14, 11-16.

CHICHESTER, C. H. JR., 12-14, 12-16.
CHICHESTER, JOHN, 12-16.
CHILD, JOHN F. JR., 12-25, 13-16.
CHILD, JOHN FRANCIS, JR., 11-11, 11-16, 11-19.
CHING, C. T. K., 12-11, 12-13.
CHIRHART, EDWARD F., 12-26, 13-17.
CHO, WHEWON PH. D., 12-23.
CHOLVIS, FRANCISCO, 12-11.
CHRISIAN, VIRGIL L., 16-12.
CHRISTENSEN, CARL C., 12-13.
CHRISTENSEN, ROBERT, 13-11.
CHRISTIAN, A. H., 24-15.
CHRISTIANSEN W. K. S., 19-15.
CHRISTOPHER, S. H., 12-11, 12-12.
CHURCH, A. HAMILTON, 13-15.
CHURCH, BYRON, 11-11, 11-13, 11-14, 11-18, 11-19, 12-24,
    13-16, 13-17, 13-19, 19-12.
CHURCH, BYRON M., 11-11, 11-12, 11-13, 11-14, 11-16,
    13-19.
CHURCH, EUGENE B., 11-11, 11-17, 11-19, 13-20.
CHURCHILL, WINSTON S., 11-11, 11-12, 11-18.
CIMELY, G., 12-11, 12-26, 22-18.
CINCINNATI, OHIO REAL ESTATE BOARD, 11-14,
    11-16.
CITIZEN'S UNION, NEW YORK CITY, 412-14.
CIVIL AERONAUTICS BOARD, 24-13.
CLARK ROBERT, 13-15.
CLARK, C. D., 11-11, 11-19, 12-24.
CLARK, COLIN, 13-11.
CLARK, EDWARD L., 12-11, 12-13, 17-12.
CLARK, FOREST F., 13-16, 13-17.
CLARK, FRANK B., 11-11, 11-14, 11-16.
CLARK, GILBERT K., 12-16, 23-11, 24-15.
CLARK, H. F., 11-13.
CLARK, HORACE F., 11-11, 11-13, 11-14, 11-16, 12-17,
    12-24, 13-11, 13-16, 13-17, 13-18, 13-19, 21-13, 22-22.
CLARK, HORACE FRISBY, 13-16.
CLARK, J. A., 13-11, 22-18.
CLARK, JOHN G., 22-18.
CLARK, KENNETH, 18-11, 18-12, 18-15, 18-16, 19-15.
CLARK, LOUIS M., 12-11, 13-19, 19-13.
CLARK, PATRICK H., 12-23.
CLARK, RALPH E., 12-13, 14-11.
CLARK, RAMSEY, 11-16, 25-11, 25-12, 25-13, 25-14, 25-15.
CLARK, ROBERT M., 12-11, 13-20.
CLARK, SIR KENNETH, 18-11, 19-15.
CLARK, W. C., 12-24, 19-15.
CLAUS, R. JAMES, 13-11, 13-15, 13-20.
CLAUSEN, DON H., 11-11, 11-12.
CLAVEL, BERNARD, 18-11, 18-12, 19-15.
CLAWSON, MARION, 12-11, 13-21.
CLAY, DEANE J., 12-14, 12-26.
CLAY, GRADY, 11-13, 13-17.
CLAY, WILLIAM, 23-11.
CLEMENS, ROBERT J., 18-11, 18-15, 19-15.
CLEMENTS, ROBERT J., 18-11, 18-13, 18-15, 19-15.
CLEMINSHAW COMPANY, 12-14, 12-15.
CLEMINSHAW, J. M., 12-11, 12-12, 12-17, 13-11.
CLEMINSHAW, J. M. CO., 12-14, 12-15.
CLEMINSHAW, WILLIAM, 12-13, 13-15.
CLENDENIN, J. C., 19-16.
CLENDENIN, S. C., 19-16.
CLEVELAND ASSN OF BUILDING OWNERS AND
    MANAGERS, 12-24, 13-20.
CLEVELAND HOUSING CO., 21-11.

# BIBLIOGRAPHY OF APPRAISAL LITERATURE

CLEVELAND REAL ESTATE BOARD, 11-14.
CLEVELAND, ALLEN L., 12-16, 13-15.
CLEVELAND, F. A, 12-25, 19-14, 24-14.
CLICKNER, EDWIN K., 12-19, 13-11.
CLIFFER, HAROLD J., 15-14.
CLIFFORD, ANN, 18-17.
CLIFFORD, ARTHUR M., 19-18.
CLIFFORD, DEREK, 18-11, 18-12, 18-13, 18-15, 19-15.
CLONTS, H. A., JR., 13-11.
CLOPPER, SIMON, 11-11, 11-14, 12-13.
CLOVER, VERNON T., 12-13, 22-18.
CLURMAN, ALBERT W., 11-11, 12-16, 21-11, 22-11.
CLURMAN, DAVID, 13-19, 19-15, 22-18.
CLYDE, GEORGE D., 17-16.
COATES, CULLEN W., 12-16.
COATES, JOHN J., 12-16.
COATES, THOMAS, 15-11, 19-13.
COBB, J, 18-15.
COBLEIGH, I. U., 13-20, 19-15, 19-16.
COCHRAN, GAIL V., 12-25, 13-15.
COCHRAN, JOHN D., 12-26.
COCHRANE, D. H., 13-17.
COCKE, RICHARD, 18-11, 18-15.
COCKERELL, SYDNEY C., 18-15.
COE, R. K., 22-19, 22-20.
COES, HAROLD V., 11-11, 11-19, 19-12.
COFFIN, GEORGE H. JR., 11-11, 11-16, 13-11, 13-20, 17-14.
COFFMAN, PAUL B., 12-11, 13-14, 13-15, 19-15, 19-16.
COGHLAN, THOMAS J., 19-11, 19-12.
COHEN, B. I., 13-17, 13-19.
COHEN, J. SOLIS, 13-18.
COHEN, LEO, 12-11, 24-14.
COHEN, MORRIS, 13-16.
COHEN, SAMUEL H., 20-11.
COHN, ALEXANDER, 13-19.
COHN, JOSEPH D., 12-16, 24-15.
COHN, WALTER W., 11-11, 12-14, 12-15, 12-20.
COLDSTREAM, J. N., 18-14.
COLE, ANN KILBORN, 18-15, 18-16.
COLE, ANNE KILBORN, 18-16.
COLE, F. M., 12-14, 17-12.
COLE, JOHN D., 11-14, 12-13, 12-14, 12-15, 12-17, 13-13.
COLE, LEE W., 22-11.
COLEAN, MILES, 21-16, 22-18, 23-13.
COLEMAN, DAN, 13-22, 22-15.
COLERIDGE, ANTHONY, 18-16, 19-15.
COLLANTE, JOSE, 12-13.
COLLARD, ELIZABETH, 18-14, 18-15, 19-15.
COLLIER, RONALD, 12-14.
COLLINS, C. F., 12-13.
COLLINS, E. R., 13-13, 13-16, 13-22, 22-17.
COLLINS, G. ROWLAND, 11-11, 11-16, 11-19, 13-16, 19-12.
COLLINS, H. G., 14-14.
COLOAN, H. BRONSON, 12-11, 22-19, 22-20.
COLORADO, 12-11, 12-13.
COLORADO ASSESSMENT METHODS COMMITTEE, 12-13.
COLORADO LEGISLATIVE COUNCIL, 12-13, 16-11.
COLORADO TAX COMMISSION, 12-13.
COLWELL, R. N., 11-14, 14-11, 22-11.
COMISKEY, E. E., 11-11, 12-24, 19-17.
COMMERCE TODAY, 13-11, 13-13, 13-15.
COMMITTEE FROM FIVE PRINCIPAL FEDERAL AGENCIES, 11-14, 11-15, 12-17.
COMSTOCK, HELEN, 18-15.

CON, J. M., 18-17.
CONAN, ROBERT J., 11-11, 11-12, 11-13, 11-14, 11-19.
CONDICT, HAROLD V., 11-11, 11-16.
CONDICT, HORACE V., 11-11, 11-14.
CONDON, JOHN A., 21-16.
CONGDON, WALTER B., 14-11, 14-12.
CONGER, GENE M., 12-14.
CONLEE, DONALD R., 12-19, 13-15.
CONLON, CHARLES F., 12-11, 12-26.
CONNAWAY, JOSEPH C., 13-15.
CONNELL, E. A., 17-13.
CONNELLY, C., 18-15.
CONNELLY, WILLIAM F., 12-11, 13-15, 23-11.
CONNERY, RUSSELL B., 12-13, 13-15.
CONNETICUT TAX COMMISSION, 12-11, 12-13.
CONNOISSEUR, 18-16.
CONNOLLY, DANIEL E., 14-11.
CONNOLLY, JOHN E., 13-13.
CONNORS, JOHN E., 16-15, 22-18.
CONRADS, ULRICH, 19-15.
CONRAN, C. L., 11-11, 11-17.
CONSER, EUGENE P., 11-11, 11-12.
CONSIDINE, CHARLES, 12-11.
CONSIDINE, CHARLES RAY, 11-11, 11-19, 12-11.
CONSTAM, E., 11-11, 11-12, 11-16.
CONVERSE, C. L., 13-11.
COOK, BILLY D, 12-11.
COOK, C WAYNE, 14-18.
COOK, D. C., 16-12.
COOK, R. M., 18-14, 19-15.
COOK, ROBERT S., 12-25, 14-11.
COOK, WALTER L., 15-14.
COOKE, A. C., 12-16.
COOKE, JOHN, 11-11, 11-12, 11-18.
COOMBE, J. P., 12-12, 12-13, 12-17.
COOMBS, DAVID, 18-11, 19-15.
COOMBS, WHITNEY, 12-11, 14-15.
COON, JEAN M., 12-14.
COOPER K. J., 11-18, 13-11, 14-11, 23-11, 23-13.
COOPER, ARTHUR PH. D., 11-11, 11-18, 19-15.
COOPER, DAVID, 18-11, 19-15.
COOPER, DOUGLAS, 18-11, 18-13, 18-15, 19-15.
COOPER, GEORGE H., 21-16.
COOPER, J. M., 11-14, 11-19.
COOPER, J. ROBERT, 12-13, 14-15, 22-18.
COOPER, JAMES, 19-13.
COPELAND, HARRY E., 13-11, 13-14, 13-17.
COPPARD CHARLES, 19-12.
COPPOCK, D. J., 11-11, 11-19.
CORDIER, HENRY K, 18-15, 18-18, 19-15.
CORDIER, HENRY K., 11-11, 11-12, 11-16, 12-23, 13-17, 13-19, 19-15.
CORMAN, R. R., 14-11.
CORNICK, PHILIP H., 12-13, 22-19, 22-20.
CORNISH, GEOFFREY S., 15-14.
CORNYN, JOHN E., 13-18.
CORUCH, WILLIAM H., 12-14, 12-20.
COSGROVE, MICHAEL HENRY PH. D., 16-14.
COSTA RICA, 22-11, 22-14, 22-18.
COTTE, SABINE, 18-11, 19-15.
COTTEN, ROBERT, 12-16, 13-22, 22-17.
COTTON, JOHN, 12-14.
COTTON, W. O., 11-11.
COTTON, W. OWEN, 13-17, 13-19.
COUGHLAN, J. D., 12-24.

COULSON, ROBERT, 11-11, 11-12, 11-18.
COULSON, ROBERT M, 11-11, 11-12, 11-18.
COURTHION, PIERRE, 18-11, 19-15.
COURTNEY, ALBERT J., 13-20.
COVEY, FRANK M. JR., 12-18, 24-15.
COWARD, WILLIAM, 13-19, 18-16.
COWIE, DONALD, 18-16.
COWLES, HERBERT V., 12-13, 13-11.
COWLEY, LEONARD M., 11-11, 11-14, 11-16, 12-15, 12-16, 13-11, 13-20, 14-18, 24-13.
COX, W. E. JR., 12-22, 13-15.
COX, WARREN E., 11-11, 11-19, 18-11, 18-12, 18-13, 18-14, 18-15, 18-17, 19-15, 19-18.
COYLE, JOSEPH A., 11-14, 11-19, 12-11.
CRAFT, D. JAMES, 13-18, 13-19.
CRAGIN, RAYMOND T., 11-11, 19-14, 19-15, 19-16, 19-17.
CRAIG, R. H., 11-11, 11-14, 11-19, 12-11, 12-13, 12-20, 13-17.
CRAIG, ROBERT H., 12-13, 12-24, 13-15.
CRAIGEN, GEORGE J., 11-14, 11-19.
CRAIGIE, EDWARD JOHN, 22-19.
CRAMER, FLOYD, 11-11, 11-19, 19-11.
CRAMER, J. J., JR., 12-23.
CRANSTONE, J. G., 21-15.
CRAWFAORD, CLAUDE O., 12-16.
CRAWFORD, CLAUDE O., 12-14, 12-15, 12-16, 12-18, 13-15.
CRAWFORD, EDWARD J., 22-18.
CRAWFORD, EDWARD J. JR., 13-20.
CRAWFORD, LOTTIE L., 13-21.
CREE, JAMES W. JR., 12-24.
CREEDY, JOHN A., 13-11, 17-16, 24-11, 24-12.
CRESPO, MANUEL, 11-14, 12-11, 12-13.
CRETIEN, P. D. JR., 19-16.
CRIPPS, WILFRED JOSEPH, 18-14, 18-15, 19-15.
CRIST, MARION, 11-11, 11-18.
CRIVELLATO, VALENTINE, 18-11, 19-15.
CROCHERON, CLARENCE, 11-11, 11-16, 12-13, 12-24, 13-15, 19-14, 19-15, 21-11, 23-11.
CROCKETT, J., 19-16.
CRONER, FRED, JR., 12-15, 12-16.
CRONHEIM, DAVID, 11-11, 11-13.
CRONK, E. A., 12-20.
CROOK, HOWARD W., 23-14.
CROOK, J. MORDAUNT, 18-16.
CROSBY, HARRY L., 11-14, 11-19.
CROUCH, WILLIAM H., 12-18, 12-19, 15-14.
CROUEN, THOMAS, 18-11.
CROUSE, EARL F., 11-14, 14-11, 22-19, 22-20.
CROWLEY, WILLIAM DAVID JR., 14-11.
CROWNINGSHIELD, ROBERT, 18-17.
CRUNDEN, ALLAN B., 16-15.
CRUTCHFIELD, JAMES A., 17-17.
CUERPO TECNICO DE TASACIONES DEL PERU, 11-11, 11-18.
CUMMINGS, J. S., 11-14, 11-16.
CUMMINGS, JOHN S., 16-11.
CUMMINGS, LAWRENCE B., 22-19, 22-20.
CUMMINS, C. R., 11-11, 11-16, 11-19.
CUMMINS, CHARLES A., 11-11, 11-13.
CUNLIFFE, H. L., 21-11.
CUNNINGHAM, F. M., 12-16, 22-12, 23-11.
CUNNINGHAM, J. B., 14-11, 14-15, 19-13.
CUNNYNGHAM, WILKIE, 12-16, 12-26, 22-16.
CURRAN, DONALD J., 12-11, 13-13, 13-17.
CURRY, CHARLES F., 11-14, 11-19.

CURTIS, S. G., 13-15.
CUSHION, J. P., 18-15, 19-15.
CUSHION, JOHN P., 18-14, 19-15.
CZOBOR, AGNES, 18-11.


D.C. STORUD, 19-15, 22-18.
D' RUGGIERO, LORENZO, 11-11, 11-16.
DADDO, DR. JEROME, 12-14.
DAGGETT, S., 16-15.
DAHLSTROM, B. P., 16-11.
DAIL, CHARLES C., 13-17, 16-16.
DALEFIELD, K. S., 12-11.
DALGETY, GEORGE S., 12-14, 13-19, 19-12, 19-13, 19-18.
DALLAVIA, L., 21-16.
DAMASE, JACQUES, 18-15.
DANA, RICHARD TURNER, 20-15.
DANAHEY, THOMAS P., 13-16, 13-17, 13-18, 13-19.
DANCE, PETER S., 18-15.
DANGE, M N, 11-11, 11-19.
DANNER, E. H., 12-11, 16-15.
DANNIEL, W. S., 13-17.
DARBY, CLEMENT H., 11-11, 11-19, 12-23.
DARIO GONZALEZ, RUBEN, 11-11, 11-13, 12-19.
DARK, TAYLOR, 12-19.
DARM, ADAM EUGENE, 11-11, 11-16, 11-19, 23-11.
DARRACH, CHARLES GOBRECHT, 16-11.
DARSEY, GLENN S., 12-14, 12-18.
DASSO, DR. JEROME, 12-25, 19-12.
DASSO, JEROME, 11-11, 11-19, 12-13.
DASSO, JEROME J., 19-13.
DAULTE, FRANCOIS, 18-11, 18-15, 19-15.
DAVENPORT, HERBERT JOSEPH, 11-11, 11-17.
DAVID, E. L., 12-11, 12-13.
DAVID, MARTIN, 12-11, 19-14.
DAVIDSON, J. B., 14-11, 21-11.
DAVIDSON, JAMES R., 13-19, 13-20.
DAVIDSON, ROBERT C., 22-16.
DAVIDSON, THOMAS LEA, 12-16, 13-15.
DAVIDSON, WILLIAM R., 11-11, 13-14, 13-15.
DAVIE, GIBSON A., 18-13.
DAVIE, MAURICE R., 13-11.
DAVIES, C. M., 14-11, 22-24.
DAVIES, CHARLES T., 11-11, 11-14.
DAVIES, CLARENCE, J., 11-11, 11-14, 11-16.
DAVIES, DAVID G., 13-11.
DAVIES, DEREK C., 18-15, 18-16, 19-15.
DAVIES, MARTIN, 18-11, 18-13, 18-15.
DAVIES, MAURICE B. T., 11-14, 12-11, 12-13.
DAVIES, WILLIAM E., 22-18.
DAVIS, ARTHUR M., 12-11.
DAVIS, CLAUDE J., 12-17.
DAVIS, D. B., 13-19.
DAVIS, DEREK C., 18-14, 18-15, 18-16.
DAVIS, DEREK C. AND KEITH MIDDLEMAS, 18-15, 19-15.
DAVIS, E. G., 13-22, 22-17.
DAVIS, H. D., 15-25, 19-15.
DAVIS, IRVING F. JR., 11-14, 14-11.
DAVIS, IRWIN, 13-19.
DAVIS, J. C., 13-20.
DAVIS, J. CLARENCE, JR., 11-11, 11-14.
DAVIS, J. TAIT, 13-14, 13-16, 13-19.
DAVIS, JERRY C., 11-12, 12-26, 22-18, 24-15.

## BIBLIOGRAPHY OF APPRAISAL LITERATURE

DAVIS, JOHN W., 12-16, 16-15.
DAVIS, N. L., 11-14, 20-11, 20-12, 20-13, 20-14, 20-15.
DAVIS, NOBLE L., 21-18.
DAVIS, R. A., 12-11, 12-14.
DAVIS, ROBERT A., 12-20, 14-15.
DAVIS, W. D., 11-11, 11-12, 11-13, 11-14, 11-16, 11-19, 12-11, 12-14, 12-16, 12-18, 13-14, 13-21, 13-23, 14-11, 14-15, 14-16, 19-12, 22-17, 22-18, 24-15, 25-11, 25-12, 25-13, 25-14.
DAVIS, W. D. MAI, 12-26.
DAVIS, W. D. SR., 14-16, 22-18.
DAVIS, WILLIAM D., 11-11, 11-17, 11-19, 21-11, 24-15.
DAVIS, WILLIAM D. SR., 13-23.
DAVIS, WILLIAM M., 11-11, 12-16.
DAWLEY, CHESTER G., 11-11, 11-14.
DAWNES, KERRY, 18-11, 18-13, 18-15, 19-15.
DAWNIE, LEONARD, 11-14, 11-16.
DAWSONS OF PALL MALL, 11-14, 18-11, 18-12, 18-13, 18-14, 18-15.
DAY DESMOND D., 11-11.
DAY, J. EDWARD, 13-16.
DAY, JOSEPH P., 22-18.
DE BELLAIGUE, G., 18-18, 19-15.
DE CANN, C. G. L., 18-11.
DE JONGE, C. H., 18-14, 18-15.
DE LEEUW, F., 13-11, 13-16.
DE LIMA H. A., 12-23, 22-19, 22-20.
DE NOYELLES F., 11-11, 11-12.
DE SALES PEREZ, FRANCISCO, 11-11, 11-16, 11-18, 13-18.
DE SALVO, J. S., 12-11, 13-18, 19-15.
DE VRIES, ROSCOE, 12-15, 12-16, 24-14.
DE WOLFE, P., 11-14, 12-24.
DEAN, J., 12-11, 19-14, 19-15.
DEBOOS, FRANK A., 11-11, 11-16, 12-15, 12-24, 13-15, 19-13, 20-14, 22-11, 22-18, 22-19, 22-20, 22-22.
DEBREU, GERARD, 11-11.
DEBUTTS, CARY E., 13-15, 19-13.
DECKER, ORVILLE, 13-17.
DECKMAN, WILLIAM L., 12-15.
DEEBLES, V. A., 18-15.
DEFFEY, SARLE M., 12-16.
DEGLER, GEORGE FREDERICK, PH. D., 15-15, 15-20.
DEGRAFF, HERRELL, 23-11.
DEGRAFF, JOHN T., 11-14.
DELGADO, CLARENCE N., 12-13.
DELIEB, ERIC, 18-14, 18-15, 19-15.
DELL, BURNHAM N., 13-11.
DEMARA, CYRIL R., 11-11, 11-16, 11-19, 19-17.
DEMICK, A., 18-15.
DEMMERY, JOSEPH, 11-11, 11-16.
DEMUS, OTTO, 18-11, 19-15.
DENAPOLI, CHARLES, 11-17, 11-19.
DENIS, J. W., 11-11, 11-14, 11-17, 11-19, 12-14.
DENISION, TONY, 18-16, 18-65, 19-15.
DENTON JOHN H., 11-14, 11-19, 12-24, 21-11.
DENTON, JOHN H., 11-16, 11-18, 11-19, 12-24, 13-11, 13-14, 22-18.
DEPARTMENT OF AGRICULTURE, 22-19, 22-20.
DERBES, JR., MAX J., 23-11.
DERBES, MAX J., 11-11, 11-19, 12-24, 22-21.
DERBES, MAX J. JR., 12-15, 12-16, 13-19, 19-15.
DERBES, MAX J. JR., 11-11, 11-14, 11-16, 11-19, 12-14, 12-15, 12-16, 12-18, 12-24, 12-26, 13-17, 13-18, 13-19, 13-22, 16-12, 22-17, 22-18.
DERBES, MAX J. JR. MAI, 12-16.
DERBES, MAX J. SR., 11-13, 21-12.
DERBY, LOUIS F., 11-19, 13-15.
DES JARDINS, RICHARD J., 13-11, 13-17.
DESALVO, J. S., 12-11, 13-18, 19-15.
DESCHARNES, ROBERT, 18-11.
DETROIT BUREAU OF GOVERNMENTAL RESEARCH, 12-14.
DETROIT REAL ESTATE BOARD, 21-11.
DEUTSCH, JOSEPH S., 12-14.
DEVELOPMENT VALUE, 11-19, 13-23.
DEWEY, EDWARD R., 11-11, 11-14, 21-18.
DEWEY, JOHN M., 12-16, 17-16, 22-21.
DEZEEUW, J. W., 22-16.
DIAMOND, JOSEF, 12-14.
DIAMOND, MAURICE, 18-11.
DIAMOND, THOMAS M., 12-14.
DIAMOND, THOMAS M. JR., 12-14.
DIEHL, PROF. CONRAD, 18-12.
DIEPENBROCK, BRAM, 12-16, 20-11, 20-15.
DIERCKS, K. J., 12-16, 22-21.
DIERKER, GERALD J., 11-19, 12-24, 16-11.
DIESSLIN, HOWARD G., 14-11.
DIETZ, P. O., 11-19, 19-15, 19-17.
DILL, ORVAL, 14-11, 19-12.
DILLE, J. M., 14-13, 14-15.
DILMORE, G., 11-11, 11-19, 12-14, 12-24, 19-15.
DILMORE, GENE, 11-11, 11-14, 11-16, 11-17, 11-19, 13-11, 22-17, 22-18.
DINGER, JULIUS J., 15-15, 22-18.
DINGMAN, CHARLES F., 21-13.
DISTELHORST, CARL F., 11-11, 11-18.
DITCHY, CLAIR W., 13-19.
DITTRICH, N. E., 11-11, 11-16.
DIX, S. M., 12-14, 20-11.
DIX, SAMUEL M., 12-14, 12-15, 20-11.
DIX, W. B., 12-11, 17-14.
DOANE, D. HOWARD, 14-11.
DOBIE, J. FRANK, TOM LEA, 18-11, 18-15.
DOCKSTADER, FREDERICK J., 18-12, 18-15, 19-15.
DODD, DAVID LE FEVRE, 16-14, 19-16.
DODD, EDWARD, 18-12, 18-15, 19-15.
DODDS, R. W., 11-14, 12-24.
DODGE, F. W. CORP., 21-13.
DODGE, JOSEPH W., 19-11, 22-18.
DODGE, RICHARD L., 13-15.
DODGSON, CAMPBELL, 18-12, 19-15.
DOELGER, WILLIAM E. P., 13-19.
DOERING, WARNER W., 19-12.
DOFSTEDT, CARL J., 23-14.
DOHERTY, RICHARD M., 12-21, 13-19, 22-18.
DOIRON, J. CLIFFORD, 11-14, 11-16.
DOLAN, HARRY T., 11-11, 11-14, 12-14, 12-18, 12-26, 20-11.
DOLAN, THOMAS A., 11-11, 13-19, 19-12, 19-15.
DOLLE, HODGE L., 12-14.
DOLMAN, JOHN P., 11-11, 11-12, 11-13, 11-14, 11-16, 11-18, 11-19, 12-19, 13-21.
DOMENECH, RAFAEL, 18-16, 19-15.
DONAHOO, JOHN W., 12-11.
DONETH, JOHN G., 14-11, 21-11.
DONNELLY, P. J., 18-15.
DONOGH, A. ORMSBY, 13-21, 22-18.
DONOGH, A. ORMSBY, JR., 11-14, 11-16.
DONOGHUE, DAVID, 17-15.
DONOVAN, J., 12-11, 12-25, 18-11.

DOODHA, KERSI D., 11-11.
DORAN, SAMUEL M, 14-14.
DORAU, HERBERT B., 11-11, 11-14, 11-16, 11-19, 13-11, 13-16, 16-11, 22-19.
DORION, GUY, 11-11, 11-12, 11-18.
DOUD, LAURENCE F., 12-22, 13-11, 17-50.
DOUGLAS, R. BRUCE., 11-14.
DOW SERVICE, INC., 11-14.
DOW, PETER, 12-16.
DOWELL, J. M., 14-13.
DOWELL, JESSE M, 14-11.
DOWLE, ANTHONY, 18-15.
DOWLING, J. W. F., 22-18.
DOWLING, ROBERT E., 22-18.
DOWNIE, LEONARD, 11-11, 11-12, 11-14, 11-19.
DOWNING, C., 17-14.
DOWNING, W. C., 17-14.
DOWNS, ANTHONY, 11-11, 11-16, 13-11, 13-13.
DOWNS, GEORGE W., 12-11, 13-11.
DOWNS, JAMES C., 11-11, 11-16, 12-13, 13-13.
DOWNS, M. D., 12-11, 12-13, 13-11.
DOXIADIS, C. A., 13-11, 13-13.
DOYLE, B. E., 13-13, 13-15.
DOYLE, JOHN P., 12-11, 12-16.
DOZIER, S. ROBERT, 12-11.
DRAKE LAW REVIEW, 12-11, 13-21.
DREANEY, LEONARD, 12-13.
DRENNAN, GEORGE W., 13-15, 23-11.
DRENNAN, SHELDON L., 13-20.
DREPPARD, CARL W., 18-16.
DRISCOLL, FRED S., 21-13.
DRISCOLL, ROBERT L., 12-14, 17-15.
DRISCOLL, T. LORIN, 13-19.
DRUCKER, E. R., 12-19.
DRUMN, EDWARD P., 13-17.
DRURY, EUELYN, 11-15, 11-18.
DUBIELZIG, R. C., 16-11.
DUBOIS, AYERS J., 11-11, 11-14, 11-16, 11-18, 11-19, 12-14, 12-24, 13-15, 13-16, 13-17, 13-19, 19-12, 19-13.
DUBY, GEORGES, 18-11, 19-15.
DUCK, BERKLEY W., 11-11, 11-12.
DUCKLIEB, BRUNO, 13-15.
DUDLEY, JAMES E., 11-11, 11-18.
DUERR, MICHAEL G., 14-11.
DUERR, WILLIAM A., 17-12.
DUFFEY, EARLE M., 12-14.
DUFFY, G., 13-16, 13-21, 16-11, 20-13, 21-13, 21-16.
DUFFY, GEORGE C., 11-11, 11-12, 12-13, 12-14, 12-16.
DUGGIN, MARSHALL E., 12-13, 13-13.
DUHAMEL, L. A., 11-11, 22-18, 22-19, 22-20.
DUKE, RICHARD D., 13-17.
DUKE, RICHARD DE LA BARRE, 24-15.
DUNCAN, KENNETH, 13-19, 19-15.
DUNHAM, HOWARD W. JR., 11-14, 11-17, 13-19.
DUNLAP, DONALD C., 12-16, 24-15.
DUNN, CECIL L., 11-11, 11-19, 22-18.
DUNN, DOMINICK R., 11-11, 11-12, 11-13, 11-14, 11-16, 11-17, 11-18, 11-19, 12-14, 12-20, 12-24, 12-26, 13-13, 13-19, 14-15, 21-11, 21-12, 21-13, 21-14, 22-18.
DUPIN, JACQUES, 18-11, 19-15.
DURHAM, WILLIAM K., 14-11.
DUSSLER. LUITPOLD, 18-11, 18-15.
DUTTON, 18-14.
DUVALL, GARNER W., 14-11.
DUVALL, LOY CLEVELAND LEE, 12-11, 12-12, 22-18.

DWYER, JAY J., 12-11, 12-24, 21-11.
DYE, DEWEY A. JR., 12-15.
DYESS, WILLIAM B., 19-15.
DYKE, JOHN B., 12-13, 13-19.
DYKSTRA, GERALD O., 11-11, 11-13, 11-14, 11-16.
DYSON, J. F., 11-14, 11-16.

EAGAN, LAURENCE J., 11-11, 12-11, 12-12, 12-13.
EAGLE, GORDON E., 13-17.
EAMER A. STANLEY, 12-13.
EARLY, ALEXANDER R., 12-12.
EAST CENTRAL REGIONAL ADVISORY COMMITTEE, 16-11, 16-12, 19-15.
EASTBURN, DAVID P., 11-11.
EASTBURN, WALTER N., 22-16, 24-14.
EASTWOOD H. W., 11-11, 11-18.
EATHERLY, BILLY J., 16-11.
EATON, J. D., 12-24.
EATON, KEITH E., 12-20.
EBERHARDT, DUANE O., 13-16, 13-19.
ECHANDIA, DEVIS HERNANDO, 12-11.
ECKER-RACZ, L LAZLO, 12-11.
ECKER-RACZ, L. L., 12-11.
ECKERSBERG, ALFRED K., 13-16.
ECKERT, FRED W., 12-11, 12-25, 13-15.
ECKHARDT, ROBERT A., 12-13.
ECKHOFF, HARRY C., 15-14.
ECKLEY, ROBERT S., 13-16.
ECKSTEIN, ARTHUR, 11-11, 11-12.
ECONOMIC OBSOLESCENCE, 11-14.
EDDINS, ROBERT E., 13-19.
EDENS, DAVID, 12-15, 19-12.
EDEY, WINTHROP, 18-15, 18-16, 19-15.
EDGERTON, W. H., 21-13.
EDGERTON, WILLIAM H., 11-14, 21-13.
EDMAN, J. J., 11-11, 11-12, 11-13, 11-14, 11-18, 11-19, 12-14, 12-15, 12-16, 12-18, 12-20, 12-23, 12-26, 13-11, 13-13, 13-15, 13-17, 13-20, 13-21, 13-22, 14-11, 14-13, 14-15, 15-12, 16-11, 17-14, 17-15, 17-16, 19-13, 19-15, 21-12, 21-18, 22-11, 22-14, 22-15, 22-18, 22-19, 22-20, 22-21, 22-22, 24-13.
EDMONDS, E. C., 19-12.
EDMONDS, M. G., 13-20.
EDMUNDS, JOHN T., 12-14.
EDWARDES, CYRIL R., 21-13.
EDWARDS, EDWARD E., 22-18.
EDWARDS, FRANK M., 11-16, 12-24.
EGERTON, J. W., 11-11, 11-12, 11-14, 11-19, 13-23.
EGGER, R. L. JR., 13-15.
EHERT, WILLIAM C., 12-23.
EHLERS, HENRY W., 12-16, 19-15.
EICHEN, C., 13-16.
EICHENBERG, EUGENE, JR., 13-15.
EICHHORN, VICTOR H., 12-16.
EIKMEYER, LEO J., 13-19.
EIKMEYER, LEO J., 13-17.
EILERTS, HOPE, 11-11, 11-13, 11-16.
EINSTEIN, EDWIN M., 11-11, 11-14.
EISENLAUER, JACK F., 11-11, 11-14, 12-11, 12-12, 12-13.
EISGRUBER, LUDWIG M., 14-11.
EITEMAN, DAVID K., 12-11.
ELDER, HERBERT W., 22-19, 22-20, 24-15.
ELIOT, ALEXANDER, 18-11, 19-15.

# BIBLIOGRAPHY OF APPRAISAL LITERATURE

ELKIN, A. DAVIS, 14-12.
ELLER, HERBERT D., 11-14, 11-16, 13-15, 13-19.
ELLIOTT ADDRESSING MACHINE CO., 12-11.
ELLIOTT, E. N. R., 12-20.
ELLIOTT, F. E., 14-11.
ELLIOTT, RALPH A., 14-15.
ELLIS, C. G., 18-16.
ELLIS, J. H., 11-11, 11-18.
ELLIS, LESTER J., 12-16, 24-15.
ELLIS, ROSS M., 12-15, 17-12.
ELLWOOD, L. W., 11-11, 11-14, 11-16, 11-19, 12-14, 13-19, 19-12, 19-15, 21-11, 21-16.
ELLWOOD, LEON W., 11-11, 11-12, 11-13, 11-14, 11-16, 11-19, 12-25, 13-15, 13-19, 19-11, 19-12, 19-18, 21-11, 22-18.
ELLWOOD, LEON, W., 22-18.
ELSE-MITCHELL, JUSTICE, 11-11, 11-12.
ELY, O., 11-19, 12-24, 16-11, 23-11.
ELY, RICHARD T., 11-11, 13-11, 22-11.
EMBREE, WILLIAM L., 11-14, 11-16.
EMERSON, DONALD M., 13-19.
EMERSON, F. C., 13-19.
EMERY, HAZEN C., 23-11.
EMMENEGGER, EDWIN F., 12-15.
EMPSON, W. JENNINGS, 12-14.
ENDELMAN, EDWARD, 11-13, 11-16.
ENEMARK, FRED, 13-17, 23-13.
ENFIELD, C. W., 12-16, 24-15.
ENFIELD, CLIFTON W., 12-14, 12-16, 20-11, 24-15. 12-18.
ENGGASS, ROBERT, 18-11, 18-15, 19-15.
ENGINEERING NEW RECORD, 21-13.
ENGINEERING NEWS RECORD, 21-13.
ENGINEERING NEWS-RECORD, 13-11, 13-12, 13-15, 13-20, 16-16, 17-16, 19-14, 20-12, 21-16.
ENGLAND, WESLEY P., 12-23.
ENGLE, NATHANIEL, 11-11, 19-14, 19-15.
ENGLEHORN, V. A., 11-11, 11-14, 11-16, 14-11, 14-15, 14-18.
ENO FOUNDATION, 13-12.
ENTREKEN, HENRY C. JR., 12-21, 13-19, 19-12.
ENTWISTLE, WALLACE E., 13-15.
EPPINK, NORMAN, 18-11, 18-12, 18-15, 19-15.
ERBACH, GEORGE H., 12-13, 19-13.
ERNANDEZ, JUSTINO, 18-11, 18-12, 18-14, 18-15.
ERNST, E. CHARLES, 13-16.
ERSKINE, R. C., 13-11, 13-15.
ETHERIDGE, KEN, 18-12, 18-15.
ETTEMAN, DAVID K., 12-11, 16-11, 19-16.
ETTINGER, VIRGIL P., 12-11.
ETTLINGER, L. D., 18-11, 18-15, 18-16.
EUROPEAN CUSTOMS UNION STUDY GROUP., 12-11.
EVANS, BERNARD G., 12-16, 14-11.
EVANS, DONALD D., 13-19.
EVANS, JOHN M., 12-18.
EVANS, LOUIS H., 17-15.
EVANS, MARVIN J., 12-15, 12-16, 16-12.
EVERETTE, C. H., 12-11, 14-15.
EVERS, CECIL C., 13-20.
EVERTS, FRANK, 12-23, 18-17.
EVERTS, HENRY P., 12-11.
EWING, JOSEPH NEFF, 12-16.
EWING, WILLIAM O. JR., 12-16.
EXPRESS PUBLISHING CO., 13-17, 13-19.
EZEKIEL, MORDECAI, 11-11, 11-14, 11-16.
F.P.C., 12-24, 16-13, 19-15.

FABIAN, ROBERT H., 12-16.
FACK, ALBERT, 18-18.
FAGG, WILLIAM, 18-14, 19-15.
FAIR, E. W., 13-12, 13-14, 24-11, 24-12, 24-17.
FALKINER, RICHARD, 18-16, 18-17, 19-15.
FALLIN, G. H., 11-11, 11-16.
FALLON, C., 11-11, 11-18.
FALLOON, WILBUR J., 11-11, 11-13.
FALUDI, E. G., 13-11, 13-13.
FANIEL, STEPHONE, 18-11.
FARM AND LAND REALTOR, 13-17.
FARM AND RANCH BROKERS MANUAL, 14-11.
FARM APPRAISAL WORK AT COLLEGE LEVEL, 14-15.
FARR JR, WILLIAM, 14-18.
FARRELL, PAUL B. JR., 11-11, 11-19, 19-15.
FARREN, JOHN R., 12-19, 13-17.
FARRINGTON WILLIAM C., 12-16, 22-21.
FARSTAD, E. K., 12-14.
FARSTAD, E. KARL, 12-20.
FAULKNER, P. G., 21-16.
FAVA, EDWARD, 11-11, 11-14, 11-16, 12-14, 12-18, 13-11, 13-15.
FAVELA, NORVEL F., 21-13.
FAY, CLIFFORD T., 13-15.
FEATHERMAN, B. E., 13-20.
FEATHERSTON, F. B., 11-14, 11-19.
FEC, 16-11, 16-12, 19-15.
FEDERAL RESERVE BANK OF KANSAS CITY, 14-11.
FEDERAL HOME LOAN BANK REVIEW, 11-11, 11-14, 11-16, 13-17, 19-13, 19-15, 22-18.
FEDERAL HOUSING ADMINISTRATION, 13-11, 13-13, 13-17, 24-13.
FEDERAL POWER COMMISSION, 16-11, 16-12, 19-15.
FEDERAL POWER COMISSION, 16-12, 16-13, 16-14, 17-15.
FEDERAL POWER COMMISION, 16-12, 19-15, 21-16.
FEDERAL POWER COMMISSION, 11-14, 12-11, 12-15, 12-16, 12-24, 12-26, 13-15, 16-11, 16-12, 16-13, 16-14, 17-15, 17-16, 17-17, 19-15, 21-16.
FEDERAL POWER COMMISSION STAFF REPORT, 16-12, 17-15.
FEDERAL REAL ESTATE BOARD, 11-11.
FEDERAL RESERVE BANK OF CLEVELAND, 14-11, 24-13.
FEDERAL RESERVE BANK OF BOSTON, 11-14, 11-16, 25-11.
FEDERAL RESERVE BANK OF CHICAGO, 11-11, 13-11, 13-16, 13-17, 13-22, 13-23, 14-15, 19-15, 22-20.
FEDERAL RESERVE BANK OF CLEVELAND, 11-11, 11-14, 11-16, 13-11, 13-17, 14-11, 19-15, 22-19.
FEDERAL RESERVE BANK OF DALLAS, 11-11, 11-19.
FEDERAL RESERVE BANK OF NEW YORK, 11-18.
FEDERAL RESERVE BANK OF PHILADELPHIA, 11-18, 13-15, 13-16, 13-21.
FEDERAL RESERVE BANK OF RICHMOND, 14-11.
FEDERAL RESERVE BANK OF SAN FRANCISCO, 11-19, 17-12.
FEDERAL RESERVE BANK OF ST. LOUIS, 11-11, 11-14, 11-18, 11-19, 14-15, 22-20, 25-11, 25-12, 25-13, 25-14, 25-15.
FEDERAL TAX ADMINISTRATION, 12-11, 13-16, 25-11.
FEDERATION OF TAX ADMINISTRATORS, 12-11, 12-12, 25-11.
FEINSCHREIBER, R., 12-11, 12-24.
FELD, CHARLES, 18-11, 19-15.
FELT, JAMES, 13-11.

FENTON, HARRY R., 11-11, 11-12, 11-14, 11-16, 12-16.
FENWICK, D. R., 12-11, 19-12.
FERBOS, JACQUES, 12-20.
FERGUSON, ABNER H., 13-13.
FERGUSON, EGBERT R. JR., 11-13, 11-14, 11-16.
FERGUSON, FRANCIS E, 14-15.
FERGUSON, HILL, 11-11, 11-14, 11-16, 12-11, 12-12, 12-13, 13-17, 19-11.
FERGUSON, W. E., 11-12.
FERNIER, ROBERT, 18-15.
FERRARI, ENRIQUE LAFUENTE, 18-12, 19-15.
FERRERO, MDRCEDES VIALE, 18-15.
FERRERO, PAUL E., 11-13, 11-16, 11-18.
FICK, H. G. E., 12-13, 14-15, 24-15.
FIEDLER, A. C., 14-16.
FIELD, RALPH V., 11-11, 11-14, 11-16, 11-19, 12-24, 13-19, 14-11, 14-15.
FIELD, SAM HOUSTON, 12-13.
FIELD, SAMUEL, 13-18.
FIELD, WAYNE, 13-21.
FIFER, LOUIS J., 11-11, 11-12.
FILLEY, ROBERT B., 13-11, 22-21.
FINANCIAL WORLD, 19-15, 19-16.
FINBURGH, BERT J., 11-11, 11-14, 19-15.
FINCH, NELSON E., 11-11, 11-16, 12-22, 13-15.
FINCH, NELSON E., 13-15.
FINEHAUM, M. L., 19-18, 22-18, 22-19, 22-20.
FINKEL, JULIUS, 12-14, 13-15.
FINNEGAN, G T, 19-15.
FINNIS, FREDERIC H., 12-13, 22-18.
FINOL, VINCENCIO BAEZ, 12-11, 14-11.
FIREY, WALTER, 13-17.
FISCHER, ERNEST M., 19-12, 22-18.
FISCHER, R. M., 11-11, 11-12, 11-14, 11-16, 11-18, 12-24, 12-25, 19-14, 19-16, 21-11, 21-18, 23-11.
FISCHER, REINHARD M., 11-14, 11-16.
FISH, JOHN C. L., 21-11, 21-16, 21-19.
FISHER, DONALD M., 12-13, 19-16, 24-14.
FISHER, E. M., 11-11, 11-16, 19-15.
FISHER, EDMOND C., 12-15, 13-11.
FISHER, ERNEST M., 11-11, 11-14, 11-16, 13-11, 13-13, 13-14, 13-16, 13-19, 13-23, 22-18.
FISHER, GEORGE L., 11-14.
FISHER, HENRY F., 12-23, 13-15.
FISHER, LEIGH, 23-12, 24-13.
FISHER, OSCAR, 22-19, 22-20.
FISHER, R. M., 11-11, 11-16, 19-15, 21-18.
FISHER, ROBERT M., 13-16.
FISHER, ROBERT MOORE, 13-20, 19-12.
FISHER, STANLEY, 18-14, 19-15.
FISHER, STANLEY W., 18-15.
FISHER, WILLIAM C., 16-11.
FISK, ELMORE A., 11-11, 11-16.
FISK, KENNETH, 12-11, 13-19, 13-20, 13-21, 17-12.
FISKE, W. P., 11-15, 23-11.
FISKEN, A. J., 11-11, 11-12.
FITZGERALD, DESMOND, 18-18.
FITZGERALD, WILLIAM F., 13-17, 22-16.
FITZPATRICK, JOHN S., 11-14, 11-16, 19-11.
FLANAGAN, CHARLES P., 19-13.
FLEET, C. J., 14-11.
FLEISCHMANN, LEON, 13-15.
FLEMING, DONALD P., 12-13.
FLEMING, HARRY D. JR., 13-15, 19-15.
FLEMING, KENNETH W, 20-11.
FLESHMAN, ROBERT M., 13-21.
FLETCHER, C. V., 11-14, 11-16.
FLETCHER, H. MORLEY, 18-14, 19-15.
FLETCHER, JENNIFER, 18-11, 19-15.
FLETCHER, ROBERT RAY PH. D., 12-16, 17-16.
FLETCHER, THELMA R., 18-15, 19-15.
FLEXNER, JAMES THOMAS, 18-11, 19-15.
FLICK, JOHN E., 12-11, 25-11.
FLICKINGER, LOWELL D., 13-17.
FLIETZE, HANS, 18-11, 18-12, 18-13, 18-14, 18-15, 18-16.
FLOODWAY COMMITTEE, 22-21.
FLORES, ORLANDO, 11-11, 11-16.
FLORIDA STATE ROAD DEPARTMENT, 24-15.
FLORIDA WORKS PROGRESS ADMINISTRATION, 12-11.
FLOY, HENRY, 16-11.
FOGARTY, F., 22-11.
FOGARTY, JAMES T., 12-11.
FOGLESONG, CHARLES W., 19-13.
FOLEY, CLETIS R., 11-11, 11-14.
FOLEY, DAVID A., 12-14.
FORBERG, FRED C., 12-13.
FORBES, 19-15.
FORD, BACON, AND DAVIS, INC., 13-15, 19-18.
FORD, JAMES, 12-14, 13-16, 13-19, 13-46.
FOREST, J., 12-16.
FORNACI, CHARLES M., 12-16, 22-16.
FORREST C. HOLVECK, 12-13, 14-11.
FORSBERG, WINIFIELD, 14-11.
FOSS, GEORGE B. JR., 13-11.
FOSSLER, DUANE M., 13-19, 21-13.
FOSTER, GEORGE, JR., 12-26.
FOSTER, HORATIO A., 16-11, 23-11.
FOSTER, JOSEPH A., 24-13.
FOSTER, JOSEPH K., 18-12, 18-15, 19-15.
FOSTER, N. LEE, 13-12.
FOSTER, R. D., 11-11, 11-16.
FOWLER, CODY, 12-26.
FOWLER, G., 13-18, 13-19, 15-15.
FOX, NORBERT J., 11-14, 11-16.
FOX, PAUL W., 12-15.
FPC, 12-15, 12-16, 12-26, 16-11, 16-12, 16-13, 16-15, 17-15, 17-16, 19-15, 20-13.
FRANCOIS, WALDO, 19-15.
FRANCOIS, WALDO E., 13-20, 19-15.
FRANKEL, EDWARD T., 11-14, 11-19, 12-24.
FRANKLAND, BAMFORD, 12-14.
FRANKLIN, R. J., 12-11, 13-15, 22-16.
FRANSES, JACK, 18-15.
FRANTZEN, HAROLD C., 13-15, 19-12.
FRANTZEN, HAROLD G., 13-19, 19-12.
FRANZEN, WILLIAM F., 13-11, 14-11.
FRANZERO, CARLO MARIA, 18-11, 18-15.
FRASNAY, DANIEL, 18-11, 18-15, 19-15.
FREDERICKS, A. A., 24-14.
FREDRICKSON, R., 13-21.
FREE, R. L., 11-14, 11-16.
FREE, ROBERT L., 11-13, 11-14, 11-16, 11-19, 12-14, 12-26, 13-15, 13-20, 19-13, 24-15.
FREE, VICTOR J., 11-11, 11-12, 11-14, 11-16, 12-24.
FREEBRUG, CHARLES H., 13-19.
FREEDLAND, FRED, 12-16, 25-11, 25-12.
FREEMAN, E. STEWART, 23-11.
FREEMAN, RAOUL J., 12-13, 22-18.
FREEMAN, ROGER A., 12-11.
FREEMAN, SEYMOUR, 18-17.

FRENVO, IVAN, 18-12.
FREUDENBERGER, JOSEPH N., 11-14, 11-16.
FREY, HERBERT O., 19-11, 19-12.
FRIBOURG, ALBERT W., 19-13.
FRIDAY, DAVID, 11-11, 11-16.
FRIDEMAN, EDITH J., 22-18.
FRIEDLAINDER, WALTER, 18-11, 19-15.
FRIEDLANDER, MAX J., 18-11.
FRIEDMAN, A. R., 19-13.
FRIEDMAN, ALBERT L., 11-11, 11-12, 11-14, 11-16, 13-17.
FRIEDMAN, EDITH JUDITH, 22-18.
FRIEDMANN, LIONEL, 12-14.
FRIES, EUGENE H., 13-15.
FRISSELL, ROBERT N., 11-11, 11-12, 12-14.
FROMKES, SAUL, 13-15, 19-12.
FROST, BENNETT H., 11-11, 11-18.
FROST, F DANIELS, 12-11, 19-15.
FROST, JACK W., 12-16.
FRUIN-COLNON CONTRACTING COMPANY, 13-15, 21-13.
FRUIN, E. G., 14-11.
FRUITS, S. C., 12-11.
FRY, PETER, 12-13.
FRYXELL, CARL A., 11-13, 11-16, 19-15.
FUHRER, MAX, 11-14, 11-19.
FULCO, ROY J., 12-16.
FULLER, R. S., 11-11, 11-18.
FULLER, ROBERT, 13-17, 22-19.
FULLER, ROBERT S., 11-14, 11-16, 13-16, 13-17, 13-22, 22-15, 22-17, 22-19, 22-20.
FULLERTON, D. H., 11-11, 11-14, 11-18.
FULLERTON, PAUL, 11-16, 11-17, 12-24, 13-19, 22-11, 23-11.
FUNARO, BRUNO, 13-15.
FUNKE, JOHN H., 23-13.
FURBAY, JOHN H., 11-18.
FURMAN, ROY E., 12-16.
FURST, H., 18-11, 18-12, 18-13, 18-14, 18-15, 18-16.


GUDE, RICHARD B., 11-16, 11-19.
GUDIN, C. R., 13-15.
GUDIN, CAMILLE R., 12-13, 13-15.
GABERMAN, HARRY, 12-11.
GABLER, L. R., 12-21, 13-11.
GADDIS, P. L., 14-11.
GADDIS, PERCY A., 11-11, 11-13, 11-16, 12-16, 23-11.
GADDIS, PORTER L., 13-23.
GADE, GEORGE, 13-17.
GAFFNEY, M. MASON, 12-11, 13-13.
GAGE, DANIEL D., 13-18, 13-21.
GAGE, DANIEL D. JR., 11-11, 11-18.
GAHR, EDMOND W., 14-15.
GAILLARD, WILLIAM E. G., 23-11.
GAKENHEIMER, RALPH A., 13-11, 24-11.
GALE, CHARLES J., 12-15.
GALE, JOHN F., 14-12.
GALIK, ALBERT R., 11-14, 11-19.
GALLAGHER, E. F., 12-24.
GALLAGHER, JOSEPH A., 12-14, 12-15.
GALLAGHER, JOSEPH A. SR., 12-16, 13-16, 13-19, 22-14.
GALLAGHER, PAUL W., 19-12.
GALLAGHER, RUSSELL B., 12-23, 13-15.

GALLAHER, JOSEPH A. SR., 11-11, 11-12.
GALUSH, ROBERT J., 13-16, 13-19.
GAMBLE, W. P., 11-11, 14-11.
GAMMON, GEORGE W., 11-11, 11-19, 13-15, 19-15.
GANNON, HENRY F., 12-15.
GANNON, JAMES F. JR., 13-15.
GARAS, KLARA, 18-11, 19-15.
GARBER, H. A., 23-13.
GARBER, HENRY A., 12-23.
GARBER, L. L., 20-14.
GARCIA PAREDES, JENARO, 14-11.
GARCIA, K., 12-12, 12-13.
GARDENER, ALAN C., 11-14, 11-16, 11-17.
GARDINER, MAC., 11-16, 12-14.
GARFIELD, PAUL J, 16-11.
GARRET, H. J., 12-15, 12-18.
GARRETT, THOMAS M., 11-11, 11-12, 11-18.
GARRISON CHARLES B., 14-11, 23-11.
GARRISON, BURL L., 11-11, 11-14, 11-16, 11-17, 11-19, 12-24, 22-19, 22-20.
GARRISON, WILLIAM L., 22-19, 24-11, 24-16.
GARRITY, THOMAS P, 12-13.
GARZON, JULIAN, 12-13, 22-22.
GASSIER, PIERRE, 18-11, 19-15.
GASTON, JAMES E., 11-14, 12-12, 12-13.
GATES, NILES, 22-19, 22-20.
GATES, NILES S., 23-11.
GATES, PHILIP B., 13-21.
GATES, W., 19-16.
GATES, WILLIAM S. JR., 11-14, 11-16.
GAUMNITZ, J. E., 19-15.
GAY, L. W., 13-17.
GAYDON, ALEXANDER THOMAS, 12-11.
GAZTAMBIDE, DR. JUAN B., 12-11, 19-13.
GEBHART, J. C., 22-18.
GEER, M. W., 13-13.
GELBAND, J. F., 13-19, 19-15, 19-16.
GELDZAHLER, HENRY, 18-11, 18-13, 18-15, 19-15.
GELFAND, J. E., 19-12.
GELFARD, J. E., 13-16, 19-12.
GELLER, CARL, 13-16, 13-19.
GELMAN, M., 13-15, 19-16.
GEMEINHARDT, ROBERT J., 15-14.
GENNACO, FRANK, 13-19.
GEORGE, ALLAN C., 11-11, 11-18, 11-19, 13-15.
GEORGE, E. O., 23-13.
GEORGE, ERNEST, 12-11, 22-18.
GEPHART, W. F., 12-23.
GERE, CHARLOTTE, 18-17.
GERE, EDWIN A. JR., 12-11, 12-13.
GERKIN, LEONARD, 13-22, 22-15.
GERMAIN, EDGAR H., 18-11.
GERRITY, HARRY, 12-24.
GERRITY, HARRY J., 12-11.
GERSON, DR. H., 18-11.
GIBBONS, F. R., 22-19, 22-20.
GIBBONS, JAMES E., 11-14, 11-16, 11-19, 12-11, 12-25, 13-19, 19-12, 19-13, 19-14, 19-15, 21-11, 21-18.
GIBLIN, EDMUND W., 12-13.
GIBSON, BLAINE C., 13-15, 17-15, 22-18.
GIBSON, BRUCE G., 11-11, 11-12, 11-18.
GIBSON, HOWARD L., 16-16.
GIBSON, K., 23-11.
GIBSON, LIOYD C., 12-11, 12-12, 12-13.
GIBSON, LLOYD, 12-11.

GIBSON, NEVILLE E., 13-11.
GIEDION, SIGFRIED, 13-11.
GIFFORD, GERALD F, 14-13.
GILBERT, DEWAYNE E., 12-13, 14-14.
GILBERT, H. M., 13-11.
GILBERT, HARRY E., 12-11, 12-14.
GILBERT, RICHARD G., 11-14, 11-16.
GILDEA, C. D., 12-11.
GILL, MCCUNE, 11-16.
GILL, WILLIAM A., 11-14, 11-16.
GILL, WILLIAM J., 13-19, 13-21, 19-11, 19-12.
GILL, WILLIAM L., 12-26, 13-15, 19-18.
GILLESPIE, JOHN, 11-11, 11-12.
GILLETTE, H P, 16-14, 17-16.
GILLETTE, H. P., 11-16, 12-24.
GILLIES, JAMES, 13-13, 22-19.
GILLIS, BRUCE D., 11-11, 11-14.
GILMORE, FRANK V., 13-17.
GIMMY, ARTHUR E., 13-21.
GINGRICH, LAVERNE, 19-13.
GITELSON, ALFRED, 12-14.
GITTERMAN, A. N., 11-11, 11-16, 13-11, 22-18.
GIVENS, HARRY, 20-12.
GLAS, HAROLD V., 11-14, 11-16.
GLADSTONE, ROBERT M., 13-11.
GLADSTONE, WILLIAM F, 19-17.
GLAESER, MARTIN G., 16-11.
GLASER, SIDNEY, 12-11, 12-13.
GLASS, EDWARD F., 11-11, 11-16.
GLASSBURNER, FRED R., 13-15.
GLAZE, BERT T., 13-18.
GLEAVES, MILNOR E., 12-15, 12-18.
GLOAG, JOHN, 18-16, 18-18.
GLOS, HAROLD V., 11-14, 11-16, 12-14, 12-20, 13-15, 13-19, 13-20, 19-13.
GLOVER, CHARLES P., 12-11, 22-19.
GLUNT, DAVID, 19-16, 21-16.
GOBLE, EMERSON, 21-13.
GODDEN, A. GEOFFREY, 18-15.
GODDEN, GEOFFREY, 18-14, 18-15.
GODDEN, GEOFFREY A., 18-14, 18-15, 18-16, 19-15.
GODFREY, RICHARD G., 13-19, 19-15.
GODGREY, EDWARD, 12-11.
GODIN, C. R., 11-11, 11-19, 12-13, 13-15.
GODIN, CAMILLE R., 11-11, 11-12, 12-13.
GODTHWAITE, G. E., 21-12.
GODWIN, HOWARD S., 12-11, 12-23.
GOHM. D. C., 18-12.
GOLBERG, M. A., 24-11.
GOLDBLATT, ABRAHAM, 13-16.
GOLDEN, G. A., 11-11, 11-19, 19-12, 19-15.
GOLDEN, GERALD A., 12-23, 13-16, 19-13, 19-15.
GOLDEN, JAY S., 22-19, 24-15.
GOLDFARB, MORRIS, 11-11, 11-16, 11-19, 13-15, 19-15.
GOLDIN, A. J., 12-23.
GOLDING, JOHN, 18-11.
GOLDING, STUART S., 13-15, 19-43.
GOLDMAN, ABRAM F., 12-11, 12-12.
GOLDMAN, ARTHUR SWORN, 13-19.
GOLDMAN, THEORDORE M., 13-19.
GOLDSCHEIDER, LUDWIG, 18-11, 18-15, 19-15.
GOLDSTEIN, GEORGE, 11-11, 12-24, 12-25, 21-11.
GOLDSTEIN, SIMEON F., 12-24, 21-11.
GOLDSTEIN, WILLEAM M., 12-11.
GOLDSTINE, HARRY, 12-14, 22-16.
GOLDSTON, ELI, 13-11, 13-17.
GOLDSTONE, BRACTON, 11-11, 11-14, 11-16, 11-19.
GOLOBIC, REX, 15-11.
GOMEZ, CARLOS EDUARDO, 12-14.
GONZALES, C. S., 11-11, 11-12, 11-18.
GONZALEZ VALE, LUIS, 11-11, 11-12, 12-14.
GONZALEZ, CONCHA J., 11-11, 22-11.
GOOD, FREDERICK H., 13-19.
GOOD, H. A., 12-14, 17-16, 22-16.
GOOD, SHELDON F., 19-15.
GOOD, WILLIAM CHARLES, 12-11, 14-15.
GOODMAN, ROBERT C., 13-14.
GOODRICH, HAROLD S., 22-16, 25-11.
GOODSPEED, M. J., 11-14, 11-16, 22-11, 22-18, 22-19, 22-20.
GOODWIN, E. F., 12-16, 16-15.
GOODYEAR, J. LEO, 22-18.
GORDON, G. W. E., 13-19.
GORDON, MYRON J., 13-15, 19-15.
GORKA, FRANCIS L., 12-23, 21-12.
GORTON, JAMES, 12-24.
GOSS, R. O., 19-15, 22-24.
GOSSELIN, JACQUES, 11-11, 11-12, 11-18, 13-15, 21-12.
GOTSCH, C. H., 14-11.
GOTTESMAN, JEROME, 13-12.
GOTTLIEB, J. R., 19-15, 22-18.
GOTTLIEB, M., 11-18, 13-11, 13-19, 13-20, 13-22.
GOTTSHALL, FRANKLIN H., 18-18.
GOULD, CECIL, 18-11.
GOULD, J. P., 13-20, 19-15.
GOULD, JAY M., 13-15.
GOURLWY, H. J. F., 16-14.
GOVERNMENT AFFAIRS FOUNDATION, INCORPORATED, 12-11.
GOVERNMENT PRINTING OFFICE, 23-11.
GOWLAND, RUSSELL W., 19-13.
GRAASKAMP, J. A., 13-15.
GRAASKAMP, JAMES, 11-14, 11-16, 19-15.
GRAASKAMP, JAMES E., 11-14, 11-19.
GRABAR, ANDRE, 18-12, 19-15.
GRACE, ARTHUR B. JR., 12-14.
GRACE, THOMAS G., 13-16.
GRACER, GENE, 19-13.
GRAF, WAYNE J., 14-11.
GRAHAM, 13-15, 19-18.
GRAHAM, BENJAMIN, 19-15, 19-18.
GRAHAM, D. H. JR., 12-13, 13-15.
GRAHAM, DAVID M., 11-14, 12-23.
GRAHAM, DONALD H. JR., 12-11, 13-15, 19-15, 22-18.
GRAHAM, J. W., 13-17, 21-12.
GRAHAM, WILLARD J., 16-11.
GRAICHEN, R. E., 12-24, 19-15.
GRAND, P. M., 18-12, 18-16, 19-15.
GRANDJEAN, BREDO L., 18-14, 19-15.
GRANDJEAN, SERGE, 18-18, 19-15.
GRANFIELD, MICHAEL EDWARD PH. D., 13-16, 13-17, 13-19.
GRANT, E. L., 11-11, 12-24.
GRANT, ROSS, 13-18, 13-20.
GRATE, PONTUS, 18-15.
GRAUGNARD, F. A. JR., 12-16.
GRAVES, GLENN F., 12-15.
GRAVES, H. WALTER, 22-18.
GRAVES, T. J., 12-11.
GRAY, A. F. B., 12-13, 13-11.
GRAY, ARTHUR L. JR., 13-13.

# BIBLIOGRAPHY OF APPRAISAL LITERATURE

GRAY, BASIL, 18-11, 19-15.
GRAY, GEORGE H., 11-11, 11-16, 12-26.
GRAY, LESLIE, 12-16.
GRAY, RICHARD J., 11-11, 23-11.
GRAYSON, HARRY, 12-21.
GREAT BRITAIN MINISTRY OF HOUSING & LOCAL GOVT, 17-14, 17-15.
GREAT BRITAIN MINISTRY OF HOUSING AND LOCAL GOVERN, 11-16, 11-18, 13-11, 13-16.
GREBLER, LEO, 11-14, 11-18, 12-24, 13-13, 13-16.
GREEN, ARTHUR W., 12-14.
GREEN, JOHN B., 11-14, 11-16, 13-15.
GREEN, WILLIAM H., 23-11, 23-13, 23-16.
GREENBAUM, IRVING PHD, 16-11, 16-12, 19-15.
GREENBAUM, MICHAEL, 11-11, 16-11.
GREENE, ALFRED J., 22-19, 22-20.
GREENE, ALFRED J. JR., 12-13, 13-19, 22-19, 22-20.
GREENE, FRED T., 19-12.
GREENE, H. D., 13-15.
GREENE, W. L., 11-14, 11-16.
GREENEBAUM, MICHAEL, 11-11, 12-23, 16-11, 22-16.
GREENESTREET, KELVIN, 11-11, 11-16.
GREENSWORD, L. H., 12-13.
GREER, D. C., 12-16, 24-15.
GREER, GUY, 12-11, 13-11, 13-14, 13-16.
GREGORIETTI, GUIDO, 18-17, 19-15.
GREGORY, E. SANFORD, 23-11.
GREGORY, R. P., 12-16.
GREY, ARTHUR, L. JR., 13-13.
GRICE, ALEXANDER P., 24-13.
GRIFFITH, C. R., 13-20.
GRIFFITH, L. B., 12-22.
GRIMES, J. A., 12-11.
GRIMES, JOHN A., 11-11, 11-16, 11-17.
GRIMES, ROBERT A., 12-13.
GRIMM, RUDOLPH J., 12-23.
GRISELLE, SHERMAN W., 13-12, 13-17.
GROETSCH, FOREST L., 14-11, 24-15.
GROGAN, JAMES J., 11-19, 12-24, 13-15, 13-19.
GRONER, ORVILLE, 19-13, 19-15, 22-18.
GRONINGER, TAYLOR E., 16-11.
GROS-GALLINER, GABRIELLA, 18-15, 18-16.
GROSS, WILLIAM J., 12-16, 22-16, 24-11.
GROSSO, ANTHONY P., 12-13, 15-11.
GROTECLOSS, EDWARD JR., 13-13, 24-15.
GROVER, RAY AND LEE, 18-12, 19-15.
GROVES, ASA B., 11-11, 11-16, 11-18.
GROVES, HAROLD M., 11-11, 11-19.
GROVES, HENRY M., 12-24, 19-17.
GROVES, RICHARD N., 13-19.
GRUELICH, RICHARD H. JR., 13-17, 13-21, 13-23, 23-11.
GRUEN, VICTOR, 13-15, 13-23.
GRUEN, VICTOR, 13-13.
GRUNDALD, ADOLPH E., 12-11, 19-16.
GRUNDMEIER, HAROLD H., 12-13, 13-19.
GRUNERT, HAROLD F., 13-19.
GRUNEWALD, ADOLPH E, 12-11, 19-16.
GRUNEWALD, ADOLPH E., 12-11, 19-16.
GRUNSKY, CARL E., 11-11, 11-13, 11-14, 11-16, 12-24, 16-11, 19-12, 21-12.
GUATEMALA AUDIENCIA, 11-11, 11-16.
GUERRERO, DANTE, 14-11.
GUERRERO, SAULO E., 14-11.
GUEST, CHRISTOPHER WILLIAM GRAHAM, 11-11, 11-16.
GUILFORD, W. S, 14-11.
GUILFORD, W. S., 13-15, 14-17.
GUINEY, JOSEPH, 13-19.
GUITTARD, CLARENCE A., 12-15.
GUMP, RICHARD, 11-11, 11-18.
GUNNING, WALTER E., 11-14, 12-15, 22-19, 22-20.
GUPTE, K. S., 12-11.
GURDIS, REYNAL AND COMPANY, 18-15.
GURNEE, MARK S., 16-11, 25-11.
GURTHIE, R. R., 12-16.
GUSTAFSON, HAROLD M., 12-16.
GUTFELD, LUDWIG, 18-11, 18-15.
GUTHMAN, H. G., 11-14, 11-16, 11-19, 19-15.
GUTHMANM, H. G., 11-11, 11-19.
GUTHRIE, R. R., 13-16.
GUTSCHENRITTER, FRANK, 14-15.

HAAGLAND, HENRY E., 11-11, 11-16.
HAALAND ARNE W., 13-22, 22-17.
HAALAND, ARNE W., 11-14, 11-16.
HAAR, CHARLES M., 24-13.
HAAS, CHARLES E., 12-15.
HAAS, DR. ROBERT BARLETT, 11-11, 11-14, 18-14, 18-15, 18-16, 18-18.
HACK, B., 18-11, 19-15.
HACKER ART BOOKS, 18-11, 18-12, 19-15.
HACKER ART BOOKS INC, 18-11, 18-13, 18-15, 19-15.
HACKETT, F. HUNTER, 13-19.
HADLEY, GEORGE C., 12-13, 12-14, 12-15, 12-26, 22-16, 24-15.
HADY, THOMAS F., 12-13.
HAEDAHE, HANS ULRICH, 18-14, 18-15, 19-15.
HAEGER, LEONARD G., 13-16.
HAGEN, O., 11-11, 11-16.
HAGENSICK, JOHN C., 12-23.
HAGES, COLIN, 18-11, 18-15.
HAGGSTROM, ROBERT J., 22-18.
HAGMAN, D. G., 12-11, 13-11.
HAGMAN, DONALD C., 12-14.
HAGNESTEIN, W. D., 12-16, 14-15, 17-13.
HAGOOD, WAYNE D., 11-11, 11-12, 11-14, 11-16, 11-18, 13-11, 13-15, 13-17, 13-19, 13-22, 22-17.
HAIDIE, MARTIN, 18-11, 19-15.
HAIG, GRAEME T., 11-11, 11-12, 11-18, 12-14.
HAIGHT, JAMES R., 11-11, 11-14, 11-18, 19-11, 19-15, 21-18.
HAINES, C. GRODON, 12-11, 22-16.
HAINES, HOWARD, 11-14, 11-16, 13-21.
HAISLOP, E. G., 12-13.
HALE, C. W., 12-11, 12-26, 13-13, 23-13.
HALE, JAMES R., 11-11, 11-12.
HALE, JUSTICE JOHN, 12-26.
HALEY, BYRON R., 13-22, 22-17.
HALEY, HARRY B., 13-16, 13-19.
HALEY, JOHN L., 11-16, 12-16, 12-18.
HALGERSON, J. R., 12-13.
HALL, A. A., 14-13, 14-15, 22-20.
HALL, ARTHUR B., 12-16.
HALL, ARTHUR F., 12-23, 19-11, 19-12.
HALL, C. W., 11-11, 11-14.
HALL, CARL B., 12-16, 22-16.
HALL, FRANK D., 11-11, 11-16, 11-18, 11-19, 12-23, 13-14, 13-15, 19-11, 19-12, 21-18, 22-18.

HALL, H. B., 23-11.
HALL, HARRY H., 11-11, 11-14, 11-16.
HALL, HENRY C., 14-15, 19-11, 22-18.
HALL, JAMES R., 13-17, 19-15.
HALL, JOHN H., 11-11, 11-12, 11-18.
HALL, JOSEPH B., 11-12, 11-13, 11-16, 11-19, 12-11, 13-14, 13-17.
HALL, JOSEPH P., 13-15.
HALL, PETER GEOFFREY, 22-19, 22-20.
HALL, ROBERT W., 11-11, 11-14, 11-16, 11-18.
HALL, T. H. 3RD, 13-15.
HALL, THOMAS H. III, 12-18, 13-21, 17-12.
HALL, THOMAS, III, 12-15.
HALL, WALTER B., 12-16.
HALLADE, MADELEIN, 18-11, 18-13, 18-15, 19-15.
HALLADE, MADELEINE, 18-11, 19-15.
HALLIDAY, C. S., 11-13, 11-16.
HAMBLETON, RAY W., 12-15, 13-15, 19-13.
HAMBURG, ALEX M., 12-11.
HAMILIN, BEN W., 13-17, 13-22.
HAMILTON, ANDREW C., 11-11, 11-13, 11-16, 12-11, 12-14, 12-20, 12-26, 13-15.
HAMILTON, H. P., 11-14, 11-16, 13-18, 16-16.
HAMILTON, HOWARD D., 12-11, 17-14.
HAMILTON, HOWARD P., 13-11.
HAMILTON, RAYMOND WARREN, 13-19.
HAMLEN, WILLIAM E., 12-16.
HAMMACHER, A. M., 18-11, 18-13, 19-15.
HAMMAN, CHARLES L., 13-13.
HAMMAR, CONRAD H., 11-14, 14-11, 22-11, 22-18, 22-19, 22-20.
HAMPTON, CHRISTOPHER, 18-11, 18-16, 19-15.
HANAO, YOCHIO, 11-14, 11-19, 19-15.
HANAO, YOSHIO, 22-18.
HANCOCK, M. L., 11-11, 11-14.
HANCOCK, MACKLIN L., 13-14, 13-23.
HANDEL, MORRIS, 12-11, 12-26.
HANDLER, ALAN B., 12-11, 12-26.
HANEMANN, H. J. F., 12-16, 12-23, 19-15.
HANES, HERMAN. L., 11-14, 11-16.
HANFMANN, GEORGE M. A., 18-13, 19-15.
HANFORD SR, LLOYD D., 13-14.
HANFORD, EDGAR C., 11-13.
HANFORD, HENRY S., 12-21.
HANFORD, JR LLOYD D., 19-17.
HANFORD, LLOYD B. JR., 11-14, 11-16.
HANFORD, LLOYD D., 11-11, 11-14, 13-19.
HANFORD, LLOYD D. SR., 11-14, 12-14, 13-14, 13-19, 19-15.
HANFORD, LLOYD JR., 11-14, 12-11, 12-24, 22-18.
HANLEY, DUDLEY J., 12-14, 12-26, 13-13, 22-16.
HANLEY, E. J., 12-24, 19-15, 23-11.
HANNAH, FREDERICK J., 13-21.
HANNAH, H. W., 14-11.
HANNOCH, FRANKLIN, 12-14, 12-18, 13-15.
HANRAHAN, DANIEL C., 12-21, 13-15, 13-17.
HANSBERGER, R. V., 11-18, 13-16, 19-11, 19-15.
HANSEN, HENRY H., 11-18, 18-15.
HANSEN, VICTOR R., 12-11, 12-14.
HANSEN, VIGGO, 11-14, 11-19.
HANSON, A. E., 13-17.
HANSON, ALDEN W., 11-11, 11-12.
HANSON, PETER, 11-11, 11-13, 11-14, 11-16, 11-19, 12-14, 12-15, 12-20, 12-23, 12-24, 13-11, 13-15, 19-11.
HARDEN, D. B., 18-14, 18-15, 19-15.

HARDIE, MARTIN, 18-11, 19-15.
HARDIN, C. M., 17-12.
HARDIN, LOWELL S., 14-11.
HARDING, CARL G., 12-14, 13-15, 13-17.
HARDS, I BLAIR, 20-15.
HARDWICK, CHARLES Z., 13-15.
HARDY, NEAL J., 13-16.
HARDY, T. F., 12-11.
HARGROVE, M. M., 11-18, 13-11.
HARMAN, GABRIEL C., 13-11.
HARRIS, CHAUNCY D., 23-11.
HARRIS, EDWARD F., 12-18.
HARRIS, ENRIQUETA, 18-11, 18-15.
HARRIS, HARWELL H., 11-14, 11-18.
HARRIS, J. R., 18-11, 18-12, 19-15.
HARRIS, KERR, 13-15, 15-13.
HARRIS, RICHARD D., 12-14.
HARRIS, STEPHEN M., 13-13, 13-15.
HARRIS, W. G., 18-17, 19-11.
HARRIS, WILLIAM W., 13-11, 13-13, 13-19.
HARRISON & SONS, 12-11.
HARRISON, DAVID C., 12-11, 13-16.
HARRISON, LOUIS A., 11-14, 11-16, 13-17, 22-19.
HARRISON, ROLAND T., 12-13.
HARRISON, SIGMUND, 13-15.
HARRISON, THOMAS, 13-15.
HARRISS, C LOWELL, 12-11, 19-15.
HART, ALAN F., 11-16, 11-18, 12-13, 12-17.
HART, FREDERICK, 18-13.
HART, GERALD T., 13-20.
HART, L. C., 13-16.
HART, LARRY C., 23-13.
HARTER, HUGH I., 14-15.
HARTMAN, FRANKLIN L., 13-17.
HARTMAN, H. H., 19-15.
HARTMAN, J. W., 12-13, 17-15.
HARTMAN, JOAN M., 18-17, 19-15.
HARTMAN, T. W., 11-14, 12-24, 13-19.
HARTNETT, EDGAR C., 13-17, 24-15.
HARTT, FREDERICK, 18-11.
HARTWIG, J. D., 12-11, 22-18.
HARTWIG, JOSEPH D, 12-11, 19-17.
HARTWIG, O. J., 11-18.
HARVARD LAW REVIEW, 12-11, 12-13.
HARVARD UNIVERSITY LAW SCHOOL, 12-11.
HARVEY, REESE, 24-15.
HARVEY, ROBERT O., 11-11, 11-14, 11-18, 11-19, 13-11, 13-17, 21-11.
HARVEY, WILLIAM A., 14-15.
HASKETT, JACK, 13-20.
HASTINGS, BYRON, 15-23.
HASTINGS, MACDONALD, 18-15, 19-15.
HASTINGS, ROD, 12-13.
HATCH, CHESTER W., 13-22, 16-12.
HATFIELD, SAMUEL M., 13-16, 13-19, 22-21.
HATFIEND, ROLLAND F., 12-11.
HATHAWAY, PAUL L., 11-16, 13-17, 22-19, 24-11.
HATWELL, CHARLES O., 12-16.
HAUSER, PHILIP M., 13-11.
HAVEMAN, ROBERT H., 17-16.
HAVERKORN, THOMAS W., 13-15.
HAWES, A. S., 11-13, 11-16.
HAWK STEPHEN L, 19-15.
HAWK, R. L. D., 13-15.
HAWKINS, GEORGE C., 12-15, 12-16.

# BIBLIOGRAPHY OF APPRAISAL LITERATURE

HAY, GEORGE C., 14-18.
HAY, LEON E, 16-14.
HAYDEN, ARTHUR, 18-15, 18-16.
HAYES, DOUGLAS, 11-11, 11-14, 11-16.
HAYES, DOUGLAS A., 11-14, 11-19, 12-24, 19-15.
HAYES, EDWARD R., 12-13, 13-13.
HAYES, H. V., 16-11.
HAYES, JOHN, 18-15.
HAYES, K., 19-15.
HAYES, R. W., 13-11, 13-12, 24-17.
HAYES, SAMUEL L. III, 19-15, 22-18.
HAYES, THOMAS J., 19-12.
HAYES, TOM JR., 12-19, 13-15.
HAYNES, DENYS, 18-11.
HAYNES, J. L., 11-11, 11-14.
HAYNES, JOHN L., 19-18, 22-18.
HAYNES, JUSTIN H., 11-11, 12-24.
HAYNSWORTH, CHARLES G., 11-14, 11-19.
HAYS, JOHN, 18-15.
HAZEN, ALLEN, 16-11, 16-14.
HEAD, GEORGE, 13-15.
HEAD, GEORGE J., 11-11, 11-12, 11-16.
HEALEY, F.J., 11-11, 11-14.
HEANEY, DONALD L., 12-15, 24-15.
HEARLE, EDWARD F. R., 11-14, 12-11, 12-13.
HEATH, J. JR., 19-14.
HEATH, SPENCER, 22-21.
HEBB, WINSTON P, 12-23, 23-11.
HECHT, KENNETH G., 12-14.
HECHT, LEE I., 12-11, 22-18.
HECHT, LESTER S., 12-14, 22-21.
HECKERLING, P. E., 12-11.
HECKMAN, J. W., 12-11, 16-11.
HEDGE, A M, 14-11, 14-13.
HEENAN, G. WARREN, 22-21, 24-19.
HEER, CLYDE W., 11-11, 11-14, 11-16.
HEER, ROBERT R., 11-14, 12-24.
HEFTI, WILMA C., 22-18.
HEGGLAND, THUROLOW M., 12-13.
HEILBRUN, JAMES, 12-11, 13-16, 22-18.
HEILBTUN, JAMES, 12-11, 13-16, 22-18.
HEILMAN, R. E., 16-11.
HEINEKE, PAUL H., 11-11, 11-12, 11-18.
HEINMULLER, CARL, 13-15.
HEINZ, DORA, 18-16, 19-15.
HELD, HARRY, 11-11, 11-16, 13-17.
HELD, JULIUS S., 18-11, 18-13, 18-15, 19-15.
HELFTS, JACQUES, 18-14, 19-15.
HELLAND, ARTHUR T., 11-14, 11-16.
HELLER, ROGER, 14-11, 19-13.
HELLMUTH, WILLIAM F. JR., 12-11.
HELM, W. P., 12-13, 13-15.
HELMBERGER, JOHN D., 12-11, 13-21.
HELSTAD, ORRIN L., 12-14, 24-15.
HEMMER, EDGAR HAROLD, PH. D., 19-15, 22-18.
HENDERER, EDMOND, 22-16.
HENDERSON AND ROSS, 13-15, 17-17, 19-12, 22-18.
HENDERSON, HAROLD W., 12-13.
HENDERSON, J.D., 11-16.
HENDERSON, JAMES D., 11-12, 11-14, 11-16, 12-14, 13-15, 13-20, 17-15, 19-13, 22-18.
HENDERSON, JAMES DOUGALD, 19-18.
HENDERSON, PHILIP A., 19-13.
HENDON, JOHN F., 13-12, 13-13.
HENDON, WS., 12-13.

HENDRICKS, FORD, 12-14.
HENDRICKS, ROBERT W., 13-13, 13-17, 13-19, 24-15.
HENDRIE, ROBERT E., 11-17, 12-24.
HENDY, PHILLIP, 18-11, 18-13, 18-15, 19-15.
HENEBERRY, WILLIAM H., 12-11, 12-13, 14-15.
HENINGTON, CHARLES R., 14-11.
HENRY FRANCHOISE, 18-11, 18-15, 18-16, 19-15.
HENRY, E. G., 11-14, 11-16.
HENRY, ERNEST E., 14-11.
HENRY, ROSS F., 12-13, 14-11.
HENSON, C. B., 11-19, 12-24.
HEPDITCH, G. D., 12-13, 17-14.
HEPDITCH, GORDON D., 12-13, 12-26.
HER MAJESTYS STATIONERY OFFICE, 18-16.
HERBERT, ROBERT L., 18-11, 19-15.
HERD, JOHN J., 13-20, 19-19.
HERRICK, ANSON, 21-12.
HERRING, FRANK W., 24-11.
HERRINGTON, F. A., 12-11, 12-13.
HERRMAN, CYRIL C., 13-17.
HERRMANN, CYRIL C., 22-21, 23-11.
HERST JR, HERMAN, 18-15.
HERTEL, HENRY, 13-20.
HERTLEIN, G. C., 11-14, 11-16, 18-11, 18-12, 18-13, 18-14.
HERTZ, CARL F., 22-19, 22-20.
HERTZMAN, IRVING L., 21-16.
HERY, ELMER G., 11-14, 11-16.
HERZ, WALTER, 18-17.
HERZER, T. O. F., 11-11, 11-12, 11-16.
HESS, RUDOLF, 12-16, 22-16, 24-11, 24-15.
HESTE, W. F., 14-11.
HEUCK, ROBERT, 13-19, 21-12.
HEWEN, LORING M., 22-18.
HEWITT, JOHN A., 11-11, 11-12, 11-18.
HEWITT, R. F., 13-14.
HIBBEN, JAMES B., 13-13, 13-19.
HICKMAN, LEON E., 13-13.
HICKS, JAMES B., 12-16.
HICKS, JOHN RICHARD, 16-11.
HIDESLEY, C. HUGH, 18-11, 18-12, 18-13, 18-15.
HIEATT, CLARENCE C., 11-13, 11-16.
HIGGINS J. WARREN, 12-11.
HIGGINS WARREN J, 11-14, 11-17, 11-19.
HIGGINS, REYNOLD, 18-16, 18-17, 19-15.
HIGGINS, REYNOLD ALLEYNE, 18-17.
HIGGINS, WARREN J., 12-11, 22-18.
HIGGS, GERALD B., 22-19, 22-20.
HIGHMARK, LOUIS A., 12-19, 12-26.
HIGHWAY RESEARCH BOARD, 12-14, 12-15, 12-16, 20-11, 24-11, 24-15.
HIGHWAY RESEARCH BOARD, NATIONAL ACADEMY OF SCIENC, 24-15.
HIGNETTE, H. W., 11-11, 11-18.
HILL, AUSTIN M., 12-16.
HILL, R. D., 12-26, 16-12.
HILLENBRAND, BERNARD F., 12-11.
HILLER BEUIS, 18-14, 19-15.
HILLER, J., 18-12.
HILLIER, BEVIS, 18-11, 18-13, 18-14, 18-15, 19-15.
HILTON, HOLLAND, 13-19.
HILTON, TIMOTHY, 18-11.
HIMMELBLAU, DAVID, 19-15.
HIMSTREET, WILLIAM C., 11-14, 11-16.
HINCKLEY, F. LEWIS, 18-16.
HIND, ARTHUR M., 18-12, 19-15.

HINDS, DUDLEY S., 11-11, 11-12, 11-18.
HINE, ROBERT V., 18-11, 18-12.
HINES, JIMMY, 15-14.
HINMAN, ALBERT G., 11-13, 11-14.
HINSHAW, ANDREW J., 12-13, 23-11.
HINTON, W. L. JR., 12-13.
HINTON, WALTER L., 12-13.
HIRMER, MAX, 18-12, 18-15, 18-16, 19-15.
HISLOP, RICHARD, 18-11.
HITCHINGS, T. C. JR., 11-11, 19-13.
HO, CHIN, 13-19.
HOAD, WILLIAM M., 13-15, 15-15.
HOAGLAND, HENRY E., 11-11, 11-14, 11-16, 12-11, 12-13, 13-11, 22-19, 22-20, 22-21.
HOBBS, W. E., 14-11.
HOBSON, A. R. A., 18-15, 19-15.
HODDESON, DAVID, 11-11, 11-16.
HODGES, M. B., 11-14, 11-16, 12-15.
HODGES, M. B. JR., 11-11, 11-12, 11-14, 11-16, 11-18, 12-11, 12-14, 12-18, 12-25, 18-11, 19-12, 19-15.
HODIN, J. P., 18-11.
HOEFER, ROLAND G., 13-16.
HOF, FREDERICK B., 19-11, 19-12, 19-15.
HOFFMAN, ARNOLD J., 11-19, 12-24.
HOFFMAN, HERBERT, 18-16, 18-17.
HOFFMAN, ISREAL, 12-13, 12-14.
HOFFMAN, JUDGE MURRAY, 11-11, 11-14, 11-16.
HOFMANN, WERNER, 18-11, 19-15.
HOGAN, HOWARD T., 12-11, 12-13, 22-18.
HOGAN, HUNTER A. JR., 23-11.
HOGAN, JOHN D., 412-11.
HOGAN, JOHN J., 11-14, 11-16.
HOGAN, LEO E., 12-13, 13-15, 24-13.
HOGAN, RICHARD A., 12-16.
HOGAN, W. T., 12-11.
HOGARTY, T. F., 12-25, 19-15, 19-16.
HOGENSON, HARRIS O., 13-14.
HOGUET, ROBERT L., 22-18.
HOGUET, ROBERT LOUIS, 11-11, 11-18.
HOLBROOK, JEFFREY, 11-11, 11-13, 11-16, 11-19, 22-19, 22-20.
HOLBROOK, M. JEFFREY, 12-14, 15-11.
HOLBROOK, MILLARD C., 19-13.
HOLCOMB, J. M., 11-11, 14-11.
HOLDEN, ARTHUR C., 12-11, 12-14, 13-11, 13-13, 13-17, 21-14, 22-18.
HOLDEN, THOMAS S., 11-11, 11-18, 13-13, 13-16, 19-11, 21-16, 22-18, 23-11.
HOLECOMB, PAUL E., 12-24.
HOLLAND, DANIEL M., 12-11, 22-18.
HOLLAND, MILTON, 12-23.
HOLLANDER, LOUIS H., 19-16.
HOLLEBAUGH, CLIFFORD W., 11-11, 11-13, 11-14, 11-16, 11-19, 12-24, 12-25, 13-15, 13-17, 13-19.
HOLLINGSHEAD, WADE C., 13-15.
HOLLOWAY, E. S., 18-18.
HOLLOWAY, JOHN P., 12-15.
HOLMAN, RALPH, 12-14.
HOLME, BRYON, 18-11.
HOLMES, DALE W., 13-15.
HOLMES, LAWRENCE G., 12-11, 13-15, 20-11, 22-18.
IIOLT, A. W., 11-14.
HOLT, DARRELL M., 11-11, 11-18.
HOLTON, JAMES L., 19-12.
HOLZ, LEFFERT, 12-14, 12-26.

HOLZHAUER, JOHN A., 11-14, 11-16, 11-19.
HOLZMAN, ROBERT S, 12-11.
HOME OWNER S LOAN CORPORATION, 11-14, 11-16, 13-19, 19-11.
HOMER, S., 19-15, 19-16.
HOMES, S., 19-15, 19-16.
HONAD, YOSHIO, 11-14, 11-19, 19-15.
HONEY, GAYLE K., 12-11.
HONEY, W. B., 18-14, 18-16.
HONOUR, HUGH, 18-18, 19-15.
HOOKER, JOHN P., 11-11, 11-14, 11-16, 22-19.
HOOKER, RAYMOND W., 12-16, 24-11, 24-15.
HOOPER, A. L., 12-16.
HOOT, WELDON, 22-18.
HOOVER, HERBERT C., 17-14.
HOOVER, I. H., 24-13.
HOOVER, RICHARD I., 11-11, 11-13, 11-16, 24-15.
HOPKINS, CHARLES I., 11-11, 11-16, 11-18, 19-11.
HOPKINS, ED W., 22-18.
HOPKINS, JON H., 18-12.
HOPKINS, ROBERT W., 12-14, 13-13, 13-19.
HOPPE, JOHN G. JR., 11-11, 11-14, 11-16.
HORAN, CHARLES J., 13-13.
HORAN, GEORGE B., 11-11, 11-16, 12-11.
HORGAN, JOHN P., 12-16, 12-26.
HORGAN, N. J, 12-24, 23-13.
HORN, RONALD R., 13-17.
HORNDOHL, FRANK, 12-23.
HORNE, ARCHIE J., 22-17.
HORNE, DONALD, 11-19, 12-24.
HORNUNG, CLARENCE PEARSON, 18-15, 18-16, 18-17.
HORRELL, ALBERT J., 12-16, 12-26.
HORTON, E. B. JR., 21-11.
HORTON, E.B. JR., 11-14, 11-19.
HORTON, GEORGE S., 11-14, 11-16, 13-19.
HORVITZ, S. A., 12-11, 12-24.
HORWATH, 13-15.
HORWATH AND HORWATH, 15-13.
HOSFORD, WANDA, 18-15, 18-16.
HOSKINS, HENRY J. B., 13-15.
HOSSACK, A. B., 11-19, 12-11, 12-24.
HOSSACK, J. E., 19-15.
HOTCKISS, L. M., 12-11, 13-17.
HOTELLING, HAROLD, 11-14, 12-19.
HOUSE & HOME, 13-15, 13-19.
HOUSE AND HOME, 13-15, 13-16, 13-17, 13-19.
HOUSE, PETER, 12-11, 12-13, 13-23, 14-11, 14-15, 15-14.
HOUSING AND REDEVELOPMENT BOARD, 13-16.
HOUSTON, SAM, 12-16, 12-26.
HOWARD, JACK M., 12-16, 12-26.
HOWARD, JEROME H., 12-15.
HOWARD, JEROME L., 13-17, 19-11, 19-12.
HOWARD, T. HOGAN, 12-11, 12-13, 22-18.
HOWARD, WILLIAM F., 12-16, 21-14, 22-16.
HOWARDS, I., 12-11.
HOWELL, BEN R., 22-14.
HOWELL, DONALD E, 14-18.
HOWORTH, PHILIP H., 12-11, 22-18.
HOYLE, FRED W., 13-17, 22-21.
HOYT, 11-11, 11-18, 22-19, 22-20.
HOYT, GEORGE H., 11-11, 11-12.
HOYT, HOMER, 11-11, 11-16, 11-18, 13-11, 13-13, 13-14, 13-15, 13-17, 13-18, 13-19, 14-11, 19-11, 19-12, 21-13, 21-16, 22-18, 22-19, 22-20, 24-11.
HOYT, JOHN R., 11-11, 11-12, 11-16, 13-15.

# BIBLIOGRAPHY OF APPRAISAL LITERATURE

HUANG, HAN LIANG, 12-11.
HUBBARD, CHARLES L., 11-11.
HUBBARD, DAVID F., 14-11.
HUBBART, J. ROY, 13-15.
HUBER, RICHARD G., 12-26.
HUBIN, VINCENT J., 11-11, 11-14, 11-16, 11-19, 12-11, 12-16, 13-11, 19-15, 22-18.
HUCK, ROBERT, 11-11, 11-14, 11-16, 22-21.
HUDE, JAMES V., 12-14.
HUDELSON, ROBERT R., 14-15.
HUDER, K. LEE, 11-11, 11-14.
HUDSEN, H. R., 11-11, 11-14, 23-11.
HUDSON, RAY M., 13-11.
HUDSON, RAYMOUND, 12-14.
HUDSON, W. J., 13-15.
HUFFMAN, WILLIAM H., 11-11, 12-14, 12-16.
HUFFTS, 12-16, 22-16.
HUGHES, C. W., 12-11.
HUGHES, EARL M., 14-15.
HUGHES, G. BERNARD, 18-14, 18-15, 18-16, 19-15.
HUGHES, GRAHAM, 18-15, 18-17, 19-15.
HUGHES, JAMES J., 11-11, 11-14.
HUGHES, JOHN D., 13-17.
HUGHES, R. G., 13-19.
HUGHES, RICHARD, 11-11, 11-16.
HUGHES, ROBERT, 18-11, 19-15.
HUGHES, THERLE, 18-16, 19-15.
HUGHES, THIRLE AND BERNARD, 18-14, 19-15.
HUHN, G. P., 11-14, 11-16.
HULLEY, ROBERT B., 24-11.
HULSE, FRED E., 12-11, 12-13, 13-23, 14-15.
HULTEM, JOHN J., 21-18.
HULTEN, JOHN J., 11-11, 11-14, 11-16.
HUMPHREY, D. E., 11-14, 11-16.
HUMPHREY, G. H., 12-11.
HUMPHREYS, LESTER W., 11-11, 12-16.
HUNNICUTT, WARREN P., 12-11, 12-26.
HUNSCHE, RALPH, 12-16, 13-15.
HUNTER, FREDERICK W., 18-15.
HUNTER, HAMILTON W., 11-11, 11-17.
HUNTER, JENEL L., 12-11, 15-17.
HUNTER, WALTER C., 11-14, 11-16.
HUNTLEY, GENE, 12-14, 13-17, 24-15.
HURD, RICHARD M., 11-11, 11-18, 13-11, 21-11, 22-19, 23-13, 24-11.
HURD, RICHARD MELANCTHON, 11-18, 13-11, 24-11.
HURLBURT, VIRGIL L., 14-15, 19-13, 22-20.
HURLBUTT, EDMUND C., 12-26.
HURLEY, JAMES J., 12-11, 17-15.
HURLEY, W. B., 13-17.
HURTADO MARTINEZ, LUIS, 11-11, 13-11, 13-16, 13-17.
HURWITT, S., 18-11, 18-12.
HUSBAND, WILLIAM H., 22-18.
HUSEMANN, FIELDING L., 11-14, 11-16.
HUTCHINS, ROBERT MAYNARD, 11-11.
HUTCHINSON, GEORGE, 12-15.
HUTCHINSON, IRA K., 12-15, 16-11.
HUTCHINSON, R. M., 14-15.
HUTTS, J. MARSHALL, 12-15, 12-16.
HUYGHE, RENE, 18-11, 19-15.
HYAM, LESLIE A., 11-11, 11-14, 11-16, 18-11, 18-12, 18-13, 18-14, 19-15.
HYDER, K. LEE, 11-11, 11-13, 11-14, 11-16, 11-17, 11-19, 12-18, 12-24, 12-26, 13-13, 13-15, 13-17, 13-20, 13-21, 19-13, 23-11, 23-14.

HYDER, LEE K., 23-11.
HYLTON, G. W., 11-13, 11-15.
HYNES, G. DEWEY, 13-19.
HYSOM, JOHN, 19-17.

I.R.S., 12-24.
IBSEN, NORM, 12-14.
ICE, WILLARD, 12-11.
IGNATYEV, G. M., 14-11, 22-20.
IICH, S. G., 13-11.
ILLINOIS DEPARTMENT OF REVENUE, 12-13, 13-15, 22-18.
ILLINOIS STATE TAX COMMISSION, 12-11.
ILLINOIS TAX COMMISSION, 12-13.
ILLINOIS UNIV, INSTITUTE OF GOVT & PUBLIC AFFAIRS, 12-13.
INDERBITZEN, ANTON L., 22-15.
INDUSTRIAL RESEARCH, 17-14, 20-13, 21-14, 22-21.
INDUSTRY WEEK, 13-13, 19-15, 24-11, 24-12.
INGERMAN, SIDNEY HERBERT, PH. D, 24-13.
INGLIS, E. R., 12-19.
INGRAM, DAVID, 12-14, 12-26.
INMAN, PETER L., 13-17.
INNARD, WILLIAM N., 13-17, 17-60.
INNOCENTI, R. E., 19-15, 19-16.
INST. OF NEWSPAPER CONTROLLERS & FINANCE OFFICERS, 13-15.
INSTITUTE FOR TAX ASSESSORS, UNIVERSITY OF TEXAS, 12-11, 12-13.
INSTITUTE OF PUBLIC SERVICE, 12-13.
INSTITUTE OF REAL ESTATE MANAGEMENT, 13-17, 22-18.
INSTITUTE ON EMINENT DOMAIN, 12-15, 12-26.
INSTITUTE'S RESEARCH COMMITTEE, 12-26, 22-18.
INSTITUTO AGRARIO NACIONAL (VZLA.), 14-11.
INSURED MORTGAGE PORTFOLIO, 13-11.
INTERART PUBLISHERS INC., 11-16, 18-11, 18-12, 18-13, 18-14, 18-15.
INTERNATIONAL ASSOCIATION OF ASSESSING OFFICERS, 11-14, 12-13, 12-15, 12-17, 13-13, 13-15, 13-19, 19-13, 20-13.
INTERNATIONAL CITY MANAGERS ASSOCIATION, 12-11, 12-12, 12-13.
INTERNATIONAL COMMERCE, 18-12.
INTERNATIONAL CONFERENCE OF ASSESSING OFFICERS, 12-13.
INTERNATIONAL COUNCIL OF APPRAISAL ORGANIZATIONS, 12-16.
INTERNATIONAL COUNCIL OF SHOPPING CENTERS, 13-15.
INTERSTATE COMMERCE COMMISSION, 12-16, 12-24, 24-11, 24-14.
INWOOD, WILLIAM, 22-18.
IOWA, 12-11, 12-13.
IOWA LAW REVIEW, 12-11, 13-11, 22-20.
IOWA LEGISLATIVE RESEARCH BUREAU, 12-11.
IOWA PROPERTY TAX DIVISION, 12-13, 22-18.
IRVING, KARL, 12-13.
IRWIM, S. C., 22-19, 22-20.
IRWIN, DAVID, 18-11, 19-15.
IRWINE, ALFRED G., 15-14.
ITTEN, JOHANNES, 19-15.

JACKS, MORRIS, 11-14, 21-16.
JACKSON, CHARLES J., 18-15, 19-15.
JACKSON, FRAND W., 11-11, 11-19.
JACKSON, FREDERICK W., 13-19.
JACKSON, HOWARD F., 11-11, 11-14, 11-16.
JACKSON, KENNETH N., 11-11, 11-14.
JACKSON, RILLA EVELYN, 18-11, 18-12, 18-13, 18-14, 18-15, 18-16.
JACOB, HERBERT, 12-13.
JACOBS, FLOR GILL, 18-15.
JACOBS, HARDY W., 12-11.
JACOBS, J. L., 12-12, 12-13, 22-18.
JACOBS, JAMES PH. D., 12-16, 12-19, 14-13.
JACOBS, THEODORE M., 11-11, 11-14.
JACOBSEN, NORMAN, 13-19.
JACOBSON, CHARLES E., 13-17.
JACOBSON, GLENN H., 12-16.
JAFFE, J. M., 11-14, 12-11.
JAFFE, L. C., 18-15, 19-15.
JAFFEE, BRUCE LEWIS PH. D., 16-11.
JAHR, ALFRED D., 12-14, 12-15.
JAMES, L. DOUGLAS., 12-16, 22-21.
JAMES, M. F., 11-11, 11-13.
JAMES, M. H., 11-11, 11-13, 11-14, 11-16, 13-17.
JAMES, PHILIP, ED., 18-13, 18-15.
JAMESON, MARY ETHEL, 11-16.
JAMIESON, J. B., 11-11, 19-12.
JANSSEN, M. R., 13-18.
JARCHON, ALFRED W., 13-16.
JARCHOW, ALFRED, 11-19, 19-12, 19-15.
JARCHOW, ALFRED W, 13-17.
JARCHOW, ALFRED W., 11-14, 11-16, 13-16.
JAROS, ALFRED L. JR., 20-13, 21-13, 21-16.
JARRETT, R. J., 11-11, 11-18.
JARRY, MADELEINE, 18-18, 19-15.
JEAN W. H., 12-25, 19-14.
JEFFERIES, RODNEY L., 11-12, 11-18.
JEFFERSON, GEORGE T., 24-15.
JEFFERY, RICHARD, 11-11, 11-16, 22-18.
JELENSKI, CONSTANTINE, 18-17, 19-15.
JELLIS, WILLIAM, 11-16, 11-19.
JEMING, JOSEPH B., 12-11, 21-12.
JEN, F. C., 12-24.
JENKINS, RALPH W., 11-11.
JENKINS, W. A., 14-11.
JENKS, ALDRO, 11-18, 12-11, 12-13.
JENKS, ALORO, 12-13.
JENNETT, C. B., 13-19, 14-15.
JENNING, JOSEPH B., 13-11.
JENNINGS, CHRISTOPHER R., 13-20.
JENSEEN, WARD J., 13-15.
JENSEN, CARL G., 12-24.
JENSEN, DANIEL LYLE, 16-12.
JENSEN, HOWARD I, 12-18, 14-11.
JENSEN, JAMES E., 17-15.
JENYNS, SOAMES, 18-15, 18-16.
JERRARD, L. P., 22-19, 22-20.
JERRARD, W. L., 13-15.
JERRETT, HERMAN D., 12-15, 13-18, 22-18, 22-19.
JERRETT, HERMAN DANIEL, 22-17.
JERSEY CITY BUREAU OF TAX ASSESSMENT, 12-11, 12-13.
JERSEY CITY, NEW JERSEY BUREAU OF ASSESSMENT, 12-13, 22-22.
JESNESS, O. B., 14-15, 22-20.
JEUDWINE, W. R., 18-15.
JEWETT APPRAISAL SERVICE, 14-17.
JEWETT, JOHN G., 19-14, 19-15, 23-11.
JIAN, C. L., 22-14.
JOACHIM, HARRY J., 11-14, 11-19, 12-15, 20-13.
JOHN, GERD, 12-11.
JOHNDROE, S. F. FR., 12-14.
JOHNS, A. B. C. JR., 12-11.
JOHNSON, ALBERT L., 12-15.
JOHNSON, B. D. L., 24-11.
JOHNSON, BARRY E, 14-11, 19-13.
JOHNSON, CLIFFORD R., 11-11, 11-14, 11-16, 12-16, 13-15, 13-17.
JOHNSON, DONAL, 14-11.
JOHNSON, E. C., 14-15.
JOHNSON, E. HOLLAND, 11-14, 11-16, 21-11.
JOHNSON, EARLE VINCENT, 12-19, 12-22.
JOHNSON, ERNEST H., 12-11, 12-13, 17-12.
JOHNSON, H. N., 12-26.
JOHNSON, HAROLD E., 12-16, 22-16.
JOHNSON, HENRY N., 12-26, 22-18.
JOHNSON, IRVING E., 19-12.
JOHNSON, JESSE W., 11-11, 11-14.
JOHNSON, LEEVERN, 13-13, 13-19, 22-16, 22-19.
JOHNSON, LOWELL C., 12-16, 17-14, 17-15.
JOHNSON, LYLE R., 12-11, 12-19, 19-15, 19-17.
JOHNSON, PHILIP M., 13-13.
JOHNSON, R W, 19-15.
JOHNSON, RALPH J., 13-16, 13-19.
JOHNSON, RALPH S., 12-11, 12-13, 17-12.
JOHNSON, RAYMOND, 12-13.
JOHNSON, RICHARD B., 22-24.
JOHNSON, ROBERT T., 17-15.
JOHNSON, RUSSELL BRUCE, PH. D., 14-11, 19-11.
JOHNSON, U. WEBSTER, 11-11, 11-16.
JOHNSTOME, W. GORDON, 15-20.
JOHNSTON, DOUGLAS, 11-11, 11-19.
JOHNSTON, EARL S., 11-14.
JOHNSTON, GEORGE C. JR., 13-19.
JOHNSTON, RICHARD STANLEY PH. D., 23-11, 23-17.
JOHNSTONE, PAULINE, 13-21, 18-12.
JOHNSTONE, W. GORDON, 13-19.
JONES, CARRIE MAUDE, 15-20.
JONES, DR. OLIVER H., 11-11, 11-18.
JONES, E., 19-15, 24-14.
JONES, E. P., 12-15, 12-16.
JONES, FRANCIS E., 11-13, 11-14, 11-16.
JONES, J. H., 11-14, 11-19.
JONES, WALTER B., 12-26.
JOPLIN, A. F., 23-11.
JOPLING, CAROL F., 19-15.
JORDAN, ROBERT D., 12-16, 22-16.
JORDON, R. D., 12-16, 22-16.
JOSEPH, MICHAEL, 18-11, 18-13, 18-15, 19-15.
JOSLIN, E. G., 12-14.
JOSLIN, EDWARD G., 11-13, 11-16.
JOUR OF AMER SOC OF FARM MGRS & RURAL APPRAISERS, 11-11, 11-12, 11-14, 11-16, 14-11.
JOYCE, W. V., 12-15.
JUDSON, A. R., 11-11, 11-18, 14-11.
JUNDT, DWIGHT W., 14-15.
JURETIE, LOUIS L., 12-23.
JURETTE, LOUIS J., 11-11, 11-12.
JUSTUS, FRED E. JR., 21-11.

KAFFENBERGER, KARL G. JR., 11-16, 11-19.
KAGANOVICH, A. L., 18-11, 18-12.
KAHN, CASE-SCHIMMEL, 19-15, 22-18.
KAHN, SANDERS A., 11-11, 11-12, 11-14, 11-16, 11-17, 11-18, 12-16, 12-24, 12-26, 13-11, 13-13, 13-14, 13-15, 13-17, 13-21, 13-23, 19-15, 22-11, 22-18, 22-19, 24-18.
KAIN, J. F., AND QUIGLEY, J. M., 12-19, 13-16.
KAIN, JOHN F., 13-17.
KAINEN, JACOB, 18-12, 19-15.
KALISH, JACOB, 11-16, 12-14.
KALTENBACH, HENRY J., 12-16, 12-18, 12-26, 22-18, 24-11, 24-15, 24-16.
KAM, WILLIAM H., 13-15, 19-15, 22-19.
KAMINS, R. M., 11-11, 11-18.
KAMLET, MARK, 11-14, 11-16, 13-15, 15-13, 17-13, 22-18.
KANE, C. V., 13-17.
KANN, BRUCE E., 11-11, 11-13, 11-16.
KANS., CITIZENS COMM ON ASSESSMENT EQUALIZATION, 12-12, 12-13.
KANSAS AGRICULTURAL EXPERIMENT STATION MANHATTAN, 12-11, 22-18.
KANSAS LEGISLATIVE COUNCIL, 12-11, 17-15.
KANSAS PROPERTY VALUATION DEPARTMENT, 12-13.
KAPLAN, R. S., 19-15.
KAPLAN, WILLIAM L., 13-11.
KAPROW, ALAN, 19-15.
KARKOW, WALDERMAR, 11-11, 11-14.
KARPE, ELMER F., 13-16.
KASCLE, E, 19-14, 19-17.
KASSAK, PETER J., 17-15.
KATES, G. M., 18-15, 18-18.
KATONA, GEORGE, 11-18.
KAUFMAN, H., 19-15, 19-16.
KAUFMAN, K. A., 12-16, 16-11, 17-11, 20-13, 20-15, 21-11, 21-16, 23-11.
KAWAHITO, KIYOSHI PHD, 20-15.
KAYLIN, S. O., 13-15.
KAZDIN, S. EDWIN, 11-11, 11-13, 11-14, 11-16, 11-19, 12-11, 12-14, 12-24, 12-25, 13-19, 19-11, 19-12, 19-15, 21-11, 22-11.
KEAN, R. GORDON, JR., 12-15.
KECK, JOHN G., 11-11, 11-14.
KEDZIERSKI, S. L., 13-17.
KEEFER, E. D., 11-14, 11-19, 12-24, 13-15, 13-19, 15-15.
KEEGAN, NORMAN J., 12-14, 13-19.
KEELY, JOSEPH F., 12-16.
KEENAN, M., 19-12.
KEENE, J., 12-12, 12-14, 12-19, 13-19.
KEENLEYSIDE, A., 12-14, 12-25, 14-18.
KEESLER, WILLIAM F., 13-20.
KEESLING, FRANK M., 12-11, 19-13.
KEEZER, DR. DEXTER M, 13-16.
KEITH, JOHN H., 11-18, 12-11, 12-12, 12-13.
KEITH, N.S., 12-13, 13-16.
KELDER, DIANE, 18-11.
KELLEHER, PAUL E., 13-21, 19-13.
KELLENBERGER, ALLEN N., 12-13, 12-16, 24-14.
KELLER, HARRY K., 11-11, 11-14, 13-11, 13-19.
KELLEY, ARTHUR C., 11-11, 11-16.
KELLEY, CHARLES B., 11-18.
KELLEY, JOHN F., 11-16, 13-15, 13-19, 18-11, 18-12, 18-13, 18-14, 24-15.
KELLEY, WILLIAM T., 11-14, 11-16, 13-16, 13-19.
KELLOG, CHARLES E, 14-11.

KELLOUGH, U. R., 12-24, 21-13, 21-16.
KELLOUGH, W. R., 11-11, 11-13, 11-14, 11-16, 12-18, 12-23, 12-25, 13-11, 13-15, 13-16, 13-17, 14-11, 19-15, 21-11, 21-12, 22-19, 22-20.
KELLY, BURNHAM, 13-16.
KELLY, ED, 12-18, 21-21.
KELLY, FRANCIS J., 13-21.
KELLY, ORR, 11-18.
KELLY, PILSON W., 19-14.
KELLY, ROB ROY, 18-12, 19-15.
KELLY, W. T., 13-19.
KELP, JOHN P., 18-11.
KENDALL, LEON T., 13-19.
KENNEDY G., 13-11.
KENNEDY, D. A., 11-11, 11-12, 11-14.
KENNEDY, DAVID O D., 13-19.
KENNEDY, DAVID H., 12-13.
KENNEDY, DONALD A., 12-19.
KENNEDY, FRANCIS H., 12-13, 24-11.
KENNEDY, HAROLD W., 12-14, 12-26.
KENNEDY, JAMES C., 12-11, 24-14.
KENNEDY, JOHN P., 12-13, 13-19.
KENNEDY, R. D., 11-11, 11-12.
KENNEDY, W. F., 12-16, 12-26, 19-15.
KENNETH, CLARK, 18-11, 19-15.
KENNY, J. M., 21-20.
KENNY, NORMAN W., 11-11, 11-17.
KENT, FRAND W., 11-11.
KENT, FRANK W., 18-11, 18-12, 18-13, 18-14, 18-15, 18-16.
KENT, FREDERICK C., 11-14, 12-12.
KENTUCKY DEPARTMENT OF REVENUE, 12-13, 22-18.
KENTUCKY LAW JOURNAL, 12-13.
KENTUCKY LEGISLATIVE RESEARCH COMMISSION, 12-11, 12-13.
KEOGH, J. VINCENT, 12-26.
KERLER, ROBERT G., 13-20.
KERN, JAMES M., 13-17, 13-19, 19-11, 19-15, 22-18.
KERR, MAX H., 12-13.
KERRISON, IRVINE L. H., 12-13.
KERSHOW WARREN W, 11-11, 11-14.
KESSLER, CHARLES S., 18-15.
KESTER, ROY B., 11-14.
KEUTNER, HERBERT, 18-13, 19-15.
KIBBEY, GERALD S., 22-18.
KIDDER, F. E., 13-13.
KILBORNE, R. D., 19-14, 19-15.
KILEY, EDWARD V., 12-16, 22-18, 24-11.
KILMORE, GENE, 22-18.
KILPATRICK, WYLIE, 12-11.
KINCAID, H. EVERT, 12-26.
KINDER, W. J., 12-23.
KING, BEN E., 11-11, 11-12, 12-26.
KING, BOWDEN V., 13-11.
KING, C. A., 13-20.
KING, PAT, 11-11, 12-14.
KING, PATRICK, 13-11.
KING, WILLFORD I., 11-11, 12-11, 13-13, 19-15, 22-18.
KING, WILLFORD ISBELL, 12-11.
KING, WILLIAM H., 12-14.
KINGSBURY, LAURA MABEL, 13-16.
KINNAID, WILLIAM N. JR., 11-11, 11-16.
KINNARD JR, W. N., 11-14, 11-19.
KINNARD, DR. WILLIAM N., 22-18.
KINNARD, DR. WILLIAM N. JR., 13-19.
KINNARD, W. N., 11-11, 11-16.

MARJASON L C, 13-15.
MARKEIM, J. WILLIAM, 12-14, 12-26, 13-17.
MARKHAM, MARION, 12-16, 22-21.
MARKLE, SHELDON E., 12-11, 12-13.
MARKS, R. E., 24-14, 24-15.
MARLYN, FRANK, 13-11.
MARPLES, RICHARD A, 12-14, 25-11, 25-12.
MARQUIS, RICHARD, 11-11, 11-14, 11-16.
MARR C. R., 13-11.
MARSELE, PETER R. AND ALFRED CALABRESE, 12-11, 22-11.
MARSH, MORITON, 18-16.
MARSHALL AND STEVENS PUBLICATION COMPANY, 21-15, 21-16, 21-20.
MARSHALL, J. W., 12-14, 13-19, 21-12.
MARSHALL, T., 13-11, 13-16.
MARSHALL, TRUETT B., 12-13.
MARSHALL, W. & YOUNG, A., 19-15, 19-16.
MARSTON, 19-19.
MARSTON, ANSON, 11-14, 11-19, 12-24, 12-26, 19-14, 19-19, 21-11, 21-16, 22-19, 22-20, 23-11.
MARTENSON, W. J., 11-11, 11-19, 12-24.
MARTIN D. W., 12-11.
MARTIN, C. VIRGIL, 13-12, 13-15.
MARTIN, E. KRANZ, 13-12.
MARTIN, HOWARD S., 13-15.
MARTIN, J. R., 18-13, 18-15.
MARTIN, JAMES M., 12-13, 13-21.
MARTIN, JAMES W., 12-11, 12-13, 12-26, 19-15, 24-14.
MARTIN, N. D., 13-12, 13-14, 24-11, 24-12.
MARTIN, NORENE DAN, 24-11.
MARTIN, PRESTON, 22-18.
MARTIN, S. J., 12-26, 19-16.
MARTIN, T. MAXMILLIAN, 13-19.
MARTIN, W. H., 22-18, 24-11, 24-13.
MARTIN, WENDELL H., 13-16, 22-18, 22-21.
MARTIN, WILLIAM MCCHESNEY, 13-16, 19-12.
MARTINDALE, ANDREW, 18-11, 18-15.
MARTINDELL, JACKSON, 11-11, 11-18.
MARTINEZ R., NESTOR, 21-18.
MARTINI, EUGENE R., 11-18.
MARTLING, W. LOCKWOOD, JR., 11-14, 21-11.
MARTZ, CLYDE O., 12-14.
MARTZKE, ARTHUR J., 19-12, 22-18.
MARX, CLAUDE ROGER, 18-11, 19-15.
MARX, LEONARD, 22-18.
MARYON, 18-13, 18-14.
MASAD, RIMON NICOLA, 12-13, 13-15.
MASHKE, D. K., 11-11, 11-12, 13-22, 21-11, 22-17.
MASON, ROBERT G., 12-13.
MASON, TOM, 22-18, 22-24.
MASON, W. BEVERLEY, JR., 13-17.
MASSACHUSETTS LEGISLATIVE RESEARCH COUNCIL, 12-11.
MASSIN, 16-15, 18-15, 19-15.
MASTER, ROBERT E. L. AND JEAN HOUSTON, 18-12, 19-15.
MATERN, RUDOLPH, 11-11, 11-18.
MATHENY, EDWARD T., 19-13.
MATHERLY, WALTER J., 11-11, 11-18, 22-18.
MATHUR, G., 12-19, 19-14.
MATSON, ARTUR J., 14-11, 14-13.
MATTER, J. AUBREY, 12-13, 13-19, 22-18.
MATTHEWS, HAROLD WILLIAM, 11-11, 11-14.
MATTHEWS, M. L., 21-13.

MATTHEWS, MYRON L., 11-11, 11-12, 11-14, 11-16, 11-18, 12-11, 12-23, 12-24, 13-20, 19-14, 21-11, 21-13, 21-15, 21-16, 21-18, 21-20.
MATTHEWS, STEWART B., 13-18, 22-18.
MATTHEWS, WILLIAM P., 14-15.
MAUCH, ARTHUR, 14-15, 22-18.
MAXWELL, GEORGE I., 12-14, 24-15.
MAY, ARHUR, 13-17.
MAY, ARTHUR A, 11-11, 11-12, 11-19, 12-24, 13-19, 22-18.
MAY, ARTHUR A., 11-11, 11-14, 11-16, 12-24, 13-17, 13-19, 22-18.
MAY, M., 13-11, 19-15, 19-16.
MAY, OLIVER, 11-16, 11-19.
MAYER, CHRISTA C., 18-15, 18-16.
MAYER, EDWIN, 11-11, 11-16, 22-11.
MAYER, GEORGE E., 13-19.
MAYER, HAROLD M., 22-18, 23-11.
MAYER, L. A., 13-11, 13-15, 13-27.
MAYER, LESTER B., 14-15.
MAYHEW, ROBERT R., 13-19.
MAYNARD, E. L., 12-11, 16-12, 16-13.
MC MICHAEL, STANLEY L., 11-11, 11-14, 11-16, 13-15, 21-11, 23-11.
MCANELLY, E. E., 14-15.
MCANLY, H. T., 11-19, 21-11, 21-17.
MCCALLUM, ANGUS, 13-19.
MCCALLUM, J. E., 16-12, 24-14.
MCCANDLESS, DONALD C., 11-11, 11-14.
MCCARTHY, CHARLES R., 13-19, 14-15.
MCCARTHY, CLARENCE F., 12-11.
MCCARTHY, EARL D., 12-16, 13-15.
MCCARTHY, GEORGE D, 19-17.
MCCARTHY, JOSEPH R., 11-11, 11-18.
MCCASLIN, A. A., 19-13, 22-18.
MCCAWLEY, PATRICIA K., 18-15, 18-16, 19-15.
MCCGARRY, THOMAS F., 13-13, 24-15.
MCCLELLAN, ELISABETH, 18-15, 18-19, 19-15.
MCCLELLAN, W A, 19-18.
MCCLELLAND, HARRY, 22-18.
MCCLINTON, KATHERINE MORRISON, 18-16, 19-15.
MCCLOSKEY, W. D., 13-15, 21-14.
MCCLOY, H. F., 13-16.
MCCLOY, HOWARD F., 22-18.
MCCLOY, WILLIAM M., 12-23.
MCCLURE, 18-16, 18-18.
MCCOOMBS, IRVINE J., 12-13.
MCCORMACK, J. E., 13-13.
MCCORMACK, JAMES E., 11-11, 13-13, 22-18, 23-11.
MCCORMICK, LORING O., 11-11, 11-16, 11-19, 12-24, 13-19, 22-18.
MCCORMICK, LORING, SCHMUTZ, GEORGE, 11-11, 11-19.
MCCORMICK, M. J., 11-11, 11-19.
MCCORMICK, MICHAEL J., 13-15.
MCCOY, CHARLES R., 12-14, 12-15, 13-11, 13-15, 19-13, 22-18.
MCCROSKY, T. T., 13-19, 13-22.
MCCURDY, ROBERT V., 12-18, 12-24, 12-25, 13-15, 13-19, 21-16, 22-18.
MCCUTCHEON, JAMES T., 12-13, 13-11.
MCCUTCHEON, W. B., 11-14, 11-19, 12-25, 13-19, 13-23.
MCDANIEL, G. A., 11-11, 17-15.
MCDIARMID, M. C., 13-22, 22-17.
MCDILL, 18-16.
MCDONALD, A. M., 11-11, 11-19, 12-24, 13-16, 13-19.

# BIBLIOGRAPHY OF APPRAISAL LITERATURE

MCDONALD, ADRIAN F., 11-11, 11-13, 11-18, 11-19, 12-14, 12-24, 12-26, 13-17, 13-19, 14-11, 19-15, 22-18, 24-15.
MCDONALD, D. L., 11-14, 11-16, 13-11, 14-11.
MCDONALD, J., 17-15.
MCDONALD, JOHN A., 12-13.
MCDONALD, LUCILLE S., 18-17.
MCDONALD, RAYMOND J., 11-11.
MCDONALD, STEPHEN L., 12-11.
MCDONNELL, N. B., 12-11, 12-13.
MCDONNELL, WILLIAM A., 13-13.
MCDOWELL, HARRY G., 12-11, 12-13.
MCELVEE, EUGENE, 19-15.
MCELWEE, EUGENE, 12-25, 13-20.
MCENTIRE, DAVIS, 13-11.
MCFADDEN, NORMAN E., 12-26, 22-18.
MCFADZEAN, JAMES, 12-15.
MCFARLEN, T. A., 11-14, 11-16, 14-11.
MCGAHEY, ROBERT L., 11-14, 11-16.
MCGARRY, D. F., 22-18.
MCGARRY, DANIEL F., 12-14.
MCGAVIN, C. T., 13-12.
MCGAVIN, CHARLES T., 13-12.
MCGLONE V. P., 11-11, 11-16.
MCGOUGH R. M., 13-11, 14-15.
MCGOUGH, B. C., 12-14, 12-15, 12-16, 12-18, 22-18, 24-15.
MCGOUGH, BOBBY C., 12-16, 24-15.
MCGOVERN, JOHN E., 13-19, 13-23.
MCGRATH, GEORGE W., 22-18.
MCGREGOR, GWENITH, 12-11.
MCGUINESS, EDWARD J., 12-13, 13-19.
MCGUINNESS, EDWARD J, 13-14.
MCGUIRE, D. C., 23-11.
MCGUIRE, JOSEPH, 22-18.
MCHENRY, D. B., 12-16.
MCINNES, N., 12-25, 18-15.
MCINTOSH, KENNETH W., 13-19.
MCIVER, C. R., 12-16.
MCKAY, CHARLES WATSON, 13-20, 20-15, 23-11.
MCKAY, E. O., 13-19.
MCKAY, GORDON A., 12-23.
MCKAY, HERNDON, 11-11, 11-14.
MCKAY, JACK F., 12-13.
MCKAY, R. J., 12-11, 22-16, 22-18.
MCKEAN, JAMES P., 11-14, 11-16.
MCKEE-BERGER-MANSUETO, 21-20.
MCKEE, D. L., 13-11.
MCKEE, GLENN M., 12-13.
MCKEEVER, J. ROSS, 13-11, 13-14.
MCKELDIN, THEODORE R., 13-19.
MCKEOWN, J. C., 19-15.
MCKEY, ROBERT M., 13-15, 22-18.
MCKIBBIN, CLIFFORD W., 13-21.
MCKIBBIN, FRANK B., 12-14, 13-19.
MCKINNEY, HOWARD C., 11-14, 11-16.
MCKINNON, NEIL J., 12-11.
MCLAUGHLIN, CHARLES J., 12-11, 22-18.
MCLAUGHLIN, FRANK, 12-14, 13-19.
MCLAUGHLIN, FRANK J., 11-11, 11-16, 11-19.
MCLAUGHLIN, GLEEN E., 23-11.
MCLAUGHLIN, WALTER W., 11-19, 14-11.
MCLEAN, E. E., 19-11, 22-18.
MCLEAN, J. G., 19-14, 19-15.
MCLEAN, W. M., 12-15, 12-26.
MCLEOD, MORTON P., 11-11, 11-14.
MCLEOD, V. W., 12-14.
MCMAHEN, D. H., 14-11, 23-13.
MCMAHON, THOMAS C., 13-14, 13-15, 13-17.
MCMANUS, G. J., 21-11, 23-18.
MCMANUS, JOSEPH F., 11-11, 11-12.
MCMICHAEL. S. L., 19-15.
MCMICHAEL, JAMES M., 11-14, 11-16, 12-11, 19-15.
MCMICHAEL, S. L., 12-11, 12-14, 13-15.
MCMICHAEL, STANLEY, 13-11.
MCMICHAEL, STANLEY L., 11-11, 11-12, 11-13, 11-14, 11-15, 11-16, 11-19, 12-14, 12-24, 12-25, 13-11, 13-13, 13-14, 13-15, 13-17, 13-18, 13-19, 13-20, 13-22, 17-13, 19-13, 20-13, 22-18, 22-22, 22-24, 23-11, 24-17.
MCMNUS, G. J., 17-11.
MCMORRAN, J. BURCH, 11-11, 11-14, 11-16, 12-11.
MCMULLIN J. A., 11-11, 11-16.
MCMURRY, ROBERT N., 23-11.
MCNAMARA, KATHERINE, 13-11.
MCNULTY, CHARLES S., 12-13, 13-19.
MCNULTY, J. W., 12-11, 20-13, 24-12.
MCPHERSON, JOSEPH F., 11-11, 11-16.
MCPHERSON, L. D., 22-22.
MCPHERSON, L. V., 22-18, 22-24.
MCREYNOLDS, TOM, 13-15, 13-23, 15-11, 19-15, 24-17.
MCSPADDEN, FRANK J, 22-18.
MCSWAIN, ROBERT H., 12-13.
MCSWEENEY, THOMAS F., 11-11, 11-14, 11-16, 11-19, 12-16, 12-24, 17-14.
MCVEAGH, J., 12-26.
MEAD, WALTER J., 12-11, 17-12, 19-14.
MEADOW, BEN, 17-12.
MEANS, ERNEST E., 12-11, 12-13.
MEANS, ROBERT S., 21-13.
MEAUZE, PIERRE, 18-13.
MEDICI, GUISEPPE, 11-11, 11-16.
MEEK, RONALD L., 11-11, 11-13, 11-17.
MEENACH, T. J., 11-11, 11-16.
MEENEN, H. J., 14-11, 21-11, 23-13.
MEER, F. VAN DER, 18-11, 18-12, 19-15.
MEHREN, GEORGE L., 14-15.
MEILACH, DONA, 18-13, 19-15.
MEISS, MILLARD, 18-11, 19-15.
MEISSNER, KURT, 18-13, 18-14, 18-15.
MELAMED, ANSHEL, 13-19, 13-23.
MELENDY, MERLE C., 11-11, 11-16.
MELICHER, R. W, 16-12, 19-15.
MELLOR, PHILLIP, 12-14, 17-16.
MELLOR, ROSS, 14-15.
MELNYK, PETER F., 12-13, 12-24.
MELOT, MICHEL, 18-12, 18-15.
MELTZER, HERMAN, 12-14, 12-26.
MENDEZ, ALFREDO, JR., 12-16, 13-16.
MERCER, ERIC, 18-16.
MERCER, GEORGE L., 11-14, 11-16, 11-19.
MERCHANTS ASSOCIATION OF NEW YORK, 13-11.
MEREDITY, L. DOUGLAS, 13-17, 19-11, 19-12.
MERREL, JOHN A., 11-11, 11-12.
MERRELL, JOHN H., 11-16, 11-18.
MERRIAM, A. O., 12-23, 19-12.
MERRIAM, ROBERT E, 12-11.
MERRILL, EUGENE S., 17-14, 19-14, 19-16.
MERTZKE, A. J., 13-17.
MERTZKE, ARTHUR J., 11-11, 11-14, 11-16, 11-19, 12-25, 13-11, 13-14, 13-19, 19-13, 22-11, 22-18.
MERTZKE, ARTHUR., 11-19, 13-15.
MESSNER, DR. STEPHEN D., 13-13.

METCALFE, C. B., 22-20.
METZ, ERIC RUDOLF, 12-23, 24-17.
MEYER, EDWIN G., 12-14, 12-16, 13-17.
MEYER, HAROLD, 12-16.
MEYER, HAROLD F., 12-11, 12-25.
MEYER, R. A. JR., 12-14.
MEYERS, ROBERT M, 19-16.
MEYRICK, SIR SAMMUEL RUSH, 18-16, 18-18.
MICAY, A. R., 12-14.
MICHALOWSKI, KAZIMIERZ, 18-11, 19-15.
MICHIGAN CITIZENS RESEARCH COUNCIL, 12-11.
MICKLE, D. GRANT, 22-21, 24-12.
MIDDLEMAS, KEITH, 18-15, 18-16.
MIDDLEMIST, W. J., 12-12.
MIELDS JR. HUGH, 13-11.
MIELDS, HUGH JR., 12-11.
MILISIEWICZ, JANINA, 11-11, 11-12, 11-14, 11-16.
MILL, JOHN STUART, 11-11, 11-14.
MILLER C. ARC, 12-16, 22-19, 22-20.
MILLER MARTIN D., 20-12, 21-16.
MILLER, ALTEN S., 17-15.
MILLER, D. C., 18-11, 18-13, 19-15.
MILLER, DULCY B., 12-24.
MILLER, GERALD W., 12-13.
H. P. MILLER, 13-11.
MILLER, HENRY, 18-11.
MILLER, HENRY S., 19-11.
MILLER, J. EARL, 14-15.
MILLER, KENNETH C. JR., 13-19, 24-12.
MILLER, M. D., 24-11.
MILLER, M. E., 12-11.
MILLER, MARTIN D., 12-11, 12-13.
MILLER, MARTIN D. M., 12-13.
MILLER, R. D., 11-11, 11-19, 12-24.
MILLER, REX K., 12-15, 12-16, 17-15.
MILLER, W. S., 12-13.
MILLER, WILLIAM STANLEY, 12-11, 22-18.
MILLIMAN, J. W., 12-11.
MILLMAN, DEANE A., 12-11, 17-14.
MILLS, DOREMUS L., 20-13.
MILLS, WILBUR D, 12-11.
MILNER, JOSEPH, 13-14, 13-20.
MILWAUKEE TAX DEPARTMENT, 12-13.
MINAYA, NICHOLAS J., 11-11, 11-14.
MINISTERIO DE AGRICULTURA Y CRIA DE VZLA., 17-12.
MINNESOTA TAX COMMISSION, 12-13.
MINOR, CHARLES, D., 17-12.
MINWEGEN ROGER P., 11-11, 11-12.
MISCHKE, ARTHUR, 12-13, 14-13.
MISFELDT, DOUGLAS E., 12-13, 16-12, 17-15.
MISSISSIPPI STATE TAX COMMISSION, 12-12, 12-13.
MISSOURI STATE TAX COMMISSION, 12-11, 12-13.
MITCHELL, A. CROMAR, 11-11, 11-12, 11-13.
MITCHELL, JACK, 14-15.
MITCHELL, KENNETH F., 13-11, 13-19.
MITCHELL, RICHARD E., 12-22, 22-20, 23-11.
MITTEN, DAVID GORDON, 18-15.
MIYAGAUA TORAS, 18-11, 18-16, 19-15.
MOAK, JAMES E., 12-11, 12-13, 17-12.
MOBILE HOMES MANUFACTURERS ASSOCIATION, 13-16, 13-17.
MOBLEY, H. H., 12-16, 24-15.
MOEBES, CARL, 12-14, 12-16, 17-14.
MOEBES, CARL G., 12-14, 12-16, 17-14.

MOHR, LARRY R., 12-13, 12-24, 16-11.
MOIXER, MIKLOS, 18-11, 19-15.
MOLINARI, GEORGE, 19-15.
MOLLAN, WILLIAM W., 11-13, 11-14, 11-16, 19-12.
MOLONEY, J. L., 15-15.
MONCUR, JAMES E. T. PH. D., 16-14.
MONDELLO, R., 13-11.
MONDELLO, ROMEO, 13-11, 22-18.
MONIESON, DAVID DANNY, 11-11, 11-19.
MONRAD, OSCAR, 23-11.
MONTANA LEGISLATIVE COUNCIL, 12-11.
MONTANO, JOSEPH M., 13-11, 14-11.
MONTGOMERY, CHARLES F., 18-11, 18-18.
MONTGOMERY, W., 12-16.
MONTGOMERY, W. R., 13-15.
MONTONNA DAVID L., 13-18.
MONTONNA, D. L., 11-11, 11-16, 19-15, 21-11.
MONTONNA, DAVID L., 11-16, 11-19, 12-24, 12-25, 13-17, 13-18, 19-15, 19-17.
MONTOYA, JOSEPH A., 12-26, 19-15.
MONTZ, A. S., 11-14, 11-16.
MONYEK, R. H., 11-19, 11-24, 12-11, 12-24.
MOORE, B. H., 12-16, 24-14.
MOORE, HANNAH HUDSON, 18-15.
MOORE, L. J., 12-16.
MOORE, MILTON W., 11-11, 11-14.
MOORE, N. HUDSON, 18-15, 18-16.
MOORE, PEYTON H., 12-15.
MOORE, ROBERT C., 19-12.
MOORE, WILLIS, 19-15.
MOORES, CHESTER A., 11-11, 11-18.
MORA FERNANDEZ, DANIEL, 12-1..
MORASSI, ANTONIO, 18-11, 19-15.
MORDEN, J. W., 12-20.
MOREHOUSE, E. W., 11-11, 11-14.
MORESCO, ENRIQUE, 12-14.
MORGAN, BELDEN, 11-11, 11-18, 11-19, 12-24, 13-17, 13-18, 13-19, 13-23, 14-11, 21-13, 22-15.
MORGAN, CECIL L., 12-12, 12-13.
MORGAN, JAMES V., 11-11, 11-12, 11-14, 11-16, 13-17.
MORLEY FLETCHER, H., 18-14, 19-15.
MORONEY, ROBERT E, 19-14, 19-16.
MORRELL, JOSEPH C., 13-15, 13-17, 13-19, 22-18.
MORRIS GUARD J., 13-15.
MORRIS, STEWART, 12-26, 19-15, 19-16.
MORRIS, VICTOR P., 22-18.
MORRISON, CHARLES W., 22-24, 23-11.
MORRISON, D. G., 19-14.
MORRISON, E. R., 11-16, 14-11, 14-13, 14-18.
MORRISSEY, THOMAS P., 11-11, 11-14, 11-16.
MORROW, R. CONRAD, 12-14, 13-15, 13-17, 19-13.
MORSE, HARRISON H., 13-15, 19-15.
MORSE, PETER, 18-12.
MORSE, ROBERT R, 14-18.
MORSE, TRUE D., 11-14, 11-16, 12-13, 14-11, 14-15, 14-16, 14-18.
MORSEY, NASHAAT, 11-11, 11-18, 17-16, 22-24.
MORSEY, NASHATT, 11-11, 11-16, 11-18.
MORSS, ELLIOTT R., 12-11.
MORSY, NASHAAT, 11-11, 11-16, 14-11.
MORTIMER, J. R., 12-16, 24-15.
MORTON, PERRY W., 12-14.
MORTON, PHILIP, 18-15, 18-17.
MORTON, WALTER A., 12-25, 19-15.
MOSBY, WILLIAM E., 13-19.

MOSELLE-, 21-20.
MOSER, A. W., 11-19, 12-24.
MOSER, LEROY C., 12-15, 19-13.
MOSES, ALEX I., 12-15, 12-16.
MOSHER, M. L., 14-15.
MOSLEY, FRED M., 12-16.
MOSORIAK, 18-15.
MOSS, DAVID S., 19-15, 22-18.
MOSS, HUNTER, 13-11, 13-15, 13-16, 24-15.
MOTT, G. M., 13-14.
MOTT, SEWARD H., 12-14, 13-15, 13-17, 13-23.
MOULTON, HAROLD G., 19-11.
MOURRAY, JAMES W., 12-12, 13-11.
MOWLL, WILLIAM L., 19-12.
MROTER, RAYMOND D., 11-16, 19-13.
MUELLER, EVA, 13-17.
MULCAHY, JOHN V., 12-15, 12-16.
MULDOON, JOSEPH, 24-19.
MULHERN, EUGENE, 13-15.
MULHERN, EUGENE S., 11-11, 11-14, 11-16.
MULLENDORE, WALTER E., 16-11, 16-12, 16-13.
MULLENIX, C. A., 13-19, 22-18.
MULLER, PRISICILLA E., 18-15, 18-17, 19-15.
MULLINS, EDWIN, 18-11, 19-15.
MUNCY, DOROTHY A., 15-20, 23-11.
MUNDY, F. W., 19-15, 24-14.
MUNIC FIN OFFCRS ASSN OF U. S. & CANADA, 11-14, 12-13.
MUNICIPAL & LOCAL FINANCE OFFCRS OF PENNSYLVANIA, 12-13.
MURCHISON, KENNETH, 12-24, 21-11.
MURILLO, ANA J. ECO., 11-11, 11-14.
MURPHY J. P., 11-11, 11-16, 12-15.
MURPHY JR, RICHARD E., 19-17.
MURPHY, ANDREW L., 13-15.
MURPHY, J. W., 22-18, 22-19, 22-20.
MURPHY, LEO A., 12-16, 12-21.
MURRAY, HENRY T., 13-17, 14-15, 14-18.
MURRAY, JOHN, 18-15, 18-16, 19-15.
MURRAY, R. F., 19-15, 19-16.
MURRAY, T. G., 19-15, 22-18.
MURRAY, W. G., 14-15.
MURRAY, WILLIAM G, 14-11.
MURRAY, WILLIAM G., 11-11, 11-14, 11-16, 12-13, 14-13, 14-15, 14-16, 14-17, 22-18.
MURRAY, WILLIAM H., 13-19.
MUSCH, HENRY JR., 11-11, 11-16.
MUSCH, HENRY, JR., 11-12.
MUSGRAVE, RICHARD A., 12-11.
MUSKIE, EDMUND S, 12-11.
MUSKIN, SELMA J., 12-11.
MUSTOE, NELSON EDWIN, 11-11, 11-14, 11-16.
MYERS, W. . I., 11-11, 11-18.

N. Y. STATE BOARD OF EQUALIZATION & ASSESSMENT, 12-12, 12-13.
N. Y. TIMES INDEX, 13-11, 13-13, 13-16, 13-17, 13-19, 14-11, 21-13, 22-18.
N.A. CONFERENCE OF APPRAISAL ORGANIZATIONS, 11-12.
NAMAVATI, ROSHAN, 11-11, 11-14, 11-16, 12-11.
NANCE, JAMES J., 11-11, 11-18.
NANNEY, L. C., 14-17, 14-18.
NARKISS, BEZALEL, 18-15, 19-15.

NASARIO, LUIS A., 11-14, 11-16.
NASH, W. W., 13-17.
NATION S CITIES, 12-11.
NATIONAL APPRAISAL FORUM, 19-12.
NATIONAL ASSOCIATION OF ASSESSING FINANCE, 12-13.
NATIONAL ASSOCIATION OF ASSESSING OFFICERS, 11-11, 11-16, 12-11, 12-13, 13-11.
NATIONAL ASSOCIATION OF BUILDING OWNERS & MANAGERS, 12-24.
NATIONAL ASSOCIATION OF COUNTY OFFICIALS, 12-11, 12-26.
NATIONAL ASSOCIATION OF MUTUAL SAVINGS BANKS, 19-12, 22-18.
NATIONAL ASSOCIATION OF REAL ESTATE BOARDS, 11-11, 11-12, 11-14, 11-16, 12-24, 13-14, 13-19, 19-11, 22-18, 23-11.
NATIONAL ASSOCIATION OF TAX ADMINISTRATORS, 12-11, 12-13, 24-14.
NATIONAL COMMITTEE OF R. R. & PUB UTIL TAX REP'S, 12-13.
NATIONAL EDUCATION ASSOCIATION OF UNITED STATES, 12-13.
NATIONAL GOLF FOUNDATION, INC., 15-14.
NATIONAL INSTITUTE OF MUNICIPAL LAW OFFICERS, 12-14.
NATIONAL INSTITUTE OF REAL ESTATE BROKERS, 13-15, 19-13, 22-18.
NATIONAL MUNICIPAL LEAGUE, 12-13.
NATIONAL PARKING ASSOCIATION, 13-12.
NATIONAL REAL ESTATE JOURNAL, 11-11, 11-14, 11-16, 12-11, 12-22, 12-26, 13-14, 13-15, 13-17, 13-19, 13-20, 13-23, 17-15, 19-13, 22-18, 23-11.
NATIONAL RESOURCES COMMITTEE, URBANISM COMMITTEE, 13-11.
NATL REAL ESTATE JOUR, ACTUAL APPRAISAL REPORTS, 14-18, 14-19.
NATTHEN, LEONARD W., 12-11.
NAYLOR, R. VELDON, 13-17.
NAYLOR, VELDON R, 15-20.
NAZARIO, LUIS A, 11-11, 11-16.
NAZARIO, LUIS A., 11-11, 11-14, 11-16, 13-18.
NEALEY, MORGAN T. JR., 12-16, 22-16, 25-14.
NEATHY, NIGEL, 18-11, 19-15.
NEBRASKA LEGISLATIVE COUNCIL, 12-11.
NEBRASKA STATE TAX COMMISSIONER, 12-11, 12-13.
NEGUS, ARTHUR, 18-15, 18-16, 19-15.
NEILSON, CHARLESWORTH K., 11-18, 16-11.
NEISWANGER, DAVID, 12-14, 12-26, 13-19, 22-18, 24-13.
NELSON, A. V., 13-11.
NELSON, ALBERT H., 14-13, 14-15.
NELSON, CONRAD J., 12-23.
NELSON, EUGENE F., 12-16.
NELSON, FORREST S., 13-21.
NELSON, H. V., 22-18.
NELSON, HENRY PH. D., 13-19.
NELSON, N. B., 11-13, 11-14.
NELSON, R. D., 11-11, 19-11, 19-15, 23-11.
NELSON, R. L., 11-14, 11-19, 13-15, 13-19.
NELSON, RICHARD L., 11-14, 11-19, 12-16, 13-13, 13-15, 24-14.
NELSON, RICHARD LAWRENCE, 12-22, 13-14, 13-15, 19-15.
NELSON, RICHRD L., 11-11, 11-12.
NELSON, ROBERT V., 13-19.

NELSON, ROLAND D., 11-11, 11-14, 11-16, 11-19, 12-11, 13-12, 13-20, 19-15, 22-18.
NELSON, T. R., 11-14, 11-16.
NELSON, W. L., 11-11, 11-19, 12-24, 20-12, 23-14.
NELSON, WALTER C., 13-16.
NESIUS, ERNEST J., 14-18.
NESS, OWEN M., 12-16, 14-15.
NESSER, RICHARD S., 11-16, 11-19, 12-13, 13-17, 13-20, 19-15, 22-19.
NETZER, DICK, 12-11, 19-11, 19-14.
NEUMAN, RONALD, 11-11, 11-12, 11-16.
NEUMANN, JAROMIR, 18-11, 18-15, 19-15.
NEUMEYER, A., 19-15.
NEUSES, DON P., 13-11.
NEUTZE, M., 13-11, 13-13, 22-19.
NEUTZMAN, R. A., 12-11.
NEVADA TAX COMMISSION, 12-13.
NEVEROV, O., 18-16, 18-17.
NEVINS, RICHARD, 12-11.
NEW JERSEY COMMISSION ON STATE TAX POLICY, 12-11, 24-14.
NEW JERSEY DIVISION OF TAXATION, 12-11, 12-12.
NEW JERSEY LOCAL PROPERTY TAX BUREAU, 12-11.
NEW JERSEY STATE TAX DEPARTMENT, 12-13.
NEW YORK CITY CITIZENS BUDGET COMMISSION, 12-11.
NEW YORK METROPOLITAN MUSEUM OF ART, 18-11.
NEW YORK STATE SOCIETY OF REAL ESTATE APPRAISERS, 12-13.
NEW ZEALAND SOCIETY OF ACCOUNTANTS, 19-16.
NEWCOMB, ROBINSON, 13-17, 19-15, 22-19.
NEWCOMBE, DEWEY, 19-12.
NEWHOUSE, WADE J. JR., 12-11.
NEWLOVE, G. H., 11-19, 12-24.
NEWLOVE, GEORGE HILLIS, 11-14, 11-16.
NEWMAN, D. K., 13-16, 21-11.
NEWMAN, J. WILSON, 13-15.
NEWTON, E. W., 11-11, 11-14.
NIBLEY, ROBERT, 12-26.
NICHOLIN, JORGE, 19-15.
NICHOLLS, CHARLES C. JR., 13-15.
NICHOLLS, D. H., 12-11.
NICHOLLS, DAVID H., 12-11.
NICHOLS, ALAN H., 12-12, 12-13.
NICHOLS, FRED W., 12-16.
NICHOLS, GEORGE L., 12-11.
NICHOLS, J. C., 13-11.
NICHOLS, PHILIP, 12-11, 12-15, 19-16.
NICHOLS, THOMAS S., 12-11.
NICOLL, JOHN, 18-11.
NICOLLS, J. P., 11-11, 11-18, 22-18.
NIEHANS, J., 16-11.
NIEHAUS, T. B., 15-15, 17-12.
NIELSON, HOWARD N., 19-11, 19-12.
NIKI, TAMON, 18-11, 18-15.
NIKOLITCH, RADOJE, 14-15.
NINDE, HARRY W., 11-14, 11-16.
NIRENSTEIN, NATHAN, 11-11, 11-18, 13-11, 13-14.
NIXON, T. CARL, 12-14.
NOEL, ALBERT, 12-15.
NOLAN, FRAND W. SR., 13-16.
NOLAN, JAMES J, 21-11.
NOLAN, JAMES J., 11-12, 11-13, 11-14, 11-16, 13-11, 14-11, 22-18.
NOLAN, PRESTON M., 11-19, 12-23, 12-24, 13-15, 13-21, 21-11.
NOONAN, ALBERT W., 12-11.
NORCROSS DR.CARL, 13-16.
NORCROSS, CARL, 11-18, 13-11.
NORE, KENNETH C., 14-11.
NORGAARD, RICHARD L., 19-14, 19-15, 19-17.
NORMAN, R. SMITH, 11-14, 11-16.
NORTH , E. G., 13-19.
NORTH DAKOTA TAX COMMISSION, 12-11, 12-13.
NORTH, E. G., 13-19.
NORTH, L. W., 11-11, 11-14, 11-16.
NORTH, LINCOLN W., 11-19.
NORTHUP, GRAHAM T., 11-19.
NORTON, FAY A., 13-15.
NORTON, L. F., 14-15.
NORVELL, JAMES R., 12-14.
NOWAK, ARTHUR M., 11-11, 11-14, 11-16.
NOWAK, F, J., 12-21.
NOWELL, R. I, 14-15, 19-12.
NOWICKI JOSEPH A, 13-11.
NOWICKI, JOSEPH A., 13-13, 13-16, 13-19.
NOYES, GEORGE I., 11-11, 11-14.
NUETZMAN, R. A., 11-19, 12-11, 21-11.
NUGENT, R. A., 12-14.
NUGENT, R. A. L., 11-11, 11-14, 12-14, 12-18, 12-20.
NURNBERG, H., 11-19, 12-11, 12-24, 19-15.
NUSBAUM, ROGER F., 24-15.
NUTTER, C. ARMEL, 11-11, 11-18, 13-13, 13-17, 21-18, 24-15.
NUTTING, WALLACE, 24-11, 24-15.
NYE, JAMES L., 13-19.

OCONNOR, THOMAS A., 12-13, 24-13.
ODELL, H. AUGUSTUS, 11-11, 11-18.
OHARE, ROBERT J. M., 24-11.
OKEEFE, PAUL T., 19-12, 19-13, 22-18.
OKEEFE, RAYMOND T., 13-19.
OLEARY, J. J., 19-12, 19-15.
OMARA, LAURENCE, 22-18.
ONEIL, THOMAS E., 11-14, 11-16.
ONEILL, JOSEPH HENRY, 12-11, 13-15.
ORORKE, T., 11-11, 11-14.
OROURRK, GERALD A., 13-22, 22-17.
O'BIER, RAY E., 12-14.
O'BRIEN, GENERAL JOHN J., 22-18.
O'BRIEN, W. H., 13-17, 21-13.
O'CONNELL, STEPHEN C., 13-15.
O'CONNOR, JAMES G, 14-14.
O'DONNELL, GEORGENE, 18-14, 18-15.
O'FLAHERTY, JOHN D., 11-11, 11-16, 21-11.
OAKLAND, CALIF. REAL ESTATE BOARD, 11-14.
OAKLAND, W. H., 12-11.
OAKLEAF, R. B., 13-11, 13-14, 13-15.
OBERBILLIG, ERNEST, 17-14.
OBERNDORF, THEODORE W, 13-13.
OCHS, HARRY T. JR., 16-11.
OCHS, HARRY T., JR., 11-14, 11-16.
ODELL, R. T., 14-13.
ODELL, RUSSELL T., 14-13.
ODOM, WILLIAM M., 18-18, 19-15.
OELAND, L. L., 13-17.
OESTERLE, HARRIS, 12-13, 24-14.

OFFICE, THE, 12-11.
OGBURN, WILLIAM F., 13-17, 13-19.
OGDEN, JAMES N., 12-11, 24-14.
OGUR, DAVID JONATHAN, PH. D., 13-18, 13-19, 13-21.
OHIO TAX COMMISSION, 11-11, 11-15.
OHMAN, ROBERT E., 11-14, 23-11.
OHNO, K., 22-19.
OLAVE, OSCAR A., 13-19, 13-23.
OLCOTT, MARGARET, 11-14, 11-15, 14-15, 22-18.
OLDAK, P. G., 11-11, 11-16.
OLDEROGGE, DMITRY, 18-11.
OLDMAN, O., 12-11, 12-13.
OLDMAN, OLIVER, 12-11.
OLIVER, RUSSELL H., 11-11, 11-19, 12-24.
OLIVER, WILLIAM FREDERICK, 12-14, 13-11.
OLMSTEAD, HAROLD M., 16-11.
OLSEN, NILS ANDREAS, 12-23, 14-15.
OLSON, IRVING J, 19-15.
OLSON, IRVING J., 12-11, 12-13.
OLSON, JAMES C., 13-15.
OLSON, LYLE H., 11-11, 11-16, 12-11, 12-17, 19-15.
OLSON, OLOF W, 19-15.
OMAHA BUILDING OWNERS AND MANAGERS ASSOCIATION, 13-15.
OMAN, CHARLES, 18-11, 18-13, 18-15, 19-15.
OMLID, KENNETH E., 12-11.
ONTARIO CHAPTER REPORT, 12-14.
ONTARIO DEPT OF AGRICULTURE, 14-11.
OPELKA, F. GREGORY, 11-13, 11-19, 12-24, 13-19, 19-11.
OPPE, A. P., 18-11.
OPPENHEIM, JACK N., 13-15.
OPPERMAN, PAUL, 12-16, 13-11.
OREGON STATE TAX COMMISSION, 12-11, 12-13, 14-15.
OREGON STATE TAX COMMISSION, VALUATION DIVISION, 11-15, 12-11.
OREGON UNIVERSITY, 12-11, 12-13.
ORGEL, LEWIS, 12-15, 12-26, 13-15.
ORMSBEE, THOMAS H., 18-16.
ORR, JOHN, 12-11, 22-19, 22-20.
ORT, ROBERT M., 13-12, 13-15.
OSBORN, FRANK K., 12-13, 13-19.
OSBORNE, HAROLD, 19-15.
OSENBAUGH, CHARLES L., 12-13, 13-16, 13-17.
OSTENDORF, E. L., 11-11, 11-12, 11-13, 11-16, 20-15, 23-11.
OSTERGREN, C. N., 11-19, 12-24.
OTIS, ARTHUR S., 12-11.
OTT, LAWSON R., 11-11, 11-16.
OTTO, 18-15, 19-15.
OUTWATER, H. G., 11-14, 11-16.
OVERDEN, DENNIS, 18-13, 18-15.
OWEN, GEORGE, 14-11, 14-15, 19-11, 19-12.
OWEN, LEROY D., 20-15, 22-18, 23-11.
OWEN, PAT, 18-15.
OWEN, THORNTON W., 13-19.
OWEN, WILFRED, 13-14, 13-19, 19-15.
OWENS-CORNING FIBERGLAS, 13-16, 13-19.
OXFORD AND ASQUITH, 12-11, 22-19, 22-20.

PAARLBERG, DON, 14-15, 22-18.
PACEY, M. D., 19-15.
PADDOCK, JAMES C., 14-11, 14-17.
PADILLA GONZALEZ, GILBERTO, 11-11, 11-12, 11-14.
PAGANO, WILLIAM B., 13-19.
PAGE, ALFRED N., 22-19, 22-20.
PAGE, GEORGE A. JR., 12-11, 19-14.
PAIGE, C. E., 16-13.
PAIGE, CLAYTON W., 12-16, 13-11, 15-14.
PAILET, GUSTAVE, 20-11, 20-12, 20-13, 20-14, 20-15.
PAINE, PAUL, 17-15.
PAL, PRATAPADITYA, 18-12, 19-15.
PALLOTTINO, MASSIMO, 18-11.
PALMA LABASTIDA, M. A., 11-11, 11-16.
PALMER, ALFRED W., 13-19.
PALMER, BROOKS, 18-15, 18-16, 19-15.
PALMER, DWIGHT, 13-11.
PALMER, EDWARD DEL, 11-11, 11-16.
PALYI, MELCHIOR, 11-18, 11-19.
PAPAGEORGIOU, GEORGE J. AND EMILIO CASETTI, 13-16, 13-19.
PAPE, LEROY F., 19-11, 19-12.
PAPER INDUSTRY, W. W., 11-13, 23-11.
PAQUET, HENRI, 11-18.
PARCHER, L. A., 12-25, 14-17, 17-02.
PARDEE, CATHERINE E., 12-13.
PARDUE, BEULAH LEA, 12-11, 12-13.
PARDUE, MORRIS HAYWARD PH. D., 13-21, 19-11, 19-17.
PARHAM, J. R., 12-11.
PARK, OLIVER W., 12-13, 13-11.
PARK, R. D., 17-14.
PARKE, FENTON M., 22-18, 23-11.
PARKER, D. W., 16-15.
PARKER, ELSIE SMITH, 11-11, 11-18.
PARKER, W. C., 12-14, 13-19.
PARKINSON, G., 11-14, 13-16, 13-18, 19-15.
PARKINSON, THOMAS I., 19-12.
PARNELL, WALLACE H., 12-13.
PARROT, ALFRED F., 13-23.
PARROTT, C. J., 12-16.
PARRY, J. F., 25-11, 25-12.
PARSON, G. E., 21-11, 21-16.
PARSONS, C. W. S., 20-15, 21-11, 21-15.
PARTAIN, LLOYD E., 14-13.
PARTRIDGE, CHARLES, 12-14, 12-26, 22-18, 22-24, 23-11.
PARVIN, ROBERT G., 11-11, 11-16, 19-15.
PASS, HENRY, 12-16.
PASSEION, ROGER, 18-11, 18-15, 19-15.
PATCHIN ASA, PETER J., 11-11.
PATINA PRESS, 18-16.
PATINKIN, DON, 11-11, 11-16.
PATON, WILLIAM A., 11-19, 12-24.
PATRICK, R. W., 12-16, 24-16.
PATT, H. B., 12-15, 14-15.
PATT, HERBERT B., 11-14, 11-19.
PATTBERG, E. J., 19-15, 19-16.
PATTEN, JOHN W., 14-15.
PATTERSON, SAMUEL A., 12-13, 13-11.
PATTERSON, SAMUEL A. JR., 12-13.
PAUL, RANDOLPH E, 12-11, 19-17.
PAUL, SAMUEL, 13-19.
PAULSEN, R. G., 13-23.
PAULSON, PHILIP A., 12-14, 21-12.
PAULSON, RONALD, 18-12.
PAULY, MARK V., 12-23.
PAVITT, 21-20.
PAWLEY, R. W., 12-14, 14-11, 22-20, 22-23.
PAWLEY, ROBERT W., 12-18, 14-15, 22-23.
PAXTON, KENNETH WAYNE PH. D, 13-11, 24-11.

PAYNE, SILAS O., 12-26, 19-13.
PEACOCK, GEORGE R., 13-19.
PEALY, ROBERT H., 12-11.
PEARCE, C. J., 19-13.
PEARCEY, F., 11-11.
PEARL, MILTON A., 11-11, 11-14, 11-16, 12-14.
PEARSON, ALBIN S., 12-16.
PEARSON, F. A., 11-11, 11-12, 11-13, 13-18, 19-16, 22-18.
PEARSON, K. G., 13-14, 19-15, 22-18.
PEARSON, KARL G., 22-18.
PEARSON, NORMAN, 14-11.
PEASE, R. R., 13-15.
PEATMAN, JOHN GREY, 19-15, 22-18.
PECK, AUSTIN, 12-14.
PECK, HOMER M., 12-16, 15-26, 24-15, 24-16.
PEDERSON, B. E., 19-13.
PELOUBET, MAURICE E., 11-13, 11-19, 12-11, 12-24, 12-26.
PENA GARCIA, M. A., 11-11, 11-12, 11-13, 11-16, 12-14, 13-11, 14-11.
PENDLETON, WILLIAM C., 12-13.
PENMAN, S. H., 19-20.
PENNA LEAGUE OF BLDG & LOAN ASSOCIATIONS, 11-14.
PENNSYLVANIA STATE CHAMBER OF COMMERCE, 12-11, 17-12.
PENNSYLVANIA STATE TAX EQUALIZATION BOARD, 12-13.
PENNSYLVANIAN, 12-13.
PENNY, A., 13-15.
PENNY, A. L., 11-13, 11-16, 11-19, 12-19.
PENNY, ALFRED L., 11-16, 11-19, 13-15.
PENROSE, ROLAND, 18-11, 18-12, 18-13, 18-15.
PEPPIATT, H. G., 11-14.
PERCIVAL, JOHN C., 12-11.
PEREIRA, WILLIAM L., 12-13, 13-11.
PERIN, RENE, 12-11.
PERK, RALPH J., 12-13.
PERKINS, CARROLL M., 12-11.
PERLMAN, LESLIE, 13-15.
PERRY, CLARENCE ARTHUR, 13-11, 13-17.
PERRY, H. B., 16-11, 19-14.
PERRY, HORACE B., 11-19, 12-24, 16-11.
PERRY, RALPH BARTON, 11-11, 11-16.
PERRY, ROBERT D., 11-14.
PERT, WOODBY X., 11-11, 11-14.
PESCHEL, J. L., 12-11, 12-15, 12-26, 17-15.
PETERS, W., 19-15, 22-16.
PETERSEN, T. A., 14-11.
PETERSON, CARL H., 11-19, 12-24, 19-15.
PETERSON, CHARLES C. M., 12-14, 12-16, 12-26.
PETERSON, CHARLES E. JR., 13-20.
PETERSON, CHARLES E. JR., 12-24, 22-24, 23-14.
PETERSON, RONALD S., 12-11, 12-13, 19-13.
PETERSON, T. A., 14-11.
PETERSON, WILLIAM H., 12-16.
PETHERICK J. P., 12-11.
PETREE, NEIL, 13-15, 13-23.
PETRIE, JOSEPH A., 17-13.
PETROLEUM REFINERY ENGINEERING, 23-14.
PETRY, ELDON H., 13-22, 22-18.
PETTY, JOHN A., 11-14.
PEURIFY, 21-13.
PFEFFERKORN, LAWRENCE G., 13-11.
PHELAN, JAMES, 12-11.

PHILIPS, F. M., 11-11, 11-13.
PHILIPS, L. A., 12-16, 16-12.
PHILLIPS, BARBARA ASHLEY, 12-11, 12-26.
PHILLIPS, C. W., 12-16, 22-16, 24-15.
PHILLIPS, GEORGE A., 13-15, 13-17.
PHIMISTER, Z. S., 11-11, 11-14.
PHINNEY, G. W., 11-11, 11-12.
PIANKOFF, ALEXANDER, 18-11, 18-15, 18-16, 19-15.
PIAZZA, COSMO C., 22-18.
PICARD, GILBERT, 18-11, 19-15.
PICK, J., 12-24.
PICKARD, JEROME P., 12-11, 12-13.
PICKARD, W. C., 11-11, 11-16, 13-17.
PICKENS, PHILIP, 12-14.
PIDOCK, W. L., 11-14.
PIERCE, J. T., 12-11, 12-12.
PIERCE, PHILIP F., 11-11, 11-12, 11-14, 11-18.
PIERRE, JOHN A., 12-12, 12-26.
PIERSALL, R. W. JR., 12-24.
PIGNATTI, TERISIO, 18-11.
PIGNATTI, TERISTO, 19-15.
PIKE, HERBERT, 14-15.
PILL, JOHN R., 12-16, 17-11.
PILLSBURY, H. WATTS, 15-19.
PILLSWORTH, W. H., 11-14.
PILMER, C. L., 12-16, 14-15.
PILMER, CHARLES L., 11-11, 11-12.
PINE, VANDERLYN R., 19-19.
PINGRY, GEORGE S., 12-14.
PINK, LOUIS N., 12-23.
PINKERTON, A. M., 11-11, 11-12.
PINNELL, W. GEORGE, 12-18, 24-15.
PINTO, EDWIN, 13-19.
PINTON, EDWARD AND EVA PINTO, 18-14.
PIO, ROBERT, 11-11, 11-16.
PIPER, JOHN, 18-14, 18-15, 18-16, 19-15.
PITMAN, HAYDEN W., 12-11, 12-13, 22-18.
PITT, JOHN E., 11-11, 11-16, 12-16, 22-24.
PITTLE, HERBERT, 12-15.
PITTMAN, VIRGIL, 12-14, 12-16.
PITTSBURGH, 12-13.
PLAGER, ALFRED R., 13-15.
PLANNING DEPARTMENT, 13-21.
PLANT, PETER B, 19-14.
PLEETER, SAUL PH. D., 13-16, 13-18.
PLENDER JOHN, 13-15.
PLETZ, C. L., 20-12.
PLEYDELL, 12-11.
PLUM, LESTER, 19-15.
PLUMMER, ALVIN S., 11-16.
PODD, GEORGE O., 13-15.
PODELL, BERTRAM L., 12-11, 13-19.
POINTER, RUSSEL A., 11-11, 11-18.
POLAK, DR. W. J., 11-11, 11-19, 12-24.
POLIS, S. N., 13-14.
POLK, JAMES K., 12-11.
POLLAK, M. I. TAFT, 13-11.
POLLARA, F., 11-18, 13-11.
POLLARD, W. L., 11-13, 12-14, 12-20, 13-11.
POLLEY, JOSEPH H., 11-14, 13-19.
POLLEYS, THOMAS A., 11-11, 11-16.
POLLOCK, WALTER W., 11-11, 11-13, 11-16.
POND, O. L., 16-11.
POOD, GEORGE O., 13-15.
POOLE, J. W., 13-13.

POPE-HENNESSY, JOHN, 18-11, 18-15.
POPE, L. E., 21-12.
POPE, LESLIE E., 11-14, 11-16.
POPE, LONNIE, 11-11, 11-14, 11-19, 12-24.
POPPER, FRANK, 18-12, 19-15.
PORTER, FRANK DAVID, III, 13-15.
PORTER, GEORGE D., 11-14, 16-11.
PORTER, JOHN W., 13-15, 14-11.
PORTER, LESTER W., 22-18.
PORTER, PAUL W., 25-11, 25-15.
PORTER, ROBERT R., 11-11, 11-16.
PORTER, STEPHEN, 13-23.
PORTER, STEPHEN L., 13-23.
PORTLAND, OREGON, REALTY BOARD, 11-14.
POS, JACOB, 14-15.
POST, EDWARD T., 11-13, 11-16.
POTTER, EDWARD, 20-15, 21-11, 23-11.
POTTER, GEORGE S., 23-11.
POTTER, J., 19-15, 19-16.
POTTER, J. C., 19-15, 19-16.
POTTER, W. E., 11-11, 17-16.
POTTS, W. T. JR., 11-11, 11-14.
POTTS, WALTER T. JR., 13-13.
POWDRELL J. D., 11-11, 11-18.
POWELL, ROGER K, 19-17.
POWERS, BENJ. M., 12-16.
POWERS, RONALD V., 12-13.
PRACTICAL LAND ECONOMIC STUDY PROGRAMS, 11-14, 12-16.
PRACTICAL USE OF OUR LAND ECONOMIC STUDIES, 11-16, 12-16.
PRATAPADITYA, PAL, 18-12, 19-15.
PRATT, DOROTHY AND RICHARD, 13-19.
PRATT, LOUIS M., 13-18, 13-19.
PRATT, ROBERT J. A., 13-16.
PRAVER, STANLEY, 13-21.
PRAZ, MARIO, 18-15, 19-15.
PREINREICH, GABRIEL A., 11-11, 11-19, 12-24.
PRENTICE HALL EDITORIAL STAFF, 11-14, 11-15.
PRENTICE, P. K., 12-11.
PRENTICE, PERRY, 11-11, 11-16, 13-19.
PRENTICE, PERRY F., 13-19.
PRESSLEY, LESTER N., 12-13, 13-19.
PRICE, JAMES R., 13-19.
PRICE, OLIN, 11-11, 11-18.
PRIEST, ALAN, 18-11, 18-13, 18-15, 19-15.
PRIESTMAN, GLYNDON, 12-26.
PRIMM, H. M., 13-18.
PRIMM, HAROLD M., 11-12, 14-11.
PRIMMER, JOHN L., 12-11.
PRINCE, W. H., 13-16.
PROCDGS OF 4TH INST ON EMINT DOM EVIDENCES OF VAL, 12-15.
PROCOS, DIMITRI, 12-17, 12-19, 12-22, 13-11.
PROKOSCH, WALTHER, 13-11, 15-17.
PROPERTY TAX BULLETIN, 12-13.
PROUDFOOT, MALCOLM J., 13-14.
PROUTY, 12-13.
PROUTY, FRANK H., 16-11, 23-11.
PROUTY, W. L., 12-15, 21-11, 21-13, 21-16.
PROUTY, W. L. AND OHTERS, 21-11, 21-13, 21-16.
PROUTY, W. L. AND OTHERS, 11-11, 11-13, 11-14, 11-18, 11-19, 12-24, 13-11, 13-15, 13-19, 13-20, 13-21, 14-11, 20-11, 21-11, 21-13, 23-11.
PRUSSIANO, JOSEPH B., 11-14.

PRYOR, FRANCIS D., 12-16, 13-11, 22-16, 24-15.
PUBLIC ADMINISTRATION SERVICE, 12-13.
PUBLIC AFFAIRS RESEARCH COUNCIL, 12-11.
PUBLIC PERSONNEL ASSOCIATION, 11-14, 11-16.
PUBLISHERS WEEKLY, 18-15.
PUGIN, A. W. N., 11-18.
PUGIN, AUGUSTUS WELBY N., 18-16, 18-18.
PULIS, ARTHUR G. JR., 22-18.
PULVER, HARRY E., 20-12, 21-13.
PURDON, JOHN, 12-23.
PURDY, LAWSON, 12-13, 22-18.
PURDY, VICTOR M., 12-11, 12-13, 12-24.
PURNELL, CHARLES G., 12-15, 19-13.
PURNELL, ROBERT L., 12-13.
PYE, G., 11-11, 11-16.

QUIGLEY IAN H., 19-15.
QUIN, GEORGE ROBERT, 11-11, 11-19, 12-25, 19-13.
QUINLAN, H. F., 17-15.
QUINN, THOMAS, 19-12.
QUINN, WILLIAM E., 13-15.
QUINTANA, ISADORO, 11-11, 11-18.
QUINTANA, ISIDOR, 11-14, 11-16.
QUINTANA, ISIDORO, 11-11, 11-16, 12-14.
QUINTO, OSCAR B., 11-11, 11-14, 11-16.

R. G. RIDKER, 13-19, 24-11.
R. WRAIGHT, 19-15.
RAAFLAUB, O. V., 13-15, 14-11.
RACKHAM, JOHN B, 12-13.
RACZ, ISTUAN, 18-12, 18-17.
RADCLIFFE, ANTHONY, 18-15, 18-17, 19-15.
RADEMACHER, HELLMUT, 18-12, 19-15.
RAETHER, HOWARD C., 13-15.
RAGAN, RICHARD, 12-13.
RAGLEY, MAX, 22-18.
RAHENKAMP, J., 13-11.
RAINEY, A. J., 12-25, 19-13.
RAINEY, ARTHUR J., 19-13.
RAISON, B. V., 11-11, 11-12.
RALEIGH, JAMES, 13-15.
RALEIGH, JAMES C., 12-14, 12-18, 13-11, 13-16, 20-15, 23-11, 23-14, 24-14.
RALSTON, JACKSON HARVEY, 12-11.
RALYA, DON L., 22-18.
RAMOS MARTINEZ, JOSE A., 12-14, 12-20.
RAMS, EDWARD M., 12-18.
RAMS, EDWIN M., 11-11, 11-12, 11-14, 11-16, 12-11, 12-16, 12-19, 13-11, 13-14, 13-15, 13-17, 13-19, 19-15, 22-21, 23-13, 24-13.
RAMSEY, L. G. G., 18-16.
RAMSEY, LIG. G., 18-16.
RANCICH, M. T., 13-11.
RANDALL, FRANK, 12-15, 12-16, 16-11.
RANDALL, ROLAND R., 11-11, 11-12, 13-16.
RANDALL, WILLIAM J., 11-14, 11-16, 11-19, 12-11, 12-14, 12-16, 12-24, 12-26, 13-12, 13-15, 13-17, 13-20, 17-14, 19-15, 21-11, 22-17, 22-18, 24-13, 25-12.
RANDELL, MURRAY E., 13-19, 13-20, 16-12.
RANGE APPRAISAL COMMISSION, 14-18.
RANKIN, DUDLEY L., 12-15, 12-16.
RAPKIN, CHESTER, 19-15, 22-18.

RAPPORT, RICHARD, 11-11, 11-18.
RASTALL, W. H., 12-24.
RATCLIFF, DR. RICHARD U., 11-11, 11-14, 11-16, 11-19, 12-14, 12-25, 13-13, 22-18.
RATCLIFF, R. U., 11-11, 11-12, 11-13, 11-14, 11-16, 11-19, 12-14.
RATCLIFF, RICHARD UPDEGRAFF, 12-14, 13-11, 22-18, 24-15.
RATCLIFF, WILBUR S. JR., 12-13, 12-17.
RATHBUN, DANIEL B., 13-16, 19-11.
RATHJE, FRANK C., 19-12.
RAUBER, EARLE L., 11-11, 11-19, 22-18.
RAUSCHENBUSCH, DR. H., 11-15, 18-11, 18-12, 18-13, 18-14, 18-15.
RAWLINGS, BROWN R., 14-15.
RAWSON, MARY, 12-11.
RAWSON, P. S., 18-11, 18-15, 18-16, 19-15.
RAY, ANTHONY, 18-13, 18-14, 19-15.
RAY, RAYMOND, 12-16, 12-26.
RAYNAL, MAURICE, 18-11.
READ, SIR HERBERT, 18-15.
READE, BRAIN, 18-11, 18-13, 19-15.
REAL ESTATE ANALYST APPRAISAL BULLETIN, 22-18.
REAL ESTATE ANALYST, THE, 11-11, 11-14, 11-16, 11-18, 12-13, 12-24, 13-11, 13-14, 13-15, 13-16, 13-17, 13-19, 13-20, 13-21, 14-15, 15-11, 19-13, 19-15, 21-11, 21-12, 21-13, 21-16, 22-11, 22-18, 22-22, 24-11.
REAL ESTATE APPRAISER, 13-19.
REAL ESTATE APPRAISER, THE, 13-15, 15-14.
REAL ESTATE BOARD OF NEW YORK, 11-14, 11-15, 12-14, 22-22.
REAL ESTATE INVESTMENT LETTER, 15-14, 19-15, 22-18.
REAL ESTATE RECORD, 13-17, 19-12, 19-15.
REAL ESTATE RECORD AND BUILDERS GUIDE, 13-23, 22-18.
REAL ESTATE RECORD, 12-24.
REAL ESTATE, ANALYST, THE, 12-24, 22-18.
REALTY BLUE BOOK OF CALIFORNIA, 22-18.
RECHT, J. RICHARD, 11-11, 11-19.
RECK, ROBERT OTTO, 17-14.
REDDING, E. D., 23-14.
REDEL, W. R., 12-16, 22-24.
REDMOND, JOHN T., 13-18.
REECE, RICHARD, 12-15.
REECE, RICHARD L., 13-11.
REED, DONNELL D., 22-18.
REED, HENRY E., 22-18.
REED, PRENTISS B., 12-23.
REED, ROBERT D., 12-14, 15-17.
REED, STANLEY, 18-15, 18-16.
REED, VERGIL D., 13-11.
REESE, LOUIE, 11-14, 12-15, 12-16.
REEVE, D. W., 12-11.
REEVE, DOUGLAS W., 11-11, 11-12, 11-16, 12-11.
REEVES, CUTHBERT E., 11-14, 11-16, 12-11, 12-13, 12-14, 12-24, 12-25, 13-14, 13-16, 13-17, 13-18, 13-19, 21-13, 22-18, 22-19.
REEVES, H. CLYDE, 12-13.
REEVES, L. T., 12-24.
REEVES, L. T. JR., 12-24, 21-11.
REEVIS, CUTHBERT E., 22-18.
REGIS, A. S., 12-13, 13-14.
REGIS, ANDREW S., 12-13.

REGISTER, J. ALVIN, 11-11, 11-14, 11-19, 12-11, 13-13, 13-15, 13-18, 13-19, 19-13, 22-18, 22-21.
REGISTER, NORMAN, 12-13, 22-18, 24-13.
REHNBERG, REX D., 14-11.
REID, GARE B., 11-12.
REID, WALT, 19-15.
REID, WILLIAM L., 16-11, 24-15.
REIDY, MAURICE F., 11-11, 11-14, 11-16, 11-18, 12-25, 13-20, 13-21, 22-18.
REILLEY, FRANK K, 19-15.
REILLY, GEORGE R., 12-13.
REILLY, JOHN A., 19-11.
REILLY, JOHN J., 16-11.
REINMUTH, J. E., 22-18.
REISS, FRANKLIN J., 14-15, 22-20.
REITLINGER, 13-21, 18-11.
REITLINGER, G. R., 11-18, 18-11, 18-12, 18-13, 18-14, 18-15.
REITLINGER, GERALD, 11-11, 11-18, 18-11.
RENAUD, CLEMENT, 24-11.
RENNE, ROLAND R., 11-11, 13-17.
RENO, E. S., 12-24.
RENO, RICHARD R., 22-18.
RENSHAW, E. F., 13-11, 13-16.
RENSHAW, EDWARD F., 11-14, 11-16.
REOK, ERNEST C. JR., 12-13.
RESIDENTIAL APPRAISER, 11-11, 11-13, 11-14, 13-16, 13-17, 13-19, 24-13.
RESNICK, WILLIAM C., 13-11.
RETF, W. E., 16-11.
REUTHER, J. L., 12-11, 12-12, 12-13.
REVIEW OF SOCIETY OF RESIDENTIAL APPRAISERS, 11-11, 11-16, 13-15, 13-17, 13-18.
REVIEW, THE, 11-11, 11-12, 11-13, 11-14, 11-16, 11-18, 13-11, 13-15, 13-16, 13-17, 13-19, 13-20, 13-21, 19-15, 21-13, 21-16, 22-18, 23-11, 24-17.
REYES, N. C., 17-15.
REYNOLDS, ANTHONY, 11-16, 11-18.
REYNOLDS, C. W., 21-13.
REYNOLDS, FRANK G., 13-19.
REYNOLDS, GRAHAM, 18-11, 19-15.
REYNOLDS, J. E., 14-15.
REYNOLDS, KIRK, 13-17, 13-19.
REYNOLDS, SAMUEL T., 12-11, 12-13.
REYNOLDS, TEMPLE A., 22-18.
REZZOLLA, JOHN R. JR., 12-16, 19-13.
RHAMSTINE, ADAM W., 13-11, 13-23.
RHOADES, ORILLE BOURASSA, 18-16.
RHODES, DANIEL, 18-12, 18-15, 19-15.
RHODES, RICHARD M., 12-16, 21-16.
RIBETH, WILLIAM C., 11-11, 11-12.
RICARDO, D., 11-11.
RICE, DAVID TALBOT, 18-11, 19-15.
RICE, DENNIS G., 18-14, 18-16.
RICE, RALPH S, 12-11, 19-16.
RICH, RICHARD C., 13-12.
RICH, RICHARD H., 13-14, 13-23.
RICH, S. G., 13-11.
RICHARD, F. DONALD, 19-11.
RICHARD, JOHN L. JR., 13-15.
RICHARDS, JOHN L. JR., 11-11, 21-11.
RICHARDS, RALPH H., 13-17, 22-18.
RICHARDSON, WILLIAM A. JR., 23-11, 23-12.
RICHMAN, RAYMOND L., 12-11.
RICHMOND, SIR IAN, 11-11, 18-13.

RICHTER, F. E., 12-16, 13-21, 19-15.
RICHTER, G. M. A., 18-11, 18-13, 18-15, 19-15.
RICHTER, GISELA, 18-12, 18-15.
RICHTER, GISELA M. A., 11-11, 18-13, 18-17, 19-15.
RICK, WILLIAM B., 13-15, 22-24.
RICKS, R. BRUCE, 11-16, 12-11, 19-13, 19-15, 19-17, 22-18.
RICKS, ROBERT, 13-17.
RIDGWAY, MAURICE H., 18-14, 18-15.
RIDLEY, MICHAEL, 18-11.
RIEFSTAHL, ELIZABETH, 18-15.
RIEMER, RICHARD L., 11-11, 12-14, 12-16.
RIEMER, SVEND, 13-16.
RIESTERER LLOYD V, 19-15.
RIGBY, DOUGLAS, 18-11.
RIGGE, ALBERT G., 19-17.
RIGGS, H. E., 12-14.
RIGHT OF WAY, 12-16, 12-26, 13-17, 16-12, 22-18, 24-11, 24-13, 24-15.
RILEY, WILLIAM H., 12-13, 15-14.
RINEHART, MORRIS L., 12-11.
RING, ALFRED A., 11-11, 11-14, 11-16, 11-18, 11-19, 12-13, 12-14, 12-24, 12-25, 12-26, 13-11, 13-17, 19-12, 19-13, 19-17, 21-11, 21-18, 22-18.
RINGER, V. P., 11-11.
RITLEY, ROGER D., 13-16, 13-19.
RIVARD, L., 19-12.
RIVAROLA, CARLOS H., 13-20.
RMAS, EDWIN M., 13-17.
ROBB, JOSEPH A., 12-24, 13-19.
ROBBINS, DONALD L., 12-23.
ROBBINS, IRA S., 13-13.
ROBBINS, PAUL, 14-18.
ROBBINS, RICHARD M., 12-19.
ROBERTS DAVID D., 13-15.
ROBERTS, AUSTIN, L. JR., 24-15.
ROBERTS, CHARLES A., 19-13.
ROBERTS, EDWIN A., JR., 11-11.
ROBERTS, FRANCIS R., 12-12, 12-13.
ROBERTS, FRANK B., 23-11.
ROBERTS, GORDON L., 12-11.
ROBERTS, JAMES O. JR., 12-11.
ROBERTS, JOHN A., 12-16, 12-26, 13-15, 23-11.
ROBERTS, NORMAN L., 12-11.
ROBERTS, RICHARD, 11-11, 11-16.
ROBERTS, SIDNEY I., 12-11.
ROBERTS, T. L., 12-15, 22-18.
ROBERTS, THOMAS L., 12-11, 12-15.
ROBERTSON, D. S., 11-11, 18-13.
ROBERTSON, FRASER, 11-11, 11-12.
ROBERTSON, GILES, 18-11, 18-13, 18-15, 19-15.
ROBERTSON, JAMES M., 12-13.
ROBERTSON, JOHN MACKINNON, 12-11, 22-19.
ROBERTSON, M., 19-15.
ROBERTSON, MARTIN, 18-11, 19-15.
ROBICHEK, A. A., 12-19.
ROBINS, PHILIP KENNETH, PH. D., 11-11, 13-16.
ROBINSON SIR DOVE-MEYER, 13-14.
ROBINSON, E. B., 14-12, 14-15.
ROBINSON, J. NATTS, 19-11.
ROBINSON, M. E., 24-14.
ROBINSON, PETER C., 13-15.
ROBINSON, W. ALFRED, 15-15.
ROBINSON, WILLIAM K., 11-11, 18-14, 18-15.
ROBINSON, WILLIAM W., 22-11, 22-18, 22-19, 22-20.
ROBY, RONALD H., 12-14.

ROCHE, JOHN K., 12-13.
RODA, FRANK, 12-16, 12-26.
RODDER, NORMAN J., 13-17.
RODDEWIG, CLARE M., 12-11.
RODEN, P. F., 19-15, 19-16.
RODEWALD, G. E. JR., 12-13, 19-15.
RODEY, B. S., JR., 11-11, 11-13.
RODGERS, RAYMOND, 22-18.
RODIL, JORGE LAMPORT (LIC), 11-14.
RODMAN, JAMES A. JR., 12-18, 13-17.
RODMAN, JOHN E., 12-23.
RODRIGUEZ, LOUIS J., 17-12, 17-15, 17-16.
RODWIN, LLOYD, 11-11, 13-16, 13-17.
ROE, G. P., 14-11.
ROE, STANLEY, 13-13, 19-13, 23-11.
ROESCH, RICHARD R., 12-13, 13-19.
ROETTGER, G. J., 12-11, 12-18, 13-18.
ROGER-MARX, CLAUDE, 18-11, 19-15.
ROGERS, 12-14, 12-26.
ROGERS RUSSELL R., 12-18.
ROGERS, C. N., 11-14, 14-11.
ROGERS, CHARLES G., 12-11.
ROGERS, GRANCES, 18-17.
ROGERS, HENRY, W., 12-14.
ROGERS, JOHN D., 12-16, 12-26.
ROGERS, JOHN V., 14-11, 22-20.
ROGERS, MICHAEL H., 13-13.
ROGERS, RUSSELL R., 11-14, 11-16, 12-14, 15-21.
ROITMAN, SOL, 20-11.
ROKES, WILLIS PARK, 12-15.
ROLL, R., 19-15, 19-16.
ROLLAND, L. G., 18-17.
ROMANOVA, M. A., 17-14.
ROMNEY, GEORGE W, 12-11.
ROSAN, R. A., 17-15.
ROSE, C. W., 11-11, 11-14, 23-13.
ROSE, J. T. SR., 12-13.
ROSE, MURIEL, 18-14.
ROSEMARY, FREEMAN, 18-15, 19-15.
ROSEN, G. R., 13-11, 13-13, 13-16.
ROSENBERG, JAKOB, 18-12, 18-15, 19-15.
ROSENBLUM, ROBERT, 18-12, 19-15.
ROSENCRANS, DAN, 12-16, 12-23.
ROSENCRANS, DANIEL W., 12-16, 24-15.
ROSENFELD, A. J., 12-15.
ROSENMAN, DOROTHY, 13-11.
ROSENWEIG, REUBEN, 11-13, 12-14.
ROSS, BYRON F., 19-15.
ROSS, CHARLES M., 23-11.
ROSS, THORSTON, 13-17.
ROSS, THURSTON, 11-14.
ROSS, THURSTON H., 11-11, 11-16, 11-19, 12-25, 13-15, 13-17, 19-12, 19-15, 22-18.
ROSS, WALTER W., 13-21.
ROSS, WILL H., 14-15.
ROSSMILLER, G. E., 14-15.
ROSTVOLD, WERHARD N., 12-11, 12-13.
ROTH, H. LING, 18-14, 18-15.
ROTH, H. LINY, 18-15, 18-16, 19-15.
ROTH, LOVIS, 19-16.
ROTH, VINCENT E., 11-14, 11-16.
ROTHCHILD, SIGMUND, 11-11, 18-11, 18-12, 18-13.
ROTHE, EDITH, 18-15, 19-15.
ROTHSCHILD, SIGMUND, 11-11, 11-14, 11-16, 12-23, 18-11, 18-12, 18-13.

ROTHSCHILD, VAL J., 22-18.
ROTHSTEIN, A. J., 22-12.
ROTI, RICHARD F., 13-12.
ROUGH NOTES CO., INC., 11-14.
ROULAC STEPHEN E, 13-16.
ROUNTREY, EDWARD, 12-13.
ROUNTREY, J. EDWARD, 12-12.
ROUSE, JAMES W., 13-11, 19-12.
ROWE, LEO S., 13-11.
ROWLAND, BENJAMIN, 18-11, 19-15.
ROWLANDS, DAVID T., 12-11, 13-17, 22-18.
ROWLSON, JOHN F., 12-19, 13-11, 13-19, 19-15, 22-18, 22-21.
ROYAL BANK, 24-12.
ROYAL BANK OF CANADA, 11-11, 11-14.
ROYAL, PEYTON K., 11-11, 11-19, 15-11, 21-11.
ROYCE, FRANK, 12-24.
ROYCE, FRANK A., 11-11, 11-18.
ROYCRAFT, D. F., 23-11.
RUAN SANTOS, EDUARDO, 11-11, 11-12.
RUBIN, WILLIAM S, 18-11.
RUBIN, WILLIAM S., 18-11.
RUBLOFF, ARTHUR, 13-15.
RUCH, PAUL E., 22-18.
RUDOLPH, MAX J., 13-13, 13-16.
RUGELES, IVAN OLIVER, 11-11, 11-14, 11-16, 11-18, 11-19.
RUGGLES, RICHARD, 11-11, 11-16.
RUHE, KARL, 12-11, 12-26, 19-19, 22-18.
RUHMER, EBERHARD, 18-12.
RUJZ SANCHES, JOSE, 12-11.
RUPERT, JOHN F., 11-16, 12-14, 12-20.
RUSH, DONALD R., 14-15, 14-18.
RUSH, RICHARD H., 18-16, 19-15.
RUSINOFF S E, 20-15.
RUSSELL, BRUCE, 14-11, 14-15.
RUSSELL, HORACE, 11-11, 11-12, 11-14, 12-26, 13-17, 19-11, 19-12.
RUSSELL, HUGH H., 13-22, 22-17.
RUSSELL, JOHN D., 11-14.
RUSSOLI, FRANCO, 18-12, 19-15.
RUTAN, HAROLD, 19-12.
RUTGERS UNIVERSITY BUREAU OF GOVERNMENT RESEARCH, 12-13.
RYAN, JAMES A., 11-14, 21-11.
RYAN, JOHN, 11-19, 12-24.
RYAN, JOHN C., 11-11, 11-16.
RYAN, JOHN L., 14-11.
RYBECK, WALTER, 12-11, 12-13, 13-11, 13-13.

SAAW, EUGENE A., 22-18, 24-14.
SAAW, JOE S., 12-18.
SABBADINI, ALEX, 12-11, 18-15, 22-18.
SABIT, JULIET, 13-14.
SACHS, EARL, 12-15, 13-22, 22-17.
SACKMAN, JULIUS L., 11-11, 11-14, 11-16, 12-14, 12-15, 19-13.
SACLES, KENNETH E., 11-11, 21-16.
SADESKY, WILLIAM V., 12-25, 19-13.
SALIERS, EARL A., 11-19, 12-24.
SALVAGE, WILLIAM L., 14-18.
SALVINI, ROBERTO, 18-13, 19-15.

SAMMON, JOHN P., 22-18.
SANDERS, CURTIS A., 13-18.
SANDERS, CURTIS A. 1, 13-17.
SANDISON, R. W., 12-11, 22-18.
SANDLIN, H. J., 14-15.
SANDO, LAURENCE, 11-11, 11-12, 11-14, 11-18, 12-15, 12-16, 13-15, 19-13, 22-16, 24-15.
SANDON, HENRY, 18-14, 18-15, 18-16.
SANDS, LAWRENCE, 12-11, 12-13.
SANFORD, GEORGE A., 13-11, 22-18.
SANFORD, RALPH S., 19-11.
SAPP, ALLAN N., 13-15, 22-18.
SARGENT, FREDERIC O., 14-11, 23-11.
SARLES, KENNETH A., 12-24.
SARLES, KENNETH E., 11-11, 11-16, 11-19, 12-13, 12-23, 13-19, 19-12, 22-22, 24-11.
SARMA, L. V. L. N., 13-20, 13-21.
SARMIENTO, EDUARDO, 12-16.
SATHER, KENT N., 13-19.
SATIE, JEAN PAUL, 18-11, 18-15, 18-16, 19-15.
SAUCIER, JOHN W., 13-17.
SAUNDERS, G. A., 23-14.
SAVAGE, G., 18-11, 18-12, 18-13, 18-15.
SAVAGE, GEORGE, 18-12, 18-13, 18-14, 18-17, 19-15.
SAVINGS BANK JOURNAL, 11-12, 11-13.
SAXE, E. B., 13-15, 22-18.
SAXON, FLOYD, 12-15.
SAXON, FLOYD M., 12-14.
SAYER, D. D. JR., 13-15.
SAYER, D. DAYTON, 13-15.
SAYRE, T. H., 12-16, 13-11.
SAZAMA, G. W., 12-11, 12-12, 13-11.
SCAARFF, MAURICE R., 11-24, 12-11, 16-11.
SCAFF, HAROLD H., 11-19, 12-24.
SCALF, RICHARD L., 13-18.
SCANLAN, E. L., 19-12.
SCARRY, DONALD M. PH. D., 12-11, 12-13.
SCHAAF, A. H., 12-11, 13-13, 13-17, 19-12.
SCHACKNE, JOHN R., 12-11, 13-14.
SCHAFF, ARTHUR, 20-11.
SCHALL, I. D., 12-13, 19-15.
SCHALL, L. D., 19-15.
SCHARF, CHARLES A, 19-14, 19-17.
SCHARFF, M. R., 11-11, 11-19, 12-24.
SCHARFF, MAURICE R., 11-11, 11-16, 11-19, 12-24, 12-25, 16-11, 16-14, 19-14.
SCHARN, WILLIAM H. JR., 14-15, 22-18.
SCHEEFLY, J E, 19-15, 19-17.
SCHEFTEL, YETTA, 12-11, 22-19, 22-20.
SCHEICK, WILLIAM H., 13-16.
SCHEIDT, JOHN, 11-14, 11-16, 11-17, 21-13.
SCHELLING, CLINTON W., 19-12.
SCHERER, L. F., 12-16.
SCHEUER, JAMES H., 13-11, 13-13.
SCHIACH, A D, 19-15.
SCHIEFFELIN, WILLIAM JAY, 12-11, 13-16.
SCHIETINGER, E. F., 13-17.
SCHIMMEL, ALFRED, 12-11, 12-13, 13-15, 22-18.
SCHLAGENHAUF, PAUL, 12-11, 13-22, 22-11.
SCHLAUCH, WILLIAM S., 11-11, 11-19.
SCHLEGEL, W. J., 13-17.
SCHLITT, CARL D., 13-19.
SCHMID, CALVIN F., 11-11.
SCHMIDT, EDWARD BENJAMIN, 12-11, 12-13, 22-18.
SCHMIDT, FRITZ, 11-19, 12-24, 21-12.

SCHMIDT, H. E., 19-16.
SCHMIDT, WALTER S., 11-14, 11-19, 13-11, 22-11, 22-18.
SCHMIED, WIELAND, 18-12, 18-15.
SCHMITT, ROBERT C., 13-11.
SCHMUTZ, GEORGE L., 11-11, 11-12, 11-13, 11-14, 11-16, 11-18, 11-19, 12-11, 12-13, 12-14, 12-15, 12-16, 12-20, 12-24, 12-26, 13-11, 13-15, 13-17, 13-18, 14-18, 17-12, 17-14, 19-13, 19-15, 19-19, 19-20, 19-21, 22-18, 24-13.
SCHNEIDER, ARTHUR A., 12-14.
SCHNEIDER, GEORGE A., 13-19, 22-18.
SCHNEIDER, JOHN S., 13-15, 13-20, 19-15.
SCHNELL, A. F., 13-15.
SCHNITMAN, L. SETH, 13-17.
SCHOEN, HARRY, 11-16, 19-15.
SCHOFER, AUGUST, 12-26, 24-15.
SCHORR, PHILIP, 13-18.
SCHROPP, T. L., 11-16, 20-12, 20-15.
SCHULTE, AUGUST B., 11-11, 11-19, 13-12, 13-17, 22-18.
SCHULTZ, CARLTON, 13-15, 22-18.
SCHULTZ, EARLE, 13-15.
SCHULTZ, MORTIMER L., 22-18.
SCHULTZ, WILLIAM J., 11-11.
SCHUMACHER, ARNOLD C., 13-23.
SCHUMACHER, DAVID T., 11-17, 11-19, 12-24, 21-12.
SCHUMACHER, ERNEST P., 13-16, 13-17, 22-22.
SCHUMACHER, RAY J., 11-19, 12-24.
SCHURAB, B., 12-24.
SCHURMANN, ULRICH, 18-14, 18-15, 19-15.
SCHWARTZ, JAY, 12-14, 22-18.
SCHWARTZ, SIDNEY M., 11-11.
SCHWINDEN, JAMES, 12-13.
SCHWINGLE, C J, 19-15.
SCHWINGLE, C. J., 11-11, 23-11.
SCHWINGLE, CLEMENT J., 13-15.
SCHWULST, EARL B., 11-11, 13-18.
SCOFIELD, WILLIAM H., 14-11, 14-15.
SCOTT, AMORET, 18-16, 19-15.
SCOTT, JOHN T. JR., 14-11, 23-11, 24-11.
SCOTT, ROBERT V., 13-17.
SCRANTON, ROBERT L., 18-12, 18-16, 19-15.
SCRIBNER, DAVID JR., 11-11, 11-12.
SCUSSEL, GEORGE P., 17-12.
SEABY, H. A., 18-15, 19-15.
SEARLES, SIDNEY Z., 12-14, 12-16, 12-26.
SEARS, G. E., 14-15.
SEASTONE, DOW, 12-11.
SEATTLE REAL ESTATE ASSOCIATION, 11-11, 13-11.
SEAVER, GUY J., 22-18.
SEEGER, WILLIAM R., 13-11.
SEELYE, EDWIN E., 11-15.
SEGAL, HERBERT I., 11-14, 11-16.
SEIDEL, A H, 19-20, 19-21, 19-22.
SEIDMAN, M. I., 16-11.
SEILERN, COUNT, 18-11.
SELDIN, MAURICE, 11-11, 11-14.
SELDIN, MAURY, 19-15, 22-18.
SELIGMAN, DANIEL, 13-13, 13-17, 13-20, 22-18.
SELL, R., 12-11, 13-15, 19-13.
SELLERS, RANDOLPH F., 13-17, 22-19, 22-20.
SELTZER, RICHARD J., 13-15.
SELWYN, A., 18-17.
SELZ, JEAN, 18-11.
SEMENZATO, CAMILLO, 18-13, 18-16.
SERBEIN, OSCAR N., 11-14.
SERBEIN, OSCAR N. JR., 11-14.
SERULLAZ, MAURICE, 18-11, 19-15.
SESTRIC, JOSEPH P., 12-13.
SEVERSON, HARRY L., 19-16, 21-16.
SEWARD, D. J., 12-14.
SEWARD, D. T., 12-26.
SEXAUER, GEORGE C., 12-25.
SEYFRIED, W. R., 12-22.
SEYFRIED, WARREN R., 13-17, 22-19.
SEYMOUR, C. F., 11-11, 11-12.
SEYMOUR, CHARLES F., 11-11, 11-16, 12-26, 13-13, 22-18.
SEYMOUR, D. D., 13-11.
SHADRAWY, BERNARD F., 12-13, 13-15.
SHAFFER, FORD G., 14-14.
SHANAHAN JOHN E, 11-14.
SHANKLAND, F. J., 11-11, 11-13.
SHANNON, FRANCIS JOHN, 12-11.
SHANNON, JOHN, 12-11, 12-13.
SHANNON, WILLIAM, 22-18.
SHAPIRO, H., 12-13, 14-11.
SHAPIRO, HARVEY, 12-11, 14-11.
SHAPIRO, IRVING D., 19-13, 19-15.
SHAPIRO, M., 11-11, 11-19.
SHAPLEY, FEIN RUSK, 18-11, 19-15.
SHARP, PHILIP D. JR., 12-11.
SHATTOCK, CHARLES B., 14-15, 16-12.
SHATTUCK, CHARLES B., 11-11, 11-12, 12-25, 13-17, 13-19.
SHAW AND SONS LTD., 16-11.
SHAW, EUGENE AIKEN, 12-16, 12-18.
SHAW, G. B., 18-11, 18-12, 18-13, 18-14, 18-15.
SHAW, J. BYAM, 18-11, 18-15, 19-15.
SHAY, HERBERT K., 12-13, 21-12.
SHEAFFER, JOHN R., 12-23.
SHEEDAN, DENNIS D., 24-14.
SHEEDY, PAUL, 12-11.
SHEEHAN, JAMES J., 13-15.
SHEFFER, H. FRAZIER, 11-13, 11-16, 22-18.
SHELGER, KURT S., 13-12, 13-15, 13-17, 13-19.
SHELL, JOE L., 12-14, 12-16.
SHELTON, J. P., 19-16.
SHENEHON, HOWARD E., 13-11, 13-17.
SHENKEL, WILLIAM M., 11-11, 11-14, 11-16, 11-19, 12-16, 12-24, 13-11, 13-13, 13-19, 19-13, 19-17, 22-18, 22-21, 23-02, 23-11.
SHENREL, WILLIAM M., 23-11.
SHEPPARD, D. W., 12-13, 14-15.
SHERIDAN, LEO J., 13-18, 13-20.
SHERIDAN, V. G., 11-16.
SHERIDAN, VINCENT GEORGE, 11-11.
SHERMAN, ARTHUR B., 11-18.
SHERMAN, H. J., 11-11, 11-13.
SHERMER, MALCOLM, 19-15, 19-16.
SHERMER, MALCOLM H., 11-11, 11-16.
SHERRINGTON C. E. M., 24-14.
SHIACH A.D., 11-19, 12-24, 19-15.
SHIACH, ALEXANDER D., 19-16.
SHIMMON, R. E., 13-15, 13-19.
SHIPLEY, ROBERT C. JR., 12-11, 19-15.
SHIPP, ROYAL, 11-19, 13-15.
SHIVELY, JOHN W., 13-13.
SHOOP, CARL S., 12-11.
SHOPLIN, AUGUST, 12-13, 22-18.
SHOWELL, BRIAN, 13-15, 13-16.
SHUGRUE, FRANK R., 11-11, 11-14, 11-16, 22-18.
SHULTIS, ARTHUR, 12-14, 14-17.

SHURBERG, MERWIN, 11-11, 11-17, 11-19, 21-11.
SHUTE, CLYDE, 21-13.
SHWAYDER, K, 12-13, 12-25, 19-14.
SIBERLING, NORMAN J., 11-11, 19-15.
SIDERMAN, DAVID, 12-14.
SIEJA, EDWARD M., 12-13, 13-11, 22-21, 24-13.
SIEMENS, HENRY J., 12-16.
SIEMENS, HENRY T., 12-15, 12-16.
SIGISMONDI, AUGUSTUS R., 12-14.
SILAS, O. PAYNE, 12-26, 19-13.
SILVERHERZ, JOSEPH D., 11-11, 11-19, 12-11, 12-13, 12-24.
SILVERHERZ, JOSEPH DAVID, 12-13.
SILVERMAN, BENJAMIN, 11-11, 11-12, 11-13, 11-14, 11-16, 11-19, 12-14, 12-24, 16-11, 16-12, 16-13, 16-14, 16-15, 16-16, 18-11, 18-12, 18-13, 18-14, 18-15, 19-19, 19-20, 19-21, 19-22, 23-18.
SIMERAL WILLIAM B, 15-24.
SIMMONDS, H. H., 11-19, 12-24.
SIMMONS, MERCER W., 12-19, 13-19.
SIMMS, S. R., 11-11, 11-14, 12-26.
SIMON, ROBERT E., 11-11, 11-13, 14-11.
SIMONEAUX, MERVIN J., 12-11.
SIMONETT, D. S., 11-14, 11-16, 14-11.
SIMONITE, C. R., 11-11, 11-18.
SIMONSON, E. M., 12-16, 13-13.
SIMPSON, DR. H. D., 12-13.
SIMPSON, HERBERT D., 13-23.
SIMPSON, HERBERT DOWNS, 13-23.
SINCLAIR, G. D., 20-15.
SINCLAIR, GEORGE D., 13-21.
SINGH, MADANJEET, 18-12, 19-15.
SINGLETON, C. G. JR., 11-11, 13-23, 19-15.
SINGLETON, CHARLES S., 18-11, 18-12, 19-15.
SINGLETON, ESTHER, 18-16.
SINNITT, PAUL, 12-14, 12-16, 12-26.
SISKA, FRNAK J., 12-13, 13-15.
SKEER, DAVID, 12-14, 19-13.
SKELLEY, LELOISE DAVIS, 18-14, 18-15.
SKELTON, JOHN E., 12-13.
SKINNER, ROBERT G, 19-19.
SKOGSTAD, TOR, 11-14, 21-11, 21-13.
SKYSCRAPER MANAGEMENT, 19-13.
SLADE, ESTER P., 13-15.
SLADE, LESTER P., 13-19.
SLATER, RONALD W., 13-17.
SLAYTON, WILLIAM L., 13-13.
SLICHTER, S. H., 11-11, 11-18.
SLICHTER, SUMNER H., 11-11, 11-18.
SLICKTER, S. H., 12-25.
SLONIM, M. J., 11-11, 11-13, 11-16, 11-19, 12-14, 12-15, 13-15.
SLOSSON, FRANK S., 19-13.
SLY, JOHN F., 12-11.
SMAILS, R. G. H., 11-19, 12-24.
SMALE, JOHN G., 12-11.
SMELLIE, R. G., 11-14.
SMETHURST, R. G., 13-17, 13-19.
SMITH, 13-11.
SMITH, ALAN H., 12-12, 19-12.
SMITH, ARNOLD R., 13-15.
SMITH, ARTHUR A., 17-15.
SMITH, BERNARD, 18-11, 19-15.
SMITH, CARL S., 24-15.
SMITH, CHARLES E., 11-14, 11-16, 13-13.

SMITH, DAN T., 12-11.
SMITH, DAVID H., 11-19, 12-23, 12-24.
SMITH, FRANK A., 12-16.
SMITH, FRED E., 13-17, 22-18.
SMITH, G. A., 13-16, 13-17, 13-19.
SMITH, GEORGE C., 13-15, 23-11.
SMITH, GILBERT A., 12-16, 22-16.
SMITH, GLENN C., 14-15.
SMITH, GRACE HOWARD AND EUGENE RANDOLPH SMITH, 18-17, 19-15.
SMITH, GUY V., 12-16, 13-15, 19-15.
SMITH, GUY-HAROLD, 19-15, 19-18.
SMITH, HALBERT C., 11-11, 11-16, 19-15, 22-18.
SMITH, J. H. JR., 11-11.
SMITH, J. J., 12-16.
SMITH, JAMES J., 11-11, 11-14, 11-18.
SMITH, JOSEPH R. III, 12-14.
SMITH, KENNETH B., 13-11.
SMITH, LAMAR, 11-14, 11-16, 12-16.
SMITH, LAMAR H., 11-14, 11-16, 12-16, 24-15.
SMITH, LARRY, 11-11, 11-17, 11-19, 13-11, 13-15, 13-23, 19-15, 22-18.
SMITH, LAWRENCE E., 13-15.
SMITH, LAWRENCE E., SR., 12-25.
SMITH, LEE THOMPSON, 19-12.
SMITH, LELAND F., 23-11.
SMITH, LEONARD C., 11-11, 11-14, 11-16, 11-17, 11-19, 12-16, 21-11.
SMITH, LEVIE D., 12-15, 13-15, 13-21.
SMITH, LEVIE D. JR., 13-19.
SMITH, LEVIE D. SR., 11-14, 11-16.
SMITH, LEWIS R., 11-14.
SMITH, PIERCE J., 12-13, 13-15.
SMITH, R. GILMAN, 24-19.
SMITH, R. S., 12-11, 12-25.
SMITH, RALPH ELBERTON, 11-18, 12-11.
SMITH, RALPH M., 11-11, 11-14, 11-16.
SMITH, ROBERT C., 18-12, 19-15.
SMITH, T. R., 12-11.
SMITH, W. J., 14-15.
SMITH, W. LAURENCE, 12-17, 19-13.
SMITH, WALLACE F., 12-21, 13-16.
SMITH, WALSTEIN FR., 11-11, 11-16.
SMITH, WALSTEIN JR., 11-11, 11-13, 12-11, 12-14.
SMITH, WALSTEIN, JR., 11-11, 11-16, 12-14, 13-11, 13-13, 13-15, 22-16, 22-18.
SMITH, WILEY W., 12-11.
SMITH, WILLIAM B., 13-19.
SMITH, WINIFRED W., 12-13.
SMYTH, W. A., 11-11, 18-11, 18-12, 18-13, 18-14, 18-15.
SMYTH, WILLIAM A., 11-12.
SNITZER, EDWARD L., 12-14, 12-15, 12-16, 12-20, 12-26, 13-12, 22-12.
SNORGRASS, G. VERN, 13-15.
SNORGRASS, VERN G., 19-11, 19-14, 19-15, 19-19.
SNOWMAN, A. KENNETH, 18-15.
SNYDER, AREAS B., 12-16.
SNYDER, BLAKE, 11-11, 11-16, 12-24.
SNYDER, DONALD E., 11-14, 11-16.
SNYDER, FREAS B., 12-14.
SOCIETY OF INDUSTRIAL REALTORS, 11-14, 11-15, 22-18.
SOCIETY OF REAL ESTATE APPRAISERS, 13-17, 13-19.
SOCIETY OF RESIDENTIAL APPRAISERS, 11-11, 11-12, 11-13, 11-16, 13-17, 13-19, 19-11.

SODERQUIST, OSCAR, 11-14, 11-16, 12-11, 12-24.
SOLARI, VIRGILIO S, 22-20.
SOLBERG, ERLING D., 11-11, 14-11.
SOLIS-COHEN, J. JR., 13-20, 19-13.
SOLO, RICHARD D., 12-15.
SOLOMON, C. FRANCIS, JR., 11-11, 11-14.
SOLOMON, R. J., 13-11, 13-14, 13-22, 22-11.
SOMBERG, SEYMOUR L., 17-12.
SOMERFELD, H. B., 14-15.
SOMERVILLE, EDWIN L., 13-18.
SOMERVILLE, H. H., 12-14.
SONNENSCHIEN, FRANK E., 19-14.
SOPHY, GERALD, 20-14.
SORTOR, CHARLES H., 14-15, 16-14.
SOTAK, ANDREW, 13-21.
SOTAVE, 11-11, 11-12, 11-16.
SOTAVE, BOLETIN, 13-15, 13-18.
SOTHEBY, 18-11, 18-12, 18-13, 18-15, 18-16.
SOULE, N. C., 13-14.
SOULE, NAT C., 11-14, 11-16.
SOUTH DAKOTA LEGISLATIVE RESEARCH COUNCIL, 12-11, 17-15.
SOUTHARD, MELVILLE, 12-14.
SOUTHERLAND, EDWIN W., 12-11.
SOUTHERN CALIFORNIA GOLF ASSOCIATION, 15-13, 15-14.
SOUTHWEST REGIONAL ADVISORY COMMITTEE, 16-12.
SPAHR, WALTER E., 11-11, 11-16, 11-17, 11-19.
SPARHAWK, HOWARD E., 14-18.
SPARKMAN, JOHN J., 13-16.
SPEARS, NATHANIEL, 18-16.
SPECK, G. E., 18-16.
SPECTOR, JACK L., 18-11, 18-12, 19-15.
SPEED, A., 11-14, 11-16.
SPEED, A. A., 11-11, 11-14.
SPEEDY SQUIRE L., 14-15.
SPEIDEL, R. E., 12-11.
SPELMAN, E. C., 13-15.
SPELMAN, EVERETT C., 13-15.
SPENCER, CHARLES E. JR., 12-14.
SPENCER, W. H., 22-18.
SPENGLER, E. H., 24-19.
SPICER, O. W., 17-13.
SPILDER, JOHN B., 11-11, 11-16.
SPILKER, JOHN B., 12-11.
SPILLER, ROBERT J., 13-17.
SPINDLE, JAMES A., 12-16, 17-15.
SPON, EDWARD, 11-11, 13-11.
SPRAY, F., 12-26.
SPREAD, K. J., 12-13.
SPRING, TERRENCE, 13-17, 13-19.
SPRINKEL, BERLY W., 11-18, 11-19, 19-15.
SPROULL, EDWARD I., 19-13.
SQUIRE, LATHAM C., 13-11, 22-18.
SREA COMMITTEE PAPER, 19-15.
SROUFE, THOMAS A., 11-11, 11-14, 11-16.
ST. PETERSBURG, FLORIDA FINANCE DEPARTMENT, 12-11, 12-12, 12-26.
ST. GEORGE, JOHN F., 11-11, 11-18, 12-12, 12-13, 12-26, 13-13.
STACER, THOMAS C., 12-16, 12-26, 17-12.
STAFF OF THE FRICK COLLECTION, 18-11, 18-15, 19-15.
STAFFORD, JAMES G., 11-14, 11-16.

STAFFORD, L. D., 11-11, 11-19, 19-15.
STAHL, SHELDON W., 11-18, 19-15, 21-18.
STALCUP, H. E., 14-15.
STAMPER, F. A., 12-16.
STANFORD, MELVIN J., 11-16, 11-19, 21-18.
STANLEY, A. L., 19-15, 19-18, 19-19, 19-20, 19-21.
STANTON, BEN E., 24-15.
STANTON, WOLCOTT P., 22-18.
STAPLES, JACK D., 19-15, 24-11, 24-15.
STAPLETON, R. C., 19-14, 19-15.
STAPLETON, THOMAS M, 19-19.
STARKE, GEORGE C., 11-14, 11-16, 11-19.
STARR, J. O., 12-23, 19-13.
STARR, ROGER, 13-13.
STARRETT, PAUL, 11-19, 12-22, 12-24, 17-15, 19-13, 22-14, 22-21, 23-11.
STATE COMMISSION OF REVENUE AND TAXATION: KANSAS, 12-13.
STATHAM, ROBERT R, 12-11.
STATISTICAL ABSTRACT OF THE UNITED STATES, 13-14, 19-15.
STAUB, WALTER A., 11-19, 12-24.
STAZZI, FRANCESCO, 18-14, 18-15, 18-17.
STEAD, WILLIAM H., 13-17.
STEARNS, EDWARD C., 13-15, 13-17.
STECHOU, W., 18-11, 19-15.
STEELE, FRANK N., 11-11, 11-12.
STEELE, J., 12-12, 12-24, 13-13.
STEELE, JOHN, 13-15, 23-14.
STEELE, ROBERT A., 11-11, 11-18.
STEGMAN, MICHAEL A., 13-13.
STEIN, H. L., 11-11, 11-14.
STEINBERGER, E. A., 21-12.
STEINER, J. JEFFERSON F., 19-13.
STEINER, JEFFERSON F., 11-11, 11-12.
STEINER, RICHARD L., 22-11, 22-18, 22-19, 22-20.
STEINGRABER, ERICH, 18-15, 18-16, 18-17, 19-15.
STEINHART, RALPH, 11-11.
STENICO, ARTURO, 18-11, 18-16.
STERLING, H. ALBERT, 12-11, 13-17, 13-19.
STERLING, R. R., 12-13, 12-17.
STERLING, RAY T., 11-13, 12-14.
STERM, JOSEPH E., 13-15.
STERN, HENRI, 18-12, 18-15.
STERN, OSCAR I., 11-11, 11-18, 13-17.
STERZER, HERBERT, 11-11, 11-12.
STEUER, AARON, 11-11, 11-12, 11-14, 22-18.
STEVENS, FRANCIS K., 11-11, 11-12, 13-15, 13-18, 13-20.
STEVENS, ROBERT W., 13-11, 13-21.
STEVENS, ROGER L., 19-15, 22-18.
STEVENS, WILLIAM T., 11-11, 11-16, 11-17.
STEVENSON, R. A., 11-11, 11-19.
STEVICK, J. C., 11-14, 11-16.
STEWARD, CHARLES L., 11-11, 11-18, 14-11, 14-15, 23-18.
STEWARD, J. A., 11-11, 11-18.
STEWARD, WILLIAM A., 12-14.
STEWART, C. L., 12-14, 14-15.
STEWART, CHARLES L., 14-11.
STEWART, CLYDE E., 14-15.
STEWART, DWIGHT A., 11-11, 11-14.
STEWART, GRAEME, 12-18.
STEWART, J. H., 12-20.
STEWART, J. I., 11-11, 11-16, 11-18, 12-20.
STEWART, J. S., 12-11.
STEWART, JAMES INNES, 11-11, 11-16.

STEWART, PHILIP O., 22-21.
STEWART, SAMUEL, 11-11, 11-12.
STEWART, SAMUEL B., 12-11, 12-13.
STEWART, TOM, 12-15.
STEWART, W. C., 12-16, 13-19, 22-24.
STILES, LYNN A., 12-11, 13-23.
STINSON, CHARLES H., 11-11.
STOCKER, FREDERICK D, 12-13.
STOCKTON, JOHN Q., 11-11, 11-16.
STOKES, CHARLES J., 12-11.
STOLINSKI, JOSEPH C., 12-13, 14-15.
STOLL, R. T., 18-13, 19-15.
STOLP, JOHN A., 13-15.
STONE, J. E, 19-16.
STONE, MAJOR EDWARD, 13-16.
STONE, PETER A., 11-11, 11-14.
STONE, ROBERT, 22-15.
STONE, ROBERT R., 12-14, 12-16.
STOREY, HAROLD, 12-11.
STORY, BEN H. JR., 12-15, 12-16.
STOTHART, JACK, 11-16, 11-18.
STOTTLE, BURR S., 11-11, 12-19.
STOVER, V. G., 12-16, 22-16.
STOWE, THOMAS C., 11-11, 11-16, 16-11.
STRASBURG, MAX, 18-17.
STRATHON, ERIC C., 11-11, 11-18.
STRAUB, ROBERT, 12-14, 12-16.
STRAUSS, GEORGE, 12-11.
STREUKENS, H. H., 12-14, 12-16, 12-18.
STREUKENS, HERBERT H., 19-13.
STRIDE, I. L., 11-11, 11-14.
STRONG, D. E., 18-15, 19-15.
STROUSE, BENJAMIN A., 13-18, 19-13.
STRUNCK, JAMES E., 12-15, 24-13.
STRUNG, J., 14-11.
STRUNK, NORMAN, 11-16.
STRUNK, NORMAN W., 11-13, 11-16.
STUART, DARWIN G., 13-23.
STUART, EDWARD, JR., 17-12.
STUART, WILLIAM N., 14-17.
STUBBS, ROBERT C., 12-13, 12-15.
STUDDARD, KENNETH E., 12-11, 13-19.
STUETZER JR, HERMAN, 12-11, 19-17.
STUNARD, EUGENE W., 11-11, 11-19, 19-11, 19-14.
SUDDERTH, WAYNE, 13-13.
SULLIVAN, J. BURKE, 12-15, 12-24.
SULLIVAN, MICHAEL, 19-15.
SULLIVAN, RICHARD B., 19-12.
SUMMER, J. D., 24-12.
SUMOWSKI, WERNER, 18-11.
SUQIURA, SEIZO, 11-11, 11-18.
SURIANO, HORACIO O., 12-11.
SURTEES, VIRGINIA, 18-11, 18-15.
SURVEY OF URBAN RENWAL LAND DISPOSITION, 13-13.
SURVEY RESEARCH CENTER, UNIVERSITY OF MICHIGAN, 13-17, 13-19, 21-15.
SUSNIR, JOHN, 13-16.
SUSSNA, DR. STEPHEN, 13-12.
SUTER, ROBERT C, 12-11, 12-13, 14-11, 19-11.
SUTER, ROBERT C., 14-11.
SUTHERLAND, C. H. V., 18-15, 19-15.
SUTHERLAND, CHARLES F., 12-11, 17-12.
SUTHERLAND, J. FREDERICK, 11-14.
SUTTE, DONALD T. JR., 12-15, 24-15.

SUTTE, DONALD T. JR. M. A. I., 24-11, 24-15.
SUTTON, FRANKLIN P., 12-12.
SVOBODA, ALBERT C., 19-15, 22-18.
SWAFFORD, EMMETT, 22-11, 24-11, 24-15.
SWAIN, H. H., 24-14.
SWAN, CLIFFORD L., 19-15, 19-17, 19-19, 19-20, 19-21, 19-22.
SWAN, HERBERT S., 13-11, 13-15, 13-16.
SWAN, J. WILSON, 11-14, 11-16, 12-26.
SWAN, ROGER H., 12-14.
SWAN, RUSSELL E., 11-13, 11-16.
SWANEY, FRED, 14-11, 15-15.
SWANSON, EARL R., 14-11, 14-12.
SWEENEY, HENERY W., 11-14, 11-16.
SWEENY, HENRY W., 11-19, 12-24.
SWEET, FREDERICK A., 18-11, 18-12, 19-15.
SWEET, GILBERT N., 13-23.
SWEET, HOLLIS A., 12-13.
SWENSSON, EARL S., 13-19.
SWEPTSON, DWIGHT C., 11-11, 11-18.
SWEZEY, WILLIAM D., 11-11, 11-14.
SWICK, E. H., 24-11, 24-15.
SWITZER, DOROTHY, 13-11, 14-11.
SYBILLE, HAYNES, 18-15, 19-15.
SYBRANDT, JOHN L., 12-14, 12-23.
SYCHRAVA, L., 12-16, 24-15.
SYDNEY, EARL OF PEMBROKE, 18-11, 19-15.
SYMONDS, WELSFORD J., 12-13.


TAEUBER, K. C., 11-11, 11-16.
TAEUBER, K. G., 11-16.
TAIT, STUART C., 11-11, 18-11, 18-12, 18-13.
TALLIN, C. K., 12-14.
TALLIN, CLIVE K., 12-14.
TALMADGE, M. P., 12-13.
TANNENBAUM, A. A., 13-17.
TANNERY, FLADGER FREEMAN, 12-13, 12-26.
TANNEY, WILLIAM W., 12-24, 13-13, 13-15, 19-16.
TAPP, JESSE W., 11-11, 11-18.
TARRANT, JOHN F., 12-11.
TATLOW, R. H. III., 13-15.
TATUM, CHARLES ALVIN, 11-14, 11-15.
TAX ADMINISTRATION NEWS, 12-11.
TAX INSTITUTE INCORPORATED, 12-11.
TAX INSTITUTE OF AMERICA;, 12-13.
TAX INSTITUTE, INCORPORATED, 12-11.
TAX POLICY, 12-11, 12-13.
TAYLOR, CARL, 11-14.
TAYLOR, DINSMORE, 22-18.
TAYLOR, FRANK, 13-15.
TAYLOR, FRANK H., 12-16, 24-14.
TAYLOR, GEORGE H., 12-23.
TAYLOR, J. J., 11-11, 11-19, 12-24.
TAYLOR, JAMES R., 11-11, 11-19, 12-24, 19-15, 19-17.
TAYLOR, LUCY B., 18-14.
TAYLOR, RICHARD H., 24-15.
TAYLOR, RICHARD., 12-16, 12-26.
TAYLOR, THOMAS L., 12-14, 12-19.
TAYNTON, M., 12-11, 12-24.
TEBBETTS, R. S., 12-23.
TECHNICAL BULLETIN, 13-19.
TECHNICAL VALUATION, 11-11, 11-16, 11-18, 12-13, 13-15.

# BIBLIOGRAPHY OF APPRAISAL LITERATURE

TECKEMEYER, E. B., 11-11, 11-14.
TECKEMEYER, EARL B., 11-11, 11-14, 11-16.
TEICHERT, C. O., 12-14.
TENNER, IRVING, 11-14.
TENNESSEE BOARD OF EQUALIZATION, 12-11.
TERBORGH, GEORGE, 11-19, 12-11, 12-24, 13-16, 20-11, 20-12, 20-14, 20-15, 21-13, 21-14.
TERON, WILLIAM, 13-11.
TESTINO G., RICARDO, 11-11, 11-16.
TEXAS COMMISSION ON STATE AND LOCAL TAX POLICY, 12-11.
TEXAS, COMPTROLLER'S OFFICE, 12-13, 12-26.
THALER, D., 13-18, 13-19, 19-11, 19-13, 21-16.
THALHIMER, MORTON G., 13-15.
THAYER, DONALD C., 11-14, 11-16, 19-12.
THE AMER INSTITUTE OF ARCHITECTS JOUR, 11-15.
THE AMERICAN INSTITUTE OF REAL ESTATE APPRAISERS, 12-15, 12-16.
THE APPRAISAL JOURNAL, 11-11, 11-16, 11-18, 12-26, 19-15.
THE ECONOMIST, 11-11, 12-24.
THE REVIEW, 11-11, 11-14.
THE UNIVERSITY OF UTAH, 22-18.
THE WEST CENTRAL REGIONAL ADVISORY COMMITTEE, 16-12.
THEIS, C KENNETH, 12-15.
THEISS, WILLIAM R., 17-14.
THEISS, WILLIAM R., 12-11, 12-12, 12-13, 12-14, 12-15, 12-16, 12-26, 13-11, 13-14, 13-15, 13-19, 13-21, 13-22, 14-11, 16-16, 19-13, 20-11, 21-16, 22-11, 22-16, 22-17, 22-21, 24-12.
THEOBALD, A. D., 11-11, 11-19, 13-19.
THEOBALD, A. E., 13-22, 22-17.
THERA, JOHN M., 13-19.
THIEL, FLOYD I., 11-14, 11-16, 12-16, 24-15.
THOMAS, BERY E., 12-13, 14-11.
THOMAS, C. L., 13-19.
THOMAS, D. L., 11-11, 11-18.
THOMAS, EDMUND E., 22-18.
THOMAS, HARRY F., 19-11.
THOMAS, P. I., 12-23.
THOMPSON, ARTHUR P., 18-16.
THOMPSON, BURTON, 11-11, 11-13, 11-19, 12-14, 12-24, 12-26.
THOMPSON, CLARE R., 12-13.
THOMPSON, GEORGE M., 12-26.
THOMPSON, GLEN, 12-13.
THOMPSON, GLENN P., 12-16, 22-18.
THOMPSON, JOSEPH SEXTON, 12-11.
THOMPSON, LOREN L., 11-14, 11-16, 11-18, 12-16.
THOMPSON, NEIL S., 12-14.
THOMPSON, PELL, 11-11, 11-14, 11-16, 22-18.
THOMPSON, PROF. WARREN S., 13-11, 22-18.
THOMPSON, R. E., 11-11, 11-14, 11-16, 11-19, 12-23, 12-25, 19-15, 22-18, 22-24.
THOMPSON, STEPHEN G., 22-18.
THOMPSON, W. E., 12-13.
THOMPSON, W. N. AND JAMES O. MELTON, 14-15.
THOMPSON, WARREN S., 13-11.
THOMSEN, C. T., 12-24.
THOMSON, CHARLES, 11-11.
THOMSON, F. L., 14-11.
THOMSON, ROBERT H., 13-17, 21-18.
THOMSON, W. F., 11-14, 11-16, 19-11, 19-12.
THOMSSEN, ROHLAND H., 11-11, 11-12, 11-16.
THORKELSON, GERALD F., 11-14, 14-11.

THORN, BURTON R., 21-11, 21-13.
THORNCROFT, MICHAEL E. T., 11-11, 11-18.
THORNDIKE, EDWARD L. AND ELLA WOODYARD, 11-11, 13-11.
THORNE, O. J., 19-17.
THORNE, OAKLEIGH J., 13-15, 17-13.
THORNTON, J., 12-25.
THORNTON, PETER, 18-15, 19-15.
THORNTON, W. B., 12-16, 17-12.
THORNTON, WILLIAM W., 17-15.
THORPE, E. EVERETT, 11-16, 11-17.
THORPE, LAYARD G., 11-14, 11-16.
THORSON, IVAN A., 11-11, 11-12, 11-14, 11-16, 11-18, 11-19, 12-11, 12-26, 13-11, 13-14, 13-17, 13-18, 19-13, 19-15, 22-18.
THORSON, J. T., 11-11, 11-13, 11-16, 12-20.
THOS, D. WOODS, E. J. MCCORMICK R. E. BLANCHARD, 14-11.
THRIFT, E. W., 13-11, 24-12.
THRIFT, ERIC W., 13-13, 24-15.
THRUN, FRED MARTIN, 14-11, 21-14.
THUDSON, F. M., 13-15.
THULMAN, ROBERT K., 13-19, 20-11.
THUROW, RAYMOND, 11-11, 11-14, 12-13.
TIDEMAN, ROBERT, 12-13, 12-26.
TIDEMANN, ARTHUR R., 14-11.
TIEGER, MAX, 13-15, 22-24.
TIERNEY, JOHN L, 11-16.
TILGHMAN-MAYER COMPANY, 13-21, 21-16.
TILLY, V. S., 13-15.
TIME, INC., 11-11, 13-11.
TIMM, WERNER, 18-12.
TINETTI, J. R. AND D. G. WARREN, 12-15, 13-11.
TIPTON, BALLARD B., 11-15, 12-13.
TISHMAN, DAVID, 19-15, 22-18.
TODD, CARL L., 12-16.
TODD, DAVID KEITH (EDITOR), 16-14.
TODD, ERIC C. E., 12-20.
TOLCOTT, M., 14-11.
TOLLER, JANE, 18-16, 19-15.
TOLTZMAN, R. J., 11-11, 11-12.
TOMPSON, GEORGE W., 11-11.
TOMSON, BERNARD, 11-11.
TONTI, D. LOUIS, 24-11.
TONTZ, ROBERT L., 11-11, 11-16.
TOOLEY, R. V., 11-14.
TORREY, WILLIAM W., 11-11, 11-14, 11-16, 19-13.
TOTH, LOUIS, 13-15.
TOURTELOT, ROBERT H., 12-13, 13-19.
TOWERS, ALBERT G., 11-11, 11-14.
TOWERS, ALBERT G. JR., 11-11, 11-12, 11-16, 21-11, 21-12, 21-13, 21-14, 21-15, 21-16, 21-18.
TOWL, BURL A. JR., 12-16.
TOWNSEND, F. S., 19-16.
TOWNSEND, F. S. JR., 13-15, 19-16.
TOWNSEND, GILBERT, 11-14, 11-16, 21-11.
TOWNSEND, T. L., 14-11, 16-16, 18-11, 19-13.
TRANSOM, G. E. JR., 11-11, 11-19, 12-24.
TRASK, ELWOOD E., 14-12, 14-17.
TRAUTMAN, PHILIP A., 12-13.
TRAVIS, BROLEY E., 12-12, 12-13, 16-11, 19-16.
TRAVIS, BROLEY, E., 16-11.
TREADWAY, F. H. JR. M. A. I., 12-16.
TREADWELL, JOHN C., 11-11, 11-19.
TREASURY DEPARTMENT, 11-11, 11-19, 12-24.

## Index of Authors

TREBING, HARRY M., 16-11.
TREDWELL, JOHN C., 11-16, 11-19, 12-24, 12-25, 13-15.
TRENDALL, A. D., 18-16.
TRENHOLM, KENNETH M., 12-15, 12-16.
TRENT, I. J., 14-11, 22-20.
TREVINO, ALBERT F. JR., 11-11.
TREWICK, HENRY, 18-11, 18-14, 18-15, 19-15.
TRITSCHLER, C. A., 11-11, 11-14.
TROAST, PAUL L., 24-11, 24-15.
TROWBRIDGE, CARL R., 11-11, 11-16, 12-14, 12-24, 16-11.
TROWELL, MARGARET, 18-13.
TROXEL JAY C, 23-11.
TROXEL, JAY C., 11-11, 11-16, 13-15, 21-11.
TROXELL, D CHASE, 19-15.
TRUE, WALLACE, 13-21, 19-11.
TRUE, WALLACE W., 11-18, 12-23, 13-11, 13-13, 13-15, 13-17, 19-11, 19-15, 23-11.
TRUEHEART, LAWRENCE G., 12-16, 22-21.
TRUMBLE, MELVIN J., 12-24, 23-11.
TUCKER, GILBERT M., 11-11, 12-11, 13-11.
TUCKER, HAROLD J., 13-17.
TUCKER, J. WALTER, JR., 19-11.
TUCKETT, HARVEY GARNETT PHIPPS, 12-11, 22-14.
TULLEY ROBERT, 12-26.
TULLEY, J. BENTON, 13-15, 19-13.
TURE, NORMAN B, 12-11.
TURNBULL, JAMES, 13-15.
TURNEAURE, F. E., 16-14.
TURNER CONSTRUCTION COMPANY, 21-13.
TURNER, EARL KENNETH, 12-13.
TURNER, HOWARD M., 12-16, 16-14.
TURNER, JOHN F. C. AND ROBERT FICHTER, 12-26, 13-11, 19-18.
TURNER, ROBERT C., 11-11, 11-18, 13-15, 19-15.
TURNEURE, F. E., 16-14.
TURPIE, A., 11-11, 14-11.
TUSKA, C D, 19-20.
TYNAN, PETER, 11-11, 11-16.

U. S. FEDERAL HOUSING ADMINISTRATION, 13-16.
U. P. A. V., 11-11, 11-12.
U. S. ADVISORY COMM ON INTERGOVERNMENTAL RELATIONS, 12-11.
U. S. AGRICULTURAL RESEARCH SERVICE, 12-11, 14-13, 14-15.
U. S. ARMY CORPS OF ENGINEERS, 11-14, 11-15, 25-11, 25-12.
U. S. BUREAU OF FOREIGN AND DOMESTIC COMMERCE, 18-17.
U. S. BUREAU OF INTERNAL REVENUE, 12-24.
U. S. BUREAU OF LABOR STATISTICS, 11-14.
U. S. BUREAU OF THE CENSUS, 12-11.
U. S. CENSUS BUREAU, 11-14.
U. S. DEPARTMENT OF AGRICULTURE, 11-14, 12-11, 12-13, 14-11.
U. S. FEDERAL HOUSING ADMINISTRATION, 13-16, 13-17.
U. S. FEDERAL WORKS AGENCY, 12-16, 22-16, 24-11, 24-15.
U. S. GOVERNMENT PRINTING OFFICE, 13-11, 13-16, 13-21, 13-23, 14-11, 17-14, 22-19, 22-20.
U. S. INTERNAL REVENUE SERVICE, 12-11, 12-24.
U. S. JOINT COMMITEE ON INTERNAL REVENUE TAXATION, 12-11.
U. S. URBAN RENEWAL ADMINISTRATION, 12-11, 13-13.
UGHETTA, HENRY L., 12-14.
UNDERWOOD, GEORGE, 21-15.
UNGER, MAURICE A., 22-18.
UNITED STATES BUREAU OF CENSUS, 12-13, 16-11.
UNIVERSITY OF PITTSBURGH, 12-15.
UNRUH, JESSE M., 12-11, 12-13.
UNTERKIRCHER, FIANZ, 18-15, 19-15.
UNTRACHT, OPPI, 18-14.
UPHAM, N. J., 13-14.
URBACH, ZSUZSA, 18-11.
URBAN LAND INSTITUTE, 11-11, 12-11, 13-11, 13-15, 13-19, 13-20.
URBAN RENEWAL ADMINISTRATION, 13-13.
USHER, THOMAS B., 11-15, 12-13.
UTAH FOUNDATION, 12-11, 12-13.

VAN BRAAN, FRED A., 18-15.
VAN BUREN, DEWITT, 11-11, 11-16, 12-15, 12-16.
VAN CLEEF, EUGENE, 11-14, 12-22, 13-14, 13-17, 23-11, 24-11.
VAN DEUSEN, FRANCIS B., 24-15.
VAN DYKE, JOHN C., 18-11.
VAN FLEET, J. B., 12-11, 17-13, 17-15.
VAN HORN, ALAN J., 12-16.
VAN HORNE, J., 12-11, 16-11.
VAN LEUVEN, KARL J., 13-11.
VAN NOY, C. W., 11-14, 23-11.
VAN RASSEL, A. JOHN, 13-17.
VAN SCHAICK, GEORGE S., 22-18.
VAN VUUREN, W., 11-11, 12-11, 12-13, 14-11, 14-15.
VANCIL, RICHARD F, 19-15, 19-19.
VANDERLIP, FRANK A., 22-18.
VANDERMARK, W. R., 12-16.
VANDERPOOL, TOM, 12-15, 12-16, 14-18, 24-15.
VARTY, LEO G., 11-11, 11-16, 23-11.
VASS, DANIEL T, 19-14.
VATTER, W. J., 19-17.
VAUGHAN JR, JOHN L, 19-15, 19-17.
VAUGHAN, G. A., 13-16.
VAUGHAN, J. H., 11-11, 11-14.
VAUGHAN, J. L. JR., 11-11, 11-16, 12-11, 12-13, 19-11, 19-14, 19-15, 19-17, 19-19, 19-20, 23-15.
VEGA, ELIAS E., 12-11.
VEGAS ROLANDO, NICOLAS, 11-11, 11-12, 11-16, 13-14.
VENNARD, EDWIN, 16-12.
VERDIER, PHILIPPE, 18-11.
VERHAGEN, A. M., 14-11, 14-15.
VERLET, PIERRE, 18-16, 19-15.
VERMILYA, SHERWOOD S., 23-13.
VERMONT TAX DEPARTMENT, 12-11, 17-12.
VERZONE, PAOLO, 18-11, 18-12.
VIEIRO, RAUL OSCAR, 12-11, 12-17.
VIELE, G. ROBERT, 15-15, 15-16.
VIESER, MILFORD A., 13-13.
VINCENT, FRED E., 11-14, 11-16.
VINCENT, G., 12-15, 14-11.
VINCENT, GERARD, 12-15.
VIZARD, RICHARD, 13-21.
VOCKE, DR. WILHELM, 11-11.
VON HAGEN, VICTOR W., 11-11.

VON LEHE, ARTHUR R., 12-11.
VOSKUIL, W. N., 16-14.
VRIESEN, GUSTAV, 18-11, 19-15.
VUKICEVICH, BENJAMIN G., 11-14, 11-16.


WALFFLIN, HEINRICH, 18-12.
WADA, S. A., 11-11, 11-19, 12-24.
WADDEL, HAROLD H., 11-11, 11-12.
WADE, G., 22-18.
WADLEY, NICHOLAS, 18-11, 18-12, 19-15.
WADLINGTON, I. L., 24-13.
WAELTI, J. J., 13-11, 15-16, 17-16.
WAGNER, C. RAY, 11-11, 12-13, 12-16, 23-11.
WAGNER, E. F., 12-16, 13-17, 24-15.
WAGNER, J. J., 11-11, 11-19, 12-24, 13-19, 14-15.
WAGNER, PERCY E., 11-11, 11-12, 11-14, 11-16, 11-19, 12-14, 12-19, 12-20, 13-15, 13-17, 13-19, 13-22, 19-12, 22-17.
WAILS, CHARLES E., 12-13, 16-11.
WALD, HASKELL P., 12-11, 14-11.
WALDEN, R. R., 12-13, 13-15.
WALDMAN, DIANE, 18-12, 19-15.
WALDO, FRANCOIS, 11-11, 13-21, 19-15.
WALDRON, ROBERT, 23-11.
WALDRON, ROBERT F., 13-11.
WALES, T. J., 11-11, 11-19, 12-24.
WALHU, R. A., 18-11, 19-15.
WALKER, FRANK R., 11-15.
WALKER, J., 12-22, 13-11, 21-13.
WALKER, JOAN MANOR, 22-18.
WALKER, MABEL, 12-11, 13-13, 22-18.
WALKER, PAUL H., 12-11.
WALKER, WILLIAM P., 12-11, 12-13.
WALL, NORBERT F., 11-14, 11-16, 13-11, 13-17, 22-16.
WALL, WILLIAM J, 12-11, 19-15.
WALLACE, DAVID A., 13-11, 24-11.
WALLACE, J. WAGNER, 12-13, 13-20.
WALLACE, JAMES J., 14-11, 14-12.
WALLACE, JOHN, 12-13.
WALLACE, JOHN C., 13-16.
WALLACE, LEW E., 12-24, 14-11, 20-15.
WALLACE, W. H., 12-13, 16-11.
WALLEY, BEN H., 12-16.
WALLEY, ERSEL, 12-14, 12-16.
WALLICH, H. C., 19-15, 19-16.
WALLINGFORT, J. WALLINGFORD, 11-11, 11-14.
WALLIS, L. J., 12-16.
WALLSTEIN, LEONARD, 12-14.
WALRATH, ARTHUR J., 12-11.
WALSH, DONALD, 12-14, 13-15.
WALSH, EDWARD V., 12-24, 13-17, 21-14.
WALSH, H. VANDERVOORT, 11-11, 11-16, 21-11.
WALSH, J. F., 12-16.
WALSH, JAMES A., 13-17.
WALSH, JAMES L. JR., 12-26.
WALSH, STUART P., 13-15.
WALSTEIN, SMITH, JR., 11-11, 11-16.
WALSTRUM, S. WILLIAM, 11-11, 11-16.
WALTEMADE, HENRY G., 12-14, 12-26.
WALTER, K. W., 24-11.
WALTHER, H. O., 12-19, 13-17, 13-19, 24-13.
WALTHER, HERMAN O., 11-11, 11-12, 11-14, 11-16, 12-11, 12-13, 12-15, 12-19, 12-26, 13-19, 24-13.
WALTON, L. ELLIS FR., 12-16, 24-11.

WALTON, WILLIAM B., 13-15.
WANENMACHER, J. M., 17-15.
WANSCHER, OLE, 18-18, 19-15.
WARD, STANLEY, 12-11, 17-15.
WARD, WILLIAM REGINALD, 12-11.
WARDEN, FRANK E., 12-13.
WARDLE, PATRICIA, 18-15, 18-16.
WARE, DORA, 11-14.
WARK, ROBERT R., 18-12, 18-15.
WARMAN, EDWIN G., 18-16.
WARNER, ARTHUR E., 4 11-11, 11-16.
WARNER, ARTHUR J., 11-14, 11-15.
WARNER, JOHN., 11-14, 11-16.
WARREN, G. F., 11-11, 19-15.
WARREN, ISABELLA, 11-11, 11-18.
WARREN, ISABELLA C, 18-15.
WARREN, J. STANLEY, 11-14.
WARREN, JOHN A., 12-13.
WARREN, S. W., 22-20.
WARREN, STANLEY W., 22-20.
WARTERFIELD, J. SOULE, 12-13.
WARWICK, SAMUEL C., 11-11, 12-11, 12-14, 13-15, 19-13.
WASHINGTON STATE TAX COMMISSION, 12-11.
WASHINGTON TAX COMMISSION, 11-15, 12-11.
WASSER, CLINTON H., 14-18.
WATERER, JOHN W., 18-14.
WATERHOUSE, ELLIS, 18-11, 18-15, 19-15.
WATERMAN, EARL W., 11-14.
WATERS, J. M., 11-11.
WATERS, L. LESLIE, 24-11, 24-12.
WATERSON, GEORGE T., 13-11.
WATKINS, J. OLIVER, 11-16, 11-18.
WATKINS, LURA WOODSIDE, 18-14, 19-15.
WATKINS, O. R., 12-13, 14-15, 22-18.
WATKINS, PHILIP L., 19-11.
WATSON, F., 18-15.
WATSON, JAIRUS H., 12-14.
WATSON, JOHN JAMES, 13-11.
WATSON, LESLIE J., 16-14.
WATSON, PHILIP E., 12-13.
WATSON, THOMAS C., 12-13.
WATSON, WILLIAM H., 11-11, 11-13.
WATTLES, GURDON H., 12-16.
WATTS, JOHN F., 12-16, 14-14.
WATTS, RICHARD C., 12-13.
WAUGH, ALEXANDER P., 12-14.
WAY, R. P., 18-16.
WAYNE, HAROLD M, 12-13.
WAYTAS, R. E., 13-19.
WEAVER, HOWARD S., 14-13, 22-20.
WEAVER, HOWARD SILAS, 13-17, 13-19.
WEAVER, J. R., 23-14.
WEAVER, ROBERT C., 13-11.
WEAVER, W. C. JR., 12-23, 19-15, 22-18.
WEBB, A. JAY, 13-20.
WEBB, CLARENCE ALBERT, 11-11, 11-16.
WEBB, JAMES A., 11-11, 11-14, 11-16, 19-13, 22-18.
WEBB, JOHN C., 11-14, 11-16, 12-16.
WEBB, WILLIAM E., 12-15.
WEBER, GUIDO L., 14-15, 22-20.
WEBER, WALTER W., 17-13.
WEBSTER, JOHN K., 13-17, 13-18.
WEBSTER, R. H., 13-11.
WEBSTER, S. S. JR., 11-19, 12-24.
WEBSTER, T. B. L., 18-13, 18-15.

WECHSLER, HERMAN J., 18-12, 19-15.
WECKSLER, A. N., 12-24, 12-25.
WEDEMEYER, KARL ERIC PH. D., 16-13.
WEDGEWOOD, JOSIAH C., 12-11, 16-11, 22-21.
WEED, KENNETH A., 11-11, 11-13, 13-15, 13-18, 13-19, 21-13, 22-18.
WEED, KENNETH A., 13-17, 13-18, 13-19, 14-13.
WEEKES, R. E., 13-11, 13-12, 13-13, 13-14, 13-15, 13-20.
WEEKES, ROBERT E., 11-19.
WEEKS, DAVID, 14-11, 22-20.
WEEKS, E. W., 13-21.
WEENEY, JAMES LEE, 13-16.
WEHER, ROBERT H., 12-16, 12-25, 17-14.
WEIL, ANDREW L., 12-13, 16-16.
WEILER, R. J., 12-11.
WEILER, ROBERT J., 12-11, 22-18.
WEIMER, ARTHUR M., 11-11, 11-14, 11-16, 13-11, 13-13, 13-19, 22-18.
WEINGARTEN, EDWARD A., 12-14, 12-26.
WEIR, T. R., 11-11, 11-18.
WEISER, FRIEDRICH, 11-11.
WEISS, E. B., 13-11, 13-13, 13-15, 19-15, 21-14, 21-15.
WEISS, H. K., 19-13.
WEISS, HAROLD G., 19-13.
WEISS, W. B., 12-11, 21-14, 24-12.
WEITZELL, E. C., 14-13.
WELCH, CHARLES E., 12-13, 12-24.
WELCH, FRANCIS Y., 16-11.
WELCH, HIRAM, U., 11-14, 21-11.
WELCH, KENNETH C., 13-12, 13-15, 13-20.
WELCH, R. B., 12-11, 12-13.
WELCH, RAYMOND F., 11-11, 11-16.
WELCH, RONALD B., 12-11, 12-12, 12-13, 17-15.
WELD, WALLACE W., 15-14.
WELHAVEN, E. R., 12-13.
WELLER, ALLEN S., 18-11, 18-13.
WELLS. H. C., 13-18, 13-19.
WELLS, GEORGE E., 13-21.
WELLS, H. C., 11-11, 11-14, 13-19.
WELLS, HENRY W., 11-11, 11-18.
WELLS, R. L., 24-11, 24-19.
WELLS, REX I., 12-16, 24-15.
WELSCH, G. A., 11-14, 19-15.
WELSH, THOMAS M., 14-18.
WELTZ, VERNON R., 12-11, 12-13.
WENDT, P. F., 12-11, 19-15, 22-18.
WENDT, PAUL F., 11-11, 11-14, 11-16, 11-18, 11-19, 12-13, 12-14, 12-24, 13-09, 13-11, 13-14, 13-16, 13-18, 13-19, 19-15, 19-16, 22-18, 22-19, 24-11.
WENGER, RALPH W., 13-13, 22-16.
WENGER, RALPH W. JR., 11-11, 12-14.
WENHORN, EDWARD, 18-14.
WENZLICK, ALBERT, 24-12.
WENZLICK, DELBERT S., 13-18.
WENZLICK, ROY, 11-11, 11-12, 11-14, 11-16, 11-18, 12-13, 13-16, 13-19, 19-12, 22-18.
WENZLICK, ROY, RESEARCH CORP., 11-15, 13-15, 13-17, 21-12.
WERNER, ALFRED, 18-13, 18-15, 19-15.
WESCOTT, T. C., 11-11, 11-14.
WESMAN, HARVEY, 12-24, 13-19.
WESSEL, R. H., 19-15, 19-16.
WEST VIRGINIA LAW REVIEW, 12-11.
WEST VIRGINIA TAX COMNISSION, 12-11.
WEST WILLIAM B. III, 12-14.

WESTBROOK, RONALD WILLIAM, 11-15.
WESTBY, R. L., 11-11, 11-14, 14-11.
WESTEBBE, R. W., 13-11.
WESTERFIELD, RAY B., 11-11, 11-18, 19-17, 22-18.
WESTERN KENTUCKY UNIVERSITY, 12-11.
WESTGATE, TEVIS T., 14-17, 22-11.
WEWEE, DEWITT, 12-14.
WEYERHAEUSER COMPANY, 12-11, 17-12, 17-13.
WHEELER, A. J., 12-15.
WHEELER, BAYARD O., 12-13.
WHEELER, BLEEKER L., 17-14.
WHEELER, MORGAN, 22-16, 25-14.
WHELDON, GEORGE T., 11-11, 11-14, 12-24.
WHINNEY, MARGARET, 18-11, 18-15.
WHIPP, DONALD V. JR., 14-15.
WHIPPLE, R. T. M., 11-11, 11-14, 12-19.
WHISTON, FRANK M., 11-11, 13-11, 13-14.
WHITE, CARL, 12-19, 16-11, 19-15.
WHITE, EDWARD L., 12-19.
WHITE, JAMES, 18-11, 18-15, 19-15.
WHITE, JOHN B., 12-13, 14-17.
WHITE, JOHN R., 11-11, 11-12, 11-14, 11-16, 11-19, 12-17, 12-26, 13-11, 13-13, 13-19, 19-12, 22-18, 22-21.
WHITE, JOHN ROBERT, 11-10, 11-11, 11-16, 11-18, 11-19, 12-13, 13-13, 13-19, 24-18.
WHITE, JON MANCHIP, 18-11.
WHITE, PHILIP H., 11-11, 11-14, 11-16, 11-19.
WHITE, RAYMOND W., 12-16, 14-13.
WHITE, ROBERT B., 12-13, 12-26, 13-19.
WHITE, WALLACE E., 12-13, 15-23.
WHITEHEAD, J. B., 11-11, 11-14.
WHITELAW, ROBERT, 14-11.
WHITESIDE, ALBA, 12-14, 12-16.
WHITLEY, B. J., 12-16.
WHITLOCK, HERBERT PERCY, 18-06, 18-17.
WHITMORE, HENRY, 13-11, 22-18.
WHITNALL, GORDON, 11-11, 11-18, 13-15.
WHITNEY, RAMEY C., 13-18.
WHITT, GLENN L., 12-16, 24-15.
WHITTAKER, THOMAS PALMER, 12-11.
WHITTEN, 11-11, 11-16, 16-11.
WHITTEN, R H, 16-11.
WHITTEN, ROBERT, 13-11.
WHITTINGTON, P. L., 12-23.
WHYNACHT, C. F., 11-11.
WHYTE, WILLIAM H. JR., 13-13, 13-19.
WHYTE, WILLIAM H., JR., 13-11, 13-16, 13-19.
WICKENDEN, W. E., 11-11, 11-12.
WICKENS, DAVID L., 13-17, 22-18.
WICKSELL, KNUT, VALUCE, 13-18.
WICKSTEAD, PHILIP HENRY, 11-11.
WIDEN, E. N., 11-16, 13-12.
WIEAND, KENNETH FRANKLIN JR. PH. D., 24-12.
WIEBE, JACOB EDWIN PHD, 17-16, 19-15.
WIGHT, WARD, 11-11, 11-18.
WILBANKS, RICHARD P., 11-11, 11-13, 12-14.
WILCOX, DONALD A., 11-11, 12-14, 12-20.
WILCOX, JOHN P., 12-15, 19-13.
WILCOX, WALTER W., 14-15.
WILDMAN, JOHN R., 11-11, 11-19.
WILDSMITH, P. D., 11-11, 11-16.
WILFRED R., 11-14, 19-15, 21-11, 23-11.
WILKEN, ARNOLD A., 19-11.
WILKINSON, F., 18-15, 19-15.
WILKINSON, FREDERICK, 18-15, 19-15.

WILKINSON, O. N., 18-15.
WILLARD, JAMES FIELD, 12-13.
WILLATT, N., 18-17.
WILLIAMS, CHARLES A. JR., 12-11, 12-13.
WILLIAMS, CHARLES H., 24-13.
WILLIAMS, D. N., 11-11, 20-13, 23-11, 24-11.
WILLIAMS, ELLIS T., 12-11, 12-13, 17-12.
WILLIAMS, HARRY G. C., 13-11.
WILLIAMS, HOWARD L., 12-15.
WILLIAMS, J. R., 12-24.
WILLIAMS, JAY, 13-17.
WILLIAMS, JOHN B., 19-15.
WILLIAMS, JOHN R., 12-24.
WILLIAMS, L., 18-16.
WILLIAMS, LESLIE, 13-11, 24-12.
WILLIAMS, PERCY R., 12-11.
WILLIAMS, ROBERT M., 12-13, 13-19, 21-20, 22-19.
WILLIAMS, SQUIRE N JR., 12-13.
WILLIAMS, VICTOR F., 12-16.
WILLIAMS, W., 19-15.
WILLIAMS, WALTER, 21-12.
WILLIAMSON, J. P., 19-15, 19-16.
WILLIAMSON, J. PETER, 11-14, 19-13.
WILLIS, H. P., 19-15.
WILLIS, REED WESTON PH. D., 16-14.
WILLIS, RICHARD S., 12-23, 22-18.
WILLISTON, W. B., 12-14.
WILLISTON, WALTER B., 12-26.
WILLNETTE, MCDONNELL, WOLCOTT, EDUCATION COMMITTEE, 14-11, 14-12.
WILLS, GEOFFREY, 18-14, 18-15, 18-16, 18-17, 19-15.
WILLS, J. E., 14-15.
WILNETT, 11-11, 11-14, 11-16, 14-13, 19-13.
WILNETTE, 11-11, 11-14, 11-16, 12-14, 14-11, 14-18, 22-18.
WILSON, D EARL, 13-13.
WILSON, D. EARL, 11-11, 11-13, 12-11, 22-24, 23-11.
WILSON, DAVID, 18-14.
WILSON, FRED, 12-13.
WILSON, GEORGE A., 11-11, 11-19, 12-24.
WILSON, JOHN W., 13-17.
WILSON, LEWIS E., 12-13.
WILSON, P. M., 11-11, 11-18, 22-18.
WILSON, PETER M., 15-17.
WILSON, RALPH G., 12-13.
WILSON, WILLIAM, 12-14, 12-26, 13-13, 20-11.
WINCHESTER, EDITH, 18-16.
WINDER, AMBROSE J., 12-14.
WINFREY, ROBLEY, 11-11, 11-14, 11-16, 19-15, 21-11, 23-11.
WINGATE, HAROLD C., 12-11, 12-13.
WINGATE, ISABEL, 18-14.
WINNER, FRED M., 12-14.
WINNICK, LOUIS, 11-11, 11-16, 13-13.
WINNING, HASSO VON, 18-15.
WINSOR, EDWARD H., 12-11, 12-25.
WINSTEAD, ROBERT W., 11-11, 11-13, 11-14, 11-15, 11-16, 11-18.
WINSTON, CAREY, 11-11, 11-12, 19-12.
WINTER, E. A., 11-14, 11-16, 13-11, 13-17.
WINTER, H. ALLEN, 13-15.
WINTERHALT, J. H., 11-11, 13-17.
WISCONSIN BOARD OF TAX APPEALS, 12-11.
WISCONSIN BUREAU OF RECLAMATION, 11-16, 15-16.
WISCONSIN LEGISLATIVE REFERENCE LIBRARY, 12-11.

WISCONSIN PUBLIC SERVICE COMMISSION, 11-11, 11-19, 12-24.
WISCONSIN TAX COMMISSION, 12-13.
WISCONSIN TAXPAYER, 12-11.
WISCONSIN, UNIVERSITY OF, 11-11, 11-12, 11-14.
WISTRAND, GLEN L., 14-17.
WITKOWSKY, JACK, 11-16.
WITTMAN, FRANK, 11-14, 11-16, 12-25.
WITZLEBEN, ELIZABETH VON., 18-15, 18-16.
WOEFF, HELMUT O., 11-11, 11-18.
WOEHLER, ELMER C., 24-20.
WOJTUSIAK, J, 18-11, 18-12.
WOLDEN, RUSSELL L., 12-13, 24-15.
WOLDEY, S. W., 18-18.
WOLF, ARTHUR L., 13-16.
WOLFE, HENRY D, 19-16.
WOLFF, F. RICHARD, 13-13.
WOLFF, LEWIS, 12-11, 12-23, 22-18.
WOLFF, LEWIS N., 12-26, 13-13, 13-14, 13-15, 13-16.
WOLFF, WILLIAM R., 16-11.
WOLFFE, LEONARD L., 13-11.
WOLFSON, HENRY, 13-15, 19-13.
WOLITZER, P., 12-11, 13-16.
WOLK, H. I., 11-11, 12-24, 19-15, 21-11.
WOLSEY, S. W., AND R. W. P. LUFF, 18-16, 18-18.
WOLTMAN, FREDERICK, 19-13, 19-18.
WOLTZ, SETH P., 11-11, 11-14, 11-16, 13-17.
WON, PHILIP W., 13-17, 19-13.
WOOD, CHARLES P., 11-18, 23-11.
WOOD, DODSON COMPANY, INC., 12-13.
WOOD, HARVEY, E., 16-11.
WOOD, IVAN D., 14-14.
WOOD, J. D., 13-20.
WOOD, RAMSAY, 13-16.
WOODHOUSE, C. PLATTEN, 18-15.
WOODHOUSE, CHARLES PLATTEN, 18-16, 19-15.
WOODLAND PIERCE CO., 13-23, 16-14.
WOODLING, GEORGE V, 19-20.
WOODRUFF, A. M., 12-11.
WOODRUFF, ARCH, 12-11.
WOODRUFF, ARCH M., 12-13.
WOODRUFF, ARCHIBALD, 12-11.
WOODRUFF, ARCHIBALD MULFORD, 11-11, 11-16.
WOODRUFF, ARCHIBALD W, 12-11.
WOODRUFF, ARCHIBALD, JR., 12-11.
WOODRUFF, WAYNE O., 19-13.
WOODWARD, DONALD B., 11-11, 11-18, 11-19, 12-11, 23-11.
WOODWORTH, LEO D., 11-11, 11-13, 21-15, 23-11.
WOOLEY, J. C., 14-15.
WOOLEY, R. J., 22-21.
WOOLLEY, R. J., 12-14.
WORCHESTER, THOMAS, 23-11.
WORKING COMMITTEE ON UTILITIES, 16-11.
WORKMASTER, H. C., 11-15, 12-12, 12-13, 12-14.
WORLEY DON, 14-14.
WORSEK, LEONARD, 13-13, 13-15.
WORSHAM, JOSEPH I., 12-14, 12-18.
WORTH, WILLARD J., 13-17.
WORTHINGTON, J. E., 11-11, 11-19.
WRIGHT, CARROLL, 11-11, 11-16, 12-16, 14-18, 24-15.
WRIGHT, CHARLES G., 13-16.
WRIGHT, FRANK LLOYD, 13-11.
WRIGHT, HENRY, 11-18.
WRIGHT, J. W., 19-15, 19-16.

## Index of Authors

WRIGHT, KARL T., 11-11, 11-18.
WRIGHT, ROBERT R., 12-16.
WRIGHT, W. P., 12-13.
WRIGHT, WALTER T., 12-16.
WULFF, EDUARDO J., 11-11.
WURFEL, LESTER E., 12-23, 19-11.
WURSTER, CATHERINE, ET AL., 13-11.
WYCKOFF, RALPH W. G., 12-14.
WYCOFF, F. C., 12-24, 12-25, 24-17.
WYER, SAMUEL S., 16-11.
WYNACHT, C. F., 11-11, 11-13.
WYNGARDEN, HERMAN, 11-14.

YALE LAW JOURNAL, 12-11, 13-19.
YANDLE, B. JR., 13-13, 13-16.
YANUS, MUHAMMAD, PH. D., 12-19, 16-14, 17-16.
YARMON, E. N., 19-12.
YARMON, ELLIOT H., 19-15.
YARMON, ELLIOT N., 22-18.
YARMON, ELLIOTT N., 11-19, 19-13.
YASHANOFF, B. A., 11-11, 11-18.
YATES, DONALD H., 12-14, 12-26.
YELLOTT, JOHN I., 13-19.
YORK, JAMES O., 13-15.
YORSHIS, STANLEY H., 15-17.
YOUNG, ELBERT A., 11-14, 12-13.
YOUNG, FRANK I., 12-16.

YOUNG, G., 24-11.
YOUNG, G. I. M., 12-14, 12-16, 12-20, 13-11.
YOUNG, GARY, 18-18.
YOUNG, H. J., 12-16, 16-12.
YOUNG, MELVIN A., 12-11.
YOUNGER, LEE B., 12-13.

ZANABONI VELAZQUEZ, DINAK, 12-11.
ZANGER, AARON, 12-23.
ZANGERIE, JOHN A., 22-18.
ZANGERLE, J. A., 11-14, 14-11.
ZANGERLE, JOHN A., 11-11, 11-14, 11-16, 12-13, 13-15, 13-19, 13-21.
ZAVIN, LOUIS B., 12-11, 22-18.
ZECKENDORF, WILLIAM, 11-11, 11-16, 13-15.
ZELITSKY, ALVIN, 13-11.
ZEPP, EDWARD G., 11-11, 11-12, 11-16, 11-18.
ZEPP, EDWARD G., M.A.I., 12-17.
ZETTEL, RICHARD M., 12-16, 24-15.
ZETTLEMOYER, CHARLES L., 12-11, 17-12.
ZIMMERMAN, EARL M., 13-16.
ZIRKEL, WILLIAM, 12-11.
ZOCK, RICHARD, 19-12.
ZUBOU, V. P., 18-11.
ZUCKER, R. P., 13-15.
ZUVER, BERT L., 12-13.

**COLOPHON — The Bibliography of Appraisal Literature**

TYPE: Century Schoolbook

NOTES ON PRODUCTION: The original data from which the body of the bibliography was developed, was keyboarded onto an 800 bpi computer tape. Additional information was merged into the tape to make the bibliography as current as possible.

Upon completion of the total data base, a chain printout was made to check for obvious machine errors, and a correction routine was established.

After completing the elimination of errors process, a new program was developed whereby the computer language could be translated into printer's or typesetter's language. This was done through a subroutine; type was set from magnetic tape on a cathode-ray tube (CRT) Linotron 505, at 160 lines per minute.

Although the typesetting was accomplished entirely through computer manipulation, it was decided to force the equipment to generate typesetting which would reflect typographic quality as though it were produced in the conventional manner. Despite the sophistication in the data collection processing, and typesetting mechanisms, the glue used to hold the book together is still an animal glue prepared according to a very old formula, which is over 100 years old, and the fabric has a cotton content!

Thus, in the production of this work, the most advanced technology is combined with some very old and traditional materials.

TYPE: Century Schoolbook

STOCK: 60lb. White Williamsburg offset

BINDING: Smythe-sewn, casebound

Technical Consultants on Printing to ASA: Paul M. Wester and Philip C. Smith, Corporate Press, Inc., 2414 Douglas Street, N. E., Washington, D. C. 20018.

**INPUT DATA BANK — ASA**
**"The Bibliography of Appraisal Literature"**

It is suggested the following be incorporated in the Data Bank, for inclusion in a Supplementary Publication:

Author (1) _____
            LAST NAME                     FIRST NAME                  MIDDLE INITIAL

Author (2) _____

Article Title _____

Publication Name _____

Publisher _____
         NAME                            CITY                       PUBLICATION DATE

Contributed by _____
                                     (your signature)

- - - - - - - - - - - - - - - - - - - - - - - - - - - - - - - - - - - - - - - - - - -

**INPUT DATA BANK — ASA**
**"The Bibliography of Appraisal Literature"**

It is suggested the following be incorporated in the Data Bank, for inclusion in a Supplementary Publication:

Author (1) _____
            LAST NAME                     FIRST NAME                  MIDDLE INITIAL

Author (2) _____

Article Title _____

Publication Name _____

Publisher _____
         NAME                            CITY                       PUBLICATION DATE

Contributed by _____
                                     (your signature)

- - - - - - - - - - - - - - - - - - - - - - - - - - - - - - - - - - - - - - - - - - -

**INPUT DATA BANK — ASA**
**"The Bibliography of Appraisal Literature"**

It is suggested the following be incorporated in the Data Bank, for inclusion in a Supplementary Publication:

Author (1) _____
            LAST NAME                     FIRST NAME                  MIDDLE INITIAL

Author (2) _____

Article Title _____

Publication Name _____

Publisher _____
         NAME                            CITY                       PUBLICATION DATE

Contributed by _____
                                     (your signature)

| Postage Will Be Paid By Addressee | **BUSINESS REPLY MAIL**<br>First Class Permit No. 35834 Washington, D.C. | No Postage Stamp Necessary If Mailed In The United States |
|---|---|---|

**AMERICAN SOCIETY OF APPRAISERS**
Dulles International Airport
P.O. Box 17265
Washington, D.C. 20041

---

| Postage Will Be Paid By Addressee | **BUSINESS REPLY MAIL**<br>First Class Permit No. 35834 Washington, D.C. | No Postage Stamp Necessary If Mailed In The United States |
|---|---|---|

**AMERICAN SOCIETY OF APPRAISERS**
Dulles International Airport
P.O. Box 17265
Washington, D.C. 20041

---

| Postage Will Be Paid By Addressee | **BUSINESS REPLY MAIL**<br>First Class Permit No. 35834 Washington, D.C. | No Postage Stamp Necessary If Mailed In The United States |
|---|---|---|

**AMERICAN SOCIETY OF APPRAISERS**
Dulles International Airport
P.O. Box 17265
Washington, D.C. 20041

Z
7164
V3
M3

MAY 19 1976

RAYMOND H. FOGLER LIBRARY